ENCYCLOPEDIA OF CONTEMPORARY SPANISH CULTURE

ENCYCLOPEDIA OF CONTEMPORARY SPANISH CULTURE

Edited by
Eamonn Rodgers

Honorary Assistant Editor
Valerie Rodgers

London and New York

First published 1999
by Routledge
11 New Fetter Lane, London EC4P 4E
Simultaneously published in the USA and Canada by Routledge
29 West 35th Street, New York, NY 10001

Typeset in Baskerville by Routledge
Printed and bound in Great Britain by TJ International Ltd, Padstow, Cornwall

British Library Cataloguing in Publication Data
A catalogue record for this book is available from the British Library

Library of Congress Cataloging in Publication Data
Encyclopedia of contemporary Spanish culture /
edited by Eamonn Rodgers.
p. cm.
Includes bibliographical references and index.
1. Spain—Civilization—20th century—Encyclopedias. I. Rodgers, E. J.
(Eamonn J.)
DP233.5.E63 1999
946.082—dc21 98-42158
CIP

ISBN 0-415-13187-1

Contents

Editorial team

List of contributors

Yaw Agawu-Kakraba
Penn State Altoona, USA

Concha Alborg
St Joseph's University, PA, USA

Gayle Allard
Madrid, Spain

Alicia Alted
UNED, Spain

Carlos Álvarez Aragüés
IES de San Juan del Puerto, Spain

José Amodia
University of Bradford, UK

Luis O. Arata
Quinnipiac College, CT, USA

Paul Bangs
University College London, UK

Gemma Belmonte Talero
London, UK

Luis Vicente Belmonte Talero
Seville, Spain

Maryellen Bieder
Indiana University, USA

Frieda H. Blackwell
Baylor University, TX, USA

Georgina Blakeley
University of Huddersfield, UK

Carlos Blanco Lou
Zaragoza, Spain

Audrey Brassloff
University of Salford, UK

Anny Brooksbank Jones
University of Leeds, UK

Rosemary Clark
University of Cambridge, UK

Daniele Conversi
Central European Univeristy, Budapest, Hungary

Kathryn Crameri
Lancaster University, UK

Catherine Davies
University of Manchester, UK

Xon de Ros
King's College, London, UK

Philip Deacon
University of Sheffield, UK

Fernando Delgado
Madrid, Spain

Chris Dixon
University of Strathclyde, UK

Enric Dolz i Ferrer
London, UK

Chris Ealham
University of Wales, UK

Michael R. Eddy
South Kent College, UK

Peter William Evans
Queen Mary and Westfield College, UK

Isidro Fadrique
Spain

Josep-Anton Fernández
Queen Mary and Westfield College, UK

Aurora F. Polanco
Madrid, Spain

John P. Gabriele
College of Wooster, OH, USA

David George
University of Wales, Swansea, UK

John P. Gibbons
Manchester Metropolitan University, UK

Luis T. González-del-Valle
University of Colorado at Boulder, USA

Jessamy Harvey
Birkbeck College, University of London, UK

David K. Herzberger
University of Connecticut, USA

Paul Heywood
University of Nottingham, UK

Leo Hickey
University of Salford, UK

Marion Peter Holt
CUNY, USA

Jonathan Hopkin
University of Birmingham, UK

Miguel Jiménez Pinilla
Madrid, Spain

Roberta Johnson
University of Kansas, USA

Barry Jordan
De Montfort University, UK

Paul Kennedy
Loughborough University, UK

Dominic Keown
University of Cambridge, UK

John W. Kronik
Cornell University, NY, USA

Teresa Lawlor
Kingston University, UK

C.A. Longhurst
Exeter University, UK

Lourdes López Nieto
UNED, Spain

Ian Macdonald
University of Aberdeen, UK

Shirley Mangini
California State University, Long Beach, USA

Roberto Carlos Manteiga
University of Rhode Island, USA

Clare Mar-Molinero
University of Southampton, UK

Emma Martinell Gifre
University of Barcelona, Spain

Jonathan Mayhew
University of Kansas, USA

Kathleen McNerney
West Virginia University, USA

Thomas Mermall
New York, USA

Stephen Miller
Texas A&M University, USA

Mihail Moldoveanu
Paris, France

Antonio Monegal-Brancos
Cornell University, USA

José Ramón Montero
Instituto Juan March, Spain

C. Brian Morris
University of California Los Angeles, USA

Michael T. Newton
Northumberland, UK

Hugh O'Donnell
Glasgow Caledonian University, UK

Helen Oppenheimer
London, UK

José Ortega
University of New Mexico, USA

Ramón Parrondo
Instituto Cervantes, Alcalá de Henares, Spain

Genaro J. Pérez
Texas Tech University, USA

Janet Pérez
Texas Tech University, USA

Chris Perriam
University of Newcastle-upon-Tyne, UK

Benny Pollack
University of Liverpool, UK

Michael Richards
University of the West of England, UK

Michael Rigby
South Bank University, UK

Eamonn Rodgers
Strathclyde University, UK

Chris Ross
Austria

Ian Campbell Ross
Trinity College, Dublin, Ireland

Keith Salmon
University of Luton, UK

Antonio Ruiz Salvador
Dalhousie University, Canada

Sandra J. Schumm
Missouri Western State College, USA

Juan Serrano
Kingston University, UK

S. Serrano
Kingston University, UK

K.M. Sibbald
McGill University, Canada

Angel Smith
University of Leeds, UK

Antonio Sobejano-Morán
SUNY Binghampton, USA

Ignacio Soldevila Durante
Quebec, Canada

Miranda Stewart
University of Strathclyde, UK

Maria Nowakowska Stycos
Cornell University – Ithaca, USA

John Sullivan
Bristol, UK

Arthur Terry
Emeritus Professor, University of Essex, UK

Gareth Thomas
Coventry University, UK

Monica Threlfall
Loughborough University, UK

Núria Triana Toribio
University of Liverpool, UK

Anthony Trippett
University of Sheffield, UK

María Francisca Vilches de Frutos
Consejo Superior de Investigationes Científicas, Spain

Gloria Feiman Waldman
York College CUNY, USA

D. Gareth Walters
University of Glasgow, UK

Nicholas Watkins
University of Leicester, UK

Phyllis Zatlin
Rutgers University, USA

Introduction

This *Encyclopedia of Contemporary Spanish Culture* reflects the expansion of interest in Spanish culture which has been a feature not only of academic life but of the general public arena during the last quarter of the twentieth century. It strives to meet the needs not only of students following traditional language and literature courses but also of those studying in the broader and more flexible programmes which have emerged in universities and further education colleges, in which Spanish is studied in the context of area studies, business studies and political and social sciences. It is also relevant to students who are not specializing in Spanish culture as such, but who nevertheless need to acquire a knowledge of contemporary Spain as part of a curriculum in, for instance, European studies, European politics, popular culture or film studies. The encyclopedia is written so as to require no knowledge of the Spanish language, or of Spanish history and institutions other than what can be acquired by an educated non-specialist reader of the quality daily or weekly press.

One reason for the widespread interest in Spain, for which the *Encyclopedia of Contemporary Spanish Culture* tries to cater, is the impressively successful and, in the main, peaceful transition since 1975 from an authoritarian political system to a modern liberal democracy, a series of profound changes which have had far-reaching cultural effects. Spain up to 1975 was an anomaly in Europe, the last and longest surviving relic of the military dictatorships of the 1930s. A mere seven years later, it not only had free elections, parliamentary government and a democratic constitution, but had installed a centre-left social democrat government. It achieved this by a combination of adaptation and modernization of existing institutions, and imaginative innovations such as the replacement of the rigid unitary structure of the Franco dictatorship with a quasi-federal constitution creating a system of autonomous communities, which recognized the cultural, political and economic diversity of the peninsula.

This blend of continuity and innovation has been the keynote of cultural developments such as contemporary music and dance, which have incorporated traditional forms like flamenco into new modes of expression which link Spain to some of the most adventurous movements in Europe and beyond. Moreover, developments in areas like poetry and the visual arts have reconnected with some of the bold insights of the avant-garde movements of the 1930s without in any sense being backward-looking. In addition, though cultural life has flourished in the freer conditions of democracy, the widely held view of the Franco dictatorship as a cultural desert, while partly true, is an exaggeration. Despite the difficulties imposed by censorship, writers, artists and filmmakers were still able to produce work of quality, and to maintain a tradition on which later generations could build. This is no less true of the distinctive cultures of Catalonia, Galicia and the Basque country, which were never completely stifled during the dictatorship, though they have undoubtedly been the beneficiaries of the resources devoted to the promotion of regional cultures by the autonomous communities.

In its presentation and coverage, the *Encyclopedia of Contemporary Spanish Culture* endeavours to break new ground. The definition of 'Spanish' includes 'all cultures present within the territorial boundaries of the Spanish state'. This means that due regard is paid to the Catalan, Galician and Basque languages and cultures. The definition of 'culture' is similarly comprehensive, reflecting the breaking-down of the barriers that have traditionally separated 'popular' and 'high' culture, a development not unique to Spain, but arguably more accentuated there, given the circumstances of recent Spanish history. The reader will find entries on architecture, cinema, the economy, education, fashion, food and drink, gay culture, intellectual life, language, literature, the media, music, politics, religion, society, sport and youth culture. Overview essays give a general picture of broad areas such as politics or literature, which are extensively cross-referenced to shorter notes on individuals or movements. These are either indicated by bold type in the text, or by 'see also' references at the end of each article. Readers can therefore navigate their own route through the various aspects of a topic, making their own connections as they go along. The longer entries are 'facts-fronted' and have suggestions for further reading which in most cases are accompanied by notes indicating their content or relevance. Where possible, sources in English have been recommended, though the dearth of published work in English on certain topics has meant that the only material available is in Spanish or Catalan.

The chronological period covered by the encyclopedia begins with the end of the Civil War in 1939, though the emphasis falls predominantly on the post-Franco period initiated by the demise of the dictator in 1975. Some references to earlier periods are included where the needs of historical contextualization seemed to warrant this. The overall balance is as comprehensive as it was possible to achieve, having regard to considerations of space, and of the need to give proper prominence to aspects neglected in other compilations. In view of the political changes that have taken place since 1975, politics has received ample coverage, since it is necessary to understand the shifting realignments of political forces to which writers, filmmakers and the media were reacting. Overview articles on the main literary genres have been supplemented with shorter pieces on individual writers, in an effort to ensure that new developments such as the expansion of women's writing or writing in Basque are given due attention.

In general, the titles of books mentioned in the encyclopedia have been translated. Where published translations already exist, the English title is given first, followed by the original in brackets; otherwise my own translation of the title is given in brackets. An exception is made for the titles of most plays and films, since it is not always possible to know whether a performance of a play outside Spain was in the original language, in translation, or whether the same translated title was used in different performances. The English title has been used for plays printed in translation, and for a small number of films, when it is reasonably clear that the film has been distributed under this title in both Britain and the US.

With the single exception of the singer Karina, for whom no available reference work yielded a date of birth, places and dates of birth and death have been given in all biographical entries. Place-names have mostly been kept in their Spanish form, save where the Anglicized form was in general use among English speakers (e.g. Andalusia, Seville). Currency presented a particular problem, both because the small size of the unit, the peseta, means that one has to handle very large figures, and also because of differences in the meaning of 'billion' (a thousand million in America, and now almost universally in Britain) and *billón* (a million million). To avoid confusion, I have opted to quote large sums as, for instance, 20,000m (twenty billion, US/UK) or $20m^2$ (twenty billion, Spain) as appropriate.

Acknowledgments

I would like to thank all the contributors to this volume, particularly those who generously took on a higher than average number of articles, and those who undertook to write on topics outside their subject areas. At Routledge, Fiona Cairns and, particularly, Denise Rea have been unstinting in their advice, practical support and encouragement.

Finally, and not least, I have an incalculable debt to my wife, Valerie, who not only provided moral support, as always, but carried out a large share of the primary research and initial drafting, and translated the articles which were submitted in French. Without this, the project would have taken two or three times as long.

How to use this book

Structure

The *Encyclopedia* contains over 700 alphabetically arranged, signed entries, ranging from concise, factual contributions to longer overview essays.

For readers with a particular interest, a thematic contents list on p. xiv groups entries according to subject, e.g. music or the visual arts. In the body of each entry direct cross-references, indicated in bold type, lead to other relevant articles, while a 'see also' section at the end suggests related topics.

Biographical entries contain dates and places of birth and death, wherever the information is readily available, followed by the profession of the subject. Place-names have mostly been kept in their Spanish form, except where the Anglicized form is in common use among English speakers (e.g. Andalusia and Seville).

To avoid ambiguity in the meaning of the term 'billion', large sums of currency are given in millions. A *billón* pesetas (in Spanish a million million) is expressed as a million squared (m^2). For instance $20m^2$ indicates twenty *billón*.

Bibliographic items

These are divided into 3 sections:

1 Bibliography/Filmography/Discography – a selection of the entrant's work.
2 References – items which are mentioned in the body of the article.
3 Further reading – suggestions for sources for further study, in most cases including annotations indicating content or relevance.

In the body of the entries, the titles of books have been translated. Where published translations already exist, the English title is given first, followed by the original in parentheses; otherwise a literal translation of the title is given in parentheses. An exception is made for the titles of most plays and films, since it is not always possible to know whether a performance of a play outside Spain was in the original language, in translation, or whether the same translated title was used in different performances. The English title has been used for plays printed in translation, and for a small number of films, when it is reasonably clear that the film has been distributed under this title in both Britain and the US.

Thematic entry list

Architecture

architects
architecture
architecture, Francoist
architecture, post-Francoist
Arribas, Alfredo
Bofill, Ricardo
Bohigas, Oriol
Calatrava, Santiago
Candela Outerino, Felix
Coderch, José Antonio
Correa i Ruiz, Federico de
Cruz, Antonio
Domènech i Montaner, Lluis
Freixes, Dani
GATEPAC
Gaudí, Antoni
Interiorism
Iñíguez, Manuel
Jujol, Josep Maria
Linazasoro, José Ignacio
Martinell, César
Masó i Valentí, Rafael
Milá i Sagnier, Alfonso
Miralles, Enric
Modernism
Moneo, Rafael
Moragas i Galissa, Antoni de
Muncunill i Parellada, Lluis
Navarro Baldeweg, Juan
Noucentisme
Puig i Cadafalch, Josep
Sáenz de Oiza, Francisco Javier
Sert, José Luis
Sostres, José María
Sota, Alejandro de la
Tusquets, Oscar

Cultural institutions/phenomena

Archaeological Museum of Tenerife
arts funding
arts policy
Ateneo
Basque culture
Canarian culture
Catalan culture
Cervantes Institute
comics
cultural institutions and movements
Dalí Museum
Diada de Cataluna
europeísmo
fiestas
fotonovelas
foundations
Francoist culture
Galician culture
gay culture
Guggenheim Museum
Institute of Catalan Studies
Juan March Foundation
kiosk literature
Law of Patronage
libraries
literacy
Ministry of Culture
Movida, la
Museum of the Canaries
museums
ONCE
pornography
Prado Museum

Economy

Education

Fashion and design

Film

Arte y ensayo
Banderas, Antonio
Bardem, Juan Antonio
Bellmunt, Francesc
Berlanga, Luis
Bigas Luna, José Juan
Bodegas, Roberto
Borau, José Luis
Buñuel, Luis
Camino, Jaime
Camus, Mario
Chávarri, Jaime
cinema law
Colomo Gómez, Fernando
Drove, Antonio
dubbing
Erice, Víctor
Fernán Gómez, Fernando
film and cinema
film festivals
Franco, Ricardo
Garci, José-Luis
García Sanchez, José Luis
Gutiérrez Aragón, Manuel
Herralde, Gonzalo
IIEC
La Iglesia, Eloy de
Landa, Alfredo
Martínez-Lázaro, Emilio
Maura, Carmen
Medem, Julio
Mira i Franco, Carles
Miró, Pilar
Molina, Josefina
Olea, Pedro
Patino, Basilio M.
Querejeta, Elías
Rabal, Francisco
Regueiro, Francisco
Rey, Fernando
Salamanca conversations
San Sebastián film festival
Saura, Carlos
Suárez, Gonzalo
Trueba, Fernando
Ungría, Alfonso
Uribe, Imanol
Zulueta, Iván

Food and drink

cafeterías
Canarian cuisine
Codorniu
fast food outlets
food and drink
Freixenet
mealtimes
merienda
regional cooking
restaurants
seafood
tapas
VIPS
wine

History

autarky
Canarian cuisine
Casas Viejas
censorship
Civil War
Fraga Iribarne, Manuel
historiography
history
La Cierva y de Hoces, Ricardo de
press law

Intellectual life

Abellán, José Luis
Aranguren, José Luis López
Ateneo
Candel i Tortajada, Francesc
Caro Baroja, Julio
Castro, Américo
exile
Fusi Aizpurua, Juan Pablo
Giménez Caballero, Ernesto
intellectual life
Laín Entralgo, Pedro
Linz Storch de Gracia, Juan José
López Ibor, Juan José
López Rodó, Laureano
Maravall Casesnoves, José Antonio
Marías, Julián
Miguel, Amando de
Ortega y Gasset, José
Pemán y Pemartín, José María

Language and national identity

Literature

Media

Music

Performing arts

Politics

Religion

minority religions
National Catholicism
Opus Dei
religion
Roman Catholicism
Serra d'Or
Suquía Goicoechea, Angel
Vida Nueva

Society

abortion law
AIDS
class
consumerism
crime
demographic indicators
drug problem
environment
family
foundations
health care
housing
marriage and divorce
military service
penal code
personal names
planning
poverty
racism
sexual behaviour
shanty towns
social attitudes
society
urbanization
women

Sport and leisure

aficionado
alternativa
athletics
Ballesteros Sota, Severiano
Barcelona FC
basketball
Benítez, Manuel ('El Cordobés')
Bruguera, Sergi
bullfighting
camping
Chenel, Antonio ('Antoñete')
corrida
cycling
fallas
ferias
fishing
football
gambling
ganadería
gardens
golf
González Lucas, Luis Miguel ('Dominguín')
holidays
hunting
Induráin, Miguel
Janeiro, Jesús ('Jesulín de Ubrique')
Martínez, Conchita
matador
Mejías Jiménez, Antonio ('Bienvenida')
motor car
motorcycle
national lottery
novillero
Ojeda González, Francisco
Olazábal, Jose María
Olympic Games
Ordóñez Araujo, Antonio
paradores
Ponce Martínez, Enrique
Real Madrid
rejoneador
rejoneo
Rivera Pérez, Francisco ('Paquirri')
Rodríguez Sánchez, Manuel ('Manolete')
Romero López, Francisco ('Curro Romero')
Ruiz Román, Juan Antonio ('Espartaco')
Samaranch, Juan Antonio
Sánchez Vicario, Arantxa
sport and leisure
sporting press
tennis
torero
zoological gardens

Visual arts

art collections
art exhibitions
Arroyo, Eduardo
Brossa, Joan
Català-Roca, Francesc
Catany, Tony

Writers

ABC

ABC is one of a very small number of older family-owned newspapers to survive the transition to democracy following the death of General Franco. It is unashamedly conservative in outlook, but is one of the most successful newspapers in Spain.

Although published in Madrid, *ABC* is a newspaper with a national readership throughout Spain. It is published by Prensa Española, one of the oldest family-owned publishing groups in the country. It is the only major national newspaper which does not provide data to the Estudio General de Medios (General Media Survey), the organization which provides statistics on readerships and the like for most Spanish publications. Despite this, it is generally believed to be one of Spain's most widely read dailies, with an average circulation of around a quarter of a million copies, placing it close behind its main national rival *El* ***País***.

ABC's appeal is not immediately apparent to the outsider. It has the smallest format of all the Madrid dailies, a feature which has the additional consequence of making it often quite bulky: it can at times total as many as 130 pages, these having the unusual distinction of being stapled at the spine. It is printed on rather poor quality paper, and features few photographs, presenting the reader with broad columns of uninterrupted text occasionally enlivened by the odd line drawing or graph. It has an overwhelmingly unmodern feel, appearing as something of a survivor from a bygone age.

Its political coverage is unabashedly conservative. It has missed few opportunities to criticize the various **PSOE** governments which have been in office since the early 1980s, and it is uncompromising in its defence of the unity of Spain against any kind of separatist tendency. During the Barcelona Olympics it argued aggressively against any degree of Catalanization of the Games, insisting that they were wholly Spanish. It has further alienated many Catalans by taking a hostile approach to the process of linguistic normalization in that community, even going so far as to accuse the Catalan parliament, the Generalitat, of 'linguistic fascism'.

Since it does not participate in the General Media Survey, it is difficult to obtain reliable data regarding the precise section of Spanish society to which *ABC* appeals. On the basis of the evidence available from its own columns, however, it seems clear that it is essentially an older person's newspaper and that it caters for those who are suspicious of change and want such change as is inevitable to be at a slow pace. As more younger readers come on to the Spanish newspaper market, it seems unlikely that *ABC* will be able to maintain its current position in the hierarchy of Spanish newspapers in the longer term.

Further reading

Mateo, R. de and Corbella, J.M. (1992) 'Spain' in B.S. Østergaard (ed.) *The Media in Western Europe*, London: Sage (a useful guide to the media situation in Spain in general, though its coverage of individual newspapers is rather slim).

HUGH O'DONNELL

Abellán, José Luis

b. 1933, Madrid

Academic and literary critic

One of the most prolific writers on the history of philosophy, Abellán is the author of the multi-volume *Historia crítica del pensamiento español* (Critical History of Spanish Thought) (1979–89), and of studies of **Ortega y Gasset**. He secured an appointment in the Faculty of Philosophy of the Complutense University of Madrid in 1966, subsequently becoming professor of the History of Spanish Thought. He co-authored, with Antonio Monclús, *El pensamiento español contemporáneo y la vida de América* (Contemporary Spanish Thought and the Life of America) (1989), for the third volume of which he was awarded the National Essay Prize.

EAMONN RODGERS

abortion law

Under the Franco regime illegal abortion had been very widely practised as a form of birth control. Until the legalization of contraceptives in 1978, numbers of abortions are estimated to have been between 300,000 and 350,000 a year in the 1970s (about 40 percent of the figure for live births). In 1985 a law decriminalizing voluntary termination of pregnancy in special cases was approved. It provided for termination on grounds of danger to the life of the mother or the child, risk of foetal malformation, and rape. Facilities for termination were made available in public centres and in accredited private clinics, of which there were 215 and 54 respectively in 1991.

Figures given in that year in an answer to parliamentary questions showed that since 1985 a total of 110,000 women had obtained legal abortions in Spain, the most frequent ground being danger to the physical or psychological health of the mother. Over 40 percent of the women were under 25, and between 1987 and 1989 10,000 operations had been performed on women between the ages of 15 and 19 years, representing 13 percent of all legal abortions. Of all the **autonomous communities**, Madrid had the highest number of legal abortions (8,238). The information also showed that there had been a significant reduction in the numbers of Spanish women seeking abortions abroad. The UK had always been the most frequent destination, with over 14,000 a year by 1978 and 22,002 in 1983. By 1989 the figure had dropped to 1,332.

A different set of figures, however, from a study financed by the **Instituto de la Mujer** and included in the World Health Organization's Special Programme of Investigation into Human Reproduction, pointed to a continuing high level of illegal abortion. These data suggested that there were in fact in the region of 105,000 terminations every year in Spain (nearly six times the admitted figure), 71 percent of which were illegal. Equally remarkable was the revelation that some 97 percent of legal terminations took place in private clinics. Though the conscientious objection clause offered an escape route to health professionals in the public sector unwilling to perform the operations, there were indications that some of those objecting were subsequently carrying out terminations in a private centre.

Reform of the law was already being discussed, and earlier in 1991 a draft proposal to extend decriminalization of abortion on socio-economic grounds had been drawn up by a commission of five experts. This was considered a moderate proposal in the face of pressure from, on the one hand, those who favoured extending decriminalization even further, and, on the other, continuing opposition by the Spanish bishops, who published in the same year *El aborto, 100 cuestiones y respuestas sobre la defensa de la vida humana y la actitud de los católicos* (Abortion: 100 Questions and Answers on the Defence of Human Life and the Attitude of Catholics).

In 1992 the Government announced it was seeking to negotiate the extension of abortion by a 'combined system of time limits and specified conditions'. In 1994 a joint proposal from the Ministries of Justice and Interior, Health and Social Affairs, was referred to the Consejo General del Poder Judicial (CGPJ – the General Council of the Judiciary). It would have permitted a woman to terminate her pregnancy in the first 12 weeks, on condition that she waited three days to hear arguments from state representatives in favour of preserving life, and received counselling on the various supports available, and on the juridical and medical aspects of termination. There was strong opposition from conservative political and judicial quarters, as well as from the Conference of Bishops, who had already in 1993 maintained that the State had no competence to legislate in favour of abortion. Feminist organizations were also unhappy with the proposal, because, since it did not tackle the problem of conscientious objection in the public health sector, it would strengthen economic discrimination. They were also concerned that counselling could become a form of coercion. In the event the proposal failed to get the expected majority approval of the CGPJ and was not pursued.

Towards the end of 1994 the government announced that it would introduce legislation to legalize abortion on socio-economic grounds the following February. However, because the socialist **PSOE** party did not have an overall majority, it was forced to make pacts with the **PP** and other conservative parties, in particular the **CiU**, which resulted in lengthy delays.

See also: National Catholicism; Roman Catholicism; sexual behaviour; social attitudes

Further reading

Hooper, J. (1995) *The New Spaniards*, Harmondsworth: Penguin (chapter 10 discusses abortion in the context of the sexual revolution).

EAMONN RODGERS

Abril, Victoria

b. 1959, Madrid

Actress

Abril is one of the best known actresses outside Spain. By 1989 she had already achieved national success and had made several films abroad, notably in France, for instance Beneix's *La Lune dans le caniveau* (*The Moon in the Gutter*) (1982). However, it was her starring role in **Almodóvar**'s *¡Átame!* (*Tie Me Up, Tie Me Down!*) which brought her international acclaim and she appeared in two more of his late films. In her roles for Almodóvar she epitomizes restrained passion, elegance and intelligence, while showing comic talent especially in later films such as Balasko's 1995 *Gazon maudit* (*French Twist*).

NÚRIA TRIANA TORIBIO

Abril Martorell, Fernando

b. 1936, Valencia; d. 1998, Spain

Politician

Abril Martorell was the key member of the presidential 'inner circle' in the years of Adolfo Suárez's UCD governments (1977–81). After a rapid career in the state administration as a specialist in agricultural matters, he became Agriculture Minister in Suárez's first government (1976–7), then Vice-President for Political Affairs (1977–8) and later for Economic Affairs (1978–80). He was sacked in a cabinet reshuffle shortly before Suárez, his close friend and political ally, was forced out of office.

JONATHAN HOPKIN

advertising

Advertising in Spain is part of the international advertising scene, with the top twenty agencies being owned, with very few exceptions, wholly or in part by multinational groups. Most of these groups became established by acquiring or associating with local agencies, though some have built them up from scratch. In international competitions Spain regularly appears among the top three countries for the quality of its advertisements.

After major increases in spending on advertising in the 1980s, the economic recession resulted in 1993 being described as the worst in the history of Spanish advertising, when there was a 7.7 percent decrease in advertising investment in the main **media**, and an overall decrease of 4.6 percent. A modest increase of around 1 percent the following year and just under 4 percent in 1995 marked the beginning of a recovery, but this was unevenly spread over the various media.

The 1980s and 1990s have seen a major change in the relative positions of the major advertising media, and the recession and the advent of newer outlets has meant fierce competition for the attention of prospective customers. **Television** began to oust the daily **press** as the medium commanding the highest revenue at the start of the 1990s and by 1993 was attracting almost 45 percent of investment in the conventional advertising media. This was due to a policy of setting very low tariffs as an answer to the pressing need to generate income (there is no television licence fee in Spain). But the resulting saturation of the medium by publicity is causing a reaction among audiences and a change in their viewing habits. Relativities have also been changing within the television sector. The advent of private companies has led to a decline in the income and market share of the previous monopoly holder TVE, to the extent that in 1994 TVE-1 lost its prime position to Antena 3 and was continuing to lose investment in 1995.

Though the other conventional media suffered from the effects of the rapid expansion of television advertising, both the press and **radio** are considered to have been successful in overcoming their difficulties and are either holding their own or marginally increasing their market share. Decentralized printing, technical advances, the strengthening of local sections and the increasing bulk of Sunday supplements have contributed to the recuperation of the press, and the radio channels have begun to tailor their programmes to specific and increasing audiences. Cinema and outdoor advertising hold on to their very small share of the market and it appears to be magazines, especially technical ones, that have suffered the most in the shifting relativities.

Other forms of advertising between them account for very slightly more than half of all investment, and chief among them are direct marketing, accounting for over 23 percent of all investment, and, some way behind at 8 percent, publicity at point of sale. For the future the Internet is being recognized as having enormous potential for advertising and direct selling, as suggested by trends in the USA, where towards the end of the 1990s the Internet attracted at least 3 percent of investment, a figure likely to rise to over 22 percent by 2002.

Although television heads the overall list of advertising media, there are quite substantial differences in the choice of media by the various sectors. In 1995, for example, advertising in culture and communication media, the sector with the largest investment, was split approximately 40 percent to television, 35 to the dailies, 12 to magazines, 8 to radio, 3 to supplements and Sunday papers, 1.5 to outdoor and a mere 0.12 to cinema. A roughly similar pattern was visible in the transport (cars) sector. The cosmetic, hygiene and pharmaceutical sector on the other hand showed a strong bias of 62 percent to television, with 19 to magazines and 13 to radio, with a mere 2.5 to the dailies and 2 to the supplements. The food sector had an even stronger bias to television of 86 percent, with only 1 percent each to the dailies and supplements, but it was the detergent and cleaning materials sector which put virtually all its advertising on television, a massive 98 percent. Construction, agriculture and industry, on the other hand, put 70 percent of their investment into the dailies and a further 14 percent into magazines. The drinks industry concentrated 49 percent of its investment on television, but also almost a quarter on radio. Tobacco, exiled from television, also put a quarter of its advertising on radio, but a further quarter on outdoor displays. The sector that put the highest percentage into the magazines was the textile and clothing industry at 36 percent, while the dailies attracted roughly half of the investment of the public and private services sector and the transport, travel and tourism sector.

Of the advertisers, the largest overall investors are regularly El **Corte Inglés**, which tends to spread its publicity widely across the media, Procter & Gamble, which concentrates virtually all its publicity on television, and various motorcar manufacturers who tend to share the best part of their investment between television and the dailies.

A General Advertising Law was first introduced in 1964 under Franco, and advertisements were regularly subjected to censorship, especially any in which an insufficiently clad female appeared. Since then there have been modifications to the general law in 1988 as well as various specific regulations or guidelines, especially with regard to television.

Since 1978, for example, it has been illegal to advertise tobacco and drinks of over 20 percent alcoholic content, and in 1990 TVE's Administrative Council issued a series of guidelines relating to the standards of behaviour and language and the uses of alcohol portrayed in publicity material. But in sexual matters the revolution has been complete. Highly suggestive and provocative images, particularly of the female figure, have been used to advertise the most improbable of products, even cough lozenges, and strong objections to the exploitation of women as sex objects have begun to be voiced in Spain, as elsewhere.

See also: consumerism; economy; food and drink; sport and leisure; standard of living

Further reading

H. Graham and J. Labanyi (eds) (1995) *Spanish Cultural Studies, an Introduction: The Struggle for Modernity*, Oxford: Oxford University Press (an indispensable handbook; chapters 15 to 22 have several references to advertising in the context of overall cultural developments since 1960).

Schubert, A. (1990) *A Social History of Modern Spain*, London: Routledge (pp. 256–64 provide an analysis of the socio-political and economic changes of the Franco regime and the transition to democracy).

EAMONN RODGERS

aficionado

This term means literally, a fan of any spectacle or activity. In **bullfighting**, it refers to a knowledgeable devotee (as opposed to an uninformed spectator).

IAN CAMPBELL ROSS

Agencia EFE

Founded by the Franco government in 1938 in the Nationalist zone during the Civil War, as the sole channel for the control of news originating from foreign agencies, EFE continued, even after the restoration of democracy, to be owned by the state, and operates, in effect, as the official news agency, with the editorial line being determined by the party in power. The largest news agency in the Spanish-speaking world, employing 1,145 people, EFE distributes information to 1,500 locations on the globe, including 137 cities in 102 countries. It releases some 300 reports daily, offering a 24-hour service to more than 2,000 journalists affiliated to EFE world-wide. Digital data is accessed through more than 1,000 terminals round the globe, linked to satellite transmitters. As well as news, EFE offers a large number of subscription services both within Spain and internationally, including sports information, photographs, a documentation bank covering the years 1939 to the present, and technical support. It markets annual compilations of information on CD-ROM.

EFE has also, through its Departmento de Español Urgente (Department for the Defence of Spanish), founded in 1982, taken on the role of protecting traditional orthographic and grammatical norms for modern Spanish, and, especially, fostering the use of 'correct' Spanish on the Internet, in opposition to the domination of English.

EAMONN RODGERS

agriculture

Spanish agriculture is characterized by diversity and unpredictability. In a good year agriculture and fisheries together account for approximately 5 percent of Spain's GDP, but lower than average rainfall from 1991 to 1995 reduced this figure very significantly. Hardest hit were cereals and crops that require irrigation. Between one-sixth and one-fifth of the cultivated land in Spain is in need of irrigation to be productive, and the issue of water transfers for agricultural purposes from areas with plentiful supplies to areas with insufficient supplies has become the subject of heated debates and public protests, worsened by the nationalistic outlook of Spain's regional governments. Although Spain has for a long time invested heavily in reservoirs, water conservation is not popular with Spaniards. Despite the problems, the agricultural sector still offers employment to 8 percent of the country's workforce (not including family members who contribute their labour to agricultural enterprises), though many labourers are underemployed or even (as in Andalusia) in receipt of a special agricultural subsidy.

The productivity of Spanish agriculture varies greatly. It is high in the production of horticultural products and low in the production of milk and cereals (except rice). The diversity of cultivation makes geographical characterization difficult, but in general livestock predominates in the north and west, cereals (except rice) in the centre, and fruit and vegetables in the south and east. Viticulture is widespread throughout the country, and there is scarcely a region which does not produce its own wine. Spain's undoubted agricultural strengths lie in citrus fruits (grown in the Mediterranean provinces, especially Valencia); in early vegetables (grown under glass and plastic in the south and southeast); in soft fruits (grown mostly in the province of Huelva); and in rice (grown in the wetlands of the Ebro and Guadalquivir basins, Valencia and Badajoz). There are, however, many other food crops produced in significant quantities. Spain is a major producer of olive oil, although production of sunflower oil now greatly exceeds that of the more traditional olive oil (some 10 percent of the olive crop is not pressed but marketed as table olives). Leguminous plants are also widely cultivated, notably chick peas, beans, lentils and peas. Alongside the usual root crops and tubers (potatoes, onions etc.) and salad vegetables (tomatoes, lettuce etc.) are grown other less common crops such as sweet potatoes, peppers, artichokes, aubergines, asparagus and garlic. For fresh fruit lovers Spain is something of a paradise: at some stage during the year there are available oranges, mandarins, grapefruit, bananas, apricots, peaches, nectarines, apples, pears, plums, grapes, figs, cherries, strawberries, custard apples, avocados, kiwis, pomegranates, quince, medlars, melons and water melons, as well as a variety of nuts. Crops which require industrial transformation include sugar beet, sugar cane, cotton, tobacco, chicory, aniseed, saffron, peppercorn, hemp and osier for wickerwork.

Spain is the world's third largest producer of wine but its production per hectare is considerably lower than those of France and Italy. Traditionally only sherry and Rioja wines have had an international acceptance, but the huge strides in vinification technology made by Spanish wineries over the past twenty years have resulted in major quality improvements and vastly increased exports. There is, however, serious overproduction, and about one-third of the wine produced is bought by intervention and distilled (uneconomically) into industrial alcohols. If the EU's proposed quota system is implemented, Spain could be badly hit, especially in the huge but inefficient wine-producing area of La Mancha, south of Madrid.

As far as meat production is concerned, pork is the most important product by both weight and value, outstripping beef several times over, this being partly due to the popularity and high price of cured ham. Chicken occupies second place. Goats have declined relative to other livestock and are no longer important, but sheep on the other hand, with some twenty-five million head, are bred extensively for wool and their milk goes into cheesemaking. The dairy sector, heavily concentrated in the north and northwest, where regular rainfall ensures adequate pastures, is inefficient, with average herd size scarcely into double figures. Spain imports substantial quantities of milk and dairy products, mainly from France.

EU entry has on the whole been beneficial to Spanish agriculture, with farm incomes having risen steadily since entry, and by considerably more than the EU average. While some of this increase in income can be attributed to improved productivity, most of it is due to the price support system of the CAP and the devaluation of the peseta against the ECU. Agricultural products account for a very significant proportion of Spain's exports (just under 20 percent) although the value of agricultural imports in the mid-1990s slightly exceeded the value of exports (largely because of the Spaniards' insatiable demand for fish and seafood). Despite improvements in the decade to 1996, Spanish agriculture remains undercapitalized and labour-intensive and suffers from inadequate market orientation. Nevertheless, given adequate rainfall and/or assured water supplies, there are sectors, such as fruit, vegetables, olives and olive oil, and wine, where Spain could easily go on to consolidate its strengths with nothing more than improved management and informed marketing.

See also: economy; labour market; land tenure; *latifundia*; migration; *minifundia*; standard of living; water supply

Further reading

Chislett, W. (1996) *Spain 1996. The Central Hispano Handbook*, Madrid: Banco Central Hispano (chapter 5 offers a succinct account of recent developments).

Salmon, K. (1995) *The Modern Spanish Economy. Transformation and Integration into Europe*, London: Pinter (chapter 3 offers an informative survey of agriculture, forestry and fishing).

C.A. LONGHURST

AIDS

Since the AIDS epidemic hit Spain in 1981 it is estimated that there may have been as many as 40,000 cases. The National AIDS Register had recorded 27,500 cases to the end of 1994 and 15,000 AIDS-related deaths, but this is generally admitted to be below the real figure, for until the redefinition of AIDS-induced illnesses many conditions and deaths were not attributed to AIDS. The most frequent cause of transmission of the virus is the intravenous use of drugs (64 percent), followed by homosexual relations (15 percent), heterosexual relations (13 percent) and foetal infection (2 percent), a pattern different from that of the rest of Europe, where homosexuality is the chief cause of transmission. Of those known to have been infected 80 percent have been male. It is officially estimated that there are some 150,000 people who are HIV-positive (0.375 percent of the population), and the incidence of AIDS is currently running at something over 4,000 new cases per annum, the worst affected areas by far being Madrid, Catalonia and the Basque country. The strong drugs connection has resulted in 30 percent of the prison population either being HIV-positive or already having developed AIDS. Although the PSOE government led by Felipe González carried out campaigns warning drug users of the dangers of infection through shared needles and urging the use of condoms as a preventive measure, this latter advice was strongly contested by the Catholic Church. The annual cost to the Spanish health service of dealing with the epidemic was running at 20,000m pesetas in 1990 and, according to some Spanish scientists, was leading to the neglect of other important diseases. Meanwhile AIDS has continued to spread, albeit rather more slowly in the 1990s, suggesting greater public awareness of the risks. Nevertheless at a rate of about 120 new diagnosed sufferers per million inhabitants Spain now has the highest incidence of AIDS in Europe.

C.A. LONGHURST

Alaska

b. 1963, Mexico

Singer

At the age of 14 Olvido Gara became the first punk girl in Spain to leap onto the stage, dressed in a leopard skin suit holding a guitar. As her real name did not possess sufficient glamour for the would-be star, she renamed herself Alaska after a song by Lou Reed. Alaska made her début in Kaka de Luxe which managed to record an EP; the group consisted of six other musicians who would go on to form some of the most acclaimed bands of new Spanish pop.

Her next group was Alaska y los Pegamoides, in which Olvido began as a guitarist. Shortly afterwards she exchanged her arrow-shaped guitar for a microphone, and sang her first single 'Horror en el Hipermercado' (Horror in the Hypermarket), redolent of the recurrent themes of her long career: narratives of everyday domestic life, combined with references to film, television, comics and science fiction. Her original look and innovative ideas carved her a prominent place in the flourishing Spanish music scene.

Alaska acted in Pedro **Almodóvar**'s first film: *Pepi, Luci, Bom y otras chicas del montón* (Pepi, Luci, Bom and All Those Other Girls), adding a touch of youthful rebellion as one of the three female protagonists.

The first and only LP recorded by Alaska y los Pegamoides had the audacious title *Grandes Éxitos* (Greatest Hits), and in it they combined different pop music formulas, written by the two composers who have worked with Alaska throughout her career: Carlos Berlanga and Nacho Canut. Personal differences between members of the group caused it to split up, and Alaska went on to form Alaska y Dinarama with Berlanga and Canut. With Dinarama Alaska reached the summit of her career: the group went to number one in Spain in 1984 with the record *Deseo carnal* (Carnal Desire), they triumphed in Latin America, they organized huge tours. Alaska became a celebrity; she presented television programmes, made commercials, wrote articles in the press and was frequently invited on to chat shows as the mouthpiece of popular culture.

Her last record with Dinarama, *Fan Fatal* (Fatal Fan), came out when acid-house music hit. More changes in the line up followed and in 1989 Alaska, together with Nacho Canut, created Fangoria, their definitive techno-pop project, with more introspective lyrics. Through Fangoria Alaska has developed ideas which hark back to the underground/cult scene. Fangoria has its own fan club which produces a fanzine, they have a studio where they can record whenever they wish to do so, they play at concerts they organize themselves; in other words they have complete control of their work, independent of the pressures of record companies. In this way Fangoria has managed to retain what many of their contemporaries have lost: public credibility.

See also: *Movida, la;* rock and pop

FERNANDO DELGADO

Alberti, Rafael

b. 1902, El Puerto de Santa María (Cadiz)

Writer

When he returned to Spain in April 1977 at the age of seventy-four, Rafael Alberti had spent over half of his life in exile. With a vigour that belies his age, he has seemed determined to maintain the *élan* embodied in the angel of haste, one of the many angels through which he expressed his complex thoughts and feelings in his masterwork of the 1920s, *Sobre los ángeles* (Concerning the Angels). As an unwavering member of the Communist party since the early 1930s, he has had to flee countries, has been refused entry to others, and has been welcomed with open arms by many more. As a candidate of the Communist party he was elected to the Spanish Senate in 1977 in the first elections after Franco's death; he resigned three months later. Prolonged exile has enabled Alberti to display an extraordinary poetic and personal stamina independent of Spain, for he had not grounded his writings in Spain and even less in his native Andalusia. His ability to detach himself and to re-attach himself, to throw down roots that grow into books of poetry, has converted his travels into a creative odyssey whose stages are clearly marked in such titles as *Baladas y canciones del Paraná* (Ballads and Songs of the River Paraná), *Sonríe China* (China Smiles) and *Roma, peligro para caminantes* (Rome, A Danger to Pedestrians). In declaring on his ninetieth birthday 'I regret nothing. Commitment has never jeopardized my work', Alberti exhibited that confidence and fortitude that have sustained him throughout his life, especially when he has been the target of vilification, from being called 'Russian' after his travels to Soviet Russia in the 1930s to the accusation in 1993 that he signed death warrants during the Civil War. The rush to defend him against a charge that was quickly withdrawn by the historian Torcuato **Luca de Tena** is testimony to the reverence he inspires in Spain, which has showered him with prizes and honours that, after a forced hiatus of almost fifty years, crown the promise of a distinguished career heralded by the award in 1925 of the National Prize for Literature for his first book of poetry, *Marinero en tierra* (Sailor on Land). The prestigious **Cervantes Prize**, the title 'hijo predilecto de Andalucía' (favourite son of Andalusia) and honorary degrees from the Universities of Granada and Cadiz acknowledge, however tardily, the status of a man whose creativity was celebrated in the international congress organized in Cadiz in 1990 to coincide with his eighty-eighth birthday and the establishment of the Rafael Alberti Foundation.

The award in 1981 of the National Prize for Theatre reminds us that Alberti, though celebrated mainly as a poet, is an accomplished dramatist. He is also a fine writer of prose, whose long awaited second volume of memoirs documents the life of a man who has been an actor on the world's stage: accounts of his escape from France, of his precarious life in Argentina, of friendships, of the fascination exercised by the shape of letters, evince a vitality that animates the many articles he has published since in *El* ***País***. It is significant that he recalls the angel of haste and quotes lines from that poem in a book of poetry written between 1979 and 1982, *Versos sueltos de cada día* (Verses Written Day by Day), where his definition of poetry as 'no estar sentado' (not to be seated) maintains his faith in the mobility that has been for him a physical reality and a psychological necessity, one that has led him to style himself 'un marinero en tierra por el aire' (an airborne sailor on land) and 'un poeta errante y callejero' (a vagabond poet of the streets). These designations allude to the many flights he has taken in his travels around the world; they also define him in relation to what he was, positing fidelity to self and continuity of self as canons that explain the allusions to *Marinero en tierra* and to a work which in the 1930s advertised the indivisibility of poet and political missionary, *El poeta en la calle* (The Poet in the Street).

Throughout his career Alberti has evinced assurance about who he is and faith in what he does, situating himself at the centre of his works and adopting manners appropriate to the role he selects: since his return to Spain, the roles are those of the common man and commentator, of the diarist, and of the exalted lover. Whatever the role, he acts it masterfully, speaking out from the printed page as eloquently as in his public appearances and recitals, where he invariably astounds his audience with his legendary memory, and in his political campaigning in verse, where, in *Nuevas coplas de Juan Panadero* (New Rhymes by John the Baker), he uses a transparent alter ego to assail social injustices and to exalt ideals of liberty and friendship in the limpid manner of Andalusian popular verse. Private rather than public concerns energize *Versos sueltos de cada día*, where despondency about his advancing years is a sad counterpoint to his buoyant insistence that his marriage, at the age of ninety-two, to María Asunción Mateo 'is for me like an injection of youth... I am ageless'. Precise echoes of *Sobre los ángeles* point to the emotional turbulence underlying *Versos sueltos de cada día*, where jottings unified by mood as well as by a confessional manner reveal a mind assailed by memories of forced activity, of political involvement and its cost, and of his first wife, María Teresa **León**, whose redemption of him in the 1920s is seen in contrast with the incapacitating illness that claimed her mind and then her life. Maintaining that line of self-deprecatory humour initiated by an early poem entitled 'El tonto de Rafael (Autorretrato burlesco)' (The Fool Rafael (Burlesque Self-Portrait)), Alberti presents himself in this work as a man who, aware of his age, defies it in words by styling himself an 'Icaro pretencioso sin edad, con las alas prestadas' (pretentious, ageless Icarus with borrowed wings).

As if to prove his vitality, he postulates survival as a positive state in *Los hijos del drago* (The Sons of the Dragon), opposing to the hideous Adefesia the eternal figure of Venus, who is named here as Beatriz. Although love has never been a strong theme of Alberti's poetry, in *Los hijos del drago*, and then in *Canciones para Altair* (Songs for Altair), he seems anxious to make up for lost time. Adopting the manner of the adoring lover wounded by love, he kneels before his mistress, whose body he celebrates with a rhetorical elegance faithful to the cultured manner he cultivated in the 1920s in homage to the seventeenth-century poet Luis de Góngora. Increasing the temperature of his passion, Alberti conjoins two venerable topics to present Altair as both Venus arising from the waves and a star that has come down from its constellation. The explicit drawings which accompanied the poems in the first edition illustrate his depiction of her as 'palpable': the woman exalted as Altair has enabled Alberti to transcend and triumph over his years, to challenge prejudices and expectations, and to extend the limits of his own poetry. Alberti's poems continue to surprise and to radiate an energy whose message is positive as they illustrate the continuing benefits for him as creator and for us as readers of the 'hambre vital' (hunger for life) he admired in Picasso.

Major works

Alberti, R. (1929) *Sobre los ángeles* (1927–8), Madrid: Castalia; trans. G. Connell, *Concerning the Angels*, London: Rapp & Carroll, 1967 (poetry).

—— (1952) *Retornos de lo vivo lejano* (1948–1952)

(Remembrances of Things Living and Distant), Buenos Aires: Losada (poetry).
—— (1959) *La arboleda perdida. Libros I y II de memorias*, Buenos Aires: Compañía General Fabril Editores; trans. G. Burns, *The Lost Grove*, Berkeley, CA: University of California Press, 1976 (autobiography).
—— (1966) *Selected Poems*, ed. and trans. B. Belitt, Berkeley and Los Angeles, CA: University of California Press (poetry).
—— (1982) *Versos sueltos de cada día* (Verses Written Day by Day), Barcelona: Seix Barral (poetry written 1979–82).
—— (1986) *Los hijos del drago y otros poemas* (Sons of the Dragon and Other Poems), Granada: Exma. Diputación Provincial de Granada (poetry).
—— (1987) *La arboleda perdida. Libros III y IV de memorias*, Barcelona: Seix Barral (autobiography).
—— (1989) *Canciones para Altair. Con seis dibujos del autor* (Songs for Altair. With Six Drawings by the Author), Madrid: Ediciones Hiperion (poetry).

Further reading

Jiménez Fajardo, S. (1985) *Multiple Spaces: the Poetry of Rafael Alberti*, London: Tamesis.
Popkin, L.B. (1975) *The Theatre of Rafael Alberti*, London: Tamesis.
Wesseling, P. (1981) *Revolution and Tradition: the Poetry of Rafael Alberti*, Valencia: Albatros Hispanófila.

C. BRIAN MORRIS

Aldecoa, Ignacio

b. 24 July 1925, Vitoria; d. 15 November 1969, Madrid

Writer

Aldecoa was one of a group of writers who experienced the Civil War in childhood, and who later formed the so-called Generación de Medio Siglo (Mid-Century Generation), which included Jesús Fernández Santos, Rafael Sánchez Ferlosio, Medardo Fraile, Alfonso Sastre and Carmen Martín Gaite. Aldecoa entered the University of Salamanca, officially to read philosophy, but neglected his studies in favour of literary pursuits. In 1944 he moved to Madrid, where he met his future wife, Josefina Rodríguez, whom he married in 1952, and who, as Josefina R. Aldecoa, was later to become a significant literary figure in her own right. In 1953 Aldecoa collaborated with Sánchez Ferlosio and Sastre in editing the *Revista Española*, founded by the distinguished scholar Antonio Rodríguez-Moñino, but in the difficult intellectual climate of the Franco era the journal folded after a year, owing to lack of subscribers.

Aldecoa's main activity as a writer was in his preferred genre of the short story, in which he gained his first laurels, winning the Juventud Prize for 'Seguir de pobres' (Always Poor). Several collections followed, of which the most notable are *Espera de tercera clase* (Third-Class Waiting Room) (1955), *Arqueología* (Archaeology) (1961) and *Pájaros y espantapájaros* (Birds and Scarecrows) (1963). His first novel, *El fulgor y la sangre* (Radiance and Blood) was short-listed for the Planeta Prize.

Unlike many of his contemporaries, Aldecoa was able to devote himself full-time to writing, after Josefina founded a private school. In the 1960s he travelled widely in the US and in eastern and western Europe, feeding his experiences into his stories. Like most of the *Generación de Medio Siglo*, his work was influenced by the neo-realism of the contemporary Italian cinema.

See also: novel

Further reading

Fiddian, R.W. (1979) *Ignacio Aldecoa*, Boston, MA: Twayne (a highly accessible overview of the writer).
Landeira, R. and Mellizo, C. (eds) (1977) *Ignacio Aldecoa*, Laramie, WY: University of Wyoming (a useful collection of critical essays).

EAMONN RODGERS

Aldecoa, Josefina

b. 1926, La Robla (León)

Writer

Aldecoa (widow of Ignacio Aldecoa), emerged as a major feminist voice in the 1980s. Two decades of silence followed her 1962 story anthology, *A ninguna parte* (Going Nowhere). Post-Franco writings include the biographical history of the 'Mid-Century Generation', *Los niños de la guerra* (War's Children), a theme fictionalized in *Porque éramos jóvenes* (Because We Were Young). Excellent feminist novels, *La enredadera* (Clinging Vine) and *El vergel* (Enclosed Garden) investigate marital discontent, while *Historia de una maestra* (Schoolmarm's Tale) pays tribute to her mother and Republic pedagogues. *Mujeres de negro* (Women in Mourning) explores exile and return.

Further reading

Perez, J. (1990) 'Plant Imagery and Feminine Dependency in Three Contemporary Women Writers', in N. Valis and C. Bradford (eds) *In the Feminine Mode: Essays on Hispanic Women Writers*, Lewisburg, PA: Bucknell University Press, pp. 79–100 (analysis of Aldecoa's *La enredadera*, plus Carmen Martín Gaite and Maria Antònia Oliver).

—— (1991). 'La madurez narrativa de Josefina Aldecoa', *Alaluz* 23, 1: 49–53 (studies *La enredadera*, *Porque éramos jóvenes* and *El vergel*).

JANET PÉREZ

Aleixandre Merlot, Vicente

b. 1898, Seville; d. 1984, Madrid

Poet

One of the most accomplished avant-garde poets of the pre-war period, Vicente Aleixandre served as a mentor to younger poets of successive generations, writing socially engaged verse in the 1950s and evolving in a more philosophical direction during the final decades of his life. The Nobel Prize awarded to Aleixandre in 1977 constituted a significant recognition of his individual achievement as well as of his crucial role in keeping literary culture alive during the Franco regime.

Aleixandre formed part of a brilliant group of poets, known collectively as the 'Generation of 1927', who came of age in the 1920s. Working alongside such notable writers as Federico García Lorca and Luis Cernuda, he originally gained recognition for the difficult surrealist-influenced poetry of books like *Espadas como labios* (Swords Like Lips) and *La destrucción o el amor* (Destruction or Love). Even in the 1930s, however, he sought to mitigate the hermeticism of his work in order to make his poetry more accessible to his readers. The results of this stylistic clarification can be seen in the books he wrote after the Civil War. In *Sombra del paraíso* (Shadow of Paradise) (1944) he evokes visionary images of his idyllic childhood in Málaga that contrast, implicitly, with the devastation wrought by the war. This book is widely considered one of the most important collections of poetry published in the 1940s, a relatively barren period for Spanish poetry.

Aleixandre's desire for clarity eventually led him to experiment with a self-consciously 'prosaic' style, seen in book such as *Historia del corazón* (History/Story of the Heart) (1954) and *En un vasto dominio* (In a Vast Dominion) (1962). While Aleixandre's earlier work dealt largely with the relation between the individual subject and the cosmos, his poetry of the 1950s takes as its central theme the idea of social solidarity. As one of the few important Spanish poets of the pre-war generations to remain in the country after the end of the Civil War, Aleixandre enjoyed an unparalleled prestige among younger poets from the 1940s to the 1970s. Some others who stayed did so because of their sympathy with the Franco regime. Aleixandre, however, was forced to remain because of his chronic ill health, and maintained his staunch opposition to the right-wing politics of the Nationalists. Aleixandre's motto 'Poetry is communication' made him an important model for the social poets of the 1950s, including Blas de Otero. It also inspired the influential theories of Carlos Bousoño, an important poet and literary theorist who wrote the first full-length study of Aleixandre's poetry.

Aleixandre's close relationship with younger poets continued throughout the 1960s and 1970s. His style often seemed to be evolving sympathetically in response to the shifting concerns of successive generations of poets. Thus the books written in the 1950s reflect the prevalence of social themes in the immediate post-war period. In the 1960s, likewise, Aleixandre's style became more complex and introspective, echoing the increasing interest among younger poets in a poetics of 'knowledge' or 'discovery'. His close friendship with poets such as Carlos Bousoño, Claudio Rodríguez, Guillermo Carnero and Antonio Colinas thus served two important functions: Aleixandre was an invaluable source of solidarity and encouragement for these writers, who in turn stimulated him in his continual artistic renovation.

The crowning achievement of Aleixandre's career is the poetry of his two final books. *Poemas de la consumación* (Poems of Consummation) (1968) contains brief reflections on the themes of old age and impending death. *Diálogos del conocimiento* (Dialogues of Knowledge) (1974), written in the same difficult style, consists of more extensive poems in dialogue form, in which the interplay of conflicting voices expresses a dialectical approach to reality. Aleixandre's unique style, defined by its short hermetic sentences and its unusual combinations of verb tenses, serves to explore the paradoxical vitality of the liminal stage between life and death. Another major concern in these works is the nature of knowledge itself: Aleixandre's complex word play leads to an epistemological investigation of the limits of human knowing in the face of the unknown.

In some respects, the final stage of Aleixandre's poetic career represents a return to the avant-garde aesthetics of his earlier works. While all of Aleixandre's poetry is significant in its historical context, the more prosaic style of books like *En un vasto dominio* suffers somewhat in comparison with the poetic intensity of Aleixandre's very best work: the surrealist poetry of the 1930s and the metaphysical reflections of these final works.

The Nobel Prize for literature, awarded to Aleixandre in 1977, recognized him not only for his poetic achievement, but also for his broader role within Spanish literary culture. As the first Nobel Prize awarded to a Spanish writer after the death of Franco in 1975, it had special significance for the emerging culture of democratic Spain.

Further reading

Daydí-Tolson, S. (ed.) (1981) *Vicente Aleixandre: A Critical Appraisal*, Ypsilanti, MI: Bilingual Press.

Hyde, L. (ed.) (1981) *A Longing For the Light*, New York: Harper & Row.

JONATHAN MAYHEW

Almodóvar, Pedro

b. 1949, Ciudad Real

Filmmaker

After early experimental work in Super-8 format, Almodóvar directed his first full feature in 1979, *Pepi, Luci, Bom, y otras chicas del montón* (Pepi, Luci, Bom, and All Those Other Girls). This film, together with *Laberinto de pasiones* (Labyrinth of Passion) (1982), identified Almodóvar with the Madrid ***Movida***, projecting through an increasingly stylized Pop-Art *mise-en-scène* a post-modernist vision of contemporary urban life. Almodóvar's aesthetic is shaped by elements borrowed from Spanish popular cinema, from comics, fashion magazines and *boleros* (a type of popular dance tune), as well as from the great comedies and melodramas of the Hollywood cinema. The films are characterized formally by colour, dynamism and visual flair, and, in their subject matter, by irreverent satire of sexual and social orthodoxies. Almodóvar's films have had spectacular success both in Spain and abroad, appealing to a wide variety of audiences, minority and mainstream. Their treatment, above all, of sexuality – both conventional and dissident – has converted Almodóvar into a cult figure. His films explore both the peaks and troughs of desire, often focusing on the solitude and despair of failed relationships in narratives that thrive on emotional intensity and excess. In this respect he is the Spanish heir to the great Hollywood director Douglas Sirk. But native Spanish traditions – for example, popular 1960s comedies directed by Pedro Lazaga or Mariano Ozores, neo-realist satires by Berlanga – have also left their unmistakable traces.

In the early and middle stages of Almodóvar's career his films were distinguished by the appearances in prominent roles of Carmen Maura and Antonio Banderas. No scatter-brained 'Almodóvar girl', Carmen Maura has often provided in these films a sharp focus for the plausible treatment –

through both comedy and melodrama – of issues affecting Spanish women. In *¿Qué he hecho yo para merecer esto?* (What Have I Done to Deserve This?) (1984), a film largely refocusing the drives and patterns of indigenous neo-realist cinema, the Carmen Maura role provides a visual register for the pressures faced by working-class women. In *Mujeres al borde de un ataque de nervios* (*Women on the Edge of a Nervous Breakdown*) (1988), to date Spain's most commercially successful film, with a host of awards to its name, the middle-class, professional woman's problems – above all in love – are addressed. Antonio Banderas' contribution to Almodóvar's films has given varied and complex representation to the constraints and vicissitudes of a masculinity both liberated and in crisis. In *¡Atame!* (*Tie Me Up, Tie Me Down!*) (1989), he portrays its darker side. In *La ley del deseo* (The Law of Desire) (1987), one of the many films concentrating on male homosexuality, he embodies the passionate sensibility of gay desire.

The laws of desire continue to feature as key areas of interest in Almodóvar's subsequent films, *Tacones lejanos* (*High Heels*), *Kika*, and *La flor de mi secreto* (The Flower of my Secret), all of which maintain, additionally, their Pop-Art mixture of high and low, straight and camp, comic and melodramatic aesthetics.

Further reading

García de León, M.A. and Maldonado, T. (1989) *Pedro Almodóvar: La otra España cañí*, Ciudad Real: Diputación de Ciudad Real.

Holguín, A. (1994) *Pedro Almodóvar*, Madrid: Cátedra.

Smith, P.J. (1994) *Desire Unlimited*, London: Verso (an important study by a leading theorist of gay aesthetics).

Strauss, F. (1994) *Pedro Almodóvar, un cine visceral*, Madrid: Ediciones de El País.

Vidal, N. (1988) *The Films of Pedro Almodóvar*, Madrid: Ministerio de Cultura.

PETER WILLIAM EVANS

Alós, Concha

b. 1922, Valencia

Writer

This transitional figure between post-war 'social' novelists and post-neo-realist experimentalism expresses many feminist concerns, reiterating typical themes and motifs including the 'war between the sexes', woman as sex-object in *Os habla Electra* (Electra Speaks) (1975), feminine alienation and oppression in *Os habla Electra* and *El asesino de los sueños* (The Assassin of Dreams) (1986), and woman as predator in *Rey de gatos* (King of Cats) 1972. Thematics range from naturalist scenes, in *Los enanos* (The Dwarves) (1962) and *La madama* (The Madam) (1969), to Civil War experiences, in *El caballo rojo* (The Red Horse) (1966), hunger and misery in *La madama*, and ecological issues in *Las hogueras* (Bonfires) (1964) and *El asesino de los sueños*. Republican refugees' perspective of the Spanish Civil War is portrayed in *El caballo rojo* (1966). Symbolic colouration, in *Argeo ha muerto, supongo* (Argeo is Dead, I Suppose) (1982), intertextual dialogues, binary oppositions, and experimental narrative techniques appear in later novels. Perhaps because she was something of a precursor, Spanish critics have neglected Alós' novels and short stories, reacting negatively to her 'unwomanly' vocabulary and topics which anticipate works written fifteen or twenty years later.

Further reading

Ortúzar-Young, A. (1993) 'Concha Alós', in L.G. Levine, Marson and G.F. Waldman (eds) *Spanish Women Writers: A Bio-Bibliographical Source Book*, Westport, CT: Greenwood Press, pp. 23–31 (very comprehensive survey of life and works and thematic analysis in English).

Pérez, Genaro J. (1993) *La narrativa de Concha Alós: Texto, pretexto y contexto*, London: Tamesis (a useful book-length study in Spanish).

GENARO J. PÉREZ

Alperi Fernández, Víctor

b. 1930, Mieres (Asturias)

Writer

Avoiding metropolitan literary centres, Alperi practised journalism and wrote criticism, novels, stories and non-fiction in northern isolation after obtaining a doctorate in law from the University of Oviedo. Characteristic novels exemplify Spain's neo-realist 'social' literature of the mid-century, featuring economic problems, attenuated naturalism, and portraits of transition from agrarianism to modernity. *Sueño de sombra* (Dream of Shadows), *Agua india* (Indian Waters) and *Cristo habló en la montaña* (Christ Spoke on the Mount), written in collaboration with Juan Mollá, preceded *Dentro del río* (Within the River) and *Una historia de guerra* (War Story), portraying regional and national civil conflict.

JANET PÉREZ

alternativa

In this ceremony a bullfighter graduates from being a ***novillero*** to a ***matador*** *de toros*. In Spain, any *alternativa* taken outside of Madrid's Las Ventas arena must be confirmed there (*confirmación de alternativa*).

See also: bullfighting

IAN CAMPBELL ROSS

Álvarez de Toledo Maura, Luisa Isabel

b. 1930, Seville

Writer

This aristocratic activist, Duchess of Medina Sidonia, promulgates humanitarian issues, denouncing economic exploitation and criticizing affluent lifestyles. Her 1972 autobiographical memoir *My Prison* criticizes Spanish justice and penal systems. The thesis novel, *The Strike* (*La huelga*) indicts 'Establishment' brutalization of Andalusian workers. *La base* (The Airbase) depicts negative effects on a fictional town from a neighbouring US-Spanish airfield: increasing corruption, decreasing autonomy and environmental degradation. In *La cacería* (The Chase), Madrid aristocrats hunting in rural Andalusia provide an opportunity for exposing high society decadence and criticizing the Franco regime's unjust social policies.

JANET PÉREZ

Alzaga, Oscar

b. 1942, Madrid

Politician and lawyer

A prominent Christian democrat, Alzaga was active in the 'tolerated opposition' to Franco and the **Tácito** movement, joining **UCD** as part of Fernando Alvarez de Miranda's PDC. Refusing several offers to join **Suárez**'s government, he used his high profile in the UCD parliamentary group to organize conservative opposition to Suárez's centrist strategy. He then left the party to create the Partido Demócrata Popular (PDP), a Christian democrat splinter group which joined **Fraga**'s Coalición Popular. His uneasy relationship with the PDP's coalition partners, which confirmed his reputation as a difficult political ally, led to his resignation in 1986.

JONATHAN HOPKIN

Amedo, José

b. 1946, Lugo (Galicia)

Police officer

Amedo moved from his native village to Bilbao at a young age. He worked for the Francoist *Brigada Social*, the political branch of the secret police, and carried out surveillance of university students. He was arrested in 1988 in connection with possible involvement in right-wing hit squad **GAL**, which had carried out several attacks on ETA members and sympathizers. He was convicted of six charges of attempted murder in 1991, but transferred to an open prison regime in 1994. Despite earlier denials, he subsequently admitted involvement in

GAL, and incriminated both his superiors in the police and government ministers.

EAMONN RODGERS

American bases agreement

The sympathy which Franco had displayed towards the Axis powers during WWII earned the regime the hostility of the western democracies, notably the United States, which in 1945 signalled its displeasure by replacing its retiring Ambassador to Spain with a Chargé d'Affaires. By the end of 1947, however, with the acceleration of the Cold War, the attitude of the US State Department and the Joint Chiefs of Staff was becoming more benevolent. The usefulness of Spain to American strategic defence plans, combined with the dire state of the Spanish economy, made a military agreement seem attractive to both countries. By 1949, American warships were making courtesy visits to Spanish ports, and in 1951 the Embassy in Madrid was restored to its former status. In the same year, the Joint Chiefs of Staff established direct contact with their Spanish counterparts with a view to co-operating on the establishment of air and naval bases in Spain.

Negotiations, however, proceeded slowly, owing in part to the unflattering view which American visiting teams had formed of Spain's military and economic capability, and in part to Franco's determination to extract the maximum benefit from the relationship. Eventually, in September 1953, the Defence Pacts were concluded, though on terms more favourable to the US than to Spain. The agreement meant that the Americans were not obliged to come to Spain's aid unless she was attacked by a communist country. American military personnel stationed in Spain were exempt from Spanish law and from paying Spanish taxes. Perhaps the clearest indication that the US gave scant consideration to Spanish interests was that air bases were established close to major centres of population, at Torrejón de Ardoz near Madrid, and at Seville and Zaragoza.

The agreement ended Spain's post-war isolation, and was presented by the propaganda of the regime as a great diplomatic success. However, the benefits flowing from the pact were less than Franco had hoped. Though Spain received some $266m in military and technical aid, general economic support was very limited. Besides, availability of equipment to upgrade the capability of the Spanish armed forces was limited by America's prior commitments to NATO, and by her involvement in the Korean War. The result was that the military hardware supplied to Spain was outdated.

The bases agreement was very unpopular with the left wing in Spain after the restoration of democracy in 1977, and when it came up for renewal in 1987, the Socialist government in power embarked on a radical renegotiation. It was eventually agreed that the 72 F-16 aircraft stationed at Torrejón would be removed by 1991. Well before then, in any case, the Defence Pacts had been superseded by the entry of Spain into **NATO**.

EAMONN RODGERS

Añoveros Ataún, Antonio

b. 1909, Pamplona; d. 1987, Bilbao

Bishop

Añoveros Ataún served as military chaplain during the Civil War, Auxiliary Bishop of Málaga (1952), Bishop of Cádiz-Ceuta (1964) and Bishop of Bilbao (1971–8). In Cádiz, he was well-known for his championship of the poor and exploited of Andalusia. In February 1974, while Bishop of Bilbao, he authorized a pastoral letter stating that the Basques were entitled to their own identity and language. The Arias Navarro government placed him under house arrest for this 'attack on national unity' and threatened to deport him, but eventually had to back down. The 'Añoveros affair' is seen by many as marking the end of the church–state alliance in Francoist Spain.

AUDREY BRASSLOFF

'ANTOÑETE' *see* Chenel, Antonio

Aranda, Vicente

b. 1926, Barcelona

Filmmaker

Aranda began his career with fantasy-horror films before producing *Cambio de sexo* (Change of Sex) (1976), a sensitive portrayal of an effeminate youth played by Victoria **Abril**. In *La muchacha de las bragas de oro* (The Girl in the Golden Panties) (1980) he both exploited the new freedom from censorship and portrayed the contrast between the older and newer Spains. He has since produced a variety of films, including thrillers like *Fanny Pelopaja* (Straw-Haired Fanny) (1984), the box-office success *El Lute, camina o revienta* (*Run For Your Life*) (1987) and an adaptation of Luis Martin Santos' *Tiempo de silencio* (Time of Silence) (1986). In 1992, he won the Goya Prize for best direction and best film for *Amantes* (Lovers) (1991).

EAMONN RODGERS

Aranguren, José Luis López

b. 1909, Avila; d. 1996, Madrid

Philosopher and essayist

Aranguren is the first prominent Catholic intellectual of the early decades of the Franco regime to encourage a more tolerant and receptive attitude to modern thought. Unlike other well-known liberal Catholics of the period, Aranguren wrote critical treatises and essays on figures considered dangerous by the official guardians of Spanish culture. His studies of Luther, Kierkegaard and Unamuno in *Catolicismo y protestantismo como formas de existencia* (Catholicism and Protestantism as Ways of Life) show an independence of mind uncommon for that time. During the 1950s and 1960s, Aranguren stressed the need for Spanish Catholics to abandon their hostility to secular thought, enter a dialogue with Protestants, atheists and Marxists, and encouraged the authorities to restore democratic institutions. In 1965, after taking part in student demonstrations in favour of the liberalization of academic life, he was removed from his Chair of Ethics at the University of Madrid, and was only reinstated on Franco's death.

Aranguren's main contribution to Spanish thought is a treatise on ethics entitled *Ética* (1958), which at the time of publication was the only book on moral science written in a rigorous, non-apologetic and contemporary philosophical language. Eschewing any notion of a normative ethics or Kant's categorical imperative, he holds that humankind is moral by virtue of an ineluctable need to interact with others. This will to coexist accrues in human beings an ethos, or character. Ethics is therefore a structure of coexistence, which is the ground and content of morality (in all its diverse forms). To accept morality as structure is to recognize that all human activity is essentially moral and that disciplines devoted to the study of human relations contain explicitly or implicitly ethical problems. Aranguren expanded his ethic of coexistence into a series of essays on human communication in an era of mass media and consumer economy.

One of the distinctive marks of Aranguren's intellectual temper is an appropriation of the English empirical tradition, the school of ordinary language analysis and varieties of neo-positivism. He also maintained a sustained dialogue with Marxism – of which *El marxismo como moral* (Marxism as a Moral System) is an example – and with the younger generation of scholars and intellectuals of all political persuasions. In sum, Aranguren was a Catholic intellectual trained in the philosophy of Aristotle and Aquinas, but equally at home with Marx, Russell and Talcott Parsons. He was admired as a fearless social critic for whom the role of the intellectual consisted in the happy marriage of theory and praxis. He was awarded the National Prize for Literature in 1989, and the Prince of Asturias Prize for Communication and Humanities in 1995.

Further reading

Aranguren, J.L. (1969) *Human Communication*, New York: McGraw-Hill (a summary of his main ideas on the basic ethical problems of human communication).

Mermall, T. (1976) *The Rhetoric of Humanism: Spanish Culture after Ortega y Gasset*, New York: Bilingual

Press (places Aranguren's thought in the context of post-Civil War culture).

THOMAS MERMALL

Archaeological Museum of Tenerife

In 1913, the Tenerife Island Council acquired part of the collections of the Scientific Society founded by Juan Bethencourt Alfonso, and established the Archaeological Museum of Tenerife. During the Franco era, the museum was the home of important work by Luis Diego Cuscoy on the pre-Spanish islanders, the *Guanches*. During the 1990s, the museum was moved to new, larger premises in Santa Cruz but gained notoriety for the 'discovery' of the 'Zenata Stone', an apparently politically inspired forgery of an inscription designed to promote the Canarian independence movement.

See also: Canarian culture; Cubillo Ferreira, Antonio; Museum of the Canaries

M.R. EDDY

archaeology

Archaeology in Spain was strongly influenced by the forty years of Franco's dictatorship. Many of the more innovative researchers of the pre-Civil War decades either went into exile or were prevented from working, and most of those who were involved in research under Franco became servants of the regime's needs. The isolation of Spanish science during the Franco period led to stagnation in archaeological methodology and theory.

Before the Civil War, the development of archaeological research in Spain closely mirrored the progress of the subject elsewhere in western Europe. The nineteenth and early twentieth centuries saw considerable work by gifted antiquarians, often working with the leading French scholars of the day. At national level, this led to the progressive institutionalization of culture and knowledge. *Comisiones de Monumentos* (Monuments Commissions) were established in 1814, and the Museo Arqueológico Nacional (National Archaeological Museum) in 1867. In the second half of the nineteenth century, the Academia de la Historia (Academy of History) took on renewed importance, and the newly created Escuela Superior de la Diplomacia began teaching archaeology and numismatics. Many regional and local archaeological societies and museums were founded and a number of key general histories written. The *Ley de Excavaciones Arqueológicas* (Archaeological Excavations Law) was passed in 1911, and a Comisión de Investigaciones Paleontológicas y Prehistóricas (Commission for Palaeontological and Prehistoric Research) founded the following year. Spanish archaeological research also took on an international dimension with the creation of the Spanish School of Archaeology in Rome.

The institutionalization of archaeological research was associated with the development of a Spanish nationalist school which attracted the more reactionary scholars. During the early twentieth century, however, regionalist institutions were also established, in the first instance in Catalonia where a Servei d'Investigacions Arqueòlogicas (Archaeological Research Service) was set up within the Institut d'Estudis Catalans (Institute for Catalan Studies) in 1915. Similar bodies were created in the Basque country in 1921 and 1925, in Galicia in 1923, and in Valencia and Andalusia in 1927.

By the 1920s, somatological anthropology (the study of the evolution of human body-types) was firmly entrenched as a research tool in several institutions, and scholars from outside Spain were attracted by the supposedly racially isolated populations of the Basque country and the Canary Islands. The social Darwinism underlying the somatological approach agreed well with the reactionary sentiments of the nationalist scholars.

With the Francoist victory in the Civil War, this nationalistic tradition came to dominate the archaeological scheme. The regional institutions were either disbanded or obliged to conform to the vision of Spanish prehistory divided chronologically into great cultures which embraced the whole of the peninsula. The appointment of Provincial Commissioners for Archaeology, during and just after the Civil War, under the Falangist national Commissioner, Julio Martínez Santa-Olalla, restricted the development of locally based cultural sequences. Despite the gradual opening-up of Spanish academia from the 1950s, regional surveys of archaeology complied with a generally pan-Iberian model. Spanish archaeology remained more or less atrophied until the 1970s when, with some influence from processual or New Archaeology, the subject became a 'narrative composed of endless lists of objects described in the most minute detail' (Díaz-Andreu 1993b: 16).

The transition to democracy allowed increased theoretical and methodological diversity. Emphasis moved from traditional historicist interpretations and from the positivist listing of artefacts to an examination of the environment, economy, and social processes. During the 1980s, a series of congresses considered archaeological methods – particularly Soria in 1981, Madrid in 1985, and Barcelona in 1986. Most Spanish archaeological literature from the late 1980s onward contains some review of epistemology and theory.

Three distinct theoretical directions were adopted by Spanish archaeologists: the Marxist, closely following the Latin American Marxist model; a neo-Marxist approach, akin to the Frankfurt School; and a form of structuralism developed by Celso Martín de Guzmán at the Complutense University in Madrid. Generally archaeologists in Spain have now taken on board, albeit not uncritically, the theoretical basis of processual archaeology.

Nevertheless, epistemological awareness and theoretical debate have not changed archaeological practice to any real extent. More excavations have been undertaken during the 1980s and 1990s, particularly as the *Ley del Patrimonio Histórico Español* (Spanish Historic Heritage Law) of 1985 came into force. More of those excavations have been accompanied by palaeo-environmental investigation and consideration has been given to social and economic factors. Yet the archaeological community in Spain 'remains more interested in the maintenance of its elitist positions and the reproduction of its privileges than in the social relevance it could claim by offering a critical view of the past in relation to the present' (Vázquez Varela and Risch 1991: 45).

The 1985 Law modernized archaeological legislation, introducing the concept of *Bien Cultural* (Cultural Property) which gave similar levels of protection to artefacts, sites and landscapes, and allowed various levels of local government to take action to conserve cultural properties. The 1985 Law enabled the Regional Governments to establish their own archaeological services and to introduce regional legislation. Where such legislation has been introduced, however, it has been directed as much at protecting the existing archaeological communities' interests as at protecting the heritage or at promoting improvements in archaeological practice.

The Spanish archaeological heritage is vast and still relatively unexplored. Much of its exploration has been carried out within inadequate and outmoded methodological and theoretical frameworks, to the detriment of Spain's heritage, and it is to be hoped that future generations of Spanish archaeologists will provide the much-needed critical view of the past in relation to the present.

Further reading

Alcina Franch, J. (1989) *Arqueología antropológica*, Akal: Madrid.

Díaz-Andreu, M. (1993a) 'Theory and Ideology in Archaeology: Spanish Archaeology Under the Franco Regime', *Antiquity* 67, 254: 74–82.

—— (1993b) 'El pasado en el presente: La búsqueda de las raíces en los nacionalismos culturales. El caso español', *Pre-Actas del Congreso Os Nacionalismos en Europa: Pasado e Presente*, pp. 1–25, University of Santiago de Compostela, 27–9 September 1993.

Martínez Navarrete, M.I. (1990) 'La prehistoria española en los últimos cincuenta años: teoría y práctica', *Hispania* 175: 439–57.

Vázquez Varela, J.M. and Risch, R. (1991) 'Theory in Spanish Archaeology Since 1960', in I. Hodder (ed.) *Archaeological Theory in Europe: The Last Three Decades*, London: Routledge.

M.R. EDDY

architects

Spain is one of the few countries where architects are found in the higher reaches of political life.

This is particularly the case in Catalonia, but since this region is one of major socio-economic importance, the effect is felt throughout the whole country. Indeed **Puig i Cadafalch**, one of the best architects of **Modernism** and of ***Noucentisme***, was President of the Mancomunitat (the autonomous government of Catalonia) between 1917 and 1924. After the death of Franco the most vigorous supporter of the socialist-controlled city council was **Bohigas**, author of Barcelona's new planning philosophy. In the opposite political camp was **Bofill**, internationally recognized for his contributions to monumental architecture. This shows the major role which architecture could play in this city, and also the extent to which architects could capture the attention of the wider public.

In the Catalonia of Modernism there were already two radically different attitudes towards political life: on the one hand **Domènech i Montaner** and Puig i Cadafalch represent the public-spirited architect, who has a real impact on community policy (following the example of the Viennese architect Otto Wagner), while on the other **Gaudí** and **Jujol** exemplify the architect as artist, working largely in isolation from society. It is the former type who are particularly responsible for the good reputation enjoyed by architects in Spain.

The activity of most distinguished Spanish architects of this century is associated with the development of the main centres of Barcelona, Madrid and San Sebastián. Another important locus is Andalusia where architecture has developed in a more random fashion, especially at Seville, Cordoba and Granada. To a lesser degree Valencia acts as a magnet for talented architects.

In Catalonia, the early years of the twentieth century were a time of great architectural ferment. The leading exponents of Modernism, together with their pupils and imitators, formed an impressive group of distinguished figures, who fuelled passionate debate on architectural matters. Luis Domènech i Montaner, Antoni Gaudí, Josep Puig i Cadafalch, Josep Maria Jujol, Eric Sagnier, Jeroni Granell and Bonaventura Bassegoda are only a few of those active in Barcelona at this time. In the following generation, which marked the transition to *Noucentisme* but also to certain forms of rationalism, we find César **Martinell**, Rafael **Masó**, Josep Pericas, Francesc Folguera, Adolf Florensa, Nicolau Rubió i Tuduri, Joaquin Guardia i Vial, Francesc Nebot, Eusebi Bona and Raimon Durán i Reynals. In the early 1930s Barcelona was the scene of some of the most important activities of **GATEPAC**, redolent in some respects of the *Esprit Nouveau* which inspired Le Corbusier in Paris. The Catalan architects of this group were **Sert**, Yllescas, Subirana and Jose Torres Clavé. It was here that after the Civil War **Coderch**, and some years later, **Correa** and **Milá**, **Moragas** and **Sostres** began their activities. The desire for modernization and openness to new ideas favoured the birth of the Grupo R in the 1950s, an intellectual discussion group on architectural issues, which included among its members the young **Bohigas**, Coderch, Moragas and Sostres. In the 1970s, there is a notable diversification of architectural production, seen in the emergence of the Studio PER, with **Tusquets**, Clotet, Bonet and Cirici, and also the *Taller de Arquitectura* around **Bofill**. In the 1980s, new names, often of partnerships, come to the fore: Bach and Mora, Pinon and Viaplana, Garcès and Soria, Bonell and Rius, **Miralles** and Pinos, Torres and Martínez Lapeña, **Freixes** and Miranda, Arribas, Morte, Ferrater, Mateo. The majority of these continue to consolidate their reputation in the 1990s, and new names start becoming known, such as Sunyer, González, Bou or Tarrasso.

While few cities match Barcelona for architectural ferment, important activity is going on elsewhere. In Madrid, turn-of-the-century architecture was represented by works in the eclectic tradition, very much influenced by French architecture of the nineteenth century. With the advent of the modern movement, GATEPAC found a staunch ally in García Mercadal, the driving force behind a group of enthusiastic architects. After the Civil War it is difficult to find a great name in Madrid architecture until the 1960s when **Sáenz de Oiza** came on the scene, followed a few years later by one of the greatest contemporary architects, Rafael **Moneo**. In the 1980s **Navarro Baldeweg** began to make his mark in Madrid.

The Basque region and Navarre have their own distinctive architectural traditions: the eclectic approach of the late ninteenth century was interpreted there in a very characteristic way. The architect Victor Eusa is a good example of this distinctive vision, as can be seen from his very original projects in Pamplona in the 1930s. The influence of this tradition can still be observed in the 1970s and 1980s with partnerships such as that of **Iñíguez** and Ustarroz (Pamplona and San Sebastián) and **Linazasoro** and Garay (San Sebastián), which are trying to revive certain features of traditional construction.

Andalusia, with its rich architectural heritage, offers fewer examples of this individualistic talent, but it was, after all, in Seville that Aníbal González worked, that great defender of regionalism and the driving force behind the Ibero-American Exhibition of 1929. At Granada three other architects remarkable for their originality are Giménez Lacal, Cendoya and Anasagasti, the creators of the Carmen de Rodríguez-Acosta. Contemporary architecture in Andalusia is fostered by architects such as Antonio **Cruz**, Antonio Ortiz and Vásquez Consuegra.

From the 1980s onward, Valencia is very well represented by Santiago **Calatrava**, an architect-engineer of international renown.

See also: architecture; architecture, Francoist; architecture, post-Francoist

Further reading

El Croquis (1985–95), Madrid.

Loyer, F. (1991) *L'art nouveau en Catalogne*, Paris: Biblio. Arts, Le Septième Fou.

Moldoveanu, M. (1996) *Barcelona: Architectures of Exuberance*, Barcelona: Lunwerg (an overview of different periods and styles, richly illustrated with photographs by the author).

Progressive Architecture (1993) New York, July 1993.

Rubió i Tuduri, N. (1927) *Diàlegs sobre l'arquitectura*, Barcelona: Cuadernos.

Zabalbeascoa, A. (1992) *The New Spanish Architecture*, New York: Rizzoli.

MIHAIL MOLDOVEANU

architecture

Architecture in Spain is an area of great complexity, exemplifying the idiosyncrasies of each region and their distinctive histories, rather than displaying common national characteristics. While Andalusia and the Basque country, for example, are both autonomous regions within present-day Spain, they differ fundamentally in their history and their aspirations, which inevitably is reflected in their architecture. The term 'Spanish architecture' therefore covers a wide range of diverse styles, something which is as true now as it was in previous centuries.

Any attempt to describe a common heritage immediately raises questions about the dominance of the centre, especially Madrid, over the peripheral regions, which often have a more clearly defined character. Undoubtedly, examples of state architecture such as the late sixteenth-century monastery/palace of El Escorial by Juan de Herrera, a typical symbol of centralized power, exercise a pervasive influence all over Spain, but their impact on the evolution of Andalusian cities like Seville or Cordoba is marginal. Here, the Moorish inheritance is too deeply rooted and cherished for it to be obliterated by others. On the contrary, the hybrid *mudéjar* style, based on Moorish architecture, which evolved in Andalusia under the *conquistadores*, became a source of inspiration for the whole of the Iberian peninsula. Towards the end of the nineteenth century, *neo-mudéjar* became very widespread throughout Spain, offering, as it were, a kind of home-grown exoticism. Catalan **Modernism** offers some splendid examples: **Gaudí** and **Jujol** too gave their seal of approval to *neo-mudéjar.*

The regions bordering the Pyrenees (Catalonia, Aragon, Navarre and the Basque country) have a very rich heritage of Romanesque and Gothic architecture, and the historicist revivals of the late nineteenth century successfully exploited this source. Gothic is very evident in Galicia in the famous pilgrim centre of Santiago de Compostela, and in Castille, Valencia, Ciudad Real and Asturias. Andalusia has its Moorish and *mudéjar* architecture, but is also the home of the best examples of *plateresco*, a Spanish variant of renaissance style, characterized by particularly elaborate decoration of the façades.

Towards the end of the nineteenth and the beginning of the twentieth century, the whole of Spain, especially the north, was affected by the changes brought about by industrialization. All the large cities acquired railway stations, some notable examples being at Valencia and Toledo, the Estación de Francia in Barcelona, the Estación de Atocha in Madrid and the Plaza de Armas in Seville. Elegant covered markets were also built in Barcelona, Valencia and Seville. Public architecture was either art nouveau or an eclectic blend of the main European styles: Catalonia, for example, was deeply influenced by the local variant of art nouveau, Catalan Modernism.

In the late 1920s two contrasting trends began to appear in Spanish architecture. One derived from the European movement towards modernity exemplified by Walter Gropius or Le Corbusier. This trend was well represented in the Barcelona International Exhibition of 1929, which featured the most typical symbol of this tendency, the German pavilion by Mies van der Rohe. From this there developed, extending during the following years to Madrid and San Sebastián, a movement associated with the **GATEPAC** group around José Luis **Sert**. By contrast, in this same year, Seville took a different path with the Ibero-American Exhibition. The complex consisting of the Parque María Luisa, the national pavilions and the Plaza de España was a splendidly successful exploitation of local traditions and the Andalusian architectural heritage. This expression of regionalism owed a great deal of its effectiveness to Aníbal González as well as to the participation of the celebrated French garden designer, Forestier. A comparable approach was adopted by Victor Eusa in Navarre, Rafael **Masó** and Francesc Folguera in Catalonia (creators of S'Agaró, a very successful garden-city on the Catalan coast) and Giménez Lacal, Cendoya and Anasagasti in Andalusia (responsible for the Carmen de Rodríguez-Acosta in Granada).

Original creative architecture came to a complete halt during the Civil War (1936–9). In the immediate aftermath, resources were scarce and the style subsequently favoured by the dictatorship was not noted for refinement. But gradually this official architecture improved under the influence of Italian 'fascist' architecture, while overall a certain relaxation of the climate allowed some very interesting projects to emerge, despite the relative isolation and apathy. It was during the post-war years that **Coderch**, one of the great figures of Spanish architecture, began to make his mark in Barcelona, together with other leading figures such as **Moragas** or **Sostres**. In Madrid, de la **Sota** began to create works of great importance, followed a few years later by **Sáenz de Oiza**, who revitalized the concept of monumental architecture. In Barcelona the intellectual debate on architectural issues was stimulated by the Grupo R, active in the 1950s and including among others Sostres, Coderch, Moragas and the young Bohigas who was to become one of the most notable influences on Catalan architecture. In fact it was Bohigas who was to redefine the bases of architectural policy in Catalonia after the end of the dictatorship (1976).

In the 1970s it was above all in Barcelona that trends were being set, and young teams of architects were becoming known. As well as a marked influence of Italian Design there was the impact of **Interiorism**, and the appeal of the neoclassical and a well-grounded rationalist school. All this created an architectural scene of great diversity, which, with the approach of the 1990s, was intensified by the huge amount of construction activity necessitated by the Olympic games of 1992.

In the last years of the dictatorship Rafael **Moneo**, soon to become a leading name in Spanish architecture after 1975, began to practise in Madrid. Moneo's very varied output displays great flair for monumental projects, as well as refinement, simplicity and erudition. The transformation which he wrought in the Atocha railway station is a measure of his talent. Also in Madrid, **Navarro Baldeweg** introduced an interesting element of plasticity with his complex architectural creations.

In the 1980s and 1990s the Basque country and Navarre pursued their own distinctive paths, characterized by greater attachment to traditional architectural values, and the use of forms deriving from historic styles: the leading names here are **Iñíguez**, Ustarroz, **Linazasoro** and Garay.

In Andalusia, the most notable architectural projects after 1985 are concentrated in Seville and Cadiz. The predominant taste among the leading contemporary Andalusian architects is heavily influenced by the Portuguese Alvaro Siza, creator in the 1990s of a remarkable Museum of Fine Arts in Santiago in Galicia. This approach involves a re-interpretation of the kind of architectural expression characteristic of the historic avant-garde (Mies, Le Corbusier etc.) which is stripped down to its essentials. It is a very pure architecture, of striking white shapes, represented mainly by Antonio **Cruz**, Antonio Ortiz and Guillermo Vásquez Consuegra. As coincidence would have it, Seville and Barcelona both witnessed major events in 1929 and in 1992, when Barcelona's Olympics were matched by Seville's **Expo-92**. The event stimulated a large number of projects: in addition to the spectacular modernization of the whole urban infrastructure, there were noteworthy new buildings, some of them designed by internationally renowned architects: for example, the new Santa Justa railway station, by Cruz and Ortiz.

In Valencia, the 1980s saw the appearance of a great architect on the international scene, Santiago **Calatrava**. He was in some respects a successor to **Candela**, an excellent architect-engineer who left his country for Mexico after the Civil War. Calatrava is the creator of a considerable number of large-scale projects of astonishing structural inventiveness, and is the Spanish architect best known abroad, with prestige buildings in France, Germany and other countries.

Architectural criticism is a development principally of the 1990s, if one excepts the writings of Rafols and Cirici Pellicer, and the impressive activity in this field of Oriol Bohigas. The most noteworthy critics are Sola-Morales, Montaner, Fernández Galiano, Lluis Permanyer and Llatzer Moix. The best-known specialized journals are *El Croquis*, *Quaderns*, *Architectura Viva*, *On* and *Diseño Interior*.

See also: architects; architecture, Francoist; architecture, post-Francoist

Further reading

El Croquis (1985–95) Madrid.

Gombrich, E. (1972) *Histoire de l'Art*, Paris: Flammarion.

Loyer, F. (1991) *L'art nouveau en Catalogne*, Paris: Biblio. Arts, Le Septième Fou.

Moldoveanu, M. (1996) *Barcelona: Architectures of Exuberance*, Barcelona: Lunwerg (an overview of different periods and styles, richly illustrated with photographs by the author).

Progressive Architecture (1993) New York, July 1993.

Rubió i Tuduri, N. (1927), *Diàlegs sobre l'arquitectura*, Barcelona: Cuadernos

Zabalbeascoa, A. (1992) *The New Spanish Architecture*, New York: Rizzoli

MIHAIL MOLDOVEANU

architecture, Francoist

Although in theory the term 'Francoist architecture' ought to apply to the architecture promoted by General Franco's regime during his personal rule from 1939 to 1975, it is not altogether meaningful to speak of a true Francoist architecture after 1960. Despite the dictatorial nature of the regime, Spain began from that date to experience, albeit in a modified form, influences from abroad, which relegated so-called Francoist architecture to second place. The term is primarily relevant, therefore, to the 1940s and 1950s.

Architectural practice underwent a radical change of direction after the Civil War of 1936–9. **GATEPAC** disbanded and most of the noted architects who were trying to modernize architectural idiom, following the example of Gropius or Le Corbusier, had to leave the country. Of those who remained, some adapted to the taste of the time, while others struggled through the first ten to fifteen years of Francoism, until they could pick up the threads of their professional lives. On the other hand, those architects who were not caught up in the modern movement found themselves suddenly in favour, because the new regime wanted large-scale monumental architecture which celebrated the grandeur of the past.

At first, Francoist architecture was massive and graceless in character, having much in common with that of Nazi Germany, but things soon began to change, partly through the efforts of a group of well-informed architects who knew how to adopt the required eclectic approach, and partly under the influence of Italian 'fascist' architecture. Mussolini's Italy experienced an enormous expansion in monumental architecture, including some very innovative creations. Long after the fall of

Mussolini, young 'Francoist' architects were going to Italy to study the work of, for instance, Terragni, Piacentini and Libera. Moreover, the central position occupied by the church in Spain meant that many of the interesting creations of this period are ecclesiastical buildings, like those of Victor Eusa in Navarre or Francesc Folguera in Catalonia. Indeed, a substantial number of architects who cultivated eclecticism continued to work on in Catalonia, reinforced by followers of ***Noucentisme*** who had survived the war. The most remarkable works produced by this group were those of Francesc Mitjans, Nicolau Rubio i Tuduri, Eusebi Bona, Luis Bonet, Adolfo Florensa and Raimon Duran Reynals. The younger generation which was trained in Catalonia during this period also produced interesting figures such as José Antonio **Coderch**, José María **Sostres** or Antoni de **Moragas**. In Madrid, Luis Gutiérrez Soto was noted for his very erudite architecture, while Francisco **Sáenz de Oiza** laid the foundations of a type of monumentalism more in keeping with international trends, which he continued to develop successfully after the death of Franco.

'Francoist architecture' also denotes the regime's policy of giving the institutions of state power an assertive physical presence in the cities, reflected in the number of new urban buildings constructed during this period. Sited for maximum impact, but with little concern for proportion, these constructions often had carved decoration, sometimes a fountain strategically placed at the entrance, a prominent balcony or a motif in bas-relief calculated to evoke civic pride. In rural settings, the legacy of the Franco era is seen in an impressive number of monuments and military barracks.

Unlike Hitler's Germany or Mussolini's Italy, Franco's Spain was never a wealthy country, and it is a matter for conjecture whether with more resources he would have evolved his own distinctive 'style', on the model of the two modern dictators who inspired him. The urge to leave his mark through the medium of architecture was just as great, but after the Civil War Spain was in such a ravaged state that mere survival had to take priority. WWII meant his abandonment by his erstwhile allies, and their subsequent disappearance from the scene. After the war, Franco lost international support, and his country was subjected for several years to an economic blockade. By the time conditions began to improve in the 1960s, Franco was too old and temperamentally disinclined to take an interest in architectural projects. Perhaps by then he had missed his vocation.

Nonetheless, in Madrid and all the larger cities there remain some fine government buildings, hospitals and military barracks which testify to what 'Francoist architecture' could have been.

See also: architects; architecture; architecture, post-Francoist

Further reading

Alomar, G. (1948) *Sobre tendencias estilísticas en la arquitectura española actual*, Madrid: Boletín de la Dirección General de Arquitectura (somewhat dated, but a useful guide to the Franco period).

Gombrich, E. (1972) *Histoire de l'Art*, Paris: Flammarion.

MIHAIL MOLDOVEANU

architecture, post-Francoist

Strictly speaking, the term 'post-Francoist architecture' would denote the development of architecture in Spain after the death of Franco in 1975. In reality, however, Francoist architecture is a somewhat vague concept as regards architectural style or approach, particularly from the 1960s onward (see also **architecture, Francoist**). The last fifteen years of Franco's dictatorship were characterized principally by the limitations imposed by censorship and self-censorship, which delayed the arrival in Spain of some forms of architectural expression. It was precisely these restrictions, indeed, which arguably facilitated the upsurge in creativity which followed the demise of the dictatorship. The fact that this took place without violence created a favourable climate for architectural work of considerable diversity. There were no 'victims': architects who had been practising in the last years of the Franco regime continued to do so, often consolidating their international reputation as the result of wider contacts, while their younger colleagues followed their own distinctive paths, willing to learn the basics from their elders, but rapidly putting them into practice in their own way. This is clearly illustrated by the fact that for the major architects of the 1960s or 1970s, such as **Coderch**, **Milá**, **Correa** or **Sáenz de Oiza**, the death of Franco made no noticeable difference to their architectural style. They received more varied commissions and enjoyed wider influence, but their creative activity as such showed no break with the period immediately before.

Nevertheless the change of regime was important. The country experienced a period of prosperity, and architects shared in the increased influence which intellectuals in general exercised on the administration. There were numerous long-term and ambitious building projects, a spectacular surge in urban renewal, and unprecedented activity in all spheres of civic and industrial architecture. Whereas in the 1960s the relative backwardness of Spanish architecture had been a matter for regret, in the 1980s and 1990s Spain became a model for other countries to follow, not simply because of the prestige of a few high-profile figures, but because the death of Franco seemed to release a burst of creativity that affected the whole country, ranging from very modest constructions to large-scale complexes. Previously it was rare to find examples of contemporary architecture outside Madrid, Barcelona or San Sebastián, but now high-quality modern works were being produced practically everywhere in Spain.

The established centres of twentieth-century architecture nevertheless reflected this new creativity more obviously than the newer ones. Thus Barcelona, where architecture had been a central concern of public life for over a hundred years, acquired an impressive number of new buildings, partly as a result of hosting the Olympic Games in 1992. The architect Oriol **Bohigas** was one of the principal instigators of urban policy in a city which was home to several teams of young architects producing work of high standard. They include Bach and Mora, Garcès and Soria, Torres and Martínez Lapeña, **Tusquets** and Díaz, **Freixes** and Miranda, Pinon and Viaplana, Ferrater, **Bofill**, **Miralles** and Arribas. Furthermore, the 'giants' of the international scene were invited to build there, for instance Isozaki, Foster, Calatrava, Gregotti, Siza, Meier, Skidmore, Owings and Merrill and Gehry.

In Madrid the trend for large-scale work is well represented by architects such as **Moneo** and **Navarro Baldeweg**, and it was also in the 1980s that the most complex works of Sáenz de Oiza, a well-known architect of the 1950s and 1960s, came to fruition. Seville also has witnessed a boom as the result of the International Exhibition **Expo-92**, involving many world-class architects: Ando, Grimshaw, Aulenti, Calatrava, Makowets, Viguier and Jodry. The major influences on contemporary Andalusian architecture are somewhat different from those in other regions of Spain. The Portuguese architect Alvaro Siza has been a major source of inspiration for Antonio **Cruz**, Antonio Ortiz and Vásquez Consuegra in particular. In the Basque region and Navarre the work of **Linazasoro**, Garay, **Iñíguez** and Ustarroz displays a regionalist approach of a very high standard, and new teams are setting up in the Balearics and Galicia.

An important factor in the flowering of the profession at local level is the network of colleges of architects. Each region has a college which enjoys a high degree of autonomy, compared with architectural organizations elsewhere in the EU. The college performs a variety of functions, acting as a professional union, bank, social security office and centre of cultural activity. In this latter role its contacts throughout the world, and the exchanges resulting from them, are impressive. All this means that the profession is better defended, better administered and better informed than ever before, and is a model of good practice.

See also: architects; architecture; Modernism; *Noucentisme*

Further reading

Loyer, F. (1991) *L'art nouveau en Catalogne*, Paris: Biblio. Arts, Le Septième Fou.

Moldoveanu, M. (1996) *Barcelona: Architectures of Exuberance*, Barcelona: Lunwerg (an overview of different periods and styles, richly illustrated with photographs by the author).

Rubió i Tuduri, N. (1927), *Diàlegs sobre l'arquitectura*

(Dialogues on Architecture), Barcelona: Cuadernos.
Levene, R.C., Márquez Cecilia, F. and Ruiz Barbarín, A. (1990) *Arquitectura española contemporánea, 1975–90*, Madrid: El Croquis Editorial.
Zabalbeascoa, A. (1992) *The New Spanish Architecture*, New York: Rizzoli

MIHAIL MOLDOVEANU

Ardanza, José Antonio

b. 1941, Elorrio (Vizcaya)

President of the autonomous Basque government

Ardanza joined the youth section of the **PNV** in 1961. He studied law and on graduating worked for the savings bank linked to the co-operative movement in Mondragón.

In 1979 he joined the PNV and was elected mayor of Mondragón, retaining that position until 1983 when he became leader of the provincial government of Guipúzcoa. He replaced Carlos Garaikoetxea as leader of the Basque autonomous government in 1985. Ardanza's tact and discretion have made him popular with nationalists and non-nationalists alike. He retired in October 1998 and is expected to be replaced by Juan Joseé Ibarretxe.

JOHN SULLIVAN

Areilza, José María de

b. 1909, Portugalete (Vizcaya)

Diplomat and politician

Though a supporter of Franco until the 1960s, Areilza became convinced of the need for reform, and evolved towards support for a conservative democratic monarchy, resigning as Ambassador to Paris in 1964 to become political secretary to the Pretender, Don Juan de Borbón. On the death of Franco, he became Foreign Minister in the Arias Navarro government, but refused to serve in the **Suárez** cabinet formed in 1976. He failed to win the leadership of **UCD**, and helped to found Coalición Democrática (Democratic Coalition), which later became one of the components of the **PP**.

EAMONN RODGERS

Argenta, Ataúlfo

b. 1913, Castro Urdiales (Santander); d. 1958, Madrid

Pianist and conductor

Argenta studied piano in the Madrid Conservatory, later moving to Belgium and Germany, where he studied conducting under Carl Schuricht. He obtained a teaching post in the Kassel Conservatory, but returned to Spain in 1939. He played piano and celeste with the National Orchestra, and began his career as a conductor with the Spanish Radio Orchestra. Argenta became conductor of the National Orchestra in 1945. During his relatively short career, he made many orchestral recordings, some of which were still being issued in the 1970s.

EAMONN RODGERS

Aritzeta i Abad, Margarida

b. 1953, Valls (Tarragona)

Writer

A professor at the University of Tarragona, Aritzeta has also worked in radio and won a number of prizes for her Catalan fiction. Her stories and novels range from realistic to delightfully unreal, exaggerated or absurd. Topics include the environment, gender changes, ageing, the Native Americans of Canada, political cover-ups, and manipulation of the media and language. She is also active in cultural journalism and literary criticism, contributing articles to numerous arts magazines in Catalonia.

Her first novel, *Quan la pedra es torna fang a les mans* (When Stone Turns to Mud in Our Hands) (1981), won the Víctor Català Prize, and *Un febrer a la pell* (A February Under the Skin), set against the background of the ***Tejerazo*** of 23 February 1981, won the Sant Jordi Prize. Aritzeta's narrative is wide-ranging in form and style as well as theme; she has successfully crafted **detective fiction**, **science fiction**, and imaginative adventures. Her public is also varied, including subway commuters, literary critics, and children.

Addressed to young people but intriguing enough for any suspense fan is *Un rock d'estiu* (A Summer Rock Band) (1992), with the narrator(s) shifting between singular and plural in the first person. Teenagers trying to launch a hard rock group and at the same time take vengeance on authority figures, especially the stodgy old English professor, find that things are not as simple as they thought, and that perhaps they bit off more than they could chew. The language is colloquial and captures the frustrations and fantasies, the hopes and disappointments of the volatile group.

A tribute to Aritzeta's great versatility and imagination, *Atlàntida* (Atlantis) (1995) draws on a number of sources: several mythologies in addition to the legend of the lost island, Catalan folklore, and the beloved nineteenth-century poet and priest, Jacint Verdaguer, who wrote a long and splendid work by the same name. An adventure novel in which humans, semi-gods, and fantastic beings cohabitate, the narration revolves around a quest for fertility: a tender shoot must be returned to a devastated land to restore it to health and well-being.

In *L'home inventat* (The Invented Man) (1996), Aritzeta plays literary games with the detective genre. The protagonist is a writer of mystery novels who proposes a macabre scheme to fend off boredom. She uses real writers and has them assassinated in her fiction, but finds more reality than she expected intruding into her plan.

Aritzeta is a prolific writer whose work offers us a puzzle for our time while exploring universal problems with humour and elegance.

Further reading

McNerney, K. (1991) 'The Feminist Science Fiction of Margarida Aritzeta', in B. Lawton and A. Tamburri (eds) *Romance Languages Annual*, West Lafayette, IN: Purdue Research Foundation, pp. 488–90.

KATHLEEN McNERNEY

armed forces

Until well into the 1980s, the armed forces in Spain constituted a political institution rather than a means of defence. Throughout the nineteenth century, the army had regarded itself as the ultimate arbiter of national life, enriching political terminology with a new term, *pronunciamiento*, which means a military rising in favour of a stated political aim. The **Civil War** of 1936–9, when Generals Mola and Franco declared against the Second Republic, can be seen as the most recent in a long line of similar ideologically motivated insurrections.

The outcome of the Civil War compounded the institutionalization of the armed forces, for they were seen, not as an organization entrusted with the defence of all citizens, but as the embodiment of the aspirations of the victorious side. The defence and armed service portfolios in Franco's cabinet were always held by high-ranking officers. Serving army officers were commonly seconded to command positions in the police and the **Civil Guard**. Military service was compulsory, and conscientious objection was not recognized, refusal to serve being punished by long terms of imprisonment. The Organic Law of the State (1967) copper-fastened the political role of the armed forces by making them responsible for 'the defence of the institutional system', which in effect meant the suppression of internal dissent. Terrorist crimes, and the catch-all offence of 'disrespect to the armed forces', were tried by court-martial, as the Catalan theatrical group Els **Joglars** found to its cost in 1977, even after parliamentary democracy had already been re-established.

Though an integral part of a highly militarized regime, the armed forces were poorly funded and equipped, even after the **American bases agreement** of 1953. In the mid-1960s, 82 percent of the armed forces budget went on pay. Total expenditure per member was one-third that of Italy, and less than one-sixth that of France or Britain. Pay and promotional structures for career officers were poor by comparison with other European countries, though better than the average wages of their civilian compatriots. Until the reforms of the 1980s, promotion was on strict seniority, which both militated against professionalism, and also created a top-heavy structure, with a high proportion of officers to other ranks: in 1975, there were 24,000 officers to 220,000 other personnel.

The political influence of the armed forces remained strong even after Franco's death, so much so that in September 1976 Adolfo **Suárez** felt constrained to submit his plan for political reform to a meeting of the armed service ministers, the Captains-General of the nine military regions, and the Chiefs of Staff. This virtually conceded to the armed forces the role of monitoring the transition to democracy. Their statement that they would support 'whatever opinion can be contained in the institutional order and its legitimate development' carried the ominous implication that they still reserved the right to veto any development which they considered excessively radical.

The interventionist instincts of the armed forces were fostered by the continuing deference shown by politicians during the years after the restoration of democracy. Provocative speeches by serving officers of extreme right-wing views went unpunished, and even blatant breaches of discipline attracted derisory sentences. For example, in October 1977, a Civil Guard commander in Málaga, **Tejero**, created a potentially lethal confrontation by sending his men to control a legal demonstration, armed with live ammunition rather than riot gear. Tejero's only penalty was a month's confinement to barracks, after which he was given a desk job. This kind of episode simply encouraged the tendency towards political plotting, compounded by the reluctance of the military intelligence service, the CESID, to pass on to the authorities evidence of military conspiracies against the elected government.

It was the attempted coup known as the ***Tejerazo*** (1981) which finally strengthened the hand of the government in asserting civilian authority over the armed forces. Already, certain reforms had been instituted in the late 1970s by the Defence Minister, General **Gutiérrez Mellado**. Restrictions on political activity were imposed, and military jurisdiction over terrorist offences was abolished. A clear line of command was established from the three branches of the armed forces to a newly-established Joint Chiefs of Staff Committee, and onward to the government. The first reform of the standing orders, the *Reales Ordenanzas* (Royal ordinances) since the eighteenth century came into force in 1979, and in the following year the jurisdiction of courts martial was restricted to military personnel. In 1981, the military authorities were given the power to remove incompetent officers from the active list, and selection procedures for promotion on merit to ranks above major were introduced. Despite some wavering in the government's resolve, and its apparent willingness to continue to bear the high cost of an over-staffed military establishment and a very generous retirement scheme, these measures indicate the attempts of successive administrations to depoliticize the armed forces and introduce greater professionalism. Much of the credit for this belongs to a civilian, Narcís **Serra**, who served as Defence Minister from 1982 to 1991.

The most effective measure, however, was the decision taken in the wake of the *Tejerazo* to press ahead with negotiations for entry to **NATO**, which was ratified in 1982. Though the Spanish armed forces are not fully integrated into the command structure of NATO, membership provided opportunities not only for modernizing equipment, but also for an internationalization of their role. Since 1989, Spanish military personnel have taken part in UN peace-keeping activities, notably in Bosnia, where they suffered casualties, and were involved in the UN-sponsored blockade of Iraq during the Gulf War of 1990–1. By 1992, Spain had the highest number of officers serving under UN auspices.

See also: Civil War; Franco Bahamonde, Francisco; *golpismo*; history; politics

Further reading

Hooper, J. (1995) *The New Spaniards*, Harmondsworth: Penguin (chapter 8 is an excellent, clear account of the political role of the armed forces, and their development since 1975).

Ross, C.J. (1997) *Contemporary Spain: A Handbook*, London and New York: Arnold (chapter 4 provides a useful summary).

EAMONN RODGERS

Armendáriz, Montxo

b. 1949, Olleta (Navarre)

Filmmaker

After a series of shorts on regional themes, such as *Rivera navarra* (Navarrese Riverside), his first film *Tasio* (1984), produced by Elías Querejeta, was well received. Since then his films have explored contemporary social problems of teenage suicide and drug addiction, as in *27 horas* (27 Hours) (1986), of immigration, as in the prize-winning *Las cartas de Alou* (Alou's Letters) (1990), and of the violent anarchic youth of Madrid in *Historias del Kronen* (Kronen Stories) (1994). With *Secretos del corazón* (Secrets of the Heart) (1996), enthusiastically received at Berlin, he has returned to the warmth and intimacy of his first film.

EAMONN RODGERS

Armiñán, Jaime de

b. 1927, Madrid

Filmmaker

Armiñán works as television director, scriptwriter and film director. In the 1970s he co-directed with **Borau** *Mi querida señorita* (My Dear Miss) (1971), a compassionate story of a transsexual, and *El amor del Capitán Brando* (Captain Brando's Love) (1974). His study of the relationship between the elderly hero and the young girl (played by Ana Torrent) in *El nido* (The Nest) (1980) was a major success. Other films of the 1980s include the comedy *Stico* (1984) and *La hora bruja* (The Witching Hour) (1985). Two films of the 1990s, *El otro lado del túnel* (The Other End of the Tunnel) and *El palomo cojo* (The Lame Pigeon) were selected for showing at Berlin and San Sebastián respectively.

EAMONN RODGERS

Arrabal, Fernando

b. 1932, Melilla (Spanish Morocco)

Writer

Although Arrabal has lived in France since 1955, his roots are profoundly Spanish, deeply marked by a poverty-stricken childhood in the years after the Civil War. His work is haunted by the presence of a domineering mother and a father whom he never really knew but idolized. His father was arrested as a Republican in 1936, and vanished from prison in 1942.

Arrabal's early works led the drama critic Martin Esslin to classify him as an absurdist playwright, a rubric which applies mainly to the form of his plays, devoid of any substantial plot or verisimilitude. In plays such as *Le Cimetière des voitures* (*The Automobile Graveyard*), and *L'Architecte et l'empereur d'Assyrie* (*The Architect and the Emperor of Assyria*), Arrabal orchestrates the action either as ceremonies or gives it an underlying structure of repetitions and inversions. His novel *The Tower Struck by Lightning* (*La torre herida por el rayo*) unfolds with the chess moves of two players, which enact the memories of two bizarre opponents who nevertheless complement each other, much as white pieces need black ones to play.

Arrabal uses simple structures like game boards to unleash a flow of episodes marked by chaos, violence, obsessions, both comic and repulsive, as if he dismembered his own life and culture to rebuild it in dreams and nightmares reminiscent of Salvador **Dalí** and Luis **Buñuel**. The substance of his plays is deeply autobiographical, but left raw, unformed, as in dreams. His films and novels also share this introspective tendency. His first film *Viva la muerte* (Long Live Death) has the repulsive grip of a nightmare. The point of view is often that of a child witnessing, with eyes that cannot make sense, the violence and ceremonies of an adult world.

The later film *Odyssey of the Pacific* is representative of the best the author has to offer, once he stops toying with frivolous excess. It is also one of his least known works, indicating that his work may appeal more for the buffoonery than for a genuine and playful human vision that comes quietly to the surface now and then and is richly satisfying.

What is always present yet often hidden in

Arrabal's work is a childlike charm, a certain uninhibited festive play with life as he sees it. The writer is at heart an anarchist, although far more prone to mischief. He confounds and celebrates this confusion for the sake of creating a fog from which a new order might emerge. Beneath the posturing are the charming views of a writer who never wants to grow up, fortunately.

Further reading

Arata, L.O. (1982) *The Festive Play of Fernando Arrabal*, Lexington, KY: University Press of Kentucky (focuses on Arrabal's theatre up to 1972 and places it in a critical historical context as a form of festive play).

Arrabal, F. (1993) *Pic-Nic, El triciclo, El laberinto*, Madrid: Catedra (this new edition by Angel Berenguer contains a thorough biographical chronology and bibliography up to 1984).

LUIS O. ARATA

Arrese y Magra, José Luis

b. 1905, Bilbao; d. 1986, Corella (Navarre)

Politician

A founder member of **Falange** in 1933, Arrese distinguished himself by his emphatically pro-Nazi stance before and during WWII, even advocating in 1943 that Spain declare war on the side of the Axis. As Secretary-General of the **National Movement** (1941), he helped to absorb and emasculate the old, socially radical Falange and subordinate it to the political needs of the Franco regime. When Director of Press and Propaganda in the 1940s, he was responsible for setting up both Radio Nacional and the No-Do (Noticias y Documentos – News and Documentaries), the sole permitted supplier of cinema newsreels, which cinema-owners were compelled to project, on pain of heavy fines (see also **censorship**). In 1956, Arrese tried to institutionalize the National Movement and give it more clearly-defined role within the state, intending that it should continue to be the dominant political force after Franco's retirement or death. This plan, however, provoked determined opposition among monarchists and the military, who persuaded Franco that the succession problem would be better dealt with by an authoritarian monarchy. Another factor in the defeat of Arrese's plan was Franco's unwillingness to allow the creation of a power-base which might threaten his personal rule. Though Franco sympathized with Arrese, he moved him sideways into the politically less sensitive post of Minister of Housing. Arrese later resigned in 1960 in protest at restrictions on public spending.

Arrese's career illustrates the tensions among the various interests and factions in the Franco regime, often wrongly supposed to have been a rigidly monolithic structure.

See also: Franco Bahamonde, Francisco; Francoist culture; history

Further reading

Preston, P. (1993) *Franco*, London: Harper Collins (an outstanding biography, which gives a profound insight into every aspect of the Franco period).

EAMONN RODGERS

Arribas, Alfredo

b. 1954, Barcelona

Architect

Arribas distinguished himself in the late 1980s with several projects in Barcelona. His futuristic designs for bars and restaurants are a significant contribution to the growth of **Interiorism**, and their sympathetic reception by the public is a powerful vindication of the movement. Important examples are the establishments Network and Velvet (both 1987), Torres de Avila (1992), and Estándard (1993). The Gran Velvet (1993) and the Hirai Museum (1993, Marugame, Japan) are his main architectural achievements. His work has won numerous prizes, and in 1995 to 1996 he completed prestigious projects in Germany, such as the interiors of the Commerzbank and the Euronet complex, both in Frankfurt.

MIHAIL MOLDOVEANU

Arroyo, Eduardo

b. 1937, Madrid

Artist

Best known for his paintings and stage designs, Arroyo is also a creative sculptor, potter and printmaker. After moving to Paris in 1958, Arroyo established himself in the 1960s and 1970s as a painter in the *Realismo Crítico* (critical realism) style. Perennially interested in the theme of power, his ironical treatments of dictators, for instance in *Los cuatro dictadores* (The Four Dictators), bullfighters, generals and Spanish gentlemen aroused considerable controversy. He directed the biennial exhibition of plastic arts in Venice in 1976 and was one of the promoters of the exhibition *España Vanguardista 1936–76*. Later styles and series include portraiture, especially of artist friends, and series of urban subjects such as *Toda la ciudad habla de ello* (The Whole Town's Talking about it). In 1982 he won the National Prize for Plastic Arts. Notable among his paintings are *Velázquez mi padre* (My Father Velázquez), *25 años de paz* (Twenty-five Years of Peace, an ironic commentary on a Francoist slogan), *Miró rehecho* (Miró Recreated) and *Treinta años después* (Thirty Years On). His sculptures include a series of bronze heads of chimney-sweeps, and his stage designs include sets for works by Calderón, Fernando Arrabal and Janacek.

See also: painting; visual arts

EAMONN RODGERS

art collections

The best-known Spanish art collection is undoubtedly that housed in the **Prado Museum** in Madrid, and is an example of a collection that owes its origin to the donation to the public of privately owned works, in this instance a large part of the royal collection formed by the Hapsburg and Bourbon kings. Similarly the Museo Cerralbo, Madrid, is named after the 17th Marquis of Cerralbo, Enrique de Aguilera (1845–1922), who bequeathed his collections to the nation. Other beneficiaries of private generosity include the Museu d'Art de Catalunya (Catalan Museum of Art), which inherited most of the collection of Francisco de Asís Cambó y Batlle, a politician and banker who specialized in schools and artists not widely represented elsewhere, the Museo de Arte Abstracto Español in Cuenca, which houses abstract paintings collected by the painter Fernando Zóbel, the **Picasso** Museum in Barcelona, the **Dalí** Museum in Figueras, and the Evaristo Valle Museum in Gijón.

Many publicly owned collections derive originally from the convents and monasteries dissolved at the end of the eighteenth and beginning of the nineteenth centuries. The Museo de la Trinidad, for instance, was created in 1837 to preserve works of art confiscated from religious establishments in Madrid, Avila, Segovia and Toledo, a collection that was later incorporated into the Prado Museum. The Museum of Fine Art in Seville, which houses the next most important art collection after the Prado, was founded in 1835 for the same reason, and another major European art museum, the Museum of Fine Art in Valencia, founded in the previous century, acquired collections from similar sources at this time.

Paintings that have been entered for examination since the founding of the **Royal Academy** in 1752 form the basis of another large collection in Madrid, and the **Queen Sofía Museum**, re-opened in 1990 after extensive refurbishment, specializes in collections of modern art.

Many privately owned collections have been made available to the public, either as the result of purchase, such as that of Luis Plandiura (1882–1956) bought by the Museu d'Art de Catalunya, or that of Baron Thyssen-Bornemisza (see also **Thyssen-Bornemisza Museum**), or by the creation of private foundations to preserve and display works of art, such as the Fundación Casa de Alba, established by the 18th Duchess of Alba in 1975 in the Palacio de Liria in Madrid, which houses an important collection of European masters, the Fundación Joan **Miró** in Barcelona, established in 1971, and the Fundación **Tàpies** established in Barcelona in 1990.

Valuable collections have also been formed by major companies, notably that of the Spanish National Telephone Company, which includes works by Juan Gris, Eduardo Chillida and Luis Fernández and was brought together into a permanent exhibition in 1993; that of the Banco Argentaria, which in 1966 comprised some 3,000 pieces from the sixteenth century to the present day; and that of ICO (Instituto de Crédito Oficial – Official Credit Institute), in which the major artists of the 1980s are represented. A large collection of contemporary art is also held by the ARCO Foundation, established in 1987 to facilitate the purchase of works from commercial galleries exhibiting at the annual ARCO International Modern Art Fairs.

See also: art exhibitions; arts funding; arts policy; museums

EAMONN RODGERS

art exhibitions

Exhibitions of art have become an important part of modern Spanish culture. A survey in 1985 showed that 20 percent of the population over the age of 14 visited museums and art galleries twice a month, and special exhibitions mounted by the **Prado Museum**, most notably those on Velázquez in 1990, Ribera in 1992 and Goya in 1994, attracted huge national and international interest.

In addition to special exhibitions organized by **museums** which house major **art collections**, such as the Prado Museum, the **Queen Sofia Museum**, and the Art Museums of Seville and Valencia, exhibitions are hosted by a wide range of public and private institutions.

The **autonomous communities** and the *Ayuntamientos* (municipal authorities) are important cultural agents and organize exhibitions, some with a strong regional or local flavour. The autonomous community of Madrid, for instance, inaugurated its newly furbished salon in 1990 with *Madrid Arte 60*, creating a highly successful series with subsequent exhibitions on the 1970s, 1950s, 1980s and 1940s, and the Ayuntamiento hosts frequent exhibitions in its three major centres, the Museo Municipal, the Centro Cultural de la Villa de Madrid, and especially the Centro Cultural del Conde Duque. The **Generalitat** de Catalunya and the Ayuntamiento de Barcelona support exhibitions in the Museum of Modern Art in Barcelona such as those on **Modernism** and Informalism and in Valencia the Instituto Valenciano de Arte Moderno (IVAM), founded in 1989, hosts important exhibitions in the region. A very successful series of exhibitions of religious art under the generic title of *Las Edades del Hombre* (The Ages of Man) began in the Cathedral of Valladolid in 1988 where it attracted over half a million visitors and has continued in the Cathedrals of Burgos, León, Salamanca, Antwerp and, in 1997, Burgo de Osma.

Other major public bodies which regularly mount exhibitions are the **Royal Academy** which celebrated its 250th aniversary in 1994 with a display of masterpieces from its own collection, the National Library, and each year since 1981 the Palacio de Velázquez in the Retiro Park in Madrid has been home to the *Salón de los 16* in which artists present their most recent works.

Private sponsors also play a very important role in the promotion of art exhibitions. As well as foundations such as the **Juan March Foundation**, the Miró Foundation, the Tàpies Foundation and the Thyssen-Bornemisza Foundation (see also **Thyssen-Bornemisza Museum**), the larger financial and business enterprises contribute enormously to the cultural life of Spain (see also **arts funding; Law of Patronage**). Prominent among these are the **Cajas de Ahorros** (Savings Banks) especially the Caixa de Pensions based in Barcelona, which is able to mount international exhibitions in both Barcelona and Madrid, and Cajamadrid which has promoted exhibitions on, for example, the Madrid School, Seven Spanish painters of the Paris School and, in conjunction with the Goethe Institute, contemporary German art. In addition to their general sponsorship of the arts, major banks such as Central Hispano, Banco Exterior and in particular the **BBV**, and companies such as Grupo Tabacalera and Mapfre Vida mount a wide range of exhibitions such as that of the BBV on the Golden Age of Dutch painting in 1994, and that of Mapfre Vida on Sorolla in 1995.

Add to this wide range of art exhibitors the increasing number of commercial galleries operating especially in Madrid, Barcelona and Valencia and it is easy to understand why a National Centre for Exhibitions and Artistic Promotion has been set up to sponsor, organize and co-ordinate exhibitions in Spain and abroad.

See also: art collections; museums

EAMONN RODGERS

arte y ensayo

This name (literally 'art and experimentation') was given to special cinemas licensed in 1967 for the showing of foreign films in undubbed and uncut versions. In tourist centres, provincial capitals, and cities with more than 50,000 inhabitants, special auditoria could be set up, to accommodate a maximum of 500 spectators. The measure was discriminatory, since ticket prices were higher than in the commercial cinema. The increasing reluctance of the authorities to permit foreign films to be shown in their entirety led to the disappearance of these cinemas by 1971.

See also: dubbing; film and cinema; Francoist culture

EAMONN RODGERS

arts funding

Funding for the arts derives from three main sources, direct subsidies from government bodies, indirect aid through tax incentives and private financing.

Direct funding from tax and other revenue is provided at three levels, by central government in the guise principally of the Ministry of Education and Culture/Arts, by the autonomous regional authorities and by municipal authorities. Central government funding supports institutions such the nineteen national **museums** most of which are in Madrid, the fifty or more state museums, the autonomous **Prado Museum** and **Queen Sofia Museum**, the National Library, the **Royal Theatre** and various theatres and concert halls. It also contributes 70 percent of the upkeep of over eighty cathedrals, makes capital grants to the regions and municipal authorities for large-scale building projects (e.g. the Valencia Institute of Modern Art (IVAM) and the Bilbao Municipal Art Museum), and subsidizes a wide range of cultural activities including the film industry (see also **film and cinema**). In the 1980s the overall arts budget increased by some 70 percent, but the 1990s have seen a series of reductions leading to cuts in arts subsidies, in capital grants to the regions, and in allocations to the museums. Building projects have had to be interrupted and 'spectacular' **art exhibitions** are less frequent in the face of diminishing funds and the rising costs of insurance and transport.

As a result of increased and increasing devolution the autonomous regions and municipal authorities are emerging as major funders of the arts, and this trend is set to continue with central government happy to transfer to them responsibility for buildings and events from which they derive tourist revenue. In 1995 the wealthy region of Catalonia and the city of Barcelona were the biggest spenders, though Madrid residents benefit from central government monies spent on national institutions in the capital.

Indirect public funding of the arts is by means of various tax reliefs. The **Law of Patronage** passed in 1994 regularized the part payment of tax by donating works of art to eligible institutions. These now include the various foundations which also enjoy a reduced corporate tax.

Finally a huge contribution is made by private individuals and institutions. Foundations such as the **Juan March** are major patrons of the arts, as are the **Cajas de Ahorros** (Savings Banks) which are required by law to devote half their profits to community works. The **Caixa** de Pensions of Barcelona funds among other things research in arts and science, chamber music recitals and a library service, and Cajamadrid and many others throughout Spain are active in the arts area. Major banks such as BBV, Central Hispano and Exterior de España and large business enterprises have set up cultural foundations and the larger universities also play an important role. Lastly the contributions of individual art lovers and societies of friends of the larger museums are valuable sources of income.

See also: art collections; arts policy

EAMONN RODGERS

arts policy

The main thrust of government policy on the arts since 1982 has been to put Spain back on the cultural map and to preserve its national heritage. This has involved the expenditure of large sums of money and the framing of new legislation.

An increase of some 70 percent in the arts budget between 1982 and 1989 funded initiatives in four main areas, and though this increase has not been maintained in the 1990s, they are still the main priorities. **Museums** have been major beneficiaries of government spending, the aim being to modernize and expand existing buildings, and increase the nation's collections, especially of contemporary works. The establishment of the **Queen Sofia Museum** in the eighteenth-century General Hospital of Madrid, and of the Thyssen-Bornemisza collection in the Palace of Villahermosa (see also **Thyssen-Bornemisza Museum**), the creation of a National Anthropological Museum in the former modern art museum, the refurbishment of the Americas Museum, the renovation of State Museums, the new Institute of Modern Art in Valencia (IVAM) and the Bilbao Municipal Art Museum are all examples of major capital expenditure.

A second priority is the funding of major **art exhibitions** and **art collections**. The Velázquez exhibition in the **Prado Museum** in 1990 attracted over half a million visitors, and art collections have been increased either directly through purchase, as of the Thyssen collection, and through sponsorship of the ARCO collection of modern art, or indirectly by tax incentives for the donation of works of art to eligible institutions.

Another priority is financial support for the film industry either directly via subsidies based on box-office receipts or for films of special merit, though these have had to be drastically curtailed, or indirectly by screen quotas, licence fees for **dubbing** foreign films and support for the showing of Spanish films abroad.

Funds have also been directed to the creation of new concert halls, such as the **Auditorio Nacional de Música** in Madrid and others throughout Spain, and to the renovation of others such as the Palau de la Musica in Barcelona. Many theatres have been refurbished, bodies such as the National Orchestras, the National Ballet, the National Dance Company (see also **national dance companies**) and the National Institute of Theatre and Music have had government backing and agreements have been set up between the regions, municipal authorities and managers of concert halls and theatres to co-ordinate their activities.

The other major concern of government is to preserve the cultural heritage of the Spanish people. Among other provisions the 1985 Law of Spanish National Heritage made it illegal to alter, sell or export without permission sites and objects listed on the General Register of Heritage Sites and Objects. This register is maintained and updated with the co-operation of the regions, and in 1986 a Board of Valuations for the Listing, Purchase and Export of Works of Art was set up under the same law. The thwarting of an attempt to auction Goya's *Marquesa de Santa Cruz* which had been illegally exported to London is the prime example of the government's determination to enforce this law.

See also: art collections; art exhibitions; arts funding; museums

EAMONN RODGERS

Arzallus, Javier

b. 1932, Azcoitia (Guipúzcoa)

President of the Basque Nationalist Party (PNV)

Javier Arzallus emerged as the **PNV**'s leading figure in the post-Franco period. Often controversial, he is seen by his opponents as exemplifying the unacceptable face of his party because of his alleged softness on **ETA** and its political wing, **Herri Batasuna**. His occasional statements emphasizing the racial distinctiveness of the Basques have led to him being portrayed by non-nationalist Basques as a nineteenth-century village reactionary. In contrast, Arzallus is immensely popular with PNV activists, who are not disturbed by his sometimes bellicose statements.

Arzallus is a native Basque speaker who entered a seminary at the age of 10. While a member of the Society of Jesus he studied in the universities of Zaragoza, Frankfurt and Berlin, and has degrees in law and political science. He left the Jesuits in 1967 and taught at Madrid University. On joining the PNV in 1968 he moved to Bilbao, where he practised law, and taught at the university of Deusto. He immediately became a leading member of the party. As the PNV revived at the close of the Franco dictatorship the surviving leaders from the Civil War period gave way to a new generation. Arzallus was elected to both the Vizcayan and the national committees in 1971. He became an MP for Guipúzcoa in 1977, and was re-elected in 1979. During the negotiations over the **constitution of 1978**, Arzallus was the main PNV spokesman in the Madrid parliament and an intransigent advocate of the restoration of the historic rights (*Fueros*) of the Basque country.

Arzallus' reputation as a hard liner dates from his reluctance to compromise on that issue, which led to him being removed from the negotiating team. At the end of 1979 he resigned from parliament to become President of the PNV, a position where his capacity for annoying rival political forces is not a handicap. In the early 1980s it was alleged that he urged leaders of ETA to continue their violent struggle in order to extract concessions from the Spanish government. In 1984 Arzallus clashed with Carlos Garaikoetxea, the charismatic leader (***lehendakari***) of the autonomous Basque government. Garaikoetxea wanted a centralized Basque country, whereas Arzallus and his supporters demanded the retention of the historic powers of the individual provinces. When Garaikoetxea was removed and broke away to form his own party, he was replaced by José Antonio **Ardanza**, a mild and conciliatory figure, whose strengths nicely balance those of Arzallus.

Those who are alarmed at Arzallus' calls for eventual Basque independence from Spain and his condemnation of state violence as terrorism pay insufficient attention to the subtlety encouraged by his Jesuit training. He is essentially a moderate politician, intensely loyal to his party. The contrast with Ardanza's caution and moderation is a division of labour and of temperament, rather than a potential division within the PNV.

JOHN SULLIVAN

Atencia, María Victoria

b. 1931, Málaga

Poet

María Victoria Atencia, one of the most accomplished Spanish poets of the contemporary period, was relatively unknown until the late 1970s. Her early books were published in small editions in her native Málaga and did not attract the attention of readers on a national level. After a long period of silence, she returned in 1976 with a remarkable book of poems entitled *Marta y María*. Her intricate poetic style would not have been widely appreciated in the literary climate of the 1950s and 1960s, a period in which most well-known poets were attempting to write in a more colloquial and less self-consciously 'literary' mode. Nevertheless, she found a ready audience in younger poets of the 1970s such as Guillermo **Carnero**, who helped to popularize her work among a select group of readers. Her work has been especially appreciated among her fellow poets. Another factor in her rediscovery was the growing interest in women poets beginning in the 1980s, when writers such as Blanca Andreu and Ana **Rossetti** began to publish books of poetry. Atencia's poetry, while benefiting from the boom in women's poetry generally, does not much resemble that of these younger women.

Atencia has been prolific in the 1980s and 1990s, solidifying her reputation with collections such as *Compás binario* (Duple Metre) in 1984 and *El puente* (The Bridge) in 1992. Her poetry is most notable for its stylistic subtlety, employing an intimate tone to present finely-tuned subjective reactions. Most of her poems are very short and employ the fourteen-syllable alexandrine line. While her poetry is not hermetic, its nuances demand a slow and attentive reading.

It is difficult to situate Atencia in relation to other contemporary Spanish poets. She wrote in isolation from the mostly male poets of the

'Generation of the 1950s' such as Claudio Rodríguez, Angel González and José Angel **Valente**. Some critics have linked her work to a specifically 'feminine' tradition, although she herself has rejected this notion. Her increasing use of literary and artistic intertexts in her books of the 1980s and 1990s suggests a connection with the 'culturalism' of Carnero and other poets of the 1970s. At the same time, however, her attitude to the literary tradition is less iconoclastic than that of these younger poets. Her style, while aiming for an almost classical perfection, is unmistakably original.

JONATHAN MAYHEW

Ateneo

Since its foundation in 1835, the Ateneo Científico, Literario y Artístico de Madrid (The Madrid Athenaeum) has hosted lectures and concerts, art exhibitions, courses and plays. The activities of its different sections gave it the character of a learned debating society that lived up to the triple mission implied in its title. With its excellent library, it was a constant channel of ideas, theories and movements, mixing seriousness and partisanship in varying proportions.

As well as the orthodox activities of an athenaeum, the Ateneo, in response to political and cultural circumstances, social mores and personalities, has been a place for members to drop into the ***tertulias*** to debate, not only abstract and academic topics, but the burning issues of the day. Like its close relative the café, the Ateneo is, above all, an oral institution where every conceivable subject is discussed, with differing degrees of knowledge. Politics have, however, coloured the Ateneo's activities to such an extent that we would have a better idea of its role if we added *político* to the three terms already in the title.

Dictatorships were never favourably disposed to the Ateneo in the past, and the period 1939 to 1975 was yet another period of intellectual darkness. Although the Ateneo remained open during the Francoist period, it was a time of silence, when certain topics could not be discussed, and of absences, when certain individuals could not be seen or heard. The story is in the names. In the years preceding the Civil War, lectures were given by Azorín, Maeztu, **Ortega y Gasset**, Gómez de la Serna, Pérez de Ayala, Benavente, Falla, Salinas, D'Ors, Menéndez Pidal, Américo **Castro**, Unamuno, Valle-Inclán, Azaña, Fernando de los Ríos, Besteiro, Indalecio Prieto, Alcalá Zamora, Madariaga, Marconi, Ludwig, Romains, Bergson, Malraux and Einstein, to name a few. By contrast, the post-1939 Ateneo was only a shadow of its past glories. And yet, dormant and muzzled as it was, the Ateneo managed to provide the student with a library, albeit a somewhat decimated one, the boarding-house dweller with heating, and old *ateneístas* with memories. It was as much as could have been expected from a cultural tomb.

More than five years after Franco's death, the Ateneo had not yet been granted its right to hold elections, an essential precondition for resuming its normal life after more than forty years of neglect. Whether it was because of its long tradition as a home for political opposition which no-one was keen to resurrect, the spirit of renewal during the transitional period did little to restore the Ateneo to the *ateneístas*.

Today, although the Ateneo's life is not threatened from outside, except by other institutions (Fundación Ortega y Gasset, Club XXI), its activities do not live up to its reputation, if one discounts nostalgia. The institution that once made history has been bypassed by history.

Further reading

Ruiz Salvador, A. (1971) *El Ateneo científico, literario y artístico de Madrid (1835–1885)*, London: Tamesis Books

—— (1976) *Ateneo, Dictadura y República*, Valencia: Fernando Torres.

ANTONIO RUIZ SALVADOR

athletics

Athletic activities are administered by the National Athletics Federation, which operates as a private entity and receives an annual government grant. Spanish athletes take part in national, European and international events, and made a strong contribution to Spain's sporting successes in the 1990s.

In the 1992 Olympic Games in Barcelona the gold medal for the 1,500 metre race was won by Fermín Cacho, who had already made a name for himself as the Spanish national champion for that distance, and for coming second in the World Indoor Championships in Seville in 1991. In 1993 he came second in the World Championships at Stuttgart and in 1994 first in the European Championships in Helsinki. He won the silver medal in the 1996 Olympics and another silver in the World Championships at Athens in 1997, a race in which Reyes Estévez won the bronze.

Another gold medal was won in the 1992 Olympics by Daniel Plaza in the 20 km walk, and bronze and silver medals in the 50 km walk were won by Valentín Massala in the 1996 Olympics and by García Bragado in the 1997 World Championships respectively. In 1995 Martín Fiz became world champion in the marathon and Abel Antón won the Berlin marathon in 1996. In the World Championships at Athens in 1997 Abel Antón won the gold, and Martín Fiz the silver, and the team was awarded the **Prince of Asturias Prize** for Sport for that year.

The World Championships in 1999 take place in Seville in a newly constructed Olympic stadium.

See also: sport and leisure

EAMONN RODGERS

Aub, Max

b. 1903, Paris; d. 1972, Mexico City

Writer

Max Aub was born to a German father and French mother who left France to live in Spain on the outbreak of WWI. On leaving school, Aub did not opt for a university education but instead became a travelling salesman. He indulged his passion for literature in the periods of leave between his business trips around Spain, which gave him an intimate knowledge of his adopted country and its linguistic diversity. Aub collaborated on the literary review *España*; his early works *Geografía* (Geography) and *Fábula verde* (Green Fable) show him to be a follower of **Ortega**'s theory of art for art's sake. However, he underwent a profound transformation when fascism loomed over Europe, inveighing against Ortega for persuading his generation to turn its back on the *pueblo* and popular culture. The outbreak of the Civil War found Aub in Madrid, and although his poor eyesight prevented him from becoming a combatant, he worked actively for the Republican cause, collaborating with Malraux in 1938 in a film version of *L'Espoir* (*Sierra de Teruel*, titled *Spanish Earth* in the UK). After the war, he was lucky to escape with his life: after fleeing Franco's Spain he was interned in prisons and concentration camps in France and Algeria for three years before finally being released to emigrate to Mexico.

Aub produced many novels, short stories, poetry and one-act plays. His enduring work, however, remains the collection of novels and short stories produced between 1943 and 1968, entitled *El laberinto mágico* (The Magic Labyrinth). Inspired by such writers as Jules Romains and Roger Martin du Gard, Aub uses the technique known as unanimism to portray the tortuous events of the Spanish Civil War and its after-effects in exile: hundreds of characters appear and re-appear – often in more than one novel – in a confused sequence of tragic events as the Second Republic is defeated in a war of attrition by the Nationalist armies. Many of the characters of *Field of Honour* (*Campo cerrado*), *Campo de sangre* (Field of Blood), *Campo abierto* (Open Country), *Campo del moro* (The Moor's Field) and *Campo de los almendros* (The Almond Grove) are taken from history and bear their real names; others ('Hope' for Hemingway) are disguised but nonetheless historical; finally, there are the myriad fictitious characters. Like the Spanish writers of the 'Generation of 1898', Aub is concerned to understand the 'problem of Spain'. His intellectual heroes debate the causes of the cataclysm that has overtaken them. A committed writer, Aub never allows his political engagement to descend into propaganda. If there is cowardice and treachery, it is just as likely to be encountered on his own side as on the enemy's. And towering above examples of human frailty and degradation amidst this holocaust are portrayals of human love, loyalty and sacrifice.

Further reading

Thomas, G. (1992) *The Novel of the Spanish Civil War*, Cambridge: Cambridge University Press (an analysis which contains frequent references to the novels and short stories of *El laberinto mágico*).

GARETH THOMAS

Auditorio Nacional de Música

Spain's National Concert Hall was begun in 1984 as part of a national plan for the construction of purpose-built concert halls throughout the country. From 1966 the **Royal Theatre** had served as Madrid's concert hall but it was to be restored to its original purpose as an Opera House. The new concert hall was designed by the architect García de Paredes and his team, who also drew up the designs for halls in Granada, Valencia, Cuenca and Murcia. The acoustics of the hall have been highly praised and were engineered by Lothar Cremer of Berlin who was also the acoustics engineer for the Berlin Philharmonia and Opera Houses. In 1990 one of the biggest organs in the world with 5,700 pipes was installed in the symphony hall. Built by Gerhard Grenzing it can function both as solo instrument and for accompaniment. A smaller one was planned for the recital room to be built by Gabriel Blancafort of Barcelona.

EAMONN RODGERS

autarky

The guiding principle of the Franco dictatorship's economic policy during the years 1939–59 was self-sufficiency or autarky. Numerous factors influenced this strategy, although historians continue to argue over the relative significance of each of them. The regime itself, and historians sympathetic towards Franco, have stressed that the country was affected by world war within months of the end of the Civil War and was then 'ostracized' by the international powers. The world conflict certainly made trade difficult. Moreover, the Allies were reluctant to provide Spain with food and other material when Franco's sympathy for Nazi Germany was so manifest. However, this ostracism was never total; Spain continued to trade with both the Axis powers and the Allies. Indeed, Britain had signed a trade agreement with the insurgents as early as December 1936. Although exports to Britain and France declined from 1939, trade with Germany and Italy rose spectacularly. In fact, considerable resentment was caused in Spain when it became known that food was being exported to Hitler's Germany in return for technical equipment.

Research on the early decades of the Franco dictatorship has drawn attention to the ideological commitment of the regime to autarky as an expression of extreme nationalism, a rejection of liberalism, a desire for national industrialization, a sympathy for fascist ideas, and a readiness to enter the war on the side of the Axis. Moreover, autarky fitted very well with a broader ideological belief in the need to seal Spain off culturally from the outside world. The making of the Francoist 'New State' was seen as being dependent upon a Catholic 'moral re-education' based upon the 'essential values of Spanishness'. The physical and psychological suffering that this largely self-imposed isolation created was seen as being a punishment for the 'sins' of those Spaniards who had questioned the social system of pre-Republican Spain.

Economic self-sufficiency was a disaster for the Spanish people. The attempt to achieve autarky in the wheat production sector was disastrous and, ironically, the country became dependent upon imports from the Perón regime in Argentina from 1946 until the early 1950s. Amid the already bleak landscape of mass executions in the immediate aftermath of the Spanish conflict, approximately 200,000 people died of hunger during the first few years of Francoism.

The regime finally discarded autarky in 1959 when a programme of economic liberalization – the so-called **Stabilization Plan** – was agreed. However, this did not signal an ideological change of course. Franco remained reluctant and was persuaded only by the manifest failure of autarky to industrialize the country.

Further reading

Harrison, J. (1985) *The Spanish Economy in the Twentieth Century*, London: Croom Helm (this deals with the strictly economic aspects of autarky).

Richards, M. (1996) 'Terror and Progress: Industrialization, Modernity, and the Making of Francoism', in H. Graham and J. Labanyi (eds) *Spanish Cultural Studies: An Introduction*, Oxford: Oxford University Press (an attempt to show the social and cultural aspects of autarky).

Viñas, A. (1984) *Guerra, dinero, dictadura. Ayuda fascista y autarquía en la España de Franco*, Barcelona: Crítica (a detailed study of the ideological roots of autarky).

MICHAEL RICHARDS

autonomous communities

Though the modern nation-state we call Spain is often dated from the union of the crowns of Castile and Aragon in 1479, there was still, up to modern times, considerable internal diversity among the different regions, in language, fiscal arrangements, and the structure of government. The **Basque**, **Catalan** and **Galician** languages remained vigorous within their own territories, Catalonia retained its own civil law in matters like inheritance, and the Basque provinces have traditionally enjoyed a large measure of administrative and fiscal autonomy.

Overall, however, political decision-making was concentrated in Castile, and Spain became increasingly centralized throughout the eighteenth and nineteenth centuries. The fact that Catalonia and the Basque country were also the most economically advanced areas of the peninsula made them increasingly resentful of domination by the centre, and when the opportunity presented itself during the Second Republic (1931–9), they achieved the status of self-governing units, with their own autonomous parliaments legislating on internal matters.

At the end of the Civil War, however, the Franco regime swept away all vestiges of autonomy and imposed a strictly centralist system of government. The militarist, Catholic tradition Franco represented was predicated on a unitary, Castilian-centred view of Spain, with no concessions made to the existence of other cultures. Four decades of rigidly authoritarian rule made it inevitable that the restoration of democracy after Franco's death would be seen in terms of self-determination, both for the people of Spain as a whole and for those regions which had historic claims to autonomy.

The democratically elected government which assumed office in 1977, dominated by the Union of the Democratic Centre (**UCD**), a broad coalition ranging from centre-right to centre-left, was not instinctively sympathetic to autonomist aspirations. Its leader, Adolfo **Suárez** was, however, shrewd enough to recognize that some concessions to Catalan and Basque sentiment were politically necessary, if the fledgling democracy was to survive. It was not only **regional nationalism** that threatened to destabilize the new parliamentary regime, but the attitudes of right-wing elements, especially in the **armed forces**, for whom any concession to 'separatism' meant the dismemberment of Spain.

The difficult task of balancing these opposing points of view fell to the working party which drafted a new constitution, approved by parliament in November 1978 and overwhelmingly endorsed by popular referendum in December (see also **constitution of 1978**). In its first article, the constitution proclaimed the essential unity of Spain, which largely calmed the fears of all but the extreme right. A later section stipulated, in very general terms, the conditions under which regions might accede to limited self-government. The specific provisions designed to solve the problems of the 'historic regions' (Catalonia, the Basque provinces and Galicia) were contained in an addendum which permitted regions which had had Statutes of Autonomy in the past to proceed immediately to assume interim powers of self-government and draft new Statutes.

Aspirations towards self-government were not, however, confined to those regions which had their own languages and a history of separate institutions, for not all the historic diversity within the peninsula was politico-cultural in this sense. There were economic imbalances which affected, principally, Andalusia, which also had its own claim to distinctiveness because of its long subjection to Moorish influence, and its geographical coherence. The constitution envisaged a number of arrangements which could enable other regions to gain a measure of autonomy if there was sufficient support within the region. What was called the 'fast route' entailed holding a referendum in which the Statute of Autonomy had to be approved in all the provinces making up the proposed region. The 'slow route' involved initial approval by the municipalities in the region, but thereafter extension of the degree of autonomy necessitated negotiation over a substantial period of time.

Faced with the prospect of a rash of autonomy demands, in 1981 the UCD government, with the support of the **PSOE**, a party with basically centralist instincts, drafted legislation which would have had the effect of slowing down the autonomy process, by giving the central government powers to override the legislative prerogatives of the regional assemblies. The Basques and Catalans successfully challenged the measure in the Constitutional Tribunal, and by the end of 1983, every province in the peninsula belonged to one of the seventeen autonomous regions: Andalusia, Aragon, Asturias, the Balearic Islands, the Canary Islands, Cantabria, Castile-La Mancha, Castile-León, Catalonia, Euzkadi (the Basque provinces), Extremadura, Galicia, La Rioja, Madrid, Murcia, Navarre, and Valencia.

This arrangement was a uniquely Spanish solution to a Spanish problem. Unlike, say, Canada, the USA or Germany, where the powers exercised by the provinces, states or *Länder* are standard across the federal territory, the competences of the individual *autonomías*, as they came to be called, vary. Certain structural features of the *Estado de autonomías* (State of Autonomies) are standard, such as the existence in each region of a prime minister, parliament and a high court of justice. In general, however, the 'historic' and 'fast route' regions have more freedom to determine their own internal affairs, while the 'slow route' regions are more regulated by central government. The system is far from tidy, but by making the relationship between each region and the centre analogous to a separate contract, it avoids the appearance of a federal state, which would have been unacceptable to the armed forces.

Though the arrangement can be described as a modest political success, albeit in an *ad hoc* way, a high price has been paid in administrative and financial terms. A further tier of bureaucracy has been inserted into the already cumbersome Spanish administration. Furthermore, the system of funding favours the regions with the largest measures of self-government, who are compensated for the range of the devolved responsibilities they fulfil by block grants from central government. A limited regulatory mechanism exists in the form of the *Fondo de Compensación Interterritorial* (Inter-Regional Compensation Fund), introduced by the PSOE government in 1985. However, since 1993, when minority governments (first PSOE, then **PP** from 1996) have had to be propped up by regional nationalist parties, the leaders of these parties, notably Jordi **Pujol**, have been able to negotiate larger transfers of fiscal independence, thereby widening the gap between the wealthier regions and the poorer ones.

See also: historiography; history; politics; regional parties; regionalism

Further reading

Hooper, J. (1995) *The New Spaniards*, Harmondsworth: Penguin (chapter 30 offers an excellent, concise account of the development of the autonomy process).

Newton, M. with Donaghy, P. (1997) *Institutions of Modern Spain*, Cambridge: Cambridge University Press (an excellent reference work).

Ross, C.J. (1997) *Contemporary Spain: A Handbook*, London and New York: Arnold (chapter 3 provides a detailed and clear account of the various issues arising from regionalism).

EAMONN RODGERS

autopistas

In the 1960s planning started on a network of motorways (*autopistas*) in the light of growing demand for road transport (see also **roads**). By the mid-1990s the total motorway network measured some 2,000 km. Motorways are built to a higher standard than highways (*autovías*) and normally require the payment of tolls for their use (*autopistas de peaje*) outside urban areas.

Motorways have been built largely by private companies with state support. These companies are granted the concession to build, maintain and operate the motorway for a given number of years. Where private companies have failed they have been taken over by the state.

KEITH SALMON

AVE

The first Alta Velocidad Española (Spanish High Speed Train) began operating from Madrid to Seville in April 1992, the first link in a network that will connect the capital of Spain with High Speed services in Europe by the beginning of the twenty-first century, reducing journey times by half (see also **railways**).

Construction of the first line, to Seville rather than Barcelona, was controversial because of the choice of route, the choice of European standard gauge of 1,430 mm rather than the Spanish gauge, the proportion of railway investment which it absorbed, the way contracts were awarded, the reliance on foreign technology, and the environmental impact.

Further reading

Banco Bilbao Vizcaya (1993) 'Alta velocidad: nueva era del ferrocarril', *Situación* 3–4 (a technical account of the High Speed line from Madrid to Seville).

KEITH SALMON

Avui

Avui (Today) is the only Catalan-language daily newspaper available throughout Catalonia. Though it has an important role to play in the process of **language normalization**, it has never in fact been able to compete successfully with its main Spanish-language rivals, *La* ***Vanguardia*** and *El* ***Periódico de Catalunya***.

Avui was founded in 1976 by Premsa Catalana, its appearance following closely on the death of General Franco at the end of 1975. It was therefore part of the wide-ranging process not just of political but also of linguistic democratization of Spanish society which followed the dictator's death, since the publication of a Catalan-language newspaper would not have been tolerated during his highly centralizing regime. Though it also includes news from the rest of Spain, *Avui* gives a clear priority to Catalonia and Catalan issues, and is partly funded by grants from the **Generalitat**. Despite this, *Avui*'s readership figures are by any standards disappointing, amounting to just over 150,000 per day, a figure which is less than one fifth of that of its main Spanish-language competitor, *El Periódico de Catalunya*.

The inability of *Avui* to make a serious breakthrough in the daily newspaper market is a cause of some concern to those who point out that, despite the process of language normalization which has been going on in Catalonia since the early 1980s, the media – both written and electronic – are heavily dominated by the use of Spanish. A possible explanation is the fact that a considerable section of Catalan society – particularly the older generation – is in fact illiterate in Catalan, never having learned to read it at school. Consequently, while Catalan radio and television present no problems for them, and are indeed highly successful, printed media in Catalan present a number of obstacles which they would simply rather avoid. This argument is not without force, but does not satisfactorily account for *Avui*'s continuing lack of success among younger Catalans, who still prefer to read *La Vanguardia* and *El Periódico de Catalunya*, or even Madrid-based newspapers such as *El* ***País***.

In fact, *Avui*'s general political position seems rather unattractive to a younger Catalan audience. It might be described as nationalist conservative, and is one of broad support for **CiU**, the leading nationalist party in Catalonia since the re-establishment of the Generalitat in 1978. While its editorials support the project of increased Catalan autonomy and increased use of the Catalan language, it is generally cautious and certainly could not be described as campaigning. Politically, like CiU, *Avui* can be seen as representing some of the views of sectors of the Catalan middle and upper-middle classes which, according to its own documentation, also form the bulk of its readership.

Further reading

Davies, J. (ed.) (1993) *The Mercator Media Guide*, Cardiff: University of Wales Press (contains short but informative entries on the main newspapers and television and radio stations in a number of minority languages, including Catalan).

HUGH O'DONNELL

Ayala, Francisco

b. 1906, Granada

Writer

A master stylist and an astute observer of human society, Ayala has won international recognition as a novelist, short story writer, and essayist, as well as a sociologist and social critic. He has received all of Spain's major **prizes**, including the 1972 Critics' Prize, the 1983 National Prize for Literature, the 1988 National Prize for Spanish Letters, and in 1991 Spain's most prestigious award, the **Cervantes Prize**. Election to the **Royal Academy** of Language in 1983 confirmed him as one of Spain's leading intellectuals. Since making Madrid his primary residence in 1980, he has contributed frequent essays on contemporary social issues to Spanish newspapers.

A native of Granada, Ayala became part of the literary vanguard of the late 1920s, when Spain was opening up to intellectual currents from across Europe, especially Germany, where he spent the year 1930. His earliest writings are two collections of short, experimental fiction, *El boxeador y un ángel* (The Boxer and an Angel) (1929) and *Cazador en el alba* (Hunter in the Dawn) (1930), marked by verbal experimentation and cinematographic techniques. Since his first novel in 1925, written while he was a law student in Madrid, he has written in a wide range of genres, including prose narrative, criticism, translation theory, sociology, cultural history and autobiography. In all these genres, he displays wide verbal scope, rhetorical authority and ironic vision.

A law professor at the University of Madrid when the Civil War began, Ayala served in the Republican government's Foreign Office. He left Spain just before Franco's victory in 1939, teaching first sociology and later Spanish literature at universities in Buenos Aires, Puerto Rico, and ultimately the United States. Although he made his first return visit to Spain in 1960, recording his impressions of post-war conditions in *España a la fecha* (Today's Spain), he continued to live and teach abroad. He discussed Spain again in a 1985 series of lectures, published as *La imagen de España* (The Image of Spain), which analyses the changes and continuities in the post-Franco era.

In the mid-1940s, Ayala began writing fiction again in Buenos Aires, where he knew such seminal figures as Jorge Luis Borges. Ayala's first post-war short story, 'El hechizado' (The Bewitched), which Borges considered one of the best in Hispanic literature, was included in the first of two collections published in 1949, *Usurpers* (*Los usurpadores*). *Usurpers* explores the abuse of power through the imaginative recreation of episodes from Spanish history. The second volume, *La cabeza del cordero* (The Lamb's Head), contains stories of fraternal conflict set in the context of the Civil War. Ayala's only full-length novels are two interrelated volumes, the 1958 *Death As a Way of Life* (*Muertes de perro*) and the 1962 *El fondo del vaso* (The Bottom of the Glass). Both examine the excesses and absurdities of political power in a Latin American dictatorship. He also founded two important literary magazines, *Realidad* in Buenos Aires and later *La Torre* in Puerto Rico. During these years, Ayala published numerous volumes on politics and sociology, including a frequently reissued textbook, *Tratado de sociología* (Treatise on Sociology).

His later volumes of short fiction continue his experimentation with narrative form and blur the boundaries between story, sketch, satire, essay, and autobiography. His ironic and at times acerbic view of contemporary life remains a constant in his 1955 *Historia de macacos* (Monkey Stories), his 1966 *De raptos, violaciones y otras inconveniencias* (On Abductions, Rapes and Other Inconveniences), and his 1971 *El jardín de las delicias* (The Garden of Delights). Ayala's complete prose narratives appeared in a single volume in 1969 in Mexico, since Spanish **censorship** still prohibited publication of his civil-war stories, *La cabeza del cordero*. Not until 1993 did Spain bring out his *Narrativa completa* (Complete Narratives).

A perceptive literary critic, Ayala was one of the first Spanish critics to analyse texts in terms of their narrative structure. In 1970 he wrote an influential early narratological study, *Reflexiones sobre la estructura narrativa* (Reflections on Narrative Structure), that helped ground Spanish criticism in a close reading of literary texts and give it a theoretical base. He himself has written penetrating analyses of the masterpieces of Spanish literature from the renaissance to the twentieth century.

In the 1980s Ayala brought out his three-volume memoirs, *Recuerdos y olvidos* (Recollections and Omissions). These superb vignettes together make up a fragmented autobiography that is by turns nostalgic and satirical. His observations on intellectual life on three continents exhibit his sharp eye for detail, and his engaging ironic style. The memoirs offer a portrait of Spain over nearly eight decades with intimate (and at times unflattering) glimpses of some of the country's best-known literary personalities.

Since his return to Spain in 1980, Ayala has been appreciated as an astute social observer and one of Spain's most accomplished living writers. Although the Civil War is a central metaphor of his fiction, his writing transcends historical and cultural specificity to offer a dispassionate and yet morally grounded meditation on human foibles and corruption. The pleasure of reading Ayala lies in the intelligence of his vision, his masterful control of narrative, the richness of his language, and his dark humour.

Major works

Ayala, F. (1930) *Cazador en el alba*, Madrid: Ulises (short fiction).

—— (1949) *Los usurpadores*, Buenos Aires: Sudamericana (short stories); trans. C. Richmond, *Usurpers*, New York: Penguin, 1996.

—— (1949) *La cabeza del cordero*, Buenos Aires: Losada (short stories).

—— (1955) *Historia de macacos*, Madrid: Revista de Occidente (short stories).

—— (1958) *Muertes de perro*, Buenos Aires: Sudamericana; trans. J. MacLean, *Death as a Way of Life*, New York: Macmillan, 1964; London: Michael Joseph, 1965 (novel).

—— (1965) *España a la fecha*, Buenos Aires: Sur (an essay on a returning exile's impressions of Franco's Spain).

—— (1966) *De raptos, violaciones y otras inconveniencias*, Madrid: Alfaguara (short fiction).

—— (1971) *El jardín de las delicias*, Barcelona: Seix-Barral (short fiction).

—— (1972) *Los ensayos. Teoría y crítica literaria*, Madrid: Aguilar (a compilation of Ayala's earlier volumes of literary theory and criticism).

—— (1982–91) *Recuerdos y olvidos*, 3 vols, Madrid: Alianza (autobiographical sketches).

—— (1986) *La imagen de España*, Madrid: Alianza (a collection of lectures on continuity and change in post-Franco Spain).

—— (1990) *El escritor y su siglo*, Madrid: Alianza (a compilation of Ayala's essays on the novel, literary theory and literature).

—— (1993) *Narrativa completa*, Madrid: Alianza (complete works of fiction).

Further reading

Bieder, M. (1979) *Narrative Perspective in the Post-Civil War Novels of Francisco Ayala*, Chapel Hill, NC: University of North Carolina (a very readable analysis of narrative strategy, irony and the role of the reader in *Muertes de perro* and *El fondo del vaso*).

Ellis, K. (1964). *El arte narrativo de Francisco Ayala*, Madrid: Gredos (an excellent introduction to Ayala's fiction).

Irizarry, E. (1977) *Francisco Ayala*, Boston, MA: Twayne (a well-written, perceptive overview of Ayala's life and writing).

Mermall, T. (1983) *Las alegorías del poder en Francisco Ayala*, Madrid: Fundamentos (a philosophical approach to Ayala's recurring preoccupation with structures of power in his fiction and essays).

MARYELLEN BIEDER

Azcona, Rafael

b. 1926, Logroño

Writer

Humourist, screenplay writer and novelist, Azcona,

part of the 'Mid-Century Generation', achieved considerable success as a satirist. *Vida del repelente niño Vicente* (That Repulsive Kid Vicente) (1955) and *Los muertos no se tocan, nene* (The Dead Aren't for Touching, Kid) (1956) belong to the genre of humour, as does *El pisito* (The Apartment) (1957), whose film version enjoyed great success. *Los ilusos* (Dreamers) (1958) satirizing Madrid's literary 'wannabes', and *Pobre, paralítico y muerto* (Pauper, Paralytic and Cadaver) (1960) present increasingly sombre humour, while *Los europeos* (The Europeans) (1960), is a soberly realistic 'social' novel, whose occasional satire gives way to critical intention and crude descriptions.

JANET PÉREZ

Aznar, José María

b. 1953, Madrid

Politician

Despite coming from a political family, Aznar did not take part actively in politics until the age of twenty-six, joining the **Popular Alliance** (*Alianza Popular*) after the general election of 1979. He was then employed as a civil servant in the Ministry of Finance regional office in Logroño, where within eight months he rose to be regional president of the Alliance. From 1981 he was appointed to different posts of the national staff. In 1982, he was elected as member of parliament for Avila. Between 1987 and 1989 he was head of the government of the **autonomous community** of Castile-León. In the following year, the party leader, Manuel **Fraga Iribarne**, appointed him Assistant General Secretary and a member of the National Executive Committee. When Fraga decided to concentrate on continuing his political career in his native Galicia, he proposed Aznar as his successor, a choice which was ratified at the tenth party conference in 1990. By then the party had changed its name to *Partido Popular* (Popular Party) (see also **PP**), which reflected its wish to throw off any lingering vestiges of its Francoist heritage.

Under Aznar's leadership, the fortunes of the PP improved slowly. Though it lost the elections of 1989 and 1993, its share of the vote increased, and in the European elections in 1994 it won 40 percent of the vote, more than the government party, the socialist **PSOE**. In regional and local elections in the same year its position also improved, making Aznar appear for the first time as a credible alternative to Felipe González. A narrow victory in the general election of March 1996 enabled Aznar to form a minority government, with the support of the Catalan **CiU** and the Basque **PNV** in the lower house (*Congreso*). The composition of the cabinet, which included four women and two independents, reflected Aznar's determination to present himself as the leader of a modernized and reformist centre-right party, representing a broad spectrum from Christian Democrat to liberal.

See also: political parties; politics

LOURDES LÓPEZ NIETO

B

balance of payments

Spain's balance of payments shows the usual cycle of oscillations between surplus years and deficit years. From the early 1960s to the early 1970s there was generally a surplus. But Spain's dependence on imported oil changed the situation drastically, following OPEC's quadrupling of the commodity price in 1973. Corrective action was not taken promptly by the Spanish authorities, and the ensuing current account deficit was not corrected until the peseta was devalued in 1977. The immediate improvement was short-lived, as OPEC imposed another price increase. The higher import bill at a time of exporting difficulties because of competition from newly industrialized countries caused deficits between 1980 and 1983, but the improving international situation and the increasing numbers of incoming tourists brought the account back into surplus between 1984 and 1987. Since then, trade relations and policy have been governed by Spain's position in the EU. Although Spain has exported much more to the EU since it joined, its import bill, encouraged by the liberalization of trade, has grown even more. Furthermore, a strong peseta policy (required by the ERM and the need to curb inflation), favoured importers over exporters. The result was a continuing current account deficit from 1988 onwards, which peaked in 1992. The turnaround did not come until 1995 after four re-alignments of the currency from 1992 to 1994.

Spain's deficit in merchandise trade can be made up by the surplus in services, essentially **tourism**. At between one-fifth and one-sixth of total income from visible and invisible exports, tourism is a major component of Spain's balance of payments: a buoyant tourist sector in 1995 and 1996 helped to bring the account back into the black. When earnings from tourism are insufficient to offset the deficit in visible trade, the gap has to be financed from the country's foreign currency reserves, from loans, or via inward foreign investment. The scale of foreign investment means that the balance on capital account consistently shows net inflows, so that despite the repeated current account deficits from 1988 to 1994 Spain's foreign currency reserves were on a rising trend. The only hiccup occurred in 1992 to 1993, when the turmoil in currency markets caused severe ERM instability of which the peseta was a major victim, the loss of confidence and three successive devaluations leading to serious capital outflows and a decline in reserves. Nevertheless by 1996 the upward trend in reserves had been re-established. With an import–export ratio in the region of 75 to 80 percent Spain is very unlikely in the foreseeable future to be able to finance its imports solely from its merchandise exports. As long as tourism remains a major earner, however, the balance of payments should never slip too damagingly into the red.

See also: economy; foreign trade; inflation; national debt

Further reading

Organization for Economic Co-operation and Development (yearly or biennial) *OECD Economic Surveys: Spain*, Paris: OECD Secretariat (a standard survey that covers all major aspects of the economy including the balance of payments).

C.A. LONGHURST

Ballesteros de Gaibrois, Mercedes

b. 1913, Madrid

Writer

Ballesteros de Gaibrois began writing journalistic articles in the 1940s. Her later collections of humorous sketches include *Este mundo* (This World) (1955), *Así es la vida* (That's Life) (1953) and *El personal* (Personnel) (1975). Although conservative and not particularly feminist, she writes of women, children and adolescents. Long novels include *La cometa y el eco* (The Kite and the Echo) (1956), *Eclipse de tierra* (Nothing is Impossible) (1954), *El perro del extraño rabo* (The Dog with the Strange Tail) (1953), *La sed* (Thirst) (1965), *El chico* (Boy) (1967), and *Taller* (Workshop) (1960), portraying seamstresses.

Further reading

O'Connor, P.W. (1985) 'Mercedes Ballesteros's Unsung Poetic Comedy: *Las mariposas cantan*', *Cuadernos Hispanoamericanos* 7, 1: 57–63 (a study of her comic drama by the leading expert on Spanish women's theatre).

Pérez, J. (1988) *Contemporary Women Writers of Spain*, Boston, MA: G.K. Hall, pp. 68–73 (overview of Ballesteros' novels and stories).

JANET PÉREZ

Ballesteros Sota, Severiano

b. 1957, Pedreña (Cantabria)

Golfer

National under-25s champion in 1974 and 1975, winner of the Vizcaya Open in 1974 and professional golf champion of Catalonia in 1976, Ballesteros began his victorious career in the major professional golf tournaments with the British Open in 1979, which he won again in 1984 and 1988, and the Augusta Masters in 1980 and again in 1983. In 1984 he won no fewer than five European tournaments, one American and one Japanese to take him to the top of the world rankings for that year. A regular player in Ryder Cup competitions, he was, after Tony Jacklin, the second youngest non-playing captain of the victorious European team in Valderrama in 1997.

See also: golf; sport and leisure

EAMONN RODGERS

Banco Argentaria

Argentaria is one of the largest and most successful of the newer banks, with 1,600 branches in Spain, shareholders' funds of 741,453m pesetas, clients' funds of 6,230m^2 pesetas, and pre-tax profits of 74,200m pesetas in 1995. Set up by the government in 1991 with a majority state shareholding and incorporating a number of state credit agencies such as the Caja Postal (Post Office Savings Bank), the Banco Exterior (Export Bank), Banco de Crédito Local (Municipal Credit Bank), Banco Hipotecario (Mortgage Bank) and Banco de Crédito Agrícola (Agricultural Bank), Argentaria quickly achieved a strong group identity. Its direct banking subsidiary, Banco Directo Argentaria, has established itself as the leading telephone bank in Spain. With some 3.5 million cards up to 1995, Argentaria is also the largest issuer of Visa Cards in Spain. The bulk of the share capital is now in the hands of institutional investors.

C.A. LONGHURST

Banco Central Hispano

BCH was created in 1991 through the merger of two of the old 'big seven' banks, Banco Central (1919) and Banco Hispano Americano (1900). It had long been felt that the interests and capital structure of these two high street banks complemented one another well and that a merger was a natural option. Banco Central held extensive shareholdings in the energy and transport sectors (including several wholly-owned subsidiaries), whilst the Banco Hispano Americano had interests in insurance and property. Earlier attempts at merger in 1965 and 1972 failed, due in part to lukewarm government support, but increasing competitive pressures in the late 1980s following Spain's entry into the EC and the attempt by the Kuwait Investment Office as leader of a group of shareholders to exert influence on the Board of Directors of Banco Central persuaded the two institutions to succeed at the third attempt. Today BCH is considered to be the third largest of the private banks in Spain. It has some 4 million retail customers within Spain and just over 2,500 branches (down from 3,600 at the time of the merger). It has the strongest international profile of any Spanish bank with 78 branches abroad and 10 commercial banking subsidiaries in various parts of the world. Unusually for a Spanish bank, 25 percent of the group's assets are outside Spain, and its shares are quoted in stock exchanges throughout the world. BCH continues to have large shareholdings in Spanish industry, including the large oil company CEPSA, the biggest of Spain's construction companies, Dragados, and the property company Vallehermoso. Its wholly owned subsidiary, Hispamer Banco Financiero, is the largest Spanish financial services company, and La Estrella and Banco Vitalicio are among the larger insurance companies. BCH also has important shareholdings in telecommunications, including cable television.

See also: banks; economy

C.A. LONGHURST

Banco de España

The Bank of Spain was established in 1856 as a private bank after the merger of two banks founded in the 1840s. In 1874 it was given exclusive rights by the government to the issue of the country's banknotes. Although the bank was not nationalized until 1962, when it ceased to have private shareholders, it had for some time been a private entity only in name, and in practice had operated under the aegis of the Ministry of Finance. Nationalization meant the loss of whatever vestiges of independence it might have had – nil in any case under the Franco regime – and its primary function was to implement the government's monetary policy and to exercise vigilance over the private banking sector. Ostensibly to impose prudent banking practices but in reality to facilitate government borrowing, the bank insisted throughout the 1960s and 1970s on the observance by the private banks of a variety of coefficients that obliged the latter to keep large deposits at the central bank. In fact the Bank of Spain's policing of the banking system failed to prevent the crisis of the late 1970s and early 1980s, when at least half of Spain's private banks became technically insolvent. The Bank of Spain's role then became one of banking doctor by arranging mergers and takeovers and administering the new Deposit Guarantee Fund created by the government to safeguard clients' monies and prevent a collapse of confidence. As late as 1993 the Bank of Spain had to intervene to prevent the collapse, as a result of fraudulent activities, of one of Spain's biggest banks, Banesto.

As a result of the Maastricht Treaty on European Union, the statutes governing the Bank of Spain were revised in the 1994 Law of Autonomy. This law modified the relationship between government and Bank, and gave the latter a degree of independence from political interference. The government cannot use the Bank of Spain to finance its budget deficits, not even in the short term; it can only call on whatever deposits it has at the bank. The Bank is charged with responsibility for controlling inflation, and to this end is free to set monetary policy, including interest rates, without being subject to instructions from the Ministry of Finance. The governor is obliged to inform the Parliamentary Committee on Economic Affairs of the Bank's policy and to declare at six-monthly intervals whether, or to what extent, established targets have been met. Less formally, the governor is expected to liaise with the private **banks** and **Cajas de Ahorros** in ensuring the smooth functioning of the financial system and has taken the initiative in trying to reconcile the different outlooks of these two types of financial institutions and preparing for the introduction of the single European currency.

Further reading

Chislett, W. (1996) *Spain 1996: The Central Hispano Handbook*, Madrid: Banco Central Hispano (chapter 2 on 'The Economy and EU Convergence' contains a section on the new role of the Bank of Spain in controlling inflation).

C.A LONGHURST

Banco de Santander

The Banco de Santander was founded in 1857 by a group of merchants in that city. The expansionary phase, from the mid-1950s to the mid-1970s, took it from being a predominantly regional bank to being a national bank with international representation throughout western Europe. Jointly with Bank of America it created the Banco Intercontinental Español (Bankinter), and later, with Metropolitan Life, the insurance company Santander Metropolitan. It also has a substantial stake in First Union, the seventh largest US bank, owns the Portuguese Banco de Comércio e Indústria, and has a cross-share agreement with the Royal Bank of Scotland. It has important shareholdings in the major electricity company Endesa and in telecommunications. But the most dramatic acquisition of recent years has been that of the crisis-ridden Banesto, one of Spain's major banks, brought down by the disastrous management of Mario **Conde**, subsequently investigated for alleged fraud. Following the discovery of massive irregularities in its accounts, Banesto was placed under the control of the **Banco de España** in 1993, and in 1994 Banco de Santander successfully bid for ownership in the face of competition from two other bidders, **BBV** and **Banco Argentaria**. One of the conditions of the purchase was that Santander had to keep Banesto as a distinct entity for a minimum of four years, after which the process of absorption would be implemented. The Santander's strategy has been to sell the large industrial interests of Banesto and convert it to its own style of commercial banking. The Santander-Banesto conglomerate is the largest Bank in Spain and the 45th in the world. A further distinctive mark in the history of the Santander is the introduction in 1989 of interest-bearing current accounts (known as *supercuentas*) virtually unknown in Spanish commercial banking until then. This marked the beginning of a marketing revolution among Spanish banks in attracting clients' deposits.

C.A. LONGHURST

Banderas, Antonio

b. 1960, Málaga

Actor

A highly successful actor in theatre, film and television, Banderas studied at the Málaga School of Dramatic Art in 1981, and became internationally known through his appearances in films by leading directors, especially **Almodóvar**, including *Laberinto de pasiones* (Labyrinth of Passions) (1982), *Matador* (1986), *La ley del deseo* (The Law of Desire) (1987), *Mujeres al borde de un ataque de nervios* (Women on the Verge of a Nervous Breakdown) (1988) and *¡Atame!* (Tie Me Up, Tie Me Down!) (1989). He also appeared in Carlos **Saura**'s *Los zancos* (Stilts) (1984), and **Trueba**'s *Two Much* (1995).

See also: film and cinema

EAMONN RODGERS

banks

The prolonged economic crisis that began in 1975 had a disastrous effect on the smaller private banks, many of which had to be rescued by the Bank of Spain (**Banco de España**) and absorbed by the bigger, healthier banks. Spain's entry into the EC in 1986 brought further dramatic change as competition from foreign banks threatened to take market share from the Spanish banks. A period of liberalization and streamlining of regulations by the monetary authorities was accompanied by mergers and new marketing ploys to attract depositors. The more than a hundred private banks of the early 1970s were reduced to just over thirty by the mid-1990s. The biggest mergers have been those between Banco de Bilbao and Banco de Vizcaya; Banco Central and Banco Hispanoamericano; the state-owned Banco Exterior with other financial institutions in the public sector (now known as **Banco Argentaria**); and the acquisition of the troubled Banesto by **Banco de Santander**. These now form the 'big four'. There is still a considerable number of small banks in Spain although some are in fact owned by the large banking groups. The move towards concentration is resulting in branch closures, inevitably, since Spain has considerably more bank branches than most countries in the EU. On the other hand, Spanish branches employ fewer staff on average than other countries, so productivity in terms of clients per employee is high. Because bank and building society deposits still account for over 50 percent of household savings in Spain, retail banking has been the mainstay of Spanish banks, but there is increasing interest among Spaniards in other forms of savings such as shares, pension funds, bonds and insurance policies, and the banks have responded to this by developing products such as unit trusts and private pension schemes.

The recession of the early 1990s had a significant impact on Spanish banks, lowering margins and creating a need to increase provision for bad loans. On the other hand, the Bank of Spain's reduction in the legal reserve requirements has released some funds, and while profitability has suffered it remains among the highest in the EU. The banking system was nevertheless rocked by the near-collapse of Banesto in 1993 as a result of huge sums having been illegally syphoned off by Mario **Conde** (see also **Banco de Santander**). The year 1995–6 saw a major improvement in bank balance sheets with a reduction in the provision for bad loans and in overheads together with a modest increase in earnings from financial operations. Net interest margins (the difference between interest paid and interest charged), however, have been squeezed by the increased competitiveness, but the ratio of capital and reserves to total assets is high by European standards and profits have recovered sharply. Spanish banks have also recently been building up their shareholdings in strategic sectors such as electricity and telecommunications.

See also: economy

Further reading

Salmon, K. (1995) *The Modern Spanish Economy*, 2nd edn, London: Pinter (a very accessible account of all the main aspects of the Spanish economy).

C.A. LONGHURST

Barcelona FC

Barcelona FC is much more than just a football club. Founded in 1899 by Joan Gamper, for most of its existence it has been synonymous with a popular Catalanism which defies the Spanish State, particularly during periods of political repression. According to **Vázquez Montalbán**, the history of Barcelona FC is 'la història de la sublimació èpica del poble català en un equip de futbol' ('the history of the epic sublimation of the Catalan people in a football team') (Artells 1972: 7). Just as Athletic de Bilbao represented Basque nationalist sentiment during the Franco period, so Barça, as the club is universally known, became the focus of popular resentment against the dictatorship in Catalonia. The pro-Catalan dimension still remains, and feelings regularly reach fever pitch during Barcelona's matches against **Real Madrid**, the football club most associated with Francoism and Spanish centralism. Those immigrants from other parts of Spain who are assimilated into Catalan life identify with Barcelona FC, while those who are not support the other Barcelona club, Espanyol. This reflects the political dimension of football in Barcelona.

Barcelona FC is one of the richest and most successful clubs in Europe, and has some 100,000 members. Over the years the club has spent vast sums of money purchasing players. By the mid-1990s, however, the team was made up of quite a number of local players, sprinkled with a smaller number of overseas stars than in the past, when the relationship with such players as the Brazilian Romário was not always a happy one. One of the most famous and durable of the imports seemed to be the Dutchman Johann Cruyff, who served the club as both player and manager, before being replaced in the latter capacity by Bobby Robson in 1996.

Football is not the only sport played at Barcelona FC. As with Real Madrid and other Spanish clubs, Barcelona has successful and popular basketball teams, while other sports played include rugby, hockey, ice hockey, cycling and tennis.

See also: football; sport and leisure

Further reading

Artells, J.J. (1972) *Barça, Barça, Barça*, Barcelona: Laia (a history of the club until the 1930s; especially interesting is the brief prologue by Manuel Vázquez Montalbán which sees the club as an important sub-cultural phenomenon).

DAVID GEORGE

Bardem, Juan Antonio

b. 1922, Madrid

Filmmaker

One of the famous three B's of the Franco period (see also **Buñuel, Luis; Berlanga, Luis**), Bardem was notorious for his strictures on Spanish cinema of the time as 'politically ineffective, socially false, intellectually abject, aesthetically non-existent and commercially crippled', a judgement delivered at the **Salamanca Conversations** of 1955.

The son of the actor Rafael Bardem and the actress Matilde Muñoz Sampedro, Bardem had studied along with Berlanga at **IIEC** and together they produced their first film, *Esa pareja feliz* (That Happy Couple) (1951). By focusing on the life of ordinary people and influenced by Italian neo-realism it exemplified the new social concerns of serious Spanish filmmaking, concerns which were to be severely hampered by **censorship**.

His films of the 1950s were powerful critiques of contemporary society, the self-absorption of urban society in *Muerte de un ciclista* (*Death of a Cyclist*) (1955) and the stifling boredom of provincial life in *Calle Mayor* (Main Street) (1956) which won him an International Critics Award when it was banned as an official entry at Venice. His next film *La venganza* (Revenge) (1957), which was to have been entitled *Los segadores* (The Reapers) as the first in an intended series depicting the lives of working people, was so mauled by the censors that it failed, causing him to abandon his plans. *Nunca pasa nada* (Nothing Ever Happens), written in 1960 but not made until 1963, because of problems with censorship, is considered his most representative and by some his best film.

In the 1960s and 1970s he experimented with a wide variety of genres, including his most openly communist-inspired film *El puente* (The Long Weekend) (1976), and in the 1980s directed television productions, in particular his long-planned series *Lorca, muerte de un poeta* (Lorca, Death of a Poet) (1988). He became President of the Assembly of Spanish Cinema and Audiovisual Directors in 1988, and President of the European Federation of Film Directors in 1993.

See also: film and cinema

Further reading

Higginbotham, V. (1988) *Spanish Cinema under Franco*, Austin, TX: University of Texas Press (one of the most comprehensive surveys of this period).

EAMONN RODGERS

basketball

One of the major spectator sports in Spain, basketball began to rival soccer in the late 1980s, attracting large audiences for live matches and for broadcasts on radio and television, especially after the Spanish team won a silver medal at the 1984 Olympics. Spanish teams compete regularly and successfully in the European League, Joventut (Barcelona), for example, winning in 1993–4, Real Madrid in 1994–5 and Barcelona in 1995–6 and for the Eurocopa which was won by Real Madrid in 1997. Within Spain teams compete in a Professional League, and for the Copa de Rey, the top teams being once again Barcelona, Real Madrid and Joventut. Women's teams compete in their own league, the leading club in 1996, for example, being Costa Naranja. In world championships Spain tends to rank in eighth or ninth place.

See also: sport and leisure

EAMONN RODGERS

Basque

Basque (*euskera*), unlike the other languages of Spain, is not a Romance or even an Indo-European language, but is one of the oldest languages spoken in Europe. Very little is known about its provenance or early development. In Spain it is spoken in the **autonomous communities** of the Basque country (Alava, Guipúzcoa and Vizcaya) and Navarre, and in France in Basse Navarre, Labour and Soule. Given the geographical isolation of Basque communities from each other, and the absence of a strong unifying written tradition, a number of distinct subvarieties emerged. These can be divided into two main groups: western Basque (Vizcayan) and central/eastern Basque (including Guipúzcoan).

Grammatically, the most distinctive feature of Basque is that it is an agglutinative language heavily reliant on affixation, e.g., *gizon-a* (the man), *gizon-a-ren* (of the man), *gizon-a-ren-a-ri* (to that of the man). These affixes may vary between varieties. Word order differs significantly from Indo-European languages, e.g. *neska bat naz* (girl a I am). Though its basic lexis is unrelated to Romance, making lexical creation difficult, Basque has borrowed extensively from Romance sources, e.g. *arbola* (Spanish *árbol*, 'tree'). Phonetically, Basque does not differ greatly from **Spanish**.

In 1968, after years of Francoist repression and even prohibition, an attempt was made to preserve the language and extend its use in education, administration and the media. *Euskaltzaindia* (The Royal Academy of the Basque Language) codified a standard Basque (called *batúa*), based on the central/eastern varieties. This choice, rejected by many as 'artificial' and discriminating against speakers of Vizcayan, was nonetheless eventually adopted by the Basque Autonomous Government in its Language Planning Law. Standard Basque is co-official with Spanish in **Euskadi** and in the Basque-speaking areas of Navarre.

Knowledge of Basque across the population is low compared with Catalonia or Galicia, with only 20 percent of the population in Euskadi as habitual users, and some 5 percent in Navarre. It is spoken in greatest proportion by agricultural workers as well as a significant number of professional, technical and managerial staff (most involved in its revival, for political reasons), and least by industrial workers, many of whom are Spanish-speaking immigrants. However, its use is retreating in rural areas and increasing among young urban populations.

The autonomous government has expended more on the promotion of Basque than has any other minority language area, owing partly to the symbolic value the language acquired during the Franco regime and partly to the difficulty of extending its use to non-Basque speakers. Educationally, its presence has extended well beyond the *ikastolas* (Basque-language primary schools). In the media, sections of the daily newspapers *Deia* and ***Egin*** appear in Basque, there are Basque-language radio stations (e.g. Radio Euskadi) and a **Basque television** channel (Euskal Telebista).

See also: language and education; language and national identity; language normalization

Further reading

García Mouton, P. (1994) *Lenguas y dialectos de España*, Madrid: Arco Libros (a clear overview).

Siguán, M. (1992) *España plurilingüe*, Madrid: Alianza (a comprehensive study of language planning in Spain).

MIRANDA STEWART

Basque culture

The Basque homeland consists primarily of the Spanish provinces of Guipúzcoa, Vizcaya and Alava, and areas North of the Pyrenees in south-western France. Navarre is claimed by Basques as part of **Euskadi**, but this inclusion is disputed by many Navarrese, who are predominantly Spanish-speaking, and who claim a distinct cultural and historical identity for Navarre. The **Basque** language, though a powerful focus for nationalist sentiment, is not the sole determinant of Basque identity, as the language was in serious decline by the end of the nineteenth century, and many of those who would regard themselves as Basques do not speak it. Nor is there a strong literary culture in Basque, though in the last quarter of the twentieth century writing in Basque underwent a revival, paralleling the modest expansion in the number of Basque speakers. Arantza **Urretabizkaia** is a notable woman author who writes in Basque, and Joseba Irazu, who writes under the name of Bernardo Atxaga, won the National Prize for Narrative in 1989, with *Obabakuak* (The People From Obaba).

Apart from the language, important expressions of cultural identity are found in traditional music and dance. As in Morris dancing, many Basque dances derive from ritual dances performed exclusively by men, such as the *ezpata-dantza* (sword-dance), with its distinctive 5/8 beat. Whereas these are usually danced in square formation by eight men, mixed dances of a more social kind are usually in a circle, and have much in common with other European folk-dances, in which, for example, the dancers change partners, or pass under arches formed by the linked hands of other dancers. In the Baztán valley in Navarre there is an unusual dance called the *jauziak* (high jumps). The musical accompaniment for all these dances is provided by a one-handed flute called the *txistu*, the performer simultaneously beating a small drum or *danbolina* attached to his left wrist. There is also the *txalaparta*, a kind of wooden xylophone, and the *alboka*, a double-reed instrument, which needs a special technique of breathing to make the sound flow continuously, as in a bagpipe.

The best-known Basque sport is *pelota*, which exists in several variants, ranging from handball to playing with racquets or the special large wicker gloves which enable the ball to be thrown at extremely high speeds. There are also various competitions involving the lifting, throwing and carrying of heavy weights.

See also: food and drink; regional nationalism; regionalism; wine

CARLOS ÁLVAREZ ARAGÜÉS

Basque Left

The Basque Left, Euskadiko Ezkerra (EE), had its origin in **ETA**-PM's decision to establish a political party which would be able to make use of the opportunities for legal activity during the transition from the Franco dictatorship to a parliamentary regime. A number of ETA members transferred their activities from the armed organization to the party, EIA, which held its founding meeting in April 1977. EIA was not intended to be a substitute for ETA, which remained in existence, ready to step in with armed force when the possibilities of legal action were exhausted.

EE was originally an electoral coalition, formed for the June 1977 elections, between EIA and the Movimiento Comunista, itself a 1960s split from ETA. The experience of parliamentary democracy persuaded EIA's leaders, and most of ETA-PM's activists, that armed struggle was counter-productive. ETA-PM disbanded in September 1982 except for a rump. When, in March 1982, EIA united with a dissident wing of the Communist Party in the Basque country, the united party took the name of Euskadiko Ezkerra.

EE was intended to be active in social and cultural movements, as well as taking part in elections. In particular, it was intended to unite the national and social struggles, overcoming what was seen as the false polarization encouraged by both the **PSOE** and the **PNV**. EE had some success in this endeavour, winning seats in the Madrid and Basque parliaments and obtaining 10.8 percent of the vote in the 1986 elections for the Basque parliament. However, involvement in extra-parliamentary activity soon petered out, while participation in coalition Basque governments drove a wedge between EE's socialist and nationalist wings, drawn towards alliances with the PSOE and PNV respectively. Instead of acting as a bridge between socialists and nationalists, EE was itself affected by the traditional divide in Basque politics.

In January 1991, EE entered an all-nationalist coalition in the Autonomous Basque parliament with the PNV and Garaikotxea's **Eusko Alkartasuna**, thereby freeing the PNV from the need to collaborate with the PSOE. The aim of combining socialism and nationalism had, effectively, been abandoned. That move produced two organized factions at EE's conference in February 1992, where the socialist tendency won by the narrowest of margins, and took the party into a new coalition with the PNV and the PSOE. Supporters of the nationalist wing were aware that the party had won few votes from the non-nationalist community, while it retained a considerable base in Guipúzcoa, the most nationalist province. Five of the six MPs in the Basque parliament refused to accept the new coalition and were expelled by the Party's leaders. The project of a party uniting socialism and nationalism was effectively dead. The socialist faction began negotiations with the PSOE, which led to a fusion shortly before the parliamentary elections of June 1993. The nationalist faction formed an electoral alliance with EA and went into decline.

See also: regional nationalism; regionalism

JOHN SULLIVAN

Basque Socialist Party

The Basque Socialist Party (PSOE-EE) was formed in 1993 by the unification of the Basque section of the Socialist Party (**PSOE**) and the **Basque Left** (Euskadiko Ezkerra), a group of nationalist origin. Traditionally, the PSOE had been hostile to Basque nationalism and had been seen as the party of workers from other regions of Spain. The unification gave the party a base in Basque cultural circles. It is the second electoral force in the Basque country and generally forms a coalition with the **PNV** (Basque Nationalist Party) in the regional government.

JOHN SULLIVAN

Basque television

There are two Basque television stations, both belonging to the publicly owned Euskal Telebista (Basque Television). The first broadcasts exclusively in Basque, and the second in Spanish. They are now both well established as irreplaceable elements of contemporary Basque culture.

Euskal Telebista (ETB) was the first television company in Spain to be set up outside the structures of the national Spanish Broadcasting Corporation, TVE (see also **television**), and effectively brought to an end the latter's nationwide monopoly. The first channel, ETB1, began broadcasting on 31 December 1982 without authorization from central government, a situation which led to considerable tension between **Euskadi** and Madrid. Its legal situation was not regularized until a year later in December 1983, along with that of the other emergent autonomous channels. Its programming was all in Basque, except for the news, which was in Spanish. The second channel, ETB2, came on stream on 31 May 1986 and broadcasts only in Spanish. This differentiates Basque television fundamentally from the other major autonomous broadcaster, **Catalan television**, both of whose channels broadcast exclusively in Catalan.

In fact, the situation for Basque television has been much more problematic than for its Catalan counterpart. While Catalan continues to be the majority language of Catalonia, is used throughout public administration and education, and is also relatively easy to learn for immigrants from other parts of Spain, Basque has not recovered to anything like the same extent from the repression of the Franco dictatorship, during which it was banned from all public use. Despite considerable official efforts to recover the lost ground – including the setting up of Basque language-medium schools – Basque is still understood only by a minority of the population. Such a situation is bound to have significant consequences for any media policy, whether in relation to print or electronic media.

Basque television has suffered considerably as a result. Despite concentrating on what are regarded as high-demand areas of television viewing – in particular sport (ETB provided its own coverage of the Barcelona **Olympic Games**, for example, concentrating on the performance of Basque sportsmen and women), but also children's programmes and cultural programmes – ETB has had difficulty consolidating the kind of audiences which would justify it commercially as well as politically. Given the relatively slow rate of recovery of the Basque language within Basque society in general, there seems little chance of a lasting solution to this problem.

A development which does seem to offer some hope for the future, however, has been the development of a Basque soap opera. Entitled *Goenkale* (Up the Street), it is in fact produced by an independent production company, Pausoka, for ETB1. Its success is undeniable, and it has become a part of everyday conversation in Euskadi, following a pattern already established by the successful Catalan soaps. It has also had a powerfully stimulating effect on Basque audiovisual production in general, employing almost 200 people and gaining the respect of television stations outside Euskadi.

See also: Basque culture; regional nationalism

HUGH O'DONNELL

BBV

Fully operational since 1989, the Banco Bilbao-Vizcaya (BBV) was created in 1988 by the agreement to merge the Banco de Bilbao and the Banco de Vizcaya, two of the 'big seven' banks, the former dating from 1857 and the latter from 1901. The merger occurred shortly after the shareholders of Banesto, led by the now disgraced Mario **Conde**, had defeated a takeover bid by the Banco de Bilbao. The largest Spanish bank by assets until the **Banco de Santander**'s takeover of Banesto in 1994, BBV still has the highest volume of clients' funds. At the end of 1995 it had over 2,800 branches, 34,000 employees and shareholders' funds amounting to 632,120m pesetas. Like the **Banco Central Hispano**, BBV has an important stake in Spanish companies through portfolio holdings, in part derived from Banco de Bilbao's traditional participation in Basque industry. It also has a large number of subsidiaries in financial services, insurance and property, as well as a variety of investment companies. It is the leader in private pension funds in Spain and is currently involved in the pensions market in Mexico through its Mexican subsidiary Probursa. BBV has also become active in the foreign banking sector, acquiring majority shareholdings in major banks in Peru and Mexico.

C.A. LONGHURST

Belbel, Sergi

b. 1963, Terrassa

Playwright

Sergi Belbel is one of a number of Catalan writers who have emerged since the 1980s, and the one who has had the greatest impact. Unlike the previous generation, for instance **Benet i Jornet** and Rodolf **Sirera**, Belbel has not been subject to Francoist **censorship**, and has never felt any obligation to deal with overtly political or social themes. He has the added advantage of beginning his career as a playwright at a time both of the recovery of text-based drama and of a relatively high level of public funding for Catalan theatre.

Belbel is perhaps unique in post-Civil War Catalan drama in his exclusive dedication to the theatre, as playwright, director, translator and teacher. He lectures at the Institut del Teatre (Theatre Institute) in Barcelona. He directs his own plays and has also directed and translated works by Heiner Müller and Georges Perec. He has translated Bernard-Marie Koltès and Samuel Beckett, and directed Shakespeare, Goldoni and Molière in translation.

Belbel's own plays are characterized by a concentration on personal relationships in a dehumanized society. In some plays these are mysterious, as in the dialogue between the two men in *En companyia d'abisme* (Deep Down) (1989). Often they are disturbing, particularly in *Carícies* (Caresses) (1991), probably Belbel's most polemical play. His frank presentation of sexual questions, particularly sexual deviance, in this and other plays, has led to criticism, although his plays have generally been the subject of critical acclaim. His plays are not set in a specifically Catalan or Spanish environment: the action of *Després de la pluja* (After the Rain) (1993), for instance, takes place on the flat rooftop of a skyscraper in an unnamed city, more reminiscent of New York or Chicago than Barcelona.

Belbel's plays are not didactic; on the contrary, his approach to the theatre is ludic. Humour, sometimes of a black or a farcical nature, is a constant feature of his drama. Belbel is highly conscious of the ambiguous nature of language. He is forever experimenting with language, theatrical form and stage space. His use of non-sequential dialogue and monologue is often both disturbing and humorous, and conveys a clear sense of the absurdist and dislocated nature of life. Belbel makes skilful use of stage space and uses minimalist scenery: for example, the rooftop setting of *Després de la pluja* variously conveys an impression of claustrophobia, agoraphobia and vertigo. Belbel's plays also make heavy physical demands on the actors. He regularly works with a relatively small group of actors, and the close rapport he has established with them is one of the main reasons for his success.

See also: Catalan culture; theatre

Further reading

Belbel, S. (1992) '*Tàlem*: Dossier', in *Tàlem*, Barcelona: Editorial Lumen/Departament de Cultura de la Generalitat de Catalunya.

George, D. and London, J. (1996) 'Avant-Garde Drama', in D. George and J. London (eds) *An Introduction to Contemporary Catalan Theatre*, Sheffield: Anglo-Catalan Society (sets Belbel in the context of post-Civil War Catalan avant-garde drama. The only introduction to his work in English).

DAVID GEORGE

Belén, Ana

b. 1950, Madrid

Actress and singer (real name María del Pilar Cuesta)

Ana Belén began in show business at 14 in the film *Zampo y yo* (Zampo and I).

A multifaceted artist with a deep social conscience, she became known during the 1970s as a protest singer. In the 1980s she appeared on stage and screen with resounding success (notably as Fortunata in the television adaptation of Galdós' *Fortunata y Jacinta*). She is married to the composer, singer and producer Víctor Manuel with whom she performed one of her best known hits, *La puerta de Alcalá* (The Gate of Alcalá).

See also: rock and pop

FERNANDO DELGADO

Bellmunt, Francesc

b. 1947, Sabadell (Barcelona)

Filmmaker

Bellmunt is the former (until 1994) President of the College of Cinema Directors of Catalonia, whose films, generally shot in and around Barcelona, some in Catalan, and with Catalan casts, include shorts (1968–71), documentaries such as *La Nova Cançó* (The 'New Song') (1976), coarse farce such as *Salut i força al canut* (Health, Lust and Fun) (1979), burlesque such as *Un par de huevos* (Nuts) (1985) and *Rateta, rateta* (1990), and biofilm such as *Monturiol* (1993). He has also worked in television: *¡Quin curs el meu tercer!* (My Third Year: What a Time!) (1994).

EAMONN RODGERS

Belloch, Juan Alberto

b. 1950, Mora de Rubielos (Teruel)

Lawyer and politician

A brilliant law graduate from the university of Barcelona, Belloch held important posts as a judge in the Basque country, and in 1990 was appointed to the General Council of the Judiciary. Between 1993 and 1996 he served as an independent member of Felipe **González**'s cabinet. He was appointed head of the Ministry of Justice which in 1994 became the Ministry of Justice and Interior. In this post he fulfilled a constitutional commitment to introduce juries. Long known for his progressive views on human rights, in 1984 Belloch founded the *Asociación Pro-Derechos Humanos* (Association for Human Rights).

See also: legal system; politics; PSOE

MICHAEL T. NEWTON

Benet Goitia, Juan

b. 1927, Madrid; d. 1993, Madrid

Writer

Juan Benet falls chronologically into the group of novelists known as the 'Generation of the 1950s'.

The realistic and *engagé* approach to literature espoused by these writers (including Jesús **Fernández Santos**, Ignacio **Aldecoa**, Carmen **Martín Gaite** and Rafael **Sánchez Ferlosio**) represents the dominant trend in Spain for nearly two decades following the Civil War. Despite Benet's chronological affiliation with the writers of this period, however, he represents a direct antithesis to their literary focus. Rather than record the observable in his narrative, Benet seeks instead to probe beneath the surface of reality and explore what he terms the 'zone of shadows'. The abstruse and often inaccessible fiction that results places Benet radically apart from social realism and from the mainstream of the post-war novel in general.

Benet sets nearly all of his novels in Región, a mythical region created in the fashion of Faulkner's Yoknapatawpha County or García Márquez's Macondo. This private narrative world stands as the most explicit symbol of the ruin and despair that form the central motif of Benet's fiction. Región is developed most fully in the author's early novels, *Return to Region* (*Volverás a Región*) (1967), *Una meditación* (A Meditation) (1969) and *Un viaje de invierno* (A Winter's Journey) (1972). To a large extent, Región is the aggregate of characters, events and social themes which for Benet constitute twentieth century Spanish society. His focus on the Civil War is particularly acute in these early novels, as well as in his later works such as *Saúl ante Samuel* (Saul Before Samuel) (1980) and his three-volume *Herrumbrosas lanzas* (Rusty Lances) (1983). In each of these novels Benet subverts the connection between political allegiance and ideological belief as a defining trait of the Civil War, but most importantly he reveals the violence and barren futility of the conflict and portrays post-war Spanish society as a diseased and moribund body.

Beyond the social and political background of Región lies the enigmatic reality of the region itself, portrayed by Benet on varying levels of complexity. On the one hand, he depicts Región and the surrounding area with scientific precision; on the other, he calls into question its correspondence with the everyday world of lived reality. For the most part he achieves this not explicitly through use of the supernatural, but more subtly by means of conflicting descriptions and recurrent suggestions of the unreal. The oxymoronic moves to the fore in his fiction and creates an amorphous world of contradiction. He portrays Región in a full state of decadence, surrounded by hostile landscapes and immersed in a threatening temperate zone, with time as the recurrent framing device of tragedy in each of his novels.

Benet's style of writing is perhaps best described as labyrinthine. His sentences are frequently the length of a full page or more, and include embedded parentheses and subordinate clauses which unite to form a syntactical web. Benet's style is a persistent maze of obstacles replete with complex obtrusions, delays, ambiguous interpolations and confusions. His narrators eschew words and linguistic structures that portray a world like our own; thus everything associated with what they say becomes part of a rarefied atmosphere aimed at precluding complete and rational understanding. Much of Benet's style and technique is part of a deliberate plan to withhold meaning from the reader. As a result, the world of Región remains ambiguous and mysterious amid the language that creates and sustains its very existence.

Benet's other fiction has generally been viewed as less accomplished than his Región works. For example, in *En la penumbra* (In the Penumbra) (1989), Benet moves outside Región to represent the meditations of two women on their lives as they await their mysterious destiny. In *El caballero de Sajonia* (The Gentleman from Saxony) (1991), his last novel published before his death, Benet evokes the sixteenth-century world of Martin Luther. Rather than write a traditional historical novel, however, Benet explores the painful shades of Luther's moral doubts and draws forth the complex nuances of political ambivalence that reside deeply in the theologian's soul.

In his essays Benet's interests range from music to linguistics, history and architecture, but his most perceptive writings are on literary theory. For example, in *La inspiración y el estilo* (Inspiration and Style) (1966) and *El ángel del Señor abandona a Tobías* (The Angel of the Lord abandons Tobit) (1976), Benet underscores the importance of style and enigma in the creation of fiction. In nearly all of his essays on literature Benet refuses to embrace either the traditional confidence of realism in the representational accuracy of language or the postmodern gloom over the fissure between language and reality. Instead, he understands how language gains meaning both within its discursive context and in the world itself. Most importantly, he shows how words both reveal and create the world.

See also: novel

Major works

Benet Goitia, J. (1966) *La inspiración y el estilo*, Madrid: Revista de Occidente (essays on style, writing and meaning).

—— (1967) *Volverás a Región*, Madrid: Destino; trans. Rabassa, *Return to Region*, New York: Columbia University Press, 1985 (novel).

—— (1969) *Una meditación*, Barcelona: Seix Barral ; trans. Rabassa, *A Meditation*, New York: Persea, 1982 (novel).

—— (1972) *Un viaje de invierno*, Barcelona: La Gaya Ciencia (novel).

—— (1976) *El ángel del Señor abandona a Tobías*, Barcelona: La Gaya Ciencia (essays on literary and linguistic theory).

—— (1980) *Saúl ante Samuel*, Barcelona: La Gaya Ciencia (novel).

—— (1983–6) *Herrumbrosas lanzas*, Madrid: Alfaguara, 3 vols (novel).

—— (1989) *En la penumbra*, Madrid: Alfaguara (novel).

—— (1991) *El caballero de Sajonia*, Barcelona: Planeta (novel).

Further reading

Cabrera, V. (1983) *Juan Benet*, Boston, MA: Twayne (an overview of Benet's life and writing up to 1978).

Herzberger, D. (1976) *The Novelistic World of Juan Benet*, Clear Creek, IN: The American Hispanist (a study of Benet's essays and novels up to 1975).

Manteiga, R. *et al.* (eds) (1984) *Critical Approaches to the Writings of Juan Benet*, Hanover: University Press of New England (essays on the novels, short stories and essays of Benet).

DAVID K. HERZBERGER

Benet i Jornet, Josep Maria

b. 1940, Barcelona

Playwright

Benet i Jornet is probably the most important Catalan playwright since the Civil War. His early plays have a clear socio-political content, and are influenced by Brecht and Epic Theatre. His first play, *Una vella, coneguda olor* (An Old, Familiar Smell), which received the Josep M. de Sagarra theatre prize in 1963, presents the hopeless life of the lower classes in post-Civil War Catalonia. It has the same importance for Catalan drama as Antonio **Buero Vallejo**'s *Historia de una escalera* (*Story of a Staircase*) did for its Castilian counterpart.

Benet's plays became more complex after the early 1970s, and there is less emphasis on social issues. A case in point is *Revolta de bruixes* (Witches' Revolt), which was first published in 1975 and which provided Benet with his first public and critical success outside Catalonia when it was performed in Madrid in 1980. The ethos of this play and of *El manuscrit d'Alí Bei* (Ali Bey's Manuscript) (1984) is different from that of social realism in that they suggest the impossibility of changing the world in which we live.

The performance of *El manuscrit d'Alí Bei* at the Teatre Lliure in Barcelona in 1988 marked the end of Benet's feud with this important theatre over their alleged favouring of foreign drama at the expense of Catalan playwrights, and finally established Benet's reputation with both public and critics. Further hits followed with *¡Ai, carai!* (Well I'm Blowed!), which was also performed at the Lliure in 1988, and *Desig* (Desire), which received the 1991 Catalan Literature National Prize, and was directed by Sergi **Belbel**. *Desig* marks the beginning of a new period in Benet's drama. It deals with the lack of communication between individuals through the creation of complex layers of time and space, and reveals the influence of Pinter, Mamet, Koltès and Beckett.

Public and critical reception of Benet's plays reflect not only their quality but also changing tastes among Catalan theatre-goers. *Una vella, coneguda olor* suited the prevailing taste for social realism, at least in left-wing circles. This taste had changed by the early 1970s, and reviewers had little sympathy with *Berenàveu a les fosques* (You Were Having Tea in the Dark) on its first professional performance in 1973. Around this time, text-based plays by individual authors were going out of fashion in favour of collective creation in which staging was given greater prominence. The rise of such performance groups as Els **Joglars** and Els **Comediants** in Catalonia parallels the relative demise of dramatists like Benet, while the re-establishment of text-based theatre in Catalonia (and in Europe generally) in the mid- and late-1980s coincided with the critical praise which has once more been afforded to Benet's work.

See also: Catalan culture; theatre

Further reading

Sirera, R. (1996) 'Drama and Society', in D. George and J. London (eds) *An Introduction to Contemporary Catalan Theatre*, Sheffield: Anglo-Catalan Society (sets Benet in the context of post-Civil War Catalan social drama; the only introduction to his work in English).

DAVID GEORGE

Benítez, Manuel

b. 1936, Palma del Río

Matador ('El Cordobés')

Born into a poor Andalusian family, and orphaned in the aftermath of the Civil War, El Cordobés transformed himself from an illiterate bricklayer to the most famous, though not the most highly regarded, **matador** of the past fifty years. Making up with undoubted courage, a winning smile, and the aid of an astute manager what he lacked in grace or technique, the long-haired ***torero*** offered bullfighting a modern face as Spain emerged from its conservative post-war phase into the more modern and increasingly outward-looking country of the 1960s. El Cordobés followed up his hugely successful career as a ***novillero*** by taking his ***alternativa*** in Cordoba in 1962 and confirming it in Madrid the following year, when he achieved a clamorous triumph at the expense of a serious goring. Notwithstanding his popular image as a member of the Marbella jet-set of the 1960s and 1970s, he gained steadily in skill, winning grudging admiration from all but his most acerbic detractors for performances in the leading arenas of Spain, France, Mexico and South America. El Cordobés twice broke the record for the number of ***corridas*** in a season, with 111 performances in 1965 and 121 in 1970. Despite several temporary retirements, he has remained active, making his most recent comeback in 1996.

See also: bullfighting

IAN CAMPBELL ROSS

Berlanga, Luis

b. 1921, Valencia

Filmmaker

One of the famous three B' s (see also **Buñuel, Luis; Bardem, Juan Antonio**) during the Franco regime, Berlanga studied at the **IIEC** from 1947 to 1950 along with Bardem and produced with him *Esa pareja feliz* (That Happy Couple) (1951). They both wrote the script for *Bienvenido, Mr Marshall* (Welcome, Mr Marshall) (1952) but when Bardem had to sell his share in the company Berlanga became sole director. Both films broke with tradition by taking as their subject the lives, dreams and disillusionment of ordinary people, and, like Bardem, Berlanga was to be the victim of harsh **censorship**.

When the script and the film of *Los jueves, milagro* (Every Thursday a Miracle) (1957), a satire on villagers' religious credulity, was severely handled by the censors, he produced nothing further until *Plácido*, originally entitled *Siente un pobre a su mesa* (Seat a Poor Man at Your Table) (1961). An exposé of the superficiality of the charity of the rich, the film was the first fruit of his collaboration with the screenwriter Rafael **Azcona**. *El verdugo* (The Executioner) (1963), a 'black comedy' considered among his best, again met with official disapproval and he produced his next (and worst) film *La boutique* (1967) in Argentina. *Tamaño natural* (Life Size) (1973), made in Paris, was banned from Spain for two years.

After the death of Franco Berlanga produced the first and most successful of a trilogy of farces featuring the Spanish aristocracy, *La escopeta nacional* (The National Shotgun) (1977). In 1985 he realized a project begun in the mid-1950s, *La vaquilla* (The Little Bull), a highly entertaining story set in Civil War times which was a box-office triumph. *Todos a la cárcel* (Everyone Off to Jail) won Goya Prizes for best film and best director in 1994.

See also: film and cinema; Salamanca Conversations

Further reading

Higginbotham, V. (1988) *Spanish Cinema under Franco*, Austin, TX: University of Texas Press (one of the most comprehensive surveys of this period).

EAMONN RODGERS

'BIENVENIDA' *see* Mejías Jiménez, Antonio

Bigas Luna, José Juan

b. 1946, Barcelona

Filmmaker

A director whose films have been described as 'bizarre, black, bawdy', 'offbeat, outrageous, steamy' and 'provocative, outrageous and entertaining', Bigas Luna produced his first full length film, *Tatuaje* (Tattoo) in 1976 after working in graphic design until 1970 and making shorts between 1972 and 1976.

His films of the 1970s and 1980s, among them *Bilbao* (1978), *Caniche* (Poodle) (1979), both based on his own short stories, *Renacer* (Reborn) (1981), *Lola* (1985) and *Angoixa* (Anguish) (1986) won him a great following in Barcelona. Of his 1990s films, *Las edades de Lulú* (The Ages of Lulu) (1990), a particularly explicit screen version of an erotic novel by Almudena Grandes, is among the top twenty Spanish box-office earners, and in 1993 *Huevos de oro* (Golden Balls) was among the top earners of the year. *Jamón, Jamón* (Salami, Salami), which starred Javier Bardem and launched him on his career, won the Silver Lion at Venice in 1993, and in 1994 his surrealist comedy *La teta y la luna* (The Breast and the Moon) won an award at Venice for the best film-script (with Cuca Canals), and in Spain the Premio Ondas for best film of the year.

See also: film and cinema

Further reading

Molina-Foix, V. (1977) *New Cinema in Spain*, London: British Film Institute (a comprehensive overview of current trends).

EAMONN RODGERS

black economy

The scale of the hidden economy is unknown, though it is generally recognized to be considerable (Benito 1987). The black economy is particularly important in the service industries, in construction and in certain manufacturing industries like textiles, toys and food. It also exists in agriculture, where part of the production is consumed by the producers themselves or distributed outside normal market channels.

The existence of the black economy is deeply embedded in social attitudes to the payment of taxes, in informal working arrangements, in people pursuing more than one job (*pluriempleo*) and in the widespread existence of small family firms. Frequently it involves deliberate fraud of the welfare system. Many people work in the visible economy for long enough to gain entitlement to unemployment benefit, then move to the black economy where they are exempt from taxation. In the black economy people are unprotected by employment legislation, frequently receive low wages, have little job security and little opportunity for promotion.

Employers have also used the black economy to bypass government regulations and the rigidities of the labour market, which have contributed in part to the failure of the economy to create legitimate jobs (OECD 1994). During the Franco era, dismissals necessitated a lengthy redundancy procedure, agreement by government and trade unions, and large redundancy payments. Businesses operating in the black economy are only kept afloat by low wages and low overheads, which enables them to compete unfairly with legitimate enterprises.

In rural areas the black economy has been associated with the welfare system, in particular the Agreement for the Employment and Protection of Agricultural Workers (*Acuerdo para el Empleo y la Protección Social Agrarios*) (1996), which incorporates public works programmes sponsored by local councils. These schemes have been widely abused, fostering corruption and patronage, with people being credited for work they have not done and public money being syphoned off into private projects.

Because part of the economy is hidden, official statistics may not always be reliable. The unemployment rate which is most often quoted is that based on the National Employment Survey (*Encuesta de la Población Activa*). Up to the mid-1990s this registered a national unemployment rate in excess of 20 percent and in some parts of Spain figures in excess of 30 percent. When employment in the black economy was taken into account, the real rates of unemployment were thought to be somewhat below these figures.

See also: agriculture; economy; labour market

References

Benito, S. (1987) 'La economía sumergida en España', *Revista del Instituto de Estudios Económicos* 1: 254–88.

OECD (1994) *OECD Economic Surveys: Spain 1993–1994*, Paris.

Further reading

Ahn, N. and de la Rica, S. (1997) 'The Underground Economy in Spain. An Alternative to Unemployment', *Applied Economics* 29, 6: 733–43.

Hooper, J. (1995) *The New Spaniards*, Harmondsworth: Penguin (see especially chapter 17 for a clear treatment of the topic).

Mingione, E. (1995) 'Labour market segmentation and informal work in southern Europe', *European Urban and Regional Studies* 2, 2: 121–44.

Thomas, J. (1992) *Informal economic activity*, LSE Handbooks in Economics, London: Harvester Wheatsheaf (an accessible general account of the black economy).

KEITH SALMON

Bodegas, Roberto

b. 1933, Madrid

Filmmaker

After an early career as assistant director in France Bodegas began making his own films in 1970 with *Españolas en París* (Spanish Women in Paris) (1970), *Vida conyugal sana* (A Healthy Married Life) (1973) and *Los nuevos españoles* (The New Spaniards) (1974). These are considered good examples of *tercera vía* (third way) films which have a wider appeal than intellectual cinema without being mere commercial fodder. The latter two films were scripted by José Luis **Garci**, for whom Bodegas acted as assistant director in the production of *Volver a empezar* (Starting Over) (1982).

EAMONN RODGERS

BOE

The official state gazette, *Boletín Oficial del Estado*, was founded in 1661 as the *Gaceta de Madrid*, and has been issued under its present name since 1939. Published daily in Madrid, it is received by public institutions throughout Spain. It contains the text of all new laws, decrees, ministerial orders and so on approved by **parliament**, the **council of ministers** and individual ministries. Since the early 1980s it has had equivalents in all seventeen **autonomous communities**; for instance Andalusia has the *BOJA* (*Boletín Oficial de la Junta de Andalucía*).

See also: politics

Further reading

Newton, M.T. with Donaghy, P.J. (1997) *Institutions of Modern Spain*, Cambridge: Cambridge University

Press (chapters 2, 4, 6 and 11 are especially useful for this topic).

MICHAEL T. NEWTON

Bofill, Ricardo

b. 1939, Barcelona

Architect

The work of Bofill rests on a number of specific assumptions. His vision of what the role of architecture should be at the end of the twentieth century embraces all aspects of the contemporary environment as well as taking account of the relevance of architectural history. Forced into exile by political circumstances during his student years, he continued his studies in Geneva from 1957 to 1960. As a young Catalan artist suffering persecution in his own country, he was welcomed with open arms in France, where his reputation was enhanced by several important projects which he either completed or set in train there. At the outset of his career, he adopted an original conception of the architect's task, creating in 1961 the *Taller d'Arquitectura* (Architects' Workshop), a team of architects, designers and intellectuals who committed themselves to a humanist approach to architecture and town planning. Multidisciplinarity and globalization became central themes. Prominent among the first constructions of the *Taller* are El Xanadu (1968, Calp, Alicante), El Castell (1969, Reus, Tarragona) and the Muralla Roja (1972–4, Calp, Alicante) as well as the group Waden 7 (1972–4). The unifying architectural idiom of these projects is the pursuit of geometric linearity, which, according to their author, gives them psychological depth: 'labyrinth' or 'intersections' are words which spring to mind when viewing these buildings. The international acclaim which greeted these early experiments, a combination of favourable circumstances, and Bofill's skill as a communicator, brought the *Taller* and its leader world renown.

Over time, Bofill's priorities have changed, becoming more focused on monumental architecture and its relationship with power. The *Taller* has become an international enterprise, with branches in Paris, Barcelona, Montpellier and New York, and with completed projects in, among other cities, Barcelona, Stockholm, Bordeaux, Paris, Moscow and Chicago. Bofill's works, like his discourse, have become more and more rhetorical, even tinged with a megalomania which sometimes affects the politicians and business people who are his clients. He often constructs monumental compositions in a neoclassical idiom, with the addition of modern industrial elements. During the 1980s the public associated him with post-modernism, especially after his combined exhibition with Leon Krier at the Museum of Modern Art in New York in 1985. His principal works are: the winning project (not, however, executed) for a new market-hall for Les Halles de Paris (1975–8), Les Arcades du Lac at St Quentin (France, 1977–87), the Antigone project, where as architect-in-chief he was responsible for the overall design and execution of the Antigone quarter of Montpellier (France, 1978–89), Les Espaces d'Abraxas, a monumental ensemble in Marne-la-Vallée (1978–83), Les Echelles du Baroque, a large-scale residential complex in Paris (1980–5), the Airport at Barcelona (1988–91) and the Teatre Nacional de Catalunya in Barcelona (1987–97).

See also: architects; architecture

MIHAIL MOLDOVEANU

Bohigas, Oriol

b. 1925, Barcelona

Architect and historian

Bohigas is a key figure for understanding the privileged position of architecture in Catalonia in the late twentieth century. Architect, historian and architectural critic, Bohigas belongs to an intellectual élite which plays a very active role in Catalan public life. Since qualifying in 1951, his output has been enormous. With his associates in the MBM studio, Josep Martorell and David Mackay, he has produced a series of prestigious architectural and town planning projects such as the Mutua Metal·lùrgica (headquarters of an Insurance Company in Barcelona), the Ecole Thau (Barcelona), and the Kochstraße-Friederichstraße redevelopment in Berlin, which won a prize in 1984. In

1977 he became Director of the School of Architecture in Barcelona (ETSAB), a position which enabled him to revitalize and renew this great institution. The high standard of teaching produced several generations of highly-qualified architects, many of them outstanding. In 1980 Bohigas was given overall responsibility for architecture and town planning by the Barcelona city council, continuing to act as consultant to the council even after relinquishing this post some years later. He is considered to be the main driving force behind the city's plan of urban renewal, which was highly praised in Spain and abroad. The rationalist roots of Bohigas' thinking were well known from his early years as an active member of the Grupo R (1953–63) alongside architects such as **Coderch**, **Moragas** and **Sostres**. The development of this thinking and the possibility of implementing some of its principles came in the 1980s with large-scale projects such as the green spaces plan, the opening up of Barcelona to the sea, and the subsequent plan for the Olympic Village designed for the 1992 games. Bohigas' active participation in the political life of the city recalls some of his famous predecessors such as **Domènech i Montaner** and especially **Puig i Cadafalch**, two famous exponents of **Modernism**, who had advocated strongly that architects had a duty to involve themselves in public affairs. By being faithful to this principle and bringing his great ability to bear on decision-making at a time when Barcelona was experiencing prosperity, expansion and the need for redevelopment, Bohigas decisively influenced the transformation of the city.

Like the Modernists already mentioned, Bohigas is also a distinguished historian and controversialist. Catalan Modernism is one of his favourite themes, but he is equally interested in the Cerdà plan, the architecture of the 1920s and 1930s and all the problems associated with teaching and with contemporary architectural practice. His activities have won him many distinctions.

See also: architects; architecture; architecture, post-Francoist

Further reading

Bohigas, O. (1968) *Arquitectura modernista*, Barcelona: Lumen.

Loyer, F. (1991) *L'art nouveau en Catalogne*, Paris: Biblio. Arts, Le Septième Fou.

MIHAIL MOLDOVEANU

Borau, José Luis

b. 1929, Zaragoza

Filmmaker and film critic

Noted particularly for his successful anti-Franco film *Furtivos* (Poachers) (1975) in which he played the role of the civil governor, Borau has always aimed to broaden the scope and influence of Spanish cinema. An admirer of classic Hollywood style, his first films in 1964 and 1965, the Spanish-Italian co-production *Brandy* (a western subtitled *El Sheriff de Losatumba*) and the psychological thriller *Crimen de doble filo* (Double-edged Crime), were aimed at the international market, but had little impact outside Spain. Realizing the need for economic independence, he founded his own production company, El Imán, in 1967, and collaborated with such filmmakers as **Zulueta**, to make *Un, dos, tres, al escondite inglés* (Hide and Seek) (1969), **Armiñán**, to make *Mi querida señorita* (My Dear Miss) (1971) and **Gutiérrez Aragón**, to make *Camada negra* (Black Brood) (1977). During this time he also taught screenwriting at the EOC (Escuela Oficial de Cinematografía; Official Film School), and is acknowleged as having exercised a major influence on his colleagues and pupils.

Hay que matar a B (B Must Die) (1974) marked Borau's return to directing and another attempt to exploit the international market. A political thriller in which the hunter becomes the prey, the film was a Swiss-Spanish co-production written by Borau and **Drove**, filmed in English with an international cast and then dubbed into Spanish. It was well received by Spanish critics, but was nevertheless a box-office failure. *Furtivos*, on the other hand, was a huge success. Described by Mario Vargas Llosa as 'one of the cruellest stories in Spanish cinema' and ending in matricide, it was seen as portraying the reality behind the Francoist image of Spain. After a battle with the censors it was shown at the **San Sebastián Film Festival** where it won the Golden Shell award.

Another commercial success, co-produced with Sweden, was *La Sabina* (1979) written with particular Spanish and foreign actresses in mind, and exploiting the clash of the different cultures represented by the characters they play. In 1984 Borau achieved his long-standing ambition to make a film in the US. *Río abajo* (*On the Line*) depicted, against a background of illegal immigration, the relationships between a young American border guard, a Mexican girl (played by Victoria **Abril**) and his rivals for her favours. But it proved difficult to distribute in America, was refused a showing at international festivals as being unrepresentative of Spanish culture, and its success in the home market was not enough to cover the costs.

In addition to directing, Borau has been professor of scriptwriting at the EOC, and of film direction in Valladolid.

See also: film and cinema

Further reading

Hopewell, J. (1986) *Out of the Past: Spanish Cinema After Franco*, London: British Film Institute (a very readable general account of contemporary trends).

Molina-Foix, V. (1977) *New Cinema in Spain*, London: British Film Institute (a comprehensive overview of current trends).

EAMONN RODGERS

Boyer Salvador, Miguel

b. 1939, St Jean de Luz (France)

Economist and politician

A graduate in physics and economics, Boyer Salvador became Deputy Director-General of the Research Department of the **National Industrial Institute**, and Director-General in 1974. A member of **PSOE** since 1960, he joined the Felipe **González** cabinet as Minister for Economy and Finance (1982–5), providing a politically useful link between government and banking interests. After his marriage to society beauty Isabel Preysler in 1985, he became identified with the 'Marbella set', and was seen as embodying the contradiction between socialist principles and the lavish lifestyles of those referred to cynically by the public as *los beautiful*.

EAMONN RODGERS

Brossa, Joan

b. 1919, Barcelona

Poet, playwight and artist

Brossa's most significant contribution to poetry lies in his ability to convey ordinary everyday events in a pleasing and challenging manner.

Born into a modest family in Barcelona, Brossa fought on the Republican side in the Civil War, and then had to endure Nationalist military service in Salamanca. On his return to Barcelona he became a committed defender of Catalan culture. He was fascinated by surrealism, the only avant-garde art form tolerated by the Franco regime, and produced two important artistic magazines, *Algol* and *Dau al Set* (The Seventh Side of the Die). Together with **Tàpies** he explored notions of transformation and change: they both admired the Italian magician, Fregoli, and they both had Buddhist leanings, rejecting Catholic absolutism. After visiting Paris in 1956, Brossa developed a lifelong passion for cinema.

Brossa's poetic output can be divided into four phases. The first (1941–9) is markedly surrealistic, exploring aspects of the unconscious, in free verse, as evidenced in *Poesia Rasa* (Plain Poetry). The second phase (1950–4) is characterized by an antipoetic stance, the use of prose and a semi-novelistic form, as in *U no es ningú* (One is No-one). In his third phase (1955–9), Brossa developed social and Catalan themes expressed in odes and sonnets, often epic in tone. His fourth phase, starting in 1960, is typified by picture poems, because of his experimentation with words, letters and mixed media. He collaborated with Tàpies on *El pa a la barca* (Bread on the Boat) and with **Miró** on *Cop de poma* (Apple Blow). Together with Tàpies he produced *Novel·la*, an ironic collection of certificates (birth, medical, military service, marriage and death) pointing to the dehumanizing effects of bureaucracy.

In Brossa's early plays we encounter figures from the Commedia dell'Arte, but we are also shown how capitalist society affects its citizens. In *Quiriquibu* women are unhappy and oppressed in marriage, and servants are treated with contempt. In the next phase of his *Poesia escènica* (Theatre Poetry), Brossa demystifies religion and shows how it is used to keep the masses under control, as in *Or i sal* (Gold and Salt). From his final phase, *El gran Fracaroli* treats us to a spectacle of magic tricks, ventriloquism and card games. Within his heartfelt belief that life is constantly changing, Brossa is also a humorist.

Brossa only became truly popular in the 1970s with the decline of Francoism. He is without doubt Catalonia's greatest living poet, having published 61 books of poetry and nearly 300 plays. In 1994 he was commissioned to make a sculpture for the Cathedral square in Barcelona, describing the original Latin name for the city: Barcino.

Further reading

Bordons, G. (1988) *Introducció a la poesia de Joan Brossa*, Barcelona: Edicions 62 (a thorough account of Brossa's poetry).

Coca, J. (1992) *Joan Brossa, oblidar i caminar*, Barcelona: Magrana (interviews with Brossa and commentary of his work).

Fuster, J. (1979) *Literatura catalana contemporánea*, Barcelona: Curial (an introduction to modern Catalan literature).

HELEN OPPENHEIMER

Bruguera, Sergi

b. 1971, Barcelona

Tennis player

Bruguera, ranked in 1994 the third male tennis player in the world, showed an early talent for the game, becoming Spanish children's champion at the age of eleven, and winning children's tournaments in Nice and Monte Carlo. He was twice Spanish junior champion, in 1987 and 1990, and between 1990 and 1995 was a member of the Spanish team for the Davis Cup. These years also saw a series of individual wins, at Estoril, Monte Carlo and Athens in 1991, Madrid and Gstaad in 1992, Paris, Monte Carlo, Gstaad, Prague and Bordeaux in 1993, and Paris in 1994.

EAMONN RODGERS

Buero Vallejo, Antonio

b. 1916, Guadalajara

Writer

Buero Vallejo, almost single-handedly, set the course for the Spanish **theatre** after the Civil War. He was the first playwright to launch a serious, oppositional theatre during the Franco regime, and his critical views continued to challenge Spanish audiences throughout the transition to democracy.

At the end of the Civil War most of the significant playwrights of the 1930s were dead or in **exile**, and the Spanish stage was given over to drawing-room comedies designed for an undemanding public. In this unpromising environment, Buero's prize-winning *Historia de una escalera* (*Story of a Staircase*) (1949) was acclaimed for its unconventional staging and its confrontation with the tragic reality of a Spain devastated by the recent conflict. It launched Buero on a career that was to accustom audiences to a socially committed, psychologically penetrating and technically accomplished theatre.

Early on Buero discovered the plays of Ibsen and Shaw and was deeply influenced by Unamuno, but an interest in painting led him to studies in fine arts, which the war interrupted. For his involvement on the side of the Republic he was condemned to death, and spent six years in prison after his sentence was commuted. Once released, he immersed himself in Madrid's intellectual life and began to write for the theatre, completing five plays by the time he won the Lope de Vega Prize in 1949. Many of his dramas, performed under renowned directors like José **Tamayo**, attracted enthusiastic audiences and elicited critical acclaim;

Buero has received honours such as the **Cervantes Prize** and election to the **Royal Academy** of Language. During the post-Franco years, Buero maintained his critical stance in plays like *Jueces en la noche* (*Judges in the Night*) (1979), *Lázaro en el laberinto* (*Lazarus in the Labyrinth*) (1986), and *Música cercana* (*The Music Window*) (1989), but younger theatregoers had different tastes, and reviewers commented that he had lost the freshness of his earlier efforts and the lustre he had carried as the voice of resistance to Franco.

As an opponent of the dictatorship, Buero faced the dilemma of the artist enchained by a rigorous yet capricious **censorship**. Despite reproaches from colleagues like **Sastre** and **Arrabal**, Buero persisted in his attempts to find new ways of challenging his audiences. In some of his works – *Historia de una escalera*, *Hoy es fiesta* (*Today Is a Holiday*) (1956), or *El tragaluz* (*The Basement Window*) (1967) – contemporary Spanish reality plays itself out directly. His first play, *En la ardiente oscuridad* (*In the Burning Darkness*), reveals the symbolic dimension that was to become such a fundamental component of his art. Classical myth is employed in *La tejedora de sueños* (*The Dream Weaver*), and elsewhere – *Aventura en lo gris* (*Adventure in Grey*) and *La doble historia del doctor Valmy* (*The Double Case History of Doctor Valmy*) – an imaginary land provides the cover for Buero's condemnation of war and political torture. In some of his finest plays Buero uses historical settings to comment on the contemporary condition, for example, *Un soñador para un pueblo* (*A Dreamer for the People*), *El concierto de San Ovidio* (*The Concert at Saint Ovide*), *La detonación* (*The Shot*), or his recreations of Velázquez in *Las Meninas* and Goya in *El sueño de la razón* (*The Sleep of Reason*).

While strongly unified thematically, Buero's plays are diversified and experimental in form. He has studiously avoided what he considers the excesses of the modern avant-garde, but he has a keen sense of the expressive power of the stage space and of non-verbal elements. Light and music are essential to his dramatic expression, and narrative frames lend depth to some of his best plays (for example, *El tragaluz*). Above all, Buero has experimented with devices that invite the spectator's empathy with an individual character's experience, such as Goya's deafness.

The guiding principle of Buero's programmatic theatre and his contribution to the Spanish stage – also expressed in essays, prologues, and interviews – is the creation of a modern tragedy resting on a foundation of hope, in which the individual is free to exercise moral choice. With this vision and with his keen sense of dramatic construction, Buero helped to rid the contemporary Spanish stage of its safe but tired formulas.

See also: intellectual life; theatre

Major works

Buero Vallejo, A. (1994) *Obra completa*, ed. L. Iglesias Feijoo and M. de Paco, 2 vols, Madrid: Espasa Calpe (vol. 1, *Teatro*, contains all of Buero's plays up to *Música cercana*).

—— (1950) *En la ardiente oscuridad*; trans. M.P. Holt (ed.), *In the Burning Darkness*, in *Three Plays*, San Antonio, TX: Trinity University Press, 1985.

—— (1952) *La tejedora de sueños*; trans. W.I. Oliver, *The Dream Weaver*, in R.W. Corrigan (ed.) *Masterpieces of the Modern Spanish Theatre*, New York: Macmillan, 1967.

—— (1958) *Un soñador para un pueblo*; trans. M. Thompson, *A Dreamer for the People*, Warminster: Aris & Phillips, 1994.

—— (1960) *Las Meninas*. *Las Meninas*, trans. M.P. Holt, San Antonio, TX: Trinity University Press, 1987.

—— (1962) *El concierto de San Ovidio*; trans. F. Anderson, *The Concert at Saint Ovide*, in M.P. Holt (ed.) *The Modern Spanish Stage: Four Plays*, New York: Hill & Wang, 1970.

—— (1967) *El tragaluz*; trans. and ed. P.W. O'Connor, *The Basement Window*, in *Plays of Protest from the Franco Era*, Madrid: Sociedad General Española de Librería, 1981.

—— (1970) *El sueño de la razón*; trans. M.P. Holt, *The Sleep of Reason*, in *Three Plays*, San Antonio, TX: Trinity University Press, 1985.

—— (1977) *La detonación*, trans. D. Johnston, *The Shot*, Warminster: Aris & Phillips, 1989.

—— (1986) *Lázaro en el laberinto*; trans. H. Cazorla, *Lazarus in the Labyrinth*, in P.W. O'Connor (ed.) *Plays of the New Democratic Spain (1975–90)*, Lanham, MA: University Press of America, 1992.

Further reading

Doménech, R. (1993) *El teatro de Buero Vallejo: una meditación española*, 2nd edn, Madrid: Gredos (an updated version of a perceptive and informative 1973 study).

Halsey, M.T. (1994) *From Dictatorship to Democracy: The Recent Plays of Buero Vallejo*, Ottawa: Ottawa Hispanic Studies 17, Dovehouse (a useful survey of Buero's production from 1974 to 1989).

JOHN W. KRONIK

bullfighting

The country's second-most popular spectacle (only football attracts a larger public), bullfighting has mirrored the broader cultural changes taking place in Spain since 1939. While a reduced number of ***corridas*** took place throughout the Civil War, in both Republican and Nationalist areas, the stock of fighting bulls was seriously diminished, with herds exterminated both for food and as political gestures against large landowners. Consequently, the bulls seen in Spanish rings after 1939 were generally smaller, younger, and less well-armed than those of previous eras. A single **matador**, Manuel **Rodríguez Sánchez** ('Manolete'), notable for his solemn, hieratic style, dominated the post-war years. Despite two seasons of competition with the spectacular Mexican, Carlos Arruza, in 1944 and 1945, Manolete was still the outstanding matador of his day when, on 28 August 1947, he was fatally gored by a Miura bull in Linares; his death the following day occasioned national mourning. Manolete's death left a void no contemporary could fill, not even the graceful Pepe Luis Vázquez, the more sober Antonio **Mejías** ('Bienvenida'), or the talented and glamorous Luis Miguel **González** ('Dominguín'). Indeed, in 1949 and 1950, bullfighting was dominated not by full matadors but by two ***novilleros***, Julio Aparicio and Miguel Báez ('Litri').

Geographically, bullfighting remained most popular throughout the 1940s and 1950s in its traditional strongholds (Andalusia, Valencia, central Spain and parts of the north) though mass-emigration from the impoverished south to Barcelona led to a resurgence of bullfighting there which endured for a quarter of a century. The 1950s also saw a new generation of matadors, including Aparicio, Litri, Manolo Vázquez and Antonio **Chenel** ('Antoñete'). Most important of all was Antonio **Ordóñez**, whose unique ability to unite the two principal classical styles of bullfighting, the sober *rondeño* and more flamboyant *sevillano*, led to his generally being considered the greatest matador since Manolete. In the late 1950s and early 1960s, popular ***toreros*** included the spectacular Antonio Borrero ('Chamaco'), the courageous Diego Puerta, the classical and gifted Paco Camino, and the solemn Santiago Martín ('El Viti'). There was also the fearful and erratic but incomparably artistic Francisco **Romero López** ('Curro Romero'), who in the 1990s still enjoyed unprecedented esteem in Seville, and who remains still active in his mid-sixties.

None of these, however, hinted at the development which would shortly transform the conservative world of the *corrida*: the appearance of Manuel **Benítez** ('El Cordobés'). An illiterate bricklayer, son of a rural labourer who died a prisoner following the Civil War, El Cordobés came to prominence following an unprecedented publicity campaign. Clumsy and technically inept, El Cordobés was initially the antithesis of the classical *torero*. Yet these very defects, allied to an overwhelmingly sympathetic personality, and a youthful, long-haired appearance very much at odds with the conformist Spain of the 1960s, enabled El Cordobés to personify the contemporary struggle for wealth and status in a still-impoverished country, turning him into a national icon, a Spanish equivalent of his contemporaries, the Beatles. As such he appealed both to younger Spaniards and the rapidly increasing number of tourists who frequented the newly-built bullrings of the Costa del Sol or Costa Brava. Although traditionalists never fully lost their mistrust of his clowning, El Cordobés gained steadily in technical security, improved his style and, the glamour of novelty past, obtained notable triumphs in the most serious and demanding arenas in Spain. More negatively, El Cordobés also helped impose on bullfighting a smaller, weaker, more docile bull, with sometimes scandalously shaved horns. It was this diminished animal which was most frequently to be seen in Spanish rings in the late 1960s and early 1970s, a period which saw the final retirement of such older matadors as Bienvenida, Dominguín, and Antonio Ordóñez and the emergence of important younger matadors, including Sebastián Palomo Linares, Francisco **Rivera** ('Paquirri'), Pedro Moya ('El Niño de la Capea'), and José Mari Dols ('Manzanares').

Partly in reaction to the bulls fought by El Cordobés, the 1970s saw a resurgent interest in the fighting bull itself. The large, well-armed, genuinely wild *toro bravo* had never entirely disappeared, as testified by the products of such bull-ranches as Miura, Pablo Romero, Conde de la Corte or Isaías y Tulio Vázquez. At a time of crisis for breeders, however, the bulls of Victorino Martín came to prominence in the Madrid plaza of Las Ventas, resulting both in the continuing popularity of that breeder and his bulls, and in the controversial predilection for huge, well-armed bulls which has come to distinguish Spain's most important bullring. The period since 1975 has also seen an increasingly scientific attitude to bull-breeding, led notably by Don Alvaro Domecq y Díez.

As in other areas of Spanish culture, the death of Franco in 1975 had important implications for bullfighting. When the Civil War ended, the victors endeavoured to harness bullfighting to their cause, by means of 'Victory' *corridas*, like that celebrated on 24 May 1939 in Madrid, and *corridas* such as that held annually in Bilbao on the anniversary of the 'liberation' of the city by Franco's troops. It was hoped that regional differences might be partly overcome by promoting the so-called *Fiesta Nacional*. Franco regularly and conspicuously attended the important charity bullfight, the *Corrida de Beneficencia*, held annually in Madrid, and in the 1960s he cultivated the acquaintance of El Cordobés (whose father had died in one of his prison-camps). However, Franco's evident lack of interest in bullfighting (his native region of Galicia having virtually no taurine tradition) meant that the spectacle was never as identified with his regime as some would have liked. Despite predictions to the contrary, bullfighting quickly shook off any association with Francoism. The long-standing ban on women performing on foot in the arena, for instance, was removed as part of the gradual liberalization of Spanish society. (The subsequent progress of women in bullfighting has been generally slow, however, though the highly regarded Cristina Sánchez took her ***alternativa*** in 1996.) King Juan Carlos, meanwhile, took Franco's place at the annual *Beneficencia corrida* and attended many other *corridas* in a notably democratic fashion, taking his place among his subjects rather than using the royal box. Even in regions such as **Euskadi**, which reacted most radically against the attempted imposition of a single 'Spanish' national identity, attempts to condemn bullfighting as a relic of Spain's reactionary past were soon dropped as politicians recognized the strength of popular support for the spectacle. Although the **Generalitat** in Catalonia has shown a lack of enthusiasm for bullfighting, only the Canary Islands have banned *corridas*. Leading socialist politicians soon became as familiar a sight in Spain's bullrings as conservative nationalists had been in previous decades.

As a whole, then, the 1970s were marked by continuity rather than any decisive break with the immediate past. The decade was also characterized by the lack of a really outstanding figure among leading matadors. It was remarkable, however, for the resurgence of ***rejoneo***, and *corridas* consisting solely of ***rejoneadores*** topped the hundred mark in six of the years between 1970 and 1978. Only with the emergence from obscurity of Paco Ojeda in 1981 was there a truly exceptional matador in Spanish rings and he never acquired the genuinely popular acclaim accorded El Cordobés, though his much-discussed style influenced virtually all younger *toreros*. One matador known far beyond the narrow circle of dedicated ***aficionados*** was Francisco Rivera ('Paquirri'). An Andalusian of humble birth, Paquirri was a skilled and popular figure in the ring and famous also for his marriages, first, to a daughter of Antonio Ordóñez and, subsequently, to one of Spain's best-known popular singers, Isabel Pantoja. When Paquirri was fatally gored in the small town of Pozoblanco in 1984, Spain reacted in a way unknown since the death of Manolete twenty-seven years earlier. That Paquirri died while being transported by car to the nearest large hospital also prompted much criticism of the inadequacy of medical facilities in the remoter corners of Spain. The death of one of Spain's most promising young matadors, José Cubero ('Yiyo'), in Colmenar el Viejo, in the following year, brought home to a wide public the danger inherent in bullfighting, sometimes lost sight of in the post-Cordobés era.

The increased popularity of bullfighting in the 1990s has resulted not from any appeal as anachronistic folklore but rather from the accommodation of the spectacle to the requirements of modern consumer society. Attendance at *corridas* is unprecedentedly fashionable, among women as well as men. Thoughts that bullfighting would soon feature among other uncomfortable aspects of a repudiated past have disappeared as intellectuals and celebrities as different as the economist and socialist mayor of Madrid, Enrique Tierno Galván, the opera singer Plácido Domingo, and the Nobel Prize-winning writer, Camilo José Cela, have all shown their interest in the spectacle. The number of bullfights has risen to unprecedented levels: there were 859 *corridas de toros* and 612 *novilladas* in 1997 (as opposed to 276 *corridas* and 204 *novilladas* fifty years previously). In Madrid, the San Isidro fair, which began with a modest four *corridas* in 1948, now runs to nearly thirty *corridas*, held on consecutive days. Television has played a crucial role, the private channels, including since 1998 digital television, finding live broadcasts of *corridas* popular additions to their schedules. Young matadors now frequently resemble teenage pop stars and some have enthusiastic followings among their female contemporaries. A number of popular matadors, including Juan Antonio **Ruiz**, ('Espartaco'), Jesús **Janeiro** ('Jesulín de Ubrique'), and Manuel Díaz ('El Cordobés') (self-proclaimed natural son of the older El Cordobés, Manuel Benítez), owe their considerable success as much to telegenic good looks as to their talents or courage in the ring. Whether this state of affairs is permanent or whether, removed from its traditional ambience of *sol y moscas* (sun and flies) to be sanitized and packaged by the media, bullfighting is vulnerable to the fickleness of consumer fashion is much debated by traditional *aficionados*. These prefer the solider artistic virtues of such younger *toreros* as José Miguel Arroyo ('Joselito'), Juan Serrano ('Finito de Córdoba'), Francisco Rivera Ordóñez (son of Paquirri and grandson of Antonio Ordóñez), Enrique **Ponce**, José Tomás and Julián Lopez ('El Juli').

Few *aficionados* have as yet devoted much attention to the impact European integration and changing attitudes to animal welfare may have on bullfighting. In Spain, animal rights campaigners are still relatively few in number and their poorly attended protests make little impact. Attempts in the European parliament to outlaw bullfighting have so far failed, largely because opponents' ignorance of the social and cultural history of bullfighting has led them to overlook the extent to which, in the south of France as well as in Spain and Portugal, the *corrida* is closely bound up with popular constructions of national and regional identity. Today, bullfighting is as strongly rooted in popular manifestations in Navarre, Valencia, or the working-class suburbs of Madrid, as in its traditional strongholds. This genuinely popular support, coupled with the economic importance of the *corrida*, not least in terms of employment, seems set to see bullfighting continue to flourish in the Spain of the twenty-first century.

See also: Francoist culture; sport and leisure

Further reading

Amorós, A. (1987) *Toros y cultura*, Madrid: Espasa-Calpe.

Cossío, J.M. de (ed.) (1943–92) *Los toros*, 12 vols, Madrid: Espasa-Calpe (the standard reference work).

Marvin, G. (1988) *Bullfight*, Oxford: Blackwell (an accessible account in English).

Moral, J.A. del (1994) *Cómo ver una corrida de toros*, Madrid: Alianza (an introduction to the structure and terminology of the *corrida*).

IAN CAMPBELL ROSS

Buñuel, Luis

b. 1900, Calanda (Teruel); d. 1983, Mexico City

Filmmaker

Buñuel occupies the most prominent position not only in Spanish film but in European surrealist film as a whole. No other Spanish director has left a comparable legacy of internationally recognized masterworks, and although he spent most of his career in exile he inspired a generation of younger directors, such as Carlos **Saura**, who started to work under Franco's dictatorship. His earlier films, *Un chien andalou* (*An Andalusian Dog*), which he wrote with Salvador **Dalí**, and *L'Age d'or* (*The Golden Age*), are unanimously considered the most genuine examples of surrealism in film. Many of the ideas for *Un chien andalou* emanated from the intellectual atmosphere of the *Residencia de Estudiantes*, the Madrid institution where both Buñuel and Dalí spent their university years, and where they knew such important figures as the poet Federico García Lorca.

In 1925, Buñuel moved to Paris to learn the craft of filmmaking with the French director Jean Epstein. The release, in 1929, of *Un chien andalou* gave both Dalí and Buñuel access to the surrealist group. Although, according to Buñuel, he and Dalí conceived *Un chien andalou* while trying to come up with images and associations that defied interpretation, the surrealists found in this short film the most accurate expression of the discourse of dreams, and of desire. It also transgresses humorously all the rules of cinematic continuity, providing a kind of metafictional commentary which makes us aware of the conventions and habits by which films are constructed and interpreted.

L'Age d'or adheres more strictly to the themes and concerns of the surrealist movement: desire and irrationality, *l'amour fou* and the gratuitous act, here become weapons of cultural revolution, with explicit political implications. The film attacks religion, family, morality and the whole fabric of bourgeois society. In this sense, it can be said to anticipate many of his later films, such as *Le charme discret de la bourgeoisie* (*The Discreet Charm of the Bourgeoisie*) and *Le fantôme de la liberté* (*The Phantom of Liberty*), which would also choose the same institutions as the targets of criticism.

Even before Franco came to power Buñuel had clashed with governmental **censorship**, as his 1932 documentary *Las Hurdes*, also entitled *Tierra sin pan* (*Land Without Bread*), was forbidden by the Republic because of the negative image of Spain it presented. The Civil War forced him into exile, first in the United States and from 1946 in Mexico. Some of his Mexican films were 'bread and butter' melodramas, which, though often neglected by the critics, complement his more original films of the period as they show the development of his style and the continuity of his surrealist concerns: dream-scenes and fantasies are interwoven with the naturalistic fabric of the narrative, erasing the limits between different levels of reality.

Viridiana was the first film Buñuel made in Spain after his exile, and it proved highly controversial, for contrasting reasons. A sector of the anti-Franco opposition feared it might mean the domestication of Buñuel by the dictatorship, which had approved the film. Despite being the official entry at the Cannes Film Festival, where it won the Golden Palm, the film ended up being banned in Spain, after protests about its content from the Vatican's *L'Osservatore Romano*. The critical acclaim which greeted the film marked the beginning of a period of increased international recognition and more abundant resources, mostly from French producers. In the 1960s and 1970s Buñuel achieved an unparalleled degree of creative independence, which allowed him to display his satire of religion, morality and social class through fluid narrative structures, where the rules of verisimilitude are constantly transgressed, in films such as *La Voie Lactée* (*The Milky Way*), *Le charme discret de la bourgeoisie* (which won the 1972 Academy Award for Best Foreign Film), and *Le fantôme de la liberté.*

Buñuel found in literature a permanent source of inspiration. In addition to classics such as *Wuthering Heights* and *Robinson Crusoe*, he adapted two novels by the nineteenth-century Spanish writer Benito Pérez Galdós, *Nazarín* and *Tristana.* Even films which are closely identified with his personal style, such as *Belle de jour* or *Cet obscur objet du désir* (*That Obscure Object of Desire*), have a literary source. In this, his last film, Buñuel, playfully undermining our habits of interpretation by using two actresses for the same role, returned to the impulse that had never ceased to drive his work since his earlier films, to the subject of desire.

See also: film and cinema; Rabal, Francisco; Rey, Fernando

Filmography

Buñuel, L. (1929) *Un chien andalou* (*An Andalusian Dog*).

—— (1930) *L'Age d'or* (*The Golden Age*).
—— (1932) *Las Hurdes / Tierra sin pan* (*Land Without Bread*).
—— (1950) *Los olvidados* (*The Dispossessed*).
—— (1955) *Ensayo de un crimen / La vida criminal de Archibaldo de la Cruz* (*The Criminal Life of Archibaldo de la Cruz*).
—— (1958) *Nazarín*,
—— (1961) *Viridiana*.
—— (1962) *El ángel exterminador* (*The Exterminating Angel*).
—— (1966) *Belle de jour*.
—— (1968) *La Voie Lactée* (*The Milky Way*).
—— (1969) *Tristana*.
—— (1972) *Le charme discret de la bourgeoisie* (*The Discreet Charm of the Bourgeoisie*).
—— (1974) *Le fantôme de la liberté* (*The Phantom of Liberty*).
—— (1977) *Cet obscur objet du désir* (*That Obscure Object of Desire*).

Further reading

Baxter, J. (1995) *Buñuel*, London: Fourth Estate (the latest biography in English).

Buñuel, L. and Carrière, J.-C. (1984) *My Last Breath*, London: Cape (Buñuel's not wholly reliable but engaging autobiography).

Evans, P.W. (1995) *The Films of Luis Buñuel: Subjectivity and Desire*, Oxford and New York: Oxford University Press (a sophisticated study that takes into account the most recent critical approaches).

Sánchez Vidal, A. (1991) *Luis Buñuel*, Madrid: Cátedra (a thorough introduction to Buñuel's work, with careful analyses of his films).

Sandro, P. (1987) *Diversions of Pleasure: Luis Buñuel and the Crisis of Desire*, Columbus, OH: Ohio State University Press (a perceptive analysis that addresses the films from a theoretical perspective).

ANTONIO MONEGAL-BRANCOS

BUP

The Bachillerato Universal Polivalente (Combined General Baccalaureat) derived from the Education Law of 1970, and was awarded after three years' study, from ages fourteen to sixteen. Entry to the course was selective, requiring the completion of primary education, or the first level of **FP**. The first two years followed a common syllabus, and the third offered an element of choice between arts and science subjects. Pupils proceeded to university after taking a further year of study (**COU**), or to the second level of FP. The **LOGSE**, enacted in 1990, envisaged the phasing-out of BUP by 2000.

ISIDRO FADRIQUE

C

Caballé, Montserrat

b. 1933, Barcelona

Opera singer

One of the great sopranos of her generation, Montserrat Caballé became a household name in the many countries of the world where she performed during her career. She made her début in 1956 with the Basel Opera, playing Mimi in Puccini's *La Bohème.* During the next ten years Montserrat Caballé toured the major opera houses of Europe, singing German and later the lyrical Italian operas. In 1965 she made a sensational New York début in Donizetti's *Lucrezia Borgia.*

As well as her extremely wide operatic repertoire, Caballé gave numerous recitals, often of Catalan and Spanish songs. In the late 1980s, she performed in the famous *Barcelona* concert with the rock singer Freddie Mercury, and she sang at the opening ceremony of the Barcelona Olympics in 1992.

Caballé earned a reputation for awkwardness which rivalled that of Callas. She had strong views on how certain operas should be played, and refused to compromise on standards. In 1973 she got her way after a major row on the performance of Bellini's *Norma* at La Scala, which proved to be one of her major successes. Possibly the biggest scandal of her career also came at La Scala in 1982. She was to play the leading role in a revival production of the 1957 version of Donizetti's *Anna Bolena,* which Visconti had prepared for Callas. The famous curse of Callas seemed to strike when Caballé failed to sing at the first night performance because of illness. However, the audience were not told of the illness until they were in their seats, and a near riot ensued. Caballé eventually performed the role ten days later, and, typically, won over her initially hostile audience. She repeated the role in a special performance staged for ITV's *South Bank Show* in 1993 at the Tower of London.

DAVID GEORGE

cafeterías

Spanish *cafeterías* trade primarily in the snack market, providing coffee-break style catering from breakfast to dinner-time. Although alcoholic beverages can be purchased, most of their sales are coffees, pastries, sandwiches and *tapas.* They are busy practically all day, serving breakfast, elevenses, aperitifs, after-lunch coffee, ***merienda*** and pre-dinner drinks. Originally, they evolved from the traditional café, but their decor reflects a faster, more functional and 'modern' approach to customer service. *Cafetería* prices are slightly higher than in bars and there is an official ratings system which determines prices within three categories; establishments are also allowed to charge more for table or terrace service.

RAMÓN PARRONDO

Caixa, La

La Caixa, or Caja de Ahorros y Pensiones de Barcelona, dates from 1844. In 1990 it merged with another Catalan savings bank, the Caja de Pensiones y de Ahorros de Cataluña y Baleares (1904). It is counted among the top five financial institutions in Spain and is the largest savings bank in Europe. It owns several other financial entities, among them the Asturian regional bank, Banco Herrero, and controls various others such as the Andalusian Banco Granada Jerez of which it owns 60 percent of the capital. It is active abroad through its subsidiaries Caixabank France and Caixabank Monaco, and has a minority shareholding in the Portuguese bank Banco Portugues de Investimento. As well as having a number of subsidiaries in insurance, property and investment services, it has a wide portfolio of shareholdings, including shares in electricity, gas and water companies, in the oil company Repsol and in Telefónica, being the biggest non-state shareholder in the latter.

In 1995 client deposits at La Caixa (including banking subsidiaries but excluding all other sectors) amounted to 7.34m^2 pesetas and net worth to 412,923m pesetas. Profits after tax were 62,454m pesetas. About half of La Caixa's lending is on a mortgage basis. Although the bulk of its 2,586 Spanish branches (2,920 including those of its subsidiaries) are still to be found in its home region of Catalonia, La Caixa has a presence throughout the national territory. This vast network facilitates the marketing of a range of products, including insurance, investment plans, leasing and factoring. As in the case of all Spanish **Cajas de Ahorros**, an important function of La Caixa lies in its contribution to welfare and community projects, which it carries out through its charitable foundation Fundación La Caixa. It has financed AIDS awareness and research, a wide range of scientific and artistic exhibitions, public libraries and educational projects, bursaries for study at home and abroad, and environmental improvement schemes.

C.A. LONGHURST

Caja de Madrid

Along with La **Caixa**, Caja de Madrid represents the epitome of the Spanish savings banks. Founded in 1838 by the *corregidor* (civil governor) of Madrid, the Caja de Ahorros y Monte de Piedad de Madrid has grown from its modest beginnings in which working class people deposited their scarce savings to one of Spain's major and most profitable financial institutions, the second largest of the **Cajas de Ahorros** with branches all over Spain and with close on 4m^2 pesetas of clients' deposits in 1995 and pre-tax profits of 48,000m pesetas. Of particular importance is the beneficent role of the Caja, both through direct participation in subsidized housing, schools and retirement homes, and through its cultural **foundation** Fundación Caja de Madrid, which provides funds for such diverse activities as architectural conservation and restoration, public concerts, lectures and exhibitions, cultural and scientific research and publication, and scholarships and study programmes across a broad spectrum.

C.A. LONGHURST

Cajas de Ahorros

Not unlike the British building societies, although less exclusively tied to house mortgages in their function, the Spanish Cajas de Ahorros or savings banks date from the 1830s when Spanish liberals returned from exile in France and England. The first major Caja was the Caja de Ahorros y Previsión de Madrid (1838) which followed the model of the Caisse d'Epargne de Paris. Some 250 local and regional Cajas have existed over the years. The Cajas are represented by the Confederación Española de Cajas de Ahorro (CECA) which acts as a crucial link between the individual Cajas and the monetary authorities of the state. Although during the Second Republic (1931–9) and the first two decades of the Franco regime the Cajas were deliberately placed at a disadvantage in relation to the more influential commercial **banks**, this situation changed in the 1960s following the 1962 Ley de Ordenación del Crédito y la Banca (Banking and Credit Regulation Law), and the gradual liberalization of the restrictions under which they had to operate enabled them to become increasingly competitive and to capture a substantial share of the nation's private savings and institutional lending. Nevertheless under Franco the Cajas remained subject to highly restrictive controls, which among other things obliged them to invest a large amount of their assets in government bonds. It was only in 1977 that a new law finally placed them on an approximately equal footing with the commercial banks. By the 1990s, after a period of mergers and further legislative relaxation allowing them to open branches outside their own regions and reducing their obligatory cash coefficients, there were some fifty Cajas and their combined deposits exceeded those of the commercial banks.

Although the Cajas are responsible for no more than half of mortgage finance in Spain, a strong presence in smaller towns and the wide range of services which they provide, including that of the crediting of state pensions, afford them a crucial role in the Spanish financial system. The Cajas do not have shareholders and are obliged by law to devote their profits to reserves and to cultural and welfare projects of benefit to the community. Some 25 percent of profits after tax are devoted to the latter. This to some extent makes up for the low rates of interest which they have traditionally paid to their depositors. The solvency ratio (ownership capital to total assets) of the Cajas, which stood at 12.87 percent in 1995, is in general well above the minimum of 8 percent required by European legislation.

The main policy thrust of the Cajas in recent years has been to increase their share of clients' deposits (not least by increasing the branch network); to introduce new varieties of mortgage loans and finance for consumer durables; and to enhance customer facilities such as debit cards, cash dispensers and credit transfers. This has been accompanied by a much more efficient clearing system in which the CECA has played a key role. Although they still lag behind the private banks in the area of attracting investment in financial products as distinct from simple deposits, they have nevertheless been moving cautiously into this area as well. Their philosophy, governed by the social aims for which they were founded, is still geared to providing a service to the family and to the family firm, but there is a recognition that the traditional operation of acting as mere deposit takers and then lending a substantial part of these funds to the financial market must be replaced by a much more diversified set of activities. Despite their strongly regional roots, reinforced to a degree by the new style of devolved government in Spain, some of the larger Cajas are now looking for an international role. The two largest Cajas are La **Caixa** and **Caja de Madrid** which together account for over one-third of savings banks deposits in Spain.

Further reading

Salmon, K. (1995) *The Modern Spanish Economy*, 2nd edn, London: Pinter (a very accessible account of all the main aspects of the Spanish economy).

C.A. LONGHURST

Calatrava, Santiago

b. 1951, Benimanet (Valencia)

Architect

Calatrava qualified as an architect in 1973 at Valencia, and studied civil engineering at Zurich where he subsequently taught. He very quickly earned international recognition and divides his time between his studios in Switzerland and Valencia and the many prestigious projects that he directs. An architect-engineer with enormous powers of expression, his works display his engineering skills in creations of great formal beauty. His best-known works in Spain are the Bridge of Alamillo (for Expo-92 in Seville) and the Montjuich Tower (also known as the Calatrava Tower, constructed for the Barcelona Olympic Games in 1992).

MIHAIL MOLDOVEANU

Calders, Pere

b. 1912, Barcelona

Writer

Artist, journalist and fervent Catalan activist under the Republic, Calders later turned to fiction, progressing from wartime political satire to **science fiction**, written while living in exile. His war diary, *Unitats de xoc* (Shock Troops), portraying the desperate reality of defeat, contrasts with the fantasy novel, *Gaeli i l'home déu* (Gaeli and the God Man), occupying a supernatural realm where miraculous powers create a harmonious utopia. Fantasy alternates with reality hereafter throughout Calders' career, accounting for his major successes.

Confined with other Republican refugees to a concentration camp in France, Calders escaped and eventually reached Mexico, where he lived for twenty-five years. Combining work as a graphic designer with establishing himself as a writer, he wrote fiction regularly for Catalan publications in exile. Short stories, often in the neglected genre of fantasy, became his primary vehicle. After returning to Spain, Calders emerged in the 1970s as a major cultivator of Catalan science fiction, with Manuel de **Pedrolo** and Pere Verdaguer. All three treat science fiction topics with humour and whimsy, usually employing as their setting not some distant planet but the landscape of Catalonia, and blending fantasy, reality and critical comment on mores with the familiar mythic patterns of the genre.

During the 1950s, Calders published many of his best short stories, collected as *Cròniques de la veritat oculta* (Chronicles of Hidden Truth). *Gent de l'alta vall* (High Valley People) and *Demà a les tres de la matinada* (Tomorrow at Three in the Morning) include stories logically reflecting the exile experience in realistic or humorous fashion, but usually Calders favours the Utopia/Dystopia mode of science fiction, portraying alternative social structures. His negative or satiric Utopias (Dystopias) closely resemble Catalonia and unfold in an immediate or foreseeable future, employing little jargon or pseudoscientific rhetoric. He often adopts the guise of news reports, profferring ironic, amusing chronicles of failed attempts, spoofs of scientific methods, or burlesques of Spain's technological backwardness.

Calders' father submitted some of his stories to competition for the prestigious Victor Catalá Prize, resulting in the first serious critical studies and contributing to his return to Barcelona in 1963. His second novel, *L'ombra de l'atzavara* (The Agave's Shadow), portraying Catalan exiles in Mexico, won the Sant Jordi Prize, spurring him on to publish *Ronda naval sota la boira* (Naval Round in Fog), a novelette composed in exile. New story anthologies appeared in Spain, but Calders waited ten years before publishing *L'invasió subtil i altres contes* (Subtle Invasion and Other Stories), and *Tot s'aprofita* (Everything is Utilized). Exploiting science fiction's satiric potential to political effect, Calders remains, with Pedrolo, among the most significant cultivators of this mode in the Peninsula.

Major works

Calders, P. (1968) *Tots els contes (1936–1967)* Barcelona: Libres de Sinera (thirty years' collected stories).

Further reading

Bath, A. (1987) *Pere Calders: Ideari i Ficció*, Barcelona: Edicions 62 (best and most complete critical study of Calders' fiction and ideology).

Pérez, J. (1984) 'Three Contemporary Cultivators of Science Fiction in Catalan', *Discurso Literario* 2, 1: 203–16 (discusses Calders, Pedrolo and Verdaguer).

JANET PÉREZ

Calvo Serer, Rafael

b. 1916, Valencia; d. 1988, Madrid

Politician

Calvo Serer was a leading member of **Opus Dei** and proponent of **National Catholicism**, which he advocated in *España sin problema* (Spain, Not a Problem, 1949), a riposte to the liberalizing and Europeanizing tendencies of **Ortega y Gasset**. As editor of the newspaper *Madrid*, he moved towards support of a democratic monarchy. This provoked the suppression of the paper, and his exile in France from 1971, where he became involved with the Democratic Junta, which demanded a break with the Franco regime and the restoration of democratic freedoms.

EAMONN RODGERS

Calvo Sotelo, Joaquín

b. 1905, La Coruña; d. 1993, Madrid

Dramatist

Born into a distinguished family of judges and politicians, Calvo Sotelo studied law at the University of Madrid, graduating in 1926. It was while at university that he developed his interest in journalism and the theatre, which he later combined with his professional activity as a lawyer. His literary achievements were recognized by election to the Royal Spanish Academy in 1955, and the award of the National Literature Prize in 1958 (see also **prizes**). His approximately sixty plays reflect a conservative stance, influenced by his own Catholicism, but at the same time critical of the Franco regime. Early performed work included *A la tierra: kilómetro 500 mil* (*To Earth: Kilometer 500,000*) (1932) and *El rebelde* (*The Rebel*) (1933), but it was not until the late 1940s that he really got into his stride, with the sentimental comedy *La visita que no tocó el timbre* (*The Caller Who Didn't Ring*) (1949). In the same year, he received the Jacinto Benavente Prize for the best play of the season. He wrote farces with improbable situations, and parodic comedies in the tradition of the *sainete* (a short, satirical sketch), as well as works like *Milagro en la Plaza del Progreso* (*Miracle in the Plaza del Progreso*) (1953), *La mariposa y el ingeniero* (*The Butterfly and the Engineer*) (1953), and *Micaela* (1962). He had considerable success with humorous sentimental comedies about the life of the Spanish bourgeoisie, including *Plaza de Oriente* (1947), *Dos hombres y una mujer* (*Two Men and One Woman*) (1949), *Una muchachita de Valladolid* (*A Girl from Valladolid*) (1957), *Cartas credenciales* (*Credentials of a Diplomat*, 1960), *Operación Embajada* (*Operation Embassy*) (1962), and *El baño de las ninfas* (*The Nymphs' Bath*) (1966). He is, however, best known for his historical and moralistic dramas, in which he explores how human beings behave in a hostile environment, and where he adopts a critical stance towards the Franco regime: *Criminal de guerra* (*War Criminal*) (1951), *María Antonieta* (*Marie Antoinette*) (1952), *El jefe* (*The Leader*), (1953), *Historia de un resentido* (*Story of a Resentful Man*) (1955), *Ciudad sin Dios* (*City Without God*) (1957), *Proceso al arzobispo Carranza* (*The Trial of Archbishop Carranza*) (1964), *La condesa Laurel* (*Countess Laurel*) (1964), *El poder* (*Power*) (1965), *El inocente* (*The Innocent*) (1968), *La amante* (*The Lover*) (1968) and *El alfil* (*The Bishop* – as in chess). One play of this historical type, *La muralla* (*The Wall*) (1955), was an instant success, and received critical acclaim. The plot enacts the struggle between an upper-middle-class man and his own family, to return money obtained in the Civil War to its rightful owner. With 5,000 performances, it was one of the longest-running plays in the history of the Spanish theatre.

See also: theatre

MARÍA FRANCISCA VILCHES DE FRUTOS

Calvo Sotelo y Bustelo, Leopoldo

b. 1926, Spain

Businessman and politician

Calvo Soleto y Bustelo was a leading member of **UCD**, and Prime Minister from 1981 to 1982. As a member of **Suárez**'s first government, he helped to organize UCD's first election campaign in 1977. As Minister for Relations with the EEC from 1978 to 1980, he began the negotiations leading to Spain's entry into the European Community. He succeeded Suárez as Prime Minister in January 1981 and was instrumental in Spain joining **NATO**. Initially successful in rebuilding inter-party consensus, he was unable to contain the factional conflict within UCD, and presided over the disintegration and subsequent electoral defeat of that formation in 1982.

JONATHAN HOPKIN

Camacho Abad, Marcelino

b. 1918, Osma la Rasa (Soria)

Trade union leader

Camacho is generally considered the outstanding leader in the Spanish **trade union** movement of the last four decades. His name is closely associated with the struggle against the state-controlled syndicates imposed on the working class by the Franco regime. After the dictator's death he played a central role in the re-establishment of free trade unions.

Camacho joined the **PCE** (Spanish Communist Party) when he was seventeen and has been a party member ever since. He fought in the Civil War on the Republican side, and at the end of the war was condemned to twelve years in prison, but in 1943 he escaped from the African labour camp where he was serving part of his sentence. After some years in exile, he was allowed back into Spain in 1957, at a time of profound social and economic change. Employed as a turner by Perkins Hispania in Madrid, he immersed himself in clandestine trade union activities, becoming a major force in the creation of **CC OO** (Comisiones Obreras). He was imprisoned on numerous occasions, and was one of the accused in the renowned *Proceso 1001* concluded on 23 December 1973, coincidentally the day **Carrero Blanco** was assassinated. Camacho received a twenty year sentence, later reduced to six years, and he was finally amnestied by the first post-Franco government.

His political and trade union involvement continued, if anything more intensively, after Franco's death. In line with the policy of PCE and CC OO, he initially supported the idea of a *ruptura* or clean break with the dictatorial past, but soon accepted the inevitability of a legal transition towards democracy. In 1976 he was appointed secretary general of CC OO and as a communist candidate in Madrid he gained a parliamentary seat in the 1977 and 1979 general elections. He took part in the negotiations of the **Moncloa Pacts**, which led to his being accused of subordinating the workers' interests to those of the party. Camacho has always rejected such suggestions and to prove his point he gave up his parliamentary seat in 1981. Throughout the 1980s he was a vociferous opponent of the policies of successive socialist governments, and was involved in the anti-**NATO** campaign in 1986.

At the 1987 congress of CC OO Camacho stepped down as secretary general. In recognition of his long career he was honoured with the post of union president. From that position he has exercised the patriarchal role of the retired charismatic leader.

See also: political parties; politics

Further reading

Camacho, M. (1976) *Charlas en la prisión*, Barcelona: Laia (autobiographical reflections).

—— (1990) *Confieso que he luchado*, Barcelona: Temas de Hoy (autobiographical work).

Gil, F. (1989), *Hay otro socialismo. Conversaciones con Marcelino Camacho*, Madrid: C.C.G.L (a good summary of Camacho's views on politics and trade unionism).

Ruiz, D. (ed.) (1993), *Historia de Comisiones Obreras (1958–1988)*, Madrid: Siglo XXI (provides a detailed background for some of Camacho's most active years).

JOSÉ AMODIA

Cambio 16

Cambio 16 is one of Spain's most successful weekly general and current affairs magazines. Though it no longer dominates this sector of the market as it once did, it remains a powerful voice in Spanish public debate. It is the longest standing of the various general information weekly magazines available in Spain, having been launched in the early 1970s, towards the end of the Franco era. It is published by Grupo 16, a publishing group which also puts out a daily newspaper, *Diario 16*, as well as a number of other more specialized magazines.

Cambio 16's prestige was high in the immediate post-dictatorship period of the late 1970s and early 1980s. Its general layout and structure are well-known to regular readers. It always opens with the Editor's Letter on the first inside page. This feature, which is peculiar to Spanish weekly magazines, combines some of the characteristics of an editorial with those of a personal column, and serves to set the general tone of the magazine. Following Letters to the Editor and a fairly lightweight 'People in the News' section, *Cambio 16* will then usually continue with a special feature of some kind. Next comes 'Este País' (This Country), one of the most read sections of the magazine and generally viewed as one of the most important forums for news and opinion in the country's weekly press. This is followed by a fairly substantial international news section and, finally, somewhat lighter culture/society articles.

Though it was originally prized as a focus for the expression of anti-Franco opinion, and subsequently as a champion of liberal-democratic views, it is perhaps fair to say that *Cambio 16* has to some extent aged along with its primary readership. It is now openly conservative in its political outlook, and its constant campaigns of criticism against members of **PSOE** governments cannot be fully explained by the desire simply to expose corruption. It now basically addresses a largely middle-aged, middle-class readership which would like Spain to be more modern and more efficient, but which would prefer any change which takes place not to threaten their own relatively privileged position.

This gradual ageing of *Cambio 16* has slowly opened up a space in the market which has now been exploited by a number of competing publications, the most important of which is Grupo Zeta's *Tiempo*, a much younger and pushier magazine which has now in fact overtaken *Cambio 16* in terms of sales. Nonetheless, *Cambio 16*'s long history of defence of democratic values, at a time when they were vulnerable, is likely to ensure the continued loyalty of its readership.

See also: media; press

Further reading

Mateo, R. de and Corbella, J.M. (1992) 'Spain' in B.S. Østergaard (ed.) *The Media in Western Europe*, London: Sage (a useful guide to the media situation in Spain in general, though its coverage of individual newspapers is rather slim).

HUGH O'DONNELL

Camino, Jaime

b. 1936, Barcelona

Filmmaker

In the 1960s Camino directed a variety of films, including *Mañana será otro dia* (Tomorrow will be Another Day) (1966), a critique of Spanish society in the form of a light farce on the theme of unemployment, *España otra vez* (Spain Once Again) (1968), based on the reactions of a man who had fought in the International Brigades returning to Spain thirty years later, and *Un invierno en Mallorca* (A Winter in Majorca) (1969), a highly praised study of the love of Chopin and George Sand. In 1988 he made *Luces y Sombras* (Lights and Shadows), a film which mixes historical and contemporary elements, moving between the court of Philip IV and the present day.

It is, however, probably for the films which deal with the outbreak, course and consequences of the Civil War that Camino is best known. Co-scripted with **Gutiérrez Aragón** in 1975, and set in a country holiday resort near Barcelona, *Las largas vaciones del 36* (The Long Holidays of 1936) drew on the reminiscences of Camino's own family. It was shown at Cannes in 1976, though unofficially, because of a controversial final scene in which, as the Republican army retreats, the Moorish cavalry which formed Franco's advance guard appear over the horizon. In *La vieja memoria* (Old Memories) (1976), Camino builds a picture of the war from old documentaries and interviews with survivors, accompanied by a dramatic sound track. In 1991, in *El largo invierno* (The Long Winter), he portrays Catalan opposition to Franco and the suppression of their autonomy and language.

See also: censorship; film and cinema

Further reading

Higginbotham, V. (1988) *Spanish Cinema under Franco*, Austin, TX: University of Texas Press (one of the most comprehensive surveys of this period).

Hopewell, J. (1986) *Out of the Past: Spanish Cinema After Franco*, London: British Film Institute (a very readable general account of contemporary trends).

Molina-Foix, V. (1977) *New Cinema in Spain*, London: British Film Institute (a comprehensive overview of current trends).

EAMONN RODGERS

camping

Of the 622,000 or so camping spaces available throughout Spain, the vast majority are in first or second grade sites, with around 3,000 in one luxury grade site and a little over 66,000 in 242 third grade sites. By far the highest concentration of camping sites is in Catalonia where Gerona, Tarragona, Barcelona and Lleida between them account for well over a third of the total provision, including all the luxury grade, and over half the first grade. This clearly reflects the region's high tourist profile, and other popular holiday centres, such as Huelva, Cadiz, Málaga, Alicante, Valencia and Castellón on the south and west coasts, Huesca, in the foothills of the Pyrenees, La Coruña and Pontevedra on the Galician coast and the region of Asturias with access to the Picos de Europa, are well provided.

EAMONN RODGERS

Camus, Mario

b. 1932, Santander

Filmmaker

A highly successful director, two of whose films continue to feature in the top twenty all-time Spanish box-office earners, Camus graduated from the **IIEC** in 1963 and was for a time screenwriter for Carlos **Saura**.

Con el viento solano (With the East Wind) (1965), *Los pájaros de Baden-Baden* (The Birds of Baden Baden) (1974) and *Los días del pasado* (Days Past) (1977) are considered among the best of his early films, but his first major success was with *La colmena* (The Hive) (1982). An adaptation of **Cela**'s novel built round the stories of participants in the ***tertulias*** at a typical Madrid café in the bleak post-Civil War years, the film skilfully recreates the atmosphere of the time and won a Golden Bear at Berlin. This film was followed by his second winner, also an adaptation, *Los santos inocentes* (*The Holy Innocents*) (1984) for which he won the National Cinema Prize. The 'Innocents' are a poverty-stricken peasant family on an aristocratic estate in the 1960s, where there are, in Camus' own words, 'just trees and birds and utterly abject beings'. Another fine adaptation was of Lorca's play *La casa de Bernarda Alba* (*The House of Bernarda Alba*) in 1987. In the 1990s he has directed *Sombras en una batalla* (Spectres at a Battle) (1993), a courageous film about a former ETA terrorist, and *Amor proprio* (Self-Love) (1994) in which a woman revenges herself on those who have humiliated her.

Among the television productions that he has directed are the highwayman series *Curro Jiménez*, *La leyenda del alcalde de Zalamea* and a series based on Galdós' *Fortunata y Jacinta*.

See also: film and cinema

Further reading

Higginbotham, V. (1988) *Spanish Cinema under Franco*, Austin, TX: University of Texas Press (one of the most comprehensive surveys of this period).

Hopewell, J. (1986) *Out of the Past: Spanish Cinema After Franco*, London: British Film Institute (a very readable general account of contemporary trends).

Molina-Foix, V. (1977) *New Cinema in Spain*, London: British Film Institute (a comprehensive overview of current trends).

EAMONN RODGERS

Canarian cuisine

Although most Canary Island restaurants are devoted to the needs of international tourism, traditional cookery reflects the three-fold origin of **Canarian culture**. Peninsular Spanish cuisine has thrived with the arrival of package tourism, while aspects of South American cookery, like *arroz a la cubana* (boiled rice with fried egg, fried banana and tomato sauce), remain well established among the urban working class and returned emigrants.

The staple of the pre-Spanish islanders was *gofio*, a finely-ground, roasted barley flour. In its modern form *gofio* is made from wheat, maize or millet, and only rarely from barley. Mixed with milk, *gofio* is an alternative to modern breakfast cereals. *Gofio* is most frequently served as a side dish, either as a powder sprinkled into broths and stews or *amasado* (kneaded) with milk, oil or stock into a stiff paste.

In traditional Canarian cookery grilled goat meat and rabbit play a major role. In some areas, like rural La Palma, meat is almost invariably served without vegetables, despite the islands' reputation for garden crops. Fish, especially sardines, *cherne* (grouper), *mero* (dusky perch) and *salmonete* (red mullet), is grilled and served with *mojo verde*, a spicy green sauce made of peppers and garlic. The dish *sancocho canario* is based on salted fish. Broths are an important element in traditional cookery, particularly *potaje canario*, made of coarse-cut vegetables with the local large-leafed water-cress, and often eaten with *gofio*. There is a wide range of goat's cheeses, such as *queso tierno* (a mild, semi-soft cheese often eaten with salt and a popular *tapa*), *queso flor de Guía* (a firm, medium cheese from Guía, Gran Canaria), and cellar-cured hard cheeses from the island of El Hierro. The potato is often the only vegetable served with meat or fish. *Papas arrugadas* (literally 'wrinkled potatoes', i.e. potatoes boiled in highly-salted water) are a popular side dish or *tapa* and are usually served with red *mojo* sauce.

The introduction of sugar cane and vines in the early colonial period gave rise to a substantial drinks industry. Cane sugar is the basic ingredient of Canarian rum, now produced on a fully industrial scale in Arucas, Gran Canaria. Smaller distilleries exist on La Palma. Mixed with locally produced honey, *ron miel* (honey rum) makes a very sweet liqueur. Wine, of varying quality, is produced throughout the islands. White wines are generally very light, whereas reds tend to be heavy and fruity.

Molasses, honey and almonds comprise the basis for local desserts. *Bienmesabe*, a syrup of honey and ground almonds, is either poured over ice cream and yoghurt or eaten on its own. The small Canarian banana, the staple local fruit, is tastier than its larger American cousin, though during the 1980s the banana industry declined and pineapples and kiwis were introduced.

Further reading

Eddy, M.R. (1989) *The Crafts and Traditions of the Canary Islands*, Aylesbury: Shire Publications (an informative introduction to the culture of the islands).

M.R. EDDY

Canarian culture

Canary Island culture is dominated by peninsular Spain, but displays relics of a pre-Spanish, Berber past and additions from returning *indianos* (migrants returning from the Americas) and, most recently, northern European tourists and business people. This mixture of traits gives the islands a unique cultural life which is further diversified by local variations on each island.

The language of the islands is Spanish, but closer to the Latin American variety than the peninsular: the lisped consonants 'z' and 'c' are pronounced 's', for example. In the colonial period, literature comprised mainly prose and poetic semi-historical or religious works. Not until the mid-nineteenth century did local writers begin to experiment with other literary forms. Many nineteenth- and early twentieth-century writers left the islands to further their careers in Madrid, Benito Pérez Galdós being the best known. Local writers who stayed in the islands, such as Tomás Morales, tended to be provincial and introspective, obsessed with the surrounding sea.

The aftermath of the Civil War witnessed considerable poetic creativity, particularly by the Arca group, founded by Pedro Lezcano and Ventura Doreste and later joined by Agustín and José María Millares Sall. The generally anti-Franco attitude of such poets placed poetry in the vanguard of artistic activity in the islands, a status which it still largely maintains. The strength of modern Canarian poetry is confirmed by Justo Jorge Padrón, whose third book of poems *Los círculos del infierno* (The Circles of Hell) brought him national recognition. The Canarian novel has matured since the 1970s through novels such as *Mararía* (by Rafael Arozarena) and *Guad* (by Alfonso García-Ramos, 1930–80).

Music in the Canaries is dominated at the popular level by folk styles and themes. Such music is normally performed by choral groups, accompanied by guitars, mandolins, drums and the *timple* (a small, three-stringed guitar). Some folk forms, such as the *sirinoque* of La Palma and the *tajaraste* of La Gomera, are reputedly pre-Spanish in origin and have much in common with the 'Canarian', a dance introduced into late medieval Europe. Both Gran Canaria and Tenerife possess their own orchestras, and a classical music festival of considerable quality has been held in the two islands every January since the 1980s.

Local religious sculpture and painting began in the seventeenth century, reaching its culmination in the work of José Luján Pérez (1756–1815). Secular landscape and portrait painting was begun in the mid-nineteenth century with the work of Cirilo Truilhé (1813–1904). In the twentieth century, Canarian painting was dominated by *indigenismo* (nativism) and surrealism, the former initiated by artists of the 'Luján Pérez school' in 1918, and based on pre-Spanish forms. *Indigenismo* experienced a revival in the mid-1960s, in the 'homoerotic' work of Pepe Damaso, evolved from that of Nestor de la Torre.

One prominent artist, Cesar Manrique, through his interest in the volcanic landscapes of Lanzarote, developed as a landscape architect and has made a major impact on the planning of his native island. An unusual aspect of Canarian vernacular architecture is the use of caves, some of which, like those in the *barrios* (neighbourhoods) of Tara and Cendro (Telde, Gran Canaria), have been occupied since pre-Spanish times. A number of Christian chapels in rural areas are to be found in artificial caves, e.g. in Guayadeque and Artenara (Gran Canaria).

Gran Canaría boasts the first golf course in Spain and the second oldest football club, both established by British traders in the nineteenth century. In the twentieth century Canarians took Olympic medals in sailing and swimming. Several pre-Spanish sports have been revived, and of these *lucha canaria* (Canarian wrestling) has a large following (see also **Canarian press and media**). Sailing lateen-rigged boats is another popular sport. The tourist industry and the islands' climate have attracted large numbers of wind-surfers to the eastern islands.

The religion of the islanders is mainly Roman Catholic, though Protestant churches have been established by the British and the Korean communities. Pre-Spanish fertility and water cults survive in Christianized form in the *Bajada de la Rama* (Descent of the Bough, in Agaete, Gran Canaria), *La Charca* (The Pool, in San Nicolás de Tolentino, Gran Canaria), or in the *Bajadas de la Virgen* (Descents of the Virgin) held every four years in La Palma and El Hierro. Carnival, banned under Franco except in Tenerife, is a popular opportunity to lampoon officialdom through disguises and *murgas* (satirical songs and the bands that play them).

In politics, tendencies towards self-determination have grown stronger since the demise of Franco. The archipelago is divided into seven *Cabildos* (island councils) which to a considerable extent pursue their own cultural policies. Pan-Canarianism has still to develop into a potent force, and inter-island rivalry, particularly between Tenerife and Gran Canaria, continues to be a powerful influence. The autonomous government is obliged to alternate parliamentary sessions between two buildings, one on Tenerife and the other on Gran Canaria. The rivalry between Gran Canaria and Tenerife was heightened in the early years of the twentieth century by the *pleito insular* (the island dispute). The *pleito*, which arose from administrative, educational, commercial and ecclesiastical differences between the islands, was temporarily resolved by the 1912 *Ley de Cabildos* (the Island Councils Law), which established the present local government system. The *pleito* was revived in the 1980s when the University College at Las Palmas, Gran Canaria, was made independent of Tenerife's University of La Laguna.

Further reading

de Béthencourt Masieu, A. (ed.) (1995) *Historia de Canarias*, Las Palmas de Gran Canaria: Cabildo Insular de Gran Canaría (a useful insight into various aspects of Canarian history).

Eddy, M.R. (1989) *Crafts and Traditions of the Canary Islands*, Aylesbury: Shire Ethnography (a comprehensive study by an ethnographer and archaeologist).

Galván Tudela, A. (1987), *Las fiestas populares canarias*, Santa Cruz de Tenerife: Ediciones Canarias (useful on popular traditions).

Hernández Bravo de Laguna, J. (1992) *Franquismo y transición política*, Santa Cruz de Tenerife: Centro de la Cultura Popular Canaria (an interesting study of the effects on the Canaries of political events on the Spanish mainland).

M.R. EDDY

Canarian press and media

Because of geographical location, international news is as important to the Canarian press as it is to the national media. On the other hand, local news can be more parochial than in the peninsular regional press, as the printed media are generally split between dailies based in Tenerife and Gran Canaria. Broadcast media are usually limited to a single island, while national radio and television are under pressure to report on the smaller islands.

The written press has been disadvantaged by the historically low literacy levels, emigration of the best educated, and the lack of a middle class. The earliest newspaper as such was the *Correo de Tenerife*, which was published between 1808 and 1810. Throughout the nineteenth century, numerous papers were launched and failed, the most successful lasting under two years. In the period 1875 to 1925, several newspapers were founded which have survived to the present day, among them the *Diario de Las Palmas*, closely associated with the liberals, and the *Gaceta de Tenerife*, originally a Catholic-conservative paper. The *Diario*, with its sister daily *La Provincia*, were linked to the Franco regime's **Falange** propaganda sheet, which later became the now-defunct *Eco de Canarias*. On Tenerife, the press is dominated by *El Día*, founded in 1910 as *La Prensa*, the *Diario de Avisos* and the *Gaceta*. The transition to democracy saw the failure of several papers for various reasons, notably the *Eco* (Gran Canaria); and *La Tarde* (Tenerife).

The first daily published for all the islands, *Canarias 7*, was established in the early 1980s. Its more straightforward reporting style and its moderate pro-self-determination stance gained it considerable popularity, particularly with younger readers. Other papers, notably the *Diario de Las Palmas* and the *Diario de Avisos*, have adopted similar formats if not similar politics. *El Guanche* (named after the original inhabitants of Tenerife), the voice of the militant independence movement, was founded in 1879 by Secundino Delgado in Venezuela, though the political viewpoint it defended was then illegal. Its first series ended in 1912 with Delgado's death but it was re-established in Cuba in 1924. Now in its fourth series, it is the mouthpiece of Antonio **Cubillo Ferreira**'s Congreso Nacional de Canarias (Canaries' National Congress).

Televisión Española en Canarias (Spanish Television in the Canaries) produces regional news and cultural programmes, the most distinctive of which are 'Tenderete' (a Canarian word meaning a get-together), dedicated to Canarian folk music, and various *lucha canaria* (Canarian wrestling) championships. Local radio has expanded considerably but, though commanding good audiences, is limited geographically because of the mountainous terrain and the distances between the islands, and relies on cheap chat-show and phone-in formats.

Further reading

Cabrera Déniz, G.J. and Reyes González, N. (1990) 'La prensa insular como fuente histórica', *VII Coloquio de Historia Canario-Americana (1986)*, 1: 701–43.

Chaves, A. (1986) *El periodista Víctor Zurita y el golpe de estado de 1936 en Santa Cruz*, Santa Cruz de Tenerife: Gráficas.

Hernández Bravo de Laguna, A. (1992) *Franquismo y transición política*, Santa Cruz de Tenerife: Centro de Cultura Popular Canaria.

M.R. EDDY

Candel i Tortajada, Francesc

b. 1925, Casas Altas

Writer, journalist and politician

Himself an immigrant who moved to Barcelona in his early childhood, Candel became a major interpreter and advocate of the immigrants' aspirations to participate fully in Catalan socio-cultural life. His best-selling *Els altres catalans* (The Other Catalans) (1964) was a solid defence of the immigrants' contribution to Catalan society. Although he did not present an overall solution to the issue of 'cultural integration', he defended the idea that it was essential for the immigrants to learn Catalan. He was elected Senator for the Entesa dels Catalans coalition (1977–9).

Further reading

Conversi, D. *The Basques, the Catalans* (see chapter 8 on immigration).

DANIELE CONVERSI

Candela Outerino, Felix

b. 1910, Madrid

Architect

Qualifying in 1936, Candela went into exile in 1939 in Mexico, where most of his works are located. He came under the influence there of the Spanish engineer Eduardo Torroja, a distinguished designer in reinforced concrete. Candela's work displays exceptional creativity, which has inspired architects worldwide. He won international acclaim with the church of Santa María Miráculos (1954, Mexico). His characteristic style is shown in the elegant concrete vaulting and the fluid movement of the columns, reminiscent of **Gaudí**. His best-known achievement is the Olympic Sports Palace (with Castañeda and Peyri, 1968, Mexico).

MIHAIL MOLDOVEANU

Cano, José Luis

b. 1912, Algeciras

Writer

This poet, critic, biographer, anthologist and editor came to maturity in Málaga under the influence of Emilio Prados and others associated with the review *Litoral*. During this time he came to know **Aleixandre**, García Lorca, Altolaguirre and **Dalí**, becoming especially friendly with Aleixandre during Cano's university years in the Madrid of the 1930s. Cano was imprisoned during the Civil War for having been a member of a leftist student group.

Critics debate whether Cano should be grouped with the poets of the pre-Civil War 'Generation of 1936', writers much influenced by the artistic experimentalism of their time, or with those who came to maturity and began to publish following their experience of the war and its aftermath. In fact, the centre of gravity of Cano's poetry seems to be located in Prados' aestheticism. Beginning in 1942 with *Sonetos de la bahía* (Sonnets of the Bay), and followed by such collections as *Voz de la muerte* (The Voice of Death), *Las alas perseguidas* (The Hunted Wings), *Otoño en Málaga y otros poemas* (Autumn in Malaga and Other Poems) and *Luz del tiempo* (Light of Time), Cano's poetry is characterized by a striving for formal beauty and concise versification. The most complete edition of Cano's poetry is *Poesías completas* (Barcelona) (1986). Also of considerable interest is his pre-war autobiography, *Los cuadernos de Adrian Dale: memorias y relecturas* (Madrid) (1981).

For many, Cano's greatest contributions to contemporary Spanish literature and poetry are his anthologies (e.g. *Antología de la nueva poesía española*, which reached its third edition in 1972), literary biographies, such as *Antonio Machado: biografía ilustrada* (Barcelona) (1975), and critical studies, such as the series of interviews with Aleixandre published in 1986 as *Los cuadernos de Valentonia*.

Equally important have been his labours as a key member of the editorial staff of ***Ínsula*** from its foundation in 1945 until publication of its 500th number in 1988. In all these activities he has distinguished himself as a truly open and liberal literary man whose devotion is to the best of what is new and old in Spanish literature. Typically courageous was the decision by *Ínsula* in 1955 to publish a commemorative number to honour **Ortega y Gasset** upon his death, despite the directive by the official **censorship** that only brief notices would mark his passing. The government suspended publication of the magazine for a year, but it began publishing again in 1957.

See also: poetry

STEPHEN MILLER

Capmany, Maria Aurèlia

b. 1918, Barcelona; d. 1991, Barcelona

Writer

One of the most important women writers in twentieth-century Catalonia, Maria-Aurèlia

Capmany published novels, plays and translations, particularly of contemporary French and Italian novelists. She was an essayist, and was involved in journalism, television and cultural politics. Her writings on feminism are especially important, and in the late 1970s she wrote a 45-part radio serial on the history of Catalonia.

Capmany was an avid reader of fiction, and was especially influenced by Woolf, Joyce, Hemingway and Faulkner, as well as by Sartrean existentialism. Her own fiction highlights the role of history in the destiny of the individual, and evokes the way in which time and memory constantly change everything. Her best-known novel is *Un lloc entre els morts* (A Place Among the Dead), which was awarded the Sant Jordi Prize in 1968.

Capmany's theatrical career dates from the late 1950s, when *Tu i l'hipòcrita* (You and the Hypocrite) was commissioned by the Agrupació Dramàtica de Barcelona (ADB) and performed at the Romea Theatre in Barcelona in 1959. In 1960 Capmany and Ricard Salvat founded the Escola d'Art Dramàtic Adrià Gual (EADAG), which became the major Catalan Brechtian centre. The imprint of epic theatre is evident in Capmany's *Vent de garbí i una mica de por* (South-West Wind and a Little Bit of Fear), which was performed by EADAG in 1965. *Preguntes i respostes sobre la vida i la mort de Francesc Layret, advocat dels obrers de Catalunya* (Questions and Answers on the Life and Death of Francesc Layret, Lawyer of the Workers of Catalonia), written by Capmany in collaboration with Xavier Romeu, is one of the best examples of documentary theatre in Catalonia. It was performed clandestinely in 1970. In 1971, Capmany's version of the medieval Catalan classic *Tirant lo blanc* was performed in Valencia, the year in which the Grup d'Estudis Teatrals d'Horta (a Barcelona-based theatre group) performed what is probably her most important work, the historical drama *L'ombra de l'escorpí* (The Shadow of the Scorpion).

Further reading

Various (1992) *Maria Aurèlia Capmany i Farnés (1918–1991)*, Barcelona: Ajuntament de Barcelona (commemorative volume).

DAVID GEORGE

Carnero Abat, Guillermo

b. 1947, Valencia

Poet

Guillermo Carnero is one of the most important of the poets who renovated poetry in the late 1960s. The self-conscious aestheticism of his first book, *Dibujo de la muerte* (A Sketch of Death) (1967), contrasts with the dominant modes of post-war poetry. The difficult and highly intellectual poetry of *Variaciones y figuras sobre un tema de La Bruyère* (Variations and Figures on a Theme of La Bruyère) and *El azar objetivo* (Objective Chance) (1975) investigates the relationship between language and reality. Carnero teaches at the University of Alicante and is a prominent scholar of eighteenth-century literature.

JONATHAN MAYHEW

Caro Baroja, Julio

b. 1914, Madrid; d. 1995, Vera de Bidasoa (Navarre)

Anthropologist, ethnographer and historian

Caro Baroja's writings embrace social anthropology, ancient history, popular culture, and ethnic minorities. Primarily a historical anthropologist, he maintains an undogmatic perspective on culture and society. Son of a publisher father and intellectual mother, his uncle, the novelist Pío Baroja powerfully influenced his intellectual development. Early education at the progressive Instituto Escuela was followed by university in pre-Civil War Madrid. However, at Pío Baroja's instigation he also studied with the Basque ethnographer, José Miguel de Barandiarán. After a doctorate in history (1941) from Madrid University, he briefly taught there in the 1940s, conscious of his family's perceived heterodoxy at a time when the universities were under the prevailing influence of the **Falange**. Initial publications focus on the ethnic variety of Spain, at odds with the state's insistence on unity: *Los pueblos de España. Ensayo de etnología* (The Peoples of Spain: An Essay in Ethnography) (1946); *Los vascos. Etnología* (The Basques: Ethnography) (1949).

Recognition came in the 1960s, with membership of the Royal Academy of History (1963). His sceptical, ironic, often pessimistic nature found more channels of expression after Franco's death. Despite a large output of books and articles, his lack of association with a recognized seat of learning meant that he created no school. Genuinely modest and rejecting the cult of personality, his inherent humanism affected many who came into contact with him.

Teaching at Coimbra University (1957–60) and the Ecole Pratique des Hautes Etudes in Paris (1960) heralded a period of great productiveness. His historical study of witchcraft, *The World of the Witches* (*Las brujas y su mundo*) (1961), combining religion, superstition and popular culture, was widely translated (English, French and German). There followed *El carnaval. (Análisis histórico-cultural)* (Carnival: Historical and Cultural Analysis) (1965) and *Vidas mágicas e Inquisición* (Magical Lives and the Inquisition) (1967). A pioneer in popular culture – embracing folklore, popular customs, rituals, and beliefs – he illuminatingly explored chapbook literature and the presence of magic in the theatre: *Ensayo sobre la literatura de cordel* (Essay on Chapbook Literature) (1969), and *Teatro popular y magia* (Popular Theatre and Magic) (1974). Parallel studies probed ethnic minorities and varieties of belief: *Los judíos en la España moderna y contemporánea* (The Jews in Modern and Contemporary Spain) (1961–2); *Las formas complejas de la vida religiosa. Religión, sociedad y carácter en la España de los siglos XVI y XVII* (The Complex Forms of Religious Life: Religion, Society and Character in Sixteenth and Seventeenth-Century Spain) (1978). His output remained prolific up to his death.

Major works

Caro Baroja, J. (1961) *Las brujas y su mundo*, Madrid: Revista de Occidente (historical anthropology).

—— (1964) *The World of the Witches*, trans. N. Glendinning, London: Weidenfeld & Nicolson.

Further reading

Caro Baroja, J. and Flores Arroyuelo, F.J. (1991) *Conversaciones en Itzea*, Madrid: Alianza (conversations on the author's life and thought).

Carreira, A. (1994) 'La obra de Julio Caro Baroja. Ensayo de clasificación temática', *Cuadernos Hispanoamericanos* 533–4: 9–31 (thematically structured listing of JCB's writings).

PHILIP DEACON

Carreras, José

b. 1946, Barcelona

Opera singer

Known the world over as one of the famous 'three tenors' (with Pavarotti and Domingo), José (Josep in his native Catalan) Carreras hails from a working-class area of Barcelona. Carreras' singing talent was recognized at an early age, and his love of opera began when he saw a film of Caruso in Barcelona in 1953. At the age of ten he played the part of the little boy who introduces the puppet show to Don Quixote in Manuel de Falla's *El retablo de Maese Pedro* (*Master Peter's Puppet Show*). This part is normally mimed by a boy actor while a soprano sings offstage, but such was the quality of the young Carreras' voice that he sang the part himself. He acquired a thorough knowledge of music at an early age, and, following a brief period during which he studied chemistry at university, he dedicated himself fully to opera, as an exponent of the bel canto style.

Carreras made his official début in 1970 at the **Liceu Theatre** in Barcelona – one of the major opera centres of Europe – playing opposite Montserrat **Caballé** in *Lucrezia Borgia*. His international career took off in the early 1970s, with performances at London's Festival Hall and the New York City Hall. He played Alfredo in *La Traviata* at London's Covent Garden in 1974. He was often typecast as the Romantic hero, and played dashing roles in *Tosca*, *La Bohème*, *Werther* and *Don Carlos*. He is best-known for the role which is his own favourite: the jealous Don José in Bizet's *Carmen*. He has also played a number of political roles (as in Giordano's *Andrea Chénier* in 1979), which Carreras has associated with his own strong sense of justice and democracy.

By the early 1980s he was famous enough to give solo concerts. He also ventured into other areas, recording *West Side Story* with Bernstein and playing the part of Rodolfo in a film version of *La Bohème*. It was while shooting this film that it was discovered that Carreras had leukaemia. He was given only a 10 percent chance of surviving the illness, but he not only recovered but, remarkably, was able fully to resume his singing career. He founded the José Carreras International Leukaemia Foundation, and raised money for it at selected concerts. The most celebrated of these was the Three Tenors concert at the Football World Cup in Italy in 1990. The tenors have subsequently repeated the experience (for example at the USA World Cup in 1994), and Carreras was musical director at the Barcelona Olympic Games in 1992.

See also: opera

DAVID GEORGE

Carrero Blanco, Luis

b. 1905, Spain; d. 1973, Madrid

Naval officer and politician

Luis Carrero Blanco was Franco's closest collaborator for more than thirty years, from May 1941 until his assassination by **ETA** in December 1973. His unconditional support contrasted with the relative independence of mind of other prominent ministers, like Ramón Serrano Suñer, who, during the brief period in which he was tolerated, was sympathetic to the **Falange**, with which Carrero had little patience. In this sense, he helped Franco to play off against each other the various groups within the regime, thereby perpetuating his rule.

A militarist, seeing Catholicism as the essence of Spanishness and the basis of stability, and intransigent in the face of any calls for change, Carrero once said that tempting the Spanish people with the attractions of liberalism and democracy was like handing the key of the liqueur cabinet to a confirmed alcoholic. The origins of this integralist worldview are to be found in the apocalyptic writings of the authoritarian Catholic ideologues of the years immediately before and after the Civil War, which depicted the conflict as a 'crusade' against a threat to Christian civilization itself.

Carrero's influence with Franco dates from the crisis of the regime in May 1941. In the attempt to curb the power of the Falangist element, the thirty-six year-old Chief of Operations of the Naval General Staff was promoted to undersecretary of the Presidency, which became a ministerial post in July, 1951. In the internal rivalry with the Falange, Carrero was firmly on the side of those who favoured a more conservative and Catholic set of ideas and eventually a monarchical solution to governing Spain.

Although Carrero was cautious about economic liberalization, he favoured economic development as long as the 'discipline' of 'the administration' was maintained and Catholic virtues perpetuated. Indeed, he supported the **technocrats** within the government, helping to set in motion the events leading to the ditching of **autarky** and ultimately to the state-led economic development plans of the 1960s. As Carrero increasingly took over the running of the country from Franco, he advanced to the vice-presidency of the Council of Ministers in 1967, becoming President in June 1973.

Both Franco and Carrero saw the future in terms of *continuismo*, an authoritarian transfer of power from the dictator, upon his death, to Prince **Juan Carlos**. In fact, Carrero oversaw the regime's disintegration during the early 1970s. As economic crisis, popular resistance and the activities of ETA threatened the dictatorship's survival, Carrero relied ever more on repression. His assassination in December 1973 removed the possibility of the regime surviving the eventual death of Franco.

See also: armed forces; politics

Further reading

Miguel, A. de (1975) *Sociología del franquismo*, Barcelona: Euros (this contains useful political biographies of Franco's ministers, including Carrero).

Preston, P. (1993) *Franco: A Biography*, London: HarperCollins (this has useful material on Carrero's relations with the dictator).

MICHAEL RICHARDS

Carrillo Solares, Santiago

b. 1915, Gijón (Asturias)

Politician

Carrillo is without any doubt the most significant figure in the history of Spanish communism. He joined the **PCE** (Spanish Communist Party) at the beginning of the Civil War, became a major influence in the organization during the 1950s, and was appointed Secretary General in 1960, a post he was to hold for the next 22 years. His outlook, like that of the party, followed a tortuous path from hard Stalinism to acceptance of liberal democracy, driven by political opportunism and ideological pragmatism. During his long years in exile he devised various plans to bring down the Francoist system, which, though unsuccessful, helped to keep alive the struggle against the dictatorship and thereby enhance the image of his party.

Carrillo returned to Spain surreptitiously at the beginning of 1976. By then he had distanced himself from the USSR and had become a different type of communist. Already in 1968 he had denounced the Soviet invasion of Czechoslovakia, and later he was to shed his adherence to Marxist–Leninist dogma, and to proclaim his and his party's acceptance of the basic principles of liberal democracy. All these transformations were encapsulated in a simple formula: Eurocommunism, of which Carrillo was, at the time, a main exponent.

With his reputation as a long-standing opponent of the dictatorship, and with his new image as a democratic communist, Carrillo was able to play an influential role in the transition to democracy in Spain. His main contribution was perhaps his success in convincing **Suárez**'s government and all the other major political forces in the country that democracy would not be possible without the legalization of the PCE. The PCE was legalized in the spring of 1977, but from that moment Carrillo had to face two very difficult challenges: parliamentary elections, and strong demands from within for democratization of the party structures. The outcome was unfavourable to him on both fronts.

Although Carrillo himself won a seat in the first three general elections, the PCE's results were disappointing, particularly as they found themselves a long way behind their main left-wing rivals, the **PSOE** (Socialist Workers' Party). Partly as a consequence of this, at the beginning of the 1980s Carrillo's authoritarian style of leadership began to be questioned by a new generation of party activists. After the electoral débâcle of 1982 he was forced to resign as Secretary General, and three years later he had to leave the party he had led for so long. In the 1990s, he moved closer to the Socialists, and spoke in favour of their policies without actually joining the party.

Further reading

Alba, V. (1986) *El Partido Comunista de España*, Barcelona: Planeta (a rather hostile history of the PCE with Carrillo as one of its main characters).

Claudín, F. (1983) *Santiago Carrillo. Crónica de un secretario general*, Barcelona: Planeta (a critical assessment of Carrillo's political career by a disillusioned communist intellectual).

JOSÉ AMODIA

cartoonists

Cartoonists, like other **media** professionals, laboured during the Franco period under the restrictions imposed by **censorship**. The principal satirical weekly, *La Codorniz* (The Quail), which was the main outlet for political cartoons, suffered frequent periods of suppression. With the greater press freedom under democracy, cartoonists like Forges came into their own. In the 1970s, his distinctive style, with its boldly defined outline figures and its use of oblique but barbed comment, appealed greatly to the liberal intellectual readers of ***Cambio 16***, who were broadly supportive of the new institutions, but wary of giving them uncritical approval. Subsequently, Forges moved to the associated daily newspaper, *Diario 16*, but left to join the staff of *El* ***Mundo*** when that paper was established in 1989. Since 1995, his work has been appearing regularly on the editorial page of *El* ***País***, displacing the more stylized and enigmatic Máximo, who nevertheless continues to contribute elsewhere in the paper. *El País* also features regularly the work of Peridis, whose spidery but instantly recognizable caricatures of leading political figures engage in quasi-surreal dialogue across a four- to six-frame comic strip. The main contributor of cartoons to *Cambio 16* is Juan Ballesta, whose vigorous, broad-brush drawings deliberately seek to present contemporary issues with dramatic impact.

See also: comics

EAMONN RODGERS

Casals, Pau

b. 1876, Vendrell (Catalonia); d. 1973, San Juan (Puerto Rico)

Cellist, conductor and composer

Pau Casals died in **exile**, stipulating that his body was not to be returned to Spain until the country had reverted to democracy and Catalonia had become an **autonomous community**. He was buried in Vendrell in 1979. This strength of resolve was the distinguishing mark of his life. Casals is often portrayed as a musical reactionary because of a professed dislike of atonal music and his almost puritan mastery of Beethoven and Bach, but the truth is that he was, in musical terms, a radical figure. A pre-eminent cellist, he questioned conventional practice at an early age, freeing the bow and rethinking the restrictive practices in relation to the fingering, technical revisions that, at the time, amounted to subversion.

As Spain offered no stable musical infrastructure, Casals spent much of his time abroad studying and, subsequently, on tour, but he always considered Barcelona his home, and his contribution to the cultural life of Catalonia has been notable. In 1919, he established and frequently conducted the Pau Casals Orchestra, which managed to survive for nearly two decades despite early financial constraints and would have continued if the Civil War had not broken out. Casals could also be seen as a successor to Josep Anselm Clavé, who started a number of choral societies for the working class in the nineteenth century, since he was involved in the founding of a working-man's concert association, so that symphonic concerts could be heard at reduced prices. This association grew from around 2,500 members to a total of 300,000 with branches throughout the region. Unfortunately, all of this disappeared with the defeat of the Republican side when Casals, like many others, was forced into exile.

Casals settled in Prades, a French Catalan town in the Pyrenees, where he devoted himself to teaching, composition and the organization of an annual festival. Although a musical event rather than a political one, the festival was inevitably linked to Catalonia's regeneration. Cultural aid had become a priority once Franco began his persecution of the region's language and heritage. Casals became a spokesman against the dictatorship but had little political influence. Nevertheless, this obsession with communicating a global message of peace led him to compose *El Pesebre* (The Manger) between 1943 and 1960. Criticized as derivative from nineteenth-century romanticism, this composition is not regarded as a high musical achievement. However, it dominated Casals' last performing years and was received with enthusiasm by audiences who found *El Pesebre* an emotional experience.

See also: Catalan culture; music festivals

Further reading

Baldock, R. (1992) *Pablo Casals*, London: Victor Gollancz (a fascinating account of Casals' life, containing a comprehensive discography of recordings available on compact disc).

Kirk, H.L. (1974) *Pablo Casals: a Biography*, London: Hutchinson (includes a discography compiled by Teri Noel Towe; the biography has been superseded by Baldock's, but nonetheless contains a complete discography of recordings on vinyl disc).

JESSAMY HARVEY

Casas Viejas

A village in Cadiz province, scene of an anarchist rising in January 1933, which was put down with great severity by a mixed force of **Civil Guard**s and Assault Guards, the new Republican police force founded in 1931. Though only one of many such incidents, Casas Viejas became a paradigm case of government repression. The subsequent withdrawal of the Socialists from alliance with Republicans, and the boycott by the anarchists of the elections of November 1933, ensured the victory of right-wing parties, which reversed many of the social and political gains of the early years of the Republic.

EAMONN RODGERS

Castellet, Josep Maria

b. 1926, Barcelona

Writer and critic

Castellet has arguably done more than most critics and editors to bring modern writing in both Spanish and Catalan to the attention of the reading public. Since 1964, he has been literary editor of the Barcelona publishing house Edicions 62. Anthologies such as *Poesia catalana segle XX* (Catalan Poetry of the Twentieth Century) (1963), with critical and historical introductions, gave a high profile to Catalan writing at a time when conditions were unfavourable for writing in languages other than Spanish. In 1970 he was awarded the Cross of St George (*Creu de San Jordi*) for services to Catalan culture.

Major works

Castellet, J.M. and Molas, J. (1963) *Poesia catalana del segle XX*, Barcelona: Edicions 62.

Castellet, J.M. (1966) *Un cuarto de siglo de poesía española, 1939–1964*, Barcelona: Seix Barral.

Castellet, J.M. and Molas, J. (1979), *Antologia general de la poesia catalana*, Barcelona: Edicions 62.

EAMONN RODGERS

Castillo-Puche, José Luis

b. 1919, Yecla (Murcia)

Writer

Castillo-Puche subscribes to the view that a serious work of fiction must contain an existential conflict. A good novel should include everything that deals with human beings and try to explain them. These views characterize his narratives, the three prevalent elements of which are conflict, technique and language. Conflict includes humanity's confrontation with destiny. Castillo-Puche's technique is shaped by the belief that the linear form of the novel does not truly reflect the human condition, for dreams, nightmares, fantasies, disorderly thinking, and unexpected incidents do not occur in chronological sequence. His novels, therefore, often experiment with point of view and chronology, and abound in lyricism and humour. His vocabulary features expressions from his native Murcia, including popular speech. *Con la muerte al hombro* (With Death on Your Back) (1954), his first novel, portrays a spiritual and physical invalid, living unhappily in his native village. Past and present are bridged by the unhappy protagonist's life. *Sin camino* (Without a Path) (1956), possibly autobiographical, shows the pitfalls of a religious vocation overwhelmed by worldly temptations. *El vengador* (The Avenger) (1956) narrates the thirst for revenge of those returning from the Civil War. *Hicieron partes* (They Divided the Spoils) (1957) received the Laurel Prize for Catholic novels and the prestigious Cervantes Prize. *Hicieron partes* emphasizes that money is the root of all evil, portraying six underprivileged families whose lives are disrupted by a large inheritance. *Misión a Estambul* (Mission in Istanbul) (1954) essays the spy thriller with mixed results. *Jeremías el anarquista* (Jeremiah the Anarchist) (1975) denounces Spain's social and political imbalances, while *Como ovejas al matadero* (Like Sheep to the Slaughterhouse) (1971) revisits the theme of priests confronting the dichotomy of spirit and flesh. This is the first volume of a trilogy, *El cíngulo* (The Priest's Girdle).

Hemingway, much admired by Castillo-Puche, was a frequent companion when the American writer lived in Madrid. Castillo-Puche's essays treat Hemingway's influence on Spanish letters and include a biography, *Hemingway entre la vida y la muerte* (Hemingway Between Life and Death) (1968).

Most of Castillo-Puche's narratives take place in Hécula, the fictional name of his native Yecla. His most studied work, the 'trilogy of liberation', comprises *El libro de las visiones y las apariciones* (The Book of Visions and Apparitions) (1977); *El amargo sabor de la retama* (The Bitter Taste of Broom) (1979) and *Conocerás el poso de la nada* (You Shall Know the Dregs of Nothingness) (1982), three novels set in Hécula and all treating religious fanaticism, ignorance and hypocrisy.

Further reading

Belmonte-Serrano J. (1993) 'La madre: Mito y realidad en la narrativa de José Luis Castillo-Puche', *La Chispa '93: Selected Proceedings*, New Orleans, LA: Tulane University Press, pp. 27–31 (an analysis of some motifs appearing in his novels).

Diez de Revenga, F.J. (1995). 'Castillo-Puche en los orígenes de su novela', *Murgetana* 91: 89–98 (a study of the origins of the author's narrative).

Roberts, G. (1973) *Temas existenciales en la novela española de posguerra*, Madrid: Gredos (chapter V studies Castillo-Puche).

GENARO J. PÉREZ

Castresana, Luis de

b. 1925, San Salvador del Valle (Vizcaya); d. 1986, Spain

Writer

Writing in Spanish but on Basque topics, Castresana's reputation rests largely on *El otro árbol de Guernica* (The Other Tree of Guernica) (1967), winner of the **Cervantes Prize** for Literature. This is an autobiographical story of Basque children evacuated during the Spanish Civil War to France and Belgium, where they undergo hardships and internal dissensions but maintain some unity until the war ends and they return home. The novel embodies archetypes like the peace-maker and the traitor, echoes the myth of paradise lost and regained, and treats the recurring Castresana theme of the uprooted tree roaming the world as a ship's mast. The title refers to the age-old oak, or succession of oaks, marking the place where the overlords of Vizcaya traditionally swore to respect the people's rights and privileges. Following the book's success, the author published *La verdad sobre 'El otro árbol de Guernica'* (The Truth About *El otro árbol de Guernica*) (1972), a personal reflection on its historical background and on the film which it inspired.

Perhaps Castresana's finest work is *Adiós* (Goodbye) (1969), a view of life from beyond the grave, as a man who has just died approaches his final examination on the subject of love. *Retrato de una bruja* (Portrait of a Witch) (1970) attempts to capture the psychologies and sufferings that drove people to become, or resemble, witches. His last major novel, *Montes de hierro* (Mountains of Iron) (1982), describes youthful love in a Basque mining community where justice is swift and uncertain.

Biographer of Dostoevsky, the bandit Candelas, Rasputin and José María Iparraguirre (1820–81), the Basque *bertsolari*, or bard, who composed the anthem 'Gernika'ko arbola' (The Tree of Guernica), Castresana received the **Royal Academy** Fastenrath Award for his historical novel *Catalina de Arauso, la monja alférez* (Catherine of Arauso, Nun and Ensign) (1968), based on the life of the seventeenth-century Basque adventuress who left her convent to sail to the Indies disguised as a boy, later to become a soldier and officer.

As a newspaper correspondent in London in the early 1960s, Castresana compiled *Inglaterra vista por los españoles* (England Seen by the Spaniards) (1965), a collection of texts written at various times, with a commentary of his own. Many of his stories, grounded in Basque legend, anecdote and myth, appeared in volumes such as *El pueblo olvidado* (The Forgotten Village) (1969). From 1972 onwards, he exhibited paintings of Basque landscapes and characters. One, *Autobiografía del éxodo 1937–9* (Autobiography of Exodus 1937–9), shows drab emptiness with a child huddled under a solitary tree, implicitly a portrait of Castresana himself, close to the roots which he never abandoned.

Further reading

Fentanes Ariño, J. (1972) *El mundo vasco en la obra de Luis de Castresana*, Bilbao: Gran Enciclopedia Vasca (a brief overview of Castresana's life and work).

Hickey, L. (1972) 'Introduction' to *El otro árbol de*

Guernica, London: Harrap (analyses this novel, with notes on other works).

LEO HICKEY

Castro, Américo

b. 1885, Cantagallo (Brazil); d. 1972, Madrid

Academic

A pupil of the leading philologist and historian Menéndez Pidal, Castro followed up his studies at the University of Granada with postgraduate work in Germany and Paris. During the Second Republic, he was Ambassador to Berlin. He left Spain after the Civil War, and taught in Latin America, and in the USA at the Universities of Princeton, Harvard and San Diego. He returned to Spain in 1964.

Most of Castro's work up to 1925 reflects his early training as a philologist and textual scholar. In addition to studies and editions of works by Juan de Mal Lara, Quevedo, Lope de Vega, Rojas Zorrilla, and Tirso de Molina, he also produced a classic study *El pensamiento de Cervantes* (The Thought of Cervantes) (1925). In the 1940s, however, he turned towards cultural and intellectual history, challenging the traditional Castilian-centred, unitary view of Spain's past by emphasizing the plural nature of medieval Spanish culture as a blend of Christian, Muslim and Jewish influences. Thus, for example, he argued that the military orders, with their tradition of combining asceticism with warfare in defence of what for them was the true faith, were a manifestation in Christian terms of an institution well established in Near Eastern Islam.

Castro's essential ideas are contained in *The Structure of Spanish History* (1954) (first published as *España en su historia*, 1948). With various additions and modifications, the book was republished in different versions up to shortly before Castro's death. Castro's approach to historiography was essentially a humanist one, in the sense that he dwelt on the experience and self-understanding of the various communities in Spain, using literary texts as a primary historical source, and was impatient with modern methodologies based on a consideration of economic, social or geographical factors. This earned him a sharp rejoinder from Claudio **Sánchez-Albornoz**, and the polemical exchanges between the two scholars enlivened academic circles in Spain and elsewhere for most of the 1950s and 1960s. By contrast, writers like Juan **Goytisolo** have paid warm tribute to Castro for his willingness to give overdue recognition to the Moorish and Jewish inheritance in Spanish culture, often underestimated by nationalist historians.

Castro is an important figure in Spanish cultural history and in the development of new historiographical perspectives, but he was vulnerable to the charge that his methodology lacked rigour and his interpretations were excessively conjectural.

Major works

Castro, A. (1925) *El pensamiento de Cervantes*, Madrid: Hernando

—— (1954) *The Structure of Spanish History*; trans. E.L. King, Princeton, NJ: Princeton University Press.

—— (1961) *De la edad conflictiva*, Madrid: Taurus.

—— (1977) *An Idea of History : Selected Essays*, trans. S. Gilman and E.L. King, Columbus, OH: Ohio State University Press.

Further reading

Surtz, R.E., Ferran, J. and Testa, D.P. (1988) (eds) *Americo Castro, The Impact of his Thought: Essays to Mark the Centenary of his Birth*, Madison, WI: Hispanic Seminary of Medieval Studies.

EAMONN RODGERS

Català-Roca, Francesc

b. 1922, Valls (Tarragona); d. 1998, Barcelona

Photographer

Català-Roca was a central figure in contemporary Spanish photography. Heir to his father's studio, Pere Català-Pic, he continued the tradition of the direct, documentary style typical of the 1940s and 1950s. Though passionately fond of colour, he was particularly known for his monochrome 'snapshots', in which he captured, with naturalness and humour, the sense of surprise and of the unusual. He concentrated on a wide variety of themes, among them 'Tauromaquia' (1962), 'Madrid' (1964), 'Barcelona' (1954), 'Personajes de los años cincuenta' (Figures of the 1950s) (1993) and 'Fotografías Acromáticas' (Black and White Pictures) (1994).

MIHAIL MOLDOVEANU

Catalan

Catalan is the most widely-spoken language in Spain, after Spanish. It is the (co-)official language of Catalonia, the Balearic Islands and Valencia, although, given the close relationship between linguistic status and political autonomy, claims are sometimes made, particularly in Valencia, for a separate linguistic identity for each of these regions.

Catalan is a romance language which developed from Latin. Though it became the language of an influential seaborne empire in the Middle Ages, it later suffered marginalization and persecution. As with other regional languages of Spain, the nineteenth century brought a revival in the use of Catalan, first as a vehicle of regional culture and artistic expression, but later as a symbol of political difference. By the turn of the century Catalan was being used in local government, the press and public life in general. This prompted work on the codification of Catalan, including the publication of a major grammar and dictionary.

The Second Republic (1931–6) saw a major increase in the use of Catalan, brutally curtailed by the Nationalists' victory in the Civil War and the resulting Franco dictatorship. Catalan was proscribed, particularly during the earlier period of the Franco regime. With the return to democracy and the 1978 constitution, Catalan was given the impetus to flourish once more. Language planning in Catalonia, and to a lesser extent in Valencia and the Balearic Islands, vigorously promotes Catalan in all public domains, from local government, administration and education, to commerce and the media. Catalan is found on street signs, official forms and advertisements. It is heard on radio, and the high-quality channel TV3, showing films and other programmes in Catalan. Catalan is increasingly used in the education system.

Over six million people live in Catalonia (with some ten million resident in the wider Catalan-speaking area), of whom over 90 percent declare themselves able to understand Catalan, and more than 60 percent competent to speak it. Enormous strides have been made to establish Catalan as the normal language of Catalonia, despite the challenge of mass communications in Spanish, and also the high proportion of non-Catalan speakers in Catalonia.

Catalan's relative success (impressive when compared with most other minority language situations) can be attributed to the high prestige it enjoys as the language of all social classes, of social mobility, and culture. More resources have been available for this language's revival because Catalonia is the wealthiest region of Spain, a position which reinforces the commonly-held view that Catalonia is a separate nation (within the Spanish state) whose identity is symbolized by its distinct language.

See also: Catalan culture; language and national identity; language normalization; linguistic policy and legislation

Further reading

Ros i García, M. and Strubell, M. (eds) (1984) *Catalan Sociolinguistics*, *Journal of the Sociology of Language* 47 (a comprehensive overview of Catalan from its history through to the early language planning activities of the post-Franco era).

Siguan, M. (1993) *Multilingual Spain*, Amsterdam: Swets & Zeitlinger (the best overview in English of the role of languages in Spain).

CLARE MAR-MOLINERO

Catalan culture

The post-Civil War culture of the *països catalans* (Catalan lands, including Valencia, the Balearic

Islands, and parts of Alicante) has been deeply marked by developments in the rest of Spain. By contrast with the 1930s, when Catalan social, political and cultural institutions were highly developed, the **Catalan** language was savagely repressed during the early part of the Franco regime in the 1940s, many Catalans being fined for using it in public or on the telephone. No public performance of a play in Catalan was allowed on the professional stage in Barcelona until 1946, and even after this Catalan playwrights and other writers experienced difficulty in having their work performed or published. The activity of independent theatre companies such as the Agrupació Dramàtica de Barcelona (founded in 1955) and the Escola d'Art Dramàtic Adrià Gual (founded in 1960 by Maria Aurèlia **Capmany** and Ricard Salvat) was both difficult and courageous.

The abnormality of this situation did not, however, totally preclude activity or development. Nor was Catalonia cut off from cultural developments in the rest of the western world, once the isolationism of Spain during the immediate post-Civil War years had passed. Major changes nevertheless had to wait for the cultural and socio-political upheavals of the 1960s.

It was also at this time that a generation gap opened up between writers and artists who were born before the Civil War and those who had not experienced the conflict. Among the former group were figures who remained in Catalonia (J.V. **Foix**, Salvador **Espriu**, Joan **Brossa** and Antoni **Tàpies**, for example), and others who worked in exile, such as Pau **Casals** and Pere **Calders**. Among the writers of the post-Civil War generation who came to prominence in the 1960s and the 1970s were the poets Narcís Comadira, Pere **Gimferrer** (the best-known poet of his generation) and Francesc Parcerisas. A particular characteristic of Catalan poetry of the late 1960s and the early 1970s – evident in all three poets – was its rejection of the realist ethos propounded by Josep Maria **Castellet** and Joaquim Molas in the early 1960s.

The two most important dramatists writing in Catalan in the 1960s and the 1970s were Josep Maria **Benet i Jornet** and the Valencian Rodolf **Sirera**. They were both influenced by social realism and Brechtianism in their early plays, but subsequently absorbed the post-naturalist and post-modernist aesthetics of the next generation of Catalan playwrights, of whom Sergi **Belbel** is the prime example.

In fiction, Manuel de **Pedrolo**, although born in 1918, wrote his main works from the 1950s to the 1970s. The best-known fiction writers since the 1960s are Terenci **Moix**, Montserrat **Roig** and Quim **Monzó**. All of these have, in their different ways, questioned the values of bourgeois culture. Moix and Monzó have incorporated elements of popular culture into their writing, while Roig has concentrated on the role of women in modern society.

Catalan music and spectacle have seen many changes since the 1960s, particularly the effects of the revolution in western pop music. The folk and protest singers of the 1960s were popular in Catalonia, especially Joan Baez and Pete Seeger. They found echoes in the **Nova Cançó** movement, in which singer-songwriters like **Raimon** and Lluís **Llach** (as well as the people who attended their concerts) risked beatings and imprisonment by Franco's police. Renewed interest in popular and folk music led to a rediscovery of Catalan popular music. Maria del Mar Bonet adapted and sang Mallorcan folk songs. There was an upsurge of interest in the traditional dance, the *sardana*, and in the *havanera*, or sea song. New songs were composed which combined traditional elements with aspects of the folk or rock culture.

The recovery of popular culture in late Francoism and during the transition to democracy is reflected in a growth of interest in festivals. Such festivals, as well as mime and dance, were given an avant-garde slant by such performance groups as Els **Joglars** and Els **Comediants**. The anti-Franco connotations of the recovery of popular culture in Catalonia were given an extra impetus by the language question and by what the Catalans call the *fet diferencial*, or sense of distinctive Catalanness. These observations apply equally to the enormously popular **Barcelona FC**, particularly in their matches with arch-rivals **Real Madrid**.

An important ingredient of the post-Franco period has been the advent of **Catalan television**. Although TV3 has done much for Catalan language and culture, there is a good deal of doubt amongst Catalans about what the future holds. There is a widespread fear that the growth of private television channels is not only lowering quality and leading to more Americanized programmes, but also that the Catalan language itself will suffer because the overwhelming majority of these programmes are transmitted in Spanish.

One other vitally important aspect of Catalan culture is the literature written in Spanish. In drama, both José M. Rodríguez Méndez and José **Sanchis Sinisterra** are Catalans writing in Spanish, but it is in fiction that Spanish-writing Catalans have made most impression. Carmen **Laforet**'s *Nada* is a well-known account of growing up in post-Civil War Barcelona. Novels by Juan **Marsé** and Juan **Goytisolo** are critical of the Catalan-speaking bourgeoisie, while Manuel **Vázquez Montalbán**'s detective fiction presents a highly original picture of modern-day Barcelona seen through the eyes of his post-modern sleuth Pepe Carvalho. Visions of Barcelona also characterize the novels of Eduardo **Mendoza**.

See also: Caballé, Montserrat; Carreras, José; Catalan television; Dalí, Salvador; Fuster, Joan; language and national identity; Liceu Theatre; linguistic policy and legislation; normalization; Pàmies, Teresa; regional nationalism; Riera, Carme

Further reading

Boyd, A. (1988) *The Essence of Catalonia: Barcelona and its Region*, London: André Deutsch (a guide for the discerning tourist).

Guitart i Agell, J. (1990) *Cultura a Catalunya anys noranta*, Barcelona: Generalitat de Catalunya.

Papo, A. (1985) *El jazz a Catalunya*, Barcelona: Edicions 62.

Termes, J. (ed.) (1986) *Catalanisme: història, política i cultura*, Barcelona: Avenç (a look at Catalanism from various angles).

Recolons, L. *et al.* (1989) *Catalunya 77–88: Societat, economia, política, cultura*, Barcelona: Fundació Jaume Bofill (the most complete overview of recent Catalan culture, society and politics).

DAVID GEORGE

Catalan Socialist Party

The tensions between socialism/communism and Catalan nationalism which characterize left-wing movements in Catalonia are nowhere more evident than in the Catalan Socialist Party (Partit dels Socialistes de Catalunya, or PSC). The PSC was formed in 1978 as an alliance of the three existing Catalan socialist parties, with Joan Raventós as its General Secretary. The party had great success in the municipal elections of 1979, capturing twenty-one mayoral offices. Their biggest prize was Barcelona City Council, which they have controlled ever since, mainly under the leadership of their charismatic mayor, Pasqual **Maragall**.

The early 1980s were characterized by the sometimes bitter rivalry between the PSC and **CiU** (Convergence and Unity). While the PSC controlled what was by far the largest local council, the **Generalitat** (Catalan Autonomous Government) was in the hands of Jordi **Pujol**'s CiU. However, the position of the PSC has weakened in recent years as support for CiU has grown. While the PSC has always won more votes than any other party in Catalonia at general (all-Spain) elections, it has always done less well at local and autonomous elections. However, its share of the vote has been in decline even at general elections. This has been due in part to its own internal divisions: for instance, the party almost split in 1980 after the more Catalanist wing led by Raimon Obiols and backed by the **PSOE** defeated the Spanish-nationalist wing, which presented itself as more class-oriented. Another reason for the relative decline of the PSC is its close association with PSOE (it presents itself as PSC-PSOE). The waning popularity of Felipe **González**'s government in Spain was reflected in the fortunes of the PSC in Catalonia. A third cause of its decline could be the growing sense that only Catalan nationalist parties (in particular the CiU) can defend Catalan gains against increasing attacks in the rest of Spain, particularly by the **PP** (Popular Party) in the period 1993 to 1996. The PSC has tended to present the CiU as a Catalan nationalist party in a negative sense, and this, to a certain extent, has rebounded on it. Having said all this, PSC-PSOE has retained a greater support in the industrial belt of Barcelona than the socialists have in practically the whole of the rest of Spain.

Further reading

Balcells, A. (1996) *Catalan Nationalism* (edited and introduced by G.J. Walker), Basingstoke: Macmillan (contains an analysis of the role of the PSC in Catalonia).

DAVID GEORGE

Catalan television

There are two Catalan-language television channels broadcasting from Barcelona, TV3 and Canal 33, both belonging to the publicly owned Corporació Catalana de Ràdio i Televisió (Catalan Radio and Television Corporation). Both have proved highly successful in their own terms, with TV3 attracting the larger audiences, and Catalan-language television has now become a fundamental element of **Catalan culture** in general.

Catalonia's first Catalan-language television channel, TV3, also known as Televisió de Catalunya (Catalan Television), first went on air in an experimental broadcast on 10 September 1983, some ten months after the setting up of the first **Basque television** channel, and in defiance, like it, of central government, which considered its use of certain terrestrial frequencies to be illegal. But the controversies surrounding its launch were not only legal. Considerable resentment was caused in Catalonia by the then head of Spanish **television**, José María Calviño, when he suggested during a visit to Barcelona that Catalan television should limit itself to things Catalan, rather than attempting to become a mainstream channel with a full portfolio of programme types (and thereby entering, of course, into direct competition with Spanish national television). Catalan television picked up this particular gauntlet enthusiastically, and has never had any doubts about its vocation to become the main television station of Catalonia as a whole, offering the entire range of programmes which viewers would expect from a mainstream television channel.

Despite the original legal difficulties, TV3's legal situation was – like that of all the television channels of the other **autonomous communities** – eventually normalized towards the end of 1984, representing a considerable political victory for the communities *vis-à-vis* Madrid. From 5 April 1989 Catalan television, together with the other autonomous channels, has also been a member of the Federación de Organizaciones de Radio y Televisión Autonómicas (Federation of Autonomous Radio and Television Organizations), in an attempt to strengthen the defence of its interests and increase its ability to bid successfully for programmes on the international markets.

In TV3's first experimental broadcast, Catalans received foreign programmes dubbed into Catalan. It moved to regular broadcasting on 16 January 1984 with a weekly service of fourteen hours, increasing to thirty-five hours on 2 April. Although the process of dubbing continues (both of foreign-language productions and of productions in Spanish), TV3 has become an important source of domestic Catalan-language production, and has indeed become one of the most dynamic and forward-looking stations in Spain, opening a new complex of four buildings in 1986, and being the first station in Spain to introduce Electronic News Gathering teams and to design a corporate image.

On 10 September 1988 a second Catalan-language television channel entitled Canal 33 came on air unexpectedly, much to the surprise of large sectors of Catalan society, including the Catalan parliament, which had not been informed of the decision to launch the new channel. A number of reasons explain this unexpected appearance. One was plans developed by central television, TVE, to launch a Catalan-language channel of its own in October of that year (a channel which never, in fact, got off the ground). Another was the desire to offset the imminent arrival of the new private channels which it was quite correctly felt in Catalonia would have the effect of increasing the amount of Spanish-language television available to Catalans. The sudden launch of this new channel caused immediate tensions between the Catalan and Madrid governments, resulting a few days later in Madrid jamming transmission of the new channel. This situation continued for a further two months as a solution to the legal problems was sought. In the end Canal 33 was able to begin broadcasting in January 1989. Its remit has been to concentrate on programmes of a more regional nature, thereby complementing TV3's more broadly based mainstream programming, as well as to provide good quality cultural productions, and extensive coverage of sport.

It would be wrong to suggest that Catalans do not watch Spanish-language television. The two most successful channels in Spain, TVE1 and Antena 3, are enjoyed by many Catalan speakers, and many of their programmes record high viewing figures in Catalonia. Nonetheless, there can be little doubt that the contribution made by the two public Catalan-language stations has been of tremendous importance to Catalonia in many ways.

TV3 is a worthy rival in all respects to all the national terrestrial channels, which it regularly outperforms, even at peak times. Some of its greatest successes have been its historical series and its domestically produced *culebrons* (similar to British or American 'soap operas', with the crucial difference that they do eventually reach a conclusion after approximately two hundred episodes). The first of these productions, *Poble Nou* (New Town), set in post-Olympic Barcelona, attracted vast audiences, its final episode in December 1994 being seen by over one and a half million people. It also represented TV3's first 'internal export', was subsequently dubbed into Spanish by the original actors, and was sold to the national station Antena 3 and beamed throughout Spain under the new title *Los Mejores Años* (The Best Years).

However, the importance of Catalan-language television is not simply the delivery of Catalan televisual products to the Catalan population. It is seen by many in Catalonia as a key element in **language normalization** in Catalonia (a process to which it undoubtedly contributes in important ways) and in strengthening the notion of Catalan identity as available to all the citizens of Catalonia, whatever their origin.

Further reading

Cardús, S. (1995) *Política de Paper: Premsa i poder a Catalunya 1981–1992*, Barcelona: Edicions La Campana (see in particular chapters 3 and 6).

Villagrasa, J.M. (1992) 'Spain: The Emergence of Commercial Television', in A. Silj (ed.) *The New Television in Europe*, London: John Libbey (a wide-ranging but very readable account of changes in television throughout Spain since the early 1980s).

HUGH O'DONNELL

Catalan United Socialist Party

The Catalan United Socialist Party, better known by its acronym PSUC (Partit Socialista Unificat de Catalunya), was formed during the early days of the Civil War with the encouragement of the Communist International. However, it was not recognized by the **PSOE** (Socialist Workers Party). The PSUC was nominally independent of the **PCE** (Spanish Communist Party), but tended to be subservient to it and to the Stalinist Communist International. The PSUC was involved on the side of the Moscow-backed Communists in their repression of Anarchists and Trotskyists during the events of May 1937 in Barcelona, which are vividly described in George Orwell's *Homage to Catalonia* (1939). Despite their ostensibly Catalan identity, the PSUC sided with the centralizing forces in the Republican Government.

After the end of the Civil War, the PSUC, like other left-wing groupings, suffered from Francoist repression. Its influence, however, grew during the 1960s, particularly in the Barcelona branch of the newly-formed **CC OO** (Workers' Committees). The success of CC OO all over Spain in the late 1960s and early 1970s was reflected in considerable working-class support for both the PCE and the PSUC.

As in all radical working-class movements in potentially nationalist situations, there was always a tension within PSUC as to whether they were primarily a Catalanist or a working-class party. In a book in 1967, Jordi Solé Tura, who later left the party and became a Minister of Culture under Felipe **González**, equated Catalanism with bourgeois values, which he naturally considered to be incompatible with socialism. However, through their opposition to Franco, and their success at building mass working-class movements, whether through trade unionism or the important residents' associations, the PSUC gained widespread grass-root support in Catalonia. They are also credited with avoiding a split between native Catalans and the large numbers of working-class immigrants from the south of Spain who arrived in Catalonia during the 1960s and the 1970s. The PSUC was rewarded with an 18.2 percent share of the vote in the 1977 General Elections.

After that date, however, their electoral strength declined sharply. The attempt by the leader of the PCE, Santiago **Carrillo**, to impose his Euro-communism on the PSUC was rejected by the 1981 Congress. This completely split the PSUC, and led to its irrevocable decline, which was heightened by the demise of the PCE and by the feeling among the working classes that a vote for the PSOE or the **PSC** (Catalan Socialist Party) was tactically more useful than one for the PSUC. Following their disastrous performance at the 1982 General Election (4.6 percent of the vote), Antoni Gutiérrez resigned as the party's General Secretary and was replaced by Rafael Ribó. The latter was the moving force behind the formation in 1987 of the **Initiative for Catalonia** Coalition (IC), which has enjoyed some limited success at recent elections.

Further reading

Balcells, A. (1996) *Catalan Nationalism*, ed. G.J. Walker, Basingstoke: Macmillan (contains an analysis of the role of the PSUC in Catalonia).

DAVID GEORGE

Catany, Toni

b. 1942, Llucmajor (Mallorca)

Photographer

Established in Barcelona since 1963, Catany first made his name through his work for *La Vanguardia* in the late 1960s. Later the film magazine *Imagen y Sonido* (Image and Sound) provided a more suitable vehicle for his development, which was influenced by internationally known photographers such as Richard Avedon or Frank Horvath. In 1977 he helped to establish the Alabern group, whose aim was to revitalize photography by seeking greater freedom of expression. Since then, the generally restrained quality of Catany's work has been increasingly marked by the search for formal purity.

MIHAIL MOLDOVEANU

CC OO

The Workers' Committees (CC OO – Comisiones Obreras) emerged as a clandestine movement during the Asturian miners' mobilizations of 1958, subsequently combining legitimate activity inside the state-run **vertical syndicates** with illegal struggles in defence of working-class interests. While its supporters viewed this approach as a tactical innovation, the exiled leaders of the 'historic unions' (**UGT** and **CNT**) dubbed CC OO 'collaborationist'. CC OO nevertheless continued to aspire towards syndical unity and hoped to attract all workers, without distinction of political or religious beliefs. This non-sectarian approach was reinforced by flexible organizational structures and workplace democracy, which favoured ideological diversity and ensured that while **PCE** (communist) members were active in CC OO, so too were Catholic workers, dissident Falangists, socialists and anarcho-syndicalists.

CC OO spearheaded a resurgence of industrial conflict during the final decade of the dictatorship and eclipsed the 'historic unions' in their traditional bastions like Andalusia, Asturias, Catalonia, Madrid and Valencia. Growth brought increased institutionalization and CC OO became a state-wide movement at its 1967 Congress, which also witnessed the ascendency of the PCE. That same year official tolerance ended, a *volte-face* provoked by CC OO success in the 1966 syndical elections and the advent of the economic crisis.

State and employer repression did not diminish the mobilizing power of CC OO in the workplace. At its 1976 Congress CC OO consolidated itself as an independent union, heralding a struggle for hegemony with the UGT. Dissenters regarded this development as a break with the traditional goal of syndical unity, and amid growing bureaucratization and PCE influence, the CC OO left wing split. The 1977 **Moncloa Pacts** highlighted the readiness of CC OO to neutralize revolutionary tendencies in order to ensure the return of democracy. While advocating socialist transformation, its statutes make an explicit commitment to the 1978 constitution, which explains its consistently reformist practice after Franco.

In 1978, CC OO claimed a membership of 1.8 million and won the first post-Francoist syndical elections with 34.5 percent of the vote. However, by the early 1980s membership was around 800,000 and CC OO was losing ground to the UGT. Nevertheless, CC OO has maintained its strongholds in Catalonia, Valencia, Andalusia and Madrid and remains the dominant syndical force in the largest factories and in the construction and metal sectors, underlining its predominantly industrial nature when compared with the UGT. Since the consolidation of democracy, CC OO has adopted a more combative stance, mobilizing jointly with the UGT from the mid-1980s against government austerity measures and unemployment.

See also: Camacho, Marcelino; political parties; politics; trade unions

Further reading

Balfour, S. (1989) *Dictatorship, Workers and the City. Labour in Greater Barcelona Since 1939*, Oxford: Clarendon (a thorough study by a leading labour historian).

Fishman, R. (1990) *Working Class Organization and the Return of Democracy in Spain*, Ithaca, NY: Cornell University Press (a comprehensive overview of labour politics during the transition).

Prevost, G. (1984) 'Change and Continuity in the Spanish Labour Movement', *West European Politics* 7, 1.

Ruiz, D. (ed.) (1993) *Historia de Comisiones Obreras (1958–1988)*, Madrid: Siglo XXI.

CHRIS EALHAM

Cecilia

b. 1948, Spain; d. 1976, Spain

Singer (real name Evangelina Sobredo)

Cecilia (Evangelina Sobredo) lived in various countries up to the age of 17 as her father was a diplomat. She returned to Spain in 1966 to read Law, and met musicians with whom she would form her first group, 'Expresión', before embarking on a solo career (adopting the name Cecilia after the Simon and Garfunkel song). Cecilia recorded three LPs and her songs are full of socio-political references. Her career was cut short in 1976 when she died in a car accident. Two posthumous collections of her greatest hits and recordings of unfinished songs have been published.

See also: rock and pop

MIGUEL JIMÉNEZ PINILLA

Cela Trulock, Camilo José

b. 1916, Iria Flavia del Padrón (Galicia)

Writer

Cela's 1989 Nobel Prize increased his already high visibility. The Madrid daily *El País* claimed that his first novel *The Family of Pascual Duarte* (*La familia de Pascual Duarte*, 1942) was the 'most translated novel of the Spanish language', followed by *The Hive* (*La colmena*, 1951). These two novels are the focus of most critical writing, with consequent neglect of twelve other novels, some eighteen short story collections, twelve novellas, a dozen travel books, poetry, theatre, more than twenty collections of essays, and numerous miscellaneous prose works. These include his unfinished memoirs, criticism, erudite lexicography of obscenity and vulgarity – the *Diccionario secreto* (Secret Dictionary) – a four-volume survey of sexuality, *Enciclopedia del erotismo*, volumes of sketches, vignettes, caricatures and limited edition works of difficult classification produced for the collectors' market. Since the Nobel, Cela has published steadily, including the novels *Cristo versus Arizona* (1988), *El asesinato del perdedor* (The Loser's Murder) (1994) and *La cruz de*

San Andrés (St Andrew's Cross) (1994). In 1995, he received the **Cervantes Prize**.

Cela's style employs alliterative, rhythmic prose, parallelistic constructions, grotesque caricatures alongside moments of tenderness, occasional lyricism with ever-present ironies, abundant taglines and popular sayings, vulgarity, and obscenities in the context of academically correct passages. He playfully examines words and language, trivializing or reducing to absurdity, producing scenes, conversations and incidents capable of standing alone, while avoiding 'closed' narrative, traditional plots, connected action and sequential chronologies.

The Family of Pascual Duarte initiated, after the Civil War, the neo-naturalistic movement known as *tremendismo*. Emphasizing violence, the repulsive and ugly, *tremendismo* lacks naturalism's scientific pretensions, employing caricature, gallows humour, and deliberate distortions. *La colmena*, deemed the prototype for the 1950s and 1960s 'social' novel, spurred Cela's 1957 election to the **Royal Academy**. Numerous picaresque elements, present in both works, constitute recurrent motifs, dominant in *Nuevas aventuras y desventuras del Lazarillo de Tormes* (New Adventures and Misadventures of Lazarillo) (1944), and reappearing in frequent portraits of beggars, the blind, prostitutes and a host of poor people in *Historias de España: Los ciegos, los tontos* (Tales of Spain: The Blind, the Idiots) (1958), *Los viejos amigos* (Old Friends) (1960), *Garito de hospicianos* (Poorhouse Inmates) (1963), *Izas, rabizas y colipoterras* (Bawds, Harlots and Whores) (1964), and the seven volume series, *Nuevas escenas matritenses* (New Madrid Scenes) (1965).

Characteristic traits include depiction of numerous mental and sexual aberrations, antiheroic figures, frequently deviant or nauseating behaviour, ugly, repugnant, malformed or mutilated characters, and the dehumanization of characters. Violent, sadistic, or irrational crimes appear in numerous short stories and novels, including *The Family of Pascual Duarte, La Catira, San Camilo, 1936, Mazurca para dos muertos* (Mazurka for Two Cadavers), *Cristo versus Arizona*, and *La cruz de San Andrés*. *Mazurca*, his second Civil War novel, awarded the 1983 National Literary Prize, reflects wartime violence, revenge and atrocities on a mythic scale. Man's inhumanity to man (and especially women and children) produces enormously shocking sexual violence and grotesque ways of dying (*La Catira, Cristo versus Arizona*), with victims fried, devoured by piranhas, entombed alive in salt, disembowelled, impaled, butchered and tortured in countless ways. Sadism, masochism, rape, voyeurism, exhibitionism, homosexuality, lesbianism, necrophilia, paedophilia and incest abound, reflecting Cela's determination to shock any lingering sense of social propriety (for example, the narrator of *Cristo versus Arizona* figures among the most assiduous patrons of his mother, a prostitute).

Alienation, despair, individual helplessness, isolation, callousness or cruelty of the strong, materialism, cynicism and absolute selfishness produce a fictional world seen as comprising only two groups, victims and executioners. Characters are typically amoral or immoral (sometimes quite zestfully so), with the few ethical or good ones appearing somewhat unintelligent. Cela's novels become progressively more experimental, moving from early traditional, confessional, picaresque formats to rambling, disjointed monologue, illustrated in the surrealistic *Mrs. Caldwell Speaks to her Son* (*Mrs. Caldwell habla con su hijo*) and in *Oficio de tinieblas, 5* (Tenebrae) which abounds in references to farce, deceit, defeat, suicide, betrayal, alienation, prostitution and death. Fully developed characters are almost nonexistent after *Pascual Duarte*, and plots become more tenuous, incomplete, or diffuse. Lyric motifs, repetition, or thematic reiteration assume the structuring functions of plot. Settings – nearly always stylized save for the travel books – grow increasingly vague, disappearing altogether in *Oficio de tinieblas*. Stylized and mythically exaggerated settings reapppear in *Mazurca* and *Cristo versus Arizona*. Chronology, 'story', and memorable characters, effaced in longer works, survive in Cela's brief fiction. Later novels, postmodern in their fluctuations, contradictions, and indeterminacy, openly criticize the Spanish 'Establishment' – the government, church, military, judicial, penal, and educational systems – while continuing to catalogue injustices, abuses, and inhumanity.

Major works

Cela Trulock, C.J. (1942) *La familia de Pascual Duarte*;

trans. A. Kerrigan, *The Family of Pascual Duarte*, Boston, MA: Little, Brown, 1964 (novel).
—— (1948) *Viaje a la Alcarria*, Barcelona: Ediciones Destino; trans. F.M. López-Morillas, *Journey to the Alcarria*, Madison, WI: University of Wisconsin Press, 1964 (travel).
—— (1951) *La colmena*, Buenos Aires: Noguer; trans. J.M. Cohen, *The Hive*, with A. Barea, New York: Farrar, Straus & Young, 1953 (novel).
—— (1953) *Mrs. Caldwell habla con su hijo*, Barcelona: Ediciones Destino; trans. J.S. Bernstein, *Mrs. Caldwell Speaks to her Son*, Ithaca, NY: Cornell University Press, 1968 (novel).
—— (1969) *San Camilo, 1936*, Madrid: Alfaguara; trans. J.H.R. Polt, *The Eve, Feast and Octave of St Camillus of the Year 1936 in Madrid*, Durham, NC: Duke University Press, 1991 (novel).

Further reading

Cela Conde, C.J. (1984) *Cela mi padre*, Madrid: Ediciones Temas de Hoy (a sometimes disconcerting biography of the writer by his son).
Foster, D. (1967) *Forms of the Novel in the Work of Camilo José Cela*, Columbia, MO: University of Missouri Press (formal approach to the early novels).
Henn, D. (1974) *Camilo José Cela. La colmena*, London: Grant & Cutler (a text-oriented study guide).
Insula (1989) 518–19 (this journal contains a bibliography of Cela's works).
Kirsner, R. (1966). *The Novels and Travels of Camilo José Cela*, Chapel Hill, NC: University of North Carolina Press (still the best study of the travel books).
McPheeters, D.W. (1969) *Camilo José Cela*, New York: Twayne (primarily a study of the first six novels, in English).
Pérez, J. (1988) '*Mazurca para dos muertos*: Demythologization of the Civil War, History and Narrative Reliability', *The Contemporary Spanish Novel: 1936–1986*, ed. K. Glenn, *et al.* (special number of *Anales de la literatura española contemporánea* 13, 1–2: 83–104 (analyses Cela's subversion of official, or Francoist, historiography and postmodern narrative 'unwriting').
—— (1991) 'Camilo José Cela: A Retrospective and Prospective Assessment', *Anales de la literatura española contemporánea* 16: 361–77 (assesses criticism on Cela up to the Nobel Prize).
—— (1996) 'Text, Context and Subtext of the Unreliable Narrative: Cela's *El asesinato del perdedor*', *Anales de la Literatura Española Contemporánea* 21 (1996): 85–100.

JANET PÉREZ

censorship

The official culture of Franco's Spain was intolerant, xenophobic, sectarian and resolutely Castilian. Any expression of Catalan, Basque or Galician culture was forbidden, but no-one, whatever his or her cultural origins, was immune from censorship. José Angel Valente had his passport withdrawn in 1972 by order of a military court for publishing a short story deemed to be insulting to the army, and his publisher was sentenced to six months' imprisonment.

Censorship bore most heavily on those forms of expression which reached the wider public, especially the press and the cinema. Any news displeasing to the government was systematically suppressed, and editors were obliged to act as channels of state propaganda. Editors who failed to comply with directives from the *Delegación de Prensa* (Press Section) of the Ministry of Education were heavily fined.

A similar balance between suppression and enforced publication existed in the cinema. No film could be shown, in public or in private, unless it received a certificate of approval from the *Junta Superior de Orientación Cinematográfica* (Higher Board of Cinematic Orientation). In 1943, it became compulsory for cinemas to include in their programmes the officially approved newsreels known as the NO-DO (*Noticiario Documental*). It was in the cinema that the influence of the Catholic Church was mainly exercised, for in addition to being represented on the *Junta Superior*, the Church had its own censorship organization, whose classifications of films were published in the press.

Whereas the main thrust of state censorship was political, the influence of the church was directed principally towards suppressing supposed sexual laxity or explicitness. Norms published by the bishops in 1959 forbade engaged couples to walk arm-in-arm, and posters displayed in church porches in the 1960s set out detailed specifications for modesty in women's dress. Newspapers and magazines employed *retocadores* (retouchers), who were responsible for painting vests on the torsos of boxers, lengthening hemlines and reducing the size of women's busts.

All of this created a climate of stifling conformity, but in practice implementation of regulations was patchy and inconsistent. This could work in either a negative or positive direction. In the 1950s writers and filmmakers complained that the operation of censorship was frequently arbitrary and unpredictable. Works permitted by the Ministry of Information and Tourism (which took over the functions of censorship on its formation in 1951) could be suppressed as a result of ecclesiatical interference or complaints from private citizens. On the other hand, personal contacts could often enable applicants to bypass the system, especially since fellow-writers were often employed as readers by the censorship apparatus.

Furthermore, censorship offered a challenge to the resourceful writer or filmmaker. An indirect and allegorical treatment of contemporary political issues could not only outwit the censor but lend depth and complexity to the work. Antonio **Buero Vallejo**'s historical plays and Carlos **Saura**'s 1965 film *La caza* (The Hunt) are notable examples of works in which the events of the plot are meant to suggest by analogy the endemic violence in Spanish society which led to the Civil War.

There were other factors, of an economic or political kind, which to some extent mitigated the rigour of censorship. At the same time as the regime was attempting to smother dissent among its own citizens, it was trying to present an acceptable face to the outside world. By the 1960s, delegations from cultural bodies like UNESCO were being shown collections of books published in Catalan, in an attempt to create the impression of an open and pluralist cultural climate, but there were still no Catalan newspapers or periodicals, with the sole exception of the monthly ***Serra d'Or***, permitted only because it was published by a church body, the Benedictine monastery of Montserrat.

In the cinema, considerations of prestige merged with economic factors to produce a balance between ideological control and concessions to popular demand which was virtually unique to Spain. The cinema was not solely an art form which could increase Spain's reputation abroad but an industry which employed significant numbers of people. In addition, in a country with the highest European ratio of seats to population, the cinema helped to forward the regime's policy of discouraging the populace from engaging in political debate by providing an unceasing stream of light entertainment. In order to cater for this demand, the authorities allowed the importation of large numbers of American films, but, by making compulsory the **dubbing** of the soundtrack into Spanish, they ensured that anything considered risqué or politically sensitive was edited out.

The mid-1960s saw a change in the apparatus of censorship with the enactment of the **Press Law** sponsored by the Minister of Information and Tourism, Manuel **Fraga Iribarne**. Prior censorship was abolished, but the authorities could still suppress or confiscate material after publication. This measure, though presented at the time as an important step towards liberalization, did little more than replace censorship by bureaucrats with self-censorship.

Censorship virtually disappeared with the death of Franco, and the years immediately after 1975 were characterized by an upsurge of sexually explicit magazines and films, but after the intensity of the post-Franco sex holiday, the availability of pornography in Spain settled back to a more moderate level. Press freedom has made an important contribution to the consolidation of democracy by exposing **corruption** and abuses of power, but state **television** (RTVE) has attracted criticism, both under the UCD administrations of 1977 to 1982 and under the Socialists post-1982, for lack of objectivity and excessive coverage of the party of government.

See also: Basque culture; Catalan culture; cinema law; Francoist culture; Galician culture; language and national identity; pornography; theatre

Further reading

Carr, R. and Fusi, J.P. (1979) *Spain: Dictatorship to Democracy*, London: Allen & Unwin (chapter 6 includes an excellent account of Francoist culture and the changes it underwent after 1975).

Gubern, R. (1981) *La censura: Función política y ordenamiento jurídico bajo el franquismo (1936–1975)*, Barcelona: Ediciones Península (an excellent and well-documented general study).

Hooper, J. (1995) *The New Spaniards*, Harmondsworth: Penguin (chapter 10 includes useful comments on censorship in the context of a general shift in social and moral attitudes).

EAMONN RODGERS

Centelles, Agustí

b. 1909, Grau (Valencia); d. 1985, Barcelona

Photographer

Centelles was very well-known in the 1930s for his direct, spare style, and for his very lively photojournalism for newspapers such as *La Vanguardia*, *Diario de Barcelona* and *La Humanitat*. He had great skill with the miniature Leica, which enabled him to follow and photograph scenes of the Civil War. His personal archives are one of the most important documentary sources for the Republican period and the war years. His involvement on the Republican side forced him to go into exile in France in 1939, from where he returned in 1944 to concentrate mainly on commercial photography. In 1984 he received the National Prize for the Plastic Arts for his life's work.

MIHAIL MOLDOVEANU

CEOE

The Confederación Española de Organizaciones Empresariales (CEOE – Confederation of Employers Organizations) is the major national organization representing business interests in Spain. The CEOE plays an important role in the labour market and a more general role in shaping government policy, in forming public opinion, in vocational training and in Spanish culture. It also represents Spanish employers in international organizations and in other countries. Since its foundation in 1977 the CEOE has been a vehicle for expressing the conservative viewpoint, contributing to the shift in Spanish politics towards the centre in the mid-1990s.

The CEOE has a membership embracing both individual companies and other employers organizations. These include those representing employers in particular areas of the country (for example the Employers Federation of Andalusia), those representing specific economic sectors of the economy (such as the private banks) and those representing specific categories of businesses such as small and medium size businesses; the latter being represented by the Confederation of Small and Medium-Size Enterprises (Confederación Española de Pequeñas y Medianas Empresas – CEPYME).

The ultimate ruling body of the CEOE is the General Assembly, composed of a large number of delegates, elected for four-year terms, representing all the organizations of the CEOE. The General Assembly elects a Chairperson and a Board of Directors, who in turn appoint the members of the Executive Committee. A number of ad-hoc advisory committees consider specific issues such as government budgets, taxation, the labour market, health and safety, infrastructure, energy and the European Union. There is a permanent secretariat to advise on, and co-ordinate the work of, the CEOE and to implement its policies.

The activities of the CEOE are, first, to represent the viewpoint of the business community in discussions with the government over public policy, including those which take place in the government's Economic and Social Affairs Committee, and with the **trade unions** over collective wage agreements and working conditions. It undertakes research into issues affecting the business community and publishes reports. For example, the CEOE carries out on-going analyses of the Spanish economy in order to offer advice on enhancing the competitive position of Spanish companies. For its members the CEOE provides a forum for discussion and a source of business information. It also runs training courses and offers some technical support. As a broader cultural organization, the CEOE Foundation promotes cultural activity, social and scientific research.

During the 'transition to democracy' and economic crisis at the end of the 1970s, the CEOE was one of the three parties involved in reaching agreements that contributed towards stabilizing the economy, the other two being the government and the trade unions. In 1984 it was a signatory to the Economic and Social Accord, along with the government and the General Workers Trade Union (**UGT**). However, despite its alignment with the ruling political party in 1996, it remained outside the agreement on pensions (initially reached in 1995 as the *Pacto de Toledo*) between the government and the trade unions, arguing that the cost to business remained too high.

During the mid-1990s the CEOE, under the presidency of José María Cuevas (in office since 1984), became the axis for conservative criticism of the socialist (**PSOE**) government. Its leadership allied with the opposition conservative Popular Party (**PP**), providing technical support in developing the PP's economic programme. Following the victory of the PP in the elections in 1996 some members of the CEOE joined the PP government.

Although the CEOE represents the business community, that community does not have a single view on all issues. Internal tensions reflect the different perspectives which emerge from the variety of businesses in the country and their regional origin, as well as personality clashes.

See also: economy; labour market; trade unions; unemployment

KEITH SALMON

Cervantes Institute

The Cervantes Institute is the overall title of a network of Institutes in various countries which provide classes in Spanish, organize cultural events, and administer the official Diploma in Spanish as a Foreign Language awarded by the Ministry of Education and Science. The Institute was established in March 1991, on the model of the Alliance Française, the British Council, and the Goethe Institut. It brought together under one umbrella the various educational and cultural activities outside Spain already supported by the Ministries of Culture, Foreign Affairs, Education and Science, Labour and Finance. For administrative purposes, the Institute functions under Foreign Affairs, which channels funds for teaching and secretarial staff, while the receiving country provides premises and equipment. The first Institute was opened in Liverpool in 1990, and by August 1991, the number worldwide had grown to forty, through the incorporation into the network of a number of existing cultural centres. The first overall Director, Nicolás Sánchez Albornoz, was appointed in September 1991.

By 1993, however, the original project to establish seventy centres worldwide was beginning to appear over-ambitious. Despite an annual budget which had risen from 2,200m pesetas in 1991 to 3,800m in 1993, ten centres were forced to close, either for lack of local demand for Spanish classes, the cost of refurbishment of older premises, or, in the case of Liverpool, because the university needed to recover the use of its building. The savings made enabled the Institute to consolidate its operations, and expand into Eastern Europe, where centres were opened in Bucharest and Warsaw in 1994. In that year, the total number of centres was 32, spread over 21 countries. The annual budget had risen to 4,194m pesetas, but this, at approximately 50 percent of Italy's expenditure on corresponding institutes, 7 percent that of Britain, and 5 percent that of France, was still insufficient for the organization's needs.

Completion of formal requirements for recognition by the host countries had, however, lagged behind even this modest expansion, and, as a result, many of the centres found themselves in an ambiguous legal situation. Unlike embassy staff, those employed in the Institutes had no diplomatic immunity, and were therefore technically subject to the requirements of the host country with regard to residence and work permits, and taxation. While the centres themselves often enjoyed a de facto tax-free status, the fact that they were not registered with the tax authorities precluded them recovering, for example, VAT payments. Over and above this, there were problems of chronic under-resourcing and management, and, in 1995, a number of controversial resignations by local Institute directors.

In 1996, Sánchez Albornoz was replaced as overall Director by a career diplomat, Santiago de Mora-Figueroa, Marquis of Tamarón, who, despite the problems of resourcing, continued to expand the Institute's operations, opening a centre in Chicago in October 1996, one in Utrecht, and one in Manchester in June 1997. In a bid to keep down costs, development began on a plan to distribute educational material on the Internet.

EAMONN RODGERS

Cervantes Prize

The Cervantes Prize is the most prestigious, though not the most valuable, literary prize in Spain, often described in the media as the Spanish equivalent of the Nobel Prize for Literature. By the mid-1990s, its value stood at 15m pesetas. It is awarded annually for major contributions to literature in Spanish, and is not confined to writers originating or domiciled in Spain. The 1996 winner was the poet José García Nieto, and the previous year it was won, somewhat controversially, by the veteran writer Camilo José Cela, who had on previous occasions made scathing remarks about the competition.

EAMONN RODGERS

Chacel, Rosa

b. 1898, Valladolid; d. 1994, Madrid

Writer

Rosa Chacel was proud of having been born in 1898, as she liked to associate herself with the iconoclastic spirit of the 'Generation of 1898'. Chacel's education, life and career, however, were very different from those of the 1898 writers, all of whom were male, although she was fortunate that her parents recognized and encouraged her artistic talents. Chacel spent her first ten years in Valladolid where, owing to a sickly constitution, she was home tutored. After the family moved to Madrid in 1908, she studied art, first in the School of Arts and Crafts (Escuela de Artes y Oficios) (1910) and then in the School of Fine Arts (Escuela de Bellas Artes de San Fernando) (1915). Chacel also frequented the Ateneo and Ramón Gómez de la Serna's vanguard enclave at Café de Pombo. Her fiction is frequently associated with vanguardism, but though she flirted with vanguard linguistic virtuosity in the 1920s and 1930s, she found a unique voice in exile after the Spanish Civil War (1936–9). Her mature style carries traces of vanguardism but it also incorporates the psychological depth and introspection we associate with high modernism.

In 1921 Chacel married the painter Timoteo Pérez Rubio and accompanied him to Rome where he had a scholarship at the School of Art. During her stay in Rome (1922–7), Chacel devoted herself to reading José **Ortega y Gasset**, James Joyce, and Marcel Proust, among many others. She also travelled, especially to the culturally avant-garde Paris. Towards the end of the Roman period, Chacel abandoned her earlier inclinations towards the plastic arts and found her vocation in fiction writing. In Rome she wrote her first novel *Estación. Ida y vuelta* (Round Trip Station) (published 1930). Chacel claims it was written under the influence of Ortega's philosophy, and it is the most avant-garde of her novels. Loosely modelled on *A Portrait of the Artist as a Young Man*, which made a great impact on Chacel when she read it in the early 1920s, the novel narrates the vicissitudes of a young man's relationships with two women and his coming into consciousness of his artistic vocation. More than a narrative, it is a series of moments in which the protagonist's consciousness is revealed.

Once re-established in Madrid in 1927, Chacel collaborated in the ***Revista de Occidente*** and other journals, where she demonstrated a philosophical sophistication equal to that of contemporary male intellectuals, with essays like her response to Georg Simmel's ideas on love, 'Esquema de los problemas prácticos y actuales del amor' (Outline of the Current Practical Problems of Love) (31 (1931): 129–80). Between 1940 and 1950, Chacel divided her time between Rio de Janeiro, where her husband worked, and Buenos Aires, where her son Carlos attended school. She published articles in prestigious Latin American journals, such as *Sur*, but her artistic production slowed.

In 1941 she published *Teresa*, a novelized biography of the romantic poet José Espronceda's mistress, originally commissioned for a biography series initiated by Ortega. In 1945 *Memoirs of Leticia Valle* (*Memorias de Leticia Valle*) appeared. While traces of vanguardism remain in the elliptical nature of the narrative, *Memoirs* represents a new kind of novel that has affinities with the *nouveau roman*. All events are revealed from the perspective of the narrator–protagonist (an eleven-year-old girl) who has apparently seduced her teacher. The novel has complex implications for gender as Leticia seems to be equally loved by and in love with her very masculine (*machista*) tutor and his feminine, musical, and intuitive wife.

Between 1950 and 1958 Chacel wrote her finest novel, *La sinrazón* (Unreason) (published in 1961). *La sinrazón* is a first-person narration from the perspective of the male protagonist, who is entangled in relationships with two women. His schizophrenia eventually destroys him, and he commits suicide, like the central male character in *Memoirs of Leticia Valle*. Thus, in retrospect, the novel is narrated by a dead man, a configuration that casts the entire novel in a singular light. *La sinrazon* is in many ways the embodiment of the philosophical ideas on eros that Chacel developed in her essay *Saturnal*, which continued the critique of love in the west she had begun in her essay in *Revista de Occidente*. There she views eros as a totality that cannot be separated from other aspects of life. (Chacel was awarded a Guggenheim Fellowship for a stay in New York from 1959 to 1961 to work on the essay; she completed it in Brazil the late 1960s.)

Chacel began to keep a diary while in exile, which was eventually published as *Alcancía, Ida* (Alcancía, Outward Journey) (1946–66) and *Alcancía, Vuelta* (Alcancía, Return Journey) (1967–81) in 1982. She also published an autobiography of her first ten years of life – *Desde el amanecer* (As Dawn Breaks) – in 1972. In 1974 Chacel returned permanently to Madrid. With the aid of a Fundación March grant she was able to complete the novel *Barrio de Maravillas* (Maravillas District), which won the Premio de la Crítica in 1976. It became the first novel in a trilogy that includes *Acrópolis* (1984) and *Ciencias naturales* (Natural Sciences) (1988). These dialogued novels centre on the subtle permutations in relations between members of different classes and genders in the lives of young girls growing up in a Spanish society.

By Chacel's own assessment, the major influences on her fiction-writing were Proust, Joyce, and Ramón Gómez de la Serna. Her modulated handling of human subjectivity (male as well as female), however, makes one think more of Virginia Woolf, who, like Chacel used sexual ambiguity in her psychological portraits. In addition to the novels mentioned, Chacel also published a book of novel projects *Novelas antes de tiempo* (Novels Before Their Time) (1981), collections of stories – *Sobre el piélago* (1952), *Ofrenda a una virgen loca* (Offering to a Mad Virgin) (1961), *Balaam y otros relatos* (Balaam and other Stories) (1962), and *Icada, Nevda, Diada* (1971), – another book of poetry, *Versos prohibidos* (Forbidden Verses) (1978), and several essays of a theoretical nature – *La confesión* (Confession) (1971), *Los títulos* (Titles) (1981), *Rebañaduras* (Parings) (1986), and *La lectura es secreto* (Reading is a Secret Activity) (1989).

Although forgotten and unread for many years in her native Spain, Chacel's work gained significant recognition towards the end of her life. Chacel comes as close as any twentieth-century Spanish woman writer to achieving canonical status. Her writing habits were slow and laborious, but the care and meticulousness of her craft paid off in works of lasting achievement.

See also: feminist writing; novel; women's writing

Major works

Chacel, R. (1930) *Estación. Ida y vuelta*, Madrid: Editorial Ulises.

—— (1945) *Memorias de Leticia Valle*, Buenos Aires: Emecé.

—— (1960) *La sinrazón*, Buenos Aires: Losada.

—— (1971) *La confesión*, Barcelona: Edhasa.

—— (1976) *Barrio de Maravillas*, Barcelona: Seix Barral.

Further reading

Ministerio de Cultura (1990) *Rosa Chacel, Premio Nacional de las Letras Españolas 1987*, Barcelona:

Anthropos (includes good biographical notes and bibliography).

Crispin, J. (1969) 'Rosa Chacel y las "ideas sobre la novela"', *Insula* 262: 10 (a study of Chacel's theory of the novel in relation to Ortega).

Johnson, R. (1986) '*Estación. Ida y vuelta*, de Rosa Chacel: un nuevo tiempo para la novela', in F. de Burgos (ed.) *Prosa hispánica de vanguardia*, Madrid: Editorial Orígenes, pp. 201–8.

Mangini, S. (1987) 'Women and Spanish Modernism: The Case of Rosa Chacel', *Anales de la Literatura Española Contemporánea* 12: 17–28 (an important study by a leading Chacel scholar).

Rodríguez, A. (1983) 'Los diarios de Rosa Chacel', *Cuadernos Hispanoamericanos* 399: 145–7.

ROBERTA JOHNSON

Chávarri, Jaime

b. 1943, Madrid

Filmmaker and film critic

A graduate of the Escuela Oficial de Cine (EOC) in 1970, Chávarri is a very versatile film director whose first major success was with *El desencanto* (Disenchantment) (1976). A study of the Francoist poet, Panero, who had died in 1962, the film was based on interviews with his wife and son, members of a right-wing family whom he described as not having known for the past four or five centuries what work was, but who are nevertheless 'disenchanted' with the regime.

The following year he directed *A un Dios desconocido* (To an Unknown God), which was greeted with rave reviews at the **San Sebastián Film Festival**. Co-scripted with **Querejeta** and produced in the immediate post-Franco period, the film takes as its subject the return to Granada of an ageing homosexual, witness to the death of Garcia Lorca.

Like other directors Chávarri has been successful with film adaptations, such as *Bearn o la sala de las muñecas* (Bearn or The Dolls' Room) (1983), set in Majorca in 1863, and the box-office winner *Las bicicletas son para el verano* (Bicycles are for Summer) (1984) based on the play by **Fernán Gómez**, set in Madrid at the outbreak of the Civil War. Also popular was his 1989 film *Las cosas del querer* (Fond Things) with its catchy musical numbers.

In addition to feature films and his early shorts and super-8 features such as *Run, Blancanieves, Run* (Run, Snow-White, Run) (1968) and *Ginebra en los infernos* (Guinevere in Hell) (1970), Chávarri has also directed many productions for Spanish television such as *La intrusa* (based on a story by Jorge Luis Borges) (1987) and *Yo soy el que tu buscas* (from a work by García Márquez) (1988). He has also successfully functioned as set designer, for instance for **Erice**'s *El espíritu de la colmena* (The Spirit of the Beehive) (1973), as actor, for instance in **Almodóvar**'s *¿Que he hecho yo para merecer esto?* (What Have I Done to Deserve This?) (1984) and as film critic for *Film Ideal*.

Further reading

Higginbotham, V. (1988) *Spanish Cinema under Franco*, Austin, TX: University of Texas Press (one of the most comprehensive surveys of this period).

Molina-Foix, V. (1977) *New Cinema in Spain*, London: British Film Institute (a comprehensive overview of current trends).

EAMONN RODGERS

Chaves, Manuel

b. 1945, Ceuta

Politician

A prominent figure in the Socialist **PSOE**, which he joined in 1968. A lecturer in labour law, he became a member of the Executive Committee of the **UGT** (General Workers Union) in 1976 and the following year was elected to parliament. Minister of Labour and Social Security from 1986, he left the cabinet in 1990 following his appointment as head of the regional government of Andalusia.

See also: autonomous communities; politics; trade unions

PAUL KENNEDY

Chenel, Antonio

b. 1934 , Madrid

Matador ('Antoñete')

After some years of success as a **matador** following his ***alternativa*** in 1953, Antoñete saw his career decline prior to his retirement in 1975. He reappeared unexpectedly in 1981 and, until a further retirement in 1985, was admired, particularly in Madrid, as the most profound stylist of the day.

See also: bullfighting

IAN CAMPBELL ROSS

Chillida, Eduardo

b. 1924, San Sebastián

Sculptor

Chillida, Spain's leading sculptor, studied architecture at the University of Madrid from 1943 to 1946 before deciding to become an artist in 1947. He moved to Paris in 1948, exhibited at the Salon de Mai in 1949, and then returned permanently to San Sebastián in 1951, feeling the need to return to his Basque roots. He denied ever having come into conflict with Franco's regime. He established a growing reputation in the 1950s, receiving the *Gran Premio Internazionale di Scultura* at the Venice Biennale in 1958. His sculptures in the 1950s, made out of forged iron with the assistance of a local blacksmith, were in the tradition of metal sculptures established by his countryman Picasso, in collaboration with Julio González, between 1928 and 1932, and also had affinities with the contemporary post-WWII vogue for abstract symbolist image making, but they were simpler and more abstract than Picasso's essentially figurative sculptures and showed little of the existential angst of sculptures by contemporaries coming to terms with war, violence, degradation and loss.

Three preoccupations run through his work: materials, space and the quest for a public sculpture. His abiding concern with the quality of his materials, an enhanced materiality, meant that his sculptures changed both form and content with changes in media. His wrought iron sculptures dramatically exploit the solidity and weight of massive units of iron, defying gravity in the exploration of space. In 1959 he experimented with wood and steel, and in 1965, inspired by a visit to Greece in 1963, with its whitewashed buildings reflecting the intense light, he began a series of sculptures in alabaster called *Elogio de la Luz* (In Praise of Light). He has worked in both stone and concrete and in 1973, with the assistance of Joan Gardy Artigas, he began a series of sculptures in terracotta. His preoccupation with the unfolding relationships between massively solid forms and space gives his sculptures an architectural character which relates back to his years studying architecture in Madrid. Form frames space, and ostensibly man-made geometric shapes, cut through naturally shaped forms, enhance the quality of the material. His wish for a public sculpture has resulted in an increasingly monumental fusion of sculpture with architecture in commissions for prestigious sites throughout the world: notably, *Comb of the Wind IV* (1969) in front of the UNESCO building in Paris; *Alrededor del vacío V* (Surrounding the Void V) (1970) in the courtyard of the World Bank in Washington DC; *Monumento* (1971) in front of the Thyssen building in Dusseldorf; *Lugar de encuentros III* (Meeting Point III) (1972–8), underneath the Castellana bridge in Madrid; *Monumento de los fueros* (Monument to Basque Law) (1975), in the main square in Vitoria which he designed with the architect Luis Peña Ganchegui; *Combs of the Wind* (1977) at Donostia Bay, San Sebastián; *Gure aitaren etxea* (1988) monument in Guernica; and *Elogio del horizonte* (In Praise of the Horizon) (1990) at Gijon.

Among numerous awards and honours, he received the Diano Marina Prize in Milan in 1974, membership of the Royal Academy, London, in 1993, the Prince of Asturias Prize in Fine Arts in 1987 and the Order for Science and Art from Germany in 1988.

See also: sculpture; visual arts

NICHOLAS WATKINS

Cho Juáa

Cartoon character Cho Juáa (Don Juan) has been described as the 'typical village opportunist' of the Canary Islands, a cartoon equivalent of Pepe **Monagas**. The creation of Eduardo Millares Sall, Cho Juáa and his long-suffering, and equally opportunistic, wife Casildita inhabit a world of goat-trading peasants, rum-drinkers, gullible *chónis* (foreigners), and *cambulloneros* (dock-side spivs). Drawn or painted in bold angular outline, Cho Juáa's paunch overhangs his broad waistband into which is tucked a *naife* (Canarian knife). Millares Sall first exhibited in 1944 and his caricatures of island life, often accompanied by brief examples of Canarian Spanish, have been published regularly in the local press.

See also: Canarian culture; Monagas, Pepe

M.R. EDDY

church finances

In Francoist times and in the early transition period, the principal source of church financing were state funds compensating for the expropriation of church property in the nineteenth century. A new three-stage funding system was envisaged by the 1979 Partial Accords (which replaced the 1953 Concordat) but was not fully implemented. Since 1988 the church has largely been financed by an annual block grant from the state coffers and revenue deriving from 0.52 percent of personal income tax when so stipulated by tax-payers. Additionally there are direct contributions, some of which can be offset against income tax. Poorer dioceses are helped by the richer via an Inter-Diocesan Common Fund. National and regional government subsidies are given for the upkeep of some church property deemed part of the national heritage. Although it is the stated aim of the church to be self-financing, dependence on the state is likely to continue in the foreseeable future.

See also: church and state

Further reading

Hooper, J. (1995) *The New Spaniards*, Harmondsworth: Penguin (see chapter 9 for a useful account of church–state relations, including financial arrangements).

AUDREY BRASSLOFF

church and state

While the early years of Francoism were marked by a renewal of the centuries-old symbiosis of throne and altar in Spain, the twilight of the regime witnessed increasing tension between them, especially regarding human rights issues. The Roman Catholic church, once the legitimizer of dictatorship, prepared to legitimize democracy. However, in the post-Franco period, a church used to enjoying a monopoly position as guardian of Spain's morals did not find democratic pluralism an easy bedfellow, particularly while the Socialist **PSOE** was in power.

Under the double pressure of the modernizing influence of the Second Vatican Council (1962–5) and of its own more progressive grassroots movements, the Spanish church started to distance itself from the Franco regime. By the 1970s, church–state relations were stretched to the limit, as evidenced by the '**Añoveros** affair' and by deadlock in the overhaul of the 1953 Concordat between Spain and the Holy See. Although the hierarchy did not make a complete break with Francoism, its political credentials were respectable enough when the transition from dictatorship to democracy came about, thanks largely to the strong leadership of the Cardinal Archbishop of Madrid, Vicente **Enrique y Tarancón**, who was also President of the Bishops' Conference (CEE) at the time.

The church entered into a positive if critical engagement with democracy, professing independence but reserving the right to issue moral judgements. Once the foundations of formal democracy had been laid in the country, this meant in practice that it would tend to favour parties whose political programmes were broadly in line with, or at least were not opposed to Catholic doctrine, though Tarancón refused to endorse any political party, even one with a Christian Democrat label. Increasing prominence was given in the hierarchy's statements to their stance on education, divorce, abortion and anti-Marxism, which worked in favour of the political centre and to the detriment of left-wing parties. Church influence was seen behind the success in 1977 and again – more blatantly – in 1979 of the Union of the Democratic Centre (**UCD**), headed by Adolfo **Suárez**.

The fundamental issue in these first post-Franco years of church–state relations concerned the future role and influence of the church in Spanish society. In the **constitution of 1978**, **Roman Catholicism** ceased to be the official **religion** of the state, though subtle wording discriminated in its favour. The constitution also unveiled a broad spectrum of political and social options for Spaniards, including divorce and abortion (see also **abortion law**), both anathema to Catholic doctrine. With the advent of a new Pope, John Paul II, in 1978, the Spanish Bishops' Conference moved progressively to the right of the 'extreme centre' position which, backed by Paul VI and the Nuncio, Monsignor Dadaglio, had characterized Tarancón's mandate. UCD's divorce law (1981) was fought to the bitter end by the church, along with the **Popular Alliance**, its champion in the Spanish parliament.

Meanwhile King **Juan Carlos I** had renounced (1976) the right of the Head of State to be involved in the appointment of bishops and the 1953 Concordat was replaced by Partial Accords (1979), covering, *inter alia*, the church's legal status, **church finances**, state subsidies for church schools, the rights of parents to choose the religious education of their children, and inclusion in all state school curricula of (optional) religious instruction in conditions comparable to those governing other core subjects.

Despite conflict over divorce, church–state relations during the UCD period of government had run relatively smoothly. With the accession to power of the PSOE in late 1982, they soon came under greater strain. 1983 was described as the 'year of the three wars of religion', with the passage of a law decriminalizing abortion in three circumstances, the publication of a church catechism condemning abortion as being as evil as terrorism and war, and the introduction of proposed new legislation on education (approved in 1984 as the **LODE**), which granted generous subsidies to church schools but with strings attached. In 1990, another education law, the **LOGSE**, prolonged the church–state education saga by challenging the position of religious instruction in schools as a core subject. Especially during the CEE Presidency of Monsignor **Suquía** from 1984 to 1993, friction between church and the PSOE government was never far below the surface, primarily regarding education, liberalization of the abortion law, and an alleged anti-clerical and anti-religious bias in the media, matched by PSOE complaints of anti-government propaganda emanating from **COPE**, the church radio station. The PSOE were also sensitive to church criticisms of corruption scandals in their midst and references to attempts to 'dechristianize' Spanish society. In 1993 Suquía was succeeded by Monsignor Elias Yanes, a CEE President more in the 'dialogue' mould of Cardinal Tarancón.

From the structural point of view, relations between the Department of Religious Affairs at the Ministry of Justice and church representatives operate at three levels: ministers/bishops, a joint technico-political commission, and working parties set up to examine specific questions.

See also: National Catholicism; religion

Further reading

Brassloff, A. (1998) *Region and Politics in Spain – the Spanish Church in Transition (1962–1996)*, London: Macmillan (gives a comprehensive account of church–state relations).

Heywood, P. (1995) *The Government and Politics of Spain*, London: Macmillan (pp. 68–74 give a useful brief summary of the evolving constitutional situation of the church).

Hooper, J. (1995) *The New Spaniards*, Harmondsworth: Penguin (chapter 9 offers a readable and reliable overview of the issue).

AUDREY BRASSLOFF

cinema law

Various measures have been taken since the mid-1950s to protect the Spanish cinema industry against competition, notably the 'screen quota', which regulated the proportion of Spanish to foreign films. Despite these measures, and generous subsidies since 1984, the number of films made in Spain continued to decline. In 1993, the then Minister of Culture, Carmen Alborch, provoked a national shutdown of cinemas by raising to one in two the quota of European Union to non-EU films, and increasing the fees paid by distributors for **dubbing** licences. The success of the Spanish film industry during 1994 to 1996, however, permitted a relaxation of restrictions, announced by the government in July 1996.

EAMONN RODGERS

Cirarda Lachiondo, José María

b. 1917, Baquio (Vizcaya)

Archbishop

Appointed Auxiliary Bishop of Seville in 1960, Cirarda became Bishop of Santander in 1968 and soon afterwards simultaneously Apostolic Administrator of Bilbao. In 1971 he became Bishop of Córdoba and subsequently Archbishop of Pamplona-Tudela from 1978 until he retired in 1993.

As Bishop of Seville, he condemned the low wages of agricultural workers and while Apostolic Administrator of Bilbao he gained a reputation for strong support of priests of his diocese in political trouble with the Franco regime, but in the post-Franco years his profile was less clearly definable.

AUDREY BRASSLOFF

Cirici Pellicer, Alexandre

b. 1914, Barcelona; d. 1983, Barcelona

Art historian

Cirici was a man of exceptional talent and intellectual energy, who brought new ideas to the world of art and design, insisting always on their social relevance and application.

Originally intending to study architecture, Cirici's career was cut short by the Civil War, after which he had to go into exile in Montpellier. He attempted to further his architectural career in Paris, but had to leave after the German occupation. He returned to Barcelona in 1941 but was unable to continue his studies because of his political activities before the war, having been a founder member of ADLAN (Amics de l'art nou – Friends of Contemporary Art) and JEREC (Joventuts d'esquerra republicana de l'Estat català – Catalan Left Republican Youth).

In the 1940s he began to publish books relating art to science, culture and lifestyle. His first important contribution *Picasso avant Picasso* gave recognition to **Picasso** while he was still disapproved of by the Franco government. Cirici organized resistance movements, MSC (*Moviment socialista de Catalunya* – Catalan Socialist Movement), and contributed to magazines, such as *Algol* and *Ariel*, identifying Catalan **Modernism** as the first unifying cultural event of Catalonia. In 1949 he founded *Club 49* with Joan Prats, which was like ADLAN before the war. In the same year he published *El surrealismo* (Surrealism), *Miró y la imaginación* (Miró and the Imagination) and *Arquitectura del siglo XX* (Twentieth-Century Architecture).

In the 1950s his own publishing enterprise ZEN reflected his interest in oriental philosophy. He published *La Sagrada Familia de Gaudí Barcelona* (Gaudí's Church of the Holy Family), and set up the Museum of Contemporary Art. Three important works appeared in the late 1950s: *La arquitectura catalana* (Catalan Architecture), *La escultura catalana* (Catalan Sculpture), and *La pintura catalana* (Catalan Painting), providing the first synthesis of Catalan art from prehistory to the present day.

By the 1960s he had merged FAD (Foment de les arts decoratives – Society for the Encouragement of Decorative Arts) with ADI (Agrupació de disseny industrial – Industrial Design Group), to form ADIFAD. The teaching branch of this enterprise, where Cirici taught design, was called ELISAVA, after a medieval Catalan artist who made the first known work of applied art. He became a member of AICA (Associació internacional de critics d'art – International Association of Art Critics) and was eventually elected its President, thus marking his worldwide reputation as an art critic. He published *Art i societat* (Art and

Society), stressing that modern art embraced a new way of thinking, to combat the past.

Always open to new ideas Cirici taught courses in visual semiotics and artistic codes at the University of Barcelona, where he became a professor. He was thrice elected senator for the Catalan Socialist Party (Partit dels Socialistes de Catalunya), in recognition of his lifelong battle for the Catalan people, socialist principles and the importance of art in everyday life.

Further reading

Badia i Margarit, A. (ed.) (1984) *Homenatge de Catalunya a Alexandre Cirici*, Barcelona: Universitat de Barcelona (biographical details and a lively collection of essays).

Gaya Nuño, J.A. (1975) *Historia de la crítica de arte en España*, Madrid: Ibérico (acknowledgement of Cirici's contribution to art history).

Homage to Cirici (1983) *Serra d'Or* vol. 25, Barcelona: Abadia de Montserrat (entire volume in praise of Cirici).

HELEN OPPENHEIMER

CiU

Convergence and Unity is the name given to the Catalan centre-right political party which has dominated Catalan politics during the post-Franco era. It is a coalition between two parties, the CDC (Convergència Democràtica de Catalunya – Democratic Convergence of Catalonia) and the UDC (Unió Democràtica de Catalunya – Democratic Union of Catalonia), which has been operative since September 1978.

The CiU has been the main political group in the **Generalitat**, or Catalan autonomous parliament, since 1980. It obtained its first overall majority in 1984, a feat it repeated in 1988 and 1992. It lost this overall majority in 1995, but still governs in the Generalitat. The CiU has also been relatively successful in elections to the Madrid parliament, increasing its representation from eight deputies and one senator in 1979, to twelve deputies and seven senators in 1982, eighteen deputies and eleven senators in 1986, to eighteen deputies and twelve senators in 1989, when it became the third political force in the Spanish state. Although it achieved one fewer deputy in 1993 than in 1989, it was by now the main Catalan political party in Madrid, and it increased its influence at state level enormously when it entered into an agreement to support the minority Socialist government of Felipe **González**. Since 1996 it has supported the minority PP government of José María Aznar.

CiU has also had success at local and at European elections, although the success is a qualified one in the case of the former. Despite its hold on many municipalities, it has never managed to wrest control of Barcelona City Council from the socialists, and in 1995 its then General Secretary, Miquel **Roca i Junyent**, failed in his attempt to become Mayor of Barcelona ahead of the incumbent Pasqual **Maragall**. CiU obtained three MEPs in 1987, and two in 1989. At the elections to the European Parliament in 1994, CiU stood in a coalition with the PSM (Nacionalistes de Mallorca – Mallorcan Nationalists) and the Unitat del Poble Valencià (Valencian People's Unity Party), obtaining three seats. One of CiU's MEPs, Carles Gasòliba i Böhm, is Treasurer of the Liberal Group of the European Parliament.

CDC has been the dominant partner in the CiU alliance, and has 30,000 members. The coalition has tended to be dominated by CDC and its charismatic leader and President of the Generalitat since 1980, Jordi **Pujol**. Nevertheless, the leader of UDC, Josep M. Duran i Lleida, has been developing a strong political profile, and is President of the Christian Democratic International group. The coalition between the two parties has held firm, although relations between the two leaders have not always been easy, particularly over CiU's support for the González Government between 1993 and 1996.

DAVID GEORGE

Civil Guard

Spain's *Guardia Civil*, the Civil Guard, is a police force whose roles and image are deeply embedded in the evolution of modern Spain. The poet García

Lorca's pre-Civil War vision of their 'patent-leather souls' reflects the origins of the Civil Guard in 1844 as a military force designed to protect the interests of landowners and of a centralizing state. By 1936 population change had led to the emergence of urban police forces with the Civil Guard specializing in rural policing. It was on this basic structure that Franco built his police system after the Civil War, and the Civil Guard underwent further militarization as part of the new regime's authoritarian social control. Its rural role continued, with heavy emphasis on political repression through its detailed files and its Intelligence Service. From the *Carabineros* with whom it was merged it inherited control over frontiers and strategic installations. In 1959 it acquired traffic control on main **roads** and by 1960 its numbers were three times those of the uniformed urban police.

With the democratic transition after 1975, **policing** became a central issue. The Civil Guard had to become a defender of the **constitution of 1978** and **civil rights**, but at the same time it was the government's most effective instrument in the struggle with **ETA**, a struggle whose violence in turn had its roots in Franco's repressive policing. These contradictions were made more difficult by the anti-democratic views of many senior Civil Guard officers and the 1981 ***Tejerazo***. The outcome by the time of the Police Law of 1986 was an accommodation that has seen the Civil Guard accept its democratic role, including the symbolic disappearance of the shiny black tricorn hat, but retain much of its special character.

The Civil Guard now polices all **municipalities** of under 20,000, and deals with customs, main roads, coasts, frontiers, ports and airports, **hunting** and forests, among other duties. It now has **women** members and takes in **military service** conscripts. It is responsible jointly to the Ministries of the Interior and Defence. It remains socially somewhat isolated from the rural communities it serves and retains much of its military ethos. In 1986 the government appointed a civilian, Luis **Roldán**, to head it for the first time, but his later flight from Spain and subsequent arrest on **corruption** charges played a part in weakening the position of Prime Minister Felipe **González**, as did allegations about the Prime Minister's connivance at illegal anti-terrorist activity (such as the **GAL**), by police, including the Civil Guard.

Further reading

Hooper, J. (1987) *The Spaniards: A Portrait of the New Spain*, Harmondsworth: Penguin (Chapter 10 includes a very readable and thorough account of the police system).

Macdonald, I.R. (1985) 'The Police System of Spain', in J. Roach and J. Thomaneck (eds) *Police and Public Order in Europe*, Beckenham: Croom Helm (the most comprehensive account available in English).

—— (1987) 'Spain's 1986 Police Law: Transition from Dictatorship to Democracy', *Police Studies*, 10, 1: 16–21 (updates the previous item).

IAN MACDONALD

civil rights

The **constitution of 1978** defines Spain as a state under the rule of law, and subscribes to the Universal Declaration of Human Rights. It proclaims equality under the law and outlaws discrimination, forbids torture and capital punishment, and guarantees freedom of conscience, expression and association. Detained persons must be brought before a court within 72 hours or released, and must be informed of their right to silence and to legal representation.

The effectiveness of these principles depends on the willingness of governments to implement them. In practice, the dramatic increase in crime, together with terrorist activity by **ETA**, has encouraged governments to prioritize effective **policing** over the protection of civil liberties. The anti-terrorist legislation introduced in 1977 permitted the detention of suspects for longer than 72 hours, and for years afterwards, there were allegations of ill-treatment, and even deaths, of suspects in custody. Furthermore, the government persistently condoned police brutality, once, in 1986, ordering **Civil Guards** facing charges of ill-treatment to ignore a court summons. In 1992, in an attempt to combat drug-related crime, the government introduced the *Ley de Seguridad Ciuda-*

dana (Public Safety Law), which would have given the police powers, in certain circumstances, to enter private homes without a warrant.

In the event, this law was declared unconstitutional by the **Constitutional Tribunal**, but the degree to which the citizen can expect protection from the **legal system** is limited by two factors. One is that the independence of the judiciary, though enshrined in law, is less respected in Spain than in other countries with a longer democratic tradition. This was underlined when, in 1997, the Prime Minister, **Aznar**, appointed as Chief Prosecutor of the Audiencia Nacional (National Court) a barrister who had been disciplined by the Council of Prosecutors. The second limiting factor is the slowness of court procedure, which can mean that accused persons face long delays before their case comes to trial.

In November 1995, the first thorough revision of the **penal code** since 1848 was enacted. It provided for suspended sentences, weekend imprisonment, and harsher penalties for corruption, and introduced the principle of diminished responsibility. The important safeguard of trial by jury, promised by the socialists since the 1980s, was not, however, implemented until May 1996, and could prove controversial in operation. In March 1997, a jury in **Euskadi** acquitted a member of ETA's youth wing of the murder of two policemen, on grounds of diminished responsibility. It was suggested in the press that the difficulty of ensuring the anonymity of juries in areas where intimidation by terrorist sympathizers is common may have influenced the verdict.

See also: GAL; terrorism

Further reading

Hooper, J. (1995) *The New Spaniards*, Harmondsworth: Penguin (chapter 16 gives a lucid account of the complexities of this issue).

Newton, M.T. with Donaghy, P.J. (1997) *Institutions of Modern Spain*, Cambridge: Cambridge University Press (a standard work of reference).

Ross, C.J. (1997) *Contemporary Spain: A Handbook*, London and New York: Arnold (chapter 9 gives a clear and succinct summary of the administration of justice and its implications for civil rights).

EAMONN RODGERS

Civil War

The Spanish Civil War was brought about by the decision of right-wing groupings, especially in the **armed forces**, to reverse what they regarded as the slide into anarchy caused by the policies of the Second Republic, and the increasing militancy of radical working-class organizations. After the victory of the Popular Front in the elections of February 1936, a group of senior officers, co-ordinated by General Emilio Mola, the garrison commander in Pamplona, began to plan a military uprising, intending that it should be a swift coup which would seize control within a short time-span. The plan was that the military commanders in the provincial capitals would declare a state of siege, and join Mola as he advanced south from Pamplona, and Franco who would be moving north with units from Spanish Morocco. The two armies would meet west of Madrid and then turn towards the capital, which they expected to fall quickly. In the event, however, the insurgents had to fight a long and bitter campaign lasting nearly three years, from July 1936 to March 1939.

What prolonged the war was the loyalty to the legitimate government of sizeable sectors of the armed forces, plus the determined resistance of the trade union militias, who made up in enthusiasm what they lacked in training and discipline. The insurgents, however, had at their disposal, in addition to those troops who joined them on the mainland, the Army of Africa, made up of the highly-experienced professional soldiers of the Foreign Legion, plus the Moorish volunteer units, who together constituted a formidable fighting force.

Under international law, the government of the Republic, as the legal authority, was entitled to purchase military supplies from other countries, but in practice this proved difficult to implement because of the complex political situation in Europe. The European democracies were fearful of provoking the Axis powers, Nazi Germany and

Fascist Italy, into intervening decisively in support of Franco. Within the first month of the war, a Non-Intervention Pact was agreed by some twenty-seven countries, though it was widely flouted. Two of the signatories, Germany and Italy, provided air support to Franco within days of the rising, which proved crucial in enabling him to ferry the Army of Africa across the Straits of Gibraltar.

In this situation, the Republic turned for assistance to the Soviet Union, which initially provided food and raw materials, and sent to Spain representatives of the Comintern, the organization which in various European countries and the US helped to recruit the International Brigades, providing the Republic with a total of 60,000 men between the beginning of the conflict and October 1938, when they were withdrawn. Military hardware and munitions began to arrive in October 1936, but the volume of Soviet aid was determined by the complexities of foreign policy. Since Stalin was following a strategy of supporting Popular Front governments, it was not in his interest that the Republic should be defeated. Neither, however, were Soviet interests served by the emergence of a victorious revolutionary regime in Spain, which would destabilize western Europe and possibly provoke Germany and Italy to attack the Soviet Union.

Military intervention by the Axis powers had dramatic and visible results when the German Condor Legion (a volunteer airforce unit) bombed the Basque town of Guernica on 26 April 1937, destroying about 70 percent of the houses. Soviet intervention, by contrast, had effects which were both political and military within the Republican zone, especially in Catalonia. The workers' militias, particularly the anarchist CNT-FAI and the Trotskyist POUM, saw their task as not only defending the Republic but bringing about a social revolution. By contrast, communists and socialists gave priority to winning the war, and were prepared to postpone political objectives in the interests of forging a disciplined and effective fighting force. Tension between these two groupings produced street-fighting in Barcelona in May 1937, with the communists decisively gaining the upper hand, an advantage which they exploited ruthlessly in a campaign of intimidation, assassination and torture against former rivals in the Republican camp. Victory in this conflict enabled the communists to reorganize the regular army, and also enhanced their political influence within the government.

In addition to bitterly-fought battles in the field, the Civil War was also characterized by atrocities and reprisals, though these arguably had a different character and source in each zone. In the early months, many deaths in the Republican zone can be attributed to an upsurge of anger against those deemed to be representatives of oppressive institutions: landowners executed by their tenants and workers; priests and members of religious orders (to an estimated total of some 6,800) shot by the militias, or victims of popular violence. To these must be added the anarchist and POUM members killed by the communists during and after the summer of 1937. In the areas occupied by the insurgents, mass executions reflected Franco's policy of systematically eliminating possible sources of opposition, so as to secure his rearguard, and determine the future political character of Spain by imposing unity through terror. Members of the Popular Front parties caught in the Nationalist zone, trade unionists, captured members of the Republican police and army, were shown little or no quarter: in Córdoba province alone, total casualties attributed to this policy are estimated at 32,000.

After the Francoist victory, these executions continued on a large scale into the early to mid-1940s. In addition, the regime itself admitted to 250,000 political prisoners, though the real figure was probably higher. All the democratic institutions associated with the Republic were systematically dismantled, and there was no attempt to achieve reconciliation between former adversaries: the propaganda of the regime systematically presented supporters of the Republic as the enemies of Spain. Post-war repression led to the **exile** of some of the most gifted professionals, academics, writers and artists, which impoverished Spanish intellectual and cultural life.

See also: Franco Bahamonde, Francisco; Francoist culture; history

Further reading

Blinkhorn, M. (1988) *Democracy and Civil War in Spain, 1931–1939*, London: Routledge (an excellent short introduction to the main issues and the course of the war).

Carr, R. (1993) *The Spanish Tragedy: The Civil War in Perspective*, London: Weidenfeld & Nicolson (a comprehensive study of the complexities of the political context).

Preston, P. (1986) *The Spanish Civil War, 1936–39*, London: Weidenfeld & Nicolson (a very accessible, concise account, usefully illustrated with photographs and maps).

Thomas, H. (1977) *The Spanish Civil War*, Harmondsworth: Penguin in Association with Hamish Hamilton (the third edition of this classic study, substantially revised and enlarged; the most reliable and comprehensive treatment available).

EAMONN RODGERS

class

In a 1993 survey of 8,500 people carried out by the Fundación FOESSA, 99.5 percent of respondents were prepared to ascribe themelves to a given social class, despite the fact that as many as 27 percent expressed the view that Spain is no longer divided into classes. It seems that perception of social stratification is still present, albeit in an attenuated form. In Spain social class is seen to be governed not only by the traditional criterion of origins (the class of one's parents) but increasingly by education and occupation. Mode of speech, which in some societies can be an important differentiating criterion, is of comparatively little relevance in Spain, where speech distinctions are much more geographical than social. Class mobility in Spain over the past thirty years has been marked by mesocratization, and specifically by the shift from working class to middle class status. At the start of the 1960s most sociological measures put the working class at about 60 percent of the population; latest estimates put it at below 40 percent, with some as low as 30 percent. In the 1993 survey carried out by the team from the Complutense University of Madrid led by Professor Amando de **Miguel** and contained in the 1995 report, the results for subjective (ie. self-positioned) social class were: upper and upper middle 9 percent; middle 57 percent; lower middle and working class 34 percent. Furthermore, identification with the lower class is far more common among older people than among younger people: 49 percent in the 65 plus category compared to 24 percent in the 18–29 category. Although the bulk of respondents believe they have stayed in their original class, 7 percent believe they have moved to a lower class and 21 percent to a higher class (17 percent moving from lower to middle class).

Spanish society appears today to be much more homogeneous than thirty years ago. Apart from the obvious factor of a more even distribution of the country's wealth (see also **national income**) helping to ensure a more comparable lifestyle, the fundamental factors promoting mesocratization have been economic development, urbanization, tertiarization and access to secondary and higher education. Spain has moved rapidly from a predominantly agrarian economy and rural society to a highly urbanized society and service economy, and this has been accompanied by a massive transfer of population from countryside to major towns and cities. The agricultural sector has gone from being the largest work provider by a very considerable margin in 1960 to being the smallest by far. The secondary sector has barely changed at all (although its share of employment increased up to the mid-1970s and decreased after that). The services sector meanwhile has doubled its importance for employment, and not only because of the expansion of tourism, but much more through the expansion of services provided by the state following the implantation of democracy and regional autonomy. By far the biggest increase in tertiary-sector jobs has been in public administration, sanitation, education and health. Alongside the loss of jobs in agriculture as a result of mechanization, in industry as a result of recession and restructuring, and in certain traditional service-sector areas such as transport, repairs and domestic services, has to be placed the creation of jobs which had till recently been the preserve of the middle classes. What has made it possible for the children of lower class urban immigrants to gain access to these middle-class jobs has been the huge increase in educational enrolments in the 1970s and 1980s, of which the concentration of population in urban centres was a pre-requisite. Thus between 1960 and 1980 there was an eightfold increase in secondary education and a fourfold increase in higher education. In the previously mentioned survey, 47 percent who had gone to university had a father who had only been to primary school, suggesting that Spain's economic development has been especially beneficial to those whose parents had had little education. It has therefore been the improvement in the educational level of the country that has made it possible for new generations of young people from working class origins to aspire to non-manual occupations. This applies to both sexes, but dramatically so to women. Thus we can observe that between 1970 and 1990 the proportion of employed women with secondary qualifications increased by a factor of ten, and those with university qualifications by a factor of eleven. Not only are occupation and educational level the two most frequently used criteria in the objective measure of social class, but furthermore there is a strongly positive correlation between educational level and subjective social class: the higher the level the more marked the tendency to place oneself in the middle or upper classes, and conversely the lower the qualification the more marked the self-ascription to a lower class. Indeed the correlation between level of education and self-declared social class is stronger even than that between occupation and class. It is interesting to note in this regard that the upward social mobility father-to-son is surpassed by that of mother-to-daughter, a clear indication of the greatly increased participation rate of women in education and the effect of this on perceived social class.

To these essential factors bringing about social change – economic development, rural exodus, tertiarization, education (especially of women) – has to be added the equalizing effect of an urban youth culture that emerged at a time of liberation following the end of the Francoist dictatorship and which showed itself to be a good deal less class-conscious and deferential than the culture of its elders, as well as displaying a more homogeneous lifestyle in its leisure activities and public comportment. Such factors, together with the role of television in promoting greater homogeneity of interests, attitudes and tastes, remain unquantifiable. But the near universal replacement of the polite form of address, *usted*, by the familiar form, *tú*, is an interesting manifestation of social equalization.

Further reading

De Miguel, A. (1995) *La sociedad española 1994–95*, Madrid: Universidad Complutense (sociological series based on yearly survey; also relevant are the 1992–3 and 1993–4 reports based on 1991 and 1992 surveys).

Longhurst, C.A. (1995) 'Calculating the Incalculable: Reflections on the Changing Class Structure of Contemporary Spain', *Journal of the Association for Contemporary Iberian Studies*, vol. 8, 2: 2–18 (an attempt to explain and re-calculate social classes in Spain).

C.A. LONGHURST

CNT

The Confederación Nacional del Trabajo (National Labour Confederation) is an anarcho-syndicalist trade union which played a major role in Spanish politics during the first forty years of the twentieth century. It was founded in Barcelona in 1910 and, from the first, in anarchist fashion, rejected political parties of the working class and advocated the adoption of militant 'direct action' tactics. Between 1910 and 1939 it vied for leadership of the Spanish labour movement with the socialist **PSOE** and its related trade union, the **UGT**. However, it entered into decline during the Civil War and, especially, under the Franco regime. At the same time, divisions within the union became increasingly bitter, leading to a split in 1945 and the foundation of two rival organizations. It is now but a pale shadow of its former self.

ANGEL SMITH

Coderch, José Antonio

b. 1913, Barcelona; d. 1984, Barcelona

Architect

Coderch's work is an important landmark in post-Civil War Spanish architecture. He studied at the Escuela de Arquitectura (School of Architecture) in Barcelona, under Josep Maria **Jujol**, which helps to explain some characteristic features of his later work. He began as town architect in Sitges and in 1943 moved to Madrid to work for the state architectural directorate. On returning to Barcelona, he began practising as an independent architect, at first in association with Manuel Valls. In 1949 he took part in a national architecture congress, where he came to the attention of two distinguished guests, Gio Ponti and Alberto Sartorius, who took a great deal of interest in his work. From then on his projects and his ideas were routinely reported in the international professional journals. The Grupo R was born in his studio in 1951, a sort of intellectual dissenting movement promoted by a group of Catalan architects. They included Coderch's contemporary José María **Sostres**, and Oriol **Bohigas** and Josep Martorell, representing the post-Civil War generation. The group was opposed to the pervasive monumentalist architecture of the period, and by means of debates, exhibitions and competitions it aimed to make public opinion aware of more modern trends. Coderch withdrew from the group in 1952, and it disbanded in 1958 when its members felt their mission had been accomplished.

In 1951 Coderch created the Spanish pavilion for the ninth Milan Triennial, consolidating his international renown with the award of a gold medal. From 1959 he attended the International Congresses on Modern Architecture (CIAM) on the recommendation of José Lluis **Sert**. Lecturing on architecture was another important part of his activity. His work was awarded numerous national and international distinctions.

Coderch's work stands out from the general architectural climate of his time by reason of a certain 'organic' quality, modified by the architectural vocabulary inherited from pioneers of modernity such as Le Corbusier or Walter Gropius. One can detect here a remote influence of Frank Lloyd Wright, but equally it could be a reflection of some of the features of Catalan **Modernism**, especially that of **Gaudí** and Jujol. A very characteristic example of this is the group of apartments he constructed in Barceloneta (1951, Barcelona). Between 1955 and 1970, he designed a large number of houses, all of which are characterized by a remarkable formal elegance. The best known is the Casa Catasus (1956, Sitges) and also the very refined Casa Ugalde (1951, Caldetas). His Casa Tàpies (1960, Barcelona), the studio-apartment of the painter Antoni **Tàpies**, is equally famous for its façade, conceived of as a complex filter between exterior and interior. Of his post-1970 pieces the best known is the Instituto Francés (1974, Barcelona) a clever variation on the theme of the curtain wall. He has also created very sensitive designs, the best known being his design for a lamp.

Coderch's sensibility continues to influence contemporary Catalan architecture.

See also: architects; architecture; architecture, Francoist; architecture, post-Francoist

MIHAIL MOLDOVEANU

Codorniu

Cordorniu was founded 1926, though it derives from a family business established in 1551. Specializing in wines, brandy and brandy spirits, it is a subsidiary of UNIDECO (Barcelona). Cordorniu is mainly known for its brand of sparkling wine, called *cava*, which it has been producing with the *Méthode Champenoise* since 1872. Its wine-cellars are the largest in the world, and were declared a national monument in 1976. Employing a workforce of just over 400 people, Cordorniu's total annual sales in 1996 were worth 22,220m pesetas, of which export sales occupied 30 percent. The group reorganized in 1994 and Codorniu S.A. absorbed Vinícola Rodel S.A. (sparkling) and Bodegas Masia Bach S.A. (still).

EAMONN RODGERS

collective agreements

This term is applied to agreements reached through the process of collective bargaining. A distinction must be made between those collective agreements resulting from the Franco regime's *Ley de Convenios Colectivos* (Law on Collective Agreements) of 24 April 1958 and those introduced under the labour reforms which were implemented following Franco's death in 1975.

Enacted following criticism of Spain by the International Labour Organization, the Law on Collective Agreements was the first item of legislation introduced by the Franco regime which specifically dealt with labour. According to its provisions, the **vertical syndicates** were allowed to engage in workplace-level collective bargaining with employers to determine wage levels and working conditions. The administrative and legal authorities retained a tight control over the negotiation and administration of collective agreements and each agreement applied to all workers and employers in the sector concerned. Workers' distrust of the official syndicates and employers' willingness to negotiate with genuine representatives of labour so as to increase productivity led to the involvement of unofficial workers' representatives in collective bargaining negotiations. These representatives formed the basis for the emergence of the **CC OO** (Comisiones Obreras – Workers' Committees), which established parallel organizations to the official syndicates.

The system of collective bargaining remained virtually unaltered until the legalization of **trade unions** in 1977 and the establishment of the 'right to collective bargaining' enshrined in article 37.1 of the 1978 constitution. The *Estatuto de los Trabajadores* (Workers' Statute) implemented on 15 March 1980 and reformulated 24 March 1995 outlines the legal framework for worker representation and the legal procedures for the collective bargaining process itself. In firms with fewer than fifty and more than ten employees, workers are represented by up to three *delegados de personal* (workers' delegates) elected by majority vote of the entire workforce. In firms with fifty or more employees, *comités de empresa* (works' councils) are elected by all employees. Depending on the size of the firm, works' councils may have from 5 to 75 members.

Essentially concerned with terms and conditions of employment, collective agreements may be negotiated at several levels, ranging from the company level through to the local, provincial or national level. At company level workers are represented by the company's works' council, whilst negotiations carried out at other levels require a negotiating committee to be formed from representatives of those unions which enjoy the status of 'most representative unions' (those which have obtained 10 percent or more of members of works' councils).

Around six million workers are covered by collective agreements. The duration of agreements is usually one to two years.

See also: industrial relations; labour law

Further reading

Martín Valverde, A. (ed.) (1991) *European Employment and Industrial Relations Glossary: Spain*, London: Sweet & Maxwell (indispensable for students of Spanish labour relations).

Miguélez, F. and Prieto C. (eds) (1991) *Las relaciones laborales en España*, Madrid: Siglo XXI de España (each chapter is followed by a comprehensive bibliography).

Newton, M.T. with Donaghy, P. (1997) *Institutions of Modern Spain*, Cambridge: Cambridge University Press (chapter 11, on trade unions, gives a useful account of the operation of the labour market and collective agreements).

PAUL KENNEDY

Colomo Gómez, Fernando

b. 1946, Madrid

Filmmaker

Colomo is best known for his modern Madrid comedies. A graduate of the Escuela Oficial de Cinematografía (State Film School) in set design he had worked as producer and screenwriter and had directed some prize-winning shorts before his *Tigres de papel* (Paper Tigers) (1977) met with huge success especially with younger audiences. Among his best films since then have been *La mano negra* (The Black

Hand) (1980), a tongue-in-cheek spy thriller co-scripted with **Trueba**, the box-office winner *La vida alegre* (A Life of Pleasure) (1987) and *Alegre ma non troppo* (1993). He founded several film companies.

EAMONN RODGERS

Comediants, Els

Formed in 1971, Els Comediants is the group which has done most to incorporate into performance theatre aspects of popular festivals such as carnival. Carnival was banned in Franco's Spain, and its recovery and the development of local festivals are part of the dynamic revival of popular culture which took place in Catalonia and in other parts of Spain after the death of Franco. Els Comediants are indebted both to Catalan popular tradition and to European and American avant-garde performance groups. For example, the Bread and Puppet Theatre spent time with them at their home base in Canet de Mar in 1977 and then, during the following year, performed several street shows in Barcelona.

One of Els Comediants' best-known shows is *Dimonis* (Devils) (1982), which has been performed in several countries. The show takes the form of a journey, derived from the Catholic *via crucis*, but using carnival techniques of inversion of values, satire and an emphasis on the macabre. It is also related to one of the oldest festivals in Europe – the Patum de Berga. A *patum* is a figure representing a fabulous animal which is paraded through the streets during popular festivals, particularly in the small town of Berga, located about 100 km to the north of Barcelona. *Dimonis* is played in the open air, preferably in the street. Spectators are led through a town by the devils, who jostle them amidst fire and music. The experience for the spectator who has not previously encountered this sort of theatre is memorable if hazardous, as the sparks from the fireworks often land on the crowd. Indeed, the fire regulations of some localities has made it impossible for a performance of *Dimonis* to take place.

Like other Catalan performance groups, Els Comediants have been involved in activities which complement their theatrical work. In 1983, the LP of their 1979 show *Sol, solet* (Sun, Little Sun) was released. It included the soundtrack of the show, made up of popular songs. Material from the show was also included in a book-object with metal covers, fold-out pages and illustrations. The book won several international prizes. Els Comediants have made a film with Carles **Mira** entitled *Karnaval* (1985), which was shot in the Municipal Theatre of Girona.

However, the company's most public work came in the 1992 Olympic Games. Els Comediants organized the closing ceremony in which the birth of life was visualized through fire and the formation of the solar system. It was a pyrotechnical *tour de force* which made planets, stars, the sun and the moon appear in a magnificent dance of the universe. This large-scale spectacle in which 850 people participated is probably the best example of Els Comediants' ability to organize macro-events where elaborate visual effects and technical perfection come together.

Further reading

Saumell, M. (1996) 'Performance Groups in Catalonia', in D. George and J. London (eds) *An Introduction to Contemporary Catalan Theatre*, Sheffield: Anglo-Catalan Society (the only full-length study of the phenomenon in English).

DAVID GEORGE

comics

As in other countries, comics are part of the contemporary consumer culture, but they show some features which are peculiar to Spain. During the Franco period, they functioned as part of the propaganda apparatus of the regime, fostering the dominant mythology of the heroic Christian crusader, especially in the series *El guerrero del antifaz* (The Masked Warrior). This figure was a kind of medieval Lone Ranger, single-handedly routing, not renegade gun-runners or corrupt sheriffs, but devious Moorish adversaries. In default of other popular diversions like television, comics fulfilled the need for escapism and entertainment in the bleak years of the 1940s and 1950s, when they enjoyed a vogue aptly summed up by one commentator who described them as 'the cinema of the poor'. The bulk of those produced fell into the usual categories of adventure stories and humour. The former was represented by, for example, the series involving the vicissitudes of the ship 'El Cachorro' and its crew, and the space voyages of Diego Valor. The latter is typified most famously by the characters Mortadelo and Filemón.

Given the cultural diversity of the peninsula, however, comics, as a popular medium, could also function as a very effective means of disseminating languages other than Spanish, something implicitly recognized by the Franco regime when comics in **Catalan** continued to be banned in the late 1950s. With the removal of **censorship**, they have become in the 1990s a significant feature of publication in **Basque**.

The ending of censorship has also meant that comics have become an important sub-genre of **pornography**, and one which is potentially very powerful, given their popular appeal, the absence of regulation, and, above all, the fact that they are readily available to children, being displayed openly in department stores and other places visited by families. Furthermore, they are, if anything, even more explicit than films or television, because the artist, not having to work with living models, has considerably more freedom to portray situations in detail.

With the diversification of culture since the restoration of democracy, and, in particular, the breaking down of the traditional distinction between popular and 'high' culture, comics continue to enjoy a significant vogue. They are one of the principal means of dissemination of **science fiction**, and reprints of *El guerrero del antifaz* have become a collectors' item.

See also: Francoist culture; kiosk literature; publishing; readership

Further reading

Cuadrado, J. (1997) *Diccionario de uso de la historieta española (1873–1996)*, Madrid: Compañía Literaria (the most comprehensive reference-work available on the genre).

EAMONN RODGERS

Conde, Mario

b. 1948, Pontevedra (Galicia)

Financier

Appointed President of Banesto, then one of Spain's seven major clearing **banks**, in December 1987, Conde became an outspoken critic of the socialist government of Felipe **González**, accusing ministers of a 'preoccupation' with European policy, especially entry into the exchange rate mechanism in 1989 and acceptance of the Maastricht Treaty in 1992. In the early 1990s a series of mergers within the banking world left Conde with considerably reduced influence, and when Banesto over-extended its loan book just as recession hit Spain, the state-run Deposit Guarantee Fund was obliged to intervene in December 1993. Conde was dismissed, arrested and subsequently prosecuted for fraud. In the aftermath of the scandal Banesto was bought out by the **Banco de Santander**.

See also: corruption; politics

PAUL HEYWOOD

conscientious objection

Conscientious objection to military service was not recognized during the Franco regime. The **constitution of 1978** makes provision for exemption from conscription on conscientious grounds, and allows those exempted to substitute civilian social service, which is also compulsory. The relevant legislation, however, was not enacted until 1984. Under this act, the onus is on those claiming exemption on conscientious grounds to apply, stating the grounds. About 90 percent of these applications are granted. By the end of 1996, the total granted exemption since the coming into force of the law was over 400,000. In that year, there were more than 93,000 applications, an increase of 28 percent on 1995. Some 91,000 of these were accepted, 22 percent more than in the previous year. By about 1990, the proportion of those seeking exemption in any one year was typically about 40 percent of those who agreed to serve, or 30 percent of the total called up.

The granting of so many exemptions, and the requirement of *prestación social sustitutoria* (alternative community service) entailed the provision of work placements on a large scale, but these lagged far behind the numbers needing to be accommodated. By the end of 1996, 130,000 recognized conscientious objectors were still waiting to complete their community service, which technically precluded them from obtaining state employment. In the same year, the government modified the 1984 law, which had in any case never been fully enforced, by introducing the *Ley Reguladora del Voluntariado Social* (Law Regulating Voluntary Social Work), which allowed work for recognized voluntary agencies to be offset against compulsory community service.

Some conscientious objectors, known as ***insumisos***, refuse even to do the alternative community service, which makes them liable to prosecution. Once again, however, the numbers concerned, and the lack of resources, have in practice often meant that most people in this category escape punishment.

See also: armed forces; military service

Further reading

Hooper, J. (1995) *The New Spaniards*, Harmondsworth: Penguin (the last three pages of chapter 8 give a clear account of the changes in military recruitment policy).

EAMONN RODGERS

constitution of 1978

Following the historic general election of 1977, the newly elected **parliament** proceeded to draw up a new constitution for democratic Spain. The first draft was prepared by a group of seven parliamentarians, representing the major political parties, appointed by the committee of constitutional affairs; this consisted of thirty-six members of the *Congreso de Diputados* (the lower house) drawn from these parties in proportion to their strength in the Congress. The draft was submitted for scrutiny and amendment, first to the constitutional committee of the Congress and then to its counterpart in the Senate. Subsequently, it was scrutinized by a joint committee of both Houses before being approved in a joint session on 31 October 1978. Finally, on 6 December, the agreed text was submitted to a direct vote of the Spanish people in a national referendum. On 28 December, King Juan Carlos signed the new constitution, which, significantly, had won the support of 98 percent of the country's parliamentarians and 88 percent of the 68 percent of the electorate which voted in the referendum.

The constitution is divided into eleven major sections, including a preliminary section laying down the principles of the new state. Article 1 proclaims that Spain is a 'social and democratic state based on the rule of law... national sovereignty resides in the people from whom all powers derive'. Article 2, while referring to the 'indissoluble unity of the Spanish nation', recognizes the 'right of the nationalities and regions of Spain to autonomy'. Article 3 recognizes regional languages as co-official in the regions alongside Spanish, which remains the official language of the state. An important principle is 'political pluralism'; in this context both **political parties** and **trade unions** are expressly recognized. Article 9.2 puts an obligation on the authorities to create the conditions in which the freedom and equality of the individual can be genuine and effective, and to remove obstacles to the full participation of citizens in the political, economic, social and cultural life of the country.

Two major provisions refer to Spain's traditional ***poderes fácticos***, the **armed forces** and the Roman Catholic Church. Article 8 states that the role of the armed forces is 'to safeguard the sovereignty and independence of Spain, defend its territorial integrity and the constitutional order', but it also makes it clear that the ultimate responsibility for national defence lies not with the armed forces but with the popularly elected government of the day. Article 16, while affirming that there will be complete religious freedom, breaks with the Franco tradition in proclaiming that there will be no state **religion**. However, clause 3 of this article goes on to say that 'the authorities shall take into account the religious beliefs of Spanish society and shall maintain consequent links with the Catholic Church and other faiths'.

Section II examines the role of the **monarchy**, laying particular stress on its role vis-à-vis the constitution. Section III outlines the composition, functions and powers of both houses of parliament. Section IV deals with the organization of the government and public administration, while Sections V and VI respectively refer to the relationship between the government, the legislature and the judicial authorities. Section VII lays down the basic principles by which the **economy** shall be run. Section VIII concerns the fundamental question of the relationship between central government and the regions and peoples of Spain – the issue which prompted the most heated debate. Section IX outlines the composition and powers of the **Constitutional Tribunal** and Section X the processes by which the constitution may be reformed. It is worthy of note that the 1978 constitution devotes much more attention than previous constitutions to such key aspects of democracy as rights, the legislature, popular sovereignty, and the rights of the regions.

The longest section of the constitution deals with rights and the obligation of the state to protect them. Article 10 affirms that such rights shall conform to those listed in the Universal Declaration of Human Rights. These rights fall into three categories: basic human or **civil rights**; political rights; and socio-economic rights. Among the basic civil rights listed are: the right to life and to personal physical integrity (article 15); the right to freedom, including *habeas corpus* (article 17); the right to equal treatment before the law for all citizens, irrespective of differences of birth, race, sex, religion or belief (article 14); and the right of free access to the courts, including the right to be defended in court and to have access to a solicitor while in detention (article 24). Among the political rights guaranteed – long denied or flouted under Franco – are: the right to freedom of expression (article 20); the right of assembly and the right to demonstrate in public (article 21); the right of association (article 22); and the right to strike, also forbidden during the dictatorship (article 28). The socio-economic rights include: the right to work, including the right of **women** to equal treatment to men in employment terms (article 35); the right to collective bargaining (article 37); and the right to education (see also **education and research**), which incorporates the freedom to choose the type of education and school one wishes as well as the right of individuals and groups to found centres of learning (article 27).

In general the 1978 constitution can be seen as a balanced document which respects the views of both traditionalists and progressives across a range of political, social and economic issues which prior to Franco and during his regime divided Spaniards in an often irreconcilable way. While legally it may be an imperfect document, politically it has enormous significance in that it reflects the political consensus of the time and the determination of a generation of political leaders of all persuasions to bring about national reconciliation.

See also: church and state; Franco; language and national identity; legal system; LODE; regionalism

Further reading

Newton, M.T. with Donaghy, P.J. (1997) *Institutions of Modern Spain*, Cambridge: University Press (chapter 2 is devoted exclusively to the constitution and there is a detailed bibliographical section).

MICHAEL T. NEWTON

Constitutional Tribunal

The Constitutional Tribunal was established under Title IX of the **constitution of 1978** and formally legislated into existence the following year. It is charged with upholding and interpreting the constitution, giving the tribunal an authority which effectively places it above the three classic powers of the state: executive, legislature and judiciary. There is no right of appeal against the tribunal's decisions, and its powers extend over the entire national territory. Any law – whether passed by **parliament** or an **autonomous community** – or executive measure may be declared unconstitutional.

Based in Madrid, the tribunal is composed of twelve members, all of whom must have at least fifteen years' legal experience. They may be nominated either by parliament, the government in power, or the CGPJ (Consejo General del Poder Judicial – General Council of the Judiciary) which is responsible for regulating the judicial system. Members of the Constititional Tribunal serve nine-year terms, with a third of the membership being renewed every three years. While in office, they are debarred both from other public posts and from professional and commercial activity.

On various occasions since 1979, the Constitutional Tribunal has been accused of excessive centralism. For example, in 1989, the Catalan politician Jordi **Pujol** claimed the tribunal was seeking to reduce the powers available to the seventeen autonomous communities. Although this charge was vigorously denied by the tribunal, suspicion of undue influence continued. Many observers believe that the tribunal was routinely exposed to political pressure during the socialist **PSOE**'s long period in office between 1982 and 1996. The problems of regionalist resentment and the suspicion of political involvement which faced the tribunal in the early 1980s were undoubtedly compounded by an excessive workload. In 1988 alone, 2,268 cases were referred for deliberation and, by the early 1990s, an average of two and a half years was taken to hear a case. A growing agreement at both national and regional level that cases should, where possible, be resolved without recourse to the tribunal has, however, led to a reduction in this previously unmanageable workload.

See also: legal system

Further reading

Heywood, P. (1995) *The Government and Politics of Spain*, London: Macmillan (pp. 105–9 give a more detailed account of the Constitutional Tribunal and its workings, as part of a general discussion of the legal system).

PAUL HEYWOOD

consumerism

The past thirty years have witnessed a radical modification of Spain's consumer structure. The steady growth of per capita income since the 1950s has increased the consumption of products other than basics such as food or clothing. In addition, the evolution of Spanish **society** since the transition to democracy has widened the range of Spanish consumer needs.

The consumer society in Spain dates from the 1960s, when economic development starts to take effect after the **Stabilization Plan**. **Industrial development**, together with the beginnings of urban modernization, favoured the introduction of consumer goods such as cars, television sets and domestic appliances. The trend towards mass consumerism became general in the 1970s, producing a proportional increase in expenditure on services and non-essential goods. During the 1980s, Spain's consumer habits came more into line with those of western European countries, with greater priority being given to spending on transport, communications, leisure, culture and services.

Purchasing decisions are conditioned by a series of factors connected with the consumer structure of Spanish households. The decrease in the rate of population growth since 1985, and the progressive ageing of the population, have meant that increasing attention is paid to what is referred to in Spain as the *tercera edad* (pensioners). Manufacturers' marketing strategies have changed accordingly towards promoting health foods and services for this clientele. Moreover, there has been an increase in the number of smaller households, by reason of, for instance, cohabitation and one-parent families. The decrease in marriage and birth rates, and the increasing frequency of divorce (see also **marriage and divorce**), have fragmented traditional households, with larger numbers of households being inhabited by a smaller number of people. In addition, the increasing incorporation of **women** into the workforce has changed traditional **family** roles, which have become more homogeneous and democratic, with more women behaving as consumers of financial services and more men as consumers of health-food and beauty products. Last but not least, the stability of consumers' purchasing power has been affected by **inflation**.

Periods of economic recession have noticeably caused consumers to look for what are called *marcas blandas* (cheaper brands imitating better ones), sacrificing the quality and prestige features of products.

Several consumer tendencies may be identified in contemporary Spanish society. The increased importance of the household as a consumption unit has stimulated new services and products for the home. The increase in free time due to **unemployment** and the progressive ageing of the population, accompanied by a generalized search for happiness, self-fulfilment and enjoyment of free time, has triggered the expansion of the leisure sector. The protection of consumers' rights has been increased by the creation of a legislative code and an arbitration system. The search for greater comfort and convenience has meant that when purchasing, for instance, appliances or pre-cooked food, consumers give a higher priority to user-friendliness, ergonomics, synergy or interactivity. The continuing importance of health and beauty issues has produced a partial abandonment of traditional foods in search of more balanced diets, and the expansion of markets related to health clubs and beauty products. The increasing prominence accorded to environmental issues has affected the images projected by companies and their marketing strategies. Underlying all these factors is the development of consumer education, which favours a more informed choice.

See also: demographic indicators; economy; food and drink; Francoist culture; legal system; sport and leisure; standard of living

Further reading

de Miguel, A. (1994) *La Sociedad Española 1993–94. Informe Sociológico de la Universidad Complutense*, Madrid: Alianza Editorial (a sociological study of Spanish society, analysing Spaniards' character and habits).

Graham, H. and Labanyi, J. (eds) (1995) *Spanish Cultural Studies: An Introduction*, Oxford: Oxford University Press (a collection of essays on different contemporary cultural issues; section 2 of Part III deals with consumerism, mass culture and developmentalism in Spain, during the 1960–75 period).

Schubert, A. (1990) *A Social History of Modern Spain*, London: Routledge (pp. 256–64 provide an analysis of the socio-political and economic changes of the Franco regime and the subsequent return of democracy).

GEMMA BELMONTE TALERO

COPE

The Cadena de Ondas Populares Españolas (Popular Spanish Airwaves Network) is a private **radio** network in which the Roman Catholic Church has a 50 percent stake, and is the second most popular after **SER**, which in 1997 had 9.4 million listeners as against COPE's 3.9 million. Like most of the major networks except Radio Nacional, COPE has increased its listener base, which has risen by more than 40 percent since 1988. During the first half of the 1990s it was noted for devoting large amounts of airtime to criticism of the socialist **PSOE** government for corruption.

See also: media; national radio

EAMONN RODGERS

Corcuera, José Luis

b. 1945, Burgos

Politician

An electrician by profession, Corcuera served as Minister of the Interior in the socialist **PSOE** government from 1988–93 and was the first minister in democratic Spain not to have a university degree. He became indelibly associated with a highly controversial security law, popularly known as the '*Ley Corcuera*'. Although successfully piloted through parliament, the law attracted intense opposition and was referred to the **Constitutional Tribunal**. In 1993, the tribunal declared as unconstitutional certain provisions of the law, notably that allowing the police access to private homes without warrants. This decision forced Corcuera to resign from government in November 1993. In 1994, following a press campaign and the prosecution of a former governor of the Bank of Spain, Mariano **Rubio**, for fraud, Corcuera – together with Carlos Solchaga, Minister of the Economy 1985–93 – resigned his seat in parliament over his failure to detect criminal irregularities.

See also: corruption; politics

PAUL HEYWOOD

'CORDOBÉS, EL' *see* Benítez, Manuel

Correa i Ruiz, Federico de

b. 1924, Barcelona

Architect

The architectural activity of Correa is closely linked to that of his associate Alfonso **Milá**. Correa is also one of the most influential teachers in the Barcelona School of Architecture, where he taught from 1959 to 1966 and again from 1977 to 1990. His teaching activity reflects his instinctive inclination towards formal perfection, which also characterizes the work of the Correa-Milá studio. The work of this partnership continues the tradition of **Coderch**, while evincing a desire for renewal. It was through the work of Correa and Milá that the new concepts of Italian design of the 1960s and 1970s reached Spain, an innovation reflected in the Olivetti head office (1968–9) and the restaurant *Giardinetto* (1974, Barcelona).

See also: architects; architecture

MIHAIL MOLDOVEANU

corrida

Corrida de toros is literally the 'running of bulls'. The English term 'bullfight' introduces an understanding of the spectacle entirely alien to Spanish culture. The *corrida* today usually consists of three **matadors** – each with a *cuadrilla* (or team) of assistants on foot (*banderilleros*) and on horseback (*picadores*) – who perform with two bulls each (the senior matador taking the first and fourth animals, the next in seniority the second and fifth, and the junior matador the third and sixth), though several variations are possible.

See also: bullfighting

IAN CAMPBELL ROSS

corruption

A stream of corruption scandals emerged in Spain at the beginning of the 1990s. Many involved politicians, financiers and public officials who were closely connected to the socialist **PSOE** administration. Four factors can help to explain this upsurge in corruption: the financing of parties; the hegemony of the PSOE from 1982 to 1996; the nature of state development; and the nature of civil society.

Political parties themselves have frequently been the protagonists of corruption cases, the most important of which was the so-called **Filesa** case, named after a Barcelona-based group of consultancy companies that allegedly financed the socialists' 1989 general election campaign. All parties, to a greater or lesser extent, have resorted to irregular financing, as without it they seem unable to meet the high expenses involved in the continuous round of municipal, regional and general elections. State budget allocations to parties are insufficient, party membership is so low that income from members' dues is negligible, and there is no mechanism for tax-deductible political donations which are, in any case, curtailed by law.

Alongside charges of corruption for financial purposes, Spanish parties, and the PSOE in particular, have been accused of abusing state resources for party purposes. This has been most apparent in the case of television, where the socialists have been charged with partisan control of appointments and news output. The 1986 referendum campaign to decide Spain's entry to **NATO** was the clearest example of the PSOE's abuse of the media and the administration. No major newspaper sympathized with the 'no' campaign, television coverage was blatantly one-sided and 'no' campaigners were sometimes denied use of meeting places.

The socialists have also been criticized for a lack of transparency in their relationship with the business community. 'Insider-trading' increased dramatically in Spain during the 1980s economic boom. The most spectacular example was the downfall of Mariano **Rubio**, the former governor of the Bank of Spain, imprisoned in 1994 on charges of fraud, tax evasion and falsifying public documents. The PSOE has also been accused of handing out favours and sinecures to party members, as well as influence trafficking. Such behaviour undoubtedly tarnished the socialists' image and contributed to their electoral decline and ultimate loss of power to the right-wing **PP** (Partido Popular – Popular Party) in the 1996 general elections.

State development in Spain has long been hampered by the persistence of patron-client networks and clientelistic practices. Although today the Spanish state more closely resembles other states in Europe than at any other time in its history, much of this previous patrimonial legacy still remains. Despite extensive reforms, the state remains an ubiquitous presence and still provides numerous opportunities for corruption. First, there has been a significant rise in public spending and an increase in government activities. Second, the establishment of the seventeen **autonomous communities** in Spain, designed to take power away from the central state, has in reality simply duplicated it at the regional level, thereby creating greater opportunities for corruption.

In sharp contrast to this ubiquitous state is a civil society which has historically lacked long-standing associational traditions. The response of civil society to the high level of corruption and the parties' excessive penetration of the state, has been one of passivity, which has encouraged the political class to act with impunity. The **press** has been the only sector really to challenge the high level of corruption. As far as the judiciary is concerned, investigations into corruption have frequently produced unsatisfactory sentences. This is because the judiciary is often far from independent of the government. A twenty-member committee known as the Consejo General del Poder Judicial (General Council of the Judiciary) regulates Spain's judicial system. As parliament has been responsible for electing all twenty members since 1985, the PSOE effectively controlled the judiciary until the loss of its absolute majority in 1993.

Until this date, the socialists also effectively gained control over the board in charge of the state-owned **radio** and **television** network, the **Defensor del Pueblo** (Spain's Ombudsman), the Tribunal de Cuentas (Audit Tribunal) which audits public-sector accounts, and even the **Constitutional Tribunal** itself. Given the use of proportional representation, the commission which drafted the 1978 constitution had made membership of such institutions dependent upon the balance of forces in parliament.

Such a wave of corruption scandals, however, should neither be exaggerated nor seen as the exclusive preserve of the socialist government. Although some claim that corruption is the hallmark of modern democratic Spain, it has long characterized Spain's political history: the Francoist regime was equally marked by high levels of corruption. One hopeful feature of democracy in Spain is that corruption, thanks to the press and to the integrity of certain individual judges, has come out into the open and is being tackled in a forthright manner. Penal measures against corruption have been introduced in Spain, albeit belatedly and hurriedly. These include a tightening-up of the penal code and increased penalties for insider trading and tax fraud. Other moves include establishing a special prosecutor's office to deal with corruption and strengthening the powers of the Audit Tribunal. Parliamentary committees have also been established to investigate party funding.

Despite such measures, most agree that corruption will continue in Spain unless there is a reform of party financing and greater transparency and accountability with regard to the activities of political parties, their relation to the state and to other interests in society, in particular, big business.

Further reading

Heywood, P. (ed.) (1994) *Distorting Democracy: Political Corruption in Spain, Italy and Malta*, CMS Occasional paper, No. 10; University of Bristol: Centre for Mediterranean Studies (a detailed analysis of corruption in Spain).

Hooper, J. (1995) *The New Spaniards*, Harmonds-

worth: Penguin (corruption is analysed in several chapters, particularly chapters 5 and 31).
Martín de Pozuelo, E. *et al.* (1994) *Guía de la Corrupción*, Barcelona: Plaza & Janes (a journalistic guide to the various corruption cases in Spain).

GEORGINA BLAKELEY

Corte Inglés, El

El Corte Inglés is a large chain of department stores, with branches in all the major cities, and employing some 37,000 people. Founded in 1940, it is the largest Spanish retail trade company by financial size, and in 1994 made a profit of over 725,000m pesetas. Gross profit in 1995 showed an increase of 4.4 percent over the previous year, but net profit was reduced by 7.8 percent, owing to large-scale investment, including the acquisition of **Galerías Preciados**. Its sales ranking among European companies was 265 in 1996, representing a small decline from 249 in the previous year. In addition to its main retailing activity, it manufactures, exports and imports ready-made clothing, and has diversified into property construction, travel agencies, and insurance. It also owns the major supermarket chain Hipercor.

EAMONN RODGERS

COU

The Curso de Orientación Universitaria (University Orientation Course) was, until 1999, the principal means of preparing students for university entrance. Established under the General Education Law of 1970, its aim was to provide an in-depth training for university work, by building on the studies undertaken for **BUP**. Entry to COU was from the third year of BUP or the second level of **FP**. Originally, the course consisted of three common subjects, Spanish language, a foreign language, and philosophy, and two options, sciences or humanities. Subsequently, the options were increased to four: science and technology, biological and health sciences, social sciences, and a linguistic and humanities option. The **LOGSE** (1990) provided for the replacement of COU with a new examination by the 1999 to 2000 academic session.

ISIDRO FADRIQUE

council of ministers

This equivalent of the British cabinet first came into being in 1714. It is the highest political and executive body in the country. Normally it consists of the prime minister, the deputy prime minister(s) and the ministers. Meetings of the council are usually chaired by the prime minister, unless the king is present or unless the premier is ill or absent abroad, in which case his or her place is taken by a deputy. The council normally meets once a week on Fridays in ordinary session but extraordinary meetings can be called at any time should the political situation demand it.

Article 97 of the **constitution of 1978**, equating government with the cabinet, affirms that 'the government directs internal and foreign policy, the civil and military administration and the defence of the state. It exercises the executive function and rule-making powers . . . ' It has both a political and an administrative role. In the latter capacity, it controls the activity of all branches of the civil service.

While the council of ministers enjoys certain legislative, judicial and defence powers, its main responsibilities are of an executive nature. Here its major function is to formulate and approve national policy over the whole area represented by the various ministries. It takes the initiative in preparing draft laws which are normally drawn up in particular departments before being approved by the cabinet and then submitted for approval to parliament. Another important power relates to appointments of high-ranking officials: these include ambassadors, under-secretaries of state, civil governors, government delegates to the **autonomous communities** and captains-general of the army. In addition, the cabinet is required to establish government standing and ad hoc committees. It also has the right to call regional and local (though not general) elections every four years.

Article 97 makes it clear that the government, through the council of ministers, is responsible for the control of military affairs and for the defence of the state. Article 104 also assigns to the cabinet responsibility for the security and **policing** of the country.

The council enjoys a number of rights relating to the autonomous communities. For example, it has the right to oblige them to carry out their functions according to the constitution and to bring a regional authority before the **Constitutional Tribunal** if it is adopting legislation which contravenes the constitution.

Since the first post-Franco cabinet was established in 1977, all councils of ministers have consisted predominantly of the members of one (ie. the ruling) party, although several cabinets have contained a few independents and technocrats with no obvious party affiliation.

See also: armed forces; González, Felipe; Juan Carlos I; politics; Suárez, Adolfo

Further reading

Heywood, P. (1991) 'Governing a New Democracy: the Powers of the Prime Minister in Spain', *West European Politics* 14: 97–115.

Newton, M.T. with Donaghy, P.J. (1997) *Institutions of Modern Spain*, Cambridge: Cambridge University Press (chapter 5.5 deals in detail with the council of ministers).

MICHAEL T. NEWTON

crafts

Spain has a long tradition of hand crafts ranging from traditional wooden agricultural implements still made in the remoter regions to world famous porcelain and damascene wares. **Pottery** is a craft practised throughout the country. Many regions have distinctive types and colours, such as the well-known wares of Talavera and Manises. The products of the **Lladró** porcelain factories are exported worldwide.

Other widespread crafts are embroidery, wooden furniture, wood carving, and basket work. Furniture ranges from sophisticated modern and reproduction antique to the so-called Castilian furniture (*madera de Castilla*), rustic styles made in centres such as Bárcena Mayor, Saja, Carmona and Almagro. Wood carving, too, takes many forms: traditional spoons from boxwood in Isaba in the Valle del Ronacal, and, in the Canaries, ornate house balconies and knives with delicately carved handles. Wicker work made from willow and hazel, ranging from baskets and panniers to chairs and armchairs, is a feature of regions such as Extremadura, Cantabria and Castilla-La Mancha.

Other crafts are somewhat more regionalized. Castilla-La Mancha has a strong tradition in textiles, producing handwoven rugs and tapestries. The Royal Tapestry Factory founded in the eighteenth century in Madrid is the only royal factory to survive, and was still in production in 1996, but with a question mark over its future. Lace is made in Lagartera and especially in Almagro, where bobbin or cushion lace is a speciality. This derives from the sale of the town in the sixteenth century by Charles V to Flemish bankers, who imported lace-makers from Bruges. Wool and linen cloth is made in the Canaries and articles made from esparto grass are among the textiles produced in Andalusia, especially in Granada and Ubeda.

Guitars are made by hand in Granada and Toledo, and all kinds of stringed instruments in Casasimarro (Cuenca province), including rebecs (*rabeles*), early lute-type violins, which are also made in Cantabria.

Some crafts are extremely localized, such as the making of *albarcas*, wooden clogs found predominantly in Cantabria, and very distinctive types of agricultural implements, often native to one or two villages, such as the *cebilla*, a kind of yoke used for controlling animals, *garios* and *garias*, different local varieties of wooden fork for winnowing grain, and various kinds of wooden vessels used in milking. Cow bells used to be made in Lamasón in this region and church bells made in Meruelo (Trasmiera) were exported worldwide.

Some individual cities have such a strong tradition of handcrafts that they have their products named after them. One of these is Granada. In addition to several of the crafts already mentioned, it specializes in embossed and engraved copperware, embossed leatherwork, a very wide range of metalwork, wrought iron, jewellery, mirrors and textiles from the Alpujarras (*tejidos alpujarreños*), but is noted above all for marquetry and inlaid mother of pearl. Another is Toledo, home to several crafts but famous particularly for its weaponry and for its damascene work, the art of inlaying baser metals such as iron, steel, bronze or copper with intricate gold and silver designs to form articles of great beauty, from rings, brooches and pendants to large plates and pictures.

Craftwork is undoubtedly a growth industry, keeping pace with demand for and interest in the products of old and new skills. In Extremadura a special Centre for the Promotion of Handcraft has been set up in Cáceres to encourage young craft workers to revive the skills in embroidery, wooden furniture making, wickerwork and gold and silver work which are traditional to the area. Craftwares are sold widely throughout Spain, and in Madrid and other large cities not only are there shops specializing in Toledo wares and Granada wares, but there are branches of Artespaña, the official Spanish government handcraft shop.

See also: Basque culture; Canarian culture; Catalan culture; Galician culture

Further reading

Feito, J.M. (1977) *La artesanía popular asturiana*, Salinas: Ayalga (a study of the traditional crafts of Asturias).

—— (1982) *Presente y futuro de las artesanías en la sociedad industrial*, Madrid: Ministerio de Industria y Energía (an important report on the future of crafts in an increasingly industrialized society).

EAMONN RODGERS

Crespo, Angel

b. 1926, Ciudad Real; d. 1995, Barcelona

Poet, critic and translator

In his first two volumes, *Una lengua emerge* (A Language Emerges) and *Quedan señales* (Signs Remain), published in the early 1950s, Crespo established himself as a highly skilled pastoral poet, working inside a narrow, but deeply felt, range of experience, without much concern for contemporary poetic movements. As he himself has explained, the feeling for country life which is at the root of many of his best early poems was a reaction of self-defence against the shortcomings of a conventional education just after the Civil War. Several of these early poems, like the much-anthologized 'Un vaso de agua para la madre de Juan Alcaide' (A Glass of Water for the Mother of Juan Alcaide) are as good as anything Crespo wrote later, and they show him already in possession of an individual language which marks him off from other poets of the *neorrealista* group with whom he is often associated. Though many of Crespo's attitudes can loosely be called 'realistic', there is also a strong element of the irrational running through his work which enables him to explore complex psychological states, as in the disturbing fantasy of 'El heredero' (The Heir), one of his most powerful poems of this phase.

These poems, together with much of his subsequent work, are contained in two large selections from smaller volumes, *En medio del camino* (In the Midst of the Journey) and *El bosque transparente* (The Transparent Forest), which between them cover the years 1949 to 1981. Though many of these poems have to do with particular places – Crespo was an inveterate traveller and lived for long periods in Puerto Rico and Sweden – they are never merely descriptive, and the ostensible subjects, more often than not, are approached from an intensely personal angle. Moreover, in a remarkable series of prose poems which began to appear in 1964 and which persisted throughout his later work, there is an increasing freedom of association, together with a subtlety of reflection which can best be described as 'metaphysical'. Part of this comes from the experience of translating Dante – a task which occupied Crespo for much of the 1970s, and which he saw as co-extensive with his work as an original poet. The results are very evident in *Ocupación del fuego* (Occupation of Fire), the collection he published in 1990. Here, fire is a complex symbol: the fire of poetic inspiration, but also the origin to which all poetic speech must aspire, an 'other' which is never fully attainable, but whose presence, however elusive, guarantees the nature of the poetic act.

Evidently, Crespo is a poet who continued to work hard on himself over the years and who remained open to new experiences. His best poems reveal a fastidiousness of language seldom found in Spanish outside the poets of the Symbolist tradition, though the sense of humanity they express is directly accessible and often very moving.

Further reading

Di Pinto, M. (ed.) (1964) *Angel Crespo, Poesie,* Rome: Sciascia (contains a long preface).

ARTHUR TERRY

crime

There is a conviction among many people in Spain that crime has risen spectacularly since the ending of the Franco dictatorship. Though the statistics indicate a considerable increase in reported crime to a peak around 1989–91, this evidence must be handled with considerable care. The apparent contrast between the relative safety of city streets during the Franco regime and the frequency of armed robberies (*atracos*) in the 1980s, conceals the fact that for most of the period of the dictatorship **censorship** of the media prevented the public from obtaining an accurate picture of crime statistics. In any case, the incidence of crime began to rise before Franco's death, and is partly attributable to the increasing social and economic pressures associated with the ending of the boom around 1973 to 1974, and the growing **drug problem**: in 1990, the head of the prison service estimated that half those in prison were there because of drug-related offences.

Drug dependency is probably one of the main explanations for the huge increase in the type of crime most likely to affect public perceptions: muggings and armed robberies. Between 1980 and 1985, according to figures from the Ministry of Justice and the Interior, reported crimes in this category rose two and a half times, from 9,918 to 27,887. There was a further increase of the same order to a peak of 71,602 in 1990, but this figure was halved to 35,170 by 1995. Over approximately the same period (1984–94), arrests for drug trafficking almost trebled, from 11,446 to 31,703, and seizures of drug consignments quadrupled, from 6,939 to 28,301. The other type of crime which directly affects the public is car theft, which has risen from its already high 1980 level. In the period 1980 to 1985, there was an increase of 30 percent in car theft, from 91,548 to 118,975, and a further 14 percent increase to 135,559 by 1990. The 1995 figure, however, shows a substantial decrease of 27 percent, to 98,847.

Though these figures suggest a substantial improvement during the period 1990 to 1995, caution is needed in interpreting the statistics because they reflect only reported crime. Police figures for 1995 suggest that the number of armed robberies may be more than double the figure quoted above. It is probable that in Spain there is a higher degree of reluctance in the population to report crime than there is in Britain, owing to the legacy of distrust created by heavy-handed **policing** in Franco's day, which has not entirely disappeared. Even allowing for this, however, the fact that the reported crime rate in Spain in 1990 was less than a third of that for England and Wales provides some grounds for claiming that the overall picture is relatively favourable. The deterioration perceived by the general population refers principally to urban-based and drug-related offences such as armed robbery and car theft, and the increase in economic crime such as fraud and embezzlement. But 88 percent of urban crime in 1995 was against property, and only 1.7 percent against the person. Crime is relatively infrequent in rural areas, and even the pessimistic estimates given by police figures show that overall crime rates have fallen by 7 percent between 1992 and 1995.

Further reading

Hooper, J. (1995) *The New Spaniards,* Harmondsworth: Penguin (chapters 15 and 16 give a concise and balanced account of law and order issues).

EAMONN RODGERS

critical theory

Critical theory in Spain can be divided into two interrelated areas: academic criticism as developed in the **universities**, and criticism disseminated by the mass **media**. Academic criticism has moved from structuralist models, which concentrate on analysing the distinctive properties of literary language and the literary text, towards a conception of the text as a communicative act, with consequent emphasis on reception theory and pragmatics, that is, the total context in which communication occurs. The effects of this shift can be seen both in the teaching of language and literature from the early years of schooling and in the consumer behaviour of readers of the literary supplements of the major newspapers, which have a considerable influence on publishers' sales figures.

The history of modern critical theory in Spain begins with **Ortega y Gasset**'s *The Dehumanization of Art* (*La deshumanización del arte*) (1925), which has had a profound influence both on criticism and on creative writing. This essay, which emphasized the distance between avant-garde works and the general public, was interpreted by the 'Generation of 1927' (Lorca, Cernuda, **Aleixandre**, **Guillén** and Dámaso Alonso) as providing the theoretical base for a highly formalist type of literature, elitist and inaccessible, akin to surrealism and indebted to the 'pure poetry' of Juan Ramón Jiménez. In the half-century to 1970, successive generations of critics, often themselves creative writers, made a huge contribution to elucidating this literature and contemporary literature in general. Highly-trained in stylistic and historical methods, they strove, often successfully, to break down the dichotomy between the formal and historical aspects, and between the stylistic and semantic dimensions of the literary work. Dámaso Alonso, like so many of his generation a poet as well as a critic, and trained in the tradition of Saussure and Bally, provides the reader, by means of a descriptive analysis of the stylistic resources of a given text, with a convincing interpretation of the work being studied, whether difficult classics like the seventeenth-century poet Góngora, or those included in his *Poetas españoles contemporáneos* (Contemporary Spanish Poets) (1958). Carlos Bousoño, also a poet, though of a younger generation, is the author of a fundamental critical study which became an essential text for students of literature. His *Teoría de la expresión poética* (Theory of Poetic Expression) analyses, from a phenomenological perspective, the most apparently obscure Spanish poetry, from St John of the Cross to the twentieth century, in an attempt to discover its interpretative codes. These critics enjoyed the advantage of wide erudition, which enabled some of them, from the 1940s on, to evolve towards structuralist, semiotic or reader-reception approaches, notably Alarcos Llorach, Lázaro Carreter and Senabre.

In the latter part of the twentieth century, critical theory has considerably broadened its scope. Academic critics, traditionally contemptuous of literary journalism, have gradually begun to write for the supplements of newspapers like ***ABC***, *El* ***País*** and *La* ***Vanguardia***. These publications have acquired increasing importance, and have tended to blur the division between academic criticism and what Northrop Frye called 'public criticism'. This type of journalistic criticism, however, often serves the interests of publishing houses, and in many instances critic and publisher are one and the same person, which is not conducive to impartial judgement.

Spain has a dearth of weeklies similar to those in France, Britain and America, which keep the general reader informed about literature. It is true that there are Spanish literary reviews, but their commercial life is precarious, and they often depend for their survival on institutional subsidy. There is no Spanish equivalent of *The Times Literary Supplement* or *The London Review of Books*, though the Barcelona-based *Lateral*, or *Libros*, in Madrid, try to fill the gap, even adopting the layout of their British counterparts. Cultural programmes on television are largely relegated to minority viewing time. The novelist Javier Marías has lamented the fact that Spain has no critic who can fulfil the role of national arbiter of taste, such as George Steiner in Britain. One possible explanation is that, both in critical theory and in creative writing, Spain has progressed too rapidly from being pre-modern to being postmodern.

With some differences of detail, critical theory is in a similar situation in Catalonia. After a long period when the language was suppressed, quality publications, especially ***Serra d'Or***, began to appear in the late 1950s, with extensive sections devoted to **Catalan culture**, as well as discussion of the latest international trends in literary theory. Gabriel **Ferrater**, an academic and poet, contributed articles to this journal in which he provided a sound, modern critical framework for new writing in Catalan, refreshingly free from self-indulgent historicism. Departments of Catalan Literature continued to expand, some outside the Catalan-speaking regions. Side by side with academic publications, new literary reviews appeared, such as *Lletra de canvi*. Within Catalonia, and, on a more modest scale, in Valencia and the Balearic Islands, the press published weekly literary supplements containing reviews and analyses of the latest literary and artistic production, as well as rediscoveries of the literature of the past, which helped to normalize the discussion of Catalan literature. **Catalan television** also has programmes on literature and the arts.

Writing in Basque and Galician is on a more limited scale. In the late 1960s, a Galician magazine, *Grial*, became a focus for the revival of **Galician culture**. Critical writing, however, tends to be generally impressionistic.

Further reading

Casado, M. *et al.* (1995) *Ínsula*, pp. 587–8 (the whole double issue is an interesting monograph on recent development in the field of Spanish literary criticism).

Labany, J. (1995) 'Literary Experiment and Cultural Cannibalization', in H. Graham and J. Labanyi (eds) *Spanish Cultural Studies: an Introduction*, Oxford: Oxford University Press (provides a good resumé of literary experimentation since the late 1950s, linked to Critical Theory).

Schneider, M.J. and Stern, I. (eds) (1988). *Modern Spanish and Portuguese Literatures*, New York: Continuum (summary of criticism on Castilian, Catalan, Galician and Basque writers; the introduction provides a useful panorama of twentieth-century Spanish criticism).

ENRIC DOLZ I FERRER

Cruz, Antonio

b. 1948, Seville

Architect

Even before qualifying as an architect, Cruz went into partnership in 1971 with his colleague Antonio Ortiz. They both completed their architectural studies in Madrid in 1974 and returned to Seville to continue their work. The architecture of Cruz and Ortiz is imbued with resonances of the modern movement, and they are particularly open to the idiom of Italian and Dutch rationalists. Scandinavian influence is also evident, especially in the meticulous approach to the design of apartment blocks, in which the partnership specializes. The complex in the Calle Doña Maria Coronel (Seville, 1978) is a good example. Their best-known work is the Santa Justa railway station (Seville, 1991–2), a large-scale composition of great simplicity, reminiscent of the Termini station in Rome.

See also: architects; architecture

MIHAIL MOLDOVEANU

CSIC

The Consejo Superior de Investigaciones Científicas (Council for Scientific Research) was set up in November 1939, a few months after the end of the Civil War. From the beginning, it bore the stamp of the victorious Francoist regime. In the early years, its character was set by the then Minister of Education, José Ibáñez Martín, and José María de Albareda. The Council took over all the functions of the old Junta para Ampliación de Estudios e Investigaciones Científicas (Council for Advanced Studies and Scientific Research), while rejecting the philosophy which had inspired its creation in 1907. It also took over the Residencia de Estudiantes, which in the 1920s and 1930s had been a powerhouse of cultural and intellectual life, with the presence of such figures as Lorca and Dalí. Adopting the motto of the fourteenth-century Catalan philosopher and theologian Ramón Llull, *Arbor Scientiae* (The Tree of Knowledge), it attempted to bring under its control all branches of human learning, grouping them in three large blocs, corresponding respectively to Spirit, Matter and Life. Each of these areas was in turn subdivided into specialized institutes.

Just as **university education** was affected by the social and economic development of Spain in the 1960s, so the CSIC was perceived as being in need of reform, in respect of its organization, personnel and functions. Although the CSIC had been founded with the intention of promoting, directing and co-ordinating scientific research in Spain, in its early years it had only scored very limited success. In the 1970s, efforts were made to re-configure it as the main vehicle of national science policy, but it was only with the accession of the socialist government, especially after the enactment of the Science Law in 1987, that the national strategy for Research and Development began to take shape. Within this framework, the CSIC is the main autonomous body responsible for the implementation of the National Research Plan drawn up by the Inter-Ministerial Committee for Science and Technology, which reports directly to the government. In 1995, the work of the CSIC was being carried on by ninety-one institutes, employing 6,400 people.

In addition to the individual libraries of the various institutes, the CSIC has an important central library, and a vigorous publishing operation, issuing, in addition to monographs, more than two hundred specialist journals, and a general periodical, *Arbor*, which has been running since 1945. The CSIC is undoubtedly the most important interdisciplinary research body in Spain. In addition, the old Residencia de Estudiantes, though it no longer has the character it had in Lorca's time, provides modestly-priced accommodation and meals for visiting researchers.

See also: education and research; Francoist culture; science; universities; university education

Further reading

Arbor (1990) *El Consejo: una visión retrospectiva* (a special number of *Arbor*, which includes contributions from past presidents of CSIC).

Carr, R. and Fusi, J.P. (1979) *Spain: Dictatorship to Democracy*, London: George Allen & Unwin (chapter 6 sets the CSIC within the context of Francoist cultural and educational policy).

ALICIA ALTED

Cuallado, Gabriel

b. 1925, Masanasa (Valencia)

Photographer

Cuallado is the best known Spanish photographer of his generation. Among the distinctions awarded to his work are that of Best European Photographer (1993) and the National Photography Prize (Spain, 1994).

His early training took place within the Afal group, which he joined in 1957. In 1959 he was a founder member of the group La Palangana, which strives to encourage a more modern approach to Spanish photography. His works are distinguished by their vigorous composition, as well as by the important role of the material objects included within the frame. The background is treated with the same care as the human subject who nearly always appears in his pictures. He employs an exceptionally varied range of grey scales in his black and white photography.

Further reading

Gabriel Cuallado (1989) Valencia, IVAM

MIHAIL MOLDOVEANU

Cubillo Ferreira, Antonio

b. 1930, La Laguna (Tenerife)

Canarian nationalist leader

Brought up in the rural north of Tenerife, Cubillo studied law at the University of La Laguna and during the late 1950s and early 1960s defended various strikers and labour organizations, most notably the port workers of Santa Cruz, dairy-workers and bus-drivers. In 1960, he co-founded a radical independence movement, Canarias Libre (Free Canary Islands), with leading communists like the lawyer Fernando Sagaseta. Shortly afterwards he was arrested but fled into exile before sentence was passed. He established contacts with the communist **PCE** in Paris, but his separatist ambitions resulted in the PCE distancing itself from him. In 1964 he moved to Algeria, where he set up MPAIAC (Movimiento Popular para la Autodeterminación e Independencia del Archipiélago Canario – Movement for the Self-Determination and Independence of the Canarian Archipelago) and began broadcasting pro-independence propaganda to the islands. The broadcasts of Radio Canarias Libre were popular among the students at La Laguna University, and prepared the ground for a growth of independence feeling in the post-Franco period. From his Algiers base Cubillo steadily built up the case for Canarian independence in the Organization of African States and among the pro-Soviet states of the United Nations. The historic connection between the Canaries and Cuba was instrumental in the acceptance of his claims.

In 1978, he was knifed in his Algiers apartment block and suffered injuries which left him almost totally paralysed below the waist. His attackers were never caught. Their identity has caused much speculation, which has centred on both the Spanish and Algerian secret services.

Cubillo returned to the Canary Islands in 1985 and has campaigned in regional and local elections, though not at national or European level. Although Cubillo still enjoys some affection among more radical elements of Canarian society, his party, re-established in December 1986 as the Congreso Nacional de Canarias (Canary Islands National Congress) regularly polls under 2 percent of the vote. Other pro-autonomy parties, however, take a good third of the vote and now dominate the regional assembly as well as many *cabildos* (island councils) and town councils. His status in the independence movement was undermined in the early 1990s by the foundation of the Las Palmas-based Coalición para Canarias Libre by his former lieutenant, Angel Cuenca Sanabria.

Apart from his purely political work, Cubillo has been actively engaged in linguistic and historical work based on the premise of the African, particularly Berber, origin of the pre-Spanish inhabitants of the Canary Islands (the *Guanches*). Research into the pre-Spanish past has been used to bolster the cause of Canarian independence ever since Secundino Delgado set up the first modern movement in the late nineteenth century. MPAIAC's manifesto, known as *El Libro Blanco* (The White Book) and published in 1970, stresses the 'scientific' basis for the uniqueness of the Canarian people, although the evidence for this is mainly derived from discredited craniometric work.

See also: Archaeological Museum of Tenerife; Canarian culture; Museum of the Canaries

Further reading

Cubillo, A. (1991) *Los Años Verdes. Semimemorias*, Sta. Cruz de Tenerife: Centro de la Cultura Popular Canaria (a rather fanciful version of Cubillo's early life and career).

Garí Hayek, D (1992) *Historia del nacionalismo canario*, Sta. Cruz de Tenerife: Benchomo (the best overview of modern Canarian nationalism).

Mercer, J. (1980) *The Canary Islanders: Their Prehistory, Conquest, and Survival*, London: Rex Collings (modern Canarian nationalism up to the death of Franco is covered in an appendix).

M.R. EDDY

cultural institutions and movements

As with other aspects of Spanish life, cultural institutions and movements have shown increasing complexity and diversification since the end of the Franco dictatorship in 1975. **Francoist culture**, characterized by Castilian-centred nationalism and an identification of Spanishness with **National Catholicism**, was an attempt to express the ideology of the faction which had emerged victorious from the Civil War. Cultural and intellectual life was controlled by a rigorous **censorship**, which encouraged a 'culture of evasion', the uncritical acceptance of optimistic views of current reality purveyed through the cinema (see also **film and cinema**), sentimental popular literature, and spectator sports, especially **football**. The attempt to impose cultural homogeneity, however, was undermined by the survival of some elements of intellectual independence among certain élites, and the continued vitality of **Basque**, **Catalan** and **Galician cultures**.

The other factor which defeated the regime's attempts to create an official culture was lack of resources, but this situation changed radically with the restoration of democracy, particularly after the victory of the socialist **PSOE** in the elections of 1982. Already in 1977 the **UCD** administration had set up a new **Ministry of Culture**, which took over some of the functions previously exercised by the Ministry of Education and the Ministry of Information and Tourism. In the 1980s, the new Ministry assumed an increasingly pro-active role in revitalizing Spanish cultural institutions, and preserving the national heritage more effectively. The Law of Spanish National Heritage (1985) set up a General Register of Heritage Sites and Objects, and made it an offence to alter, sell or export without permission any art object or site listed in this register. The arts budget was increased by around 70 percent between 1982 and 1989, and though there were cutbacks in the 1990s, considerable advances were made. **Museums** and art galleries were among the major beneficiaries of government spending, and the results were seen in the modernization and expansion of existing buildings, and the enhancement of national art collections by a programme of acquisition of contemporary works. Generous support was given to the film industry, which also enjoyed a measure of protection under the 'screen quota' system (see also **cinema law**). New concert halls were built, notably the **Auditorio Nacional de Música** (National Concert Hall, 1984–90), and the refurbished **Royal Theatre** was re-opened in its original character as an opera house in October 1997. In the same month, the spectacular results achieved through private finance were exemplified in the inauguration of the Guggenheim Museum in Bilbao, which not only provides an outstanding venue for the display of contemporary art, but is itself a strikingly modern architectural statement.

The budget of the Ministry of Culture was reduced in the 1990s as more and more activity was undertaken by the governments of the various **autonomous communities**, though the central authorities continued to be involved in supporting regional projects, such as the refurbishment of regional theatres, and the construction of new concert halls. New music festivals have been inaugurated in Alicante and Cuenca, and few regions are now without their own orchestras. Public art galleries have been opened, notably the Instituto Valenciano de Arte Moderno (Valencia Institute of Modern Art).

In parallel with, but independently of these developments at official level, the popular 'culture of evasion' continued to flourish, helped by an increasingly active publishing industry which flooded the market with new books and magazines, usually categorized as **kiosk literature**. Nevertheless, the interest of the wider public in more challenging cultural manifestations such as art exhibitions has burgeoned. The International Festival of Contemporary Art held in Madrid in 1983 attracted huge numbers of visitors. A survey carried out by the Ministry of Culture in 1985 indicated that 20 percent of all Spaniards over the age of fourteen visit an art gallery at least once a fortnight. A major exhibition of Velázquez's paintings in the **Prado Museum** in 1990 attracted a total of half a million people. Figures produced for 1995 show that reading (55 percent) and listening to music (70 percent) are the favourite leisure activities of more people than watch spectator sports or go to discos (25 percent each).

In addition to this expansion of what came to be called *la demanda cultural* ('cultural demand'), there were various alternative movements, with a strong current of non-conformity, which derived largely from the heady experience of freedom after the stifling climate of the Franco years. The most symptomatic of these was the Madrid-based phenomenon called *la* ***Movida***, an untranslatable term which carries connotations of excitement, experimentation and excess, akin to the climate of the 'swinging London' of the 1960s. From about 1980, discos, bars and clubs proliferated, and new punk bands and **independent record companies** sprang up to feed the taste of a youth clientele in reaction against the **rock** music of the 1970s. The cinema also provided an outlet for the movement, one of its most representative figures being the director Pedro **Almodóvar**.

Almodóvar is also a link to the other main alternative movement, **gay culture**. The first Gay

Pride march was held in Barcelona in the same month as the first democratic elections since the Civil War (June 1977), though it was not until 1995 that discrimination on grounds of sexual orientation was made an offence under the new Penal Code. As with *la Movida*, music plays a central role in gay culture, not only in the large number of gay bars and clubs which have sprung up in major cities since the late 1970s, but also in some aspects of the *Nova cançó*, notably in the work of Lluís **Llach**.

While it would be untrue to say that the Franco regime stifled cultural endeavour completely, it is clear that since 1975 a new balance has been struck between élite cultures and the cultures of previously neglected groups such as gay people, the young and the inhabitants of peripheral regions.

See also: film and cinema; flamenco; language and national identity; music; novel; performing arts; poetry; theatre; visual arts

Further reading

Graham, H. and Labanyi, J. (eds) (1995) *Spanish Cultural Studies, an Introduction: The Struggle for Modernity*, Oxford: Oxford University Press (see part IV, chapters 18–22, for an authoritative account by various specialist authors of the cultural changes since 1975).

Hooper, J. (1995) *The New Spaniards*, Harmondsworth: Penguin (chapters 23 and 24 offer an excellent overview of the development of cultural life since 1975).

EAMONN RODGERS

'CURRO ROMERO' *see* Romero López, Francisco

cycling

Cycling is one of the most popular sports in Spain, both as a participator and a spectator sport, whether viewed from the trackside or via the very ample televised coverage. The major event is the Tour of Spain (*Vuelta a España*) which takes place from September to October each year. It is typically a twenty-three day event with one rest day, and the route varies from year to year. The 1996 route began with a circular stage of 162 km in Valencia, and the remaining days' stages were: Valencia–Cuenca (205 km); Cuenca–Albacete (184 km); Albacete–Murcia (160 km); Murcia–Almería (210 km); Almería–Málaga (210 km) Málaga–-Marbella (150 km); Marbella–Jerez de la Frontera (205 km); Jerez de la Frontera–Córdoba (204 km); rest day; El Tiemblo–Avila (46 km against the clock); Avila–Salamanca (197 km); Benavente–Alto del Naranco (188 km); Oviedo–Lagos de Covadogna (170 km); Cangas de Onís–Parque Naturaleza de Cabárceno (170 km); Parque Naturaleza de Cabárceno–Alto Cruz de la Demanda (210 km); Logroño–Sabiñánigo (222 km); Sabiñánigo–Ampriu (158 km); Benasque–Zaragoza (222 km); Getafe–Avila (212 km); Avila–Destilerías DYC (204 km); Segovia–Destilerías DYC (44 km against the clock); finishing with a circle of 165 km in Madrid. The total of 3,898 km includes a number of arduous mountain stages, especially in the Pyrenees in northern Aragon. The 1997 route broke with tradition by starting from outside Spain in Lisbon and omitting the Pyrenees.

In addition to the Tour of Spain, fifteen other shorter events such as the Tour of Andalusia, the Tour of Asturias etc. are held each year, as well as a series of one-day events.

The Tour of Spain has been won by many Spaniards since it began in 1935, but it was a series of victories in the Tour de France which both created enthusiasm for cycling within Spain and brought Spanish professional cyclists to world attention. The Tour had been won by Bahamontes in 1959, by Ocaña in 1973, and by Delgado in 1988, but **Induráin**'s victories from 1991–5 made him one of only three to have won five times, and the only one to have done so consecutively. Spanish cyclists have also been successful in world championships (Indurain and Olano, for example, were world champions in 1995, and won gold and silver medals respectively in the 1996 Olympics) and the Spanish teams of ONCE and Banesto feature frequently among the top five professional teams worldwide.

See also: sport and leisure

EAMONN RODGERS

D

Dalí, Salvador

b. 1904, Figueras; d. 1989, Figueras

Artist

Dalí's interest in Freud and psychoanalysis led him to develop the paranoic critical method of painting, whereby images are broken down visually and by free association. Millet's *Angelus*, depicting a man and a woman standing in a field, may be associated with two large rocks filling a space, but also with a pair of cherries, because they are two.

Dalí was the second son of a strict but progressive notary from Figueras in Catalonia. His elder brother had died, and being given the dead brother's name, he felt himself to be a substitute, leading to ferocious ambition coupled with morbid sensitivity. Tensions with his father are amply explored in Dalí's William Tell paintings, where the Swiss archer is associated with Abraham and even God, in his willingness to sacrifice his own son. Dalí's castration complex is evidenced in *Dismal Sport* and *The Great Masturbator.* But the landscape of his childhood never left him. The vast plain of the Ampurdán blistering under bright light, is a constant reference.

Unusually gifted from a very early age Dalí went to study at the Madrid School of Fine Art but would not accept his professors' competence to judge him. A strong and artistically productive friendship with the poet Lorca ended when Dalí collaborated with **Buñuel** on the surrealist film *Un Chien andalou.* Using techniques of montage and dissolving frames to explore the transformation of objects, Dalí claimed the film was anti-aesthetic and signified nothing.

While the surrealists wanted to fuse dream and reality into a surreality, Dalí wanted to sustain the opposition, so that his imagination would substitute, not extend, reality. His emphasis on tradition, albeit decadent, combined with his highly skilled near photographic technique, eventually distanced him from the French surrealists and their communist leanings. They disapproved of his marriage to Gala and anagrammed his name to Avida Dollars.

Pronouncing himself apolitical Dalí nevertheless painted in 1936 *Soft Construction with Boiled Beans: Premonition of Civil War,* wherein one giant set of leprous limbs tear themselves apart, simultaneously victim and aggressor. Much influenced by the writings of Jacques Lacan on paranoia, Dalí strove to systematize confusion, so that his compositions could sustain multiple interpretations depending on focus and association, as in *Apparition of Face and Fruit Dish on a Beach.* In *The Metamorphosis of Narcissus* Dalí plays further on reality and illusion since Narcissus fell in love with his own reflection but drowned trying to reach it. The image of Narcissus doubles up as a hand holding a cracked egg.

Dalí is one of the most famous artists of this century. His work can be seen at major art galleries throughout the world and at the **Dalí Museum** in Figueras.

See also: painting; visual arts

Further reading

Ades, D. (1995) *Dalí*, London: Thames & Hudson (an excellent study of Dalí's life and work).

Descharnes, R. (1984) *Salvador Dalí, The Work, The Man*, New York: Harry Abrams (an informed critical study).

Secrest, M. (1986) *Salvador Dalí, The Surrealist Jester*, London: Weidenfeld & Nicolson (an interesting biography).

HELEN OPPENHEIMER

Dalí Museum

The 'Theatre of Memory', as Dalí named it, opened in 1974 in Figueras (Girona), the painter's birthplace. The museum itself and its setting attract as much interest as the collection – mostly works made from the 1960s onwards. Under Dalí's supervision it was built on the remains of a former playhouse. Its reticulated dome, baroque decorations, surreal paraphernalia and installations, all embody the eccentric spirit of the artist's legacy to his homeland. In 1983 the Torre Galatea annexe was added in homage to Gala, his lifelong companion and muse, who figures prominently in the museum's paintings.

See also: visual arts

XON DE ROS

dance

Despite the richness of the Spanish dance tradition, both in its academic and folk manifestations, it was not until the 1990s that the state made a serious effort to structure dance education so as to provide a qualification of the same status as other university degrees. This was particularly paradoxical in a country which has produced so many brilliant dancers, and which, particularly since the transition to democracy, has discovered contemporary dance, and has seen a revolution in the understanding of dance, blending traditional forms such as **flamenco** with other styles.

By contrast with the academic rigidity of formal dance (*danza*), folk-dance (*baile popular*) is a much freer form, enabling people to externalize their feelings, especially during spring and summer ***fiestas*** such as those of St John, St Peter, St James and a host of other local patron saints, which offer a welcome break from daily toil. Autumn and winter festivals such as the Day of the Dead or All Souls' Day, Christmas and Carnival also have their characteristic dances. The medieval Danse Macabre survives in many parts of Spain, with dancers performing in cemeteries on All Souls' Day, though this custom has disappeared in Castile. All the **autonomous communities** share the traditional dance-forms of the *jota*, the *fandango* and the *seguidilla*, though the latter two are not found in León.

Though the tradition of classical dance goes back to the nineteenth century, it has never given rise to dance companies with the same international impact as flamenco or folk-dance groups. After the restoration of democracy, an attempt was made to fill this gap by the creation of the Spanish National Classical Ballet Company (Ballet Nacional de España Clásico). However, despite the efforts of successive Directors such as Víctor Ullate, María de Ávila and Maya Plisetskaya, it never acquired a distinctive character, owing in part to the absence of clear political direction about the role of dance in the new Spain. Several voices advocated emphasizing contemporary dance as the appropriate means of expression for a society which was undergoing rapid modernization after forty years of stagnation. In the various regions, small companies sprang up, with the support of town councils and other official bodies, such as the Zaragoza Classical Ballet Company, which has been struggling to survive since 1982, or the short-lived Basque Ballet Company, founded in 1989. In addition, there were smaller companies which catered for the demand of artistically conservative parents, who sent their daughters to private ballet schools for social rather than professional reasons. The creation of Víctor Ullate's company in 1988 brought a breath of fresh air, with his idiosyncratic creations blending neoclassical and folk dance. María de Avila, later Director of the National Ballet Companies, founded Young Ballet as an outlet for her pupils, but despite the presence of future international stars such as Trinidad Sevillano, Antonio Castilla and Amaya Iglesias, lack of official support, and the short-sightedness of government cultural policy eventually caused it to collapse.

By contrast, contemporary dance has undergone spectacular development, led by heroic figures determined to modernize the taste of a public deprived of this form of art during the Franco regime. The movement has been spearheaded by Catalonia and Valencia, which have produced the best companies and the best creators of new forms. The foundation of the independent Ballet Contemporani de Barcelona in 1977 set new standards of professionalism. The Factory (La Fàbrica) has revolutionized the teaching of the new style, and has been the inspiration for numerous subsequent developments, among others *Ananda Dansa*, *Danat Dansa*, *L'anònima Imperial*, *Mudanzas*, *Malpelo* and *10 & 10*, the latter the only significant contribution from the Spanish-speaking interior. Of particular note is the work of choreographers such as Cesc Gelabert, who won the National Dance Prize in 1996. Together with Lydia Azzopardi, he has been active since 1980 in introducing new trends and creating brilliantly original dance routines for their companies. Ramón Oller and his Metros company are fulfilling their early promise, and, together with other small groups, some of them amateur, are building up an enthusiastic and knowledgeable following. The return of Nacho Duato, and his controversial transformation of the National Classical Ballet Company into the National Dance Company (Compañía Nacional de Danza), which in a mere six years he turned into a world-class contemporary dance company, has made art dance a mass phenomenon.

The regulation of dance education via conservatories enabled students to obtain recognized qualifications as classical (ballet) or traditional (Spanish) dancers. But the system also had an important role in the renewal of Spanish dance by combining the spontaneity and natural talent of its earlier products with a more sophisticated technique, which helped to launch the careers of Antonio Canales and Lola Greco, who continued the innovative work of Antonio Gades and Cristina Hoyos. The explosive irruption onto the scene of Joaquín Cortés, who fuses various styles with flamenco and traditional dance, has made him the most charismatic figure in the public's eyes since Duato. Besides, since 1992, the government has been phasing in various educational reforms which finally recognize art education as a legitimate university course (see also **LOGSE**). This has put pressure on the conservatories and private dance schools. The conservatories offer three programmes, classical ballet, contemporary dance and Spanish dance, which includes flamenco, *escuela bolera*, classical Spanish dance, and regional dance. In theory, the latter embraces all manifestations of folk-dance, but this genre is facing severe difficulties owing to the lack of government support, and survives thanks to the enthusiasm of small research groups and regional organizations such as town and provincial councils, which sometimes subsidize Folklore Schools.

The study of dance history is a relatively recent development, and has usually been carried on from within a musicological perspective. This is gradually giving way to research conducted by scholars with a specifically dance background, such as Ana Yepes, María José Ruiz and Carlos Blanco, who are striving to rediscover the historical roots of what has become in contemporary Spain a rich and vibrant phenomenon.

See also: Basque culture; Canarian culture; Catalan culture; Galician culture; national dance companies; performing arts

Further reading

Abad Hernán, P.P. (1989) *Cancionero popular de Castilla y León: Romances, canciones y danzas de tradición oral*, Salamanca: Centro de Cultura Tradicional (a comprehensive compilation of traditional music, including dance music).

Aznar, J. (ed.) (1994) *Dansa : noves tendències de la coreografia catalana*, Barcelona: Diputació de Barcelona (illustrated with numerous photographs).

Caballero Bonald, J.M. (1959) *Andalusian Dances*, trans. C.D. Ley, Barcelona: Noguer (somewhat dated, but one of the few studies available in English).

Durand-Viel, A.M. (1983) *La sevillana : datos sobre el folklore de la Baja Andalucía*, Sevilla: Servicio de Publicaciones del Ayuntamiento de Sevilla (a study of this characteristic dance-form).

El Sac de Danses (research group) (1987) *El Risto: Danses catalanes que encara es ballen*, Barcelona: Alta Fulla (a description of one of the major regional dance traditions).

Miguel Lara, M.J. de (ed.) (1994) *La danza en la escuela*, Sevilla: Diputación Provincial (considers the implications of the introduction of dance into the school curriculum).

Río Orozco, C. del (1993) *Apuntes sobre la danza española*, Córdoba: Tip. Artística (pp. 155–7 contain a useful bibliography).

Wingrave, H. (1972) *Spanish Dancing, A Handbook on Steps, Style, Castanets and Dancing*, Speldhurst: Planned Action (a practical manual).

CARLOS BLANCO LOU

De la Rosa, Javier

b. 1947, Barcelona

Financier

A Catalan financier who was accused in 1994 of fraud and misappropriation of public funds which included re-routing part of a loan guaranteed by the **Generalitat** towards his own private businesses rather than towards saving the subsequently bankrupt holding company, Grand Tibidabo, which he had acquired in 1991. His arrest prompted opposition calls for the resignation of senior members of the Generalitat who had previously blocked an investigation by Catalonia's regional parliament into de la Rosa's affairs. He also faced a separate investigation by the Kuwait Investment Office into his running of the Spanish investment arm of the Office – Group Torras – following serious financial losses.

See also: corruption; politics

GEORGINA BLAKELEY

Defensor del Pueblo

The People's Defender is the title given in Spain to the ombudsman charged with defending the rights guaranteed in Title I of the **constitution of 1978**. The office is not technically part of the judiciary and was given a formal existence only in May 1981. The first ombudsman, Joaquín Ruiz Giménez, served from 1982–7, in line with the statutes governing the post, which determine that the ombudsman serves for five years. The ombudsman is appointed by a majority vote of at least three fifths of each chamber of parliament, and acts both to supervise the activities of the Spanish administration and to investigate citizens' complaints against abuses of their rights. An annual report is made back to parliament.

Since the post was created, there has been concern over some overlap in function with the attorney general's office, as well as inadequate budgetary provision and an overwhelming case load. Doubts have surfaced on occasion as to whether a proper distance was being kept between the ombudsman's office and the government; this was particularly true towards the end of the **PSOE**'s long term of office (1982–96) and formed part of a more general concern at a blurring of the lines between government and state. Despite such reservations, however, the office continues to play both a constitutional and a political role.

PAUL HEYWOOD

Delibes Setién, Miguel

b. 1920, Valladolid

Writer

In 1975, Miguel Delibes was named member of the **Royal Academy** of Language. In his acceptance speech, Delibes spelt out what have constituted the thematic components of his works: the myth of progress, solidarity, ecology, childhood, death, the city versus the country, ethical and moral concerns. A social realist, Delibes' mission in his novelistic discourse has been to grasp the essence of Spanish life in order to explore human experience in post-Civil War Spain.

Delibes launched his career with two undistinguished novels, *La sombra del ciprés es alargada* (The Long Shadow of the Cypress) (1947), and *Aún es de día* (It Is Still Daylight) (1949). The former, which won the 1947 **Nadal Prize**, explores the horrors of war and the question of isolation and death. However, his most definitive novel based on the

Spanish Civil War, *The Stuff of Heroes* (*337A, madera de héroe*), would not be published until forty years later (1987). *The Stuff of Heroes* undermines the Nationalist government's myth of a crusade in which Francoists attempted to justify the regime's excesses during the Spanish Civil War and its subsequent efforts to stifle opposition in the name of an authentic Spanish identity.

The novelist, nevertheless, discovered his true voice in *The Path* (*El camino*) (1950), a *Bildungsroman* that recounts a small boy's childhood experiences on the eve of his forced departure to go to school in the city. Two contending points of view, the young boy's and that of narrator's, explore on the one hand, a vision of the present and the past, and on the other, a realization that the past must be abandoned for a future of progress. What Delibes questions is the kind of progress that the young boy's education is supposed to engender.

Delibes explores and subverts indirectly the Francoist rhetoric of economic and social progress in the late 1950s and early 1960s in *Smoke on the Ground* (*Las ratas*, 1962) and *Los santos inocentes* (The Holy Innocents) (1981). Set in rural Spain, both novels highlight the horrid living conditions of the rural folk. The child-protagonist and his father in *Smoke on the Ground* live in a cave and make a living by killing water rats and selling them to be eaten in the local tavern. The village oracle, the protagonist is remarkably knowledgeable about the natural world, based on careful observation of his environment and nature. The same idea of living in harmony with nature runs through *Los santos inocentes* as well as *El disputado voto del señor Cayo* (The Fight for Señor Cayo's Vote) (1978). Closely linked with the theme of nature is that of solidarity among individuals. Delibes demonstrates this idea effectively in *La hoja roja* (The Red Leaf) (1962) in which an old man finds himself completely abandoned by society after his retirement. The novelist believes that if human beings have lost their ability to be in solidarity with each other, it is because of unmediated technological and industrial progress devoid of moral and ethical concerns. The writer's preoccupation with the reckless quest for technological progress is evident in *Parábola del náufrago* (Parable of the Shipwrecked Man) (1969). As in the anti-Utopian novels such as Aldous Huxley's *Brave New World* and George Orwell's *1984*, Delibes analyses the nightmare associated with the annihilation of human will and reason. *Parábola del náufrago* underlines individuals' automatization in a technologized world to the extent that they lose their identity. Like other post-war novelists such as Juan **Benet**, Juan **Goytisolo**, **Torrente Ballester** and **Martín-Santos**, who have attempted to criticize some of the Francoist myths and policies, Delibes also challenges some of the Nationalist government's myths. He, however, discloses alternative ways of comprehending human reality by proposing a possible world for the Spaniard. Delibes substitutes his own vision of a world distinct from the Francoist ideologically constructed one in *Five Hours with Mario* (*Cinco horas con Mario*, 1966) in which the ideals of the defunct protagonist become a blueprint for a new Spain. The new Spain in Delibes' view is not one in which progress is defined as the physical and material well-being of a few in the society who exploit and dehumanize others. Progress is the sensible balance between the traditional and the modern. It also signifies for Delibes the individual who lives in close collaboration with nature and emerges as an integral part of it.

Major works

Delibes Setién, M. (1947) *La sombra del ciprés es alargada*, Barcelona: Ediciones Destino (novel).

—— (1950) *El camino*, Barcelona: Ediciones Destino; trans. J. and B. Haycraft, *The Path*, London: Hamilton; New York: John Day Co, 1961 (novel).

—— (1962) *Las ratas*, Barcelona: Ediciones Destino; trans. A. Johnson, *Smoke on the Ground*, Garden City, NY: Doubleday, 1972 (novel).

—— (1966) *Cinco horas con Mario*, Barcelona: Ediciones Destino; trans. F.M. López-Morillas, *Five Hours with Mario*, New York: Columbia University Press, 1988 (novel).

—— (1969) *Parábola del náufrago*, Barcelona: Ediciones Destino (novel).

—— (1987) *337A, madera de héroe*, Barcelona: Ediciones Destino; trans. Frances M. López-Morillas, *The Stuff of Heroes*, New York: Pantheon Books, 1990 (novel).

Further reading

Agawu-Kakraba, Y.B. (1996) *Demythification in the Fiction of Miguel Delibes*, New York: Peter Lang (a well documented study of some of the Francoist myths and how those myths are undermined).

Alonso de los Ríos, C. (1971) *Conversaciones con Miguel Delibes*, Madrid: Magisterio Español (based on conversation with Delibes, this work deals with issues that concern him in life and their representation in his novels).

Díaz, J.W. (1972) *Miguel Delibes*, New York: Twayne (provides biographical information on Delibes and analyses some of his novels and short stories).

Rey, A. (1975) *La originalidad novelística de Miguel Delibes*, Santiago de Compostela: Universidad de Santiago de Compostela (scrutinizes themes, style and the originality of Delibes' artistic creation).

YAW AGAWU-KAKRABA

demographic indicators

In 1995 Spain had a population very close to 40 million. At 78 inhabitants per km^2, its population density is well below those of France (103 per km^2), Italy (192 per km^2) or the UK (235 per km^2), but the population is very unevenly spread. 60 percent of the country's inhabitants are to be found in the periphery and the archipelagos, with only a few large population centres in the interior (Madrid, Zaragoza, Valladolid). Spain is highly urbanized: 50 percent of the population lives in cities of more than 100,000 inhabitants, or 80 percent if we include those of more than 50,000 inhabitants.

After strong population growth in the 1960s and 1970s there was a marked deceleration in the 1980s. The strong growth of the 1960s and early 1970s was due to both a high birth rate and a falling mortality rate. In the 1980s, however, the birth rate fell dramatically from a high point of twenty-two per thousand in 1960 to ten per thousand by 1991. In the late 1990s the fertility rate (average number of children born per woman), at 1.2, was the lowest in Europe. The fall in the fertility rate has been accompanied by a marked rise in the age at which women have children. As the mortality rate creeps up again because of the changing age structure of the population (by the year 2020 there are likely to be more Spaniards aged over 60 than under 16), the low fertility rate, if sustained, must mean a gradual decline in population. Nevertheless life expectancy at birth remains very high (78 years, higher than in most EU countries) and infant mortality is lower than ever and comparable to that across the EU, so both factors together should ensure population stability for several decades, although the potentially active population (16 to 64) will decline and the dependency ratio will rise. Population stability is also helped by the fact that immigration exceeds emigration (a reversal of the trend of the 1960s and early 1970s), but it is impossible to quantify because much of it is illegal (see also **immigrants**). Although legal foreign residents number just over half a million, the total figure is thought to be in the region of 800,000. Many of the illegal immigrants come from North Africa and the poorer countries of Latin America.

Further reading

De Miguel, A. (1992) *La sociedad española 1992–93*, Madrid: Alianza Editorial, pp. 35–147 (the first volume in a series based on yearly surveys; a highly useful sociological tool).

Puyol Antolín, R. (1988) *La población española*, Madrid: Editorial Síntesis (adopts a predominantly geographical or spatial approach to population questions).

V Informe sociológico sobre la situación social de España (1994) Madrid: Fundación FOESSA, vol. 1, pp. 145–413 (the most complete social survey of Spain and an indispensable source of sociological information).

C.A. LONGHURST

design

During the Franco dictatorship, when the climate was unfavourable to design, demand from industry was scant, and the few intellectuals who believed in progressive design, excluded as they were from political and economic influence, had to make a heroic effort to produce even a few creations, which are now almost museum pieces. As with other areas of cultural life, designers strove to organize themselves in professional associations and to develop infrastructures. Significant efforts in this direction were made by various Madrid-based groups, especially those which came together in the SEDI (Sociedad de Estudios sobre el Diseño Industrial – Society for Studies in Industrial Design). An important role was also played by the architect Carlos de Miguel, editor of the *Revista de Arquitectura* (Architecture Review), and his partners Javier Carvajal and Luis Feduchi.

It was, however, in Barcelona, with its industrial and commercial culture, that the modernization of design, which had begun under the Second Republic, was given a new lease of life. Antoni de **Moragas** and Oriol **Bohigas** set up the Grupo R, which tried to recreate the spirit of the pre-Civil War **GATEPAC**. Under the stimulus of a visit from Gio Ponti, editor of the Italian journal *Domus*, the IDIB (Institut de Disseny Industrial de Barcelona – Barcelona Institute of Industrial Design) was set up. Subsequently, in 1960, the Industrial Design Group of the old FAD (Foment de les Arts Decoratives – Institute for the Encouragement of Decorative Arts, founded in 1903) was created, followed in 1961 by the Graphic Design and Visual Communication Group. Also in 1961, the first Delta Prizes for industrial design were awarded.

Education and training in design was the work of specialized schools, of which the most important are the Elisava school, the oldest, founded in Barcelona in 1959, and the Eina school, opened in 1967. Traditional schools such as Massana and La Llotja were simultaneously including design in their courses. Miguel Durán Lóriga founded the first school in Madrid of industrial design, and by 1982 the Faculties of Fine Arts had begun incorporating the teaching of design into their programmes.

The 1960s saw the beginning of a period of intense activity, of collaboration with other humanistic disciplines, foreign contacts and conferences (e.g. Valencia, 1967; Ibiza, 1971). In 1973, the Fundación BCD (a foundation linked to the Barcelona Centre for Industrial Design) was set up to foster design in both the public and private sectors. That same year, however, saw the oil crisis, which led to a slowing-down of industry, an increasing conservatism, and a neglect of design, which put in jeopardy the achievements of the 1960s. Nevertheless, the death of Franco in 1975 provided the opportunity to begin laying the foundations of a new culture of taste. Design became the means of creating the image which the young democracy wished to display to the world.

The profession began discussions with the administration, inevitably tentative because of the transitional situation. There was no shortage of designers who had received a specialized training, and both the central government and those of the **autonomous communities** saw them as attractive allies, but the infrastructure was lacking, as was a deeper generalized awareness in society at large. In 1982, the Ministry of Industry and Energy asked BCD to design and mount a travelling exhibition with the aim of educating the public. In 1984, the AEDP (Asociación Española de Diseñadores Profesionales – Spanish Association of Professional Designers) was set up. Design benefited from the increasing international interest in Spain in the mid-1980s, and in 1987 the government financed an exhibition *El Diseño en España* (Design in Spain) in Brussels, as part of the *Europalia* programme. Official support for design was confirmed in the same year with the award of the first National Design Prizes.

Graphic design

The re-establishment of democracy revitalized visual culture: new logos for political parties and institutions, new communications media, products, brands and services. Alberto Corazón was one of the first to realize that the characteristic field of operation of the designer is the public sector, and he worked hard to convince others of the importance of graphic design for creating a social identity. This idea had also been vigorously defended since the 1960s by José María Cruz Novillo, who was commissioned to design many of the symbols of the new democratic Spain, including those of the Madrid autonomous region, the Posts and Telegraphs service and the **PSOE**. Corazón designed the new imagery of the Ministry of Public works, as well as the Madrid suburban rail network. Josep Maria Trias performed a similar task for the Barcelona Metro, and designed the logos for the Barcelona Olympics of 1992. América Sánchez was responsible for the Picasso Museum.

In the field of book design, Corazón has done memorable work for his own publishing-house, while Daniel Gil has earned distinction as a designer for Alianza Editorial, as has Diego Lara in Alfaguara. Graphic work was pioneered in Catalonia by Jordi Fornas and Giralt Miracle, who found a worthy successor in Enric Satué, in his work for the ***Diari de Barcelona***, the magazines *Arquitecturas Bis* and *CAU*, and books published by La Gaya Ciencia.

Several talented figures have contributed to the development of design in the various autonomous communities, among them Audeva and Pepe Barro (Galicia), Antonio Pérez Escolano (Seville), Severo Almansa and Vicente Martínez Gadea (Murcia). Illustrator-designers such as Peret, Javier de Juan, Fernando Medina and Montxo Algora have given some of the symbols a ludic, comic-strip quality, of which the most notable example is Mariscal's mascot for the Barcelona Olympics.

Interior and industrial design

Industrial design was pioneered during the years of reconstruction after the dictatorship by a group of individual designers, many of them self-taught, or by **architects**. A significant contribution to the modernization of the everyday environment has been made by André Ricard (product design), Miquel Milá (furniture design), Fernando Marquina (household design), Tous y Fargas (industrial and technological design), Alfonso **Milá** and Federico **Correa** (interior design). The foundation of Bocaccio Design in 1972 was an important landmark in the establishment of quality design, with the launch not only of their own products, such as the 'Seville' table and chair and the 'Hialina' bookcase, but also of prestigious foreign brands. The Sala Vinçon in Barcelona, opened in 1973, was not only the first design shop in the style of Habitat, but also ran exhibitions, and generally encouraged creativity.

The 1980s were both a period of great ferment and a time when Spain had to compete in Europe, which, partly as a result of the international renown of the ***Movida***, had high expectations of change. Spain, which had lost out on large sections of the modern movement, threw itself wholeheartedly into the most advanced versions of postmodernism. The whole environment, ranging from the clothes people wore, hairstyles, where they spent their free time, small consumer goods, to political programmes and market strategies, became the subject of the most detailed attention on the part of designers. New magazines devoted entirely to design began to appear, including *ON*, *De Diseño* and *ARDI*, edited by Juli Capella and Quim Larrea, not to mention those more specifically associated with *la Movida*: *Sur Exprés*, *El Europeo* and *La Luna*. Without moving from their own homes, readers could study pictures of newly-designed bars such as *El Gambrinus* (Javier Mariscal and Alfredo **Arribas**, 1988), *Network* and *Velvet* (Samsó and Arribas, 1987). The boom in design during this decade embraced fashion (Jesús del Pozo, Adolfo Domínguez, Antonio Miró and Roberto Verino), costume jewellery (Chus Bares, Joaquín Berao and Chelo Sastre) and footwear (Sara Navarro).

It is during this period that there emerges what was referred to as *diseño de autor* ('author' design), in keeping with the general reaction against the rigid austerity of minimalist and functionalist approaches. The banal styles imported from Italy took on a warm and ludic character, almost like a permanent *fiesta*, after many years of gloomy obscurantism. The joyful and sensual quality of Mediterranean design merged with the reaction against the strict canons of the modern movement.

The roots of this spectacular expansion of design are to be looked for in the new social prestige of the profession, its links with other branches of artistic culture, and the new needs of industry, which had a vested interest in co-opting designers. The media and advertising also had an important role in creating this new perception. However, the very success of the profession, and the blurring of the distinctions among different modes of artistic expression, were to create tensions in the 1990s. Though Javier Mariscal, in collaboration with Fernando Salas, had designed the popular 'Duplex' stool for a bar in Valencia, he was known only as a comic-strip artist. At the first show organized by the Memphis Group (Milan), he collaborated with Pepe Cortés to present the 'Colón' coffee table and the 'Hilton' trolley. His collection *Muebles Amorales* (Amoral Furniture) was displayed in the Sala Vinçon, Barcelona. Many of these designers do not think of themselves as industrial designers, but as creative artists, sculptors of shapes, or draughtsmen of items of furniture.

There is a risk that the volume of Catalan design will result in the undervaluing of design in other parts of Spain, though in the 1990s the work of Iosu Rada, Carlos Lalastra and Miguel Angel Ciganda in the Basque country make this less likely. Valencia shows considerable vitality, with Vicent Martínez, Pedro Miralles and the La Nave group playing a leading role. Andalusia has fewer professionals than Barcelona or Valencia because of its lower level of industrial development, but a large amount of creative work is being done by people linked to the plastic arts or to architecture: Diego Santos and Julio Juste, who head the City and Design group, the painter Guillermo Pérez Villalta and the painter, architect and sculptor José Ramón Sierra.

If the 1980s were characterized by rapid growth and a certain element of overvaluing of design, the task of the 1990s is to complete the process of convincing public and private institutions, and, above all, industry, that design is an indispensable necessity.

Further reading

Diseño España. Europalia 85 (1985) Madrid (catalogue of this important exhibition).

'25 años de diseño gráfico español' (1996) *Experimenta* 13–14.

ADP (1989) *Plural Design*, Barcelona: Ediciones del Serbal.

Arias, J. (1996) *Maestros del diseño español*, Madrid: Experimental.

Capella, J. and Larrea, Q. (1991) *Nuevo diseño español*, Barcelona: Gustau Gili.

Dent Coad, E. (1990) *Spanish Design and Architecture*, London: Studio Vista.

—— (1995), 'Designer Culture in the 1980s: The Price of Success', in H. Graham and J. Labanyi (eds) *Spanish Cultural Studies, an Introduction: The Struggle for Modernity*, Oxford: Oxford University Press, pp. 376–80 (a very useful brief introduction to the designer boom).

AURORA FERNÁNDEZ POLANCO

detective fiction

Spain had no significant indigenous tradition of detective fiction until the 1970s. Though stories of crime were popular in the nineteenth century, these usually appealed to sensationalism, and lacked the key elements of the detective novel. There is no equivalent of the classic British model represented by Sherlock Holmes, the brilliant amateur who solves difficult cases with an elegance which makes the police appear slow-witted. Nor is there any direct impact in the 1930s and 1940s of the American 'hard-boiled' genre, in which the private eye is the lone defender of integrity in a society seen as overwhelmingly impersonal and corrupt.

The **censorship** practised during the Franco regime was inimical to both these models. Cynicism about the inherent benevolence of the state, or the portrayal of large-scale crime or corruption were officially discouraged, and there was no question of showing the police as incapable of clearing up cases. Nevertheless, several forces for change were at work. One was the influence, beginning in the 1950s, of Italian neo-realist cinema, with its unsentimental portrayal of human behaviour. American detective novels like those of Dashiell Hammett and Raymond Chandler were turned into films in the 1940s and 1950s, which became something of a cult among French intellectuals, who in turn influenced a younger generation of writers in Spain.

Given the climate of censorship, it was somewhat less risky to write detective fiction on the British model, with its predominant emphasis on problem-solving, and this inspired some of the earliest attempts in Spain. In 1953, Francisco García Pavón won a prize for a short story, the protagonist of which was a rural detective, nicknamed Plinio. García Pavón later expanded the idea into a series of novels published between 1965 and 1975. Prior to this, Rafael Tasis had published in Catalan his Superintendent Vilagut trilogy, *La Bíblia valenciana* (The Valencian Bible) (1955), *És hora de plegar* (Time to Pack It In) (1956), and *Un crim al Paral·lel* (Murder on the Parallel) (1960). There were also early examples of American-style fiction by Manuel de **Pedrolo**, who had not only translated Chandler, Hammett and other authors of the 1930s, but had worked as a private detective, and had direct experience of the underbelly of Barcelona society. In 1954, he published *Es vessa una sang fàcil* (Easy Blood is Spilt), and *L'inspector fa tard* (The Inspector is Late).

When censorship was relaxed after 1975, there was a receptive readership for translations of detective fiction in English, and new Spanish writing in the genre often acknowledged the influence of American novels and films. For example, the Gálvez novels of Jorge Martínez Reverte contain references to Chandler and to Robert Mitchum, who played the private eye Philip Marlowe in a film version of Chandler's *The Big Sleep*. It would be a mistake, however, to conclude that Spanish detective novels were derivative, for the political and cultural situation after 1975 had some special characteristics. Manuel **Vázquez Montalbán** was one of several writers of detective novels who began their careers as journalists in the 1960s, thereby acquiring an informed and critical view of the workings of society. Julio Gálvez, for example, the protagonist of novels by Jorge Martínez Reverte, is not strictly a detective but an investigative reporter. The novels in which he appears, though written in the late 1970s and early 1980s, contain scarcely-veiled references to corruption cases and political events during the Franco period. The Serpico property investment company in *Demasiado para Gálvez* (Too Much for Gálvez) (1979) recalls the real-life Sofico, which collapsed in 1974, causing thousands of investors to lose their savings. *Gálvez en Euskadi* (Gálvez in Euskadi) shows the protagonist undergoing a learning process when his assignment forces him to get to know **ETA** from the inside.

This political dimension to the post-Franco detective novel finds one of its most characteristic expressions in the work of Manuel Vázquez Montalbán. As a left-wing activist, he had looked forward to a radical change in the structure of Spanish society following the disappearance of the dictatorship. His disillusionment with the materialism of post-Franco society is portrayed through the cynical detachment of his protagonist, the Galician detective, Pepe Carvalho. A typical example is the sardonic analysis of the internal tensions of the Communist Party in *Asesinato en el Comité Central* (Murder in the Central Committee) (1981) by Carvalho, here portrayed as an ex-member of the party, which in turn reflects Vázquez Montalbán's own ambivalent relationship with the Catalan Communist Party.

Vázquez Montalbán and Eduardo **Mendoza** have not only made distinguished contributions to the boom in the detective novel, but have developed the possibilities of the genre in original ways. Both have wide literary experience, which enables them to engage in self-conscious and often humorous reflection on the activity of writing. Vázquez Montalbán's *Los mares del sur* (South Seas) (1979) contains a scene in which Carvalho blunders into a university seminar on the thriller, and in another part of the novel, there is an encounter with a living literary critic, Sergio Beser. Two of Mendoza's novels, *El misterio de la cripta embrujada* (The Mystery of the Enchanted Crypt) (1979) and *El laberinto de las aceitunas* (The Labyrinth of Olives) (1982), are constructed as deliberate parodies of the detective genre. The protagonist is an inmate of an asylum, who is released from time to time, to help the police solve cases that they cannot clear up. The fact that once he has exhausted his usefulness he is returned to captivity without a word of thanks is the kind of cynical comment on contemporary society which has become one of the distinctive features of the detective novel in Spain.

See also: Francoist culture; kiosk literature; novel; publishing; readership

Further reading

Hart, P. (1987a) *The Spanish Sleuth: The Detective in Spanish Fiction*, London and Toronto: The Associated University Press (the standard study in English).

—— (1987b), 'An Introduction to the Spanish Sleuth', *Monographic Review/Revista Monográfica* 3,2: 163–181 (a compact and clear summary of the previous study).

Rix. R. (ed.) (1992) *Thrillers in the Transition: Novela negra and political change in Spain*, Leeds: Trinity and All Saints' College (a very useful collection of papers on different aspects of the genre).

EAMONN RODGERS

Diada de Catalunya

This is the name given to the Catalan national day, which marks not a joyous event but the beginning of one of the blackest periods in Catalan history. Following Barcelona's surrender to French and Spanish troops on 11 September 1714, Philip V abolished all Catalan political institutions, and imposed Castilian laws, absolutism and centralism. During the twentieth century, the Diada has become a symbol of Catalanism and of defiant resistance to the Spanish state. The first attempt during the Franco era to celebrate the national day came in Barcelona in 1964. In 1977, nearly two years after the death of Franco, over a million people joined a peaceful street demonstration in Barcelona to demand the restoration of Catalan autonomy.

See also: history; regional nationalism; regionalism

DAVID GEORGE

Diari de Barcelona, El

The *Diari de Barcelona* was the penultimate, and unfortunately somewhat short-lived, phase of one of the oldest newspapers in Spain. Its untimely (and to some extent unseemly) demise highlights the serious problems facing Catalan-language publications in Catalonia.

For the bulk of its existence, this paper was in fact known as *El Diario de Barcelona*. It was founded in 1792 and was, as its title suggests, published exclusively in Spanish. This situation continued until 1936, when for a period of two years it was written in Catalan. Following Franco's victory in the Spanish Civil War, it reverted to Spanish as its language of publication, and continued in this vein until 1984, although it occasionally featured articles in Catalan towards the end of this period. In 1984 it disappeared for a period of three years, re-emerging in 1987 as the *Diari de Barcelona*, now using Catalan as its language of publication. Sales during this period were extremely modest, averaging around 25,000 on weekdays and 35,000 on Sundays, and it was only a question of time before it was restructured in some way.

In April 1993 the title *Diari de Barcelona* disappeared, and the newspaper reappeared as part of the newly formed *Nou Diari* group. Local editions of the *Nou Diari* outside Barcelona also replaced a number of smaller Catalan-language newspapers in, for example, Reus, Lleida, Girona and Tarragona.

The *Nou Diari* newspapers were linked in their origins with leading members of the **Catalan Socialist Party**, and in particular with the mayor of Barcelona, Pasqual **Maragall**, and were seen by many as an attempt to provide a Catalan-language daily newspaper for the Catalan left. They therefore combined a linguistic Catalanism with a political *españolismo* (a belief in the unity of Spain), a potentially contradictory stance which they were unable to maintain in the longer term.

The Barcelona edition of the *Nou Diari* folded on 28 January 1994 after a lifespan of less than a year, owing to financial collapse, and amidst bitter recriminations between its then owners, the Dalmau brothers, and its previous owner the National Organization for the Blind – **ONCE** – which had held a 97 percent share in the *Diari de Barcelona* at the time of the original takeover. The Girona edition would subsequently cease on 2 March of the same year, and the Lleida edition on 29 March, though both the Reus and the Tarragona editions have soldiered on.

The collapse of the *Nou Diari* newspapers in Barcelona and elsewhere testifies – as do the relatively poor readership figures of Catalonia's other Catalan-language daily newspaper ***Avui*** – to the continuing problems facing the process of **language normalization** within Catalonia as far as print media are concerned, problems to which there appears to be no immediate solution.

See also: language and national identity; press; press ownership

Further reading

Davies, J. (ed.) (1993) *The Mercator Media Guide,*

Cardiff: University of Wales Press (this guide contains short but informative entries on the main newspapers and television and radio stations in a number of minority languages, including Catalan).

HUGH O'DONNELL

dictionaries and encyclopedias

The 1990s have seen a huge increase in the creation and publication of reference works under the titles of dictionaries, encylopedic dictionaries and encyclopedias.

Perhaps the greatest undertaking is the compilation by the **Royal Academy** of Language, with financial support from the **Ministry of Culture** and Education, of a database of all Spanish words, expected to reach 150 million by the end of 1997. 100 million of these will be those in use during the previous twenty-five years, forming CREA, the *Corpus de Referencia del Español Actual* (Reference Corpus of Contemporary Spanish). These are drawn from a wide variety of written materials and 15 percent from oral/spoken Spanish. The other 50 million will be words no longer current, forming CORDE, the *Corpus Diacrónico del Español* (Historical Corpus of Spanish).

The Academy is the ultimate authority for accepted usage and compiles a *Diccionario de la lengua española* (Dictionary of the Spanish Language). The twenty-first edition since the publication of a *Diccionario de autoridades* (Dictionary of Authorities) by the printing house of Francisco de Hierro in 1726, was published in 1992. In 1995 this edition was also produced in CD-ROM format, structured like the printed version with 83,014 entries, but also with an inverse dictionary and with facilities for conducting searches under a wide range of categories, such as grammatical function and dialectal usage. In 1996 an edition for secondary pupils appeared, the *Diccionario Escolar de la Real Academia*, and a CD-ROM version is planned. A new edition of the standard dictionary was planned for 1998.

Also aimed principally at students of both secondary and university levels is the *Diccionario esencial de la lengua española* (Essential Dictionary of the Spanish Language) published by Santillana in 1991. Drawn from written materials such as official publications and textbooks and especially from the everyday language of the media, the entries include etymologies, examples of usage, current expressions and phrases, synonyms and antonyms, word families, loan words and numerous grammatical notes.

After English, Spanish is the second most popular acquired language and the teaching of Spanish to foreign students has become big business in Spain, especially in Salamanca. In 1996 Santillana, as part of its agreed co-operation with the University of Salamanca in this field, published the *Diccionario Salamanca de la Lengua Española* (the Salamanca Dictionary of Spanish). Concentrating on modern Spanish it includes such elements as grammatical aids, syntax notes, usages and acronyms.

Examples of more specialized types of linguistic dictionary are the *Vocabulario científico y técnico* (A Vocabulary of Scientific and Technical Terms) produced by the Royal Academy of Science and published in 1996 by Espasa-Calpe, and a *Diccionario etimológico indoeuropeo de la lengua española* (Indo-European Etymological Dictionary of Spanish) written by E.A. Roberts and B. Pastor and published by Alianza, which traces the routes by which words have come into Spanish and the relationships between words of the same family.

Dictionaries devoted to topics other than the Spanish language have also become very popular. During 1995 alone, for example, Espasa-Calpe published a dictionary of famous women and a dictionary of nature, Planeta published a series of single-authored *Diccionarios de Autor* (Author's Dictionaries), such as the *Diccionario de Filosofía* by Savater, the *Diccionario de Historia* by Valverde and the *Diccionario de Política* by Tecglen, Alianza published the *Diccionario Oxford de la mente* (Oxford Dictionary of the Mind) and Muchnik published a series of dictionaries dedicated to topics such as jazz, the Bible and cookery.

The same year saw the completion of the first ever *Diccionario Enciclopédico de la Música Española e Hispanoamericana* (Encyclopedic Dictionary of Spanish and Latin American Music) in twenty-two volumes. It is an example of an increasingly popular hybrid of dictionary-type definitions and encyclopedia-type entries devoted either, as here, to a specific topic, or, as in the case of the ten-volume *Diccionario Enciclopédico Santillana* (The Santillana Encyclopedic Dictionary) published in 1991, to general knowledge. A shorter, two-volume example is the *Diccionario Enciclopédico* published by Espasa-Calpe in 1995.

Encylopedias too come in various shapes and sizes, but generally fall into two types, containing information either on all branches of knowledge, or on one specific branch. The most famous example of the first category is the annually updated (since 1934) multi-volume *Enciclopedia universal ilustrada europeo-americana* (Universal Illustrated Euro-American Encyclopedia), published by Espasa-Calpe, which is the Spanish equivalent of the Larousse (France), Treccani (Italy) and Brockhaus (Germany) encyclopedias. Two widely respected examples of the second are the *Enciclopedia de la historia de España* (Encyclopedia of Spanish History) (1988–93), edited by Miguel Artola, and arranged in seven volumes by theme, and the *Enciclopedia del arte español del siglo XX* (Encyclopedia of Spanish Art of the Twentieth Century) (1991–2), edited by Francisco Calvo Serraller and published by Mondadori.

With the expansion of the **publishing** industry, the number of encyclopedias has expanded dramatically. In one year in Madrid alone (1995), fourteen encyclopedias were published, some of them Spanish versions of foreign works, such as the *Women's Encyclopedia of Health and Emotional Healing*, the *Macmillan Illustrated Animal Encyclopedia*, the *Lan Times Encyclopedia of NetWorking*, and a French encyclopedia of religious affairs, *Le Fait religieux*. Spanish-produced encyclopedias also ranged over a wide area, reflecting the diversification of reader demand. There were practical handbooks such as *El cómo del porqué: guía práctica del saber cotidiano: enciclopedia visual* (A Visual Encyclopedia of Everyday Knowledge), and reference works on specialized areas such as the *Enciclopedia de ecología y medio ambiente: preservación de la naturaleza* (Encyclopedia of Ecology and the Environment: The Conservation of Nature), the *Enciclopedia de electrónica moderna: del átomo al microprocesador* (Encyclopedia of Modern Electronics: From the Atom to the Microprocessor), the *Enciclopedia de las plantas medicinales* (Encyclopedia of Medicinal Plants), the three-volume *Enciclopedia iberoamericana de psiquiatría* (Ibero-American Encyclopedia of Psychiatry), and the *Enciclopedia jurídica básica* (Basic Encyclopedia of Law).

See also: education and research; readership

EAMONN RODGERS

Diego, Gerardo

b. 1896, Santander; d. 1987, Madrid

Writer

Gerardo Diego is an enigma within the context of contemporary Spanish poetry. Although well-respected and widely read, his work has received scant critical attention. A member of the famed 'Generation of 1927', Diego is perhaps best known for his role in shaping and promoting the literary movements known as *Creacionismo* and *Ultraísmo.* The passion and vigour with which he pursued these new art forms earned him the title of *enfant terrible* of the Spanish avant-garde. His *Manual de espumas* (Manual of Foam) (1924) and *Versos humanos* (Human Verses) (1925) are widely recognized as two of the most significant contributions to the genre. He would remain the lone standard-bearer of the Creationist movement in Spain after the death of the movement's founder, the Chilean poet Vicente Huidobro, in 1948.

Following the Spanish Civil War, Diego settled in Madrid and quickly became immersed in the social and cultural life of that city. A devoted catholic and political conservative, Diego enjoyed a privileged status under the Franco regime. In 1948 he was elected to membership in the Spanish **Royal Academy** of Language.

The publication of *Angeles de Compostela* (Angels of Compostela) and *Alondra de verdad* (Lark of Truth) in 1940 and 1941, respectively, established Diego as one of the premier poets of the post-war period. *Angeles de Compostela* is a carefully sculpted and polished collection that evokes the spiritual symbolism of the baroque structure that inspired it, the *Pórtico de la Gloria* of the Cathedral of Santiago de Compostela. The poems of *Alondra de verdad* exemplify the harmonious fusion of poetry and music, Diego's two greatest passions. Other collections include *La suerte y la muerte* (Luck and Death) (1963), colourful compositions that evoke the beauty and pageantry of the ***corrida***; *Poesía amorosa* (Love Poetry) (1971), a collection of the poet's love poems written between 1918 and 1969; and *Poesía de creación* (Poetry of Creation) (1974), Diego's Creationist works. The later *Soria sucedida* (Soria Revisited) (1977), *Poemas mayores* (Major Poems) (1980), *Poemas menores* (Minor Poems) (1980), round out a poetic collection which is among the richest in Spanish letters. But Diego is recognized also for his journalistic talents. His articles number hundreds, and range from literary theory to essays on art, music, history and religion.

For his work, Diego has received nearly every major literary prize, including the National Prize for Literature, the Literature Prize of the **Juan March Foundation**, The Grand Cross of Alfonso X and the **Cervantes Prize** for Literature (see also **prizes**).

An inquisitive traveller, astute critic, accomplished pianist, and, above all, a sensitive poet, Gerardo Diego could rightfully be called a man for all seasons. His work, as King Juan Carlos stated when presenting Diego with the Cervantes Prize, adds immortality to us all.

See also: journalism; music; poetry

Further reading

Gallego Morell, A. (1956) *Vida y poesía de Gerardo Diego*, Barcelona: Editorial Aedos (examines the poet's work up to 1950, and includes important biographical information and a good but not conclusive bibliography).

Villar, A. del (1981) *Gerardo Diego*, Madrid: Ministerio de Cultura (the most comprehensive study on the poet to date).

ROBERTO CARLOS MANTEIGA

Domènech i Montaner, Lluis

b. 1850, Barcelona; d. 1923, Barcelona

Architect

Domènech i Montaner was the moving force behind Catalan **Modernism**, which has left such an important architectural heritage in contemporary Catalonia. The enormous influence that he exercised between 1880 and 1910 was due primarily to his work as an architect, but he also participated in the community life of his time as political leader, teacher and stimulator of Catalan cultural life. In his erudition and his forward-looking vision of the development of architecture in Catalonia, he was well ahead of his time. As early as 1878, at the age of 28, he published in the journal *La Renaixansa* the founding text of Catalan Modernism 'In Search of a National Architecture'. The three major themes of Domènech's thinking are: to maintain a creative contact with past traditions in the plastic arts of previous periods, to support technical progress and to invent new global forms which both embrace other artistic disciplines and adapt to changes in society. As Director of the Architecture School of Barcelona from 1901, Domènech was in a strong position to mould future generations of architects in accordance with his principles, and he trained a large number of pupils.

His architectural work developed from an eclectic approach, with a strong *mujédar* (Moorish) influence, exemplified in the head office of the publishing firm Montaner i Simon (1880, Barcelona), towards a purer and more formally adventurous style. The best known of his creations is the Palau de la Musica (Barcelona Concert Hall, 1905–8), situated in the heart of the Gothic quarter of the city. Domènech intended the building, functional in design and innovative in construction, to be a demonstration of the 'fusion of the arts', which made it a symbol of European Art at the dawn of the new century. The best artists and craftsmen of the day came together to decorate it with a great wealth of sculptures, paintings, mosaics, panelling, works in metal and especially glass, the centrepiece being a huge glass sculpture which dominated the recital hall. Domènech's influence is felt to this day, and determines the architectural character of several Catalan towns and cities, where he designed other buildings based on similar aesthetic principles, the most remarkable of them being the Casa Lleó Morera (1903–5, Barcelona), the Casa Navas (1901–7, Reus) and the Gran Hotel of Palma de Mallorca (1902–12). Other creations demonstrate a modern understanding of the problems of town planning: the café-restaurant of the Parc de la Ciutadel·la (1888, Barcelona, now the Museum of Zoology), the *Casa Fuster* (1908, Barcelona) and in particular two large hospitals conceived as independent urban units, the Institut Pere Mata of Reus (1897–1919) and the Hospital de Sant Pau of Barcelona (1902–12).

See also: architects; architecture

Further reading

Loyer, F. (1991) *L'art nouveau en Catalogne*, Paris: Biblio. Arts, Le Septième Fou.

Moldoveanu, M. (1996) *Barcelona: Architectures of Exuberance*, Barcelona: Lunwerg (an overview of different periods and styles, richly illustrated with photographs by the author).

MIHAIL MOLDOVEANU

Domingo, Plácido

b. 1941, Madrid

Tenor

Plácido Domingo began his singing career in Mexico where his family lived from 1950, appearing in ***zarzuelas*** and then in opera in 1961. That was also the year in which he made his début in the USA as Arturo in a performance of Donizetti's *Lucia di Lammermoor* in Dallas. He sang with the Israeli National Opera from 1962 to 1965 and in that year made his New York début as Pinkerton in Puccini's *Madam Butterfly* at the City Opera. Three years later he appeared for the first time at the Metropolitan as Maurizio in Cilea's *Adriana Lecouvreur*, the next year at La Scala, Milan, in the title role of Verdi's *Ernani* and two years after that at Covent Garden as Cavaradossi in Puccini's *Tosca*. During his career he has mastered a very wide-ranging repertory, has conducted operas – his first being a production of Verdi's *Attila* in Barcelona in 1973 – has made recordings and played Verdi's Otello, a role for which he became especially noted, in the Zeffirelli film, and has appeared before huge audiences as one of the 'Three Tenors' performing in concert. His autobiography, *My First Forty Years*, was published in New York in 1983.

Further reading

Snowman, D. (1985) *The World of Plácido Domingo*, New York: McGraw-Hill.

EAMONN RODGERS

'DOMINGUÍN' *see* González Lucas, Luis Miguel

Drove, Antonio

b. 1942, Madrid

Filmmaker

A graduate of the Escuela Oficial de Cinematografía (Official Film School), Drove directed his first medium length film in 1969, *¿Qué se puede hacer con una chica?* (What Can You Do With a Girl?). His most important films are *Tocata y fuga de Lolita* (Lolita's Toccata and Fugue) (his first full length in 1974), *Nosotros que fuimos tan felices* (We Who Were So Happy) (1976), *La verdad sobre el caso Savolta* (The Truth about the Savolta Case) (1980), a political film which made little impact in Spain and *El túnel* (The Tunnel) (1987). He has also written for the screen and directed productions for Spanish television. He is the founder of *Griffith* magazine.

EAMONN RODGERS

drug problem

The relatively indulgent approach of the Spanish authorities to drug-taking resulted in a massively increased consumption in the 1980s. Although drug trafficking has always been illegal, public consumption was not made so until 1992, while private consumption remains perfectly legal. Evidence of drug-taking is to be seen virtually everywhere in the larger cities in the form of addicts in parks and doorways, pushers in streets and bars, and discarded syringes and needles openly visible in public places. One direct result of the spectacular growth in drug-taking via intravenous injection has been the equally spectacular increase in **AIDS**, with about two-thirds of HIV-positive cases being drug addicts. Heroin has been responsible for the deaths of some 700 people a year out of an estimated addicted population of 80,000, i.e. two addicts per thousand inhabitants. This tends to be the drug of marginalized youth and is strongly associated with urban crime and delinquency. However, in the 1990s while the consumption of heroin began to decline, that of cocaine rose. As many as one in ten Spaniards have tried cocaine and over half a million consume it regularly. Crack, the synthetic form of cocaine, has not gained as wide an acceptance among drug takers. The so-called soft drugs, cannabis, LSD, Ecstasy and amphetamines are also in widespread use among young people. The government has conducted lacklustre publicity campaigns warning of the dangers of addiction and, more positively, has set up treatment centres. In the late 1990s there were forty-seven hospitals with drug addiction units, 411 special outpatient departments, 147 methadone treatment clinics, ninety-one group therapy centres, and twenty-one other day centres. Nevertheless, the ease with which drugs can be smuggled into Spain makes control of the problem doubly difficult. The two major points of entry are the southern ports, because of the intense traffic with Morocco, and Galicia in the northwest, whose many coastal inlets makes effective vigilance a virtual impossibility. It is well known that this previously backward northern part of Spain has witnessed an economic boom as a result of money-laundering activities derived from drug profits.

See also: social attitudes; youth culture

Further reading

Hooper, J. (1995) *The New Spaniards*, Harmondsworth: Penguin (chapter 14 gives a clear and reliable account of the drug problem in the context of other social changes).

C.A. LONGHURST

dubbing

The compulsory dubbing of foreign films into Spanish was introduced in 1941, and provided the **censorship** apparatus of the Franco regime with an additional means of controlling the content of films by manipulating the dialogue. References to the Civil War were excised from the soundtrack of *Casablanca* (1942), and in other films, lovers were converted into spouses, and passionate declarations into lofty spiritual reflections.

There was also an economic aspect to dubbing, for the removal of the linguistic barrier made it difficult for the Spanish film industry to compete against foreign productions. In 1943, the state introduced incentives for Spanish producers, in the form of licences to import and dub foreign films. Spanish distributors and those involved in dubbing were also protected by the automatic banning of any foreign film dubbed into Spanish prior to importation. The granting of dubbing permits, however, had the unexpected side-effect of creating a lucrative black market in resold licences, resulting in the drafting of new protectionist measures in 1952.

By the early 1960s, however, the opening up of the economy to international trade, and the development of tourism, produced a slight relaxation in the restrictions on foreign-language films, and some films were being shown in major cities in their original versions. This did not, however, prevent references to the economic importance of the tourist industry being cut from the Spanish soundtrack of Jaime **Camino**'s *España otra vez* (*Spain Again*) (1967). In 1966, Francesco Rosi, the Italian director of an Italo-Spanish co-production, *El momento de la verdad* (The Moment of Truth) (1965), publicly dissociated himself from the film, because the original Spanish soundtrack had been changed without consultation. Nor were soundtracks in other languages immune from interference, as was shown in the case of Bernardo Bertolucci's *Prima della rivoluzione* (Before the Revolution) (1964), where a phrase in the Italian dialogue referring to Franco, which would not have been understood by a significant proportion of the audience, was cut. Furthermore, translations of parts of the soundtrack in the subtitles were either omitted or distorted. Even as late as the beginning of the 1970s, the habit of providing a 'correct' interpretation of the ending by means of a voice-over commentary had not disappeared, as occurred with Sam Peckinpah's *The Getaway*, where it is made clear that the fugitive bandits received their just deserts.

Though censorship lapsed after the death of Franco, the charging of fees to importers and distributors of foreign films continued to provide much-needed income to support subsidies to the Spanish film industry, though these were less necessary as the industry recovered in the late 1990s.

See also: cinema law; film and cinema; Francoist culture; Salamanca Conversations

Further reading

Gubern, R. (1981) *La censura: función política y ordenamiento jurídico bajo el franquismo (1936–1975)*, Barcelona: Ediciones Península (the most thorough study of the legal framework of censorship and its practical operation).

Hooper, J. (1995) *The New Spaniards*, Harmondsworth: Penguin (chapter 23 offers an excellent overview of the cultural politics of Francoism).

EAMONN RODGERS

Dúo Dinámico, El

El Dúo Dinámico, formed in Barcelona by Ramón Arcusa and Manuel de la Calva, was one of the first groups to experiment with rock music sung in Spanish towards the end of the 1950s. At first their songs were versions of songs by Paul Anka, Neil Sedaka or Ricky Nelson, but they soon began to compose their own material which gave them hit singles like the evergreen '*Quince años tiene mi amor*' (My Love is Fifteen Years Old) (c. 1960). Their success continued until the mid-1960s, after which they worked as producers and composers for other important artists (e.g. Julio **Iglesias**). The Dúo's records are frequently re-released and they recorded a new album in 1986, sixteen years after retiring officially from the stage.

See also: music; rock and pop

MIGUEL JIMÉNEZ PINILLA

Duque, Aquilino

b. 1931, Seville

Writer

Cosmopolitan poet, novelist and translator who studied in Cambridge and worked in Italy for the United Nations, Duque began publishing poetry collections with *De palabra en palabra* (From Word to Word) (1967), winning the 1968 Leopoldo Panero Poetry Prize. Two novels, *La operación Marabu* (Operation Marabu) (1966) and *Los consulados del más allá* (Consulates of the World Beyond) (1966) preceded the brief fiction collection, *La rueda de fuego* (Wheel of Fire) (1971), winner of the 1970 Washington Irving Prize. Long novels, *La linterna mágica* (The Magic Lantern) (1971) and *El mono azul* (Blue Coverall) (1973), received more attention, but Duque's forte is the short story.

JANET PÉREZ

E

economy

The Spanish economy is a modern western-style economy based principally on the services sector, which generates just over 60 percent of the country's wealth, compared to about one-third generated by industry and construction combined, and about 5 percent by agriculture and fisheries. GDP per capita, estimated at $13,660 in 1996, has oscillated between 75 and 80 percent of the EU average. Regional imbalances are, however, more marked in Spain than in other EU countries, with a few regions (the Balearics, Madrid and Catalonia) being above the EU average whereas many others are far below. While the Spanish economy shares many characteristics with other western European economies, it offers certain moderately distinctive features. The **services** sector, despite a normal diversity and range of activities, is unusually reliant on the hotel and catering industry because of the exceptional importance of **tourism**. The industrial sector, of modest size overall, is dominated by **motor manufacture**, and the sector as a whole is largely in the hands of foreign multinationals. The **agriculture** and **fisheries** sector is the least typical, with an unusual diversity of cultivation (and a correspondingly large variation in productivity), and an unusually large fishing fleet that almost matches those of all the other EU countries put together. Agricultural development has been adversely affected by traditional **land tenure** systems, with farms that were either excessively large and under-exploited or too small to be economic (see also ***latifundia*; *minifundia***).

The modern Spanish economy has been characterized by rapid change, although it has been only partially successful in adapting to a changing international environment. Following the **Stabilization Plan** of 1959, the 1960s saw rapid and sustained growth up to the first oil shock of 1973, but Spain's dependence on imported oil and her excessive reliance on energy-intensive heavy industry meant that she could not absorb the increased **energy** costs. The state-owned **National Industrial Institute**, which had played the leading role in Spain's industrial expansion, found itself having to subsidize ailing industries to avoid large-scale industrial collapse (see also **industrial development**). The ten-year recession was followed by another period of growth during the second half of the 1980s promoted by a wave of foreign investment, in turn induced by Spain's entry to the EEC in 1986. The need to adapt the economy to European legislation and to a much more competitive environment brought about a massive shake-out, with liberalization, deregulation and privatization becoming the order of the day. Some sectors have undergone substantial transformation, for example the banking and financial services sector, which has seen mergers and takeovers as well as significant foreign penetration in what had been an inward-looking enterprise (see also **banks; Cajas de Ahorros**). State monopolies, for example in oil refining and distribution, have had to be broken up.

The modernization of the Spanish economy has therefore occurred in two wholly distinct stages: first, a period of rapid but uneven expansion during the last fifteen years of the Franco regime when the international climate was favourable; and second, a period of retrenchment, reform and restructuring when the international climate was much harsher. This second stage – which took place largely in the 1980s but which continued into the 1990s – has been difficult, as Spain struggled to modernize her ailing industries, solve her energy problem, control **inflation**, cope with growing **unemployment**, yet at the same time create the welfare state that the population expected and a socialist government wished to provide. That Spain emerged by the second half of the 1990s as a low-inflation, internationally solvent economy, close to fulfilling the Maastricht convergence criteria, is perhaps as much of an 'economic miracle' as that of the 1960s which gave rise to the phrase. The achievements since the near-collapse of the late 1970s have been substantial, especially when we consider the highly protective environment in which the Spanish economy developed even after the partial trade liberalization of Franco's **techno-crats**. The degree of openness of the Spanish economy today is remarkable, even if achieved at the cost of greatly increased foreign ownership of productive assets. Spanish **industry** has had to be scaled down with great job losses, but it is today more competitive than it has ever been. Loss-making state-owned companies have been greatly reduced in number, and some of these have good prospects of a return to profitability, notably the national airline **Iberia**. A gradual transfer of the state's interests in vehicle manufacture, oil and gas, telecommunications, banking, tobacco and electricity to the private sector has been successful both in raising revenue and in maintaining or improving profitability. Investment in the country's infrastructure has been very considerable, especially in the **transport** network, with major improvements to the country's primary road system through the construction of fast dual carriageways to add to existing privately-run toll motorways or ***autopistas*** (see also **roads**), as well as electrification of the **railways** and the development of a new high-speed line or **AVE**. In energy distribution electricity supplies are assured although still heavily reliant on imported oil for power stations; and a natural gas national grid is being developed, although, again, the gas itself has to be imported (see also **nuclear energy**). **Water supplies** are plentiful in years of normal rainfall but dry years cause shortages in the southern half of the country because of the enormous difficulty of transferring water between river systems.

Spain's international trade has also experienced unprecedented growth since it joined the EEC, with a trebling of its value in ten years. Trade with the EU now accounts for 70 percent of Spain's international trade. This is attributable not merely to invisible trade (because of the importance of tourism) but much more significantly to the increase in trade of manufactured goods, Spain having become a major car exporter. In the four years from 1993 to 1996 goods exports went up by an average of 12 percent per annum. In addition to vehicles Spain exports a fairly wide range of manufactured goods, including building materials and fittings, nuclear reactors, machinery of all kinds, and processed foods. Despite the continuing significance of exports of wine, fruit and vegetables, Spain can no longer be regarded as primarily an exporter of agricultural products. Exports of manufactured goods now make a very important contribution to Spain's **balance of payments**, and although imported manufactures are higher, the gap is made up by earnings from tourism (see also **foreign trade**).

Notwithstanding the emergence of Spain as one of the world's economic powers, occupying ninth or tenth place in the ranking, the Spanish economy displays a number of weaknesses and enduring problems. Chief among these is the high rate of unemployment, which at 22 percent in 1996 was the worst in the EU and double the EU average. It is probable that up to one-third of the allegedly unemployed do in fact find work in the '**black economy**', but unemployment nevertheless remains a major blackspot. The rigidity of the Spanish **labour market** has persisted despite partial attempts at dismantling Francoist labour laws, so that an increase in the labour force (the result of the 1960s baby boom and of a much increased demand for jobs on the part of women) has not been met by an equivalent increase in jobs: the number of persons employed has changed very little in twenty years, despite the growth of the economy. The result, inevitably, has been that unemployment has shot up from under half a million in 1974 (just before the first oil crisis had its full impact) to over three million in the 1990s. It is young people who have been hardest hit, and especially those with limited educational qualifications who have little chance of finding permanent employment. Labour market reforms in 1984 and 1994 were meant to encourage employers to take on labour by allowing fixed-term contracts and lowering dismissal costs on economic grounds, but the bureaucratic procedures involved have made employers wary, so that the end result of the new labour legislation has been greater insecurity of employment without a counterbalancing increase in jobs.

Another troublespot is to be found in the heavy burden imposed on the Spanish economy by a generous welfare state and by a burgeoning public administration, the latter being largely the result of the seventeen regional governments creating a whole new tier of bureaucracy. Since the restoration of democracy the number of civil servants has gone up from under 1 million to 1.7 million. At the same time the vast improvements in **health care**, education (see also **education and research**) and **social security** provision have resulted in public expenditure racing ahead of income and increasing the budget deficit (see also **national debt**). Indeed overshooting the budget became a regular feature of the socialist administration that governed Spain from 1982 to 1996 and which showed scant regard for setting realistic targets for government income and expenditure. Controlling expenditure on health and social security is a major challenge. An ageing population, coupled to a low birth rate and an employed population that is stubbornly static, means that the ratio of pensioners to those in work is rising, creating problems in the state financing of pensions. The proportion of social security contributors to pensioners has already worsened from 3 to 1 to 2 to 1 in twenty years and this trend seems likely to continue. The health service is even more of a burden on state expenditure and has experienced rising costs which the government is trying to rein in by reducing the pharmaceuticals bill.

Tax evasion and the underground economy remain areas where progress has been limited. Strict new directives to banking institutions and the introduction of personal identification numbers for fiscal purposes have made money laundering a little more difficult, but the prevalence of a cash economy greatly facilitates the conversion of illegal monies: many legal businesses in Galicia are widely thought to have been set up with profits from drug smuggling. Unemployment fraud is also thought to be high, but the very nature of the black economy with its myriad family and backstreet businesses which appear and disappear with lightning speed and where many find intermittent work, makes it virtually impossible to track down. More harmful is the relative ease with which perhaps two million Spaniards, many of them comparatively affluent self-employed business men and professionals, are able to defraud the tax authorities by not declaring their true income or cheating on VAT (see also **taxation**). This fraud by the better-off ultimately results in higher tax bills for those who, being on a payroll, have tax deducted at source.

A further area of concern for the Spanish economy is that of geographical inequalities of wealth, a long-standing problem that had shown some modest signs of improvement but which the new emphasis on devolved regional tax-raising powers will make far more difficult to tackle from the centre. The poorest regions and provinces lag far behind the wealthiest ones, and only strong redistributive policies, transferring resources from the latter to the former (through investment and tax incentives as well as direct subsidies) could hope to narrow the gap. The political situation of the 1990s, in which renegotiation of regional financing became the price of support of the government by Basque and Catalan nationalists, as well as the need for reduced central government spending, made it difficult to implement policies of this kind (see also **national income**).

Despite these various problems, none of which can be solved in the short term, the Spanish economy is in better shape – unemployment apart – than it has been since 1973. The internationalization phase, which has undoubtedly cost jobs, is more or less over and the economy has emerged strengthened. Labour costs remain on the high side but are moderating, while the budget deficit is gradually being reduced although public sector debt remains high and servicing it is costly. Within the **European Union**, the Spanish economy is a medium-size economy which has profited from membership through increased trade, a high measure of foreign investment, and aid from the EU's structural funds. A strong foreign presence in the economy makes it susceptible to decisions taken in distant multinational headquarters, but this is a modern-day inconvenience that applies to many other economies, including the British. Spanish business culture is not accustomed to operating in a highly competitive international environment, but developments, for example in banking or in the hotel industry, suggest that a more enterprising outlook is beginning to emerge (see also **Caixa, La**). Spain also continues to derive considerable benefit from a tourist sector which, despite previous gloomy prophecies of environmental disaster and tourist desertions, remains vibrant. Most Spaniards enjoy a **standard of living** comparable to that of the British and a quality of life that many consider to be higher. With the fourth highest life expectancy in the world, high educational indices, and a respectable per capita income, the 1996 UN ranking of human development accorded Spain tenth place out of 174 countries, the fifth of the fifteen EU countries and ahead of Germany, Italy, and Britain.

Further reading

Chislett, W. (1996, 1997) *Spain 1996. The Central Hispano Handbook* and *Spain 1997. The Central Hispano Handbook*, Madrid: Banco Central Hispano (by far the best yearly survey of economic developments in Spain: lucid, accessible and informative).

Newton, M.T. with Donaghy, P.J. (1997) *Institutions of Modern Spain. A Political and Economic Guide*, 2nd edn, Cambridge: Cambridge University Press (geared to political rather than economic structures but does offer an excellent descriptive summary of public sector enterprises, financial institutions and economic relations with the EU).

Salmon, K. (1995) *The Modern Spanish Economy. Transformation and Integration into Europe*, London: Pinter (the best, most comprehensive general survey of the contemporary Spanish economy and its evolution).

C.A. LONGHURST

education and research

Education has undergone major development in Spain since 1970, when it was first made free and compulsory for all to age 14 with the introduction of **EGB**. In the ten years to 1995, expenditure in absolute terms increased three-fold, rising to 5 percent of GDP. While significant, however, this expansion began from a low base by comparison with other developed countries. By the early 1990s, expenditure per student at primary and secondary levels in the state sector was still only $2,840, as against the OECD average of $4,700. Spending per third-level student was $3,770, compared to an OECD average of $10,030. The combined participation rate for all forms of education stood at 86 percent in the mid-1990s, equal to that of France, and higher than Japan's. Nevertheless, the underdevelopment of previous decades was still having an effect on the general educational level of society. Though a larger proportion of the young population was benefitting from education than in 1970, and adult illiteracy had virtually disappeared, only 25 percent of the population in the age group 25 to 64 had completed secondary education, as against 80 percent in Germany and the US.

The organization of the educational system is a combined activity of national and regional governments. Central government is responsible for the validation of qualifications, syllabuses and progression requirements. The **autonomous communities** with the largest measures of self-government (e.g. Catalonia, the Basque country and Andalusia) enjoy considerable independence in the internal administration of the system within their areas, including universities. Other regions work directly under the control of the central government.

The period since 1970 has been punctuated by several important, and sometimes controversial, legislative measures designed to increase access to education. Despite considerable opposition from the Church, right-wing political interests and middle-class parents, the **LODE** (1984) attempted to create an integrated system by extending state subsidies to private schools, thereby reducing the economic and social barriers between them and the public sector. It stipulated that all schools receiving state subsidies must offer free education, apply the same admission criteria as state schools, observe minimum standards, to be monitored by government inspectors, and establish school councils, on which parents and pupils would be represented. This act increased state control of primary and secondary education, but left untouched the question of quality, widely perceived as deficient. In 1994, a survey of pupils between the ages of 13 and 16 showed that 45 percent saw themselves as deriving little benefit from the education system, owing to the high examination failure rates, and the frequency with which years were repeated.

The **LOGSE** (1990) attempted to address the issue of quality by initiating a series of reforms, due to be phased in fully by the year 2000. The main provisions were the raising of the age of compulsory schooling to 16, the breaking-down of the barrier between academic and vocational education, and the diversification and modernization of the curriculum. The other main effect was the virtual secularization of education. In 1979, classes in ethics were made available to pupils who did not wish to attend religious instruction, which had been compulsory under Franco. In the event, only about 10 percent of primary school pupils and 20–30 percent of secondary pupils availed themselves of these. The LOGSE did away with the ethics classes, leaving religious instruction in a somewhat exposed position as an optional activity, though the conservative **PP** government elected in March 1996 considered reintroducing religion as an academic subject into the core curriculum.

The introduction of greater flexibility in the curriculum as a result of the LOGSE was an attempt to correct the traditional bias of the secondary school system towards academic study. In 1992, only 3 percent of the workforce between the ages of 25 and 64 had received professional training, as against 27 percent in Germany and France. Overall, 80 percent of workers have no professional qualification. The new curriculum allows for the teaching of manual skills as well as management and languages, the latter to begin at age 8. Language learning, indeed, has been one of the most successful developments in the 1990s, with 92 percent of pupils learning a foreign language, predominantly English. Opportunities for language acquisition by adults are provided by a national network of **official language schools**.

The availability of free education does not extend beyond secondary school. When the student goes to university, registration and tuition fees are payable, and there is no comprehensive national system of higher education grants, though scholarships are available for those whose parental income falls below about £15,000 per annum. Fee levels, however, are modest by comparison with Britain and the US, though student organizations have frequently demonstrated in favour of a reduction in fees.

About 1.4 million students nationally are enrolled in higher education, the effect of a rapid expansion which has led to complaints of *masificación* ('massification', or over-expansion). Though over twenty new universities have been founded in Spain since 1970 (about half the total), some of the older institutions are very large by British standards: the Complutense in Madrid, for example, has 130,000 students. Overcrowding in classrooms, lack of contact with teaching staff, and poor facilities have led to student demonstrations and boycotts. There is a clear perception that expansion has not improved the quality of education, though when the government introduced selective examinations for university entrance in the late 1980s, students protested vigorously. Spain, in fact, has the highest drop-out rate in the EU, with only 45 percent of students completing their degrees within the normal time-span, as compared with 90 percent in the UK, and 70 percent in Germany.

Like primary and secondary education, the tertiary sector has been the subject of legislative reform, mainly through the **LRU** (1983), which codified the basis of academic freedom and university autonomy. Universities draw up their own statutes and budgets, and elect their own governing bodies. Within the terms of a national curricular framework, they have a certain freedom to introduce new degree programmes, which are of four years' duration rather than the traditional five. This act, however, made no change in the status of tenured staff, who continue to be classified as civil servants. In common with established staff in state schools, they enter the profession by competitive public examination (*oposiciones*), and can then, subject to merit and length of service, seek to transfer to other institutions within the system.

Although the LRU sought to modernize university curricula and introduce more flexibility, universities still remain dominated by generalists taking traditional degrees. Even allowing for the possibility that the figures may be distorted by the weight of numbers in the older and larger institutions, it is a fact that, in the session 1994–5, law still had 28 percent more students than faculties of economics and business, more than three times as many as languages, and more than six times as many as chemistry. Medicine accounts for fewer than 4 percent of all students in university faculties, while the EU average output of graduates in medicine is 17 percent. Only 17 percent of all students of information technology follow courses in university faculties, but even when one adds to these all the IT students studying in vocationally oriented *escuelas universitarias*, law students still outnumber them four and a half times. A similar pattern may be observed even in the Open University, the **UNED**, where five times as many students study in the general area of law and social sciences as in humanities, and six times as many as in science and engineering combined.

University departments are active in research and publication, and have produced work of high quality in all fields, though most of the internationally recognized contributions to research have been in the humanities. Despite the **exile** of many of the best intellects in the country after the Civil War, fundamental work of great distinction has been done in history (by, for instance, Menéndez Pidal, Artola, **Maravall**, Domínguez Ortiz, **Vicens Vives** and **Fusi**), philosophy and history of philosophy (**Abellán**, **Aranguren**, Elías Díaz and **Marías**), language (Alvar and Lapesa), literature (Mainer and Rico) and sociology (Amando de **Miguel**).

The prominence of the humanities is in part due to past under-investment in **science** and technology, which only began to be made good on a significant scale in the 1980s. Spending on research and development in the decade to 1994 increased from 0.6 percent of GDP to 1 percent, the highest proportional increase in the OECD. In absolute terms, total investment in research has increased five-fold between 1982 and 1994, but as a percentage of GDP, R & D expenditure is still less than half that of the UK, France, Italy and Germany. As in other countries, the bulk of the expansion in research has been in science and technology. Between 1985 and 1994, the number of research scientists and engineers doubled, to 42,000.

Research activity is dispersed over a large number of public and private institutions, of which the most important is the **CSIC**. Private foundations and institutes have also had an important role. For example, the Juan March Institute for Study and Research runs the Centre for Advanced Study in the Social Sciences (CEACS) and the Centre for International Meetings on Biology. CEACS, founded in 1987, and recognized by the Ministry of Education, carries out postgraduate teaching and research, specializing in comparative studies in European politics, economics and sociology. It awards its own Masters degrees and prepares students for doctoral qualifications validated by one of the state universities.

By the early 1980s, the government became convinced of the need to focus research effort and implement a national strategy. The Science Law of 1986 provided for an institutional framework to coordinate the activities of the universities, CSIC, the National Industrial Institute and a large number of other bodies dependent on the Ministries of Agriculture, Industry, and Defence. A National Research Plan was drawn up, to be overseen by an interdepartmental Science and Technology Committee. Beginning in 1988, various stages of the plan have been implemented, including investment, training, evaluation, and integration with international programmes under European Union auspices.

See also: intellectual life; universities; university education

Further reading

Alted, A. (1995), 'Educational Policy in Democratic Spain', in H. Graham and J. Labanyi (eds) *Spanish Cultural Studies, an Introduction: The Struggle for Modernity*, Oxford: Oxford University Press, pp. 320–5 (an excellent overview of the changes in educational structure and policy since 1970).

Chislett, W. (1996), *Spain 1996: The Central Hispano Handbook*, Madrid: Central Hispano, pp. 32–5 (a brief but clear summary, illustrated with useful graphs).

Spain 1995 (1995) Madrid: government publication, pp. 347–81 (a useful overview of education and research policy).

EAMONN RODGERS

EGB

Basic General Education (Educación General Básica – EGB) emerged from the enactment of the Education Law of 1970. It embraced what had previously been primary education and the first cycle of secondary school. It established free compulsory education until age 13, and its avowed intention was to provide a comprehensive, egalitarian education, which would develop the individual pupil's capacity for reflexion, observation and imagination. Successful completion of the eight-year programme led to the award of the *Graduado Escolar* (School Graduate) certificate, which qualified the pupil to proceed to secondary school and continue studies up to the level of **BUP**. Those who did not receive this qualification obtained a *Certificado de Escolaridad* (School Attendance Certificate), which allowed them to proceed to **FP**.

EGB was originally divided into two phases, from 6 to 10 years, and from 11 to 13. In the 1970s, the syllabus was modified by the introduction of 'ethical and civic education' as an alternative to religion, and English as an alternative to French. In their respective regions, **Catalan**, **Basque** and **Galician** were introduced. By the early 1980s, it became obvious that the rapid changes which the country had experienced necessitated further reforms, and in 1981 the **UCD** government replaced the two-stage curriculum with a three-stage one. The initial cycle included the first two years, the intermediate cycle years three to five, and the higher cycle years six to eight. In accordance with the articles on education in the **constitution of 1978**, minimum requirements for the initial cycle were laid down. The object was to guarantee a common cultural foundation to all Spanish children, though there was provision for this to be extended and diversified in the various **autonomous communities**.

Pupils' progress was monitored by a combination of continuous assessment and examinations, and all subjects in a cycle had to be passed before proceeding to the next stage. In 1983 the **PSOE** government introduced remedial education to control the high failure rate, especially among the economically and geographically disadvantaged.

Towards the end of 1990 new reforming legislation was introduced, the **LOGSE**, with the intention of restructuring the entire educational system. It began to be implemented in stages in 1991, and EGB was phased out by 1997.

See also: education and research; language and education; language normalization; nursery education

Further reading

Alted, A. (1995), 'Educational Policy in Democratic Spain', in H. Graham and J. Labanyi (eds) *Spanish Cultural Studies, an Introduction: The Struggle for Modernity*, Oxford: Oxford University Press, pp. 320–5 (an excellent overview of the changes in educational structure and policy since 1970).

Chislett, W. (1996), *Spain 1996: The Central Hispano Handbook*, Madrid: Central Hispano, pp. 32–5 (a brief but clear summary, illustrated with useful graphs).

ISIDRO FADRIQUE

Egin

The title of this ultra-nationalist and left-wing newspaper comes from a **Basque** word meaning 'to do'. The paper has often been accused of acting as a mouthpiece for the terrorist organization **ETA**. It contains sections on regional politics, economic affairs, news from what it calls 'the Spanish state', international news, sport and culture. The bulk of the material is written in Spanish, apart from the Basque titles of the sections, and a few items in Basque.

During the transition to democracy after the ending of the Franco dictatorship in 1975, *Egin* tried to project itself as the voice of the *abertzale* (nationalist) left, and some of its editorials came out against violence as a means of achieving political freedom for the region. This commitment to peaceful means, however, was short-lived, since it soon became clear that ETA regarded itself as at war, not solely with Francoism, but with the Spanish state which, in their view, was unlawfully occupying and oppressing **Euskadi**.

In the 1980s, the **Herri Batasuna** coalition, regarded as the political wing of ETA, gained control of the paper. The editorial line in the 1990s is determined by KAS (Koordinadora Abertzale Sozialista – Socialist Patriotic Co-ordinating Committee), the umbrella organization to which ETA belongs, and which many people, including certain nationalist leaders, suspect of singling out individuals who later become ETA targets. To be named in hostile terms in *Egin* is guaranteed to inspire fear.

The presentation of ETA actions in the pages of *Egin*, even when these are indiscriminate, pay little attention to the consequences for the victims and their families, but instead emphasize that such operations are a response to state violence against the Basque people. Nevertheless, the authorities have not been able to take effective action against *Egin*, since courts have ultimately asserted the principle of freedom of expression.

CARLOS ÁLVAREZ ARAGÜÉS

elections

After the long dictatorship of Franco, the elections of 1977 successfully established a democratic regime in which the ballot box served its usual functions of government control, parliamentary representation, and political legitimation. Since then, elections have been held at regular intervals to elect the bi-cameral **parliament**, formed by the 350 members of the Congress of Deputies and the approximately 200 members of the Senate. These are regarded as the most important, and have the highest electoral turnout. Elections are also held for the parliaments of the seventeen **autonomous communities**, the 8,000 municipal councils, and the Spanish seats in the European Parliament.

The general elections held since 1977 display three distinct phases. The first, extending from 1977 to 1982, and including the general election of 1979, was characterized by a moderate pluralist party system, and minority government by the centre-right **UCD** led by Adolfo **Suárez**, which steered through the transition to democracy. Facing them was a fragmented opposition, dominated by Felipe **González**'s socialist **PSOE**. The second phase (1982–93) dates from the extraordinary electoral result of October 1982, when with the collapse of UCD the PSOE was able to win an absolute majority, and become the dominant party. The PSOE went on to win the next two elections, maintaining a considerable lead in terms of both votes and seats over the **Popular Alliance**, the staunchly conservative party led by Manuel **Fraga**. The 1993 elections brought the socialist supremacy to an end, though González, by then the longest-serving Prime Minister in Spanish history, was still able to form a minority PSOE government. However, greater competition on the left between the PSOE and the **United Left**, the coalition centred on the **PCE** led by Julio Anguita, and on the right between the PSOE and the **PP**, paved the way for the political changeover which eventually took place in 1996. For the first time, José María **Aznar**'s PP won an electoral contest, although his minority government depended, as had the PSOE since 1993, on the support of the Catalan and Basque nationalists of, respectively, **CiU** and **PNV**.

Throughout these changes there has been a certain continuity in electoral behaviour. First, electoral and parliamentary fragmentation (that is, the number of significant parties) has remained low. Despite the presence of numerous nationalist and **regional parties** in parliament, the two main **political parties** have generally won over 70 percent of the vote and more than 80 percent of the seats. Second, the ideological polarization between the principal parties has been relatively limited. The majority of voters have opted for centre-right or centre-left parties; the extremist parties (with the exception of **Herri Batasuna** in **Euskadi**) are insignificant. Finally, electoral volatility (that is, changes in voting choices in successive elections) has shown some unusual features. It was relatively low in the first elections (1977 and 1979) and exceptionally high in 1982, when more than 40 percent of citizens changed parties in what is considered to have been one of the biggest swings in European electoral history. Since then, however, swings have remained within narrow limits, comparable to those found in the most stable European party systems.

In the light of the various general elections held since 1977, Spaniards' electoral behaviour can be described as stable, and the overall framework of the party system has been institutionalized. The principal characteristics of electoral behaviour are (i) the weakness of party identification, amongst the lowest in Europe; (ii) the virtual absence of social or political organizations serving to anchor votes; (iii) the limited role of class conflict, due to the typically catch-all strategies adopted by all the parties; (iv) the even weaker impact of the religious cleavage, in the wake of an intense process of secularization; (v) the extraordinary importance, by contrast, of the regional cleavage in some autonomous communities, especially the Basque country, Catalonia, and Navarre; and (vi) despite the absence of sharp polarization between the two main parties, the decisive importance of ideological preferences between left and right, which are stronger than party loyalties.

The proportional system used for elections to the Congress of Deputies is sometimes described as a 'strong' system because of its capacity to restrict voter behaviour and exert a restraining influence on parties. The combination of the highly uneven distribution of seats in thinly populated provincial districts, its small magnitude (the majority have six seats or fewer), and the use of the D'Hondt 'additional member' formula, have favoured the emergence of strong majority parties. Any imbalances in the system have been compensated for by its capacity to produce governability, reduce parliamentary fragmentation, contribute to stability, respect party pluralism, and foster political integration, in a situation characterized by profound territorial differences.

See also: political parties; politics; regional nationalism; regional parties

Further reading

Del Castillo, P. (ed.) (1994) *Comportamiento político y electoral*, Madrid: Centro de Investigaciones Sociológicas (a thorough and useful symposium volume on Spanish elections and electoral behaviour).

Gunther, R., Sani, G. and Shabad, G. (1986) *Spain after Franco: The Making of a Competitive Party System*, Berkeley, CA: University of California Press (an excellent and well-documented account of the 1977 and 1979 elections).

Linz, J.J. and Montero, J.R. (eds) (1986) *Crisis y cambio: electores y partidos en la España de los años ochenta*, Madrid: Centro de Estudios Constitucionales (a very detailed analysis of the 1982 elections and their consequences).

JOSÉ RAMÓN MONTERO

energy

The grave repercussions which the oil-shock of 1973 had on the Spanish economy (repeated in the early 1980s) eventually persuaded the government to introduce an energy plan in order to reduce the country's dependence on imported oil. Despite an oil-substitution policy Spain still depends on oil for over 50 percent of its primary energy needs (or two-thirds of final energy consumption). Increasing use is being made of natural gas (replacing town gas), although this also has to be imported, mostly from Algeria. Just under 20 percent of the primary energy consumption is derived from coal, but Spanish coal is both expensive to mine and highly polluting. Four-fifths of the coal mined is directly consumed by the steel and cement industries. Nuclear power accounts for a little over 15 percent of primary energy consumption (see also **nuclear energy**), while hydraulic power and wind-generated power together account for some 5 percent. In terms of electricity production (as distinct from primary energy consumption), thermal electricity (from coal, oil and gas-fired power stations) accounts for almost half of all electricity generated, nuclear for just over one-third, hydroelectricity for about 15 percent, and other renewable resources for less than 2 percent. Because of rainfall variations, hydraulically produced electricity can undergo wide fluctuations. The fourth National Energy Plan, 1991–2000, seeks an improvement in energy savings, a diversification of supplies, better use of domestic (including renewable) resources, and improved environmental protection. Dependence on external energy sources has not changed, nor is likely to change, very significantly.

The electricity supply industry is dominated by two very large companies, Endesa and Iberdrola, each of which consists of a number of regional subsidiaries. There are in addition a number of smaller independent companies, while the high tension national grid is run by Redesa. The main gas supply company is Gas Natural, which supplies 90 percent of the market, while the distribution of oil products is dominated by Repsol, now under increasing competition from BP, Elf, Shell and other foreign multinationals.

See also: industrial development; industry

Further reading

Salmon, K. (1995) *The Modern Spanish Economy. Transformation and Integration into Europe*, London: Pinter (chapter 5 offers a full account of the energy sector).

C.A. LONGHURST

Enrique y Tarancón, Vicente

b. 1907, Burriana (Castellón, Valencia); d. 1994 Villarreal (Valencia)

Cardinal Archbishop

The outstanding contribution to Spain's modern history made by Cardinal Tarancón was in seeking to reconcile a society whose Civil War divide between victors and vanquished remained unhealed, as he steered a reactionary Spanish Church into the more progressive Catholicism of the Second Vatican Council, into disengagement from Francoism, and into easing the country's passage from dictatorship to democracy.

From his personal experiences as a young priest in the Second Republic, in the Civil War and its aftermath, and as Bishop of Solsona (1945–64) and subsequently Archbishop of Oviedo (1964–9), Tarancón acquired a robust social conscience and political awareness. Pope Paul VI (1963–78), who wanted a strong man in position to lead the Spanish Church in the twilight of Francoism and in the post-Franco era, appointed him in 1969 Archbishop of Toledo and Primate of Spain, and two months later gave him his cardinal's hat. In 1971 Tarancón was translated to the key post of Archbishop of Madrid and elected President of the Spanish Bishops' Conference. In this capacity he used his considerable diplomatic skills over the next ten years to keep the Spanish Church at the 'extreme centre' of Catholicism and of national politics.

The Cardinal had to disengage the institutional church from its close alliance with the Franco regime, which brought him into conflict not only with the Spanish government but also with right-wing bishops, priests and laity. When he officiated at the funeral service for Admiral **Carrero Blanco** in 1973, he was met with shouts of 'Tarancón to the firing squad'. In March 1974 he was ready to excommunicate the government if it carried out its threat to expel Monsignor Antonio **Añoveros** of Bilbao. Yet, although relations with the Franco regime were tense, they were never broken: Tarancón was ever a man of dialogue and moderation, in a style which came to be known as 'taranconismo'.

Preaching during the Mass marking the accession of King **Juan Carlos I** on 27 November 1975, Tarancón called for a democratic programme for the nation, and mutual independence in Church–State relations. Aware that Spain was now pluralist and increasingly secularized, he ensured that there would be no church-endorsed 'Catholic' political parties, though his preference was for those that were imbued with 'Christian humanism'. When issues arose such as the definition by the 1978 constitution of the church's future role in society, or the introduction of divorce, or church schools and religious education in schools, his defence of church demands was firm but never confrontational: in this he carried most of the hierarchy with him, to the chagrin of the 'maximalist' bishops.

Having enjoyed the support of Paul VI, Tarancón incurred the displeasure of Pope John Paul II (1978–) through his perceived failure to fight more tenaciously for what the Vatican saw as the church's 'rights' in the constitution and in the 1979 Partial Agreements between Spain and the Holy See. On his retirement in 1983 he retained his independent openness of spirit regarding both intra-ecclesial and national affairs, a major concern being the need for positive ethical values in democracy.

See also: church and state; National Catholicism; religion

AUDREY BRASSLOFF

environment

Unlike most of Europe, Spain has retained an extraordinarily rich natural environment, owing to geographical and historical factors. A crossroads between Atlantic and Mediterranean, Europe and Africa, it is a region where historical, cultural and sociological diversity has shaped the landscape almost as much as geographical location. One of the first countries to designate National Parks, Spain has, however, failed to ensure that some of Europe's most important habitats are adequately protected. Though there is no shortage of protective legislation, administration has been inadequate, leading to patchy enforcement.

In the rush to develop economically during the 'Spanish Miracle' of the 1960s and 1970s, scant attention was paid to the environment, so pollution and habitat destruction harmed many areas of great ecological value. New threats have appeared – especially since Spain joined the **European Union** – although advances have been made in protection, mainly through pressures from non-governmental agencies.

Habitats

Spain is a mountainous country, which, coupled with low population density, has helped to preserve many areas – as in the Mediterranean forests of the Tagus valley, mountain areas of the Picos de Europa and Sierra de Gata, and the almost African landscapes of the Coto de Doñana. But it has undergone dramatic transformation by human activity, leaving wilderness areas alongside agricultural landscapes which entailed clearance of the vast Mediterranean forest which once covered most of Spain. Few areas of climax forest are left, and the dry, open plains of the steppes and mesetas are covered with cereal production or grazing, both on an extensive basis and with low use of pesticides and fertilizers until the 1990s. Mountain pastures have seen continuing transhumance systems of grazing over centuries. The agro-sylvo-pastoral system of the *dehesa*, a parkland created from semi-cleared Mediterranean evergreen oak forests, forms the world's largest oak forest in western Spain. These and other semi-natural areas are important repositories of wild life.

The importance of Spain's natural environment cannot be overestimated, with large numbers of unique species of flora and fauna. European lynx, brown bear, Egyptian mongoose, black vultures, imperial eagles and black storks find their last refuge in Spain, whilst new species of plants are still discovered in remoter mountain areas. On the migration route towards Africa, millions of migrating birds pass through, many wintering in Spain itself. It is therefore of European and world importance.

Protection

The National Parks, though well established, allow economic activity to threaten their very existence: Teide in the Canary Islands, affected by soil erosion and tourist disturbance; the Tablas de Daimiel (La Mancha), a wetland which is rarely wet; and the internationally important Coto de Doñana (southwest Andalusia), with its wetlands, dunes, forest and coastline, vital for migrating and wintering birds, is under threat from water extraction and from disturbance by agriculture and mining and tourist developments.

Many areas have been designated Nature Parks, mainly through local pressures, which have been facilitated by the creation of the **autonomous communities**. The most important example was Monfragüe in Extremadura, the only large expanse of Mediterranean forest under strict protection in Europe, and one of the world's great reserves. Others followed, campaigners initially preferring this form of protection, with control exercised at regional, not national level, even though this sometimes led to embroilment in local/national political disputes, as in the case of the Santoña marshes. In spite of inadequate regional resources, this seemed preferable to the creation of National

Parks, given the history of failures attributed to the institution supposed to protect them, the Institute for Nature Conservation (ICONA). This body was also largely responsible for reafforestation with non-native species, a disastrous policy which, though largely dormant, could be revived, given pressures on paper prices. Improvements in the 1990s have led to greater faith in the central administration, with some Nature Parks converted into National Parks, including plans for Monfragüe itself.

Regional devolution suited the rise of pressure groups in a country with little tradition of this kind of community action. More local control has empowered them to achieve significant results, especially when conservation is shown to benefit local people. Although a national 'green' movement never established itself, the successful conservation groups tended to remain apolitical, such as the largest, ADENEX in Extremadura. Bodies like ADENA, (the Spanish WorldWide Fund for Nature), were regarded as too closely linked with the very 'establishment' considered to have fostered many of the problems.

Spain's membership of the European Union has had mixed effects in the area of conservation. Support for environmental protection measures has improved, even involving a 'greening' of the Common Agricultural Policy (CAP). Pressure groups have had success in referring to European law and directives. But Structural Funds have had a devastating impact on the environment. The CAP, applied to a climatically distinct area of Europe for which it was not designed, has led to losses of habitat and wildlife as farmers struggle to gain short-term benefits with intensive methods ill-suited to the landscape, involving clearances, irrigation and the use of chemicals. However, measures like set-aside (if applied logically) and Environmentally Sensitive Areas might enable traditional agricultural methods to survive and thus protect valuable habitats. The Regional Development Fund supports many ill-considered projects, often without the relevant checks of impact assessments.

Conclusions

Spain is at a crucial point in its environmental history. Pressures have never been greater, but neither has awareness been so high. The tensions thus created will be difficult to resolve, and likely to be further complicated as global warming increases climatic change. Spain is in danger of desertification, and years of drought highlighted this. Inappropriate agriculture and unnecessary developments will bring disasters for wildlife and citizens, and this may encourage the radical policy changes needed to ensure better protection of Spain's natural heritage, above all, by protecting traditional extensive agricultural methods.

Further reading

Bangs, P. (1985) 'Monfragüe, a Conservation Success in Spain', *Oryx* xix, July: 140–5.

—— (1985) 'Regionalism and Conservation', *Iberian Studies* 14, 1–2: 29–43.

—— (1988) 'Doubt Over *Dehesa*', *Environment Now* 11, December: 30–2.

—— (1995) 'The European Union and the Spanish Environment', in T. Cooper (ed.) *Spain in Europe*, Leeds Iberian Papers, pp. 169–90.

Grunfeld, F. (1988) *Wild Spain*, London: Ebury Press.

PAUL BANGS

Erice, Víctor

b. 1940, San Sebastián

Filmmaker and scriptwriter

Erice is one of the most respected *auteurs* in Spanish cinema despite the sparseness of his productions: three films in twenty years. His cinema is characterized by a poetic, introspective quality and formal accomplishment, though at times it may suffer from a certain hermeticism. Initially associated with the producer Elías **Querejeta**, his subsequent career has followed a distinctively individual trajectory. A well-informed film critic, co-founder of the leftist magazine *Nuestro Cine* and a collaborator in *Cuadernos de Arte y Pensamiento* (Studies in Art and Thought), Erice has also co-written a book on Nicholas Ray and adapted a series of Jorge Luis Borges' stories for **television**, as well as working in television advertising. His films are criss-crossed with cinematic as well as literary references. His full-length début, *El espíritu de la colmena* (*The Spirit of the Beehive*) (1973) was a box-office success acclaimed by audiences and critics alike: it was the first Spanish film to win the Golden Shell at the **San Sebastián Film Festival**. Set in a small Castilian village in 1940, it is the story of a young girl literally mesmerized by the image of Frankenstein's monster, after seeing James Whale's 1932 classic in the cinema. The film is not only a powerful evocation of childhood and a reflection on the compelling make-believe power of cinema, but also by capturing the desolate mood of the post-war era in its gloomy atmosphere and pervasive silence, it becomes an understated indictment of Franco's oppressive regime. Evasion and family dynamics are further explored in *El Sur* (The South) (1983), whose release was surrounded by expectation and controversy since part of the original script was left unshot due to production pressures. In a long flashback, an adolescent girl recounts the events from the arrival of her family in a provincial town of northern Spain in the late 1940s to her father's suicide in 1957. The film, superbly photographed, explores the psychological processes in the relation between father and daughter.

El sol del membrillo (*The Quince Tree Sun*) (1992) is a departure from the feminine voice of the previous two films. In an experimental mixture of documentary and fiction we witness the real-life contemporary painter Antonio López at work trying to capture in his canvas the fleeting splendour of a quince tree planted in his backyard. An essay on the nature of representation and artistic endeavour, the film is also concerned with the themes of communication, urban environment and its audiovisual landscape.

See also: *arte y ensayo*; film and cinema; Francoist culture

Further reading

Evans, P. and Fiddian, R. (1987) 'Víctor Erice's *El Sur*: A Narrative of Star Cross'd Lovers', *Bulletin of Hispanic Studies*, 64: 127–35 (an interesting discussion of the role of ideology in the film in the light of melodrama conventions).

Kinder, M. (1983) 'The Children of Franco in the New Spanish Cinema', *Quarterly Review of Film Studies* 8, 2: 57–76 (an examination of the symbolism of children in film narratives of the period with special reference to *El espíritu de la colmena*).

de Ros, X. (1995) 'Víctor Erice's 'voluntad de estilo' in *El espíritu de la colmena*', *Forum for Modern Languages Studies*, 23,1: 74–83 (a study of the film's relation to contemporary cinema traditions).

Smith, P.J. (1993) 'Víctor Erice Painting the Sun: Whispers and Rapture', *Sight and Sound*, April issue, 26–9 (a brief but illuminating essay on politics and art in the films of Erice, preceded by an interview with the filmmaker by Rikki Morgan).

XON DE ROS

Escobedo, Joana

b. 1942, Barcelona

Writer

Escobedo belongs to the academic world as author of **Catalan** language textbooks, and to the cultural world of museums and libraries as curator of special collections at the Biblioteca de Catalunya. As critic, she has authored numerous erudite articles for professional journals. Her wider visibility results from cultivation of imaginative fiction in the feminist vein coinciding with the post-Franco vogue of vernacular writing. *Silenci endins* (The Silence Around) (1979) explores via interior monologue the female protagonist's memories of rigid, repressive conditioning; *Amic, Amat* (Friend, Lover) (1980) employs multiple time planes to sketch and dissect problematic relationships.

See also: feminism; feminist writing; women's writing

JANET PÉREZ

Escrivá de Balaguer, José María

b. 1902, Barbastro (Aragon); d. 1975, Rome

Priest

The son of a bankrupt cloth-merchant, Escrivá entered the Seminary of Logroño in 1918, transferring to that of Zaragoza in 1920. In 1923, he embarked on a law degree at the University of Zaragoza. Ordained priest in 1925, he began his ministry in a rural parish in the Zaragoza diocese, but moved to Madrid in 1927 to work with slum-dwellers. In 1928, he founded **Opus Dei**, an organization of lay Catholics, to which was added, in 1943, the Priestly Society of the Holy Cross, to provide pastoral care for members. During the Civil War, he narrowly escaped execution at the hands of the Republicans, being saved through the intervention of the Interior Minister, Julián Zugazagoitia, who was himself executed on Franco's orders in 1940.

Escrivá's influence was initially disseminated through a collection of moral maxims entitled *The Way* (*El camino*), published in 1939, but the real expansion of Opus Dei activity began in the 1940s. In 1946, Escrivá moved to Rome, where he remained until the end of his life, directing the work of his organization, which by the time of his death had grown to 60,000 members worldwide, covering some eighty nationalities. The title of *Beatus* (Blessed) was conferred on him by Pope John Paul II in 1992, somewhat controversially, as the honour was bestowed within a very short time of his death. Comparisons were made with the slowness with which the cause of the saintly Pope John XXIII, who had died twelve years earlier than Escrivá, was advancing. Moreover, the traditional procedure of allowing adversarial testimony was not followed in Escrivá's case, and some ex-members of Opus who wished to give evidence were excluded from doing so.

When plans for Escrivá's beatification were announced, Cardinal **Enrique y Tarancón** expressed doubts about whether he was a suitable role-model for Christians. This view was supported by Escrivá's own nephew, and by former senior members of Opus, who attributed the uncritical loyalty to *el padre*, as he was called by his followers, to the fact that he had encouraged a personality cult, and accused him of adopting a bullying attitude towards his subordinates. Escrivá enjoyed frequenting aristocratic circles, and changed his birth-name, Escribá Albás, to the more noble-sounding Escrivá de Balaguer, eventually acquiring the title of Marquis of Peralta. The criticism which greeted this latter move, however, was so great that he transferred the title to his brother.

EAMONN RODGERS

'ESPARTACO' *see* Ruiz Román, Juan Antonio

Espriu, Salvador

b. 1913, Santa Coloma de Farners (Gerona); d. 1985, Barcelona

Writer

Although born in a village in the province of Gerona, Espriu will always be associated with Arenys de Mar, a small fishing town on the Costa Brava where he spent his boyhood summers, and which figures as Sinera in much of his work. By his mid-twenties he had published several works of prose fiction, notably the novels *El doctor Rip* (Dr Rip) (1931) and *Laia* (1932). At the end of the Civil War, Espriu turned to drama with his *Antígona* (Antigone) (written 1939, published 1955), a reconciliatory vision of a war between brothers. Although he had also written poetry before the end of the Civil War, it was only with *Cementiri de Sinera* (Sinera Cemetery) (1944–5) that he opted decisively for poetry. Its clandestine publication in 1946 at a time when publishing in Catalan was prohibited ushered in a period of predominantly poetic creativity. The cycles of the 1940s and 1950s are taut and integrated works, and in each the struggle for identity and recovery is enacted. The opening of the cycle is invariably bleak and negative: the silences and the lack of identity in *Cementiri de Sinera*, the image of the waters of the abyss confronting the self in *Les hores* (The Hours) (1951), the weary puppets and the cacophonous music in *Mrs Death* (1952), the dark prison cell of both *El caminant i el mur* (The Wanderer and the Wall) (1955) and *Final del laberint* (End of the

Labyrinth) (1955). But each time there is a sense of gain, whether in individual identity or, increasingly, in a collective awareness or the articulation of a collective voice. In *Cementiri de Sinera*, for example, individual observation leads to social observances, and the political or civic concerns implicit in the earlier collections culminate in *La pell de brau* (The Bull-Hide) (1960). This collection contains a clear rebuke to Franco and marks the involvement of Espriu with the Catalan nationalist and democratic aspirations of the 1960s, seen in the adoption of his poetry by the singers of the ***Nova Cançó***, and in his arrest after participating in the student sit-in at the Monastery of Sarrià in 1966. In the 1960s, too, Espriu's works were adapted for dramatic presentation: *La pell de brau* was performed at the Mataró Glassworks, while a more ambitious project involved the reworking of several texts into the *Ronda de Mort a Sinera* (Patrol of Death in Sinera). A poet of impressive lyrical restraint and ethical sobriety, Espriu has been justly described by Manuel **Vázquez Montalbán** as one of the symbols of Catalan cultural and moral resistance to Francoism.

Further reading

Bogin, M. (1988) *Selected Poems of Salvador Espriu*, New York and London: W.W. Norton (a small selection of Espriu's poetry with facing translation and a short but informative introduction).

Castellet, J.M. (1971) *Iniciación a la poesía de Salvador Espriu*, Madrid: Taurus (the best overview of Espriu's poetry).

Walters, D.G. (1994) ' "Sense cap nom ni símbol": recovery and identity in Salvador Espriu's *Cementiri de Sinera*', *Modern Language Review* 89, 4: 889–901 (a detailed study of Espriu's first cycle drawing attention to its integral and dynamic character).

D. GARETH WALTERS

ETA

ETA (Euskadi ta Askatasuna), whose name is **Basque** for '**Euskadi** and Freedom', was founded to resist the Franco regime's repression of Basque national consciousness. Yet the restoration of democracy, and the wide-ranging Basque autonomy that followed, did not signal an end to ETA's violent activities. Although the number of its victims declined from the peak of the early 1980s, the increasingly indiscriminate nature of ETA's violence – and the rise in intimidation and vandalism by its supporters – meant that it remained a major problem for the Basque country and for Spain as a whole.

ETA was formed in 1959 by elements of the youth wing of the moderate **PNV** and a radical nationalist splinter group Ekin. As the latter's name – the Basque for 'action' – suggested, ETA was a response to the passivity of mainstream nationalism at the time; its aim was an independent Basque state. From 1961 the group undertook armed actions against property. In 1968, after the shooting of one of its activists by a police patrol, it committed its first assassination – typically for this early period, of a member of the Francoist security apparatus. ETA became generally known in 1970, when sixteen activists were tried by a military tribunal in Burgos. Six were condemned to death, but their sentences were commuted after international protests. In 1973 ETA assassinated Franco's Prime Minister and likely successor, Admiral **Carrero Blanco**, by blowing up his car in Madrid.

In 1965 the organization had officially adopted leftist ideas alongside its nationalist principles. During the following decade it suffered various rifts involving their proponents and activists for whom nationalist ideas remained paramount. Underlying these, however, was a further question: the relation between 'military' – that is, armed – and political activity, the legalization of which brought differences to a head. In 1976, the then leadership decided to give political activity equal priority with the 'armed struggle'. This provoked the breakaway of a 'military' wing, ETA-m. The 'politico-military' faction, ETA-pm, after promoting the creation of **Basque Left**, renounced violence in 1982. Since then ETA-m, rejoined by those ETA-pm members who rejected this course, has been the only active part of the organization.

During the primacy of more leftist-oriented groups, including ETA-pm, ETA's targets were extended to Basque businessmen allegedly exploiting the 'Basque Working Class' which ETA claimed to represent. Kidnappings of such figures continued into the 1990s. By then the range of targets had widened to include politicians and civilian employees of the central and regional governments. Moreover, in addition to killing and maiming members of the public with letter and car bombs 'intended' for others, ETA has planted devices in public places such as department stores.

ETA's core of activists always depended on a wider network of sympathizers. Since 1975 it has used the freedoms afforded by democracy to develop this network, known collectively as the Basque National Liberation Movement (MLNV), the political wing of which is **Herri Batasuna**. The MLNV's leadership is the so-called Socialist Patriotic Co-ordinating Committee (KAS), consisting of representatives of various groups linked to ETA. The most prominent are the Gestoras Pro-Amnistía (support groups for ETA prisoners) and KAS' own youth wing, Jarrai, which has been increasingly active in the 1990s, harassing police officers, burning buses and organizing pro-ETA demonstrations.

Under the dictatorship ETA enjoyed considerable prestige, not merely among nationalists but also among opponents of the regime throughout Spain. However, acceptance of the new constitutional order, and revulsion at the indiscriminate use of violence, increasingly restricted sympathy for ETA to its own diehard supporters. Yet these form a significant minority of Basque society, and the pressures they exert, especially in the more rural areas long meant that the majority's opposition to ETA was muted. That is one reason why the authorities have found it so hard to put an end to ETA. Another is the abortive use of counter-terrorist groups, most notoriously the **GAL**, which provided ETA with a powerful propaganda weapon. Consequently the organization was repeatedly able to survive the arrest of activists and even its leaders. Attempts at clandestine negotiation, both by the Spanish government and by the leadership of the PNV, have always foundered on the intransigence of ETA's demands.

ETA's persistence has been seen as reflecting the deep-rooted importance of ideas of martyrdom in Basque collective consciousness. It reflects also the contemporary fact that the Basque country – and especially its youth – suffers in aggravated form various ills common in declining industrial regions, most notably chronic unemployment. Moreover, for over twenty years it has been in social and political turmoil, with direct action a constant factor. Under these circumstances ETA's anti-state rhetoric provides a ready-made channel for frustrations possibly unrelated to nationalism, and constantly generates a climate propitious to its continuing violence.

Recently, however, hopes of an end to violence have risen. A series of successful police operations, begun in 1996, were crucial in breaking the deadlock. In July 1997 ETA reacted by assassinating Miguel Angel Blanco, a councillor for the ruling People's Party (see also **PP**) in the town of Ermua. This action in turn triggered popular rejection of violence on a hitherto unknown scale, which further killings of PP representatives served only to heighten. The pressure on ETA increased with more arrests of key activists, and the closing by the courts in July 1998 of the newspaper *Egin*, long notorious as its mouthpiece. By then ETA had begun to seek a political escape route through contacts with the PNV. On 16 September its leadership announced the first 'indefinite' ceasefire in the organization's history. In November the Spanish government declared its willingness to negociate directly with ETA.

See also: González Cataráin, María Dolores; regional nationalism; *reinserción*; revolutionary tax; terrorism

Further reading

Clark, R. (1984) *The Basque Insurgents: ETA 1952–1980*, Madison, WI: University of Wisconsin (insight into the social milieu from which activists emerged).

—— (1990) *Negotiating with ETA: Obstacles to Peace in the Basque Country, 1975–1988*, Reno, NV: University of Nevada (covers in detail all the most important initiatives).

Llera, F. (1992) 'ETA: ejército secreto y movimiento social', in *Revista de Estudios Políticos* 78 (statistical summary of violence and assessment of its social significance).

Sullivan, J. (1988) *ETA and Basque Nationalism: the*

Fight for Euskadi, 1890–1986, London: Routledge (the definitive account of ETA's development to the mid-1980s).

Zulaika, J. (1989) *Basque Violence: Metaphor and Sacrament*, Reno, NV: University of Nevada (discusses socio-anthropological roots of violence).

CHRIS ROSS

European Union

There has been enthusiastic support in Spain since the 1960s for greater integration into Europe, in part as a reaction against what was perceived as the cultural, political and economic isolation of the country, particularly during the Franco regime (see also ***europeísmo***). The first application for membership of the then European Economic Community was made in 1962, but was rejected because of the absence of democratic institutions in Spain. Nevertheless, a preferential trade agreement was signed with the EEC in 1970. The first democratically elected government of the post-Franco period applied formally for membership in July 1977, and in November Spain joined the Council of Europe and adopted the European Convention on Human Rights.

Both economically and politically, post-Franco governments were faced with a number of daunting tasks in preparing for EC entry. By 1975, Spain's economy was still one of most protected in Europe. Furthermore, the **UCD** government had perforce to devote most of its attention to political and constitutional issues related to the transition to democracy. Consequently, when **PSOE** came to power in 1982, major restructuring of the economy was long overdue. Its election promise to create 800,000 jobs had to be subordinated to the pursuit of greater competitiveness. One of the first illustrations of this was the Law on Reconversion and Industrialization (1984), which attempted to modernize industries like shipbuilding, steel manufacture and textiles, creating in the process serious job losses in these industries.

The negotiations over entry were complicated, partly because of Spain's long tradition of protectionism, partly because of her level of industrial development. In 1983, industrial output in Spain was only 60 percent of the EC average. Though there had been vigorous investment in certain heavy industries in the 1970s, this sector, particularly steel production, was out of phase with the rest of Europe, and was achieving high levels of productivity precisely at the time when demand in the rest of the world was falling off. A further problem was the low cost and high productivity of Spanish agriculture, which was regarded with some apprehension by other member-states with similar Mediterranean economies. Had special conditions not been applied, Spanish agricultural production would, by itself, have made the pre-1986 nine-member Community self-sufficient in wine, fruit and vegetables, and created a surplus of 10 percent above self-sufficiency in olive oil. In addition, with more than double the EC average per capita consumption of fish, and the largest fishing fleet in Europe (the third biggest in the world), which provided 20 percent of all employment in Spain, imposition of EC quota rules was inevitably going to create severe difficulties (see also **fisheries**).

Spain's entry in 1986 was therefore agreed on somewhat unusual terms. The government was required to press ahead with the programme of ***reconversión industrial***, and the Spanish motor manufacturing industry was given the protection of import tariffs for three further years after accession. A seven to ten-year period was allowed for the adjustment of agricultural prices and industrial tariffs, and the full integration of the Spanish fishing fleet was postponed for ten years.

The adaptation strategy followed by PSOE between 1985 and 1990 was economically successful in achieving growth and productivity, and reducing inflation. But there were social costs in the shape of high unemployment and reductions in spending on public services, leading to industrial unrest. In the period 1986–90, Spain had, second only to Greece, the highest EC rate of working days lost through strikes, five times as many as Britain. Also, the very speed of growth produced the renewed threat of inflation in the early 1990s. Increased energy costs and the slowing-down of industry internationally meant that by 1991, GDP per capita was still less than 80 percent of the EU average. In addition, the pressure to meet the Maastricht convergence criteria after 1992 (strict control of inflation, interest rates, exchange rates and budget deficits) reduced the government's freedom of action with regard to social expenditure and job creation.

As against this, Spain is the highest net gainer from transfers of EU funds, receiving 7,500m ecus in 1995, more than twice as much as the next highest, Greece, and three times as much as Portugal. A major source of subsidies has been support for environmental projects, for which Spain received 30,200m pesetas in 1991 from the European Regional Fund. The 'cohesion fund' set up under the Maastricht treaty yielded, in 1994, nearly 19m ecus to support 162 environmental projects in Spain.

Despite the political costs incurred by increased industrial tension, EU membership has also brought political benefits. Not the least of the reasons why the **armed forces** are unlikely to intervene again in politics is that any future military coup would lead to Spain's expulsion from the EU, with serious economic and social consequences. The opportunities for increased co-operation with other European police forces has been an important factor in reducing **terrorism** in Spain. The reluctance of some EU partner countries to extradite members of **ETA** prompted the Prime Minister, José María Aznar, to propose at a summit in Dublin in October 1996 that the EU should become a single jurisdictional area, with free movement of police officers, the development of Europol into a federal force comparable to the FBI, and the removal from EU citizens of the right of asylum in member states.

Not everyone in Spain would go so far as Aznar in advocating this level of integration, in view of economic and social consequences such as the hardship suffered by fishing communities in Galicia and the Basque country. It is also true that in common with other member states, Spain has less control over her own economic policy than before EU accession. In 1995, for example, the European Commission threatened to exclude Spain from participation in a new round of cohesion funds unless the government reduced public spending and employment in the public sector, and pressed ahead with privatization programmes.

Nevertheless Spain's general commitment to the consolidation of the EU, shared by successive governments, business and the populace at large, cannot be in doubt. It is reflected in the wide support, particularly in Catalonia, for the concept of 'Europe of the regions'. The Catalan President, Jordi **Pujol**, is chair of the Assembly of European Regions, to which all Spain's **autonomous communities** belong, except for Navarre and Castilla-La Mancha. Pasqual **Maragall**, the socialist mayor of Barcelona, founded in 1989 the Council of European Municipalities and Regions, which brings together representatives of major European cities.

See also: economy; foreign policy; NATO

Further reading

Heywood, P. (1995) *The Government and Politics of Spain*, London: Macmillan (chapter 12 is an admirably lucid account of the effects of EU membership).

Newton, M.T. with Donaghy, P.J. (1997) *Institutions of Modern Spain: A Political and Economic Guide*, Cambridge: Cambridge University Press (chapter 15 is an indispensable overview of the relations between Spain and the EU).

EAMONN RODGERS

europeísmo

Spain, which in the sixteenth century was the most powerful nation in Europe, has had an ambivalent relationship with her neighbours since at least the middle of the eighteenth century. On the one hand, progressive intellectual élites thought of social and political modernization as 'catching up' with Europe, but on the other, these same élites, together with their more conservative compatriots, viewed external influences, particularly from France, as threatening Spain's cultural and, especially, religious distinctiveness.

In the present century, this ambivalence persisted throughout and beyond the Franco regime. The support which Italy and Germany had given to Franco during the Civil War encouraged the dictator to believe that Spain would in due course join a club of powerful militaristic nations which would create a new European order, but his enthusiasm for this idea cooled when the tide of WWII turned in favour of the Allies. In the 1940s, the western democracies remained aloof from Spain because of Franco's support of the Axis powers during WWII: Spain was not, for example, admitted to the **United Nations** until 1955.

Francoist rhetoric fostered the notion that this isolation was a mark of Spain's moral superiority to what were described as the decadent and corrupt democracies. Simultaneously, however, the regime made sedulous efforts to ingratiate itself with the international community, and commercial and other links with Europe were cultivated, especially after the **Stabilization Plan**, which opened Spain to foreign investment. The increasing prosperity of the 1960s, together with more frequent contacts with the rest of Europe stemming from **migration** of workers and **tourism**, encouraged awareness among both the political élites and the populace at large of the benefits of membership of the European Economic Communities (see also **European Union**), which led to Spain's first application for membership in 1962. Accession to the EEC was, however, precluded by the absence of a democratic system in Spain until after the death of Franco in 1975. Even after this date, negotiations were difficult and protracted, and Spain did not finally join until 1986.

Independently of the economic arguments for European Community membership, however, attitudes towards European integration among the populace at large have been very positive for at least the last twenty-five years. This has been intensified under successive **PSOE** governments, who have consistently emphasized Spain's destiny in Europe, at the expense of the close ties with the US fostered by Franco. This emerged clearly in 1986 in the referendum on membership of **NATO**, when government propaganda gave pre-eminent importance to solidarity with European partners, largely glossing over the reality of American leadership of the alliance.

On a day-to-day basis, visitors to Spain can see ample evidence of assimilation to general European patterns in such matters as quality of main **roads**, **transport**, cost of living, availability of consumer goods, **architecture** and **fashion**.

See also: European Union; foreign policy; history

Further reading

Heywood, P. (1995) *The Government and Politics of Spain*, London: Macmillan (chapter 12 is an admirably lucid account of the effects of EU membership).

Newton, M.T. with Donaghy, P.J. (1997) *Institutions of Modern Spain: A Political and Economic Guide*, Cambridge: Cambridge University Press (chapter 15 is an indispensable overview of the relations between Spain and the EU).

EAMONN RODGERS

Euskadi

Name invented by Sabino Arana, founder of Basque nationalism, for Basques' supposed national territory. Originally spelt 'Euzkadi', the form with 's' is now usual. In this sense, Euskadi consists of seven 'historic territories': the provinces of Alava, Guipúzcoa, Navarre and Vizcaya (Euskadi Sur), and the French districts of Labourd, Basse Navarre and Soule (Euskadi Norte or *Iparralde*). The term is now used also, even by some nationalists, to mean the Basque **autonomous community** created in 1979, consisting of Alava, Guipúzcoa and Vizcaya.

CHRIS ROSS

Eusko Alkartasuna

Eusko Alkartasuna is **Basque** for 'Basque Solidarity', a party formed in 1986 by dissident elements of the **PNV**. It is closely identified with its leader Carlos Garaikoetxea, ***lehendakari*** from 1980 to 1984. Initially the EA enjoyed considerable success but after 1987 its support declined. In the Basque regional election in 1994 it won 10 percent of the votes, thereafter joining a coalition government as in 1990–1. In Navarre, where its vote share is 5 percent, EA is also a coalition partner.

Further reading

Llera, F. (1994) *Los Vascos y la Política*, Bilbao: Universidad del País Vasco (overview of the Basque political system, giving electoral statistics).

CHRIS ROSS

exile

The greatest exodus from Spain this century was that resulting from the Civil War of 1936–9. The collapse of the Catalan front at the end of January 1939 caused a massive flow of Republican refugees across the French border, with 470,000 people entering France between 27 January and 10 February. Another 15,000 left for north Africa, and 6,000 for the Soviet Union, in addition to the 3,000 children already evacuated there in 1937. Among Latin American countries, Mexico received the largest number of Republican refugees: some 22,000 settled there between 1939 and 1948.

Though the cohort entering France contained men, women and children from all age groups, there was a predominance of young men from the defeated Republican army, mostly from Catalonia and Aragon. A large proportion consisted of civil servants from the central and autonomous regional governments, and the upper echelons of the political parties and the trade unions, including Republicans, socialists, communists and members of the **UGT** and **CNT**.

The scale of the exodus constituted a serious problem for the French government, which tried to force as many as possible to return to Spain or move on to other countries. In addition, after 1940, the Vichy regime arrested prominent Republicans living in France and handed them over to face execution by Francoist firing squads, the most notorious case being that of the former President of the Catalan **Generalitat**, Lluis Companys. Many others were picked up by the Gestapo and sent to their deaths in concentration camps, except for the few who were fortunate enough to survive, such as Jorge **Semprún**. The combined effect of deportations and voluntary departures was that by 1945 the initial cohort was reduced to 150,000.

In Mexico, in August 1945, the Republican government in exile had been reconstituted, and remained in being until 1977, enjoying official recognition by Mexico and Yugoslavia. The political parties in exile were also reorganized, especially in France and Mexico. One of the most abiding legacies of the exodus, however, was the enrichment of literary, scientific and artistic life in other countries, notably Britain, France, the US, and the states of Latin America, by the presence, either temporary or permanent, of leading Spanish academics, writers and intellectuals, such as Max **Aub**, Francisco **Ayala**, Américo **Castro**, José **Ortega y Gasset** and Antonio Rodríguez-Moñino. These were supplemented by a younger generation of those who had spent their formative years in Spain, but found the repressive atmosphere of the Franco regime intolerable, such as Juan **Goytisolo**.

See also: censorship; Francoist culture; history; politics

Further reading

Abellán, J.L. (1976) *El exilio español de 1939*, Madrid: Taurus, 6 vols (a basic reference work).

Cuesta, J. and Bermejo, B. (1996) *Emigración y exilio. Españoles en Francia, 1936–1946*, Madrid: Eudema (papers of a 1991 conference on the topic, giving an up-to-date account).

Rubio, J. (1977) *La emigración de la guerra civil de 1936–1939*, Madrid: San Martín, 3 vols (a classic study; the third volume includes a very interesting documentary appendix).

Various authors (1982) *El exilio español en México, 1939–1982*, Mexico: Fondo de Cultura Económica (an important symposium by various authors, including historical articles and personal testimonies, as well as a biobibliographical section on Republican intellectuals in Mexico).

ALICIA ALTED

Expo-92

The sixty-fifth Universal Exhibition, Expo-92, took place on the island of La Cartuja, in the Guadalquivir river facing the historic centre of

Seville, from 20 April to 12 October 1992. Together with the Barcelona **Olympic Games** and Madrid's tenure as European City of Culture, this was one of the three major international events held in Spain to commemorate the ***Quinto Centenario*** (five-hundredth anniversary) of Columbus' first voyage to the Americas in 1492.

In the run up to the exhibition, five years of publicly and privately financed construction work produced 70 km of new roads, including the SE30 motorway, eight new bridges over the river, a new train station to accommodate the high-speed **AVE** Madrid–Seville link instituted to coincide with the event, and numerous new hotels, apartment blocks and car parks. The airport was modernized and historic buildings, including those which had housed the 1929 Hispano-American Exhibition, were restored. The development of the site itself, with its 68 pavilions, 96 restaurants, 150 shops and 70 bars, completely transformed the city's appearance and left it better linked to the rest of the country and the international community than it had ever been in its long history.

Represented in the exhibition, the theme of which was the Age of Discovery, exemplified in the five pavilions (the Fifteenth Century, the Discoveries, Navigation, Nature and the Future), were 102 countries, 58 having their own national pavilions, with smaller countries sharing five collective pavilions. Although the exhibition strove to live up to its publicity slogan of *Todo el mundo está en una isla* (The whole world on one island), the 12 million visitors who came at a rate of over 200,000 a day were significantly less than the 14 to 15 million budgeted for, and many of the 55,000 cultural events were rather poorly attended.

Well-publicized disruptions caused by sporadic protests from Native American rights activists, two major fire scares and subsequent suggestions of political nepotism by the **PSOE** government, plus allegations of financial impropriety in the allocation of building contracts, have not ultimately undermined the overall judgement that the event was a success. The effects of the world recession of the time, which contributed to the shortfall in meeting projected visitor targets and income budgets, were less marked in Andalusia, historically one of Spain's poorest areas. A joint venture known as Cartuja-93, between the event organizer and the local authorities, has successfully recouped some of the capital investment, through the sell-off of much of the real estate, and the exhibition site has been redeveloped as a theme park, the Parque de los Descubrimientos (Discovery Park), which has continued to attract tourist trade to the area. Furthermore, the improved infrastructure and communications resulting from the exhibition are expected to offer significant long term benefits to the local economy.

See also: arts funding; Olympic Games; *Quinto Centenario*

CHRIS DIXON

F

Falange

The Falange (literally 'phalanx') was founded in 1933 by José Antonio Primo de Rivera as a uniformed organization on the model of the Italian fascists. It began in reaction to the left-leaning policies of the Second Republic, and adopted a strongly nationalist rhetoric, as well as displaying a readiness to engage in street violence against socialists and other radical groupings. In 1934 it merged with an overtly pro-Nazi organization, the Juntas de Ofensiva Nacional-Sindicalista (Committees of the National Syndicalist Offensive). In the Civil War, it provided volunteer companies for the Francoist rising. Partly to further the war effort on the Nationalist side by providing a unified command structure, partly to bolster Franco's personal hegemony, the Falange was merged with the Carlists in 1937 to form what became known as the **National Movement**.

From this date on, the name 'Falange' is used, somewhat confusingly, to designate the new merged organization (usually designated as FET), the original core of the 'old' pre-1937 Falange, and the National Movement which became institutionalized as a bureaucratic organization within the post-war Franco state. Though the slogan of the original Falange, *España, Una, Grande, Libre* (Spain, One, Great and Free), and the symbol of the yoke and arrows, were adopted by the Franco regime, old Falangists soon found themselves marginalized after the Civil War. One of Franco's titles was *Jefe Nacional* (National Leader) of the Falange, and he frequently wore the uniform when addressing veterans' rallies, but he had little time for the anti-bourgeois populism of the old Falange, nor had he any intention of allowing it to challenge his personal power. His only departures from this policy occurred when he temporarily favoured the Falange in order to check the political influence of the monarchists. Franco's instinctive personal sympathy with some of the nationalistic and authoritarian elements in Falangist rhetoric was far outweighed by his characteristic pragmatism, as José Luis **Arrese** found to his cost when he tried in 1956 to institutionalize the organization within the structures of the state.

See also: history; politics

Further reading

Payne, S.G. (1976) *Franco's Spain*, London: Routledge & Kegan Paul (an excellent brief overview, with a clear treatment of this topic).

Preston, P. (1993) *Franco*, London: Harper Collins (an outstanding biography, which gives a profound insight into every aspect of the Franco period; an exceptionally detailed index makes it easy to follow through particular topics).

EAMONN RODGERS

Falcón, Lidia

b. 1935, Madrid

Feminist writer

Lidia Falcón is the mother of contemporary Spanish feminism. She is both Betty Friedan and

Simone de Beauvoir in one: thinker, activist, novelist, dramatist, essayist and journalist, she has authored twenty books. Since the 1960s she has been Spain's most outspoken feminist. Her political activism and militant commitment to women earned her both public recognition and persecution by the Franco regime. She was arrested and jailed on numerous occasions and spent nine months in Madrid's Yeserías prison, accused of pro-ETA activity and implicated in both the assassination of Luis **Carrero Blanco** and the bombing of the Cafetería Rolando in Madrid, a spot frequented by the Civil Guard.

She founded the magazine *Vindicación Feminista* (Feminist Vindication), the theoretical journal *Poder y Libertad* (Power and Freedom) and the publishing house Vindicación Feminista Publicaciones to encourage open debate, offer a feminist point of view on national and international issues and stimulate the creation of a feminist culture. Falcón's most dramatic contribution to Spanish feminism is founding the first feminist party in Spain, the Partido Feminista.

Falcón's production is truly prodigious and still growing, comprising a serious theoretical exploration. Falcón writes scholarly, elaborately researched and thoughtful books that discuss the hard questions of contemporary feminist theory and political thought. She moves easily between fiction and non-fiction, and between a strong critique of inherent structures of male dominance found in Spanish society and a sense of optimism towards possibilities for future change. Her overtly feminist theatre dramatizes the plight of Spanish women, often taking its plot line from her own legal cases or from prominent cases reported in the press.

For Falcón, feminism is the revolution of the 1990s, the only coherent political philosophy to lead us into the twenty-first century. The central question that is first posed in *Mujer y sociedad* (Women and Society) is why women, independently of their religious beliefs, geographic situation or the period in which they have lived, have found themselves and still find themselves without civil, political and social rights. Falcón continues to address this question and expand upon it in later tomes where she considers violence against women, women's relation to political power and the apoliticization of the feminist movement.

One of Falcón's major contributions to Spanish feminism is the internationalization of its struggle. Her speaking engagements at academic centres throughout the United States and in other parts of the globe have served to present not only her controversial theses but also the Spanish female circumstance to new audiences. Tireless, she fights with the zeal of a true revolutionary, building daily on the acts of the past. Persistently maintaining women's issues in the public eye, Falcón continues to espouse vanguard positions that have yet to be embraced by the mainstream.

Further reading

Waldman G.F. (1993) 'Lidia Falcón O'Neill', in *Spanish Women Writers: a Bio-bibliographical Source Book*, Westport, CT: Greenwood Press (thorough introduction to Falcón: biography, major themes, criticism and complete bibliography).

GLORIA FEIMAN WALDMAN

fallas

The *fallas* are an annual festival celebrated in the city of Valencia in March, which probably owes its origin to an ancient spring rite. In the Middle Ages, the guilds of carpenters ceremonially burned, on St Joseph's day (19 March), the wooden candle-brackets which they had used to light their workshops during the winter. Nowadays huge, grotesque figures made of wood and papier mâché are constructed in the streets, usually making some satirical comment on a topical subject, and often including caricatures of well-known public figures. After several days of carnivalesque festivities, street-theatre and similar diversions, the figures are burned in a spectacular fireworks display.

See also: *fiestas*

EAMONN RODGERS

family

Historically, the family has been an extremely important institution in Spain, as one would expect in a society which for so long was traditional,

Catholic and hierarchical. During the Franco regime, the family was enshrined in basic legislation as one of the 'organic' institutions of the state, and between 1945 and 1958, the position of male head of the family (*cabeza de familia*) was given legal status. From the late 1960s, heads of families formed one of the colleges for the controlled elections to the **parliament**. Family planning was illegal (though increasingly practised during the 1960s), and there were special bonuses payable to large families, and even prizes (*premios de natalidad*) for exceptionally large numbers of children.

Despite the speed of modernization in structures and attitudes since the late 1970s, the family is still very influential. Some 80 percent of respondents to surveys in the 1990s declared that the family was the most important element in their lives, and the strength of family loyalties can lead to nepotism and **corruption**. Though there has been a decrease in the number of marriages, from 7.36 per thousand in 1970 to 5.59 in 1991, this is accounted for partly by the tendency to postpone marriage, and for young people in Spain to stay on in the parental home later than elsewhere in Europe. In the 1970s, the average age of marriage was 24 for women and 26 for men, but in the 1990s these figures have risen to 26 and 28 respectively. Cohabitation has become increasingly common since the 1970s, but in all but a very small minority of cases, it is followed by marriage. Though the proportion of births to single parents increased by a factor of eight between 1970 and 1990, from just over 1 percent to 9 percent, this figure is still low by comparison with most European countries. Despite the availability of legal divorce since 1981, divorce rates, at ten percent of marriages, are also low.

This is not to say that nothing has changed, for even during the Franco era, family size declined for economic reasons during the 1940s and 1950s. This trend increased throughout the 1960s and 1970s owing to the increased, though unofficial, availability of contraception, better levels of education, and improvements in the status and independence of **women** through greater employment opportunities. From a level of just over three children per household in the 1950s, the average had gone down by the second half of the 1980s to 1.2. Another departure from traditional patterns is the decrease in the number of elderly people living with married offspring. In the early 1990s, slightly over one in five persons over 65 were living in extended families: twenty years earlier, nearly three-quarters did so. That the family unit in Spain, though comparatively stable and solid by the standards of some other countries, is coming under the kind of pressures experienced elsewhere is suggested by the increasing evidence presented in the media of wife-battering, even murder, as well as cruelty and sexual abuse of children. The sacrosanct status which the family has enjoyed in the past, indeed, may well make it more difficult for public agencies to deal with this kind of problem.

See also: abortion law; marriage and divorce; sexual behaviour; social attitudes; society

Further reading

Hooper, J. (1995) *The New Spaniards*, Harmondsworth: Penguin (chapters 11 and 12 give an excellent overview of the issues connected with family life).

Lawlor, T., Rigby, M. *et al.* (1998) *Contemporary Spain*, London and New York: Longman (pp. 304–8 contain a useful digest of relevant statistics).

EAMONN RODGERS

fashion

Two major fashion shows are held each February and each September, the Pasarela Cibeles in Madrid and the Salón Gaudí in Barcelona. These are the shop-window for an industry which in 1995 was employing up to 180,000 personnel and producing articles worth over 1m^2 pesetas, putting Spain into fifth place in Europe. The majority of the 5,500 or so businesses involved are small and medium enterprises, three quarters of them employing fewer than twenty people. Spain also regularly hosts specialist international trade fairs, such as Pielespaña, one of the most important exhibitions in the world for fashions in leather, and the Feria Internacional de Moda Infantil (FIMI, the International Exhibition of Fashions for Young People).

The great fashion designer of all time associated with Spain is undoubtedly Balenciaga, the centenary of whose birth was celebrated in 1995. Born in Guetaria, he met with great success in Paris and was the creator of, among other things, the Dolman sleeve, and was noted for his fondness for large buttons. National Balenciaga Prizes are awarded annually, with several classes, including ones for best Spanish designer and best new entrant.

In the 1990s the leading designers included Victorio & Lucchino of Seville, whose house regularly furnished the final display of the Madrid shows, Javier Larrainzar of Madrid, designer of dresses for the aristocracy, Roberto Verinno, Jesús del Pozo, Modesto Lomba and Luis Devota (Devota & Lomba), Lydia Delagado, Palacio y Lemoniez, Francis Montesinos (Valencia), Paco Casado, Jordi Cuesta, Manuel Piña, Adolfo Domínguez (Galicia), Pedro Morago, Angel Schlesser, Antonio Pernas and Purificación García.

The fortunes of fashion houses in the 1990s were affected by a number of factors, chief among them the economic crisis, and changes in the climate. Designers have commented since 1988 that very cold springs and hot autumns have effectively reduced the seasons, and therefore the types of clothing required, from four to two. Consumer demand was further diminished by economic recession, and this resulted in noticeable changes in the fashion industry. Some houses closed down, others completely restructured their businesses, and overall there was a much greater awareness of the new realities. It was recognized that, while there was still room for the fantastic and the glamorous, commercially successful designs had to be adaptable to the retail market. As one designer was quoted as saying, 'Frivolity has gone; this is a business and we can't allow ourselves to produce works of art.'

One result of this new sense of realism was the move to direct retailing of designer clothing. Among the leading fashion houses who opened shops in Spain and abroad were Javier Larrainzar, Roberto Verinno, Antonio Pernas, Angel Schlesser, Adolfo Domínguez, Manuel Piña and Mila and Tucho Balado's label *A Menos Cuarto*. Retail lines are usually either cheaper versions of models shown at the shows, or collections intended for immediate sale, and prices vary according to the particular design and material used. One very noticeable trend of fashions in the 1990s was the 'revival' of styles from earlier decades, especially the 1960s and 1970s.

The outstanding name in accessories is undoubtedly that of Loewe, famous for the design and production of leather goods. A Spanish firm in origin, it celebrated its 150th anniversary in 1996 with exhibitions in Madrid, Seville and Barcelona.

A *Dictionary of Fashion* was published in 1996 to coincide with the Madrid show, written by Margarita Riviere and illustrated by the designer Antonio Miró.

EAMONN RODGERS

fast food outlets

Street vendors traditionally provided 'food to go' in busy urban thoroughfares and at festive events, and they still do, especially selling *churros* (deep fried dough shaped into ribbed sticks, coated with sugar), roast chestnuts, *garrapiñadas* (syrup-coated dry roasted almonds) or *perritos* (hot dogs), mostly regarded as snacks rather than proper food.

Demographic changes during the 1950s and 1960s saw the emergence of a primarily urban population whose hectic lifestyle demanded catering outlets specializing in promptly served, inexpensive fare. Snack bars and ***cafeterías*** started to fill the niche in the market, offering fixed menus of *platos combinados* all day. Whereas ***tapas***, small portions of food consumed at the bar with drinks, tend to be ordered when socializing with a group of people and are normally shared, the *plato combinado* is an individual one-dish meal consisting of meat, fish or eggs, vegetables and potatoes or rice.

American-style burger bars (*hamburgueserías*) and *pizzerías* started to appear in the late 1970s and early 1980s, but the presence of large catering multinationals was not evident until the mid-1980s. While they command a good share of the fast food market, especially among teenage consumers, the Spanish taste for *bocadillos* (filled baguettes), *tapas* and other traditional dishes has offered opportunities for small local businesses to evolve (*bocaterías*), especially those that provide a delivery service.

Spaniards may like their food served fast, but they do not normally like to consume it on the hoof; even if there has been a growth in the take-away sector, which only started in the late 1980s, most people will consume the food at home. Some restaurants offer the possibility of ordering full traditional meals (e.g. *paella*, roast lamb or seafood), including wine, and having them delivered.

See also: food and drink; regional cooking; restaurants

RAMÓN PARRONDO

feminism

Early Spanish feminism was weak and conservative, although socialist and anarchist feminism was important between 1920 and 1930. The greatest reforms concerning women's emancipation were introduced in the 1931 constitution, which stipulated absolute equality before the law (universal male suffrage dates from 1890). In 1933 women voted for the first time, but they were blamed for the fact that a right-wing government came to power. After the outbreak of the Civil War women's groups, newspapers, and conferences flourished, but once Franco came to power, women (like men) lost all their civil rights in the authoritarian, Catholic regime. Feminist organizations were out of the question. The official women's organization, the Sección femenina (Women's Section) of the **National Movement** was run by Pilar Primo de Rivera, the sister of the leader of the **Falange**. In 1938 divorce and civil marriage were outlawed in the Nationalist zone, and in 1941 abortion was made a criminal offence. In the 1960s there were no feminist organizations in Spain although the conditions for the future success of feminism (industrialization, consumerism, secularization and higher education) were being laid down, and women became active in trade unions, political parties and housewives' associations (both legal and illegal).

The women's movement (second-wave feminism) emerged late in Spain compared with the rest of Europe. It blossomed rapidly after Franco's death between 1975 and 1979, then split into small groups. After the Socialist victory of 1982 it lost its radical edge and political leverage. Throughout the 1970s second-wave feminism was closely involved with the anti-Franco and anti-capitalist movements, with the result that feminism was not a priority on the programmes of the political parties introducing key democratic reforms. Feminist objectives had always been subordinated to class politics in Spain. This led to the phenomenon of double militancy (women participating in both left-wing political parties and feminist or women's organizations) which became both Spanish feminism's strength and its Achilles' heel. In 1975, International Women's Year, the Sección femenina was charged with the official representation of Spanish women. In response to the lack of activity a non-governmental organization was set up in Barcelona to prepare for the celebrations. This gave rise to the first *Jornadas Nacionales por la Liberación de la Mujer* (National Women's Liberation Conference), celebrated illegally in Madrid in December 1975 (just over two weeks after Franco's death). It was attended by five hundred women from all over Spain and was the first feminist meeting of its kind since 1939. It was followed by the *Les Jornades Catalanes de la Dona* (Catalan Women's Conference) held in October 1976. The focus of this conference was still primarily anti-capitalist. Shortly after, the Associació Catalana de la Dona (Catalan Women's Association) was founded; it was the first democratic, independent, feminist organization embracing women of all classes and ideologies. The first militant feminist magazine, *Vindicación feminista* (Feminist Vindication), was started up by Lidia **Falcón** in 1976. After the elections of June 1977, twenty-two new women MPs took their seats in parliament, including a **PSOE** feminist, Carlota Bustelo. However, in 1977 the Catalan women's movement split leading to the founding of the Revolutionary Feminist Organization and, in 1979, to the Marxist–feminist Feminist Party of Spain, led by Lidia Falcón.

After the constitution of 1978, which declared women's equality before the law, it seemed feminism could free itself from the political parties of the left and go its own way. The *Jornadas de Granada* (Granada Conference) of 1979, attended by 3,000 women, opted for radical or difference feminism in order to distance feminism from political parties. From then on a rift opened between difference feminism (based on grass-roots, independent collectives) and equality or Marxist/Socialist feminism. Radical feminism was concerned with the individual objectives, personal problems and sexuality of women and aimed to reform patriarchal ways of thinking rather than encourage collective effort against capitalism. After 1979 the women's movement fragmented, reflecting diverse ideologies and strategies and regional and national cultural differences. Meanwhile, women continued to be very active in the trade unions, particularly Comisiones Obreras (**CC OO**). Between 1981 and 1984 the annual *Jornadas de Mujeres Independientes* (Independent Feminists' Conference) took place, although the aims of the radical feminists (to encourage self-awareness, implement non-hierarchical organization and reject dual activism) were vague. The *Jornadas Diez años de lucha del Movimiento Feminista* (Ten Years of Struggle by the Feminist Movement Conference) was held in Barcelona in 1985.

Meanwhile, democratic reforms (for example, the legalization of contraception (1978) and laws ensuring equality in the workplace (1980)) were taking the edge off political feminism. In 1981 the mutual assent divorce law was approved, although there were no provisions for alimony payment, and abortion was depenalized in 1983, although the **abortion law** – delayed until 1985 – was restrictive and made no provision for clinical facilities. The **Instituto de la Mujer** (Women's Institute), now a part of the Ministry of Social Services, was established in 1983 with a budget of £3.5m to encourage equal opportunities and legal equality in all aspects of women's lives. In a 1987 catalogue, however, only seventy out of six hundred women's organizations defined themselves as feminist. In 1989 there were nine hundred registered women's groups in Spain but only a tiny percentage of the female population belonged to such a group. In 1994 women MPs constituted only 16 percent of the total in parliament.

Spanish feminism was undermined because of the lack of a suffragette movement, the lack of a democratic institutional framework, and the rejection of women-only sex-segregated organizations. Key reforms regarding women's emancipation are seen to have been the work of the centre-left rather than the women's movement. The Socialist victory of 1982 saw the implementation of much necessary legislation but, arguably, the greatest obstacle to women's independence in the 1990s was women's unemployment. In 1987 Spain had the largest percentages of unemployed and non-active women in the EU.

See also: Falcón, Lidia; feminist writing; Instituto de la Mujer; women; women's writing

Further reading

Acklesberg, M.A. (1991) *Free Women of Spain. Anarchism and the Struggle for the Emancipation of Women*, Pennsylvania: Indiana University Press (one of the most scholarly studies of this topic).

Brooksbank Jones, A. (1997) *Women in Contemporary Spain*, Manchester: Manchester University Press (the most thorough and detailed account concentrating on the transition period until the mid-1990s).

Graham, H. and Labanyi, J. (1995) *Spanish Cultural Studies: An Introduction*, Oxford: Oxford University Press (several good essays on women in Spain).

Scanlon, G. (1976) *Polémica feminista en la España contemporánea (1868–1974)*, Madrid: Siglo XXI (a detailed survey of feminism from 1868 until Franco's death; the original thesis is available in English in the University of London).

Slaughter, J. and Kern R. (eds) (1981) *European Women on the Left*, Westport, CT: Greenwood (includes chapters on socialist Margarita Nelken and anarchist Federica Montseny).

Threlfall, M. (1985) 'The Women's Movement in Spain', *New Left Review*, 151: 44–73 (the most complete short overview of the Spanish women's movement between 1975 and 1985).

CATHERINE DAVIES

feminist writing

Feminist writing in Spain can be divided into three categories in order of importance: socio-historical studies; creative literature; and theoretical studies.

Since the 1970s there has been a concerted effort (mainly on the part of women journalists and academics) to study the situation of women in

Spain and to chart Spanish women's history (including the history of **feminism**). Interest has focused predominantly on the current social status of **women**, examined from diverse points of view (economic, political, cultural, demographic and educational) with special emphasis on the legal position of women and equal opportunities in the work place. These sociological studies are generally fully documented and rigorous in their analyses. Historical studies are not so plentiful, although there is growing interest among researchers, particularly with reference to women's work, education, demography, art and politics during the nineteenth and twentieth centuries. Mary Nash (1983) is typical in this respect. Leading researchers in the field of sociological and historical studies, including Carmen Alcalde, Concepción Borreguero, María Campo Alange, Rosa María Capel Martínez, and María Angeles Durán, often work in collaboration with the Women's Studies Centres set up in the Universities of Barcelona, Madrid and San Sebastián among others. Further interest has been fomented by numerous conferences and seminar series such as the *Jornadas Interdisciplinarias* (Interdisciplinary Conferences) organized by the Autonomous and Complutense Universities in Madrid and the Spanish Association of Research into Women's History, presided over by Mary Nash. The Documentation Centre at the **Instituto de la Mujer**, established in 1983, is invaluable and the Institute also makes funding available for publications, conferences and similar events. In addition to the above, recent editions of the virtually unknown works of early feminists (for example, Concepción Arenal, Clara Campoamor and Margarita Nelken) are being published in increasing numbers. Several bibliographical studies, essential tools of research, have appeared since 1980. An impressive example is María del Carmen Simón Palmer's research on nineteenth-century Spanish women writers who, she discovered, published widely on all subjects, from medicine to poetry. A sizeable bibliography of social and historical studies now exists covering all aspects of women's lives in Spain.

The popular texts of the 1970s and early 1980s which traced the development of the feminist movement in Spain and elsewhere (authored by, for example, Maria Aurèlia **Capmany**, Anabel González, Anna Mercade, Magda Oranich and Montserrat **Roig**) have given way to more theoretically oriented studies of feminism, gender and sexuality. Spanish feminist thinkers have developed interesting new directions in feminist theory and are fully briefed in important debates abroad thanks to the plethora of translations of foreign feminist texts published in, for example, Cátedra's 'Feminisms' Collection in collaboration with the Instituto de la Mujer. Perhaps the most prominent feminist writer since the 1970s has been the militant feminist Lidia **Falcón** whose theory of feminism as a political instrument to vindicate women as a social class is expounded in several works. The philosopher Celia Amorós (1985) writes on feminism and ethics. In her later work she traces a feminist philosophical memory in seventeenth-century Enlightenment thought. Similarly, the philosopher Alicia Puleo (1992) inserts the themes of gender and sex in discussions on contemporary philosophy. Victoria Sau (1986) proposes a 'matristic' model in which binaries (love/war, nature/culture) are annulled in a femino-centric synthesis. Radical feminist Victoria Sendón de León (1981) develops the ideas of Luce Irigaray and defends the concept of an uncompromising Ginandria which is neither an Androginia nor feminism but the rejection of the pretence of integration.

Concurrent with these factual and theoretical studies exists a substantial corpus of feminist fiction which has blossomed since the 1970s. The long but somewhat sporadic tradition of female-authored feminist fiction (particularly short fiction) which, following the fortunes of the feminist movement, flourished in the 1920s and 1930s (in the work of Carmen de Burgos, Margarita Nelken, Eva Carmen Nelken and Federica Montseny) but almost disappeared in the 1940s and 1950s, re-emerged with a vengeance after Franco's death. The early post-Franco fiction of authors such as Rosa **Montero**, Montserrat Roig, Carme **Riera** and María Xosé Queizán examines contemporary feminist topics such as divorce, abortion, double militancy (see also **feminism**) and relationships between women usually within the framework of individual women's experiences and lifestories, set in the present or the past. In much of the fiction published by feminist authors after 1980 emphasis is placed on women as subjects of (erotic) desire and female sexuality, thus giving rise to an important current of female-authored erotic fiction describing heterosexual or lesbian relationships. Important in this respect is the novelist Esther **Tusquets**. Spanish women writers, however, have not been keen to be labelled feminists and few (if any) would describe their work as exclusively feminist. As is the case in the other disciplines mentioned above, the unjustly neglected work of feminist novelists, poets and dramatists of the past is now being brought to light and published in modern editions, in collections such as Castalia's 'Women Writers' Series produced in collaboration with the Instituto de la Mujer.

See also: Falcón, Lidia; feminism; women; women's writing

References

Amorós, C. (1985) *Hacia una crítica de la razón patriarcal*, Barcelona: Anthropos.

Nash, M. (1983) *Mujer, familia y trabajo en España 1875–1936*, Barcelona: Anthropos.

Puleo, A.H. (1992) *Dialéctica de la sexualidad*, Madrid: Cátedra/Instituto de la Mujer.

Sau, V. (1986) *Aportaciones para una lógica del feminismo*, Barcelona: La Sal.

Sendón de León, V. (1981) *Sobre diosas, Amazonas y vestales: utopías para un feminismo radical*, Madrid: Zero ZXY.

Further reading

Aguado, A., Capel, R. and Glez, T. *et al.* (eds) (1994) *Textos para la historia de las mujeres en España*, Madrid: Cátedra (includes a substantial section on the twentieth century).

Capel Martínez, R. (ed.) ([1982] 1986), *Mujer y sociedad en España 1700–1975*, Madrid: Instituto de la Mujer.

Davies, C. (1991) *Contemporary Feminist Fiction in Spain. The Work of Montserrat Roig and Rosa Montero*, Oxford: Berg.

—— (1998) *Spanish Women's Writing 1849–1996*, London: Athlone.

Folguera, P. (ed.) (1988) *El feminismo en España. Dos siglos de historia*, Madrid: Editorial Pablo Iglesias.

CATHERINE DAVIES

ferias

Well over a hundred trade fairs take place annually throughout Spain and are hosted by Fair Organizations in some fourteen centres. In Madrid the Fair Institution (IFEMA), comprising the Autonomous Region, the City Hall, the Chamber of Commerce and Industry and Cajamadrid, operates from Parque Ferial Juan Carlos I, a purpose-built exhibition ground. It hosts twenty or more fairs on contemporary art (ARCO), footwear, musical instruments, optics, antiques, sporting goods, tourism, jewellery, leather, fur, fashions, scientific instruments, education, furniture, gifts, office equipment and the **Madrid Book Fair**, many of them international in scope.

Outside the capital an International Samples Fair operates from Valencia and hosts over twenty fairs including modern and contemporary art (Interart), musical instruments (Intermusic), fashions, furniture and so on, as in Madrid, but also international fairs in areas such as ceramics, paper, toys, lighting, agricultural and meat industries, hunting and fishing, and pharmaceuticals. The Fira de Barcelona also hosts over twenty fairs in many of the trades already mentioned and in wines and spirits, packaging, catering, cars, sports and computer science, among others. Bilbao's trade fairs are biennial and concentrate principally on industries such as machine tools, machine systems, foundries, welding, electrical and electronics, new technologies, naval, maritime and fishing, and forestry. Other major trade fair centres include The National Official Fair Institute based in Zaragoza, which hosts over fifteen fairs, among them civil defence, robotics, a gardening and floral art show and a water fair, and FIBES, the Ibero-American Trade Fair in Seville which also hosts fairs in building and public works, stone working and agricultural machinery.

A special trade exhibition **Expo-92** was held in Seville in 1992 in conjunction with the **Quinto Centenario**.

EAMONN RODGERS

Fernán Gómez, Fernando

b. 1921, Lima (Peru)

Actor and filmmaker

Hugely successful as a film actor, Fernán Gómez is also a noted film director, novelist, dramatist and poet. Born in Peru but brought up in Spain from a very early age, he began his acting career in the theatre when the Civil War interrupted his studies. In 1951 he played the husband in *Esa pareja feliz* (That Happy Couple, directed by **Berlanga** and **Bardem**) and continued to work with leading directors. In the 1970s he played roles in films such as **Saura**'s *Ana y los lobos* (Anna and the Wolves) (1972), **Erice**'s *El espíritu de la colmena* (The Spirit of the Beehive) (1973), **Armiñán**'s *El amor del capitán Brando* (The Love of Captain Brando) (1974) and Juan Estelrich's *El anacoreta* (The Anchorite) (1976) for which he was awarded the prestigious Silver Bear at Berlin. In the 1980s he appeared in films by **Gutiérrez Aragón** such as *Maravillas* (1980), *La noche mas hermosa* (The Most Beautiful Night) (1984) and *La mitad del cielo* (Half of Heaven) (1986), in Saura's *Los zancos* (Stilts) (1984) which he co-scripted, and in Armiñán's *Stico* (1984) for which he again won a Silver Bear at Berlin. In the 1990s he appeared in **Trueba**'s Oscar winning film *Belle Epoque* (1993).

As well as acting in well over a hundred films he has also directed many films of his own since 1952. *Mambrú se fué a la guerra* (Marlborough Went to War) (1986) and *El viaje a ninguna parte* (Journey to Nowhere) (1986), in which he also stars, are good examples of his gentle, subtle humour, the latter being described as 'the most distinguished film of the year'.

As a dramatist he won the Lope de Vega Prize in 1977 for his play *Las bicicletas son para el verano* (Bicycles are for Summer) which was adapted for the screen by **Chávarri** in 1984. He has also written, produced and acted in several television series such as *El Pícaro* (The Rogue) (1973) and *Juan Soldado* (Soldier John) (1973), and in 1990 published a two-volume work, *El tiempo amarillo* (Time in Yellow).

See also: film and cinema; theatre

EAMONN RODGERS

Fernández Cubas, Cristina

b. 1945, Arenys de Mar (Barcelona)

Writer

Since publication in 1980 and 1983, respectively, of collections of fantastic tales, *Mi hermana Elba* (My Sister Elba) and *Los altillos de Brumal* (The Attics of Brumal), Fernández Cubas has figured among the most admired authors of her generation. Novels and later stories sometimes continue in the fantastic mode but also explore more realistic approaches. Her narratives typically include some combination of the following: parody, intertextuality and metafiction, including emphasis on oral storytelling; humour and irony; a fascination with language, the non-verbal, and the failure of communication systems; identity crises, madness, and other psychoanalytical concerns. In 1995, she published the novel *El columpio* (The Swing).

PHYLLIS ZATLIN

Fernández de la Reguera Ugarte, Ricardo

b. 1916, Barcenillas (Santander)

Writer

Popular for his direct realistic style, Fernández de la Reguera achieved commercial success first with the hard-hitting 1950 novel, *Cuando me voy a morir* (In the Darkness of My Fury), recipient of the City of Barcelona Award. His success continued in 1952 with *Cuerpo a tierra* (Reach for the Ground), based on his experiences in Franco's army during the Spanish Civil War. He writes primarily novels, but also short stories, literary critiques and histories. In the 1960s, he and his wife, the poet Susana **March**, collaborated on *Episodios nacionales contemporáneos* (Contemporary National Episodes), a series of ten novels on contemporary Spanish history.

FRIEDA H. BLACKWELL

Fernández-Miranda, Torcuato

b. 1915, Gijón (Asturias); d. 1980, London

University professor and politician

Fernández-Miranda was a key figure in the democratizing process which followed Franco's death in 1975. He designed the master plan which facilitated the legal transition from dictatorship to democracy. In a very apt metaphor that process of transition has been likened to a dramatic play in which the King was the producer, **Suárez** the main actor, and Fernández-Miranda the playwright.

Fernández-Miranda is often described as an enigmatic figure. There are undoubtedly some very mystifying contradictions in his biography. Before 1975, both his political activity and his writings convey the impression of a complex and reactionary politician, loyal to the dictatorship, and always inclined to oppose any liberalizing attempt during the Franco years. And yet, when the dictator died, Fernández-Miranda was to provide the formula that made democracy possible in Spain. This is the great paradox in his life, a paradox which until now nobody has explained convincingly.

Until 1969 Fernández-Miranda's presence in Spanish public life was not particularly prominent. He had fought in the Civil War on Franco's side. At the end of the war he completed his law degree, and at the age of 30 he became professor of Politics at Oviedo University, and later, in 1951, rector of the same institution. His political career started at about this time. As university rector he had a seat in parliament, and subsequently occupied several posts in the Ministry of Education and the National Movement. At the beginning of the 1960s he was chosen as one of Prince Juan Carlos' tutors. This appointment was to have a lasting effect on both tutor and pupil.

Given his relative political obscurity until then, and the fact that he did not have close links with any of the political groups in the Franco system, his appointment as Secretary General of the **National Movement** in the government reshuffle of October 1969 came as a surprise. However, his position was further strengthened when **Carrero Blanco** was appointed Prime Minister in the summer of 1973: Fernández-Miranda not only kept his post as head of the National Movement, but became Deputy Prime Minister. During his years in government he was seen as a clear opponent of any proposal which might have pushed Spain towards liberal democracy. Such a political stance was in line with the ideological principles defended in many of his writings: a curious mixture of idiosyncratic **Falange** ideology and traditional Catholicism.

Nevertheless, a profound transformation was to follow. After the assassination of Carrero Blanco by the Basque terrorist group ETA, Fernández-Miranda became acting head of government for a few days, but he must have felt profoundly hurt when Franco finally chose Arias Navarro rather than him to replace the assassinated Prime Minister.

Fernández-Miranda returned to the political arena after Franco's demise. One of the first decisions taken by Juan Carlos after his coronation was to appoint his old tutor as Speaker of Parliament and Chairman of the Council of the Realm, one of the most powerful posts in Franco's political system. From such a position and over a period of less than eighteen months, a completely transformed Fernández-Miranda was to carry out a quiet, efficient, and in some respects Machiavellian operation which would make possible the 'miracle' of turning the dictatorship into a democracy without major upheavals. During those eighteen months Fernández-Miranda advised the King in moments of crisis; he contributed to the downfall of Arias Navarro, the inflexible Prime Minister left behind by Franco; together with the King he skilfully manipulated the levers of power to secure the appointment of Adolfo Suárez to replace Arias Navarro; he offered Suárez and his new government the blueprint for the *Ley para la Reforma Política* (Law of Political Reform), which was the key to constitutional change; and, finally, he succeeded in steering this bill through a Francoist parliament, forcing upon most of its members the acceptance of political suicide.

Apart from his influence on the King, which was no doubt considerable but impossible to ascertain in objective terms, Fernández-Miranda's greatest political achievement was the *Ley para la Reforma*

Política, a brief and intentionally ambiguous legal text with enormous constitutional implications. Its final approval in a referendum held on 15 December 1976 made unworkable most of the political institutions left behind by Franco and, formally at least, gave sovereignty back to the Spanish people so as to enable them to build a new democratic system. Fernández-Miranda's plan had to do with means, not ends; it did not predetermine the nature of political reform, it just made it possible.

From the beginning of 1977, relations between the Prime Minister and Fernández-Miranda started to deteriorate. Suárez, who until then had relied so heavily on him, realized he no longer needed his political mentor. For his part, Fernández-Miranda did not like some of the changes brought about by Suárez: there was a major disagreement between them over the legalization of the communist **PCE** in the spring of 1977. Disenchantment led to his resignation as Speaker of Parliament at the end of May, two weeks before the first democratic elections were due to take place. His services were rewarded by the King with a dukedom.

From that moment on Fernández-Miranda's political career declined rapidly. He was appointed senator by King Juan Carlos and considered becoming a parliamentary candidate for the **Popular Alliance**. Little by little he withdrew from public life and did not make the headlines again until the announcement of his death during a private visit to London.

Further reading

Alcocer, J.L. (1986) *Torcuato Fernández-Miranda. Agonía de un estado*, Barcelona: Planeta (an analysis of Fernández-Miranda's political career through the eyes of a friend and admirer).

Amodia, J. (1992) 'Torcuato Fernández-Miranda: El taumaturgo de la transición', *ACIS* 5, 2: 40–51 (an evaluation of TFM as an academic, a politician and a monarchist).

Fernández-Miranda, P. and A. (1995) *Lo que el Rey me ha pedido*, Barcelona: Plaza & Janés (a fundamental study based on TFM's private papers, though partly marred by the proximity of the authors to their subject).

Vilallonga, J.L. de (1993) *El Rey. Conversaciones con D. Juan Carlos I de España*, Barcelona: Plaza & Janés (the best source to get some insight into the King's views on TFM).

JOSÉ AMODIA

Fernández Santos, Jesús

b. 1926, Madrid; d. 1988, Madrid

Writer

Jesús Fernández Santos was a prominent member of a group of Spanish novelists commonly known as the 'Generation of the 1950s'. The realistic orientation and *engagé* approach to literature espoused by these writers became the predominant literary force in Spain during the 1950s and 1960s. Fernández Santos' 1954 novel *Los bravos* (The Untamed) is widely considered the first important novel of social realism of the post-war period and serves as a model for the development of social realistic fiction over the next fifteen years. With its emphasis on a collective protagonist and detailed portrayal of the harsh daily life in rural Spain, the novel conflicts sharply with the representation of the national identity promoted by the Franco regime during the same period.

During the 1960s and 1970s Fernández Santos' narrative development paralleled the general movement in Spain towards a more diversified form of writing. His novels and short stories of this period reflected a growing concern for the existential dilemma of individuals rather than the social problems of the masses. His works also embodied many of the innovative stylistic and technical devices aimed at enhancing the complexity of structure and language. In his 1969 novel, *El hombre de los santos* (The Man of the Saints) and in *Libro de las memorias de las cosas* (The Book of Memorable Events), winner of the 1970 **Nadal Prize**, Fernández Santos probes the despair and emptiness of characters who are shaped by psychological rather than historical time and whose memory affords the only possible escape from solitude.

In the final decade of his career Fernández Santos began to pursue a life-long interest in historical fiction. In *Extramuros*, for example, winner of the National Literary Prize in 1979, he explores the incestuous relationship of two nuns in sixteenth-century Spain who seek to save their convent from pestilence and drought through the contrivance of a miracle: the wounds of Christ's stigmata that one of the nuns inflicts upon the other. Fernández Santos also explores the psycho-historical dilemmas of women protagonists in other novels of this period, such as the 1982 **Planeta Prize** winner *Jaque a la dama* (Check the Lady), set in Spain and Italy before and after WWII, and *La que no tiene nombre* (The One Without a Name), which takes place primarily in medieval Spain.

Throughout his career Fernández Santos worked to revivify his writing and to progress towards heightened psychological representation and technical sophistication. He stands as one of the most versatile writers of post-war Spain, but his most important contribution to Spanish letters are his early novels and short stories of social realism and his belief that fiction is an able vehicle for promoting social change.

See also: censorship; Francoist culture; literature; novel

Further reading

Alborg, C. (1984) *Temas y técnicas en la narrativa de Jesús Fernández Santos*, Madrid: Gredos (a thorough study of themes and techniques in Fernández Santos' fiction, with a strong bibliography).

Herzberger, D. (1983) *Jesús Fernández Santos*, Boston, MA: Twayne Publishers (a detailed overview of Fernández Santos' fiction and essays up to 1981).

DAVID K. HERZBERGER

Ferrater, Gabriel

b. 1922, Reus; d. 1972, Sant Cugat del Vallés

Poet, critic and linguistician

Ferrater burst on the Catalan literary scene in 1960 with his first book of poems, to be followed in quick succession by two further volumes, all of which were collected in 1968 under the title *Les dones i els dies* (Women and Days). In the atmosphere of the 1960s, with its emphasis on 'social realism', Ferrater's poems could not fail to be disconcerting: though they dealt to a great extent with everyday life, they were concerned, not so much with 'realism' as such, but with what goes to make up an individual life. This is partly a moral undertaking; as Ferrater himself once wrote:

> When I write a poem, the only thing which concerns me – and which gives me trouble – is to define as clearly as possible my moral attitudes, that is to say, the distance between the feelings the poem expresses and what one might call the centre of my imagination.
>
> (epilogue to *Da nuces pueris* (Nuts for the Boys), 1960)

In his two longest poems, *In memoriam* (1960) and *Poema inacabat* (Unfinished Poem) (1966), memory forms a crucial part of this exercise. In the first, a series of anecdotes from a wartime adolescence alternate with more reflective passages in an attempt to grasp experience which was not understood at the time, but which, seen from an adult point of view, seems to make up some sort of pattern. And in *Poema inacabat*, though anecdote is not so prominent, the fact that the poem is addressed to a girl much younger than himself enables Ferrater not only to look back on his *own* past but to advise his addressee on how to conduct her own life. Above all, he argues, she has a 'right to be happy', though this can only be achieved against enormous odds – the odds he explores in a series of remarkably clear-sighted love poems.

Ferrater's moral attitudes do not depend on any transcendental system of beliefs; like Thomas Hardy, one of his favourite poets, he writes simply from his own life, concerned with capturing the perceptions – the 'moments of vision' – which unexpectedly interrupt the surface of everyday existence. Though his aims are strictly rational, he also makes due allowance for the irrational – something which accounts for the metaphorical richness of his poems and his willingness to face up to ambiguities. Few poets have left such a vivid record of what it was to live through the atmosphere which followed the Civil War, something which emerges almost incidentally from what are essentially personal poems. Above all, Ferrater writes about a recognizable world; his poems are a serious and many-sided attempt to show what it means to live in this world – one which is accessible to anyone with eyes to see it.

Further reading

Macià, X. and Perpinyà, N. (1986) *La poesia de Gabriel Ferrater*, Barcelona: Edicions 62.

Perpinyà, N. (1991) *'Teoria dels cossos' de Gabriel Ferrater*, Barcelona: Editorial Empúries (on Ferrater's final collection).

Terry, A. (1979) 'Preface' to G. Ferrater, *Mujeres y días*, Barcelona: Seix Barral.

ARTHUR TERRY

FEVE

In 1965 the state-owned railway company Ferrocarriles Españoles de Via Estrecha (FEVE) was formed to take control of the publicly owned narrow gauge railway system (see also **railways**). Some parts of the narrow gauge system were transferred to the regions in 1978, leaving FEVE free to operate a network which in 1996 extended over some 1,100 km in the north of Spain. Passenger traffic is concentrated on urban commuter lines, discouraged from using longer distance routes by slow speeds resulting from single track working, sharp curves, steep gradients and circuitous routes (although these characteristics have been taken advantage of in operating a tourist train, the 'Transcantábrico').

Further reading

Wais, F. (1987) 'Ferrocarriles de via estrecha', in *Historia de los ferrocarriles españoles*, 3rd edn, vol. 2, chapter 18, Madrid: Editora Nacional for the Fundación de los Ferrocarriles Españoles (discussion of the development of the narrow gauge railway system in Spain).

KEITH SALMON

fiestas

Each of the approximately 8,000 villages and small towns in Spain has its own annual *fiesta*, which in the smaller and poorer villages can last a few days, and in the larger towns anything from a week to a month. Despite the long-standing pattern of migration from the villages to the major cities, many people return to their family's place of origin to take part in the *fiesta*. These occasions originated in religious festivals, though increasingly they have come to be combined with civic celebrations. Typically, there is a solemn religious ceremony attended by the village dignitaries in full regalia, and a series of secular events celebrating regional dress, food, music and sports. There are often literary competitions, plays, ***corridas***, all emphasizing their distinctively local character, as well as special events for particular groups, such as senior citizens, children, guilds and civic and religious fraternities. A raffle, where the prize is a lamb or a calf, is sometimes used to finance a banquet specifically for the single young men and women of the village. All of this takes place to the accompaniment of music and *verbenas*, that is, open-air dancing, especially at night.

The importance of **tourism** has led many towns and villages to invest a great deal of effort in enhancing the beauty and distinctiveness of their *fiestas*. Some are officially designated as events of 'International Tourist Interest', such as the Carnivals of Santa Cruz de Tenerife and Cadiz, the **Holy Week Processions** of Seville, Valladolid, Málaga, Cuenca and Zamora, the April Fair in Seville, the Pamplona *Sanfermines* (the running of the bulls, widely publicized by Hemingway), the ***fallas*** in Valencia and Alicante, the festival of Corpus Christi in Toledo, the mock battle between Moors and Christians in Alcoy, the Elche Mystery Play and the Wine Harvest in Jérez de la Frontera.

Many towns have, in addition to their major festival, a second one, primarily for local people, without the overwhelming presence of tourists, such as the unpublicized 'Little San Fermín' in Pamplona. There are also less elaborate festivals marking particular events in the agricultural calendar, such as the blessing of the animals on St Anthony's day, the celebration of the wine harvest at Michaelmas, and the *Cruz de mayo* (The

May Cross) to mark the culmination of spring. The Day of the Dead is celebrated throughout Spain on 2 November. Many places in Spain have their local pilgrimage or procession in honour of the Virgin, the most famous being the *Rocío* (Our Lady of the Dew) in Almonte (Huelva, Andalusia), which brings together up to a million people, and the *Virgen del Pilar* (Our Lady of the Pillar) in Zaragoza, the latter a brilliant spectacle of colour from the huge quantity of flowers carried in procession.

To these traditional *fiestas* have been added in modern times public holidays marking events of national significance, such as the National Day on 12 October, and Constitution Day on 6 December. Spain has also adopted international secular festivals of a more commercial character, such as Father's Day and Mother's Day.

See also: Basque culture; Canarian culture; Catalan culture; Galician culture

CARLOS ÁLVAREZ ARAGÜÉS

Filesa

This was a corruption case in which the socialist **PSOE** was accused of illegally financing itself in the late 1980s by selling phantom consulting services to big business. Named after a Barcelona-based group of consultancy companies, Filesa allegedly financed the PSOE government's 1989 general election campaign. In particular, it was suspected that the Filesa group received a sum of 1,000m pesetas (approximately $8.4m) from leading domestic banks, principally the **BBV** and the Banco Central, and several companies including Catalana de Gas, and the Pryca supermarket chain, in return for fictitious consultancy reports. Filesa was controlled by Carlos Navarro, a member of parliament and former treasurer of the PSOE parliamentary party and by Senator José María Sala, administrative secretary of the **Catalan Socialist Party** and a member of the party's national executive.

Filesa then supposedly made direct payments to service companies supplying the PSOE campaign headquarters, but in order to disguise the payments it took receipts, not from party suppliers, but from a group of companies, called 2020, controlled by Aida Alvarez, a former national co-ordinator of the PSOE's finances. Moreover, the 2020 group of companies itself was linked in press reports to large consultancy payments made by Germany's Siemens group in exchange for obtaining a contract in 1989 to provide the electrification for the high-speed train link between Madrid and Seville.

The PSOE reacted to the scandal by criticizing the judge in charge of the case, Marino Barbero, arguing that the investigation was politically motivated and part of a wider conspiracy to undermine the PSOE administration. The government narrowly avoided a special parliamentary investigation into the Filesa affair and established instead a parliamentary commission charged with investigating the financing of all political parties since 1979, when the first local elections were held under the new democratic regime. In this way, the socialists limited the damage to themselves by focusing on the problem in general rather than concentrating on any particular cases.

The fact that the right-wing **PP** found itself embroiled in a similar scandal to the Filesa affair, which forced it to sack its national treasurer for allegedly organizing illicit funding in 1990, does suggest that the question of irregular party financing is one that affects all parties in Spain. In particular, it highlights the difficulties parties face in meeting the ever-growing financial costs arising from the continous round of municipal, regional and general elections with their ever-greater stress on advertising and the mass media, as well as the costs of financing large party bureaucracies staffed by paid officials.

See also: corruption; political parties; politics

Further reading

Heywood, P. (ed.) (1995) *Distorting Democracy: Political Corruption in Spain, Italy and Malta*, CMS Occasional Paper, No. 10; University of Bristol: Centre for Mediterranean Studies.

Hooper, J. (1995) *The New Spaniards*, Harmondsworth: Penguin (corruption is analysed in several chapters, particularly chapters 5 and 31).

Martín de Pozuelo, E. *et al.* (1994) *Guía de la Corrupción*, Barcelona: Plaza & Janes (a journalistic guide to the various corruption cases in Spain).

GEORGINA BLAKELEY

film and cinema

In 1996 Spain celebrated the centenary of its film industry. During these hundred years, individual directors, actors and films had local and international successes, but the industry as a whole had also more than its fair share of troubles.

Closely linked to the political and cultural life of the country and its regions, Spanish filmmaking is very susceptible both to constitutional and policy changes within Spain and to influences from without. The victory of Franco that brought an end to the Civil War ushered in a lengthy period of rigorous **censorship** that had long-term effects on Spanish cinema. Portraits of an ideal Spain in historical epics, religious dramas and folkloric productions, such as those produced by Cifesa (Compañía Industrial Film Español) in the 1930s and 1940s, were the order of the day. Franco himself scripted and oversaw the making of a notorious film called *Raza* (Race) (1941), and from 1942 all news and documentary films were produced by the official film company Noticiarios y Documentales Cinematográficos, or NO-DO as it was commonly known. Scripts had to be submitted to the Board of Censors before filming could even begin, and the finished film resubmitted. All foreign films were reviewed and either completely banned, or underwent compulsory **dubbing**. This procedure was to prove particularly detrimental to local production, since licences to import and dub were granted preferentially to production companies whose Spanish films most reflected Francoist orthodoxy. There was therefore a strong financial incentive both to ensure that native-produced films confined themselves to reflecting the prevailing ideology, and to minister to the popular demand for foreign films. From 1952, the rewards for political orthodoxy took the form of a sliding scale of subsidies, which could mean rebates on production costs of as much as 50 percent for films considered 'of national interest'.

Among the many artists and intellectuals who went into **exile** in this period was **Buñuel**, whose iconoclasm had already got him into trouble. He eventually settled in Mexico and became internationally known in the 1960s and 1970s for films such as *The Discreet Charm of the Bourgeoisie* (1972). It was ironic that *Viridiana*, a film produced by him in Spain in 1960 in response to an invitation, was not only passed by the Spanish censors but was Spain's official entry at the Cannes Film Festival in 1961, and was immediately banned until 1977, having incurred the wrath of the Roman Catholic Church. But not all dissident voices were silenced, and by dint of various ruses, such as submitting a different version to the censors, many fine films were produced in defiance of the regime, such as **Bardem**'s powerful critiques of contemporary society, *Muerte de un ciclista* (Death of a Cyclist) (1955) and *Calle Mayor* (Main Street) (1956), **Berlanga**'s black comedy *El verdugo* (The Executioner) (1963), **Erice**'s acclaimed *El espíritu de la colmena* (The Spirit of the Beehive) (1973), Ricardo **Franco**'s *Pascual Duarte* (1974), and **Borau**'s anti-Franco film *Furtivos* (Poachers) (1975). **Saura** in particular was able, through reminiscence, symbolism and other oblique forms of reference, to evoke the tensions of the Civil War and the oppressive nature of the Franco regime in films such as *La Caza* (The Hunt) (1965), *Ana y los lobos* (Anna and the Wolves) (1972), *La prima Angélica* (Cousin Angelica) (1973) and *Cría cuervos* (Raise Ravens) (1975).

With the death of Franco and the transition to democracy came a freedom both to explore the past and to set out in new directions. Already in preparation in 1975 was **Camino**'s *Las largas vaciones del 36* (The Long Holidays of '36) based on reminiscences, from the Republican viewpoint, of the outbreak of the Civil War. The old animosities nevertheless ran deep: the coda to that film, in which a detachment of Moorish cavalry is seen riding menacingly towards the viewer during the final credits, was cut by the censors. **Gutiérrez Aragón**'s *Camada negra* (Black Brood) (1977), a study of a fascist terrorist family, also proved highly controversial. The atmosphere of the times was frequently recreated through adaptation of literary works, among the best examples being **Camus**' *La colmena* (The Hive, 1982, based on **Cela**'s 1951 novel), set in a Madrid café in 1942, and **Chávarri**'s *Las bicicletas son para el verano* (Bicycles are for Summer, 1984, based on the play by **Fernán Gómez**), set in Madrid at the outbreak of the Civil War. **Garci**'s *Volver a empezar* (To Begin Again) (1982) exploited the theme of the returned Republican exile, which was already appearing in films towards the end of the Franco regime, such as **Armiñán**'s *El amor del Capitán Brando* (Captain Brando's Love) (1974). Documentary films began to make their appearance, including those of **Patino** made in secret in the 1970s: *Canciones para después de una guerra* (Songs for After a War) (1971), described as 'one of the most evocative films ever made in Spain', and *Caudillo* (Military Boss) (1976); Camino's *La vieja memoria* (Old Memories) (1976), **Herralde**'s *Raza, el espíritu de Franco* (Raza, the Spirit of Franco) (1977) and Pilar **Miró**'s *El crimen de Cuenca* (The Cuenca Crime) (1979), released only in 1981, after an attempt at suppression by the military authorities. Then in 1985 **Berlanga** made *La vaquilla* (The Little Bull), a comedy set in the Civil War, which had been turned down several times by the censors. The film created a box-office record, and established that, more than forty years after the tragic events of that period, audiences could laugh as well as weep at them.

Relaxation in censorship also opened the door to more explicit treatment of sexual matters, and of the social mores both of the older and of the younger, more 'liberated' urban Spain. In 1977 Berlanga produced the first and most successful of a trilogy of farces featuring the Spanish aristocracy, *La escopeta nacional* (The National Shotgun), **Aranda**'s *La muchacha de las bragas de oro* (The Girl in the Golden Panties) (1980) exploited the contrast between the older and newer Spains, and **Almodóvar**'s early films reflected the Madrid urban lifestyle known as *la* ***Movida***.

No sooner were Spanish filmmakers freed from ideological control, however, than they came face to face with the harsh realities of the marketplace, for the easing of censorship also released a flood of foreign films into Spain, especially from America and Italy. Spanish producers' share of local box-office receipts, which was almost 30 percent in 1977, declined rapidly to just over 16 percent in 1979, never rose again above 23 percent, and since 1989 has been around 10 to 12 percent, though occasionally dropping to little more than 7 percent. Added to this has been the overall drop in cinema attendance from 255,785,000 in 1975 to 94,600,000 in 1995, due in some measure, as elsewhere, to increased private viewing of videos and television productions.

The response has been two-fold: protectionist measures against non-Spanish films, and state subsidies to bolster the indigenous film industry. Screen quotas, governing the ratio of Spanish to foreign films shown in cinemas, and control of licences to dub and distribute non-Spanish films had to be speedily reintroduced in 1980 and have continued with modifications since then (see also **cinema law**). Spain's entry into the European Community in 1986 adversely affected the ratios, since films made in the other member states had to be included in the Spanish quota. A system of state subsidies, in the form of generous advances against potential box-office receipts, devised by Pilar Miró in 1983, favoured 'quality' and large-budget films in the 1980s, but thereafter economic pressures led to much tighter government budgets and stricter controls. From the early 1990s, too, financial support deriving from sales to Spanish Television (RTVE) began to fail as the state company lost a large proportion of its audience and advertising revenue to the new private channels. By then, many film directors were minimizing the risks by producing for the small screen and/or making domestic comedies, which have always been the most popular form of cinema entertainment in Spain. Other film professionals such as photographers and set designers were also supplementing their living by working in television.

From the mid-1990s, however, the industry was strengthened by new alliances between film and television companies. Two major groupings emerged: the consortium including Sogepaq, Iberoamérica, Polygram, Canal + and Warner España; and the conglomerate of Atrium, Antena 3 television, Cartel and Origen. This resulted in a growth in internal commercial investment, and increasing access to external finance especially through co-productions, which have always formed a sizeable part of the industry. Cinema attendance, too, began to rise as older cinemas were converted into multiple units, and new ones were built in suburban shopping centres, especially round Barcelona and Madrid.

Not all films produced in the 1980s and 1990s proved successful by any means, and government policy towards the industry was often determined by the desire to discourage what have been described as 'forgettable films of minimal audience interest'. But beleaguered though the industry was, many films of national and international repute were produced in a wide range of styles and content. The events of the Civil War and the Franco period still inspired films, many of them adaptations of literary works which themselves took a critical stance towards conservative Spain: Saura's *¡Ay, Carmela!* (1989), based on a 1986 play by **Sanchis Sinisterra**; Camus' *Los santos inocentes* (The Holy Innocents) (1984), derived from a novel by **Delibes**; his film version of Lorca's *La casa de Bernarda Alba* (The House of Bernarda Alba) (1987); Aranda's *Tiempo de silencio* (Time of Silence) (1986), based on the novel by **Martín-Santos**; and Miro's *Beltenebros* (1991). Family relations were explored in Erice's *El Sur* (The South) (1983), and urban life and social problems in films by the Basque directors **La Iglesia**, with *Navajeros* (Knife Fighters) (1980), *Colegas* (Mates) (1982) and *El pico* (The Shoot Up) (1983), and **Armendáriz**, with *Las cartas de Alou* (Alou's Letters) (1990) and *Historias del Kronen* (Kronen Stories) (1994). Directly concerned with Basque political matters were **Uribe**'s *La muerte de Mikel* (Mikel's Murder) (1983) and *Dias contados* (Running Out of Time) (1994) (see also **Medem, Julio; Olea, Pedro**), while in a different vein altogether were the bawdy and bizarre films of the Catalan director **Bigas Luna**, including *Jamón, Jamón* (Salami) (1992) and *Huevos de oro* (Golden Balls) (1993) (see also **Bellmunt, Francesc**). Spain's **flamenco** tradition inspired a series of musicals by Saura, beginning with *Bodas de sangre* (Blood Wedding) (1980) and including *Carmen* (1983), and it was also in the early 1980s that the new and very popular genre of Madrid comedies was born. Among the earliest was **Trueba**'s *Opera prima* (First Effort) (1980), the first of his many successful comedies, in particular *Belle Epoque* (1993), for which he won an Oscar. **Colomo**, the producer of Trueba's first film, himself directed *La mano negra* (The Black Hand) (1980), a tongue-in-cheek spy thriller co-scripted with Trueba, and the box-office winner *La vida alegre* (A Life of Pleasure) (1987). But the best known director of modern Spanish comedy in the 1980s and 1990s has undoubtedly been Almodóvar, whose *Mujeres al borde de un ataque de nervios* (Women on the Edge of a Nervous Breakdown) (1988) continues to head the list of Spain's 'best sellers', followed closely by his *Tacones lejanos* (High Heels) (1991), and not far behind by his *¡Atame!* (Tie Me Up, Tie Me Down!) (1989).

A major contribution to the success of Spanish films has been the talent of producers such as **Querejeta** (associated especially with Saura and Erice and described as one of the most innovative and imaginative in the history of Spanish cinema), and Vicente Gómez (an extremely active producer for many leading directors) and of actors such as Victoria **Abril**, Antonio **Banderas**, Ana **Belén**, Fernando Fernán Gómez, Alfredo **Landa**, Carmen **Maura**, Francisco **Rabal**, and Fernando **Rey**.

See also: film festivals; Salamanca Conversations

Further reading

Besas, P. (1985) *Behind the Spanish Lens: Spanish Cinema under Fascism and Democracy*, Denver, CO: Arden Press (a comprehensive information source).

Higginbotham, V. (1988) *Spanish Cinema under Franco*, Austin, TX: University of Texas Press (one of the most comprehensive surveys of this period).

Hopewell, J. (1986) *Out of the Past: Spanish Cinema After Franco*, London: British Film Institute (a very readable general account of contemporary trends).

Kinder, M. (1993) *Blood Cinema: The Reconstruction of National Identity in Spain*, Berkeley, CA: University of California Press (a psychological approach to the thematic aspects of films).

Molina-Foix, V. (1977) *New Cinema in Spain*, London: British Film Institute (a comprehensive overview of current trends).

EAMONN RODGERS

film festivals

The diversity of film festivals, together with the lack of a coherent policy on the part of the central administration, makes generalization difficult. The most prestigious is **San Sebastián**, followed by Valladolid and the Iberian-American Film Festival of Huelva, all three receiving official funding. Many others, such as those of Barcelona, Valencia or Madrid, are supported by the governments of the **autonomous communities**. Of the specialized types, the oldest are Bilbao (1958), devoted to documentary and shorts, and Sitges (1969) devoted to the fantastic and horror film.

See also: arts funding; film and cinema

Further reading

García Fernández, E.C. (1985) *Historia ilustrada del cine español*, Madrid: Planeta (contains a section devoted to the issue).

XON DE ROS

fisheries

With nearly 20,000 vessels of varying size capable of unloading well over a million tons of fish a year from near and distant waters, the Spanish fishing fleet is the largest by far in the EU. Three-quarters of the fleet is based in the Atlantic and Canarian ports, with Galicia having the lion's share. This region, which includes Vigo, the largest fishing port in Spain, lands half of the country's catch, and fishing remains critically important in providing employment, with one in five jobs dependent on the industry. The very size of the Spanish fishing fleet has occasioned severe problems for itself after the European Community's extension of its territorial waters from 12 to 200 miles on 1 January 1977 and the decline of fish stocks in Spain's traditional fishing grounds. Joining the Community in 1986 (with full integration in the fisheries sector in 1996) has not proved to be a salvation: only a small proportion of Spanish vessels have been granted licences to operate in Community waters, and the Common Fisheries Policy, with its insistence on strict quotas and enforced mooring periods, has been a bitter pill for Spanish fishermen. Particularly badly hit have been the fishing communities of the Cantabrian and Galician coasts.

Increasing restrictions over access to what had been traditional fishing grounds have led to friction and serious incidents between Spanish fishermen and the authorities and/or fishermen of other countries, notably Morocco, France and Canada. Desperate to maintain their threatened livelihood, Spanish fishermen have attempted to re-adjust in a variety of ways: by seeking new, but inevitably more distant, difficult and costly, fishing grounds in international waters; by registering their vessels perfectly legally in other EU countries (and thereby provoking much adverse criticism, especially in the UK); and by flouting Community regulations through landing fish in excess of quota and using illegal nets. The industry clearly faces a difficult future and the process of contraction through the scrapping of older vessels is set to continue. Despite its size the Spanish fishing fleet is much less efficient than those of its main competitors both in terms of catch per boat and catch per crew member, so employment prospects in the industry look bleak. A programme of aid, funded by both the Spanish government and the EU, for modernization and restructuring was begun in the 1990s. Fish farming is considered the only viable long-term response to the crisis caused by depletion of fish stocks, and the government is supporting investments in this sector.

Nevertheless, despite the problems of access to fishing grounds, overcapacity and dwindling fish stocks, demand for fish in Spain continues unabated, requiring increasing amounts of imports and bringing about an overall deficit in international trade in food products. At over 40 kilograms per inhabitant per annum, Spanish consumption of fish is double the European average, and is the second food item by cost (after meat products) of Spanish households. Spanish imports of fish and seafood amount to not much less than half of the country's consumption; exports, including canned products, are approximately one-third of the value of imports.

C.A. LONGHURST

fishing

Spain is a noted venue for fishing enthusiasts. The sport is regulated by the Spanish Fishing Federation, and there are well over a thousand fishing clubs. In 1995, 66,645 licences were issued to men, and 4,251 to women, with the largest numbers by far being issued in the regions of Catalonia (14,345) and Valencia (13,463), with Aragon (9,306) and Andalusia (8,561) as runners up. The total, however, reflects the huge reduction there has been in the overall number of licences, from a peak in late 1970s of over 700,000 to just over 70,000 in the mid-1990s. Drought and pollution in the lower and middle reaches of rivers have taken their toll, but measures to combat declining numbers of fish include re-stocking, fish nurseries and the return of captured fish to the water.

With her long sea coasts, marshes and numerous rivers Spain offers a very wide range of fishing environments, several regions being especially well-known for their good freshwater fishing. In Cantabria the Gorge of La Hermida on the river Deva is noted for trout and salmon, and the village of La Hermida is a celebrated meeting place of anglers. Extremadura boasts excellent trout rivers and marshes that are rich in coarse fish, and the area has produced a good number of records in carp and black bass. In Castilla-La Mancha carp, barbel, black bass, pike, crayfish, salmon and trout, both common and rainbow, are among a very wide variety of fish to be found in rivers and reservoirs. The Upper Tagus and its tributaries in Guadalajara and Cuenca in particular attract large numbers both of native Spaniards and tourists each year, and several of the reservoirs are noted fishing reserves.

World Championships in sea fishing have been won by individual Spaniards and by Spanish teams, and National Championships are held annually in sea fishing, beach-casting and freshwater fishing.

See also: environment; sport and leisure

EAMONN RODGERS

flamenco

Flamenco, a type of Spanish music and dance, first crystallized in its present form in the early eighteenth century, in the gypsy communities of southern Andalusia, particularly in the areas of Seville, Jerez and Cadiz. The origin of the word flamenco is uncertain. One theory is that it is derived from the Arabic words *felamengu* (itinerant peasant) or *flahencon* (collection of songs). Another theory is that it was the term used in the sixteenth century to refer to the Flemish ('flamenco') retinue that Charles I brought from Flanders to Spain. Nor is there complete consensus among flamencologists as to the meaning of flamenco or gypsy song commonly called *cante jondo*, though the majority hold that *jondo* is a variant of the Spanish word *hondo* (deep), and thus means deep song. Others believe it is derived from the Hebrew *jontoh*, referring to songs sung on festive or rest days.

Cante jondo has clear traces of Arabic and Spanish folk melodies, as well as vestiges of Byzantine, Christian and Jewish religious music, the *saeta* being an example of the latter. The music expresses the sorrows and joys (though the former predominate) of daily life, and the songs often commence with a prolonged, plaintive *¡Ay!*, echoing the nocturnal lament of a tribe wandering in unknown lands. There are many sub-species of flamenco song and these different styles are sometimes divided into *cante grande* (grand song) and *cante chico* (small song), though some reject this classification, as each of the various styles has its own inherent difficulties. However, examples of *cante grande* would include the unaccompanied *tonás*, the *fragüeros* or *martinetes* (originating in the blacksmiths' forges, with the beat of the hammer and anvil), *siguiriyas*, *soleares* and the prison songs, or *carceleras*. Examples of the brighter *cante chico* include *bulerías*, *tangos*, *alegrías*, *fandangos*, *sevillanas* and *malagueñas*, the last two named after their places of origin.

The male or female flamenco singer is called *cantaor* or *cantaora* respectively. One of the most heralded singers until his death in 1992 was the diminutive *Camarón de la Isla* (The Shrimp of San Fernando). Over the years *payos* (non-gypsies) have entered flamenco circles and some, like Silverio, Chacón or Pepe de la Matrona became acclaimed performers. Sometimes a singer is said to possess *duende*, an indescribable and illusive inspirational spirit that elevates a performance to high art.

By the mid-1900s much that was being passed off as flamenco was a debased spectacle delivered as cheap tourist entertainment. However, true flamenco is still alive in the intimate gatherings and spontaneous communal *juergas* (parties) held in family patios, local flamenco *peñas* (clubs), or the prestigious Andalusian *cante jondo* festivals.

Further reading

Caba Landa, C. and P. (1988) *Andalucía, su comunismo y su cante jondo*, Cadiz: University of Cadiz.

Pohren, D.E. (1984) *The Art of Flamenco*, UK: Musical New Services Ltd.

Ríos Ruiz, M. (1988) *Introducción al Cante Flamenco*, Madrid: Ediciones Istmo.

JUAN SERRANO

Flores, Lola

b. 1923, Jerez de la Frontera; d. 1995, Madrid

Flamenco singer

Lola Flores was a flamboyant figure who created her own legend and became a popular icon for nearly half a century. The daughter of a bar-owner and a half-gypsy mother, she began singing and dancing **flamenco** round the cafés of Jerez at the age of ten. By the time she was fifteen, she was touring Andalusia with a variety company, and in 1940 she settled in Madrid. At a time of stifling conformity, she defied convention with a long and much publicized affair with the flamenco singer Manolo Caracol, the first of many lovers, reportedly including football stars, bullfighters and film directors. In addition to touring Spain and South America with flamenco shows, she appeared in many films, and by the late 1950s was reputed to earn a million pesetas per picture, a fabulous sum at that time. Her nickname *La Faraona* (a gypsy term meaning 'the Queen' (of flamenco)), derived from one of her songs, aptly encapsulated her lifestyle.

In 1957, she married an impoverished Catalan singer, Antonio González ('*El Pescaílla*'), with whom she lived happily for nearly forty years, and had three children, Lolita, Antonio and Rosario, who also made careers in music and the cinema, though with somewhat more modest success. Her later years were marred by difficulties over unpaid arrears of tax, when she was prosecuted in 1989 for failing to declare her income for the years 1982 to 1985.

Lola Flores became a national institution to the extent that she was frequently asked to perform for Franco on 18 July, the anniversary of the military insurrection which began the Civil War. After the dictator's death, she had to defend herself against a wave of criticism for apparently compromising with the regime, but in the long run her popularity remained undimmed. When she died from cancer in May 1995, she lay in state in an auditorium in the *Centro Cultural de la Villa* (the Madrid city Cultural Centre), and some 150,000 people filed past her coffin amid scenes of great emotion. Her son Antonio was unable to come to terms with her death, and committed suicide two weeks later.

EAMONN RODGERS

Foix, J.V.

b. 1893, Barcelona; d. 1987, Barcelona

Poet

Foix is one of the three outstanding Catalan poets of his generation, along with Carles Riba and Josep Carner. Though he begins from the same basic premises as the other two – the need for an officially sponsored revival of Catalan culture and for a new blend of tradition and modernity – he quickly diverges from them in his conception of the old and the new. The spectrum of Foix's poetry, in fact, is much wider than that of any of his contemporaries: at one end of the scale, he goes back through the fifteenth-century poet Ausias March to the poems of the troubadours and the philosophy of Ramon Llull, and at the other he is closer to Apollinaire and the futurists than to

Mallarmé. Yet the more one reads his poetry, the more one is made to realize the unexpected links which join the two ends of the spectrum. More than once he has described his prose poems as *semblances* (a term he takes from Llull): fantasies which nevertheless are 'real' to the extent that they reflect, however tangentially, the personality of the writer.

Something like half of Foix's work consists of six collections of prose poems grouped under the general title of *Diari 1918*. The fact that he has chosen to refer this part of his work to a particular year, though it is clear that many of the pieces must have been written much later, suggests that the later work, both poems and prose poems, represents a steady unfolding of the possibilities implicit in his very earliest writing. Especially in his earliest collections of prose poems, *Gertrudis* and *KRTU*, Foix seems very close to certain techniques of surrealism, yet the total effect is anything but arbitrary. If their narratives often seem to take place on the frontiers of dream, it is a waking dream in which the poet never abandons his control.

In his book of sonnets, *Sol, i de dol* (Alone and in Mourning), published in 1947, though written before the Civil War, the assumptions which lie behind the prose poems are more clearly defined. In the best of these poems, the sense of a free-ranging mind which is nevertheless rooted in a particular time and place leads Foix to a sense of human solidarity, so that his feeling for the Catalan language becomes a feeling of being anchored in a community which still maintains its traditional dignity. Thus, it comes as no surprise to find that Foix has written several of the most moving poems to have come out of the Civil War. In them, however, there is no sense of compromise: as ever, Foix continues to question his own identity, not in any narcisstic sense, but as a guarantee of his right to speak for others in a common situation. Though he describes himself modestly as an 'investigator in poetry', Foix's protean gifts and inflexible integrity make his work one of the most exciting achievements in modern Catalan poetry.

Further reading

Gimferrer, P. (1974) *La poesia de J.V. Foix*, Barcelona: Ediciones 62 (the best general study).

ARTHUR TERRY

folk music

Spanish folk music falls into three broad categories, which are not always clearly delineated. In the first place, there is the musicological definition of folk music, that is, the popular musical and poetic heritage of the various cultures and regions of the peninsula, reflecting the rhythm of the seasons in an agricultural society. The late arrival of industrialization in Spain has facilitated the preservation and transmission of this tradition. The second category consists of more widely disseminated popular music, prior to the Anglo-American invasion of the 1960s, in which traditional forms are re-worked and adapted to the taste of a mass public. Third, the 1960s see the emergence, mainly in university circles, of a movement deriving from American folk music, which evolves either towards musicological research, or towards **protest songs**.

The first systematic study of Spanish folk music was carried out by the Andalusian Antonio Machado Álvarez, the father of the poets Antonio and Manuel Machado. In 1883, Machado Álvarez published an inventory of all aspects of folklore, a kind of ethnographical catalogue, which included traditional popular music. From that date on, several musicologists have collected, catalogued and studied documentary evidence on the enormous variety of folk music, placing it in the context of Mediterranean Europe, as defined by ethnomusicologists.

The most widespread form in the Spanish folk-music repertoire is the song, especially the *cuarteta*, a stanza of four verses of eight syllables, with an alternating rhyme (a b a b), which can be either assonantal or consonantal. The popular name for this form is the *copla*. This term is also applied to the commonest musical form, where a single melodic phrase takes in a stanza of the text, divided into two periods, which are each divided into two sub-periods. The *canción* is formed by a *copla* and an *estribillo* (refrain), stanza and refrain alternating. Another very characteristic form in the traditional repertoire is the *romance*, or ballad, an eight-syllable narrative form, in which a well-known story is set to music. Ballads were still being handed down among the rural population in the mid to late twentieth century.

The essentially agricultural character of Spanish society remained unchanged, in many regions, until the early 1960s. This not only ensured the survival of traditional melodies and words, but also provided a stable environment in which new compositions could take root in the collective memory alongside older forms, a process which requires the passage of about a generation. The songs of Antonio Machín or Concha Piquer, popularized via the radio, were some of the earliest examples of this commercialization of popular music, which simply used traditional tunes which would have been familiar to their listeners.

The Catalan novelist Manuel **Vázquez Montalbán** has studied the history of the Spanish popular song, and has coined the phrase *canción nacional* to describe the blend of stage-music and traditional song which made its appearance in the 1920s, and became firmly entrenched in the period after the Civil War. According to Vázquez Montalbán, the success of this kind of music is partly due to the poets of the 'Generation of 1927', many of them Andalusians, and keen students of folklore. Manuel Machado, Villalón, García Lorca and **Alberti** were fascinated by the Andalusian *cante hondo* or *cante jondo* (literally 'deep song'), and by motifs from the ballads. In this respect they stand within a tradition of sophisticated popularization which goes back to the great lyric poets of the seventeenth century.

The type of music described by Vázquez Montalbán has a metrical scheme very similar to that of the ballad. Andalusian pronunciation is virtually obligatory, and images and themes are taken from traditional lyric. It is, in fact, a music which fosters the conventional idea of 'typically Spanish', which made it particularly congenial to **Francoist culture**. The image of Spanishness derived from British and French romantic travellers of the nineteenth century was overlaid with the Francoist ethos of individualism versus communism, of the Hispanic race and the much-vaunted 'historical destiny' of Spain, the whole blend having a strong undercurrent of sensuality. Crimes of passion are a frequent theme of these songs, and, despite its compatibility with Francoism, there is in this music a savage, inchoate revolt against the sexual and social norms laid down by church and state, a safety valve against the political repression of the time, the roots of which nevertheless reach far back into the past.

Industrial development in the 1960s facilitated the appearance of a new kind of 'folk', deriving from Joan Baez and Pete Seeger, rather than from the indigenous music of the countryside. The father of this tradition of Spanish folk music is Joaquín Díaz, who, nevertheless, devoted a great deal of time and effort to the study and popularization of the Spanish popular music heritage, as Machado had done before him. The group 'Nuestro Pequeño Mundo' (Our Small World), which produced its first recording in 1968, was initially heavily influenced by American examples, especially 'The Weavers', but gradually moved towards a greater concentration on Spanish traditional song.

Another Castilian group, from Segovia, 'Nuevo Mester de Juglaría' (New Minstrels), developed away from the Angloamerican instrumentation and harmonies of 'Nuestro Pequeño Mundo' towards an effort of popularization of motifs collected in the villages of Old Castile, which were then worked into new compositions which used traditional patterns and rhythms. A similar activity was carried out in Andalusia by 'Jarcha', while in 1967 in Catalonia the 'Grup de Folk' emerged, closely connected with the ***Nova Cançó***. Other regions produced similar groups: in the Canaries, 'Los Sabandeños'; in Galicia, 'Voces Ceibes'; in **Euskadi**, 'Ez Dok Amairu'; and in Valencia 'Al Tall'. In general, these groups have a strong element of nationalism, insisting on using their own language, **Catalan**, **Galician** or **Basque**, and rediscovering characteristic melodic forms as markers of national identity. The greater normalization of regional cultural and political life since the transition to democracy has brought about a decline in their influence, though it is still present.

Further reading

Crivillé i Bargalló, J. (1983) *Historia de la música española. Vol. 7. El folklore musical*, Madrid: Alianza (the best account of Spanish folk from a musicological point of view; deals with traditional repertory, song and dances as well as flamenco).

Ordovás, J. (1991) 'Pop music', in A. Ramos Gascón (ed.) *Spain Today: In Search of Modernity*, Madrid: Cátedra (gives a summary of the *copla* in its development until 1990).

Vázquez Montalban, M. (1970) *Crónica sentimental de España*, Barcelona: Lumen (provides a very lively and striking panorama of the relationships between folklore, subculture and the age of dictatorship).

ENRIC DOLZ I FERRER

Fontcuberta, Joan

b. 1955, Barcelona

Photographer

Fontcuberta is the standard-bearer of a new and radical understanding of the social role of the photographer. In 1977 he was co-founder of the Alabern group of Barcelona. Shortly after, he became editor-in-chief of *Photovision*, which he had also helped to found, and taught in the Faculty of Fine Arts of the University of Barcelona between 1979 and 1986. The essence of his approach is his absolute rejection of the notion that photography has a documentary role. He sees himself as an artist, on the same level as painters or sculptors. His sometimes surrealistic creations are reminiscent of the work of artists like Cindy Sherman, Jenny Holzer or Joseph Kossuth.

See also: photography; visual arts

MIHAIL MOLDOVEANU

food and drink

The increasing pace of life, which is a feature of modern and especially urban Spain, together with cultural influences from outside the country, have effected many changes in eating and drinking habits.

Traditional Spanish dishes are mainly the products of **regional cooking**, which owes its variety to a range of historical, economic and especially geographical factors. The *Meseta*, the central plain of Castile, a wheat-producing and pastoral region, is the home of roast lamb. The northern coastal regions are rich in fish and meat, and the Ebro valley in trout and market garden vegetables. Catalonia, and especially Valencia and Murcia, are renowned for dishes such as the famous *paella*, which depend on rice, one of several commodities first introduced by the Arabs. Typical of Andalusia is the cold vegetable soup, *gazpacho*, and the region is also famous for *pescaíto frito* (mixed fried fish).

In addition, the quality and authenticity of many local products are protected by guarantees of origin (*Denominaciones de Origen*), including eleven types of cheese (those made from the milk of cows, sheep and goats are the ones most commonly eaten in Spain), three of the huge variety of locally produced hams (those from Teruel, Guijuelo and Dehesa de Extremadura), four kinds of fresh meat, two kinds of rice, various varieties of fruit and vegetables, four brands of olive oil, honey from La Alcarria and *turrón* (a form of nougat made from honey and almond etc.) from Jijona.

These originally local cuisines and products have become increasingly 'nationalized', helped in no small measure by the phenomenal growth in the publication and sales of cookery books, and the development of cookery sections in magazines, all of which reflect the greater interest in culinary matters in the 1980s and 1990s. This phenomenon, together with the virtual disappearance of domestic help, has also led to the establishment of high-class **restaurants** throughout the country and to an increase in the frequency of dining out.

Spain is also experiencing the effects on its cuisine and diet of various socio-economic and cultural changes. One of these is the increasing 'internationalization' of food and eating habits. French, German, Italian, Chinese, Japanese, Indian and Mexican are only some of the many types of restaurant to be found, especially in the largest cities, and 'exotic' imported foods from regions such as Latin America, the Caribbean and Asia are increasingly common. At the other end of the scale, cornflakes and other cereals have begun to oust the traditional breakfast, margarine is increasingly used instead of olive oil for cooking toasted sandwiches and eggs, and the bottle of ketchup is the modern substitute for *tomate frito*, the traditional condiment based on fried tomatoes.

Especially noticeable have been the general increase in the pace of life and the growing number of women who go out to work, developments which have both contributed to and been encouraged by the availability of **fast food outlets** and 'convenience food'. A study of the typical 'shopping basket' of the mid-1990s showed, by comparison with that of the mid-1970s, that foods requiring long preparation, such as chickpeas, had virtually disappeared from it, while frozen foods and pre-cooked dishes, easy to store and cook with the advent of freezers and microwave ovens, were very popular. It is reckoned that the time spent preparing a lunchtime meal has shrunk from sixty minutes to fifteen.

The contents of the modern Spanish shopping basket are not, however, determined solely by speed and convenience. Chicken and salmon, once prohibitively expensive, are examples of foods that have become commonplace because they are much cheaper relative to other meat and fish, while the popularity of salads and other light food reflects an increased concern for healthy eating.

There have been marked changes too in preferred drinks. Spain is the producer of a huge range of **wines**, and wine was still the most likely accompaniment to the foods in the 1976 shopping basket, together with Spanish sparkling/mineral water such as La Casera. But by the middle of the 1990s they had been ousted by beer and American soft drinks, especially among the younger generation. Many well-known brands of German beer are brewed under licence in Spain, and are often preferred to the traditional bottle of wine. Besides, changes in work-patterns have begun to make inroads on the custom of having a heavy meal with wine in the early afternoon, followed by a *siesta*.

See also: mealtimes; *merienda*

Further reading

Andrews, C. (1989) *Catalan Cuisine: Europe's Last Great Culinary Secret*, London: Heathline.

Aria, P. (1992) *Essential Food and Drink: Spain*, Basingstoke: Automobile Association (a useful general guide).

Casas, P. (1985) *The Foods and Wines of Spain*, Harmondsworth: Penguin (a handy compendium).

—— (1991) *Tapas: The Little Dishes of Spain*, London: Pavilion (one of the few studies of this very distinctive feature of Spanish cuisine).

Read, J., Manjón, M. and Johnson, H. (1987) *The Wine and Food of Spain*, London: Weidenfeld & Nicholson (co-authored by one of the leading writers on Spanish food and wine).

Ríos, A. (1992) *The Heritage of Spanish Cooking*, London: Ebury Press.

EAMONN RODGERS

football

Rivalled only by basketball as the major spectator sport, football has been described as a national religion. Under Franco it was encouraged, along with other sports and other diversions such as the cinema, radio and **kiosk literature**, as a sort of 'opium of the people', but also as a means of enhancing the image of the regime abroad as it basked in the glory of Spanish victories, especially by **Real Madrid** in European Cup matches. It was during this period that huge stadia were built in Madrid, Barcelona and Valencia, but Franco's policy of favouring the Madrid team had the effect of turning the regional teams of **Barcelona FC** and Athletic de Bilbao and their colours into foci of nationalist aspiration.

Football clubs operate as private sports companies linked to a national federation, and are members of the Professional Football League (the *Liga*). The Spanish League is considered among the best in the world, attracting players of the highest international ranking, but there is literally a price to pay. At the beginning of the 1997 season, for example, the clubs invested 571,000m pesetas, representing an increase of 22,000m pesetas over the previous year, for 130 players, with Real Betis creating a world record for the highest transfer fee. Not surprisingly many clubs are heavily in debt, despite significant revenue from the granting of television rights, and a crisis meeting of First and

Second Division clubs in 1997 welcomed with some relief the proposal that their share of the income from football pools be increased from 8.5 to 10 percent, representing something over 8,000m pesetas per season.

Another aspect of the international market in players is that a substantial number of the members of the top Spanish teams are from outside Spain and the other EU countries, Brazil, Argentina and Uruguay being well represented, together with the former Yugoslavia, Croatia and Bosnia. This was already true to a limited extent even under Franco – witness the quarrel between Barcelona and Real Madrid over the Argentinian Alfredo di Stefano in 1952 – but the practice has become much more prevalent, to the extent that in 1991 a restriction was placed on the numbers of non-EU players. Only six licences are allowed per club and four players per match, though this can be circumvented if necessary by naturalization. In 1997 a strike by footballers in favour of a reduction in the numbers of such players was only brought to an end by the promise of an enquiry into the matter in the year 2000, when the 1991 agreement ends. Moreover, in the highly competitive world of league and international football such international stars are often birds of passage, not always completing even one season. Coaches, too, suffer the effects of increasing competitiveness: sixteen were dismissed in the 1994–5 season, fourteen the following season and fifteen in 1996–7, so that the average 'life' of a coach had become a mere six months and twenty days (compared with two years and five months in the English league).

Within the League are First, Second, Second B (further divided into four groups) and Third Divisions (further divided into seventeen groups). The number of clubs in the First Division has gradually increased over the years from ten in 1928–9 to twenty-two from 1995–6. From 1984–5 to 1994–5 Real Madrid and Barcelona shared the leadership between them, Madrid achieving a run of five consecutive wins 1985–6 to 1989–90, a feat it had also achieved in the 1960s. Internal crises in the two clubs, including the dismissal or resignation of their coaches, resulted in first and second place going to Atlético Madrid and Valencia in 1995–6.

The clubs also compete annually for the King's Cup (*Copa del Rey*) – Athletic Bilbao, Barcelona and Real Madrid among the most successful – and for the *Supercopa*, a match between the winners of the League and the King's Cup. National teams compete regularly and with considerable success in Europe, and since 1978 have regularly qualified to play for the World Cup.

The intense interest of Spaniards in football is reflected in the sales of daily newspapers devoted entirely to sport and mainly to football. By 1995 *Marca* had become the best selling daily, beating even *El País* into second place, and accounting for nearly 12 percent of circulation. *As*, the leading sports daily until the end of the 1980s, ranked eighth, accounting for another 2.8 percent, and *Sport* and *El Mundo Deportivo*, both published in Barcelona, ranked tenth and twelfth, accounting for a further 4.5 percent between them. Televised matches likewise attract huge audiences, leading to fierce competition between companies for television rights. In 1997 a controversial law, dubbed the football law (*ley de fútbol*) was passed to control the freedom of subscriber television companies to exercise exclusive rights to football coverage. On the grounds that football is a 'matter of public interest' it will permit transmission of matches on non-subscription channels on days and at times of the government's choosing, most probably on Sundays.

See also: sport and leisure

Further reading

MacClancy, J. (1996) 'Nationalism at Play: The Basques of Vizcaya and Athletic Club de Bilbao' in J. MacClancy (ed.) *Sport, Identity and Ethnicity*, Oxford: Berg (focuses on football as an expression of Basque identity).

Shaw, D. 'The Politics of "Fútbol"', *History Today* August 1985: 38–42 (a useful brief account of the political significance of football during the Franco regime).

EAMONN RODGERS

foreign policy

There exist two main debates regarding Spain's foreign policy under the Franco regime. First, the regime was remarkably opportunistic in exploiting the global divisions of the Cold War. Second, the Foreign Ministry was considerably more progressive than might have been expected from a right-wing authoritarian dictatorship. The fact remains that the isolation experienced by the Franco regime has remained relevant to the shaping of contemporary Spain's foreign policy. It was only in 1986 that Spain formally exchanged ambassadors with Israel and, in 1989, Spain was the only **NATO** member to condemn the US invasion of Panama in the UN General Assembly. The Madrid NATO summit, held in July 1997, failed to achieve the full integration of Spain into NATO's Integrated Military Command. This was partly a result of ongoing disputes regarding the status of the Canary Islands and Gibraltar within the NATO commands.

Spain's foreign policy still exhibits aspects of its colonial legacy within the Spanish-speaking world. The much-maligned term *Hispanidad* has given way to the *Comunidad iberoamericana de naciones* (Spanish-American Community of Nations), a group of countries tied by common history to the Iberian peninsula. Since 1991, a series of annual summits have become a valuable public relations opportunity for Spanish and Latin American governments alike.

In spite of this ongoing linkage to Latin America, Spain has sought status not only as a Spanish-speaking power, but more significantly as a major participant on the European stage. Since the treaty of accession to the European Communities was signed in June 1985, Spain has consistently pursued a policy of support for the federalist model of integration. Despite economic hardship in the form of **unemployment** for many Spaniards, the **PSOE** governments under Felipe **González** pursued a decidedly neo-liberal programme of restructuring. This economic policy, whilst being highly controversial with **trade unions** like the **UGT**, underlined a desire for membership of the European mainstream. Such a domestic agenda has dominated foreign policy. In the case of European Monetary Union (EMU), a successful accession in the first wave is as much a foreign policy goal as an economic target. Spanish foreign policy, dominated by European integration, represents a continuation of Spain's ongoing historical dilemma. There exists a choice between whether or not it should pursue and compete as a medium-sized European nation, or seek a Hispanic role based upon its historical linkages.

The fact remains that Spain is among the poorer EU member states. The European vocation so dreamt of by modernizers is by no means a certainty and carries some risks. While successive governments remain committed to the concept of a European Union, the direction of integration and the opportunities hoped for by Spain are more likely to be decided by the actions of the biggest EU member states. Achievement of the convergence criteria for EMU may admit Spain to the first wave of a single currency, but the full realization of the project will depend on the actions of Germany and France.

Spain still remains subordinated to the security policy of the Atlantic-looking powers of western Europe. NATO's reputation was subject to suspicion for a substantial period within Spain, and in spite of considerable efforts, a European defence and security identity remains distant. Despite a prolonged and largely successful campaign to play a significant role in Europe, notable diplomatic successes for Spain have been few and far between.

The Mediterranean remains the largest security concern for Spain. While most of Europe has been preoccupied by the scale of the restructuring of Eastern Europe and the former Soviet Union, the depth of poverty and the fragility of peace in North Africa constitute a serious problem. The 'Mediterranean Partnership' programme of the EU offers little by way of aid, compared to what is available to aspirant EU applicants in Eastern Europe. Only when the rhetoric is matched by the resources of Europe can Spain say that its policies towards its particular areas of concern have been a success.

Foreign policy within a democratic framework has seen considerable change since the early 1980s. The efforts by the then Foreign Minister Fernando **Morán** to pursue a progressive foreign policy (1982–5) reflected an attempt to maintain some of the Franco regime's dubious successes. The *puente*, that is, the bridge between Europe and Latin America, was revitalized to indicate or even demarcate the victory of the Socialists in 1982. Towards Central America, sympathy and moral support in the face of active US policy caused Spain to evolve a position visibly distinct from the rest of the European Community. While this position may have been politically expedient, it did little to improve Spain's standing in either Europe, Latin America or the world. By the time of the NATO referendum (1986), Morán had been replaced. His successors have focused their energies more on Europe than Latin America, though Spain enjoyed an obvious advantage in leading Europe's opening towards the continent.

Spain's more prominent international role has been a product of the democratic transition. This does not mean that the legacy of isolation has been lost, but that the adoption of foreign policy positions remain conditioned by its experience of the twentieth century.

See also: American bases agreement; economy; European Union; *europeísmo*; foreign trade

Further reading

Barbé, E. (1996) 'The External Dissenter: Spain' in S. Stavridis and C. Hill (eds) *Domestic Sources of Foreign* Policy, Oxford: Berg (a handy brief introduction to foreign policy issues).

Cortada, J. (ed.) (1980) *Spain in the Twentieth Century World*, London: Aldwych (a comprehensive study of the Franco period).

Gillespie, R., Rodrigo, F. and Story, J. (eds) (1995) *Democratic Spain: Reshaping External Relations in a Changing World*, London: Routledge (an excellent symposium of essays, covering all aspects of the topic).

Heywood, P. (1995) *The Government and Politics of Spain*, London: Macmillan (see chapter 12 for a lucid and concise account of Spain's international relations).

Pollack, B. (1987) *The Paradox of Spanish Foreign Policy*, London: Frances Pinter (a key study of the complexities of foreign policy).

BENNY POLLACK

foreign trade

Although Spain's foreign trade cannot be compared to that of traditional trading nations such as Germany or the UK, it is nevertheless among the top twenty in the world, with about 2 percent of visible global trade by value (compared to about 9 percent for Germany and 5 percent for the UK). In invisibles or services Spain is in the top ten countries because of the importance of its tourist sector. After a period of limited (though not negligible, as is sometimes assumed) growth during the years of political isolation in the 1940s and 1950s, Spain's foreign trade grew more rapidly following the introduction of a new tariff as a result of negotiations with the OECD under the reformist Minister of Commerce Alberto Ullastres. This trade liberalization was only partial, however, and was followed ten years later by a further relaxation under the Luxembourg Accord with the EEC which offered a substantial reduction of the latter's external tariff to Spanish exporters. Further lowering of trade barriers followed after agreements with EFTA and GATT. Between 1985 and 1995 Spain's foreign trade virtually trebled, much of it being associated with the EC. Already during the 1970s Spain's major trading partners were countries in the EC, especially as far as exports were concerned. On the eve of accession (1 January 1986) Spain's exports to the EC had already breached the 50 percent mark; nevertheless this geographical shift in trade was given a further boost after accession, so that today the EU accounts for well over two-thirds of Spain's foreign trade, with the value of her exports to the EU exceeding the value of imports from the EU by some 5 percent of Spain's total international trade. Within the EU, Spain's biggest trading partner by a considerable margin is France, followed by Germany, Italy and the UK. Outside the EU, Spain's biggest trading partner by far is the US, from whom Spain imports almost twice as much as she exports.

As well as a change in the geographical distribution of Spain's foreign trade there has been a change in its composition. Whereas thirty years ago Spanish manufactures were only just beginning to challenge agricultural products as the major type of export, now they are six times more important by value (not counting leather goods and textiles). The reason for the large shift is not hard to find. The biggest export by far is that of road vehicles, for Spain is a major car manufacturer and some 70 percent of her production is exported. Also important are industrial machinery and equipment; other metallic manufactures; and chemicals. These four types of manufactures account for well over half of Spain's exports compared to about 12 percent for non-processed agricultural products, 5 percent for processed food, drinks and tobacco, and a similar percentage for leather goods and textiles. Nevertheless agricultural products are still very significant, the most important items being fresh fruit (especially oranges) and vegetables. In processed foods the most important exports are alcoholic drinks and preserved fruit and vegetables.

Turning now to imports, Spain is also a major importer of manufactures. The four types of manufactures referred to above account for almost exactly half of Spain's imports. Other important items on Spain's shopping list are fuels, at about 11 percent of the total shopping bill the most expensive item other than machinery and vehicles; animal products, especially fish and crustaceans (about 5 percent of imports); processed foods and drinks (5 percent); textiles (5 percent); plastic and rubber products (4 percent); vegetable products, especially cereals and animal feed (4 percent); precision instruments (3 percent); and paper products (3 percent).

Spain's international trade is to a very significant degree in the hands of Spanish subsidiaries of foreign companies. In 1993 the top ten exporters were: Seat-Volkswagen, GM-Opel, Renault, Ford, Citroën, Michelin, IBM, Repsol Petroleum, Peugeot and Nissan (of which only Repsol is Spanish). The top ten importers were: Repsol Petroleum, Renault, GM-Opel, Ford, Seat-Volkswagen, CEPSA, Petronor, Citroën, IBM and Peugeot (Repsol, CEPSA and Petronor are importers of crude oil). These ten companies accounted for 23 percent of Spain's total foreign trade in merchandise.

The cost of Spain's merchandise imports exceeds that of her exports, thereby creating a deficit in visible trade. In invisible trade, however, Spain has a healthy surplus which makes all the difference to the **balance of payments**. It should be pointed out, however, that the surplus in invisible trade applies to tourism services only; in non-tourist services there is normally a small deficit.

Further reading

Chislett, W. (1996) *Spain 1996. The Central Hispano Handbook*, Madrid: Banco Central Hispano (chapter 3 surveys recent developments in foreign trade, investment and balance of payments).

Harrison, J. (1993) *The Spanish Economy: From the Civil War to the European Community*, London: Macmillan (chapter 8 offers a succinct survey of foreign trade).

Ministerio de Economía y Hacienda (annual series) *Estadística del comercio exterior de España*, Madrid (trade statistics).

C.A. LONGHURST

Fórmica Corsi, Mercedes

b. 1918, Cadiz

Writer

Unusual in being lawyer, journalist, feminist and novelist, Fórmica began as a member of the ultraconservative **Falange** before the Civil War but eventually campaigned for legal and professional equality for women. Her 1950 novel, *Monte de Sancha* (Sancha's Mountain), is considered the first post-war Spanish view of the civil conflict to present both sides. *La ciudad perdida* (The Lost City) (1951), set in the 1950s, sympathetically portrays an anti-Franco guerrilla. *A instancia de parte* (Upon Petition of the Third Party) (1955), her most profeminist novel indicts *machismo*, while the two memoir volumes, *Pequeña historia de ayer* (Brief History of Yesterday) (1982, 1984) are gems.

Further reading

Pérez, J. (1988) *Contemporary Women Writers of Spain*, Boston, MA: G.K. Hall, pp. 102–4 (overview of the novels and memoirs).

JANET PÉREZ

fotonovelas

A sub-genre of **comics**, these 'photonovels' consist of a series of posed photographs with speech balloons added to make up continuous stories. Usually romantic and sentimental in theme, they were part of the escapism characteristic of **Francoist culture**, and remained popular throughout the 1950s, though sales gradually declined from the 1960s on.

See also: kiosk literature; press; readership

EAMONN RODGERS

foundations

Foundations (*fundaciones*) are charitable organizations founded, often by commercial enterprises, but also by individuals, for a wide variety of social and cultural purposes. Regulated by the **Law of Patronage**, they benefit from a reduced corporate tax, and are eligible to receive works of art donated by individuals and corporate bodies in part payment of tax liabilities. Among the more than 2,700 foundations registered are the **ONCE** Foundations for providing work for the blind and for training guide-dogs, the Savings Banks (**Cajas de Ahorros**), which are required by law to devote half their profits to community works, and major banks such as BBV, Central Hispano and Exterior de España, and other large business enterprises. The **Juan March Foundation** was instituted by the financier of that name to promote scientific education, and the Fundación Ramón Areces exists to encourage and develop scientific and technical research. The Fundación Universidad-Empresa has the mission of maintaining dialogue and co-operation between universities and industry in the Madrid region. The García Lorca Foundation, presided over by the poet's sister Isabel, was created to promote interest in the life and works of Lorca. It has a library and photographic archive, and publishes a biennial bulletin on the work of Lorca and the 'Generation of 1927'. The Ortega y Gasset Foundation, headed by the writer's daughter, Soledad Ortega Spottorno, promotes the social sciences and humanities, and publishes the ***Revista de Occidente***.

See also: cultural institutions and movements

EAMONN RODGERS

FP

Formación profesional (vocational education), designed to provide pupils with job-related skills, is part of the system of secondary education, parallel to, but of a lower standard than **BUP**, and imparted in special vocational schools. There are two stages: the first consists of two years of compulsory schooling for those who have failed to obtain the *Graduado Escolar* certificate (see also **EGB**). This leads to certification as a *técnico auxiliar* (auxiliary technician), and qualifies the recipient for entry into the second grade of BUP or the second stage of FP. The latter has two strands, a general two-year course or a specialized three-year programme, leading to qualification as a *técnico especialista* (specialist technician). This specialized course admits to the first year of university.

See also: LODE; LOGSE

ISIDRO FADRIQUE

Fraga Iribarne, Manuel

b. 1922, Villalba (Lugo)

Politician

Conservative politician Fraga was a dominant figure on the Spanish political scene from the 1960s to the beginning of the 1990s. After a meteoric academic career, Fraga came to prominence as Minister for Information and Tourism (1962–9), with his advocacy of political *apertura* (opening), particularly through the Press Law of 1966, which he presented as a liberalization of **censorship**. A prominent opponent of the **Opus Dei**, he was forced out in 1969, and sent to London as ambassador from 1973 to 1975, where he cultivated his reformist reputation and prepared his return.

On Franco's death, he was appointed Minister of the Interior in Arias Navarro's last government. His inflexible approach to the question of public order, and the failure of the Arias government to present a coherent programme of reform, severely damaged his reputation and he was excluded from Adolfo **Suárez**'s reformist government. He responded by courting hard-line Francoists and integrating them into a conservative political grouping **Popular Alliance** (AP) under his leadership, contributing to their acceptance of the new democratic regime. Strongly backed by financial circles, AP seemed to misjudge the reforming mood of the times, and polled a miserable 7 percent of the vote in the 1977 elections. Fraga ditched the reactionary rhetoric of the 1977 campaign to become, as a member of the drafting committee, one of the seven 'fathers of the constitution' (see also **constitution of 1978**), and his support for the text led the more reactionary elements of AP to leave the party. However, his more moderate approach in the 1979 elections failed to improve AP's 1977 performance.

The decline of Suárez's **UCD** after 1979 presented Fraga with an opportunity to recover, which he seized eagerly. Latching on to the discontent in conservative circles at the UCD's centrist policies, Fraga launched fierce attacks on Suárez whilst secretly negotiating with the UCD's conservative wing to force Suárez into a centre-right coalition, the so-called 'natural majority'. UCD's electoral collapse in 1982 allowed AP, in coalition with conservative defectors from UCD, to make a quantum leap to 26 percent of the vote, becoming the main opposition to the Socialists. However, his inability to improve on this performance in 1986 led the party's backers in the business world to put pressure on Fraga to make way for a younger leader less tainted by involvement with the Franco regime. He resigned in December 1986, but the disastrous outcome of the battle for the succession led to his taking over again, briefly, from 1988 to 1990. He then made way for José María **Aznar**, and entered regional politics in his native Galicia, where he became President of the **Xunta de Galicia** (regional government) from 1990.

Fraga's main contribution to Spanish political life was to reconcile democratic reform with conservative values, acting as a democratic point of reference for erstwhile Francoists. His genuine commitment to democracy was, however, undermined by his temperamental approach to politics.

Further reading

Dávila, C. and Herrero, L. (1989) *De Fraga a Fraga. Crónica secreta de Alianza Popular*, Barcelona: Plaza y Janés (journalistic account of Popular Alliance's travails in the 1980s).

Preston, P. (1986) *The Triumph of Democracy in Spain*, London: Methuen (Fraga's political trajectory is thoroughly examined in this account of the transition from dictatorship to democracy).

JONATHAN HOPKIN

Fraile Ruiz, Medardo

b. 1925, Madrid

Writer

Mainly known as a prolific short-story writer, Medardo Fraile has also written a play, *El hermano* (The Brother) (1948), two volumes of journalism, four books of literary criticism, and a translation of Robert Louis Stevenson's *The Weir of Hermiston* (1995). With Alfonso **Sastre**, he was one of the founders of the Arte Nuevo theatre group in the mid-1940s, and between 1957 and 1964 was deputy editor in chief and drama critic of *Cuadernos de Agora*. After a period in the Spanish Department at the University of Southampton, he secured a lectureship at the University of Strathclyde (Glasgow), retiring with the title of emeritus professor in 1986.

His first volume of short stories, *Cuentos con algún amor* (Stories with a Little Love), was published in 1954. Between then and 1994, he published eleven further volumes, including five of stories for children. His collected stories came out in an edition of *Cuentos completos* (Complete Stories) in 1991. His work attracted awards and distinctions from an early stage, including the Sésamo Prize for Short Story and the Critics' Book of the Year Award (1965), the Estafeta Literaria Prize for Short Story (1970), and the Hucha de Oro Prize for Short Story (1971). In 1988 he won the Ibáñez Fantoni Prize for Journalism.

See also: literature; novel; performing arts; theatre

EAMONN RODGERS

Franco, Ricardo

b. 1949, Madrid; d. 1998, Madrid

Filmmaker

After working as assistant director to his uncle and directing shorts and an experimental but largely unsuccessful film *El desastre de Annual* (The Massacre at Annual) (1970), Franco made his name in 1974 with *Pascual Duarte*, based on the novel by **Cela**. Depicting the unrelieved poverty, ignorance and cruelty of life in rural Spain, the film ends with the execution of Duarte by garrotting in all its stark reality. *Despues de tanto años* (After So Many Years) (1994) takes an equally hard look at physical disintegration and death. Featuring the Panero brothers, it functions as a sequel to **Chávarri**'s *El desencanto* (Disenchantment) (1976). At the time of his sudden death from a heart attack in 1998, Franco was in the process of making *Lágrimas negras* (Black Tears).

EAMONN RODGERS

Franco Bahamonde, Francisco

b. 1892, El Ferrol (Galicia); d. 1975, Madrid

Soldier and Head of State

Franco's early military career was mainly associated with Spanish Morocco, where he acquired a reputation for personal bravery and stern discipline, and achieved rapid promotion, becoming in 1926 the youngest Brigadier in Europe. During the turbulent period of the Second Republic (1931–6), though instinctively conservative in his views, he refused to become involved in the attempted right-wing coup by General Sanjurjo, showing evidence, not so much of the professional soldier's loyalty to the legal government, as of the caution and pragmatism which he would later display during the Civil War and his years as Head of State.

This caution made him hesitant about joining the military conspiracy of 1936, which led to the Civil War. As late as 12 July, six days before the military insurrection, Franco had still not committed himself. The murder by the police of a right-wing member of parliament, however, precipitated matters, and Franco assumed command of the Moroccan and southern wing of the movement, subsequently becoming overall *Generalísimo* of the rebel ('Nationalist') forces by September 1936. A dogged rather than brilliant strategist, he was determined that his troops would suffer no harassment in the rearguard, and, once he had secured a stretch of territory, he proceeded to eliminate potential enemies by systematic executions of Republicans.

This policy of repression was also designed to ensure that when the war was won, there would be no significant political opposition to Franco's exercise of personal power. Executions of political dissidents continued on a large scale into the 1940s (and sporadically into the 1970s), and large numbers of Republicans were held in prison camps in the immediate post-war years. Catch-all offences of 'military rebellion' and 'illegal propaganda' meant prison sentences for distribution of leaflets or possession of banned publications. Franco also created a legal framework which consolidated his personal dictatorship. Though the Succession Law of 1947 defined Spain as a kingdom, it confirmed Franco's de facto wartime position as Head of State, with the power to nominate his own royal successor. Though he had no intention of respecting the rights of the legitimate heir, Don Juan, Count of Barcelona, this law enabled Franco to retain the support of monarchists by holding out the hope of an eventual restoration.

The other purpose of the Succession Law was to present a façade of respectability to the democratic world by fostering the notion that the current dictatorship was a transitional arrangement. Though Spain had been formally neutral during WWII, Franco's speeches, and the controlled press, gave overt sympathy and moral support to Germany and Italy. This resulted in Spain being ostracized by the Western Allies, and excluded from membership of the United Nations until 1955. With the growing tension of the Cold War, however, the US came to regard Franco as a reliable ally against Soviet expansionism, and in 1953 an agreement was concluded which permitted the Americans to establish bases in Spain (see also **American bases agreement**), in return for $226m in military and technical aid.

This pursuit of international prestige and the flattering of military vanity were to be important elements of Franco's policy. The attempt to balance these goals produced some characteristic ambiguities. On the one hand, the idea of a crusade against godless communism was perpetuated as a national ideal. Furthermore, the unitary conception of Spain, dear to the armed forces and conservative interests generally, was fostered at the expense of the non-Castilian regions. Demands for recognition of cultural distinctiveness were treated as 'separatism', and as an attack on the integrity of the 'nation'. Catalan books were publicly burned in Barcelona in 1939, and the more than two hundred periodical publications which had existed before the war were suppressed. Speakers of minority languages could be fined for conducting telephone conversations in their own tongue. As against this, the need for acceptance by the international community produced some token relaxation of restrictions, enabling the regime to disarm criticism to some extent. From the late 1940s on, the volume of publications in Catalan increased, though they were nearly always of minority interest. It remained extremely difficult to publish anything in Catalan which was likely to have a mass appeal; there was no Catalan radio or television, and no newspapers.

The simplicity of Franco's political outlook was matched by a profound ignorance of economics. For several years, he continued to pursue a policy of **autarky**, which was adopted from sheer necessity after the Civil War, but which was subsequently turned into a Nationalistic creed of self-sufficiency. Moreover, despite his authoritarian personality, and his capacity for swift and vindictive action against individuals whom he considered a threat, Franco exercised little real oversight over the activities of his various ministers, with the result that there was no overall control of government spending. By 1956, rising inflation and an adverse balance of payments was threatening the economy with collapse. A cabinet reshuffle in February 1957 brought into the government the so-called **technocrats**, many of them members of the secretive Catholic organization **Opus Dei**. By 1959, they had elaborated a **Stabilization Plan**, which froze wages and opened Spain to foreign investment, resulting in rapid industrialization and expansion of the economy. In the 1960s, Spain's annual growth rate, at 7 percent, was the second highest in the capitalist world. There was little real attempt, however, to alter the distribution of wealth, property ownership, or the structure of society, and this decade witnessed a level of industrial and political unrest unequalled since the 1930s.

The propaganda of the Franco regime presented him as a wise and firm leader, but in reality he was often passive and played a waiting game, in the hope that crises would be solved by time. His guiding principle was the determination to remain in power as long as possible, which often entailed playing one faction off against another, so as to neutralize any possible challenges to his own position. Thus the cabinet reshuffle of 1957 can be seen as an attempt to promote the technocrats so as to reduce the influence of the **Falange**, which, throughout the previous year, under its energetic and ambitious Minister Secretary-General, José Luis **Arrese**, had been striving to assert greater control over the government.

Although Franco had been sympathetic to the plan to give greater prominence to the Falange, of which he was Jefe Nacional (National Leader), he was also conscious of the need to avoid alienating other political interests. Critics of the Franco regime often describe it excessively loosely as 'fascist', a label which does not account for the complexities of the situation. If the description were accurate, it would give Franco credit for a more developed and coherent political ideology than he actually possessed, and for success in imposing it. The reality was that, at different times, he was subjected to different pressures from the various factions which supported his rule, pressures with which he coped by giving the impression that he was making meaningful concessions to the interest group concerned, while in fact he was reserving his freedom of manœuvre. A large section of the political élite, including, significantly, most of the senior military officers who had supported his assumption of the role of Head of State during the Civil War, remained monarchist: Franco's curbing of the Falange in 1957 was due, as much as anything, to fear of a challenge from this lobby.

The cabinet reshuffle of 1957 also marks the beginning of Franco's gradual withdrawal from direct involvement in government, though he never completely relinquished control. In the last fifteen years of his rule, the affairs of state were increasingly left to the relevant ministers, while Franco spent more and more time in his favourite occupations of shooting and fishing. This was due not only to advancing age, but also to the increased complexity of running a state which stood in need of rapid modernization, and required the kind of professional competence which the technocrats were well placed to provide. Franco's own naïve expectation that security of employment and firm policing would produce a docile and depoliticized populace was proved to be inadequate as early as 1951, when Barcelona witnessed a transport boycott, caused by an increase in fares, which quickly developed into a general strike. The increased prosperity of the 1960s did not filter down into the working class rapidly enough to prevent serious industrial unrest, prompted by an amalgam of specific demands for improvements in wages and working conditions, and political aspirations towards greater liberalization. The very success of the regime's economic policies, particularly in encouraging **tourism**, had created expectations of change which made the structures of Francoism seem obsolete even to some of its most loyal supporters. Franco, however, could only respond with harsher security measures, including the setting up of the Public Order Tribunal in 1963, specifically to deal with political offences. One of his last official acts, a month before his death, was to confirm death sentences passed by court martial on members of various terrorist organizations.

Franco's reluctance to contemplate relinquishing power caused him to put off making arrangements for a successor, until advancing years and failing health made it inevitable. Moreover, his well-founded suspicion that the legitimate heir to the throne, Don Juan, would restore a liberal constitutional monarchy made him hesitate about using the provisions of the Law of Succession. In 1969, however, when he was 76, he agreed to a suggestion from his long-term ally, Admiral Luis **Carrero Blanco**, that Don Juan's son, **Juan Carlos**, should be formally nominated his successor as Head of State in the event of his death. The basic structure of the regime would, however, remain largely unaffected. Juan Carlos was made to swear allegiance to the Principles of the **National Movement**, and was, significantly, designated 'Prince of Spain' rather than 'Prince of Asturias', the title traditionally bestowed on the heir to the throne. Franco thereby wished to signal a break in continuity with the previous monarchy, a process which he compounded by using the term *instaurar* (to install) rather than *restaurar* (to restore).

Franco's intention was that real political control would be exercised after his demise by Carrero Blanco, and he had, indeed, ceded more and more of the day-to-day running of the government to him, appointing him Vice-President of the Council of Ministers in 1967, and President in 1973. In December 1973, however, Carrero was assassinated by **ETA**. His successor, Carlos Arias Navarro, was a deeply conservative but indecisive civilian who was unlikely to influence Juan Carlos in the same way. Subsequent events were to prove, in any case, that Juan Carlos not only had a mind of his own, but was deeply committed to democratization, despite the training in the military ethos of the regime which, at Franco's insistence, he had received.

This was only one of several respects in which Franco's efforts to perpetuate his regime were, ironically, frustrated by the very measures he had taken. The prosperity which he had hoped would depoliticize the populace only heightened aspirations for greater freedom. The oscillation between inward-looking nationalism and the desire for international recognition inevitably opened Spain to liberalizing influences, a process hastened by the need to increase foreign earnings through tourism. The ultimate enigma of Francoism, how such a mediocre person could survive in power for so long, is explicable in terms of his ability to manipulate the rivalries among the different factions in the political élites, and to play on the public's fear of a return to the chaos of the Civil War, and the hardship of the 'years of hunger' of the early 1940s.

See also: censorship; Civil War; Francoist culture; historiography; history; National Catholicism

Further reading

Ellwood, S. (1994) *Franco*, London and New York: Longman (an excellent, readable shorter study).

Fusi, J.P. (1985) *Franco: Autoritarismo y poder personal*, Madrid: Ediciones El País (a useful analysis by a leading Spanish contemporary historian).

Preston, P. (1993) *Franco*, London: Harper Collins (the standard and most comprehensive biography in English).

EAMONN RODGERS

Francoist culture

The cultural complexion of Franco's Spain is one of the outcomes of the Civil War and its aftermath. The propaganda of the Francoist side fostered the notion that in overcoming the 'red hordes' they were also redressing the effects of two centuries of negative and alien influence deriving from the Enlightenment, nineteenth-century liberalism and modern democracy. The educational system and the media, heavily controlled by **censorship**, were therefore pressed into service to create an official culture which, in the eyes of the regime, would be truer to Spain's authentic character and heritage. The title of the Ministry of National Education, which had been used since the early nineteenth century, took on a new force, the word 'National' denoting not only the territorial scope of the department's activities, but also its mission to act as a channel of Nationalist ideology. One of the first acts of the new post-war Ministry was to establish, in November 1939, the **CSIC** (Higher Research Council), the aim of which was stated in its founding charter as 'the restoration of the classic and Christian unity of the sciences, which was destroyed in the eighteenth century'.

The rhetoric of the regime was not, however, backed by resources sufficient to enable the government to patronize official culture on a large scale, and in this situation a key role was played by **National Catholicism**. Catholicism was seen not only as closely bound up with the current political system, but as the essence of Spanish nationality, and the unifying force which had made Spain great in the past. In iconography, **architecture** and **historiography**, pride of place was given to the symbols of imperial Spain. The titles of periodicals published by the **Falange** both during and after the Civil War illustrate this eloquently: *Jerarquía* (Hierarchy), *Vértice* (Apex), and above all, *Escorial*, which took its name from the huge monastery-palace built by Philip II. Historical research on the modern period was discouraged, and attention was paid primarily to the 'Reconquest' of Spain from the Moors in the late Middle Ages, the unification of the crowns of Castile and Aragon and the achievement of religious uniformity by the 'Catholic monarchs' Ferdinand and Isabella at the end of the fifteenth century, and the imperial expansion of the sixteenth and seventeenth centuries. Church influence on the content of teaching at all levels of the educational system was profound: conservative Catholic opposition to any attempt at liberalization could even bring about the dismissal of a Minister of Education, Joaquín Ruiz Giménez, in 1956.

The attempt to impose a distinctive Catholic-Nationalist culture, however, met with limited success. Though the secretive Catholic organization **Opus Dei** acquired considerable influence in the Higher Research Council, in practice the Council avoided becoming a crude instrument of government propaganda, and soon earned a well-merited reputation for supporting serious scholarly research. This illustrates the ambiguous nature of Francoist culture. On the one hand, many scholars active prior to the Civil War stayed on in Spain, and co-operated with the regime, partly because it was the only way in which they could function professionally (the alternatives being silence or **exile**), partly because the values manipulated by the regime (the glory of Spain in former times, the distinctiveness of the national character) made a powerful appeal to patriotic sentiment. At the same time, however, the international contacts necessary to effective research, coupled with the regime's efforts to present a respectable face to the rest of the world, meant that the enterprise of creating a restrictive conception of national culture was ultimately doomed to failure. By the 1950s, promising young researchers were studying in the US and in various European countries.

Moreover, even within the permitted area of investigation, the application of rigorous scholarship had the effect of undermining the received view of the past. Economic historians like Ramón Carande, as early as 1942, demonstrated that the supposed imperial grandeur of Hapsburg Spain rested on an extremely weak financial base. The application of modern quantitative methods, especially in the hands of **Vicens Vives**, challenged the supremacy of traditionalist narrative approaches, and, from the 1950s, encouraged historians to look for the origins of modern Spain, not in the imperial past, but in the economic and political developments of the eighteenth and nineteenth centuries.

The official culture of the regime was ultimately unsuccessful in garnering the support of the intellectual community, but the spirit of critical independence, albeit muted, which existed in intellectual circles had little or no effect on the populace at large. One result of the Francoist system was to produce a large measure of depoliticization among the population, both by playing on fears of a return to the turmoil of the Civil War, and by fostering what has been aptly called a 'culture of evasion'. The stifling of overt criticism by censorship was complemented by the promotion of an optimistic view of conditions in Spain, and of life in general. In this process a key role was played by the cinema (see also **film and cinema**), **radio**, **kiosk literature** and spectator sports, especially **football**. In the late 1940s Spain had the highest number of cinema seats per capita of any country outside the US. Despite the poverty of the years after the Civil War, both Madrid and Barcelona saw the building of huge football stadia. Radio soaps attracted audiences of millions.

All these genres provided entertainment of an uncritical kind which reinforced the general absence of intellectual curiosity outside élite circles. Nevertheless, the influx of foreign films, in a ratio of four or five to each Spanish one in the 1940s and 1950s, offered the public images of a glamorous lifestyle which, however superficial, exposed the austerity of life in Spain and created a discontent which was to fuel the demand for change after Franco's death.

See also: consumerism; *fotonovelas*; history; *¡HOLA!*

Further reading

Carr, R. and Fusi, J.P. (1979) *Spain: Dictatorship to Democracy*, London: George Allen & Unwin (chapter 6 is an excellent overview of culture during the Franco period).

Hooper, J. (1995) *The New Spaniards*, Harmondsworth: Penguin (a very readable and informative guide to the Franco and post-Franco eras).

EAMONN RODGERS

FRAP

The Frente Revolucionario Antifascista y Patriota (Revolutionary, Anti-fascist and Patriotic Front) was a left-wing terrorist organization which emerged from obscurity around 1973. It was responsible for the murders of various members of the security forces, but was largely dismantled by a series of arrests in 1974. It was revealed long afterwards that it had been heavily infiltrated by the police, and is an example of the sinister overlap which occurred in the 1970s between left-wing groups and elements in the security forces acting as *agents provocateurs* in order to justify repressive measures.

EAMONN RODGERS

freemasonry

The supposed existence of an international masonic conspiracy to destabilize Spain was one of the staples of right-wing rhetoric throughout the nineteenth century and the Franco period. The reality was that even during the Second Republic, total numbers in Spain were only around 5,000. These numbers declined drastically during the Franco regime as a result of official persecution, which is estimated to have affected, during and after the Civil War, three times as many people as there were actual members. The Law for Repression of Freemasonry (March 1940) established heavy penalties for membership, or for advocating the benefits of masonic activity. Franco's speeches, up to and including his last public one, a few weeks before his death, reflected his obsession with freemasonry as a sinister international plot against Spain.

In 1979, following on the legalization of freemasonry by the Supreme Court two years earlier, Spanish lodges were re-founded under the auspices of French masonry, and the independent Grand Lodge of Spain was established in 1982. In 1996, there were reported to be 2,000 adherents of mainstream freemasonry in Spain, plus another 300 members of unaffiliated groups. This compares with 3 million members in the US and 800,000 in Britain. Approximately a third of the membership in Spain consists of British and other foreign residents. Outside the main centres of Madrid and Catalonia, membership is most numerous in areas where British expatriates have settled: the Canaries, Balearics and the south coast, especially around towns like Marbella.

The Roman Catholic church was implacably hostile to freemasonry until the 1960s, but in the early 1990s the Vatican lifted the ban on church members joining the masons. The Grand Lodge of Spain requires belief in some religion as a precondition of membership, which has helped to smooth over traditional differences. Luis Salat, a former Grand Master, was buried with full Catholic obsequies. The Grand Symbolic Lodge, affiliated to French masonry, has a more secular character, but admits believers and agnostics alike. Unlike the mainstream Grand Lodge of Spain, it admits women, and in May 1997 elected the first woman Deputy Grand Master, Ascensión Tejerina.

Further reading

Ferrer Benimeli, J. (1980) *Masonería española contemporánea*, vol. 2 *Desde 1868 hasta nuestros días*, Mexico and Madrid: Siglo Veintiuno de España Editores (chapters 5 and 6 cover the contemporary period; there is a useful appendix of relevant documents, and a very full bibliography).

Pérez Díaz, S. (1996) 'Los masones salen a la luz', *El País Internacional*, 15 April.

EAMONN RODGERS

Freixenet

Freixenet is an internationally known label for a light sparkling cava **wine**. The Freixenet company was founded at the beginning of the twentieth century producing cava using the Méthode Champenoise and marketing its products under a variety of labels until it adopted the Freixenet label exclusively from 1915. The company produces 70 percent of the cava sold outside Spain in some 120 countries. It has subsidiaries in the UK, Germany, the USA (producing one million bottles from its own vineyards annually) and Mexico (producing 400,000 bottles annually from its own vineyards). In 1985 the company acquired the French champagne producer, Henri Abelé, and in Spain it owns three cava producing and two winemaking companies. Its turnover in 1994 was 35,000m pesetas, of which 12,500m came from exports.

EAMONN RODGERS

Freixes, Dani

b. 1946, Barcelona

Architect

Dani Freixes often succeeds in infusing architecture with a distinctive breath of the poetical: functional and constructional features blend effortlessly with artistic ones. His association since 1972 with Vicente Miranda has produced works which are both rational and playful. The projects executed in collaboration with Pep Angli and Eulalia González include the Parc Clot (1986, Barcelona), the extension to the **Dalí Museum** (1994, Figueras) and the Faculty of Communication Sciences (1996, Barcelona). In the area of **Interiorism** their great successes are the two bars Zsa-Zsa (1989, Barcelona) and Seltz (1993, Barcelona) and the club-restaurant Magic Barça (1996, Barcelona).

MIHAIL MOLDOVEANU

Frühbeck de Burgos, Rafael

b. 1933, Burgos

Conductor

One of Spain's most distinguished and internationally well-known conductors, Frühbeck de Burgos was appointed musical director of the Vienna Symphony Orchestra in 1991, general musical director of the Deutsche Oper, Berlin, in 1992 and musical director of the Rundfunk Symphony Orchestra, Berlin, in 1994. He had begun his musical studies in Spain, studying piano, violin and harmony in Bilbao and composition under Julio Gómez at the Royal Conservatory of Music, Madrid. Between 1953 and 1956 he was director of music for the army. Subsequently, he attended the School of Music at Munich for specialized courses in conducting under Lessing and Eichorn, and was appointed director of the Municipal Orchestra of Bilbao in 1958. Then in 1962 he became director of the National Orchestra of Spain, a post which he held until 1978, though he was already much in demand abroad, acting as general musical director of the Düsseldorf Symphony Orchestra from 1966 to 1971, and musical director of the Montreal Symphony Orchestra from 1974 to 1976. He was principal guest conductor for many leading orchestras abroad, holding an appointment with the New Philharmonia in London between 1969 and 1973, with the National Symphony Orchestra, Washington DC from 1980 to 1990, and with the Yomiuri Nippon Symphony Orchestra, Tokyo, becoming its honorary conductor in 1991. A wide range of recordings includes Falla's *Atlántida*, *La vida breve* and *The Three-Cornered Hat*, Orff's *Carmina Burana*, Mendelssohn's *Elijah*, and Mozart's *Requiem*.

Frühbeck de Burgos' services to music were recognized by the award of the Grand Cross, Order of Civil Merit by the Spanish government, an honorary doctorate from the University of Navarre in 1994, and the Gold Medal of the City of Vienna in 1995.

See also: music; opera; orchestras

EAMONN RODGERS

Fuentes Quintana, Enrique

b. 1924, Carrión de los Condes (Palencia)

Politician and academic economist

Distinguished economist, Vice-President for Economic Affairs following the general election of June 1977, and author of many books and articles, Fuentes Quintana played a significant role in the elaboration of the **Moncloa Pacts** and introduced an important series of reforms aimed at liberalizing the Spanish banking and financial system. His resignation in February 1978, on account of the government's apparent lack of support for his initiatives, was one of the events which gave the **UCD** government a more right-wing complexion. He is emeritus professor at **UNED**.

See also: economy; politics

PAUL KENNEDY

Fuertes, Gloria

b. 1918, Madrid; d. 1998, Madrid

Poet, writer and editor

An unconventional figure, Gloria Fuertes actively refuses to fit any mould – either as a poet or as a woman. In her introduction to *Obras Incompletas* (Incomplete Works) published by Cátedra in 1975, she expresses the angry suspicion that a minority, composed of critics and academics, will now descend upon her poems to classify them according to existing literary or social categories. Fuertes has always preferred to project the image of a popular poet in direct communication with a majority: the people.

Born to a working-class family who lived in a poor quarter of Madrid, her writing is steeped in the slang and colloquialisms of this setting. The Civil War marked the beginning of her adult life, and anti-war sentiment became a thematic constant. However, it was not until after Franco's death that Fuertes made open references to her own experience of the war and the subsequent dictatorship.

Her poetry began to appear in journals during the 1940s, and she progressed through a series of occupations until becoming, remarkably for a poet, financially self-supporting through her writing. Despite her current disavowal of being influenced by other poets, it can be seen that Fuertes developed within various traditions to emerge with a singular voice and style after decades of writing. Her initial connection with surrealism was interrupted by another idea which came into play in the 1950s, when a group of poets focused on the common man. Alongside Celaya and others, Fuertes' main objective was to draw attention to the injustice of the social system. They believed this was possible through the revolutionizing of poetic language, so they began exploring the potential richness in everyday speech. From now on Fuertes' background was to feed into her poetry, as she demonstrated an ability to record and transform the ordinary with pathos and humour. Eventually she moved on in a more personal direction, recording her experience as a woman and a writer in poems that are exceptionally short, a form she herself dubs 'mini-poems'. Though not wishing to be considered a feminist, Fuertes often reminds interviewers that she and other women poets gathered weekly in the 1950s for an alternative ***tertulia*** called 'Poetry in Skirts'.

The presence of social concerns continues unabated into the 1990s, and a deeper exploration of the sensory and ludic potential of language is revealed in her collections: *Historia de Gloria: Amor, humor y desamor* (Gloria's Story: Loving, Laughing and Unloving) (1980) and *Mujer de verso en pecho* (Woman with Poetry Within) (1995).

Further reading

Capuccio, B.L. (1993) 'Gloria Fuertes frente a la critica', *Anales de la literatura contemporanea* 18, 1: 89–108 (this overview of critical approaches to Fuertes' poetry is an indispensable bibliography).

Sherno, S.R. (1989–90) 'The Poetry of Gloria Fuertes: Textuality and Sexuality', *Siglo XX* 7, 1–2: 19–23 (valuable study of the relationship between poetry and gender, though overly informed by universal feminist categories).

JESSAMY HARVEY

Fura dels Baus, La

La Fura may be described as the Catalan performance group of the rock age. Founded in 1979, they include artists from various disciplines, including music and dance. As with Els **Joglars**, the acting style of La Fura is physically very demanding on the actors. They have been innovative in their use of different urban spaces for the performance of their shows. These include markets, train stations and disused factories. They have adapted their performances to the particular setting in which each individual performance takes place. These settings are extremely varied: for instance, *Suz/o/Suz* has been performed in locations as different as a Madrid morgue and a Sydney garage.

An Artaudian primitive ritualism is an essential ingredient of La Fura's shows, some of which are characterized by destructive violence, as when the performers destroy a car with sledgehammers in *Accions*. The Who's smashing of guitars on stage comes to mind. Like other Catalan performance groups, La Fura dels Baus have marketed products related to their shows. They have made a maxi-single 'Ajoë' (1986) and two LPs, *Suz* (1988) and *Noun* (1990) (the LP *Noun* was produced before the show of the same name, in collaboration with the flamenco singer Ginesa Ortega). The video *Ulelé* (1987), made by Francisco Montoliu, includes fragments of the production of *Suz/o/Suz* relocated in open landscapes. La Fura's interest in machinery led them to organize Autòmates (Automata) in 1988, a dynamic exhibition of machines and sound contraptions used in *Suz/o/Suz* and *Tier mon*.

Like Els **Comediants**, La Fura participated in the Barcelona Olympic Games in 1992 by organizing the opening ceremony, *Mar Mediterrània* (Mediterranean Sea). It was conceived as a spectacular cosmogonic fight, derived from the ancient Roman *naumachia* (naval battle), between ignorant irrationality on the one hand (represented by animals and fantastical monsters like the hydra) and civilization on the other (represented by the sea, a ship and Hercules). This plot was introduced through a sophisticated, pre-recorded video portraying the movement of masses and set to music by Ryuichi Sakamoto. The result was a kind of gestural 'score' which created a new conceptual and aesthetic precedent for Olympic ceremonies of the future.

See also: Catalan culture; *Movida, la*; performing arts; rock and pop

Further reading

Saumell, M. (1996) 'Performance Groups in Catalonia', in D. George and J. London (eds) *An Introduction to Contemporary Catalan Theatre*, Sheffield: Anglo-Catalan Society (the only full-length study of the phenomenon in English).

DAVID GEORGE

Fusi Aizpurua, Juan Pablo

b. 1945, San Sebastián

Historian

After taking his doctorate at the Complutense University of Madrid, Fusi worked at St Antony's College, Oxford (1970–4 as Research Fellow, and 1976–9 as Director of the Iberian Centre), collaborating with Sir Raymond Carr on an important and influential study of the post-Franco transition, *Spain: Dictatorship to Democracy* (1979). From 1987 to 1990 Fusi was Director of the National Library of Spain, and since 1990 has been professor of Contemporary History at the Complutense. He has been a visiting professor at the University of Wisconsin at Madison (1981). His publications include studies of labour politics in the Basque country, and a biography of Franco (1985). He holds an honorary doctorate from New York University.

EAMONN RODGERS

Fuster, Joan

b. 1922, Sueca (Valencia); d. 1992, Sueca

Historian and critic

Joan Fuster is without doubt one of the most eminent figures to emerge from the País Valenciá in the twentieth century. His stature in the Catalan cultural and ideological sphere is comparable to that enjoyed in literature by his fellow-Valencian Vicente Blasco Ibáñez. Fuster's long career, which could best be described as one of 'creative belligerence', may be outlined by his involvement in a series of activities which take the form of, in ascending order of significance, poet, journalist, essayist, literary critic and historian.

After an initial flirtation with poetry, Fuster rejected the rarified atmosphere of poetic experience in the early 1950s to involve himself more directly in the progressive struggle against Franco's dictatorship and its state machinery. His tireless struggle against all aspects of Francoist repression is repeatedly articulated within the framework of speculation on the nature of Valencian identity, and outspoken defence of the rights of ethnic minorities. With this in view, he embarked on a journalistic career which would last for four decades, and include an enormous number of high-quality contributions to the local and national **press**. The logical corollary of this activity was the writing of reflective essays on ethical issues. In collections such as *Diccionari per a ociosos* (Dictionary for Idlers) (1964) and *Rebeldes y heterodoxos* (Rebels and Heretics) (1972), he displays the progressive humanism and respect for scientific procedure which he derives from Montaigne and the major writings of the French Enlightenment.

It is, however, in the field of literary criticism that Fuster's intellectual muscle shows to best advantage. The high-quality scholarship displayed in his anthology of Valencian poets (1956) was also reflected in his studies of Ausias March, Isabel de Villena Espriu, Salvat-Papasseit, and Estellés, and culminated in 1972 in his *Literatura catalana contemporània* (Contemporary Catalan Literature). This volume provides both a comprehensive overview of twentieth-century Catalan letters and a sensitive synthesis of underlying currents. It is regarded as the authoritative starting-point for any prospective study of this field.

Fuster's most perceptive and polemical writing is to be found in his reflections on the Valencian character and heritage. In an era typified by rigid centralism and the imposition of a Castilian-based view of Spanish nationhood, he became the champion of Valencian cultural identity. Over a period of four decades, he produced over a dozen volumes, epitomized by *Nosaltres els valencians* (We

Valencians) (1962), which demonstrate, with substantive evidence and impeccable clarity, the Catalanity of the País Valencià. In this regard, Fuster was one of the first to trace the nature of the polemic, over the previous three centuries, between those who saw the place of Valencia as firmly within the Catalan cultural and linguistic world, and those who attempted to argue for linguistic secessionism, which he saw as politically motivated by regressive centralism.

With the restoration of democracy, Fuster's lifelong dedication to the promotion of Valencian culture was recognized by awards from the **Generalitat** of both Catalonia and Valencia. After receiving an honorary doctorate from the University of Barcelona in 1984, he became professor of Catalan at the University of Valencia in 1986. He also attracted unwelcome attention from local far-right elements. Effigies of him were burnt in the 1962 ***fallas***, and his home was bombed in 1981.

See also: regional nationalism

DOMINIC KEOWN

G

GAL

The Grupos Antiterroristas de Liberación (Anti-terrorist Liberation Groups) were clandestine right-wing hit squads formed in the early 1980s, with the alleged connivance of government ministers, and involving senior figures in the police, in an attempt to strike at key members of the command structure of the Basque organization **ETA**. GAL is believed to have been implicated in twenty-three murders of persons associated with ETA between 1983 and 1986.

Though undercover execution squads existed during the **UCD** government, the creation and funding of GAL as such was the work of forces closely identified with the **PSOE** administration which assumed power in 1982. The existence of the organization came to light when a Basque businessman (who happened to be a French citizen), Segundo Marey, was kidnapped in mistake for an ETA activist. A statement released by his captors claimed responsibility for the incident on behalf of a hitherto unknown entity, Grupos Antiterroristas de Liberación. In April 1987, during the trial in Lisbon of Portuguese nationals who had been involved in attacks on suspected ETA members, the accused claimed that they had been contracted by a Spanish police superintendent, José **Amedo**. Investigations carried out in December showed that between 1985 and 1987 Amedo had spent 27m pesetas for which he could not satisfactorily account. Together with a colleague, Michel Domínguez, he was arrested in 1988, and the two officers were charged with the murder of Juan Carlos García Goena, who had been assassinated in Hendaye in July 1986.

Though Amedo denied the charge, some of the evidence given in the case was compelling. For example, staff from a hotel in San Sebastián testified that Amedo had been seen there several times in the company of people later identified as GAL mercenaries, at dates which coincided closely with the attacks. An alibi claim by Amedo was demolished when documentary evidence showed that he was in Irún under a false identity at the time of the murder of Goena. On the other hand, witnesses contradicted each other, and handwriting experts could not agree. The prosecution recognized that the evidence was largely circumstantial, and Amedo and Domínguez were acquitted of the murder charge. They were, however, convicted of the attempted murder of six people wounded in a machine-gun attack on two bars in St Jean de Luz frequented by ETA members, and sentenced to seventeen years on each charge, a total of 108 years.

It was clear by then, however, that the case had much wider ramifications. A number of questions remained unanswered, particularly regarding the ultimate responsibility for the foundation and organization of GAL, and the source of the funds controlled by Amedo. Witnesses were evasive under questioning, especially when asked about secret funds available to the security services (the *fondos reservados* which were to become an important element in the affair). The Prime Minister of the day, Felipe **González**, was forced to provide a written statement to the court, denying that he had known about the activities of GAL, or that he had discussed them with the French authorities.

The case refused to go away. Amedo's name surfaced again in another trial in May 1993, when a person accused of the murder of the **Herri Batasuna** leader Santiago Brouard, claimed that Amedo had been present when this murder was planned. There was consequently great surprise in legal circles, and among the public at large, when the authorities announced in May 1994 that Amedo and Domínguez would benefit from the so-called 'third degree' prison regime, normally applied only to those who are deemed to have served three-quarters of their sentence. This would allow them freedom during the day and at weekends. For reasons which, it subsequently appeared, were far from disinterested, the proposal was supported by the former Interior Minister, José Barrionuevo, and by the ex-Director of Security, Julián Sancristóbal, both of whom were later the subject of judicial investigation by the judge Baltasar **Garzón**.

Garzón's tenacity in following up the GAL affair has unearthed a complex network of intrigue, corruption and political manœuvering. As a result of statements taken from Amedo and Domínguez in December 1994, three of their superiors were imprisoned pending further enquiries. In parallel with the judicial investigation, Amedo and Domínguez began giving interviews to the newspaper ***El Mundo***, in the course of which it was alleged that Rafael Vera, the former Secretary of State for Security in the Interior Ministry, had offered them sums up to 100m pesetas each in return for their silence, and that these had been paid into a Swiss bank account in 1991, with the knowledge of the then Minister, José Luis Corcuera. By January 1995, Garzón had established that two numbered accounts in Switzerland, in the names of the respective wives of Amedo and Domínguez, contained funds in excess of this amount. Vera and his secretary, Juan de Justo, were arrested on charges of misuse of state funds, being an accessory to crime, and forgery.

Garzón's zeal in pursuing the case earned him, not surprisingly, the hostility of much of the political class, especially senior members of the ruling PSOE. In addition, he was the victim of a press campaign, notably by the right-wing ***ABC***, which in February 1995 alleged that the secret funds controlled by the Interior Ministry had paid for a holiday taken by Garzón in Santo Domingo. Garzón was, however, able to disprove this, and his impartiality was defended by the Council of the Judiciary.

Public interest in the affair, already high, was raised to a new emotional pitch when concrete evidence of the fate of some of GAL's victims emerged dramatically in the same month. In 1985, the bodies of two men shot through the head and buried in quicklime had been discovered in the Alicante area. It was assumed at the time that they were the victims of a mafioso killing, and the investigating magistrate had closed the case for lack of evidence and ordered their burial. The pathologist who had examined the bodies, however, was not satisfied with this explanation, and took it on himself to preserve them in the morgue. Information which Amedo provided in the course of Garzón's investigation enabled the pathologist to identify the bodies as those of José Antonio Lasa and José Ignacio Zabala, members of ETA, who had disappeared in 1983, and, as subsequently emerged, had been tortured and killed, probably around January 1984, in the Intxaurrondo Civil Guard barracks (San Sebastián). The commander of this barracks at the time, Enrique Rodríguez Galindo, whose anti-ETA activities would later earn him the highest number of decorations awarded to any military officer, and who was ultimately promoted to General, was eventually arrested and charged on 23 May 1996.

A month after the discovery of the bodies, in April 1995, Garzón formally indicted Rafael Vera and others, including a member of the Basque branch of PSOE, García Damborenea; the former Civil Governor of Vizcaya, Julián Sancristóbal; the chief of police in Bilbao, Francisco Alvarez; and the head of intelligence in Bilbao, Miguel Planchuelo. In the indictment, they were described as the founders of GAL. Vera was released in July on bail of 200m pesetas, paid by PSOE. At the same time, however, Planchuelo confirmed the testimony given by Amedo and Domínguez, and accused the former Interior Minister Barrionuevo of being in ultimate control of GAL. Damborenea admitted his involvement in the Marey kidnapping, but alleged that Felipe González had approved of the use of illegal methods for dealing with ETA.

At the end of July 1995, Garzón notified the Supreme Court that there was *prima facie* evidence of the involvement in GAL of González, Barrionuevo, former Deputy Prime Minister Narcís Serra and the leader of the Basque socialists, Txiki Benegas. The Congress of Deputies agreed to lift Barrionuevo's parliamentary immunity so that his case could be investigated by the Supreme Court, and in the event only he was proceeded against. On 12 January 1996, he was indicted on charges of complicity in the kidnapping of Marey, and, twelve days later, for involvement in the establishment of GAL and misuse of public funds.

By then, a further bizarre twist had been given to the affair. In September 1995, it was reported that the disgraced banker, Mario **Conde**, who was being prosecuted for fraud in connection with the collapse of the Banesto bank, had for some months been threatening to publish sensitive information, potentially damaging to the government. He had apparently obtained copies of documents belonging to the State Security Services (CESID), illegally removed by a former Security Service officer, Colonel Perote, and claimed that they contained what came to be referred to as the 'founding document' of GAL. The government at first refused to declassify the 'CESID papers', as they were called, but at the end of January 1997, the Supreme Court demanded that they be handed over. In March, they were examined by the court, and deemed to be harmless to state security. Any possible dramatic effect consequent on their release was diminished by the fact that they had already been made public in *El País* and *El Mundo*. Though they appeared to confirm that the planning of illegal actions was carried out jointly by CESID and the Civil Guard, there was no mention of GAL by name, and in any case the papers presented to the court were copies of copies, and therefore not wholly conclusive as evidence. Felipe González was, however, definitively cleared of any involvement.

It is difficult to overestimate the influence of this 'dirty war' episode on the political atmosphere of Spain since the late 1980s. The complex interaction of corruption, arbitrary action, personal vendetta and cover-up has raised serious questions about how far the rule of law has really taken root in Spain since the ending of the Franco dictatorship. The efforts of conscientious judges to ensure that the servants of the state are not immune from the law have been obstructed by powerful interests in financial and political circles. Furthermore, the absence of a sound tradition of jurisprudence in cases of this nature makes it difficult to determine where the line is to be drawn between preventing arbitrary and illegal action, and allowing some discretion to the state in dealing with the problem of terrorism. It has also meant that some members of the judiciary, notably Garzón, lay themselves open to the accusation of acting beyond their remit, or pursuing personal ambition. A further problem which needs to be resolved is the freedom which the media enjoy to comment on cases while they are still before the courts, which creates what has been called 'parallel trials'. The entire episode, indeed, offers a classic illustration of how changes in political culture, dependent as they are on personnel and attitudes, lag behind the structural transformations effected during the post-Franco transition to democracy.

See also: corruption; legal system; politics

EAMONN RODGERS

Gala, Antonio

b. 1936, Córdoba

Writer

Playwright, television writer, novelist and journalist, Gala was born in the first year of the Civil War, grew up during the most restrictive years of the Franco era and was the first of his generation to write successfully for the theatre. After receiving multiple university degrees in Law, Philosophy and Letters, and Political Science, he entered a monastery for a time. In 1963 his first produced play, *Los verdes campos del Edén* (*The Green Fields of Eden*), was warmly received by critics and audiences. With its concern for the dispossessed, its symbolic elements and poetic overtones, this realistic drama about a group of homeless people who take up residence in a cemetery crypt set the tone for many of his later plays. His next performed work, *El sol en el hormiguero* (The Sun on the Anthill) (1966), was a complex treatment of Swift's Gulliver and the political effects of his arrival among the Lilliputians. The critical reception was mixed, with one respected reviewer attacking both play and production.

Gala's reputation grew with *Los buenos dias perdidos* (*The Bells of Orleans*), which ran for more than five hundred performances after its première in 1972. *Anillos para una dama* (Rings for a Lady) (1973), a revisionist treatment of the Cid legend from the point of view of his widow Jimena, and *Petra Regalada* (1980), an allegorical depiction of the end of the Franco era, were two major successes that followed. All of these plays deal with the struggles of women or minorities for identity and survival. After the end of censorship, Gala introduced sympathetic gay characters who were thwarted by homophobia in *La vieja señorita del Paraíso* (The Old Lady of the Paradise Cafe). *Samarkanda* (Samarkand), staged in 1985, was one of the rare Spanish plays that focuses on, and deals explicitly with, a homosexual relationship.

Throughout his career Gala has written for television, beginning with twenty-six scripts for the series *Y al fin, esperanza* (And at the End, Hope) in 1967. The following year he wrote his first film script for director Mario **Camus**. He also wrote the successful musical *Carmen, Carmen* and the libretto for Leonardo Bolada's opera *Cristóbal Colón*, which was commissioned to commemorate the quincentennial of the discovery of America. In the 1980s Gala became disenchanted with theatrical production and began to write increasingly for periodicals. Because of a long-running newspaper column and frequent essays and articles for the Madrid press, his name is familiar to many Spaniards who may never have seen any of his plays. A first novel, *El manuscrito carmesí* (The Crimson Manuscript) (1990), won the **Planeta Prize** in 1990, and *Más allá del jardin* (Beyond the Garden) became a best seller in 1995.

See also: performing arts; theatre

Further reading

Díaz Padilla, F. (ed.) (1981) *Obras escogidas*, Madrid: Aguilar (an edition of twelve of Gala's plays with a lengthy introduction in Spanish by the editor).

Zatlin, P. (ed.) (1981) *Noviembre y un poco de hierba; Petra Regalada*, Madrid: Cátedra (an edition of two of Gala's plays with an excellent study of his life and theatre).

MARION PETER HOLT

Galerías Preciados

An important chain of department stores, though not as powerful financially as El **Corte Inglés**. Founded in 1934, it has branches in major provincial cities like Valladolid and Bilbao, as well as five stores in Madrid and two in Barcelona, and employs 7,600 people. In 1995 it was acquired by El Corte Inglés. Its European sales ranking in 1996 was 3,067.

EAMONN RODGERS

Galician

Galician, a Romance language closely related to Portuguese, is spoken by approximately 1.5 million inhabitants of northwestern Spain principally in the **autonomous community** of Galicia, but also in parts of Asturias and Castilla y León. While Galician enjoyed a rich written tradition during the Middle Ages, it was subsequently ousted by **Spanish** in religious and administrative life and amongst the more affluent classes of society. Spanish thus became the prestige language with the use of Galician increasingly restricted to rural areas and the home, a process which culminated in the nineteenth century when the language, like the region, became associated with backwardness and poverty. Despite a literary revival at the end of the nineteenth century (led by writers such as Rosalía de Castro) which gave rise to the founding of the Academy of the Galician Language in 1906, and a brief period when it almost achieved co-officiality with Spanish under the Second Republic, Galician had to wait for the **constitution of 1978** and the Language Planning Law of 1983 to receive official protection and sponsorship.

Despite the fact that there are two main subvarieties of Galician (the eastern, covering the provinces of Orense and Lugo and the zones of contact with Asturian and Leonese dialects, and the western, covering La Coruña and Pontevedra) differences are not significant enough to prove a barrier to the codification of a Galician standard. Rather, conflict has arisen between two views of the status of Galician: the official position held by the 'isolationists' (including the Academy and the Institute of Galician Language of the University of Santiago) who seek to establish 'pure' Galician norms; and the 'reintegrationists' who see Galician as a subvariety of Portuguese (albeit contaminated through contact with Spanish) and therefore wish to align Galician orthography with that of Portuguese. Thus endings such as *-ción*, *-sion* or *-xion* are rejected by the reintegrationists on the grounds that they are calques of the Spanish *-ción;* they propose *-çom* or even the Portuguese *-ção.* What was initially a linguistic debate has become political as the government, parliament and main political parties have adopted the isolationist position while nationalist and radical sectors have espoused the reintegrationist cause (which does not appear to have found favour with Galician society at large).

Although Galician is proportionally much more widely spoken than **Basque** and **Catalan** (with 90 percent of the population able to speak it), this may be due to low inward migration. Mainly spoken in rural areas, it is nonetheless increasingly being adopted among professional urban sectors of the population for nationalist reasons. The Galician government is not as active as its Basque or Catalan counterparts in promoting its language although it often takes its lead from them. Galician has gained in prestige in education and public administration, although a diglossic situation remains in which Spanish is still frequently seen as the prestige language to be used in the public arena. Publishing in Galician has increased significantly over recent years, Spanish-language newspapers have sections in Galician and there is a Galician-speaking television and radio channel.

Further reading

García Mouton, P. (1994) *Lenguas y dialectos de España*, Madrid: Arco Libros, S.L. (a clear overview of language varieties in Spain).

Siguán, M. (1992) *España plurilingüe*, Madrid: Alianza (a comprehensive study of language planning).

MIRANDA STEWART

Galician culture

Shaping influences on Galician culture include: *galego*, the **Galician** language closely related to Portuguese, dialects of which (including *castrapismo*, a part-Castilian dialect) are used by the vast majority of its population; a medieval legacy of religious patronage, associated notably with *El Camino de Santiago* and rapid monastic expansion; identification with a Celtic prehistory inspired by folklore and archaeological studies; a strong emotional attachment to the land (see also ***minifundia***) and sea, and the related experiences of human loss, through famine, drowning and emigration; resistance to the Franco regime through the persistence of Galician cultural activism; the institutionalization and subsidy of culture by the **Xunta de Galicia**; and intermittent openness to ideas emanating from across the peninsula and abroad.

The recovery of the Galician past was a key project of a national cultural movement in the nineteenth and twentieth centuries. One early exponent was Rosaliá de Castro who expressed in poetry that most Galician of emotions, *saudade*: the sense of longing left behind by loss. The *rexurdimento* (renaissance) was reinforced by the success of the literary magazine *Nós* before the Civil War and rekindled after 1950 by the Galaixa publishing house. A key figure was Alfonso Castelao whose life (as author, artist and politician), death (exiled during the Franco era) and posthumous return (reburied in Galicia after democratic change) encapsulated the experience of his generation (*Xeneracion Nós*).

Feeding the past into contemporary Galician culture has taken place along many paths. These vary in form from the hints of pagan iconography evident in the shapes and painted patterns of modern Sargadelos ceramics to the special personal requests made to the spirits of the dead at the *romérias* (festivals) held annually in the village of San Andreas de Texido. The most ubiquitous cultural symbol of the past is probably the *gaitas* (bagpipes) from the Celtic-inspired folk music scene, and popularized particularly by groups such as Milladoiro in recent decades. In literature, Alvaro Cunqueiro's writings re-enter the magical world of the Galician medieval troubadours through journeys into the myths and legends of the past. Carlos Casares is one of those post-war poets and novelists who helped to open Galician writing to international and 'avant-garde' influences. The poetry and novels of young writers, notably Manuel Rivas, display a new self-confident exploration of Galician identity whose works confront the traditional past of Galicia with experiences of modern consumerism and technology-shaped change. Such writers have re-explored old Galician literary themes of migration, longing and loss, albeit less hidebound by traditional imagery.

The Xunta de Galicia has subsidized cultural activities across the *autonomía*. Most notably, it has implemented education policies to extend the use of *galego*, established RTVG (Radio and Television Galego) in 1985, published a wide range of Galician archaeological, historical and literary works and funded art exhibitions. While arguably more successful at preserving the cultural past than stimulating current cultural production, the Xunta's support for the Museo de Arte Contemparanea, opened up alongside the Museo do Pobo Gallego (folklore museum), symbolizes its awareness of the various facets of Galician culture today.

JOHN GIBBONS

gambling

It is estimated that Spaniards are the biggest gamblers in Europe and the third biggest in the world, after Americans and Filipinos. Among the figures on which this judgement is based is one showing that in 1991 gamblers lost a total amounting to a sixth of what was spent on food and 50 percent more than the total spent on alcohol and tobacco. In the same year, on average, every Spaniard over sixteen years of age staked the equivalent of over US $500 or £300, not counting what was spent on slot machines.

Outlets for legal gambling are private casinos, bingo halls and slot-machines (all controlled by the Ministry of the Interior), public lotteries and the football pool (controlled by ONLAE), and the lottery organized by **ONCE**. The relaxation of gambling laws in 1977 has increased by a factor of five the gross amount spent on legal gambling, compared with the Franco era. Of the twenty-six casinos registered in 1996, eighteen were opened between 1979 and 1981, and, according to figures from the Ministry of the Interior, they accounted for about 5 percent of the money gambled. Bingo halls, by comparison, have proved enormously popular, with 752 authorized by 1984, a figure which had dropped to 539 by 1996, when they accounted for just over 19 percent of gambling. The ubiquitous slot-machines, appropriately named *tragaperras* ('money-eaters'), attracted a massive 34 percent of gamblers' money, a good deal more than individual lotteries (such as the **national lottery** at over 17 percent and ONCE at about 12 percent), and second only to lottery sales as a whole, which stand at over 38 percent. The official football pool, known as the *Quiniela* and dating back to the Franco era, trailed far behind at just over 2 percent.

The extension of legal gambling has not meant the end of illegal gambling. In the 1980s, it was estimated that something like 500,000m pesetas were staked on activities like card and domino games in bars, and, in the Basque region, sporting and cultural events.

See also: sport and leisure

Further reading

Hooper, J. (1995) *The New Spaniards*, Harmondsworth: Penguin (chapter 13, 'High Stakes', gives a very informative account of the subject).

EAMONN RODGERS

ganadería

A *ganadería* is a cattle ranch, especially for raising fighting bulls (*toros bravos*).

See also: bullfighting

IAN CAMPBELL ROSS

Garci, José-Luis

b. 1944, Madrid

Filmmaker

Garci began his career in film as a critic, writing for *Signo*, *Aún* and *Cinestudio*, and acting as editor-in-chief of *Reseña* and *Revista SP* for two years. In 1970 he began writing scripts for films such as *La cabina* (The Telephone Booth) (1972), a prize-winning short directed by Antonio Mercero, and *Vida conyugal sana* (A Healthy Married Life) (1973) and *Los nuevos españoles* (The New Spaniards) (1974) both directed by **Bodegas**.

Following his success with the short *Mi Marilyn* (My Marilyn) (1975) about the American film star, he directed an all-time box office winner *Asignatura pendiente* (Pending Exam) in 1977. Depicting the unsuccessful attempt by a left-wing lawyer and his former girlfriend to recapture the excitement of their earlier relationship the film was seen as representing the lost and irrecoverable opportunities of the Franco years. In similar vein *Solos en la madrugada* (Alone at Dawn) (1978) depicted with wit and humour the humdrum middle-class lives of former college radicals.

Las verdes praderas (Green Pastures) (1979) and *El crack* (The Crack) (1981), both starring Alfredo **Landa**, brought him further success, as did *Volver a empezar* (To Begin Again) (1982). A moving portrait of a former Republican soldier, now an ageing professor in America, returning to Spain for a last visit to his native town, it was the first Spanish film to win an Oscar for best film in a foreign language. *Canción de cuna* (Lullaby) (1994) also won him international recognition. Based on a story by Martínez Sierra about nuns who adopt a child left on their doorstep, the film deliberately recreates an older classic style and gained him an award for best director in Montreal.

EAMONN RODGERS

García Sánchez, José Luis

b. 1941, Salamanca

Filmmaker and writer

In addition to his numerous children's stories and scripts for television, García Sánchez wrote scripts for important films in the 1970s such as *Habla, Mudita* (Speak, Mute Girl) (1973) and *Camada negra* (Black Brood) (1977) by **Gutiérrez Aragón**, and *Queridísimos verdugos* (Dearest Hangmen) (1973) for **Patino**. As director he shared the Golden Bear award at Berlin in 1978 for his art film *Las truchas* (The Trout).

In the 1980s and 1990s films such as *La corte de Faraón* (Pharaoh's Court) (1985) and *La noche más larga* (The Longest Night) (1990) deal with episodes of censorship and violence in Franco's Spain, while *El vuelo de la paloma* (The Flight of the Dove) (1989) takes a more satirical look and *Tranvía a la Malvarrosa* (Tram to Malvarrosa) (1996) a brighter look at those times. Among successful screen adaptations are his *Divinas palabras* (Divine Words) (1987) and *Tirano Banderas* (Banderas the Tyrant) (1993) based on plays by Valle-Inclán.

EAMONN RODGERS

García Serrano, Rafael

b. 1917, Pamplona

Writer

Journalist, novelist and essayist, García unfailingly propagandizes for the Falangists (see also **Falange**), exalting their heroics in *Eugenio o la proclamación de la primavera* (Eugene, or Proclaiming Springtime) (1938), and *La fiel infantería* (The Loyal Infantry) (1943) which crudely depicts life in the trenches. This resounding popular success received national recognition, but *Plaza del Castillo* (Castle Square) is literarily superior. *Los ojos perdidos* (Lost Eyes) (1958) and *La paz dura quince días* (Peace Lasts Two Weeks) (1960) truculently promote fascist ideology.

Further reading

Nora, EG. de (1967) *La novela española contemporánea*,

vol. 3, Madrid: Gredos, pp. 89–94 (good literary history which places García Serrano and his works in context).

Pérez, J. (1989, 1992) 'Fascist Models and Literary Subversion: Two Fictional Modes in Postwar Spain', *South Central Review* 6, 2: 73–87; repr. in *Fascism/Literature/Aesthetics*, ed. R.J. Golsan, University Press of New England, 128–42 (compares fiction of García Serrano with subversive treatment by Torrente Ballester).

JANET PÉREZ

gardens

Gardens may be divided into formal, botanical, public and private, each illustrating in different ways many of the influences that have formed Spanish culture.

Formal gardens

The oldest and some of the best known formal gardens are in the south of Spain in an area dominated for centuries by Arabs and Moors. The Patio de los Naranjos (Patio of the Orange Trees) in Córdoba was laid out in the tenth century, the orange trees being planted in the twelfth and thirteenth centuries. The Patio de los Naranjos in Seville dates from the twelfth century, and the gardens of the Alhambra and those of the Generalife from the thirteenth and fourteenth, all displaying features derived from the Islamic garden. Typical are the paved courtyard enclosed by high white stucco walls and divided by intersecting paths into geometrically shaped beds, usually square or rectangular, linked by irrigation channels; formalized planting such as rows of trees; water features such as pools and low level fountains; decorative coloured glazed ceramic tiles (*azulejos*) used particularly on the lower half of walls, fountains and benches; ironwork grilles (*rejas*) covering the exterior of windows and acting as gates in doorways.

Nor did Moorish influence on the design of formal gardens end with the loss of political dominance. The gardens of the Alcázar in Seville were built for Peter the Cruel in the middle of the fourteenth century by craftsmen from Granada and Toledo and were essentially Islamic in character. Over the centuries, however, the influence of European styles became more prominent. At first, they were frequently amalgamated with Moorish styles, a combination known as *mudéjar*, as in the sixteenth-century gardens of the House of Pilate and the House of the Sisters in Seville with their classical sculptures, Gothic balustrades and renaissance fountains. Alternatively, they were added to existing gardens, such as Charles V's pavilion, with its renaissance features, in the Alcázar gardens and his two additional courtyards in the Alhambra. In purer forms they were the inspiration for the gardens of the Casa de Campo and of the Palace of El Pardo in Madrid and the Island gardens at Aranjuez, all laid out by Charles V in Italian style with square beds, geometric patterns of planting, and sculptures and fountains at path intersections. Similarly, the garden of La Granja, begun in the eighteenth century by the Bourbon King Philip V, is in French style with parterres, avenues, pavilions, fountains and cascades.

The many monastic and cloister gardens in Spain also provide good examples of formal styles, and in general in Spain these styles lasted longer than in France or England.

Botanical gardens

A wide variety of trees, shrubs and flowers are known to have been grown by the Arabs in their gardens. Lists include orange, lemon, citron, bay and cypress trees; myrtle and arbutus; and roses, irises, gillyflowers, violets, lilies and narcissi among the flowers. Jasmines were introduced from Persia and at least one species of lilac. Also introduced were lavender and several herbs, among them dill, fennel and savoury.

From the sixteenth century onward, botanical expeditions were sent from Spain to the New World; cacao, cocoa and various spice trees; tagetes, nasturtium, fuschia, passionflower and the dahlia; and, of course, tobacco, are but a few of the huge range of new plants brought back from that region. Attempts were made to establish botanical gardens at various sites, the first by Philip II at Aranjuez, until the Royal Botanical

Garden of Madrid was created in 1755 under Ferdinand VI from the gardens of the royal apothecary at Migas Calientes, and then moved by Charles III to its final location at the Prado and officially opened in 1781. In 1981, after long periods of neglect, it was restored by Leandro Silva and re-inaugurated with the dual purpose of promoting scientific research and providing a public amenity. It was also Charles III who in 1788 commissioned the Marquis of Villanueva to create the Acclimatization Garden of Tenerife in La Orotava, which specializes in tropical plants. Other important botanical gardens are at Valencia and Barcelona.

Public gardens

Modern public gardens in Spain are largely the work of architects. Some of them were originally private gardens that have been remodelled, some are better classified as parks, and others are a direct result of the tourist trade. Several hotel and apartment schemes on the coast have substantial architect-designed gardens, for example, Los Monteros with its woodland garden, Puente Romano with its series of gardens and courts leading to the sea, and the Jardines de las Golondrinas with swimming pools, palms and exotic Strelitzia plants.

Private gardens

The styles of private gardens vary greatly from the simplest of courtyards with terracotta pots planted with cinerarias or geraniums, to the lavish planting of country or suburban villas. Many Islamic features are still common, notably that of the garden as an enclosed space with white walls, iron railings and grilles, planting beds, ornamental tiles and low fountains. New plants have continued to be introduced, but it is beginning to be recognized that the modern fascination in Spain, as elsewhere, with novelties is leading to the creation of gardens costly to maintain in terms of water usage, fertilizers and pesticides and to the exclusion of native species almost to the point of extinction.

Further reading

Casa Valdés, M. de (1987) *Spanish Gardens*, Woodbridge: Antique Collectors' Club (an expert view of Spanish gardens).

Correcher, C.M. (1993) *Gardens of Spain*, New York: Harry N. Abrams.

EAMONN RODGERS

Garrigues Walker, Antonio

b. 1934, Madrid

Businessman and politician

A business leader with political ambitions, Garrigues Walker played a significant part in the reorganization of the political parties on the centre and right during the late 1970s and 1980s. In 1980 to 1981 he garnered support in business circles for the conservative critical movement within the **UCD** party. A key figure in attempts to promote a liberal party in Spain particularly after the death of his brother, (see also **Garrigues Walker, Joaquín**), he was also instrumental in setting up the ill-fated Partido Reformista, led by Miquel **Roca**, which aimed to recreate a centre-right alternative to the Socialist Workers' Party (**PSOE**).

JONATHAN HOPKIN

Garrigues Walker, Joaquín

b. 1933, Madrid

Politician and businessman

The charismatic leader of the liberal faction in the **UCD** party from 1977 to 1980, Joaquín Garrigues Walker never disguised his prime ministerial ambitions and was an important figure in the campaign to overturn Prime Minister Adolfo **Suárez**. Despite a brief and unimpressive ministerial career (Minister of Public Works 1977–9), he managed to present himself as Prime Minister-in-waiting, and like his brother Antonio **Garrigues Walker**, used his extensive business connections to good effect in promoting his political views. His early death from leukaemia in September 1980 deprived the Spanish right of one of its more popular leaders.

JONATHAN HOPKIN

Garzón, Baltasar

b. 1955, Jaén

Judge

The judiciary played a prominent role in the fight against corruption in the early 1990s both in terms of investigating and prosecuting cases of political corruption. This central role adopted by the judiciary had the effect of catapulting many judges into high-profile public roles. One judge in particular, Baltazar Garzón, achieved such notoriety that the press dubbed him 'Super Garzón'.

Garzón gained a high public profile principally as head of the investigation into the activities of the **GAL**, an anti-**ETA** group which engaged in a dirty war campaign against the Basque terrorist organization between 1983 and 1986. The group was allegedly set up by two senior Spanish police officers and was authorized and financed from within the Interior Ministry. Although the case was supposedly solved with the sentencing of the two police suspects, José Amedo and Michel Domínguez, the GAL case was reopened by Garzón following a series of interviews with Amedo and Domínguez, published in the newspaper ***El Mundo***, which implicated senior government officials. Garzón was temporarily suspended from the case in January 1995 owing to allegations from a former member of the Interior Ministry that he was involved in a deliberate campaign to undermine the socialist **PSOE** administration. The government was considerably embarrassed when these allegations were unfounded and Garzón was subsequently reaffirmed in his position as investigating magistrate for the case.

Garzón also gained a high political profile by standing as an independent candidate in the 1993 general election. He appeared on the PSOE's list for Madrid as the number two candidate behind Felipe **González** in what was widely regarded as a deliberate move by the socialists to show that they were taking the fight against corruption seriously. Regarded as a political trump card at the time, Garzón was duly elected, only to resign in May 1994 in protest against what he regarded as the government's reluctance to tackle corruption directly, as well as the government's overt interference in the judiciary. Indeed, the blurring of the boundaries between executive and judiciary in Spain is clearly a problem. All too often the judiciary is viewed as simply another branch of the executive, something which can be seen in the increasing overlap in personnel between the executive and the judiciary of which Garzón is simply the most notorious example.

See also: corruption; legal system; politics

GEORGINA BLAKELEY

GATEPAC

The Grupo de Arquitectos y Técnicos Españoles para el Progreso de la Arquitectura Contemporánea (Group of Spanish Architects and Technicians for Progress in Contemporary Architecture) was an organization which owed its origin mainly to the architect José Luis **Sert** of Barcelona. There is no doubt that sooner or later Spain would have experienced the impact of the European avant-garde, but the process was hastened by Sert's impatience with existing conventions. GATEPAC provided a fruitful breeding-ground for the ideas of Walter Gropius and Le Corbusier, which were being promoted at this time through the CIAMs (Congresos Internationales de Arquitectura Moderna – International Congresses of Modern Architecture). Founded on 26 October 1930 in Zaragoza, GATEPAC brought together three groups of young architects, from the Basque region, Madrid and Catalonia, where Sert had already formed the group GATCPAC (where the 'C' stands for Catalan) in 1929 in Barcelona. After qualifying, Sert had worked for a year in the studio of Le Corbusier in Paris in 1928, and had returned to Spain determined to spread the ideas of the modern movement. Meanwhile in Madrid the architect Fernando García Mercadal had begun, single-handedly but with great conviction, a campaign in support of European modernity after meeting Peter Behrens, Poelzig, Mies van der Rohe, Le Corbusier and the group associated with the journal *L'Esprit Nouveau*. In fact it was on the invitation of García Mercadal that Le Corbusier came to Madrid in 1928 to give some lectures, and Sert seized the opportunity to invite Le Corbusier to give an impromptu lecture in Barcelona on his way home. Le Corbusier's collaboration with Sert and the Catalans proved to be very productive. A third group was formed in the Basque region, headed by the architects Vallejo, Labayen and Aizpurua. José Manuel Aizpurua was the main driving force behind the group, and his Club Nautique in San Sebastián (1929–30, with Labayen) is a good example of the direction the theory was taking. The Barcelona group was more prolific, with Sert, Yllescas, Subirana and the very talented Josep Torrés-Clavé, a victim of the Civil War in 1939 at the age of 32. The Central Dispensary for Tuberculosis (1935, Barcelona) is a good example of their approach. GATEPAC's most representative product was the journal *AC* (*Actividad Contemporánea*) published between 1931 and 1937. Its pages display a unity of purpose and combativeness in spreading the group's ideas, opposing official architecture and publicizing their projects. Articles were contributed not only by the founder-members of the group but by other significant figures of the period, such as Raimon Duran Reynals, Antoni Bonet and Francesc Folguera.

The Civil War and certain ideological differences led to the disbanding of the group in 1937, but its example continued to exercise considerable influence in the post-war period, especially through pupils and younger colleagues of the original members.

See also: architects; architecture

MIHAIL MOLDOVEANU

Gaudí, Antoni

b. 1852, Reus; d. 1926, Barcelona

Architect

A mythical figure of Catalan **Modernism**, Gaudí is the most celebrated Iberian architect of all time. From his student days, he showed exceptional talent for design and for the mathematics of structures. In his youth he was influenced by the ideas of Viollet-le-Duc on the scholarly use of historic styles, ideas which were defended in Barcelona in the second half of the nineteenth century by Elias Rogent. Gaudí never forgot Rogent's teaching, though its importance diminished over the years. Moreover, his work as a whole becomes increasingly distanced from the modernist movement, despite the fact that it was Gaudí who provided the most spectacular examples of it. His idiosyncratic style defies easy categorization. In the early period of his activity, *mudéjar* (Moorish) influences are recognizable, despite his fervent Catholicism, as well as some elements derived from Mackintosh, the pre-eminent representative in Britain of the 'Modern Style'. In the second phase of his career, his buildings express a complex vision dominated by a quasi-organic sculptural 'tectonics'. Among the manifestations of this are the links between natural and built structures, decoration based on complex geometry, polychromy, unusual juxtapositions of materials, historical allusion, the metaphor of myth, and the representation of the spiritual.

Apart from some isolated projects, his activity was centred on Barcelona and its environs. As a young architect, Gaudí gained the support of a rich aristocratic patron, Eusebi Güell, who became more and more involved in the bold enterprises proposed by his protégé. This relationship goes some way to explain Gaudí's development, since it fostered his idiosyncrasy and caused him to reflect even more deeply on questions of creativity. His individualism, the result of a growing mystical fervour, helped to turn him into an *artiste maudit* in the romantic tradition.

Among his first creations the most notable are the Casa Vicens (1883–5, Barcelona), the Palau Güell (1886–8, Barcelona) the Casa Calvet (1898–1902, Barcelona) the façade of which was to become a model for other modernist architects, and the Torre Bellesguard (1900–9, Barcelona). The church of the Sagrada Familia, emblematic of Barcelona, is a work of colossal proportions, which absorbed him from 1883 until his death in 1926. This building, where he lived for the last twelve years of his life, remained unfinished at the end of the twentieth century, having been worked on sporadically in the 1980s and generated considerable controversy about the appropriateness of continuing the work. Equally famous are the Casa Batlló, an extraordinary zoomorphic creation on the most elegant avenue in Barcelona, the Passeig de Gràcia (1904–6), the very sculptural Casa Milà known as La Pedrera situated on the same avenue

(1906–10), the internal refurbishment of the Cathedral of Palma de Mallorca (1904–14), the Parc Güell (1900–14, Barcelona) and the Cripta Güell (1908–16, Colonia Güell, Barcelona). Among his associates and followers are the noted architects **Jujol**, Francesc Berenguer and César **Martinell**.

See also: architects; architecture

Further reading

Bohigas, O. (1973) *Arquitectura Modernista*, Barcelona: Lumen (an important study by a leading Catalan architect).

Loyer, F. (1991) *L'art nouveau en Catalogne*, Paris: Biblio. Arts, Le Septième Fou (a comprehensive overview).

Moldoveanu, M. (1996) *Barcelona: Architectures of Exuberance*, Barcelona: Lunwerg (an overview of different periods and styles, richly illustrated with photographs by the author).

MIHAIL MOLDOVEANU

gay culture

While in many western countries the emergence of lesbian and gay cultures in the 1970s was quickly linked to a reclamation of homosexual social and cultural histories which were relatively easy to unearth, the Spanish situation – at least until the symbolic moments of 1978 (the new constitution) and 1979 (the general election) – has meant that a tradition of lives lived beyond heterosexuality is only slowly becoming visible, and in a fragmentary way. On the other hand, as much **gay writing** in Spain suggests, a plurality of queer cultures now exists and is rapidly proliferating across the regions and languages of the Spanish state. In the broadest terms, and from an Anglo-Saxon perspective, it is now possible to be in any major centre for a night or two and identify distinctive manifestations of 'lesbian' and 'gay' culture in two familiar areas, that of issue-based politics and that of recreation.

The first Gay Pride March in Spain was held in June 1977 in Barcelona, when some 4,000 took to the streets, a figure since then only rarely matched. A lesbian and gay politics concerned with rights and single issues has remained predominant, with recent campaigning focusing on homophobic attacks by ultra-right skinheads, rights of tenure and inheritance for cohabiting same-sex couples, parenting, and discrimination on grounds of sexual orientation (finally outlawed in the Penal Code of December 1995). If this seems to correspond to the Anglo-Saxon model of gay and lesbian politics, the many radical and theoretically sophisticated publications in circulation (certainly more of their type than in the United Kingdom) and the groupings behind them suggest a considerable overlap with queer politics and culture too. In Madrid *De Un Plumazo* (At a Stroke of the Pen), *Nosotras* (Us), *InformaLES* (Outsiders) and *Non grata* (Not Wanted), in Valencia the wide-circulation *El Paper Gai* (The Gay Paper) and in Bilbao *Gay Hotsa* all theorize sex, the body, culture, and political engagement from what look like queer perspectives. The terminologies of 'gay' and 'queer' are, however, significantly problematic. Guasch (1991) prefers the widely used *entender* (literally 'to understand' or 'to be in the know') for men who have sex with men to the imported and culturally inappropriate 'gay model' (43–6 and 159–65). Cultural difference notwithstanding, *lesbiana* and *lésbico/a* do signify a clear set of political and cultural practices in Spain, although it is something of a commonplace for these to be ignored or overlooked. For instance, while the May/June 1995 issue of the now practically mainstream lesbian and gay bi-monthly *¿Entiendes?* (Are You in the Know?) in Madrid asked 'Where Are All the Lesbians in This Country?', at the same time Marta Balletbò's lesbian-themed film comedy *Costa Brava* had become a hit in Catalonia and *Lambda* – the Catalan equivalent of *¿Entiendes?* – was able to discuss with the director the film's successful if light-hearted 'normalization' of lesbian issues.

In the social spaces of the extremely numerous gay cafés, bars and clubs of the major cities, music plays a key role in the construction of non-heterosexually identified cultures. In the clubs the sounds are predominantly those of the New York, Manchester and London scenes and the out-of-town club cultures of France and Italy. Scandinavian and German tastes are added in at the gay super-resorts at Playa de Inglés, Ibiza and Sitges. Beyond the clubs there is a distinctly homosexual resonance to the *copla*, the *bolero*, and latin beat for some, and for others the camper forms of **flamenco** rock make an obvious transgressive point. Among those who have cult status are Catalan singer-songwriter Lluís **Llach** who came out in the 1970s with 'Cançó d'amor' ('Love Song') and settings of Cavafy, and Paco Clavel who performs camp renditions of hits of the 1960s and 1970s. In 1975 Eduardo Haro Ibars' *Gay Rock* had responded to a glamorously transgressive strain in musical and performance culture which, along with punk makes its appearance in scenes in **Almodóvar**'s early movies and feeds into the ***Movida*** (whose gayness is easy to chart, for example, in the art work of the two-man Costus partnership). Super-icon **Alaska** carried the torch of transgressive tradition in the 1980s, and Javier Gurruchaga with the Orquesta Mondragón, along with Miguel Bosé, were points of reference for men. For women in the 1990s Marina Rossell, with her looks and her settings of poems by lesbian poet Maria Mercè Marçal, has a considerable following, one of Spain's biggest bands, **Mecano**, has brought out the lesbian-themed 'Mujer contra mujer', and the Catalan band Els Pets has had a minor hit with 'S'ha acabat' ('It's Over Now') on a gay love affair.

In cinema the Filmotecas of Madrid, Valencia and Barcelona (which has also hosted lesbian and gay theatre seasons) give prominence to films by or for lesbians and gay men, and commercially released Spanish queer cinema is beginning to make an appearance in the late 1990s. Established stars are serving to keep the non-straight on screen (in the tradition of films by Jaime **Chávarri**, Eloy de **La Iglesia**, Pedro **Olea**, and Almodóvar) with Jorge Sanz convincingly playing a rent-boy in *Hotel y domicilio* (In Calls or Out) and Javier Bardem pretending to be hot for men as a telephone sex-line worker who gets embroiled in a complex murder plot in *Boca a boca* (Mouth to Mouth). Super-star Victoria **Abril**'s role in the French production *Le Gazon maudit* (*French Twist*) (1995) brings issues concerning the representation of lesbianism to the top of new cultural agendas.

Further reading

Alas, L. (1994) *De la acera de enfrente. Todo lo que se debe saber de los gays y nadie se ha atrevido a contar*, Madrid: El Papagayo.

Bergmann, E.L. and Smith, P.J. (1995) 'Introduction' in Bergmann and Smith (eds) *¿Entiendes? Queer Readings, Hispanic Writings*, Durham and London: Duke University Press.

Guasch O. (1991) *La sociedad rosa*, Barcelona: Anagrama.

Smith P.J. (1992) *Laws of Desire. Questions of Homosexuality in Spanish Writing and Film 1960–1990*, Oxford: Oxford University Press.

CHRIS PERRIAM

gay writing

Gay and lesbian writing in Spain has many histories and displays a complex variety of identifications and non-identifications with the notions of homosexual culture, community, politics and sensibilities.

As elsewhere in Europe, pre-1960s Spain had its more or less veiled homosexual voices; in this case mostly male and poets. A quiet, aestheticizing homoerotic strain is taken up by Pablo García Baena and Ricardo Molina. Luis Cernuda's austere but sensual and explicit explorations of homosexual desire in *Poemas para un cuerpo* (Poems for a Body) serve in the 1950s to link an older gay generation of writers to the new: there are echoes of Cernuda in poems of the 1960s onwards by Francisco Brines; and Luis Antonio de **Villena** in the 1970s and early 1980s mingles outrageousness and decadentism with Cernuda's ethics and aesthetics of desire.

In prose narrative, Villena's parallel vocation as a narrator-chronicler of Madrid gay life is matched by Terenci **Moix**'s treatments of Barcelona as a scenario for a postmodern sentimental education, and the archetypal story of growing up lesbian or gay, used by Moix, also provides the framework for Andalusian Eduardo Mendicutti's highly successful 1991 novel *El palomo cojo* (The Lame Dove) – now a screenplay directed by Jaime de **Armiñán**. The title story of Carme **Riera**'s still popular collection of 1975, *Te deix amor la mar com a penyora* (I Leave You, My Love, The Sea as a Token), in its depiction of an intense relationship between a younger and an older woman, shares common thematic if not stylistic ground with the difficult and self-conscious narratives of unpoliticized lesbianism and bisexuality of Esther **Tusquets** to which the feminist writings of Maria Mercè Marçal provide an enlivening contrast.

Mendicutti, like Villena and novelist Álvaro Pombo, is interested in the dynamics of age and power inequalities in non-gay identified relationships: his *Los novios búlgaros* (Bulgarian Boyfriends) (1993) explores issues of exploitation, empowerment, and national identity while the hilarious and astute *Una mala noche la tiene cualquiera* (Anyone Can Have Bad Night) (1982) looks at sexual and gender politics through the eyes of a communist-sympathizing transvestite narrating the events of the night of Colonel Antonio **Tejero**'s coup attempt of February 1981.

Resonances of the gay liberation movement in the early 1970s, Spain's emergence from Francoism, and later the impact of HIV and **AIDS** have led, not unexpectedly, to the formation of a distinctively resistant tradition of gay writing, especially in those from Catalan-speaking territories. Juan **Goytisolo**'s literary career is as exemplary in its refusal to conform to type as is his polyfaceted life. Some of the anti-establishment directness and radical sexual politics of Valencian Lluis Fernández's novel of 1978, *L'anarquista nu* (The Naked Anarchist), is to be traced in his parodic melodrama of 1993, *Espejo de amor y lujo* (A Mirror of Love and Luxury), and Catalonia has until the mid-1990s been the principal site for the production of alternative lesbian and gay discourses through small-circulation magazines, with the Madrid lesbian and gay collective's magazine *¿Entiendes?* (Are you in the Know?) now beginning to take centre-stage.

See also: gay culture

Further reading

Fernández, J.A. (1995) 'Death and the Angel in Lluis Fernández's *L'anarchista nu*', *Neophilologus* 79: 263–71.

Perriam, C.G. (1995) *Desire and Dissent: An Introduction to Luis Antonio de Villena*, Oxford: Berg (a well-received monograph by a leading researcher in this field).

Smith, P.J. (1992) *Laws of Desire: Questions of Homosexuality in Spanish Writing and Film, 1960–90*, Oxford: Oxford University Press (an important study by a distinguished scholar).

CHRIS PERRIAM

Generalitat

Originally formed in 1359 for the purpose of collecting war tax (itself called the *generalitat*), this entity became the major institution of government in Catalonia in the fifteenth century. Its power was reduced by Ferdinand the Catholic, and it was suppressed by Philip V following Barcelona's surrender during the War of Succession. The Generalitat was re-established in the 1930s during the Second Spanish Republic, and it took over most central government services and the running of the war effort during the early part of the Spanish Civil War. It was abolished by General Franco following the Nationalist victory.

In 1977 a provisional Generalitat was restored, with Josep Tarradellas as its President. One of its tasks was to draw up a new Autonomy Statute, as laid out in the **constitution of 1978**. It produced the Statute of Sau, which in 1979 was approved by the Catalan people in a referendum and was ratified by the Madrid parliament. The Generalitat consists of the Catalan parliament, the President of the Generalitat and the Executive Council. It has 135 deputies, who are chosen in elections held every four years.

The Generalitat possesses legislative and certain tax-raising powers, and is responsible for, among other things, education, language policy, culture and the autonomous police force. In European terms, the **autonomous communities** in Spain have fairly wide powers and responsibilities, and the Generalitat is a large organization, employing many people. Since 1980, the main party in the Catalan parliament has been **CiU** (Convergència i Unió – Convergence and Unity), and the President of the Generalitat has been the charismatic leader of CiU, Jordi **Pujol**.

Further reading

Cruanyes, J. and Ortiz, R. (1986) *Història de Catalunya*, Barcelona: Jonc, pp. 75–6, 211–23, 227–31, 247–50 (deals with the foundation and subsequent development of the Generalitat within the general history of Catalonia).

DAVID GEORGE

Gil de Biedma, Jaime

b. 1929, Barcelona; d. 1990, Barcelona

Writer

Gil de Biedma is one of the best-known members of the 'Generation of the 1950s', also referred to as the 'children of the Civil War'. Born into a wealthy Catalan family, he was a precocious child who witnessed the onset of the war, but, unlike others of his generation, he was whisked off to the family estate in Segovia where he would not suffer its ravages. As a young man he studied law in Barcelona, but became far more interested in literature, especially after a stay at Oxford in 1953. There he discovered the poets T.S. Eliot and W.H. Auden who would greatly influence his literary style.

In the same year, Gil de Biedma published his first book of poetry, *Según sentencia del tiempo* (According to Time's Verdict). In 1955 the poet began his life-long career as an executive in the General Company of Filipino Tobacco and also published a translation of Eliot's *The Use of Poetry and the Use of Criticism*; but a bout of tuberculosis was to take him to the family's country estate in 1956, where he kept a diary that was published in 1974. Entitled *Diario del artista seriamente enfermo* (Diary of a Seriously Ill Artist), it describes the artist's journey towards the mastery of his poetic style. Most of the poetry written during his convalescence can be found in the first section of his book *Compañeros de viaje* (Fellow Travellers), published in 1959. In the book he emphasizes his commitment to protest poetry. The political and literary activities he shared with his 'fellow travellers' are retold in his 1966 *Moralidades* (Moralities), where he also reveals himself to be an erotic poet. Two years later, in *Poemas póstumos* (Posthumous Poems), the poet reflects the disillusionment he grappled with because of the loss of youth and love. Most of his poetry was published in 1969 under the title *Colección particular* (Private Collection), but it was banned by the state **censorship**. A new edition entitled *Las personas del verbo* (The Personae of the Word) did not appear on bookshelves until the death of Franco in 1975.

In spite of Gil de Biedma's small body of work, by the time he died of **AIDS** in 1990, he had become something of a cult figure among young Spanish poets. His interest in literary criticism and English literature, in both erotic and social themes, his ironic, self-deprecating, guilty tone, in addition to his intellectual stature and sophisticated life style, set him apart from his contemporaries and distinguished him as a wordly poet whom the younger generations wished to emulate.

See also: gay culture; gay writing; poetry

Further reading

Mangini González, S. (1980) *Gil de Biedma*, Madrid: Júcar (the first anthology and critical study of Gil de Biedma's poetry).

Rovira, P. (1986) *La poesía de Jaime Gil de Biedma*, Barcelona: Mall (an essential study for understanding the poet's work).

SHIRLEY MANGINI

Giménez Arnau, José Antonio

b. 1912, Laredo (Santander)

Writer

Novelist, playwright and career diplomat, Giménez Arnau usually treats psychological or moral crises, or deals with global political issues such as 'Cold War' allegiances, exile, intrigue or atomic holocaust (this aristocratic conservative served the Franco regime in several major international diplomatic posts). Major novels include *La colmena* (The Beehive) (1945), *La hija de Jano* (Janus' Daughter) (1947), *El puente* (The Bridge) (1941), *De pantalón largo* (In Long Pants) (1952), *Luna llena* (Full Moon) (1953), *El canto del gallo* (Cock's Crow) (1954), *La tierra prometida* (Promised Land) (1958), *Este-Oeste*

(East-West) (1961), *La mecedora* (Rocking-chair) (1964) and *El distinguido delegado* (The Distinguished Delegate) (1970).

JANET PÉREZ

Giménez Caballero, Ernesto

b. 1899, Madrid; d. 1988, Madrid

Writer and politician

An avant-garde writer in the 1920s, founding *La Gaceta Literaria* (The Literary Gazette) in 1927, Giménez Caballero soon turned towards fascist politics, and was one of the founders of the **Falange** in 1933. He fought on the side of the pro-Franco insurgents in the Civil War, and was instrumental in helping Franco and Serrano Suñer to force a merger between the Falange and the Carlists, creating an umbrella organization which evolved into the **National Movement**. One of most determined propagandists of the Nationalist camp, he helped to build up the idea of the continuity between Franco and the military leaders of Spain's crusading past.

EAMONN RODGERS

Gimferrer, Pere

b. 1945, Barcelona

Poet, essayist, critic and novelist

Gimferrer's first collections of poems were written in Spanish. In them he shows a remarkable freedom from contemporary influences; instead, he adopts a much more cosmopolitan range of models, from Rimbaud and Darío to Eliot, Wallace Stevens, St-John Perse and Octavio Paz. The results of this can be seen at their best in *Arde el mar* (The Sea is Burning), published in 1966, where the use of certain cinematic techniques – montage, abrupt transitions – is combined with a kind of metapoetry in which the poem is made to reflect on its own composition.

From 1970 onwards, all Gimferrer's poetry is written in Catalan, a transition which he describes as the need to write in a language in which the 'I' of the poems could coincide with himself. In his first three collections in Catalan, *Els miralls* (The Mirrors), *Hora foscant* (The Darkening Hour) and *Foc cec* (Blind Fire), the preoccupations of the earlier poems – notably, the search for identity – are continued, along with an exploration of those elements in the Catalan tradition – popular poetry, the Baroque – which are still valid for a contemporary poet. In *Tres poemes* (Three Poems), first published in 1974, Gimferrer extends the erotic dimension already apparent in some of his earlier works: sexual love, not seen as an end in itself, but as a means of access to a higher reality. These themes and others come together in *L'espai desert* (Deserted Space) (1977), Gimferrer's most ambitious poem to date. Here, for the first time, he investigates the possibilities of poetry within the context of a specific time and place. Much of this investigation depends on language itself; Gimferrer sees the poem as an activity, rather than as a means of expression: the complex transformations of the poem are brought about by the pressures of the actual language in such a way that the identity of the poet is destroyed and reformed through glimpses of a truer reality.

In *Aparicions* (Apparitions) (1981), the long sequence which followed *L'espai desert*, the question of individual identity is approached from a more inward direction, from the connection between the act of writing and the possibility of living an authentic life. Thus the poem moves between a state of pre-consciousness associated with dream to a 'centre of consciousness' in which individual identity is merged in a reciprocal movement between particular lives and the life of the earth.

Since *Aparicions*, Gimferrer has published two further collections, *El vendaval* (The Whirlwind) (1988) and *La llum* (The Light) (1991). In contrast to the free verse of much of the earlier poetry, many of these poems are strict sonnets, in which Gimferrer's virtuosity reaches new heights. He himself has described these poems as 'Symbolism taken to its final limits': if they constantly lament the gap which separates words from the objects they attempt to designate, their formal perfection serves to undermine what, at first sight, might seem a depressing conclusion.

Gimferrer is also the author of an outstanding novel, *Fortuny* (1983), as well as two books of criticism and diaries and essays in both Spanish and Catalan.

Further reading

Gracia, J. (1994) 'Preface' to P. Gimferrer, *Arde el mar*, Madrid: Cátedra.

Terry, A. (1995) 'Introduction' to P. Gimferrer, *Obra catalana completa I: Poesia* (Complete Catalan Works: Poetry), Barcelona: Ediciones 62.

ARTHUR TERRY

golf

Since 1979, when Seve **Ballesteros** won the British Open, golf has attracted increasing numbers of players both from within Spain and from abroad. Within Spain it has become the third national sport in terms of the number of members of the Golfing Federation, partly as the result of a decrease in fees for most greens. At international level the world famous course at Valderrama in the province of Cadiz was host to the Ryder Cup in 1997, the first time it was played outside its traditional venues in the USA and the UK, and with over sixty courses in the area, more per square kilometre than anywhere else in Spain, and some of them able to be played by night, the Costa del Sol has justifiably been nicknamed the 'Costa del Golf'. A record number of some 6,000 played on the greens each day in the 1996 season, bringing in huge revenues to the area, and as demand continues to outstrip provision, the tourist authorities of Costa del Sol and Andalusia are increasing and promoting the facilities they offer, especially as it is reckoned that each golfer has three times as much purchasing power as the average tourist.

International competitions held in Spain include the Spanish Open, the Turespaña Masters and various regional Opens such as those of Catalonia, the Balearics, Andalusia and the Canaries, and Spanish professional players such as Ballesteros and **Olazábal** have featured among the top world players and earners.

See also: sport and leisure

EAMONN RODGERS

golpismo

Golpismo, a tendency to engage in *golpes* or *coups d'état*, was the word used in the Spain of the 1970s and 1980s to designate the attitudes of hard-right elements in the **armed forces** towards the emergent democratic state. The armed forces had long been suspicious of civilian politicians, and regarded themselves as the ultimate arbiters of political development, reserving the right to intervene when events were taking a course of which they disapproved. The reluctance of successive governments during the transition to democracy to grasp the nettle of military subversion, combined with the failure of the intelligence services to keep the civil authorities informed about the existence of conspiracies against the state, encouraged the 'ultras' in the armed forces to believe that they could plot with impunity.

In addition to these political attitudes, certain general features of military culture fostered the *golpista* mentality. The networks of personal loyalty among those who had served together created strong bonds which extended not only through and across military units, but also linked these units to right-wing civilian groups. Furthermore, the command structure of the armed forces meant that small numbers of politically committed officers could mobilize large numbers of personnel, independently of whether those under their command shared their superiors' views. It was reported at the time of the ***Tejerazo***, for example, that the rank-and-file members involved did not know that their objective was the parliament building until they actually arrived there.

The ultra-right press, too, had a role in creating a climate favourable to a military take-over. The newspaper *El Alcázar* (The Citadel), whose main readership was composed of serving members of the armed forces, and whose editorial line was uncompromisingly anti-democratic, carried on a virulent campaign against the reforming Minister for Defence, Manuel **Gutiérrez Mellado**. In the months before the *Tejerazo* (between December 1980 and February 1981), the paper published a series of articles under the signature of the Colectivo Almendros (the Almond-Tree Group), advocating military intervention. It has been suggested that the reference to almond-trees was a coded warning that a major action was planned for late February, when the almond-blossom appears.

The *golpistas*, however, were ultimately not to have it all their own way. The vast majority of armed forces and security personnel were loyal to the new democratic system. Besides, the same features of military culture which favoured conspiracy could work in the opposite direction. The command structure made it relatively easy to remove disloyal officers from key positions and replace them with others committed to the defence of the constitution, some of whom had a crucial role in aborting illegal actions. For example, in November 1978, General Antonio Pascual Galmés ensured the failure of the attempted coup which became known as *Operación Galaxia* by preventing a crack armoured division from joining other units involved in the conspiracy. At the time of the *Tejerazo* in 1981, the police, then under the command of a seconded army officer, José Sáenz de Santamaría, surrounded the Cortes building, and prevented other units from joining Tejero's force.

Two other key factors in the eventual decline of *golpismo* were the fact that the conspirators had offended against a cardinal principle of the military ethos by disobeying orders from their superiors, and also the fact that their repeated failures drove them to increasingly desperate measures which alienated all but their most hardline supporters. In acting against democratic institutions, they were also rebelling against their ultimate military superior, King Juan Carlos, in his capacity as Commander-in-Chief of all the armed forces, a point underlined by the King himself when he appeared on television on the night of the *Tejerazo*. While the plan in February 1981 had been to install a 'government of national salvation', a further plot discovered in June of that year would have entailed much more violent measures, including the bombing of the Camp Nou stadium in Barcelona during a Catalan nationalist rally, the deposition of the King and the elimination of democrats, whose names were already on prepared death-lists. Another plan to seize control prior to the 1982 elections would have involved the execution of senior staff officers who refused to join the rising.

The process of bringing the armed forces finally under civilian control was consolidated by the reforms carried out by the Minister of Defence, Narcis **Serra**, and by the decision to press ahead with **NATO** membership. Gradual replacement of hardline personnel, as well as increasing professionalism and involvement in international peacekeeping, finally brought about the depoliticization which successive governments had failed to achieve since the early nineteenth century.

See also: *poderes fácticos*; politics

Further reading

Hooper, J. (1995) *The New Spaniards*, Harmondsworth: Penguin (chapter 8 is an excellent, clear account of the political role of the armed forces, and their development since 1975).

Preston, P. (1986) *The Triumph of Democracy in Spain*, London and New York: Methuen (a highly readable and well-documented account of the events of the transition; for the military conspiracies, see especially chapters 5–8).

Ross, C.J. (1997) *Contemporary Spain: A Handbook*, London and New York: Arnold (chapter 4 provides a useful summary).

EAMONN RODGERS

Gómez Ojea, Carmen

b. 1945, Gijón

Writer

Poet, innovative novelist and short story writer, Gómez Ojea accumulated an extensive unpublished œuvre before winning the 1981 **Nadal Prize** with *Cantiga de agüero* (Canticle of Omens). Like feminist writers seeking women's past unrecorded by history, she deals with witchcraft, superstition, 'wise women', myth, magic and folklore. This blend appears variously in her published works, including the story collection *Otras mujeres y Fabia* (Other Women and Fabia) (1982) and *Los perros de Hécate* (Hecate's Hounds) (1985). More realistic depiction of her generation's repressive upbringing combines fantasy and authentic student rebellions in *La novela que Marien no terminó* (Marien's Unfinished Novel).

Further reading

Boschetto, S.M. (1992). 'Double-Voiced Tales in Carmen Gómez Ojea's *La novela que Marien no terminó*', *Hispania* 75, 3: 500–7 (studies double narration in storytelling by characters who both act and narrate).

Castillo, D. (1990) 'Frame Tale: Carmen Gómez Ojea's *Otras mujeres y Fabia*', *In the Feminine Mode: Essays on Hispanic Women Writers*, eds N. Valis and C. Maier, London: Associated University Presses (emphasis on role of patriarchy and condition of women).

Ordóñez, E. (1988). '*Los perros de Hécate* as a Paradigm of Narrative Defiance', *Anales de la Narrativa Española Contemporánea* 13, 1–2: 71–81 (emphasizes the character of Tarsiana plus reader–text relationships).

JANET PÉREZ

González, Felipe

b. 1942, Seville

Politician

Prime Minister from 1982 until 1996, Felipe González is one of the most emblematic political figures of Spain's new democracy. If Adolfo **Suárez** is regarded as the politician who contributed most to the Spanish transition to democracy, González is arguably the politician who has contributed most to the consolidation of democracy.

Trained as a labour lawyer in Andalusia, he was one of the so-called 'young turks' of the interior who in 1972 finally wrested control of the Socialist Party (**PSOE**) from the exiled leadership, based in Toulouse since 1947. Henceforth, González, with the support and help of his closest friend Alfonso **Guerra**, built the Socialist Party into a formidable electoral machine. It was a political marriage made in heaven: whilst González became a high-profile charismatic leader, Guerra worked diligently behind the scenes to establish a unified and disciplined party which would ensure the PSOE's electoral dominance throughout the 1980s.

Following a landslide victory in 1982, González's first term in office represented a large leap forward in the process of democratic consolidation. Although in many respects the Socialists' policies were simply building upon the groundwork laid by the previous **UCD** administrations under Adolfo Suárez, their overwhelming popular and parliamentary majority gave them a mandate and authority to tackle longstanding problems, which the previous minority UCD governments had lacked. Thus, the **armed forces**, the regional question, political violence and the **economy** were all policy areas tackled with remarkable success and acumen by the Socialist administration.

In 1986 González easily won a second term in office on the back of an economic boom for which his first administration had laid the foundations. Domestic policy successes were matched by recognition on the international stage as Spain became reintegrated into the international community by first joining the **European Union** in 1986, and subsequently **NATO** in that same year. Spain's longstanding political and economic isolation was thus brought to a close.

However, despite these evident successes both domestically and internationally, 1986 marked the turning point in the PSOE's fortunes. González was increasingly accused of governing in a high-handed manner which fostered an atmosphere of **corruption** and abuse of power. In particular, the Socialists' policy volte-face on NATO and their orchestration of a referendum campaign in 1986 in which they unashamedly abused their position in power and the resources at their disposal to secure Spain's entry into NATO, marked the starting point of the Socialists' precipitous descent from the moral high ground in Spanish politics which they had previously occupied unchallenged.

González himself appeared to become increasingly bored by domestic politics during his second administration. He was frequently absent from parliamentary sessions despite his undisputed oratorical skills and ability to dominate debate. Perhaps foreseeing a future career on the European stage, he preferred instead to adopt the role of international statesman, a role he played with considerable aplomb. Consequently, González declared that the 1989 election would be the last he would fight at the helm of the Socialist Party. By this stage, however, the leader and the party had become so intertwined that it was difficult to separate the one from the other. González had become the PSOE's electoral trump card to the extent that, for much of the electorate, a vote for the Socialists was as much a vote for Felipe as it was for the party. González's decision to stand down unleashed such a bitter struggle within the party that he was eventually forced to retract his decision.

González's third administration continued the downward trend in the PSOE's fortunes with the loss of its absolute majority by one seat. Alfonso Guerra's resignation as Deputy Prime Minister in early 1991, following a corruption scandal involving his brother Juan **Guerra**, was evidence of a growing personal and ideological rift between himself as deputy leader of the Socialist party machine which remained committed, in theory at least, to socialism, and González as leader of a Socialist government which had drifted to the right.

Thus, the early collaboration between González and Guerra which was key to the organizational unity and discipline of the PSOE throughout the 1980s, was replaced by an increasingly bitter division, both personal and ideological, between the two politicians. This division was crystallized after the 1993 general election when, following an election campaign which González himself personally masterminded, the Socialists won a surprise fourth term in office. This time, however, they were forced into coalition with the Catalan and Basque **regional parties** after falling short of an absolute majority by sixteen seats. The more orthodox left-wing '*guerrista*' faction within the party headed by Guerra was duly purged from the 1993 government and the liberal market-oriented faction within the Socialist Party, the so-called '*renovadores*' ('renewers') led by Carlos **Solchaga**, minister of the economy from 1985 to 1993, and backed by González, gained ascendancy.

More seriously, the Socialists' fourth administration became mired in corruption scandals which even cast doubt on González's personal integrity. The most serious accusation against the government was of involvement in a dirty war against **ETA** terrorists during the 1980s, masterminded by a shadowy organization called **GAL** which allegedly received government funds. Although González escaped personal charges, the taint of corruption undoubtedly became an obstacle to his future career hopes, despite being widely tipped to succeed Jacques Delors as President of the European Commission in 1995. In addition, accusations of corruption undoubtedly played a part in the Socialists' defeat in the 1996 elections which brought to a close their period of political dominance.

The PSOE's share of the vote remained substantial enough, however, to allow them to claim the election as a 'sweet defeat'. Soon after this election, González stood down as party leader. The legacy he has left his successor is a mixed one indeed. However, the accusations of corruption and abuse of power which characterized the Socialists' last term in office should not detract from González's stature as a politician and a statesman or his undisputed contribution to the consolidation of democracy in Spain.

Further reading

Fuente, I. (1991) *El Caballo Cansado: el largo adiós de Felipe González*, Madrid: Temas de Hoy (a journalistic account of the political career of Felipe González).

Tusell, J. and Sinova, J. (1992) *La decada socialista: el ocaso de Felipe González*, Madrid: Espasa Calpe (a well-documented account of the role played by Felipe González during the Socialists' first decade in power).

GEORGINA BLAKELEY

González Cataráin, María Dolores

b. 1954, Ordizia (Guipúzcoa); d. 1986, Ordizia

Political activist (*nom de guerre* 'Yoyes')

González Cataráin was a member of **ETA**'s 'military' wing, exiled in France (1973) and later Mexico (1979). In the late 1970s she joined the organization's leadership, one of very few women to do so. She subsequently regularized her situation under the ***reinserción*** measures, returning to Spain in 1985. On 10 September 1986, while walking her 3-year-old child, she was assassinated by an ETA commando because, having availed herself of the government's ***reinserción*** scheme, she returned to her home village in defiance of death-threats from her erstwhile comrades. Her killing was condemned by all sectors of Basque opinion other than supporters of **Herri Batasuna**, and marked a turning-point in attitudes towards ETA among more moderate nationalists.

CHRIS ROSS

González Lucas, Luis Miguel

b. 1926 , Madrid; d. 1996, Sotogrande

Matador ('Dominguín')

The son and brother of **matadors**, Dominguín was a successful child bullfighter (*becerrista*) after 1937. Having renounced an ***alternativa*** taken in Colombia in 1941, he took a second in Spain in 1944. Present in the ring when 'Manolete' (Manuel **Rodríguez Sánchez**) was killed, Dominguín briefly inherited his role as Spain's leading matador, performing in one hundred *corridas* in 1948. Accomplished and versatile, Dominguín remained active into the 1960s and reappeared successfully between 1971 and 1973. A friend of Picasso and Alberti, Dominguín was the subject of Hemingway's *The Dangerous Summer.* Formerly married to the actress Lucia Bosé, he is the father of the singer Miguel Bosé.

See also: bullfighting

IAN CAMPBELL ROSS

Goytisolo, Juan

b. 1931, Barcelona

Writer

In the first volume of his autobiography, *Forbidden Territory* (*Coto vedado*, 1985), Goytisolo refers to his long experience of exile, emphasizing the sense of 'unrootedness' from all social, racial or ideological ties which he feels in every cultural environment, especially that of western Europe. Goytisolo's conviction of always being an outsider stems in part from his rejection of his family background, partly from his detestation of the Franco regime, and partly from his acceptance, when he was in his early thirties, of his homosexuality. The theme of family tradition is an important one in *Marks of Identity* (*Señas de identidad*, 1966), and the attack on Franco's Spain emerges most clearly in *Count Julian* (*Reivindicación del conde don Julián*, 1970). In the long run, however, his alienation proved positive, for it gave him a sense of total liberation from national, cultural and moral ties, and facilitated the evolution of a literary style of great originality and satirical power. This detachment from his roots is compounded by the fact that he has not lived permanently in Spain since 1956, when he chose voluntary exile in Paris. Since 1964, he has usually spent half the year in Paris and half in Morocco.

Goytisolo came from a family of Basque extraction resident in Catalonia for four generations, and grew up with Castilian, rather than **Catalan**, as his mother tongue. His first forays into fiction-writing date from the early to mid-1950s, with *The Young Assassins* (*Juegos de manos*, 1954), *Children of Chaos* (*Duelo en el Paraíso*, 1955), his first major novel, and *Fiestas*. Goytisolo submitted *Juegos de manos* for the **Nadal Prize** in 1954, but it was rejected by the jury on the grounds of its leftward-leaning sympathies. *Duelo en el Paraíso* touches on the sensitive subject of the Civil War, and although passed by the censors, the novel contains, in the figure of Doña Estanislaa, a powerful evocation of the selfishness and irresponsibility of the right-wing Francoist bourgeoisie, which, Goytisolo makes clear, is largely to blame for the conflict.

In later works, such as the novels *Señas de identidad* and *Reivindicación del conde don Julián*, and the collection of essays *Furgón de cola* (The Brake-van) (1967), the anti-Franco stance is much more explicit, but the novels are not mere works of polemic, for their political and psychological themes are closely associated. Although *Duelo en el Paraíso* is set in a small village near the French border in Upper Catalonia during the last days of the Civil War, there is very little explicit detail about location, chronology, comparative military strength, or even the issues being fought over. For the most part, the war is heard merely as a distant rumble, largely because Goytisolo is concerned with more fundamental issues.

Chief among these is the whole question of personal identity and the authenticity of the self. Abandoned by their elders, the boys in *Duelo en el Paraíso* revert to a semi-savage state and paint their faces, in a way comparable to the situation portrayed in William Golding's *Lord of the Flies*. The adoption of masks is, in fact, a common practice among Goytisolo's characters, and indicates a deep-rooted desire to protect the kernel of one's genuine being from scrutiny or possession by others.

Goytisolo's preoccupation with questions of personal identity leads him logically towards the uncompromising pursuit of personal freedom: the family tie, and the related ideas of tradition and authority, are all resolutely rejected. Furthermore, the deadening influence of authoritarianism is seen as exercised simultaneously, and to their mutual benefit, by the family and the militaristic regime. The rejection of Nationalist culture thus comes to be centred on the figure of the dictator himself, who is portrayed in *Coto vedado* in quasi-Freudian terms as the castrating Father.

This pursuit of personal authenticity and freedom is reflected at the level of language. Goytisolo's belated discovery, in 1957, after taking up residence in Paris, of the Spanish classics neglected during his formal education resolved his linguistic and cultural hesitations (between Catalan and Castilian) in favour of Castilian. What he later described in *Coto vedado* as his fierce struggle with the Castilian language gave him access to a satirical weapon of apparently inexhaustible inventiveness with which he could pursue, in ever more original ways, his attack on the values of the regime, and ultimately, in *John the Landless* (*Juan sin tierra*, 1975), *Makbara* and *Landscapes after the Battle* (*Paisajes después de la batalla*), on the whole of western bourgeois society. Furthermore, his cosmopolitan situation, and the widening of cultural and linguistic horizons which this entailed, not only gave him a specially acute awareness of what was unique about the Spanish linguistic and literary heritage, but also gave him a redoubled sense of freedom from facile categorizations.

Another event which proved to be liberating and formative for Goytisolo's career as a writer was his discovery, late in 1957 or early in 1958, of the austere, 'African' beauty of the arid southeastern part of the peninsula, especially Almería, which was to prove a bridge to North Africa, and in turn to the whole of the Arabic and Islamic world. In Morocco, as in Almería, Goytisolo found the same elemental qualities of natural dignity, earthiness and spontaneous friendship which, in his somewhat romantic view, underlie the essential Spanish character, increasingly threatened by commercialization and international tourism.

The beginnings of Goytisolo's turbulent love-affair with the Spanish language were, then, followed within less than two years by a spontaneous upsurge of affection for a majestic and impoverished landscape, which modified his alienation from Spain, and offered a glimpse of a possible alternative sense of cultural identity. The combined effects of these experiences, however, would not be fully assimilated until Goytisolo had come to terms with another major area of inner conflict, his sexual ambiguity. His long-standing liaison with Monique Lange, whom he eventually married in 1978, was both passionate and fulfilling, but he also had various affairs with Arab men, and by about 1964 the latent conflict could no longer be concealed. In the second volume of his autobiography, *Realms of Strife* (*En los reinos de Taifa*, 1986), he gives a moving account of how he staked his whole relationship with Monique on an open declaration, and of how they reconstructed their future together.

It was the resolution of this crisis which enabled Goytisolo to integrate in his writing all the diverse political and cultural elements summarized above. He himself described this integration as the entry of the Maghreb (the North African desert) into his life. Goytisolo's Maghreb is simultaneously a real place and an imagined society, natural, spontaneous and tolerant of everything that lies *extramuros* (outside the walls) of the sanitized middle-class culture of western Europe.

The effect on his writing was profound. From *Reivindicación del conde don Julián* onwards, the surface realism of earlier novels is largely abandoned in favour of a ludic exuberance of language, often richly comic, by contrast with the almost complete absence of humour in previous works. No subject is taboo, no cherished assumption is immune from his gleeful iconoclasm. *Reivindicación del conde don Julián* takes the form of a drug-induced fantasy in the mind of the narrator, in which he sees himself as the reincarnation of the arch-traitor Julian, execrated for centuries by nationalistic Spaniards as the person who allegedly invited the Moors into Spain in the eighth century. The novel is an imaginative recreation of a new Moorish invasion which, in a glorious orgy of destruction, razes every hallowed institution, even the Castilian language itself. The fragmentary and hermetic nature of these later works, in which fictional and non-fictional texts, invented scenes and historical details are intermingled, makes them impossible to classify, still less to summarize, but two themes predominate.

One is the celebration of the body in all its aspects, especially those conventionally regarded as taboo: not only the sexual vitality of the slaves evoked at the beginning of *Juan sin tierra* but also defecation, natural odours, dirt and disease. By defiantly making explicit what is usually silenced, Goytisolo is metaphorically embracing the world of the pariahs and outcasts, whose capacity to disturb the ordered, asceptic lives of 'respectable' people gives them a freedom and dignity which those imprisoned within bourgeois convention conspicuously lack. A recognition of common biological humanity, even in its ugliest and most abject form, has the potential (albeit usually unrealized) to transcend barriers of all kinds between people.

The second recurrent theme is that of writing itself, closely linked to the theme of the body, since writing is seen as an extension of sexual activity. Goytisolo's acceptance of his homosexuality, and his rejection of all inherited assumptions and values, implied his acceptance of his status *extramuros*, and the complete isolation which this entailed. Since in this situation personal identity cannot be defined in terms of nationality, class, creed or profession, sex and writing become the only two reference points in the writer's life, and are, indeed, his identity, as Goytisolo repeatedly says. Writing *Reivindicación del conde don Julián* was almost an erotic physical struggle to wrest new possibilities and pleasures from language. The identification of writing and sex means that just as his sexuality is by definition of the kind that produces no offspring, his writing, at least at the level of professed intention, is self-sufficient and has no purpose beyond itself. Nevertheless, though it would be inappropriate to try to pin down any specific political, or indeed other message, it is precisely the playful and irreverent quality of his writing that makes the anti-Francoist satire of *Reivindicación del conde don Julián* and the attack on western European consumerism in *Juan sin tierra, Makbara* and *Paisajes después de la batalla* so effective.

Goytisolo could almost be said to court incomprehension and marginalization, but can nevertheless claim rich literary rewards. In distancing himself from officially approved literary coteries, and cultivating a view of writing as a self-sufficient, onanistic and largely unlawful activity, he opens for himself a gateway into limitless creative and expressive freedom. In this way he avoids the narrow ideological consistency which is often the price paid by the practitioners of more conventional approaches to fictional narrative.

See also: gay culture; gay writing; language and national identity; novel

Major works

Goytisolo, J. (1954) *Juegos de manos*, Barcelona: Ediciones Destino; trans. J. Rust, *The Young Assassins*, London: McGibbon & Kee, 1960 (novel).

—— (1955) *Duelo en el Paraíso*, Barcelona: Ediciones Destino; trans. C. Brooke-Rose, *Children of Chaos*, London: McGibbon & Kee, 1958 (novel).

—— (1966) *Señas de identidad*, Mexico: Joaquín Mortiz; trans. G. Rabassa, *Marks of Identity*, London: The Serpent's Tail, 1988 (novel).

—— (1967) *Furgón de cola*, Paris: Ruedo Ibérico (collection of essays on various aspects of Spanish culture, politics and literature).

—— (1970) *Reivindicación del conde don Julián*, Mexico: Joaquín Mortiz; trans. H. Lane *Count Julian*, New York: Viking Press, 1975; London: Serpent's Tail, 1989 (novel).

—— (1975) *Juan sin Tierra*, Barcelona: Seix Barral; trans. H. Lane, *John the Landless*, New York: Viking Press, 1975 (novel).

—— (1985) *Coto vedado*, Barcelona: Seix Barral; trans P. Bush, *Forbidden Territory*, San Francisco: North Point Press, 1989 (autobiography).

—— (1986) *En los reinos de Taifa*, Barcelona: Seix Barral; trans. P. Bush, *Realms of Strife*, San Francisco: North Point Press, 1990 (autobiography).

Further reading

Jordan, B. (1990) *Writing and Politics in Franco's Spain*, London and New York: Routledge (a very readable analysis of the social novel in the 1950s and 1960s).

Lee Six, A. (1990) *Juan Goytisolo, The Case for Chaos*, New Haven, CT and London: Yale University Press (an excellent study of Goytisolo's critique of conventional literary and other categories in the later novels; contains a bibliography of all his writings up to 1988).

Pérez, G.J. (1979) *Formalist Elements in the Novels of Juan Goytisolo*, Madrid: José Porrúa (a useful study of structural features in Goytisolo's novels).

Ugarte, M. (1982) *Trilogy of Treason: An Intertextual Study of Juan Goytisolo*, London: University of Missouri Press (a perceptive and highly regarded monograph).

EAMONN RODGERS

Goytisolo, Luis

b. 1935, Barcelona

Writer

Since his early beginnings as a writer, Goytisolo has wrestled with and placed special emphasis on narrative structure as a way to universalize the content of his literary works. Even in his early novels, oriented towards realism, such as *Las afueras* (The Outskirts) (1958) and *Las mismas palabras* (The Same Words) (1962), narrative fragmentation and juxtaposition play an important role, which Goytisolo carried to its limits in his tetralogy *Antagonía* (Antagony), *Fábulas* (Fables) (1981), *Investigaciones y conjeturas de Claudio Mendoza* (Claudio Mendoza's Inquiries and Conjectures) (1986) and later works. However, starting with *Antagonía*, his most ambitious narrative project, Goytisolo assumes a new stance towards literature. Now he gradually replaces his engagement with the socio-political realities of Spain with a preoccupation with the inner self and a search for personal authenticity. Concurrently, he reflects on the mechanics of the writing and reading process, flaunting and laying bare the nature and conventions of narrative, and becomes one of the metafictional writers par excellence in Spain.

Although Goytisolo was born in Barcelona and has resided there ever since, he has adopted Spanish, rather than Catalan, as his literary language. His first steps into fiction-writing date from the late 1950s and early 1960s, with *Las afueras*, winner of the Biblioteca Breve Prize in 1958, and *Las mismas palabras*. The action in *Las afueras*, as in most of his narrative, takes place in Barcelona or its whereabouts, and it depicts the disenchantment of those who won the Civil War, the marginalization of the poor, and social class confrontations.

In *Recuento* (Recount) (1973), the first of *Antagonía*'s novels, Goytisolo pursues and expands his social concerns and provides a parodic representation of the Catalan bourgeoisie, the overall Catalan culture, the Francoist establishment – the church, the family, the army and so on – and, even, of Marxist ideology. The turning point in the novel, and in Goytisolo's literary career, arises when the narrator-protagonist is imprisoned because of his clandestine activities within the Communist Party (PCE) against the Francoist government. This experience, which parallels Goytisolo's own in 1960, marks the end of the protagonist's struggle for social justice and the beginning of his career as a writer. From this point on, Goytisolo's narrative becomes extremely self-conscious, exposing the conventions involved in the writing and reading processes.

In each of the remaining novels that compose *Antagonía*, Goytisolo will place special emphasis on a specific metafictional activity. In *Los verdes de mayo hasta el mar* (The Greens of May Down to the Sea) (1976) Goytisolo unveils the complexities involved in the writing process. In *La cólera de Aquiles* (The Wrath of Achilles) (1979) the text becomes the product of the different manipulative readings furnished by the narrator-protagonist; and *Teoría del conocimiento* (Theory of Knowledge) (1981) focuses on the appropriation and agency of the word.

Goytisolo carries on his self-reflective ruminations in *Estela del fuego que se aleja* (The Fire Wake that Recedes) (1984), winner of the Critics Prize in 1984, where he uses the metaphor of the book to equate it to a life written by somebody else. In *La paradoja del ave migratoria* (The Paradox of the Migratory Bird) (1987), Goytisolo portrays the intermingling of various texts created imaginatively by the protagonist in the instant that precedes his death. And in *Estatua con palomas* (Statue with Pigeons) (1992), winner of the National Narrative Prize in 1993, Goytisolo creates a pseudo-autobiography which, in fact, is everybody's autobiography.

The pervasive use of metaphor in Goytisolo's fiction serves to encapsulate the meaning of his narrative creation. Some metaphors, as the description of one of Velázquez's paintings in each of the novels of *Antagonía*, reflect the narrative structure of the novels themselves. Others – the sea, the garden, the portrait of the Ideal City, the Old Wise Man or the bronze eagle – purport to be, among other things, archetypal representations of inner realities that include the unconscious, the anima, or repressed feelings. And with another cluster of metaphors – the eye, the number three, concentric circularity or the book – Goytisolo enlarges the narrative horizons of his narrative to pursue a cosmogonic and theogonic vision of the world.

One of Goytisolo's key narrative motifs is the voyage. Sometimes, as in *Recuento* or *Los verdes de mayo hasta el mar*, it takes the form of an initiatory descent into areas of the protagonist's unconscious in order to achieve individuation and regenerate himself as a writer or as a new human being. Sometimes, as in *Estela del fuego que se aleja* or *La paradoja del ave migratoria*, the journey functions as a metaphor for the course of life. In fact, travelling seems to be one of Goytisolo's favourite hobbies. In 1987 he took a trip to several Asiatic countries and to the USA, and as a result of this experience he published a series of articles for six weeks in *El País*. In 1989 and 1991 he visited several African countries and filmed a documentary series for Spanish television (RTVE) entitled 'Indico'.

Goytisolo has emerged as one of the most astute practitioners of metafiction, and his narrative has gained him the reputation of being hermetic and complex. Nevertheless, he articulates a view of literature that reconciles metafictional theory and practice with an existential search for self-authenticity.

Major works

Goytisolo, L. (1958) *Las afueras*, Barcelona: Seix Barral (novel).

—— (1962) *Las mismas palabras*, Barcelona: Seix Barral (novel).

—— (1973) *Recuento*, México: Seix Barral (novel).

—— (1976) *Los verdes de mayo hasta el mar*, Barcelona: Seix Barral (novel).

—— (1979) *La cólera de Aquiles*, Barcelona: Seix Barral (novel).

—— (1981) *Teoría del conocimiento*, Barcelona: Seix Barral (novel).

—— (1981) *Fábulas*, Barcelona: Bruguera (fables).

—— (1984) *Estela del fuego que se aleja*, Barcelona: Anagrama (novel).

—— (1986) *Investigaciones y conjeturas de Claudio Mendoza*, Barcelona: Anagrama (novel).

—— (1987) *La paradoja del ave migratoria*, Madrid: Alfaguara (novel).

—— (1987) *Luces del Pacífico* (collection of travel articles on different Asiatic countries and the USA published in *El País*).

—— (1992) *Estatua con palomas*, Barcelona: Ediciones Destino (novella).

Further reading

Spires, R.C. (1984) *Beyond the Metafictional Mode. Directions in the Modern Spanish Novel*, Lexington, KY: The University Press of Kentucky (a very perceptive analysis of twentieth century Spanish metafiction, including *Antagonía*).

Clotas, S. (1983) *El cosmos de 'Antagonía'*, Barcelona: Anagrama (an excellent collection of critical essays centred on *Antagonía*).

Sobejano-Morán, A. (1993) *La metaficción creadora en 'Antagonía' de Luis Goytisolo*, Lewiston, NY: Edwin Mellen Press (a useful study of *Antagonía's* metafictional techniques).

ANTONIO SOBEJANO-MORÁN

Goytisolo Gay, José Agustín

b. 1928, Barcelona

Writer and lawyer

The elder brother of Juan and Luis **Goytisolo**, José Agustín Goytisolo is known primarily, though not exclusively, as a poet. After studying Law, he became editor in a publishing house, and was active as an essayist and translator. Professorial appointments followed in Mexico, Havana and at Notre Dame, Indiana. He is the author of critical studies such as *Poetas catalanes contemporáneos* (Contemporary Catalan Poets) (1968) and *Nueva poesía cubana* (New Cuban Poetry) (1970).

It is, however, on his considerable poetic production that his significance mainly rests. Between 1955 and 1995, he published fifteen collections of poetry. *El retorno* (The Return) (1955), *Salmos al viento* (Psalms to the Wind) (1957) and *Claridad* (Brightness) (1961) established his reputation. *Años decisivos* (Years of Decision) (1963) was followed by *Algo sucede* (Something is Happening) (1967). After a period of relative silence, the 1970s were productive years, with *Bajo tolerancia* (On Suffrance) (1973), *Taller de arquitectura* (Architect's Office) (1976), *Del tiempo del olvido* (From the Time of Forgetfulness) (1978), *Palabras para Julia* (Words for Julia) (1979) and *Los pasos del cazador* (The Hunter's Footsteps) (1980). He has remained writing into his middle and late sixties, with *Novísima oda a Barcelona* (New Ode to Barcelona) (1992) and *Como los trenes de la noche* (Like the Night Trains) (1995).

Goytisolo's work received early recognition with the award of the Adonais Prize (Madrid 1956), the Boscán Prize (Barcelona 1958) and the Ausias March Prize (Valencia 1960). Further honours followed, including the Gold Medal of the City of Florence (1970) and the Critics' Prize for Poetry (1993).

Goytisolo has continued his work in publishing, and edits the *Colección Marca Hispánica* published by Ediciones del Mall.

EAMONN RODGERS

Grand Tibidabo

This large holding company was acquired in 1991 by Javier **de la Rosa**, with subsidiaries in the leisure and insurance sectors, and went bankrupt in 1994, causing 9,000 small investors to lose their savings. Auditors found that losses were at least five times those declared by the management, and that various irregularities appeared to have been committed, such as the transfer of unsecured credits to de la Rosa, and between companies in the group.

See also: corruption

EAMONN RODGERS

GRAPO

The Grupos de Resistencia Antifascista Primero de Octubre (Anti-Fascist Resistance Groups of the First of October) were a supposedly left-wing terrorist organization which took its name from the date in 1975 when Franco, only a few weeks before his death, made a speech to a large rally of the **Falange**, which was held to express support for tough law-and-order policies. The timing of bombings and shootings claimed by GRAPO, however, gave rise to suspicion that the organization had been infiltrated by far-right groups, who were using it to further a deliberate policy of destabilization. GRAPO's activities intensified, for example, just before the passage of the Law of Political Reform in November 1976, and in the aftermath of the ***Tejerazo*** in 1981.

EAMONN RODGERS

Guerra, Alfonso

b. 1941, Seville

Politician

Together with his life-long friend, Felipe **González**, Alfonso Guerra played a key role during the transition process in rebuilding the Spanish Socialist Party (**PSOE**) which had been left seriously weakened by the Civil War and the subsequent Francoist dictatorship. He was one of the so-called 'young turks' within Spain who mounted a sustained assault against the exiled socialist leadership, based in Toulouse since 1947, who had failed to respond to the changes occurring within Spanish society. Control of the party was finally wrested from the exiled leadership when official recognition was granted by the Socialist International to the 'renovators' of the interior in 1972.

From that moment onwards, Guerra became the perfect partner to González. Whilst González adopted a much higher public profile befitting the charismatic leader he was to become, Guerra, a meticulous organizer and strategist, worked diligently behind the scenes to establish a dynamic party machine. He masterminded the organizational changes within the PSOE at the XXVIII Congress in 1979 which dramatically reduced the number of delegations represented (50 as opposed to 1,000) and introduced a form of block vote. These organizational changes consolidated power within the leadership and turned the PSOE into a highly centralized, disciplined organization, closely controlled by Guerra himself. The largest delegation which controls 25 percent of the total vote, the Andalusian, has been seen almost as Guerra's personal fiefdom. This unity and discipline paved the way for the PSOE's subsequent electoral successes throughout the 1980s.

Following the first Socialist victory in the 1982 general elections, Guerra was appointed Deputy Prime Minister, in addition to his position as Deputy General Secretary of the party. Shortly after the 1989 general elections, however, when the Socialists were returned to office only one seat short of an absolute majority, his brother, Juan **Guerra**, was accused of peddling influence and using government resources to amass a personal fortune. As a result Alfonso Guerra was forced to resign as Deputy Prime Minister in early 1991, though he remained deputy General Secretary of the party. His departure exacerbated a division which had been growing for some time between the socialist party machine which remained committed, in theory at least, to **socialism**, and a socialist government which had drifted to the right.

Guerra's departure was also evidence of a personal and ideological rift between himself and González. Guerra heads a more orthodox left-wing '*guerrista*' faction within the party which espouses a populist leftist rhetoric. This faction, purged from the 1993 government, has frequently clashed with the other main faction within the Socialist Party led by Carlos **Solchaga**, minister of the economy from 1985 to 1993, and backed by González: the so-called '*renovadores*', who advocate a liberal market-oriented version of social democracy. Thus, the early collaboration between González and Guerra which was the key to the organizational unity and discipline of the PSOE throughout the 1980s, has been replaced by an increasingly bitter division within the party between '*guerristas*' and '*renovadores*' led by Guerra and González respectively.

Further reading

Fernández Braso, M. and Guerra, A. (1983) *Conversaciones con Alfonso Guerra*, Barcelona: Planeta (an interesting account exploring Guerra's personal views on a wide range of topics).

Miralles, M. and Satue, F. (1991) *Alfonso Guerra, el conspirador*, Madrid: Temas de Hoy (a journalistic, lively account of Alfonso Guerra).

GEORGINA BLAKELEY

Guerra, Juan

b. 1943, Seville

Businessman

The brother of the former Deputy Prime Minister and deputy **PSOE** leader, Alfonso **Guerra**, Juan Guerra was accused in 1990 of influence peddling to further his business interests whilst occupying a local government office and working as an 'adviser' to his brother. The accusations brought about the resignation of Alfonso Guerra as Deputy Prime Minister in 1991.

GEORGINA BLAKELEY

Guggenheim Museum

The Guggenheim Museum of Bilbao houses part of the large art collection of the New York Guggenheim Foundation, together with purchases of its own. The permanent exhibition represents twentieth-century art from Kandinsky to the present day, with special attention paid to abstract expressionism and minimalist art; purchases include works by Anselm Kiefer and sculptures by Eduardo **Chillida**. The architecturally stunning building, largely clad in titanium, was designed by Frank O. Gehry, and financed by Basque public institutions as part of a plan to revitalize an otherwise largely industrial area. Opened in October 1997, the museum has nineteen galleries and a central glassed atrium giving panoramic views of river, city and mountains, as well as an auditorium and other facilities. It attracted 100,000 visitors in the first month, and surpassed the record for a single day's visitors previously held by the **Dalí Museum**, Figueras.

See also: architecture; art collections; art exhibitions; museums; visual arts

EAMONN RODGERS

Guillén, Jorge

b. 1893, Valladolid; d. 1984, Málaga

Poet

Castilian by birth, European in taste and education, this true cosmopolitan spent nearly forty years in voluntary exile in America before definitively returning to Spain to become, with the award of the **Cervantes Prize** in 1977, the acknowledged doyen of Spanish poetry in the post-Franco era. A founder member of the 'Generation of 1927' with friends and fellow-poets Pedro Salinas and Federico García Lorca, Guillén clearly exemplifies the gradual move in twentieth century Spanish poetics away from high modernism to poetry whose themes and expression are grounded in the shifting realities of daily life. Nowhere is this more evident than in the distance between the ordered vision of the natural world in *Cántico* (Canticle) (first published 1928) and the vignettes of human existence, bound by the specifics of time and space and recorded in the more discursive, often ironic, style of *Clamor* (Clamour) (1957). Not a prolific poet, Guillén devoted himself with rare dedication to his art. Ever conscious of his own debts to a rich and varied literary tradition, he tried, with signal success in *Homenaje* (Homage) (1967) and his literary criticism in *Language and Poetry*, to connect modern readers with significant prior works. Ultimately, his search for life's essences in language led Guillén to view the poetic process as a continual act of discovery and both *Y otros poemas* (And Other Poems) (1973) and *Final* (The End) (1987) are implicit invitations to his readers to continue that process, thereby eloquently foregrounding the exceptionally organic nature of all his work.

Guillén began writing *Cántico* in 1919. The volume grew steadily from the original seventy-five poems of 1928 through second, third and fourth editions published in 1936, 1945 and 1950, respectively, to a final, densely worked structure of 334 poems notable for their profound beauty of language and ethical idealism. In the first two editions, particularly, Guillén attempted to embody an essential vision of reality in which the poem would become an icon of perfection, reflecting the timeless order, geometrical archetypes and symmetrical harmonies of the natural world in an expression of wonder and joyous affirmation. For some this flawless precision seemed cold, cerebral and too close for comfort to the ideal of pure poetry constructed by the French poets so admired by Guillén, Stéphane Mallarmé and Paul Valéry. To be fair, however, if Guillén had deliberately excised the minutiae of anecdote and sentimentality from his poetry, his epiphanies of love and being-in-the-world must rank among the most sensuous amatory verse ever written.

In the difficult circumstances of the aftermath of war in Europe and exile after 1938, Guillén continued to pursue his dual vocation as 'poet-professor', notably at Wellesley College between 1940 and 1957. Nevertheless, rather than forging verbal incarnations, Guillén now dealt more and more with specific events and situations in the variety of verse forms and stylistic techniques that would become the hallmark of his later work.

Despite such obvious differences, Guillén never missed an opportunity to insist that his trilogy *Clamor* was a true complement to the testimony to life portrayed in *Cántico*. Thus, under the new rubric of his subtitle 'Historical Time', Guillén focused his attention in the trilogy upon the incidence of evil, disorder, fate and death in contemporary life as opposed to the orderly pattern of the well-made natural world. Collective social and political turmoil provided the point of reference in 1957 for poems in *Maremágnum* (Confusion) dealing with dictatorship, the Holocaust, the atomic bomb and the Cold War. Three years later, Guillén's meditations on the destructive passage of time centred on a personal elegy for his first wife, Germaine Cahen, in *... Que van a dar en el mar* (... That Lead into the Sea). By 1963, in *A la altura de las circunstancias* (In Keeping with One's Circumstances), he was stressing the ethical imperative of resisting defeatism in order to make a collective effort towards human plenitude. Despite Francoist **censorship** this principled response won Guillén acclaim within Spain from younger poets like **Gil de Biedma** and Jaime Siles, who acknowledged his moral ascendancy and consummate craftsmanship.

Poetry's fundamental role in this discovery of the wider patterns of harmony and affirmation in modern life was the dominant theme in *Homenaje*. Here the representative function of traditional liberal humanism allowed Guillén to focus upon the contemporary relevance of past literary works. He continued this rich play of perspective until his death, poignantly identifying his own poetic evolution in complex re-readings of his earlier texts in *Y otros poemas* in 1973 and in both the 1983 and the posthumous versions of *Final*.

First used in 1968, *Aire nuestro* (Our Air) is now the title for all Guillén's poetry, spanning nearly seventy years of rigorous creative endeavour. If it is convenient to divide his poetry into stages, it is no less true to acknowledge the marvellous coherence of the world view of this poet deeply committed to the celebration of life made meaningful by love and art, in harmony with nature, yet fully cognizant of the vicissitudes of human existence.

See also: exile; poetry

Major works

Guillén, J. (1961) *Language and Poetry: Some Poets of Spain*, Cambridge, MA: Harvard University Press (literary criticism).

—— (1987) *Aire nuestro*, eds Claudio Guillén and Antonio Piedra, 5 vols, Valladolid: Centro de Creación y Estudios Jorge Guillén.

Further reading

Debicki, A.P. (1994) *Spanish Poetry of the Twentieth Century: Modernity and Beyond*, Lexington, KY: Kentucky University Press (a very readable analysis of modern Spanish poetry which situates Guillén well).

Díez de Revenga, F.J. (1993) *Jorge Guillén: el poeta y nuestro mundo*, Barcelona: Anthropos (studies all Guillén's poetry and contains a basic bibliography).

Havard, R. (1986) *Jorge Guillén: Cántico*, London: Grant & Cutler (an excellent introductory study of the four editions).

MacCurdy, G.G. (1982) *Jorge Guillén*, Boston, MA: Twayne (a useful overview with bibliography and English translations).

Mathews, E. (1985) *The Structured World of Jorge Guillén*, Liverpool: Francis Cairns (a competent comparison of *Cántico* and *Clamor*).

K.M. SIBBALD

Guillén, Rafael

b. 1933, Granada

Poet

Thematically Guillén's poetry falls into three categories: existentialist poetry, represented by collections such as *Antes de la esperanza* (Before Hope) (1956); love poetry, as in *Moheda* (1979); and social poetry, typified by *Vasto poema de resistencia* (Vast Poem of Resistance) (1981).

Guillén's poetry evolves from an early preoccupation with form towards moral commitment, and an engagement with the transcendental problem of time, death and nothingness. His love poem *Moheda* is the best example of a fusion of the ethical and the aesthetic. His poetry is clear, rich and precise, and he makes skilful use of classic metres and free verse. He received the National Poetry Prize in 1994.

Further reading

Muñiz-Romero, C. (1979) 'Rafael Guillén, misterio y límites' in 'Moheda', *Litoral* 85–7: 7–23 (contains an excellent in-depth introduction).

JOSÉ ORTEGA

guitar music

The two main varieties of Spanish guitar **music** are the classical guitar and the **flamenco** guitar. Nevertheless, the historical development of the guitar, the instrument most widely identified with Spain, brings together both eastern and western traditions, and its popular character has caused it to figure in virtually all periods of musical history. Despite its great antiquity, however, it is only during the last hundred years that the guitar has been established in its modern form and its technique has been developed.

The first music specifically composed in Spain for the guitar did not appear until *Pasacalles y Obras por Todos los Tonos Naturales y Occidentales* (Passacaglias and Pieces in all Natural and Western Keys) (1734) by Santiago de Muriza, a follower of Campion, Corbetta and De Visée. During his stay in Madrid, Boccherini used the guitar for his chamber music, thus stimulating the revival of the instrument during the eighteenth century. With Mauro Giuliani (1781–1829) and Fernando Sors (1778–1839), the author of a guitar tutor published in 1830, the instrument achieved full recognition, which was consolidated by Graciano Tarragó, María Luisa Anido and Francisco Tárrega (1852–1909).

It was Tárrega who initiated the development of modern classical guitar technique. His earlier transcriptions of works by Bach, Mozart and other composers formed the basis of the concert repertoire for guitar. Tárrega's work in developing guitar technique and writing arrangements of music composed for other instruments paved the way for two performers who are considered to be the architects of the instrument's twentieth-century renaissance Miguel Llobet and, especially, Andrés **Segovia**, who collected and expanded Tárrega's discoveries. Segovia, (1893–1987), the most remarkable guitar maestro of all times worldwide, is popularly acclaimed to be the best exponent of Spanish music. Segovia's art is gifted with a very personalized and pleasant sound, his technique is complete and rich in resources of all kinds. Always looking to expand his repertory, he investigated the music of the seventeenth- and eighteenth-centuries. Segovia gave the guitar further prominence as a concert instrument, and his artistry has been a source of inspiration for both players and composers.

Music is pervaded by folk tradition, and this is particularly true of guitar music. A Spanish composer who is especially in touch with the traditions of his own land is Joaquín **Rodrigo**, who, though primarily a virtuoso pianist rather than a guitar-player, writes for the instrument with great understanding and sympathy. The *Concierto de Aranjuez* (*Aranjuez Concerto*), the most famous of his compositions, is one of the first guitar concertos to be written in the twentieth century and one of the most popular for any instrument. Other composers drew heavily on popular and regional music for their inspiration, such as Joaquín Turina (1882–1949) and Manuel de Falla (1876–1946), who always wrote a guitar part into their large-scale instrumental works.

As well as accomplished guitarists such as Emili Pujol and José Tomás, one of the most outstanding guitar soloists of the twentieth century was Narciso Yepes (1927–97), who modified the basic form of the instrument by developing a ten-stringed version. The twentieth-century repertoire exhibits a wide variety of styles, from the romantic works inspired by Segovia to avant-garde compositions. Influences from **folk music**, flamenco and jazz have introduced unexpected tone-colourings, extending the instrument's expressive resources. The importance of modern guitar music has grown outside Spain, and leading performers such as Julian Bream and John Williams have made a significant contribution to the repertoire.

Flamenco guitar music, mainly based on improvisations, started as an accompaniment for *cante* (flamenco song), or as part of a *cuadro flamenco* (a group of flamenco singers, dancers and guitarists performing together). Flamenco dance, indeed, began in the same way, as it initially used movement to embellish the singer's performance. Even virtuosos like Paco de Lucía and Sabicas, who are famous for their solo work, would probably define flamenco in terms of *cante* rather than of guitar technique. Flamenco guitar has become increasingly popular and it has been responsible for the worldwide interest in flamenco music.

Paco de Lucía is one of the most innovative flamenco guitarists in Spain, who gained stardom by accompanying the *cante* of Camarón de la Isla. His album *Fuente y Caudal* (Fountain and Flow) revolutionized the world of flamenco guitar, by broadening the frontiers of traditional flamenco culture. Another guitarist who also won fame by accompanying Camarón is Tomatito. He is an outstanding technician as well as a sophisticated musician, and is deeply influenced by jazz. After Camarón's death, Tomatito developed his solo playing and accompanied various other *cantaores* (flamenco singers).

Flamenco guitar in the late 1990s achieved new effects through a fusion with other rhythms such as the blues, rock or jazz. The Amador brothers, Raimundo and Rafael, are good examples of this new era of flamenco music.

See also: music festivals; orchestras

Further reading

Ordovás, J. (1991) 'Pop Music', in A. Ramos Gascón (ed.) *Spain Today: in Search of Modernity*, Madrid: Cátedra (pp. 453–67 offer a panoramic view of the contemporary music scene in Spain).

White, J. (1995) 'Music and the Limits of Cultural Nationalism', in H. Graham and J. Labanyi (eds) *Spanish Cultural Studies: an Introduction*, Oxford: Oxford University Press (pp. 225–8 provide a lucid account of the evolution of the musical situation in Spain since the Civil War).

GEMMA BELMONTE TALERO

Gutiérrez Aragón, Manuel

b. 1942, Torrelavega (Santander)

Filmmaker

After graduating from the Escuela Oficial de Cinematografía (Official Film School) in 1970 Gutiérrez Aragón collaborated on the scripts of films such as **Borau**'s *Furtivos* (Poachers) (1975), **Camino**'s *Las largas vacaciones de 1936* (The Long Holidays of '36) (1975) and **García Sánchez**'s *Las truchas* (The Trout) (1978) as well as launching a successful career as director with *Habla, mudita* (Speak, Mute Girl) in 1973 which won him a Critics' Prize at Berlin.

His next film, *Camada negra* (Black Brood) (1977) produced and co-scripted by Borau, for which he was awarded the Director's Prize at Berlin in 1979, proved to be highly controversial. Made less than two years after Franco's death it was a study of a fascist terrorist family, ending with the brutal murder of his girlfriend by the 15-year-old son. Three 'bewildering symbol-laden films', *Sonámbulos* (Sleepwalkers) (1977), *El corazón del bosque* (The Heart of the Forest) (1978) and *Maravillas* (Wonders) (1980), were followed by two films which appealed to a much wider audience and sold well abroad. *Demonios en el jardín* (Demons in the Garden) (1982), in which three women, his mother, his aunt and his grandmother, fight for the affection of a young illegitimate boy, has been described as a film of great beauty and sensitivity. Claimed to be in part autobiographical, it is set in the wooded northern region of Spain which features in several of his films. *La mitad del cielo* (Half of Heaven) (1986), a 'touching, lyrical and beautiful' film about a country girl who buys and runs a restaurant in Madrid with the help of a rich benefactor, won him a Golden Shell at the **San Sebastián Film Festival**.

In the 1990s Gutiérrez Aragón worked for television, winning an award at Cannes in 1992 for his production of *El Quijote*. His film *El rey del río* (The King of the River) was the sole Spanish entry in the 1995 Berlin Film Festival, and was one of the ten selected for showing in Los Angeles in February 1996 in an exhibition of Recent Spanish Cinema.

See also: film and cinema

EAMONN RODGERS

Gutiérrez Mellado, Manuel

b. 1912, Madrid; d. 1995, Guadalajara

Army officer

Gutiérrez Mellado had a key role in the transition to

democracy in Spain, when as Minister for Defence he initiated the liberalization and depoliticization of the armed forces. During the Civil War, while sympathizing with Franco's rising, he remained in Madrid under an assumed identity, smuggling Nationalist sympathizers out of the Republican zone. He later joined the Franco forces and worked in the Nationalist propaganda services.

By the time of the formation of the first **Suárez** cabinet in 1976, Gutiérrez Mellado was known in the army as a liberal, and was consequently unpopular with the 'ultras' or the 'bunker', as the hard right came to be called. When this group circulated a dossier on him, in an attempt to discredit him, his intended appointment as Minister of Defence had to be postponed, and he became Chief of Staff, only acceding to a cabinet seat on the resignation of the hardline Santiago y Díaz de Mendívil. Despite the hostility of the bunker, Gutiérrez Mellado embarked on a series of important reforms, promoting liberal officers over right-wingers, and thereby breaching the traditional rigid system of promotion strictly on length of service. This earned him virulent abuse in public speeches by ultras, and in leaflets distributed in military housing areas. During the attempted coup of 23 February 1981, he showed considerable courage in confronting **Tejero** in the parliament building, when his rank did not prevent him being roughly manhandled.

Gutiérrez Mellado withdrew from the government in 1981 on Suárez's resignation. Although the next cabinet was entirely civilian, the pace of military reform was slowed down. Nevertheless, the changes introduced by Gutiérrez Mellado were the foundation for two measures enacted by Suárez's successor, Calvo Sotelo, which made it easier to remove unsuitable officers, and made promotion dependent on merit. The programme pursued by Narcís **Serra** built further on this foundation, introducing stringent tests of professional competence for promotion to senior ranks, and considerably slimming down the officer corps.

In later life, Gutiérrez Mellado engaged in charitable work, becoming President of the Foundation for Help Against Drug Addiction. In 1994, he was created Marqués de Gutiérrez Mellado. He died as the result of a road accident, on the way to Barcelona to deliver a lecture to a student audience.

See also: armed forces; politics

Further reading

Preston, P. (1986) *The Triumph of Democracy in Spain*, London and New York: Methuen (a lucid account of Gutiérrez Mellado's role in reforming the armed forces).

EAMONN RODGERS

Gutiérrez Torrero, Concepción

b. 1909, Córdoba

Writer (pseudonym 'Concha Lagos')

Primarily a poet, Gutiérrez Torrero also founded and directed *Cuadernos de Agora* (1956–64). Cultivating personal poetry in the Andalusian tradition, she employs classic metres with some popular forms. Later works become more meditative, philosophical and metaphysical. Characteristic collections blend transcendent speculation with existential concern for daily life, human solitude and anguish. *Antología 1954–1976* represents varied aspects of a quarter century's output. Significant collections include *Agua de Dios* (Water from God) (1958), *Luna de enero* (January Moon) (1961), *Tema fundamental* (Fundamental Theme) (1961), *Campo abierto* (Open Country) (1959) and *Teoría de la inseguridad* (Theory of Insecurity) (1980). She also writes prose fiction.

Further reading

Newton, C. (1990) 'Signos poéticos en Concha Lagos como indicios de una aventura mística', *Cuadernos Americanos* 4, 1 (19): 120–206 (analysis of imagery and relationships to mysticism).

Pérez, J. (1996) *Modern and Contemporary Spanish Women Poets*, New York: Twayne Publishers, pp. 121–4 (overview of themes and techniques).

JANET PÉREZ

Halffter, Cristóbal

b. 1930, Madrid

Composer

The nephew of Ernesto and Rodolfo Halffter, Cristóbal Halffter has worked in Spanish radio, taught at the Madrid Conservatory and conducted the Orquesta Manuel de Falla. His later work uses contemporary techniques, including electronic media. His son Pedro (1971–) has continued in the family tradition.

Further reading

Rodríguez, G. (1995) 'Segunda generación', *El País* (supplement, 17 September): 67–71.

JESSAMY HARVEY

Halffter, Ernesto

b. 1905, Madrid; d. 1989, Madrid

Composer

Ernesto Halffter studied with Manuel de Falla, composing a number of pieces whilst still a young man. Upon Falla's death, he undertook to complete the composer's unfinished work *Atlántida*, premièred in Milan in 1962. Like his brother Rodolfo, he left Spain after the Civil War, and settled in Portugal, where he continued composing and worked as conductor of a chamber orchestra.

JESSAMY HARVEY

Halffter, Rodolfo

b. 1900, Madrid; d. 1987, Mexico City

Composer

A member of a distinguished musical family, Rodolfo Halffter, brother of Ernesto, was largely self-taught as a composer. Some of his works were lost during the Civil War. After the end of the war in 1939 he lived in exile in Mexico for the remainder of his life, becoming a leading musical figure in that country.

JESSAMY HARVEY

health care

Spain has had a comprehensive health service only since 1986, when the **PSOE** government introduced the General Health Law. Previously, cover was provided under a compulsory health insurance introduced by the Franco regime in 1942, which by 1975 covered nearly 80 percent of the population. By the early 1990s, health care (except dental care and psychiatric treatment) was available free to 99 percent of the population, though anyone not receiving a state pension has to pay 40 percent of the cost of prescriptions. The overall administration of the health service at national level was entrusted to INSALUD (Instituto Nacional de la Salud – National Health Agency), which had been set up in 1978 in an attempt to co-ordinate health provision. In the years after the 1986 legislation, the seven **autonomous communities** with the largest measures of self-government (containing some 60 percent of the total population of the state) assumed responsibility not only for the administration of health care within their territories but also for policy and funding.

With the setting up of a comprehensive public health service, and a vigorous hospital building programme undertaken in the 1980s, the relative importance of private health care has decreased. Private hospitals, however, still represent 30 percent of all hospitals, and provide 20 percent of the beds. Private hospitals can receive state funding, but only if they sign an agreement with the authorities, specifying the conditions under which they provide care. About 80 percent of state health funding goes to public health care, though at 6 percent of GDP, public health expenditure is low by EU standards.

The massive increase in publicly funded health care from the mid-1980s was accompanied by a surge in demand. Hospital waiting lists increased threefold, there is a chronic shortage of hospital beds, especially long-stay beds, and there is no adequate system of aftercare. The problem is compounded by a shortage of qualified nurses and dentists, and by the inadequacy of medical training. By contrast, there is considerable overproduction of doctors, with consequent scarcity of permanent posts, a factor which has created serious unrest in the profession, reflected in a series of strikes in the first half of the 1990s.

Though Spain has one of the highest ratios of doctors to population, geographical distribution is uneven, reflecting general resource imbalances in the system as a whole. The largest share of public funding is directed towards acute hospital and specialist care, with a consequent neglect of primary care, health education and preventive medicine. To some extent this is a legacy of the past, for disease prevention was regarded by the Franco regime as essentially a public order issue, and came under the control of the Interior Ministry.

Fortunately, the general level of health in the population is good. Infant mortality rates stood at 7.8 per thousand in 1989, compared to 9.7 for the US and 8.4 for the UK. Life expectancy is 80 for women and 73 for men, the highest in the EU.

See also: AIDS; drug problem; social security

Further reading

Hooper, J. (1995) *The New Spaniards*, Harmondsworth: Penguin (chapter 18 gives a good account of health care in the context of overall social security provision).

Ross, C.J. (1997) *Contemporary Spain: A Handbook*, London: Arnold (chapter 8.2 is a well-documented and clear account of the problems faced by the health service).

EAMONN RODGERS

Herralde, Gonzalo

b. 1949, Barcelona

Filmmaker

Herralde was the director in 1977 of *Raza, el espíritu de Franco* (*Raza*, the Spirit of Franco), a documentary about the making of *Raza* (Race), a 'biographical' film whose making had been supervised by Franco in 1941. Herralde combined clips from the original film with interviews with the film's director, with the actor Alfredo Mayo and with Franco's sister, to show how film could be manipulated for propaganda purposes. Since then Herralde has produced mainly local films in Catalonia, including *Laura* (1987) and *Gold Fever* (1992), based on the 1880s novel *La febre d'or* by Narcís Oller. He has also released others in the USA, such as *Jet Lag* (*Vértigo en Manhattan*, 1980).

See also: film and cinema

EAMONN RODGERS

Herrero Rodríguez de Miñón, Miguel

b. 1940, Madrid

Politician

A major figure on the Spanish right after Franco's death, Herrero was elected on the **UCD** (Union of the Democratic Centre) list in 1977, and became one of the seven 'Fathers of the Constitution' who drafted the 1978 text (see also **constitution of 1978**). Unhappy with **Suárez**'s centrism, Herrero led a movement of internal opposition. In 1981 he left UCD to join the **Popular Alliance**, where he enjoyed some prominence despite his difficult relationship with **Fraga**. His attempt, in 1986, to succeed Fraga as leader of the Alliance provoked fierce internal opposition and he was quickly replaced. He never recovered his influence and in 1993 he retired from parliament, disillusioned with the party's direction under its new leader José María **Aznar**.

See also: political parties; politics

JONATHAN HOPKIN

Herri Batasuna

Herri Batasuna (HB) – **Basque** for 'People's Unity' – is **ETA**'s political wing. It was founded in 1978 by four left-wing nationalist parties, two of which had themselves emerged from ETA, together with a number of prominent independents without party links. Unlike **Basque Left**, HB was a purely nationalist grouping and was sponsored by the 'military' wing of ETA. Originally formed as an electoral alliance to fight the 1979 general election, HB has in theory retained that form, as well as a decision-making structure based on open assemblies. In practice, however, it is controlled by the representatives of ETA, through the agency of the Socialist Patriotic Co-ordinating Committee (Koordinadora Abertzale Sozialista – KAS). The original party components have withdrawn or declined into insignificance, and leading figures showing any tendency to criticize ETA have been removed in successive purges.

HB's programme remains based on the so-called KAS alternative, the main points of which are: withdrawal of the Spanish security forces from **Euskadi**; release of all ETA prisoners; unification of Navarre with the Basque **autonomous community**; and recognition of Basques' right to self-determination. The nature of these demands, clearly unacceptable to any Spanish government, reflects HB's purpose; to perpetuate conditions under which ETA's 'armed struggle' can be presented as a legitimate – indeed the only viable – means of achieving Basque aspirations, and to undermine the legitimacy of the Spanish state. Thus HB opposes both the **constitution of 1978** and the 1979 Basque Statute of Autonomy. It continues to boycott the Spanish and Basque parliaments, except under 'exceptional circumstances'. HB seeks also to foment a constant atmosphere of confrontation with the authorities, especially through street demonstrations, manipulating to this end a wide variety of issues not necessarily linked to that of Basque self-government.

HB has consistently scored 15–18 percent at elections in the Basque Autonomous Community and some 10 percent in Navarre. Its electoral highpoint was reached in 1986–7, when it won 13 seats in the Basque Parliament, five in the Spanish and one in the European. Thereafter its support fell slowly but inexorably; a decade later the equivalent figures were 11, two and none. Futhermore, its unquestioning support for ETA increasingly isolated HB even from other nationalist groupings. In December 1997 HB's leadership was imprisoned for an election broadcast featuring a statement on behalf of ETA. Along with the changes occurring inside ETA, this allowed new leaders, including previously expelled moderates, to begin political contacts with other nationalists. In September 1998 a joint declaration was signed at Lizarra (in Spanish, Estella), reaffirming the goal of ultimate independence; four days later ETA announced a ceasefire. Meanwhile, HB had formed a new organization, *Eusko Herritarrok*, to fight the upcoming regional election, at which it obtained 14 seats, a performance construed as an endorsement of the new course.

See also: regional nationalism; regional parties; terrorism

Further reading

Llera, F. (1994) *Los Vascos y la Política*, Bilbao: Universidad del País Vasco (overview of the Basque political system, giving electoral statistics).

Sullivan, J. (1988) *ETA and Basque Nationalism: the Fight for Euskadi, 1890–1986*, London: Routledge (chapters 7–9 include details of HB's relationship with ETA).

CHRIS ROSS

historiography

The writing of Spain's history was a particularly sensitive issue during the period of the Franco dictatorship, especially since the regime sought its legitimization in carefully selected precedents from the past. Franco's rising against the Second Republic was, at an early stage, dubbed a 'crusade' by the then Bishop of Salamanca, and Francoist propaganda thereafter strove to see the Civil War as the defence of Catholicism against 'godless communism', continuous with the medieval reconquest of Spain from the Moors, and with the struggle against Protestantism in Europe in the sixteenth and seventeenth centuries. Nationalist historiography therefore concerned itself primarily with the periods of Spain's past greatness, the union of the crowns of Aragon and Castile under Ferdinand and Isabella, and the 'imperial Spain' of the Hapsburgs.

The corollary of this concentration on the medieval and early modern periods was that the eighteenth and nineteenth centuries were comparatively neglected. The Enlightenment, modern European liberalism, and the bourgeois and proletarian revolutions experienced by other countries in the nineteenth century were regarded as an aberration, a source of foreign contamination, and the cause of all the evils of the present age. Consequently, any attempt to examine these phenomena from anything other than a censorious point of view was systematically suppressed. Juan López-Morillas' pioneering study of the influence on nineteenth-century Spain of the minor German idealist philosopher Krause, *El krausismo español* (1956), had to be published in Mexico, and was not reprinted in Spain until 1980, five years after Franco's death. An even more dangerous area for historians was the Civil War, where the official view was the only one tolerated. Hugh Thomas' classic study, *The Spanish Civil War* (1961), which set new standards of thoroughness and objectivity, appeared in Spanish translation in Paris shortly after publication, but was not published in Spain until 1976.

Since Franco's death, there has been a huge output of monographs on the modern period, and on previously forbidden subjects like the Civil War, the Second Republic, and the Franco regime itself. Historians like José María Jover Zamora, Miguel Artola, Manuel **Tuñón de Lara** and Juan Pablo **Fusi** have done fundamental work in these areas, characterized by scholarly rigour and impartiality, thoroughness, and the application of modern quantitative approaches. The seven-volume *Enciclopedia de la historia de España* (completed 1993), edited by Artola, devotes an entire volume to statistical information and maps.

This activity did not, however, arise in a vacuum, nor is it the case that prior to 1975 serious historiography was only being done outside Spain, despite the existence of justly acclaimed work by, for instance, J.H. Elliott, John Lynch, Noël Salomon, Richard Herr, Raymond Carr, and Stanley Payne. Within the constraints of the prevailing culture, modern revaluations of official interpretations of the past could and did take place. As early as 1942, Ramón Carande published a critical study of the financial structure of Hapsburg Spain. Jaume **Vicens Vives**' deceptively modest 1952 volume *Approach to the History of Spain* (*Aproximación a la historia de España*) provided a much-needed corrective to the conventional Castilian-centred view of the Spanish past by emphasizing Catalonia's distinctive contribution to the cultural and political evolution of the peninsula. It also questioned one of the key assumptions of Castilian nationalist views of the past, the notion that a fully-fledged 'reconquest' mentality existed in the immediate aftermath of the Moorish invasion in the eighth century.

This kind of revisionist historiography reflects the willingness of new generations to learn from methods and approaches developed in other countries, notably France, where the *Annales* school had encouraged the use of quantitative techniques, thereby shifting emphasis away from traditional diplomatic and constitutional history to social and economic history. This shift entails detailed analysis of a new range of primary sources, which in turn requires the abandonment of restrictive practices with regard to access to archival material. It was not uncommon during the Franco period and before for important collections of documents in private ownership to be inaccessible to researchers, either because the figure or movement to which they referred was politically controversial, or because they contained unflattering information, or through sheer possessiveness. Since 1975, the more relaxed intellectual climate has assisted greater openness and accessibility, and important collections such as the personal papers of the nineteenth-century Democrat leader Emilio Castelar, and Manuel Azaña, Prime Minister and, later, President of the Second Republic, have been deposited in the National Library and the National Historical Archives. Primary material is also being made available in print: collections like the *Bases documentales de la España contemporánea* (Documentary Sources for Contemporary Spain) have proved an invaluable resource.

There are 34,000 archives in Spain, of which 14,000 belong to the church. The remainder are divided among central, regional and local government bodies, law courts, trade union and other organizations, and private owners. Of the national total, 68 are in the care of the Ministry of Culture, of which six are state archives. The largest of these is the General Administration Archive in Alcalá de Henares, which has 160,000 linear metres of holdings, 9 million documents, and 15,000 books.

In 1990, after concerns were expressed in a report about staffing levels and facilities, the Ministry embarked on a comprehensive plan to rehouse the National Historical Archive (Madrid), and to upgrade all the major archives, including the Archive of the Indies (Seville) and the Archive of the Crown of Aragon (Barcelona), by introducing computerized cataloguing and retrieval systems, and improving arrangements for conservation and reproduction of documents. The application of advanced technology to the Indies Archive won it the Erasmus Prize in 1992. Reorganization of archives has not, however, been free of controversy. In 1995 a plan, approved by the cabinet, to move the archive of the wartime Generalitat (regional government of Catalonia) to Barcelona met with stiff opposition from the city authorities in Salamanca, home to the section of the National Historical Archive where documentation referring to the Civil War is centralized. The desire to respect the wishes of the **autonomous communities** thus conflicts with the principle stated by UNESCO, that where possible major collections should be kept together, with copies of documents being made available in other locations where appropriate. In an attempt to resolve some of these problems, a Junta Superior de Archivos (Supreme Council for Archives), composed of a small group of leading historians, was set up in 1995.

See also: history; censorship; Francoist culture

Further reading

Rodgers, E. (1989), 'The Reconquest of Spain', *THES*, 869 (30 June): 18.

EAMONN RODGERS

history

The history and culture of contemporary Spain have been deeply affected by the emergence, in the late eighteenth and early nineteenth century, of what came to be called 'the two Spains': one reformist, secularizing, liberal and European; the other traditional, Catholic, authoritarian and nationalist. Though these categories are not watertight, the deep divisions within Spanish society which they attempt to describe were very real, and had consequences which continued to reverberate up to the end of the Franco regime in the 1970s. Closely allied to this division, and compounding its effects, was the isolation of the ruling élites from the populace at large. Between 1837, when a liberal constitution was enacted, and 1890, when universal (male) suffrage was implemented for the first time, all governments were elected on a restricted property or income franchise. The proportion of the population entitled to vote hovered around 5 percent, and even after 1890 it was only 25 percent. Thus the rift between élite and populace was paralleled by a further division within the latter, between those who belonged to the political nation and participated in its processes, and those who did not. Politics was therefore largely a matter of different oligarchies competing for office and the control of access to patronage, a situation portrayed in vivid detail in the novels of Benito Pérez Galdós (1843–1920). Liberal revolutionary movements such as that of 1868, which overthrew the monarchy of Isabella II, depended on a mass following for their success, but when those who had helped to bring about political change saw no real alteration in the distribution of power or wealth, frustration could boil over into bursts of generalized violence connected only tenuously, if at all, with any structured programme or ideology. Professedly liberal regimes, therefore, often found themselves implementing stern law-and-order measures against their erstwhile allies: the post-revolutionary government of 1868 soon found itself having to cope with armed insurrection by extreme radicals, as did the short-lived Republican government of 1873, and that of the Second Republic after 1934.

This situation was further complicated by the politicization of the army. Military leaders who had been successful in the War of Independence against Napoleon, or had later won fame in the Civil Wars of 1833–9 and 1872–6, were encouraged to see themselves as the only group capable of bringing about structural change. Orderly transfers of power between different political interests were rare until 1875, more commonly being effected by army coups, of varying levels of violence, leading to the installation of a military strongman. Only after the monarchy ousted in 1868 was restored in the person of Isabella's son, Alfonso XII, with a new constitution (1876), did political hegemony pass to civilian parliamentarians. Even then, however, the oligarchic character of political life continued, with changes of government being effected by means of the *turno pacífico* (the managed alternation of the two main parties, Conservative and Liberal), rather than in response to the true wishes of the electorate.

The artificial compromises represented by the *turno pacífico* reflected a belief among the élite that modernization could only proceed slowly in a country where political culture was grossly underdeveloped. In this respect, the Restoration settlement of 1876 was the logical consequence of various attempts throughout the century to preserve the assumptions of a conservative constitutional monarchy, working in partnership with the Catholic church, though not dominated by it, and carefully controlling the degree of permitted political activity. The result was that Spain never had a fully fledged bourgeois revolution. The bourgeoisie could arguably have achieved hegemony in the 1880s and 1890s, but by then the growth of working-class radicalism caused the middle classes to retreat from the full assumption of power. Anarchist-inspired terrorism, including the assassination in 1897 of the architect of the Restoration settlement, Antonio Cánovas del Castillo, was symptomatic of the rejection of a system which had failed to tackle serious social and economic problems.

The confidence of the élite was further shaken when the last remnants of the overseas empire were lost after war with the US in 1898. Throughout the last quarter of the century, there had been a growing sense of unease at the rise of new, energetic economies such as the US and Germany, particularly among Catalan industrialists. By the mid-1890s, 60 percent of Catalonia's export trade was to Cuba, a large proportion being occupied by cotton textiles, the volume of which increased nearly fourfold between 1892 and 1897. By 1904, this had been reduced to a third. The importance of Cuba, however, and of the remaining colonies, Puerto Rico and the Philippines, was not only economic but psychological. Their loss produced a major intellectual and cultural upheaval, with a great deal of introspective analysis of Spain's history, character and future direction, as well as sharp criticism of the corruption and artificiality of the Restoration system, by writers such as Angel Ganivet (1862–98), Miguel de Unamuno (1864–1939), Pío Baroja (1872–1956) and Ramiro de Maeztu (1875–1936).

This atmosphere of crisis was accompanied by increased working-class militancy. By 1917, industrial concerns had come increasingly to be accompanied by the pursuit of revolutionary aims, especially with the greater prominence of the National Confederation of Labour (Confederación Nacional del Trabajo – **CNT**). Founded in 1911, it increased its membership from 15,000 in 1915 to 600,000 by 1919. It constituted a political phenomenon almost unique to Spain, anarcho-syndicalism, that is, a militant anarchist movement channelled into an industrial trade union organization. The ending of the boom which Spanish industry had enjoyed during WWI, with the consequent fall in prices, made the employers determined to oppose union demands for higher wages, which in turn strengthened the willingness of relatively moderate unions such as the socialist **UGT** (Unión General de Trabajadores – General

Union of Workers) to support the revolutionary strategy of the CNT. The period 1919–23 was one of considerable bitterness, which saw a ten-fold increase in assassinations and attempted assassinations, as armed gangs employed by both employers' and union organizations vied with each other in violence.

The apparent inability of the government to control events led to disillusionment with civilian rule, and when General Primo de Rivera staged a coup in Barcelona, which had been the main centre of unrest, there was little interest among the public at large in defending the parliamentary system. Primo de Rivera was politically unsophisticated, and had no clear philosophy or agenda, but in the period of his dictatorship we may see some of the origins of the corporativist and authoritarian rhetoric of which Franco was later to make extensive use. Individual rights had to be subordinated to the state, which was defined in unitary, Castilian-centred terms. As Franco was to do later, Primo redefined democracy as something independent of parliamentary institutions, and rooted in traditional, pre-political communities. Unlike Franco, however, he did not succeed in repressing political life completely, nor did he have the complete loyalty of the army. By 1929, an alliance of conservative politicians and army officers was putting pressure on King Alfonso XIII to dismiss Primo, and in January 1930 he resigned. The monarchy did not long survive his departure, for it had been discredited by its association with, and tacit approval of, the regime. The municipal elections of April, 1931 produced an overwhelming victory in the provincial capitals, where the bulk of the popular vote was concentrated, for an alliance of Republican and socialist parties, and two days later the King left Spain for good.

The new Republican government faced a series of daunting tasks, not least achieving consensus among the various political groupings of which it was composed. The Republican parties, characterized mainly by a blend of anti-clericalism and political moderation, appealed to middle-class liberal intellectuals, but lacked a strong working-class following. Socialists and anarcho-syndicalists, on the other hand, had as their main priority the improvement of workers' conditions, particularly those of landless labourers in rural areas. The potential for conflict between the different agendas was therefore high.

There was, nevertheless, one major area of agreement, though it did not embrace Catholic Republicans, which was the project of creating a secular state. Once the constitution was approved in December 1931, containing the declaration that Spain had no state religion, the government embarked on a programme of legislation over the next eighteen months which, among other things, legalized divorce, abolished state support for clergy salaries, dissolved the Jesuit order and nationalized its property, and excluded other religious orders from taking part in industry, commerce or education. Attempts to tackle the agrarian problem, however, proved more divisive. The Agricultural Reform Law (September, 1932) was intended to break up the large estates and redistribute the land, but its effectiveness was impaired by lack of finance. Furthermore, it proved all too easy for landowners to circumvent or ignore its provisions, and it failed to win support from smallholders and middle-ranking tenant farmers. Though too radical for conservatives, it was regarded by left socialists and anarchists as too slow and patchy in its operation, and in poorer rural areas there were illegal occupations of land and unauthorized timber-cutting, leading to clashes with the police and Civil Guard. In one notorious incident, at **Casas Viejas**, eleven workers were killed.

The fury provoked by this and similar incidents caused the abandonment of the Republic by the anarchists, who boycotted the elections held in November, 1933. In a parallel reaction, the socialists withdrew from electoral pacts with other parties and fought the election alone, an action for which they paid a high price, owing to the system of proportional representation adopted, which made such alliances a practical necessity. The result was a landslide victory for CEDA (*Confederación Española de Derechas Autónomas* – Spanish Confederation of the Independent Right), and the Radicals, who, despite their name, were politically conservative.

The period November 1933 to February 1936 is known as the *Bienio negro* (The Two Black Years), when the Republic took a decisive turn to the right, and attempted to reverse some of the democratic gains which had been made between 1931 and

1933. Both socialists and anarchists therefore adopted a more revolutionary stance, culminating in the general strike of September, 1934, which in Asturias developed into an armed insurrection by miners, put down with great severity by the government. Tough law-and-order policies drove socialists and anarchists into alliance once more, and led to the formation of the Popular Front, which won a majority of seats in the elections of February, 1936.

The victory of the Popular Front convinced right-wing elements in the armed forces that they should intervene to prevent what they regarded as the disintegration of the country. The failures of the Republic had been in those areas which were most calculated to provoke hostility among the military: the agrarian reforms could be presented as an attack on private property; the growing disorder was evidence of the Republic's failure to impose law and order; and the concession of autonomy to Catalonia and the Basque country seemed like the break-up of Spain. A number of senior officers therefore conspired to bring down the government by a military coup, and on 18 July, 1936, the garrisons in the north and in Spanish Morocco declared against the Republic, initiating a three-year **Civil War**.

The war resulted in the victory of the insurgent forces led by General Franco, and the installation of a dictatorship which lasted until Franco's death in 1975. Though the regime was not totally monolithic, political life in the normal sense came to a virtual standstill. Trade unions and political parties, other than the **National Movement**, were illegal, and a rigorous system of **censorship** maintained a large measure of state control of intellectual and cultural life. The regime lacked a clear ideology, but one consistent strand of policy was the effort to ensure the continuing depoliticization of the masses by improving material prosperity. The attempt to achieve this by **autarky** in the economic sphere ended in failure, and new policies fostered by the **technocrats** associated with **Opus Dei** were implemented in the **Stabilization Plan** of 1959. In the 1960s, Spain's growth rate of 7 percent was second only to that of Japan, among developed capitalist nations.

Well before Franco's death, public opinion was already pressing for political change. Increased prosperity, foreign travel, and inward tourist traffic, together with the prospect of entry into the European Economic Community (later the **European Union**), made the structures of Francoism seem glaringly anomalous in the modern world. Though there was potentially a danger of acute polarization and a recrudescence of the conflicts which had led to the Civil War, the shrewd political judgement of Adolfo **Suárez** and King **Juan Carlos I** ensured a relatively peaceful transition to democracy. In 1977, the first free elections since before the Civil War were held, and in 1982 democracy was further consolidated by the peaceful handover of power to the socialist opposition, the **PSOE**, after their overwhelming victory in the elections of that year. Despite the attempted military coup known as the ***Tejerazo*** in 1981, and the continuing problem of **ETA terrorism**, Spain is now a modern, pluralist state with solid democratic institutions, a member of **NATO** since 1981, and of the European Community since 1986.

See also: Francoist culture; historiography; intellectual life

Further reading

Carr, R. (1980) *Modern Spain, 1875–1980*, Oxford: Oxford University Press (a concise history of the period since the Restoration).

—— (1982) *Spain, 1808–1975*, Oxford: Oxford University Press (a revised and expanded edition of this classic study, first published in 1966 as a volume in the Oxford History of Modern Europe).

Grugel, J. and Rees, T. (1997) *Franco's Spain*, London: Arnold (an excellent account of the political and economic issues during the regime, with a good bibliography).

Hooper, J. (1995) *The New Spaniards*, Harmondsworth: Penguin (one of the most accessible and comprehensive accounts of the political, social and cultural developments since the restoration of democracy).

Preston, P. (1986a) *The Spanish Civil War*, London: Weidenfeld & Nicholson (a lively, compact account, with a very useful bibliographical essay).

—— (1986b) *The Triumph of Democracy in Spain*,

London and New York: Methuen (an indispensable guide to the politics of the transition).

EAMONN RODGERS

¡HOLA!

Founded in 1944 by Eduardo Sánchez and Mercedes Junco, *¡HOLA!* magazine continues to be designed entirely in Spain, under the management of their son, Eduardo Sánchez Junco, and is considered something of a sociological phenomenon.

Though the magazine has changed in format and content over the years, the accuracy of the items covered has always been held in such high esteem by readers that they believe that if the news has not appeared in *¡HOLA!* then it has not happened at all. Sales and readership figures for *¡HOLA!* increase almost by the day. With a print run of 800,000 copies per week, the magazine is available in two different versions, one for the Spanish-speaking world, the other (*HELLO!*) for the English-speaking world, and is sold in 108 countries.

One of the secrets of *¡HOLA!*'s success lies in the fact that it always meets the expectations of its readers. The magazine has a standard structure, consisting of regular sections, such as 'Panorama', with short news and curiosities; 'Seven Days', which reports on news with minimal or no photographs; 'Main Stories', covering a main story or event; 'Society', containing major social events or news about celebrities; 'Health and Beauty'; 'Cookery'; and 'Flora and Fauna', among others.

The other main reason for the magazine's success is the fact that it is produced by a family firm whose aim is family entertainment. The magazine was created by the Sánchez-Junco family with a clear – although not publicly expressed – intention of highlighting family values. In this respect, the magazine is renowned for the excellence of its coverage of the Spanish Royal family and royal events. On a wider plane, *¡HOLA!* always aims to present famous people in a favourable light, and tries to show their most positive aspects in all facets of life.

The magazine's graphic design is another of its strengths. *¡HOLA!* is said to be mainly a visual magazine, where photographs receive more prominence than the accompanying text. Indeed, the photographs are very carefully displayed, and are sometimes touched up for improved effect, by an inhouse team of photographers and editors. Photographs are occasionally bought from other agencies, but the news items accompanying them are always edited in *¡HOLA!*'s inhouse editorial style. This style is in line with the journalistic tradition established by the international news agency, **Agencia EFE**, especially as regards the condensing of information and good photographic practice.

¡HOLA! has been so successful since its launch that it has been copied in Latin America, encouraging other publishers to produce magazines similar in style and content. In Britain, *OK!* magazine is the one that has tried to imitate *¡HOLA!*'s style most closely. However, *¡HOLA!* stands out from any other magazine of its kind, holding the copyright of their brandname, *¡HOLA!*, and the translation of this title into any other language.

See also: Francoist culture; journalism; media; monarchy; *prensa del corazón*; press; society

Further reading

Bernández, A. (1991) 'The Mass Media', in A. Ramos Gascón (ed.) *Spain Today: In Search of Modernity*, Madrid: Cátedra (an essay on the role and importance of the mass media in Spain).

de Miguel, A. (1994) *La Sociedad Española, 1993–94. Informe Sociológico de la Universidad Complutense*, Madrid: Alianza Editorial (a sociological study of Spaniards in different facets of life, covering aspects such as reading habits and attitudes to the mass media).

Hooper, J. (1995) *The New Spaniards*, Harmondsworth: Penguin (chapter 21, on the press, has a section on magazines, pp. 300–2).

GEMMA BELMONTE TALERO

holidays

Though the continuing economic crisis has affected the way people think about holidays, one of the most significant results of increased free time in the Spain of the 1990s has been the emergence of what one could describe as a 'leisure culture'. The working week has been steadily reduced, owing to pressure from **trade unions** and concerns about **unemployment**. With the increase in total annual holiday periods, the traditional four-week August holiday is gradually being replaced by several shorter breaks of one to three weeks spread over the year. Furthermore, increased life expectancy has resulted in the emergence of a population referred to as the *tercera edad*, the active retired, who enjoy both leisure and significant spending power. In addition, the automation of domestic chores has increased free time for those women who are not active in the **labour market**. Also, the fact that young people are joining the job market much later than before has helped to extend their training period and their leisure time.

The increase in free time has been accompanied by a generalized search for improved quality of life, which has led to a growing emphasis on broadly educational leisure-time activities: visits to theme parks, membership of sports clubs, attendance at events run by cultural institutions, and enrolment in training centres, have all given rise to burgeoning businesses designed to cater for increased leisure. Though the seaside still plays a leading role as a place to relax during the day and to enjoy night-life, an interest in other forms of holiday-making has started to develop. Concern for environmental issues has helped to promote holiday visits to 'green' locations, such as natural parks and reserves, and the *Camino de Santiago* (the famous pilgrimage route along the North of Spain) attracts increasing numbers of people in search of physical as well as spiritual health. The countryside is now a favourite holiday destination for many Spaniards who live and work in the city during the week, and *parcelas* (plots), *casas de campo* or *fincas* (country houses) are favoured by those who want to enjoy the tranquillity of nature.

Major cities have become increasingly important as tourist destinations since the 1980s. Historic cities such as Toledo or Cáceres; capitals such as Madrid or Barcelona; cultural centres such as Alcalá de Henares; or cities offering a variety of amenities such as Seville, offer an attractive alternative to the seaside resort. Moreover, cities like Granada or Córdoba could almost be considered museums for the complex cultural and architectural legacy of Spain, and this has generated interest in hitherto neglected locations in the interior of the country.

Foreign vacations have also become quite common. Shopping trips to London, Paris, and other European capitals are widely organized for the two or three *puentes* (long weekends) occurring in the year, thanks to new transport facilities across Europe. Teachers and students have been increasingly taking part in EU-funded exchange programmes, and learning a foreign language, especially English, has become an international business since the 1970s, with many young people and professionals attending intensive residential language programmes during the summer.

See also: consumerism; demographic indicators; inflation; labour market; land tenure; *latifundia*; *minifundia*; sociology; women

Further reading

Priestly, G.K. (1996) 'City Tourism in Spain', in C.M. Law (ed.) *Tourism in Major Cities*, London: International Thompson Business (a study of the recent trend towards visiting cities as a modern alternative to more traditional tourism).

Schubert, A. (1990) *A Social History of Modern Spain*, London: Routledge (an analysis of the social development of Spain since 1800, examining the changing role of consumerism and economic prospects in modern society).

Vellas, F. and Bécherel, L. (1995) *International Tourism*, London: Macmillan Press (a socio-economic study of worldwide tourism trends, covering Spain).

GEMMA BELMONTE TALERO

Holy Week Processions

Given that **religion** in Spain is as much a cultural manifestation as an expression of personal commitment, it is not surprising that the processions held in the last three days of Holy Week often have a large element of spectacle, which threatens at times to overcome their devotional aspect. In these processions, which go back at least to the Middle Ages, images of the Virgin and of Christ carrying the cross are borne through the streets of nearly every village and town on heavy wooden litters, often elaborately carved and painted, which need as many as sixteen men to carry them. The images are accompanied by a brass band and drums. In some villages, such as Hellín in Albacete province, the drumming goes on round the clock for the duration of the festival. In the larger cities, notably Seville and Madrid, the litters are escorted by robed and hooded members of the confraternities attached to the various churches. Often they are joined by anonymous penitents walking barefoot and dragging chains attached to their ankles. The most famous of these processions is held in Seville, where the lavishly adorned image of the Virgen de la Macarena is processed to the accompaniment of the impromptu devotional song typical of Andalusia called the *saeta* (literally 'arrow').

So deeply embedded is this tradition in Andalusian culture that in 1978 some Andalusian workers in the Catalan industrial town of Hospitalet improvised their own secular variant of the Holy Week Procession, which has become an annual event, and is attended by up to 200,000 people. The same religious figures are carried, and outwardly the procession has all the appearance of a traditional one, but the difference is that it is not held under church auspices, is centred on municipal buildings, and is sponsored by a confraternity made up of professed agnostics.

The medieval origins of the processions are most clearly seen in those few places where the practice of self-flagellation is perpetuated, the most notable example being the village of San Vicente de la Sonsierra (Logroño), where hooded figures whip themselves, and their weals are then pricked with pieces of glass to make the blood flow. This practice is rare, however, and overall the processions are characterized by a mixture of religious fervour, festive rejoicing and local rivalry.

See also: National Catholicism; Roman Catholicism

EAMONN RODGERS

Hormaechea, Juan

b. 1939, Santander

Politician

Hormaechea first took office in 1977 as mayor of Santander. After ten years' service he was elected regional president of the **autonomous community** of Cantabria, serving from 1987–90 and from 1991–4. Despite being associated with the centre-right **PP** between 1987 and 1990, he was subsequently disowned by the PP – in part, because of his habit of insulting his fellow politicians – and stood for re-election in 1991 only after forming his own, Cantabrian, party. He was re-elected despite having previously lost a motion of censure brought by both the PP and the socialist **PSOE**. A political career marked by scandal came to a head in 1994 when, despite still being in office, Hormaechea was convicted of abuse of trust and misappropriation of public funds and sentenced to six years in gaol. Though technically able to continue as regional president pending the ratification of his sentence by the **Constitutional Tribunal**, he succumbed to popular and media pressure and resigned two months after being found guilty.

See also: corruption; political parties; politics

PAUL HEYWOOD

housing

Housing in Spain runs the entire gamut of housing types, from the rudimentary shacks of the **shanty towns** to opulent detached villas located on the outskirts of towns, or in prestigious suburbs like the nineteenth-century Salamanca district of Madrid. In older towns and cities there are traditional dwellings constructed around an attractive inner patio, often with an elegant upper gallery supported by pillars. The predominant urban housing type, however, is the apartment block, a category which itself includes considerable variety. The nineteenth-century expansion of towns and cities produced a range of medium-scale constructions of four to six stories, of varying levels of building quality. Many of these, especially in the inner suburbs of Madrid and Barcelona, are still in good condition, occupy a relatively expensive band of the **housing market**, and are much sought after by high earners. In smaller provincial cities, however, some of these traditional tenements are in a poor state of repair. In the mid-1990s, it was estimated that there were over half a million buildings in poor condition in Spain, notably in the Basque country, where since 1992 some 130,000m pesetas has been invested in refurbishment.

The urban landscape in Spain is, however, dominated by high-rise apartment blocks of relatively recent construction. Demand for housing in the 1960s and 1970s stimulated rapid building programmes, the legacy of which is seen in poorly planned developments of high-density, low-quality dwellings, with inadequate infrastructure and services. In 1970, for example, the suburb of Moratalaz in Madrid had the population of a sizeable town, with 90,000 inhabitants. In developments like these, especially in provincial towns, basic domestic operations like cooking depended to a large extent on bottled gas rather than main services, and travel to and from work involved substantial expense and investment of time.

The quality of housing in the 1990s reflects the greater prosperity of the country at large, and the higher expectations of home-owners for a better standard of comfort and decor. In addition, concerns about personal security have made some form of controlled entry, including video-screening, a basic feature of new apartment blocks. Occupiers no longer rely on bottled gas for cooking: by 1996, 2.5 million homes were connected to main supplies of natural gas. Higher safety standards have required the provision of automatic cut-off devices for gas supply, and smoke detectors in each apartment.

Homeowners display greater awareness and sophistication with regard to decor and furnishings. In 1996, there were ten monthly magazines catering for the taste of this clientele, for instance *El Mueble* (Furniture), *Nuevo Estilo* (New Style) and *Casa y Jardín* (House and Garden). With an increasing proportion of the female population in employment, the emphasis is on ease of maintenance, with duvets replacing blankets, and increasing reliance on easy-to-clean surfaces such as vinyls and fungicide-treated paints. In the kitchen, built-in appliances, ceramic surfaces and the use of microwave ovens have become the norm.

Over and above this, many of the changes simply reflect aesthetic rather than functional criteria. The pressure for modernization on all fronts since the end of the Franco regime expressed itself in, among other things, an increased interest in interior design, with both official and private bodies striving to heighten public awareness of developments in design both within Spain and elsewhere.

See also: consumerism; design

EAMONN RODGERS

housing market

The housing market is characterized by the relatively high cost of buying and renting; one of the highest levels of home ownership in the European Union; the small proportion of housing for rent; and the large proportion of second and vacant homes. These characteristics have raised a number of important issues: notably access to housing by those people with limited resources, the extent to which the housing market limits the geographical mobility of labour, the poor quality of many urban residential environments, and the relationship between the land market and local authority finance.

The paradox of the housing market is that although Spain has a low density of population (73 per km^2), and only 6 percent of its area is urbanized, land and property prices are high by west European standards. Unravelling this paradox requires knowledge of the complex processes working in the land and property market.

Demand for housing arises from residents and non-residents, who in turn view housing as both a form of shelter and a form of investment. In the 1960s and 1970s there was a huge increase in the demand for housing in cities, on the back of relatively high population growth rates, rising incomes and a substantial migration of people from rural to urban areas. At the end of the twentieth century increased demand for housing came primarily from a decline in household size, as people delayed marriage, had smaller families and lived longer. Around the coast and in rural settlements house prices are frequently influenced by demand from non-local residents seeking second homes. For investment purposes housing has been seen as a convenient method of securing tax concessions or of otherwise reducing tax liabilities.

Demand is also influenced by institutional factors, notably the availability of finance. Traditionally, the level of downpayment on a house has been relatively high (20 percent) and the repayment period of a mortgage relatively short (15 years). An expansion of credit in the late 1980s contributed to the property boom at that time. Very high interest rates helped to slow the economy and bring this boom to an end in the early 1990s.

The supply of land and property is regulated through the law and through the **planning** system. There is also extensive intervention by a variety of institutions. Housing development is undertaken by both the public and the private sectors. In the private sector it is undertaken by individuals, groups (*cooperativas*) and commercial developers.

Controls on building development imposed through the planning system reduce the quantity of land available for housing development and thus push up land costs. Simultaneously, these controls have been inadequate to provide quality residential environments in cities. In the mid-1990s 90 percent of the land area in Spain was classified as unavailable for building (*suelo no-urbanizable*) and only carefully specified areas were designated for early housing development. Urban development plans are frequently very long in gestation and when published may then be partially revised, causing uncertainty in the land market. Moreover, acquiring development permission has frequently been a time-consuming and costly business. A more liberal land development regime runs the risk of uncontrolled urban growth lacking adequate public services. Yet this occurred anyway in the 1960s and 1970s as the planning system was either unable or unwilling to control development. Nevertheless, there has been widespread agreement on the need to simplify and increase the flexibility of land management.

Apart from intervention through the planning system, the government has intervened in the housing market to encourage the achievement of targets for the provision of housing through National Housing Plans (*Planes Nacionales de Viviendas*) and to subsidize housing for sale rather than to provide large numbers of houses for rent. Subsidized housing (which represented about 5 percent of all housing starts in the early 1990s) is designated as either Officially Protected Housing (*Viviendas de Protección Oficial* – VPO) or as Fixed Price Housing (*Viviendas de Precio Tasado* – VPT, introduced in the 1992–5 National Housing Plan). Subsidies are provided through soft loans (low rates of interest and longer repayment periods), tax measures and grants towards construction. In general, the level of subsidy to buyers depends on their income level and the floor area of the house, with some groups such as the young attracting special assistance. Although the objective of housing promoted by the public sector has been to improve access to housing by the less well-off, the financial and administrative obstacles involved in acquiring such housing have remained too high for some people.

Only a small proportion of the housing stock in the mid-1990s was available for rent. The 1991 Census of Housing recorded a total of 17.1 million dwellings (*viviendas*), of which 11.7 million were the principal homes of the occupiers. Of these principal homes, only 1.8 million (15.4 percent) were rented, the lowest proportion in the European Union. From this historic low, the proportion of rented homes climbed to around 18 percent in 1995, due largely to more liberal legislation on property rental.

The explanation for the small rental sector lies in the tight restrictions which have been placed on landlords in the past in respect of tenancy agreements (very secure tenancies and frozen rents), the limited volume of public housing for rent and the encouragement given to people under the Franco regime and after to buy their own property. Ossified rents enabled low income families to remain in city centres along with small family businesses and may have protected city centres from wholesale redevelopment.

The first steps to liberalize the rental market

were introduced by the Minister of Finance, Miguel Boyer, in 1985. By the early 1990s there were enormous differences between new and old rents. More extensive measures were introduced in January 1995 under the Urban Property Rent Law (*Ley de Arrendamientos Urbanos*). Broadly, this law began the process of bringing rents into line with current market values over a period of between five and ten years.

Spain has one of the highest levels of second-home ownership in Europe. Many of these homes represent the rural origins of people now living in the cities. Others have been bought for tax and investment reasons, and as an escape from the noise and congestion of urban living. There are few villages in Spain where refurbishment, rebuilding or new building cannot be seen. There are also a large number of vacant dwellings; 2.5 million (excluding weekend and holiday homes) according to official estimates in the early 1990s. In part this is a reflection of rural depopulation, but the explanation for this number also lies in property market speculation and second home ownership.

The principal social issue associated with the housing market is that it has not enabled the constitutional guarantee of access to good quality housing to be met. The problem is most acute for those with limited resources, notably young people and the poor. For young people the difficulties are compounded by very high rates of youth unemployment. Hence the tendency for young people to continue living with their parents for longer than in many other countries and to delay marriage.

The frantic pace of house building in the 1960s and early 1970s overwhelmed the planning authorities, resulting in poor quality residential environments. City centres were ringed with densely spaced and poorly built tower blocks, frequently accompanied by inadequate public services and infrastructure. Pressure on housing was also reflected in developments which were built without planning consent, including some **shanty town** communities, especially in the south of Spain. The planning system has since been strengthened, but the impress of the 1960s and 1970s is clear in cities across Spain.

One final but crucial point concerning land and property is that it provides an important source of local government income (exploited to its full in the municipality of Marbella in the mid-1990s). In the mid-1990s local taxes included those on property, on construction work and a land value appreciation tax. In addition, local authorities gain income from granting building licences and from other related land transactions. Hence, there are benefits to local authorities when land and property prices are rising. There is even an inducement for local authorities to manipulate the market to create higher prices. Simultaneously the government spends large sums of money helping people gain access to housing.

Further reading

Alberdí, B. and Levenfeld, G. (1996) 'Spain', in P. Balchin (ed.) *Housing Policy in Europe*, London: Routledge (a concise account of the characteristics of the housing market in Spain).

Hooper, J. (1995) *The New Spaniards*, Harmondsworth: Penguin (chapter 20 offers a succinct and lucid account of the social effects of changes in the housing market).

Keogh, G. (1994) 'Land Law and Urban Planning in Spain: An Economic Perspective', *European Planning Studies*, 2, 4: 485–95.

McCrone, G. and Stephens, M. (1995) *Housing Policy in Britain and Europe*, London: UCL Press (chapter 6 is specifically relevant and the book includes discussion of a number of general topics applicable to housing in Europe, including housing and labour mobility).

Riera, P. and Keogh, G. (1995) 'Barcelona', in J. Berry and S. McGreal (eds) *European Cities: Planning Systems and Property Markets*, London: Spon (commentary on land law and planning).

KEITH SALMON

hunting

Spain, widely regarded as the hunting reserve of Europe, has more land area devoted to hunting than any other EU country, provides more than 20,000 permanent jobs in gamekeeping alone, and employs around two million temporary workers during the hunting season. Hunting is worth around 400,000m pesetas annually to the Spanish economy.

Spain, with its rich variety of game, is one of the few countries where hunting is practised all year round. Hunting terminology distinguishes between *caza mayor* (big game) and *caza menor* (small game). Nine of the ten big game species are native: wild boar, red deer, roe deer, fallow deer, chamois, ibex, wolf, lynx and bear. The other, the moufflon, was introduced into the *Coto Nacional de Cazorla y Segura* (Cazorla and Segura National Game Reserve) in 1953. The lynx is a protected species and may not be hunted.

Among small game, the most important species are: red-legged partridge, turtle dove, wood pigeon, quail, great bustard, capercaillie, rabbit, pheasant, hare, wildfowl and predators such as hawks, the latter being considered an endangered species and protected by a permanent hunting ban. Spain is the only country in Europe where the *avutarda* (great bustard) exists in large numbers, especially in Extremadura – a hunting region *par excellence*. The largest European bird, and relatively rare, it is much sought after by hunters.

The most numerous species, and the object of special attention by hunters, are the wildfowl: geese, and ducks such as mallard, teal and goosander. Much of Spain is covered by water: rivers, lakes, reservoirs, ponds and lagoons. Some of the wetlands, such as the Ebro Delta in Catalonia, the Albufera lagoon in Valencia, the ponds of Extremadura and the Guadalquivir marsh are renowned worldwide for wildfowling (i.e. duck hunting). The latter is close to the Coto de Doñana, considered to be the most important bird reserve in Europe.

Conservation of hunting, and the administration of parks and national game reserves are the responsibility of the Servicio de Pesca Continental, Caza y Parques Nacionales (Fishing, Hunting and National Parks Service), which currently administers two national game reserves, five national parks, and twenty-three conservation areas, including that of Anayet which is closed to hunting under an international agreement. The Dirección General de Montes, Caza y Pesca Fluvial (Office for Hunting and River Fishing), issues guidelines which are implemented in the annual *Orden de Vedas* (Close Season Orders), which are designed to ensure species conservation, and establishes regional prohibitions, with the aim of allowing populations to re-establish themselves, thereby providing increased sporting opportunities. The Dirección General de Promoción del Turismo (Office for the Promotion of Tourism) administers three national hunting reserves, which are among the finest in Europe because of their facilities, the variety of species found, and the size of their game stocks. Lastly, the Patrimonio Forestal del Estado (State Forest Trust) administers the Coto Nacional de Cazorla, the largest and best-stocked hunting reserve, where most of the top ten big game species can be found.

It is, however, in private reserves that a great deal of hunting is carried out. There are over 230 private big game reserves, which offer ample facilities, including about seventy-five high mountain locations, and a huge number of small game reserves, distributed evenly over the national territory. The importance of private reserves may be due to the fact that more than 90 percent of the demand is for small game, especially the red-legged partridge, which is hunted by the favourite method of beating-up (*ojeo*). The national game reserves offer only big game, with the exception of the Delta del Ebro and the Tablas de Daimiel lakes in La Mancha, which have a concentration of wildfowl. Besides, national reserves offer only the method known as *rececho*, which involves taking up a position in one place, whereas most hunters prefer the active pursuit characteristic of the classic Spanish *monterías*, which are regarded as more enjoyable.

Hunting is important for stimulating low-season **tourism** which not only earns foreign currency but also brings specialized tourist traffic to more remote areas, creating job prospects, increasing the standard of living locally, and enabling new initiatives.

See also: agriculture; Civil Guard; Delibes Setién, Miguel; economy; environment; labour market

Further reading

Durantel, P. (1993) *Nuevo Manual de la Caza*, Barcelona: Editorial Planeta, S.A (an introductory guide to hunting in Spain: techniques, licence requirements and organizations).

Graffi, R. (1993) *El Gran Libro del Cazador*, Barcelona: Editorial De Vecchi, S.A (an introduction to the world of hunting and falconry in Spain).

GEMMA BELMONTE TALERO

I

Ibercorp

The financial group Ibercorp was first founded, as Invesbank, in 1986 by Manuel de la Concha and Jaime Soto. Registration difficulties forced the change of name, and in 1987 Ibercorp began trading as a bank. Other limited companies were created around the bank, such as Ibercorp Leasing, Ibercorp Cataluña, and Ibercorp Bolsa. After initial spectacular success – two of these companies were bought out for 5,235m pesetas in 1990 – the shakiness of Ibercorp's foundations was revealed and the Bank of Spain was forced to intervene in March 1992. In March 1994 Ibercorp bank suspended payments. The case acquired considerable notoriety because of the number of public figures who were clients of Ibercorp, among them Miguel **Boyer**, Minister of the Economy 1982–5, and his wife, Isabel Preysler, a former wife of Julio **Iglesias**.

See also: corruption

PAUL HEYWOOD

Iberia

Although state-owned Iberia, the national airline of Spain, is one of the country's biggest companies, it was a significant loss-maker for some years. In 1995 it had an operating surplus of 25,117m pesetas but this became a loss of 61,084m pesetas after financial costs and other items were taken into account. Of its passenger income 25.2 percent was generated within Spain, 42.7 percent in the rest of Europe, and 32.1 percent in intercontinental flights. Iberia's fleet (excluding aircraft belonging to subsidiary companies), consists of some 113 aircraft, including twenty-five Boeing 727, seven 747, eight 757, eight Airbus A300, twenty-two Airbus A320, seven DC9, four DC10 and twenty-four MD87. Its first Airbus A340 was delivered in March 1996, followed by seven more in the ensuing two years. A further ninety-three aircraft belong to the subsidiaries Aviaco, Viva Air and Binter, or are rented from other companies.

Iberia has a number of wholly owned subsidiaries such as Binter Canarias, Binter Mediterráneo, Viva Air, an 83 percent shareholding in Aerolíneas Argentinas, a 45 percent shareholding in the Venezuelan airline Viasa, a 38 percent shareholding in the Chilean airline Ladeco, and a 33 percent shareholding in the Spanish airline Aviaco. It also owns or controls a number of cargo and catering companies. Iberia's route network is extensive, with around 100 destinations of its own rising to over 300 if those of its subsidiaries are included. It is the European airline with the largest number of destinations to Latin America and with the biggest network in Latin America itself. It also flies from Spain to most of the major cities of Europe, to North Africa, the Middle East, the USA, Japan, New Zealand, Australia and Equatorial Guinea, a total of forty-six countries. Iberia's average of daily flights is 850, with a carrying capacity of 90,000 seats. In 1997 it carried 24.4 million passengers.

Iberia employs over 24,000 people, and its pilots are among the highest paid in the world. In the early 1990s, the management's attempt to stem the losses by reducing staff and by other cost-cutting measures resulted in poor industrial relations with consequent disruptions. The European Commission's authorization for an injection of capital of 87,000m pesetas in 1995, to be followed by a further 20,000m in 1997, allowed the company to fend off financial collapse and introduce a three-year productivity plan to prepare it for privatization. Results for 1997 showed a modest pre-tax profit of 16,091m pesetas. Part of the restructuring was to involve the sale of some of its subsidiaries (in particular Aerolíneas Argentinas). Better management, a more streamlined employment structure, and more aggressive marketing are likely to increase profitability after the severe losses of the early 1990s.

See also: transport

Further reading

Iberia (1998) *Annual Report 1997*, Madrid.

C.A. LONGHURST

Iglesias, Julio

b. 1943, Madrid

Singer

Julio Iglesias' meteoric career began when, as a complete unknown, he won the 1968 Festival de Benidorm with the song '*La vida sigue igual*' (Life Remains the Same). One vignette at the time described him as a timid, insecure lad from Madrid who studied law and played in goal. Then a car accident forced him to rest for long months in bed, with only a guitar for company, and this was how Julio Iglesias, the singer was born.

His singing career was assured in 1970 when he performed 'Gwendolyne', Spain's entry to the Eurovision Song Contest. Although he only came fourth, his record company seized the opportunity to open the doors to the European market. In the next four years Julio Iglesias became a household name in Italy, Germany and France. From here he set out to conquer the world market with the help of well-known composers of ballads and love songs (for instance Danny Daniel, Ramón Arcusa and Manuel Alejandro) and a highly successful marketing campaign, especially after he signed a contract with the CBS in 1976. A string of number one singles and albums followed.

In 1981 he broke into the English speaking market, after a spectacular promotional campaign, with his rendition of Cole Porter's 'Begin the beguine'. After a much publicized divorce, Iglesias moved to Miami, from where he orchestrated the conquest of the far corners of the world. His first record made in America, *1100 Bel Air Place*, was released in 1984, in collaboration with Diana Ross, Willie Nelson and The Beach Boys. Sales of the album made Iglesias the most successful Spanish artist in the world market. Thereafter, his career is punctuated by attempts to recover his Hispanic audience with records like *Libra* or *Tango*, as well as his efforts to consolidate his position in the American music industry. Iglesias won a Grammy in 1987 for *Un hombre solo* (A Man Alone). He has recorded over sixty records and sold over one hundred million records in more than eighty countries. From the very beginning of his career Iglesias' private life has been in the public domain and he has managed to use the glare of publicity to enhance his celebrity status.

MIGUEL JIMÉNEZ PINILLA

IIEC

The Instituto de Investigaciones y Experiencias Cinematográficas (Institute for Film Research and Experiment) was set up by the Vice-Secretariat of Popular Education in 1947, as part of the Franco regime's attempt to control all aspects of cultural life. Like many institutions of Francoism, it went beyond the original intentions of the government, and it was the training-ground for many of the most creative and adventurous film directors produced in Spain.

EAMONN RODGERS

ikurriña

This is the **Basque** name of the flag which forms the best-known symbol of Basque nationalism.

Designed by the anglophile Sabino Arana, founder of the movement and of the Basque nationalist **PNV**, its design is based on the Union flag of the United Kingdom, incorporating the Basque national colours. The flag accordingly consists of a white cross and green saltire on a red ground. Banned by General Franco, it was adopted by the nationalist resistance to his regime centred on **ETA** and is now generally accepted as the national flag. The *ikurriña* is the official flag of the Basque **autonomous community**.

CHRIS ROSS

immigrants

Apart from the long-standing two-way traffic with Spanish America, Spain had no significant immigration from other countries until the 1980s. On the contrary, in the 1950s and 1960s the trend was for Spanish workers to leave in search of employment in the more developed economies of western Europe. In the 1980s, however, the flow of qualified professionals such as dentists and technicians from, for instance, the Dominican Republic and Argentina began to be replaced by female domestic servants from these and other Latin American countries. Between 1989 and 1991, the number of foreign residents in all categories in Spain doubled from 200,000 to 400,000, and some estimates suggest that the figure doubled again to 800,000 by 1996. This represents about two percent of the indigenous population, as against seven to eight percent in Germany and France. As in other European states, however, immigrants tend to concentrate in certain centres of population, especially Madrid (20 percent of the total immigrant population), Catalonia (18 percent), Andalusia (13 percent), Valencia (12 percent) and the Canary Islands (10 percent).

About 500,000 of the non-Spaniards resident in Spain are there legally, of whom about half come from other EU countries, 16 percent from Latin America, and 20 percent from Africa, mainly from Morocco. This leaves up to a possible 300,000 who are in Spain illegally. It is often difficult for these people to regularize their situation. In 1993, it was estimated that the Ministry of Social Affairs was receiving some 15,000 applications annually for residence permits, of which only four percent were granted. In 1996, it was announced that the regulations would be relaxed to allow the possibility of full legal status to anyone who had once had a work or residence permit, or who was related to someone in either of these categories. Only 50,000 people, however, were expected to benefit from this measure.

Conditions for illegal immigrants, and even for some legal ones, are often harsh. In 1992, the Madrid suburb of Peña Grande had 1,000 Moroccans living in a **shanty town** of 200 dwellings, the biggest concentration of its kind in Europe. Immigrants often carry a heavy burden of debt, mainly to pay off the loan provided by the person who organized their travel to Spain, but also because of the need to send back most of their earnings to their families. They are vulnerable to exploitation and discrimination, often being paid less for the same work than Spanish workers. Though there is arguably less racial antagonism in Spain than in other European countries, immigrants have nevertheless been the victims of violence, the most notorious case being that of a woman from the Dominican Republic, Lucrecia Pérez, who was murdered as she slept in a disused discoteque. The authorities, too, have sometimes dealt with illegal immigrants in a heavy-handed way, notably in the highly controversial expulsion in June 1996 of 103 illegal immigrants from Africa. Not only was it alleged that the deportees had been given no opportunity to have their applications properly processed, but the government admitted that they had been drugged prior to their expulsion.

See also: black economy; labour market

EAMONN RODGERS

independent record companies

Popular music was one of the key elements of *la* ***Movida*** at the beginning of the 1980s. Influenced by the independent spirit of the punk movement, groups flocked to the new independent record labels which had been set up to cover the ground largely ignored by multinational companies. At first, the records released tended to be limited edition singles brought out by labels such as Tres Cipreses, DRO (Discos Radioactivos Organizados), Lollipop, Nuevos Medios or GASA (Grabaciones Accidentales). Many of the groups of *la Movida* had highly improbable names such as Derribos Arias (Arias Demolition), Glutamato Ye-Ye, Parálisis Permanente (Permanent Paralysis), Radio Futura (Future Radio), Loquillo y los Trogloditas (Loquillo and the Troglodytes) and Gabinete Caligari (The Cabinet of Dr Caligari). The type of music they produced varied immensely; from the obscurity of Parálisis Permanente to the elegance of Los Esclarecidos, or from the fresh pop of Los Bólidos to the industrial fantasies of El Aviador DRO or **Almodóvar** and McNamara's cabaret act.

The focus of *la Movida* was Madrid, home of fanzines such as *Editorial del Futuro Método* (Future Method Publishers) and *La Pluma Eléctrica* (The Electric Fountain Pen) and magazines like *La Luna* (The Moon) and *Madrid me Mata* (Madrid Kills Me) which reflected what was happening in the clubs (such as Rock-Ola and El Jardín). The influence of the movement spread to other cities creating *la Movida* de Vigo, Barcelona and Valencia.

Independent labels were supported by the most progressive commentators on popular culture in the media. Radio programmes in the 1980s played a vital role in promoting new groups nationwide, especially 'Diario Pop' (Pop Diary)/'Esto no es Hawai' (This is not Hawaii) on RNE 3. Popular music programming on television, 'Caja de Ritmos' (Rhythm Box) and 'La Edad de Oro' (The Golden Age) reached an even wider audience.

From 1983 onwards sales multiplied and the small independent labels entered into serious competition with multinational companies. The commercial interest shown by major labels in bands from *la Movida* became more evident, and it was not long before some of these combos would feel tempted by promises of fame and fortune and transfer to the big record companies, who catapulted them to chart success.

Some independent companies survived throughout the 1980s, and there were even a few labels set up mid-decade (e.g. La Fábrica Magnética), but the golden days had passed and the majority of the small labels disappeared by the end of the decade.

See also: *Movida, la*; rock and pop

Further reading

Gallero J.L. (1991) *Sólo se vive una vez*, Madrid: Ardora Ediciones.

Márquez, F (1981) *Música moderna*, Madrid: Ediciones Nuevo Sendero.

MIGUEL JIMÉNEZ PINILLA

Induráin, Miguel

b. 1964, Villava (Navarre)

Cyclist

Among the greatest names in professional international cycling, Indurain became amateur champion of Spain in 1983 and turned professional in 1985, winning various Spanish 'Tours' in the succeeding years, the Paris–Nice Cycling Classic in 1989 and 1990, and the Tour de France in 1991. In 1994 he held the world record of 53.040 km/hr. By the time he retired in February 1997 he had become one of only three to have won the Tour de France five times (1991–5), and the only one to have done so consecutively. A member of the Banesto team, he had also won the Giro de Italia twice (1992–3), a World Championship in 1995 and an Olympic gold medal in 1996.

Indurain was convinced he could win the Tour de France for the sixth time, but collapsed during the Alps stage on 8 July 1996 and was unable to complete the tour. He was reluctantly persuaded by Banesto to take part in the circuit of Spain (*Vuelta a España*) for the eighth time in September 1996, but abandoned the race on 20 September with breathing problems. In February 1997 he announced his retirement from professional cycling at the age of 32. Despite the difficulties of his last months as a professional competitor, his reputation as the best ever Spanish sportsman remains intact.

See also: cycling

EAMONN RODGERS

industrial development

Broadly speaking, it is possible to divide Spain's industrial development into two phases: one slow, partial and lengthy, that took place during most of the nineteenth and part of the twentieth centuries; another, short and intense, that belongs essentially to the 1960s.

Despite the lack of investment capital, which most economic historians ascribe to an inefficient agriculture, there was some modest degree of industrial development in nineteenth-century Spain (textiles, mining, iron and steel, and railways), but the process of industrialization was not maintained in the twentieth (except briefly during the dictatorship of Primo de Rivera in the 1920s). At the time of the Civil War (1936–9), Spain was still predominantly an agrarian country, and industrial production, which had peaked in 1929, did not regain those levels until the early 1950s. Spain's poor industrial performance during the post-Civil War years can be ascribed not just to the destructive effects of the war, but even more to her isolation during and after WWII and to the sheer economic incompetence of Franco and his ministers during the first fifteen years of the regime. **Autarky**, protectionism and import-substitution, to some extent forced by Spain's exclusion from the Marshall Plan, led to a stagnant economy which lasted until the advent of US aid in the 1950s and a reorientation of economic policy. Initial expansion, however, only produced inflation and balance of payments crises in the later 1950s, and it was only with the implementation of the 1959 **Stabilization Plan** by the so-called **technocrats** of **Opus Dei** that sustained and intense industrial growth took place. From 1960 to 1974 Spain's industrial output averaged a year-on-year increase of over 11 percent, while the economy as a whole was averaging a 7 percent per annum increase.

The change of economic orientation at the heart of the regime with the arrival of the new, less ideologically motivated ministers and their advisers, provided the framework for industrial take-off. But what actually made it possible was the happy coincidence of a number of factors external to Spain: US aid, foreign currency earnings from a tourist boom, emigrants' remittances from abroad, and the availability of cheap labour for foreign investors. All these factors together led to a huge increase in the capital available for investment purposes, and increasing earnings fuelled a consumer boom. The fact that Spain started from a retarded position meant that the possibilities for growth were that much greater, while the concurrent expansion of international markets and buoyant prices for industrial products favoured Spanish exports, which in turn made possible a greater volume of technological imports, especially of much needed capital equipment.

Although the development of the 1960s and early 1970s temporarily turned Spain into the ninth industrial power in the world, it was not an unqualified success, and the roots of future problems were laid down in the very process of industrialization. First, there was excessive concentration on just a few sectors: iron and steel, shipbuilding, the metal-bashing industries in general, chemicals and cement. Second, all these industries were energy-intensive, and Spain was heavily dependent on imported oil. Third, industrialization was led by the state through its industrial arm, INI (**National Industrial Institute**), which, although successful in promoting industrial development, was more concerned with output figures than with efficiency. Fourth, there was excessive spatial concentration of industry: to the traditional industrial centres of Catalonia, the Basque country and to a lesser extent Asturias, were added the eastern provinces of Valencia and Alicante, the northern city of Valladolid, a few Atlantic ports for shipbuilding, and Madrid. Vast areas of southern, central and western Spain did not directly benefit from industrial development, despite the Franco regime's attempt at establishing development zones. Finally, Spanish industry was allowed to develop within a protectionist atmosphere in which the import of manufactured goods was controlled by tariffs or quotas and exports were encouraged by a variety of subsidies; such cosseting resulted in a lack of competitiveness.

The effects on the cost of oil of the OPEC price rises of the 1970s, together with intense competition from newly industrialized countries, had such a severe impact on Spanish industry that Spain was threatened with de-industrialization as firms, both public and private, recorded huge losses. From 1975 to 1979 Spanish industrial output stagnated as shipyards and steel mills found themselves with few orders and households stopped replacing electrodomestic consumer goods. Forced eventually to take remedial action, the centre-right **UCD** government and its successor the socialist **PSOE** administration implemented a policy of so-called industrial reconversion (***reconversión industrial***) in the 1980s which applied compulsorily to public sector companies and voluntarily to the private sector. Essentially the policy was one of a temporary propping up to enable companies to shed labour, modernize and become more competitive. Much of the government aid went in providing for early retirements and redundancy compensation as well as to write off losses, but some aid was also channelled into more positive aspects such as research and development, re-equipment, and rationalization through mergers. Just how effective the industrial reconversion programme was in saving great swathes of Spanish industry from total collapse remains a matter of debate. Ultimately the real saviour was to be foreign investment as Spain's long-drawn out negotiations to join the EC concluded in agreement. But it would be fair to say that with about a million jobs shed between 1975 and 1985, and with new foreign markets having been found to make up for sluggish demand at home, Spanish industry emerged from the ten-year crisis leaner, fitter and more competitive. The price paid for the lop-sided industrial development of the 1960s had been heavy – poor competitiveness leading to loss of jobs and import penetration in an increasingly liberalized international trading system – but in any case the fortunes of Spanish industry were finally and inevitably to be dominated by European circumstances.

Further reading

Harrison, J. (1993) *The Spanish Economy. From the Civil War to the European Community*, London: Macmillan (chapters 2 and 5 offer a good summary).

Salmon, K. (1995) *The Modern Spanish Economy. Transformation and Integration into Europe*, London: Pinter (chapters 1 and 6 provide excellent syntheses).

C.A. LONGHURST

industrial relations

The Franco regime prohibited **trade unions**, establishing instead the so-called '**vertical syndicates**' (*sindicatos verticales*), which, purporting to make class conflict irrelevant, grouped workers, managers and employers together on an industry by industry basis. The law on **collective agreements** of 1958 allowed collective bargaining on wage settlements in individual enterprises, but in the late 1950s and early 1960s, specifically industrial demands for improvements in earnings and conditions of work were frequently inseparable from politically motivated aspirations for greater democracy in trade union organization and in the political system as a whole.

The restoration of democracy after the death of Franco saw a sharp rise in trade union activity and membership. The consultation between government and unions which produced the **Moncloa Pacts** established a precedent for partnership in tackling the serious problems of inflation and balance of payments deficits, and led to a series of wage agreements in the years up to 1986. Little was done, however, to tackle the high rates of unemployment, and relations between government and unions deteriorated to the point where the whole country was brought to a standstill by a very successful general strike in December 1987.

This gave the unions considerable power in the early 1990s: for example, an agreement for an extra 400,000m pesetas for pensions was concluded on 25 January 1990. By that time, however, the initial surge of enthusiasm for union membership had fallen off. From 58 percent of salaried workers in 1978, active membership had fallen to 10 percent by 1994 (compared to 40 percent in Britain and over 80 percent in Sweden). The effect of this is somewhat mitigated by the fact that voting in union elections is open to non-members, but overall the result has been a substantial weakening of union power. This has enabled both **PSOE** and **PP** governments to press ahead with deregulation measures similar to those being pursued elsewhere in Europe. In 1994 a legislative package was approved which curtailed job protection, introduced greater flexibility into the **labour market**, and increased the proportion of temporary and part-time contracts.

Apart from local industrial disputes, there has been a decline in the traditional militancy of the Spanish labour movement, reflected in a steady reduction since 1980 in the number of working days lost through strikes.

Further reading

Heywood, P. (1995) *The Government and Politics of Spain*, London: Macmillan (see especially chapters 10 and 11 for a lucid account of the modernization of the economy and the corresponding changes in the role of unions).

EAMONN RODGERS

industry

Spain became a fully industrialized nation much later than most other western European nations. Although Catalonia and the Basque country could be considered industrialized regions by the end of the nineteenth century, the rest of Spain was predominantly agricultural until the rapid industrial expansion of the 1960s. Even today large areas of western Spain have little industry; indeed 60 percent of Spanish industry is located in just five provinces: Barcelona, Vizcaya, Madrid, Valencia and Alicante. The rapid **industrial development** of the 1960s was followed by an equally rapid de-industrialization in the late 1970s and early 1980s as energy-intensive industries found they could not absorb the vastly increased energy costs brought about by the OPEC increase in the price of oil. Spanish industry, at one time dominated by the public sector, is now dominated by foreign-owned companies, which generate more than half of manufacturing output. Although the public sector still retains a presence, privatization is proceeding apace as the state divests itself of profitable enterprises to raise revenue or of unprofitable ones to reduce losses. Some industries, however, such as coal and shipbuilding, are such heavy losers that there is little prospect of the private sector taking them over. Among the big public corporations to be successfully privatized have been the telecommunications company Telefónica, the oil company Repsol, and the electricty company Endesa, with the Spanish commercial **banks** having been encouraged to become major shareholders in order to keep control at home. Among the best known foreign companies with an important stake in Spanish industrial enterprise, either directly or through shareholdings, are Elf-Aquitaine, BP, Shell, Total, IBM, Hewlett-Packard, Rank Xerox, Olivetti, Digital, Fujitsu, GEC-Alsthom, Bosch, Siemens, Dow Chemical, Henkel, Hoechst, Procter & Gamble, Bayer, Ciba-Geigy, Unilever, Nestlé, Allied Lyons, Danone, Guinness, as well as the vehicle manufacturers Volkswagen, Renault, General Motors, Ford, Citroën, Nissan, Peugeot, Mercedes Benz and Fiat-Iveco, the motor-cycle manufacturers Honda and Yamaha, and tyre manufacturers such as Michelin and Firestone. There are some 10,000 companies operating in Spain which have 50 percent or more of their share capital in foreign hands.

Large loss-making industrial companies that remain in the public sector include Hunosa (mining), Astilleros Españoles and Bazán (shipbuilding), Santa Bárbara (defence equipment), Ensidesa and Altos Hornos (steel). There is little the government can do except try to stem the losses by a gradual process of cutbacks, outright closure being a political impossibility as long as the current high unemployment persists. Previous attempts at redundancies provoked such violent protests that the proposed figures had to be scaled down.

Industrial output (excluding construction) accounts for about 22 percent of Spain's GDP, down from about 27 percent in the late 1980s. Looking at broadly defined industrial sectors, the largest by output value is the metallic industries sector (which includes all machinery and vehicle manufacture) with 28–9 percent of the total value of industrial production. In second place comes the food processing industry (including drinks and tobacco), which contributes about 20 percent. In third and fourth places come non-energy minerals and chemical industries with 17–18 percent, and the water and primary energy sector (which includes petroleum refining and electricity production and distribution) with about 14.5 percent of total industrial output. These are the four major industrial sectors, after which come the paper production and publishing sector (6 percent), the rubber and plastics sector (3.5 percent), the wood, cork and furniture sector, the footwear and clothing sector, the textile (i.e. cloth) and leather sector (each of which contribute approximately 3 percent), and finally other manufactures (e.g. jewellery, toys and sports equipment) with less than 1 percent. If we compare value of production with value added, the figures change little except for two sectors: with 19 percent of the total value added the water and primary energy sector shows itself to be highly efficient (relative to the prices it can command in the market place), whereas the food processing sector, with just 15 percent of the total value added, shows itself to be relatively inefficient. It must be pointed out that the high efficiency of the energy sector is due entirely to the electricity sub-sector, where the difference between production costs and the prices obtained at the point of sale is huge. No other industrial sector (except water supply) enjoys such a monopolistic advantage. This explains the popularity of electricity supply companies with Spanish shareholders. Finally, with an employed population of between 2.0 and 2.2 million out of a total employed population of some 12.4 million, Spanish industry as a whole is relatively more efficient in its use of labour than either agriculture, construction or services. This, however, has been achieved at the cost of shedding some three-quarters of a million jobs between 1990 and 1993.

See also: industrial development; *reconversión industrial*

Further reading

Chislett, W. (1996) *Spain 1996. The Central Hispano Handbook*, Madrid: Banco Central Hispano (chapter 4 offers a clear, succinct account of recent developments).

Salmon, K. (1995) *The Modern Spanish Economy. Transformation and Integration into Europe*, London: Pinter (chapter 6 offers an informative survey of Spanish industry by sector).

C.A. LONGHURST

inflation

Spain has had on the whole a high inflation economy both before, during and after the period of rapid development of 1960–74, and it was only in the 1990s that the monetary authorities at last appeared to be on top of the problem. Already towards the end of the 1950s inflation was hitting 15 percent but was brought under control following the **Stabilization Plan** of 1959. During the 1960s inflation was held down to single figures, but the quadrupling of world oil prices in 1973–4 and official and private sector yielding to trade union pressure for high wage increases resulted in spiralling costs and consequent price rises. Neither the government nor the employers knew how to stand up to the new power of the unions and the latters' explosive wage claims: in 1976 alone the total wage bill went up by 22 percent and the following year inflation hit the roof with an official rate of 24.5 percent and unofficial estimates of 30 percent. The remorseless rise in unemployment from 1975 to 1985 also paradoxically added to the inflationary pressures by forcing the government to borrow in order to meet its ever-increasing commitments to the burgeoning welfare state.

The **Moncloa Pacts** of 1977 between government, opposition, unions and employers did not help the government's fight against inflation as it was meant to do. As the price of their support for the pact, the socialist opposition and the unions insisted that the government contain the threat of rising unemployment by maintaining high levels of public expenditure, which made the control of inflation that much more difficult. The prices and wages policy had little effect, partly because the wage norm was too high and not even adhered to in the private sector, and partly because the

Spanish retail price index: average yearly percentage change

1968	4.9	1975	17.0	1982	14.4	1989	6.8
1969	2.2	1976	17.6	1983	12.2	1990	6.7
1970	5.7	1977	24.5	1984	11.3	1991	5.9
1971	8.2	1978	19.8	1985	8.8	1992	5.9
1972	8.3	1979	15.7	1986	8.8	1993	4.6
1973	11.4	1980	15.5	1987	5.3	1994	4.7
1974	15.7	1981	14.6	1988	4.8	1995	4.7

government itself approved huge price rises in many of the areas which it controlled (e.g. public transport). The oil price increases of 1979 also added to inflationary pressures.

It took ten years from the time of the Moncloa Pact to bring inflation down to the 5 percent mark, but the continuously high interest rates that this required proved a serious disincentive to investment by private businesses and may help to explain in part the lack of job creation in Spain. The boom of the late 1980s induced by Spain's entry to the EC and the renewed foreign investment that this attracted threatened to push inflation up again, but a new climate of moderation in wage claims and the pressures on the government to meet the convergence criteria laid down at Maastricht have ensured a less permissive atmosphere. By 1996 headline inflation was down to 3.2 percent, the lowest for thirty years. Nevertheless the higher level of inflation in Spain as compared to most of its international competitors has inevitably meant that over the years the exchange value of the peseta has fallen, and indeed the loss of value measured against more stable currencies such as the German mark and the US dollar has been substantial.

Further reading

OECD (published annually or bi-annually) *OECD Economic Surveys: Spain*, Paris (sober and reliable regular surveys of the Spanish economy including all macroeconomic indicators).

C.A. LONGHURST

Initiative for Catalonia

Initiative for Catalonia (Iniciativa per Catalunya – IC) was formed in 1987 by Rafael Ribó – who had replaced Antoni Gutiérrez as General Secretary of the communist **Catalan United Socialist Party** (PSUC) after the 1982 Spanish general election – in alliance with left-wing nationalists. Its sister organization within the Spanish state is the **United Left** (Izquierda Unida – IU), but the old tensions between Catalanism and communism remain. The leader of the Spanish communists and of IU, Julio Anguita, has rivalled José María **Aznar** in his anti-Catalanism, which has led to a desire on Ribó's part to distance himself from IU. In the 1996 Spanish general elections IC won two seats.

DAVID GEORGE

Institute of Catalan Studies

The Institute of Catalan Studies (*Institut d'Estudis Catalans*) was founded in 1907 by the leader of *Solidaritat Catalana* (Catalan Solidarity), Enric Prat de la Riba. It was an academic body dedicated to scientific research in the fields of Catalan history, literature, archaeology, art history and law. One of its remits was to establish the norms of written Catalan, a task which was undertaken by the engineer-turned-grammarian, Pompeu Fabra. Its activities were interrupted by Francoism, but it secretly resumed them in 1944 under its best-known post-Civil War head, R. Aramon i Serra. The Institute of Catalan Studies groups together several Catalan academic bodies, and awards a series of annual prizes.

See also: Catalan; Catalan culture; regional nationalism

Further reading

Aramon i Serra, R. (1975) *L'Institut d'Estudis Catalans*, Barcelona (a history of the Institute).

DAVID GEORGE

Instituto de la Mujer

From 1983 to 1996 the Institute was the central government department responsible for promoting gender equality under the socialist **PSOE** administration. Responding to pressure from the party's feminist caucus Mujer y Socialismo (Women and Socialism), the socialist government established the Institute (Law 16/1983) as an autonomous body of the **Ministry of Culture**. In 1988 it became a key arm of the new ministry of social affairs. Its functions were to promote the social advancement of women and gender equality in politics, employment, health, education, the family and the media.

The Institute obtained cabinet approval for its detailed Equality Plans (1988–90 and 1993–5) so as to ensure their implementation throughout the administration. Though the goal of equality was advanced through reform of laws governing abortion, rape, marriage, divorce, pensions, maternity leave and education, the government failed to amend its restrictive **abortion law** to include social grounds before it lost power.

The Institute supported similar bodies set up in the seventeen autonomous governments and also funded local women's associations, to which it gave between 140 and 260 grants per year. It ran eleven women's advice bureaux which dealt with over 50,000 consultations, as well as a 24-hour hotline which took 80,000 calls per year. It ran television campaigns challenging the gender stereotyping of jobs and used street hoardings to promote safe sex through condom use, with the slogan: 'Póntelo, pónselo' ('Put it on, put it on him'). Its social programmes ranged from creating refuges against domestic violence, to training women in rural communities, to running holiday camps for single mothers and their children. The Institute commissioned research to identify the needs of particular groups such as workers, prostitutes and the elderly, making statistics on gender differences widely available. Attempting to reach a wide audience, it distributed over half a million information leaflets annually. It created a 10,000 document library and promoted women's contribution to the arts through touring exhibitions and literary prizes. Total staffing varied from 170 to 220 people, and its annual budget in the early 1990s was 2,300m pesetas.

From 1983 to 1996 the Institute's directors were socialist-feminists from within and from outside the governing party: Carlota Bustelo, Carmen Martínez Ten, Purificación Gutierrez and Marina Subirats. Public opinion widely supported the Institute's work and welcomed the new cultural image of a modern, well-educated woman exercising choice over her fertility and working life. Nevertheless, critics levelled charges of élitism and lack of attention to the needs of ordinary women. Some feminist organizations voiced concerns about the Institute's perceived dominance over the wider women's movement.

See also: feminism

Further reading

Threlfall, M. (1996) 'Feminist Politics and Social Change in Spain' in M. Threlfall (ed.) *Mapping the Women's Movement*, London and New York: Verso, pp. 115–51.

Valiente, C. (1995) 'The Power of Persuasion: the *Instituto de la Mujer* in Spain' in D.M. Stetson and A. Mazur, *Comparative State Feminism*, Thousand Oaks, CA: Sage, pp. 221–36.

MONICA THRELFALL

Ínsula

A Madrid-based monthly literary magazine first published in January 1946, *Ínsula* was associated also with a bookstore and a publishing house of the same name, as well as a famous ***tertulia*** in Madrid. Two periods of the review suggest themselves. The first extended from 1946 until 1988, and included the first 500 numbers of the publication. It was mainly presided over by the founding editor Enrique Canito (1902–92), a high school professor of French who was deprived of his position for political reasons by the Franco regime. The poet José Luis **Cano** participated in the founding of *Ínsula*, and over the next forty-two years occupied the posts of secretary, associate editor and, upon Canito's retirement in January, 1983, editor. The greatness of the first epoch of *Ínsula* derives from its role in maintaining a forum and spirit of cultural and literary dialogue during the worst years of Francoism. It kept its readers in contact with the Spanish intelligentsia in **exile** that wrote for its pages, and published material by and about virtually all the greater and lesser figures of contemporary and classic literature in Spanish, and, to a notably lesser extent, in other languages. Its format was similar to that of the leading Spanish dailies. Hence in the tradition of **Ortega**, it made high culture attractive and accessible to both the literary professional and to the educated general reader. An emblematic event in the history of *Ínsula* during the worst of the **censorship** was its defiance of a prohibition against giving prominence to Ortega on the occasion of his death. In response the editors dedicated the November 1955 number to his memory. As a result the magazine was not allowed to publish again until January 1957. In June 1987 Cano became President of the magazine and was succeeded in the editorship by Víctor García de la Concha, a professor at the University of Salamanca.

The unofficial second epoch of *Ínsula* begins with the publication of number 501: Cano's name disappears from the editorial team of *Ínsula*; the characteristic green of the masthead and highlight lettering of the magazine is replaced by red; the review is printed on a heavier, more expensive stock; and the traditional sections or departments of the magazine disappear. While the Canito–Cano *Ínsula* was characterized by a policy of informing its readership of new developments in national and international literature, culture and related research, the new *Ínsula* is more professorial and academic. It depends heavily on the publication of partial and total monographic issues under the rubric 'El Estado de la Cuestión' (The State of Current Research). Critics, usually university-based, study specific Spanish and Spanish-American writers, movements and genres.

Further reading

Abellán, M.L. (1984) 'La revista *Insula* y el exilio español', *Revista Nacional de Cultura* (Caracas) 255: 33–40.

Cano, J.L. (1988) 'Breve historia de *Insula*', *Insula* 499–500: 1–2.

Gómez Sempere, J. (1983) *Indices de la revista 'Insula' (1946–1980)*, Madrid: Dirección General del Libro y Bibliotecas.

STEPHEN MILLER

insumisos

'Insumisos' is the name given to those who refuse to do both military service and *prestación social sustitutoria* (alternative community service). Conscientious objection to military service is recognized, but refusal to do the civilian alternative is a criminal offence, though lack of resources often means that in practice the law is not enforced. The new penal code of 1995 reduced the penalties for *insumisión* by making the refusal to do social service punishable by fine rather than imprisonment. The main consequence of *insumisión*, however, is disqualification from state employment for 10 to 14 years.

EAMONN RODGERS

intellectual life

Spain in the 1920s and 1930s displayed considerable intellectual vitality, not only because of the presence of an exceptionally gifted generation of writers and artists (such as Rafael **Alberti**, Luis **Buñuel**, Salvador **Dalí**, Federico García Lorca and Jorge **Guillén**), but also because of the revitalization of critical enquiry stimulated by the work of the philosopher José **Ortega y Gasset**, whose editorship of the *Library of Twentieth-Century Ideas* helped to familiarize the reading public with some of the main currents of European thought.

This development was, however, truncated by the outbreak of the **Civil War** in 1936. Given that the main university cities of Madrid and Barcelona remained in Republican hands, most of the leading intellectuals found themselves in Republican territory, and initially supported the elected government. Ortega was among those who signed a manifesto in favour of the Republic, as was the historian Ramón Menéndez Pidal. The atrocities carried out by Republican militias in the early days of the war, however, and the increasing influence of the communists in the government, alienated this support, and most of the leading intellectuals left Spain either during or at the end of the war, some not returning until many years later.

The victorious Franco regime was deeply suspicious of intellectual activity, and strove to control intellectual and cultural life through a rigorous system of **censorship**, and by state and church tutelage of **university education**. According to the official ideology, the traditions of critical enquiry deriving from the eighteenth and nineteenth centuries were subversive and anti-Spanish. The founding charter of the institution set up to co-ordinate and oversee research in post-

Civil War Spain, the **CSIC**, stated as its purpose 'the restoration of the classic and Christian unity of the sciences, which was destroyed in the eighteenth century'. Many of those intellectuals who had survived the war and remained in Spain found the climate uncongenial, and eventually joined their colleagues in **exile**, for instance, Manuel **Tuñón de Lara**. Others who grew up in Franco's Spain, such as Juan **Goytisolo**, found that by the mid-1950s they needed to breathe the freer air of other countries.

The intellectuals who remained can be grouped into three categories. In the first place, there were those who consciously and deliberately applied their energies to the difficult and ultimately ineffective enterprise of providing a theoretical framework for the Francoist system, notably José María de **Areilza**, José Luis **Arrese y Magra**, Rafael **Calvo Serer**, Dionisio Ridruejo and, above all, Eugeni D'Ors. Many of these became disillusioned and either moved towards opposition (Ridruejo as early as 1940), or were driven into opposition by incurring Franco's disfavour (Calvo Serer). With the exception of D'Ors, all the above functioned primarily in the political arena, but bridges between politics and academia were provided by figures like the Benedictine monk, Justo Pérez de Urbel, who as well as being a very distinguished medieval historian was a member of the Francoist Cortes (see also **parliament**), adviser to the Women's Section of the **National Movement**, and the first Abbot of the Valley of the Fallen, the monument to the (Nationalist) dead of the Civil War, constructed by the labour of Republican prisoners.

The second category includes conservative academics such as Ricardo del Arco, José Antonio **Maravall** and Pedro **Laín Entralgo**, who, while not systematically propagandizing on behalf of the regime, generally shared its Castilian nationalist view of Spanish history (see also **historiography**), and were instinctively hostile to political radicalism of the left. Members of this group would have viewed themselves, not as the front line of defence of the regime, but as professional educators working within the only system available. Some, including Maravall and Laín Entralgo, were liberal Catholics who hoped for a gradual opening up of Francoism to modernizing tendencies, and became increasingly disillusioned at the continuing entrenchment of the regime.

The third group were, broadly speaking, liberal Catholic dissidents, within the narrow field of manœuvre that the climate of censorship and repression allowed to dissenting views. The fact that they were able to function at all was largely due to their courage and intellectual integrity, but also to the skill with which they could steer a careful course among the various reefs, and thereby preserve a measure of intellectual independence. An important contributory factor was the inefficient operation of the censorship, and its inconsistency in application, which often meant that work of a specialist or technical nature could be published. Philosophy in particular benefited from this, and José Luis L. **Aranguren** published in his *Catolicismo y protestantismo como formas de existencia* (Catholicism and Protestantism as Ways of Life) (1952) a collection of essays on Luther, Kierkegaard and Unamuno, as well as other essays on Marxism, all topics which would have been considered taboo in the 1940s. Julián **Marías**, a disciple of Ortega, continued to occupy his chair throughout the Franco period, and to develop Ortega's insights in his published writing. Enrique **Tierno Galván**, despite having fought on the Republican side during the Civil War, and having been interned after the war in a Francoist concentration camp, held a chair of Public Law in Murcia and subsequently in Salamanca, and published articles in the *Revista de Estudios Políticos* (Political Studies Review), the organ of the Instituto de Estudios Políticos (Political Studies Institute).

In any case, it proved impossible in practice for the regime to exclude intellectual currents from abroad, or to interfere effectively with the network of international contacts characteristic of academic research. Besides, the increasing desire on the part of the authorities to present an acceptable face to the rest of the world helped to mitigate some of the potential rigours of censorship. Nevertheless, there was still a clear dividing-line between toleration of certain kinds of intellectual activity and continued suppression of any direct criticism of the regime, as Aranguren and Tierno Galván found to their cost in 1965 when they were sacked from their chairs for joining a student demonstration in favour of liberalizing the university system.

The regime also proved unable to rely on the uncritical support of the Roman Catholic Church, which for most of the dictatorship had been one of the principal mechanisms of social and intellectual control. Though the official position remained that all teaching in educational establishments, including universities, had to conform to Catholic dogma, in practice the church, from about the mid-1950s, and, more particularly, the 1960s, outpaced the political institutions in its development towards more progressive and tolerant attitudes. The relative modernization of the church, especially after the Second Vatican Council (1962–5), undermined **National Catholicism**, distanced the church from Francoism, and provided intellectual and moral support for liberal Catholics such as Aranguren.

The survival of intellectual dissent during the Franco regime ensured there was already a foundation on which to build when democracy was restored. Even before Franco's death, some exiled academics returned, and continued to exercise a positive influence in semi-retirement, for instance, Américo **Castro**. Others returned after 1975, and occupied university posts with success and distinction (Tuñón de Lara) or contributed to intellectual and cultural life through their writing (Francisco **Ayala**). The main element of continuity, however, was provided by the institutions which, despite state control, had enabled some modicum of independent intellectual life to subsist. In addition to figures like Aranguren, Marías and Tierno Galván, a younger generation trained during the dictatorship, including, among many others, Miguel Artola and Juan Pablo **Fusi** (history) Francisco Rico (literature), José Luis **Abellán** and Elías Díaz (history of philosophy), carried on the work of maintaining intellectual integrity and professionalism in the universities. The Law of University Reform of 1983 (**LRU**) finally freed the universities from state control, and provided greater security of tenure for academic staff. The CSIC has also developed well beyond the original intentions of its founders, and since 1987 has been the main body entrusted with the elaboration of the National Science Plan. Though the **Royal Academies** remain relatively conservative institutions, they retain a key role in fostering academic debate through their activities in organizing seminars, lectures and conferences, and in promoting publication.

Perhaps the dominant element, however, in intellectual life since the mid-1970s has been the democratic transition itself, which has given rise to a spate of books and articles on the nature of Spanish society, Spanish identity, and the problems raised by these and related issues. The evolution of Spain into a quasi-federation of **autonomous communities** has changed the terms of social and political debate, much of which is now carried on, not in the institutions mentioned above, but in the **press**, particularly the quality press which has emerged since the early 1970s, represented by *El **País***, *El **Mundo*** and ***Cambio 16***. Though gross **readership** figures for newspapers are lower than those in France, Germany and Britain, it is likely that proportionately as many people read the quality press in Spain as in Britain (see also **media**). Readership of serious novels has increased dramatically since the mid-1980s. Even a challenging novelist like Juan **Benet**, who makes heavy demands on the reader, could command a print run of 25,000 copies, and the playwright Antonio **Gala**'s first novel had a print run of 200,000 in 1990.

All these developments are symptoms of the widening of access to education since 1970, the development of mass communications, and the burgeoning of **literature** and the arts, which have revitalized the intellectual climate and broken down some of the barriers between élite intellectual groups and an increasingly sophisticated public.

See also: education and research; Francoist culture; university education

Further reading

Aranguren, J.L.L. (1975) *La cultura española y la cultura establecida*, Madrid: Taurus (a stimulating study by one of the leading participants in the cultural and intellectual debate).

Díaz, E. *Etica contra política: Los intelectuales y el poder*, Madrid: Centro de Estudios Constitucionales (a fundamental analysis by an eminent historian of philosophy).

—— (1992) *Pensamiento español, 1939–73*, Madrid:

Tecnos (the second edition of an important study first published in 1974; still relevant).

—— (1982) *El exilio español en México, 1939–1982*, México: Fondo de Cultura Económica (an important symposium by various authors, including historical articles and personal testimonies, as well as a biobibliographical section on Republican intellectuals in Mexico).

EAMONN RODGERS

Interiorism

'Interiorism' in its strictest sense is a specialist activity akin to interior design, and is concerned with planning indoor living or recreational spaces. In Catalonia, however, the term has taken on a different connotation, and denotes an approach to architecture which was originally influenced by interior designers. This development can be attributed to the importance of the prizes awarded annually by the Barcelona FAD (*Foment de les Arts Decoratives* – Institute for the Encouragement of Decorative Arts, a private body founded in 1902), to the best architectural designs. There are two distinct categories: architecture and interior architecture ('interiorism'). In the 1970s several of the entries presented by 'interiorist' architects were much more courageous and imaginative than those in the 'architecture' category. 'Interiorism' consequently became the research laboratory for new forms of expression, and by the 1980s strictly 'architectural' works began to display characteristics previously exclusive to the 'interiorists'. It is an approach which borrows some of the methods and attitudes of visual spectacle, avoiding the conformism of much contemporary architecture, and cultivating effects of surprise. 'Interiorism' stimulated a counter-current within contemporary Catalan architecture, and its results are particularly noticeable in Barcelona in the 1980s and 1990s.

The FAD prizes provide very interesting evidence of the changes in Catalan culture. Though they were first awarded in 1958, the intention behind them goes back a long way. In 1899 the *Ajuntament de Barcelona* (Corporation of Barcelona) decided that a panel consisting mainly of architects would adjudicate on the award of a prize to the best building constructed that year. The prize for 1900 was awarded to **Gaudí** for his *Casa Calvet*, which continued to serve as a model for a long time after. From 1902 onwards the Corporation created a special prize for the interiors of public buildings, awarded in 1903 to **Domènech i Montaner** for his *Fonda España*. These panels continued to function under the auspices of the city council until 1912, and their activities coincided with the great creative period of **Modernism**. The FAD's purpose in reviving these annual competitions in 1958 was to revitalize architectural practice by trying to recapture the heady excitement of Catalan Modernism. The fact that Barcelona is once again, at the end of the twentieth century, a city in which architectural debate is uniquely intense, suggests that this purpose has been achieved. By giving international prominence to the originality of Catalan architecture, the FAD Prizes highlight the extent to which it has been influenced by 'Interiorism'.

See also: architects; architecture; design

Further reading

Moldoveanu, M. (1996) *Barcelona: Architectures of Exuberance*, Barcelona: Lunwerg (an overview of different periods and styles, richly illustrated with photographs by the author).

MIHAIL MOLDOVEANU

Interviú

Interviú is a highly successful weekly magazine which combines soft pornography with by and large serious reporting on a wide range of issues. It offers a combination of appeals which, in western Europe at least, seems to exist only in Spain.

Interviú belongs to the Zeta publishing group, and was launched in 1976, coinciding with a particular period of Spanish political and cultural history known commonly as *el destape*, an almost untranslatable term which can mean either 'taking off' or 'uncorking the bottle' (see also **pornography**). This period was a direct reaction to the repressive attitude of the Franco regime to anything relating to sex, and brought a relatively short-lived but fairly intense surge of interest in pornography and indeed nudity in general. The effects of *el destape* can still be felt even in good quality Spanish magazines today, where pictures of at least partly naked women (and less frequently men) are much more likely to appear than they are in equivalent publications elsewhere in Europe.

While nudity will normally be introduced into other mainstream magazines within the framework of articles on tourism, fashion or so on, *Interviú*'s particular strategy consists in being entirely open about its pornographic content, regularly featuring a naked model on its front pages, and promising viewers two soft-porn photo-features in every issue. While some might argue that there is no such thing as 'tasteful' pornography, however soft, it is fair to say that *Interviú* avoids the more contrived poses often adopted by models in magazines from the harder end of the soft-porn industry. As far as *Interviú* is concerned, pubic hair and bosoms are in, but genitalia are definitely out.

Alongside its two regular soft-porn features, *Interviú* includes articles covering an astonishing range of issues, from the social to the political to the cultural. Nor are these articles – nor the adverts which accompany them – aimed at an exclusively male readership, since they can cover, for example, the advantages of breast milk as opposed to formula or various fashions for expectant mothers. Leading political figures will often allow themselves to be interviewed by, or otherwise feature in, the magazine, knowing that it will do nothing to harm their reputation.

Interviú is a complex cultural product, and can only be understood against the backdrop of the repressive sexual politics of the Franco regime and the subsequent free-for-all of *el destape*. It unabashedly disseminates very soft pornography to a primarily – but by no means exclusively – male readership without the fumbling embarrassment of top-shelf pre-sealed 'classic' soft-porn publications, and, by providing reasonably serious coverage of current issues, allows the reader to claim, not entirely mendaciously, that he (or even she) has bought it primarily on its journalistic merits. It shuns the pseudo-intellectual pretensions of American publications such as *Playboy*, and at the same time avoids the truly tacky feel of down-market soft-porn publications in a number of other European countries. It is no doubt frowned upon by a number of sectors of Spanish society, but there are no immediate prospects of a decline in its fortunes.

HUGH O'DONNELL

Iñíguez, Manuel

b. 1948, Pamplona (Navarre)

Architect

Working in partnership with Alberto Ustarroz (also born in Pamplona in 1948) Iñíguez teaches at the School of Architecture in San Sebastián, which was founded in 1977 with the mission of improving architectural practice in the region. Iñíguez and Ustarroz have made a distinguished contribution to this enterprise, which won them the first European Prize for Urban Renewal awarded by the Brussels Architectural Foundation. The regionalism displayed in their early projects has gradually been replaced by a tendency towards rationalism. Their best known work is the conversion of an old rural building into a restaurant (1980, Cordobilla, Navarre), a harmonious blend of restoration and modernization. Another notable building of theirs is the town hall at Lesaca (1987, Navarre).

See also: architects; architecture

MIHAIL MOLDOVEANU

J

Janeiro, Jesús

b. 1974, Ubrique

Matador ('Jesulín de Ubrique')

Having taken his ***alternativa*** aged 16 in 1990, Jesulín soon gained an unrivalled popularity, not least among his female contemporaries. Less admired by traditional ***aficionados***, Jesulín nevertheless established new records for the number of ***corridas*** fought in a season: 153 in 1994 and 161 in 1995.

See also: bullfighting

IAN CAMPBELL ROSS

Janés, Clara

b. 1940, Barcelona

Writer

Although of a **Catalan** publishing family, Janés writes poetry, novels and essays largely in Spanish. She has lived abroad extensively and translates from several central European languages. Her studies of comparative literature enhance the cosmopolitan, cultured ambience of her writing. Existentialist, anguished and introspective in poetry collections including *Las estrellas vencidas* (Conquered Stars) (1964), *Límite humano* (Human Limitations) (1973) and *Libro de alienaciones* (Book of Alienations) (1980), she introduces increasingly frank eroticism in *Kampa* (1986), *Eros* (1981) and *Creciente fértil* (Fertile Crescent) (1989). *Desintegración* (1969) and *Los caballos del sueño* (Dream Horses) (1989) are major 'generational' novels.

Further reading

Pérez, J. (1991) 'The Novels of a Poet: Clara Janés', in L. González del Valle and J. Baena (eds) *Critical Essays on the Literatures of Spain and Spanish America*, pp. 197–207 (a special number of *Anales de la Literatura Española Contemporánea* which compares portraits of Janés' generation written three decades apart).

—— (1994) 'Clara Janés', in *Twentieth Century Spanish Poets: Second Series*, ed. J.P. Winfield, vol. 134 of the *Dictionary of Literary Biography*, pp. 205–12 (panorama of life and works to 1992, emphasizing poetry).

JANET PÉREZ

'JESULÍN DE UBRIQUE' *see* Janeiro, Jesús

Jiménez Lozano, José

b. 1930, Luaga (Avila)

Writer

This journalist, novelist and historian specializing in ecclesiastical topics possesses a uniquely personal accent, a voice of tolerant, dispassionate equilibrium in treating Spain's spiritual schism (fanaticism versus anticlericalism). As editor of the venerable Valladolid daily, *El Norte de Castilla*, he followed novelist Miguel **Delibes**, whom he cites as a significant antecedent and model. He accepted the challenge of writing objectively on highly emotional, controversial matters – from religious freedom to the crisis of church authority, conflicts between church and state, satanic cults and inquisitorial persecutions – in response to Vatican II's aspirations towards social justice which divided the Spanish church between its traditional, conservative hierarchy and liberal younger priests, alienating official Spanish Catholicism from Rome and providing the conflictive context of his writings. The essay, *Meditación española sobre la libertad religiosa* (Spanish Meditation on Religious Freedom) (1966), and historical fiction including *Historia de un otoño* (Autumnal History) (1971), dramatizing the eighteenth century struggle of Jansenists and Jesuits plus many articles collected in *La ronquera de Fray Luis y otras inquisiciones* (Friar Luis' Hoarseness and Other Inquisitions) (1973) reflect these themes, as does his protracted series of columns in the Barcelona weekly *Destino*. These examine the fortunes of Erasmus in Spain, analyse ideas of Pascal, pay tribute to Cardinal Newman, discuss Galdós' thesis novels with understanding, and meditate upon the singular nature of Spanish Catholicism. Witchcraft and superstition, sexuality and challenges to faith, implications of space travel for Christianity, similarities between St Francis and the hippies inspire other essays. Among his most fascinating writings are those on the history of 'civil' burial in Spain, reflecting the profound intolerance that segregated the unorthodox from 'true believers' even in death: *Los cementerios civiles y la heterodoxia española* (Civil Cemeteries and Spanish Heterodoxy) and *Sobre judíos, moriscos y conversos* (Concerning Jews, Moors and Converts) (second expanded edition 1982).

The historical novel *El sambenito* (The Saffron Tunic) (1972) examines the Inquisition's last years from perspectives of friends and relatives of the condemned Pablo de Olavide, whose guilt is doubtful but whom no one dares defend. In *La salamandra* (The Salamander) (1973) two geriatric villagers, thrown together in an asylum, reminisce about their past, recalling six decades of events significantly marked by ideological conflict. Religious themes also appear in the novel *Duelo en la casa grande* (Mourning in the Big House) (1982) and *Parábolas y circunloquios de Rabí Isaac Ben Yehuda* (Rabbi Isaac Ben Yehuda's Parables and Circumlocutions) (1985). Further orientalism and still more ancient settings appear in *Sara de Ur* (Sarah of Ur) (1989) recounting the Egyptian travels of a spoiled young Chaldean noblewoman. Short story collections include *El santo de mayo* (May's Saint) (1976), tales of varied themes and techniques set in earlier times which establish parallels between remote events and present problems, and *El grano de maíz rojo* (The Grain of Red Corn) (1989), some thirty stories varying in language and setting but united by their peculiar outlook, which won the 1989 National Critics Prize for Narrative in Spanish.

Further reading

Higuero, F.J. (1993) 'Los códigos metanarrativos en *Los grandes relatos* de José Jiménez Lozano', *Ojáncano* 8: 52–68 (studies narrative and metatexts in Jiménez Lozano's so-called *episodios nacionales*).

Sherzer, W.M. (1992). 'José Jiménez Lozano: Tale Telling in Old Castile', *Revista Hispánica Moderna* 45, 2: 310–17 (draws parallels with social history, emphasizing archaism, nostalgia).

JANET PÉREZ

Joglars, Els

It was Els Joglars who first put Catalan performance groups on the international map. Els Joglars were formed in 1962, and since 1966 have been led by the charismatic Albert Boadella. Like other performance groups and exponents of the ***Nova Cançó***, Els Joglars took a radically anti-Francoist stance in their earlier work. Ironically, they had greater problems with **censorship** after the death of Franco than during Francoism. In 1977, when censorship was apparently over, Els Joglars performed their satire against torture, *La torna* (Left Overs), which was a homage to Salvador Puig Antich, the anarchist executed by the Francoist government in 1974. The production caused the imprisonment of some members of the group (including Albert Boadella) and the enforced exile of others. The resultant protests, both inside and outside theatrical circles all over Spain, were part of a wider struggle to establish normality in the wake of Francoism.

Some of Els Joglars' shows have caused offence amongst conservative sections of Spanish society. An example is *Teledeum*, which provoked widespread protest because of its satirical treatment of the Catholic Church. Although they have asserted Catalan national identity in their work, Els Joglars have also attacked and offended conservative Catalan nationalists.

Els Joglars have been innovative in technical as well as in socio-political questions. They included mime in a number of their early shows. European and American performance groups were influential in this respect, but it was also a way of circumventing the limitations imposed by censorship. Gesture and physical movement are an integral part of Boadella's conception of the actor's art, and, like Grotowsky and others, he makes huge physical demands upon his actors. Music has also been included in Els Joglars' shows, as in *Mary d'Ous* (Egg Mary), which was constructed like a musical canon. In the 1970s, Els Joglars worked closely with the innovative Catalan set designers Iago Pericot and Fabià Puigserver. The latter was responsible for the sets of *Alias Serrallonga* and *M-7 Catalònia*.

Like other Catalan performance groups, including El Tricicle and La Cubana, Els Joglars have worked in television. Among their shows is a parody of the documentary genre for TV3 (Catalan Television) entitled *Som una meravella* (We Are Simply Marvellous). Their *Ya semos europeos* (sic) (Now, Let's Be European) is a similar series for Spanish television.

See also: Comediants, Els; Fura dels Baus, la; performing arts

Further reading

Ayesa, G. (1978) *Joglars, una història*, Barcelona: La Gaya Ciencia (a history of the early years of the group).

Bartomeus, A. (d.) (1987) *Mester de joglaria: Els Joglars 25 anys*, Barcelona: Edicions 62.

Boadella, A. (1985) *Els Joglars, 23 años, mayoría de edad*, Madrid: Centro de Documentación Teatral (evaluation by the founder of the group).

Saumell, M. (1996) 'Performance Groups in Catalonia', in D. George and J. London (eds) *An Introduction to Contemporary Catalan Theatre*, Sheffield: Anglo-Catalan Society (the only full-length study of the phenomenon in English).

DAVID GEORGE

journalism

Because of the operation of **censorship** during the Franco regime, the profession of journalism was seen by the authorities as a virtual arm of the state apparatus. Significantly, one of the earliest Schools of Journalism in Spain was at the University of Navarre, a private foundation controlled by the right-wing Catholic organization **Opus Dei**. Though some courageous journalists risked fines and imprisonment for publishing news which the regime wished to suppress, in practice the pressure to conform was very powerful, particularly in view of the so-called *consignas*, official instructions which obliged editors to publish items emanating from the Ministry of Information and Tourism.

Nevertheless, the closing years of the regime saw the beginnings of a more independent, liberal kind of journalism, represented notably by ***Cambio 16***, founded in 1972, and committed from its inception to democratic principles, a stance which earned it frequent penalties, including suppression and alteration of articles on, for example, the elections for the **vertical syndicates**, or the capital charges against members of **ETA** in 1975. With the launching of *El* ***País*** in 1976, the standard of journalism in Spain rapidly began to be assimilated to the best practice followed in other democratic countries: serious, critical and informed, with due attention paid to international affairs, the economy and cultural matters. *El País* in particular provided a forum for intensive discussion of the kind of democratic society which it hoped would emerge from the dismantling of the apparatus of the dictatorship.

With the appearance of *El* ***Mundo*** in 1989, a new style of investigative journalism was inaugurated, more combative and tenacious in uncovering evidence of corruption in government circles. *El Mundo* kept up unremitting pressure on the socialist

PSOE administration over alleged influence-peddling, financial corruption, and, most notoriously, its involvement in the **GAL** affair. From the mid-1990s, however, rumours of contacts between the editor and the disgraced banker Mario **Conde** raised questions about the paper's independence of vested interests.

El Mundo, indeed, illustrates one of the special features of journalism in Spain in the last quarter of the twentieth century, which in turn is a function of the rapidity of political change since 1975. Inevitably, the system of checks and balances which in other countries has evolved over a longer period of time is less robust in Spain, particularly with regard to institutional constraints on the power of the executive, and protection for the independence of the judiciary. In default of effective checks and balances, the function of control has been assumed by journalists, who consequently wield considerable political influence, particularly since the profession is dominated by university graduates, who see themselves as an intellectual élite writing for the other élites who make up the political class. The absence of effective libel legislation, or laws protecting privacy, often means that investigative journalism takes the form of personalized attacks on individuals. Moreover, there is no developed concept of 'contempt of court' to prevent what has been described as *instrucción paralela* ('parallel depositions'), that is, the open and detailed discussion of legal cases in the media, particularly the press, while court proceedings are in train.

There is no doubt that press freedom has made a crucial contribution to the evolution of a democratic culture in Spain. Further development will depend both on the willingness of journalists to exercise a measure of self-discipline and also on the readiness of the government to relax its control of the sources of information. It remains the case, even under democracy, that the largest news agency in the Spanish-speaking world, **Agencia EFE**, is owned by the Spanish government, and its editorial line reflects the priorities of the party in power.

See also: media; press; press ownership; radio; television

EAMONN RODGERS

Juan Arbó, Sebastián

b. 1902, Sant Carles de la Ràpita (Tarragona); d. 1984, Barcelona

Writer

Exemplifying the dilemma of bilinguals pressurized into using only Spanish by the Franco regime, Arbó wrote several novels in **Catalan** before 1936, published another simultaneously in both his languages in the 1940s and concentrated on Spanish from 1948 to the mid-1960s, before reverting to his mother tongue.

Educated largely through reading books borrowed from the family for which his parents worked as servants, Arbó's early writings describe the hardships of life on the land near the mouth of the river Ebro, where he was born. *Terres de l'Ebre* (Lands of the Ebro) (1932), the dramatic story of an obsessive worker whose wife is drowned, whose son abandons him to migrate to the city and who, on being evicted from his land, reacts so insanely that he is locked up and hangs himself, is typical of this first period, showing the misery of humans in conflict with a desolate, hostile environment, where loneliness, hunger and tragedy are daily realities.

Published in two languages, *Tino Costa* (Tino Costa) (1948), a harsh tale of passionate love, similarly ends in violence when the protagonist kills an innocent girl and is stoned to death by the villagers, after which his mother goes insane and his lover kills herself. *Sobre las piedras grises* (On the Grey Stones) (1948), winner of the **Nadal Prize**, initiates the author's Spanish phase. Less violent but no less pessimistic than his previous fiction, it depicts a simple civil servant who is cheated out of a small inheritance, humiliated at work and then unfairly dismissed. The only positive events in his sad life are his wedding to an admirable girl, attracted by his extreme innocence, and his daughter's marriage to a reformed anarchist whom her parents had saved and harboured when he was on the run from the police. The novel received little critical acclaim, mainly because of its lack of verisimilitude and the protagonist's unrealistic naïvety.

Considered, on the contrary, to be his finest work, *Nuevas y viejas andanzas de Martín de Caretas* (New and Old Adventures of Martin from Caretas)

(1959) is a charming picaresque tale of an innocently mischievous child's early life and journey from his native village to Barcelona, describing various adventures along the way to the big city. With *Narracions del Delta* (Stories from the Delta) (1965) and other late writings, the author returns to Catalan and to themes of his childhood. Apart from his fiction and countless contributions to prestigious newspapers, Arbó is known as the biographer of Cervantes, Pío Baroja, Oscar Wilde and the nineteenth-century tragic priest Jacint Verdaguer, only the last of whom is directly reflected in his own writings.

Further reading

Alborg, J.L. (1962) *Hora actual de la novela española*, Madrid: Taurus, vol. 2, pp. 269–88 (a critical survey of Arbó's work up to 1959).

Arnau, C. (1984) 'Prologue' to *Terres de l'Ebre*, Barcelona: Edicions 62 (a Catalan overview of Arbó's work).

LEO HICKEY

Juan Carlos I

b. 1938, Rome

King of Spain

Juan Carlos de Borbón is the grandson of the last reigning monarch, Alfonso XIII, who left Spain on the declaration of the Republic in 1931, and abdicated in 1941 in favour of his son, Don Juan, Count of Barcelona. Don Juan was known to favour a restoration of the monarchy in its constitutional, pre-Civil War form, which meant that his relations with Franco were at best cool and often became strained. By an agreement reached in 1948 between Don Juan and Franco, Juan Carlos was sent to be educated in Spain, while his father continued to live in exile in Portugal. Don Juan would have preferred his son, on completing his secondary education, to go to a university elsewhere in Europe, but Franco wished him to have a military education. Juan Carlos accordingly spent four years at the Military Academy in Zaragoza, and graduated in 1959 with commissions in each of the three services. In 1962, he married Princess Sophia, daughter of King Paul and Queen Frederika of Greece.

The 1947 Succession Law had defined Spain as a monarchy governed by a regent, and had envisaged an eventual restoration of the monarchy on Franco's demise, with the future Head of State having very considerable powers. It had also given Franco the right to nominate his successor, though by the time he was seventy in 1962 he had still not done so. It became obvious to the public, however, throughout the 1960s that Franco was grooming Juan Carlos to assume the role, which earned the prince considerable unpopularity on some of his travels around Spain when, on occasion, he and Sophia were pelted with overripe fruit. Eventually, in July 1969, Franco publicly nominated Juan Carlos as his successor, significantly withholding the title Prince of Asturias, traditionally held by the heir to the throne, and conferring instead the new title of Prince of Spain. This was to reinforce the point he had made both in article 11 of the Succession Law and in many public speeches, that the institution which succeeded him would not be a restoration of the previous constitutional monarchy, but a new one created by him (an *instauración* rather than a *restauración*).

The succession arrangements were not calculated to raise expectations of greater democratization after Franco, particularly when the appointment of the hard-line **Carrero Blanco** as Head of Government suggested that Franco's intention was that Juan Carlos would continue to be controlled by a military strongman when he acceded to the throne. Although Juan Carlos was not widely credited with much political acumen in the last years of the regime, and though the assassination of Carrero Blanco in 1973 removed any hope of the survival of Francoism after Franco, the clear judgement and strength of character which Juan Carlos revealed after his accession suggest that he would not have allowed himself to be manipulated by a military hardliner. In any case, the Organic Law of the State (1967) had not only reinforced the succession provisions of the 1947 legislation, but had conferred wide executive functions on the Head of State, which in the event Juan Carlos was to use creatively to bring about reform. His choice of Torcuato **Fernández-**

Miranda as President of the Cortes made possible the appointment as Prime Minister of Adolfo **Suárez**, who was the key agent in the transition to democracy.

Though crucial during the period 1975–8, most of these powers were considerably watered down by the **constitution of 1978**, leaving the Spanish Head of State with even more limited functions, in certain respects, than the British monarch. Official documents are not issued in the King's name alone, but have to be countersigned by the Prime Minister or other relevant member of the cabinet. The role of Commander-in-Chief of the Armed Forces, however, became much more than purely ceremonial when on the night of the attempted coup of 23 February 1981 (see also ***Tejerazo, El***), Juan Carlos appeared on television in uniform and confirmed his commitment to the constitution, having previously telephoned all the regional commanders and reminded them of their oath of allegiance.

The King's resolute defence of democracy is probably the most significant reason for the popularity which he and the royal family continue to enjoy. Over and above this, however, their lifestyle and general demeanour in public have enabled them to avoid alienating public opinion in a country where anti-monarchism, though nearly always a minority view, was nevertheless held, at various times in the past, with vehement conviction. Even before his accession, Juan Carlos decided not to move to the grandiose Oriente Palace, which is only used for large state occasions, but to stay in the more modest Zarzuela, the house he and Sophia had occupied since their marriage. The royal family pay taxes like other citizens, and the informality cultivated on public appearances, especially by Juan Carlos, together with his sense of humour, have ensured a high degree of personal loyalty and affection from the populace at large, whatever the long-term prospects for the institution of monarchy as such.

See also: history; monarchy; politics

Further reading

Heywood, P. (1995) *The Government and Politics of Spain*, London: Macmillan (see pp. 83–8 for a lucid brief account of the role of monarchy in Spain).

Hooper, J. (1995) *The New Spaniards*, Harmondsworth: Penguin (chapter 7 is an excellent historical contextualization of Juan Carlos' accession, and of how he is perceived by the public).

Newton, M.T with Donaghy, P.J. (1997) *Institutions of Modern Spain: A Political and Economic Guide* (chapter 3 is the best account available of the evolution of the monarchy before and after the constitution).

EAMONN RODGERS

Juan March Foundation

Founded in 1955 by the financier Juan March Ordinas the foundation exists primarily to promote scientific education, by funding post-doctoral fellowships in Spain and abroad, visits to Spain by leading scientists, international seminars and prizes. The Juan March Institute for Study and Research established in 1986 comprises the Centre for Advanced Study in the Social Sciences and the Centre for International Meetings on Biology. The Foundation also sponsors a wide range of cultural events including **art exhibitions** and concerts, and publishes book reviews, news bulletins, reports and summaries of research. In the area of social assistance it makes donations to recognized relief and charitable institutions.

See also: education and research; foundations; science

EAMONN RODGERS

Jujol, Josep Maria

b. 1879, Tarragona; d. 1949, Barcelona

Architect

Josep Maria Jujol, an architect and artist who worked mainly in and around Barcelona and Tarragona, is especially noted for his brilliant association with Antoni **Gaudí**, first as a favourite pupil and later as full-time collaborator. His own independent work remains little known, though it shows clear evidence of his individual talent. This is partly due to the prestige which surrounds Gaudí, but partly also because by the time Jujol was practising alone, the great period of **Modernism** was over, and the taste of the public had changed. Jujol remained the only significant creative architect who was trying to remain faithful to his modernist inheritance while at the same time pioneering new forms of expression. This unusual decision meant that he remained rather marginalized, being passed over for prestigious commissions and working with very limited resources, by contrast with the more lavish provision characteristic of Modernism. On the other hand, the artistic originality which Gaudí so much admired in him reached new heights precisely because of these unfavourable conditions. Richness achieved in poverty is the paradox of all Jujol's work. The fact that he was also a painter greatly influenced his creations, and artists such as **Miró** and **Dalí** recognized in him an inspirational source of the first order.

Other distinctive features of Jujol's work are his liking for collage and the unusual juxtaposition of materials, the use of strong colour, reworkings of Gothic style, which often produced very complex compositions, and a passion for intervening in his capacity as an artist in his architectural constructions.

The compositions in *trencadís* (a collage of pottery shards) on the famous Parc Güell and the paintings on the panelling of the Cathedral of Palma de Mallorca are the foremost results of his association with Gaudí. Notable independent works are the Torre de la Creu (1913), Can Negre (1915) and Casa Planells (1923) in Barcelona and its environs. Tarragona and the surrounding area also boast some very interesting buildings by him, the most notable being the Teatro del Patronato Obrero (Workers' Foundation Theatre) (1908), Casa Bofarull (1914), the Vistabella church (1918) and the Montferri shrine (1926). Though unjustly neglected, Jujol's work is an important legacy of the avant-garde in twentieth century art, and some of his preoccupations are found again in the conceptualist art of the 1960s.

See also: architects; architecture

Further reading

Loyer, F. (1991) *L'art nouveau en Catalogne*, Paris: Biblio. Arts, Le Septième Fou.

Moldoveanu, M. (1996) *Barcelona: Architectures of Exuberance*, Barcelona: Lunwerg (an overview of different periods and styles, richly illustrated with photographs by the author).

Jujol i Gilbert, J.M. (1989) *Josep Maria Jujol, Arquitecto, 1879–1949*, Barcelona: Colegio de Arquitectos de Cataluña (a collective symposium on Jujol by contemporary practitioners and scholars).

MIHAIL MOLDOVEANU

K

Karina

Spain

Singer

Karina was the leading female vocalist in Spanish pop music during the second half of the 1960s and the early 1970s. She dominated the charts and records sales, through a solid repertoire of cover versions of well-known European and American songs and compositions by the most prestigious Spanish songwriters. Her greatest hits include 'Abergavenny' (La fiesta), 'Little Arrows' (Las flechas del amor), 'El baúl de los recuerdos' (The Chest of Memories), 'Romeo y Julieta' (Romeo and Juliet). She won over Spanish audiences with her sweet, angelic, ingenuous air and became the ideal girlfriend for adolescents of her generation. Karina's fame waned in the 1980s, although periodically she performs her old hits as a last act of nostalgia.

See also: rock and pop

FERNANDO DELGADO

KIO

The Kuwait Investment Office became the symbol both of the boom in the Spanish economy in the 1980s and of the prevalence of **corruption**. KIO was the largest foreign investor in Spain, via a holding company called Grupo Torras. It began in 1984 to buy into paper manufacturing, chemicals, food production, real estate and banking, and its empire was said to be worth 700,000m pesetas. By late 1992, however, Torras had debts of 250,000m pesetas, of which 150,000m was owed to KIO itself. KIO's suspension of payments in December 1992 was reported at the time to be the largest ever in Spain. KIO estimated that its total losses in Spain between 1984 and 1992 amounted to 450,000m pesetas, and accused the former director of Torras, Javier **de la Rosa**, of maladministration.

EAMONN RODGERS

kiosk literature

Literatura de quiosco is a phrase used since the late nineteenth century to designate a type of popular light reading-matter sold from kiosks in streets, parks and railway stations. In the second half of the twentieth century, the phrase simply meant literature with a mass appeal, independently of where it was sold, though street kiosks continue to be one of the main retail outlets, along with stationery shops, department stores, and newsagents in stations and airports. As with other aspects of contemporary cultural life, however, traditional distinctions have become blurred, and while escapist romantic novels predominate in this sector of the market, it is also a means of disseminating 'serious' literature, both classical and contemporary, through the increasing number of pocket and paperback series.

Much of the output of this kind of literature is targeted at young readers. A survey carried out by the Instituto Nacional de Estadística (INE –

National Statistical Institute) and the **Ministry of Culture** in 1987 suggested that the sector of the public which reads most is the age group between 14 and 24, that this cohort is more likely to read books than newspapers, and that its reading is a leisure-time rather than a functional activity. In the bottom half of this sample (14–19 years), 70 percent read books. When questioned about their preferences for different kinds of novel, 84 percent reported having read adventure novels, 83 percent comic-strip books, 66 percent **detective fiction**, 59 percent **science fiction**, and 55 percent humorous novels. Romantic novels and novels by contemporary writers were read by 39 percent of respondents, and classic novels by 38 percent. In non-fiction, 45 percent reported having read practical manuals or books about hobbies, 43 percent poetry, 30 percent biography, 21 percent art and 18 percent discursive prose. Though publishers have not had much success with collections and series devised specifically for this young clientele (largely because potential readers tend to think of them as 'children's literature'), many contemporary authors have managed to appeal to this readership by careful choice of subject and style (see also **novel**).

Kiosk literature is also the main source of translations of foreign best-sellers, with Agatha Christie heading the list. Other popular authors include Jules Verne, Jane Austen, the Brontë sisters, Conan Doyle, Stephen King, John le Carré, J.R.R. Tolkien, Stanley Kubrick, John Steinbech and Frederick Forsyth. Perhaps surprisingly, many editions of Shakespeare are also sold through this outlet.

Romantic novels are still very popular, though the genre of the ***novela rosa***, which had its heyday in the 1920s and 1930s, has declined in popular esteem. Nevertheless, reprints of works from that period are still sold in substantial numbers, and the romantic novel owes much for its survival to the enormous popularity of the works of Corín **Tellado**.

See also: comics; *fotonovelas*; pornography; publishing; readership

Further reading

Hooper, J. (1995) *The New Spaniards*, Harmondsworth: Penguin (chapters 21 and 24 give an excellent overview of the cultural changes of the 1970s and 1980s).

CARLOS ÁLVAREZ ARAGÜÉS

L

La Cierva y de Hoces, Ricardo

b. 1926, Madrid

Historian

After taking his first degree in Rome, and doctorates in Chemistry and Letters at the University of Madrid, La Cierva entered the Official School of Journalism. As professor of Geography and Contemporary History at the Complutense University of Madrid, he developed a specialism in the history of contemporary Spain, with particular reference to the Civil War, and came to be regarded as virtually the official historian of Francoism, with studies like *Historia de la Guerra Civil española* (History of the Spanish Civil War) (1969), *Francisco Franco, un siglo de historia* (Francisco Franco, a Century of History) (1973), and *1939, agonía y victoria* (1939, Agony and Victory) (1989). In the final years of the Franco regime, he was associated with a reformist group within the administration, and was one of those who resigned in sympathy with the sacked Minister of Information, Pío Cabanillas, in October 1974.

La Cierva's later career is an interesting example of the fluid nature of political loyalties during the transition to democracy. After the elections of 1977, he became a member of the UCD parliamentary coalition led by Adolfo Suárez, whose nomination as Prime Minister by King Juan Carlos he had described in 1976, in a memorable newspaper headline, as 'a huge mistake'. He served as senator for Murcia from 1977 to 1979, and sat as a member of the lower house between 1979 and 1982. During the second of these periods, he was appointed Minister of Culture, an event which was greeted with considerable surprise, given the fact that he had not only been an apologist for the Franco regime, but had worked for the censorship apparatus, acquiring in the process a well-merited reputation for severity. He was particularly notorious for creating difficulties for writers who wished to publish on the Civil War from a point of view sympathetic to the Republican side.

EAMONN RODGERS

La Iglesia, Eloy de

b. 1944, Zarauz (Guipúzcoa)

Filmmaker

Director of *El pico* (The Shoot Up), the box-office success of 1983, Eloy de la Iglesia is known for his no-holds-barred films, such as *Los placeres ocultos* (Hidden Pleasures) (1976), *El diputado* (The Deputy) (1978), *Navajeros* (Knife Fighters) (1980) and *Colegas* (Mates) (1982), about prostitution, homosexuality, drug addiction and the whole seamier side of modern culture.

EAMONN RODGERS

labour law

Labour law was consolidated as a **legal system** in Spain during the period of Primo de Rivera's Dictatorship (1923–9) and the Second Republic

(1931–6). The constitution of the Second Republic (1931) provided the foundation for a systematic approach to labour law by enshrining the basic principles of free association and the right to organize trade unions, and adopted a progressive approach to certain economic and social rights. In the spirit of this constitution, two important pieces of legislation were enacted in 1931: the *Ley de Contrato de Trabajo* (Employment Contract Act), and the *Ley de Jornada Máxima Legal* (Maximum Legal Working Hours Act).

During the Civil War and the Franco regime further amendments to the labour legislation were approved, especially with regard to **social security**, working hours, **holiday** entitlement and employment contracts. However, the most significant amendments to labour legislation occurred after Franco's death, as a result of the political and social reforms introduced during the transition to democracy. The 1931 *Ley de Contrato de Trabajo* was supplemented by two Industrial Relations Acts: the *Ley de Relaciones Laborales* (Law of Labour Relations) of 1976, and the *Real Decreto-Ley de Relaciones de Trabajo* (Royal Decree on Labour Relations) of 1977, which attempted to establish the legal framework for labour disputes and strikes. Likewise, the *Ley Reguladora del Derecho de Asociación Sindical* (Trade Union Rights Act) of 1977 provided for a restructuring of the **trade unions** system.

The **constitution of 1978** laid down the principles of a new legal framework for **industrial relations**, by ratifying the right to full employment, social security, professional training and promotion, health and hygiene at work, paid holidays and the participation of employees in the company. The constitution also protects the right to join a union, to strike, to enter into **collective agreements**, to earn a minimum wage and, lastly, to exercise professional freedom.

These provisions, together with Spain's membership of the EU, have produced a set of regulations which control all aspects of legal-industrial relations, and which are embodied in the following acts: the *Estatuto de los Trabajadores* (Workers' Statute, 1995); the *Ley Orgánica de Libertad Sindical* (Law of Trade Union Freedom, 1985, which regulates the organization and structure of trade unions); the *Ley de Procedimiento Laboral* (Law of Labour Procedure, 1995, which regulates requirements and procedures in industrial matters); the *Ley de la Seguridad Social* (Law of Social Security, 1994); and two very innovative laws, the *Ley de Prevención de Accidentes Laborales* (Law for the Prevention of Accidents at Work, 1995) and the *Ley de Empresas de Trabajo Temporal* (Law for the Regulation of Temporary Work Agencies, 1994). In addition, the **Constitutional Tribunal** has fulfilled an important role in revising the existing labour law to bring it into line with constitutional guarantees on fundamental rights.

See also: CEOE; CC OO; Francoist culture; vertical sydicates

Further reading

de Miguel, A. (1994) *La Sociedad Española, 1993–94. Informe Sociológico de la Universidad Complutense*, Madrid: Alianza Editorial (see pp. 623–75 for a sociological study of the structure of labour, membership of trade unions, working hours, work conditions and attitudes to work).

Heywood, P. (1995) *The Government and Politics of Spain*, London: Macmillan (chapters 10 and 11 give an excellent overview of the current state of the labour market).

Montoya Melgar, A. (ed.) (1995) *Enciclopedia Jurídica Básica*, Madrid: Editorial Civitas (volume 2 contains ample information about the Spanish legal system, covering aspects such as: labour law, working hours, retirement, National Insurance, employment and workers' right to strike).

GEMMA BELMONTE TALERO

labour market

Since the mid-1970s the Spanish labour market has been characterized by high unemployment and a virtually continuous rise in the labour force. Whereas the employed population has changed little overall (except for normal fluctuations associated with boom and recession), remaining around the 12 million mark, the active population (those in work or seeking work) has risen from 12.5 million to 15.5 million. This increase is largely explained by two factors: the baby boom of the 1960s, which brought increased numbers to the labour market in the 1980s, and a sharply increased tendency among women to look for employment. Thus, the female participation rate (workforce as a percentage of the population of working age), which stood at about 23 percent at the beginning of the 1970s, had risen to 36 percent by 1995, the bulk of the increase having taken place in the 1980s. Between 1980 and 1994 the male workforce went up by about 540,000 and the female workforce by about 2,100,000. The Spanish economy has been unable to create sufficient jobs to absorb all the additional job seekers. This is not a wholly new phenomenon, because the very low unemployment during the 'miracle' years of the 1960s is in part explained by the substantial number of Spaniards who emigrated at a time when finding a job in the powerful economies of Europe was comparatively easy. When the European economic crisis of the mid-1970s forced many of them out of their jobs, Spain found herself with inbound waves of migrants returning to a country in the throes of the deepest industrial recession in her history. Unemployment was made worse by this return migration, although some migrants had a cushion of accumulated savings or redundancy monies that enabled them to open small businesses. Both agriculture and industry shed large numbers of jobs during the crisis-ridden years of 1975–84 (about 840,000 and one million respectively). In agriculture this was part of a long-term trend; in industry and construction it was the result of poor competitiveness once the energy price increases began to bite. Despite rigid labour laws making dismissal of employees exceedingly difficult, redundancies were inevitable if any Spanish industry was going to survive, something which was recognized by the government in their programme of ***reconversión industrial***: much of the government-subsidized restructuring aid went to meet the costs associated with redundancy and early retirement compensation.

The unemployment problem caused by agricultural mechanization and industrial restructuring at a time of return migration and increasing job-seekers would have been even worse but for the sustained growth of the **services** sector of the economy, which continued to create jobs throughout the crisis years with an average yearly growth of 0.5 percent, well short of what was needed to compensate for losses in the other sectors, but clearly indicative of a marked trend in employment patterns. This process of tertiarization is a key characteristic of the contemporary Spanish economy and therefore of the labour market. From employing about 30 percent of the labour force in the 1960s, the services sector has gone on to employ 60 percent in the 1990s, with the largest proportional increase occurring in the 1980s, but even during the years of **industrial development** in the 1960s it was the tertiary sector that showed the highest increase in employment, a difference that became far more marked in the years after 1979 when industry was subjected to a rapid slimming down process. Later still, during the recovery phase of 1985–90, three times as many jobs were created in services as in industry (972,800 and 325,000 respectively). In effect what has happened is that since 1960 there has been a massive transfer of manpower from agricultural activity to employment in the services via, to some extent, a temporary stopover in the industrial sector during the boom years of 1960–73.

This shift from agriculture and industry to services has been accompanied by a greatly increased presence of the public sector in the labour market. Many of the new jobs were created in state-run services, so that whilst the private sector of the economy was contracting and shedding jobs, the public sector was expanding and creating them. The trend towards an ever-increasing presence of the public sector in the labour market came to an end following the escalating government deficit and the public expenditure crisis of the 1990s, but nevertheless the government's impact on the jobs market has been considerable. First, government spending clearly helped to contain the burgeoning unemployment problem by creating half-a-million jobs in Public Administration, Education, Health, Social Security and Sanitation. Second, whilst jobs were being lost in areas associated with the humbler, less skilled sectors of society (e.g. shop assistants, repairers or transport workers), they have by contrast been created in areas more generally associated with the higher skilled (e.g. teachers, health workers or administrators). Third, and consequentially, the labour market has become much kinder to the better educated and more highly trained and very much harsher to those who are poorly educated or unskilled. In this respect the change has been little short of dramatic: in 1970 the proportion of the employed who had post-compulsory educational qualifications was 6.5 percent for males and 5.9 percent for females; by 1991 the equivalent figures were 48 percent for males and 68.6 percent for females. The employment trend in favour of the more educated is unmistakeable.

The need to encourage job creation in the private sector has persuaded the government to introduce labour market reforms by dismantling the rigid Francoist labour laws that were thought to inhibit employers from taking on workers. The first package of measures came in 1984, when new labour legislation allowed firms to use part-time and temporary contracts more freely than before, as a result of which one-third of all employees are now on fixed-term contracts. This legislation, however, had no measurable impact on employment, in view of which further liberalizing measures were introduced in 1994 under the slogan of *flexibilización*. This greater flexibility is meant to allow firms to react more quickly to changes in the economic cycle. Reasons for both individual and collective dismissals are now much more broadly defined than before; severance payments have a maximum of one year's salary, provided the dismissal is for approved reasons, higher levels of compensation applying in cases of unfair dismissal; within certain constraints, an employer can impose geographical and functional redeployment on employees; temporary contracts may be extended beyond the previously permissible limits; part-time contracts no longer have stipulated hours or entitlement to the usual welfare benefits if below 12 hours per week; the qualifying age for apprenticeship contracts is raised from 20 to 25 and there is no compulsory compensation upon dismissal. Trades unions, whose agreement is no longer required on a variety of issues after emendation of the Workers' Statute, denounced these measures as a 'hire-and-fire' approach to labour and an attack on the rights of workers, but whatever the appropriateness of this approach to eliminating labour market inefficiencies, the fact remains that labour courts in Spain retain very significant powers and that dismissal costs remain comparatively high. Nor is it entirely clear whether curtailing restrictive union practices and reducing employee protection is a sufficient incentive to employers. Some recognition of this in official circles is indicated by a new emphasis on the importance of adequate training of the workforce to ensure the international competitiveness of Spanish firms.

Further reading

Chislett, W. (1996) *Spain 1996. The Central Hispano Handbook*, Madrid (chapter 1 gives a clear summary of recent developments).

De Miguel, A. (1992) *La sociedad española 1992–93*, Madrid: Alianza (chapter 8 is an interesting commentary on occupation based on the results of a survey).

Fundación FOESSA (1994) *V Informe sociológico sobre la situación social en España*, Madrid (a detailed sociological analysis of employment and unemployment).

Longhurst, C.A. (1995) 'The Spanish Labour Market: Recent Trends and Current Problems', in *Leeds Papers on Spain in Europe*, Leeds: Trinity and All Saints, pp. 9–37 (surveys broad developments from c. 1970 to 1994).

C.A. LONGHURST

Laforet Díaz, Carmen

b. 1921

Writer

Carmen Laforet burst upon the post-Civil War literary scene at the age of 23 with the novel *Andrea* (*Nada*), which won the Nadal Prize in 1944. Laforet's life spanned two radically different periods in Spanish cultural and political history. She experienced the freer social attitudes towards women that the Republic (1931–9) brought during her adolescent years in the Canary Islands. The end of the Civil War (1936–9), however, found her as a student in Barcelona, where she first experienced the backlash against women's freedom that the victorious Franco regime inspired.

Laforet's fiction, which includes four long

novels, seven novellas and a number of short stories, exemplifies the conflicting pressures caused by the abrupt shift from the liberal ambience of the 1920s and 1930s to the repression of the Franco regime. Laforet's first novel *Andrea* reflects these two worlds. The protagonist Andrea arrives in Barcelona from a Catalan village to live with relatives, whose formerly comfortable bourgeois lives have been disrupted by the war. The events of the household reflect the tensions and repression of post-Civil War Spain, while on the other hand Andrea's university friends and milieu capture some of the pre-war freedom and artistic promise. *Andrea* marked an important milestone in Spanish fiction; it was a model for treating the Civil War and Franco's Spain in an oblique way that could pass the censors, and it opened the doors for the large number of women writers who have now become part of the Spanish literary canon.

Shortly after the publication of *Andrea*, Laforet married the journalist Manuel Cerezales. The demands of motherhood (she has five children) and the unfavourable position of women during the 1940s and 1950s slowed Laforet's production, but she continued to publish until 1963 when, inexplicably, she stopped writing fiction. *La isla y los demonios* (The Island and the Devils) (1952) reflects the pre-war years Laforet spent in the Canary Islands and captures the more liberated milieu that allowed young girls to develop artistic talents. *La mujer nueva* (The New Woman) (1955) and *La insolación* (Sunstroke) (1963) both focus on post-War Spain and the restraints on men's and women's roles imposed by the Franco regime. Although *La mujer nueva* deals ostensibly with a personal religious (mystical) crisis that Laforet herself experienced in the early 1950s, the novel provides a general view of life in 1950s Spain – the pseudo-religiosity, the materialism, the lack of choices for women in society. *La insolación*, amazingly for its day, deals with the theme of homosexuality in a rigidly *machista* and patriarchal system.

Much of Laforet's fiction centres on personal freedom. Her work has much in common with French existentialism, which influenced European thought during the years she was writing.

See also: feminist writing; novel; women's writing

Major works

Laforet Díaz, C. (1945) *Nada* (*Andrea*), Barcelona: Destino.

—— (1952) *La isla y los demonios*, Barcelona: Destino.

—— (1955) *La mujer nueva*, Barcelona: Destino.

—— (1957) *Novelas I*, Barcelona: Planeta.

—— (1963) *La insolación*, Barcelona: Planeta.

Further reading

El Saffar, R. (1978) 'Structural and Thematic Tactics of Suppression in Carmen Laforet's *Nada*', *Symposium* 28: 119–29.

Johnson, R. (1981) *Carmen Laforet*, Boston, MA: Twayne (an accessible overview in English).

Ordóñez, E. (1976) 'Nada: Initiation into Bourgeois Patriarchy', in L.E. Davis and I.C. Tarán (eds) *The Analysis of Hispanic Texts: Current Trends in Methodology*, Jamaica, NY: Bilingual Press (a feminist reading of Laforet's major novel).

ROBERTA JOHNSON

'LAGOS, CONCHA' *see* Gutiérrez Torrero, Concepción

Laiglesia González, Álvaro de

b. 1922, San Sebastián; d. 1981, Manchester (England)

Writer

Gaining fame as a comic writer in the *tremendismo* movement of the 1940s, in which brutal realism and gratuitous violence predominated, Laiglesia served many years as the director of the weekly newspaper *La Codorniz*. He published more than thirty novels and collections of short stories, as well as collaborating on theatrical pieces, all in a comic vein. His writings are characterized by a humorous, agile style, and often ironically satirize social mores. Several pieces incorporate unconventional subject matter that ranges from Spain's tourism industry, heavily regulated during the Franco regime, to life in the hereafter. All of his works have enjoyed wide popular success, often having three or four printings the first year and going into some twenty editions. Laiglesia's career as a writer began early as he sent off narratives to children's magazines, and soon thereafter expanded to articles submitted to a humour periodical published in the Nationalist zone during the Spanish Civil War. He later served as a soldier and newspaper correspondent in Franco's army before beginning his novelistic career. Some of his more popular works include *La mosca en mi sopa* (The Fly in My Soup), which appeared in 1944, *La gallina de los huevos de plomo* (The Hen Who Laid Lead Eggs), *Todos los ombligos son redondos* (All Bellybuttons are Round) from the 1950s and his last novel from 1980, *Morir con las medias puestas* (Dying with Your Stockings On), an appropriate final work from a writer who continued producing up until his death. He also contributed frequently to the series entitled *Maestros de humor* (Masters of Humour). In many cases, his incorporation of slang and popular language into titles such as *Dios le ampare, imbécil* (God Help You, Idiot) (1957) and *Tú también naciste desnudito* (You Too Were Born Naked) (1961), make abundantly clear the humorous intent of the novelist, as well as explain his appeal to a wide audience. He began writing dramas in 1946, collaborating with Miguel **Mihura**, to stage *El caso de la mujer asesinadita* (The Case of the Slightly Murdered Woman). This rather off-beat murder mystery received favourable critical commentary for its originality. In the late 1940s he again collaborated to produce the farce, *Los sombreros de dos picos* (The Two-Cornered Hat), supposedly aimed at the chaos of modern society. The comedy *El drama de la familia invisible* (The Drama of the Invisible Family) (1949), a collaborative effort with Janos Voszany, featured the novelty of leading characters who never appear on stage. *'La Cordorniz' sin jaula. Datos para la historia de una revista* ('The Quail' Without a Cage. Facts for the History of a Magazine), published the year of his death, offers readers a history of Laiglesia's years as editor of this publication. While critics have admired Laiglesia's original, lively, and funny style, they have dedicated no in-depth study to his works, labelling them amusing and entertaining, with great popular appeal, but lacking in transcendental value or high literary quality.

FRIEDA H. BLACKWELL

Laín Entralgo, Pedro

b. 1908, Urrea de Gaén (Teruel)

Medical historian and writer

Laín Entralgo was professor of the History of Medicine in the Complutense University of Madrid 1942–78, and rector 1951–6. He was a member of an intellectual minority within the **Falange** which contributed to the journal *Escorial*, and in the 1950s a supporter of the liberalizing policies of the then Minister for Education, Joaquín **Ruiz Giménez**. In addition to works on the history of medicine, he wrote *La generación del 98* (The Generation of 98) (1945), and *España como problema* (The Problem of Spain) (1949), which drew a riposte from Rafael **Calvo Serer**, *España sin problema* (Spain: No Problem) (1949). He was general editor, 1972–5, of the seven-volume *Historia Universal de la Medicina* (Universal History of Medicine).

ALICIA ALTED

land tenure

Land tenure is a crucial factor in the operation of rural land markets, influencing the pace and direction of agricultural development. Since land tenure systems govern access to the means of production in agriculture, they have also been an intensely political subject in rural societies, being one of the factors contributing to the Spanish Civil War. As recently as 1960, over 40 percent of the labour force in Spain were engaged in agriculture. Since that date employment in agriculture has fallen to less than 10 percent of all employment. With fewer people depending on agriculture for their livelihood, land tenure as a political issue has largely disappeared from the national political agenda.

In the south of Spain the existence of large estates (see also ***latifundia***) has prevented many people from acquiring viable farms. In other areas of Spain, for example in parts of Galicia, the land tenure system has allowed property to be divided and sub-divided, leaving very small and fragmented farms (see also ***minifundia***) quite unable to compete effectively or support a family.

The net result of the division of land is a distorted farm size structure, where a large proportion of all holdings are very small and cover only a small proportion of the total land area, while a small proportion of all holdings are very large and occupy a large proportion of the land area. Moreover, statistics on farm size conceal the extent to which individuals own large areas of land through ownership of more than one farm.

These characteristics of land tenure have led people to argue for land reform at least since the late eighteenth century when Jovellanos published his report on agriculture (Andrés Alvarez 1955). Where the land tenure system is deficient, land reform may be necessary to restore equity and/or efficiency. However, in a democracy where private property is respected, such reform can only be slow.

During the twentieth century the redistribution of land from large estates was begun under the Republic but then reversed under General Franco. Land reform during the Franco regime concentrated on irrigation projects, settlement schemes and land consolidation supervised by state agrarian organizations (the last of which was the National Institute for Agrarian Reform and Development, IRYDA). Following the institution of democracy and the emergence of regional governments, responsibility for land reform was transferred to the regions, where policy has continued to avoid the division of large estates.

Contemporary patterns of rural land tenure are complex, varying from one part of Spain to another, reflecting events which stretch back into history. Nevertheless, three principal forms of rural land tenure are recognized in official statistics: owner occupation, tenancy and share-cropping (*aparcería*). These statistics show some 95 percent of all farms as being owner occupied. Three-quarters of the total agricultural land area is under owner occupation and a little over one-fifth under various forms of tenancy (INE 1995). The conditions of tenancies vary, for example in respect of the length (five years being quite common in the early 1990s), frequency of rent reviews and rights to have tenancy agreements extended. There may even be different rights of use (usufruct) in the same piece of land (for example for hunting or for cropping).

Although security of tenure is regarded as being of fundamental importance on both equity and efficiency grounds, inflexible tenancy regulations can discourage land owners from renting out land. Hence, measures have been sought which will increase the flexibility of the land market through more flexible leases. Other factors such as the taxation system, the nature of government intervention, agricultural product prices, the possibilities for conversion to non-agricultural use and the age structure of land owners (the majority being aged 55 and over) also effect the operation of the agricultural land market.

Over half the moorland and woodland (*bosque*) is under private ownership and about two-fifths belongs to local authorities (this land is frequently upland and unsuitable for agricultural use). Less than 10 percent belongs to the state and regional governments. Apart from their commercial use woodlands provide an invaluable leisure facility; as such they require careful management. Exploitation of the woodlands threatens not only the woodlands themselves but the whole ecosystem. However, while many woodland areas are now designated as protected areas, the pattern of woodland ownership offers only limited opportunity for the state and regional governments to become directly involved in woodland management. In part this explains the extensive planting, sometimes unauthorized, of fast growing eucalyptus trees.

See also: agriculture; labour market; migration

References

Andrés Alvarez, V. (1955) *Informe sobre la Ley Agraria 1785, por Gaspar Melchor de Jovellanos*, Madrid: Instituto de Estudios Políticos.

Instituto Nacional de Estadística, INE (1995) *Encuesta sobre la estructura de las explotaciones agrícolas 1993*, Madrid.

Further reading

Bosque Maurel, J. (1973) 'Latifundio y minifundio en Andalucía Oriental', *Estudios Geográficos*, 132–3: 457–500 (a detailed discussion of *latifundia* and *minifundia* in eastern Andalusia).

King, R. (1973) *Land Reform: the Italian Experience*, London: Butterworth & Co (an interesting comparative study).

Malefakis, E. (1970) *Agrarian reform and peasant revolution in Spain*, New Haven, CT: Yale University Press (deals with the political issue of land reform).

Naylon, J. (1973) 'An Appraisal of Spanish Irrigation and Land Settlement Policy Since 1939', *Iberian Studies*, 2, 1: 12–18.

KEITH SALMON

Landa, Alfredo

b. 1933, Pamplona (Navarre)

Actor

In his career as a film actor Landa has worked for a wide variety of directors including, in the 1970s and 1980s, **Bardem** in *El Puente* (The Long Weekend) (1976), **Garci** in *El crack* (The Crack) (1981), **Camus** in *Los santos inocentes* (*The Holy Innocents*) (1984), and **Patino** in *Los paraísos perdidos* (The Lost Paradises) (1985). In the 1990s he has appeared in films and television productions such as *El Quijote* (1991), Cuerda's *La marrana* (The Pig) (1992), for which he won the 1993 Goya Prize for best actor, the 1993 television series *Lleno por favor* (Full Up), and **Gutiérrez Aragón**'s *El rey del río* (King of the River) (1995). He was awarded the Gold Medal for Fine Arts in 1992.

See also: film and cinema

EAMONN RODGERS

language and education

Given the different sociolinguistic circumstances surrounding each of Spain's minority languages, attempts to increase their educational status have varied according to circumstance. Perhaps the most complex response has been that of the **autonomous community**, faced with the lowest proportion of proficient speakers and the greatest linguistic distance between **Basque** and **Spanish**.

Despite Franco's prohibition of minority languages, in the 1960s a number of Basque-medium schools (*ikastolas*) were set up clandestinely and in the 1970s these came to be tolerated by the regime. However, real efforts both to introduce Basque to the curriculum and to increase its use as medium of instruction did not start until the enactment of the **constitution of 1978**. In addition to the prevailing situation in which Basque did not figure anywhere in the curriculum (unofficially referred to as Model X), three new models of education were offered from 1979–80 onwards: Model A (instruction in Spanish with Basque as a subject); Model B (some subjects delivered in Spanish and some in Basque); and Model D (instruction in Basque with Spanish as a subject). While initially some 75 percent of pupils continued to be taught according to Model X with a small fraction receiving instruction through Basque, by the end of the 1980s Model X had virtually disappeared and by the mid-1990s Model A accounted for less than half of the intake. Indeed, Model A may disappear entirely from the province of Guipuzcoa by the year 2000. In the Basque-speaking areas of Navarre progress has been less marked and the autonomous community makes provision for what is called Model G (the equivalent of Model X).

In Catalonia, since the 1978 constitution, the **Generalitat** has followed a robust policy of promoting **Catalan** as the medium of instruction. There has been rapid Catalanization of both public and private education, supported by massive investments in materials creation and teacher retraining. One of the most successful innovations has been immersion in Catalan, an idea adopted from French Canada and implemented from pre-school education onwards. Furthermore, Catalan has been adopted as official language of the main universities and while members of staff may opt to give classes in the language of their choice, this is increasingly Catalan. In the autonomous communities of Valencia and the Balearics, progress has been much less swift, partly due to a lack of political will and partly, in the case of Valencia, due to a reluctance, for reasons of linguistic and regional identity, to import staff and materials from Catalonia.

In Galicia a lack of political will on the part of the Xunta and a certain hostility on the part of a population sensitive to the lack of social prestige of **Galician** meant that its introduction into education was initially very slow. Subsequently, however, as the language has gained in status and more teachers have been trained, the teaching of **Galician** as a subject has become widespread. Nonetheless, teaching is, for the most part, carried out through the medium of Spanish.

In all areas resistance has been noted on the part of some parents and pupils anxious for a greater concentration on the learning of 'world' rather than minority languages.

See also: language and national identity; language normalization; linguistic policy and legislation

MIRANDA STEWART

language and national identity

The relationship between language and identity is perhaps clearest in the debates in Spain and Latin America over the term used to refer to the principal official language: *español* or *castellano*. The **constitution of 1978** chose to adopt the term *castellano* to avoid the implication that **Spanish** (*español* can be used to refer to both the language and the state) enjoys a privileged status compared with that of the other languages of Spain (for instance **Catalan**); in parts of Latin America, the term *castellano* is also preferred to avoid connotations of Spanish colonialism; in other parts *español* is seen, for the same reasons, to be the more neutral term. That this and other language-related issues have the power to inflame passions and ensure a constant stream of 'letters to the editor' in the Spanish press testifies to the importance of language to notions of identity in contemporary Spain.

Throughout the twentieth century language has been central to discussions about national and regional identity in Spain, a country where more than 40 percent of the population lives in an area where a minority language is spoken in addition to Spanish. Interest in minority languages had been gaining force since the end of the nineteenth century, and it was hoped that these languages might gain official status under the Republic of 1931–9, but this hope was quickly brought to an end with the victory of Franco's Nationalist troops. Franco was to make the Spanish language his symbol of national unity, and systematic efforts were made to prohibit the use of languages other than Spanish and, if possible, actually to eradicate them. For example, not only was all public use of Basque prohibited, including the baptism of children with Basque names, but books in Basque were publicly burnt and inscriptions in Basque on public buildings physically effaced. Thus it is not surprising that the minority languages came to symbolize not only regional identity but anti-Franco resistance. This was particularly evident in the case of the Catalan **protest song**, the ***Nova Cançó***. While, over the course of the Franco regime, repression gradually lessened, it is interesting to note that it had little effect in reducing the numbers of speakers of minority languages.

With the constitution of 1978 and the creation of a quasi-federal state, the commitment by the **autonomous communities** where minority languages are spoken to the promotion of these languages has proved a reliable index of nationalist feeling. Indeed, such has been the importance of language as a badge of identity that, in addition to the principal minority languages of Basque, Catalan and **Galician**, attempts have been made to gain independent status for Aranese (a Gascon dialect spoken in North West Catalonia), Aragonese (*fable*) and Asturian (*bable*) and to raise the status of different varieties of Spanish (for example, Andalusian, Extremaduran). Even within minority language areas, conflict may arise over questions of regional identity. The most striking example of this is the case of *valenciano*, the minority language spoken in the autonomous community of Valencia. Opinion is divided over whether *valenciano* is a variety of Catalan (a view held by linguists) or a language in its own right (a view held by Valencian regionalists who fear what they see as the cultural and linguistic imperialism of Barcelona) and this particular language 'war' has even given rise to serious acts of violence in post-constitution Spain.

In the 1990s there has been a clear attempt to promote the Spanish language at home and abroad as a symbol of national unity; abroad, through the creation of the **Cervantes Institutes** (to promote Spanish language and culture) which has enhanced Spain's presence in Europe; at home, through the decision to fund the compilation of a descriptive dictionary of Spanish using information technology (see also **dictionaries and encyclopedias**).

Defenders of the Spanish language perceive a dual threat: on the one hand, from the success of **language normalization** programmes in prosperous minority language areas (most particularly Catalonia); and from increasing globalization with the concomitant ascendancy of the English language.

Perhaps the greatest pressure on Spanish comes from the vast amount of new terminology, particularly in the fields of science and technology, which enters the language each year, principally from English and also from French. Unlike other countries (for example, France which has sought to protect its language from a 'foreign invasion' through legislation), Spain, notwithstanding the presence of a **Royal Academy** of Language, has adopted a more pragmatic perspective. Given the pace of change and in view of the absence of adequate descriptive dictionaries, the 1980s and 1990s witnessed the growth of the 'style guide'. Initially produced by the Spanish news agency **Agencia EFE** to safeguard standards in the written media, these guides have extended first to cover individual newspapers and later radio and television and also areas of professional discourse (e.g. Clinical Medicine). A principal concern is to provide indigenous equivalents for imported terminology (e.g. *liquidación de activos* for 'asset-stripping') and, if this proves difficult, to standardize the integration of loans into Spanish (e.g. *scanner* becomes *escáner*). Also advice may be given on how to avoid the use of English language constructions. For example, in the field of medicine, whereas in English compound nouns abound such as 'methicillin-resistant disease', doctors in Spain are enjoined to use the unwieldy Spanish construction, *una enfermedad resistente a la metacilina.*

Another area of concern in the late twentieth century has been the implications of globalization for the Spanish alphabet. International alphabetical reference does not recognize the separate entry, adopted in Spanish dictionaries, of digraphs Ll, Ch, and international keyboards do not always include the diacritic *ñ* (tilde). Proposals to align Spanish with international practice brought public outcry and a heated defence of the language in the face of perceived Anglo-Saxon hegemony. In the case of the digraphs, Spanish practice has come into line with that of the wider international community; in the case of *ñ* (even more clearly a symbol of national identity in Spain given its presence in *España*), its defence continues to be vigorous and its survival an indicator of the importance of language to identity.

See also: language and education; linguistic policy and legislation

MIRANDA STEWART

language normalization

The **constitution of 1978** establishes the framework for significant language planning activities, particularly in **autonomous communities** where minority languages are spoken. This framework has been further defined in the Statutes of Autonomy of certain regions, with specific language articles and, in a few specific cases, with laws of linguistic normalization.

The concept 'normalization' (*normalización*) is peculiarly Spanish. It appears originally to have been used by Catalan sociolinguists, as the result of their direct translation of the similar French term, which, however, was being used to convey the English idea of 'standardization'. The Catalan writers (such as Aracil, Ninyoles and Vallverdú) extended its meaning to encompass goals which include both status and corpus language planning. Some argued that this inevitably requires a certain political sovereignty and right to self-determination. They stress that normalization involves putting languages on an equal footing with one another, neither higher nor lower, by developing the language both in its corpus elaboration and in its use and ultimate spread. Cobarrubias (1987) elaborates on the difference between normalization and standardization, known as *normativización* in the Spanish context. According to Cobarrubias, normalization entails functional, demographic and geographic spread of a language.

This interpretation of normalization has formed the basis of the goals of language planning in Catalonia, the Basque country, Galicia, Valencia and the Balearic Islands. Besides implying the promotion of **Catalan**, **Basque** and **Galician** to equal status with **Spanish**, 'normal' is also understood to refer to their previous historical status. This is especially true for Catalan, a high-prestige language in the Middle Ages and widely-used during the 1930s. In this way, then, normalization encompasses both the idea of linguistic equality for minority Spanish languages, and their role as identity markers for their communities.

However, there is a certain degree of ambiguity about the meaning of this term, reflecting both its origin and the tensions which lie under the surface of current language planning in Spain. For example, *La Ley de la Normalización del Uso de Euskera* is translated by the Basques themselves as 'The Law of the Standardization of the Use of Basque'. The Catalans and Galicians translate their laws by 'normalization'. This may reflect the fact that of the three languages, the one still most in need of dialectal standardization at the time of these laws was Basque.

Similarly, the emphasis on *normativización* as a part of the normalization process has been far more apparent in Galicia where the term has, above all, been used to define orthographic rules for the use and teaching of Galician. This in turn arises from the significant debate which continues to take place over whether Galician is, and therefore should be written as, a separate language, or is a variety of Portuguese, with Portuguese spelling. Arguably the most important effect that the linguistic normalization law has had in Galicia has been the publication by its local government of the norms of orthography to be followed in the use of Galician.

The programmes that have been followed in the different linguistic minority communities vary in terms of emphasis, level of participation and funding, and overall success. However, the model is basically the same. The Catalans, as the largest and wealthiest of the linguistic minorities, have led the way with the fullest programme and, undeniably, with the greatest success.

The normalization programmes are run by a department of the region's local government, usually a language policy directorate. Most language issues in school-age education are addressed by departments of education, but in close liaison with the language planners. A major part of the work is to promote the language by active campaigns of consciousness-raising, creating positive images and attitudes to the language. If the languages are to be promoted and revived the local administrations of these regions must lead the way in using the local language. All local civil servants must be competent bilinguals. The degree to which local government debates, internal memos, public enquiries, etc. are dealt with in the regional language varies enormously across the three minority language communities. While in the Basque country the use of Spanish is frequent, in Catalonia it is rare to hear Spanish spoken in the offices of the **Generalitat**.

Besides this official use, the language planners are targeting sectors such as trade unions and professional associations to persuade them to promote the local language in their documents and discussions. Banks, restaurants, and commerce in general are encouraged to use the local language in dealings with the public and in their publications. Public notices, and particularly road signs and transport information, are in the local language.

The media is a particularly important area for language planners, both for the use of the language – on television, radio and the press – and as a vehicle of propaganda and persuasion. The increased used of the local languages on television is considered one of the most productive ways of encouraging its acceptance and improving competence in it. Given the lower levels of literacy in the regional languages than oral use (particularly in the case of Basque), the written press plays a smaller role.

However, the written language is promoted through the efforts of the section of the language planning departments which elaborates and develops vocabulary and corpora of terminology. Particularly in Catalonia, this has often consisted of the production of posters and signs to be displayed in the relevant establishments using appropriate terms and phrases for different activities and sectors of society. Campaigns take place to persuade people to say things 'correctly' in their local language. In areas where Castilian-speaking immigration is high, adult education classes are also available to teach the local languages.

By far the most influential area of language planning is without doubt the education system. The teaching of the regional languages in the schools and colleges of their communities is viewed as the prime target. In all regions where languages other than Spanish are spoken, there is a basic entitlement of three hours' teaching of the regional language, plus one hour when the regional language is used as the medium of instruction for another curricular subject. This applies equally to Spanish in the event of the language of the school being predominantly the regional language. Different models of language provision in the schools have emerged, with the most radical being the Immersion method, largely promoted in Catalonia. Here, children whose mother-tongue is Spanish are immersed in the target regional language for the first few years of their schooling, with little or no contact with Spanish until they are seven or eight. The overall aim of all the education programmes is to allow children to have an equal command of both community languages by the time they finish their compulsory schooling. The results so far are patchy, with, once again, the greatest success in Catalonia.

The normalization programmes have, inevitably, encountered mixed success to date. In general, attitudes are more positive to the minority languages and the use of them has increased. Such programmes, however, are expensive, raising political and moral questions over the prioritizing of these languages, above all as markers of identity, given that the other function of language, that of communication, is clearly catered for through the use of Spanish.

References

Cobarrubias, J. (1987) 'Models of Language Planning for Minority Languages', *Bulletin of the CAAL*, 47–70 (this is the most comprehensive discussion of the concept of 'normalization').

CLARE MAR-MOLINERO

latifundia

Latifundia are large agrarian estates often associated with extensive farming especially in the South (in Andalusia, Castilla-La Mancha and Extremadura), frequently involving a monoculture based around pasture in mountainous areas and arable crops or olives in the lowlands. Their presence has had a profound political and social significance in the development of Spain, creating on the one hand a deeply conservative landed nobility, frequently absent from their farm holdings, and on the other, an impoverished landless peasantry denied access to the ownership of viable farms. *Latifundia* were part of a system of class domination and suppression, a feudal society, fostering militant labour organization and precipitating rural emigration (see also **land tenure**), a stumbling block to agricultural modernization and broader economic development.

Many of the large estates can be traced back to the Reconquest when land was granted in perpetuity to the nobility, the military orders and the church. Large tracts of land also became the common lands of municipalities. A number of factors led to increased concentration of land in the hands of a small number of owners, the neglect of land and the loss of tax revenue by the state: the exemption of church property from taxes; the conversion of arable land to pasture as part of the sheep-rearing economy of the pastoral brotherhood of the *Mesta* (owners of sheep herded back and forth across Spain who gained significant privileges and monopolies from the late thirteenth century); the system of inheritance of entailed estates by primogeniture (*mayorazgo*), by which a great house could ensure that its possessions passed intact from one heir to the next; and matrimonial alliances which consolidated great blocks of land into the hands of a powerful few. This prompted the disentailment laws of the mid-nineteenth century under which church and municipal lands were expropriated by the state and sold at auction. The effect of disentailment, however, was to transfer land from corporate owners to wealthy individuals.

Under the Second Republic measures were implemented to break up large estates, but these measures were disrupted by the Civil War. The

Franco regime then reversed the process of expropriation and switched the emphasis in land reform to irrigation, land settlement schemes and land consolidation.

In the latter part of the twentieth century the issue of *latifundia* faded from the national political agenda as fewer people sought a livelihood from agriculture, with the modernization of agriculture and the European Common Agricultural Policy, and with the welfare state. Outward migration during the 1950s and 1960s released pressure on the land and diverted attention away from discontent over land ownership. By the time migration slowed in the 1970s, and a political regime was installed that was more sympathetic to the problem, the problem itself had partly evaporated. Modern large estates are essential in areas of low yield grain growing such as the *meseta* of central Spain, and in many areas they are company farms practising the most modern agro-industrial techniques.

Nevertheless, the break-up of large estates may still offer opportunities for a more productive use of the land and the creation of employment (in 1989 farms of 500 hectares or more occupied one quarter of land used for agriculture in Spain). Following the establishment of democratic government in the 1970s, a number of laws were passed permitting the expropriation of large estates where land could be shown to be under-utilized. In Andalusia (where it is written into the Statute of Autonomy that the government should pursue agrarian reform), the process of identifying such estates was begun in 1984. However, little expropriation had occurred by the mid-1990s.

See also: agriculture; land tenure

Further reading

Giner, S. and Sevilla, E. (1977) 'The Latifundio as a Local Mode of Class Domination: the Spanish case', *Iberian Studies* 6, 2: 47–57 (a discussion focusing on the definition of *latifundia*).

Maas, J. (1983) 'The Behaviour of Landowners as an Explanation of Regional Differences in Agriculture: Latifundists in Seville and Córdoba (Spain)', *Tijdschrift voor Economische e Sociale Geografie*, 74, 2: 87–95 (an indication of the changing use of large estates).

Martínez Alier, J. (1971) *Labourers and Landowners of Southern Spain*, London: George Allen & Unwin (a specific case study from the province of Córdoba in the 1960s).

KEITH SALMON

Lavilla Alsina, Landelino

b. 1934, Lleida (Lérida)

Politician

A prominent member of the **Tácito** group of Christian Democrats who argued for democracy from within the Franco regime. As Minister for Justice in **Suárez**'s first government (1976–7) he drafted the Law for Political Reform, the centre-piece of the Suárez reform programme, and was Speaker of the Congress of Deputies from 1979–82. Initially close to Suárez, as nominal leader of the UCD's internal opposition, he stood against him at the Palma Congress of 1981. He later adopted a more conciliatory stance, and dutifully took on the hopeless task of leading UCD into the 1982 elections, retiring from the political scene soon afterwards.

JONATHAN HOPKIN

Law of Patronage

The Law of Foundations and of Fiscal Incentives for Private Participation in Activities of Public Interest, better known as the Law of Patronage (*Ley de mecenazgo*), was finally passed in 1994 after several years of negotiation. Individuals and corporate bodies can receive rebates of up to 20 percent of their tax liability by donating works of art (including contemporary works) to institutions whose chief purpose is to promote civic, educational, cultural, sporting or health initiatives, among them the non-profitmaking **foundations**, which also benefit from a reduction in the *Impuesto de Sociedades* (Corporate Tax). In 1995, for example, the Queen Sofia Museum received 112 such works.

Private universities and bodies concerned with **language normalization** are excluded from the scope of the law.

See also: arts funding; arts policy; cultural institutions and movements; museums

EAMONN RODGERS

legal system

Following the approval of the new **constitution of 1978**, the Spanish legal system, which under Franco was not only anachronistic but largely dependent on an all-powerful executive, was modernized and brought more in line with that of other western European democracies. This process was carried out mainly in the mid-1980s under the reforming administrations of Felipe **González**. The present system is largely governed by two major laws, the Organic Law of the Judiciary (1985 and 1995) and the Law of Staffing and Demarcation (1988).

Justice is administered within a single national system structured according to territorial and functional criteria. The state is organized into municipalities, *partidos judiciales* (two or more municipalities), provinces and **autonomous communities**, each level with its own institutions, and the system is divided according to five branches of justice, each regulated by its own specific codes (*códigos*). These branches are civil, criminal, administrative, social and military (the latter normally applying only to members of the armed forces). In spite of moves towards decentralization in Spain, the legal system remains largely centralized and hierarchical.

The General Council of the Judiciary is the highest governing body of the judiciary. Its powers lie mainly in the area of appointments, including the right to propose its own president, two members of the **Constitutional Tribunal** and judges serving in the Supreme Court. It also has responsibility for the training, location and promotion of judges, as well as disciplinary affairs.

The Department of the Attorney General of the State (*Ministerio Fiscal*) has two basic functions. First, it ensures that the system of justice functions in accordance with the law and in the interests of the general public; and, second, it ensures that the courts are independent. The department is entrusted with the protection of the **civil rights** of citizens in the constitution; thus, it is empowered to initiate appeals for protection before the Constitutional Tribunal. Moreover, it oversees the bureaucracy of the prosecution service and the nationwide career structure of the public prosecutors, which is quite separate from that applying to judges. At its head is the attorney general of the state, who is responsible for the operation of the whole system and nominally in charge of the entire corps of prosecutors.

The administration of justice operates at four levels, national, regional, provincial and local. At the national level, the major institutions are the Supreme Court (Tribunal Supremo) and the National Court (Audiencia Nacional). The Supreme Court, which has jurisdiction throughout Spain, is the highest court of justice in the land for all except constitutional matters. The Supreme Court is composed of five divisions, each headed by its own president, and consisting of a fixed number of judges. These are the civil, criminal, administrative, social and military divisions. One of the major functions of the civil and criminal divisions is to hear complaints against the prime minister, the presidents of both houses of parliament and other high-ranking public servants. The administrative division hears complaints made about high-ranking public bodies as opposed to individuals. Among other things, social courts deal with labour disputes.

The National Court is divided into three divisions: criminal, administrative and social. The first is the court of last appeal in such cases as crimes committed abroad (involving possible extradition), the forging of foreign currency, drug-trafficking and criminal acts against the monarchy and other state institutions. In the 1990s, the National Court has been involved in high-profile cases such as the **GAL** affair.

Courts were first established in all regions only after the creation of the autonomous communities post-1979. High courts of justice (*tribunales superiores de justicia*) are composed of three divisions: joint civil/criminal, administrative and social. Acting as a civil division, the joint court is a court of sole instance in complaints against the president and ministers of the regional parliament and government. The administrative division hears cases against acts or decisions of the regional government, its president and ministers. Administrative, social and juvenile courts also function at the provincial level.

Local courts operate at the provincial, subprovincial and municipal levels. The provincial courts (*audiencias provinciales*) are located in provincial capitals. They deal only with civil and criminal matters. The civil division deals largely with appeals against sentences passed by lower level courts in the province, while the criminal division covers both serious criminal offences referred to it directly and appeals against sentences of lower criminal courts. It is in these courts that the jury system began to be implemented in 1996.

Many local courts (*juzgados*) are located in the main town of a *partido judicial*. These include the courts of first instance, which deal with civil affairs and normally hold the local civil register, and the courts of instruction, which deal with minor criminal offences as well as *habeas corpus* matters. In small towns, these two types of court function as one. The equivalent of English magistrates' courts, the so-called 'peace' courts, are located in every municipality, where there is not already a court of first instance or instruction. In practice, they are to be found in most municipalities with populations of under 6,000. These courts deal with minor civil and criminal offences. One of their other civil functions is to maintain the civil register if this has been delegated to them by the appropriate court of first instance.

The Ministry of Justice (*Ministerio de Justicia*) is quite separate from the institutions described above, but is required to liaise with them and to ensure that all the legislation in this area serves to protect fundamental rights. It is also its responsibility to initiate legislation in the whole range of areas related to the administration of justice. Over the last decade, one of its main tasks has been to ensure that Spanish legislation conforms to European law.

See also: European Union; labour law; politics

Further reading

Heywood, P. (1995) *The Government and Politics of Spain*, London: Macmillan (one of the most authoritative accounts available).

Newton, M.T. with Donaghy, P.J. (1997) *Institutions of Modern Spain*, Cambridge: Cambridge University Press (the standard reference work on this topic).

MICHAEL T. NEWTON

Leguina, Joaquín

b. 1941, Villaescusa (Santander)

Politician, economist and writer

After graduating in economics from Bilbao and taking higher degrees in Madrid and the Sorbonne, Leguina joined the socialist **PSOE** in 1977 and became MP for Madrid in 1982. The following year, he was elected president of the **autonomous community** of Madrid, a post he held for eight years. A member of the more critical section of the party, Leguina holds strong views on unemployment, drugs, crime and NATO, and has often been a controversial figure, while remaining basically loyal to the governmental programme of his longtime friend, Felipe **González**.

See also: Guerra, Alfonso; socialism

MICHAEL T. NEWTON

lehendakari

This is the Basque name for the prime minister of the Basque **autonomous community** (previously *lendakari*). It was first applied to the head of the Basque government during the Civil War and subsequently in exile, José Antonio Aguirre. On his death the post was assumed by Jesús María de Leizaola. The first post-Franco *lehendakari* was Carlos Garaikoetxea, elected in 1980. His resignation in 1984 led to the appointment of José Antonio **Ardanza**. Like the three previous holders of the title he is a member of the Basque nationalist **PNV**.

The *lehendakari*'s official residence is the mansion of *Ajuria Enea*, in Vitoria.

C.J. ROSS

León, María Teresa

b. 1904, Logroño; d. 1988, Madrid

Writer

Rejecting her conservative, upper-middle-class background, León – an early feminist – joined the ranks of social revolutionaries during the years of the Second Republic. She married the poet Rafael **Alberti**, whose avant-garde beginnings and renunciation of 'art for art's sake' in favour of committed literature match her own artistic trajectory. Early experimentalism imbues *La bella del mal amor* (The Beauty Wrongly Loved) (1930), brief tales blending traditional and rural themes and medievalism, and *Rosa-fría, patinadora de la luna* (Cold Rosa, Skater of the Moon) (1934), which combines fantasy with lyricism. Aesthetics give way to ideological combativeness, Naturalism and Marxism in *Cuentos de la España actual* (Tales of Spain Today) (1937), realistic stories of class struggle, street clashes, arson, violence and hatred, clearly Marxist in depicting proletarian revolt, bourgeois indolence, and pervasive social injustice. These stories and those of *Una estrella roja* (A Red Star) (1979) reflect León's own ideological awakening: in one, an upper-class girl watches with mixed feelings as Anarchists torch her convent school; in another, the death of the pre-adolescent daughter of a terrorist, trained to plant bombs, is commemorated by communist workers who award her a red star. León also wrote the documentary *Crónica general de la Guerra Civil* (General Chronicle of the Civil War) (1937) early in the conflict, and a more abstract novel reflecting wartime experiences, *Contra viento y marea* (Against Wind and Tide) (1941), which views life as a struggle against overwhelming odds.

León collaborated in defending the Republic, working with Antonio Machado and the National Council for the Theatre. She campaigned in support of workers and the poor, and with Alberti founded a short-lived popular theatre, recounted in the wartime autobiographical novel *Juego limpio* (Playing Fair) (1959). The short story collection, *Morirás lejos* (You'll Die Far Away) (1942), treats war and exile, while *La historia tiene la palabra* (History Has the Final Word) (1977) recounts efforts, in which Alberti and León participated, to save national artistic treasures from bombardments and capture by Falangists. At the end of the war she accompanied Alberti to exile in France and Argentina, then moved in the 1960s to Rome where they remained until convinced in the 1980s that Spain's democracy would last.

In exile, León wrote fictional biographies of Cervantes and the post-Romantic poet, Gustavo Adolfo Bécquer, plus historical fiction for juvenile readers starring *El Cid Campeador* (The Warrior Lord) (1962) and *Doña Jimena Díaz de Vivar* (1960). *Las peregrinaciones de Teresa* (Teresa's Pilgrimage) (1950) explores feminine psychology in nine stories linked by the symbolic character of Teresa, while *Fábulas del tiempo amargo* (Bitter Times Fables) (1962) and *Memoria de la melancolía* (Melancholy's Memoir) (1970) recreate exile experiences. *Sonríe China* (China Smiles) (1958) records a visit with Alberti to the People's Republic.

Major works

The commemorative volume *María Teresa León* (1987), Valladolid: Junta de Castilla y León, contains a useful bibliography.

Further reading

Bauer, B.W. (1993) 'María Teresa Leon (1904–1988)' in L.G. Levine *et al.* (eds) *Spanish Women Writers: A BioBibliographical Source Book*, Westport, CT: Greenwood Press, 253–63 (a useful brief overview).

Pérez, J. (1988) *Contemporary Women Writers of Spain*, Boston, MA: G.K. Hall, 45–9 (life and works survey emphasizing narrative volumes).

Pochat, M.T. (1989) 'María Teresa León, memoria del recuerdo en el exilio', *Cuadernos hispanoamericanos* 47,374: 135–42 (treats exile experience and its role in her writings).

Torres Nebrera, G. (1984) 'La obra literaria de María Teresa León (cuentos y teatro)', *Anuario de Estudios Filológicos* 7: 361–84 (literary history plus rather detailed examination of León's theatrical works and brief fiction).

JANET PÉREZ

libraries

In addition to its two largest libraries, the Biblioteca Nacional (National Library) and the Biblioteca de Catalunya (National Library of Catalonia), Spain has a range of facilities including public libraries, university and school libraries, libraries of learned bodies such as the **Royal Academies**, and various private and special libraries.

The Biblioteca Nacional

Originally a Royal Library established by Philip V in the early eighteenth century (1711), the Biblioteca Nacional is the legal deposit library for Spain, with all the problems of space and resources that that position entails. Extensive reconstruction of the building it has occupied in Madrid since 1892 was begun in 1986, with two phases completed by 1994. A new building in Alcalá de Henares, at first intended for a separate Inter-library Loan Service, functions as a second book repository. A programme of automation begun in 1988 has resulted in the formation of the ARIADNA data-base which facilitates the compilation of the national bibliography for which the library assumed responsibility in 1986, and other computerised bibliographical projects. In a major administrative reorganization in 1991 it became an autonomous body, with a president (the Minister of Education) and a general director.

With total holdings of some eight million items, including important collections of material from the Inquisition, from the Madrid convents and monasteries dissolved in 1837, and from the many private libraries donated during the nineteenth century, it provides a range of services, including a General Information Service, a Library Documentary Service and a Periodicals Documentary Service.

The Biblioteca de Catalunya

Originally founded in 1907 as the library of the Institute of Catalan Studies and established as a national library in 1914, the Biblioteca de Catalunya is the legal deposit library for books printed or published in Catalonia. Housed since 1936–9 in the former Hospital de la Santa Creu it regained its national status with the creation of the Autonomous Region of Catalonia in 1979 and the first Catalan Libraries Act in 1981. Its functions were further defined in the Catalan Library System Law of 1993, and include the creation of a Catalan national bibliography and union catalogue. The process of automation, using Catalan software (SICAB), was begun in 1990, and major reconstruction of the original building and the creation of new storage space was started in 1993.

Among the important holdings in its total of some two million items are the Cervantes Collection, the Verdaguer Collection, the Torres Amat Library, the Biblioteca Romàntica Tusquets de Cabirol and the Arxiu Joan Maragall Collection.

Public libraries

There has been a very noticeable extension and improvement of the public library system since the mid-1980s and a corresponding growth in the number of readers and loans, which increased by the best part of a million each between 1992 and 1995 alone. A project to integrate the libraries into a single automated system (PROIN) was begun in 1989 and has resulted in the creation of the REBECA database.

Other libraries

University and special libraries have also developed their own union catalogues, facilitating joint cataloguing and interlibrary loans, and along with the national, public and Royal Academy libraries are represented on the Library Coordination Council which is attached to the Ministry of Culture and is chaired by the director of the Biblioteca Nacional. Cathedrals and religious houses often have rich holdings of interest to scholars, and there are valuable private research collections such as that in the Menéndez y Pelayo

Library in Santander, formed from the personal library of the nineteenth-century polymath Marcelino Menéndez y Pelayo, and open to bona fide scholars. The **Ateneo** has extensive holdings, as has the Cortes, though their use is normally restricted to members of these bodies.

See also: cultural institutions and movements; education and research; intellectual life

Further reading

Girón, A. (1994) 'The Biblioteca Nacional of Spain', *Alexandria*, 6 (2): 91–105 (a very detailed and informative article by a former director of the National Library).

Panyella, V. (1993) 'The Biblioteca de Catalunya – National Library of Catalonia', *Alexandria*, 5 (2):127–42 (a very detailed and informative article by the library manager).

EAMONN RODGERS

Liceu Theatre

The Gran Teatre del Liceu (Great Theatre of the Liceu) in Barcelona, is in the process of reconstruction after being completely gutted by fire in January 1994. The oldest active opera house in Spain and among the most important world-wide, it was the brain child of Joaquim de Gispert, who financed its construction on the site of a former monastery by selling the theatre boxes (*palcos*) as shares. Opened in 1847, and reconstructed after a fire in 1861, it became the venue for productions of opera, ballet, music and drama performed by world class artists. It was so closely identified with the leisure pursuits of the wealthy Barcelona bourgeoisie in the 1890s that it became the target of a notorious anarchist bomb attack, in which twenty-one people were killed. On a more positive note, it was the scene of José **Carreras**' professional début in 1970.

Owned and financed until 1980 entirely by the Society of Owners with some 400 members, some of them direct descendants of the original share/box holders, and from 1980 by a consortium of the Owners, the **Generalitat**, the City Council and the Provincial Council of Barcelona, and the Ministry of Culture, the theatre passed completely into public ownership after the 1994 fire and is governed by the Liceu **Foundation**.

In the reconstruction plan outlined in 1995 the general appearance of the theatre was to be restored with its red plush stall seating and gilded mouldings. The stage, stall and dress circle boxes were also to be rebuilt for the use of the original owners and for the consortium of banks and businesses which was expected to contribute as much as 45 percent of the cost of reconstruction, estimated at 9,680m pesetas. But advantage was to be taken of the rebuilding to remove the boxes on the upper circles, to improve the view of the stage by reducing the overall seating and heightening the proscenium arch, to provide for vertical scene shifting and to facilitate television filming by improved lighting. It was planned to have the reconstruction completed in 1997 for the 150th aniversary of the theatre.

See also: music; opera; performing arts

EAMONN RODGERS

Linazasoro, José Ignacio

b. 1947, San Sebastián

Architect

Linazasoro is particularly active in the field of architectural theory. Qualifying in 1972, he gained his doctorate in 1976 and went on to lecture on architecture first at Valladolid and then at the Escuela Técnica Superior de Arquitectura in Madrid. He is the author of an important contribution to the debate about post-modernism in the 1980s: *El proyecto clásico en Arquitectura* (The Classical Project in Architecture) (1984). He is heavily involved in the promotion of Basque culture, and his work offers a very sophisticated modern interpretation of Basque regional traditions. In addition, he has been greatly inspired by the neo-classical architectural heritage, which gives his creations a feeling of balance and simplicity. Among his best known works are the Economics Faculty building in Madrid (1991–3) and the restoration of the Hospedal del Rey at Melilla (1995–6).

See also: architects; architecture; Modernism

MIHAIL MOLDOVEANU

linguistic policy and legislation

One of the most distinctive features of post-Franco Spain is its emergence as a decentralized and plurilingual country after a period during which severe, albeit lessening, repression of minority languages was exercised in the interests of achieving a centralized, monolingual state. As a reaction against the linguistic illiberalism of this period, the **constitution of 1978** sought to redress the balance and offer a measure of protection to minority languages, henceforth seen as part of Spain's rich cultural diversity. While the constitution established **Spanish** as the official state language, in article 3.2 it provided for the co-officiality of the various minority languages or *lenguas propias* within their **autonomous communities**.

Those who drafted the constitution were careful to avoid specifying exactly how many languages exist in Spain and chose to leave such tasks of self-definition to the autonomous communities themselves. Thus, in the legislative framework provided by the Statutes of Autonomy, in addition to Spanish, reference is made to the following minority varieties: **Catalan**, Valencian, **Galician**, **Basque**, *bable* (spoken in Asturias) and the different dialects of Aragon and Andalusia. The articles of the Statutes relating to language are further developed in the *Leyes de Normalización* (Language Planning Laws) passed between 1982 and 1986 (Basque country, 1982, Catalonia, 1983, Galicia, 1983, Valencia, 1983, Balearic Islands, 1986 and Navarre, 1986). These essentially build on the notions of linguistic rights enshrined in the constitution, that is, the minority language's status of co-officiality with Spanish, the right of citizens to know and use that language in all circumstances and the right to freedom from discrimination on linguistic grounds. Some also specify the geographical area in which the law applies, for example, Navarre identifies three zones (Basque-speaking, Spanish-speaking and mixed) in each of which different provisions of the legislation will apply. The legislation typically refers to the responsibilities of the government of the autonomous community in promoting the minority language in both stages of the planning process; corpus planning and status planning. Thus, the legislation specifies the code (language variety) to be adopted (e.g. *el euskera* – Basque) and may name the institution responsible for the formal codification of grammatical and orthographic norms and for updating the lexicon of the language (e.g. *Euskaltazaindia* – The Royal Academy of the Basque Language); second, it lays down the ways in which the knowledge and use of the language are to be promoted (principally in the areas of Public Administration, Education and Culture and the Media). Furthermore, most autonomous communities with minority languages have created specific departments to assist in the implementation of the legislation.

Significant parts of this legislation have proved a site for conflict, for example, the selection of Valencian rather than Catalan in the autonomous community of Valencia and the absence of reference to an authority responsible for its codification; the perception by some Spanish-speakers in, for example, Catalonia that their rights are not respected; and the perception by minority language speakers of the inequality of status between their language and Spanish.

See also: language and education; language and national identity; language normalization

Further reading

Siguán, M. (1992) *España plurilingüe*, Madrid: Alianza (chapter 2 includes an excellent overview of language policy and legislation; there is also an extensive thematically organized bibliography).

MIRANDA STEWART

Linz Storch de Gracia, Juan José

b. 1926, Bonn

Sociologist

Linz Storch de Gracia moved to Madrid in 1932, and studied Economic and Political Sciences and

Law, followed by postgraduate work in Columbia University, New York. His doctoral thesis was entitled *Las bases sociales de los partidos políticos en la República Federal alemana* (The Social Bases of Political Parties in the Federal German Republic) (1958). He carried out his first empirical research into Spanish business between 1958 and 1961, subsequently in collaboration with his pupil Amando de **Miguel**. He was appointed professor in Yale in 1969. His work has concentrated on the social, political and economic conditions of Spain, and on contemporary political movements, including a comparative study of the transition to democracy in southern and eastern Europe and in Latin America.

ALICIA ALTED

literacy

In a Ministry of Education Survey of 1993 the rate of illiteracy was given as 3.5 percent. This figure compares with a figure of 32 percent, or by some estimates even 40 percent in 1930, and is evidence of the concern of successive regimes to increase the rate of literacy for cultural and economic reasons.

Literacy campaigns were a marked feature of the Second Republic, though hampered by a shortage of schools and teachers, and during the Civil War the Republicans provided literacy classes and **libraries** to soldiers at the front via Cultural Militias, and to civilians via Flying Brigades. An era of **censorship** was ushered in with Franco's victory, but the propaganda value of the 'right kind' of reading was not ignored, and the Women's Section of the **Falange** in particular were involved in the provision of literacy classes. By 1960 it is reckoned that the rate of illiteracy had dropped to some 15 percent. But this was still a high rate, and a successful literacy campaign was inaugurated in 1963 by the Minister of Education, Lora Tamayo. Priority was given to primary education, which was made free in 1965, the school-leaving age having been raised to 14 the previous year.

As educational expenditure and participation in education increased, so the levels of illiteracy continued to drop, aided by government initiatives such as the Adult Education Service, which by 1985–6 was catering for nearly 150,000 students with a teaching staff of over 3,000. By the time of the 1993 survey, illiteracy was confined largely to those over 45 years of age who had not had the benefits of universal education, and had become a contributor to the generation gap, especially in families with children at university.

See also: education and research; EGB; LODE; LOGSE; readership

EAMONN RODGERS

literary journals

Despite the constant complaints from writers and literary critics about the limitations of **readership** in Spain, there is a substantial number of literary journals, of varying degrees of durability and financial health. Of those which have shown a capacity for survival over time, and have acquired a certain prestige, perhaps the most widely read is ***Insula***, founded in 1946. *Ínsula* played a key role in disseminating literary culture during the Franco dictatorship, and defied government **censorship** by giving prominence to dissident writers, many of them living in **exile**. The ***Revista de Occidente***, founded in 1923 by José **Ortega y Gasset**, is of greater antiquity, but has not enjoyed the same unbroken continuity, having been in abeyance between 1936 and 1963, and again between 1975 and 1980. The **CSIC** publishes the *Revista de Literatura*, formerly *Cuadernos de Literatura*. Founded in 1942, it covers a wide range of aspects of literary study, including documentary research, literary history and literary theory. A similar academic publication is *Cuadernos Hispanoamericanos*, published since 1948 by the Instituto de Cooperación Iberoamericana.

A lively modern addition to the range is *El Urugallo*, which first appeared between 1970 and 1975, and was relaunched in 1986. It has extensive coverage of literary and cultural events in Spain and abroad. Though there is no exact equivalent in Spain of the *Times Literary Supplement* or the *New York Review of Books*, *El Urugallo* and other publications such as *Saber Leer*, a relatively new journal (1987–) published by the **Juan March Foundation**, help to keep readers abreast of cultural life both in

Spain and elsewhere. It should also be noted that the literary supplements of the major national dailies make an important contribution towards fulfilling the same role.

Outside the capital, ***Serra d'Or***, published since 1959 entirely in Catalan, by the Benedictine monks of Montserrat, has ample coverage of literature, film and drama, in addition to its main task of promoting discussion of theological topics. Despite its important role in the defence of Catalan culture and language, its focus is not purely regional, but European and international. Regional publications properly so-called include *Nordes*, a Galician journal of poetry and criticism launched in La Coruña in 1975, *La Página* (La Laguna, Tenerife), and the Basque *Urruzuno Literatur Lehiaketa* (Vitoria).

The **Royal Academies** and the **universities** also produce several titles, though some are sporadic in their appearance. The *Boletín de la Real Academia Española* is one of the most prestigious. The University of Santiago de Compostela produces *Estudios de Literatura Contemporánea*, and the University of Alicante *Anales de Literatura Española*. Modern developments in literary theory and cultural studies have stimulated new journals such as *Tropelías* (University of Zaragoza, 1990–).

In terms of circulation, the most successful journals are the *Revista de Occidente* and *Saber Leer*, each with 20,000 subscribers, though in the case of the former it should be noted that many copies are sold to institutions and individuals outside Spain. *El Urogallo* and *Serra d'Or* each have a circulation of around 15,000. This compares at one end of the scale with the relatively low circulation of *Cuadernos Hispanoamericanos* (2,000), and that of a medium-circulation non-literary monthly such as *Comercio e Industria*, which has around 80,000 subscribers.

See also: cultural institutions and movements; literature; media; press

EAMONN RODGERS

literature

The development of literature since the end of the Franco regime in 1975 is characterized by a blend of continuity and rapid innovation. Though **censorship** and the general ideological climate of the regime provided inauspicious conditions for literary and cultural activity, some of the most notable literary achievements of the twentieth century in Spain were realized during the dictatorship. This was particularly the case in the **novel**, with the work of **Cela**, **Laforet** and **Matute** marking decisive formal innovations and offering a critique of the official version of reality purveyed by the regime. In the **theatre**, too, **Buero Vallejo**, **Sastre** and **Gala** courageously challenged the prevailing authoritarianism with plays which criticized cruelty and injustice, sometimes obliquely, but often explicitly. **Poetry** also flourished, owing to the efforts of an exceptionally gifted succession of poets from the 1950s on.

Three factors combined to enable writers to achieve some successes, even within the limited field of manœuvre allowed by censorship. In the first place, the functioning of censorship itself was often inefficient, inconsistent, and prone to manipulation by personal contacts and influence. Moreover, writers themselves developed considerable skill in exploiting the limits of what was permitted: Buero, for example, wrote several ostensibly historical plays, in which the implied parallels with the Franco dictatorship were clear enough to perceptive audiences, but insufficiently explicit to allow the censors to invoke the criteria, however vague and general, by which they operated. Poetry, appealing to a limited readership, was comparatively unmolested by censorship. Though José Angel **Valente** suffered harassment from the authorities, it was not because of his poetry, but because of a short story which the censors regarded as critical of the **armed forces**. In any case, by the 1960s, the regime's anxiety to present itself to the world as a modern, quasi-democratic polity had the effect of mitigating some of the more severe effects of censorship, though there were still limits to what could be written. The explicit comments on the Civil War and on police brutality during the regime in Juan **Goytisolo**'s *Marks of Identity* (*Señas de identidad*, 1966) meant that the book was first published in Mexico, and did not appear under a Spanish imprint until after Franco's death.

Second, it proved impossible in practice for the regime to isolate Spain from intellectual and cultural currents from outside, owing to the importance of **tourism** and the growth of international communications. The discovery of Italian neo-realism in the 1950s had a profound effect on both the Spanish cinema and, more notably, on the novel. By the 1960s, the increasing availability of foreign works of **critical theory**, plus the growth of innovative fiction in Latin America, represented, among others, by the 'magical realism' of Gabriel García Márquez, was encouraging experimentation among Spanish writers.

The third factor was the traditional, humanistic character of **university education**, which, while limiting its practical relevance to a society in need of rapid technological modernization, kept alive interest in literature in general, and in the literary heritage of the various cultures of Spain in particular. Admittedly, for most of the Francoist period, it is meaningful to speak of a cleavage between élite and mass cultures. Academic critics tended to be dismissive towards literary journalism, and the reading public for serious creative literature remained relatively limited until the 1980s. Nevertheless, it was university graduates, including many from disciplines other than arts, who staffed the **literary journals**, started brave and precarious **publishing** ventures, and, indeed, produced much of the creative writing, some of which, like the early work of Cela, was partly influenced by the sixteenth- and seventeenth-century picaresque novel, a genre in which Spain had excelled.

The role of education in the sphere of literature became increasingly important after 1970 (see also **education and research**), when the first of several legislative measures was enacted, which had the effect of widening participation in education and, in the long run, creating a more sophisticated and demanding **readership**. In parallel with this, the publishing industry has expanded and diversified, aided by the penetration of the Spanish market by international firms like the German-based Springer group, and the adoption of aggressive marketing strategies. One consequence of this has been to foster an approach to literature similar to the **consumerism** which determines attitudes towards other products.

The effects of this on the cultural and literary environment have been complex. At one level, the escapism which characterized **Francoist culture** has been compounded, producing a burgeoning of what is referred to as '**kiosk literature**' (*literatura de quiosco*). Already, during the dictatorship, the reading public had developed a taste for translations of English and American novels of adventure, romance and **detective fiction**, as well as indigenous genres such as the ***novela rosa*** and the ***fotonovela***. To this has been added a proliferation of other kinds of reading matter, such as practical manuals, **comics**, gossip magazines coming under the general rubric of ***prensa del corazón***, and **pornography**. Newspaper kiosks located on the street and in railway and bus stations, stationers, large department stores, and even fast food chains such as **VIPS** (see also **fast food outlets**), all provide retail outlets for a much more diversified mass literature. Figures produced by the National Statistical Institute show that in 1995 reading was more than twice as popular a leisure-time activity as watching spectator sports or going to discos.

The increasing tendency of readers to behave as consumers has, however, been beneficial to more serious kinds of literature as well. Though readership of the **press** is overall among the lowest in Europe, readership of the quality press (***ABC***, ***El País***, ***El Mundo***, ***La Vanguardia***) is comparable to that in the UK (see also **media**). The lack of specialist weeklies such as the *Times Literary Supplement* or the *New York Review of Books* is compensated for by the literary supplements of the Spanish quality papers, which exercise considerable influence over reader preferences, and also have an impact on the sales figures of publishing houses. The traditional disdain of academic critics for anything smacking of popularization has been broken down, and many now write willingly for the newspaper supplements. Writers like the novelist Francisco Umbral and the dramatist Antonio Gala have earned a secondary reputation as literary and political journalists with a wider public than they commanded through their creative work. In addition to prolonging the 'culture of evasion' characteristic of Francoism, the retail outlets mentioned above have also been a means of disseminating low-cost editions of foreign and Spanish classics, as well as work by serious contemporary writers. Whereas in the 1950s and

1960s a quality novel by a Spanish writer might have a print-run of a few thousand, from the mid-1980s, it was not uncommon for leading novelists like Juan **Benet** to have initial print-runs of several tens of thousands.

Part of the reason for this is that serious writers often adapted their style and subject-matter (judiciously, it must be said) to the demands of the market. Poetry, a genre identified in the public mind with the concerns of an élite minority, has not shared in the general expansion to the same extent as the novel, though a survey of young readers carried out on behalf of the **Ministry of Culture** in 1987 showed that in the late teens and early twenties age-group, 40 percent reported having read a volume of poetry. The same survey suggested that it was this age-range that accounted for the largest single cohort of the reading public, and this group was more likely to read books than newspapers. It is to the interests of this sector, with its desire to understand contemporary society and its antecedents in the Civil War and the Franco dictatorship, that many of the most successful novelists have been able to appeal. This is, for example, why the detective novel, especially in the hands of one of its most successful exponents, Manuel **Vázquez Montalbán**, has displayed some unusual features in Spain since 1975, with implied political and social commentary being accorded as much importance as the solution of the crime.

The other major development since the 1980s has been the expansion of **women's writing**. Though novelists like Rosa **Chacel**, Carmen Laforet and Ana María Matute enjoy a well-merited reputation as a result of work published in the difficult Franco years, relatively few women were writing in the social-realist mode which won favour with influential critical opinion in the 1950s and 1960s. The situation of women writers in all genres has been transformed by general changes in the social status of **women**, the expansion of the publishing industry, the more favourable critical climate, and the multiplication of sub-genres, including erotic literature, to which many women writers have contributed.

Literature since 1975, therefore, has reflected the expansion of the reading public in numerical terms, the increasing commercialization of the publishing industry, and the blurring of the distinctions between 'high' and 'popular' cultures, with the consequent diversification of activity and interests by writers and readers alike. Traditionalist critics, in Spain as elsewhere, continue to deplore what they see as the decline of literature, particularly in competition with the audiovisual media, but the complexity of the situation does not warrant such pessimistic judgements.

See also: cultural institutions and movements

Further reading

Debicki, A.P. (1994) *Spanish Poetry of the Twentieth Century: Modernity and Beyond*, Lexington, KY: University Press of Kentucky (contains especially useful overviews of Spanish poetry of the 1970s and 1980s).

Graham, H. and Labanyi, J. (eds) (1995) *Spanish Cultural Studies, an Introduction: The Struggle for Modernity*, Oxford: Oxford University Press (the index can be used as a guide to the references to literature which appear through the book, and to individual writers).

Hooper, J. (1995) *The New Spaniards*, Harmondsworth: Penguin (see chapters 24, 28 and 29 for a concise overview of the main trends).

Jordan B. (1990) *Writers and Politics in Franco's Spain*, London: Routledge (one of the most lucid studies in English of the novel in relation to its socio-political context).

Ruiz Ramón, F. (1989) *Historia del teatro español. Siglo XX*, Madrid: Cátedra (a history of the Spanish theatre in the twentieth century).

EAMONN RODGERS

Llach, Lluís

b. 1948, Verges (Girona)

Singer and songwriter

One of the major figures of the Catalan ***Nova Cançó***, Llach became famous in the 1970s for his **protest songs**, including 'En Maurici' and 'Cal que neixin flors a cada instant' (Let All the Flowers Bloom). More recently his work reveals the influence of music from Arab countries.

See also: Catalan culture; folk music; gay culture; *Movida, la*; music

DAVID GEORGE

Lladró

In 1951 three brothers set up a workshop in their own house, making flowers, vases and figurines, first in earthenware and later in porcelain. Eight years later they moved to Tavernes Blanques where, by incorporating sculptors, chemists and decorators into the team, they developed new styles and especially the new technique of single-firing pre-decorated pieces (by contrast with the normal triple-firing technique). They began to export and in 1969 built the first of the Lladró factories, which became known as *La Ciudad de la Porcelana* (Porcelain City), with over 1,500 employees, most of them women. By the 1990s the enterprise had expanded to five factories which export porcelain figures to over 120 countries and have diversified into leather goods.

The elongated style which became world famous was developed in the 1960s, principally by the sculptor Fulgencio Garcia López (1915–94). Born in Valencia, he had trained at the San Carlos School of Fine Art, and in 1945 had won a prize in the National Exhibition of Fine Arts, Madrid. He later directed the Lladró Sculpture Workshop, in which specialists are trained in the techniques of decorative porcelain. Many pieces have become part of private and museum collections, especially the Lladró Museum opened in New York in 1988, and among the most notable are *Triste Arlequín* (Sad Harlequin), *Amparito con cesta* (Amparito with a Basket), *La Virgen de los Desamparados* (Our Lady of the Destitute), *Ciervos perseguidos* (Stags in Flight), *Violencia* (Violence), and *Don Quijote*.

See also: design; pottery; sculpture

EAMONN RODGERS

LODE

The *Ley Orgánica de Derecho a la Educación* (Law of Entitlement to Education) was an attempt to give legislative effect to certain provisions of the **constitution of 1978**, which imposed on the state the obligation to provide free compulsory elementary education at public expense. The constitution established the right to found schools, the rights of parents to choose the kind of moral and religious education they wished for their children, and protected academic freedom and freedom of conscience. The state, for its part, was obliged to guarantee access to education for all citizens. The LODE (1984) provided for management and control structures for schools and distinguished between public, private and maintained schools, thereby attempting to achieve equality of opportunity within a mixed system.

See also: BUP; COU; FP; LOGSE

Further reading

Bosch, F. and Díaz, (1988) *La educación en España. Una perspectiva económica*, Barcelona: Ariel.

ISIDRO FADRIQUE

LOGSE

The *Ley de Ordenación General del Sistema Educativo* (Law for the General Reform of the Educational System) (1990) was an attempt to address issues such as the need to rationalize the relationship between **FP** and **BUP**, introduce greater flexibility in the curriculum and avoid early specialization. The law envisaged the phasing-in over ten years of a new syllabus and examination structure, replacing **COU** by the year 2000.

ISIDRO FADRIQUE

López Ibor, Juan José

b. 1908, Sollana (Valencia); d. 1991, Madrid

Psychiatrist and writer

López Ibor studied medicine at the University of Valencia, and in 1932, was appointed to the Chair of Forensic Medicine in Santiago de Compostela, becoming professor of Psychiatry in Madrid in 1960. He wrote fourteen books on psychology and was a significant figure in cultural history because of his forays into what he called 'collective psychology'. His attempts to define and analyse the Spanish character in *El español y su complejo de inferioridad* (The Spaniard and his Inferiority Complex), which went through five editions by 1960, place him firmly within the ambit of **Francoist culture**, with its emphasis on essential values, austerity, nationalism, and the identification of Spanishness with Catholicism.

EAMONN RODGERS

López Rodó, Laureano

b. 1920, Barcelona

Politician and academic

An administrative lawyer who obtained a Chair at the University of Santiago de Compostela at the age of 25, López Rodó was typical of a new breed of highly gifted civil servants who came to prominence in the 1950s. He received his first political appointment in 1956 through the patronage of **Carrero Blanco**, who made him Technical Secretary of the Office of the Council of Ministers. In this capacity López Rodó had considerable influence on the crucial cabinet reshuffle of 1957 which brought into the government the so-called **technocrats**, many of them, like López Rodó himself, members of **Opus Dei**. This was the beginning of the gradual realignment of the regime in response to contemporary economic realities, the main result of which was the **Stabilization Plan** of 1959.

Energetic and hard-working, López Rodó initiated a reform of the structure of government which gradually began to shift the day-to-day administration away from Franco towards a network of committees serviced by a new Office of Economic Co-ordination and Planning. This was part of a cautious evolutionary strategy on the part of López Rodó to move towards a system of government which would ultimately not depend on the person of Franco, but which would preserve the essential lineaments of authoritarianism, albeit in a modernized form. Symptomatic of this strategy was López Rodó's drafting of the *Principles of the **National Movement*** in 1957, a document which paid lip-service to the ideals of the old **Falange**, but which was sedulously vague about how these were to influence the form of the state. The eventual nomination of Prince **Juan Carlos** as successor to Franco in 1969 was one of the most significant long-term results of López Rodó's activities.

López Rodó's power and influence increased even further when in 1962 he was appointed to head the Commissariat for the Development Plan, which gave him a key role in formulating economic policy. In 1965 he was made Minister without Portfolio, and has been credited with much of the economic success which Spain achieved in the 1960s. His indispensability to the regime for nearly two decades after his first government appointment is revealed by the fact that although implicated in the **Matesa** scandal in 1969, he retained his post while other ministerial colleagues lost theirs. With the increasing physical and mental incapacity of Franco, however, and the return to repression during the closing years of the regime, he was moved to the less influential post of Minister of Foreign affairs in 1973. After Carrero Blanco's assassination and the appointment of Carlos Arias Navarro as Prime Minister, he was dropped from the cabinet and became Ambassador to Austria. In the elections of 1977 he gained a seat for the **Popular Alliance** in Barcelona, which he held until 1979.

López Rodó was not an instinctive democrat: he was one of the *siete magníficos*, the 'magnificent seven', involved with Manuel **Fraga Iribarne** in the foundation of the Popular Alliance, which they hoped might preserve the essential features of Francoism. Nevertheless, his career illustrates the important role played by a particular kind of academically brilliant and ambitious career bureaucrat in modernizing the economic and administrative structure of the regime in ways which, whatever their long-term intentions, helped to smooth the transition to democracy.

See also: history

Further reading

Preston, P. (1993) *Franco*, London: Harper Collins

(the standard and most comprehensive biography in English; the index enables the reader to trace López Rodó's career and relate it to contemporary historical events).

EAMONN RODGERS

López Rubio, José

b. 1903, Motril; d. 1996, Madrid

Writer and filmmaker

Playwright, film director, and television writer, whose active career spanned more than five decades, López Rubio grew up in Granada, where he attended performances of touring companies with his parents, who were devotees of the theatre. His first important literary achievement was a collection of short stories, *Cuentos inverosímiles* (Improbable Tales), in 1924; his only novel, *Roque Six*, was published in 1928. After initial successes in 1929 and 1930 with two plays written with Eduardo Ugarte, he worked in Hollywood for five years, first as adapter of several early talking pictures for Spanish versions at MGM and then as a leading screen-writer for Fox's Spanish division. López Rubio became a close associate of Charles Chaplin and attended the gatherings of celebrities at Chaplin's home. He returned to Spain after the Civil War and directed six full-length films, including an adaptation of Benavente's tragedy *La malquerida* (*The Passion Flower*) (1940). Resuming playwriting in 1949, he became a master of serio-comic theatre with *Celos del aire* (*In August We Play the Pyrenees*) (1950), *La venda en los ojos* (*The Blindfold*) (1954), and *La otra orilla* (*The Other Shore*) (1954); he also translated more than twenty foreign plays and musicals for the Spanish stage; his last play, *La puerta del ángel* (The Way of the Angel), was performed in 1985. Many of his nineteen plays are highly self-reflective in the manner of Evreinov and Pirandello and reflect the humoristic techniques of the so-called 'Other Generation of 1927', a group of young playwrights who shared common interests and Madrid's literary gatherings in the 1920s, especially those of the brilliant but eccentric Ramón Gómez de la Serna. Several of his comedies were written as vehicles for the prominent stage and film comedienne Conchita Montes. Although some critics have dismissed his comedies as escapist entertainment, revivals of his plays in the post-Franco period have been met with critical respect, and the rebellion of his female protagonists against social norms reveals far more social commentary than was originally attributed to these subtle and sophisticated plays. A notable atypical drama is *Las manos son inocentes* (Our Hands are Innocent) (1958), a stark study of moral decay and guilt resulting from economic deprivation.

López Rubio's first series of television plays, *Al filo de lo imposible* (At the Edge of the Impossible) (1968–9), received the National Prize for Television in 1971. These short scripts offered the familiar serious comedy of his works for the stage as well as a darker humour and irony. A second series, *Mujeres insólitas* (Exceptional Women) (1976), utilizes an innovative distancing technique to question the legends surrounding some thirteen famous women from Cleopatra to Lola Montes. A stage manager called Pepe appears in each episode and assumes various roles as the protagonist steps in and out of the action to comment on the interpretations others have made of her life. In 1986 the veteran writer was elected a member of the **Royal Academy**.

See also: film and cinema; television

Further reading

Holt, M.P. (1980) *José López Rubio*, Boston, MA: Twayne (a concise study of the writer's life and career, with analyses and plot descriptions of his plays).

MARION PETER HOLT

Los Ángeles, Victoria de

b. 1923, Barcelona

Singer

Born Victoria Gómez Cima, Victoria de los Ángeles displayed a talent for music from an early age, and was sent to the Liceo Conservatory in Barcelona, where she studied voice with Dolores Frau, making such rapid progress that she completed the six-year course in half the time. She made her concert début as a soprano in Barcelona in 1944, and sang her first operatic role, as the Countess in *The Marriage of Figaro*, at the Barcelona Lyric Theatre in 1946. Further operatic roles in *Lohengrin*, *Die Meistersinger*, *Tannhäuser*, *Faust* and *Der Freischütz* followed from 1947–9. In 1948 she married Enrique Magriñá Mir, who became her manager. Her career developed rapidly in the 1950s, when she sang at Covent Garden, the New York Metropolitan Opera and La Scala, taking leading roles in, among other works, *La Bohème*, *Madame Butterfly*, *Manon Lescaut* and *Otello*. Reviewers consistently praised the natural purity of her voice, and her apparently effortless control, which made her particularly suitable for lyrical roles in operas by composers such as Puccini, rather than the heavy dramatic roles demanded by, for example, Wagner's *Ring* cycle.

Her reputation and virtuosity were still undimmed when she sang the title-role in *Carmen* at the New York City Opera in 1979. Since the 1970s, however, she has concentrated more on recital work, which has also earned her enthusiastic praise. Her recorded repertoire is extensive, including opera and song recitals. She is arguably among the top five female singers in the world this century.

EAMONN RODGERS

LRU

The *Ley de Reforma Universitaria* (Law of University Reform) was enacted on 25 August 1983, in an attempt to deal with the crisis which had plagued the universities since the mid-1960s, when the rapid growth of the student population had created huge pressure of numbers, leading in turn to infrastructural problems and staff shortages. In addition, the atmosphere of discontent was intensified by the fact that most staff had no security of tenure. The intention of the legislation was to implement the principle of university autonomy by sharing responsibility among the state, the **autonomous communities**, and the universities themselves in respect of organization, government, financing and academic affairs. An important provision of the act was the creation of private universities, for which detailed regulations were finally drawn up in 1991. The act also provided for the assessment of the teaching and research competence of academic staff.

Though the LRU has been criticized, and has not met all the expectations which it aroused, its effects on university life have been visible and positive. Universities are now much freer from official control, and there have been significant increases in funding.

See also: education and research; LOGSE; science; student life; UNED; universities; university education

Further reading

Capitán Díaz, A. (1994) *Historia de la educación en España. II: Pedagogía contemporánea*, Madrid: Dykinson (pp. 841–59 contain a detailed commentary on the act).

Hooper, J. (1995) *The New Spaniards*, Harmondsworth: Penguin (chapter 19 gives a good overall account of the development of education at all levels).

ALICIA ALTED

Luca de Tena y Brunet, Torcuato

b. 1923, Madrid

Writer

Journalist, novelist, dramatist and poet, Torcuato Luca de Tena has continued the literary tradition of his father, dramatist Juan Ignacio, Marquis of Luca de Tena, and his grandfather, founder of the newspaper ***ABC***. Although Luca de Tena studied law, he began working as a correspondent for *ABC* in 1945, travelling to several countries including England, the USA, the Middle East, Hungary and Mexico. In 1962, he became editor of *ABC*. He maintains a special interest in Latin America, having founded *ABC de las Américas*, which focuses on that region.

Luca de Tena's literary career began in 1945 with a modest book of poems entitled *Espuma, nube, viento* (Foam, Cloud, Wind), followed in 1948 by a journalistic chronicle, *El Londres de la postguerra* (Post-War London) which won the Larragoiti Journalism Award. His first novelistic effort, *La otra vida del Capitán Contreras* (The Second Life of Captain Contreras) (1953) recounted the disillusionment of a seventeenth-century soldier, resurrected in the twentieth century. His second novelistic effort, published in 1955, was *La edad prohibida* (The Forbidden Age), memoirs of adolescence, which won both the National Literary Award and the Málaga-Costa del Sol Award. His 1961 novel of adultery, *La mujer del otro* (Another Man's Wife) received the **Planeta Prize**. *La brújula loca* (The Crazy Compass) (1964) and *Pepa Niebla* (1970), more mature works, present psychological profiles of, respectively, a child during the Civil War and a schizophrenic. Novels from the 1970s and 1980s include *Cartas de más allá* (Letters from Beyond) (1978), *Los renglones torcidos de Dios* (God's Twisted Pages) (1979), *Escritos en las olas* (Written on the Waves) (1979), and *Los hijos de la lluvia (a.C.)* (Children of the Rain, B.C.) (1985). Luca de Tena's novels have enjoyed wide popularity with the reading public, going into several editions, but have received scant critical attention, perhaps because they conform to traditional novelistic forms, and have occasionally been labelled superficial.

Luca de Tena's dramatic production began in 1967 when he and his father collaborated to adapt his novel *La otra vida del Capitán Contreras* to the stage. The 1975 drama *Hay una luz sobre la cama* (There's a Light Over the Bed) featured the same protagonist as his novel *Pepa Niebla.* Other dramas include *El triunfador* (The Victor) (1975), *Una visita inmoral* (An Immoral Visit) (1975) and *El extraño mundo de Nacho Larranga* (Nacho Larranga's Strange World) (1979).

Luca de Tena has also produced non-fiction works. He collaborated in 1955 with Captain Teodoro Palacios, held in Russian prison camps for eleven years, to produce *Embajador en el infierno* (Ambassador in Hell) (1955) which received both the National and Army Literary Awards. The results of his historical investigation appeared in *Los mil y un descubrimientos de América* (The Thousand and One Discoveries of America) and also in the biography *Yo, Juan Domingo Perón* (I, Juan Domingo Perón) in 1976.

Luca de Tena was elected to the Royal Academy of the Spanish Language in 1972.

FRIEDA H. BLACKWELL

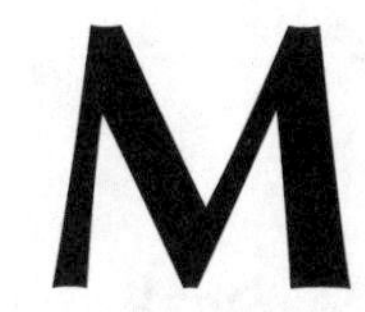

Madrid Book Fair

Held annually from the end of May to the middle of June in the Retiro Park, the Madrid Book Fair, with some 450 stands, attracts two and a half million visitors. Leading authors attend to sign copies of their latest works, and sales of the most popular individual titles run into several thousand each, with well over a quarter of a million all told. Children's literature and activities receive special promotion, and braille and multimedia productions have been a feature since 1995. Many new publications are launched in conjunction with the fair, which is also accessible via the Internet.

See also: publishing; readership

EAMONN RODGERS

Manent, Albert

b. 1930, Premià de Dalt

Writer

Manent began as a poet, but soon turned to journalism and literary criticism. His critical writing avoids dogma and eschews eclecticism. His major contributions to Catalan literary criticism are three books on major figures of ***Noucentisme***, including *Carles Riba* (1963), *Josep Carner i el noucentisme: vida, obra i llegenda* (Josep Carner and Noucentisme: Life, Work and Legend) (1969), and *Jaume Bofill i Mates Guerau de Lliost: l'home, el poeta, el polític* (Jaume Bofill i Mates Guerau de Lliost: The Man, the Poet, the Politician) (1979). Another of Manent's notable contributions is his huge bibliography of Catalan writers who wrote in exile after the Spanish Civil War, *Literatura catalana a l'exili* (Catalan Literature in Exile) (1976). Manent's *Escriptors i editors del Noucents* (Writers and Editors of the 1900s) (1984) is a collection of articles on various Catalan authors, as well as his reflections on cultural resistance under Franco and aspects of the development of book publishing during the twentieth century.

Further reading

Medina, J. (1988) 'La crítica literaria i la història de la literatura' in M. de Riquer, A. Comas and J. Molas (eds) *Història de la literatura catalana*, 11 vols, Barcelona: Ariel, XI (contains an introductory section on Manent).

DAVID GEORGE

'MANOLETE' *see* Rodríguez Sánchez, Manuel

Mar Bonet, Maria del

b. 1947, Palma de Mallorca

Singer and songwriter

One of the leading exponents of the ***Nova Cançó***, Maria del Mar Bonet's music is based on sources as varied as folk songs from the Balearic islands, French poets and contemporary Catalan poets. A strong North African influence is evident in a number of her songs.

DAVID GEORGE

Maragall, Pasqual

b. 1941, Barcelona

Politician

Pasqual Maragall is a law graduate from the University of Barcelona, from which he obtained his doctorate in economics. He was active in Catalan socialist groups during the Franco era, and was a **Catalan Socialist Party** (PSC) candidate at the local elections in 1979. He quickly rose to prominence in local government, and was Mayor of Barcelona from 1982 to 1997. His most important achievement was his part in the staging of the 1992 Barcelona Oympic Games.

DAVID GEORGE

Maravall Casesnoves, José Antonio

b. 1911, Játiva (Valencia); d. 1986, Madrid

Historian and political theorist

Although most of José Antonio Maravall's career was spent under the Franco regime, his importance extends beyond its confines. He entered the University of Murcia in 1927 to read Philosophy and Letters and Law, continuing his studies in Madrid. In the 1930s he collaborated in journals such as *Cruz y Raya* (Plus and Minus) and ***Revista de Occidente*** (The Western Review). During the Civil War, he took the side of the Francoist insurgents, as one of a minority within the **Falange** which aspired to direct the cultural destinies of Spain, by constructing a fascist state with 'liberal' or 'Orteguian' elements (see also **Ortega y Gasset, José**), and which later clustered around the journal *Escorial* and the *Revista de Estudios Políticos* (Political Studies Review). Becoming editor of *Cuadernos Hispanoamericanos* in 1948, he lived in Paris from 1949 to 1954 as director of the Spanish College within the Sorbonne. On returning to Spain in 1955, he was appointed to the Chair of the History of Spanish Political and Social Thought in the Faculty of Economic and Political Sciences in the University of Madrid, where he remained until his retirement. His work was mainly concerned with the theory of the state, but covered many other aspects of Spanish cultural history.

Maravall is also significant as a representative of those who initially supported the Franco regime but later advocated liberalization. In 1970, along with other leading intellectuals such as **Tierno Galván**, Ruiz Giménez, **Aranguren**, **Laín Entralgo**, **Marías** and **Tamames**, he signed a document advocating reform of the political system, free trade unions, freedom of association, and the revision of the *Plan de Desarrollo* (Development Plan) and the 1953 Concordat with the Vatican.

ALICIA ALTED

March Alcalá, Susana

b. 1918, Barcelona

Writer

Poet, novelist and short story writer, Susana March, who achieved her mature style in the 1950s, explores the solitary struggle of women who aspire to autonomy in a patriarchal society. March has not received the critical attention she deserves from feminist critics, though she anticipates many of the concerns of feminism. In addition, the experimental novels of the 1960s have eclipsed her traditional realistic style. Representative of her best work are collections of poems, *Esta mujer que soy* (The Woman I Am) (1959), *Poemas: Antología: 1938–59* (Poems; Anthology: 1938–1959, 1966) and the novel, *Algo muere cada día* (Something Dies Within Us Every Day) (1955), translated into French (*Les ruines et les jours*).

In the semi-autobiographical novel, *Algo muere cada día*, the narrator-protagonist, María, develops her potential as a writer, raises her children and becomes financially independent, in the absence of her husband. (He is in political exile during the early years of the Franco regime.) However, her autonomy is ultimately thwarted by her husband's return. As María knows, the norms of the patriarchal order will be re-established, with her happiness, pleasure, convenience and personal destiny fading into insignificance. María's resignation, modified only by her unspoken non-conformity and her ability to endure, may seem too tame to modern readers, but the novel reflects the social circumstances of the early post-war years, before the reform of the Spanish civil code in 1970, when there was no divorce and women were treated as minors, dependent on the male head of the family.

March places women in a network of relationships: family, extended family and friends. Her themes are represented by poems in the 1966 anthology. Among them, 'Mi madre y yo' (My Mother and I) and 'La madre' (Mother) capture a daughter's devotion to her mother and their mutual understanding as a profound life force. Maternal tenderness for a son is poignantly expressed in 'Mi hijo ha crecido este verano' (My Son Has Grown This Summer). 'A un hombre' (To a Man) is a thoughtful statement of the unfulfilled desire for friendship and mutual respect between men and women. Like Gloria **Fuertes**, March uses colloquial language to evoke emotion or criticize social norms that stifle women's aspirations. However, March's tone is more controlled, and her language more lyrical. In 'Una señora' (A Lady), ladylike behaviour becomes a form of self-censorship, communicated through the paradox of a silent scream.

March has written ten books of verse, four novels, two collections of short stories and with her husband, Ricardo **Fernández de la Reguera Ugarte**, has co-authored nine historical novels. These were published by Editorial Planeta (1963–72) in a series entitled *Episodios Nacionales Contemporáneos* (Contemporary National Episodes).

Further reading

Cavallo, S. (1990) 'The Quiescent Muse of Susana March', *Monographic Review/Revista Monográfica, Odessa, IX* 6: 81–92 (an overview and analysis of March's poetry).

Patterson, H.W. (1965) *Antología Bilingüe (Español-Inglés) de la Poesía Española Moderna*, Madrid: Cultura Hispánica (includes translations of two poems, 'Long, Long Ago' and 'Threshold').

Pérez, J. (1988) *Contemporary Women Writers of Spain* Boston, MA: Twayne Publishers (an overview of writing by Spanish women authors through the 1980s, containing useful socio-political information).

MARIA NOWAKOWSKA STYCOS

Marías, Julián

b. 1914, Valladolid

Philosopher and essayist

A leading disciple of José **Ortega y Gasset**, Marías has expanded his master's theories of vital and historical reason into his own system of 'the empirical structure of human life'. Ortega's vital and historical reason assumes that the task of philosophy is to serve human needs in their concrete social and cultural immediacy; it therefore reflects our attempt to find meaning and direction within a specific historical circumstance. Marías has assimilated this principle as well as ancillary categories crucial to Ortega's understanding of human life – such as the role of narrativity, the importance of beliefs, and his theory of generations – into his own science of reality. This science acquires for the author a metaphysical status: it recognizes the primacy of concrete personal existence, conditioned by historical forces as the foundations of all reality. To paraphrase an important passage in the author's work, the structure of human life assumes that past and future are *present* in the life of one and all, and that these features are implicated in the *why* and the *for what* of our actions.

Also noteworthy is the author's study of Unamuno, and of Spain during the reign of Charles III.

See also: cultural institutions and movements; intellectual life; philosophy

THOMAS MERMALL

marriage and divorce

A public opinion poll of 1981 produced in Spain a 23 percent agreement with the statement that marriage was an outdated institution, the second highest positive response rate (after France at 29 percent) in ten western European countries. The subsequent drop in marriage indices has confirmed the decline in the popularity of marriage in Spain, although whether the causes are predominantly economic (long recession accompanied by high unemployment from 1975 to 1984) or predominantly social (a shift in attitudes and a decline in the influence of the church) is unclear. The number of marriages per thousand inhabitants has dropped from 7.5 in the 1960s to an average of 5.4 in the 1980s. Although it has crept up in the 1990s to 5.7, this is still very much lower than we might expect given the high number of people reaching marriageable age as a result of the baby boom of the 1960s. It is clear that co-habitation and even single parenthood have become more acceptable, the illegitimacy rate having climbed from a low point of 1.3 percent of births in 1971 to over 9 percent of births by the end of the 1980s (still much lower than in most other western European countries). As far as the average age of contracting partners is concerned there was a significant drop in the 1970s to 24 for women and 26 for men, but it has since risen to 26 for women and 28 for men.

Divorce in Spain has been possible since 1981. Far from the predicted avalanche of applications to the courts from estranged couples, the take-up rate was low at just 16,000 dissolutions during the first year after the divorce law was enacted, climbing gradually to a peak of 27,500 in 1991. This gives a divorce rate among the Spanish population of 0.5 per thousand, or roughly one in ten marriages, substantially lower than in most other western European countries. Legal separation has increased faster than divorce in the 1980s to reach 40,000 by 1992. Both divorce and separation can be obtained by mutual consent or through application by one partner with a legally justified cause. Although the latter type of application still outnumbers the former, there has been a clear tendency for joint applications to increase, and they now account for 45 percent of divorces and virtually 50 percent of separations.

Further reading

Hooper, J. (1995) *The New Spaniards*, Harmondsworth: Penguin, 176–85 (entertaining, perceptive and mostly accurate).

V Informe sociológico sobre la situación social de España (1994) Madrid: Fundación FOESSA, vol. 1, pp. 173–4, 433–45 and 491–7 (the social survey of Spain par excellence and an indispensable sociological tool).

C.A. LONGHURST

Marsé Carbó, Juan

b. 1933, Barcelona

Writer

Marsé left school at thirteen, worked as a jewellery-maker and started writing short stories in 1959. His first and most autobiographical novel, *Encerrados con un solo juguete* (Shut In With Only One Toy), was published in 1961.

Like many writers of the mid-twentieth century, he depicts with stark realism the sense of hopelessness expressed either in apathy or in revolt by the young growing up under Francoism. Passive or dissident, his protagonists adopt stances establishing an ironic distance between them and the situations they encounter. Through them Marsé explores the social, political and religious myths behind the reigning ideologies of the period. In *Ultimas tardes con Teresa* (Last Evenings with Teresa) (1966) the student activist Teresa, from a wealthy middle-class family, tries to help Manuel, whom she idealizes as a working-class militant. In fact, he is unemployed, a thief, and sees Teresa as his passport to social advancement. Through their relationship Marsé exposes the deceptive fictional nature of the mythic identities they create for one other.

In *La oscura historia de la prima Montse* (Montse's Dark Story) (1970) the narrator, Paco, is implicated in the story he tells. Attempting to reconstruct events eight years after they occurred, Paco offers various interpretations complicated by hindsight and his need for self-justification, exploring the potential for deception in subjective narration. *The Fallen* (*Si te dicen que caí*) (1973), also told in retrospect, consists of fictions consciously created and constantly altered by children who draw on experience, rumour, films and imagination, combining stark realism with extravagant fantasy in playfully contradictory confusion. The manipulation of information is central to the narrative in *La muchacha de las bragas de oro* (The Girl with the Golden Panties) (1978), in which a former Falangist historian tries to make the past more acceptable as he writes his autobiography, discovering, however, that the fiction he creates is closer to the truth than the memories he tries to deny. Then, in mocking self-parody Marsé focuses on the ambivalence of language itself in *El amante bilingüe* (The Bilingual Lover) (1990). His virtual homonym Juan Marés tries to become the gipsy-like lover for whom his wealthy Catalan wife has left him. Marés' personality disintegrates, his bilingualism degenerates into meaningless babble and narration itself is destroyed.

Writing about the repression and hardship of the 1940s, student and worker movements of the 1950s, the economic boom and progressive ideals of the 1960s, and the re-emergence of democracy and Catalan nationalism in the 1970s, Marsé undermines the credibility of history, of those who tell it, and of language itself. Dreams, myths and fantasies, and the collective memory of a community, provide a provocative alternative reading of the Franco years.

Further reading

Barral, C. (1975) *Años de penitencia*, Madrid: Alianza Editorial (an autobiography providing useful points of comparison with Marsé's novels).

Labanyi, J. (1989) *Myth and history in the contemporary Spanish novel*, Cambridge: Cambridge University Press (an illuminating discussion of *The Fallen* as 'corrupt narrative').

ROSEMARY CLARK

Marsillach, Adolfo

b. 1928, Barcelona

Actor and theatre director

One of the most prominent directors in Spain, Marsillach began his acting career in radio plays. His first stage role was in *Cyrano de Bergerac*, and he went on to play in works by Calderón, Sartre and Tennessee Williams. In 1953, he made his début as a theatrical director, and in the early 1960s added cinema and television direction to his portfolio, a mixture which he maintained throughout the succeeding three decades. He has also written plays, including *Mata-Hari* (1983) and *Feliz aniversario* (Happy Anniversary) (1991). His main importance, however, is that he was one of a small number of directors interested in heightening awareness among Spanish audiences of theatrical developments in other countries, and also in revitalizing the classic Spanish theatre of the seventeenth century through his leadership, since 1986, of the National Classical Theatre Company. Since 1989 he has been Director-General of the Instituto Nacional de Artes Escénicas y Música (INAEM – National Institute of Theatre Arts and Music). He is a recipient of the National Prize for Theatre and the Gold Medal for Fine Arts (1992).

See also: performing arts; theatre

EAMONN RODGERS

Martín Gaite, Carmen

b. 1925, Salamanca

Writer

Carmen Martín Gaite, who won the **Nadal Prize** for the best Spanish novel of 1958 with her first full-length narrative, *Behind the Curtains* (*Entre visillos*), has achieved recognition as one of Spain's major novelists. She was awarded the prestigious National Prize for Spanish Letters in 1994.

In 1950 Martín Gaite moved from her native Salamanca to Madrid where she joined a group of young writers who would come to be known as the 'Generation of the 1950s'. The world in which this group moved is analysed in her essay *Esperando el porvenir* (Waiting for the Future) (1994). Italian neo-realist cinema influenced the early work of this group which included Josefina Rodríguez, who married Ignacio **Aldecoa** and writes as Josefina R. **Aldecoa**, and Rafael **Sánchez Ferlosio**, to whom Martín Gaite was married.

On the basis of her first novel, her short stories and other texts, Martín Gaite's work has been labelled by critics as social realism. In fact, it is much more than this. Her texts are those of a woman writer who usually prefers to describe the lives of women, as in *Variable Cloud* (*Nubosidad variable*) (1992), and she often mixes novelistic fiction with the essay or even the historical study. In *The Back Room* (*El cuarto de atrás*), with which she won the National Prize for Literature in 1978, the reader finds autobiographical allusions inter-mingled with elements of the mystery novel in a text which is, above all, a reflection on the act of writing.

While she was awarded the **Prince of Asturias Prize** in 1988, it is above all since the publication of the two lengthy novels *Variable Cloud* and *La Reina de las Nieves* (The Snow Queen) (1994) that she has achieved considerable popularity. In 1996 she publishes *Lo raro es vivir* (Being Alive is Unusual) and in 1998 *Inse de casa* (Leaving Home). She participates frequently in the literary events organized by the **Juan March Foundation** in Madrid and she has become a much sought-after figure in the annual **Madrid Book Fair**. In the opinion of critics her novels attest to a genuine mastery of the colloquial registers of Spanish and of the techniques of dialogue. It is thus not surprising to find in her work a persistent interest in the question of human communication, a topic she analysed from a theoretical viewpoint in the essay *La búsqueda del interlocutor y otras búsquedas* (In Search of an Interlocutor, and Other Searches) (1974).

Several texts by Martín Gaite have been adapted for television and for the cinema. She has also written original scripts for two successful television series: one on the life of St Teresa of Avila (with Víctor García de la Concha, 1983), and the other, *Celia*, based on the work of Elena Fortún (with José Luis **Borau**, 1993).

Further reading

Brown, J.L. (1987) *Secrets from the Back Room: The Fiction of Carmen Martín Gaite*, University of Mississippi, MS: Romance Monographs (an important study by a leading scholar).

Fernández, L.M. (1992) *El neorrealismo en la narración española de los años cincuenta*, Santiago de Compostela: Universidade de Santiago de Compostela (sets the novel in the context of neo-realism in literature and the cinema).

Martinell, E. (1995) *Carmen Martín Gaite. Hilo a la cometa. La visión, la memoria y el sueño*, Madrid: Espasa-Calpe.

—— (1996) *El mundo de los objectos en la obra de Carmen Martín Gaite*, Cáceres: Universidad de Extremadura.

Servodidio, M. and Welles, M.L. (eds) (1983) *From Fiction to Metafiction: Essays in Honor of Carmen Martín Gaite*, Lincoln, NB: Nebraska Society of Spanish and Spanish-American Studies (a useful symposium of different views).

EMMA MARTINELL GIFRE

Martín-Santos, Luis

b. 1924, Larache (Morocco); d. 1964, Vitoria

Psychiatrist and novelist

Luis Martín-Santos (not to be confused with a less well-known novelist of the same name, without the hyphen, born in 1921) was born in a Spanish outpost in Morocco, where his father was a medical officer in the army. In 1929, the family moved to San Sebastián. Luis studied medicine at the University of Salamanca, graduating in 1946. Postgraduate studies in Madrid, from 1946 to 1949, were followed by a period as a researcher in the **CSIC**, where he collaborated with Juan José **López Ibor** and Pedro **Laín Entralgo**. After a period as a surgeon, Martín-Santos decided to specialize in psychiatry, and secured a post as director of a mental hospital in Ciudad Real. After further research in Germany, he returned to Spain in 1951 to head the psychiatric hospital in San Sebastián.

Martín-Santos' professional career developed in parallel with his involvement in the cultural and political ferment of the 1950s. Despite the restrictions imposed by **censorship**, the first half of the decade saw the foundation of the Madrid literary review, *La Revista de España* and the Barcelona periodical *Laye*, as well as increasing demands among young intellectuals for reform of the university system and of political structures in general. Martín-Santos was drawn into the literary café society of Madrid, where he met novelists such as Rafael **Sánchez Ferlosio**, Juan **Benet**, Ignacio **Aldecoa**, and the dramatist Alfonso **Sastre**. Inevitably, however, this intellectual ferment led to renewed repression by the Franco regime, especially after the student disturbances in Madrid in 1956, and the dismissal of the relatively liberal Minister of Education, Joaquín **Ruiz Giménez**. As an active member of the clandestine socialist **PSOE**, Martín-Santos was arrested several times between 1957 and 1962, and in 1958 was imprisoned for four months.

These events, and his earlier experience as a medical researcher, flowed together into his only finished novel, *Time of Silence* (*Tiempo de silencio*, 1962). Whereas other writers, such as Aldecoa, Jesús **Fernández Santos** and Juan **Goytisolo** in his early novels, criticized the regime indirectly through starkly realistic portrayals of life under the dictatorship, Martín-Santos adopted a boldly innovative style, akin to the 'stream-of consciousness' writing associated with James Joyce. The nightmarish and partly nocturnal perambulations of the protagonist, Pedro, echo those of Leopold Bloom in *Ulysses*. Although the scenes through which he passes depict various representative aspects of Spanish society (Pedro's under-resourced laboratory, the indifferent and self-indulgent bourgeoisie, the miserable inhabitants of the shanty-towns), they do so in a grotesque and exaggerated way. Rather than criticize the regime through an objective portrayal of its failures, as his neo-realist contemporaries did, Martín-Santos uses symbolism and parallels with ancient myths to undermine the myths which sustained the dictatorship. The subject of Pedro's research, cancer, comes to stand for the moral disease at the core of society, which, as the deeply pessimistic ending of the novel implies, is incurable. His ambition of winning the Nobel Prize is seen to be absurdly unrealistic, and to stem as much from his own lack of energy and initiative as from the social and moral context.

Between 1962 and his early death in a car accident in 1964, Martín-Santos worked on a second novel, edited and published posthumously in 1975 by José-Carlos Mainer as *Tiempo de destrucción* (Time of Destruction). As with *Time of Silence*, the attack on the myths of Francoism is built around the trajectory of a single protagonist, Agustín. Mainer skilfully reconstructed most of the novel from a partly-finished typscript, with the aid of an outline provided by Martín-Santos' brother Leandro. A collection of shorter writings was published, also posthumously, in 1970 under the title *Apólogos y otras prosas inéditas* (Fables and Other Unpublished Prose Writings). In addition to his literary work, Martín-Santos also published sixteen scientific papers and a book on mental illness.

The fact that Martín-Santos left only one finished novel before his untimely death at the age of forty belies his importance. *Time of Silence* had reached its twentieth edition by 1983, and had a profound influence on the subsequent development of prose fiction in Spain. The neo-realism of the mid-1950s gave way to a more evocative, less directly referential style, emphasizing the role of memory and subjective perception in the creation of reality, represented typically by Juan and Luis **Goytisolo**, Juan **Marsé** and Juan **Benet**.

See also: Francoist culture; novel

Major works

Martín-Santos, L. (1962) *Tiempo de silencio*, Barcelona: Seix Barral; trans. G. Leeson, *Time of Silence*, New York: Harcourt, Brace & World (1964).

—— (1975) *Tiempo de destrucción*, Barcelona: Seix Barral.

Further reading

Labanyi, J. (1989) *Myth and History in the Contemporary Spanish Novel*, Cambridge: Cambridge University Press (chapter 3, 'Fiction as Mask: *Tiempo de silencio*' is a very perceptive analysis of the use of myth in this novel).

Mainer, J.C. (1975) 'Introduction' to *Tiempo de destrucción*, Barcelona: Seix Barral (the most useful general overview of Martín-Santos' work, as well as a very interesting account of the reconstruction of *Tiempo de destrucción*).

Palley, J. (1971), 'The Periplus of Don Pedro: *Tiempo de silencio*', *Bulletin of Hispanic Studies* 48: 239–54 (a detailed analysis of the structure of the novel).

EAMONN RODGERS

Martín Villa, Rodolfo

b. 1943, Santa María del Páramo (León)

Politician

After graduating in engineering at Madrid, Martín Villa spent the period 1965–74 in Franco's official trade union bureaucracy. In 1975 he was appointed Minister of Union Relations and subsequently served Adolfo **Suárez** and **Calvo Sotelo** as Interior Minister (1976–9) and as Minister of State for Regional Affairs and Vice-premier (1980–2). He joined the newly formed centre-right **PP** in 1989 and was elected as MP for Madrid in all subsequent elections. He was a somewhat controversial and authoritarian figure of Christian Democratic leanings, who nonetheless played an important role in the transition to democracy.

See also: National Movement; politics; UCD

MICHAEL T. NEWTON

Martinell, César

b. 1880, Valls (Alt Camp); d. 1973, Barcelona

Architect

César Martinell is both architect and art historian, whose work shows the influence of his mentor Antoni **Gaudí**. A member of the Barcelona School, Martinell displays great inventiveness in structural design and technique, as well as a creative interpretation of the aesthetic idiom of **Modernism**. Among his varied creations his industrial farm buildings occupy a special place in the development of architecture. Thirty wine-growing co-operatives in various parts of Catalonia are constructed in a quasi-ecclesiastical style: temples of industry, one might say. The skill of the engineer is complemented by great artistic interventiveness.

MIHAIL MOLDOVEANU

Martínez, Conchita

b. 1972, Monzón (Huesca)

International tennis player

Martínez is one of a distinguished generation of young Spanish sports personalities, who won the Wimbledon Ladies' Championship in 1994, when she was ranked third in the world. She retained her ranking in the top five in the world in the mid-1990s, when she had a particularly successful career, winning many titles.

See also: Sánchez Vicario, Arantxa; tennis

EAMONN RODGERS

Martínez-Lázaro, Emilio

b. 1945, Madrid

Filmmaker

Martínez-Lázaro is the co-scriptwriter of Ricardo **Franco**'s *Pascual Duarte*. From 1976 he has combined a versatile film career with extensive television work, including the full-length television feature *Todo va mal* (Everything's Going Badly) (1984).

EAMONN RODGERS

Marxism

The influence of Marxist–Leninist ideology in Spain has been relatively weak, despite the professed adherence to it of the communist **PCE** and the left wing of the socialist **PSOE** during the Civil War. During the Franco regime, the spectre of a supposed Marxist–Masonic conspiracy against Spain provided a convenient set of clichés with which to keep alive the fear of a return to the conflicts which had brought about the war. With the re-establishment of democracy, particularly in the context of the first post-Franco general election in 1977, both parties evolved towards a more moderate, social-democrat position. Although the legalization of the PCE was bitterly resented by the **armed forces**, it was welcomed by the political community as a whole, not least because the party had agreed to work within the structures of constitutional monarchy. The new, post-exile leadership of the PSOE, represented by Felipe **González** and Alfonso **Guerra**, adopted a similar stance, though the membership as a whole resisted attempts to remove the explicit commitment to Marxist–Leninism in the party manifesto.

The PSOE's success in the local and municipal elections of 1979 convinced González and Guerra that there was considerable grass-roots support for the party, and that the Marxist label was the only factor deterring the electorate from giving PSOE power at national level. González therefore staged a tactical resignation from the post of Secretary-General at the XXVIII Congress in May 1979, and spent the summer touring the country and winning over the support of rank-and-file members in the provinces. At an extraordinary congress in September, he secured overwhelming endorsement for his modernization plans, and PSOE, freed from its Marxist legacy, won a landslide victory in the general elections of 1982.

Subsequently, PSOE continued on its moderate path, prompting in 1986 the creation of the **United Left** coalition, made up of disaffected ex-members of PSOE's left wing, and PCE members striving to rebuild the party's shattered electoral support. Insofar as remnants of Marxism survive in Spain, it is found in the United Left, though despite its name, the grouping lacks ideological and organizational coherence.

See also: socialism

EAMONN RODGERS

Masó i Valentí, Rafael

b. 1880, Girona; d. 1935, Girona

Architect and writer

Masó is the key figure in the development of **Noucentisme** in Girona. He founded the literary society *Athenea* and was an architect of great originality. His earlier work belongs stylistically to **Modernism**, as exemplified in the Harinera Teixidor (1910–11, Girona), an industrial building in which modernist vocabulary is used with great flair. After 1912 his work became noucentist, combining new influences in original ways. The Casa Masramon (1913–4, Olot) and the Casa Ensesa (1918–22, Girona) are the best examples of this period. From 1924 until his death he was involved in the construction of a striking urban residential development, S'Agaró, which still influences the architectural character of the Costa Brava.

MIHAIL MOLDOVEANU

matador

Properly called *matador de toros* – literally, a killer of bulls – the matador is the principal, that is, the most admired and best-paid, performer in the modern bullfight, which uses four to five-year-old bulls.

See also: bullfighting

IAN CAMPBELL ROSS

Matesa

Matesa was the most famous corruption case under the Franco dictatorship, centring around a textile firm of the same name, *Maquinaria Textil del Norte de España Sociedad Anónima* (North of Spain Textile Machinery), which manufactured textile machinery in Pamplona. The **technocrats** of **Opus Dei** who had enjoyed political ascendancy in the Francoist regime since the beginning of economic liberalization in the 1950s, were implicated in the scandal which involved the fraudulent use of government funds for the export of textile machinery.

The Director of Matesa, Juan Vilá Reyes, had presided over the development of a shuttleless loom which was successfully exported to Europe, Latin America and the USA and as such was highly regarded by the technocrats. Vilá Reyes was himself a member of the Opus Dei as well as being a close friend of Laureano **López Rodó**, the Minister for the Development Plan. However, financial irregularities came to light in 1968, when it was alleged that Matesa had fraudulently obtained government export credits by setting up subsidiary companies in Latin America which had then ordered large quantities of the shuttleless looms. In addition to López Rodó several other ministers, all members of Opus Dei, were implicated in the scandal.

Although it seems that Franco himself was not particulary concerned by what he regarded as merely the sidestepping of regulations in order to encourage much needed exports, the Matesa scandal was used as political fodder in the **Falange**'s fight to end what they regarded as the excessive dominance of the Opus Dei in the government. José Ruiz Solís, Secretary of the Falange, unleashed a bitter press campaign with the support of Manuel **Fraga Iribarne**, the Minister of Information and Tourism, against the technocrats in an attempt to break the hegemony of the Opus Dei group.

However, the campaign, which was feasible partly as a result of the new relaxed **Press Law** elaborated by Fraga, seriously backfired. Franco was far more concerned with the damage to Spain's international credibility caused by the press campaign, and by the debilitating power struggle between the Falange and the Opus Dei, than with the original fraud itself. Ultimately, the two ministers involved in publicizing the scandal, Solís as Secretary of the Movement and Fraga as Minister of Information, were forced to leave their posts, whilst the Opus Dei technocrats escaped rather lightly. The scandal, however, did mark the beginning of the end of the Opus Dei's dominance in the Francoist regime.

GEORGINA BLAKELEY

Matute, Ana María

b. 1926, Barcelona

Writer

Interviews by Matute during the 1950s, 1960s and 1970s reiterate the significance of childhood experiences of the Civil War and her own marginal, outsider status. Both profoundly mark her writings, producing pervasive feelings of alienation, solitude and melancholy. Matute's family owned a factory in Barcelona but resided alternately between Madrid and Barcelona for business reasons; consequently, she recalls always being 'from elsewhere': Catalan in Madrid, Castilian in Barcelona. Her maternal grandparents' mountain estate in Old Castile bordered La Rioja, Logroño and Navarre, near the village of Mansilla de la Sierra ('Hegroz' and 'Artámila' in her fictions) and in this remote, rugged, primitive area, Matute enjoyed her childhood summers. When eight years old, convalescing from a near-fatal illness, she spent a year here, attending the one-room country school with the barefoot children of tenant farmers. Spain's cultural and economic contrasts imprinted themselves indelibly upon her sensibility, awakening the socio-political conscience that characterizes her writings. The Civil War, erupting just before her tenth birthday, trapped the family in Barcelona for the duration. With schools closed and many former teachers (nuns and priests) executed or in hiding, Matute, her siblings and young cousins remained indoors behind closed shutters, hearing the sounds of fighting in the streets, taking shelter during bombardments, frequently witnessing atrocities when allowed to venture forth. Her father's factory was 'nationalized' (appropriated by the Popular Front) and their home occupied by militia during the social revolution which accompanied the war in Barcelona. Adolescent experiences of class conflict taught Matute the arbitrary nature of social values and structures, inspiring lifelong commitment to social justice. Further insights appear in *A la mitad del camino* (Halfway Down the Road) (1961), *El río* (The River), and *Historias de la Artámila* (Tales of Artámila).

Los Abel (The Abel Family) (1948) introduces for the first time a theme which was to reappear in several of Matute's works: fratricidal strife, articulated through a reworking of the biblical myth of Cain and Abel, an emblem of the Civil War for Matute and many other writers. Years after the Abel siblings mysteriously disappeared, an acquaintance discovers evidence of internecine rivalries for lands and loves, motifs reiterated in Matute's monumental masterpiece, *Los hijos muertos* (The Dead Children), winner of the Critics' Prize for the best novel of 1958, and of the 1959 Miguel de Cervantes National Literary Prize. In these works, as in *Fiesta al noroeste* (Celebration in the Northwest) (1952) – sombre, dark chronicles of the decadence and downfall of rural gentry – Matute explores the underlying causes of the Civil War: socio-economic exploitation, abuse, indifference by powerful landholders to the welfare and rights of the poor, tenants and day-labourers. Updating the myth of Cain and Abel, Matute creates characters not only symbolic of social conditions and political ideologies but solitary and alienated individuals, frustrated by hostile environments and their own weaknesses. Unlike many post-war neo-realists, Matute conveys her social criticism not through impassive objectivity, but through a combination of lyricism, occasional pathos, interior monologue with its psychological insights, moments of intense drama, occasional surprise endings and sudden, sometimes grotesque violence.

Matute's short stories contain similar themes: *El tiempo* (Time) (1957), *El arrepentido* (The Repentant One) (1961), and *Historias de la Artámila* (Tales of Artamila) (1961) treat primarily lower-class characters, victimized by poverty, exploitation and indifference, or depict the loneliness of the old, the deformed, the ugly or timid. Another pervasive theme involves the private worlds of children and adolescents, their fantasies, disillusionments, and occasionally cruel adaptations: *Los niños tontos* (The Stupid Children) (1956), termed by Camilo José **Cela** the most important book by a woman since Emilia Pardo Bazán, sensitively paints fantasy sketches of children who die, mature, or otherwise escape harsh reality, while *Libro de juegos para los niños de los otros* (Book of Games for Others' Children) (1961), undisguised social criticism, combines essay and short story modes. These sketches, which are neither about games nor intended for children, depict fantasy outlets for repressed resentment, class hatred and deprivation. Matute also cultivates juvenile fiction, writing Andersen-inspired fairy tales for younger children, plus novels of passage such as *Paulina, el mundo y las estrellas* (Pauline, the World and Stars) (1960) and *El polizón del 'Ulises'* (The Cabinboy of the 'Ulysses') (1962) intended for adolescents. *Tres y un sueño* (Three (Fantasies) and One Dream) (1961) paints three people's private fantasy worlds filled with fairy-tale elements, while *El río* (The River) (1963) nostalgically evokes childhood experiences following the submerging of Mansilla de la Sierra beneath a reservoir.

For some critics, Matute's crowning achievement is her trilogy *Los mercaderes* (The Merchants) , comprising *Primera memoria* (First Memoir, winner of the Nadal Prize) (1960), *Los soldados lloran de noche* (Soldiers Cry by Night) (1964); and *La trampa* (Trap) (1969), which re-examines conservative class structures and political *caciquismo* (bossism) as root causes of Spain's civil conflict. These independent novels, spanning some three decades, reiterate themes of betrayal, loss of innocence, idealism versus materialism, solitude, disillusionment, self-sacrifice, and the (usually evil) power of entrenched position, hereditary wealth, and the past. Biblical symbols and the modernized Cain and Abel myth blend with sordid adult sexuality as young idealists encounter repeated disillusionment. Matute's last significant work, *La torre vigía* (The Watchtower) (1971), an apocalyptic work in the style of the chivalric romance, depicts the death or frustration of youthful idealism, desolation and resignation. In *Olvidado Rey Gudú*, another millenial and apocalyptic, neo-chivalric chronicle, Matute continues many many themes of *La torre vigía* but adds fairy-tale motifs and characters and one of her most intriguing heroines. This dynastic chronicle, some four times the length of its predecessor, emphasizes the mindless cruelty of war, subtly drawing parallels between the close of the first millennium and the second.

During the 1960s Matute ranked among Spain's most prominent novelists, being selected as one of five representative writers (and sole woman) required by the 'Advanced Placement' Spanish programme in US secondary schools. Declining health and changing post-Franco aesthetics brought problems with publishers, with novels announced, then withdrawn. While any comeback to prominence seems unlikely, Matute continues among the most artistic and admired of the mid-century 'social realists'.

In January 1998 Matute became a member of the **Royal Academy**.

See also: censorship; Francoist culture; literature; novel

Major works

Matute, A.M. (1948) *Los Abel*, Barcelona: Ediciones Destino (novel).

—— (1952) *Fiesta al noroeste*, Barcelona: Pareja y Borrás (novelette).

—— (1956) *Los niños tontos*, Madrid: Ediciones Arión (stories).

—— (1958) *Los hijos muertos*, Barcelona: Editorial Planeta (novel).

—— (1960) *Primera memoria*, Barcelona: Ediciones Destino; trans. J. Mason, *Awakening*, London: Hutchinson, 1963; also trans. E. Kerrigan, *School of the Sun*, New York: Pantheon Books, 1963 (novel).

—— (1961) *El arrepentido*, Barcelona: Editorial Rocas (stories).

—— (1961) *Historias de la Artámila*, Barcelona: Ediciones Destino (stories).

—— (1963) *El río*, Barcelona: Editorial Argos (sketches).

—— (1964) *Los soldados lloran de noche*, Barcelona: Ediciones Destino; trans. R. Nugent and M.J. de la Cámara, *Soldiers Cry by Night*, Pittsburgh, PA: Latin American Literary Review Press, 1995 (novel).

—— (1968) *Algunos muchachos*, Barcelona: Ediciones Destino (stories).

—— (1969) *La trampa*, Barcelona: Ediciones Destino (novel).

—— (1971) *La torre vigía*, Barcelona: Editorial Lumen (novel).

Further reading

Díaz, J. (1971) *Ana María Matute*, New York: Twayne (a biobibliographical study analysing all works except *La trampa*).

Jones, M.E.W. (1970) *The World of Ana María Matute*, Lexington, KY: University of Kentucky Press (an excellent study of biblical allusions, childhood and adolescence, and stylistic devices).

Pérez, J. (1991) 'The Fictional World of Ana María Matute: Solitude, Injustice and Dreams', in J. Lipman Brown (ed.) *Women Writers of Contemporary Spain*, Newark, DE: University of Delaware Press, pp. 93–115 (analysis of motifs listed, paying special attention to *La torre vigía*).

Roy, J (ed.) (1993) *The Literary World of Ana María Matute*, Miami: Iberian Studies Institute (contains four essays).

Thomas, M.D. (1978) 'The Rite of Initiation in Matute's *Primera memoria*', *Kentucky Romance Quarterly* 25, 2: 153–64.

JANET PÉREZ

Maura, Carmen

b. 1945, Madrid

Actress

One of the most versatile and successful actresses of her generation, Maura is internationally renowned for her work with **Almodóvar**, starring in roles such as Pepa in *Women on the Verge of a Nervous Breakdown* (*Mujeres al borde de un ataque de nervios*, 1988) or Tina in *La ley del deseo* (Law of Desire) (1987). Already, however, she had had a continuous career in Spanish film and television and had worked widely in performing roles throughout the 1960s. She became a charismatic television presenter for a popular chat show in the 1980s and continues to work in Spain and abroad.

NÚRIA TRIANA TORIBIO

Mayoral, Marina

b. 1942, Mondoñedo (Lugo)

Critic and writer

An established literary critic, who teaches Spanish literature at the Universidad Complutense in Madrid, Mayoral has written extensively on two Galician writers of the nineteenth century, Rosalía de Castro and Emilia Pardo Bazán. Since the publication of her first novel in 1979, *Cándida otra vez* (Once Again Cándida), she has published five novels, a collection of short stories, *Morir en sus brazos y otros cuentos* (To Die in His Arms and Other Stories) (1989) and several other fictional works of shorter length. Among them, Mayoral has published three in her native Galician, *Unha árbore, un adeus* (A Tree, a Goodbye) (1988), *O reloxio da torre* (The Tower Clock) (1988), and *Chamábase Luis* (His Name was Luis) (1989), thus joining the group of contemporary writers who have started to publish in their vernacular language.

Mayoral's novels reveal common themes: some of the same characters reappear, story lines continue, and all have the presence of Galicia as an unmistakable characteristic. She has created, in the fashion of Juan **Benet**, a fictitious town, Brétama, which exemplifies Galicia's semifeudal society. It is evident in Mayoral's works that inequities exist between the working class and the privileged class, illustrated in *Contra muerte y amor* (Against Love and Death) where all the characters are Galician by birth, even though the novel takes place in Madrid.

Other themes in Mayoral's novels are the traditional ones of liberty, death and love which border on the melodramatic. Often violent, untimely, or mysterious endings are the fate of many of her characters. Her approach to love, marriage and other relationships, involving homosexuality and incest, as is the case in *La única libertad* (The Only Liberty), show a marked change from the **censorship** of the Franco era.

Mayoral's novels, like *Al otro lado* (On the Other Side), tend to have involved, intricate action with an element of mystery and intrigue reminiscent of **detective fiction**. She also incorporates different narrative points of view and the use of humour, which is a fundamental aspect of her writing.

The strength of Mayoral's novels lies in the richness and originality of her characterizations. A wide range of characters from different social classes, ages and occupations relate to each other in a weblike pattern. Strong female protagonists are of special interest in all her novels, but she also portrays substantial male characters. Although Mayoral does not proclaim herself a militant feminist, in her novels she defends a better position of women in society. All her female characters are unique personalities who serve as models to the female reader.

Marina Mayoral shows a definite development in her fiction; not only have her novels grown in length, but they have also grown in complexity. *Recóndita armonía* (Hidden Harmony) of 1994 is a case in point for its parallel structure. Mayoral has earned an important place among contemporary writers; she has been praised by critics and is appreciated by her readers, both in Spanish and Galician. Since 1994 Marina Mayoral has published two important works: a novel, *Dar la vida y el alma* (Madrid, 1996), with the parallel structure of a double love story, and *Recuerda cuerpo* (Madrid, 1998), a collection of clever short stories.

Further reading

Alborg, C. (1991) 'Marina Mayoral's Narrative: Old Families and New Faces from Galicia', in J. Brown (ed.) *Women writers of Contemporary Spain: Exiles in the Homeland*, Newark, DE: University of Delaware Press (a review of Mayoral's themes and most memorable characters).

Mayoral, M. (1992) *Cándida otra vez*, ed. G. Gullón, Madrid: Castalia (a useful edition with an introduction and bibliography).

Zatlin, P. (1987) 'Detective Fiction and the Novels of Mayoral', *Monographic Review/Revista Monográfica* 3, 1–2: 279–87 (an excellent study relating Mayoral's novels to detective fiction).

CONCHA ALBORG

mealtimes

The times of the midday and evening meals in Spain tend to be later than in many other parts of Europe, and are usually even later in the south of Spain than in the north. During the working week, *el desayuno* (breakfast) is around 7.30 a.m., though many people postpone this until the mid-morning break, around 10.30 a.m. Lunch, called *la comida* or *el almuerzo*, is the main meal of the day and is usually eaten between 2–3 p.m. ***Merienda*** (equivalent to teatime) is around 6.30 p.m., and *la cena* (dinner), normally a light meal, is sometime between 9–10 p.m. During the summer months, these times can be even later.

JUAN SERRANO

Mecano

Mecano's first record was released in 1981 and Ana Torroja and brothers Nacho and José María Cano, instantly became pop idols for adolescents. Mecano has enjoyed lasting commercial and artistic success. The group produced six LPs where more frivolous tracks written by Nacho, like 'Maquillaje' (Make-up), 'Me colé en una fiesta' (Uninvited Guest), are mixed with more reflective and mature songs by José María, like 'Aire' (Air), 'Un poco loco' (A Little Crazy) or 'Mujer contra mujer' (Woman Versus Woman).

See also: rock and pop

FERNANDO DELGADO

Medem, Julio

b. 1958, San Sebastián

Filmmaker

Medem belongs to the generation of Basque filmmakers which made a forceful début in the early 1990s and brought Basque cinema to the forefront of the Spanish international market. Eschewing a nation-building agenda, his films explore the parameters of a plural cultural identity and tradition in ways that are both innovative and self-confident. If *Vacas* (Cows) (1992) offers a dissection of the rural saga film, *La ardilla roja* (The Red Squirrel) (1993) awarded the Youth Prize in the Directors' Fortnight in Cannes, adopts different generic conventions to reflect on issues of identity and memory. The stunning camera work in *Tierra* (Earth) (1996) confirms Medem's talent for creating a haunting atmosphere in film. The formal accomplishment of his filmmaking, together with a suggestive symbolism and complex narrative style, single out Medem as a representative of the new European cinema.

See also: film and cinema

Further reading

Ros, X. de (1997) '*Vacas* and Basque Cinema', *Journal of the Institute of Romance Studies*, 5: 225–34.

XON DE ROS

media

During the first thirty years of the Francoist dictatorship, the media were subjected to severe **censorship**, under the 1938 *Ley de Prensa* (Press Law), which gave the government absolute control over the media. Publishers were required to provide the censors with all material prior to publication, and government nominees were appointed to executive positions in media companies. In 1966, the *Ley de Prensa e Imprenta* (**Press Law**), unofficially known as the *Ley de Fraga* (**Fraga** Law), was passed. Though this measure abolished prior censorship, publications which transgressed the (still ill-defined) limits of freedom of expression, or attacked the founding principles of the regime, could be fined, suspended and even closed down. The limited nature of this act may be gauged by the number of clandestine publications which were launched in its immediate aftermath.

The **constitution of 1978**, which recognized and protected freedom of expression (article 20), changed this situation dramatically. From the 1970s onwards, the media were revitalized, and favourable market conditions in the 1980s have produced an unprecedented expansion in the amount of information and cultural discussion on offer. The **press** was augmented with new titles, mostly at regional or local level, though in many cases these were local editions of existing national publications. Readership figures for the weekday editions of the daily newspapers rose to 2.5 million by 1994, with substantially higher figures for the weekend editions.

The three leading newspapers in terms of sales, *El* ***País***, ***ABC*** and *El* ***Mundo***, are national dailies published in Madrid, with regional editions in some of the **autonomous communities**. All three compete with each other in news coverage and also in the **readership** at which they aim. They are followed by *La* ***Vanguardia*** and *El* ***Periódico de Catalunya***, published in Barcelona and read essentially in Catalonia. Among the daily newspapers, some of the highest readership figures are commanded by the **sporting press**, especially the two papers exclusively devoted to sport, *Marca* and *As*, which in 1992 ranked third and eighth respectively. Another area of increasing importance in the Spanish press is economics, which is covered by new publications devoted exclusively to this topic, such as *Actualidad Económica* and *Expansión*, as well as by the business supplements included in the most important newspapers.

Though annual average readership of the daily press has shown a slight increase since 1993, levels of readership are still among the lowest in Europe. In 1992, 10 percent of Spaniards regularly bought a newspaper, compared to 15 percent in France, 35 percent in Germany, and 40 percent in Britain. It is true that because of the Spanish habit of sharing reading matter in bars, private clubs or libraries, real readership figures are probably of the order of 25–30 percent. Nevertheless, the corresponding rate for France is over 50 percent, and for Britain 85 percent. On the other hand, readership of the quality press is probably comparable in Spain and the UK: there is no equivalent in Spain of the sensationalist popular tabloid press which commands such a large share of the market in Britain. Nor do Spaniards have the habit of taking out regular subscriptions, preferring to purchase directly from news stands (*kioscos*) and local shops.

Within the print media, the most vigorous area is, undoubtedly, *revistas periódicas* (regular magazines), a high-profit sector with a increasing number of publications, many of them Spanish editions of foreign magazines. The most successful publications of the 1980s have been the so-called ***prensa del corazón*** (romantic press). The most famous of these magazines are ***¡HOLA!***, *Semana*, *Lecturas*, *Diez Minutos* and more recently, *QMD*, which is based on a television programme containing news about the rich and famous. These magazines have been successful because they fill the gap left by the daily newspapers, which, unlike those in Britain and the US, do not have personal and gossip columns.

During the last years of the dictatorship and the transition to democracy, newspapers seemed reluctant to publish items on current affairs, and this gap was also successfully filled by the magazine sector. The first real news magazine was ***Cambio 16***, which started production in 1972. Similar in style to *The Times* or *Newsweek*, *Cambio 16* set a new standard of professionalism. However, with the increasing modernization of the style and content of newspapers, most of these magazines gradually disappeared, except for *Cambio 16* and *Tiempo*, the latter having a more sensationalist character. However, the magazine that best reflects the liberal spirit of the years that followed the dictatorship is ***Interviú***, which combines an explosive mixture of free coverage of politics and photographs of naked women.

The most characteristic feature of the structure of mass media in Spain is the outstanding importance and influence of the very heterogeneous medium of **radio**. Radio has the advantage of being ubiquitious, is practically free, and can be listened to in public. It satisfies a general cultural need, which is the Spaniards' liking for conversation, and the interest in things local and close at hand. The two main varieties of radio found in Spain are: *onda media* (medium wave) and conventional radio on the one hand, and *frecuencia modulada* (FM) and *radio fórmula* (specialized radio) on the other, the latter being the preferred medium of the younger age-groups.

New licences granted in 1990 by the central government and the six autonomous communities, which enjoy devolved powers in the area of electronic communication, increased the number of radio stations to nearly 1.5 million. There are another 400 municipal radio stations and around 100 community radio stations, which are not restricted by the current legislation.

Although the first radio stations began to operate in 1924, the number of listeners was not large until the mid-1930s. After the Civil War, radio became the most effective of all propaganda tools. Broadcasting was regulated by the 1939 Statutory Order, which gave the government-controlled Radio Nacional de España (RNE) (**national radio** of Spain) the exclusive right to broadcast news. Only groups which were close to the regime were given licences, and in 1960 all radio stations were legally required to broadcast simultaneously the news programme of *RNE*. This order was only repealed in 1977.

Radio underwent a radical change in structure and outline during the 1970s, when broadcasting was deregulated, and more licences for FM stations were granted. News broadcasts were liberalized, and radio became a means of expression for the political transition to democracy, and subsequently a provider of entertainment. Radio is still considered very influential, its successful combination of news, music and current affairs winning it an audience which in the 1990s has remained stable at approximately 16 million listeners, much larger than in any other European country.

Radio is structured commercially around a mixed system of public and private stations. The biggest public network is RNE, which has the widest coverage, reaching all over the world with its Radio Exterior de España station, the first to broadcast outside Spain. Among the private networks, **SER**, **COPE**, Antena 3 and Onda Cero are the leading groups in terms of listeners and publicity. With the development of the autonomous communities in Spain there appeared during the 1980s a number of regional and local radio networks run by the various autonomous governments. The highest audiences for radio programmes are achieved by the early morning news programmes and the ***tertulias*** (discussions), both of them being popularly broadcast between 9–10 a.m. The sports programmes also attract a large following.

Television is the communication medium which has experienced the largest increase in variety and services in Spain. It began to operate as a state service in 1956, under the strict control of the regime. The present structure of the public television system dates from 1980, when the *Estatuto de Radio y Televisión* (Radio and Television Statute) was passed. This statute established various parliamentary groups for control of the medium, as well as a Consejo de Administración (administration board) for regulating and managing its functioning.

In 1994 public television adopted a new strategy in order to reaffirm its public identity and differentiate it from its private competitors. The competition for audience share between the state-run channels and the three main private channels, and the need to adapt to the new technology, especially cable, satellite and digital television, have inaugurated a new era for television in Spain. Of the two state-run channels, TVE1 is directed to a general public, offering uninterrupted programming from early morning to late at night and has the largest overall audience, despite the intense competition of the private television channels for specific programmes and times. TVE2 has a more flexible programming, which pays special attention to sports broadcasts and live broadcasts of important cultural events.

The 1980 Statute also allowed the establishment of a third regional channel, dependent for control and financial support on the autonomous communities, in order to enable them to express their own identities. In **Euskadi**, Euskal Televista was set up in 1983, broadcasting in Basque. Subsequently, Catalonia developed its own channel, TV3, followed by the Galician TVG. Since then, other regional channels have developed, including: Canal Sur in Andalusia, with 2.1 million viewers in 1993, TeleMadrid with 1.2 million viewers and Canal 9 in Valencia, with 1.2 million spectators. Moreover, Euskadi and Catalonia have created their own fourth territorial channel, ETB2 and Canal 33 respectively, and other regions have begun negotiations for creating their own channels.

Private television networks began in 1990. Licences were granted on condition that ownership of the private channels was predominantly Spanish and that at least 15 percent of the output was home-produced. Antena 3 was the first channel to operate, followed by Tele 5, and finally by Canal + in 1990. The programming of these channels is mainly based on a combination of news, games and films. Their emphasis is more on entertainment than on information and, except for Canal + (which is supported by subscriptions), all channels, including the state-run ones, depend financially on **advertising** revenue.

Spanish viewers' preferences hardly differ from those of other western European countries. In order to retain audiences, television networks compete with a very similar mix of programming, mostly composed of news, sports, Latin American *telenovelas* or *culebrones* (soap operas) broadcast at midday, quiz shows and repeats. Films made for television, mostly imported from the US, dominate prime time hours and attract the largest audiences. Spanish programmes such as *La Clave*, *Informe*

Semanal (Weekly Report) and *¿Quién sabe dónde?* (Who Knows Where?) have gained a loyal audience throughout years. In this context, it is worth mentioning that the only originally Spanish idea to have crossed the borders with success has been the game-show *Un, Dos, Tres* (One, Two, Three).

The attempt by the Spanish media to respond to the trends set in other western European countries has resulted in a number of fundamental structural changes from the mid-1980s to the mid-1990s, in particular the attempt to reach specific market sectors and also the increasing penetration of the media market by foreign capital, with consequent influence on the Spanish cultural industry. From the 1980s onwards, the communication business in Spain has maximized its profits by adapting to market globalization and to the diversification of **consumerism**. The enormous attention paid by the big communication groups to the Spanish media market has been mainly due to the steady increase in per capita income and consumer indices in Spain, and the relative saturation of communications markets in northern Europe, which have shown a level of growth well below that of southern Europe. Spain has therefore become an attractive country for their acquisition and expansion strategies.

See also: Basque television; Catalan television; kiosk literature; publishing; regionalism; social attitudes; society; youth culture

Further reading

Aguilera Moyano, M. de (1991) 'Las Comunicaciones Sociales', in J. Vidal Beneyto (ed.) *España a Debate*, Madrid: Editorial Tecnos (a theoretical analysis of the media as a politicized and commercial industry).

Bernández, A. (1991) 'The Mass Media' in A. Ramón Gascón (ed.) *Spain Today: In Search of Modernity*, Madrid: Cátedra (pp. 431–54 offer an informative account of the changes which have occurred in the Spanish media, from the Francoist censorship to the globalization of the 1980s and 1990s).

de Miguel, A. (1994) *La Sociedad Española 1993–1994. Informe Sociológico de la Universidad Complutense*, Madrid: Alianza Editorial (see pp. 679–736 for a sociological study of Spanish attitudes towards the media, covering aspects such as: reading habits, radio audiences, the importance of television, popularity and the use and abuse of language in the media).

Graham, H. and Labanyi, J. (eds) (1995) *Spanish Cultural Studies: An Introduction*, Oxford: Oxford University Press (pp. 356–73 contain several articles dealing with the evolution and modernization of the media in Spain, from the dictatorship up to the mid-1990s, with an expanded analysis on television).

Hooper, J. (1995) *The New Spaniards*, Harmondsworth: Penguin (chapters 21 and 22 provide a detailed sociological view on the Spanish media, from Franco's dictatorship to the1980s, including some useful statistics).

GEMMA BELMONTE TALERO

Mejías Jiménez, Antonio

b. 1922, Caracas; d. 1975, Madrid

Matador ('Bienvenida')

Son of Manuel Mejías Bienvenida, a leading **matador** of the early decades of the century, Antonio Bienvenida was one of five brothers who became matadors, the others being Manolo, Pepe, Angel Luis and Juan. After taking his ***alternativa*** in 1942, Bienvenida was much admired for his classical style and remained active until 1966. After a triumphal return to the rings in 1971, he finally retired in 1974. A veteran of over 800 ***corridas***, he died the following year in a freak accident on a bull-ranch.

See also: bullfighting

IAN CAMPBELL ROSS

Mendoza, Eduardo

b. 1943, Barcelona

Writer

Emerging as a novelist in the post-Franco period, Mendoza has become one of the most significant exponents of the detective genre while also parodying this form to criticize social ills.

In 1973 he moved to New York, living there until 1982 while supporting himself as a translator. His novels depart from the experimentalism of the Spanish 'new novel' (popular during most of the 1960s and 1970s) since he accords relatively little importance to discourse and instead brings back plot and story to the narrative. *The Truth about the Savolta Case* (*La verdad sobre el caso Savolta*, 1975) propelled Mendoza into the national limelight when the novel – acclaimed by both critics and readers – was awarded the prestigious Critics' Prize in 1976. This work, narrated retrospectively by a first-person narrator who is not the protagonist, contains numerous intertexts in the form of newspaper clippings and excerpts from other narratives, plus the registers of cross-examination and the argot of the lower classes.

The two novels that follow, *El misterio de la cripta embrujada* (The Mystery of the Enchanted Crypt) (1979) and *El laberinto de las aceitunas* (The Olives Labyrinth) (1982), are essentially parodies of 'tough guys' fiction. These novels, set in contemporary Barcelona, depict and implicitly denounce the poverty and crime overwhelming the lower classes. Both feature the same protagonist and satirize the social injustice and moral shortcomings of Barcelona society. In *The City of Marvels* (*La ciudad de los prodigios*, 1986) Mendoza returns to an epoch which he as author knows only through documentation. The events take place between two World Fairs held in Barcelona, in 1888 and 1929 respectively. This critically acclaimed work reconstructs the career of Onofre Bouvila, a man who rises from an obscure, lower class and socioeconomic background to fabulous wealth. From his beginnings as a street urchin, he attains inordinate wealth thanks to his keen mind and unabashed cynicism. Onofre could be considered a picaresque figure whose social ascent results from a myriad of questionable activities such as gangsterism, real estate speculation, illicit arms production and trafficking, and political manipulations. Onofre acquires dimensions beyond those usual for a fictional character, since apparently the author meant him to symbolize the rise of the Barcelona bourgeoisie; his activities mirror the acquisitive pursuits of this class during the same period. *Sin noticias de Gurb* (Without News from Gurb) (1991) concerns the search for an extra-terrestrial who, after assuming the identity of the singer Marta Sánchez, has disappeared without trace in the urban jungle of Barcelona. This setting affords the author the opportunity to reveal the underbelly of the city and expose all its blemishes and injustices.

Further reading

Hickey, L. (1990) 'Deviancy and Deviation in Eduardo Mendoza's *Enchanted Crypt*', *Anales de la literatura española contemporánea* 15, 1–3: 51–63 (an illuminating analysis of the novel).

Resina, J.R. (1994) 'Money, Desire, and History in Eduardo Mendoza's *City of Marvels*', *PMLA* 109, 5: 951–68 (a detailed analysis of the underlying theme of the novel, the acquisition of power through wealth).

Rodríguez-García, J.M. (1992–3) 'Gatsby Goes to Barcelona: On the Configuration of the Post-modern Spanish Novel', *Letras Peninsulares* 5, 3: 407–27 (compares Fitzgerald's novel with *La verdad sobre el caso Savolta* in parallel principles of constructive narratology, non-literary intertexts and spatiotemporal similarities, viewing the later work as postmodern pastiche).

GENARO J. PÉREZ

merienda

Merienda, the afternoon snack equivalent to teatime, is taken at around 6.30 p.m. and usually consists of coffee, or sometimes tea, and some type of cake, bun or biscuit. For growing children *merienda* is an important meal and is generally more substantial. It usually comprises either a glass of milk (often flavoured with chocolate), or yoghurt, *un bocadillo* (a sandwich) containing either a savoury filling or eaten with chocolate or a chocolate spread. This can be followed by cake and/or biscuits. Sometimes, more frequently during the winter months, *la cena* (the evening meal) is brought forward and combined with the *merienda* to form a hearty *merienda-cena*, eaten at around 8.30 p.m.

JUAN SERRANO

migration

Spain has experienced very substantial population movements since the 1950s, both internal and external. By far the most important were those of the 1950s and 1960s involving the transfer of at least four million people from a rural or backward milieu to the developing cities. By the mid-1980s a quarter of all Spaniards lived in a province other than the one in which they were born; additionally there was a population shift from villages and towns to the capital of the same province, which in many cases (e.g. Málaga, Seville) absorbed tens of thousands from other parts of their own provinces. During the years of rapid development in the 1960s the provinces with the highest number of immigrants were Madrid, Barcelona, Valencia and Vizcaya; and those with the highest number of emigrants were provinces in the regions of Extremadura, the two Castiles (excluding Madrid), Andalusia and Galicia. At a time when the population of Spain grew by 10 percent, 23 of the 50 Spanish provinces lost population. This led to the abandonment of entire villages and the depopulation of large areas of the interior. This mass migratory movement only came to an end following the onset of the long recession from 1975 to 1984, although even during this period of reduced economic activity there were 20 provinces which lost inhabitants, in part no doubt because of the ageing structure of their populations. Among the provinces with the highest absolute losses were Badajoz and Cáceres in Extremadura, Ciudad Real and Cuenca in Castile-La Mancha, León and Zamora in Castile-León, Jaén and Córdoba in Andalusia, and Teruel in Aragon. The one characteristic these provinces have in common is that they are all in the interior rather than on the littoral. In Galicia, for example, the two seabord provinces Pontevedra and La Coruña experienced net immigration, whereas the two interior provinces Lugo and Orense had net emigration.

In the 1980s migratory movements were less marked and in some cases reversed. A comparison of the 1981 and 1991 population censuses reveals that the regions with the highest net gains of population in relative terms were the Canaries (19.7 percent), the Balearics (13.7), Andalusia (9.3), Comunidad Valenciana (7.6), Madrid (7.3) and Murcia (7.3). The highest net losers were Galicia (-3.3), Asturias (-2.7) and the Basque country (-1.5). Given that the natural population growth between the two censuses was 3.1 percent, these changes can be ascribed in substantial measure to migratory movements. In absolute rather than relative terms, the regions with the highest net increases were Andalusia (c. 600,000) and Madrid (c. 344,000). Latest figures, however, suggest that densely populated provinces (Barcelona, Madrid, Vizcaya and Guipúzcoa) are now experiencing low level emigration: in 1993 Barcelona had a net migratory loss of 12,240 and Madrid of 6,362. But Valencia, another province with a relatively high density, has not so far shown the same tendency.

External migration, though not as pronounced as internal, was important in the 1960s. Emigration was probably given a boost by the sharp deflationary shock of the 1959 **Stabilization Plan** and was able to benefit from a general European prosperity. This wave of emigration perhaps goes some way towards explaining the low unemployment in the Spain of the 1960s. 1,310,424 Spaniards (of whom a majority were Galicians and Andalusians) are recorded as having left their country to go and work abroad, mostly in other countries of western Europe (especially France, Germany and Switzerland). However, what is frequently forgotten is that most of these emigrants returned after just a few years, so that in the four years 1965–8 return migration exceeded outmigration by some 233,000. For the period 1960–73 as a whole, net emigration (ie. emigrants minus returnees) was just 151,500, a figure far from the 'millions' often cited in uninformed accounts. The years 1974–80 saw a marked reduction in emigrants owing to the world economic recession induced by the first oil shock of 1973, and during this period returnees exceeded leavers by 291,500. In something over twenty years the external migratory activity had balanced out. The early 1980s saw modest net balances in favour of emigration, but the late 1980s again established a trend in the opposite direction, with arrivals exceeding leavers. It is thus perfectly clear that the vast majority of Spaniards who emigrate do so on a temporary basis only. The 1990s have confirmed the trend that Spain is now a country of net immigration. Some of the immigrants are

Spaniards returning home to retire after working abroad, some are foreigners seeking a milder climate for the same reason, and an unknown number are illegal arrivals from the poorer countries of North Africa and Latin America. Spain is no longer an exporter of labour: despite high unemployment, Spaniards are choosing to stay at home.

Further reading

Fundación FOESSA (1994) *V Informe sociológico sobra la situación social de España*, Madrid (vol. 1, chapter 2.2 is devoted to 'Movimientos migratorios en España' (Migratory Movements in Spain) and contains much information, especially for the 1980s).

C.A. LONGHURST

Miguel, Amando de

b. 1937, Zamora

Sociologist

Studied in Columbia University, New York, and has occupied chairs in Barcelona, Valencia and Madrid. A specialist in the structure of Spanish society, his work is greatly influenced by American sociology. Has published more than sixty books, several hundred monographic studies, and more than a thousand articles of various kinds. His 1995 volume *La España de nuestros abuelos. Historia íntima de una época* (The Spain of our Grandparents: The Intimate History of an Epoch) combines his sociological training with his interest in nineteenth-century and contemporary Spanish literature. A book which had a considerable impact at the time of its publication was *Sociología del franquismo. Análisis ideológico de los ministros del regimen* (The Sociology of Francoism: An Ideological Analysis of the Ministers of the Regime) (1975).

ALICIA ALTED

Mihura Santos, Miguel

b. 1905, Madrid; d. 1977, Madrid

Writer

Mihura is considered contemporary Spain's leading comic playwright. In addition to writing for the stage, he was a director and a screenwriter. During his youth, he worked as an actor but abandoned acting to dedicate himself entirely to writing. Mihura's first dramatic compositions were written in collaboration with other playwrights of his generation such as Joaquín **Calvo Sotelo** and Álvaro de **Laiglesia**. He wrote his first play, *Tres sombreros de copa* (Three Top Hats), in 1932. It had its début in 1952 and was a commercial success, winning its author critical acclaim. Similar recognition continued in conjunction with subsequent works almost without interruption until 1968, the year of Mihura's last play, *Sólo el amor y la luna traen fortuna* (Only Love and the Moon Bring Good Luck) and after which he gave up writing because of failing health. Mihura was awarded the National Theatre Prize three times, in 1953 for *Tres sombreros de copa*, in 1956 for *Mi adorado Juan* (My Beloved Juan), and in 1959 for *Maribel y la extraña familia* (Maribel and the Strange Family). In 1964, he was awarded the prestigious Calderón de la Barca Prize for *Ninette y un señor de Murcia* (Ninette and a Gentleman from Murcia). In all, Mihura wrote twenty-three plays.

Characteristically described as light-hearted comedy, Mihura's theatre is not without its transcendental artistic and social significance. In both form and technique, his drama reflects many of the avant-garde trends of the twentieth century. For example, the play within the play that pervades *Tres sombreros de copa*, and the question of identity in *El caso del señor vestido de violeta* (The Case of the Gentleman Dressed in Violet) (staged 1954) are metatheatrical devices that call our attention to the phenomenological implications of theatre as a self-referential art. There is also a discernible absurdist vein in Mihura's theatre. Such is the case in *Carlota* (staged 1957), where cause and effect are discounted through Mihura's clever use of language, and in *La bella Dorotea* (The Fair Dorotea) (1963), where he resorts to the ritual-like use of subplots to undermine audience anticipation and stress the subjectivity and unpredictability of reality. In other plays, such as *El caso de la señora estupenda* (The Case of the Stupendous Lady) (1953), *Las entretenidas* (Ladies of the Night) (1962), and *Milagro en casa de los López* (Miracle at the López House) (1965), Mihura dramatizes the quasi-existential confrontation of self and society by relying exclusively on mystery and intrigue.

Mihura's theatre constitutes a unique brand of social satire. On the surface, his protagonists appear frivolous. Yet as their otherwise trivial predicaments evolve, they ultimately strike a pathetic note *vis-à-vis* the world they inhabit. As a result, Mihura succeeds in questioning the very arbitrary, if not capricious nature, of reality while parodying social conventions. His critical objective masked by farce, Mihura proves that light-hearted comedy can be a vehicle for social as well as artistic insight.

Further reading

Holt, M.P. (1975) *The Contemporary Spanish Stage (1949–1972)*, Boston, MA: Twayne Publishers (chapter 2 discusses Mihura's theatre in conjunction with the work of other leading dramatists of the 1930s, 1940s and 1950s).

McKay, D.R. (1977) *Miguel Mihura*, Boston, MA: Twayne Publishers (an excellent general introduction to Mihura's theatre).

Miguel Martinez, E. de (1979) *El teatro de Miguel Mihura*, Salamanca: Universidad de Salamanca (a comprehensive study of the themes and formal elements of Mihura's theatre).

JOHN P. GABRIELE

Milá i Sagnier, Alfonso

b. 1924, Barcelona

Architect

Milá qualified as an architect in Barcelona in 1952 and became the associate of Federico **Correa**. Their work has greatly influenced architecture and **Interiorism** in Barcelona and opened up new possibilities for Spain as a whole. La Talaia (1972, Barcelona) is a good example of this new departure, and another well-known work of theirs is the headquarters of the Barcelona Provincial Council (1985–7). In conjunction with the Italian Vittorio Gregotti they also designed the series of constructions put in place for the Barcelona **Olympic Games** of 1992. Their most characteristic artistic statement is the 'interiorist' restaurant Flash-Flash (1970, Barcelona).

MIHAIL MOLDOVEANU

Milans del Bosch, Jaime

b. 1915, Madrid; d. 1997, Madrid

Army officer

Milans del Bosch came from a very old and military family, and had a very successful career under the Franco regime. He commanded some of the most important operational units, such as the crack Brunete Armoured Division, and was appointed Captain-General of the military region of Valencia. It was during this command that he took part in the attempted military coup against the democratic government in February 1981, known as *El* ***Tejerazo***, bringing tanks onto the streets, and imposing a curfew on the city. He was sentenced to 26 years in prison and dismissed from the army, but benefited from remission on grounds of age and was released in 1990.

LOURDES LÓPEZ NIETO

military service

During the Franco regime, compulsory military service was seen as a way of inculcating the ideology of the regime, rather than training an effective defence force. There was no provision for conscientious objection, and refusal to serve in the armed forces led to severe penalties. Despite the increasing professionalism of the armed forces under the socialist **PSOE** administrations of the 1980s and early 1990s, the government was reluctant to abandon conscription, seeing it as a way of ensuring 'social cohesion'. In any case, the high cost of moving to a fully professional army provided a powerful disincentive to a socialist government committed to keeping defence expenditure down. In the mid-1990s defence spending, at 1.26 percent of GDP, was the second lowest in NATO, after Luxembourg.

Despite the lack of resources, the idea of a fully professional army began to be discussed in political and military circles from around 1990. By 1993, the government had adopted a plan which envisaged that by the year 2000, 50 percent of the armed forces would be composed of volunteers. In December 1996, the government announced that compulsory military service would be abolished by 2002. After that date, the army would consist of professional soldiers, supplemented by volunteers enlisting for fixed periods, normally one year. The additional costs were estimated at $780m per annum.

This scheme involved certain difficulties, outlined in a report by the Ministry of Defence at the end of 1996. The needs of national defence, as well as obligations to NATO and the United Nations, could be jeopardized by possible shortfalls in personnel, caused by the increase in numbers of conscientious objectors, which had risen some 22 percent in the previous year. In addition, nearly a million persons liable to call-up had successfully applied for postponement of their military service. If they were exempted, it could leave a serious deficit in numbers. On the other hand, the government was committed to increasing gradually the numbers of career professionals, which left proportionally less room for conscripts, and made it next to impossible to allow them to complete their service within the time remaining before its abolition.

Possible solutions outlined in this report included extending the grounds for exemption, and reducing the period of service from nine to six months. A further incentive to complete military service was to give ex-recruits priority in appointments to state jobs.

See also: armed forces; conscientious objection; *insumisos*

EAMONN RODGERS

minifundia

Very small farms (*minifundia*) are a common feature of the size structure of agricultural holdings throughout Spain (see also **land tenure**). Under intensive **agriculture** (horticulture or the factory farming of livestock) they can offer a reasonable or good livelihood, but a few head of cattle or a few hectares of arable land are entirely inadequate to support a full-time family farm. The best they can offer is a source of part-time employment, a complementary income or a leisure opportunity. In areas of activity other than agriculture, the term *minifundismo* has come to be applied to all very small businesses.

Small farms are often fragmented into numerous dispersed plots (although fragmentation is also present on large farms), giving a variegated aspect to the landscape. In addition, there may be multi-ownership of single plots and different use-rights in the same plot. Efficiency is precluded by limitations on economies of scale: difficulties of mechanization, the loss of land in field boundaries, the restrictions placed on raising loans to finance improvements and the time lost in moving from one plot to another. However, the possession of plots on different types of land (irrigated land, land on south facing slopes, etc.) allows for a range of crops to be produced.

Minifundia have their origins partly in land tenure systems which have allowed for the division and sub-division of land on inheritance (partible inheritance), common under Roman law and customary law, and upheld in the Napoleonic Code. They have also arisen from population pressure on available agricultural land, with large swathes of productive land being occupied by ***latifundia***.

The survival of small farms has been made possible by the extension of irrigated areas and by various forms of protectionism, including that offered by the Common Agricultural Policy of the European Union. The latter, while encouraging land consolidation and early retirement, has viewed support to farmers with small farms as part of the mechanism for ensuring the survival of rural communities and managing the rural environment.

Progress in reducing the number of farm units

has been slow, barely reflecting the enormous decline in labour from the agricultural sector in the twentieth century. Programmes designed to improve the size structure of holdings through the consolidation of farms and dispersed plots of land have been in operation since the early 1950s and are now supported by the Common Agricultural Policy. The aims and scope of these programmes have varied from the limited rearrangement of properties to wholesale rural development. Most progress has been made in the grain lands of the central plateau (the Meseta), but even here consolidation has frequently left farms too small to support a family. There is some evidence that apart from intensive farming (where the number of farms has been increasing), the number of small holdings is declining, but the process is slow. While people have moved to towns, families have been reluctant to sever their rural roots, modest rural homes being transformed into modern second homes with accompanying land.

Further reading

Guedes, M. (1981) 'Recent Agricultural Land Policy in Spain', *Oxford Agrarian Studies*, 10: 26–43.

Naylon, J. (1959) 'Land Consolidation in Spain', *Annals of the Association of American Geographers*, 49: 361–73.

—— (1961) 'Progress in Land Consolidation in Spain', *Annals of the Association of American Geographers*, 51: 335–8.

O'Flannagan, P. (1980) 'Agrarian Structures in North Western Iberia. Responses and their Implications for Development', *Geoforum* 2, 157–69 (on the problems of small farms and the process of consolidation in Galicia).

—— (1982) 'Land Reform and Rural Modernization in Spain: a Galician Perspective', *Erdkunde*, 36: 48–53 (on the problems of small farms and the process of consolidation in Galicia).

KEITH SALMON

mining

Spain possesses a rich and diverse variety of mineral resources that have supported mining and quarrying activities throughout the country, embracing sources of energy (coal, oil, gas and uranium), metallic minerals (copper, iron, lead, mercury, pyrites, tin, wolfram, zinc, silver and gold), non-metallic minerals (including potash and salt), and quarry products (such as limestone, sand and gravel, granite, marble and slate).

In the last quarter of the twentieth century coal and metallic mineral mining were in decline, a process slowed by government subsidies, direct government intervention and the remnants of protectionism. Weak prices, shifting patterns of demand, liberalization of markets and increased international competition, rising production costs, low-grade deposits, exhaustion of deposits and more stringent environmental regulations, combined to reduce these activities to a fraction of their former size. A recovery in mineral prices, new prospecting techniques and production technologies may enable output of some of these minerals to recover but there is unlikely to be any increase in employment. Quarry products, on the other hand, continue to respond to the cyclical pattern of demand in the construction industry.

Apart from problems endemic to mining itself, domestic markets for many minerals have shrunk. In some cases raw material processing industries have closed or raw materials have been displaced by new production technologies (for example in iron and steel). The liberalization of other markets, such as electricity generation, metal manufacturing, heavy chemicals and fertilizers, has enabled manufacturers to buy raw materials more cheaply on the open market. The consequent decline of raw material production has left the country dependent on imports, especially of energy and metals. In the mid-1990s there was a trade deficit in energy, metallic and non-metallic minerals, with a surplus only on quarry products.

Energy products have represented the largest component of the mining industry by value of output, while quarry products account for the majority of mineral workings. Within the energy sector, coal and lignite account for most of the value of output and employment. In metallic minerals, zinc and precious metals (gold and silver) are the principal products followed by iron and mercury. Almost all lead, copper, pyrites and tin production had ceased in the mid 1990s. Of non-metallic minerals, potash and salt remain important products. Limestone is the most important quarry product, both in terms of value of output and the number of people employed in its extraction, followed by sand and gravel, granite, marble and slate.

Mining activities have attracted settlements dependent on the mines. Mine closures have threatened these communities, prompting stiff union opposition and government intervention at regional, state and European Community level. The problems have been most serious in the coal mining areas of Asturias and León and in the metal mines of Huelva. In many of these communities the population has declined, undermining their viability through the selective out-migration of working-age people and the closure of services.

In former mining areas, centuries of mining have left a legacy of old mine workings, environmental degradation and pollution that will challenge the environmental industry well into the twenty-first century. However, these old mine workings also constitute a resource in themselves, part of the industrial heritage of Spain, which can be adapted to form the basis of alternative employment in local tourism (as for example around the Rio Tinto mines in Huelva). This is one avenue which may lead to the regeneration of mining areas.

Further reading

Checkland, S. (1967) *The Mines of Tharsis*, London: George Allen & Unwin (a company history).

García Guinea, J. and Martínez Frías, J. (1992) *Recursos minerales de España*, Madrid: CSIC (a detailed inventory of mineral resources).

Harvey, C. (1981) *The Rio Tinto Company*, London: Alison Hodge (a company history).

Salmon, K. (1995) *The Modern Spanish Economy*, 2nd edn, London: Cassell (chapters 4 and 5 include references to the mining industry).

Tamames, R. *Estructura económica de España*, Madrid: Alianza Editorial (the content of the discussion varies according to the edition).

KEITH SALMON

Ministry of Culture

Established in 1977 by the centre-right **UCD** administration to take over some of the functions discharged by the Ministry of Education and the Ministry of Information and Tourism during the Franco regime, the Ministry of Culture continued as a separate entity under the socialist **PSOE** government from 1982, but was merged into the Ministry of Education and Culture as part of the reorganization of Ministries under the centre-right **PP** in May 1996.

The Ministry performs two major and interrelated functions, that of exercising financial control over its portion (in the region of 0.4 percent) of the state budget, and of contributing to the formulation and implementation of government policy on cultural matters. On the financial front it dispenses grants of public monies to a wide range of cultural institutions such as national and state **museums**, the autonomous **Prado Museum** and **Queen Sofia Museum**, the National Library (see also **libraries**), the **Auditorio Nacional de Música**, the National **Orchestras**, the **Royal Theatre** and various other theatres and concert halls; to the upkeep of cathedrals; to the Spanish film industry (see also **film and cinema**), and to the Institute of Conservation and Restoration of Cultural Goods, the Institute of Cinematography and Audiovisual Arts and the National Institute of Performing Arts and Music. As a result of increased devolution, however, the autonomous regions and municipal authorities are emerging as major funders of the arts, and this trend is set to continue with central government happy to transfer to them responsibility for buildings and events from which they derive tourist revenue.

With regard to policy, the 1980s and 1990s saw the creation of central agencies, such as the Centre for Exhibitions and Artistic Promotion, the formulation of plans, such as the Architectural Plan for the Renovation of State Museums, and the introduction of important legislation, especially the 1985 Law of Spanish National Heritage, which made it illegal to alter, sell or export without permission sites and objects listed on the General Register of Heritage Sites and Objects.

The merger with Education in 1996 was

attended with considerable controversy. Academics, writers and other prominent figures connected with cultural activity saw it as an indication of lack of commitment to culture on the part of the government. Moreover, the public statements of the Education Minister, Esperanza Aguirre, particularly about the teaching of history from a 'national' perspective, were regarded in those **autonomous communities** which had a distinctive regional culture as a return to the unitary, centralist vision of Spain which had been dominant under the Franco regime.

See also: arts funding; arts policy

EAMONN RODGERS

minority religions

Since 1492, when most of the Muslim and Jewish population in Spain was forced to leave, the predominant religion in Spain has been **Roman Catholicism**. Furthermore, the vigilance of the Inquisition during the sixteenth and seventeenth centuries prevented the Reformation from taking root to any significant extent. After the revolution of 1868, a degree of relative tolerance was introduced, which permitted the growth of small evangelical groups. Total numbers were, however, tiny, and these groups suffered further serious decline as a result of the religious conformity imposed under the Franco regime after the Civil War and reinforced by the Concordat between Spain and the Vatican in 1953.

The Concordat nevertheless followed the 1945 *Fuero de los Españoles* (Charter of the Spaniards) in guaranteeing that no-one would suffer discrimination for their beliefs, or for the private practice of non-Roman Catholic religions. As an expression of religious tolerance, this was of somewhat limited scope, for Protestant denominations could not, for example, advertise services or publish literature. Moreover, the legislation was often applied rather unevenly across the country. Whereas in provincial towns and cities Protestant centres of worship could, as late as 1958, be arbitrarily closed by the police, in Madrid, where official action was carried out under the eyes of foreign embassies, the authorities were more circumspect. The Cathedral church of the Spanish Reformed Episcopal Church (Iglesia Española Reformada Episcopal), has functioned continuously in the capital since 1894.

A significant thawing of the climate occurred in the late 1960s, partly as a result of the liberalizing declarations on religious freedom adopted by the Second Vatican Council (1962–5), partly through the efforts of the Foreign Minister, Fernando María Castiella, who was sympathetic to the plight of religious minorities in Spain. The 1967 Law of Religious Freedom, however, still contained provisions which the leaders of the Protestant minorities found vexatious, such as the requirement to register as 'legal associations', and to keep a record of their members, demands with which many of them refused to comply.

The constitution of 1978 finally abolished religious discrimination, including the requirement to declare one's religious affiliation. This has not led to a great surge in membership of non-Catholic religions, largely because of the worldwide drift towards secularization. Nevertheless, in 1985, the annual digest published by *El País* listed 373 addresses of religious organizations of various kinds. Statistics on membership are difficult to obtain, but the various denominations count their numbers in thousands rather than hundreds of thousands. The most important are the Evangelical Church (Iglesia Evangélica Española), largely Methodist in character, the Reformed Episcopal Church, which is a member of the Anglican Communion, the Federation of Evangelical Free Churches (Federación de Iglesias Evangélicas Independientes de España), the Evangelical Baptist Union (Unión Evangélica Bautista Española), the Seventh-Day Adventists, the Jehovah's Witnesses, and the Jewish community. It is unlikely that the total number of active adherents of non-Catholic religions (as distinct from agnostics and atheists) exceeds 0.1 percent of the population.

See also: church and state; National Catholicism; religion; Roman Catholicism

Further reading

Hughey, J.D. (1970) *Religious Freedom in Spain: Its Ebb and Flow*, Freeport, NY (a highly-regarded historic source).

Vilar, J.B. (1994) *Intolerancia y libertad en la España contemporánea: los orígenes del protestantismo español actual*, Madrid: Istmo.

EAMONN RODGERS

Mira i Franco, Carles

b. 1947, Valencia; d. 1993, Valencia

Filmmaker

Carles Mira's short film career was characterized by his abiding interest in the popular festivals of his native Valencia, as well as in the rich Moorish past of Spain. His first full-length film, the 1978 *La portentosa vida del Padre Vicente* (The Wondrous Life of Father Vicente), provoked great scandal in right-wing Valencian circles, and his irreverent presentation of Spanish history in films such as *Jalea Real* (Royal Jelly) was similarly polemical. Mira worked closely with major figures from Catalan and Valencian drama, as in the 1985 *Karnaval*, which he made with Els **Comediants**.

DAVID GEORGE

Miralles, Enric

b. 1953, Barcelona

Architect

Miralles' sculptural gifts are very visible in all his work. His large-scale designs for street furniture, many of them done in collaboration with Carme Pinos, display an interesting range of architectural idiom, the best known being the Avenida Icaria in Barcelona (1992).

The Centro Cultural La Mina (1992), his contributions to the Camy-Nestlé factory at Villadecans (1994) and to the La Llauna school at Badalona (1986 and 1995) are the most notable examples of his work within Catalonia. He is also responsible for some remarkable creations outside Catalonia such as the Círculo de Lectores in Madrid (1993). His work won him the Golden Lion at the Venice Architecture Bienniale in 1996.

MIHAIL MOLDOVEANU

Miró, Joan

b. 1893, Barcelona; d. 1983, Palma de Mallorca

Artist

Miró claimed that he never intended to create symbols, yet his childlike images remind us of prehistoric shapes that reflect basic life forces such as growth, movement, attraction and repulsion.

Early inspiration came from a farm near the hill town of Montroig. Miró was influenced by the use of colour in Fauve painting, and developed an interest in detail and the rhythmic patterns of traditional Catalan art. *The Farm* is like an inventory of typical rural objects, and the very enlarged feet of *The Farmer's Wife* emphasize his belief that energy rises from the earth before transfiguring reality.

After 1920 Miró worked in Paris, where he met leading surrealists and responded to their appeal to the imagination. He began to combine phantasmagoria with his depiction of external reality. In *The Ploughed Field* we find giant ears and eyes growing on trees. Thereafter Miró developed an entire pictorial language, a kind of visual shorthand. In *Catalan Landscape (The Hunter)* we recognize remnants of a moustache, the partial flame of an exploded gun, but never the entire object. This dismemberment is repeated in *Portrait of Madame K* where he selects images to convey the presence of a woman: head, breasts, heart, pubic hair.

The surrealists favoured exploring the subconscious and also chance. Spontaneity was successfully harnessed in Miró's 'dream paintings', but as oil and tempera proved limiting for the ideas of surrealism, Miró declared that he wished to 'assassinate painting'. He turned to collage, using string, random objects and a variety of textured surfaces. His images were often based on the abstraction of items advertised in illustrated catalogues, yet in the finished artwork such as *Painting, 1933*, they achieve the status of symbols. But what are they symbols of? Once more we find our reference in the stars and circles of archetypal iconography.

Miró's work darkened with the advent of the Spanish Civil War. He used pastels to accentuate violent distortions in his 'peintures sauvages', wherein the sky is often red or black. The now famous poster *Aidez l'Espagne*, descibes an immense clenched fist symbolizing the heroism and strength needed to defeat fascism.

During the difficult years of WWII, Miró returned to Spain from occupied France, and retreated into detail. Swarms of tiny emblems fill the gently coloured spaces of his 'constellation paintings', and are given long poetic titles like, *Woman Beside a Lake Whose Surface Has Been Made Iridescent by a Passing Swan.*

Miró achieved worldwide recognition by the late 1950s. He continued to experiment with ceramics and lithography from his studio in Calamayor, Mallorca. Much of his painting and sculpture can be seen at the Fondation Maeght in St Paul de Vence, France, and at the Fundació Miró on Monjuich in Barcelona.

Further reading

Dupin, J. (1962) *Miró*, London: Collins (a sensitive account of Miró's development).

Lassaigne, J. (1963) *Miró*, Lausanne: Skira (a competent study).

Penrose, R. (1995) *Miró*, London: Thames & Hudson (a clear and insightful study of Miró's life and work).

HELEN OPPENHEIMER

Miró, Pilar

b. 1940, Madrid; d. 1997, Madrid

Filmmaker

Pilar Miró studied law and journalism and in 1968 graduated in scriptwriting from the Escuela Oficial de Cine (EOC). Later she taught scriptwriting and montage at the EOC. In the 1960s she became the first woman to direct programmes and feature films for Spanish **television**, with over 300 programmes to her credit, ranging from literary adaptations to news bulletins and including drama and magazines. In 1982 she was made Under Secretary for the Cinema, the first woman ever to hold that post in Spain. During her years in office she issued the 'Miró Law' which attempted to kickstart the Spanish film industry (never very strong hitherto), by instigating a state-funded system of advances against receipts. These measures launched the careers of such directors as **Almodóvar** and were of great benefit to the country's cinema.

In 1986, after leaving this post she became Director of Spain's only public television channel, and her years in office were regarded as highly successful. However, as a woman in a high position she encountered much misogynistic criticism. She resigned from the post after being charged with spending public funds on her own clothes, a charge from which she was cleared in 1992.

Miró maintained a strong and independent stance, but never considered herself to be a feminist. Nevertheless, her film career allows an insight into the difficulties and opportunities for a woman director in a country in which the position of women – not only in the cinema but in society in general – had been pushed back to quasi-medieval conditions under the right-wing dictatorship of Franco and his strongest ally, the Roman Catholic church.

The moral repression of Miró's generation and the stiff censorship rules of the regime led several filmmakers in the mid 1970s – including Miró herself, Josefina **Molina** and Vicente **Aranda** – to make use of the tradition of gothic horror films as a vehicle for the problematic topic of sexuality. In Miró's films, images of sexuality are often intertwined with transgression, sadism and an awareness of sin. Her first film, *La petición* (The Engagement Party) (1976), shows a heroine (played by Ana **Belén**), sexually active and drawn to sadism. However, we can detect here a difference from other productions of the genre, in that the heroine is not a passive victim but an agent: her sexual passion kills her first lover and after the next has helped her dispose of the body, she despatches him with an oar. In her second film, the *El crimen de Cuenca* (*The Cuenca Crime*) (1979), the sadistic characters are men. It is based on an actual event at the turn of the century, when, following a suspected murder, the two accused were brutally tortured by corrupt members of the Civil Guard in order to extract a confession. The film consequently became the subject of the last act of political censorship in Spain, generating media attention and popular debate, which distracted audiences from the undisputable merit of the film.

Like many of her contemporaries, Miró was also drawn to literary adaptations, while consciously rejecting popular genres. *La petición* itself was an adaptation from Zola. In 1986 she filmed her personal version of Goethe's *Werther* and, in 1991, the award-winning thriller *Beltenebros* from the novel by Vicente Muñoz Molina. The book, a thriller in which an undercover communist agent (played in the film by Terence Stamp) investigates the death of several members of the party's Spanish underground branch in the early dictatorship years, is intrinsically cinematic. Miró simply used the conventions of *film noir*, and hence the film is problematic in its treatment of women, who are portrayed as sirens casting a shadow of moral ambiguity. It is nevertheless true that, through the use of those very rules, the film succeeded in recreating the dark years of repression and mystery.

Her *Gary Cooper que estás en los cielos* (Gary Cooper Who Art in Heaven) (1980) and *El pájaro de la felicidad* (The Bird of Happiness) (1993) focus on the struggle of women artists. In both cases Miró concentrates on a professional woman's moment of awareness of her fragile world as a note of defeat pervades an otherwise successful life. In the former, the heroine discovers that she has a serious illness and is thrown into an assessment of her life, and in the latter it is an assault and attempted rape which prompts the heroine to embark on a journey of self-discovery.

There are moments of lyricism in Miró's films (*El pájaro* is a remarkable example), where it is the treatment of landscape, rather than the script, which illustrates a character's alienation. Her style is more reliant on European art cinema traditions (like many of her contemporaries she aims to direct films of ***arte y ensayo***) than on Hollywood, which she, like other directors of her generation, often associates with mere populism and commercialism.

Miró's high standards of professionalism were also reflected in her work for television. Her last major project was the live coverage of the wedding of Princess Cristina in Barcelona, two weeks before her sudden death from a heart attack.

Further reading

García de León, M.A. (1994) *Elites discriminadas (Sobre el poder de las mujeres)*, Barcelona: Ántropos (analysis of the sociological relevance of Miró from the perspective of a Spanish pioneer in women studies).

Hopewell, J. (1986) *Out of the Past: Spanish Cinema after Franco*, London: British Film Institute, pp. 112–4.

Pérez Millán, J.A. (1992) *Pilar Miró: Directora de cine*, Valladolid: Semana de Cine de Valladolid (renowned Spanish critic's biased, though informed, account of the director's life and work).

Schwartz R. (1986) 'Pilar Miró' in *Spanish Film Directors (1950 – 1985) Twenty-one Profiles*, Metuchen, NJ: Scarecrow Press (slightly dated but one of the early studies on the director).

NÚRIA TRIANA TORIBIO

Modernism

One of the forms assumed by 'fin de siècle' art is Modernism, which can be regarded as the Catalan variant of the radical innovating currents which appeared all over Europe in the late nineteenth and early twentieth century: art nouveau, art 1900, modern style, *Sezession*, *Jugendstijl* or Liberty. Catalan Modernism is one of the most complex forms of this movement, and expresses itself with particular force in the richness of Catalan architecture, because of the distinctively political flavour which European modernism acquired in the region (e.g. the synthesis of the arts, empathy with nature, the free manipulation of historical reference, etc.). Architecture was seen as having a major role in nation-building, by emphasizing one of the most glorious periods of Catalan history, the Middle Ages. From the beginning, the new approach was marked by its abundant use of Romanesque and Gothic elements, in which medieval solidity was subtly blended with softer interiors, adapted effectively to 'modern' life and often sumptuously decorated.

In its origin Modernism was essentially a literary movement, as was the movement which followed it, ***Noucentisme***. The term Modernism was, indeed, adopted contrary to the wishes of the architects and artists concerned, by association with the literary group of the same name, which was promoting the idea of a general renewal. Nevertheless, the differences in attitude were considerable, notably with regard to history. Whereas the literary group advocated a total break with the past, the architects and artists proposed, on the contrary, to use the heritage of earlier cultures as the starting point for the exercise of their creative freedom. The architect **Puig i Cadafalch** preferred the label, 'The Barcelona School', but the works in question were already known as 'Modernist'.

Given the hostility of the Franco regime to any expression of nationalism other than Spanish, Modernism, as a powerful manifestation of Catalan cultural identity, had become politically marginalized by the 1940s and 1950s. The name nevertheless survived, with two distinct meanings, which continued to coexist: one, which has wide currency in the History of Art from the 1920s on, describes the evolution of art and architecture around Cubism and abstract art. The other refers to Art Nouveau as practised in Catalonia, which was at its height between the years 1880 and 1915. Catalan Modernism, in essence, denotes an aesthetic peculiar to the city of Barcelona, encapsulating a whole cluster of ideas and cultural attitudes which have deep roots in the Catalan context.

The theoretical framework of Modernism took shape long before the heyday of the movement, in a programmatic essay published in 1878 by Luis **Domènech i Montaner**. Domènech's later activity as Director of the School of Architecture, political leader and author of a series of influential writings, enabled him to disseminate his ideas among a large group of disciples, including Josep Puig i Cadafalch, himself in turn leader of a school, and an important figure in the first two decades of the twentieth century. The best-known Modernist is Antoni **Gaudí**, whose spectacular work occupies a special place in the history of European art, and who gave Catalan Modernism an international reputation. Among Gaudí's many disciples was Josep Maria **Jujol**, who collaborated in Gaudí's masterpieces such as the Parc Güell or the Casa Milá. Jujol himself developed Modernism a stage further by blending the idiom of Modernism with new forms of artistic expression, thereby giving a new boost to the movement. His work is regarded today as an important moment in the evolution of the twentieth-century avant-garde.

The legacy of Catalan Modernism is what gives contemporary Barcelona much of its distinctive atmosphere and character, in the form of well-preserved buildings which make up the greatest collection of Art Nouveau in the world. They are eloquent testimony to how seriously the 'synthesis of the arts' was taken at the time of their construction. The combined efforts of sculptors such as Eusebi Arnau or Miquel Blay, painters such as Santiago Rusiñol or Ramón Casas, cabinet-makers like Gaspar Homar and other craftsmen, ensured the success of Modernist architecture as a collective project. Moreover, the whole subsequent development of Catalan architecture was influenced by the liveliness of the debate stimulated by Modernism, its willingness to experiment, and its openness to new ideas.

See also: architects; architecture; Catalan culture

Further reading

Bohigas, O. (1973) *Arquitectura Modernista*, Barcelona: Lumen (an important study by a practising architect).

Cirici Pellicer, A. (1951) *El Arte Modernista Catalán*, Barcelona: Aymà.

Domènech i Montaner, L. (1878) *A la recerca d'una arquitectura nacional*, Barcelona: La Renaixansa (the foundation text of Modernism).

Loyer, F. (1991) *L'art nouveau en Catalogne*, Paris: Biblio. Arts, Le Septième Fou (the most up-to-date study of the movement).

MIHAIL MOLDOVEANU

Moix, Terenci

b. 1942, Barcelona

Writer

The emergence of Terenci Moix in the Catalan literary scene of the 1960s is widely regarded as little short of a Copernican revolution: while his contemporaries were still coming to terms with the consequences of Francoism for **Catalan culture**, he introduced radically new themes and attitudes, such as an interest in perverse sexuality (he was in fact the first ever openly gay author in Catalan literature), a taste for mass and pop culture, and a cosmopolitan outlook. His popularity, however, vividly contrasts with the critical neglect of which he has been the object.

A self-taught man, winner of important literary prizes, and media personality, Moix is the author of many novels as well as journalism, theatre plays, books on film and comics, and travel literature. Moix's narrative works use two distinct registers. In novels like *El dia que va morir Marilyn* (The Day Marilyn Died) (1969), voted best Catalan novel of the period 1964–70, or *La increada consciència de la raça* (The Uncreated Conscience of the Race) (1974), Moix adopts a realist style to narrate provocative stories that bring together the bourgeois family, Catalonia's history and identity, and homosexual desire. In other books, such as the collections of short stories *La torre dels vicis capitals* (The Tower of Capital Vices) (1968) and *La caiguda de l'imperi sodomita* (The Fall of the Sodomite Empire) (1974) and the novel *Món Mascle* (Macho World) (1971), he combines, in a distinctively postmodern fashion, a camp sensibility with an interest in fantasies derived from mass culture and in the myths of pop culture.

In 1983, Moix decided to write in Spanish only and became Spain's best-selling author. In his novels of this period he pursues to a large extent the camp penchant he had explored in Catalan, either in historical melodramas set in a Hollywoodesque Egypt, like *No digas que fue un sueño* (Don't Say it was a Dream) (1986), which was awarded the **Planeta Prize** in 1986 and sold over a million copies, or in a high camp parody of lesbian life, *Garras de astracán* (Astrakhan Claws) (1991). In 1990 he started the publication of his autobiography *El peso de la paja* (The Burden of Masturbation) (1989), and in 1992 returned to the Catalan language with his highly praised novel *El sexe dels àngels* (The Sex of the Angels).

See also: gay culture; gay writing; language and national identity

Further reading

Bou, E. (1988) 'La literatura actual', in M. de Riquer, A. Comas and J. Molas, *Història de la literatura catalana: Part moderna*, vol. 11, Barcelona: Ariel (contains a section on Moix's writing in Catalan).

Fernández, J.A. (1998) 'Perverting the Canon: Terenci Moix's *La caiguda de l'imperisodmita*', *Journal of Iberian and Latin American Studies* 4: 67–76.

Forrest, G.S. (1977) 'El mundo antagónico de Terenci Moix', *Hispania* 60: 927–35 (a dated but useful account of Moix's writing of the 1960s and 1970s).

Smith, P.J. (1992) *Laws of Desire: Questions of Homosexuality in Spanish Writing and Film 1960–1990*, Oxford: Clarendon (chapter 1 includes an excellent section on Moix's autobiography).

JOSEP-ANTON FERNÁNDEZ

Molina, Josefina

b. 1936, Córdoba

Filmmaker

In 1968 Molina became the first woman in Spain to graduate from the Escuela Oficial de Cine in film-directing. She works for television and has been responsible for highly acclaimed series such as *Teresa de Jesús* (1984). She combines her career in television with theatre and film direction. In 1993 she revived a classical popular text *La Lola se va a los puertos* (The Flamenco Singer) for contemporary audiences and explored Spain's recent changes in social attitudes in her 1990 *Lo más natural* (The Most Natural Thing).

Further reading

Hopewell, J. (1986) *Out of the Past*, London: British Film Institute (an accessible and informative account of developments in Spanish cinema since 1975).

NÚRIA TRIANA TORIBIO

Monagas, Pepe

The creation of journalist Pancho Guerra (Francisco Guerra Navarro) (1909–61), the fictional character Pepe Monagas has come to epitomize the picaresque in the Canary Islander. *Los cuentos famosos de Pepe Monagas* (Famous Tales of Pepe Monagas), first published in the daily press, have since been re-issued in book form together with Guerra's *Memorias de Pepe Monagas* (The Memoirs of Pepe Monagas) (1958) and his posthumous *Siete entremeses de Pepe Monagas* (Seven Interludes with Pepe Monagas, 1962). In part the literary character and the speech idioms of Pepe Monagas were inspired by Canarian comedian and actor José Castellano (1904–67) who, as a fellow member of the *Sociedad de Amigos del Arte Nestor de la Torre* (Nestor de la Torre Society of Friends of the Arts) with Guerra, also portrayed Pepe Monagas on the stage.

M.R. EDDY

monarchy

Monarchy is one of the most powerful social and above all political myths circulating in Spanish society today. It revolves centrally around the figure of the King, **Juan Carlos I**, but in the second half of the 1990s it came also to include some of the younger members of his family.

The Spanish royal family was in a state of suspended animation for most of the twentieth century, following the abdication of Alfonso XIII in 1931, the introduction of the Second Republic shortly thereafter, and the establishment of a dictatorship in 1939 by General Franco following his victory in the Spanish Civil War. Juan Carlos was proclaimed King after Franco's death in November 1975.

The development of the particular myth of monarchy which has emerged in Spain can be seen to revolve crucially around a few highly symbolic dates, these being 1975, 1981, 1992 and 1995.

The first of these, 1975, includes by extension the following two years of 'transition to democracy'. Juan Carlos is routinely described in all branches of the Spanish media as the 'architect of democracy', and is credited with having steered Spain from dictatorship to democracy almost single-handed. There can be little doubt that the path chosen by Juan Carlos was not the one which Franco had planned for him; but the simplification of history involved in this kind of personalization of complex historical processes condemns to oblivion the long and at times dangerous struggles undertaken by people from all walks of life against the Franco regime, and also fails to acknowledge the level of sacrifice – including in some cases imprisonment and even death – which many had to suffer.

The second key date is 23 February 1981. This was the day of the ***Tejerazo***, when a group of Civil Guards stormed the parliament building in Madrid and called for the reinstatement of a military dictatorship. During the tense hours which followed, Juan Carlos made a brief appearance on national television – a matter of a few minutes – wearing his uniform as Commander-in-Chief of the Armed Forces, and stated his personal commitment to a democratic system in Spain. The dominant analysis of this key turning point in the history of contemporary Spain is that it was the King himself who saved democracy by refusing to play the insurgents' game. It is true that his statement in favour of democracy was clear, and the situation would have become much more complex had he either said nothing or expressed any kind of willingness to compromise with the attempted coup, but it is a gross oversimplification to suggest that this brief intervention was the reason why the coup failed. In retrospect, there seems little likelihood that this attempted coup could ever have succeeded, even in the medium term, since it lacked anything like the necessary social or political base, and was certainly not supported by Spain's business sector, which had seen for itself the limitations inherent in dictatorial regimes. On the level of myth, however, this event served to strengthen Juan Carlos as the ultimate guarantor of democracy, as the protector of the Spanish nation against all attempts to undermine its basic freedoms.

1992 was a crucial year not just for Spain, but also for the Spanish monarchy. Seville's **Expo-92**, and in particular the Barcelona **Olympic Games** brought Spain on to the world stage. Not only Spaniards, but indeed viewers from across the world were able to see the Spanish monarch in shirt sleeves attending Olympic events in Barcelona, looking very much like any other Spanish citizen, and they were also able to view him and other members of his family warmly embracing and congratulating those Spanish athletes who won medals in different events. This served to consolidate a further strand of the Spanish monarchic myth – that of the citizen king, living not above his people but among his people, and closely in tune with their wishes and aspirations.

However, the most important event of 1992 for the Spanish monarchy took place, not in Spain, but in the United Kingdom. This was the announcement of the separation of the Prince and Princess of Wales. This event was seized upon by the Spanish media to sing the praises of their own monarch by comparison, stressing the modesty of his court and his closeness to his people, and introducing on a major scale two further elements of the contemporary myth. The first of these was that of the *working* king: being King of Spain was firmly established at this point as a job, done well by a family of professionals who were contrasted favourably with the amateurs of the British court. Second, a clear attempt was made to link the current monarchy with its historic predecessors. Monarchy thus became a means of bypassing the Franco regime, of relegating it to the level of historical mistake, of establishing dynastic monarchy as the historical truth about Spain.

March 1995 added an important new chapter to this narrative: this was the month of the marriage of the King and Queen's second daughter, the infanta Elena. Media coverage of this event – which was on a truly massive scale – consolidated all the previously existing elements and simultaneously associated all of them with the up-and-coming generation of future royals.

The myth of monarchy in Spain is one of the most successful myths of modern times. It would be incorrect to say that it is accepted uncritically by all Spaniards, but its general level of social approval is high – so much so that many in Spain believe that their monarchy offers the ideal model for the future: more glamorous than the bicycling monarchies of Scandinavia, more modern than the anachronistic monarchy of the United Kingdom – a job well done on behalf of one's fellow citizens.

Further reading

Blain, N. and O'Donnell, H. (1994) 'Royalty, Modernity and Postmodernity: Monarchy in the Spanish and British Presses', *ACIS: Journal of the Association for Contemporary Iberian Studies*, 7, 1.

HUGH O'DONNELL

Moncada, Jesús

b. 1941, Mequinensa

Writer

A gifted storyteller, widely regarded as one of the greatest talents in contemporary Catalan writing, Moncada began publishing in the 1980s with two collections of short stories. His first novel, *The Towpath* (*Camí de sirga*, 1988), won widespread acclaim and several literary prizes; it was based on the destruction of his own riverside birthplace as part of a damming project in 1970.

Further reading

Bou, E. (1993) 'Jesús Moncada: A World Saved by Literature', *Catalan Writing* 10: 61–3 (interesting general article followed by a bibliography and translations of two short stories).

KATHRYN CRAMERI

Moncloa Pacts

The Moncloa Pacts, which derive their name from the prime minister's official residence where the discussions took place, were a series of agreements signed on 25 October 1977 by representatives of the political parties which had recently been elected to the **parliament** in June 1977. The pacts were initiated by the Vice-President in charge of Economic affairs, Enrique **Fuentes Quintana**, as a way of controlling the economy which, in the early years of democracy, was suffering from spiralling wage costs, high inflation and the adverse effects of the oil crisis on the balance of payments. The importance of the Pacts, however, transcends the economic: they represented the first attempts at a political consensus stretching across all the parliamentary parties. They also acted as a precursor for the model of social partnership which was to be adopted subsequently by employers and **trade unions** and which was to lead to a series of national bargaining agreements from 1980 to 1986, in which collective responsibility and wage restraint were to be prevailing features.

The Pacts, while best remembered for their economic measures, also included political reform. On the political side they swept aside many of the constraints which still remained from the Franco legacy, addressing for example the need for increased freedom of speech and association and the reorganization of the police. At the same time the economic proposals sought to modernize the economy and included reforms in public spending, taxation and the financial system, measures to improve foreign trade and proposals for a new framework for industrial relations. Some measures were short term and others, such as industrial restructuring, were seen as much longer term. They asked for moderation and constraint by all groups in the interests of democracy and although, on the Left, the **PCE** and **PSOE** subscribed to them, critics in later years were to say that the working classes bore a disproportionate amount of the sacrifice and gained little from them.

The success of some of the measures was immediate and far reaching: inflation levels dropped from 26.4 percent in 1977 to 16 percent in 1978 and monetary reserves doubled. Moreover, the restructuring which was to go on throughout a large part of the 1980s brought efficiency gains to industry. The price of this, however, was continuing high unemployment.

Nevertheless, there is no doubt that the improvements in the Spanish economy that were achieved as a result of the Pacts, together with the political consensus, provided the economic and political stability over the following year which enabled the parliamentary parties to concentrate on drawing up the **constitution of 1978**, finalized in December. Hence it can be seen that the Pacts played an important role in helping to consolidate the fledgling democracy.

Further reading

Carr, R and Fusi, J.P. (1979) *Spain: Dictatorship to Democracy*, London: Allen & Unwin (a clear analysis of the transition, including the Moncloa Pacts).

Preston, P. (1986) *The Triumph of Democracy in Spain* London: Methuen (an exceptionally readable and lively account of all aspects of the transition).

TERESA LAWLOR

Moneo, Rafael

b. 1937, Tudela (Zaragoza)

Architect

Moneo began his career working under two great architects, **Sáenz de Oiza** in Madrid and Jorn Utzon in Denmark. He won a scholarship from the Spanish Academy in Rome in 1963 and remained there for the next two years, a period which was to have a decisive influence on his formation. On returning to Spain he began teaching architecture in Madrid, subsequently (1970–80) joining the staff of the Barcelona School of Architecture. He returned to Madrid in 1980 as lecturer in composition, a post which he held until 1985 when he became Dean of the prestigious Graduate School of Design at Harvard, where he stayed until 1990.

The first of his works to attract international attention was the Museum of Archaeology at Mérida (1986). The most important aspect of this design was the harmonious relationship he achieved with the surrounding Roman ruins. An equally good modern interpretation of the ancient world is his work on the headquarters of the Col·legi d'Arquitectes at Tarragona (1983–92), also constructed on top of ancient remains. The heritage of the past is integrated smoothly, but at the same time respectfully, into modern daily life. The refurbishment of the Villahermoso Palace in Madrid to house the Thyssen collection (1991) is a masterpiece of design, in which the distribution of space is handled with great effectiveness and simplicity (see also **Thyssen-Bornemisza Museum**). The Joan **Miró** Museum in Palma de Mallorca (1992) is a bold composition, laid out in the shape of a star, as a sort of homage to the painter. Seville Airport (1991) represents a very personal contribution to the built environment, as does the transformation of the Atocha railway station in Madrid (1992), a striking design of great simplicity. The head office of the La Previsión Company in Seville (1988) is an original interpretation of the fabric of the city. In the 1990s he constructed a huge edifice on the Avinguda Diagonal in Barcelona, La Illa, a horizontal skyscraper which despite its size is well adapted to the site. In 1996 he designed the new Conference Centre and Concert Hall, the Kursaal, in San Sebastián.

Moneo's tenure of the Deanship in Harvard consolidated his international reputation, and he won commissions for, among other distinguished buildings, the Museum of Fine Arts in Houston, Texas. In 1996 he became the first Spaniard to win the Pritzker Prize, the most prestigious international award for achievement in architecture.

See also: architects; architecture

MIHAIL MOLDOVEANU

Montero, Rosa

b. 1952, Madrid

Writer

Many of Rosa Montero's best-selling novels focus on women's identity, but they also ponder broader existential and ethical concerns in the modern world. Montero's training as a journalist and in psychology are evident in the forthright, reportorial style of her first novels and in her witty exploration of human nature. Later narratives are increasingly imaginative and creative.

Although Montero wrote stories as a child, she later felt she had nothing original to say in a fictional work, and concentrated on journalism. She contributed to a variety of presses as a teenager, began working for *El País* in 1976, and has won awards for her interviews and journalistic style. Several of Montero's publications are collections of columns previously published in *El País*. In the collection *Historias de mujeres* (Stories of Women), Montero explains her interest in **feminism** as an introduction to biographical sketches of intriguing women throughout history.

Montero's novelistic publication emerged from an editor's request for a book of interviews with women. Wanting to diverge from interrogative reporting, Montero wrote a narrative documentary, *Absent Love: A Chronicle* (*Crónica del desamor*, 1979), which glimpses at the daily life of four women in the transitional period after Franco's dictatorship. These women express opinions about abortion, birth control, marriage and divorce, homosexuality, and other formerly taboo topics. *The Delta Function* (*La función Delta*, 1981) is thematically similar, but features a dying woman in the year 2010 recalling her life in the 1980s. The humour, spontaneity, and popularity of these texts attenuate criticism that they are predominately feminist propaganda.

Succeeding novels are more diverse. *Te trataré como a una reina* (I'll Treat You Like a Queen) (1983) is a parody of the murder mystery genre that probes society's unequal treatment of the sexes, while *Amado amo* (Beloved Master) (1988) focuses on male identity and insecurity in Spain's increasingly capitalistic environment. Both works paint a pessimistic view of patriarchal culture.

Montero's use of fantasy in later novels suggests that creativity facilitates identity formation in a changing world. *Temblor* (Trembling) (1990), an allegory in a future post-holocaust age; *El nido de los sueños* (The Nest of Dreams) (1991), a children's novel; and *Bella y oscura* (Beautiful and Dark) (1993) all feature young female protagonists who employ imagination to improve their lives. In *Bella y oscura*, Baba's arrival by train to live with relatives after her mother's death is hauntingly similar to the situations in Carmen **Laforet**'s *Nada* and Ana María **Matute**'s *Primera memoria*. The setting, however, is a 1990s city plagued with poverty, child abuse and pollution. A magical Lilliputian's fantastic tales inspire Baba to create her own identity and to shield herself against adversity. These partially chimerical novels with ontological implications promise Montero continued popularity among a widening audience.

Further reading

Amell, A. (1994) *Rosa Montero's Odyssey*, Lanham and London: University Press of America (an exploration of ontological themes in Montero's novels).

Davies, C. (1994) *Contemporary Feminist Fiction in Spain: The Work of Montserrat Roig and Rosa Montero*, Oxford and Providence, RI: Berg (a feminist analysis of Roig's and Montero's novels).

SANDRA J. SCHUMM

Monzó, Quim

b. 1952, Barcelona

Writer

One of Catalan culture's most colourful characters, Monzó first burst onto the scene in 1976, with a novel entitled *L'udol del griso al caire de les clavegueres* (The Howl of the Wind Beside the Sewers), which won a major Catalan Prize. Based on the events and atmosphere surrounding the student riots in Paris in May 1968, the novel narrates the antics of young Catalans in Paris and London and their reactions to this time of political militancy and personal indulgence. While this first novel tends to mythicize the culture of the '1960s generation', subsequently Monzó has adopted a much more ironic perspective. It is this ironic humour for which he is best known, and which he employs to full effect in his collections of short stories. His narratives are original, laced with dry humour and often constructed around one central joke or startling resolution. They show a constant exploration of the possibilities of new form and themes, often use erotic scenes or sexual vocabulary, and are designed to provoke the reader into realizing that there exist many alternative ways of viewing the world. Other major publications include *O'Clock* (*Olivetti, Moulinex, Chaffoteaux et Maury*, 1980), *Benzina* (Petrol) (1983), *La magnitud de la tragèdia* (The Magnitude of the Tragedy) (1989) and *El perquè de tot plegat* (The Reason for Everything) (1993). Some of his work has been translated into Spanish and French, as well as English, and he has himself translated English-language literature into Catalan.

Monzó had no significant academic background – he never finished his secondary education, and instead trained as a graphic designer – and so came to writing from a slightly unusual direction, heavily influenced by popular culture (including cinema, television and various forms of art). His literary influences include Latin American writers, especially Julio Cortázar, and the Catalan Pere **Calders**, whom he read purely for enjoyment. It was this 'self-preparation' which led him to choose writing in general, and the short story in particular, as a medium for expression. However, Monzó's activities have certainly not been confined to literary media. His work has taken him into areas as diverse as journalism, graphic design, advertising, song-writing, amateur cinema and radio. In his contributions to ***Avui*** and other newspapers, Monzó has consistently taken real events and treated them ironically or from highly original perspectives. Many of these events are related to Catalan culture and politics, on which he has strong views, as evidenced by his statement that 'If you look at things coldly, you realise how much rubbish is spoken in the world of culture' (Cònsul 1988: 41).

Further reading

Cònsul, I. (1988) 'Quim Monzó: Interview', *Catalan Writing* 1: 39–47 (interview followed by a chronology of Monzó's life, a bibliography and translations of two short stories).

KATHRYN CRAMERI

Moragas i Galissa, Antoni de

b. 1913, Barcelona; d. 1985, Barcelona

Architect

Nephew of one of the great figures of **Modernism**, Antoni Gallissa, Antoni de Moragas qualified as an architect in 1941. He was deeply committed to avant-garde architecture which was struggling to establish itself in Spain at the time. The work which best expresses his sensibility and convictions is the renovation of the Cinema Fémina (1950–2, Barcelona) a building which displays great purity of form. A founder member of the Grupo R in 1951, along with **Coderch**, **Sostres** and **Bohigas** and others, he was subsequently elected Dean of the Col·legi d'Arquitectes de Catalunya i Balears from 1964–6 and from 1972–4. Notable among his many creations are the Hotel Park (1950–3, Barcelona) and Les Cases dels Braus (1961, Barcelona).

MIHAIL MOLDOVEANU

Morán, Fernando

b. 1926, Avilés, Asturias

Diplomat and politician

A distinguished diplomat, Morán took part in the opposition to the Franco regime as one of the founder members of **Tierno Galván**'s PSP. In 1982, Felipe **González** appointed him Foreign Minister in his first Cabinet, and he presided over the preparations for two important landmarks in recent Spanish history: entry into the European Economic Community (in January 1986) and the referendum on Spain's continuing membership of **NATO**. Unsympathetic to NATO membership, Morán was replaced by Francisco Fernández Ordóñez in 1986. Since 1987 he has been head of the PSOE Group in the European Parliament. He has published novels, poetry and works of literary criticism.

JONATHAN HOPKIN

motor car

As in other countries, the motor car has come to dominate urban and, to a lesser extent, rural life, though, since Spain started out from a relatively low incidence of car ownership before the 1960s, the growth has been all the more noticeable. In 1995, there were 14.2 million cars in Spain, an increase of 3.5 percent over the previous year, and 870,487 new registrations were added. In the twenty years up to 1996, the number of driving licences issued doubled, from 8 million to more than 16 million. The annual figure for new licences is around 700,000, which is close enough to the total of new car registrations to suggest that a large number of first-time owners are entering the market.

Parking has become a major problem in the larger cities, where huge underground parks have been excavated, though this has not altogether solved the congestion caused by on-street parking: city life, especially in Madrid, is carried on to the accompaniment of constant sounding of horns by frustrated motorists hemmed in by double- and even triple-parked vehicles. Fines are in theory levied for illegal parking, but many motorists consider that they can safely ignore them because they are rarely followed up.

Public holidays are notoriously a time not only of serious road congestion, but of a high frequency of fatal accidents, a statistic which has shown no improvement in the period 1976–96, when deaths in road accidents rose from 3,959 to 4,220. Fatalities peaked in 1990 at 5,736.

Since 1993, only unleaded fuel has been available, and the state-owned petroleum company Campsa has had to compete against other suppliers. The fitting and wearing of seatbelts has been compulsory since 1992. The standard speed-limit in urban areas is 50 km/hr, and in some towns this is enforced by the phasing of traffic lights, which are programmed to turn to red if the limit is exceeded.

Though a larger number of middle-of-the-range and upmarket models has become available, the preference of the car-owning population is predominantly for the smaller family saloon, and for certain makes which have remained consistently popular. The top six sellers in the first nine months of 1996 were the Seat Ibiza (36,715 units), Citroën ZX (32,654), Ford Fiesta (30,349), Opel Corsa (29,885), Ford Escort (28,176) and Renault Clio (27,173).

See also: autopistas; motor manufacture; motorcycles; roads

EAMONN RODGERS

motor manufacture

The motor-vehicle industry has been a leading sector in Spanish industrial development in the second half of the twentieth century, with car-manufacturing capacity around two million units a year. In addition, there is a significant truck, bus and motor-cycle industry together with parts and ancillary industries, all of which make a substantial contribution to employment, total industrial production and exports. Exports of vehicles represented over one-fifth of the value of all merchandise exports in the mid-1990s, 80 percent of cars produced in Spain were exported and many of the leading export companies in Spain were motor-vehicle manufacturers.

Foreign multinational companies dominate the sector, controlling all car, truck and bus assembly and most other major motor-vehicle and component manufacturers. Their investment transformed a backward industry oriented to the domestic market into a modern internationally integrated industry incorporating the latest production techniques. It also left the industry exposed to the changing strategic considerations of these multinational companies headquartered outside Spain with their own corporate goals.

Following the Civil War, the government adopted a policy of import substitution, directing output to the protected domestic market. Two public companies were established in the 1940s, the bus and truck manufacturer ENASA (Empresa Nacional de Autocamiones) in 1946 and the car manufacturer **Seat** (Sociedad Española de Automóviles de Turismo) in 1949, both in Barcelona. During the 1950s and 1960s the domestic industry expanded and some foreign manufacturers secured production facilities (including Citroën and Fasa-Renault).

The emphasis in motor vehicle production shifted towards exports from the 1970s onwards. Relatively low labour costs, a protected and expanding domestic market, access to component suppliers and government assistance attracted further European investment and the giant American and Japanese manufacturers Ford, General Motors, Honda, Nissan, Suzuki and Yamaha. Membership of the European Community in 1986 provided a further impetus to inward investment and opened the way for greater integration into the European motor-vehicle industry, though as a concession to ease the transition to full competition, Spain was allowed, for three years after accession, to levy a special tariff of 17.4 percent on cars imported from other EC countries.

During the first half of the 1990s international competition for new investment increased and the domestic market contracted from its peak in the late 1980s. All manufacturers sought ways of further reducing costs and increasing efficiency, frequently through shedding labour. Component supply was reorganized with global component system manufacturers emerging with their own supply chains. Component supply complexes developed around the major vehicle assembly plants in response to 'just-in-time' or 'immediate' delivery systems and closer co-operation between assemblers and suppliers in design and quality assurance.

Many towns across Spain have experienced the beneficial effects of the industry in the form of direct employment, income and business development. These towns include the centres of vehicle assembly such as Barcelona, Madrid, Linares, Palencia, Pamplona, Valencia, Valladolid, Vigo and Zaragoza, plus those towns dependent on motor-vehicle component and ancillary industries. Apart from Madrid, Valencia and a few important locations in the south, the industry is concentrated in the north. All these communities must face the challenge of ongoing restructuring in a global industry subject to rapid technological change.

See also: motor car

Further reading

Hawkesworth, R. (1981) 'The Rise of Spain's Automobile Industry', *National Westminster Bank Review*, February: 37–48 (deals with the development of the industry).

Lagendijk, A. (1994) 'The Impact of Internationalisation and Rationalisation of Production on the Spanish Automobile Industry, 1950–90', *Environment and Planning A*, 26, 11: 321–43 (covers the re-organization of the industry).

—— (1995) 'The Impact of Foreign Investments in the Automobile Industry on Local Economic Development in Spain', *Area*, 27, 4: 335–46 (deals with the impact of the industry on local development).

Lagendijk, A. and van der Knaap, B. (1995) 'The Impact of Internationalisation on the Spatial Structure of Automobile Production in Spain', *Tijdschrift voor economische en sociale geografie*, 86, 5: 426–42 (deals with the impact of industrialization of the industry on the geography of motor vehicle production in Spain).

Salmon, K. (1995) *The Modern Spanish Economy*, 2nd edn, London: Cassell Publishers, pp. 192–202 (a good synthesis of the motor-vehicle industry in Spain).

KEITH SALMON

motorcycles

In Spain, motorcycles are mainly used for sporting activities, although they also function as alternatives to cars in urban and intercity transport. The two most characteristic varieties of motorbikes for urban use are the scooter and the moped, which has an engine capacity of less than 50 c.c., a power output of 2 h.p., and a maximum speed of 40 km/hr.

Motorcycle production in Spain began in earnest in 1920. In the 1950s, the scooter and the Vespa, introduced in 1946, invaded the market. In the 1960s, demand for the scooter began to decline, and motorcycles took over. The late 1970s saw the appearance of the Japanese superbikes. By 1977, 200,000 motorcycles were manufactured in Spain.

The 1980s marked the great motorcycling revolution, with the emergence of a new clientele composed of young people born during the years of political and economic change. In Spanish **youth culture**, motorbikes are a symbol of power, enabling young people to experience new sensations such as speed and physical risk, which has, tragically, increased accident rates. Motorcycle ownership and all that it entails (engine tuning, display, maintenance, reading of specialist magazines), satisfies the younger generation's need for freedom, self-affirmation and pursuit of their own distinctive lifestyle.

Motorcycle racing is uniquely exciting, because of the high speeds involved as well as the risk run by riders. The sport depends heavily on corporate sponsorship, and the huge prizes are financially supported by revenue from **advertising** material displayed on the machines themselves, overalls and circuits. The most important international competition is the *Campeonato del Mundo de Velocidad* (World Speed Championship), which covers a series of *pruebas puntuales* (points trials) to select the best rider of the year. Since 1949 this championship has been divided into classes, according to the cylinder capacity of the motorbikes. The introduction of the 50 c.c. category enabled Spanish riders such as Santiago Herrero and Angel Nieto to win many triumphs. In 1969, Nieto became the first Spaniard to win a championship, going on to a further twelve victories. Other noteworthy Spanish riders are Jorge Martínez Aspar, with four championships, and Sito Pons, Carlos Lavado and Ricardo Tormo with two each. In the various classes, the most prominent riders are Crivillé, Checa and Puig (500 c.c.), D'Antin, Gavira, Cordoso, Alzamorra and Sainz (250 c.c.) and Aspar, Maturana, Sarda and Nieto Jr. (125 c.c.).

Other specialized activities in which Spain has participated with increasing success are: *trial* (on rough surfaces, without the foot touching the ground), *motocross* (on irregular surfaces), *enduro* or *todo terreno (TT)* (mountain rally), Dakar rally, and *raids* or *rallies* (such as the Atlas). Annual events such as the *Salón de Barcelona* (Barcelona Showroom) or the famous *concentraciones moteras* (motorcycling rallies) organized by supporters' clubs, which include races, visits to places of interest, and discussions, contribute to the increasing popularity of the sport.

See also: consumerism; industrial development; industry; motor car; motor manufacture; social attitudes; society; standard of living; student life

Further reading

Agostini, S. and Patrignani, R. (1972) *Conducción deportiva de la moto*, Barcelona: Editorial Biblioteca Deportiva De Vecchi (a study of how the different motorbike models and categories have evolved through time).

Tomasellli, J. (1995) *MOTO: Official Grand Prix Book 1995*, Brussels: IHM (a lavishly produced yearbook on motorcycling, containing the main events of the year, championships and race winners).

LUIS VICENTE BELMONTE TALERO

Movida, la

At the start of the 1980s, concurrent with the social and cultural shock waves that the advent of democracy brought to Spain, there was a renaissance in the arts with its centre of gravity in Madrid, which some commentators defined as the *la Movida madrileña*, shortened to *la Movida*.

Music was a thriving part of the movement, with new groups imitating punk and new wave sounds, as a rejection of the Spanish rock scene of the 1970s. The FM radio stations played a decisive role in extending the appeal of songs of undiscovered bands like Radio Futura, **Alaska** y los Pegamoides, Paraíso, Nacha Pop, Rubí y los Casinos and Ejecutivos Agresivos, who sent their demo tapes to the most innovative programmes. The significant air play devoted to these bands meant that many went on to become figureheads of *la Movida*. Fanzines and music pages of several newspapers showed a similar interest in promoting the novelty of this sudden avalanche of young groups. Most multinational record companies did not want to let this opportunity pass them by and decided to launch some of the up-and-coming bands. Other groups, whose work did not sit so easily in the catalogues of multinationals, released tracks with **independent record companies**, some of whom where created by the groups themselves. This was how the labels DRO (Discos Radioactivos Organizados), GASA (Grabaciones Accidentales) and Lollipop came into being and they launched the first records by El Aviador Dro, Los Esclarecidos, Décima Víctima, Derribos Arias and Los Nikis.

Initially, the movement appeared to be a passing and marginal fashion but it gradually gained acceptance and ended up attracting a wide audience and a few of the bands went on to secure the top positions in the charts in the mid-1980s. In the midst of this euphoria a multitude of discoteques, clubs (Rock-Ola became a mecca for followers of *la Movida*), and bars were opened which helped to project the image of Madrid as a city with a vibrant nightlife, though other cities such as Vigo, Barcelona or Valencia attempted to imitate the movement in the capital.

The main impact of *la Movida* was on the music scene, but the visual arts revived at the same time and dozens of artists began to make a name for themselves by jumping on the cultural bandwagon: Ceesepe, El Hortelano, Fanny McNamara and Las Costus in **painting**; Ouka Lele, Alberto García Alix and Pablo Pérez Mínguez in **photography**; Antonio Alvarado, Adolfo Domínguez, Manuel Piña and Jesús del Pozo in **fashion** design.

The national press decided to increase the cultural content of their pages, devoting lengthy monographs to any artistic event in the capital. Specialized magazines appeared willing to cover any happening which might add a degree of modernity to the impoverished cultural state of the country and profile any personage who stood out in any way within it. Some of these magazines, for instance *La Luna* (The Moon), became the voice of *la Movida*. Other publications from this period include *Madrid me Mata* (Madrid Kills Me) and *Total*.

Television also played a significant role in the the promotion of new artistic tendencies. One of the most important programmes in this respect was *La Edad de Oro* (The Golden Age), presented and directed by Paloma Chamorro, which offered live music from the latest Spanish and foreign groups, as well as interviews and footage of up and coming bands and established ones.

Public institutions collaborated in *la Movida* by promoting a wide range of events in order to heighten Madrid's fame as a centre of modernity. They sponsored competitions, organized exhibitions and edited a large number of publications. Enrique **Tierno Galván**, the socialist mayor of Madrid in the early 1980s, stood out as one of the most emblematic political figures the capital has ever had, as he made every attempt to bring Madrid up to the level of the leading European capitals.

Cinema was another show case for *la Movida*. A new type of urban comedy emphasizing the vertiginous pace of Madrid life in the 1980s proved popular with cinema-goers. Pedro **Almodóvar** is the most prominent director of film genre. After shooting a series of short films, he surprised cinema audiences with his first full length feature: *Pepi, Luci, Bom y otras chicas del montón* (Pepi, Luci, Bom and All Those Other Girls) (1979) with his provocative style, outlandish sense of humour, bad taste and kitsch. However, a second feature film *Laberinto de* *pasiones* (Labyrinth of Passions) (1982) is arguably the best representation of underground cultural life in the Madrid of the early 1980s. The film includes cameo performances from many of the leading lights of *la Movida* and a star turn by Almodóvar himself with his muse Fanny McNamara, with whom he recorded a handful of records.

See also: gay culture; rock and pop

FERNANDO DELGADO

Muncunill i Parellada, Lluis

b. 1868, Fals (Barcelona); d. 1931, Terrassa (Barcelona)

Architect

After qualifying in 1892, Muncunill established himself at Terrassa where he was town architect, and where virtually all his work is to be found, determining much of the character of the town to this day. An exponent of Catalan **Modernism**, he was at first influenced by **Domènech** and **Puig**: his earliest important creations incorporated historicist elements. After 1905, however, he began to develop his own idiom, based on the elliptical arch so characteristic of **Gaudí**. By using it unadorned, he was able to achieve great visual impact, the best example being the Masia Freixa (1907–10). He was also very successful as an industrial architect, producing buildings of great beauty, such as the factories of the companies Aymerich, Amat y Jover (1908) and Vapor Amat (1909).

MIHAIL MOLDOVEANU

Mundo, El

El Mundo, a daily newspaper published in Madrid with a national readership throughout Spain, is attempting to establish itself as a source of modern investigative journalism.

El Mundo was founded in 1989 and is, therefore, by some distance the youngest of Spain's national daily newspapers. It is clearly attempting to define itself as the most modern and forward-looking of the national dailies, as evinced by its current masthead *El Mundo del Siglo Veintuno* (The World of the Twenty-First Century). It is, like most Madrid dailies, roughly tabloid in format and is a substantial read, often totalling as many as eighty pages. It combines extensive international coverage with in-depth reporting on Spain, as well as fairly hefty business and sports sections.

Although it could not be described as sensationalist, *El Mundo* has a clear preference for controversial issues. In fact, it has attempted to establish a reputation as a newspaper committed to fearless investigative journalism. It attracted considerable opprobrium from many sectors of Spanish society for critical reports on certain activities of King **Juan Carlos I** at a time – shortly after the Barcelona **Olympic Games** – when the King's popularity throughout Spain, and the general level of adulation in the media, was at an all-time high. *El Mundo* has resolutely refused to apologize for these reports, and has defended them as its right in an open and democratic society. It has also been much involved in the unmasking of political corruption in Spain, sometimes in operations reminiscent of the unravelling of the Watergate conspiracy, a process which has gained its editor, Pedro **Ramírez**, both fame and notoriety. Though the targets of these investigations have been politicians from the socialist **PSOE**, there seems little doubt that *El Mundo* would have pursued these issues whichever party had been in power.

As well as counting some of Spain's best known journalists on its staff, *El Mundo* also features some of the country's best known columnists – notably Francisco Umbral – whose highly literate and linguistically innovative pieces are often viewed as a model of pioneering journalistic style. Indeed, Umbral's back-page column is often breathtaking in its manipulation of the Spanish language, and likewise presupposes a generally highly educated and linguistically responsive reader.

There is little doubt that *El Mundo* is something of a success story in Spanish print journalism. Despite its recent entry into the market, its current sales are just under 400,000 per day, putting it very much in the top flight of daily newspapers in Spain. To read *El Mundo* is to some extent to define oneself as up-to-date, unencumbered not only with the Francoist past, but even with the more recent past of the transition to democracy, and to be committed to a critical attitude to all social institutions, however revered they may be by other sections of society. Despite its occasional lapses into somewhat overheated reporting, its future would seem to be assured.

See also: journalism; media; press; press ownership

HUGH O'DONNELL

municipalities

Municipalities, of which there are some 8,022 represented in the country's town and city halls (*ayuntamientos*), have a long history in Spain, many of them possessing ancient royal charters. They vary enormously in size, from those of cities like Madrid and Barcelona, with roughly four and two million inhabitants respectively, to small villages with no more than a hundred citizens.

Article 140 of the **constitution of 1978** states: 'The constitution guarantees the autonomy of the municipalities. They shall enjoy full legal status. Their government and administration are the responsibility of their respective town halls, made up of the mayors and councillors.' The basic institutions are the full council (*pleno*) and the commission, each headed by the mayor (*alcalde*). While the existence of these is a legal requirement, only the larger ones tend to set up additional bodies, such as administrative departments and advisory committees.

The *pleno* is the rule-making, elected body of the *ayuntamiento*. It is made up of councillors (*concejales*) who are elected by direct, universal suffrage. In accordance with the law of 1985, the number to be elected is determined on the basis of proportional representation, modified to allow for a minimum of five councillors per municipality. The D'Hondt system is employed for the allocation of seats between the competing parties. Electors vote, not for individual councillors, but for municipality-wide lists on which there is a pre-determined ranking order headed by each party's candidate for mayor. Councillors serve for a period of four years and there is no limit to the number of terms they may serve. The council cannot be dissolved mid-term and the regular elections are controlled by central government.

The council has no authority to draft major laws, only to issue regulations (*ordenanzas*) which must conform to legislation emanating from either the national or relevant regional parliament. Among the major responsibilities of the *pleno* are: to approve the annual budget; to prioritize expenditure; to approve the accounts; and to control and oversee the work of the commission

The services carried out by a municipal council depend on its population size. All are required to provide public lighting, cemeteries, refuse collection and street cleaning; those with a population of over 5,000 are also responsible for public parks, libraries, markets, water supply and sewage treatment; those with a population of over 20,000 are also required to provide social services, police and fire services; and only those with a population of over 50,000 are also expected to have systems of urban transport and environmental protection. While councils can earn some revenue from a council tax (*comunidad*) and such things as car-parking charges and fines, the bulk of funding for the municipal authorities comes from central government.

See also: elections; taxation

Further reading

Bosch i Roca, N. (1988) 'Spanish Local Government: Territorial Organization and Financing', *Planning and Administration*, 15 (1): 6–17.

Newton, M.T. with Donaghy, P.J. (1997) *Institutions of Modern Spain*, Cambridge: Cambridge University Press (chapter 8.3 deals with most aspects of municipal administration).

MICHAEL T. NEWTON

Museum of the Canaries

The Museo Canario (Canarian Museum) in Las Palmas de Gran Canaria, housing the largest collection of pre-Spanish artefacts in the Canary Islands, still remains a private museum. Founded in 1879 as an academic society, the museum was established in the house of Dr Gregorio Chil y

Naranjo who, with the first curator Dr Victor Grau Bassas, led collecting expeditions to the pre-Spanish burial caves of the Guayadeque basin and elsewhere in Gran Canaria. After Chil's death in 1903 the museum stagnated, though it was already renowned for its collection of human skulls. With the renovations of the 1980s under the direction of Julio Cuenca Sanabria, the museum's displays have improved, though problems of access to the collections remain.

See also: Archaeological Museum of Tenerife; Canarian culture; Cubillo Ferreira, Antonio

M.R. EDDY

museums

Museums play a very important role in the preservation of Spanish culture, both ancient and modern. They range from the largest art galleries to the smallest municipal and subject-specific museums, and from institutions that are financed wholly from public monies to ones that depend entirely on private funding.

Museums which are funded from the public purse include the semi-independent trustee-governed **Prado Museum** and **Queen Sofia Museum**; national museums, such as the Museum of Decorative Arts, Madrid, the Museum of Roman Art, Mérida, and the Museum of Ceramics, Valencia, which are controlled directly by the Ministry of Education and Culture (see also **Ministry of Culture**); national subject-specific museums which are run by the relevant Ministries, such as Defence (military museums), Industry (geology) and Transport (railway); state museums jointly financed by central government and the autonomous regions; and municipal museums financed by the city councils.

These publicly funded museums were major beneficiaries of the **arts policy** and **arts funding** arrangements of the 1980s and 1990s, whereby existing buildings were modernized and expanded, and new ones built. The Queen Sofia Museum, for example, was established in the refurbished eighteenth century General Hospital of Madrid, and the **Thyssen-Bornemisza Museum** in the renovated Palace of Villahermosa. A National Anthropological Museum was formed by fusing the National Museums of Ethnology and the Spanish People in the former Modern Art Museum and the Americas Museum was refurbished. An architectural plan was devised for the renovation of state museums: the Institute of Modern Art in Valencia (IVAM) is a prime example of major new projects.

As a result of the **Law of Patronage** passed in 1994, income from private institutions and individuals is playing an increasingly important role in the economies of both older and newer museums. Some of the major public museums are supported by associations of friends, and there are many museums which are largely or wholly financed by private monies. These include museums instituted by **foundations**, such as the Miró and Tàpies Foundations; by business enterprises, such as the Museum of Contemporary Art, Barcelona, and the **Guggenheim Museum**, Bilbao; by the church, such as the Cathedral Museum, Burgos; and by individuals, such as the Lázaro Galdiano Museum, Madrid, and the Museo del Barça, Barcelona. Many of these belong to the Spanish Association of Curators, which publishes a journal, the *Revista de Museología*.

As well as the modernization, refurbishment and creation of musem buildings there has been a noticeable expansion in the number of collections, especially local and ethnological ones, and changes in the style of presentation. More rigorous selection of representative pieces and arrangements by theme or chronological development have contributed not just to the aesthetic pleasure of visits, but to the important educational function of museum collections.

See also: art exhibitions; arts funding; arts policy; cultural institutions and movements; sport and leisure

Further reading

Wright, P. (1992) 'State of the Nation', *Museums Journal*, June 1992: 25–33 (a very informative and wide-ranging article on the situation in the early 1990s).

EAMONN RODGERS

music

Musical culture in Spain has had a certain impact internationally through the work of opera singers like José **Carreras** and Plácido **Domingo**, instrumentalists of a previous generation such as Pau **Casals**, and composers such as Manuel de Falla. Like other cultural activities, however, music has not been well-supported financially by the state, especially during the Franco period. It is only since the transition to democracy, and the relative increase in prosperity, that music has enjoyed proper facilities in the form of concert-halls (see also **Auditorio Nacional de Música**) and the creation of regional **orchestras**. Musical education has been enhanced by the establishment of local conservatories, and the new syllabuses drawn up in the 1990s (see also **LOGSE**) include plans for the introduction of music at all levels of primary and secondary schools. Shortage of funds, however, and the lack of political will on the part of the conservative **PP** government elected in 1995, raise a question mark over how effectively these plans will be implemented.

Although few musicians lost their lives as a direct consequence of the Civil War, the generation which had been active in the 1920s (essentially the heirs of Falla) went into **exile**, and disappeared from the musical scene in Spain, with a few exceptions such as Joaquín **Rodrigo**. The members of this generation had been concentrated in two main groups, both going by the name of 'The Group of Eight'. In Madrid, the 'Grupo de los Ocho' included Rodolfo and Ernesto **Halffter**, while the Barcelona 'Grup dels Vuit' contained probably the most significant Spanish composer of the twentieth century after Falla, Roberto Gerhard (1896–1970). Gerhard was more popular in the UK than in his native country, and spent the last thirty years of his life in Cambridge, where he composed some of his best work, such as the *Violin Concerto* (1947) and the *Fourth (New York) Symphony* (1967). His music combines traditional Spanish elements with the twelve-tone scale which he acquired from his teacher, Schönberg, whose work he introduced into Spain. Of the Halffter brothers, the most prominent is probably Rodolfo, who emigrated in 1939 to Mexico, where, over a lengthy period of time, he developed his individual style of piano music. His direct influence on music in Spain began to be felt again in the 1960s, when he returned to teach in his native country.

As with other areas of cultural life, exile, or the stifling of the creativity of those who remained in Spain, have had long-term effects on music, not only on composition, but on performance and criticism. The Franco regime largely ignored music, apart from bringing it within the administrative ambit, and did not even attempt, as it did in other areas, to impose official standards of taste (see also **Francoist culture**). It was only in the 1950s that Spanish musicians began to develop an awareness of musical life in other countries, through the importation of books from Argentina, and scores and recordings from central Europe. The two orchestras which had existed prior to the Civil War virtually disappeared. In 1940, the National Orchestra of Spain was formed in Madrid, though it was not fully operational until 1942, adopting a conventional repertoire which excluded new trends and paid little or no attention to Spanish composers and performers. Other orchestras included the RTVE Symphony Orchestra, and those founded in Barcelona, Valencia and Bilbao, as well as a few short-lived ventures in other cities. The **music festivals** in Granada and Santander, started in 1952, did little to stimulate creativity. The state of **opera** was no more encouraging. Apart from short amateur seasons organized, with a minimum of official support, in various cities from around 1960, only the **Liceu Theatre** in Barcelona offered regular opera seasons until its destruction by fire in 1994. Spain was then without a major opera house until the re-opening in 1997 of the **Royal Theatre** (Teatro Real) in Madrid, which had provided opera performances in the nineteenth century, but subsequently concentrated on plays. In the conservatories, the effects of the Civil War were not immediate, as, despite the general dispersal of intellectuals and professionals, many of the teaching staff remained at their posts. The problem arose later, at a time when the pre-Civil War generation would have been expected to succeed to these posts. The lack of new blood meant that the conservatories stagnated, and musical education became divorced from musical practice. The exile of musicologists such as Adolfo Salazar left a gap which was difficult to fill.

Though the music composed during the Franco period tended to reflect an inward-looking nationalism, there were a few composers who were aware of the need for renewal of the musical idiom, though, given the conditions of the time, they were relatively isolated and did not in any sense form a school. Xavier Montsalvatge began under the influence of Stravinsky, but later moved towards a more neoclassical idiom in *Partita* (1958), and an expressionist style in what is probably his best work, *Cinco invocaciones al Crucificado* (Five Invocations to the Crucified Christ) (1969). The Salamanca-born composer Gerardo Gombau (1906–71) initiated, with *Doce canciones de Rafael Alberti* (Twelve Songs by Rafael **Alberti**) (1959) an experimental style which differentiates him markedly from his contemporaries. In the 1960s, works like *Cantata para la inauguración de una losa de ensayo* (Cantata for the Inauguration of a Testbed) (1967) revealed him as one of the foremost exponents of electronic music.

The inevitable opening up of cultural horizons, after the isolation of the immediate post-Civil War period, brought about significant changes in music, reflected, for example, in the emergence of the 'Generation of 1951', a loosely-organized group, held together, not by a common programme, but by the experience of similar problems and by occasional artistic collaboration. Their main aim was to make up for lost time by familiarizing themselves with the latest works by Stravinsky and Bartok, atonal expressionism, the twelve-tone scale, open and unstructured forms, and electronic techniques. Without abandoning their characteristic individual style, Spanish musicians assimilated these new trends with remarkable rapidity. The label 'Generation of 1951', apparently invented by Cristóbal Halffter, derived from the year in which most of this group, all of whom were born around 1930, finished their training. They included Antón García Abril, Luis de Pablo, Manuel Moreno Buendía and Alberto Blancafort. One of the most prominent members of the group was Juan Hidalgo, who was encouraged to explore experimental forms by the American composer John Cage. In 1964, Hidalgo founded *Zaj*, a movement committed to artistic experiment, which had a revolutionary impact not only on Spanish music, but on other cultural spheres, such as the **theatre**. Cristóbal Halffter, from having been originally influenced by his uncles, Rodolfo and Ernesto, gradually moved towards avant-garde positions, reflected, for example, in *Secuencias* (Sequences) (1964), followed by the cantata *Symposium* (1966), the first modern Spanish work to receive wide acclaim. His *Violin Concerto* (1979) is one of his finest works.

Luis de Pablo has produced a large output, characterized by considerable experimental innovation, which led him from serialism to open-ended improvisational techniques, and speculative re-workings of traditional musical forms. He is also an active promoter of cultural activities, being the prime mover behind the biennial Festival of Contemporary Music in Madrid (1964), and the 'Pamplona Encounters' (1972), a showcase for the most avant-garde currents in contemporary music and art. Carmelo Bernaola, a composer with an exceptionally disciplined approach, soon moved away from serialism to embark on an individual journey of exploration, characterized by a high degree of technical perfection. His *Relatividades* (Relativities) (1971) was followed by his *Symphony in C*, which, despite its title, does not imply a return to traditional tonalism, but the construction of a series of polarities around this note and its harmonics, a trend developed further in his *Second Symphony* (1980). Side by side with the more avant-garde members of this generation is a more conservative, or at least eclectic group, which strives to widen the possibilities of the tonal system, without abandoning it completely. Their models are Falla, Bartok, Stravinsky and Shostakovich. They include Manuel Castillo, Antón García Abril, and Amand Blanquer.

Inevitably, younger composers emerging in the mid-1960s began their careers under the shadow of serialism and atonalism, despite the fact that their training in the conservatories concentrated, in general, on traditional forms. Miguel Ángel Coria's compositions break both with older tradition and the contemporary avant-garde. The composer and musicologist Tomás Marco has forged a personal style linked to the psychology of perception. The movement towards electronic music begun by Hidalgo is continued by the Barcelona-based

Andrés Lewin-Richter. The Valencian Carles Santos has developed a distinctively ironic style, linked to the American avant-garde, repetitive music, and the incorporation of the composer or performer's own voice into the composition.

The 1980s and 1990s display a huge variety of trends, though there is a certain convergence on, for instance, computerized music, the revival of the influence of Cage, experiments in action music, and repetitive music. Spanish music has shown a capacity for development and assimilation which has reintegrated it into the mainstream of international musical life, though composers still complain of the difficulties of achieving a coherent and consistent national output of quality. Many of the conservatories consider that the boundary of the modern is to be set at impressionism, and dismiss atonalism as excessively advanced. It is only rarely that orchestras perform contemporary works by Spanish composers. The financing of orchestras continues to be a problem in Spain, though from the 1980s on, new performing groups were founded with the assistance of the governments of the **autonomous communities**, and the refurbishment of auditoria and the construction of new ones have been put in train.

Early music, an essential historical element in the development of contemporary music, has been promoted commercially in the 1990s, and a significant number of instrumental and vocal groups have emerged which have brought the repertoire of Spanish medieval, renaissance and baroque music to the attention of a public which is increasingly rediscovering its pride in its own musical heritage.

See also: folk music; guitar music; music festivals; rock and pop

Discography

García Abril, A. (1984) *Sonatas para orquesta*, Madrid Symphonic Orchestra, dir. E. García Asensio, 1994 (MARC).

—— (1966–94) *Concierto para piano y orquesta*, G. González, Madrid Symphonic Orchestra, dir. E. García Asensio, 1994 (MARC).

Gerhard, R. (1952–3; 1960) *Symphonies Nº 1 & 3*, Tenerife Symphonic Orchestra, dir. V. Pablo Pérez, 1994 (AUDIVIS).

—— *Don Quixote; Pedrelliana; Albada, interludi i dansa*, Tenerife Symphonic Orchestra, dir. V. Pablo Pérez, 1992 (AUDIVIS).

Halffter, C. *String Quartet Nº 3*, Arditti Quartet, 1991 (MONT).

Halffter, E. (1969) *Guitar Concerto*, N. Yepes, ORTVE, dir. O. Alonso, 1972 (DG).

Halffter, R. (1940) *Violin Concerto*, H. Szeryng, Royal Philarmonic Orchestra, Dr.: E. Bátiz, 1980 (ASV).

Marco, T. (1973) *Concierto Guadiana for Guitar and Orchestra*, W. Weigel, European Master Orchestra, dir. P. Schmeizer, 1992 (SCHW).

—— (1987) *Espejo desierto*, Arditti Quartet, 1991 (MONT).

Montsalvatge, X. (1953) *Concierto breve para piano y orquesta*, Morales, Madrid Symphonic Orchestra, dir. E. García Asensio, 1993 (MARC).

—— *5 canciones negras para voz y piano*, Victoria de los Ángeles, Paris Conservatory Orchestra, dir. R. Frühbeck, 1988 (EMI).

Further reading

Marco, T. (1993) *Spanish Music in the Twentieth Century*, Cambridge, MA: Harvard University Press (provides the most comprehensive account available on Contemporary Spanish music up to the 1980s; for post-war developments, chapters 10–19).

ENRIC DOLZ I FERRER

music festivals

A large number of music festivals take place regularly in Spain. Wide ranging International Festivals are held in several cities, the two most important being those of Granada and Santander which were instituted in 1952, and music forms part of several seasonal festivals, such as the Madrid Autumn Festival, the GREC Barcelona Summer Arts Festival and the Burgos Summer Festival, which incorporates the Antonio de Cabezón Music Week. More specialized festivals are devoted to areas such as religious music (especially Cuenca), jazz (especially San Sebastián), contemporary music (Alicante, Barcelona, Granada, Madrid and Pamplona), **guitar music** (e.g. Córdoba, Alicante and Laredo), organ (e.g. León and Mallorca) and early music (e.g. Seville and Pamplona).

See also: folk music; music; performing arts

EAMONN RODGERS

N

Nadal Prize

An annual prize of 3m pesetas, offered for an unpublished novel of not less than 150 pages. The winner is guaranteed publication, and the prize money is treated as a royalty advance. It is one of the most hotly contested literary prizes in Spain: in 1996, over 500 manuscripts were submitted.

EAMONN RODGERS

national anthem

The Royal March (*Marcha Real*), an anonymous piece of music dating from the eighteenth century, was adopted officially as the Spanish national anthem in 1976. It had, however, been commonly used since at least the early nineteenth century on state occasions, and had acquired a *de facto* status.

EAMONN RODGERS

National Catholicism

Despite its authoritarian character, the Franco regime had no clear political ideology, but instead used **religion** as a force for national cohesion, building on the long-standing identification of Spanish nationality with **Roman Catholicism**. The Catholic hierarchy had overwhelmingly supported the Francoist insurgents during the Civil War as a defence against 'godless Communism', and in the years after the war provided the main legitimization for the regime, more important even than the **Falange**. Franco in turn accorded the church legal status as a fundamental institution of the state. Though there was some limited toleration for **minority religions**, the state was defined as officially Catholic. Bishops had seats in the parliament and in the Council of the Realm, and the church was given a large measure of control over education. Catholic religious instruction was obligatory in all educational institutions, whether state-run or private.

In addition, the civil and criminal law embodied Catholic moral teaching. Divorce was banned, and couples who wished to marry were obliged to do so in church if either party had been baptized, even if they were no longer practising their religion. Adultery was an offence under the Penal Code, though it was more frequently enforced against women than against men, and the offences of 'blasphemy' and 'public scandal', which could lead to prosecution for kissing in public or wearing a bikini on the beach, were only removed from the Penal Code in 1987, though the economic importance of international tourism had long since caused them to fall into abeyance.

The church also exercised a wide measure of control over intellectual and cultural life. The founding charter of the state-sponsored research body, the **CSIC**, declared that its mission was to restore the unity of Christianity and science. State **censorship** of films and printed material was supplemented and reinforced by ecclesiastical censorship, which was stricter, and could sometimes lead to the banning of works which had been passed by the state censors.

The symbiosis between church and state had been a feature of Spanish life for centuries, and had been codified most recently in the Concordat of 1857. The provisions of this document were restated and extended in the Concordat of 1953, which gave Franco, as Head of State, virtual control over nominations to vacant bishoprics. The state also granted the church other privileges, such as the immunity of clergy from prosecution on criminal charges except by permission of the bishop. Throughout the 1950s and 1960s, however, relations between **church and state** underwent a gradual transformation, culminating in the **constitution of 1978**, which confirmed the separation of church and state, and established a non-denominational polity.

Though *nacionalcatolicismo* as a concept is dead, Catholicism as a cultural identity marker is still deeply rooted in Spanish life. Official state occasions retain a religious character, and the Virgin of Pilar (Zaragoza) is honoured as patron of the **armed forces**. Football teams sometimes offer the trophies they have won at the shrine of their local madonna. Furthermore, the centre-right **PP** government elected in 1996, reported to contain several members of **Opus Dei** in its ministerial team, has attempted to reverse the secularization of the state by, for example, re-introducing religion as an examinable school subject.

See also: history; politics

Further reading

Carr, R. and Fusi, J.P. (1979) *Spain: Dictatorship to Democracy*, London: Allen & Unwin (pp. 28–31 provide a succinct summary of the influence of the church under Franco).

Lannon, F. (1987) *Privilege, Persecution and Prophecy: The Catholic Church in Spain, 1875–1975*, Oxford: Oxford University Press (a classic study of the cultural and political significance of the church).

EAMONN RODGERS

national dance companies

The national dance companies have undergone many changes since their foundation. Whereas the company specializing in traditional Spanish **dance**, the Spanish National Ballet (Ballet Nacional de España) has remained true to its origins, that which offered classical ballet has been completely transformed, becoming one of the foremost exponents of contemporary dance.

The Spanish National Ballet was created by the **Ministry of Culture** in 1978, with Antonio Gades as the first Director. Gades' plan was to recreate the most representative works by Spanish artists, one of the most notable examples being his choreography for a ballet version of Lorca's *Blood Wedding* (*Bodas de Sangre*), filmed by Carlos **Saura**. In 1980 Antonio Gades was replaced by Antonio, while Víctor Ullate was appointed Artistic Director of the Spanish National Classical Ballet Company (Ballet Nacional de España Clásico), whose repertoire emphasized neoclassical dance, the Dutch School and new routines produced within the company. In 1983, the Music and Theatre Directory of the Ministry merged the two companies, and appointed María de Avila director. This marked a period of radical innovation for the Spanish Dance section, in which for the first time, musical composition, choreography, script and scenic direction were combined to produce a programme of original works which included Alberto Lorca's *Ritmos* (Rhythms), *Medea* (script by Miguel Narros, choreography by José Granero), Felipe Sánchez's *Los Tarantos*, Mariemma's *Danza y Tronío* (Dance and Extravagance), and Victoria Eugenia's *Danza IX*. This programme was presented in 1988 in the New York Metropolitan Opera House, winning the Critics' Prize for the best foreign production of the year. The classical ballet section of the merged company continued with Balanchine, Tudor, and a limited repertoire.

In 1986 the two sections once again became independent companies. José Antonio became Artistic Director of the Spanish National Ballet, and created a number of new works, including a version of Falla's *The Three-Cornered Hat* (*El sombrero de tres picos*), with a reconstruction of the original stage designs by Picasso. In 1993, the company came under the joint management of Aurora Pons, Nana Lorca (responsible for programming) and Victoria Eugenia (dance training). Meanwhile, the Classical Ballet Company was directed by Maya Plisetskaya until 1990, when the post was offered to

Nacho Duato, a distinguished young dancer and choreographer. Under Duato, the company, now renamed the National Dance Company (Compañía Nacional de Danza), developed its own distinctive identity, specializing in contemporary dance, and offering new expressive possibilities to democratic Spain, through the work of one of its most innovative young choreographers. As a result, dance became a central part of the socio-cultural scene, with each new programme being eagerly awaited by the public, which was never disappointed. Nacho Duato has created more than fifteen ballets for the company, and its repertory also includes works by Jiri Kylián, Hans van Manen, Mats Ek, William Forsythe, Ohad Naharin and Ramón Oller.

As a result of all these developments, both companies have acquired clearly defined identities, and have achieved worldwide success.

See also: cultural institutions and movements; dance; performing arts

Further reading

Aznar, J. (ed.) (1994) *Dansa : noves tendències de la coreografia catalana*, Barcelona: Diputació de Barcelona (illustrated with numerous photographs).

Miguel Lara, M.J. de (ed.) (1994) *La danza en la escuela*, Sevilla: Diputación Provincial (considers the implications of the introduction of dance into the school curriculum).

Río Orozco, C. del (1993) *Apuntes sobre la danza española*, Córdoba: Tip. Artística (pp. 155–7 contain a useful bibliography).

CARLOS BLANCO LOU

national debt

In order to join the European Monetary Union on 1 January 1999 Spain must first fulfil the convergence criterion for public debt, which states that the budget deficit must not exceed 3 percent of GDP and total public sector debt 60 percent of GDP. The latter figure was breached in 1994 at the end of three years of recession. More significantly, the yearly budget deficit had been well above the convergence limit for a number of years, with a peak of 7.5 percent in 1993. It declined to 6.7 percent in 1994 and to 6 percent in 1995. Medium-term deficit projections suggested that the fulfilment of the 3 percent criterion would be possible if proceeds from privatizations were satisfactory, planned spending cuts were enacted, and tax elasticity remained as before, with the upturn in the economy producing a corresponding increase in revenues. In trying to control the deficit, the central government faced a number of major problems: the constant revenue shortfalls of the **social security** system, which necessitated transfers from central funds; the huge salary bill of civil servants with security of tenure; and the tendency of regional governments to run up their own deficits. Indeed the latter phenomenon has been the chief reason for the breaching of the 60 percent limit referred to above, 10 percent of the national debt having been incurred by regional governments and municipal authorities. The bulk of the loans taken out by these governments and municipalities have not required central government authorization, and although the law on the financial regime of autonomous communities (LOFCA) is supposed to limit regional indebtedness by imposing a ceiling on financial costs of 25 percent of current revenue, several regions have ignored this limit without corrective action being taken against them, owing to the political weakness of the central government. Similarly, the requirement that all long-term borrowing be used for investment has been widely ignored, thereby illustrating the difficulty of imposing fiscal prudence on seventeen regional governments of different political persuasion facing different kinds of problems.

At the level of central government the management of the national debt is done by wholly orthodox means, without recourse to direct financing by the central bank (**Banco de España**), which the Treaty of Rome expressly forbids. Treasury IOUs (*pagarés del Tesoro*), sold at a discount on their face value, were popular in the 1980s because they enjoyed favourable tax treatment, but were phased out in the early 1990s. Instead greater use has been made of short-term Treasury Bills (*letras del Tesoro*) and medium- and long-term government bonds. About one-third of the national debt is in the form of three-month, six-month and twelve-month bills and just under 50 percent in three-year, five-year, ten-year and fifteen-year bonds. Borrowing in denominated foreign currency amounts to about 10 percent of the total. Financial markets have favoured government bonds in recent years, enabling the Treasury to finance the deficit comfortably. Additionally, the Treasury holds a sum equivalent to about 5 percent of total debt at the Bank of Spain which it can call upon to iron out short-term differences between outgoings and revenues at moments of unfavourable market conditions.

Further reading

Chislett, W. (1996) *Spain 1996. The Central Hispano Handbook*, Madrid (chapter 8 explains how the public deficit is financed).

C.A. LONGHURST

National Employment Institute

Until the mid-1990s the National Employment Institute (Instituto Nacional de Empleo, INEM), an agency of the Ministry of Labour, had a monopoly over employment brokerage in Spain. The agency was also responsible for distributing unemployment benefits and was one of the public agencies concerned with training. By the 1980s INEM was seen as part of the overall rigidity of the labour market, while increasing labour market flexibility became part of orthodox economic policy.

Abolition of the job brokerage monopoly of INEM was set in train by a decree passed in December 1993. Private employment agencies were legalized, though they are required to be non-profit making and to have prior authorization from INEM.

The new role of INEM concentrates on providing an employment service, especially for certain priority groups. It is no longer responsible for the payment of unemployment benefit.

KEITH SALMON

national income

According to the Statistical Office of the European Community, Spain's GDP in 1992 was 444,000m ecus and GDP per capita was 11,354 ecus (for the UK 805,600m ecus and 13,926 ecus respectively). Spain's net national income per capita was 10,014 ecus (UK 12,315). The average for the EC in the same year was 15,617 ecus for GDP per capita and 13,514 ecus for net national income per capita. On the basis of these figures we can say that the wealth of the average Spaniard is 75 percent of that of the mythical average European and 81 percent of that of the average UK citizen. At factor cost the proportion of national income accruing to employees is slightly lower than that for most other western countries and that accruing to entrepreneurial and corporate entities slightly higher. Regional disparities of income in Spain are substantial, with the richer regions (the Balearics, Madrid and Catalonia) having roughly twice the GDP per capita of the poorer regions (Galicia, Castilla-La Mancha, Andalusia and Extremadura), an inequality mitigated to some extent by the higher cost of living in the richer regions. There are also large disparities even within the same region between the more urbanized and the less urbanized provinces. The disposable income of households also reveals major differences between rich and poor households, but these differences have been narrowing slowly over the past twenty to thirty years, as the accompanying table shows. Although the top 10 percent of households still command a quarter of the country's wealth, there is much less disparity among the bulk of the population, with 52 percent of the country's disposable income going to the 60 percent of households in the middle and the differences in this large group being rather less marked.

Further reading

Fundación FOESSA (1994) *V Informe sociológico sobre la situación social de España*, Madrid: Fundación FOESSA, vol. 2, 1,413–549 (hugely informative but highly technical).

Longhurst, C.A. (1993) 'Regionalism and Economic Disparities: Three Perspectives', *ACIS: Journal of the Association for Contemporary Iberian*

Percentage distribution of disposable income of households

Decile by level of income	1970 %	Cum. %	1980 %	Cum. %	1990 %	Cum. %
1st	1.44		2.41		3.22	
2nd	3.13	4.57	3.98	6.39	4.96	8.18
3rd	4.31	8.88	5.20	11.59	5.96	14.14
4th	5.29	14.17	6.31	17.90	6.92	21.06
5th	6.42	20.59	7.48	25.38	7.87	28.93
6th	7.90	28.49	8.80	34.18	8.99	37.92
7th	8.59	37.08	10.01	44.19	10.32	48.24
8th	9.90	46.98	11.53	55.72	12.08	60.32
9th	12.26	59.24	15.05	70.77	14.99	75.31
10th	40.76	100.00	29.23	100.00	24.69	100.00

Studies, 6, 1: 32–41 (a straightforward account of regional and provincial disparities of income).

C.A. LONGHURST

National Industrial Institute

The state holding company Instituto Nacional de Industria, or INI, was finally broken up in 1995 after an existence of over half a century, during which time it played a key role in the state-led industrialization of Spain, though not a wholly successful one, since many of its companies eventually became major loss-makers. Its industrial interests have covered a vast range: iron and steel, aluminium, coal, electricity, shipbuilding, air and sea transport, oil refining, chemicals and fertilizers, vehicle and aircraft manufacture, armaments, wood pulp, and electronics. INI was for many years counted among the top twenty industrial conglomerates in Europe and accounted for 5 percent of Spain's GDP. When the world recession induced by the first oil shock hit Spain somewhat belatedly in 1975, the effect on her industrial base was devastating, and INI's role rapidly became that of throwing a lifeline to insolvent companies by providing massive subsidies from tax revenues. Teneo, set up by the **González** government in 1992 to look after those INI companies which could survive without subsidies and prepare them for privatization, was to be dissolved by the new administration of José María **Aznar**, its companies being passed over to the *Sociedad Estatal de Participación Industrial* (SEPI), which in effect is a new, leaner version of INI run from the Ministry of Industry and incorporating the state's highly profitable shareholdings in Repsol (oil) and Endesa (power), the earnings from which are being made available to subsidize and restructure the loss-makers with a view to privatization. Those INI companies for which there is no hope of profitability (shipbuilding and coal mining) have been regrouped under the aegis of the Agencia Industrial del Estado and, subject to EC regulations, have a call on the state budget. It is essentially EC rules on state subsidies that have spelt the end for INI, but INI's two biggest loss-makers, the shipbuilder Astilleros Españoles and the coal producer Hunosa, pose a problem of major proportions, outright closure appearing politically and socially unacceptable because of the scale of job losses involved.

Further reading

Salmon, K. (1995) *The Modern Spanish Economy*, 2nd edn, London: Pinter (a very accessible account of all the main aspects of the Spanish economy).

C.A. LONGHURST

national lottery

The national lottery (Lotería Nacional) in its present form was first held in metropolitan Spain (as distinct from the colonies) in 1812, though there had been one-off special purpose lotteries as far back as the sixteenth century. Regular state-run lotteries had become common in Europe in the eighteenth century, and took root in Spain when Ciriaco González de Carvajal brought the idea back from the Spanish colony of New Spain, which included what is now Mexico.

The national lottery is based on the purchase of numbered tickets and accounts for some 18 percent of all monies gambled in the country. The largest draws are the first and last of the year, called respectively the *Niño* (the 'Child') held on the eve of Epiphany (5 January) and the legendary *Gordo* ('Fat One') held close to Christmas. In 1985 a second and different type of lottery was instituted. This was called the Original Lottery (*Lotería Primitiva*), as it reinstated the model which had existed between 1763 and 1811, based on the selection or 'forecasting' of a number by the player. Not as popular as the national, the *Primitiva* accounts for between 7 and 8 percent of gamblings. A third lottery, the Bono Loto, was established in 1988 and accounts for under 2 percent of gamblings.

The state lotteries are managed by the Organismo Nacional de Loterías y Apuestas del Estado (ONLAE – National State Organization for Lotteries and Gambling) through a network of outlets with distinctive logos and interior design, and with the aid of publicity and modern technology.

See also: gambling; ONCE

EAMONN RODGERS

National Movement

The *Movimiento Nacional*, more often known simply as the *Movimiento*, was the amalgam of political forces which supported the Spanish dictatorship from 1939 to 1975. It was designed, in the propaganda of the regime, to be the institutional and political embodiment of Franco's victory in the Civil War. The roots of the regime's political organization (as well as the dictatorship's economic and cultural policies) can be traced back to the political and social crisis of the 1930s. It was to be composed of those organizations and social groups which opposed, both overtly and covertly, the democratic Second Republic, proclaimed in 1931. The most significant of these were the ultra-monarchist catholics of Acción Española and the Comunión Tradicionalista, members of the fascist **Falange**, and diverse groups of rebellious army officers, clerics, economic élites, and largely middle class or lower middle class Catholics. The most significant move to unite these groups forcibly from above was Franco's wartime unification decree of April 1937, the main effect of which was to unite the Carlist *tradicionalistas* formally with the Falange.

In essence, Franco's *Movimiento* was the body to which one had to adhere in order to participate in the narrowly confined arena of official 'politics' during the dictatorship. However, the use of the term '*Movimiento*' came to be interchangeable both with the name of the state party itself, Falange Española Tradicionalista y de las Juntas de Ofensiva Nacional-Sindicalista (FET y de las JONS – Traditionalist Spanish Phalanx and Committees of the National Syndicalist Offensive), and with the regime in a general sense. This ambiguity was typical of the overlapping structures of Francoism; it permitted a grandiose falsifying terminology to be employed, for example, when the so-called Law of the Fundamental Principles of the Movement was proclaimed in 1958. In reality, the National Movement was always distanced from economic and political decision-making.

The absorption of previously distinct political organizations and tendencies continued to define the place of the *Movimiento* within the Francoist state. While the war was still being fought a considerable influx of members into the state party began. This was to become a flood in the post-war years as people affiliated to the party in order both to demonstrate their adherence to the new regime and to seek employment within the state bureaucracy, run by the Movement. Indeed, the *Movimiento* increasingly developed into a bureaucratic entity rather than a political one. The state unions, or **vertical syndicates** (*sindicatos verticales*), were officially under the control of the secretariat of the *Movimiento* until the 'Organic Law' of 1966. This had guaranteed the appearance of Falange influence over labour policy, although, in reality, employers dealt directly with the Ministry of Labour and increasingly with 'clandestine', unofficial bodies of workers. Nevertheless, the Movement continued to exist. It was supposedly a symbol of national unity and progress, and, although it was drained of political significance, it had appropriated for itself a huge budget employed, usually in a very corrupt fashion, in the areas of state welfare, housing, and local administration. In the process it had also acquired substantial properties, originally forcibly expropriated from the democratic unions of the Republic, and dispersed again within the state bureaucracy when the *Movimiento* was finally abolished in 1977 as part of Spain's transition to democracy.

Further reading

Ellwood, S. (1987) *Spanish Fascism in the Franco Era*, London: MacMillan (the only book to date which deals with the institutions of the regime).

MICHAEL RICHARDS

national radio

The first state **radio** network in Spain, Radio Nacional de España, was set up by Franco in 1937, during the Civil War, to counter the propaganda efforts of broadcasting stations on the Republican side. During the period of his dictatorship, RNE functioned essentially as the mouthpiece of the state, and exercised a virtual monopoly, though particular interest groups such as the **National Movement**, the **vertical syndicates**, and the Roman Catholic Church were permitted to operate their own networks. RNE's monopoly was ended by the new democratic government in 1977, but it continued to occupy a commanding position, since excessive competition for space on the airwaves forced the administration to curtail the number of medium-wave networks. In 1988, RNE absorbed Radio Cadena Española, the network which grouped the stations formerly owned by the National Movement and the syndicates.

RNE runs two medium-wave channels, Radio 1, mainly broadcasting general interest and current affairs material, and Radio 5, a sports and entertainment channel with local variations. It also has two FM services, Radio 2, mainly offering classical music, and Radio 3, devoted to **rock and pop** music. Radio 1 commands by far the highest number of listeners, 1.5 million, nearly twice that of Radio 5, and more five times that of Radios 2 and 3 together. Its programmes produced for the home market, and some specially made ones, are broadcast worldwide on its short-wave service, Radio Exterior de España.

Within Spain, however, RNE's listener base has steadily declined since 1988, from 3.5 million to 2.6 million in 1997, a fall of 25 percent. This contrasts with the other major networks, **SER**, **COPE** and Onda Cero, all of which have increased their number of listeners.

See also: media

EAMONN RODGERS

NATO

The international ostracism of Spain by democratic states after WWII meant that Spain was not included in the North Atlantic Treaty Organization when it was established in 1949. Though Franco himself was favourable to membership, Britain and France were opposed, as was US President Truman. Opposition in the US was soon eroded, however, by the interest of the military establishment in having a reliable ally against the threat of Soviet expansion during the Cold War. As early as 1948, the State Department broached the question of establishing a military presence in Spain, and by 1953 the **American bases agreement** had been signed. This bilateral arrangement was the only feasible one, given the continued hostility to the Franco regime of most of the European members of NATO, and the issue of membership did not become active again until 1981.

It was internal politics, rather than global strategic considerations, which prompted the centre-right **UCD** government under Leopoldo **Calvo Sotelo** to speed up the negotiations for NATO membership. The attempted military coup of February 1981, known as the ***Tejerazo***, had convinced the government of the need to provide the **armed forces** with improved equipment, resources, career opportunities, and, above all, to foster greater professionalism and a sense of purpose, which would diminish the temptation to engage in political conspiracy. Spain's entry was formally ratified in 1982, though Spain remained outside the military command structure of NATO.

NATO membership was, however, deeply unpopular, especially among leftist political groupings, partly because of their tradition of anti-militarism, partly also because external military alliances were seen as characteristic of the Franco regime. The resounding victory of the socialist **PSOE** in the general election of 1982 was in no small measure due to its promise to hold a referendum to seek approval for leaving the alliance. Once in office, however, it became clear that leaving NATO would be costly, not least because it would jeopardize the negotiations currently in train over membership of the European Community. The issue was shelved until 1986, when the approach of the next elections made it necessary to carry out the undertaking to hold a referendum. By now, however, with Spain a member of the EC, the PSOE government was vigorously campaigning in favour of remaining in the alliance. Though the result was a decision to remain in NATO, the margin was only 12.7 percent, and the abstention rate was 40 percent. In the ensuing general election, PSOE's share of the vote fell significantly.

What is important about the government's referendum campaign was the lack of attention given to security implications, though NATO staff officers continued to regard Spain as strategically significant until the collapse of the Soviet Union. Government rhetoric concentrated on the economic and political costs of leaving the alliance, and emphasized the notion of European solidarity, almost as if NATO were an exclusively European organization, rather than one led and dominated by the US. At the same time, however, the new security context provided by NATO made it possible to reduce the dependence on direct American military presence in the peninsula. From 1987, the US air force was required to begin a phased withdrawal of its F-16 fighters from bases in Spain.

The European dimension continues to dominate discussion of NATO in Spain. In April 1996, King **Juan Carlos I** visited NATO headquarters, and made a carefully worded speech in which, while recognizing the role of the US, he chose to dwell on the importance to European integration of an autonomous defence system, and, most significantly of all, hinted that the European members of NATO could engage in military operations without the participation of the US. The ultimate significance of NATO to Spain, however, has less to do with military issues than with the stimulus which membership provides to defence-related industrial activity within Spain, and with economic and political relations with the rest of Europe. Despite the presence of a Spaniard, the former Foreign Minister Javier **Solana**, in the post of Secretary-General of NATO since 1995, Spanish politicians have been reluctant to endorse full integration into the military command structure of the organization, insisting that even in an emergency overall military command of Spanish forces must remain with Spanish officers.

See also: European Union; *europeísmo*; foreign policy; *golpismo*

Further reading

Heywood, P. (1995) *The Government and Politics of Spain*, London: Macmillan (pp. 264–70 give a very lucid account of the significance of NATO membership in the context of Spanish policy towards Europe).

Preston, P. and Smyth, D. (1984) *Spain, the EEC and NATO*, London: Royal Institute of International Affairs (a thorough account of the issues as they were perceived in the early 1980s; includes consideration of the strategic aspects).

EAMONN RODGERS

Navarro Baldeweg, Juan

b. 1939, Santander

Architect

Navarro Baldeweg has the unusual distinction of having scored notable successes as both architect and painter. His academic career embraces both these fields. After studies at the Escuela de Bellas Artes San Fernando (School of Fine Arts) in Madrid, which he entered in 1959, he qualified as an architect in 1967. Subsequent to completing his doctorate in 1969, he was appointed to a Chair in the School of Architecture in Madrid, and became associate professor at the Massachussets Institute of Technology from 1971–5. He was also visiting professor at Yale in 1990. Despite the predominantly architectural emphasis in his academic career, he won the *Premio Nacional de Artes Plásticas* (National Prize for the Plastic Arts) in 1990 for his achievement as a painter. Most of his architectural creations consist of prize-winning projects which he frequently submits to closed competitions. One example is the town-planning project Ordenación de San Francisco el Grande (1982, Madrid), followed, a few years later, by the Social Centre Puerta de Toledo (1986–8, Madrid). This work displays the chief characteristics of Navarro Baldeweg's architectural taste: elements of modern tradition, a feeling for structure and a liking for more personal shapes combined with sculptural artistry.

His best-known work is the Salamanca Conference and Exhibition centre (1987–91), a massive piece of architecture intended to merge harmoniously with the old quarter of the city. The external elevation is visually in keeping with the old frontage, and the choice of materials helps to achieve a sympathetic blend with this homogeneous cluster of historic buildings. The interior displays both inventiveness and flexibility in the spatial geometry. The main auditorium is covered by a huge circular vault, which, despite the rectangular shape of the room, rests directly on the outside walls, leaving the interior space completely free and making the building even more spectacular.

Navarro Baldeweg's painting is characterized by a great spontaneity of line, composition and colour, and is generally abstract in style, displaying something of the liveliness of a Raoul Dufy or a Pierre Alechinsky.

See also: architects; architecture; painting; visual arts

MIHAIL MOLDOVEANU

Niño Bravo

b. 1945, Valencia

Singer

Niño Bravo (Luis Manuel Ferri) began his career in a series of local bands and after an unpromising start, he shot to number one in Spain and Latin America with songs by well-known composers like Augusto Algueró or Juan Carlos Calderón, such as 'Libre' (Free) or 'Te quiero, te quiero' (I Love You, I Love You). He is often described as the Spanish Tom Jones because of his powerful voice.

Unfortunately, in 1973, at the peak of his success, he was killed in a road accident. Posthumous records, cover versions and imitators abound.

See also: music; rock and pop

MIGUEL JIMÉNEZ PINILLA

Noucentisme

Noucentisme, is a Catalan cultural movement which takes its name from the '1900s' (Catalan *noucents*), and is associated with the early years of the twentieth century. Chronologically, it succeeded Catalan **Modernism**, and was in many respects an extension of it, though it claimed to be something quite different. As with Modernism, the origins of *Noucentisme* are literary, and derive from certain ideas of Eugeni d'Ors, which were then taken up by other writers and poets, by painters, sculptors and architects and finally by politicians. The *Almanac dels Noucentistes* (1911) sets out a programme for raising Catalan national awareness, modelling the enterprise of nation-building on what was best in ancient Greece. Modernism had also emphasized that Catalonia was 'different', but the *Noucentistes* criticized the individualistic, anarchic character of Modernism, its obscure medievalism, and its overblown, florid decoration. *Noucentisme*, on the other hand, gave pride of place to Greek classicism, which it upheld for its high didactic value. The new Catalonia of which the *Noucentistes* dreamed would be inspired by civic sense, reason and logic, rather than feeling and spontaneity. Underpinning this 'official culture', as it may appropriately be called, was the politically-motivated desire to lay the institutional foundations of a modern European state.

The most visible effects of this outlook were reflected in the face of Barcelona, with new monuments, large-scale vistas and grandiose constructions, symbols of power which strove to project an image of harmony and permanence, appropriate to a great capital city. Rural Catalonia, too, felt the impact of this approach, and villages were transformed with new buildings proclaiming the importance of work as a civic activity: agricultural co-operatives often rivalled churches in their dimensions and magnificence. A new vision was born: Catalunya ciutat (Catalonia City), in which rural features were injected into the city (witness especially the romantic attitude towards nature, evident in the gardens and parks of this period), while country life was enriched by elements of urban construction.

In architecture, the work of Josep **Puig i Cadafalch** sums up this approach. The leading light of Modernism, his work nevertheless changed direction noticeably between 1910 and 1920. His project for the renovation of the Plaça Catalunya in Barcelona, the Casa Pich which fronts onto it and his own house in the Carrer Provença show how far *Noucentisme* took root in the Catalan capital. Josep Goday, a disciple of Puig, was influenced by his 'white architecture', and the work of Enric Sagnier, a Modernist architect of Puig's generation, followed a similar trend. Purity of form '*à la Brunelleschi*' was the watchword of a new generation of architects, including notably Raimon Duran Reynals and Nicolau Rubio i Tuduri, whose gardens are justly admired to this day. In Girona, the centre of the *Noucentiste* movement was the *Athenea* group led by the architect Rafael **Masó**, whose works display great originality. The work of Cesar **Martinell** combines Modernist elements with *noucentiste* compositions. Francesc Folguera and Adolfo Florença represent the last generation of Noucentist architects with work that shows a highly eclectic approach.

In literature, apart from Eugenio d'Ors, the crucial work is that of Pompeu Fabra: his establishment of norms of Catalan language usage in 1913 was a decisive moment in the recovery of national identity.

See also: architects; architecture; Catalan culture; language and national identity; language normalization

Further reading

Moldoveanu, M. (1996) *Barcelona: Architectures of Exuberance*, Barcelona: Lunwerg (an excellent overview of different periods and styles, illustrated with stunning photographs by the author).

MIHAIL MOLDOVEANU

Nova Cançó, La

La Nova Cançó, or New Song, is the name given to the movement, dating from the second half of the 1950s, which re-established popular musical forms in the Catalan-speaking parts of Spain. The seeds of what was to be an enormously influential musical and social movement were sown in 1956, when Jaume Armengol, Lluís Serrahima and Miquel Porter formed a group which sang songs in Catalan. These early songs were performed during the intervals at the Teatre Viu (Living Theatre), an experimental theatre group headed by Porter and Ricard Salvat. A key moment in the early development of the *Nova Cançó* was the formation in 1959 of Els Setze Jutges (the Sixteen Judges, a name which derives from a well-known Catalan tongue-twister). The original members of this group were Remei Margarit and Josep M. Espinàs, and they were soon joined by Delfí Abella and one of the best-known exponents of *Nova Cançó*, Francesc Pi de la Serra. Most of the famous figures of *La Nova Cançó* were, at one time or another, members of Els Setze Jutges. Apart from Pi de la Serra, they include **Raimon**, Guillermina Motta, Maria del **Mar Bonet**, Lluís **Llach** and Joan-Manuel **Serrat**.

It was during the 1960s and early 1970s that the *Nova Cançó* developed into a nationally and even internationally recognized movement. In 1963 Salomé (Maria Rosa Marco i Poquet) and the Valencian Ramon Pelegero i Sanchis (Raimon) obtained the Grand Prix at the Fifth Mediterranean Song Festival. In the previous year, the song which perhaps really popularized the *Nova Cançó* phenomenon appeared: Raimon's *Al vent* (To the Wind). The rise of *La Nova Cançó* coincides with a period in which principally young Catalans (and young people all over Spain) strove to recover their popular traditions and festivals, which had been stifled by Francoism.

As the movement developed, so it diversified. Its more 'purist' strains were counterbalanced by the growth of **protest songs**. With its emphasis on music as social and political protest, on the recovery of popular music forms and on the central role of the singer-songwriter, or *cantautor*, the *Nova Cançó* owed much to the American folk-pop movement of the 1960s. The most influential American singers were Bob Dylan, Joan Baez and Pete Seeger. Catalans developed a particular regard for the latter who, significantly, was invited to sing at the concert which was held in Barcelona in 1992 to commemorate the thirtieth anniversary of Raimon's *Al vent*.

The attraction between the *Nova Cançó* singers and Seeger was mutual. He felt a particular affection for Spain, and was responsible for the diffusion of Civil War Republican songs like *¡Viva la Quince Brigada!* (Long Live the Fifteenth Brigade) outside their native country. He identified with the anti-Franco cause, reminding us that the social protest song movement of the 1960s had a particular resonance in Spain, where artistic and political **censorship** were very real, and in Catalonia, where to these problems was added the language question. Indeed, *La Nova Cançó* survived and thrived despite the severe restrictions placed on performers. Like the Catalan performance groups Els **Joglars** and Els **Comediants**, the *cantautors*, as well as their audiences, displayed considerable bravery and ingenuity in defying repression. Franco's police frequently intervened in concerts, which often took on the character of political events.

The singers sang exclusively in Catalan in the early years, but later Spanish was used as well. The best-known bilingual exponent of *Nova Cançó* is Joan-Manuel Serrat, one of its most enduring and popular figures both inside Catalonia and throughout the Spanish-speaking world. Serrat has sold many recordings of his own songs in both Catalan and Spanish, but one of his most famous records is his musical version of four twentieth-century Spanish poets which appeared in 1978.

Serrat's venture into poetry is paralleled by Raimon's musical settings of medieval Valencian poetry and of the twentieth-century Catalan poets Salvat-Papasseit and **Espriu**, and is illustrative of the broad cultural diversification of the *Nova Cançó*. Performers from all the regions of the *països catalans* (Catalan Lands) are included in the movement. The Valencian region is represented by Ovidi Montllor, as well as by Raimon. Maria del Mar Bonet is as celebrated for her arrangements of Mallorcan folk music as she is for her own compositions. Her music has expanded to include the Mediterranean area in general, as in her 1982 LP *Cançons de la nostra Mediterrània* (Songs of our Mediterranean). There is a marked influence of North African sounds in some of the records both she and Lluís Llach have made in recent years.

See also: Catalan culture; folk music; music

DAVID GEORGE

novel

The establishment of the Franco regime at the end of the Civil War had negative consequences for all cultural activity, not least the novel. Those pre-war novelists who were not dead or exiled found themselves, for the most part, reduced to silence, leaving the field open for those who accepted the regime. These included figures from earlier generations such as Wenceslao Fernández Flórez, Foxá and Claudio de la Torre, who were joined by younger writers like Gonzalo **Torrente Ballester** and Camilo José **Cela**. The novelists who received the most ample coverage in the official press had either fought on the Franco side in the Civil War or were members of the **Falange**: Cecilio Benítez de Castro, Ignacio Agustí, Torrente Ballester, Rafael **García Serrano** and Juan A. Zunzunegui. Nevertheless, this did not guarantee them immunity from political and ecclesiastical **censorship**, as Torrente Ballester and García Serrano found to their cost.

The reading public, however, preferred translations of English and American novels, which were published in large numbers, exploiting the upheaval created by WWII, and the difficulty of enforcing copyright. Nevertheless, independently of official approval, Spanish novelists did achieve some resounding successes, notably Cela, with *The Family of Pascual Duarte* (*La familia de Pascual Duarte*, 1942), which was rejected by several publishers, and Carmen **Laforet**, whose *Nada* (*Andrea*) won the 1944 **Nadal Prize**, which for many years was to enjoy the same prestige as the Prix Goncourt in France. Critical reception was hostile because of what was regarded as the defeatist atmosphere of these novels, and the absence of spiritual values. It was precisely this, however, which enabled them to make such an impact in a society unsettled by the horrors of the Civil War and the abject misery which characterized the early years of the regime.

By contrast, the official ideology, inspired as it was by Nazism and Fascism, was optimistic. A new, triumphant, imperial age had dawned, and the creative artist was required to adopt the attitude of Adam in the Garden of Eden: with no previous history, and a brilliant future before him, he was to renounce the forbidden fruit, that is, liberal and left-wing ideas, the consumption of which had, for two centuries, visited all kinds of calamities on Spain. Literature, however, needs to draw nourishment from its roots, and, since writers were officially prevented from seeking these in the recent past, they looked back to the imperial period of the 'Catholic Monarchs', Ferdinand and Isabella and Philip II. The picaresque novel of the sixteenth and seventeenth centuries, together with the works of Cervantes, provided not only a literary model, but also a critical vision of human experience. It is therefore not surprising that the novelists who, in good faith, sought to connect with these roots produced writing which was completely in tune with the sensibility of their readers, but opposed to the official ethos. The portrayal of subhuman behaviour in Cela's first novel *Pascual Duarte* gave rise to a literary term, *tremendismo*, which came to be applied to novels of a similar tone and content. An intense period of novel-writing about the Civil War, of a documentary or 'testimonial' kind, was followed by one in which existential works, with emphasis on personal dilemmas rather than social or political issues, predominated. Miguel **Delibes**, who won the Nadal Prize in 1947 with *La sombra del ciprés es alargada* (The Long Shadow of the Cypress), is the most talented and successful exponent of this pessimistic literature.

Those few novelists who were able to continue working in exile were, by contrast, not inhibited from dwelling on the recent past. Abandoning the avant-garde techniques he had practised as a member of the 'Generation of 1927' (the generation of Lorca, **Dalí** and **Alberti**), Max **Aub**, in most of his work written between 1943 and 1968, collected under the title *El laberinto mágico* (The Magic Labyrinth), cultivated a documentary approach which has, over the years, enhanced his reputation as the major novelist of the Civil War. In similar vein, Francisco **Ayala** published in 1949 two collections of short stories which offer a detached view of human experience and of the evils of the Civil War, *Usurpers* (*Los usurpadores*) and *La cabeza del cordero* (The Lamb's Head). Ramón J. **Sender**, who had written socio-political fiction before 1936, continued to produce in exile a vast output, in which the recourse to fantasy is the vehicle of critical reflection on the recent past. Masterpieces like *Requiem for a Spanish Peasant* (*Réquiem por un campesino español*, 1953), *A Man's Place* (*El lugar del hombre*, 1939), *The King and the Queen* (*El rey y la Reina*, 1949), or the pseudo-autobiographical volumes of *Chronicle of Dawn* (*Crónica del alba*, also translated as *Before Noon*), are important landmarks in Spanish fiction. Of equal importance is the work of Eduardo Blanco Amor, beginning with *La catedral y el niño* (The Cathedral and the Child) (1948). When he returned from exile, his *Los miedos* (Fear), shortlisted for the Nadal Prize in 1962, was greeted in official circles with a deafening silence, as was the lyrical, meditative *Concierto en mi menor* (Concerto in E Minor) (1964), by another early returnee, the poet Juan Gil Albert. As well as writing on Spanish themes, the exiles reflected their experience of their adoptive communities in Europe and North and South America, in novels published mainly in Mexico and Argentina, and subsequently smuggled into Spain: Ayala's *Death as a Way of Life* (*Muertes de perro*) and *El fondo del vaso* (The Bottom of the Glass); Sender's *Epitalamio del prieto Trinidad* (1942), Aub's *Cuentos mexicanos* (Mexican Stories) (1959), and his famous literary-pictorial joke, *Jusep Torres Campalans* (1958); and Esteban Salazar Chapela's *Desnudo en Piccadilly*

(Naked in Piccadilly) (1957) and *Perico en Londres* (Perico in London) (1947).

In Spain, meanwhile, a new generation of writers who experienced the Civil War as children was coming to maturity, and rediscovering pre-war Marxist-inspired social-critical fiction, an aspect of literary history suppressed by **Francoist culture**, as well as Italian neo-realism in both the cinema and in the novel. These writers cleverly cultivated a feigned objectivity and a series of rhetorical devices which enabled them to evade censorship, producing a vast range of social-critical literature which won considerable acclaim with the public, and was awarded several literary prizes. Ignacio **Aldecoa** won the Juventud Prize in 1953 for his short story 'Seguir de pobres' (Always Poor), and in 1962 there appeared *Time of Silence* (*Tiempo de silencio*), by Luis **Martín-Santos**, a novel which occupies a similar place in the evolution of the genre as that held by Don Quixote in the development of the novels of chivalry. The most important landmarks are: Rafael **Sánchez Ferlosio**'s *The One day of the Week* (*El Jarama*), which won the Nadal Prize and the Critics' Prize in 1955; Aldecoa's *El fulgor y la sangre* (Radiance and Blood) (1954); Jesús López Pacheco's *Central Eléctrica* (Power Station); Ana María **Matute**'s *Awakening*, also translated as *School of the Sun* (*Primera memoria*, Nadal Prizewinner, 1959) and *The Lost Children* (*Los hijos muertos*, Critics' Prize, 1959); Jesús **Fernández Santos**' *En la hoguera* (At the Stake, 1957; Gabriel Miró Prize); and José M. Caballero Bonald's *Dos días de setiembre* (Two Days in September, Biblioteca Breve Prize, 1962). The strength of this movement was such that it carried along with it some of the leading novelists of the previous generation, such as Cela, whose *The Hive* (*La colmena*, 1951) is regarded, somewhat questionably, as marking the beginning of neo-realism. Delibes' *Smoke on the Ground* (*Las ratas*, 1962) and Elena **Quiroga**'s *Algo pasa en la calle* (Something's Happening Outside) (1954) also exemplify this trend. This whole group of novels is characterized by an expressive richness and lyricism which give the lie to any facile assumptions about the allegedly prosaic nature of the writing. This poetic density derives not only from the satirical mode employed in *Time of Silence* but also from the emergence of a hitherto unknown novelist who would be the standard-bearer of this generation, Juan **Benet**. His work is demanding and difficult, mixing fantasy and allegorical substitution in the manner of Kafka, but nevertheless offers a metaphorical interpretation of the contemporary history of Spain, especially in *Return to Region* (*Volverás a Región*, 1967), and the series *Herrumbrosas lanzas* (Rusty Lances) (1983–6).

Social criticism of this kind inevitably put younger writers at odds with the previous generation, and Benet came to be seen as the protector or patron of those who were seeking to mark out a territory for themselves in the highly circumscribed field of literature. The new censorship law of 1966 abolished prior censorship of manuscripts but still prescribed heavy penalties for published work considered critical of the Franco regime. The first attempts to take advantage of the new law cost authors and publishers substantial fines. Ecclesiastical censorship, however, was abolished, which opened the way to the reappearance of eroticism in the novel. The risks inherent in this were avoided by emphasizing formal experimentation and minimizing references to current social and political realities, making a virtue of what was actually a pressing necessity, given the persistence of censorship. Experimentalism drew in some long-established writers like Cela, author of *Oficio de tinieblas, 5* (Tenebrae) and Torrente Ballester, whose *La saga/fuga de J.B.* (The Saga/Flight of J.B.) (1972) was loudly acclaimed by the younger generation. Alvaro Cunqueiro, a neglected novelist with a playful imagination, won the Nadal Prize in 1968 with *Un hombre que se parecía a Orestes* (A Man who Looked Like Orestes), which prompted the reprinting of his earlier work. Juan **Goytisolo** continued his earlier vein of socio-political criticism, intensifying the satire by incorporating it into a more deliberately experimental framework in *Marks of Identity* (*Señas de identidad*, 1966), *Count Julian* (*Reivindicación del conde don Julián*, 1970), both published in Mexico, and *John the Landless* (*Juan sin tierra*, 1975).

With the death of Franco and the disappearance of censorship, publishers abandoned experimentalism in favour of a return to classic narrative and the rediscovery of history. The first notable example of this trend was *The Truth About the Savolta Case* (*La verdad sobre el caso Savolta*, 1975), by Eduardo **Mendoza**, which won the Critics' Prize in 1976.

Many of the novelists of the mid-1960s adapted to the new situation: for instance, Manuel Vázquez Montalbán, J.M. Guelbenzu, Javier Marías, J.J. Armas Marcelo, V. Molina Foix, and Félix de Azúa. After 1975, a huge range of sub-genres was cultivated: historical, adventure, erotic and **detective fiction**, and a mixture of all these, including some innovative experiments. This development was in part the effect of changes in publishing, which, influenced by American models, moved towards more aggressive marketing, stimulating demand and turning the novel into a product, the acquisition of which became a marker of cultural standing. The publication of best-seller lists was a marketing ploy to persuade the public to equate sales figures with literary value.

Though the sheer volume of material published in the 1980s and 1990s makes it impossible for even the professional critic to arrive at an overview of the entire genre, certain features stand out. The survivors of earlier generations are still remarkably productive. Francisco Ayala published *Recuerdos y olvidos* (Recollections and Omissions) in 1982, and Rosa **Chacel** *Acrópolis* in 1984 and *Ciencias naturales* (Natural Sciences) in 1988. Cela, winner of the Nobel Prize for Literature in 1989, published *Mazurka for Two Dead Men* (*Mazurca para dos muertos*) in 1983, and *Cristo versus Arizona* (Christ Against Arizona) in 1988. Torrente Ballester's creativity has shown no sign of flagging: *La isla de los jacintos cortados* (The Island of Plucked Hyacinths) appeared in 1980, *Dafne y ensueños* (Daphne and Dreams) in 1983, *La rosa de los vientos* (The Compass Rose) in 1985, and *Yo no soy yo, evidentemente* (I Am Apparently Not Me) in 1987. Miguel Delibes' critical vision of society is sustained in *El disputado voto del señor Cayo* (The Disputed Vote of Mr. Cayo) (1978) and *Los santos inocentes* (The Holy Innocents) (1981). José Luis **Sampedro**'s best work dates from the post-Franco period. The mature Juan Goytisolo has produced *Makbara* (1980), *Paisajes después de la batalla* (Landscapes After the Battle) (1982) and *Las Virtudes del pájaro solitario* (The Virtues of the Solitary Bird) (1988), as well as his autobiographical volumes *Forbidden Territory* (*Coto vedado*, 1985) and *Realms of Strife* (*En los reinos de taifa*, 1986). Carmen **Martín Gaite** achieves a perfect blend of memory and fantasy in *The Back Room* (*El cuarto de atrás*, 1978), and, after two decades of silence, Ana María Matute has brought out *Olvidado rey Gudú* (The Forgotten King Gudu) in 1996.

The younger members of this generation reached full maturity in the 1990s. Juan **Marsé**, whose bitter satire on Francoism, *The Fallen* (*Si te dicen que caí*), was published in 1973, painted in other novels, up to and including *El amante bilingüe* and *Ronda del Guinardó*, a vast fresco of Barcelona society. Luis **Goytisolo** has followed up his monumental *Antagonía* (1973–81), based on Dante's *Divina Commedia*, with *Estatua con palomas* (Statue with Doves) (1992), a complex mixture of autobiography and historical fiction. Francisco Umbral, who made his name with his satirical newspaper commentary on current events, is also a successful novelist, whose production is to Madrid what Marsé's is to Barcelona, and includes *Travesía de Madrid* (Across Madrid) (1966), *A Mortal Spring* (*Mortal y rosa*, 1975), *Los helechos arborescentes* (The Tree Ferns) (1980) and *Leyenda del César visionario* (Chronicle of the Visionary Caesar) (1991). Equally popular is Manuel Vázquez Montalbán, whose commentary on society is more ideologically consistent than Umbral's, and who has written a very successful series of detective novels from *Yo maté a Kennedy* (I Shot Kennedy) (1972) to *El premio* (The Prize) (1996). Antonio Muñoz Molina, in *Beatus Ille* (Happy the Man) (1986) and *El jinete polaco* (The Polish Rider) (1991), with absolute technical mastery and great lyrical depth, constructs a mythologized version of the story of his forebears. Javier Marías has been very successful in adapting to the new conditions of the market, and is widely respected outside Spain, as the conferring of the Impact Prize in Dublin in 1997 confirms. Publishers' statistics suggest that Arturo Pérez-Reverte, with his unrepentant return to the pleasures of the classic adventure novel of the nineteenth century, is the most widely read of the 1990s novelists.

This rich and varied production, however, lives on the edge of the abyss. The flight from literature in educational syllabuses reflects a general lack of interest, paradoxical in view of the huge expansion of the reading public in absolute terms. Readership figures, however, cannot be considered in isolation from the expansion of the population and the spread of formal schooling. As in the last days of

Pompeii, we may be seeing the final splendid fluorescence of the novel in book form before it is finally extinguished.

See also: cultural institutions and movements; detective fiction; Francoist culture; intellectual life; science fiction

Further reading

Amell, S. (1996) *The Contemporary Spanish Novel: An Annotated, Critical Bibliography, 1936–1994*, Westport, CT: Greenwood (a valuable guide to the study of the field).

Jordan B. (1990) *Writers and Politics in Franco's Spain*, London: Routledge (one of the most lucid studies in English of the novel in relation to its socio-political context).

Labanyi, J. (1989) *Myth and History in the Contemporary Spanish Novel*, Cambridge: Cambridge University Press (an indispensable study).

Soldevila Durante, I. (1998) *La novela desde 1936*, 3 vols, Madrid: Cátedra (an updated edition of one of the most comprehensive studies of the contemporary Spanish novel).

Spires, R.C. (1984) *Beyond the Metafictional Mode: Directions in the Modern Spanish Novel*, Lexington, KY: University Press of Kentucky (sets the discussion of the Spanish novel in the context of contemporary critical theory).

Thomas, G. (1990) *The Novel of the Spanish Civil War (1936–1975)*, Cambridge: Cambridge University Press (a very comprehensive survey of the genre).

IGNACIO SOLDEVILA DURANTE

novela rosa

Literally the 'rose-coloured novel', this genre is the Spanish equivalent of Mills and Boon or Barbara Cartland. It had a considerable vogue in the 1920s and 1930s, and was given a new lease of life by the work of Corín **Tellado**, who began writing in 1946 and continued into the late 1990s. Its typical format is that of a short volume of about 100 pages, which lends itself to rapid assimilation by the reader and a high level of demand for new titles. Romantic but reticent, charged with sexual tension but shrinking from explicitness, and with the inevitable happy ending, it was particularly successful during the Franco regime, when hardship, repression and the general impoverishment of cultural life created what has been aptly described as the 'culture of evasion'. Even after the abolition of **censorship**, improvements in education, and the general increase in demand for more complex and sophisticated material, there is clearly still a market for literature which offers escapism and entertainment. In this respect, though largely dismissed by critics as an inferior genre, the *novela rosa* constitutes an important sociological phenomenon, analogous to the television soap-opera and the ***fotonovela***. Furthermore, it reflects the increasing commercialization of all cultural products in the 1990s: titles from the 1940s and 1950s are not infrequently reissued in new covers, and form a sizeable proportion of the material referred to collectively as **kiosk literature**.

See also: literature; novel; publishing; readership

Further reading

Hooper, J. (1995) *The New Spaniards*, Harmondsworth: Penguin (chapters 21 and 24 give an excellent overview of the cultural changes of the 1970s and 1980s).

Juana, J.M. de (1998) 'Novelas a destajo', *Cambio 16* 15 June: 60–3 (a useful brief overview of the life and work of Corín Tellado, one of the major exponents of the genre).

EAMONN RODGERS

novillero

This is the more common term for ***matador*** *de novillos-toros* (bullfighters, who perform with three to four-year old animals, and who have not yet taken the ***alternativa***).

See also: bullfighting

IAN CAMPBELL ROSS

nuclear energy

Nuclear energy raised the possibility of cheap, pollution-free energy of almost infinite duration that would diversify and revolutionize the traditional energy base. In practice, the application of nuclear energy to the generation of electricity was accompanied by serious technological and cost problems, raising public concern over the risks of this form of power. As a result, the nuclear energy programme in Spain was frozen in the 1980s leaving electricity companies with a mountain of debt. Nevertheless, in the mid-1990s nuclear energy constituted about half of all primary energy production in Spain and provided the source of power for about one-third of all electricity generation.

In 1963 a law was passed that opened the door to the development of nuclear energy in Spain. In the same year authorization was given for the development of the first nuclear power station (José Cabrera Zorita), which began operating in August 1969. In 1971 Santa María de Geroña, and in 1972 Vandellós 1, started operating; these three power stations represented the first generation of nuclear power stations in Spain.

The main push towards the development of nuclear energy came at the beginning of the 1970s with the authorization in 1973 of a further seven nuclear power stations. The escalation of oil prices during the 1970s led to support for nuclear power in the First National Energy Plan, which envisaged a major expansion of nuclear power to 56 percent of electricity generation by 1985. These figures were later revised downwards but support remained for continuing work on the second generation of reactors and for a third generation of plants.

Enthusiasm for nuclear energy waned in the 1980s, initially in the light of slackening demand and high construction costs, but increasingly amidst worries over safety (inflamed in the mid 1980s by accidents at Three-Mile Island and Chernobyl and then by a fire at Vandellós 1 in 1989), technical problems (including the disposal of nuclear waste), the problems and costs of decommissioning, and lower conventional energy prices. In 1984 a number of construction programmes were suspended leaving electricity utilities with a substantial debt burden, which became a factor in electricity industry restructuring and led to a surcharge on consumers. Under the Fourth National Energy Plan the moratorium on nuclear energy continued with the contribution of nuclear power anticipated to fall to only 23 percent of all electricity generation by the year 2000. At the beginning of 1998 there were nine nuclear power stations in operation (mostly pressurized water reactors) with an installed capacity of 7,580 megawatts.

Nuclear power stimulated development of the uranium industry in Spain. The National Uranium Company (Enusa) was constituted in 1972 to develop uranium mining, ensure uranium supplies to power stations and provide nuclear technology services. Uranium mineral has been mined in Salamanca and in Badajoz.

As in other countries, there is concern over the storage of nuclear waste and the dismantling of nuclear power stations. Currently, nuclear waste is stored at power station sites, although some low-level waste is stored at the El Cabril mine in Córdoba. The task of dismantling power stations began with Vandellós 1. Control over nuclear waste and responsibility for dismantling nuclear power plants is in the hands of the public company Enresa.

Further reading

Salmon, K. (1995) *The Modern Spanish economy*, 2nd edn, London: Cassell (chapter 5, especially pp. 156–9, deals with the role of nuclear energy in electricity generation).

Tamames, R. *Estructura económica de España*, Madrid: Alianza Editorial (the topic is covered in Spanish in each of the numerous editions).

KEITH SALMON

Nuevo Flamenco

Paco de Lucía, Enrique Morente and Camarón de la Isla were the first artists to break away from traditional **flamenco** (gatherings with singer-songwriters and guitar) and a new generation of musicians has continued to extend the parameters of flamenco music. Flamenco is no longer the exclusive domain of a marginal Andalusian collective; in the last two decades it has entered into mainstream youth culture through the addition of new rhythms, ranging from jazz, pop, blues and disco (with echoes of Eric Clapton or The Stones), and modern instruments including synthesizers, pipes, flutes and electric guitars.

After the death of Franco there was a flamenco-pop boom with artists like Las Grecas, Amina, Peret, Los Chunguitos, Los Chichos, Triana, Paco de Lucía, Veneno, Los Chorbos and Manuel Sanlúcar who all developed their own distinctive style. A new wave of artists followed their lead: Lole y Manuel, Camarón and Caño Roto, combining traditional flamenco with modern influences. Pata Negra, Ketama and La Barbería del Sur amongst others continued to experiment with flamenco sounds, enjoying considerable chart success. Without abandoning their roots, *Nuevo Flamenco* artists breathed new life into the art through their provocative lyrics and attitude. Andalusia ceased to be the only centre of flamenco music, as groups formed in other cities like Barcelona and Madrid and even outside Spain (as in the case of the Gypsy Kings). From the 1980s clubs designed for rock concerts began to book new flamenco artists in response to the interest shown by young people.

Another key element in flamenco is **dance**, and there has also been an innovative movement in this area. Artists have moved away from traditional performances in *tablaos* (improvised stages) to large-scale flamenco spectaculars. Pastora Imperio and Carmen Amaya were in the vanguard of a fusion of modern choreography and classical ballet which was developed by Antonio Gades, Mario Maya, Joaquín Cortés and Antonio Canales.

Nuevo Flamenco is a growth area, as shown by the success of young artists like Niña Pastori, Tomatito, Navajita Plateá, Potito and Vicente Amigo and it has become a highly exportable commodity round the world.

See also: folk music; music; rock and pop

Further reading

Calvo, P. and Gamboa, J.M. (1994) *Historia-Guía del Nuevo Flamenco*, Madrid: Guía de Música.

MIGUEL JIMÉNEZ PINILLA

nursery education

Spain has an exceptionally extensive system of nursery schools. Over 90 percent of children receive at least a year of nursery schooling before they proceed to primary education or **EGB**, as it was called before 1991. Although the bulk of nursery education is provided by the state, approximately 40 percent of the schools are fee-paying, which creates a bias in favour of middle-class families, and means that poorer children who have not attended nursery school are sometimes at a disadvantage during the first year of primary school. Under the reforming legislation known as the **LOGSE** (1990), it became the responsibility of the state to provide nursery education free of charge for children aged between four and six, though attendance is not obligatory.

See also: LODE

EAMONN RODGERS

official language schools

Official language schools are a network of centres for the teaching of foreign languages. The first school was founded by the Spanish ministry of education in 1930. The major growth of official language schools took place in the 1980s, in response to the increasing interest in modern foreign languages in Spain. Seventeen languages are taught, European and Spanish regional languages being predominant. Entry requirements are that students have at least completed the first level of **secondary education**. Teachers of the official language schools qualify after passing a national examination. Advanced and elementary level courses are taught, with an option for distance learning. Tuition is also offered to teachers and other specialized groups. The schools have a policy of fostering active use of the target language in real-life contexts.

ISIDRO FADRIQUE

Ojeda González, Francisco

b. 1955, Sanlúcar de Barrameda

Matador

After his ***alternativa*** in 1979, Paco Ojeda seemed destined for rapid obscurity until his career revived remarkably in 1982. For more than a decade subsequently, he enjoyed a huge following in Spain and France. Criticized by a minority of ***aficionados***, Ojeda's profound, static style has been the most influential in changing **bullfighting** in the past thirty years. He began performing as a ***rejoneador*** in 1996.

IAN CAMPBELL ROSS

Olazábal, José María

b. 1966, San Sebastián

Sportsman

Winner of the Masters Golf tournament in Augusta, Georgia, and ranked fifth in world in 1994, Olazábal began his professional career in 1986 after a series of victories in children's, boys' and amateur championships from 1979 onwards. His other successes include the Swiss Open (1986), the Belgian Open (1988), the Ryder Cup (1989) and the Ireland Open (1990). Absent from the 1996 season because of illness, he returned in 1997 to win the Turespaña Masters and to play in the European team which won the Ryder Cup in Valderrama.

See also: golf

EAMONN RODGERS

Olea, Pedro

b. 1938, Bilbao

Filmmaker and producer

Olea's work veers between the commercial and the art cinema, with a long-standing career in television. His film *Pim, pam, pum,... fuego* (Ready,

Aim...Fire!) (1975), started the trend of political melodramas dealing with the post-war years. In the late 1970s he joined the Basque cinema movement: *Akelarre* (The Witches Sabbath) (1983), was one of the first films subsidized by the autonomous government. His talent for political parable and atmospheric period reconstruction already manifest in his adaptation of Galdos' novel, *Tormento* (Torment) (1974), reappears in *El maestro de esgrima* (*The Fencing Master*) (1992), based on Arturo Pérez Reverte's novel, which was nominated for an Oscar.

See also: Basque culture; film and cinema

Further reading

Angulo, J., Heredero, C.F. and Rebordinos, J.L. (eds) (1993), *Un cineasta llamado Pedro Olea*, San Sebastián: Filmoteca Vasca (an informative monograph containing an interview with the filmmaker).

Martínez Torres, A., (ed.) (1984) *Spanish Cinema: 1896–1983*, Madrid: Ministerio de Cultura (a good historical overview, particularly of the period 1967–83).

XON DE ROS

Oliart, Alberto

b. 1928, Mérida (Badajoz)

Businessman and politician

One of the many prominent members of the business community who participated in **Suárez**'s **UCD** governments. He has sat on the boards of some of Spain's biggest **banks**, as well as those of a number of public and private industrial companies. Close to **Calvo Sotelo**, he took on the sensitive post of Minister of Defence after the ***Tejerazo***, where he soothed military anger to the extent of being accused of appeasement. However, his conciliatory approach in the face of numerous rumours of military conspiracy succeeded in avoiding a repeat of the *Tejerazo*.

JONATHAN HOPKIN

Olmo Gallego, Lauro

b. 1922, Barco de Valdeorras, Orense; d. 1994, Madrid

Writer

Though Olmo's fame as a writer depends primarily on his dramatic production, recognition as an author came initially as the result of his prose works, with *Doce cuentos y uno más* (Twelve Short Stories Plus One), awarded the 1955 Leopoldo Alas Prize, and *Ayer, 27 de octubre* (Yesterday, October 27), for which Olmo was a finalist for the **Nadal Prize** in 1957.

Olmo's work is deeply rooted in the emerging socially conscious literature of the 1960s. The oppressive social condition and widespread economic deprivation that characterized the country led Olmo to oppose the Franco dictatorship. His work, like that of other writers of his generation such as Carlos Muñiz and José María Rodríguez Méndez, seeks to condemn social injustice and champion individual freedom. He displays a penchant for popular scenes, colloquial language and archetypal characters. Documentary in style, his plays are essentially social allegories that bring the defects of Spanish society into sharp focus.

Olmo's name is synonymous with *La camisa* (The Shirt) for which he was awarded the Valle-Inclán Theatre Prize in 1961, the Larra and National Theatre Prizes in 1962, and the Alvarez Quintero Prize in 1963. The play dramatizes vividly the plight and the aspirations of Spain's working class, and introduces several themes of national importance to which Olmo returns repeatedly throughout his career. Impoverishment, emigration and **socialism** are important themes in *English Spoken* (1968), *Pablo Iglesias* (1984) and *La jerga nacional* (National Jargon) (1984). *La condecoración* (The Medal) (1985) and *Leónidas el Grande* (Leonidas the Great), are among the playwright's most explicit anti-Francoist satires.

In other plays such as *El cuarto poder* (The Fourth Power) (1984), the thematic concern is **censorship** in journalism and its effects on the freedom of speech. Olmo's preoccupation with the plight of working class women, witnessed initially through Lola's character in *La camisa*, evolves to encompass the general notion of feminine oppression in *La* *señorita Elvira* (Miss Elvira) (1982) and *El cuerpo* (The Body) (1966). Fantasy is yet another recurring theme in such works as *José García* (1981) and *Cronicón del medioevo* (Short Chronicle of the Middle Ages). Combining his fascination for allegory and didactic social commentary, Olmo has co-authored numerous dramatic works for children with his wife Pilar Enciso.

By revealing in realistic fashion the oppression that accompanies authoritarian political ideologies and its negative effects on the freedom of individuals, Olmo's work raises pertinent moral and ethical questions about the individual and society, both in post-Civil War Spain and in society at large.

See also: Francoist culture; migration; poverty; society

Further reading

Fernández Insuela, A. (1986) *Aproximación a Lauro Olmo: vida, ideas literarias y obra narrativa*, Oviedo: Servicio de Publicaciones de la Universidad de Oviedo (a useful account of Olmo's personal life and study of his non-dramatic works).

Oliva, C. (1979) *Disidentes de la generación realista en la escena de hoy*, Murcia: Universidad de Murcia (slightly dated but excellent overview of the thematic concerns of Olmo's theatre and that of other writers of his generation).

—— (1989) *El teatro desde 1936*, Madrid: Alhambra (chapter 5 provides a comprehensive summary of the artistic and ideological concerns of Spain's socially committed theatre).

JOHN P. GABRIELE

Olympic Games

According to Juan Antonio **Samaranch**, President of the International Olympic Committee (IOC), the announcement in October 1986 that the twenty-fifth modern summer Olympics were to be held in his native Barcelona was one of the proudest moments of his life. Together with **Expo-92** and Madrid's tenure as European City of Culture the Olympic Games were one of the three major international events held in Spain to commemorate the ***Quinto Centenario*** (five-hundredth anniversary) of Columbus' 1492 voyage to the Americas.

Co-ordinated support from the **CiU**-controlled **Generalitat**, the civic administration of Barcelona's Socialist mayor, Pasqual **Maragall** and the Catalan financial sector attracted investment of over 800,000m pesetas from the public and private sectors to finance construction of venues in Diagonal, Vall d'Hebron and Montjuic, and an Olympic Village of two thousand flats along the waterfront. Major improvements were also undertaken in communication, sanitation and the local road and rail networks.

Over 10,000 contestants represented 164 countries in the games, held between 25 July and 9 August 1992, which reflected recent changes in the international situation with the re-admission of South Africa and the former Soviet Republics represented by a 'Unified Team'.

The games started controversially when King **Juan Carlos I** used **Catalan** in his address at the opening ceremony and, although many on the right railed against the prominence given to Catalan over Spanish in all official communications, the unprecedented performance of the national team led the games to be generally hailed as an outstanding success. Spain won 22 medals, 13 gold, 7 silver and 2 bronze, notably in the football competition and the prestigious 1,500 metres, won by Fermín Cacho. The effective sponsorship enjoyed by Spain's athletes in preparing for the games and the trust funds established as virtual prizes for gold medallists, contributed to Barcelona being the last games at which the IOC attempted to maintain their officially amateur status.

The *Olimpiada Cultural* (Cultural Olympics), held to coincide with the sporting festivities, attracted a number of artists and companies involved in the celebrations in Madrid and Seville, and was criticized in some sectors as attempted one-upmanship in the historic rivalry between Barcelona and Madrid.

Since the games, locals and visitors alike have continued to benefit from Barcelona's vastly improved sports facilities and public transport. Furthermore, the Galería Olímpica (Olympic Visitor Centre) in the Montjuic Stadium has become a major tourist attraction. Most analysts agree, however, that Barcelona has coped less well than Seville with the after-effects of 1992.

Although the games served to delay the effects of the international recession at a local level, the effects of the subsequent rise in unemployment have been more marked, with a larger proportion of itinerant workers choosing to remain in Catalonia, which traditionally attracts much of its workforce from elsewhere in Spain. The project to sell off or re-use real estate in the Olympic village has also proved problematic, with criticism levelled at the pricing structure and the poor quality of some of the property.

See also: athletics; regional nationalism; sport and leisure

CHRIS DIXON

ONCE

The National Organization for the Blind (Organización Nacional de Ciegos Españoles) was set up in 1938 by Julio Osuna Fajardo and Javier Gutiérrez de Tovar, to provide employment for blind people as ticket-sellers for local lotteries. Some 90 percent of blind people in Spain (about 40,000 persons) belong to this organization, which since 1950 has provided a welfare system for its members. By the early 1980s, however, commitments began to exceed income, particularly since sales of lottery tickets were competing with the other opportunities for gambling provided by the state lottery, casinos and fruit-machines located in bars. In an attempt to reverse the loss of support, the organization, with government approval, replaced in 1984 the various provincial lotteries with a single national one. By the late 1980s, ticket-sellers were earning nearly twice the average national wage, and ONCE had become a powerful and wealthy force on the financial scene, investing in banks, supermarket chains, television and radio. By the early 1990s, ONCE's investment portfolio was worth 70,000m pesetas. It has a 25 percent stake in Tele 5, and owns Onda Cero, a network of about 160 radio stations. It publishes a high-quality glossy magazine, *Perfiles*.

The expansion of ONCE into the investment marketplace has not been without controversy, particularly since it enjoys tax-free status on its profits, a privilege which it is able to transfer partially to any commercial concern in which it has a large stake. Government regulation since 1985 has brought it under ministerial control, but it continues to be a highly successful competitor to the **national lottery**, which is one of the state's main sources of revenue.

Further reading

Hooper, J. (1995) 'High Stakes', in J. Hooper *The New Spaniards*, Harmondsworth: Penguin.

EAMONN RODGERS

opera

Considering the fame of Spanish operatic singers such as Victoria de **Los Ángeles**, Plácido **Domingo**, and José **Carreras**, there is a surprising lack of opera houses in Spain. The closure of the **Royal Theatre**, Madrid, in the 1920s left the **Liceu Theatre**, Barcelona, as the only dedicated venue in the country, and when that theatre was burnt down in 1994 during renovation, there was none until the eventual reopening of the refurbished Royal as an opera house in 1997.

However, Madrid and other centres were not completely deprived of operatic performances, since individual productions and limited operatic seasons were staged at various theatres. In Madrid, for example, the Zarzuela Theatre was a frequent venue from 1955, and the Madrid Opera Festival was held annually from 1964. Elsewhere the Associations of Friends of the Opera (Asociaciones de Amigos de la Opera) were responsible for organizing short festivals in the major cities. In the late 1980s and the 1990s venues for opera seasons increased as theatres were either refurbished or built as the result of joint investment by the state and the autonomous regions and city councils. In Seville, for example, the Teatro de la Maestranza was inaugurated in 1991, and an extended opera season organized for **Expo-92**.

Although the classical repertoire predominates, new operas by Spanish composers have included Luis de Pablo's *Kiú* (1983) and *El viajero indiscreto*

(The Indiscreet Traveller) (1990), both at the Zarzuela, J.L. Turina's *Ligazón* (Liaison) (1982) in Cuenca, Joan Guinjoan's *Laudí* (1992) on the occasion of the Barcelona **Olympic Games**, and García Abril's *Divinas Palabras* (based on Valle-Inclán's play Divine Words) (1997) at the Royal Theatre.

See also: music; performing arts; *zarzuela*

EAMONN RODGERS

Opus Dei

Founded in 1928 by José María **Escrivá de Balaguer** as an organization of lay Catholics, Opus Dei (The Work of God) merged in 1943 with the Priestly Society of the Holy Cross. It has 75,000 lay members in eighty countries and 1,500 priests, and is known by its members simply as *La Obra* (The Work). Some 28,000 members are based in Spain, representing 35 percent of the total worldwide. The Director since 1994 is Javier Echeverría, who entered the organization at the age of 16 in 1948.

In terms of Roman Catholic canon law, the official status of Opus Dei is that of a 'secular institute', but in practice it has many features of a religious order, with the highest category of membership, the numeraries, living mostly in community and taking vows of poverty (e.g. holding property in common), celibacy and obedience. The difference from the traditional religious orders is that the vast majority of its members are not ordained, do not wear a special habit, and work in various paid occupations in the outside world.

The other difference from most orders, and the church at large, is that Opus Dei is much more theologically conservative, and has refused to embrace the liberalizing trends in **Roman Catholicism** which appeared in the early 1960s. This has caused it to be specially favoured by the Vatican under the highly conservative pontificate of Pope John Paul II, who in 1982 conferred on the organization the status of a personal prelature, which makes it virtually independent of the control of the local bishop, and gives it an equal right of direct access to the Vatican. This move was controversial even within the church, as it involved the highly unusual application of a procedure devised for a totally different purpose, that is, to enable, in case of need, the exercise of episcopal functions separately from territorial jurisdiction, for example, in military chaplaincies.

The conservative and authoritarian traditions of Opus Dei are reflected in the hierarchical relationships which operate within the organization. These hierarchies are determined in the first place by the power wielded by the small minority of priests, and thereafter essentially by academic achievement and earning potential. The numeraries are all graduates, many with postgraduate qualifications. Below them in importance rank the associates (formerly oblates), who observe the rule of celibacy, and supernumeraries, who are not required to do so. Though many women occupy the highest rank of numerary, the 'auxiliaries', who are assigned permanently to domestic duties, are nearly all female. Testimonies from ex-members suggest that discipline within the organization is strict, with censorship of personal correspondence and control of reading matter. There have been persistent reports that those who leave continue to be subjected to pressure, direct and indirect, to prevent them publishing accounts of their experiences, and there have even been allegations of smear campaigns against individual ex-members.

Opus Dei has consistently claimed in public to be a purely religious organization engaged in what it calls the 'intellectual apostolate', but article 202 of its statues declares that the most appropriate way to exercise this apostolate is through the holding of public office. The exact extent of the order's influence is, however, difficult to determine because of its secretive character. Though it has frequently repudiated this accusation, article 191 of its statutes imposes what it describes as a 'prudent silence' regarding the identity of members.

What is certain, however, is that it has wielded considerable power in the educational, political and economic spheres in Spain. During José Ibáñez Martín's tenure of the Ministry of Education between 1941 and 1951, Opus members were appointed to a large number of university chairs, and in 1962 the organization set up a private university in Pamplona. By the 1990s, there was hardly a city in Spain which did not have at least one secondary school owned by Opus Dei. The **technocrats** who achieved control over economic policy after the 1957 cabinet reshuffle, such as **López Rodó**, were predominantly members of the order, as was Franco's deputy **Carrero Blanco**. Several of those who helped to engineer the transition to democracy after 1975, notably Adolfo **Suárez**, were associated with the order. Though Opus Dei's influence has declined since 1975, the year which saw the death both of Franco and of Escrivá, it still has a not inconsiderable presence in the higher ranks of the centre-right **PP** which came to power in 1996, and counts two ministers, Isabel Tocino (Environment) and José Manuel Romay (Health) among its supernumeraries, as well as the Chief Public Prosecutor, Jesús Cardenal.

See also: church and state; National Catholicism

Further reading

Hooper, J. (1995) *The New Spaniards*, Harmondsworth: Penguin (pp. 140–3 give an excellent summary of the character and influence of the order).

Moncada, A. (1987) *Historia oral del Opus Dei*, Barcelona: Plaza y Janes (a first-hand account by an ex-member).

San Segundo, G. (1997) 'Opus Dei, una secta en el poder', *Cambio 16*, 2 June: 12–15 (see also pp. 16–20 of this number for other interesting material on the organization).

EAMONN RODGERS

orchestras

Though Spain has not had a strong orchestral tradition, the 1980s and 1990s saw considerably increased public investment in orchestras and concert halls throughout the country.

While the Symphony Orchestras of the **Liceu Theatre** (1847), of Madrid (1904), of Bilbao (1922) and of Tenerife (1935) pre-date the Civil War, those of Barcelona and Valencia together with the National Orchestra date from the 1940s, the Radiotelevision Symphony Orchestra from 1965, and as many as sixteen theatre, city and regional orchestras, together with the National Youth Orchestra, date from the 1980s and 1990s. To this period also belong the building of new concert halls, in particular the **Auditorio Nacional de Música** in Madrid, the renovation of others such as the splendid **Palau de la Musica** in Barcelona, and the refurbishment of many older theatres, which also act as concert venues, notably the **Royal Theatre** in Madrid. Increased funding has also facilitated visits abroad, such as that by the National Youth Orchestra to the London Proms in 1996.

See also: music; opera

EAMONN RODGERS

Ordóñez Araujo, Antonio

b. 1932, Ronda; d. 1998

Matador and bull-breeder

Brother of the **matadors** Cayetano, Juan, José and Alfonso, Antonio is son of Cayetano Ordóñez, El Niño de la Palma, model for Pedro Romero in Hemingway's *The Sun also Rises*. Having taken his ***alternativa*** in 1951, Ordóñez retired in 1962 but reappeared with huge success between 1965 and 1971 and is widely considered the finest, most artistic matador of the post-war period. The subject of Kenneth Tynan's *Bull Fever* and Hemingway's *The Dangerous Summer*, Ordóñez was made a Chevalier of the Légion d'Honneur by the French government in 1995.

See also: bullfighting

IAN CAMPBELL ROSS

Ortega y Gasset, José

b. 1883, Madrid; d. 1955, Madrid

Philosopher

After taking his degree at the Central University of Madrid in 1904, Ortega undertook postgraduate study in Marburg with the neo-Kantian Hermann Cohen. In 1910, he became professor of Metaphysics at Madrid, and in the same year married Rosa Spottorno-Topete. A prolific writer (his complete works fill eleven volumes), he published his first major work *Meditations on the Quixote* (*Meditaciones del Quijote*) in 1914. His widely read and influential study of the lack of direction and leadership in Spanish political life, *Invertebrate Spain* (*España invertebrada*) appeared in 1922, followed in 1925 by his equally important contributions to aesthetics and the theory of the novel, *The Dehumanization of Art* (*La deshumanización del arte*), and *Notes on the Novel* (*Ideas sobre la novela*).

In 1931, Ortega became a member of the Cortes (parliament) of the Second Republic, but his mixture of radicalism and authoritarian élitism made him unpopular with both right and left, and he was advised to leave Spain at the beginning of the Civil War in 1936. He did not return until 1948, after spending periods in France, the Netherlands, South America and Portugal.

Ortega's philosophy is far from systematic, but it had considerable appeal in a country with no strong tradition of rigorous speculative thought. Ortega's concept of 'vital reason' (*razón vital*) is an attempt to occupy a position midway between positivist empiricism and abstract idealism. Reality, in Ortega's view, cannot be defined in terms either of external phenomena or of abstract laws, but is a complex interaction between objective facts and their perception by the observer, which is determined by the total ambient situation in which the observer is placed.

Ortega's lasting contribution to Spanish culture does not, however, consist in his philosophical system, such as it is, but in his encouragement of intellectual debate, and his dissemination of the work of European philosophers and scientists. In 1923, he founded the ***Revista de Occidente***, which provided a forum for political and philosophical discussion. Publication was suspended at the outbreak of the Civil War, but the journal was relaunched in 1963, devoting itself thereafter mainly to the discussion of Ortega's work. He was also the General Editor, from 1922, of the *Library of Twentieth-Century Ideas*, published by Espasa-Calpe, which helped to familiarize the Spanish reading public with the works of Hegel, Husserl, Spengler and Freud.

Ortega, nevertheless, was no populist, and his view of culture had a strong element of élitism. Only a minority, he claims, are gifted with sufficient aesthetic sensibility to appreciate works of art for their own sake. The majority are interested in works of art or literature only insofar as they are relevant to their own lives. Ortega's definition of culture, therefore, excluded mass culture, though he did not necessarily equate this solely with working-class culture. In *The Revolt of the Masses* (*La rebelión de las masas*, 1930) his targets were the unthinking consumers of culture (including scientific culture), who took for granted their right to the benefits of progress, without recognizing the effort expended by various educational, artistic and professional élites to achieve the current level of civilization.

This undercurrent of élitism also appears in Ortega's political thinking, which is marked by an ambivalence characteristic of many intellectuals of his generation. By the early 1920s, he had become disillusioned with the ineffectual politics of nineteenth-century liberal parliamentarianism, and did not initially oppose the dictatorship of Primo de Rivera (1923–30). But he was outraged by what he regarded as Primo's attack on intellectual freedom through his imposition of censorship, and resigned his chair in 1929 as a protest against the enforced exile of Miguel de Unamuno. Though he travelled widely in Germany during the early years of the Hitler regime, his writings contain little criticism of Nazism, despite the fact that by 1934 its violent and repressive character was clear to most observers.

Conservative Spain had a similarly ambivalent attitude towards Ortega. On the one hand, he was looked at askance for his championship of intellectual enquiry, and his attempts to popularize non-Spanish philosophical movements. On the other, his undoubted distinction, particularly the reputation he enjoyed in Germany, was regarded, however reluctantly, by the right as enhancing the international prestige of Spain. In the last few years of his life, Ortega travelled and lectured widely in Germany, became a member of the Bavarian Academy of Fine Arts, and received honorary degrees from the Universities of Marburg and Glasgow. Despite his lifelong stance as a religious sceptic and free-thinker, he was granted a Catholic funeral. The conservative newspaper ***ABC***, together with other organs of the controlled press, gave extensive coverage to his life and work, but within a few months of his death, he was being attacked in the Catholic media for his alleged materialism and atheism.

See also: Francoist culture; intellectual life; philosophy

Major works

Ortega y Gasset, J. (1937) *Invertebrate Spain*, trans. M. Adams, New York: W.W. Norton.

—— (1968) *The Dehumanization of Art; and Other Essays on Art, Culture, and Literature*, Princeton, NJ: Princeton University Press.

—— (1985) *The Revolt of the Masses*, trans. A. Kerrigan, Notre Dame, IN: University of Notre Dame Press.

—— (1992) *The Mission of the University*, trans. H.L. Nostrand, New Brunswick, NJ: Transaction Publishers.

Further reading

Dobson, A. (1989) *An Introduction to the Politics and Philosophy of José Ortega y Gasset*, Cambridge: Cambridge University Press (a good general overview of Ortega's work).

Donoso, A. and Raley, H.C. (1986) *José Ortega y Gasset: A Bibliography of Secondary Sources*, Bowling Green, OH: Philosophy Documentation Center, Bowling Green State University (an essential source for Ortega scholarship).

Marías, J. (1983–4) *Ortega*, 2 vols, Madrid: Alianza (a fundamental study of Ortega by one of his most prominent pupils).

Orringer, N.R. (1979) *Ortega y sus fuentes germánicas*, Madrid: Gredos (an important study of the German sources of Ortega's thought by a leading Ortega scholar).

Ouimette, V. (1982) *José Ortega y Gasset*, Boston, MA: Twayne (an accessible introduction to Ortega's life and most important works).

EAMONN RODGERS

P

painting

In 1990, the largest exhibition of Velázquez's paintings ever held was mounted by the **Prado Museum** in Madrid, and was visited by half a million people. Further exhibitions on Ribera in 1992 and in honour of the 250th anniversary of Goya's birth in 1996 attracted similar numbers of visitors (see also **art exhibitions**). These facts suggest important implications for the state of Spanish cultural life in the last quarter of the twentieth century. One is the increase in the general public's interest in painting and the **visual arts** generally since the early 1980s, an interest not confined to the great artistic achievements of the past. Already in 1983, the International Festival of Contemporary Art, sponsored in Madrid by the ARCO Foundation, had generated huge interest in both viewing and purchasing works of modern art, and was only one of a very large series of exhibitions and regular art fairs held in the 1980s and 1990s.

Undoubtedly, some of this bourgeoning interest was speculative, and reflected the international trend towards acquisition of works of art for investment purposes. There was nevertheless a more generalized desire, reflected also in other areas of cultural life, to make up for the stagnation and neglect of the past. The Velázquez exhibition of 1990, which displayed seventy-nine of the more than ninety canvases he is known to have executed, was the first occasion on which so many works of one of the greatest Spanish painters of all time had ever been on view together. The volume of interest in this exhibition, and the protests of those members of the public unable to gain entry, can be seen as a reaction against cultural deprivation, official inertia and chronic under-resourcing: only a small percentage of the 7,000 or more paintings owned by the Prado are normally on permanent view. Despite a 70 percent increase in state funding for the arts in the 1980s, by 1995, the costs of transport and insurance were making it more difficult to mount exhibitions. Though it is true that most European Union states, with the exception of Italy, cut their arts budgets in 1996, Spain did so by the biggest margin, 13 percent.

Fortunately, however, the arts do not depend solely on state or regional government support, as collecting and exhibiting is an important activity of banks, business firms and private **foundations** (see also **arts funding**). This has often made it possible to bring together the work of important artists, some of them Civil War exiles, which has been dispersed through various collections in Spain and other countries. In 1993, for example, Telefónica, the state-owned telephone undertaking, consolidated its collection of paintings in a central location in Madrid, enabling it to give proper recognition to artists who had been marginalized by the Franco regime, such as Juan Gris and Luis Fernández. In the same way, the Mapfre insurance conglomerate mounted an important exhibition in 1993 of the work of the neglected Extremenian artist Juan Baroja, and a retrospective of Julián Grau Santos.

The expansion of interest in painting in the 1980s and 1990s is not confined to the work of Spanish artists, but has taken on an international dimension, especially through the acquisitions policy of the **Queen Sofía Museum** and the **Thyssen-Bornemisza Museum** housed in the Villahermosa Palace. Together with the Prado, the private foundations, commercial galleries, and the annual *Arco* fairs, Madrid can claim to have as rich and varied a concentration of art as any city in the world. Other centres, however, have also acquired a well-merited prominence, particularly Bilbao, where the **Guggenheim Museum** is not only an important artistic focus but also an outstanding contribution to the **architecture** of the city, and Valencia, home of the Instituto Valenciano de Arte Moderno (IVAM – Valencian Institute of Modern Art).

The rehabilitation of neglected artists, and the promotion of contemporary art, can also be seen as a reaction against the academicism which characterized painting during the Franco dictatorship. Perhaps the most representative example of this tradition is Zuloaga, who, despite his association with radical figures like Lorca in the 1920s, became an establishment painter after the Civil War, and portrayed Franco in the heroic pose of a medieval knight. Figurative and representative art of this kind was favoured by the regime, which was determined to eclipse the symbolic, politically charged products of the Second Republic, such as Joan **Miró**'s poster *Aidez l'Espagne.* Nevertheless, despite the politically radical stance of most of the surrealists of the 1920s and 1930s, with the possible exception of **Dalí**, surrealist art was the only form of avant-garde painting tolerated by the regime, because it was seen as élitist and relatively apolitical, though this latter assumption was erroneous. In the 1940s, interest in surrealism was revived by, among others, Joan **Brossa** and Antoni **Tàpies**, who collaborated on the art magazine *Dau al Set* (The Seventh Side of the Die). Continuity with French surrealism was provided by the influence of Pablo **Picasso**, living in exile in France, and Miró, who returned to Spain in 1940.

As these names suggest, a large part of the stimulus for developments in contemporary painting came from Catalonia, but *Dau al Set* had a counterpart in Madrid in the shape of the El Paso group, associated with Antonio **Saura**, which was active in the 1950s and 1960s. This group, together with Equipo 57 and the Valencia-based Equipo Crónica, which emerged in 1964 and remained active until the early 1980s, became increasingly politicized, and, in particular, hostile to what they saw as the commercialism and élitism of the gallery system. Satirical pastiches by Equipo Crónica of famous paintings of the past, such as the 1973 reworking of the portrait of Philip II traditionally attributed to Sánchez Coello, and the 'modernized' version of Velázquez's *Las Meninas* (1970), served to link contemporary painting with national tradition, while simultaneously satirizing artistic convention and inaugurating new kinds of pictorial language.

A comparable approach is represented by Eduardo **Arroyo**, associated with the trend referred to as *Realismo Crítico* (critical realism). His ironic treatment of figures of power (e.g. military dictators or Spanish gentlemen) earned him the hostility of the Franco regime. A somewhat different tendency is represented by the neorealism of Eduardo Naranjo, and especially Antonio López, with his stark, almost photographic portrayals of humble everyday objects, as in *Lavabo* (The Water Closet), which shows a wash-hand basin, with a shelf above holding a shaving-brush and other typical bathroom accoutrements. The 1993 exhibition in the Queen Sofía of 189 of his works, including paintings, drawings and sculpture, symbolized the final accolade accorded to one who had been viewed askance by the academicists as too avant-garde, and by contemporary artists as too traditional. The exhibition closed an unfortunate chapter which had begun in 1992, when López withdrew a display of his works from the Queen Sofía, as a protest at what he saw as the tendency to define the contemporary in exclusively avant-garde terms, with consequent neglect of realist painting.

See also: art collections; arts policy

Further reading

Bozal, V. (1991) *Historia del arte en España*, vol. 2, Madrid: Ediciones ISTMO (one of the most respected standard histories).

Dent Coad, E. (1995) 'Painting and Sculpture: The Rejection of High Art', in H. Graham and J. Labanyi (eds) *Spanish Cultural Studies, an Introduction: The Struggle for Modernity*, Oxford: Oxford

University Press, pp. 299–304 (a useful brief overview of the main trends since the Civil War).

Hooper, J. (1995) *The New Spaniards*, Harmondsworth: Penguin (chapter 23, 'Art and the Possible: The Politics of Culture', places 'art fever' in the context of general changes in the cultural climate).

EAMONN RODGERS

País, El

El País is without any doubt Spain's leading national daily newspaper. Despite growing competition from a number of quarters, it is still the market leader in terms of circulation, and is an obligatory reference point for all serious public debate within the country.

El País was founded in 1976 by PRISA, one of the main communications groups within contemporary Spain which also owns the radio network **SER** and is part owner of the subscription television channel Canal +. Its establishment therefore followed close on the death of General Franco in 1975, and responded to a growing demand for independent newspapers not compromised in any way by having lived through the previous repressive regime, championing liberal democratic values and having as their aim the investigation and analysis of all aspects of Spanish life. *El País* attracted a number of journalists and writers associated with various earlier publications which had been critical of the Franco regime, but which had not survived the transition to democracy. One of these was Eduardo Haro Tecglen, previous editor of the now defunct *Triunfo*, who writes the daily television and radio review *Visto y Oído* (Seen and Heard) for the paper.

El País quickly established itself as the newspaper of modern, liberal-democratic Spain, in contrast to publications such as ***ABC*** which continued to be steeped in a conservative ideology and in some ways never quite managed to shake off entirely the implications of their ability to live with dictatorship, even if they had never fully supported its methods. *El País* continues to attract major thinkers, intellectuals and literary and cultural figures either as regular or as occasional contributors to its columns. Its daily **readership** is well in excess of one million per day – a remarkable figure in a country which by and large has a relatively low rate of newspaper consumption – and this figure can more than double on Sundays.

Like its other major competitor *El* ***Mundo***, *El País* is roughly tabloid in format, and is a substantial read, with individual issues at times totalling as many as seventy pages, not counting any special supplements which might accompany the main part of the paper. While the front page will cover what is seen as the major event of the day – whether national or international – page two always opens the international section of the newspaper, in clear contradistinction to the bulk of Spanish dailies which will normally lead with national news first and international news later. This foregrounding of international news is in no sense a coincidence in a newspaper which sees itself – with some justification – as a major player on the European journalistic stage, and which has in fact signed co-operation agreements with a number of other European newspapers, such as the *Independent* and *La Repubblica*. Its international coverage is usually a mixture of agency material with other pieces provided by its own overseas correspondents, or, in the case of particularly important events, by journalists sent specifically by *El País*.

Following the international section are two pages of editorial and opinion. It is no exaggeration to say that these are the most important – and indeed most extensive – daily editorials in Spain. No one who makes any claim to be up-to-date with current events and debates can afford to miss these pages. Their influence in setting the agenda for public debate cannot be overstated, and many people who in one way or another do not agree with the paper's general position on a number of issues will still read the editorial since they know that it will define the broad framework of debate in a number of fields and activities. As well as the editorial strictly speaking, the accompanying – and at times very lengthy – opinion articles are often written by major public figures from a number of different spheres, many contributions having been made, for example, by the Peruvian novelist and former Presidential candidate, Mario Vargas Llosa.

After the editorial comes coverage of Spanish news, while the rest of the paper is variously given over to business, culture, sport and entertainment. Sunday editions contain a sizeable business supplement printed on pink paper, as well as a colour magazine.

El País has from the outset – in keeping with its generally liberal stance – championed the cause of a pluralistic view of Spain as regards the **autonomous communities**. This feature contrasts *El País* strongly with *ABC*, which has gained a certain level of notoriety for the virulence of its attacks on what it sees as the 'excesses of Catalan nationalism', but also from *El Mundo*, which has been to some extent unsupportive of the policy of **language normalization** within Catalonia as a whole. In keeping with this pluralistic view, *El País* publishes a number of regional editions, which combine the main paper with a supplement covering news from the community in question. Examples of these regional editions are *El País Andalucía* as well as the Barcelona edition, though the latter eventually ceased publication in the face of the strength of the local Catalan dailies (see also ***Vanguardia, La***; ***Periódico de Catalunya, El***).

The growing popularity of *El Mundo* does represent something of a threat to *El País*, though certain fairly clear differences in style will probably mean that the two papers will continue to attract rather different types of readers rather than necessarily steal them from each other. While *El Mundo* occasionally flirts with a mildly provocative headline, any hint of sensationalism, however faint, would be anathema to *El País*. And, although both types of approach are clearly present in both publications, the emphasis in *El País* is rather more on analytic rather than investigative journalism. This is a subtle but important difference, and presupposes a more thoughtful and more sophisticated relationship with the reader, a presupposition which is entirely in keeping with *El País*' view of itself and of its role within Spanish society.

See also: cultural institutions and movements; journalism; media; press; press ownership

Further reading

Mateo, R. de and Corbella, J.M. (1992) 'Spain' in B.S. Østergaard (ed.) *The Media in Western Europe*, London: Sage (a useful guide to the media situation in Spain in general, though its coverage of individual newspapers is rather slim).

HUGH O'DONNELL

Palau de la Musica

The Palau de la Musica (literally, 'Palace of Music') was inaugurated in 1908 as the headquarters of the Orfeó Català (Catalan Philharmonic Society), founded by Lluís Millet as part of that revitalization of **Catalan culture** which took place in the late nineteenth and early twentieth century. It was extensively remodelled in 1987–9 with an investment of 2,000m pesetas, and offers facilities for a wide range of activities, including concerts, recitals, congresses and receptions. The range of music covered is very varied, from the classical repertoire to popular and light music, jazz and **flamenco**. The main auditorium has seating for 2,200 people, and there is a chamber music hall, which seats 180 and provides perfect acoustics regardless of the number attending. Within the premises there is a music library and an important archive.

In 1990 a foundation (called the Orfeó Català-Palau de la Musica Catalana) was created, financed by donations from business and individuals. By 1994 the income from this source totalled 500m pesetas. The Palau de la Musica has an annual budget of 2,000m pesetas a year, which pays, among other things, for the forty-eight permanent staff, and provides 80m pesetas for the maintenance of the halls. The Palau supports the Orfeó Català, its own resident Chamber Choir, and the Youth Choir of the Orfeó Català. In 1994, 260 concerts were held in the Palau, of which 110 were sponsored by the foundation. The Palau also has the mission of promoting new talent by supporting singers and songwriters and organizing series of concerts for young performers and composers.

See also: cultural institutions and movements; foundations; music; orchestras; Royal Theatre

EAMONN RODGERS

Pàmies, Teresa

b. 1919, Balaguer, Lleida (Lérida)

Writer

An important contributor to contemporary **women's writing** in Catalan, Pàmies was forced into exile after the Civil War, but returned to Catalonia in 1971 after writing the successful *Testament a Praga* (Testament in Prague), based on her father's life. She subsequently published a number of novels drawing mainly on her experiences of the Civil War and exile, or on her later travels around Spain, contributed articles to ***Avui*** and other periodicals, and broadcast on Catalan radio. She is an original political thinker, especially concerning Marxist feminist theory.

See also: feminism; feminist writing; Marxism

KATHRYN CRAMERI

'PAQUIRRI' *see* Rivera Pérez, Francisco

paradores

Originally denoting an inn intended for the use of 'respectable' travellers, the term *parador* is now applied to a member of a network of well over ninety state-run hotels. The network was initiated in 1926 by the Marquis of Vega-Inclán as a way of increasing high-class tourist accommodation by renovating disused castles, monasteries and palaces. The first to be opened, in 1928, had been built as a hunting lodge for Alfonso XIII in the Sierra de Gredos.

Particularly impressive is the Hotel de los Reyes Católicos in Santiago, which started life as the mother house of the military Order of Santiago in the twelfth century and was greatly embellished according to the plans of King Ferdinand the Catholic in the sixteenth century. The *paradores* of León and of Cuenca were originally the monasteries of San Marcos and of San Pablo respectively, while the *parador* of Granada, the former monastery of San Francisco in the grounds of the Alhambra, is especially popular with tourists. The *parador* of Sigüenza was once a fortress, and that of Alcañiz a twelfth-century castle-monastery.

There are also a very large number of *paradores* of modern construction, such as the Cañadas del Teide in the national park on Tenerife, and together with the *paradores* situated in historic buildings they offer a wide range of good value accommodation from five-star rating downward.

See also: camping; holidays; tourism

Further reading

Hoyt Hobbs, A. (1998) *Paradors, Pousadas and Charming Villages of Spain and Portugal*, California: Fielding Worldwide (a travel guide with individual entries).

Sauvage, C. and Brown, C. (1998) *Karen Brown's Spain: Charming Inns and Itineraries*, Travel Press (a travel guide with individual entries, distributed by Fodor Travel Publications).

EAMONN RODGERS

parliament

Article 2 of the **constitution of 1978** makes it clear that 'national sovereignty resides with the Spanish people, from whom all the powers of the state derive'. This sovereignty is expressed through parliament, the elected members of which are the trustees and representatives of the will of the people. Parliament is the supreme institution of the state and, significantly, even the **monarchy** – quite deliberately defined as a 'parliamentary monarchy' – is, in the last resort, subject to its will.

The term *Cortes* has come to refer to the national parliament as a whole, whether unicameral or bicameral. Spain has a bicameral system, consisting of a lower house or Congress (*Congreso de los Diputados*) and an upper house or Senate (*Senado*). As in the UK, the lower house has precedence in most matters, including legislative affairs; this is symbolized at sessions of the joint houses of parliament, which are presided over by the president of the Congress.

In line with the constitution, the election law of 1985 established that the Congress should consist of 350 deputies. Elections are held through universal, free, direct, equal and secret suffrage, and all citizens over the age of eighteen are eligible to vote. Votes are cast, not for individual candidates, but for a party list in which candidates appear in a ranking order fixed in advance by the parties concerned. The constituency for elections is normally the province. Article 68.3 establishes a system of proportional representation for allocating seats to the provinces and the details of this are spelled out in article 162 of the election law. Article 163 specifies the method by which votes are distributed among candidates in each province: this is the D'Hondt system, which is also used in regional and local elections and which tends to favour larger parties. The life-span of the Congress is four years, after which an election must be called.

The Senate is described in article 69 of the constitution as 'the chamber of territorial representation', which in theory means that it should represent the interests of the **autonomous communities**. However, while a number of senators are, indeed, indirectly elected from among the members of the regional assemblies, the vast majority of them, 208 out of total of 256, are elected from the province which, as with the Congress, provides the normal constituency. Each province elects four senators, with each elector casting only three votes, in a first-past-the-post system, which makes no allowances for enormous population variations between the provinces. The life-span of the Senate is also four years.

Since 1994 a joint parliamentary working group has been studying ways of reforming the Senate to make it a Chamber which, both in composition and powers, more genuinely reflects the interests of the autonomous communities.

See also: elections; provincial administration

Further reading

Newton, M.T. with Donaghy, P.J. (1997) *Institutions of Modern Spain*, Cambridge University Press (chapter 4 is exclusively devoted to a detailed examination of the role, functions and operation of parliament and several Spanish works are quoted in the select bibliography).

MICHAEL T. NEWTON

Patino, Basilio M.

b. 1930, Lumbrales (Salamanca)

Filmmaker

Founder of the Salamanca University Film Club and organizer, with **Bardem**, of the 1955 film congress known as the **Salamanca Conversations**, Patino studied at the **IIEC** and produced his first film *Nueve cartas a Berta* (Nine Letters to Berta), a study in black and white of the monotony of provincial life, in 1965. His *Canciones para después de una guerra* (Songs For After a War) (1971) combining Civil War documentary footage with recordings of popular songs of the time, banned for five years as anti-Francoist, has been described as 'one of the most evocative films ever made in Spain'. *Queridísimos verdugos* (Dearest Executioners) (1973) and *Caudillo* (Military Boss) (1976) had to be made in secret, documentary footage for the latter being smuggled in from France and elsewhere. *Los paraísos perdidos* (Lost Paradises) (1985) conveys a sense of disillusionment with post-Franco Spain.

See also: censorship; film and cinema; Francoist culture

Further reading

Besas, P. (1985) *Behind the Spanish Lens: Spanish Cinema under Fascism and Democracy*, Denver, CO: Arden Press (a comprehensive information source).

Hopewell, J. (1986) *Out of the Past: Spanish Cinema After Franco*, London: British Film Institute (a very readable general account of contemporary trends).

EAMONN RODGERS

PCE

When in April 1995 the *Partido Comunista de España* (Spanish Communist Party) commemorated the seventy-fifth anniversary of its foundation, the party had few reasons, other than longevity, to celebrate the occasion. Electoral results have relegated the party to a very secondary role, its identity is largely diluted in an ambiguous coalition known as the **United Left**, and its survival appears under threat.

The truth is that, numerically at least, the PCE was never a major force in Spanish politics, even though it did exercise considerable influence during certain periods. At the time of the Civil War, both Soviet support for the Republican cause and Franco's mythical anti-communist crusade afforded the PCE a prominence well beyond the size of its membership at the time. During the long years of dictatorial rule the PCE became the spearhead of the opposition movement. Though most of its grandiose projects to bring down Franco's regime – guerrilla warfare, the National Reconciliation Plan, or the call for a peaceful general strike – did not bring about the expected result, they did give the party a leading role in many areas of clandestine activity – **student protest** movements, intellectual circles, illegal **trade unions**, and so on – and endowed it with democratic credentials.

The PCE, however, found it difficult to be accepted as a partner in the democratizing process which followed Franco's demise. Although the party had been unexpectedly legalized in the spring of 1977 and made a valuable contribution to the transition, it did not become a major protagonist in it. In the first democratic election in June 1977 it only managed to gain twenty seats – a meagre yield after so much struggle – and two years later only twenty-three. Worse was to follow. In the 1982 election they suffered a real débâcle, gaining only four seats in the new parliament. An ageing leadership out of touch with the new Spain, the difficult transition from clandestine struggle to open political contest, the ideological tensions generated by Eurocommunism, an electorate fearful of lending support to a party which might have produced radical changes in Spanish society, are some of the reasons which can be adduced to explain its failure.

In consequence the veteran leader **Carrillo** was forced to stand down in favour of a younger generation represented by Gerardo Iglesias. He set up the new electoral coalition, the United Left, in 1986, with the PCE as its central axis, and two years later handed over power to Julio **Anguita**, a politician with greater charisma, authority and dogmatism. In 1996 the party gained twenty-one seats, but it is difficult to ascertain what electoral support the communists might have without the protective cover of the United Left.

See also: Marxism; political parties; socialism

Further reading

González-Hernández, J.C. (1989) 'El PCE en el proceso de transición', in J.F. Tezanos *et al. La transición democrática española*, Madrid: Sistema (a clear and succinct analysis of the PCE's role in the transition to democracy).

Hermet, G. (1971) *Les Communistes en Espagne*, Paris: Armand Colin (the first successful attempt at an objective history of the PCE; brief and informative).

JOSÉ AMODIA

Pedrolo, Manuel de

b. 1918, L'Aranyó (Segarra); d. 1990, Barcelona

Writer

A prolific writer of novels, plays, short stories, press articles and poetry, Pedrolo was one of the few authors to write exclusively in **Catalan** throughout the Franco regime. He never compromised his principles, preferring to reach a limited audience in Catalan rather than abandon his native tongue in order to gain wider recognition. Politically, Pedrolo despised the Franco regime and all it stood for: he was a high-profile advocate of Catalan independence, and was especially prominent in the debates on autonomy which took place between 1975 and 1979, writing numerous articles on the subject which were published in the Catalan newspaper ***Avui***. This does not mean that Pedrolo's fiction was entirely conditioned by political considerations: on the contrary, aesthetic criteria were high on his agenda, and he wrote many of his works in innovative or experimental styles which were inspired by diverse influences from American and European literatures.

Critical responses to Pedrolo's writing have always been varied, and many of his works have never been closely appraised, which is not surprising given his prolific production. Some publishers refused his work because of doubts about its quality. Readers also varied in their response to him, some becoming avid fans, others remaining indifferent. His science-fiction novel *Mecanoscrit del segon origen* (Typescript of the Second Origin) (1974) is one of the best-selling Catalan novels of all time. The Catalan critic Jordi Arbonès distinguishes three phases of Pedrolo's novelistic development: 1949–56 – experimentation with narrative forms and a preoccupation with universal themes such as sex, death, freedom and identity; 1956–71 – socio-political themes; and 1971 until his death – concentration on the technical possibilities of the novel as a means of expression (Arbonès, 1980: 28–31). The distinction is not entirely clear-cut, for socio-political themes are always present in Pedrolo's fiction, even if they are subordinate to technical experimentation. As far as other genres are concerned, Pedrolo wrote many plays which have been identified with the European 'Theatre of the Absurd', and would perhaps have enjoyed widespread European recognition if they had not been written in Catalan.

Ironically, in the more conservative climate of the 1980s, Pedrolo's militant articles became an embarrassment to publications such as *Avui* which had once avidly accepted them. This, coupled with a long illness, increasingly unfavourable critical receptions of his last novels, and the dashing of his hopes for a fully independent Catalonia, meant that Pedrolo died somewhat disillusioned. Since his death there has been renewed interest in his work, with Catalan critics seeking to fill the gaps in their appraisal of him and of his contribution to Catalan literature.

See also: autonomous communities; censorship; languages and national identity

Further reading

Arbonès, J. (1980) *Pedrolo contra els límits*, Barcelona: Aymà (a thorough examination of Pedrolo's novels to 1980).

García, X. (ed.) (1992) *Rellegir Pedrolo*, Barcelona: Edicions 62 (interesting collection of articles: contains a comprehensive bibliography of works both by and concerning Pedrolo).

KATHRYN CRAMERI

Pemán y Pemartín, José María

b. 1898, Cadiz; d. 1981, Spain

Writer

A former member of the right-wing monarchist group *Acción Española* in the 1930s, Pemán was a prolific writer whose reputation was initially based on his work as a propagandist for the Francoist insurgents during the Civil War, when he was appointed to head the wartime Committee of Culture and Education. One of his most representative works of this period is the *Poema de la Bestia y el Angel* (Poem of the Beast and the Angel) (1938), an allegorical representation of the characteristic Nationalist conception of the war as a struggle between good and evil. As part of the Franco regime's purge of cultural and intellectual life, he was made Acting President of the Royal Academy between 1939 and 1940, a post which he subsequently occupied in his own right by election in 1944–7 (see also **Royal Academies**).

Like many intellectuals who had originally supported Franco, however, Pemán began in the 1950s to distance himself from the dictator, and gradually moved back towards a monarchist position, becoming an advisor to the Pretender, Don Juan de Borbón between 1957 and 1969. Though never considered by critical opinion to be a writer of genius, his presence on the literary scene could not be ignored because of the sheer volume of his output. By the time of his death, his complete works filled some seven volumes. He wrote more than sixty plays, covering the genres of historical drama in verse, thesis drama, farce and commentaries on contemporary mores. His translations and adaptions of classical plays such as *Oedipus Rex* were performed in the Roman Theatre in Mérida, and he also scored a notable success with his television series *El Séneca*. His articles in ***ABC*** in defence of the Catalan language won him a prize awarded by the Madrid Catalan Circle in 1971, and in 1981 he was awarded the Order of the Golden Fleece by

King **Juan Carlos I**. As well as plays, he wrote poetry, novels, essays and memoirs, including *Mis encuentros con Franco* (My Encounters with Franco) (1976), containing many shrewd and witty observations on the dictator and his associates.

See also: Francoist culture; history; literature; politics

EAMONN RODGERS

penal code

Criminal legislation in Spain until 1996 was governed by the Penal Code of 1848. In 1995, the **parliament** approved a completely revised code, designed to bring together the various modifications enacted since 1848, and to adapt the criminal law to the realities of a modern democratic society, and to the provisions of the **constitution of 1978**, which, among other things, had abolished the death penalty and guaranteed certain basic **civil rights** such as *habeas corpus*. The new code came into force on 25 May 1996.

In general, the thrust of the new code was to move from an approach to sentencing based on retribution to one based on rehabilition of the offender, to reduce the length of imprisonment, and to adopt a stricter approach towards corruption and 'white-collar' crime. The maximum length of prison terms was reduced from thirty years to twenty, except in cases of multiple convictions leading to concurrent sentences. Prison sentences of less than two years could be suspended for periods of two to five years, and shorter sentences could be served by weekend detention or replaced by fines or community service. Alcohol or drug dependency was accepted as a ground for the defence of diminished responsibility, and a points system was introduced for traffic offences. On the other hand, more extensive prison terms and larger fines, as well as longer periods of disqualification from public office, were introduced for bribery and **corruption**, as a response to the prevalence of these offences during the preceding decades.

Two important features of the code provided enhanced protection for civil rights. One was the provision that decisions on remission of prison terms in cases of persons serving concurrent sentences were transferred to judges, who were empowered to give the accused person the benefit of the total remission attaching to all the periods of imprisonment taken together. The other was that it was no longer necessary to prove individual criminal responsibility in cases where citizens had suffered loss or injury as the result of actions by agents of the state. Under the new code, it is sufficient to prove that the loss or injury resulted from the operation of a public service, the underlying principle being that the state and its administrative agencies could incur civil liability for actions carried out by individual agents.

The new code, however, can only function effectively if a proper infrastructure is provided for its implementation. There is a shortage of, for example, detoxification centres for drug addicts, which are essential to the rehabilitation measures envisaged for those committing drug-related offences. Though the age of adult criminal responsibility is now set at 18 years, the code makes no specific provision for young offenders, and in the absence of separate juvenile detention centres, persons over 16 years of age can find themselves incarcerated with hardened criminals. Many of those serving their sentences by means of weekend detention may in practice have to travel long distances, given the insufficiency of appropriate accommodation near their places of residence. Furthermore, as has become clear with regard to **military service**, inadequate resources will make it difficult to implement the articles referring to community service.

Above all, by transferring responsibility for trying certain categories of criminal cases from the first-instance *juzgados* to the provincial courts, the new Penal Code will compound an already serious problem of overloading of the **legal system**, which has led to long delays.

Further reading

de la Cuadra, B. (1995) 'Nace el Código Penal del siglo XXI', *El País*, 13 November, pp. 14–15 (a useful summary of the main provisions).

—— (1996) 'El nuevo Código Penal, ante la hora de la verdad', *El País*, 27 May, pp. 18–19 (an incisively critical view of the limitations of the new code).

EAMONN RODGERS

performing arts

The performing arts are arguably one of the areas in which the contradictions of the **censorship** practised by the Franco regime are most obvious. On the one hand, carnival was banned as pagan and subversive, and the cultivation of regional cultural forms like the Catalan dance, the *sardana*, was discouraged, at least in the early years of the dictatorship. The exponents of the ***Nova Cançó*** had to struggle hard against official harassment, and popular songs with radical lyrics deriving from the Civil War were suppressed. In general, any cultural manifestation likely to have a mass appeal was scrutinized more severely than those which represented only minority interests.

On the other hand, the claim of the Francoist establishment to represent all that was most authentic in Spanish tradition made it logically impossible to disapprove of traditional popular **folk music** and **dance**, especially where these could be perceived as untainted by political claims for regional autonomy. In any case, something as vital and deep-rooted as popular culture was not readily amenable to state control, and villages in some regions have even preserved the medieval *Danse Macabre* into the 1990s. Moreover, many of these traditions were capable of being exploited as tourist attractions, one of the many factors which boosted the already considerable popularity of **flamenco**.

The **theatre**, too, displayed similar paradoxes. In the years immediately after the Civil War, the theatre was dominated by slight, domestic comedies, psychological melodramas and other manifestations of what has aptly been called the 'culture of evasion'. Authors and producers were obliged to submit for approval not only scripts but also costume designs, and censorship officials attended dress rehearsals and performances to ensure that the text had not been changed. Nevertheless, as early as 1949, Antonio **Buero Vallejo** produced, in his *Historia de una escalera* (The Story of a Stairway), a bleak and critical portrayal of life in working-class Madrid. This was the first of a long series of works by Buero, written throughout the dictatorship and on into the 1980s, which uphold values such as freedom, responsibility and compassion, diametrically opposed to the ethos of Francoism. His near-contemporary Alfonso **Sastre**, even more radical and outspoken than Buero, founded the Arte Nuevo (New Art) theatre group in 1945, and was involved in the movement known as the Theatre of Social Agitation in the early 1950s. Nor was all innovative work in the theatre necessarily the work of opposition groups, for in 1954 the government sponsored the creation of the Teatro Nacional de Cámara y Ensayo (National Chamber Theatre).

One of the most important influences, however, in the development of the performing arts during the Franco period was the pioneering work of the director José **Tamayo**. Tamayo revived the tradition of the *Autos Sacramentales*, morality plays on eucharistic themes dating from the Middle Ages and the early modern period, the greatest exponent of which was the seventeenth-century dramatist Calderón. This archaic and highly stylized genre, which had largely fallen out of favour with theatre-going audiences, was given a new lease of life by being brought back into the public arena to which it had originally belonged, being performed in cathedral squares and monastery cloisters. Tamayo also brought to a wider public many of the classics of the Spanish theatrical tradition, long the preserve of élite audiences in the major cities, by performing them in large open-air venues such as the Roman theatre at Mérida. Tamayo's main achievement, however, was to introduce Spanish audiences to world theatre, especially the work of American dramatists such as Arthur Miller and major European figures like Ionesco. As director of the Teatro Español from 1955 to 1962, he enriched the repertoire of the theatre and contributed to a substantial widening of intellectual horizons.

A different kind of innovation, destined to remain productive well beyond the end of the Franco regime, was the blending of traditions of mime, dance, parody and political satire in the work of the Catalan group Els **Joglars**. Founded in 1962, it was consciously anti-Francoist from the beginning, and suffered frequent difficulties over censorship, falling foul of the authorities even in 1977, after the end of the regime, for criticizing the armed forces. Els Joglars initiated a movement which came to full maturity in the closing years of the dictatorship and the period immediately following, when Els **Comediants**, founded in 1971, and La **Fura dels Baus** (1979) combined in their performances elements of carnival and other popular festivals, pyrotechnics, music, acrobatic turns and features derived from avant-garde groups in Europe and the US.

The experience of these groups, particularly Els Joglars, demonstrates the extent to which the seeds of future developments already existed during the period of the Franco regime. There is no doubt, however, that the demise of the dictator in 1975 unlocked the pent-up energies of decades, and led to a surge of innovation and experimentation which lasted at least fifteen years. In addition to the activities of Els Comediants and La Fura dels Baus, a hitherto relatively conventional public was introduced to new blends of traditional and contemporary dance, which were seen as one of the appropriate means of expression for a young democracy seeking to make up for past stagnation and re-forge links with other cultures. Official recognition and support for this development was slow to materialize, but by the late 1980s the reorganization of the **national dance companies** had provided favourable conditions for both contemporary and traditional dance. Government action had already facilitated in 1985 the foundation of the Instituto Nacional de las Artes Escénicas y de la Música (National Institute for Performing Arts and Music), with four distinct divisions: the Centro Dramático Nacional (The National Drama Centre); the Centro Nacional de Nuevas Tendencias Escénicas (The National Centre for New Theatrical Trends); the Compañía Nacional de Teatro Clásico (The National Classical Theatre Company), and the Teatro Nacional Lírico de la Zarzuela (The National Zarzuela Lyric Theatre).

Though much of the cultural development of the 1980s and 1990s has involved building on national tradition, while at the same time opening Spain to new currents from abroad, some movements, such as the ***Movida*** of the mid-1980s, have been associated with a rejection of the past and the pursuit of open-ended experimentation in both art forms and lifestyle. *La Movida* was, among other things, a rejection of the commercialization of pop culture by multinationals, one of its manifestations being the proliferation of **independent record companies** (see also **rock and pop**).

An important role in the development of the performing arts has been fulfilled by the governments of the various **autonomous communities**, which have assumed increasing importance in **arts policy** and **arts funding** as the resources provided for the arts by the central government have decreased. Theatres in regional centres have been refurbished and new concert venues have been provided. This has had the dual effect of promoting distinctive regional cultures such as **Basque**, **Catalan** and **Galician cultures**, and has also ensured that the performing arts are no longer the preserve of a middle-class élite in Madrid and Barcelona, but are accessible to a mass public in every area of the peninsula.

Perhaps the most symptomatic event in the sphere of the performing arts in the post-Franco period was the allegorical pageant which opened and closed the Barcelona **Olympic Games** of 1992. The games provided the opportunity for an assertion of national pride on an all-Spain basis, but in effect became the locus for a demonstration of Catalan nationalism. The opening ceremony included a performance by La Fura dels Baus, which grafted modern spectacular onto the ancient classical model of the Roman sea-pageant. The closing event was a celebration by Els Comediants of the birth of the universe, in which an ancient myth was re-created with the aid of the most up-to-date pyrotechnic gadgetry.

See also: cultural institutions and movements; Francoist culture; music

Further reading

George, D. and London, J. (eds) (1996) *An Introduction to Contemporary Catalan Theatre*, Sheffield: Anglo-Catalan Society (the only full-length study of the subject in English).

Vilches de Frutos, M.F. (1992) 'Tendencias predominantes de la escena española en la década de los ochenta: Algunas reflexiones', *Anales de la*

Literatura Española Contemporánea/Annals of Contemporary Spanish Literature, 1–3: 207–220.
—— (1994) 'Spain: Artistic Profile; Theatre for Young Audiences; Puppet Theatre; Design; Theatre Space and Architecture; Criticism, Scholarship and Publishing', in D. Rubin (ed.) *The World Encyclopedia of Contemporary Theatre. Europe*, London and New York: Routledge, pp. 790–804.
Wingrave, H. (1972) *Spanish Dancing, A Handbook on Steps, Style, Castanets and Dancing*, Speldhurst: Planned Action (a practical manual).

EAMONN RODGERS

Periódico de Catalunya, El

El Periódico de Catalunya is published in Barcelona and is the most widely read daily newspaper in Catalonia. It is somewhat brash and even populist in style, but is clearly responding to a demand for a less formal style of journalism among a broader and more socially differentiated readership.

El Periódico de Catalunya was founded in 1979 by Grupo Zeta, a publishing group with extensive written and electronic media ownership throughout Spain. It is, therefore, a relatively young publication, and lacks both the tradition and the weight of its arch-rival *La* ***Vanguardia***. Despite its relative youth, it is by any standards a very successful newspaper, having a daily readership of over 850,000, a figure which rises to almost one and a quarter million on Sundays.

El Periódico de Catalunya is written uncompromisingly in Spanish, and can indeed at times take a somewhat aggressive stance in relation both to the increased use of the **Catalan** language within Catalan society (see also **language normalization**), and to the more general notion of increased autonomy or independence for Catalonia. Despite this it is in many senses very much a Catalan newspaper, giving extensive coverage to events in Barcelona and elsewhere in Catalonia, and combining this with good international coverage, a detailed business section, and the considerable attention to sport required of any mass audience newspaper. Like *La Vanguardia* it is broadsheet in format, and it is a substantial read, with individual issues reaching as many as seventy pages in length.

Despite its Catalan credentials, *El Periódico de Catalunya* must also be seen as part of a broader Spanish enterprise publishing daily newspapers in other parts of Spain (including *El Periódico de Aragón* and *La Voz de Asturias*, with which it pools not only information, but also a number of its most controversial columnists), and which also owns a number of weekly and monthly Spanish magazines, the best-known being *Tiempo* and ***Interviú***. Thus, despite its editorials and articles written in Barcelona and its very considerable coverage of Catalan events, *El Periódico* tends to place Catalonia clearly within a more general Spanish framework. Its political position is generally (though seldom stridently or exclusively) sympathetic to the mainstream Spanish right, with a corresponding emphasis on the overriding unity of Spain, even while recognizing the specificities of its individual **autonomous communities**. Its style and presentation are also notably more populist than those of *La Vanguardia.*

To some extent *El Periódico* represents the limit beyond which a more popular style of journalism in Spain cannot go. Publications with a more overtly down-market appeal have been short lived, whereas *El Periódico* has clearly exploited a niche in the Catalan market which the more serious *Vanguardia* had left untouched.

Further reading

Mateo, R. de and Corbella, J.M. (1992) 'Spain' in B.S. Østergaard (ed.) *The Media in Western Europe*, London: Sage (a useful guide to the media situation in Spain in general, though its coverage of individual newspapers is rather slim).

HUGH O'DONNELL

personal names

First names in Spain have traditionally been drawn from the calendar of saints observed by the Roman Catholic church, and, for women, from local shrines to the Virgin Mary (Pilar, Rocío) or from attributes of Christ or the Virgin (Asunción,

Encarnación). Sometimes male and female names can be combined in the same person (a man might be called José María, a woman María José). Parents wishing to choose names free from religious connotations are in practice faced with restricted choice. Even the famous communist leader La Pasionaria was called Dolores, and names derived from abstract terms like Equidad (Equity) have never become fashionable to any significant extent in Spain.

Surnames are made up of a patronymic (the father's surname) followed by a matronymic (the mother's surname), sometimes linked with *y* ('and'), which is a convenient way of distinguishing among members of the same family. Despite the patriarchal character of Spanish society in the past, married women usually kept their own surname for official purposes, adding *de* plus the husband's surname, though this latter custom is rapidly dying out.

EAMONN RODGERS

Perucho, Juan (Joan)

b. 1920, Barcelona

Writer

Poet, novelist, narrator and art critic, Perucho has been active in **Catalan** literature since the 1940s, although he received little attention until the 1980s. Inspired by a strong love of fantasy and imagination – seen as a way of introducing magic into our otherwise excessively rational lives – he combines literary, cultural and historical references with fantasy to produce highly original narratives, which have little in common with prevailing Catalan trends.

Further reading

Gillamon, J. (1990) 'Joan Perucho, Metaphors of the End of the World', *Catalan Writing*, 5: 9–23 (interesting article, followed by chronology, bibliography, and translations of three short stories).

KATHRYN CRAMERI

philosophy

Philosophy in the early years of the twentieth century was heavily influenced by two different traditions. On the one hand, there was the legacy of the Europeanizing movement known as Krausism, a kind of secular humanism with a religious tinge, which took its name from a minor German idealist, Karl Christian Friedrich Krause, who died in 1832. On the other, the soul-searching produced by the loss of the colonies in the war with the United States in 1898 would leave its imprint on a whole generation of writers, the so-called 'Generation of 1898'. One of the main representatives of Krausism, Francisco Giner de los Ríos, founded in 1876 the Institución Libre de Enseñanza (ILE – Free Institute of Education), which upheld the idea that the thorough reform of education was a precondition for changing Spanish society and its way of thinking. The ILE continued to exercise an influence on the educational and cultural policy of successive governments in the first third of the twentieth century, which earned it the increasing hostility of conservatives and Catholics.

The Europeanizing tradition of the Krausists was carried on in the 1920s by the most prominent Spanish thinker of the time, José **Ortega y Gasset**. The notion of the individual immersed in his or her historical circumstances is the central idea of his philosophy. This 'historicity' of the individual is complemented by a conception of social relations in which a select minority would rule the emergent masses, who had been acquiring greater prominence since the mid-nineteenth century. The 'revolt of the masses' was, in Ortega's view, the greatest danger which faced western society in the 1930s.

After spending the Civil War in **exile**, Ortega returned to Spain in 1945, where three years later he founded the Instituto de Humanidades (Institute of Humanities). Until Ortega's death in 1955, he continued to occupy a key position in contemporary philosophy within Spain, together with Xavier Zubiri, Manuel García Morente, Eugenio D'Ors, and Julián **Marías**, his pupil and the co-founder of the Instituto de Humanidades. Simultaneously, those exiled philosophers who were heirs of Ortega found their work greatly enriched by contact with the cultures of Spanish America, which gave a new dimension to their reflections on Spanish culture, Spanishness, and the problem of the 'two Spains' (ie, liberal and conservative). These concerns are reflected in the work of Francisco **Ayala**, María **Zambrano**, Luis Recaséns Siches and especially José Gaos. The disastrous effects of the Civil War in causing an exodus of intellectuals can be measured if we add to this list the names of Américo **Castro**, Manuel García Pelayo, José Ferrater Mora, Juan David García Bacca, Adolfo Sánchez Vázquez, Luis Araquistain, Fernando de los Rios, José Antonio Balbotín, José Castillejo and Salvador de Madariaga.

In the early years after the Civil War, most of the officially approved philosophy was scholastic in character. It was not until 1961 that the first post-war book on **Marxism** appeared, *Introducción al pensamiento marxista* (Introduction to Marxist Thought), which brought together a series of lectures given in the University of Santiago de Compostela in the autumn of 1958. From that date on, the process of rediscovery of Marxist thought was forwarded not only by philosophers but by scholars in various branches of the social sciences. This process was assisted by the rise of revolutionary movements in the Third World, and the growth of the New Left.

This period also saw the rediscovery of Krausism and the thinking which inspired the ILE, a tradition to which the Franco regime had been implacably hostile. The earliest contribution to this development was the doctoral thesis of Eloy Bullón, *La filosofía krausista en España* (Krausist Philosophy in Spain) (1958), which was followed by Vicente Cacho Viu's *La Institución Libre de Enseñanza* (The Free Institute of Education) (1962), and Dolores Gómez Molleda's *Los reformadores de la España Contemporánea* (The Reformers of Contemporary Spain) (1966).

In parallel with this, Marxist thought was reconceptualized as a 'practical humanism', which could provide a basis for a truly democratic socialism and a genuine socialist democracy. At the same time, the evolution of the Roman Catholic Church in the 1960s facilitated a dialogue between Marxism and religion. The issue is treated in works such as Tomás Malagón's *El marxismo y la 'Populorum Progressio'* (Marxism and the Papal Encyclical *Populorum Progressio*) (1967) or in the collective work *Cristianos y Marxistas: Los problemas de un diálogo* (Christians and Marxists: The Problems of Dialogue) (1969). All these elements: Krausism, the influence of the ILE, socialism, Marxism, and later anarchism, are aspects of the gradual rehabilitation of the philosophical traditions of the left, which had been rejected and ignored by the Franco regime.

See also: Francoist culture; politics; universities; university education

Further reading

Abellán, J.L. (1979–89) *Historia crítica del pensamiento español*, Madrid: Taurus, 5 vols (a very extensive and well-documented source).

Díaz, E. (1983) *Pensamiento español en la era de Franco (1939–1975)*, Madrid: Tecnos (an indispensable classic study).

Díaz Díaz, G. (1980–95) *Hombres y documentos de la Filosofía Española*, Madrid: CSIC (a large multi-volume work which has now reached its fifth volume, corresponding to the letter 'Ñ').

Ferrater Mora, J. (1994) *Diccionario de Filosofía*, Barcelona: Ariel, 4 vols (an updated edition of a basic reference text).

ALICIA ALTED

photography

Photographic societies began to flourish in Spain around 1900. Between 1839, when the first daguerreotype in Spain was developed in Barcelona by Ramon Alabern, and the second half of the nineteenth century, when photography came to be used for a wide range of applications, photography developed along similar lines in Spain as in the rest of Europe. At one level, photography was used for administrative, technical and scientific purposes. At the same time, it began from a very early date to follow divergent paths and take on some of the character of an art form. What was called 'pictorialism' aimed to raise photography to the same level of prestige as painting, and to win for it the respect normally given to unique works of art, an undertaking which was constantly threatened by the enormous popularity of the craft and the growing number of amateur practitioners. The pictorialists approached every plate and every shot with a series of elaborate procedures intended to make the finished product resemble an engraving or a watercolour. The best-known pictorialists in Spain are Miguel Goicochea de Jorge (1894–1983) of Navarre and José Oriz-Echagüe (1886–1980), who worked in Madrid.

A somewhat less sophisticated offshoot of pictorialist approaches was *costumbrista* (*'costumbres'* meaning popular customs, traditions or mores) photography, which concentrated on the observation of the picturesque. The extensive production of Joan Pereferrer (1889–1974) of Girona is a good example of this trend. A completely different approach, originating in advertising and in the work of avant-garde figures like Moholy-Nagy, is denoted by the term *Nueva Objetividad* (New Objectivity). This movement proclaimed the independence of photography from other arts, and aimed to highlight the 'objective' beauty of what was depicted, using only the 'logical' power of the camera. Emili Vila (1887–1967) and Josep Masana (1894–1979), who worked in Barcelona, are the first significant representatives of this trend, which would be followed by a large number of distinguished photographers. The influence of the avant-garde is very obvious in the work of Nicolas Lekuona (1913–37), a great Basque creative artist who died at the age of 24 in the Civil War.

Photo-journalism also became increasingly important, one of the earliest exponents being the Barcelona photographer Agustí **Centelles** (1909–85), who was active on the Republican front throughout the Civil War. The Civil War and the Franco regime created a long hiatus in the development of avant-garde experimentation, and many photographers from the Republican side had to go into exile. The work of Jalon Angel (1898–1976), the official photographer of Franco and his entourage, fostered a style firmly anchored in classical composition, with elements of 'glamour' derived from the cinema.

Until the 1970s **censorship** and isolation from the international community determined the course of Spanish photography, as well as the other arts. Nevertheless, there was no shortage of great photographers in this period, and their work was affected by the major developments taking place in photography worldwide. Thus the work of Francesc **Català-Roca** and Gabriel **Cuallado** shows the influence of the Italian neo-realism of the 1940s and 1950s. The 1970s saw a great change, with the genuine opening-up of Spain to the outside world and the progressive disappearance of censorship. The journal *Nueva Lente* (New Lens) and the work of Jorge Rueda (born Almería, 1943), mark the appearance of a more radical vision. The new generation of photographers, despite their different approaches, shared a rejection of 'photogenic' reality. Notable among them are Cristina García Rodero (born Ciudad Real, 1949), Juan Urrios (born Barcelona, 1962), Carles Fargas (born Tarragona, 1961) and Rafael **Vargas**.

See also: visual arts

MIHAIL MOLDOVEANU

Picasso, Pablo

b. 1881, Málaga; d. 1973, Mougins (France)

Painter and sculptor

Picasso's name conjures up an image of creative freedom and protean energy, epitomizing the spirit of twentieth-century art. The stylistic versatility of his œuvre, which opened the way to many artistic movements of the first half of the century, encompasses a wide range of artforms: painting, sculpture, drawing, collages, prints and ceramics. His work has often been explained and judged in terms of his life. In particular his relationship to women – both within and outside his canvases – has been the object of critical scrutiny.

Picasso attended art school in Barcelona where his family had moved in 1895, and frequented the city's artistic circles such as that around the tavern of Els Quatre Gats (The Four Cats), a centre for modernist culture in whose premises Picasso had his first exhibition in 1900. That same year he travelled to Paris for the first time. The trip was followed by longer stays in the French capital with occasional visits to Spain to see family and friends, among whom was the Catalan poet Jaume Sabartés who was later to become Picasso's personal secretary until his death in 1968. Picasso immersed himself in Parisian bohemian life, getting acquainted with Leo and Gertrude Stein, Guillaume Apollinaire and Max Jacob. His early work is characterized by a melancholic lyricism and a subdued palette (blue and rose periods, 1901–6). A growing interest in primitivism – African masks and Iberian sculpture – together with the rediscovery of Cézanne, prompted the development of his career, which was also spurred by his rivalry with Henri Matisse. In 1907 he painted *Les Demoiselles d'Avignon* which revolutionized the concept of form and space in painting, despite access to it being restricted for many years to the artist's friends. By then Picasso had already acquired a certain notoriety but it was the German dealer Kurt Kahnweiler who freed the painter from financial difficulties and thereby enabled him to experiment in this, one of his most innovative periods. Together with Braque, Picasso made his greatest contribution to modern art with cubism, which in many ways anticipated abstract expressionism. With their invention of collage in 1912, analytic cubism was transformed into synthetic cubism and Picasso, true to his Spanish inheritance, became one of the greatest still-life artists. After WWI he returned to figuration in a neoclassical mode which gradually acquired a quality of surreal expressionism, particularly in his series of women bathers. In the early 1920s and as his reputation grew he became interested in performance and collaborated, together with Cocteau, Satie and Stravinsky, in Diaghilev's Ballet Russe designing decor and costumes. The presence of the surrealist movement began to be felt in the Paris art scene, and Picasso's drawing *Le Minotaure* appeared on the cover of the first number of their review *La Révolution Surréaliste*. However, his relationship with Breton's acolytes never went beyond a cordial mutual acknowledgement. In the 1930s he made a series of a hundred etchings: the enigmatic and erotic Suite Vollard. At the same time his painting acquired a darker, more violent tone. With his personal life in turmoil he entered a creative crisis coinciding with the political malaise which preceded the Spanish Civil War.

After 1936 he settled permanently in France, for the most part in the French Midi, in self-imposed exile, and was never to return to Spain, becoming a member of the French Communist party in 1944. However, he never abandoned his interest in things Spanish as is attested by his homages to Velázquez and Goya, in the variations on *Las meninas* (1950s), and in the *Tauromaquia* aquatints series (1960), respectively. His Spanishness is particularily evident in the constant presence in his work of **bullfighting**, of which he was a life-long ***aficionado***. The imagery of the bullfight is present in one of his most famous works: *Guernica*. The bombing of the Basque town of Guernica by the German Luftwaffe in April 1937, gave Picasso the subject matter for the mural that had been commisioned by the Republican Government for the Spanish Pavilion at the Paris International Art and Techniques Exhibition which was to open in June 1937. Surrounded by controversy from its inception for its ambiguous symbolism, it became a powerful statement against war crimes and fascism in particular. After a nomadic period, the mural was finally housed in the Museum of Modern Art in New York. Its return to Spain in September 1981 was a boost to the young Spanish democracy still shaken by the ***Tejerazo*** in February of the same year. From the Casón del Buen Retiro, an annexe to the Prado, *Guernica* was moved in 1992 to the permanent collection of the new **Queen Sofia Museum** in Madrid.

One aspect of Picasso's work that has been reassessed is his sculptures, on which he worked assiduously from 1906, but which were hardly exhibited until late in his life. The sculptural work consists mainly of Cubist constructions and assemblages, but also of odd, discarded objects, like *Bull's Head*, made from a bicycle seat and handlebars. Here, his collaboration with the Catalan sculptor Julio González, as earlier with Braque, brought a surge of inspiration into his work.

Extraordinarily prolific right up to the end of his life, his œuvre is scattered among the world's major collections, but there are also some institutions devoted entirely to his work. The Museu Picasso in Barcelona, housed in the Palacio Aguilar in the city's old town, opened in 1963 and contains among some 3,000 pieces (drawings, lithographs, engravings and sculptures) many youthful works donated by the artist and Sabartés; the Antibes Museum, which Picasso used as his studio for a while, was renamed Musée Picasso in 1946, and contains a large series of ceramics made from the late 1940s;

and the Musée Picasso in Paris, which contains the artist's personal collection and his legacy to the French government after his death in 1985.

See also: exile; visual arts

Further reading

Brown, J. (1996) *Picasso and the Spanish Tradition*, New Haven, CT: Yale University Press (a superb collection of essays, including one by Jonathan Brown, which deal with Picasso's reworkings and debts to the Spanish Old Masters).

Chipp, H.B. (1988) *Picasso's Guernica: History, Transformations, Meanings*, Berkeley, CA and London: University of California Press (includes a chapter by Javier Tusell on the vicissitudes of its return to Spain).

Daix, P. (1993) *Picasso: Life and Art*, London: Thames & Hudson (comprehensive account and excellent discussion; very readable).

Richardson, J. (1991–6) *A Life of Picasso*, 2 vols, London: Jonathan Cape (authoritative, scholarly biography, offering a sympathetic view).

Museu Picasso, Musée Picasso and Musée Bonnat (1993) *Picasso: toros y toreros*, Paris and Barcelona: Editions de la Réunion des Musées Nationaux/ Ajuntament de Barcelona (this catalogue for the exhibition held by Museu Picasso, Barcelona, Musée Picasso, Paris and Musée Bonnat, Bayonne includes a series of interesting essays on the use and significance of bullfighting imagery in Picasso's work, and contains related documentary material).

Warncke, C.P. and Walther, I.F. (1994) *Picasso*, 2 vols, Köln: Benedikt Taschen (comprehensive *catalogue raisonné*; a forceful attempt to map out Picasso's entire output: paintings, drawings, etchings, lithographs, sculptures and ceramics).

XON DE ROS

Pla i Casadevall, Josep

b. 1897, Palafrugell (Girona); d. 1981, Llofriu (Girona)

Writer and journalist

Josep Pla was one of the best and most prolific Catalan prose writers of the twentieth century. Essentially a modern-day chronicler of the numerous places he visited both in Catalonia and abroad, he was a shrewd and profound observer of human beings in all their guises, a kind of successor to moralist writers of previous centuries. His prose is both rich and vivid and he is a consummate stylist.

Josep Pla began to study medicine at university before switching to a course in law. After completing his studies, he took up a career in journalism, and was for many years a correspondent with the well-known Catalan newspaper *La Veu de Catalunya*. He also wrote occasional columns in Spanish for such Madrid-based newspapers as *El Sol*. Between the two World Wars Pla's work entailed him spending long periods in European capitals, where he acquired much of his broad cultural knowledge. He was a firm supporter of political Catalanism, particularly of Francesc Cambó and the *Lliga Regionalista* (Regionalist League). He was out of Spain when the Spanish Civil War broke out, and did not return to his native Catalonia until 1939. Because of Francoist **censorship** of the Catalan language, Pla published in Spanish until 1945. After that date he began publishing in Catalan once more.

The publishing company Editorial Selecta published 29 volumes of Pla's complete works in the 1950s, of which *Homenots* (Little Men) (the first series was published in 1958) is probably the outstanding example. *Homenots* is a 'gallery of illustrious Catalans', from writers such as Josep Carner, Carles Riba and Salvador **Espriu**, to painters like Salvador **Dalí**.

Then in 1966 the publishers Destino began to bring out the definitive version of his complete works. It is difficult to pick out individual titles from Pla's vast corpus, although the first, *El quadern gris* (The Grey Notebook) (written 1936–9, published 1966), an autobiographical vision of his early years, is perhaps his masterpiece. *El quadern gris* is a rich compendium of memories of people and places, observations on how individuals can rise above the prevailing mediocrity of society, and the discovery of the inner self of the protagonist within this panorama. The work is replete with references to literary figures (including Stendhal, Goethe, Kierkegaard and Nietzsche), which, in Marina Gustà's words, are Pla's response to 'readings of that period and his search for a moral dimension, based on his own experience, which would support his observations of reality' (author's translation) (Gustà 1987: 188).

See also: Catalan culture; language and national identity

Further reading

Gustà, M. (1987) 'Josep Pla' in M. de Riquer, A. Comas and J. Molas (eds) *Història de la literatura catalana*, 11 vols, Barcelona: Ariel, X (a perceptive overview of Pla's life and works).

DAVID GEORGE

Planeta Prize

The most valuable (50m pesetas) of the literary **prizes** offered in Spain, it is awarded annually by the Planeta publishing house, for the best new novel of the year. In 1996, it was won by Fernando Schwartz, and in 1993 by Mario Vargas Llosa.

EAMONN RODGERS

planning

Town and country planning is based on the Land and Urban Planning Regulatory Act of 1956, revised in 1975 and again in 1990 by the Urban Regulatory and Land Appraisal Act. In essence the Acts (a) provide for the establishment of general municipal plans (which 'zone' land into urban, urbanisable and non-urban areas) and of more detailed sub-plans for development areas, and (b) grant building rights to landowners on condition of their fulfilling certain obligations.

Central to the 1956 Act, and to subsequent reforms, are two fundamental principles: the allocation of a substantial percentage of a development to various public uses including public housing development, and 'the fair distribution of the costs and benefits of planning'. This latter principle entails allocating the building rights, and with them the costs of the infrastructure and construction, as well as the profits from the same, to the owners of the land to be developed in proportion to their holding, but not to where it is sited in relation to the plan. This means that the original owner of land planned for a public park or school is not at a disadvantage compared with the owner of land planned for luxury housing. In addition, a particular provision of the 1990 Act discourages land speculation by allowing for compulsory purchase of land not developed within a fixed time-scale, with only 50 percent of its developmental value being returnable to the original owner.

In practice, however, planning regulations have frequently been ignored. This was particularly true of the urban, second home, and especially tourist developments of the 1960s and 1970s which took place with more regard for profit than for quality of life and environment. The tourist resort of Torremolinos is a prime example of chaotic growth which was allowed to outrun the zoning, public use and infrastructure regulations, so that in the 1990s, when upgrading became essential to its competitiveness, deficiencies in sewage disposal and in public amenities such as parks, promenades, theatres, sports and other leisure provisions had to be remedied. The 'congested and sterile' environment of cities, as the result of untrammelled growth on the outskirts and unsympathetic redevelopment in the centre, had similarly to be tackled by urban renewal plans, the most spectacular examples being slum clearance projects in Madrid, and the upgrading of Seville and Barcelona for **Expo-92** and the **Olympic Games** respectively.

See also: housing market; shanty towns; urbanization

Further reading

France, L. and Barke, M. (1992) 'Torremolinos: Then and Now', *Geographical Magazine Supplement*, January 1992: 4–7 (a brief overview of the development of the resort).

García Bellido, J. (1991) 'European Viewpoint: A (R)evolutionary Framework for Spanish Town Planning', *Town Planning Review*, 62 (4): v-viii (a description of the 1990 Act with a brief historical background).

Pollard, J. and Domínguez Rodríguez, R. (1995)

'Unconstrained Growth: The Development of a Spanish Resort', *Geography* 80 (1): 33–44 (a very informative and detailed analysis of the relationship between expansion and planning in the growth of Torremolinos).

Wilson, G. (1993) 'Regenerating Barcelona', *Planner*, 79 (7): 24.

EAMONN RODGERS

PNV

The Partido Nacional Vasco (Basque Nationalist Party) was founded at the end of the nineteenth century by Sabino Arana in order to protect the native Basque population from what he saw as contamination by immigrants from other regions, who had come to work in a rapidly industrializing area. Arana thought that the native population's best defence was its language, **Basque** (*Euskera*), which would be a barrier against the horrors of a foreign invasion by people whom he considered racially inferior, immoral and atheistic. To make matters worse the immigrants formed branches of the socialist **PSOE** and its associated trade union, the **UGT**.

Surprisingly, given that history, the PNV has become a moderate Christian Democratic party, the dominant force in the Basque country, and a power in the Spanish state. The party's orientation changed in the 1930s when the Second Republic granted the Basque country a Statute of Autonomy. As a result, the PNV and the newly created Basque government were on the losing side in the Civil War. During WWII, while the PNV-dominated Basque government in exile waited for the Allies to restore their democratic rights, the victorious Franco regime persecuted the Basque language and culture. A section of the PNV's youth grew dissatisfied with their elders' inactivity, and broke away in 1959 to form **ETA**, which aimed to achieve independence through armed struggle.

In the early 1970s, the PNV, now led by people such as Javier **Arzallus**, revived, much to the surprise of the new generation of anti-Franco activists. In the parliamentary elections held in 1977 the party emerged as a strong force whose co-operation would be necessary if a new constitution was to be agreed. The PNV leaders welcomed the **constitution of 1978**, which made an Autonomy Statute possible, but as they did not want to be seen to accept either the monarchy or Basque inclusion in the Spanish State, its MPs left the chamber before the crucial vote. In the referendum held to ratify the constitution the PNV recommended abstention.

The PNV leaders do not, in practice, think it possible to break away from Spain, but many of their members want independence. The party continues to promote Basque, but the function of the language is no longer to differentiate natives from immigrants, but to serve as a mark of identity for the whole Basque population. The PNV has been the leading force in the Basque parliament, established in 1980 to administer the Basque **autonomous community**, although it has usually had to govern as part of a coalition. The Basque government runs education and health and has its own police force and television channels (see also **Basque television**). Opponents complain that the PNV hardly distinguishes between the party and government, so that PNV membership is helpful in gaining public office. 'Spanish' parties still feel a measure of distrust about the PNV's loyalty to Spain and its constitution, although they have great respect for the head of the government, PNV member José Antonio **Ardanza**.

See also: regional nationalism; regional parties; regionalism

JOHN SULLIVAN

poderes fácticos

This phrase, which means 'the *de facto* powers', was used during the transition to democracy in the late 1970s to refer to the non-elected institutions within the state which were in a position to exercise considerable influence over the course of political life, without being accountable to the **parliament**. Initially, these were defined principally as the **armed forces** and the Roman Catholic Church. The army in particular was accustomed to seeing itself as the ultimate arbiter of political developments, a position which was implicitly recognized by Adolfo **Suárez** in September

1976, when he submitted his plan for political reform to a meeting of senior officers. By the 1980s, however, particularly after the failure of the ***Tejerazo***, the armed forces had increasingly come to accept the ultimate authority of the elected civilian government.

The church had exercised considerable power during the Franco regime (see also **church and state**), but had gradually begun to distance itself from the dictatorship from the mid-1950s, and did not attempt to impede the movement towards democratic politics after Franco's death. Nevertheless, the church has clearly been more comfortable with right-of-centre governments such as those of **UCD** (1977–82) and **PP** (1996–). During the socialist **PSOE** administration (1982–96), there was tension over such matters as the place of religious teaching in schools, and proposed legislation over divorce and abortion. Though the church can no longer be considered a *poder fáctico* in the sense in which the term was used in the 1970s, the presence of a significant number of Christian Democrats and members of **Opus Dei** in the ranks of the PP give it considerable indirect influence.

Some commentators, particularly since the late 1980s, have begun to apply the term to the **media**, particularly the **press**, which, though it has acquired a healthy independence under democracy, has not always exercised its considerable political power in a disciplined manner. Discussions of policy often rank a poor second to personalized attacks on individuals holding public office. Furthermore, open discussion in some sections of the press of prominent criminal and civil cases while they are before the courts has undermined respect for the presumption of innocence and the independence of the **legal system**.

A further agency to which the term *poder fáctico* might appropriately be applied is the security services. Whether the police officers involved in the operations of **GAL** are eventually proved to have acted independently, or whether they were operating under the authority of senior members of the government, the fact remains that parliamentary control over the security services is weak. This is particularly true of the military intelligence agency, the CESID (Centro Superior de Información de la Defensa – Centre for Defence Information). Though in the nature of things its operations have to remain secret, it has often acted in ways prejudicial to good government. In the late 1970s it withheld from the cabinet information about military conspiracies, and in 1995 was found to have tapped illegally the telephones of senior public figures, including the King. In 1998, it was revealed that for the previous six years it had had listening devices planted in the headquarters of the ultra-nationalist Basque party **Herri Batasuna**, without judicial authority.

Further reading

Heywood, P. (1995) *The Government and Politics of Spain*, London: Macmillan (chapter 3, 'The Institutional Legacy of Francoism', gives an excellent account of the *poderes fácticos*).

EAMONN RODGERS

poetry

The trajectory of Spanish poetry in the years 1939–90 is complex, beginning with the relatively impoverished poetic landscape of the aftermath of the Civil War. The social and existential themes of the 1940s and 1950s eventually gave way to a spirit of aesthetic experimentation, culminating in the 'culturalism' of the late 1960s. The period since 1975 has witnessed competing tendencies, including the emergence of a number of important women poets.

Contemporary Spanish poets are the heirs to one of the richest poetic traditions in western Europe. With the close of the Civil War in 1939, however, most of the brilliant figures of the pre-war period were either exiled, like Juan Ramón Jiménez, Luis Cernuda and Pedro Salinas, or dead, like Antonio Machado and Federico García Lorca, one of the first Spanish intellectuals to be killed in the conflict. The loss of so many important poets in so brief a time left a vacuum in the immediate postwar period: in contrast to the avant-garde style of the poets of the 1920s, José **García Nieto**, associated with the magazine *Garcilaso*, championed a more traditional style, emphasizing religious and patriotic themes. Existential and socio-political concerns were also characteristic of post-war poetry. The 1950s saw the rise of the socially engaged verse of Vicente **Aleixandre**, Blas de Otero, and Gabriel Celaya, as well as the testimonial poetry of José Hierro.

The dominance of politically engaged poetry, which was often perceived to be aesthetically deficient, provoked a reaction among some of the younger poets of the 1950s. In contrast to the propagandistic tone of social poetry, which implied that the poet was communicating a previously formulated message, these young writers envisioned writing as an exploration of the creative process. The result was the visionary poetics of Claudio Rodríguez, the minimalism of José Angel **Valente**, and the sombre metaphysical poetry of Francisco Brines. Gloria **Fuertes**' innovative colloquialism links her to the humorously incisive poetry of Angel González. Valente's 'poetics of silence' has been extremely influential on the work of younger poets of the 1970s and 1980s. Jaime **Gil de Biedma**'s ironic explorations of his own life experiences have had equal importance for other poets of this same period. María Victoria **Atencia**, another poet of this age-group, only began to receive her due in the 1980s, when her work began to appear for the first time outside of her native Málaga.

The *novísimos*, a group of poets who came of age around the year 1968, broke in more radical fashion with the postulates of the social and existential poetry of postwar Spain. What is most striking in their work is the combination of intellectual excitement, aesthetic ambition and cultural ferment. Poets like Guillermo **Carnero**, Ana María **Moix**, Leopoldo María Panero, and Pere **Gimferrer** commanded a vast knowledge of both traditional 'high culture' and twentieth-century popular culture, from Hollywood movies to rock 'n' roll. The so-called 'culturalism' characteristic of their poetry consisted of the ostentatious citation of literary and cultural intertexts. In their flamboyant eclecticism, the *novísimo* group reflected the rebellious spirit of the international **youth culture** of the late 1960s, although some, like Luis Antonio de **Villena**, later denounced the excesses of 'culturalism'.

There were two or three notable developments in Spanish poetry in the years following the death of Franco in 1975. One is a reaction to what is often perceived as the excessive intellectualism and avant-garde spirit of the *novísimo* poets writing during the years 1968–75. In their desire to connect more directly with the reading public, poets such as Luis García Montero and Felipe Benítez Reyes proposed a return to the 'poetry of experience' of the poets of the 1950s, especially Jaime Gil de Biedma. Others, including Andrés Sánchez Robayna and Amparo Amorós, have practiced a minimalist 'poetics of silence' in the manner of José Angel Valente. Perhaps the most important development in the 1980s is the emergence of an important group of women poets, who have taken centre stage in Spanish poetry for the first time in history. Ana **Rossetti**, Blanca Andreu and Luisa Castro have written formally and thematically audacious poetry that often challenges accepted attitudes towards gender and sexuality. Rossetti's erotically explicit poems have had an especially great impact.

There is a sense among some poets and critics that lyric poetry has become a relatively 'minor' genre in comparison with the novel and with film; poetry no longer occupies the cultural centre in the way it perhaps did in the 1920s. This apparent diminution in the overall significance of the genre does not reflect any lack of quality or vitality among contemporary Spanish poets. It is the result, rather, of poetry's continued identification with 'high culture' in a period in which audiovisual media have taken centre stage. At the same time, however, writers like García Montero and Rossetti have continued to find new ways to connect with the reading public. While the audience for poetry may be small in absolute terms, it remains a vital part of the culture of contemporary Spain.

See also: cultural institutions and movements; feminist writing; literature; novel; theatre; women's writing

Further reading

Debicki, A.P. (1982) *Poetry of Discovery: The Spanish Generation of 1956–1971*, Lexington, KY: University Press of Kentucky (important studies of Rodríguez, Valente, Gil de Biedma, etc.).

—— (1994) *Spanish Poetry of the Twentieth Century:*

Modernity and Beyond, Lexington, KY: University Press of Kentucky (contains especially useful overviews of Spanish poetry of the 1970s and 1980s).

Mayhew, J. (1994) *The Poetics of Self-Consciousness: Twentieth-Century Spanish Poetry*, Lewisburg: Bucknell University Press (includes studies of major poets from the 1920s to the 1980s).

JONATHAN MAYHEW

policing

It seemed at the time that reform of the police system after the death of Franco in 1975 was agonizingly slow. It had to be transformed from the repressive instrument of an authoritarian regime into a system that would protect the constitutional rights, freedoms and safety of citizens. Yet with hindsight the difficult task of changing the ethos of a complex set of large organizations was with some exceptions accomplished by 1986, the year of the completion of the new legal framework through the Organic Law of the Security Corps and Forces.

Spain's oldest national police force is the *Guardia Civil*, the **Civil Guard**, created in 1844 to protect landed property, and essentially a military force. As Spain became more urbanized newer forces emerged, some local, others national and divided into quite separate plain-clothes and uniformed branches, the latter concerned essentially with public order and officered by the military. When in 1941 Franco reshaped the police forces to suit his regime, he was following tradition in formalizing a tripartite system of Civil Guard as rural police, Armed and Traffic Police as a uniformed urban public order force (both under total military control), and the General Police Corps as plain-clothes investigative police, with an essentially political function and popularly known as the secret police.

Until 1975 police and regime were as one and the security forces became the decisive element in the thirty-six year survival of the regime. During the early years after the Civil War the more than 100,000 executions and the imprisonment of perhaps 300,000 suggest clearly the major role of the police forces. Throughout, strikes remained illegal, **censorship** was strict, party political activity was banned and meetings were carefully controlled. Political control overshadowed more run-of-the-mill police duties, but defenders of the system pointed to the – by European standards – low **crime** rates.

Franco's death in 1975 left two policing problems whose resolution was not always easy to reconcile: reform and the ending of violence in the Basque country. Franco's security forces had acted as an alien army of occupation and the intractable nature of the situation in **Euskadi** was his legacy to democratic Spain. The violence of **ETA** continued, backed by massive demonstrations, and the government discovered that its security forces, with their harsh methods of maintaining order and their frequent use of torture, were counterproductive. The years 1978 and 1979 saw a series of measures to deal with these problems: on 4 December 1978 an interim Police Law was passed, ahead of the constitution of 29 December (see also **constitution of 1978**). In the New Year General Sáenz de Santa María was placed in charge of reforming the hated Armed Police, the '*grises*' ('greys'), now in new khaki (later blue) uniforms and renamed the National Police. In December 1979 the Basque Autonomy Statute appeared, giving devolution to the Basque provinces, including potential devolution of aspects of policing. This twin-track policy of devolution and reform did not, however, produce immediate results: in 1978–80 235 deaths were caused by ETA, about three-fifths of them members of the security forces. The survival of the whole democratic process was at stake, dramatized by the ***Tejerazo*** of 23 February 1981 when a senior officer of a force legally bound to uphold constitutional order was seen trying to overthrow that order because of a supposed government softness towards the Basque problem.

While the attempted coup bolstered determination to consolidate democracy, ETA's continuing violence slowed the completion of reform: the Civil Guard was felt to be needed as a counter-terrorist force, and some of the murkier areas of police activity could survive (and haunt Felipe **González** in the 1990s). Nevertheless, 1986 saw the completion of the legal framework for the police system. Spain now has two national police forces, the Civil Guard, and, by combining the plain-clothes and uniformed urban forces, the Cuerpo Nacional de Policía (National Police Corps). There is also a multiplicity of municipal police forces, now much better trained and equipped, who do much of the day-to-day public urban police work. But between the national and municipal forces there have emerged the so-called autonomous police forces, the forces of the **autonomous communities** into which Spain has divided itself, a development foreshadowed in the 1978 constitution and first embodied in the Basque Statute of 1979.

The National Police Corps, responsible to the Ministry of the Interior, deals with **municipalities** of over 20,000 people, with identity cards, immigration matters, gambling, drugs and private security forces. The Civil Guard, responsible to the Ministries of the Interior and Defence, deals with smaller municipalities, customs, main roads, coasts, frontiers, ports and airports. There is scope for overlap, and careful liaison is needed to make the system work. It is complicated further by the autonomous police, though few regions have substantial forces. The major and most interesting case is that of the Basque police, where continuous development has led to a new force, the Ertzaintza, built afresh on democratic and community principles. It now controls most policing functions in Euskadi, only 'extra- or supra-communitary functions' being excluded. As before, potential for conflict over definitions remains. While Spain has made huge strides towards improving efficiency and eliminating militarism, it remains to be seen whether the possibilities for confusion that history and compromise have created will be overcome.

See also: armed forces; GAL; *golpismo*; terrorism

Further reading

Greer, S. (1995) 'De-centralised Policing in Spain: The Case of the Autonomous Basque Police', *Policing and Society*, 5: 15–36 (an excellent account of a remarkable experiment in policing).

Hooper, J. (1987) *The Spaniards: A Portrait of the New Spain*, Harmondsworth: Penguin (chapter 10 includes a very readable and thorough account of the police system).

Macdonald, I.R. (1985) 'The Police System of Spain', in J. Roach and J. Thomaneck (eds) *Police and Public Order in Europe*, Beckenham: Croom Helm (the most comprehensive account available in English).

—— (1987) 'Spain's 1986 Police Law: Transition from Dictatorship to Democracy', *Police Studies*, 10, 1: 16–21 (updates the previous item).

Morales Villanueva, A. (1988) *Administración policial española*, Madrid: San Martín (a full account of the structures of the police system).

IAN MACDONALD

political parties

Spanish political parties are characterized by several factors, most of which can be explained by the legacy of the Franco regime and the nature of the subsequent élite-led transition to democracy. These factors are: low levels of membership resulting in a weak party-electorate bond; an oligarchic structure and nature; the importance of personalities as opposed to policies or issues; and a tendency towards ideological vagueness.

The Spanish party system can be classified as a limited multi-party system given that although there are numerous parties in existence, only four or five are protagonists on the national political scene, either in roles of government or opposition, or as vital actors when forming pacts. Despite its multi-party nature, however, the Spanish party system clearly rests on two positions, namely the centre-right and the centre-left. The parties which make up this system are the socialist **PSOE** and the **United Left** (Izquierda Unida), the centre-right **PP** and the conservative regional parties of the Basque country (**PNV**), and Catalonia (**CiU**). These **regional parties** are strong, both in their own particular region as well as at the national level.

The major political parties in Spain have relatively few members compared to their European counterparts. Public reluctance to become a party member is understandable given that all party political activity was outlawed during the almost forty years of dictatorship under Franco. Moreover, the fact that parties were legalized only shortly before the first general **elections** in June 1977 meant that they themselves had little time to develop their organizational bases, as all other objectives were sacrificed to the priority of winning electoral support.

The oligarchic nature of Spanish political parties, that is to say the concentration of power within the party leadership at the expense of grass-roots participation, is favoured by a number of factors. First, political parties in Spain today are relatively new organizations, since even those which can lay claim to historical roots – the communist **PCE**, the PSOE and the PNV – virtually had to recreate themselves from the top downwards under the new democracy. Thus, the party executive was already firmly established before local and provincial party structures could be developed. Second, the electoral system of 'closed' lists (which prohibits the introduction or suppression of names) and 'blocked' lists (which prevents the selection of candidates in the order of preference) obliges the electorate to choose between lists of candidates offered by the party apparatus. The prospective candidate is thus dependent on the party leadership for selection and financial support, thereby ensuring that candidates show more allegiance to the party oligarchy than they do to the rank-and-file members. This relationship is further strengthened by state-financing of parties. Third, the internal organization of most parties reflects the dominance of the party leadership as compared to their small memberships. Closely approximating Michel's Iron Law of Oligarchy, the command structure is firmly regulated and hierarchical and there is little space for independent initiatives by the rank-and-file membership. Lastly, the oligarchic nature of the parties is exacerbated by the dominance of the core executive over the **parliament**. The formal rules governing the *Cortes* and the way in which they have been interpreted mean that it is generally the party spokesmen who dominate the opportunities for public speech. The initiatives available to the ordinary member of parliament are thus reduced to the simple approval or disapproval of measures by pressing the appropriate voting button.

The importance of individual leaders also reinforces this oligarchic tendency. The stress on élite-level negotiations during the transition to democracy meant that political parties frequently became identified with their high-profile leaders rather than with their party programmes. The increasing role of the mass **media** in election campaigns also emphasizes the public image of leaders, helping to establish a direct relationship between them and the electorate at the expense of the role of party activists and of the party itself in reaching public opinion.

This emphasis on personalities tends to push issues and party programmes to the background. This leads to a high degree of ideological vagueness and a situation where the public discourse of the major parties, characterized by much rhetoric, often bears little resemblance to their actual behaviour. Ideological imprecision was especially evident during the transition when parties frequently underwent dramatic shifts in their ideological and programmatic positions as they continually tried to adapt their strategies to the changing nature of the transition.

Such ideological imprecision is consonant with the catch-all strategies used by Spanish parties. Parties compete for the largest number of votes possible by making electoral appeals to numerous, and often opposed, social sectors. Ideological differences are thus minimized and electoral promises are vague. The logic of democratization in Spain meant that parties were obliged to move towards the centre in order to achieve electoral success given that public-opinion surveys demonstrated emphatically that the bulk of the electorate placed themselves in the centre of the political spectrum.

Many of these characteristics are of course common elsewhere in Europe, but what most differentiates Spanish parties from their European counterparts is that the above characteristics are more exaggerated in the former, given that the longevity of the Franco regime meant that Spain never experienced the age of mass-membership parties. Instead, Spanish parties have gone directly from being élite parties to vote-maximizing parties.

Further reading

Gunther, R., Sani, G. and Shabad, G. (1987) *Spain After Franco. The Making of a Competitive Party System*, Berkeley, CA: University of California Press (a comprehensive account of the evolution of the party system in contemporary Spain).

Heywood, P. (1995) *The Government and Politics of Spain*, London: Macmillan Press (includes excellent chapters on political parties and the party system).

Linz, J. and Montero, J. (eds), (1986) *Crisis y Cambio: Electores y Partidos en la España de los Años Ochenta*, Madrid: Centro de Estudios Constitucionales (an excellent and well-documented general study).

GEORGINA BLAKELEY

politics

Throughout the latter part of the nineteenth century and much of the twentieth century, Spanish politics has been characterized by the struggle to establish a democratic polity: a struggle which was far more protracted and bloody than that experienced by the majority of other western European countries. One of the main reasons for this democratic tardiness was that Spain long remained economically underdeveloped, thereby condemning both state and society to chronic weakness. Democracy in Spain thus remained elusive precisely because capitalist development also remained elusive. Such a situation led to the well-known maxim that Spain was somehow different from her European neighbours.

In particular, Spanish politics was characterized by a series of fault-lines which, broadly speaking, divided the political community into two main antagonistic blocs – the forces of reaction and tradition on the one hand, and the forces of reform and modernity on the other. Within these two broad camps other polarities could be discerned: centralists against regionalists; monarchists against Republicans; the church against anti-clericals; workers against employers. One of the sharpest divisions was the perennial conflict between the need to establish a unitary, centralized state on the one hand, whilst satisfying regional differences on the other.

The attempt to reconcile state and nation played a key role in the struggle between the two main antagonistic blocs – the traditionalists and the modernists – for hegemony. This struggle resulted in a permanent, and seemingly unbreakable, cycle whereby periods of authoritarianism and centralized government were followed by attempts at democratization, generally accompanied by some form of regional autonomy. Thus the formal democratic façade of the Restoration Monarchy (1875–1923) was followed by the dictatorship of Primo de Rivera (1923–31). In turn, this period of centralized dictatorial rule was followed by the Second Republic (1931–6) – Spain's first period of genuine democratization which was accompanied by a limited process of regional devolution. This democratic interlude was followed by one of the longest, most centralized, dictatorships in western Europe under General Franco. Only with the successful establishment of democracy in the 1970s would this dynamic between authoritarianism and democracy, reaction and modernity, centralism and regionalism, be broken.

To understand the success of democratization in the 1970s, however, it is necessary first to examine the reasons for its failure in the 1930s. In this sense it is impossible to overestimate the importance of history in understanding the politics of contemporary Spain. During the Second Republic the struggle between traditionalists and modernists reached its zenith. The forces of reaction – the church, the **armed forces** and the landed aristocracy – reacted vehemently against the alternative value system articulated by the Republican forces, mainly the working class and its political allies at the time, the urban middle class and the intelligentsia.

The Second Republic put forward a programme to modernize and democratize Spanish politics and society. It was not a socialist programme, nor was it a revolutionary one (although it was perceived by many as such); rather the Second Republic represented the desire simply to bring Spain into line with the rest of western Europe. However, in many senses the Second Republic was a premature political development which could not be sustained given the existing balance of power in Spain at that time. The cardinal error of the governments of the Second Republic was above all the attempt to change the balance of political power without changing the economic and social *status quo* which underpinned it.

The most powerful class – the large landowners – were the staunchest opponents of democracy. At the other end of the spectrum, the urban middle and working classes, who were most favourably inclined towards democracy, were numerically weak and fragmented. The only other numerically significant class, able to provide a counterpoint to the strength of the landed élites, was the class of impoverished landless day labourers. Such a class configuration was not conducive to the establishment of a parliamentary democracy and resulted instead in a hostile and increasingly polarized class struggle between the landless day labourers on the one hand and the large landowners on the other. The latter would be most consistently hostile to democracy whilst the former were inherently revolutionary. Such a class structure could not support a modernizing reform programme like that proposed by the Republic. Its programme was at once too radical for the landowners yet too reformist for the landless. Thus, the Second Republic collapsed into a series of confrontations between the two value systems – tradition and modernity – which became so bitter and polarized that, by 1936, the Second Republic's descent into a bloody three-year **Civil War** seemed, to many observers, inevitable.

Controversy surrounding the Spanish Civil War has led to a variety of conflicting interpretations, partly inspired by the intense social divisions which underpinned the struggle, partly because of the international interest which it aroused. Thus, the Spanish Civil War has been viewed through many different lenses: first, it has been seen by many as an ideological war, a fight between fascism and communism. Alternatively it has been seen as a religious war, a Catholic crusade against atheism. Third, it has been seen as an international war, a testing ground for WWII which was looming on the horizon. But, valid as many of these interpretations may be, the Civil War in Spain was above all a Spanish war fought by the forces of reaction against the forces of reform. It was a final attempt on the part of the conservative pillars of Spanish society – the **monarchy**, the military, the church and the landed élites – to preserve their interests against the sudden emergence of mass politics.

The Francoist dictatorship (1936–75) kept alive the division of Spain into two antagonistic blocs, but with the added dimension that the forces of reaction became the permanent victors, and the forces of reform the eternally vanquished. Yet although Franco was able to maintain Spain in a kind of political stasis owing to a combination of passive tolerance and indifference to authoritarian rule by much of the population, and a policy of selective repression for the remainder, he was unable to stop socio-economic progress and the consequences that would ensue from it. Ironically, it was the inability of the regime to cope with the transformations wrought by the period of exceptional economic growth and social change in the 1950s and 1960s, which the dictatorship itself had deliberately promoted, which led to the political weakening of the regime.

Economic growth, which had been intended to maintain the *status quo* simply served to highlight the inability of an anachronistic political system, established in an agricultural and rural world, to meet the challenges of an increasingly industrialized and urban society. Thus, in sharp contrast to democratization in the 1930s, social and economic transformation and the change in values and attitudes which that implied, both preceded and facilitated the subsequent political transformation in the 1970s.

Following the death of Franco in 1975, therefore, Spain did not undergo a political revolution, but rather an evolution from dictatorship to democracy. Arguably a revolution had already occurred in social and economic terms during the 1950s and 1960s, thereby obviating the need for a political upheaval. The Spanish economy had become integrated into the western market-based capitalist framework, thereby simultaneously strengthening state and society and changing the balance of classes within Spain. Capitalist development thus produced a class configuration which was far more conducive to the establishment of democracy. Neither the landowners nor the landless peasantry were any longer of any significance. Instead, they had been replaced by the burgeoning urban working and middle classes. Thus, by 1975, Franco's death represented little more than the last symbolic blow to a regime which had been disintegrating for years. As such, there was no real need for a clean break from the past, but rather a continuation of the process of slow transformation and evolution which had already been taking place for decades.

Continuity, not change, thus facilitated the Spanish transition to democracy, making it one of the most successful models of political transition from dictatorship to democracy which subsequent regimes in eastern Europe and Latin America would attempt to emulate. Spain's authoritarian regime was literally dismantled from within by the very people who had worked to uphold its maintenance for many years. Indeed, many of the leading actors of the transition were successful precisely because they emphasized their links with the previous regime. Adolfo **Suárez**, the main architect of the transition, had occupied several important positions in the Francoist system. The other actor who contributed invaluably to the transition process, King **Juan Carlos I**, had been hand-picked by Franco to succeed him and, with that purpose in mind, had been brought up and educated under the dictator's guidance.

It is precisely this continuation between the two regimes, in respect both of personalities associated with the previous regime and of the maintenance of existing policies, political structures and institutions, which explains the speed and relative ease with which Spain moved from dictatorship to democracy. By 1977, not even two full years after Franco's death, general elections had been held and Spain was a functioning parliamentary democracy. The new democratic **constitution of 1978** was accepted overwhelmingly by popular vote in a referendum of that year. By 1979 local elections had been held and a process of significant regional devolution, which would eventually lead to the establishment of a quasi-federal state of **autonomous communities**, was well under way. Although many problems were still to be faced in the coming years – not least an attempted military coup in 1981 – they would be tackled with the same skills employed in the transition. Negotiations, pacts and the élite cohesion which these imply, continued from the transition period into the period of democratic consolidation.

The benefits of such a transition through transaction were immediately apparent. A high degree of élite consensus and cohesion which came from a shared desire to learn from the failed democratic experiment in the 1930s, facilitated the series of agreements and pacts negotiated by élite elements from both the authoritarian regime and the democratic opposition. In a relatively peaceful manner, élites were able to reach agreement on the most important issues that have traditionally divided Spanish society, thereby resolving the historic polarization between two antagonistic blocs. Consensus has thus replaced confrontation in contemporary Spain.

Ironically, though, the very continuity which facilitated the transition has also meant the continued existence of authoritarian proclivities within Spain's political system, evident in such diverse aspects as an excessively dominant core executive, the shallow roots which political parties have put down in society, a relatively toothless parliament and an underdeveloped democratic political culture. The fact that Spain's transition was evolutionary rather than revolutionary also explains the lack of ideological content in much of Spain's contemporary politics. Consensus, so essential to achieving democracy, has almost become an ideology in itself which means that there is often a lack of genuine debate on many of the important questions which face the country.

Nevertheless, although such costs may cast doubt on the quality of democracy in Spain, its existence is beyond question. It does seem, therefore, as if the cycle between dictatorship and democracy at long last appears to have been broken. Although Spain's political system displays distinguishing traits, many of which are a product of the country's particular historical legacy, it also shares features in common with any other established European democracy. In particular, the social, political and economic problems now facing Spain are the same as those faced by the majority of countries in western Europe. If differences still exist they are now those of degree rather than kind. Spain, in political terms at least, is no longer different.

Further reading

Bell, D.S. (1983) *Democratic Politics in Spain*, London: Frances Pinter (a well-documented study which covers a range of issues on the Spanish transition to democracy).

Carr, R. and Fusi, J.P. (1991) *Spain: Dictatorship to Democracy*, London: Allen & Unwin (an excellent book which covers both the historical back-

ground to the transition as well as the actual transition process itself).
Heywood, P. (1995) *The Government and Politics of Spain*, London: Macmillan Press (the most up-to-date and comprehensive account of the government and politics of Spain under democracy).
Preston, P. (1986) *The Triumph of Democracy in Spain*, London: Methuen (the most comprehensive guide to the Spanish transition to democracy).

GEORGINA BLAKELEY

Ponce Martínez, Enrique

b. 1971, Chiva

Matador

The most admired younger **matador** of the 1990s, Ponce took his ***alternativa*** in 1990 and has founded his career on a consistent combination of classic artistry and immense technical security. His performance in over one hundred ***corridas*** in each of seven consecutive Spanish seasons between 1992 and 1998 is unparallelled.

See also: bullfighting

IAN CAMPBELL ROSS

Popular Alliance

The Alianza Popular (AP) was a coalition of different groups on the right and centre-right. Founded in 1976 by an ex-minister of the Franco regime, Manuel **Fraga Iribarne**, it was widely perceived as the political heir of the dictatorship. Its showing in the general elections of 1977 and 1979 was poor, with 8 and 5 percent of the votes respectively, and 16 and 9 seats. It did better in some regional elections, however, and by the next general election in 1982, won decisively by **PSOE**, it had become the main opposition party, owing to the eclipse of **UCD**: its share of the vote was 26 percent, and it had 107 seats. For several years afterwards, it had difficulty breaking through what Fraga Iribarne called its *techo electoral* (electoral ceiling), but gained in credibility after its re-launch in 1989 as **PP**.

LOURDES LÓPEZ NIETO

Porcel, Baltasar

b. 1937, Andratx (Mallorca)

Novelist, playwright and journalist

Baltasar Porcel is one of the leading Catalan writers of the post-Franco period. He wrote theatre early in his career, but largely abandoned this genre after the 1960s. His 1959 play *Els condemnats* (The Condemned), which received the Ciutat de Palma de Teatre Prize, is an existential tragedy. *La simbomba fosca* (The Dark Zambomba) (1961) is closer to the Theatre of the Absurd. Like *Waiting for Godot*, it is subtitled 'a tragicomedy' and has as little progressive dramatic action as Beckett's play. In common with other avant-garde plays in Franco's Spain, *La simbomba fosca* received an unfavourable critical reception. Porcel's 1962 play *Èxode* (Exodus) is one of a number of Spanish and Catalan plays of the 1960s and the 1970s to display the influence of Brecht.

In his first novel, *Solnegre* (Blacksun) (1961), the recipient of the 1961 Ciutat de Palma Prize, Porcel combines a Sartrian existentialism with a sensuous evocation of a primitive Balearic community. It is the forerunner of his mature novels, in which he creates a mythicized vision of his native Andratx, rather as Salvador **Espriu** did with his native Arenys de Mar. Porcel has described the mythification process as follows: 'it began by being Andratx, my town, and now I don't know what it is: a mythical microuniverse which exists only in my mind, a mixture of reality, imagination, barbarism and poetic gentleness' (author's translation) (quoted Bou 1988: 367).

Those works in which Porcel creates this mythical world are characterized by a brilliant, baroque prose style, and also by the presence of an occasionally gratuitous violence which recalls the *tremendismo* associated with **Cela**. A case in point is the 1968 novel *Els argonautes* (The Argonauts). The Andratx series culminates in *Difunts sota els ametlles en flor* (Dead Men Beneath the Almond Tree), which won the 1970 Josep Pla Prize. *Difunts sota els ametlles en flor* lacks a novelistic thread and is rather a series of portraits of eccentric human types set against the background of the mythicized Andratx. The term 'background' is something of a misnomer in this case, as the setting acquires a central importance in the work. It is perhaps in *Difunts sota els ametlles en flor* that Porcel's delight in storytelling for storytelling's sake is most evident.

Since the death of Franco, Porcel has attempted to make his fiction more cosmopolitan, for example in his 1984 work *Els dies immortals* (The Immortal Days). In addition to prose fiction and plays, Porcel has written travel books, as well as numerous press articles, in *La* ***Vanguardia***, *Destino*, *Tele-estel* and **Serra d'Or**. He has written on polemical international issues, for example in *El conflicto árabe-israelí* (The Arab-Israeli Conflict) (1968), and in 1977 published a bibliography of politicians, including Josep Tarradellas and Jordi **Pujol**.

Further reading

Bou, E. (1988) 'La literatura actual', in M. de Riquer, A. Comas and J. Molas (eds) *Història de la literatura catalana*, 11 vols, Barcelona: Ariel, XI (a general introduction to the work of Porcel).

Marfany, J.-L. (1988) 'El realisme històric', in M. de Riquer, A. Comas and J. Molas (eds) *Història de la literatura catalana*, 11 vols, Barcelona: Ariel, XI (sees Porcel as an exponent of historical realism up until the end of the 1960s).

DAVID GEORGE

pornography

The ill-defined threat of an invasion of 'pornography', usually linked to communist subversion, was one of the themes of right-wing propaganda during the Franco regime and the years immediately afterwards. This was the terminology used by **Carrero Blanco**, in a report to Franco in October 1969, when he complained about what he saw as the excessive liberalization introduced by **Fraga Iribarne**'s **Press Law** of 1966. That the Press Law was a restrictive measure which still provided for **censorship** was not enough to assuage right-wing fears.

Carrero did not live to see his fears realized, as they undoubtedly would have been, given the increase in sexually explicit magazines and films which flooded the market after the lifting of censorship restrictions in the late 1970s. To those belonging to the generation which as recently as 1972 had had to travel across the border into France to see *Last Tango in Paris*, the change seemed either exhilarating or catastrophic, depending on one's point of view. The perception that the sexual revolution in Spain was particularly dramatic, aptly summed up by the use of the term *el destape* (the uncorking of the bottle), derives from the fact that it contrasted so radically with what had gone before. It is probably true to say, however, that within a relatively short time the volume of pornography had settled down to a level comparable to that in most countries in western Europe.

Compared to countries like Britain, however, there are fewer controls to protect the young from exposure to pornographic material, except in the cinema. The socialist **PSOE** government which came into office in 1982 decided to regulate films, and in 1984 the first 'X' cinema, specializing in sexually explicit and violent material, was opened, which largely obviated the need for classification. The situation with regard to television, however, is rather different. Though some norms designed to avoid advocacy of violence and protect standards of taste were introduced for advertising in 1990, these are rather general, and there is no provision for preventing the screening of 'adult' material in advertisements at any time of the day. Other forms of television output are largely unregulated. Pornographic material in the form of **comics** is openly displayed in department stores and **fast food outlets** such as **VIPS**, which commonly cater for family parties.

See also: kiosk literature; *Movida, la*; sexual behaviour; social attitudes

Further reading

Hooper, J. (1995) *The New Spaniards*, Harmondsworth: Penguin (chapter 10 gives a reliable overview of various aspects of the sexual revolution).

EAMONN RODGERS

Portal Nicolás, Marta

b. 1930, Nava (Asturias)

Writer

Professional academic, journalist, essayist and novelist, Portal won the 1966 **Planeta Prize** with a pseudo-feminist novel of male philandering, *A tientas y a ciegas* (Blindly and Gropingly). Her collected novelettes comprise *El malmuerto* (Murdered). Study in Latin America resulted in scholarly essays on corn and on novels of the Mexican Revolution. *A ras de las sombras* (Level with the Shadows), fiction, preceeded another adultery novel, *Ladridos a la luna* (Howling at the Moon), again showing the woman trapped in a failed marriage. Later titles include *La veintena* (Twenty Stories) and *El buen camino* (The Good Road).

Further reading

García Viñó, M. (1984) 'Marta Portal: De la estética al conocimiento', *Arbor* 117: 127–31 (concerns her 1984 novel, *Pago de traición* – Payment for Treachery).

Pérez, J. (1988) *Contemporary Women Writers of Spain*, Boston, MA: G.K. Hall, pp. 164–5 (brief panorama of life and works).

JANET PÉREZ

pottery

Spain has a very long tradition of ceramic crafts, producing earthenware, decorative tiles and fine porcelain, often with distinctive regional variations.

Potteries were already flourishing in Castile, Aragon, Catalonia, Andalusia and Valencia at the time of the reconquest of Spain from the Moors, and the modern beautifully coloured Manises, Teruel, Granada, Talavera, and Puente del Arzobispo (Toledo) wares all derive ultimately from these long-established centres of production. In addition to its traditional forms, which included, especially in earlier periods, large decorated storage jars (*tinajas*), Spanish pottery has also been influenced by styles from abroad, particularly in the eighteenth and nineteenth centuries. Artistic movements have also had an impact, especially in Catalonia, where the advent of **Modernism** and later ***Noucentisme*** was exemplified in the work of potters such as Antoni Serra i Fiter (1869–1932), Francesc Quer (1853–1933), Josep Aragay (1889–1969) and Josep Guardiola (1869–1950). Of particular importance for the development of modern art pottery was Josep Llorens Artigas (1892–1980). Trained in Barcelona and returning there in 1941 after some years in Paris, he won international recognition and major awards for his work, which was particularly noted for the quality of the glazing. He collaborated with major artists, and especially with Joan **Miró**, producing pots, sculptures and large ceramic murals, such as those in the UNESCO building in Paris (1958), Harvard University (1960) and Barcelona Airport (1971).

The use of decorative glazed ceramic tiles (*azulejos*) on the lower half of walls, fountains and benches was a typical Moorish feature of the earliest formal gardens in the south of Spain, and examples of various types used as architectural decoration are to be seen in the Alcázar and the cathedral and churches of Seville, and the Alhambra in Granada. As new techniques developed, especially for easier mass production, so did the use of tiles for coats-of-arms over gateways, for panels such as the blue and white ones in the Alcázar and the Escorial, and for ceilings, floors and kitchens. As with traditional wares, there were distinctive regional styles of tile decoration, as well as changes in fashion under influences from abroad. In Catalonia **Gaudí**, **Domènech i Montaner** and **Puig i Cadafalch** made extensive and effective use of tiles in the Modernist style. Tile production continues to be an important industry in Spain, accounting for some 14 percent of the world total for paving and wall covering, with Porcelanosa tiles being particularly well known abroad.

Among the treasures remaining from earlier centuries is the fabulous Porcelain Room in the Royal Palace at Aranjuez, the walls and ceiling of which are fully decorated with porcelain plaques crafted between 1760 and 1765 by Giuseppe Gricci of the Royal Buen Retiro Factory, Madrid. This was established in 1759 by Charles III with the help of Italian artists, and continued production with changes of style until 1808 when it was occupied by the French. Porcelain was also produced between 1775 and 1895 at the Alcora factory which had been opened for the production of earthenware in 1727. In 1951 three brothers set up a workshop in their own house in Almácera, Valencia, moving eight years later to Tavernes Blanques, and in 1969 building the workshop known as La Ciudad de la Porcelana (City of Porcelain) and thus establishing the first of the world famous **Lladró** factories which export their distinctive figurines to well over one hundred countries.

Particularly fine collections of Spanish ceramics are to be seen in the Museum of Decorative Arts, Madrid; the Ceramics Museum of Manises, which traces the history of the local industry from the fourteenth century to the present day, and the Ceramics Museum of Valencia, which houses collections from the thirteenth to the nineteenth century, including tiled floors from Valencian mansions and five pieces of Picasso pottery.

See also: crafts; visual arts

EAMONN RODGERS

poverty

Unlike Britain, where disparities in income have been growing wider, the gap between rich and poor in Spain has gradually been narrowing. In Britain the poorest 40 percent of the population receives 14.6 percent of the national income; in Spain the same proportion receives 21 percent. The difference between the disposable income of the poorest 10 percent of households and the richest 10 percent has narrowed significantly, largely as a result of the redistributive effect of fiscal and social welfare legislation (see also **national income**). Nevertheless as the accompanying table indicates there is still a marked disparity of disposable income between the poorest households and the richest.

While the poverty threshold in a given society cannot be objectively established, if we take half of average income as the dividing line between poverty and sufficiency, a Spanish family in which

Income levels of Spanish households and population according to FOESSA

Monthly income per person in pesetas	*Families*		*Population*	
	%	*cumulative*	%	*cumulative*
Up to 15,000	1.25	1.25	2.10	2.10
15,000–19,000	1.22	2.47	1.82	3.92
19,000–26,000	3.78	6.25	4.78	8.70
26,000–38,000	11.12	17.37	12.52	21.22
38,000–47,000	11.68	29.05	12.15	33.37
47,000–57,000	12.85	41.90	12.62	45.99
57,000–66,000	9.56	51.46	9.54	55.53
66,000–75,000	8.74	60.20	8.66	64.19
75,000–94,000	12.53	72.73	12.04	76.23
94,000–113,000	8.96	81.69	8.39	84.62
113,000–132,000	5.60	87.29	5.25	89.87
132,000–151,000	3.46	90.75	3.09	92.96
151,000–170,000	2.44	93.19	1.94	94.90
170,000–189,000	1.80	94.99	1.56	96.46
189,000–227,000	2.28	97.27	1.71	98.17
227,000–265,000	1.38	98.65	0.92	99.09
265,000+	1.35	100.00	0.91	100.00

the income per person is below 38,000 pesetas per month at 1992 prices could reasonably be classed as poor in relation to the bulk of the population. As we can see from the table, applying this basic criterion would mean that some 17 percent of Spanish households (accounting for about a fifth of the population) would be classified as poor, a slightly lower proportion than in Britain (although in neither case can we speak of destitution), and some allowance may need to be made for the fact that the FOESSA survey was carried out in 1993, a time of severe recession when unemployment in Spain had reached an historic high of 3.6 million.

Inadequate material means by reference to a given norm is by definition what characterizes poverty, but both the level of poverty and the conditions which produce it vary substantially. In Spain, according to the Fifth FOESSA Report of 1993, 3.6 percent of the population lives in what the authors term severe poverty (below one quarter of average income) and 16.5 percent lives in relative poverty (between one quarter and one half of average income). The condition of poverty invariably displays concomitant features of which the following are the most common: long-term unemployment; temporary, poorly remunerated employment; large families subsisting on state benefits; elderly people on minimum pensions; lack of educational qualifications; illegal immigrant status; drug addiction; and social marginalization. Finally, it is worth noting that regional differences in wealth are very marked in Spain, with poorer regions having a GDP per capita half that of the richer regions. Income differentials are often spatially conditioned, with incomes in rural areas being far below those in urban areas, whilst migration into the cities has contributed to the creation of an urban underclass lacking in means. Despite the general atmosphere of prosperity and wealth, begging is an extremely common sight in Spanish cities.

Further reading

Córdoba Ordóñez, J. and García Alvarado, J.M. (1991) *Geografía de la pobreza y la desigualdad*, Madrid: Editorial Síntesis (less complete than the FOESSA report but more readable).

Fundación FOESSA (1994) *V Informe sociológico sobre la situación social de España*, Madrid: Fundación FOESSA, vol. 1, pp. 273–334 (the social survey of Spain par excellence and an indispensable sociological tool). Longhurst, C.A. (1997) 'Poverty Amidst Affluence in Contemporary Spain', *International Journal of Iberian Studies*, Vol. 10: 3, 133–146 (a review of the problem for the non-specialist).

C.A. LONGHURST

PP

The Partido Popular (Popular Party) emerged from the **Popular Alliance** in 1989, at which date José María **Aznar** succeeded Manuel **Fraga Iribarne** as leader. This marked a decisive stage in its development into the main opposition party during the later stages of socialist (**PSOE**) hegemony between 1982 and 1993. Internal reorganization and a change of image were intended to increase PP's credibility as an alternative government, and it was rewarded with success in municipal elections, and in elections to the parliaments of the various **autonomous communities**. Though it narrowly failed to win a majority in the general elections of 1993, by 1995 it was the governing party in three-quarters of the autonomous communities and in all the large cities except for La Coruña in Galicia, and the cities in the Basque country and Catalonia. It won enough votes in the general elections of 1996 to form a minority government, with the support of the Basque and Catalan nationalist parties, the **PNV** and **CiU**.

The advance of PP is partly explicable in terms of a combination of strong central organization and widely disseminated local groups. Its change of name in 1989 reflected a desire not only to assimilate it to other mainstream European parties of the centre-right, but also to emphasize structural coherence, rather than the notion of a coalition which its previous title had suggested. The adoption of new symbols, reflecting an increasing emphasis on marketing of its image, was an attempt to forge links with various social constituencies, and develop external relations. In economic affairs, PP adopted a neo-liberal approach, which won support from the employers' organization,

CEOE. Relations with other interests have been institutionalized via a specific section of the Executive Committee, and the party has displayed greater professionalism in cultivating the media. Expert professional help has been sought for planning party activities and training leadership cadres. This new professionalism, and its change of image had as much to do with its electoral victory in 1996 as had the recession, the exhaustion of PSOE after fourteen years in power, and the prevalence of corruption during the socialist mandate.

In 1990 PP formally applied to join the European Popular Party, the Christian Democratic grouping in the European Parliament, and since then has increased its international participation in centre-right politics, both in Europe and Latin America.

See also: political parties; politics

Further reading

Heywood, P. (1995) *The Government and Politics of Spain*, London: Macmillan (see pp. 203–8 for an excellent brief account of the rise of the 'new right' in Spain).

López Nieto, L. (1998) 'The Organizational Dynamics of AP–PP' in P. Ignacio and E. Ysmal (eds) (1998) *The Organization of Political Parties in Southern Europe*, Westport, CT and London: Praeger, pp. 254–69.

Ross, C.J. (1997) *Contemporary Spain: A Handbook*, London: Arnold (pp. 63–8 offer a lucid summary of the evolution of PP in relation to its predecessors and right-wing partners).

LOURDES LÓPEZ NIETO

Prado Museum

The Prado Museum, Madrid, houses a world-famous art collection, which includes masterpieces by Velázquez, Goya, El Greco, Bosch and Murillo, to name but a few.

Founded by Ferdinand VII to make public a large part of the royal collection formed by the Hapsburg and Bourbon kings, the Prado opened as the Royal Museum of Paintings in 1819, in a building designed originally for an Academy and Museum of Natural Sciences by Juan de Villanueva. Its original holding of 311 paintings was later augmented by the incorporation of the Museo de la Trinidad, a collection of works of art that had passed into state control from religious establishments in Madrid, Avila, Segovia and Toledo. Further purchases, the New Acquisitions, form the third section of the total collection of some 7,500 paintings, a photographic record of which was completed in 1990, and forms the basis of the three-volume catalogue. A new catalogue of the 900 or so pieces of sculpture which it also houses was published in 1994.

By 1994 pressure on space was such that only about 1,000 of the paintings could be exhibited in the original Villanueva building and in the Casón del Buen Retiro. Some 4,000 were in store, the so-called 'Hidden Prado', and the rest, the 'Dispersed Prado', was on loan to embassies, museums and churches. That year the head of the trustees was driven to speak openly of leaks in the roof, rats in the cellars, shortages in exhibition space, and totally inadequate security arrangements (not to mention space for only twenty umbrellas), a situation which had not been helped by inadequate funding and rather frequent changes in the directorship of the Museum.

In the same year submissions of projects for the expansion of the Museum were invited to an open international contest to be held in 1996, though it was the considered view of a previous director that a more rigorous selection for the permanent collection would make more effective use of the existing space. The expansion was to incorporate the Army Museum building and the ruined Hieronymite Cloisters, since the nearby Villahermosa palace had been dedicated to the **Thyssen-Bornemisza Museum**. In the meantime it was decided in 1995 to rationalize the Museum's holdings by transferring some 500 post-1881 works to the **Queen Sofia Museum**, to which **Picasso**'s *Guernica* had already been moved amid great controversy in 1992.

In 1996, following a change of government, a new director was appointed who promised to strengthen the scientific and research aspects of the Museum, creating five new curatorships, and giving the trustees new managerial powers. After a surprise failure of the judges to award a first prize in the international contest, it was decided to proceed with the plans for expansion, which had been set in train by the decision to transfer the Army Museum exhibits to Toledo. The use of the Hieronymite Cloisters site was sanctioned in November 1977, following protracted negotiations with the Archbishop of Madrid.

See also: art collections; art exhibitions; arts funding; arts policy; cultural institutions and movements; Ministry of Culture; museums; painting; visual arts

EAMONN RODGERS

Prados, Emilio

b. 1899, Málaga; d. 1962, Mexico City

Writer

Emilio Prados is one of the lesser-known figures in contemporary Spanish poetry, whose work only began to receive the critical acclaim it deserves after his death, owing to its combination of breadth and complexity. Prados' opus includes nearly two dozen published collections of poetry, in addition to several unpublished collections that appeared for the first time in his posthumous *Poesías completas* (Complete Poems) (1975–6), as well as hundreds of individual compositions published in anthologies, journals and newspapers. The deeply philosophical nature of Prados' poetry makes it difficult to penetrate. A study of the poet's manuscripts reveals a myriad of theological and philosophical influences, ranging from Heraclitus, to the Bible, to St John of the Cross. Despite these multifarious influences, Prados' philosophical digressions coalesce into one internalized ideological struggle which was a constant source of torment for him over the course of his life: the struggle between his unrelenting search for a Platonic ideal or absolute truth, and his strong sense of commitment to the betterment of humanity. Prados' work, from his earliest collections, *Tiempo* (Time) (1925) and *Vuelta* (Return) (1927), to the later *Circuncisión del sueño* (Circumcision of a Dream) (1957) and *La piedra escrita* (The Written Stone) (1961) is a kind of poetic odyssey, a tireless search to find himself in what he called 'signs of being', or elements from the material world which, in a metaphorical sense, represent his own metaphysical aspirations. This search, Prados believed, would one day culminate in the discovery of his true identity.

Prados was noted for his unflagging commitment to the cause of the Spanish Republic. During the Civil War he collaborated with María **Zambrano** on the journal *Hora de España*, and in 1937 was awarded the National Prize for Poetry for his collection of Civil War poems, *Destino fiel* (Faithful Destiny) (written 1937, first published in *Poesías completas*). Prados left Spain just prior to the Nationalist takeover and went into exile in Mexico. Emotionally and financially destitute, he relied on the help of his brother Miguel and friends like Octavio Paz to help him through those difficult years. But it was his poetry that gave Prados a real sense of purpose. In *Jardín cerrado* (Confined Garden) (1946), hailed as Prados' masterpiece, he likens himself to a sapling poplar transplanted into foreign soil and yearning for his lost garden, Spain. The poet would remain sentimentally attached to his *querida patria* (beloved homeland), decorating the walls of his apartment with photographs of past acquaintances, and maintaining correspondence with some of the fishermen from Málaga to whom he had preached **Marxism** in the early 1930s.

Prados spent his final years living as a recluse. Those who knew him during this period described him as excessively maudlin and uncommunicative. In 1962 he died of a bronchial illness that had plagued him most of his adult life.

See also: poetry

Further reading

Blanco Aguinaga, C. (1960) *Emilio Prados: Vida y obra*, New York: Columbia University Press (a biography of the poet; appears also as the Introduction to Prados' *Poesías completas*).

Hernández Pérez, P. (1988) *Emilio Prados: La memoria del olvido*, 2 vols, Zaragoza: Prensas Universitarias (a comprehensive study of one of Prados' most significant works).

Sánchis-Banús, J. (1987) *Seis lecciones: Emilio Prados, su vida, su obra, su mundo*, Valencia: Pre-Textos (the most complete study to date by the premier Prados scholar).

ROBERTO CARLOS MANTEIGA

prensa del corazón

This phrase, which means literally 'press of the heart' is the generic description of the magazines which fill the gap created by the absence of society or gossip columns in newspapers. They are represented most characteristically by ***¡HOLA!***, which gave rise in 1988 to an English-language edition, *Hello!*. A product initially of the escapist attitude fostered by **Francoist culture**, publications of this type, which include *Pronto*, *Lecturas*, *Semana* and *Diez Minutos*, continue long after the demise of the regime to minister to the seemingly insatiable fascination of the Spanish public with the rich and famous, particularly if they are women: Isabel Preysler, the princesses Stephanie and Caroline of Monaco, and film personalities like Ana **Belén** have received ample coverage. Sales figures fluctuate greatly, owing to the Spanish preference for buying from newsstands rather than taking out subscriptions, but these publications are among the best-selling items in the periodical market, with sales of several hundred thousand copies per week.

See also: kiosk literature; press; readership

EAMONN RODGERS

press

History

After the Civil War, Franco decreed the expropriation of all newspapers owned or run by parties, unions or individuals with Republican sympathies, and by 1940 they had all become the property of the **National Movement**, the only legal political party in Franco's Spain. Thus the Madrid daily *El Sol* became the **Falange** newspaper *Arriba*, and many provincial newspapers of liberal leanings became mouthpieces for fascism. New titles were also added, notably the organ of the **vertical syndicates** (Falangist-inspired unions), *Pueblo*, a Madrid evening paper. In all, some forty titles made up the state-owned stake in the newspaper industry, including the bigger of Spain's two news agencies, **Agencia EFE**. The only titles in the private sector were mostly Catholic (e.g. *Ya*) and monarchist (e.g. ***ABC***). **Censorship** and strict government control of the written press was relaxed slightly in 1966, when a **Press Law** was passed by Manuel **Fraga Iribarne**, then Minister of Information. The law, although restrictive by western standards and very unpopular in its day, gave newspaper editors a greater degree of freedom: restrictions on criticism of the principles of the National Movement or political institutions or leaders still remained, but the concept of adherence to 'truth and morals' allowed for a certain flexibility in interpretation.

Until the 1970s, most of the government-controlled newspapers were profitable or required only small subsidies, but by the end of Franco's regime (1975), their circulation had plummeted and they became a serious financial liability as well as a political embarrassment to successive governments of the democratic transition. The 1975 watershed marked the appearance of new general dailies: *El* ***País*** and *Diario 16* (Madrid), and ***El Periódico de Catalunya*** (Barcelona). There are marked differences between these newspapers and those which were published under the dictatorship: the new papers have liberal leanings and a cleaner, more modern look whereas the old ones are more conservative and retain antiquated methods of presentation. Also, several non-Castilian language dailies appeared, notably ***Avui*** (written entirely in Catalan), and *Deia* and ***Egin*** (written partly in Basque). By the late 1970s, a series of economic crises (paper prices, heavy losses in advertising and circulation revenue) affected the industry badly, particularly the well-established, traditional titles, which had been losing ground steadily to the newcomers. An exception to this was probably the ultra right-wing *El Alcázar*, whose circulation (largely among the **armed forces**) trebled and peaked in the early 1980s, though it closed in the early 1990s.

In 1981, the centre-right **UCD** government passed a bill authorizing the auction of the bulk of the Movimiento titles to the private sector. Later, successive socialist administrations sold off the remainder, mainly to local businessmen and institutions. From the mid-1980s, Spain's daily press has undergone a process of technological modernization, partly aided by financial support from the administration, which subsidized some initiatives and developed a joint programme to encourage **readership** among students. The next strategy was internationalization. Many of the larger circulation papers own shares or have agreements involving the exchange of news with the foreign press and no fewer than a dozen newspapers, including most notably *ABC*, ***La Vanguardia*** and *El País*, have established a strong presence in the Internet.

The daily press

One of the most salient features of the Spanish written media is the low circulation of the daily press. However, in spite of the fact that only one in ten people buy a daily paper, 25 percent of the country's citizens read the daily press. The explanation for this lies in the Spanish habit of sharing reading matter, particularly in public and social venues, such as bars, cafés and clubs, in the absence of a 'popular' British tabloid-style press, and in the perception that newspaper reading is essentially a middle-class habit.

The profession is indeed dominated by middle-class intellectuals, who have been unable to create products that would appeal to the working class, as shown by the unsuccesful ventures of dailies such as *Diario Libre* in 1978. *El Periódico de Catalunya* and *Diario 16*, which purport to fit into this market, largely because of their larger headlines and abundance of photographs, have been successful because their news coverage is essentially still 'serious', with political and economic news taking precedence over stories of crimes, the lives of celebrities or scandals. Spaniards prefer to read about these issues in weekly or fortnightly glossy publications, which enjoy much popular acclaim and high profits, plugging the coverage gaps left by the newspaper industry.

In Spain, there are some 155 dailies, the majority of which are local or regional. The daily papers, which increased their circulation by two and a half million from 1989 to 1994, were able to maintain these readership figures for the Monday to Friday editions throughout 1994, while registering a sharp rise in demand for the weekend editions. The organization which controls and monitors the readership of the written media (96 percent of newspapers, 90 percent of the large-circulation magazines and 52 percent of technical and professional publications) is the Oficina de Justificación de la Difusión (OJD) (Circulation Audit Office). It is the only reliable source uniformly respected by advertisers and media professionals. According to their figures for 1994, the leading national daily was the newspaper *El País*, with an average readership of 408,267 per day in 1994, an increase of just over 7,000 copies on the 1993 figure. In second place was *ABC*, with an average of 321,517 copies a day. The newspaper with the third largest readership in Spain was ***El Mundo***, with a circulation of 268,748, followed by the Catalan dailies *La Vanguardia* (207,112) and *El Periódico de Catalunya* (193,576), although most of their readership is exclusively Catalan. The sales leaders, *El País*, *ABC* and *El Mundo*, are national dailies published in Madrid, although they publish regional editions in some of the **autonomous communities**.

Readership of Sunday supplements is also led by *El País Semanal* (1,058,584 copies weekly, a record figure in the history of Spanish journalism), compared with 632,649 for *Blanco y Negro* (*ABC*), 436,242 for *La Revista* (*El Mundo*) and 338,629 for *La Vanguardia*. The OJD has also certified an average distribution of 11,170 copies for *El País Internacional* and 3,515 for *ABC Internacional*, which are sold worldwide mainly through subscription.

The daily press also includes sports newspapers, noted for their very high readership. Among the ten most widely sold dailies, two papers are exclusively dedicated to sports, *As* and *Marca*.

Another type of newspaper which has experienced great success is the economic journal. A large number of new publications devoted to this field appeared in the late 1980s and early 1990s, including dailies, and the most important national newspapers publish special supplements on economic issues.

See also: media; press ownership

RAMÓN PARRONDO

Press Law

The *Ley de Prensa e Imprenta* (1966) was an attempt by the then Minister for Information and Tourism, Manuel **Fraga Iribarne**, to introduce a modest liberalization of the laws affecting printed matter. The Press Law abolished *censura previa* (pre-publication censorship) for newspapers, but this did not mean complete removal of restrictions. Criticism of Franco, the Falange, the armed forces or the basic structure of the regime was still outlawed, and publishers, editors and journalists could face stiff fines if they were deemed to be in breach of this prohibition. The main effect of the law was to turn newspaper editors into censors by obliging them to engage in self-censorship prior to publication. The prospect of heavy fines and the financial loss resulting from confiscation of published editions meant that they tended to err on the side of caution. Furthermore, not only was the new law unclear as to the limits of permitted discussion, but it empowered the minister to classify certain information as 'reserved', a definition which in 1970 was used to suppress reporting of University matters, and of Franco's travel arrangements.

Although it was no longer compulsory to refer books and journals to the censors prior to publication, in practice most authors and publishers continued to do so. Despite the exercise of prior self-censorship, the proportion of works of all kinds in which cuts were required before authorization went up from an average of 6.5 percent in the decade prior to 1966 to 8.8 percent in the following decade, though the annual figure went down to 1.4 percent in 1975. The highest annual figure in the decade prior to the enactment of the Press Law was 9.8 in 1965, but in the four years after the act, the average annual percentage of works subjected to cuts was 12.9, with a peak of 15.9 in 1968.

These figures, however, give an over-pessimistic picture of the situation if taken in isolation. They certainly testify to the continuing vigilance of the censors, but also suggest that authors and publishers were being more adventurous in testing the limits of the freedoms made available by the new law. In this connection, it is relevant to note that the annual average number of publications submitted to the censors went up by over 80 percent, from 610 in the period 1955–65, to 1,102 between 1966 and 1975. This reflects an increase in the absolute numbers of publications appearing, which suggests that the new law did have some effect in creating a more flexible and vital cultural climate. But perhaps the most telling piece of evidence is that Franco became so enraged by the increasingly critical tone of the press, especially in exposing government corruption, that he sacked Fraga Iribarne in 1969.

See also: Francoist culture

Further reading

Abellán, M.L. (1980) *Censura y creación literaria en España (1939–1976)*, Barcelona: Ediciones Penísula (chapters 6 and 7 of Part 2 give a clear account of the content and operation of the Press Law).

Gubern, R. (1981) *La censura: Función política y ordenamiento jurídico bajo el franquismo (1936–1975)*, Barcelona: Ediciones Penísula (the first part of chapter 6 gives a useful short account of the context and effects of the law).

EAMONN RODGERS

press ownership

The diversity of press ownership in Spain before 1936 gave way after the Civil War to rigid state control, which allowed only sympathizers or governmental institutions to run newspapers. After Franco's death, the return of democracy, accompanied by a free-enterprise economic system, restored proprietorial freedom. In the new democratic Spain, newspapers increasingly constitute one component in diversified media groups, while the nation's European outlook has attracted the presence of international companies, especially in the expanding special-interest market.

Under the Second Republic (1931–6), ownership ranged from private individuals and families to trade unions and the Roman Catholic church. In the ensuing Civil War (1936–9), the victorious rebel forces appropriated newspapers in occupied areas, while the consequent Press Law (1938) made them the servants of an authoritarian state which restricted ownership to sympathizers. Confiscated publications reappeared under new titles as part of the subsidized press of the **National Movement**, established in 1940.

Papers previously owned by monarchist interests, ***ABC*** and *La* ***Vanguardia***, were returned to their owners, but with editors imposed or approved by government. The other permitted independent interest group, the church, controlled the national daily *Ya*, as well as regional and weekly publications. The ascendancy of the Catholic organization **Opus Dei** from the late 1950s encouraged the existence of periodicals owned or influenced by leading members. From a reader's perspective, though, ownership seemed secondary, because of state control of the contents via **censorship** and directives. Conditions moderated somewhat in the 1960s as a result of the regime's wish to seem less repressive (see also **Press Law**). Journals owned by interests favouring pluralism appeared, notably *Cuadernos para el Diálogo* and the re-launched ***Revista de Occidente***.

Radical change awaited Franco's demise. *El* ***País***, whose origins stretched back to 1972, finally appeared in May 1976, with shareholders of diverse political opinions, and, as the democratizing project of Adolfo **Suárez** took shape, other new titles were launched. The populist *Diario 16* was spawned in October 1976 by ***Cambio 16***, the magazine set up by sixteen progressive businessmen and journalists in 1971. Regional political interests in Catalonia and the Basque country inaugurated dailies in Catalan and Basque, ***Avui*** (1976) and *Deia* (1977). On the abolition of the National Movement (1977), its newspapers reverted to the state, which unhurriedly sold them to private, often regionally-based, interests.

At national level the increasing play of market forces brought commercial criteria to the fore. Established papers under family ownership (*La Vanguardia* and *ABC*) were restructured. Narrowly based political and general interest magazines, not only the outstanding *Cuadernos para el Diálogo* and *Triunfo*, but also *Doblón*, *Mundo*, *Posible*, and various others, folded when abandoned by their readers. Successful companies diversified: ***Interviú***, a weekly with pin-ups launched in May 1976 by a group led by Antonio Asensio, gave rise to the daily, *El* ***Periódico de Catalunya***, in 1978. The football newspaper *Marca*, previously part of the National Movement press, was bought by Punto Editorial (which later became Recoletos) in 1984, and, after modernization, greater professionalism, and support from the British Pearson group, it became in the early 1990s the most read daily paper. Other foreign-based multinational groups – Bertelsmann, Hachette, Haymarket, Rizzoli and Springer – entered the market, encouraged by Spain's European aspirations, launching special-interest periodicals or setting up joint ventures with Spanish groups.

Several prominent or established players experienced failures, as national dailies competed for an intractably static readership. The Roman Catholic Church, owner of *Ya*, sold its newspapers in 1988 to the business group Bilbao Editorial/Comecosa. Further owners and difficulties ensued and the title even closed briefly in 1996. *El Independiente*, launched as a weekly in 1987, became a daily in 1989, but after a controlling interest was sold to the **ONCE**, and despite subsequent rescue attempts, it finally disappeared (1991). Germán Sánchez Ruipérez, majority shareholder of book publisher Anaya, launched a national daily, *El Sol*, in May 1990, which folded after twenty-two months. Shorter-lived still was the sensationalist daily, *Claro*, the result of collaboration between *ABC* and the German publisher Springer; born in April 1991, it was defunct four months later.

The only success among new national dailies has been *El* ***Mundo***, created in 1989 by Spanish interests centred on a previous major shareholder in the 16 Group, Alfonso de Salas; within two years the Italian company Rizzoli-Corriere della Sera owned 45 percent of the paper. The ailing 16 Group, under administration after being taken over by the financier José Luis Domínguez, reverted in August 1996 to its founder and former chairman, Juan Tomás de Salas. Only PRISA, owner of *El País*, has grown consistently, to embrace **radio**, **television** and publishing interests, its originally broad ownership subsequently concentrating around Jesús de Polanco.

Since the late 1980s there have been constant changes of ownership or control in Spain's press, with Spain's principal banks as covert leading protagonists. Precise, up-to-date information is not easy to obtain; most companies are not listed on the Spanish stock exchange, and in certain instances, the outstanding case being the Luca de Tena family who control *ABC*, ownership disguises control. Readership remains low, while titles come and go. Successful innovation has centred primarily on special-interest publications. The most buoyant have concerned hobbies, finance and sport, particularly football. A successful group may own a national daily, a sporting and financial title, as well as special-interest magazines. Current forecasts predict increased concentration of ownership, based on internationally oriented multimedia companies.

See also: Agencia EFE; cultural institutions and movements; journalism; kiosk literature; media; *prensa del corazón*; readership

Further reading

Barrera, C. (1995). *Sin mordaza. Veinte años de prensa en democracia*, Madrid: Temas de hoy (the fullest account of the press since 1975).

Deacon, P. (1995). *The Press as Mirror of the New Spain*, Bristol: Department of Hispanic, Portuguese and Latin-American Studies, University of Bristol (the press from political, economic and social perspectives).

Edo, C. (1994) *La crisis de la prensa diaria. La línea editorial y la trayectoria de los periódicos de Madrid*, Barcelona: Ariel (focused on policies, ownership and circulation).

Hooper, J. (1995). *The New Spaniards*, Harmondsworth: Penguin (chapter twenty-one traces general and specific trends in the media).

PHILIP DEACON

Prince of Asturias Prizes

The Prince of Asturias Prizes are administered and conferred by the Prince of Asturias **Foundation**, set up in 1980, whose President is the heir to the throne of Spain. There are eight prizes, each consisting of a sum of 5m pesetas, plus a reproduction of a sculpture by Joan **Miró**. The categories are arts, communication and humanities, international co-operation, literature, peace, scientific and technical research, social sciences and sport.

The Prince of Asturias Prize is one of the most prestigious **prizes** awarded in Spain, and is often used to honour distinguished international figures as well as Spaniards. Previous winners have included the Spanish writers Camilo José **Cela** and Francisco **Umbral**, the Mexican novelist Juan Rulfo, and the Peruvian writer and former presidential candidate Mario Vargas Llosa; in the field of politics, Mikhail Gorbachev, Nelson Mandela, Isaac Rabin and Yasser Arafat; in sport, Sebastian Coe and Martina Navratilova; in the arts, Antoni **Tàpies**, Eduardo **Chillida** and Joaquín **Rodrigo**.

The prizes are not confined to individuals, but may be awarded to groups and institutions. For example, the United Nations High Commission for Refugees has been honoured, as has Médecins sans Frontières and an AIDS research foundation set up by Elizabeth Taylor. In 1998, a group of women who had worked for the advancement of women in various countries received the International Co-operation Prize. They included Graça Machel, Rigoberta Menchu and Emma Bonino.

The 1997 winners were, for arts: Vittorio Gassman; communication and humanities: Václav Havel, for his writing and his contribution to peace, and the Cable News Network (CNN), for the quality of its reporting; international co-operation: the Government of Guatemala and the organization National Guatemalan Revolutionary Unity, for bringing to an end a thirty-six-year Civil War; literature: the Colombian writer Alvaro Mutis; peace: Yehudi Menuhin and Mstislav Rostropovich; scientific and technical research: the team investigating fossil remains at the Atapuerca site (Burgos, Spain); social sciences: the Catalan philologist, historian and literary scholar Martín de Riquer; and sport: the Spanish marathon team, for its performance in the Athens Games in 1997.

The Prince of Asturias Foundation also fosters cultural and scholarly activity in other ways. It sponsors three choirs, funds activities specifically directed at preserving the cultural and environmental heritage of the Asturias region, provides grants for research and organizes conferences.

See also: arts funding; cultural institutions and movements; education and research

EAMONN RODGERS

prizes

One of the principal methods of promoting cultural activity in Spain is the award of prizes, of which there is a very large number, ranging from the highly prestigious **Prince of Asturias Prizes** to those awarded by local government bodies and small private foundations. The most prestigious literary prize is the **Cervantes Prize**, followed by the *Premio Nacional de las Letras Españolas* (National Prize for Literature), worth 5m pesetas, awarded for lifetime achievement in literature. Some are offered by publishing houses (e.g. **Planeta**), as a way of identifying and promoting writers with a high sales potential. The publisher Espasa-Calpe offers the Espasa essay prize (5m pesetas), won in 1996 by Manuel Leguineche for a study of the effects of war on children. The newspaper *El **País*** awards two prizes in memory of **Ortega y Gasset**, for reporting and photography respectively, endowed at 2m pesetas each. The *Premio de la Crítica* (Critics' Prize) for the novel is purely honorific, and carries no endowment. Patronage of culture and the arts is recognized by the award of the Juan Lladó Prize jointly by the Business Foundation and the Ortega y Gasset Foundation; it was won in 1994 by Jesús de Polanco, President of PRISA group, the publishers of *El País*.

The broadcast media also have access to a number of prizes, including the *Premio de Las Ondas* (Airwaves Prize), instituted by the radio network SER in 1953. Achievement in the film industry is marked principally by the Goya Prizes, awarded by the Academy of Cinema Arts and Sciences; as with the Oscars, there are prizes in numerous sections, such as directing, scriptwriting, camera-work, acting, and overall best film. The *Premio Nacional de Cinematografía* (National Cinematography Prize) (2m pesetas) was won jointly in 1993 by the director Víctor Erice and the film critic José Luis Guarner (posthumously).

EAMONN RODGERS

protest songs

Protest songs are essentially identified with the latter years of the Franco dictatorship, in the mid- to late 1960s. Though most of the repressive apparatus of the state remained in being, the relative relaxation of the **censorship** laws by **Fraga Iribarne** in 1966 encouraged a few singers, mostly from university and left-wing backgrounds, to begin evolving a new type of music, written and performed in semi-underground conditions. The roots of this new movement are to be found in American folksong and in poems by French singer-composers such as Leo Ferré, Jacques Brel or Georges Brassens. The targets of protest were the social injustices deriving from capitalist development, particularly acute in Spain, where there were no free **trade unions**, and more specifically political issues such as arbitrary arrest and the lack of **civil rights**. In those regions with a distinctive language and culture, especially Catalonia, protest songs focused on the denial of linguistic freedoms. Neither the singers nor their public were greatly concerned about the quality of the texts or the music, or the technical virtuosity of the performance, but welcomed the new development with an enthusiasm comparable only to the fervour of the persecuted Christians in the catacombs. By the 1960s, the regime was not in a position to repress such cultural manifestations completely, but frequently texts were censored, concerts were banned or broken up by the police, sometimes violently, and performance of the songs on radio or television was forbidden.

One of the most important centres of this kind of protest song was the Catalan-speaking regions, which produced their own brand, the ***Nova Cançó***. In the 1950s Catalonia already had a modest but significant recording industry, and, both there and in Valencia and the Balearic Islands, there was a long-standing commitment to the restoration of civil and cultural freedoms. Some songs became so popular that they virtually became hymns, which would be taken up even by Spanish-speaking audiences, who, though not sharing the language in which they were written, nevertheless identified with the rejection of the dictatorship and neoliberal capitalism which they expressed.

The protest song is not, however, exclusively Catalan. Paco Ibáñez, brought up in France by Spanish parents, became enormously popular, setting to music and performing, in Spanish, the works of 'social poets' such as José Agustín

Goytisolo or Blas de Otero, or classical authors like Góngora, Quevedo, and Juan Ruiz, whose satire against the moral corruption of their own age could be applied to the contemporary situation.

With the restoration of democracy, the protest song experienced a decline, though it has never been eclipsed completely. A few singers formerly active in this genre have continued working, such as Lluís **Llach**, whose music has evolved from explicit political commitment towards more personalized themes, and **Raimon**, who composes settings of classic poems. The phenomenon of the *cantautor*, the singer who composes and performs his own songs or settings, which was characteristic of the protest song movement of the Franco period, subsists in certain figures more tenuously connected with the tradition, such as the ever-popular Joan Manuel **Serrat**, an exponent of the *Nova Cançó* who now sings in Spanish. Víctor Manuel progressed from a mild, pastoral version of the protest song to a more overtly committed stance, as an active member of the **PCE**. Other representatives of the *cantautor* movement are José Antonio Labordeta, Luis Pastor, Carlos Cano, Hilario Camacho and Mikel Laboa.

Further reading

Boyle, C. (1995) 'The Politics of Popular Music: On the Dynamics of New Song', in H. Graham and J. Labanyi (eds) *Spanish Cultural Studies: An Introduction*, Oxford: Oxford University Press (a brief and interesting account of protest songs, with inevitable emphasis on Catalan singers).

Ordovás, J. (1991) 'Pop Music', in R. Gascón (ed.) *Spain Today: In Search of Modernity*, Madrid: Cátedra (a summary of the *Nova Cançó* and *cantautor* movements in Spain since the 1960s).

ENRIC DOLZ I FERRER

provincial administration

Spain's provinces were first established as entities of local administration in 1833. Until the new decentralized structure of the state was ushered in during the early 1980s, the country had fifty provinces, but following the creation of six single province **autonomous communities**, this number was reduced to forty-four. For national and regional elections, the province is the normal constituency.

Article 141.1 of the **constitution** states: 'The province is a local entity with its own legal status, consisting of a group of municipalities and representing a territorial division designed to carry out the activities of the state'. Thus, on the one hand, it clearly has a local function, and one of its major roles, via the *diputaciones provinciales* (provincial councils), is to provide a range of services not available to the smaller municipal authorities within its ambit. On the other hand, through the civil governor, appointed directly by the central government, the provinces continue to administer some functions traditionally delegated to them by Madrid. However, as the state has progressively devolved power to the autonomous communities, the latter function has tended to diminish in importance; provincial offices of regional ministries are now assuming more importance than those of central ministries. The funding for the regional offices comes from regional government while that for the other two areas of responsibility comes from central government.

The basic institutions of the *diputación provincial* are the full council (*pleno*) and the commission, the executive arm of the council. Each is headed by the president. The *pleno* is made up of provincial deputies who are normally elected indirectly from the councillors elected at the municipal elections. Seats are allocated according to a modified system of proportional representation. The president, usually the leader of the majority party, is elected at the first meeting of the council. The normal term of office for the president and deputies is four years.

The councils have no authority to draft major laws, only to implement those approved by national and regional parliaments. However, they can draft regulations (*ordenanzas*) which must conform to national/regional law. Among the main functions of the full councils are: to control and oversee the work of the commission; to approve annually a provincial plan for works and services in the municipalities; and to approve the annual budget drafted by the commission.

According to the law of 1985, among the major

responsibilities of the *diputación* are: to co-ordinate municipal services; to give legal, economic and technical assistance to the municipalities, particularly those of limited resources; and to provide province-wide services such as roads and bridges.

No post-Franco government has adequately tackled the problem of the serious duplication of administrative responsibilities at provincial level.

See also: elections; municipalities

Further reading

Newton, M.T with Donaghy, P.J. (1997) *Institutions of Modern Spain*, Cambridge: Cambridge University Press (chapter 8.4 deals with most aspects of provincial administration).

Solé-Vilanovas, J (1989) 'Spain: Regional and Local Government' in R.J. Bennett (ed.) *Territory and Administration in Europe*, London: Pinter, pp. 205–29

MICHAEL T. NEWTON

PSOE

The Partido Socialista Obrero Español (Spanish Socialist Workers' Party) was founded in 1879 in Madrid by a group of typesetters, led by Pablo Iglesias, a serious and austere man, who dominated the party until his death in 1925. The party initially grew slowly, particularly because it remained tied to its geographical base in Madrid. It thereby found it difficult to gain a foothold in the most industrialized region of Spain, Catalonia, where it faced strong competition from regionalist parties and the anarchist movement.

Although by the time of the Second Republic (1931–6), the PSOE had become the dominant party in Spain, its progress remained hampered by its organizational rigidity and a tension between its theoretical pronouncements, which were drenched in Marxist revolutionary rhetoric, and its practice, which was fundamentally reformist in nature. This tension led the Socialist Party to misinterpret the socio-economic context of 1930s Spain with the result that they placed too much faith in their ability to push through progressive social and economic reforms by parliamentary means. When it became apparent that all reforms, however mild in manner, would be resisted ferociously by the established order, the PSOE was unable to provide a response which might have forestalled the military revolt which heralded the beginning of the Civil War.

During the conflict itself the bitterly divided PSOE was sidelined by an increasingly dominant Communist Party (**PCE**) which benefited from the financial and logistical resources provided to the Republican government by the Soviet Union. By the end of the war the PSOE was split asunder by bitter divisions and recriminations leaving it a broken and defeated organization.

The divisions which had split the PSOE apart during the Second Republic were transferred wholesale into exile with the result that the exiled Socialist leadership remained embroiled in bitter recriminations concerning the causes of the Civil War. As a result, it became increasingly isolated from the party's grassroots militants remaining in Spain. Their inability to respond to the changing reality of events unfolding within Spain became especially evident from the 1960s onwards when young socialist groups within Spain forming the so-called Seville–Bilbao–Asturias triangle, began to challenge the exiled leadership for control of the party.

Once official recognition had been granted to these 'young Turks' of the interior by the Socialist International in 1972 the renovation of the party began in earnest. Led by Felipe **González**, who was elected to the post of first secretary in October 1974 at **Suresnes**, and his right-hand man, Alfonso **Guerra**, the PSOE initially emphasized its radical Marxist heritage. At its XXVII Congress in December 1976, the party adopted a radical Marxist stance and explicitly demanded a radical break with the present system.

However, following a negotiated transition to democracy under the guiding hand of Adolfo **Suárez** and the first general elections in 1977, the party leadership quickly realized that its Marxist identity would be an obstacle to further electoral progress. In particular, the need to consolidate Spain's still fragile democracy, especially following the military coup in 1981, became the raison d'être of the party and its main reason for dropping **Marxism** from the party's statutes. Electoral success could only be achieved by occupying the centre ground where the majority of the Spanish electorate placed itself and by adopting a catch-all strategy.

The ideological transformation of the Socialist Party into one of the most cautious social-democratic parties in Europe was accompanied by a series of much less publicized, though arguably more significant, organizational changes masterminded by Alfonso Guerra as deputy Secretary General of the party. At the PSOE's XXVIII Congress the number of delegations was dramatically reduced (50 as opposed to 1,000) and a form of block vote was introduced. These organizational changes consolidated power within the leadership and turned the PSOE into a highly centralized, disciplined party machine.

This unity and discipline is the key to explaining the PSOE's significant electoral success. By 1982 the PSOE had succeeded in becoming associated with the three things that seemingly mattered most to the Spanish electorate: moderation, modernization and democracy. It thus won its first absolute majority in 1982 when it moved to occupy the centre ground left by the dramatic collapse of the Union of the Democratic Centre (**UCD**) and its second absolute majority in the 1986 general elections. Its hegemony within the political system only began to fade in 1989 when it lost its absolute majority by one seat. In the 1993 general elections it lost a further seventeen seats which forced it into coalition with the Catalan nationalists. The PSOE's final defeat came in the 1996 general elections won by the right-wing Popular Party (**PP**). The PSOE's share of the vote remained substantial enough, however, to allow it to claim the election as a 'sweet defeat'.

Throughout its period of hegemony, the PSOE made a positive contribution to the consolidation of democracy, particularly through its subordination of the **armed forces** to the authority of civilian governments, and the consolidation of the quasi-federal structure of the Spanish state, initiated under UCD with the establishment the **autonomous communities** provided for under the 1978 **constitution**. Its relatively successful economic policies transformed Spain into the fastest growing economy in Europe in the late 1980s. The PSOE also led Spain into the **European Union** and confirmed its membership of **NATO**, thereby ending the longstanding political and economic isolation of the country.

On the negative side, the PSOE in power was accused of governing in a high-handed manner which fostered an atmosphere of **corruption** and abuse of power. The PSOE was also accused of neglecting its grassroots support and leaving a significant percentage of the centre-left electorate unrepresented due to its ideological shift to the right. The PSOE's right-wing economic policies earned it the nickname the 'Marbella Socialists' and led to a breakdown in the party's relationship with its union, the **UGT**. A one-day general strike in 1988 successfully pressurized the party into a slight ideological shift back to the left, thereby setting in motion a process of ideological renewal within the party which was strengthened by its period in opposition following the 1996 general election defeat.

See also: political parties; politics; socialism

Further reading

Gillespie, R. (1989) *The Spanish Socialist Party. A History of Factionalism*, Oxford: Clarendon Press (the most comprehensive and detailed account of the history of the Socialist Party in English).

Graham, H (1991) *Socialism and War. The Spanish Socialist Party in power and crisis, 1936–39*, Cambridge: Cambridge University Press (an excellent account of the PSOE during the years of the Second Republic).

Heywood, P. (1990) *Marxism and the Failure of Organised Socialism in Spain, 1879–1936*, Cambridge: Cambridge University Press (a comprehensive, well-documented account of the early development of the PSOE).

Mateos, A (1993) *El PSOE contra Franco*, Madrid: Editorial Pablo Iglesias (an excellent account of the PSOE's fight against the Franco dictatorship).

GEORGINA BLAKELEY

publishing

Publishing has always been an important industry in Spain, and continues to thrive and expand, benefiting from huge potential markets in the Spanish-speaking regions of the world, especially Latin America, to which it sends over half its exports. Centred on Madrid and Barcelona and employing about 10,000 people, it ranks fifth in the world and third in Europe with approximately 50,000 new publications per year, which range from the smallest pamphlet to multi-volume encyclopedias, and comprise official publications (16+ percent), commercial publications (74 percent), non-profit items (4+ percent) and self-published material (4+ percent).

Nevertheless the industry is not without its problems, some peculiar to the country, and some common to the book trade elsewhere in Europe. Despite the huge number of titles on offer – it is reckoned that there are some 170,000 in print – Spain has the lowest level of **readership** (50 percent) in Europe. The situation is being remedied partly by expanding and improving the provision of school and public **libraries** to encourage the habit of reading, and partly by the production of cheaper pocket editions to bring books within reach of a wider public.

The impressive quantity of publication also masks a number of more general trends in the industry, not all of them universally welcomed. Much of the increase in production and export comes from fascicules (works published as cumulative serials), **kiosk literature** and Bibles for Bible Societies. Though titles have increased in number, average print runs have tended to decrease, a trend which is closely linked to another factor increasingly visible in Spain as elsewhere, the 'commodification' of the book. Under the combined pressure of the need for profitability and the sheer number of new titles, the shelf-life of books has decreased rapidly, sometimes to as little as three weeks. Of the 50,000 publications in 1996, over 39,000 were first editions, compared with some 8,000 reissues and a mere 1,200 second editions and 350 third editions. This makes it more difficult for publishers to maintain an extensive or high-quality backlist, and for traditional bookshops to function in competition with chains such as Crisol and Fnac, and with outlets such as El **Corte Inglés** and **VIPS**.

Also obvious is the increasing concentration of the industry both horizontally and vertically. Of the 3,300 publishing houses in Spain, only about 700 publish more than ten books a year, and of these, six or seven large publishing groups account for over 53 percent of commercial production. Takeovers have consolidated this trend in the industry: Santillana has acquired Alfaguara; Planeta has taken over Seix Barral, Espasa Calpe and Destino, though Tusquets resumed independent status in 1998; Siruela was acquired by Anaya, and Lumen by Plaza y Janés, which in turn became part of the Bertelsmann group. Though several publishing houses have welcomed the take-overs as the only means of survival as distinct editorial entities, the smaller independent houses complain of their inability to compete with the groups, who can, for example, offer large advances to popular authors and acquire rights to complete works. These smaller firms feel at a particular disadvantage compared with large vertically integrated communication groups such as PRISA (publishers of *El* ***País*** and owners of Canal +), who publish, promote in their dailies and sell in their bookshop chains.

But while the industry is subject to general international trends of this kind, it also responds to the specific interests of the reading public and the needs of speakers of other languages. Novels (Spanish and international), **detective fiction**, travel literature, humour, biographies, dictionaries, multimedia and CD-ROM products have become increasingly popular, and though 77 percent of new titles are published in Spanish, books are increasingly published in all the other regional languages, especially Catalan (12 percent), Basque (2.5 percent) and Galician (2.5 percent).

See also: kiosk literature; literacy; literature; Madrid Book Fair; novel; press; prizes; readership; women's writing

Further reading

Fernández, J. (1995) 'Becoming Normal: Cultural Production and Cultural Policy in Catalonia', in H. Graham and J. Labanyi (eds) *Spanish Cultural*

Studies, an Introduction: The Struggle for Modernity, Oxford: Oxford University Press, pp. 342–6.
Lasagabaster, J.M. (1995) 'The Promotion of Cultural Production in Basque', in H. Graham and J. Labanyi (eds) *Spanish Cultural Studies, an Introduction: The Struggle for Modernity*, Oxford: Oxford University Press, pp. 351–5.
Toro Santos, X. de (1995) 'Negotiating Galician Cultural Identity' in H. Graham and J. Labanyi (eds) *Spanish Cultural Studies, an Introduction: The Struggle for Modernity*, Oxford: Oxford University Press, pp. 346–51 (three very useful articles on the situation in the non-Castilian regions).

EAMONN RODGERS

Puértolas Villanueva, Soledad

b. 1947, Zaragoza

Writer

Born into a middle-class family, Soledad Puértolas moved to Madrid at the age of 14 in 1961, where she took a degree in journalism, followed by a Master's in Spanish Literature at the University of California, Santa Barbara. Returning to Spain, she devoted herself to writing fiction, and won the Sésamo Prize with her first novel, *El bandido doblemente armado* (The Twice-Armed Bandit) (1980). This was followed by *Burdeos* (Bordeaux) (1986), *Todos mienten* (Everyone Lies) (1988), *Queda la noche* (The Night Remains) (1989), *Días del arenal* (Quicksand Days) (1991), and *Si al atardecer llegara el mensajero* (If the Messenger Came at Dusk) (1995). She has also produced two collections of short stories, *Una enfermedad moral* (A Moral Disease) (1982) and *La corriente del golfo* (Gulf Stream) (1993), and two volumes of children's stories, *La sombra de una noche* (The Shadow of a Night) (1986), and *El recorrido de los animales* (The Animals' Journey) (1988). Non-fictional work includes the essay *La vida oculta* (The Hidden Life) (1993), for which she won the Anagrama Prize, and an early study of the fiction of Pío Baroja (1872–1956), published in 1971.

Unlike many of her female contemporaries, Puértolas is not regarded primarily as a feminist writer, though some of her novels portray the oppression of women. She is, however, less interested in large issues concerning the structure of society than in individuals' search for identity and meaning in their lives, an issue which affects male and female characters equally.

See also: novel; women writers

EAMONN RODGERS

Puig i Cadafalch, Josep

b. 1867, Mataró; d. 1956, Madrid

Architect, historian and politician

Puig i Cadafalch excelled in all the areas which his mentor **Domènech i Montaner** had made his own: architecture, history of art and politics. In architecture he became leader of a group which espoused views similar to Domènech's, initially fostering a version of **Modernism** which was scholarly and open to technical progress, and later becoming chiefly instrumental in the transformation of Modernism into ***Noucentisme***. His long-standing interest in the history of architecture became his main concern after the coup d'état of Primo de Rivera (1923), and was intensified after the Civil War, in 1939, when he was permanently banned from practising as an architect. His contributions to art history, focusing principally on Romanesque and Gothic art, are known worldwide. Among his distinctions were honorary doctorates from several prestigious universities, and membership of the Institute of France. His political career was equally distinguished; he was the principal collaborator of Prat de Riba, first president of the *Mancomunitat* (the autonomous government of Catalonia) whom he succeeded in 1917, retaining the position until 1924. His activism earned him constant political persecution from then until his death in 1956, including a lengthy period of exile in France.

His first notable work as an architect was the Casa Martí (Barcelona, 1895), a building later made famous by the success of the bar-restaurant on the ground floor, Els Quatre Gats (The Four Cats), the rendezvous of the intellectuals and artists who gravitated towards Modernism. Puig did not hesitate to introduce Scandinavian elements into his architectural idiom, something previously unheard of in a quintessentially Mediterranean city like Barcelona. This peculiarity is seen in his best-known achievements, the large town-houses such as the Casa Terrades ('Puntxes', Barcelona, 1903–5), the Casa Macaya (Barcelona, 1898–1900), the Can Serra (1907), and the Casa Baró de Quadras (Barcelona, 1905). The Casa Amatller on the Paseo de Gracia (1898–1900) notoriously forms part of what Barcelona wags called the *manzana de la discordia* (a punning reference to the 'apple of discord', which started the Trojan war; *manzana* means 'apple', but also 'block of flats'). With its 'medieval Dutch' façade it is a landmark in a cluster of buildings by the three greatest modernist architects, which includes **Gaudí**'s Casa Batlló and Domènech's Casa Lleó Morera. All these houses share an ornateness which derives from the fusion of the decorative arts with architecture, a notion associated with the Art 1900 movement; Puig often favoured decoration with sgraffito (*esgrafiat*, a Catalan speciality). A different sort of project is the Fàbrica Casarramona (1909–11), showing the application of a modified Modernism to an industrial building. Apart from Barcelona, he designed buildings in Mataró (Casa Coll i Regas, 1897–1898), Argentona (Casa Garí, 'El Cros', 1899–1900, and his own highly original holiday home, 1897–1905) and in the wine-growing region of Sant Sadurní d'Anoia, where he designed the Codorniu wineries (1901–4) famous for their geometric purity. Of his *Noucentiste* buildings, the most remarkable are: his own home in Barcelona, his studies for the Plaça Catalunya in the city (1915–22), and his design for the Exhibition of Electrical Industries which served as the basis for the International Exhibition of Barcelona in 1929.

Further reading

Loyer, F. (1991) *L'art nouveau en Catalogne*, Paris: Biblio. Arts, Le Septième Fou.

Moldoveanu, M. (1996) *Barcelona: Architectures of Exuberance*, Barcelona: Lunwerg (an overview of different periods and styles, richly illustrated with photographs by the author).

MIHAIL MOLDOVEANU

Pujol i Soley, Jordi

b. 1930, Barcelona

Politican and writer

Since the re-establishment of democracy, Jordi Pujol has been one of the most influential political figures not only in Catalonia but in Spain as a whole. As leader of the majority party in Catalonia, Convergence and Unity (**CiU**), Pujol became President of the **Generalitat** in 1980. He has also played a major role in Spanish politics, particularly since 1993, when first Felipe **González**'s and then José María **Aznar**'s minority governments have depended on CiU support for their survival.

Pujol is a graduate in Medicine, and in 1946 became active in youth and nationalist Catholic groups. He was imprisoned for organizing pro-Catalan democratic campaigns, and spent two years in prison in the early 1960s. Following his release, he dedicated himself to projects which prepared the ground for an autonomous Catalonia. These ranged from the creation of a bank to the preparation of an encyclopedia and other publishing initiatives. In the 1960s and 1970s Pujol published several books, including *Fer poble, fer Catalunya* (Making a People, Making Catalonia) (1965) and *Construïr Catalunya* (Constructing Catalonia) (1979).

With the advent of democracy in the 1970s, Pujol threw himself wholeheartedly into the political fray. In 1977, he was elected to serve as a member of the **parliament** in Madrid. He was re-elected in 1979, but resigned in 1980 in order to stand as a candidate at the 1980 elections to the new Catalan parliament. He was elected President of the Generalitat in 1980. He has worked tirelessly to promote Catalan business, language and cultural interests both within the Iberian peninsula and abroad. He is a keen supporter of the **European Union**, and was elected President of the European Regional Assembly in 1992.

Further reading

Faulí, J. (ed.) (1988) *El pensament polític de Jordi Pujol (1980–1987)*, Barcelona: Planeta.

DAVID GEORGE

Queen Sofía Museum

The Queen Sofia Art Centre (Centro de Arte Reina Sofia – CARS), Madrid, houses a permanent collection of modern art from 1881, and is the successor to the former Museo Español de Arte Contemporáneo.

Situated near the **Prado Museum** and the **Thyssen-Bornemisza Museum** in a refurbished eighteenth-century hospital building, it opened for the display of temporary exhibitions of modern art in 1986, though work continued on a second phase until 1990, when an official reopening was celebrated with an exhibition of twentieth-century Italian art. The organization of its permanent collection continued well into 1992, and in that year, amid much controversy, **Picasso**'s famous *Guernica* was moved to the Centre from the Casón del Buen Retiro, an annexe of the Prado Museum. The permanent collection has been increased by purchase, including some international works, and by the transfer from the Prado Museum of some fifty pieces after the rationalization of the holdings of the two museums in 1995. Organized chronologically by artist and/or styles, it includes works by **Miró**, **Dalí** and Picasso and, since 1996, the **Buñuel** legacy, comprising books, objects, photographs (among them the celebrated one by Man Ray), correspondence and scripts.

See also: art collections; art exhibitions; arts funding; arts policy; museums

EAMONN RODGERS

Querejeta, Elías

b. 1935, Hernani (Guipuzcoa)

Film producer and scriptwriter

Madrid-based Basque producer and promoter of art cinema, Querejeta was associated with the most representative movements of dissident cinema in the 1960s and 1970s: the New Spanish Cinema and the Madrid Independents, among them the award-winners Carlos **Saura** and Víctor **Erice**. His shaping influence extends to the generations of Basque filmmakers of the 1980s and 1990s. Querejeta's distinctive style is characterized by expressive silences, austere scenography and a metaphorical use of the camera. He is also the father of the filmmaker Gracia Querejeta (Madrid, 1962) who made her début in 1993 with *Una estación de paso* (A Passing Season).

See also: film and cinema

Further reading

Angulo, J., Heredero, C.F. and Rebordinos, J.L. (1996) *Elías Querejeta: la producción como discurso*, San Sebastián: Filmoteca Vasca (excellent monograph which includes an interview with Querejeta).

Molina Foix, V. (1977) *New Cinema in Spain*, London: British Film Institute (factual account of the period highlighting the different tendencies with brief accounts of the main filmmakers).

XON DE ROS

Quinto Centenario

On 12 October 1492, Christopher Columbus landed on a Caribbean island on his first transatlantic voyage. His landfall is generally recognized as the European discovery of America. The five hundredth anniversary of this event was known throughout the Spanish speaking world as the *Quinto Centenario* (Quincentenary).

This anniversary was regarded as so important that detailed planning of commemorative events began as early as 1973, when Spain was represented at an international forum in Trujillo, Mexico, attended by delegates from various Latin American countries. In 1984, as a result of a series of subsequent meetings, participating countries, including Canada, Israel, Japan, Portugal and the United States in addition to Spain and the Latin American countries, each established a National Commission for the Quincentenary, representatives of which met annually to co-ordinate their activities as the International Commission for the Quincentenary. In Spain's case, the national organization was the *Sociedad Estatal V Centenario* (State Body for the Quincentenary), headed by Luis Yáñez.

In the early planning stages, the emphasis was quite clearly on the idea of 'celebration' and 'discovery', but as this terminology was unacceptable to a number of Latin American governments and indigenous groups, because of the triumphalist connotations of Spain's imperial past, the International Commission for the Quincentenary officially adopted the terms 'commemoration' and 'encounter' in 1987. Despite this more conciliatory language, the Latin American Episcopal Conference and various human rights groups were consistently critical of preparations for the Quincentenary and in Spain a protest movement calling itself the Comisión contra la Celebración del V Centenario (Commission against the Celebration of the Quincentenary) was established.

Under the aegis of the various commissions, research projects were established, films, television programmes, books and magazines were subsidized, conferences, exhibitions and other cultural events were organized and two satellites were launched to enable Spanish television and radio to be broadcast to Latin America. In addition to these, three major events took place in Spain to mark the *Quinto Centenario.*

Madrid was European City of Culture, **Expo-92** was held in Seville, and Barcelona played host to the games of the XXV Summer Olympiad. In each of these the note of celebration was clear, in contrast to the agreed international tone of commemoration. Spain's official logo for the Quincentenary was also criticized as imperialistic because it was topped by the symbol of the Spanish Crown.

The year 1992 was the five hundredth anniversary of three further events of less international significance than Columbus' voyage which were important to the development of Spain's national culture. January 1492 saw the fall of Granada, marking the conclusion of the process of *Reconquista* (Reconquest), by which the Moors were expelled from the Iberian peninsula; March saw the expulsion of the Jews from Spain; in August, Antonio de Nebrija published his *Gramática sobre la lengua castellana* (*Grammar of the Castilian Language*), the first grammar of a modern European language. Many cultural events and publications marking these anniversaries were sponsored by the *Sociedad Estatal V Centenario.*

See also: arts funding

CHRIS DIXON

Quiroga, Elena

b. 1921, Santander; d. 1995, La Coruña

Writer

One of several major women novelists to emerge in the early postwar period, Elena Quiroga gained national recognition when her second novel, *Viento del norte* (North Wind), was awarded the Nadal Prize for 1950. Although atypical of her work, it is still Quiroga's most widely read novel and one that also gained popularity as a film. The action takes place in rural Galicia and is written in a traditional novelistic structure, with an omniscient third-person narrator. Despite her birth in Santander, Quiroga always identified herself with Galicia, her father's region. She married historian Dalmiro de la Válgoma in 1950; the couple moved to Madrid but spent summers in Galicia.

Viento del norte marked the beginning of a fifteen-year period of great literary productivity; the publication of eight full-length and three short novels culminated in two fictional autobiographies: *Tristura* (Sadness), winner of the national Critics' Prize in 1960, and *Escribo tu nombre* (I Write Your Name) (1965), chosen in 1967 to represent Spain in the international Rómulo Gallegos novel contest. Her final novel, *Presente profundo* (Deep Present) appeared in 1973, and her election to the Spanish Royal Academy of Language in 1983 doubtless came as a surprise to some because of growing silences between works (see also **Royal Academies**).

Her novels from the mid-1950s were increasingly experimental and Faulknerian, in opposition to Spain's dominant current of social realism. *Algo pasa en la calle* (Something's Happening in the Street) (1954) and *La careta* (The Mask) (1955) utilized such strategies as stream-of-consciousness, multiple perspectives and temporal fluidity. Their inaccessibility to many readers facilitated her treatment of subjects generally prohibited by official censorship: divorce, sexuality, wartime atrocities, and post-war political retribution and moral degeneracy. *La última corrida* (The Last Bullfight) (1958) is a rare and much acclaimed novelistic examination of the inner world of bullfighters.

Given its linear structure, *Tristura* appears deceptively simple but in fact requires a sophisticated reader, capable of filling in gaps and silences. The perspective is that of a young child who provides only the information known to her and who is unable to communicate, even to herself, the loss she feels from the absence of love. By her adolescent years in the sequel novel, *Escribo tu nombre*, Tadea has become rebellious; the name she wishes to write is that of Liberty.

Quiroga's final novel, *Presente profundo*, returns to the complex, multiple-perspective structure of *Algo pasa en la calle* and, like *La careta*, is related to existential psychiatry in its approach to time. In dealing with society in the early 1970s, Quiroga explores marital, parent–child, and love relationships, developing both traditional and non-traditional female characters; the action shifts between Galicia and cosmopolitan Madrid, providing a full view of contemporary Spain.

Further reading

Zatlin-Boring, P. (1977) *Elena Quiroga*, Boston, MA: G.K. Hall (the only book-length study.)

Zatlin, P. (1991) 'Writing against the Current: The Novels of Elena Quiroga', in J.L. Brown (ed.) *Women Writers of Contemporary Spain. Exiles in the Homeland*, Newark, NJ: University of Delaware Press; London and Toronto: Associated University Presses, pp. 42–58 (up-to-date overview of complete works).

PHYLLIS ZATLIN

R

Rabal, Francisco

b. 1925, Aguilas (Murcia)

Film actor

After a series of films in the 1950s, including *Luna de sangre* (Blood Moon) (1950), *Murió hace quince años* (He Died Fifteen Years Ago) (1954) and *Prisionero del mar* (Prisoner of the Sea) (1957), it was his appearances in **Buñuel**'s *Nazarín* (1958), *Viridiana* (1961) and *Belle de jour* (1966) which brought Rabal international recognition. In the 1960s and 1970s he also worked with such directors as Carlos **Saura**, in *Llanto por un bandido* (Lament for a Bandit) (1963), and **Camino**, in *Las largas vacaciones de 1936* (The Long Holidays of 1936) (1976). His films of the 1980s and 1990s include **Camus**' *La colmena* (The Hive) (1982) and his *Los santos inocentes* (*The Holy Innocents*) (1984) in which Rabal played the half-mad uncle, a role for which he shared a prize for best actor with Alfredo **Landa**, and won the National Cinematography Prize; **Patino**'s *Los paraísos perdidos* (Lost Paradises) (1985), in which he played an ageing intellectual; **García Sánchez**'s *Divinas palabras* (Divine Words) (1987); **Almodóvar**'s *¡Atame!* (*Tie Me Up, Tie Me Down!*) (1989); *L'autre* (The Other) (1991) and *El hombre que perdió su sombrero* (The Man Who Lost His Hat) (1991). In 1984 he was best male actor at the Cannes Film Festival, and in 1991 he won prizes as best actor in Montreal and Gijón. In 1994 he published his memoirs under the title *Si yo te contara* (If I Told You).

See also: film and cinema

EAMONN RODGERS

racism

Spain has arguably a less severe problem of racism than other European countries, which may be due to the relatively lower proportion of **immigrants**. Nevertheless, there is a traditional antagonism towards gypsies on the part of the settled community, despite the fact that these nomadic groups have been in Spain for at least five hundred years, and have enriched popular culture with, for example, **flamenco** music and dance. Plans by town councils to provide fixed accommodation for gypsy communities have on occasion provoked opposition from residents, intensifying the tendency for gypsies to concentrate in **shanty towns** near big cities, where they are forced to live in very unfavourable conditions. Intermarriage between the gypsy and settled communities (the *payos*, as the gypsies call them) is rare, which perpetuates the mutual feeling of separateness and impedes the breaking-down of prejudice on both sides. In an effort to discourage stereotyping, voluntary organizations, and government agencies such as the Youth Institute of the Ministry of Social Affairs, have mounted advertising campaigns on television to outlaw the use of words like *gitano* as a term of abuse or mockery.

Prejudice against gypsies is probably the only major area in which community attitudes continue to have primarily an ethnic or cultural base. It is true that historically antagonism towards Muslims and Jews on religious grounds was deep-rooted, and traces of this remain. Apart from gypsies, however, hostility towards particular groups tends to be primarily economic in origin. Since the early

1980s there has been a marked increase in immigration from the poorer strata of countries in North Africa and Latin America. Immigrants from North Africa come mainly in search of seasonal work during the grape, olive or fruit harvests, and some of the most important fruit-growing areas have witnessed attacks on immigrant workers by gangs of local youths. Arrivals from sub-Saharan Africa have apparently encountered less hostility, since, engaged as they are predominantly in small-scale street-trading, they are not perceived as constituting a large homogeneous group concentrated in a particular locality, and in any case contact with the resident population is minimal.

In theory, immigrants from Latin America should find it easier to be accepted and integrated, because of the shared linguistic and cultural inheritance. In practice, however, this applies more readily to well-educated professionals, and since the early 1980s these have increasingly been replaced by women from poorer backgrounds who come in search of employment as domestic servants. Some of these people have been subjected to violent attacks, sometimes with fatal consequences, by small ultra-right groups analogous to the skinheads and football hooligans found in every western European country.

See also: social attitudes; society

CARLOS ÁLVAREZ ARAGÜÉS

radio

Spain has, in proportion to its population, the largest radio audience in Europe, with more than half the adult population listening every day. Over 18 million people listen to the four major networks, the state Radio Nacional de España (RNE: see also **national radio**), and the private networks **SER**, **COPE** and Onda Cero. These three account for some 80 percent of the total radio audience.

The intensity of competition among the networks, and the sheer number of different stations available, is a function of the liberalization of broadcasting which accompanied the transition to democracy. Between the end of the Civil War and 1977, when RNE lost its monopoly, state radio was the only source of news, which was subject, like other aspects of **publishing** and the **media**, to **censorship**. Bodies closely identified with the regime, such as the **National Movement**, the **vertical syndicates**, and the Roman Catholic church, were permitted to establish their own networks, but had to take their news from the state agency, **Agencia EFE**. Within these networks, local stations proliferated, until in the mid-1960s, some 450 were competing for space on medium wave. This figure was halved within the succeeding ten years, and by 1978, there were four medium-wave networks: RNE, Radio Cadena Española (RCE: the chain of stations belonging to the *Movimiento* and the *sindicatos*), COPE and SER. RCE merged with RNE in 1988. By then, the development of FM radio made it possible both to diversify the output of the major networks, and to increase local provision without overcrowding the medium band. The result has been a proliferation of FM stations, with some 600 new licences, at a conservative estimate, issued during the 1980s, giving Spain the largest number of radio outlets in Europe in relation to its population. In addition, several hundred unlicensed transmitters exist, many run by the municipal authorities in small towns. The government's willingness to acquiesce in this situation is illustrated by the fact that in 1988 Agencia EFE agreed to supply regular news bulletins from its own service to some of these illegal stations.

Much of the programme content is characterized by informality and spontaneity, which contrasts markedly with the more staid style to which listeners were accustomed during the Franco regime. Though RNE is still an important national institution, it has been steadily losing listener share to the private networks since the early 1980s. Though radio as a whole played an important role in keeping the nation informed during crises such as the attempted coup of 1981 (see also ***Tejerazo, El***), the fact that SER had already pioneered the provision of uncensored news in the early years of the transition may account for the fact that it is by far the most popular network.

One of the most significant aspects of the diversification of radio broadcasting has been the increased output in languages other than Spanish. Radio has played a role alongside other media in consolidating a sense of confidence and identity in those **autonomous communities** with distinctive cultural traditions. Euskadi Irratia (Basque Radio) broadcasts in Basque throughout the whole Basque territory. RTVG (Galician Radio and Television), inaugurated in 1985, transmits exclusively in Galician. Though RNE created a Catalan station in 1976, coverage was limited. With the foundation in 1983 of the Corporació Catalana de Ràdio i Televisió (CCRTV: Catalan Radio and Television Corporation), radio provision in Catalan was considerably enhanced, and Catalunya Ràdio has the largest share of the global audience in Catalonia.

Further reading

Bernández, A. (1991) 'The Mass Media', in A. Ramón Gascón (ed.) *Spain Today: In Search of Modernity*, Madrid: Cátedra (pp. 431–54 offer an informative account of the changes which have occurred in the Spanish media).

Hooper, J. (1995) *The New Spaniards*, Harmondsworth: Penguin (chapter 22 considers radio as part of a general discussion of the broadcast media).

EAMONN RODGERS

railways

The contemporary railway system in Spain comprises, first, the Spanish standard gauge system operated by the Spanish state railway company **Renfe**; second, the High Speed service operating on European gauge track (see also **AVE**); third, the narrow gauge systems operated by the state enterprise **FEVE**, regional public enterprises and private companies; and fourth, the underground railways in Barcelona, Bilbao and Madrid.

There are a number of inherent weaknesses in the railway system. These stem partly from the mountainous topography, a thinly populated interior with widely spread traffic centres, and a densely populated coastal fringe. The standard gauge system radiates out from Madrid over a distance of some 12,700 km, with an important transverse link through the Ebro valley and a high capacity route along the Mediterranean coast from the French frontier to Valencia. This radial network restricts cross-country rail travel, and not all the major urban industrial areas of Spain have direct connections with Madrid.

The standard gauge of 1,672 mm (6 *pies castellanas*), established in 1844, is relatively wide in comparison with other national railways, which rendered direct rail communications between Spain and France impossible until the introduction of the cumbersome technology of trains with variable axles in the 1960s. Other weaknesses which afflict the system in the late twentieth century are the extent of single line working, relatively steep gradients, low radius curves and on some routes the poor condition of the track, all the result of under-investment in the past and all contributing to relatively slow speeds over the network.

In the late twentieth century investment in the railways was directed at upgrading the system especially on commuter routes and on long distance inter-city routes. Commuter networks, especially those around Barcelona and Madrid, handle the largest volume of passenger traffic. Inter-city routes offer opportunities for capturing traffic from both the roads and air. The most notable example of inter-city route investment has been in the High Speed Train service, and in plans to expand this service to connect it with the High Speed railway network being developed across Europe. Investment has also gone into upgrading other routes, through for example new rolling stock (including the fast 'Talgo' trains of Spanish design and manufacture that run on standard gauge track), improved track, double track, electrification and new signalling, notably along the Mediterranean corridor. Such developments are shifting the network towards a more axial pattern based on a central corridor Seville – Madrid – Barcelona/Bilbao and a Mediterranean corridor.

Apart from the high density traffic routes, many lines have only been kept open through government subsidies and in some cases operating agreements with regional governments. Such arrangements raise the important political question of how far railway services should be seen as public services and open up the whole issue of transport policy.

See also: transport

Further reading

Martin Aceña, P., Comín, M., Muñoz Rubio, M. and Vidal Olivares, J. (1998) *150 Años de los Ferrocarriles Españoles*, 2 vols, Madrid: Fundación de los Ferrocarriles Españoles (history of Spanish railways from 1848 to 1998).

Boag, G.L. (1923) *The Railways of Spain*, London: The Railway Gazette (covers their development up to the early twentieth century).

Izquierdo, R. (1993) 'Breve evolución histórica del ferrocarril en España', *Situación* 3/4: 7–19, Bilbao: Banco Bilbao Vizcaya.

Wais, F. (1987) *Historia de los ferrocarriles españoles*, 3rd edn, vols 1 and 2, Madrid: Editora Nacional por la Fundación de los Ferrocarriles Españoles (a detailed account of the development of the railways can be found here and in publications by Renfe).

KEITH SALMON

Raimon

b. 1940, Xàtiva (Community of Valencia)

Singer and songwriter (pseudonym of Ramon Pelegero i Sanchis)

Raimon was one of the leading exponents of the ***Nova Cançó***. His 1962 song *Al vent* (To the Wind) was a landmark in the development of the movement.

DAVID GEORGE

Ramírez, Pedro J.

b. 1952, Logroño

Journalist

After a degree in journalism at the University of Navarre, and a period teaching in the US, Ramírez worked initially on the magazine *La Actualidad Española*, subsequently joining the editorial staff of ***ABC***, and was also the Madrid correspondent of the Barcelona evening paper *El Noticiero Universal*. Between 1980 and 1989 he was Editor-in-Chief of *Diario 16*, and succeeded in almost tripling its sales. In 1989, however, he was dismissed after a dispute with the board about editorial style. He immediately co-founded a new paper, *El Mundo del Siglo XXI*, usually referred to as *El* ***Mundo***, to which he managed to entice many of his former colleagues, and which by 1993 had reached sales of 200,000, placing it third in importance behind *El* ***País*** and *ABC*.

Ramírez has been determined to turn *El Mundo* into a lively investigative newspaper with a sharp nose for **corruption**, and has persistently harassed government figures, notably over the **GAL** case. He was often presented in other publications as carrying on what amounted to a personal crusade against Felipe **González**.

See also: journalism; *poderes fácticos*; press

EAMONN RODGERS

Raphael

b. 1946, Linares (Jaén)

Singer

At the age of 16, Rafael Martos arrived at the studio of his present manager in search of fame and fortune and this was start of his artistic career. His preciousness earned him the sobriquet *El niño de Linares* (The boy from Linares). He performed in the most prestigious international song festivals and at the peak of his career he played the lead in five successful films. Raphael's histrionic and impassioned delivery has spawned generations of imitators.

See also: rock and pop

FERNANDO DELGADO

readership

Despite the buoyancy of the **publishing** industry and the vast improvement in levels of **literacy**, the level of readership in Spain is the lowest in Europe, both of books (around 50 percent of population) and of newspapers (in the mid 1990s, 105 copies sold per 1,000 inhabitants, compared with the European average of 232).

A number of factors contribute to this somewhat contradictory situation. One is the very common practice of reading newspapers freely supplied in the many bars that are a focus for much of the leisure activity outside the home. Another very obvious factor is that the huge improvement in levels of literacy in the 1960s largely coincided with the arrival of **television** and its rapid growth in popularity, so that the habit of book reading came to occupy proportionately less of people's leisure time.

Reading is being encouraged by an improvement in the provision of school and public **libraries**; by state grants and financial aid for such things as cultural magazines, bookshops, and lectures and conferences in schools and universities; and by the promotion of books through trade fairs, radio and television programmes and magazines such as *Qué leer* (What to Read). The price of books is yet another factor, but one that is being met by the production of cheaper pocket editions that are within reach of a wider range of the population. Nevertheless, it remains true that the average price of a book increased by 25 percent between 1997 and 1998, from 2,000 pesetas to 2,500 pesetas.

Levels of readership are noticeably increasing among women and especially among the younger generation that has had the benefit of universal education since 1970 (see also **education and research**). Much of the cheaper **kiosk literature** sold in a variety of outlets is aimed at this section of the market. Among the older generation there has been a particularly marked increase in the readership of **novels**, especially those by younger authors, and there is also a sizeable readership for **detective fiction**, travel literature, humour, and biography and history. Nevertheless, apart from 'best-sellers', average print runs are declining, and it is generally agreed that too many titles continue to chase too few readers. Although some 2.5 million people visited the **Madrid Book Fair** in 1998, 50,000 more than the previous year, book sales at the fair fell over the same period from 475,600 to 444,143, a drop of 6.6 percent.

See also: cultural institutions and movements; literature

EAMONN RODGERS

Real Madrid

Founded in 1902, Real Madrid began to overtake **Barcelona FC** and Athletic de Bilbao as the leading Spanish football team in the early 1950s, and especially after it acquired the Argentinian player Alfredo di Stefano in 1952 in somewhat controversial circumstances. Favoured by Franco, to the extent that it was known as 'Franco's team', it became identified with the regime, while the Barcelona and Bilbao clubs and colours became synonomous with Catalan and Basque separatist aspirations. A special stadium had been built for the club in the Chamartín district of Madrid in 1947, a few years after Santiago Bernabéu became president in 1943, and was named after him in 1955 after it had been extended to hold 100,000 spectators. The team won its first League Championship in 1954, and won the European Cup five years in succession between 1956 and 1960.

Real Madrid continued to maintain a dominating position in First Division football, being especially successful in the 1960s, when it won all but two of the championships, and in the second half of the 1980s, when it again won five times in succession, so that by the end of the 1994–5 season it had surpassed its nearest rival, Barcelona, by twenty six titles to its fourteen. In 1996, however, a series of crises, resulting in the departure both of its coach, Jorge Valdano, and of its president, Ramón Mendoza, together with the financial problems common to many Spanish clubs, resulted in a drop to sixth place. It recovered its premier position in 1997, but its debts continue to mount alarmingly, due in part to the spiralling cost of transfer fees. The club has also had many successes in the annual competition for the King's Cup (*Copa del Rey*) within Spain (though Barcelona and Atlético Madrid have a better record in this particular contest), and is among the record holders for victories in the European Teams Cup (known as the *Recopa* in Spain).

See also: football; sport and leisure

EAMONN RODGERS

reconversión industrial

The Reconversion and Industrialization Law of 1984 was one of many attempts by the socialist **PSOE** government to tackle structural problems in the **economy** in order to prepare Spain for membership of the European Community (see also **European Union**). In particular, the traditional industries, shipbuilding, textiles and especially steel, were out of step with those of other industrialized countries, and were increasing output just at the time when demand elsewhere was falling off. Greater liberalization of these industries included the introduction of increased flexibility in the **labour market**, which did little to improve the high **unemployment** figures. This was a controversial issue in **industry** as a whole, but in the sectors in which *reconversión* was most urgent, there was the added difficulty that the programme had to be carried out in areas which were politically sensitive for other reasons, such as the Basque country.

See also: industrial development; industrial relations; labour law; trade unions

Further reading

Heywood, P. (1995) *The Government and Politics of Spain*, London: Macmillan (pp. 220–5 give a clear and succinct account of the issues posed by restructuring).

EAMONN RODGERS

Redondo, Nicolás

b. 1927, Bilbao

Trade union leader

Nicolás Redondo was the strong man of the socialist trade union, the **UGT**, between the early 1970s and his retirement in 1993.

He was born in Barracaldo, an industrial suburb of Bilbao, into a socialist working-class family, the son of a leading anti-Francoist labour militant. Nicolás, who had taken up work in the shipbuilding plant La Naval, joined the **PSOE** and UGT in 1945. Over the next two decades he became intensively involved in the clandestine political and union struggle against the dictatorship, and by the early 1970s, as de facto leader of the party and union's most powerful regional organization, based in the Basque country, he had become the most influential figure in the socialist movement. He strongly supported the 'renovators' against the ageing exiled leadership of the PSOE, and with the transfer of the UGT and PSOE back to Spain between 1971 and 1972 he joined the leadership teams of both organizations. Redondo saw himself as carrying on what he viewed as the democratic Marxist traditions of the Spanish socialist movement. Hence, he argued that at the PSOE 'renovators' congress of August 1972 the organization had rediscovered its roots. Nevertheless, he saw himself as essentially a trade union organizer and not a politician, and at the **Suresnes** congress of October 1974 he turned down the offer of the post of first secretary, and instead supported Felipe **González**'s candidature. His decision to concentrate on union work was confirmed in 1978, when he resigned his post on the PSOE executive committee in order to integrate part of the independent labour confederation, the Workers' Trade Union (Unión Sindical Obrera), into the UGT.

Relations between Redondo and Felipe González deteriorated, however, after the PSOE came to power in 1982. Under Redondo the UGT participated in several institutional pacts between the Employers' Federation, the **CEOE**, government and trade unions, but from 1985 he became increasingly critical of the PSOE's failure, as he saw it, to defend the interests of the working class. Divisions came to a head in 1988, when Redondo, who had been elected to parliament on the socialist ticket in 1982, resigned his seat, and forged an alliance with the pro-communist **CC OO**. The schism culminated on 14 December when the UGT and CC OO carried out a one-day general strike against government economic and social policy. Redondo felt increasingly betrayed by his old friends, arguing that while he had remained faithful to the socialists' social-democratic legacy, this had been abandoned by the government. Once crossed, he proved a tenacious foe, maintaining links with CC OO, and continuously pressing the government to pursue more pro-labour policies. He was able to marginalize pro-government voices in the UGT itself, and is not without friends within the PSOE. In 1993 he retired as general secretary of the UGT to be replaced by his protégé, Cándido Méndez.

Further reading

Gillespie, R. (1989) *The Spanish Socialist Party: A History of Factionalism*, Oxford: Clarendon Press (the most detailed history of the Spanish socialist movement between 1939 and 1982).

Guindal, M. and Serrano, R. (1986) *La otra transición: Nicolás Redondo: el sindicalismo socialista*, Madrid: Unión Editorial (the only biography of Nicolás Redondo).

ANGEL SMITH

regional cooking

Spanish cooking enjoys a marked regional character although, as in other Mediterranean countries, certain staple ingredients such as olive oil, flat-leafed parsley, garlic, tomatoes, onions, lemons and wine, are found in most Spanish kitchens. Spain's very diverse history, geography and climate, have all contributed to her culinary heritage. Paella, one of the country's national dishes, would not be what it is without the saffron, introduced into Spain by the Phoenicians, the oil and fruit of the olive trees planted by the Greeks and extended by the Romans, and short-grain rice and lemons brought by the Arabs. Also, chickpeas used in the traditional stew *cocido* owe their appearance in Spain to the Carthaginians.

Cocido is a dish which, with slight variations, can be found in all corners of the peninsula. *Cocido*, *olla*, *pote* or *escudella* as it is variously known has its roots in the *olla podrida*, or rotten pot mentioned in *Don Quijote*, and was a Christian adaptation of the ancient Jewish dish *adafina*, in which the hard boiled eggs of the latter were replaced by pork. *Cocido* consists of meat, sausages, pulses and vegetables – whatever is typical locally. It is usually served in three courses: first the soup, consisting of the strained broth, then the vegetables and pulses, and finally the meat. Chickpeas are generally used in the stews from the areas of Madrid and Andalusia, while *alubias* (white beans) are preferred in the north, the Galician *pote gallego* invariably contains turnips, and the Asturian *fabada* uses local beans called *fabes*.

The cuisines of the northern coastal regions display an abundance of fish and shellfish, and the meat from this area, which has year round green pasture, is of good quality. Galicia is renowned for its *empanadas* (meat and fish pies), and *lacón con grelos* (salted ham with turnip tops), often cooked with sausage and potatoes called *cachelos*, which give the dish a slightly bitter taste. Specialities include *nécoras* (small orange crabs), and scallops, usually baked and served in the shell – the emblem worn by pilgrims who visited the shrine of St James in Compostela. Fish and shellfish are combined in the Asturian *caldereta* (casserole), or served independently, usually accompanied by corn bread and cider – the national drink of Asturias. Salmon and the veined cheese, *cabrales*, are other local favourites. A speciality of the Santander area of Cantabria is rice and salmon cooked in milk, and a plate of anchovies in a rich egg and butter sauce is highly regarded. The Basque country is famed for the excellence of its cuisine and gastronomic societies flourish. Food here is generally uncomplicated and subtly flavoured. The region has many great dishes such as hake Vizcaya style, or *bacalao al pil-pil* (cod cooked with oil, garlic and a little chilli pepper). Baby eel and *marmitako* (tuna and potato stew) are also of note.

Aragon, Navarre and Rioja are all watered by the Ebro, Spain's longest river. Trout is plentiful here and that from Pyrenees rivers is excellent, either soaked in wine, stuffed with ham and baked Navarre style, or simply fried. A notable feature of the Ebro Valley area is *chilindrón* sauce, made with tomatoes, garlic, onions, cured ham and red peppers, in which meat is cooked, particularly chicken and rabbit. Other specialities are partridge in chocolate sauce, and quail cooked in fig leaves.

Catalonia is renowned for its sauces such as *ali-oli* (garlic mayonnaise), *romescu* (red pepper and almond sauce) and *samfaina* (a mixture of tomatoes, peppers and aubergine). Rice, fish and local sausages are used in many dishes here, often accompanied by bread rubbed with tomato and sprinkled with olive oil and salt. *Habas* (broad beans), noodle casserole, cod fritters and the local *zarzuela de mariscos* (literally operetta of seafood) are all popular.

The central Castilian plateau area is famed for its meat dishes, particularly suckling pig, and baby lamb roasted in a clay dish. Chickpeas are generally used in stews, and *Manchego* (sheep's milk cheese) accompanies many meals. Trout and river crabs are delicacies of Castile-León, and the robust Castilian soups containing ham, bread, garlic and, often, a poached egg are common.

The central east region of Valencia and its southern neighbour Murcia is the land of rice and oranges. Rice cooked *en caldero* (blended fish stock), or served with green beans and snails, vegetable stew, or seafood and meats – as in the famous paella – are typical of this area. Oranges, either served as a dessert or used in a sauce for chicken and rabbit are a major feature of Levantine cooking.

Andalusia is often called the frying pan of Spain, both for its high temperatures and cooking habits. Typical of this region is *pescaíto frito* (mixed fried fish), and *bienmesabe* (marinated fried shark). Anchovies, sardines, grey and red mullet and whiting feature regularly, as does the cold soup *gazpacho*, made with bread, garlic, oil, water and tomatoes. The excellent local hams and sherry wines are often used in distinctive sauces for fish and meat.

Extremadura has some of the country's best *embutidos* (sausages) and pork is a major feature of the local cuisine. This hunting territory offers a profusion of rabbit, quail and partridge, and a speciality is the festive dish *la caldereta*, in which pieces of fried kid are served in a sauce of chopped liver, garlic and red peppers.

Fish is a major feature of the cuisine of the Spanish islands. In the Canary Islands this is often accompanied by *el mojo* (spiced vinaigrette), which is also used with meat and vegetables. The exotic stew of the Canaries contains such ingredients as yam, pumpkin, sweet potato, potato and chickpeas. Pork and soup are a regular feature of meals in the Balearic Islands. The hearty Majorcan cabbage-and-bread soup has the consistency of a light pudding. Pork is often stuffed with liver, fruit, spices and bread and then roasted. A popular vegetable dish is *el tumbet*: a layered potato and aubergine pie, covered with tomatoes and peppers. The sweet *ensaimada*, made with a light dough and filled with cream or custard, is another local speciality.

Spanish desserts generally consist of fresh fruit, but sweets made with eggs and sugar, usually in the form of rich custards, meringues, fritters or mousse are very popular, as are fruit and almond tarts, *pudín* (a type of bread pudding), *tocino de cielo* (literally fatty bacon from heaven, but which is a rich sweet made with egg yolks and sugar), ice cream and ice cream tarts.

See also: fast food outlets; food and drink; wine

Further reading

Ortega, S. (1991) *1080 Recetas de Cocina*, Madrid: Alianza Editorial.

Passmore, J. (1995) *The Complete Spanish Cookbook*, Boston, MA and Australia: Little Brown.

Serrano, J. and S. (1993) *A Spanish Family Cookbook*, New York: Hippocrene.

S. SERRANO

regional nationalism

The **constitution of 1978** 'guarantees the right to autonomy of the *nationalities* and regions which form [the Spanish Nation]', without being specific about the distinction between nationalities and regions. In practice, the term 'regional nationalism' normally refers to the three so-called 'historic nationalities', those of Galicia, Catalonia and the Basque country (Euskadi).

Catalanism slowly evolved in the nineteenth century from moderate regionalism and a cultural revival (the *Renaixença*) into a fully fledged nationalism. Its class base, initially bourgeois, expanded during the Second Republic, when a party representing the Catalanist left gained control of the **Generalitat**. Under Franco, all political manifestations of Catalan culture were silenced, though a slow underground revival began. By the time of Franco's death, Catalanism had become a movement transcending classes, parties, and generations, which led to the re-establishment of the Generalitat in 1977. Since then, even centralist parties in Catalonia have had to reshape their names and agendas to accommodate regional aspirations. After the approval of the Statute of Autonomy and the ensuing regional elections (1980), the Generalitat became dominated by the centre-right nationalist coalition **CiU**. The **Catalan** language has been the core of most aspects of Catalan nationalism, and has experienced a revival unparalleled among other stateless nations. A law of **language normalization** was passed in 1983 to regulate its public use.

By contrast, Basque nationalism lacked since its beginnings a similar cultural cohesiveness. The nationalist **PNV** focused initially on language, race and religion as unifying principles, but the debate was radically altered by the emergence of the younger militants of **ETA** in 1959. In practice, it was difficult to mobilize support on a purely ethnic-cultural basis, since only a minority spoke – and still speak – **Basque**. As ETA turned to Marxism and class mobilization, appeals to ethnicity became impracticable, since most workers were non-Basque immigrants. ETA's support, however, increased as the Franco regime's legitimacy declined, and the organization recruited its members on the basis of patriotic commitment and resistance to repression, rather than ethnic considerations. Nevertheless, differing conceptions of Basque identity led to internal conflicts within ETA and nationalist circles. Basque nationalism dramatically expanded its basis of support during the transition to democracy (1975–82). By the time the Statute of Autonomy was approved in 1980, one section of ETA (ETA-pm) had virtually abandoned the armed struggle, and it confirmed this stance in 1982. By 1986, four main nationalist parties were competing for the electorate: the far-left pro-independence **Herri Batasuna**, the left nationalists of Euskadiko Ezkerra (**Basque Left**), the more moderate **Eusko Alkartasuna** and the historic centre-right PNV. Together they normally secure the majority of votes, at least in Vizcaya and Guipúzcoa (where they often win over 70 percent).

Galician nationalism, on the other hand, has never been a mass movement until quite recently. Its origins lie in the nineteenth-century *Rexurdimento* (Renaissance), a largely urban literary revival which rediscovered the Galician roots of Portuguese, and mythified the region's Celtic past. With urbanization and modernization, nationalism slowly expanded, but only in the 1990s has the *Bloque Nacional Gallego* (BNG – Galician National Bloc) gained consistent percentages at regional elections (18.7 percent and thirteen seats in the 1993 elections).

See also: autonomous communities; regional parties; regionalism; terrorism

Further reading

Conversi, D. (1997) *The Basques, the Catalans, and Spain: Alternative Routes to Nationalist Mobilization*, London: Hurst.

Hooper, J. (1995) *The New Spaniards*, Harmondsworth: Penguin (chapters 26–30 give an excellent account of the dynamics of regional nationalism).

DANIELE CONVERSI

regional parties

Although regionalist groups have existed since at least the First Republic (1873–4), their proliferation and institutionalization is largely a consequence of the transformation of Spain into a quasi-federal state following the approval of the **constitution of 1978**. By the mid-1990s, regionalist parties had gained seats in nearly all the parliaments of the seventeen **autonomous communities**.

Regionalist movements received a considerable boost from the example of Catalonia. Over one million people marched in Catalan streets in the *Diada de Catalunya* of 11 September 1977 demanding 'freedom, amnesty and the Statute of Autonomy'. Similar demonstrations soon sprang up in other regions: over 800,000 people turned out in Valencia on 9 October with comparable slogans. On December 4, nearly a million marched throughout Andalusia demanding Andalusian autonomy.

Nevertheless, despite their self-legitimation as 'nationalists', there is a clear distinction between the aspirations of regionalist parties and **regional**

nationalism proper, represented by organizations such as the **PNV**, **Herri Batasuna** and **CiU**. Except in Andalusia, there is often only a token emphasis on cultural distinctiveness, and little attempt to claim common descent or separate historic identity. Indeed, many of these regional parties are fundamentally conservative, oriented towards an all-Spain perspective, and affirm regional identity either as protection against more assertive varieties of nationalism (Catalan and Basque), or in pursuit of economic interests.

This is the case with the Aragonese Regionalist Party (Partido Aragonés Regionalista – PAR), which was founded in 1977 by Zaragoza's conservative élites formerly linked to Francoism. Until 1986, it remained an electoral partner of the right-wing Popular Coalition, but subsequently ran alone. Its regionalism originally reflected a concern over the rise of Catalanism, which prompted demands that Aragon be granted a similar degree of autonomy. A new name, Aragonese Party (Partido Aragonés), was chosen in February 1990 to stress its 'nationalist' credentials while retaining the older acronym (PAR).

The archetype of 'pro-centralist' regionalism which emerged in response to the ethno-nationalist challenge is Valencian Union (Unión Valenciana – UV). With its anti-intellectual overtones and absence of a coherent programme, it easily enlisted popular support for a crusade against perceived pan-Catalanist threats to merge Valencia with Catalonia proper. In the 1982 elections it stood together with Popular Coalition, securing two MPs. In 1986 it gained one seat, and two in 1989. There is a comparable movement in the Basque province of Alava, where Unión Alavesa has emerged in the 1990s in opposition to the radical nationalism of PNV and Herri Batasuna.

The Partido Regionalista Cántabro (PRC) was founded in 1978 with the aim of making Cantabria a region separate from Castile. A similar aim was sought by the Partido Riojano Progresista (PRP) also founded in 1978. Both Cantabria and La Rioja were granted Statutes of Autonomy.

By far the most intricate case is that of the Canary Islands. Coalición Canaria Nacionalista (Nationalist Canarian Coalition – CCN) was born in February 1993 from the merging of five local parties. Its main component was AIC (Agrupaciones Independientes de Canarias – Independent Canary Island Groups), itself an umbrella coalition of seven insular parties formed in the early 1980s. In the 1986 general elections AIC won one deputy and two senators, and in 1989 one deputy and one senator. In the June 1993 general elections, CCN gained four seats in the Congress and five in the Senate. CCN became the majority party in the 1995 regional elections. The first CCN-led government was formed in April 1993, after the collapse of a coalition in which AIC had shared power with the socialist **PSOE**. After its 1995 victory, CCN was again entrusted with the task of assembling the regional government. CCN also controls most town councils and three of the seven *cabildos* (island councils).

Once in power, CCN obtained several concessions from Madrid, including the regional government's authority to levy its own taxes and an Economic Law introducing a sort of 'compensation' for the islands' distance from the mainland. This brought an unprecedented boost in subsidies and investments, particularly in road construction. Official rhetoric stresses Canarian unity, in an effort to overcome the islands' legacy of political fragmentation and reciprocal insularity (known as *pleito insular*). CCN's long-term goal is the maximum of autonomy within the Spanish state, short of independence. Its aims include a reform of the Statute of Autonomy, the development of Fiscal Economic Status (*Regimen Económico Fiscal* – REF) and a 'permanent status' within the European Union as an extra-peripheral (*ultraperiférica*) region. The new Autonomy Statute should define the islands as a 'nationality', equating the Canaries to the three 'historic nationalities'.

Though Andalusia was the only region to take advantage of the 'exceptional' route to autonomy envisaged in article 151 of the constitution (which permitted any region to bid for the same measure of autonomy as the historic regions), regional parties in Andalusia are relatively weak. The Andalusian Socialist Party (Partido Socialista Andaluz – PSA), separate from the PSOE, emerged in 1979–80, later renaming itself the Andalusian Regionalist Party (Partido Andalucista – PA), but its development has been impaired both by internal wrangles and by the strength of PSOE in the region, its traditional heartland. After the

1996 general election, Andalusia had a socialist administration while the central government was conservative. There is nevertheless a strong sense of regional distinctiveness, and research on all aspects of Andalusian culture, economy and politics has boomed in recent years.

Further reading

Heywood, P. (1995) 'The Government and Politics of Spain', London: Macmillan (see chapter 1 on 'Reconciling State and Nation').

Ross, C.J. (1997) *Contemporary Spain: A Handbook*, London: Arnold (chapter 3 gives an excellent overview of the whole regionalist question, and the emergence of regional parties).

DANIELE CONVERSI

regionalism

The distinction between **regional nationalism** and regionalism is largely a matter of differing levels of political intensity, historic antecedents and cultural distinctiveness. The term 'nationalism' is certainly appropriate to the so-called 'historic nationalities': Galician, Catalan and Basque. By contrast with these, regionalist movements have never posed a serious challenge to the unitary conception of Spain.

The post-Francoist transformation of Spain from a highly centralized to a quasi-federal state was due primarily to pressure from Catalan and Basque nationalists, which led, under the **constitution of 1978**, to the creation of seventeen **autonomous communities**, some of which had little or no historic identity. For instance, Cantabria and La Rioja, each founded from a single pre-existing province (Santander and Logroño respectively) belong firmly to the Castilian cultural sphere. On the other hand, in some regions, such as Aragon, Valencia and Navarre, traditional local loyalty developed overnight into a heightened sense of distinctiveness, as a counterweight to the perceived assertiveness of Catalan and Basque nationalism.

Regionalism is also expressed through the proliferation of local research in the field of history, anthropology, economy, social issues and culture in general, often sponsored by official bodies in the region. These efforts often result in a substantial amount of publication on local knowledge, comprehensive reference works, and book series. For example, each autonomous community has now its own encyclopedia, mostly conceived on the model of the twenty-five-volume *Gran Enciclopèdia Catalana*, initiated in 1969 under the direction of Jordi Carbonell and completed in 1993.

Municipal and regional historians have been highly active, and philologists have embarked on a quest for archaic lexicons, revitalizing lost languages, as well as inventing new ones, such as the 'Cantabrian language' supposedly spoken in the region before Castilianization, an enterprise which has not caught the imagination of the public. Attempts to revive the *fabla aragonesa*, still spoken in a few Aragonese Pyrenean valleys, have met with mixed results. More successful has been the case of Asturian (nicknamed *bable*), spoken by less than 300,000 people and made co-official in the 'Principate' of Asturias (Principau d'Asturies). The language is actively promoted by the Conseyeria d'Educacion, Cultura, Deportes y Xuventu (Department of Education, Culture, Sports and Youth) through its own Serviciu de Politica Llinguistica (Language Policy Unit). Its corpus has been systematized by the Academia de la Llingua Asturiana (Asturian Language Academy) and its **language normalization** is supported by grassroots movements such as the Xunta pola Defensa de la Llingua (Committee for the Defence of the Language). Simultaneous efforts in the northern areas of León, where an *asturiano-lleonés* variant (also known as *asturianu de Llеón* or *asturleonés*) is spoken, have been carried out in parallel with the Oviedo groups.

Where language is not the distinctive regional element, other aspects of local culture have gained various degrees of institutional support. Yet, the revival has often been at the grass roots, and local artists have had to cope with dire economic conditions in order to survive. For instance, while the Andalusian government has promoted theatre, literature and **flamenco**, artistic activity has also proliferated spontaneously in gypsy communities without institutional patronage.

Overall, however, though all regions have engaged in a process of cultural revival and community-building, regions do not share the sense of separate identity experienced by Basques, Catalans and Galicians, and elaborating a distinctive culture is likely to be a long and slow process.

See also: Basque culture; Canarian culture; Catalan culture; Galician culture; regional parties

DANIELE CONVERSI

Regueiro, Francisco

b. 1934, Valladolid

Filmmaker and writer

A graduate of the **IIEC** in 1961, Regueiro began his career with the film *El buen amor* (Good Love) in 1963. Since then he has been active in several fields as a director of films for the cinema. His *Madregilda* (1992) is a brillant satire about Franco and the screening of Rita Hayworth's *Gilda*. He has also made films for television, including parts of the series *Pintores del Prado* (Painters of the Prado) and has worked as a painter and a writer, whose works include film scripts and humorous stories for *La Codorniz*.

See also: film and cinema

Further reading

Higginbotham, V. (1988) *Spanish Cinema under Franco*, Austin, TX: University of Texas Press (one of the most comprehensive surveys of this period).

Molina-Foix, V. (1977) *New Cinema in Spain*, London: British Film Institute (a comprehensive overview of current trends).

EAMONN RODGERS

reinserción

A general term for 'rehabilitation of offenders', *reinserción* is applied specifically to alleged or convicted terrorists, particularly **ETA** activists. The first such measures, negotiated in 1981–2 by representatives of the **Basque Left** and the **UCD** government, allowed over one hundred ETA members to emerge from hiding or exile. Subsequent programmes, in which the Basque regional government has acted as mediator, have been concerned with the early release of those already jailed. *Reinserción* has met both with opposition from the right, when applied to those accused of blood-crimes, and with resistance from ETA, which has taken reprisals against its beneficiaries.

See also: González Cataráin, María Dolores

C.J. ROSS

rejoneador

A *rejoneador* is a bullfighter who kills bulls from horseback. Descendants of the pre-eighteenth-century aristocratic bullfighters (*caballeros en la plaza*) who predated the modern foot-performers, *rejoneadores* are not to be confused with *picadores*, who assist **matadors** in normal ***corridas***.

See also: bullfighting; *rejoneo*

IAN CAMPBELL ROSS

rejoneo

This term refers to **bullfighting** performed wholly from horseback, by a ***rejoneador***, employing a stable of highly schooled horses. A throwback to the pre-eighteenth-century aristocratic bullfight, *rejoneo* has enjoyed renewed popularity in recent decades, thanks to such *rejoneadores* as Alvaro Domecq Díez and his son Alvaro Domecq Romero, the brothers Angel and Rafael Peralta, Fermín Bohórquez and his son, also Fermín, Manuel Vidrié, Javier Buendía, Luis and Antonio Domecq, Ginés Cartagena, his nephew Andy Cartagena and Pablo Hermoso de Mendoza. Many *rejoneadores* still come from the upper reaches of Spanish society.

IAN CAMPBELL ROSS

religion

With the exception of the small numbers adhering to **minority religions**, the predominant affiliation of Spaniards has for centuries been to **Roman Catholicism**, so much so that it has come to be seen almost as a mark of national identity. It was certainly regarded in this way in the late Middle Ages, when the long-standing, but uneasy co-existence of Christian, Muslim and Jew was finally shattered with the imposition of religious uniformity under the 'Catholic Monarchs', Ferdinand and Isabella, in 1492. The Protestant Reformation of the sixteenth century largely passed Spain by, and departure from strict orthodoxy, particularly if this involved public profession of other religions, was treated until the late nineteenth century virtually as a public order issue. The experience of George Borrow, whose much-reprinted volume *The Bible in Spain* records his work on behalf of the British and Foreign Bible Society in the 1840s, is eloquent testimony of this.

The net effect was not only that 'religion' was defined as co-terminous with Roman Catholicism, but also that those unable to accept the doctrinal framework of Catholicism found themselves labelled as unpatriotic or anti-Spanish. This made it virtually impossible to gain a hearing for a multi-denominational, pluralist concept of Spanishness, and rejection of Catholicism, in the absence of other religious alternatives, led logically to agnosticism or atheism. Religion, as embodied in the Roman Catholic church, came to appear as the principal obstacle to political modernization, particularly since the church aligned itself, until the 1960s, with conservative regimes and property-owning élites. Inevitably, therefore, the public manifestations of religion attracted deep hostility, both from the state, during the Second Republic, and from outbursts of popular anger, as illustrated by the burning of churches and religious buildings in the early 1930s, and the executions of priests and members of religious orders by Republican militias during the Civil War.

The logical outcome of this situation was that the church, with the exception of sections of the Basque clergy, threw its support behind the Francoist insurgents at the outset of the war. The insurgents in turn were thereby enabled to present themselves as the champions of religion and true Spanishness, and to characterize defenders of the Republic as hell-bent on imposing alien ideologies such as democracy and secularism. The victory of the Francoist forces compounded this symbiosis of religion and reactionary politics. Though as a young man Franco was not particularly pious, he saw considerable political advantages in identifying unambiguously with Catholicism, and he rewarded the Church for its role in legitimizing his armed insurrection and the authoritarian style of government to which it gave rise, by according it a privileged position as an institution of the state. Franco retained the power to nominate bishops, and the state supported the salaries of the clergy; the church, for its part, gained control of education, and the civil and criminal law reflected Catholic discipline in matters of marriage, divorce and private morality (see also **National Catholicism**).

This essentially political process was distinct from, and to some extent independent of religion as personal conviction, and, combined with the identification of religious affiliation with nationality mentioned above, it has had the effect of distorting the statistical evidence of religious belief. In the immediate aftermath of the Civil War, open profession of atheism, or even non-attendance at religious services, was at best disadvantageous in terms of employment prospects or eligibility for social benefit, and at worst dangerous. Though there was undoubtedly a genuine national upsurge of Catholic fervour after the war, there were strong incentives to make a token profession of loyalty to the state religion, whatever one's private views. In addition, however, the importance of Catholicism as a socio-cultural force cannot be overestimated. Even in the 1960s, when atheism could be confessed more openly, it was not unknown for non-believers to insist on their children being baptized. Even in the 1990s, the figures for those describing themselves as Catholic were considerably higher than for actual church attendance. A survey carried out by the Episcopal Conference in 1995 showed that although 90 percent of the respondents declared themselves to be Catholic, 45 percent never or hardly ever attended mass, and only 30 percent attended with moderate regularity.

This is only one of several respects in which the

situation of religion in Spain has become more complex since at least the 1950s. However close the symbiosis between the church and any particular political system, the church always reserves the right to pursue its own mission independently. In the aftermath of WWII, when communist participation in the struggles against fascism and nazism had garnered considerable prestige and support for communism among the industrial working classes, the Roman Catholic hierarchy worldwide, and especially in Europe, mounted a drive to 're-Christianize' the workplace by creating Catholic workers' organizations. In Spain, these emerged as the HOAC (Hermandades Obreras de Acción Católica – Workers' Catholic Action Brotherhoods) and JOC (Juventud Obrera Católica – Catholic Worker's Youth Organization). These bodies strove to articulate and defend Catholic teaching on social justice, which in time brought them into conflict with the regime, and, ultimately, with the hierarchy, which by the late 1960s was steadily reducing the scope of their activities.

Curtailment of the activities of HOAC and JOC ran counter, however, to the new insights on social and political rights which emerged from the Second Vatican Council (1962–5), a synod of all the bishops worldwide. Documents issued by the Council, such as the *Pastoral Constitution on the Church in the Modern World*, raised serious questions about how far the actions of repressive regimes, however much they professed to be Catholic, were compatible with the teachings of Christianity. It is, indeed, from the years following the Council that we may date the growing distancing of the church from the Franco regime. Though the Spanish bishops took a characteristically conservative line during the Council's deliberations, they showed some capacity to assimilate the new climate of openness and to re-examine traditional positions. At the end of the last Council session, in December 1965, they issued a statement expressing regret at the way in which they had been lulled into complacency by the protection of the state.

Many of the younger clergy wished to move further and faster than their leaders, and became increasingly radicalized, supporting workers' demands from the pulpit, and some even joining the communist-led **CC OO**. A survey carried out in 1970 showed that nearly half the diocesan clergy described themselves as socialists. Liberal bishops began to criticize the regime explicitly in pastoral letters and other public statements, with the result that the repressive machinery of the state came to be used against the church. The encyclical letters of Pope John XXIII, in which he had endorsed, among other things, free and democratic trade unions, were censored in Spain. A special prison for priests was set up in Zamora in the late 1960s, and in 1974 Bishop **Añoveros** of Bilbao was briefly placed under house arrest.

By the end of the Franco regime, the institutional status which the church had enjoyed had long since ceased to be sustainable, and the church was ready to embrace democracy, not only for reasons of expediency, but also as a result of the increased emphasis, in theological discussion after Vatican II, on the centrality of freedom as an element of religious commitment. The articulation of the church's mission in the changed conditions of society after 1975 fell largely to one of its most able and liberal figures, Cardinal Vicente **Enrique y Tarancón**, who, while defending traditional church teaching on divorce and religious education, nevertheless committed himself publicly to the consolidation of democracy, to acceptance of pluralism, and to the principle of mutual recognition of the autonomy of church and state.

This was a laudable attempt to normalize relations in a way appropriate to a democratic polity, but in any case there was little else the church could do, since the increasing secularization of Spanish society, in common with societies elsewhere, had considerably diminished the influence which religion exercised on people's lives. It is true that some generalizations about the classic urban/rural religious divide do not apply in Spain to the same extent as elsewhere. Catholicism remains strong in the industrialized north, especially in the Basque country. Conversely, rural Andalusia has a long tradition of anti-clericalism. Nevertheless, the well-established patterns of migration to the cities, together with increased affluence, foreign travel, and the impact of inward tourism have led to a decline in active church membership, as measured by mass attendance.

The other significant indicator is the decline in numbers entering the priesthood and religious orders. During the first two decades of the Franco period, the numbers entering the ministry were exceptionally high, and the decline in vocations was correspondingly greater when secularism began to make inroads into the traditional religious culture. In 1961, there were 825 ordinations to the priesthood; this figure had declined to 395 by 1972, and declined further to 163 in 1981. The 1995 survey quoted above showed that the shortage of clergy had become acute: the church could not provide a diocesan priest for every parish. There were 22,000 parishes, but only 20,000 priests, though there were a further 20,000 members of male religious orders, a substantial proportion of them ordained, and some of these could be called upon to help out in parish ministry from time to time. Only 1,950 seminarists were preparing for ordination, which includes students in all years of the (normally) seven-year training, and many of those would leave before completing the course. The average age of clergy was 57 and rising. Numbers of female religious, at 70,000, were substantial, but this had little impact on pastoral needs. It is also noteworthy that Spain had, in the 1980s, one of the highest rates of application from those seeking to leave the priesthood because of the celibacy rule. In the first ten years of the pontificate of Pope John Paul II (1978–88), 8 percent of the applications worldwide for release from vows (500 out of 6,000) originated in Spain. This figure has gone down markedly, reflecting the church's turn to the right during this pontificate, which has put a decisive damper on liberalizing tendencies, not least in Spain.

Spain, therefore, has witnessed something comparable to the secularization which has occurred elsewhere, but it must be recognized that the point from which the decline in religion started was different from that which existed in other countries. The influence of the Roman Catholic church remained stronger in Spain, and lasted until a later date, than almost anywhere else on the globe, except Ireland, Malta and some countries in Latin America. Although the degree of secularization has been correspondingly greater, the fact remains that, despite the diminution in the importance of the church as an institution, the cultural influence of Catholicism, especially among middle-class parents, is strong. The opposition of conservative lay people to the educational reforms of the **LODE** and the **LOGSE**, plus the proposal by the centre-right **PP** government elected in 1996 to re-introduce religion to the school curriculum as an assessable subject, suggest that, whatever the level of individual belief and commitment, religion as a socio-cultural force still retains a certain power.

See also: church and state; church finances; Opus Dei

Further reading

Carr, R. and Fusi, J.P. (1979) *Spain: Dictatorship to Democracy*, London: Allen & Unwin (pp. 28–31 provide a succinct summary of the influence of the church under Franco).

González Blasco, P. and González-Anleo, J. (1992) *Religión y sociedad en la España de los 90*, Madrid: Fundación Santa María (the most up-to-date overview of Spanish attitudes towards religion).

Grugel, J. and Rees, T. (1997) *Franco's Spain*, London: Arnold (well indexed, which makes it easy to trace the various references to the situation of the church).

Lannon, F. (1987) *Privilege, Persecution and Prophecy: The Catholic Church in Spain, 1875–1975*, Oxford: Oxford University Press (a classic study of the cultural and political significance of the church).

EAMONN RODGERS

Renfe

The Spanish state-owned **railway** company Red Nacional de Ferrocarriles Españolas (Renfe) was created by law in January 1941 to run the standard gauge railway system, which was nationalized under the same law. Renfe inherited a system with fundamental weaknesses, exacerbated by the destruction caused during the Civil War and years of under-investment. From the beginning Renfe began to accumulate losses, inflated by the paternalistic nature of this public enterprise monopoly, leaving the company with substantial debt payments. From the late 1970s the company has sought to reduce operating losses through rationalization and modernization.

Rationalization has included the closure of lines and reductions in services. The labour force has been cut from around 140,000 in 1950 to close to 36,000 in 1998. Finally, the substantial property portfolio of Renfe has been mobilized through, for example, the development of office and retail space at railway stations, the release of land for non-railway use (including housing) and the provision of new services such as telecommunications.

In 1994 Renfe was reorganized into distinct operating divisions, some of which could be floated off in a process of partial privatization. Private capital has played a role in the railways for some time, for example in the supply of rolling stock (from both national companies such as Talgo and CAF, and from foreign multinationals such as GEC-Alsthom and Siemens, which provided much of the technology and rolling stock for the High Speed line, **AVE**), in providing specialist services (for example Wagon Lits had a contract with Renfe to operate sleeping car services from 1967 until the contract was taken over by the French Accor group in 1994), and even in the running of specialist freight trains.

As with many other public enterprises, the government has tried to encourage increased efficiency by tying subsidies to the achievement of performance targets through 'contract programmes'. Where lines are uneconomic and justified only by their public service role, Renfe has sought to secure funding and operating assistance from regional governments.

Against a background of privatization and public expenditure restraint in the last decade of the twentieth century, it is probable that private finance will play an increasing role in the activities of Renfe and that mechanisms will be found to increase competition.

See also: transport

Further reading

Ferner, A. (1988) *Government Managers and Industrial Relations. Public Enterprises and their Political Environment. A Comparative Study of British Rail and Renfe*, Oxford: Basil Blackwell (discusses industrial relations in Renfe prior to the late 1980s).

Wais, F. (1987) 'Los años de la Renfe', in *Historia de los ferrocarriles españoles*, 3rd edn, vol. 2, Madrid: Editora Nacional por la Fundación de los Ferrocarriles Españoles (deals with the emergence of the company).

KEITH SALMON

restaurants

Restaurants of all kinds, from the cheap to the deluxe, from the long established to the most recent arrival, and from the traditional and regional to the ethnic and international, are to be found throughout Spain, but with the greatest variety in the largest cities.

The *Casa Botín*, which dates from 1725 and features in Hemingway's *The Sun Also Rises*, is said to be the oldest restaurant in the world, and is certainly the oldest in Madrid, which is famous for individual traditional and high-class establishments such as *Lhardy*, dating from 1839, and *La Bola*, dating from 1870, as well as *El Amparo*, *Clara's*, *Horcher*, *Jockey* and *Zalacaín*. Particularly characteristic are the concentrations of restaurants such as those occupying the former inns (*posadas*) in the Cava Baja, and the *mesones* off the Plaza Mayor, which take their names from their particular speciality. But changes within Spain, such as the disappearance of domestic help and an increasing 'interregionalism', together with influences from abroad, have resulted in a marked increase in the creation of new high-class restaurants throughout Spain, and in the variety of regional and ethnic restaurants available in the larger cities.

All restaurants are classified on a range between one and five forks, are regularly inspected, and are obliged, along with other public establishments, to keep a register of complaints. They are also theoretically obliged to offer a three-course *menú del día*, or tourist menu, at 80 percent of the cost of the courses taken individually, but the practice is becoming less common, and can easily be made unattractive.

See also: cafeterías; fast food outlets; food and drink; regional cooking

EAMONN RODGERS

Revista de Occidente

Founded in 1923 by José **Ortega y Gasset**, the *Revista de Occidente* celebrated its seventieth anniversary by publishing a special edition. Under the title *La recepción de lo nuevo* (The Reception of the New) it took the form of an anthology of texts from its first period of existence from 1923 to 1936, demonstrating the interest of contributors and readers in all things new in the intellectual world outside Spain: in literary styles, forms of music, and philosophies. Having ceased publication at the beginning of the Civil War, it was revived in 1963 by the founder's son, José Ortega Spottorno until 1975, and then relaunched again in 1980 by his daughter, Soledad Ortega when the Ortega y Gasset **Foundation** was created. Published eleven times a year by the Foundation, it is a leading intellectual and literary review covering the social sciences and the humanities, with a circulation of some 20,000.

See also: cultural institutions and movements; Francoist culture; intellectual life

EAMONN RODGERS

'revolutionary tax'

The name applied to the payments extorted by **ETA**, under threat of reprisals, from businessmen and others in the Basque country, the 'revolutionary tax' is so called because it is supposedly a levy on profits made through exploitation of the 'Basque Working Class', whose representative ETA claims to be. Despite the success of the police force (*Ertzaintza*) of the Basque **autonomous community** in capturing a number of those responsible for such extortion, the practice has continued to be widespread, although by its nature difficult to quantify.

See also: regional nationalism; regional parties; terrorism

C.J. ROSS

Rey, Fernando

b. 1917, Corunna; d. 1994, Madrid

Actor

Son of a general who fought on the Republican side in the Civil War, Fernando Casado Arambillet adopted the pseudonym Fernando Rey, the name by which he became known throughout the world as a highly talented and successful film actor – and known not only by name. The beard he wore for his role in **Buñuel**'s *Viridiana* (1961) became an equally permanent part of his image. As well as starring in other Buñuel films, *Tristana* (1969), *The Discreet Charm of the Bourgeoisie* (1972) and *That Obscure Object of Desire* (1977), he worked with major international directors in the USA, UK, Italy, France and Germany in such films as Orson Welles' *Chimes at Midnight* (1965) and Friedkin's *French Connection* (1971). But he never abandoned Spanish film, acting with characteristic subtlety in films produced by directors such **Drove**, **Regueiro**, **Camus**, **García Sánchez** and **Armiñán**. His last roles were as Don Quijote in the television series directed by **Gutiérrez Aragón** and as the protagonist in **Armiñán**'s *Al otro lado del túnel* (At the Other End of the Tunnel) and Regueiro's *Madregilda*.

See also: film and cinema

Further reading

Higginbotham, V. (1988) *Spanish Cinema under Franco*, Austin, TX: University of Texas Press (one of the most comprehensive surveys of this period).

Molina-Foix, V. (1977) *New Cinema in Spain*, London: British Film Institute (a comprehensive overview of current trends).

EAMONN RODGERS

Ribalta, Xavier

b. 1943, Tàrrega, Lleida (Lérida)

Singer

A significant figure in the early stages of the

Catalan ***Nova Cançó*** movement in the 1960s, Ribalta performed traditional songs, drawn from all periods, from the Middle Ages up to the nineteenth century, and wrote his own musical settings for poems by such major figures as Joan Maragall, Joan Salvat-Papasseit, and Salvador **Espriu**. He fell victim to state **censorship** in the late 1960s, leaving Spain for France in 1968, and only returning after the death of Franco in 1975. He performed widely in Spain and North America and made various recordings, some of them of live tour performances.

See also: Catalan culture; music; regional nationalism; regionalism

EAMONN RODGERS

Riera, Carme

b. 1948, Palma de Mallorca

Writer

Since graduating in Spanish Philology from the University of Barcelona, Riera has carved out for herself two equally successful niches in Spanish literature: one as a Lecturer in Spanish Literature at the Autonomous University of Barcelona, with a special interest in poetry; the other as a much-read writer of short stories and novels in **Catalan**. In the former capacity she has edited a collection of poetry by Carlos Barral and published his diaries, as well as writing on the poet José Agustín **Goytisolo** (among others) and contributing articles to literary journals. She has also written for television and the theatre. However, it is as a writer of fiction that she is best known to the majority of Catalans.

Her first collection of short stories, published in 1975, proved a great success with the public, and has since been reprinted more than thirty times. *Te deix, amor, la mar com a penyora* (I Leave You, My Love, the Sea as a Token) begins with a story of the same name which recounts a sensual relationship between a fifteen-year-old girl and her Maths teacher: it is not until the very last paragraph that the reader is led to realize that this is in fact a lesbian relationship. Indeed, relationships in all their varied forms are a vital component of Riera's fiction, as is an interest in female psychology. Women's lives, hopes, fears and aspirations in all their complexity are explored in a sensitive and often sensual fashion. Riera's prose is lyrical and often poetic, and one of its most distinctive features is the way she mixes different registers and even dialects of language. For example, she uses everything from very colloquial to very formal language, and employs the Mallorcan dialect of Catalan alongside standard Catalan. Not only does the Mallorcan dialect figure strongly in her work, Mallorcan life and landscapes also play a vital role.

Riera's first novel, *Una primavera per a Domenico Guarini* (A 'Primavera' for Domenico Guarini) won the prestigious Prudenci Bertrana Prize in 1980. Other successful novels followed, along with more collections of short stories. Riera has translated some of her own work into Spanish, although there are often major differences between the Catalan and Spanish versions: she has said that if the translation seems not to convey the meaning she wants, she writes a new version in Spanish. Some of her work has also been translated into other languages, including English.

See also: women's writing

Further reading

Aguado, N. (1991) 'Carme Riera or The Suggestive Power of Words', *Catalan Writing* 6: 53–6 (followed by biographical notes, bibliography, and translations of two short stories, including 'I Leave You, My Love, the Sea as a Token').

Glenn, K.M. (1994) 'Conversation with Carme Riera', *Catalan Review* 8, 1–2: 203–9 (interview).

KATHRYN CRAMERI

Rivera Pérez, Francisco

b. 1948, Tarifa; d. 1984, Pozoblanco

Matador ('Paquirri')

For almost two decades after his 1966 ***alternativa***, Paquirri was one of Spain's most versatile and popular ***toreros***. Formerly married to a daughter of Antonio Ordóñez, Paquirri subsequently married the popular singer, Isabel Pantoja. Wounded in the ring at Pozoblanco on 26 September 1984, Paquirri died en route to hospital; his remarkable composure after the goring, captured on video and repeatedly shown on television, made a profound impression on a wide public. His son, Francisco Rivera Ordóñez, took his *alternativa* in 1995.

See also: bullfighting

IAN CAMPBELL ROSS

roads

In the absence of significant inland waterways, and with a deficient rail network (see also **railways**), roads have come to carry the bulk of all land-based passenger and freight traffic in Spain. Across the system the quality of road connection varies from unsurfaced tracks to motorways, endowing different locations with different degrees of accessibility, so influencing the attraction of locations for settlement and economic development. Investment in the road infrastructure, therefore, by reducing unit transport costs has been seen as a necessary, if not a sufficient, requirement for development. Hence, from the early 1980s onwards there was an enormous investment in new roads, including the construction of a motorway system (see also ***autopistas***).

The public road network comprises those main roads carrying international traffic and linking the different regions of the country, which are the responsibility of the state (labelled as N roads, *nacionales*, forming the *Red de Interés General del Estado* – National Interest Network); those main roads providing high volume traffic movements within regions, which are the responsibility of the regions (labelled with the prefix of the region); those roads providing links within each province, which are the responsibility of the provincial authorities (labelled C roads, *comarcales*); and those local roads within municipalities which are the responsibility of the town councils. In addition, various public agencies have built road systems which are their responsibility (such as the Water Authorities and Environmental Agencies). High volume and high speed routes are provided by highways (*autovías*) and motorways (*autopistas*), the latter normally requiring the payment of tolls. Where roads form links in the European-wide system they are labelled as E roads.

At the time of Franco's death in 1975, there were only 1,134 km of highway and motorway and neither Madrid nor Barcelona had motorway connections. Road construction increased during the 1980s, guided by the First National Road Plan (1984–91) and the plans of the regional governments, and supported by co-financing from the European Community. The First National Road Plan emphasized the radial network based on Madrid, while regional plans concentrated on improving intra-regional connectivity. Cuts in public finance delayed completion of the Plan, but by the mid-1990s road systems throughout the country had been substantially improved, the network of motorways and highways having increased from 2,300 km in 1984 to 5,800 km (MOPTMA 1994).

Under the Second National Road Plan (1993–9) the priority shifted to linking all provincial capitals by high capacity roads and improving urban access roads to the motorway system. This second plan was also designed to fit within a broader National Infrastructure Plan (*Plan Director de Infraestructuras*, 1993–2007). As with the First Plan, restraints on public expenditure delayed implementation and forced a review of how investment in roads should be financed, with a view to a greater private sector participation.

Road building in Spain is made more difficult by the mountainous topography of many areas. Around the coast, where there is a high density of population and hence a large volume of traffic (swollen in summer by tourists), land for road-building is also limited in availability and very expensive. As a result road construction is exceptionally costly.

Apart from cost, two further considerations have gained importance in relation to investment in roads: the environmental impact of road construction and the wisdom of further investment in the light of increasing road traffic congestion as the volume of road traffic rises. Traffic congestion, especially in towns and on urban motorways, is coupled with growing concerns over air pollution. Despite these considerations, roads will continue to provide the dominant passenger and freight transport infrastructure in Spain.

See also: transport

References

MOPTMA (1994) *Plan Director de Infraestructuras, 1993–2007*, 2nd edn, Madrid (MOPTA is the Ministerio de Obras Públicas, Transportes y Medio Ambiente – the Ministry of Public Works, Transport and Environment).

Further reading

Tamames, R. *Estructura económica de España*, Madrid: Alianza Editorial (a discussion of the development of roads and road policy is available in each of the editions).

KEITH SALMON

Roca i Junyent, Miquel

b. 1940, Cauderan (France)

Politician

Miquel Roca comes from a family with a strong political tradition. He was born while they were living in exile from the Franco regime, although they returned to Barcelona one year after Roca's birth. He is a law graduate of Barcelona University, and defended people imprisoned under Franco. He lectured at Barcelona University, before being expelled in 1967 because of his political activity. He was a founding member of the centre-right nationalist coalition **CiU** in 1974, and was its General Secretary from 1989 to 1996. He was President of the Catalan parliamentary group in Madrid from 1977 to 1994. After failing to be elected Mayor of Barcelona in 1995, he became President of the Municipal Group of CiU in Barcelona. He is also the head of a law firm in Barcelona.

Further reading

Cortés, J.M. (1996) 'Miquel Roca: abogado y político', *El País Negocios*, 21 April 1996 (interview with Roca).

DAVID GEORGE

rock and pop

The trajectory of rock and pop music in Spain is a reflection of political and social circumstances. Until the 1950s popular music mainly consisted of songs with folk roots: *cuplés* and flamenco, as an expression of the Nationalist spirit promoted by the Francoist regime. Radio stations on American military bases were in large part responsible for introducing rock and pop music to Spain, playing records which, owing to socio-political constraints, were new to the majority of the Spanish audience. In the 1950s Spanish versions of Paul Anka or Elvis Presley tracks, sung by artists like El **Dúo Dinámico** began to appear. Covers of film tracks, recorded by stars like Gloria Lasso, became immensely popular. However, it was ballads, like those performed by José Guardiola, which triumphed in the commercial market.

In the 1960s modern music established a firm foothold in Spain, and this decade was rich in songs which later became classics of popular music. The groups that formed in the 1960s often copied what was happening in other countries. Spain had its own version of The Platters called Los 5 Latinos, and Los Mustang tried to emulate the distinctive sounds of the Beatles. With a few notable exceptions, for instance **Raphael**, solo artists made way for groups like Los Brincos and Los Bravos. Music festivals and *guateques* (dances) also became popular in this period.

The 1970s saw the return of solo artists, with strong vocal abilities and huge followings, including **Niño Bravo**, Camilo Sexto and Juan Bau. This was also the decade of singer-songwriters with committed political affiliations, like Joan Manuel **Serrat** and **Cecilia**. After 1975 censorship rules were relaxed, and songs with overt socio-political messages proliferated, for example Jarcha's hit *Libertad sin ira* (Freedom Without Rage). Another tendency to emerge at this time was progressive rock exemplified by the music of Medina Azahara. The permissive society of the late 1970s gave rise to the birth of the so-called 'new wave' as a reaction against progressive rock. Tequila and Ramoncín typified the aggressive attitude of this movement, and they revolutionized the music scene with their electric guitar playing, short tracks and direct lyrics.

There was an explosion of popular music in the 1980s as an essential part of *la* ***Movida*** which started in Madrid and spread across Spain. Groups sprang up overnight (Gabinete Caligari, **Alaska** y los Pegamoides, Radio Futura, and numerous others) and a new phenomenon in the Spanish music industry emerged: **independent record companies**.

After the euphoria of the 1980s, the music industry suffered the effects of recession. In the early 1990s many independent Spanish labels disappeared or were taken over by multinational record companies. However, other independent labels have since taken their place (e.g. Siesta, Elefant and Subterfuge), whose releases often reflect international tendencies (e.g. grunge, noise and dance). Spain has also seen a resurgence of flamenco music with a modern edge, known as ***Nuevo Flamenco***.

See also: folk music; music

Further reading

Pardo, J.R. (1988) *Historial del pop español*, Madrid: Guía del Ocio.

MIGUEL JIMÉNEZ PINILLA

Rodoreda, Mercè

b. 1908, Barcelona; d. 1983, Gerona

Writer

In 1980, Mercè Rodoreda was the first woman writer to receive the prestigious *Premi d'Honor de les Lletres Catalanes* (Prize of Honour in Catalan Letters). She wrote exclusively in **Catalan**, mainly prose fiction with the occasional foray into poetry and short plays.

Born into Barcelona's Catalan nationalist bourgeoisie, Rodoreda received little formal education. Nevertheless, during the cultural revival of the Second Republic she worked with the *Institució de les Lletres Catalanes* (Institute of Catalan Letters), contributed to several magazines and worked on her first novel *Aloma*, a psychological study of the eponymous heroine's progression from adolescence to womanhood. The numerous autobiographical references in the novel established the pattern for most of her later work.

Together with much of the Catalan intelligentsia she went into **exile** in 1939 as a result of the Republican defeat in the Civil War. She first moved to France and subsequently to Geneva, where she worked as a translator for UNESCO. While in France she became involved with Armand Obiols, a leading member of a group of Catalan writers known as the Grup de Sabadell (Sabadell Group). This relationship, which lasted until his death in 1971, proved vital for Rodoreda's career, for her creative powers had been seriously threatened by the trauma of exile. It was Obiols who encouraged her to continue writing, and who subsequently became her editor.

In the 1940s and 1950s her poetry and short fiction won several literary awards, and in 1962 she published her major novel *The Time of the Doves* (*La plaça del diamant*). Foregrounding both feminist and Catalan nationalist themes by presenting the city of Barcelona as a symbolic mirror of the protagonist Natàlia's struggle against repression, the complex interplay of interior and exterior alienation reflects many aspects of Rodoreda's own experience of exile. Gabriel García Márquez has described this as the best novel to come out of post-war Spain.

In the mid-1960s she revised her production for a complete works, published by *Edicions 62*. This led to a re-writing of her first novel on both thematic and stylistic grounds. The definitive 1968 edition of *Aloma* is in many ways a separate work from that of thirty years earlier.

Returning from exile after the death of Franco, she set up home in Romanyà de la Selva, Gerona, rather than her native Barcelona, living and working there until her death in 1983, at which time she was revising an earlier work, *La mort i la primavera* (Death and Spring) and writing a novel *Isabel i Maria* (Isabel and Maria), both of which were published posthumously.

See also: Catalan; exile; feminist writing; women's writing

Further reading

Arnau, C. (1979) *Introducció a la narrativa de Mercè*

Rodoreda, Barcelona: Edicions 62 (a thorough introduction to Rodoreda's work).
McNerney, K. and Vosburg, N. (1994) *The Garden Across the Border: Mercè Rodoreda's Fiction*, London and Toronto: Associated University Presses (a useful collection of essays on various aspects of Rodoreda's fiction).

CHRIS DIXON

Rodrigo, Joaquín

b. 1901, Sagunto

Composer

Joaquín Rodrigo characterized his compositional aesthetic by drawing a comparison between his *Concierto de Aranjuez* (1938–9) and a graceful move of the ***torero***'s cape in the bullring, thus linking his most succesful piece to a quintessentially Spanish image. As Rodrigo has been blind from the age of three, the reference to the cape's movement through the air must be understood not visually but metaphorically, an indication of his attraction towards traditional values in vogue during the later part of the nineteenth century and revived by the Franco regime as an intrinsic part of the nationalist spirit. From the time of this composition onwards, his style was fixed.

Rodrigo first studied music in Valencia with Eduardo Lopez Chararri, who may have transferred his enthusiasm for **folk music** to his pupil. He went on to study composition with Paul Dukas at the Ecole Normale de Musique in Paris. As with many composers before him, the role Paris played in his development is of great importance, for it was there that Rodrigo strengthened his resolve to write music rooted in Spanish tradition. He has written only one composition that has a definite regional character, the symphonic poem *Per la flor del lliri blau* (By the Flower of the Blue Lily) (1934) which is based on a Valencian folk song, otherwise Rodrigo's music is far more concerned with a centralized image of the nation. The *Concierto de Aranjuez* was intended to evoke the spirit of a mythical and glorious past, and made the composer a leading exponent of the Nationalist movement. Its success led him to repeat the formula again and again, though without achieving the same results until *Fantasia para un gentilhombre* (Fantasy for a Gentleman), composed in 1954. This piece, based on music by Gaspar Sanz (1640–1710), also tended towards a nationalist outlook.

After Falla's death, Rodrigo was acknowledged to be Spain's foremost living composer and was honoured with a number of medals including the Grand Cross of the Order of Alfonso X in 1953. His major works include ballets, opera, chamber music and compositions for guitar, piano, voice and orchestra. Rodrigo settled in Madrid after the Civil War, where he not only composed and wrote musical criticisms, but was attached to the **national radio** and became professor of musical history at the university. In 1996 he became the first composer ever to be awarded the Prince of Asturias Prize for the Arts.

See also: Francoist culture

Further reading

Kamhi de Rodrigo, V. (1992) *Hand in Hand with Joaquín Rodrigo: My Life at the Maestro's Side*, trans. E. Wilkerson, Pittsburgh (a personal biography by his pianist wife).
Marco, T. (1993) 'Nationalism and Casticismo', in C. Franzen (trans.) *Spanish Music in the Twentieth Century*, Harvard, MA: Harvard University Press (an excellent overview, which takes into account the impact of national culture on composition).

JESSAMY HARVEY

Rodríguez Sánchez, Manuel

b. 1917, Córdoba; d. 1947, Linares

Matador ('Manolete')

The son of a **matador** of the same name, Manolete took his ***alternativa*** in 1939 and from then until his death was virtually unchallenged as Spain's leading ***torero***, admired for his pure, solemn style and remarkable technique. He performed in more *corridas* than any other matador in the 1943 and 1944 seasons. Gored by a Miura bull in Linares on 28 August 1947, he died the following day; his death occasioned national mourning.

See also: bullfighting

IAN CAMPBELL ROSS

Roig, Montserrat

b. 1946, Barcelona; d. 1991, Barcelona

Writer

Montserrat Roig grew up in the elegant middle-class area of Barcelona known as the Eixample about whose inhabitants she wrote so knowledgeably. After attending the Adrià Gual School for Dramatic Arts she studied at the University of Barcelona, involving herself in student politics. Most of her life was spent in that city, except for periods in Britain teaching at the universities of Bristol and Strathclyde and extended visits to the Soviet Union in 1980 to research for a book on the siege of Leningrad in WWII, and to Arizona, where she was a visiting professor, in 1990. Her historical interests are evident in the painstakingly researched survey on the fate of Catalan prisoners in Nazi Germany, *Els catalans als camps nazis* (Catalans in Nazi Concentration Camps) (1977).

In addition to writing for a wide variety of Spanish- and Catalan-language newspapers and magazines Roig also worked on **Catalan television**, mainly as an interviewer. By her mid-twenties she had secured a number of literary prizes, including one for a collection of short stories, *Molta roba i poc sabó* (Many Clothes and Little Soap) (1971), that anticipate the themes, settings and characters of her five novels. The first three, written in the 1970s, could be regarded as a feminist trilogy. In *Ramona, adéu* (Farewell, Ramona) (1972) the experiences of women from three generations are juxtaposed to highlight the limitations of their lives. It is the conflict between generations, principally between the pseudo-narrator Natàlia and her father Joan, that comes to the fore in the second novel, *El temps de les cireres* (Cherry Time) (1977). Here, too, Roig relates the repression of women by men to a political dimension, conspicuously to Franco's attack on **Catalan culture**. In the next novel, *L'hora violeta* (The Violet Hour) (1980), seemingly structured as an act of recovering 'lost' texts, the reader is confronted by an array of texts – diaries, notes, jottings, letters – that are symptomatic of the marginal nature of women's writing. The final two novels, written in the 1980s, strike out in new directions. *L'òpera quotidiana* (The Daily Opera) (1982) contains a tale of desperate sexuality and jealousy. The cowardice of Horaci Duc, a Catalan nationalist, is highlighted by the bravery of his wife Maria, an immigrant from Andalusia. The final novel, *La veu melodiosa* (The Melodious Voice) emerges as a positive response to *L'òpera quotidiana*, embodying discovery and redemption: the protagonist Espardenya, rejected by his peers because of his grotesque appearance, discovers a social role while a student activist in the demonstrations of the 1960s. Ultimately he acquires not only an identity but a voice, for he has become a poet – an apt swansong for a writer obsessed by the injustices of thwarted aspirations and unheeded voices.

See also: feminism; feminist writing; women's writing

Further reading

Bellver, C.G. (1991) 'Montserrat Roig and the Creation of a Gynocentric Reality', in J.L. Brown (ed.) *Women Writers of Contemporary Spain: Exiles in the Homeland*, London and Toronto: Associated University Presses (a lucid account of the feminist issues in the novels).

Davies, C. (1994) *Contemporary Feminist Fiction in Spain: the Work of Montserrat Roig and Rosa Montero*, Oxford: New Directions in Critical Writing (an excellent survey of the themes and narrative processes of the novels).

D. GARETH WALTERS

Rojo Duque, Luis Angel

b. 1934, Madrid

Economist

Rojo studied law and economics at the University of Madrid and the London School of Economics, where he became an admirer of John Maynard

Keynes. He was a popular and innovative economics professor at the University of Madrid until 1985, where his students included the future Minister of the Economy, Carlos **Solchaga**. He entered the **Banco de España** in 1971 as head of the research division, and was named deputy governor in 1988. He assumed the governorship in 1992 when his predecessor, Mariano **Rubio**, departed following the **Ibercorp** financial scandal. Rojo is the first head of a truly autonomous Spanish central bank, following the 1994 legislation.

See also: banks; economy

GAYLE ALLARD

Roldán, Luis

b. 1943, Zaragoza

Police commander

Roldán was the first civilian ever appointed as head of the **Civil Guard**. He served as Director-General of this formerly militarized police force from 1986 to 1993, and his appointment was seen as an attempt to bring to a close the troubled history of the Civil Guard, a force much associated with the Franco dictatorship. However, suspicions of **corruption** forced his resignation. In 1994, following lengthy investigations, criminal charges, including perverting the course of justice, defrauding the treasury, and embezzling public funds, were brought against him. Though detained, he succeeded in evading police custody and became a fugitive from justice, before finally being detained in Thailand in February 1995. His escape from Spain and subsequent exile prompted the resignations of one serving and two former government ministers. He stood trial in July 1995, together with his wife, an ex-lover, and his former second-in-command, Manuel Llaneras.

PAUL HEYWOOD

Roman Catholicism

Roman Catholicism, which for centuries was considered to be an essential part of Spanish identity, has not only ceased to be the established religion but has also increasingly lost adherents as society becomes more secularized, to the point, some claim, of neo-paganism. Even during the religious triumphalism of Franco's time, the church–state symbiosis (see also **National Catholicism**) did not mean that all Spain was truly Catholic and was often counter-productive: rejection of institutional religion was bound up with the fact that the church had legitimized the Franco regime, allowed itself to be used as an instrument of social control and shared the values of the then ruling élites. Furthermore, fundamental changes in Spanish society, linked to increased migration, urbanization and economic development, coincided with a new freedom of conscience blessed by the Second Vatican Council. This led in the late 1960s to an awareness of a crisis in Spanish Catholicism in which religious practice declined, priests left the ministry in huge numbers and vocations to the priesthood slumped. A modest rise in ordinations has not compensated for the declining number of priests, as they approach retirement age.

Catholicism, which ceased to be the official religion of the state with the promulgation of the 1978 **constitution**, is still the religion of the majority of Spaniards – over 90 percent – but membership is not the same as practice: only 30 percent go to mass with any degree of frequency and 45 percent never or hardly ever attend; the decline is even higher in the 18 to 35 age group. Spain is no exception to the pattern of waning attachment to institutional religion found generally in the west, and to a 'supermarket' selectivity regarding church doctrines; inroads have also been been made by relatively new sects. Even so, Catholicism as represented by the institutional church is still a significant force in Spain. Of the principal lay religious movements, the influential **Opus Dei**, founded by José María **Escrivá de Balaguer** in 1928, and the Neocatechumen Communities, founded by Kiko Argüello in 1962, enjoy the special favour of the Vatican. The workers' arm of Catholic Action (HOAC) was notable for its struggles against socio-political injustices during the Franco period until reined in by the Catholic hierarchy in 1967; it never recovered the dynamism of its heroic period.

Popular religion is characterized by devotion to the Virgin Mary or other patronal saints; processions, especially those of Holy Week in which emotional piety blends with the superstitious; and pilgrimages to shrines often made in an atmosphere of exuberant, even pagan, festivity (see also **Holy Week Processions**).

Spain has 103 bishops governing thirteen ecclesiastical provinces, 20,000 priests, 20,000 men and 70,000 women in religious orders, some 2,000 seminarians, as well as over 7,000 missionaries abroad. There are over 43,000 Catholic schools, five Catholic universities, ten university colleges, and other higher education establishments. Charitable and social work is undertaken by members of religious orders and lay organizations such as *Cáritas* (committed to helping Spain's needy and marginalized) and the Third World solidarity group, *Manos Unidas* (Hands Together).

See also: church and state; religion; theology

Further reading

Brassloff, A. *Religion and Politics in Spain – the Spanish Church in Transition* (1962–1996), London: Macmillan (discusses the secularization of Spanish society).

González Blasco, P. and González-Anleo, J. (1992) *Religión y sociedad en la España de los 90*, Madrid: Fundación Santa María (survey of Spanish attitudes towards religion).

AUDREY BRASSLOFF

Romero, Luis

b. 1916, Barcelona

Writer and historian

A well-known Spanish and Catalan novelist, the neo-realist Romero was awarded the **Nadal Prize** and **Planeta Prize**. He has also published a poetry collection, short stories, and art and travel books. Among his best works are *La Noria* (The Treadmill) and *El Cacique* (The Boss). His journalistic essays have appeared in ***Diari de Barcelona*** and *La* ***Vanguardia***. For many years he was a close friend of Salvador **Dalí**, a painter he studied in numerous articles and in several books. Recipient of the Espejo de España Prize, Romero began in 1967 to write on the Spanish Civil War in such books as *Tres días de julio* (Three Days in July) (1967) and *Por qué y cómo mataron a Calvo Sotelo* (Why and How They Killed Calvo Sotelo) (1983).

LUIS T. GONZÁLEZ-DEL-VALLE

Romero, Pepe

b. 1944, Málaga

Guitar soloist, concerto performer and ensemble player

Originally a member of the guitar quartet Los Romeros, alongside his father Celedonio (1918–95) and brothers Celín (1940–) and Angel (1946–), Romero has created a celebrated solo career with over fifty recordings to his credit. His family emigrated to the US in 1958, since when Los Romeros, either as a group or solo, have maintained successful international careers. Pepe Romero's delivery is admired for its control, accuracy and purity in a repertory including both **flamenco** arrangements and classical pieces.

See also: folk music; guitar music

JESSAMY HARVEY

Romero López, Francisco

b. 1935, Camas

Matador ('Curro Romero')

Following his 1959 ***alternativa***, Curro Romero has enjoyed a legendary career of frequent fiascos interspersed with occasional but huge triumphs. Though the latter have become increasingly scarce, Curro Romero is unsurpassed on inspired afternoons and retains a loyal following, above all in Seville, where he has performed on nearly 200 occasions.

See also: bullfighting

IAN CAMPBELL ROSS

Rosales Camacho, Luis

b. 1910, Granada; d. 1992, Madrid

Poet and literary critic

A member of the Royal Academy of Language (see also **Royal Academies**), Rosales Camacho received numerous prizes including the National Poetry Prize and the **Cervantes Prize**, and was secretary of the literary magazine, *Escorial*, a publication that played an important role in the post-war rehabilitation of liberal writers. Rosales directed the literary journals *Cuadernos Hispanoamericanos* and *Nueva Estafeta Literaria* and produced a number of works dealing with the literature of the sixteenth and seventeenth centuries, such as *Cervantes y la libertad* (Cervantes and Freedom) and *Pasión y muerte del conde de Villamediana* (The Passion and Death of the Count of Villamediana). A member of the 'Generation of 1936', he attempted to restore the lyric tradition of the renaissance in response to neo-Gongorism. His collection *Abril* (April) is a manifesto for Catholic humanism in reaction to the pure poetry of the 'Generation of 1927'. In *La casa encendida* (The Burning House) daily experience, especially loneliness and disillusion, is raised to universal dimensions. Stylistically he fuses narrative and lyric, colloquial speech with surrealism. *El contenido en el corazón* (The Content of the Heart) constitutes a poetic search into love and friendship, and *Diario de una resurrección* (Diary of a Resurrection) his best collection of poems, is a brilliant synthesis of conceptual and linguistic clarity concerning man's search for freedom. Rosales' lyrics capture the pulse of life with simplicity. Linguistically his work reflects a direct and spontaneous communication with the reader.

See also: poetry

Further reading

Various (1971) 'Homenaje a Luis Rosales', *Cuadernos Hispanoamericanos*, 257–8; May–June (an overall assessment by several critics of Rosales' works).

JOSÉ ORTEGA

Rossetti, Ana

b. 1950, Cadiz

Poet

Since the publication of *Los devaneos de Erato* (Erato's Deliriums) in 1980 and *Dioscuros* in 1982, Ana Rossetti has been recognized as one of the most accomplished and strikingly original poets of the post-Franco period. Her work is well-known both in Spain and among students of Spanish literature abroad, especially in the United States. Rossetti's poetry is distinguished, in the first instance, by its transgressive eroticism and by its luxuriant style. Another facet of her work that has attracted a great deal of notice is her appropriation of images from advertising in poems like 'Chico Wrangler' and 'Calvin Klein, Underdrawers', from the collection *Indicios vehementes* (Vehement Signs) (1985). The sexual explicitness of her work was made possible by the lifting of censorship that occurred with the end of the Franco regime. In this respect, it participates in the *destape* (uncovering), an explosion of repressed sexual expression beginning in Spain in the late 1970s. At the same time, the high esteem in which her poetry is held owes at least as much to its stylistic brilliance and to its profound explorations of the nature of human desire.

Two of Rossetti's collections merit special mention. *Devocionario* (Devotionary) (1986) is a transgressive exploration of the erotic undercurrents of Catholicism, with especial reference to hagiographical literature. In a striking sequence of poems, engravings of martyred saints awaken the sexual imagination of a young girl. *Punto umbrío* (Shady Point) (1995) consists of a complex and tightly integrated series of poems on the theme of desire. In this last book the erotic explicitness of some of Rossetti's previous works gives way to a more introspective look at the loss and devastation inherent in frustrated love. Here, the stylistic sensuality of Rossetti's writing serves, not to shock the reader by transgressing sexual taboos, but rather to render emotional states with striking vividness and power.

In addition to her books of poetry, Rossetti is the author of several works of prose fiction on erotic themes, including *Plumas de España* (Feathers of Spain) (1988) and *Alevosías* (Treacheries) (1991), and an opera libretto, *El secreto enamorado* (The Secret Admirer) (1993). While her prose works have helped to lend legitimacy to erotica as a genre, her poetry ranks among the best written in Spain in the 1980s and 1990s. The scope and variety of her literary activities make her one of the most fascinating figures in contemporary Spanish letters.

See also: cultural institutions and movements; *Movida, la*; women writers

JONATHAN MAYHEW

Royal Academies

The official role of the eight Royal Academies is to act as advisors to the government on their particular areas of responsibility, but in practice they have turned into free-standing learned societies, which devote themselves to organizing conferences, seminars, public lectures and courses, to conferring prizes and to specialized publishing. Membership is for life and, since the Academies are predominantly financed by the state, the official status of the members is that of civil servants, though the only remuneration is an allowance for attending meetings. Candidates for vacant seats are sponsored by Academy members, and the final selection is made by ballot of the academicians. The candidate gaining an absolute majority of votes is assigned the seat vacated by the deceased member, and is expected to deliver a learned discourse on his or her area of expertise, which normally includes a tribute to the previous occupant of the seat. Election to one of the Royal Academies is regarded as among the highest honours which can be achieved in a profession. A few particularly distinguished individuals are members of more than one Academy, a notable example being Pedro **Laín Entralgo**, who belongs to the Academies of Medicine, History and Language.

Membership of the Academies is predominantly male, women occupying a mere 2.2 percent of the seats. In 1997, of a total of 312 members, there were seven women, spread over six of the eight institutions. Only the Academy of Pharmacy has more then one woman member, and the Academies of Medicine and Jurisprudence are exclusively male: the latter in particular has the reputation of being the most conservative. The women academicians best-known outside Spain are the operatic mezzo-soprano Teresa Berganza (Academy of Fine Arts) and the novelist Ana María **Matute** (Academy of Language).

The Academies function under an umbrella organization, the Institute of Spain (Instituto de España). This body was founded during the Civil War, when the existing Academies were unable to function, and initially provided a framework and a meeting-place for academicians in the Nationalist zone. Subsequently, it acquired the role of co-ordinating the activities of the Academies. In 1997, the Minister for Education and Culture, Esperanza Aguirre, announced that the Institute would soon be put on a new statutory footing, and that the annual budget of the Academies would be increased by 37 percent, from 643m pesetas in 1997 to 881m in 1998.

The oldest of these bodies is the Royal Spanish Academy of Language (Real Academia Española de la Lengua, often simply referred to as the Real Academia Española, without qualifier), founded in 1714, which has forty-six members. It is arguably the one with the highest profile, as it compiles and publishes the various editions of the Academy Dictionary (*Diccionario de la Real Academia*), long regarded as setting the authoritative standard for acceptable language use, reflected in the original title of its 1726 predecessor, *Diccionario de autoridades* (Dictionary of Authorities). Traditionally, the Academy Dictionary took a conservative attitude towards the development of the language, and was slow to include new items, even when these had been in common use for a considerable time. Since 1993, however, the Academy has enjoyed the support of a foundation, with a capital of 800m pesetas, raised by donations from banks, businesses and the **autonomous communities**, which has enabled it to proceed to the establishment of a computerized database of the contemporary language, reflecting more comprehensively and accurately the use of new vocabulary in areas such computing, marketing and environment. The CREA project (*Corpus de Referencia del Español Actual* – Reference Corpus of Contemporary Spanish) was formally inaugurated in October 1995 with the signing of an agreement with the Ministry of

Education. In 1995 a CD-ROM version of the twenty-first (1992) edition of the large standard dictionary was produced. This was followed in 1996 by an edition for secondary schools, the *Diccionario Escolar de la Real Academia*, a CD-ROM version of which was also planned.

Despite this rapid modernization in its philosophy and practice, the Academy continues to see its role as that of defending the purity of the Spanish language, in accordance with its motto, *Limpia, fija y da esplendor* (Purify, codify and enhance). Its President, Fernando Lázaro Carreter, has frequently made public statements deploring the inroads of Anglo-American influence, and expressing anxieties about the position of Spanish in relation to the other languages of Spain, particularly in view of the policies of **language normalization** followed in the autonomous communities.

The Academy of Language is also the body which rewards distinction in creative writing. Several prominent novelists are members, including Miguel **Delibes**, Luis **Goytisolo** and Camilo José **Cela**. This is one of the factors which has earned the Academy the reputation of being the most liberal and innovative of what remains a very conservative group of institutions.

Next in antiquity, according to the generally accepted dating, is the Academy of History, founded in 1738, which has thirty-six members. The St Ferdinand Academy of Fine Arts (Real Academia de Bellas Artes de San Fernando) dates from 1744, and is the largest, with fifty-seven members. The expansion of scientific and philosophical investigation in the nineteenth century saw a wave of new foundations: the Academies of Exact, Physical and Natural Sciences (Real Academia de Ciencias Exactas, Físicas y Naturales) (1847), Moral and Political Sciences (Real Academia de Ciencias Morales y Políticas) (1857), Medicine (Real Academia Nacional de Medicina) (1861, but deriving from an earlier institution founded in 1733) and Jurisprudence and Legislation (Real Academia de Jurisprudencia y Legislación) (1882, but based on an earlier foundation of 1730). The Academy of Pharmacy (Real Academia de Farmacia) was the latest to assume its present form, in 1946, though it is actually one of the most ancient, deriving from an institution founded by Philip II in 1589.

Although members of the various Academies complain from time to time that they are not consulted by the government, as envisaged in their foundation statutes, the slowness with which they conduct their deliberations has led to their being by-passed when major programmes of expansion require to be implemented. Significantly, they have had little or no input into the various National Science Plans (see also **science**), where the running has been made by the **CSIC** and the **universities**.

See also: dictionaries and encyclopedias; education and research

EAMONN RODGERS

Royal Theatre

The Royal Theatre (Teatro Real), Madrid, was re-opened in 1997 as an opera house after a complete, but also a contentious and costly, refurbishment begun in 1988.

The saga of the restoration of the theatre provides a good example of the negative as well as the positive aspects of political involvement in Spanish cultural matters. Originally opened in 1850, with a production of Donizetti's *La Favorita*, the Royal was closed in the 1920s, blown up in the Civil War and eventually re-opened in 1966 for concerts and recitals only. The project to restore it as an opera house was initiated as part of the generous **arts policy** and **arts funding** of the 1980s, and work began on it as soon as a purpose-built concert hall, the **Auditorio Nacional de Música**, had been completed. But precisely because it was publicly financed, and because key positions in state cultural institutions are political appointments (see also **cultural institutions and movements**), the project suffered a number of serious setbacks, postponing the opening of the theatre from 1992 to 1997.

In 1993, when costs had already risen to three times the original estimate, and the orchestra director, Antoni Ros Marbà, had been contracted and paid from 1989, the Minister of Culture appointed a new architect, Francisco Rodríguez de Partearroyo, who proposed substantial changes to the plans of the the original architects, Verdú (who had died suddenly at the beginning of 1992) and González Valcárcel. These were criticized for contravening the provisions of the approved Special Plan, for involving the demolition of some of the original and some of the new building, and for adding a highly controversial semi-circular vaulted roof to the cirumference of the theatre.

Then in 1995 the Madrid City Council found that its share of the annual running costs of the Royal Theatre and the Zarzuela together was going to be well beyond its arts budget, and withdrew from the Lyric Theatre Foundation, formed to finance the operation, leaving the **Ministry of Culture** and the Madrid Region to share the costs between them. By then the reconstruction cost had risen to 20,000m pesetas, compared with the initial estimate of 5,800m pesetas.

When in November 1995 the huge chandelier (a reconstruction of the original design by Pedro Tendero, a famous glazier of the mid-nineteenth century) weighing 2,700 kilograms and several metres in diameter, fell into the auditorium, reducing itself to splinters and destroying some seating and flooring, the event was described as only the latest in a long line of disasters. Reconstructed a second time by the Royal Glass Factory in La Granja, it was re-installed in time for the gala opening.

Among the many changes of key personnel in the arts world that followed the change of government in 1996, Elena Salgado, the director appointed by the previous Minister of Culture, was dismissed, and her functions taken over by a two-member executive committee, the new director of the Institute of Drama and Music (Instituto de las Artes Escénicas y de la Música – INAEM) and a representative of the Madrid Region. The artistic director, Stéphane Lissner, was retained, but resigned later in the year, accusing the director of INAEM and the Secretary of State for Culture of continual obstructionism and interference. His resignation led in turn to cancellations of two operas for the opening season by leading international conductors.

Finally opened in October, 1997, with performances of Falla's ballet *The Three-Cornered Hat* (*El sombrero de tres picos*) and his opera *La vida breve* (Life is Short), the Royal Theatre provides Spain, and Madrid in particular, with a venue primarily for opera, but also for ballet, concerts, conferences and other public events.

See also: Liceu Theatre; music; opera

EAMONN RODGERS

Rubio, Mariano

b. 1931, Spain

Economist

Rubio became Governor of the Bank of Spain (see also **Banco de España**) in 1984, a position he held until 1992. He had worked at the bank since 1965 and had served seven years as a sub-governor before his appointment to head the institution. In 1992, however, he was implicated in the banking scandal surrounding **Ibercorp**, then headed by a close friend of his, Manuel de la Concha, who was charged with investment irregularities. In 1994, Rubio was arrested and imprisoned on charges of fraud and the falsification of public documents; he was released on bail after a fortnight behind bars.

See also: corruption

PAUL HEYWOOD

Ruiz Giménez, Joaquín

b. 1912, Hoyo de Manzanares (Madrid)

Politician

One of the 'historic' leaders of the moderate opposition to Francoism, Ruiz Giménez began his political career in the service of the Franco dictatorship in its National Catholic phase, as Ambassador to the Holy See and Minister of Education (see also **National Catholicism**). After a crisis of student unrest in 1956, he was dismissed from the latter post, and began his move towards the opposition. The move was inspired in part by Pope John XXIII, with whom Ruiz Giménez had close contacts, and took the form of involvement with the social Catholic group *Izquierda Democrática* (ID – Democratic Left). In 1963 he established the magazine *Cuadernos para el*

Diálogo, which became one of the most important foci for non-communist opponents of Franco, with contributions from moderate socialists as well as Christian Democrats.

In February 1964 Ruiz Giménez severed his last ties with the Franco regime by resigning from his parliamentary seat. The increasing involvement of the left in *Cuadernos* reflected his move towards a more radical opposition to Francoism, which led to tensions between ID and more conservative Christian Democrats associated with the **Tácito** movement. This division was confirmed by Ruiz Giménez's decision to join the socialist **PSOE** in the Plataforma de Convergencia Democrática (Platform for Democratic Convergence), an opposition alliance committed to the immediate dismantling of the Franco regime and the establishment of a provisional government to construct a new democratic state. This uncompromising position was rejected by a number of more conservative members of ID, such as Oscar **Alzaga** and Fernando Alvarez de Miranda, who preferred to support the Tácito movement's attempt to bring about a more gradual democratic reform from within the state structure. The Plataforma later joined forces with the communist-led Junta Democrática (Democratic Council) to form the so-called Platajunta, from which Ruiz Giménez emerged as a representative prepared to negotiate with Adolfo **Suárez**'s reformist government.

The period approaching the 1977 elections marked his decline as one of the most important figures in the Spanish political centre. The Christian Democrat formation formed by ID in coalition with Gil Robles' Federación Popular Democrática (Popular Democratic Federation), the Equipo de la Democracia Cristiana (EDC – Christian Democratic Team), was comprehensively out-manœuvred by Adolfo Suárez, who had integrated conservative Christian Democrats into his centre-right **UCD**. Aware that Suárez's popularity and control over the state machinery would make him impossible to beat, Ruiz Giménez tried to persuade Gil Robles to ally with Suárez to give Christian Democrats greater weight within the UCD. Gil Robles refused, and the EDC stood alone in the elections, failing to win a single seat. This was the effective end of Ruiz Giménez's political career, although he did occupy the post of ***Defensor del Pueblo*** from 1982 to 1987.

Further reading

Alvarez de Miranda, F. (1985) *Del contubernio al consenso*, Barcelona: Planeta (autobiography which details the history of the Christian Democratic opposition to Franco and its reorganization in the transition period).

Carr, R. and Fusi, J.P. (1979) *Spain: Dictatorship to democracy*, London: Allen & Unwin (outlines Ruiz Giménez' activity in the opposition to Franco).

JONATHAN HOPKIN

Ruíz-Mateos, José María

b. 1931, Cadiz

Financier

A right-wing financier and maverick politician, Ruíz-Mateos faced charges of fraud following the sequestration of **RUMASA** by the socialist **PSOE** government in 1983. Fleeing from justice, he was extradited from Germany after a brief period of imprisonment, but continued to evade custody, on one occasion strolling out of the high court in disguise. In 1989, in an attempt to acquire immunity from prosecution, he stood in the Euro-elections for a party which bore his own name and which won two seats. He then stood in the general elections of 1993 as part of his campaign to win back the companies he claimed had been stolen from him by the government, but went back into hiding following reports that he had been shot at during a campaign meeting. His electoral success was widely taken to be symptomatic of disillusionment with mainstream political parties. He was acquitted over RUMASA in 1997.

See also: corruption

PAUL HEYWOOD

Ruiz Román, Juan Antonio

b. 1962, Espartinas

Matador ('Espartaco')

After a successful start and an ***alternativa*** taken in 1979, Espartaco seemed set to abandon the ring when his failing career was revived overnight by a triumph in Seville, televised live in 1985. Since then he has enjoyed remarkable success, his once-superficial style improving as his technical mastery increased. He led the list of **matadors** in the number of ***corridas*** performed in every year between 1985 and 1991 – an unequalled feat.

See also: bullfighting

IAN CAMPBELL ROSS

RUMASA

The RUMASA group was a huge financial and business empire presided over by José María **Ruiz-Mateos**. In its heyday in the early 1980s it was the largest privately owned concern in Spain, bringing together some 400 separate enterprises, including seventeen banks, and employing 60,000 people. The group collapsed amid allegations of scandal and a rash of criminal prosecutions, and was nationalized by the socialist **PSOE** government in 1983.

RUMASA was a paradigm case of the need to balance socialist rhetoric against the reality of high unemployment and the requirement to restructure the economy in preparation for EC membership. Eventually, the government decided to break up the group and re-privatize the various individual enterprises.

See also: corruption; economy; European Union

EAMONN RODGERS

S

Sáenz Alonso, Mercedes

b. 1917, San Sebastián

Writer

As professor at the University of Navarre, critic and essayist, Sáenz produced voluminous essays including *Don Juan y el donjuanismo* (Don Juan and Donjuanism) (1969), studies on renaissance poetry, witchcraft and the Spanish novel. Her novels often portray the horrors and destruction of war, as in *Bajos fondos* (The Depths) (1949) and its sequel, *Altas esferas* (Upper Sphere) (1949), both set in London around WWI. *El tiempo que se fue* (Time Now Past) (1951), with greater autobiographical substrata, studies the role of war in the decline of a noble Basque family. Loss of family and spiritual values likewise inspire *La pequeña ciudad* (Small Town) (1952).

Further reading

Pérez, J. (1988) *Contemporary Women Writers of Spain*, Boston, MA: G.K. Hall (contains a brief overview of her life and works).

JANET PÉREZ

Sáenz de Oiza, Francisco Javier

b. 1918, Caseda (Navarre)

Architect

Even before beginning to practise, Sáenz de Oiza won the National Prize for Architecture in 1946, the year he qualified. In 1954 he won again, this time with some striking constructions to his credit. His architectural style is generally ambitious, using the idiom of modern architecture to produce uncompromisingly large-scale buildings. The tower block of the Bank of Bilbao in Madrid is one of his great successes, and other representative works are the Festival Palace of Santander (1984–91) and the head office of the Autonomous Government of Andalusia in Seville (1991–6).

See also: architects; architecture; Modernism; *Noucentisme*

MIHAIL MOLDOVEANU

Salamanca Conversations

The *Conversaciones Cinematográficas de Salamanca* was the name given to a conference held in that city in 1955, to discuss the much-needed revitalization of the Spanish cinema. The organizers represented a broad spectrum of opinion, ranging from the journal *Objetivo*, which included on its editorial staff clandestine members of the Spanish Communist Party, to the SEU (Sindicato Español Universitario), the state-sponsored student union. The fact that the participants included Catholics and members of the **Falange**, and that the event enjoyed official sponsorship, with the presence on the platform of dignitaries from central and provincial government and the university, gave it a moderate and pragmatic character, which did not, however, protect it later from official criticism.

Although the inaugural address by Basilio **Patino** and a later paper by Juan Antonio **Bardem** contained trenchant criticism of the intellectual and artistic sterility of the Spanish cinema, there was no demand for the abolition of censorship, which would have been both futile and politically risky in the circumstances of the time. Attention focused rather on the need to ensure transparency and consistency in the operation of the system. The main complaint was that in the current situation it was impossible to know which subjects were taboo, especially since Spanish films seemed to be subjected to more stringent criteria than foreign productions.

The conclusions adopted at the end of the conference included demands that film professionals should be involved in the drafting of a new censorship code, that there should be a clear statement of guidelines as to what subjects were permissible, that an appeal procedure should be instituted, and that decisions on individual films should be binding. This was to avoid the all too common situation which arose when films permitted by the state authorities were subsequently censored as the result of intervention by the church or by private interests on the extreme right.

Despite the moderate nature of these demands, the very fact that sensitive topics were discussed in a critical atmosphere provoked an adverse reaction from the authorities. Some of those who had participated, such as the former Director-General of Cinema and Theatre, José María Escudero, began to speak of a 'communist plot'. A virulent campaign against the organizers was conducted in the state-controlled press in Spain, and the current Director-General, Manuel Torres López, was dismissed for 'tolerating' the event. The journal *Objetivo* was banned. The accusation of communist infiltration was predictably wide of the mark, for the **PCE** itself dismissed the Conversations as a piece of timid 'bourgeois' reformism.

Limited as the impact of the Salamanca Conversations was, they are important for illustrating the tense and polarized atmosphere of Spanish cultural life during the Franco period. They also represent the stirring of a critical spirit which would in the long run prove irresistible, and would bring about a significant relaxation of restrictions even in Franco's lifetime.

See also: censorship; film and cinema; Francoist culture

Further reading

Gubern, R. (1981) *La censura: Función política y ordenamiento jurídico bajo el franquismo (1936–1975)*, Barcelona: Ediciones Penísula (an excellent and well-documented general study).

EAMONN RODGERS

Salom, Jaime

b. 1925, Barcelona

Writer

The most successful Catalan playwright on the contemporary Madrid stage, he achieved his first hit in 1964 with the metatheatrical farce *El baúl de los disfraces* (The Trunk of Disguises). *La casa de las Chivas* (The House of the 'Chivas') (1968), a moralistic view of the Spanish Civil War from behind Republican lines, broke box office records. More recently, he has taken liberal social stances and experimented with innovative theatrical structures. His revisionist drama on Bartolomé de las Casas, *Una hoguera al amanecer* (*Bonfire at Dawn*), was premièred in Mexico in 1991 and was performed in Washington, DC and in France during the 1992 ***Quinto Centenario***.

See also: performing arts; theatre

PHYLLIS ZATLIN

Samaranch, Juan Antonio

b. 1920, Barcelona

Sports administrator

After a career in finance and the diplomatic service, culminating in a period as Spain's ambassador to the USSR from 1977–80, Juan Antonio Samaranch Torrello, Marqués de Samaranch, turned to full-time sports administration when elected President of the International Olympic Committee in 1980. A member of Spain's Olympic Committee since 1954, its President from

1967–70, he was nominated to the International Olympic Committee in 1966. The Summer **Olympic Games** were held in his home city of Barcelona in 1992.

See also: *Quinto Centenario*

Further reading

Miller, D. (1992) *Olympic Revolution: The Biography of Juan Antonio Samaranch*, London: Pavilion.

CHRIS DIXON

Sampedro, José Luis

b. 1917, Barcelona

Writer

An eminent economist, Sampedro began writing novels in the 1940s, treating themes reflecting his cosmopolitan travels: *Congreso en Estolcomo* (Conference in Stockholm) (1952), *El río que nos lleva* (The River that Carries Us) (1961) – depicting logging and its folk culture – and *El caballo desnudo* (Naked Horse) (1970). *Octubre, octubre* (October, October) (1981), his most noted novel, presents a cultured, exotic, cabalistic world. Subsequent novels include *La sonrisa etrusca* (Etruscan Smile) (1985) and *La vieja sirena* (Ancient Mermaid) (1990). *Mar al fondo* (Marine Background) (1992) and *Mientras la tierra gira* (As the World Turns) (1993) are story collections.

Further reading

Quiroga Clérigo, M. (1986) 'Las novelas de José Luis Sampedro', *Cuadernos hispanoamericanos* 428: 144–56 (general survey of Sampedro's first five novels).

Sánchez Arnosi, M. (1982) 'José Luis Sampedro y su novela *Octubre, octubre*: una teoría del conocimiento', *Insula* 424, 5.

JANET PÉREZ

San Sebastián Film Festival

The country's most prestigious international film platform, created in 1953 by a group of San Sebastián traders to prolong the summer season, is run by a consortium of local, regional and national authorities. In 1957 it was granted the A category by the IFFPA (International Federation of Film Producers Associations). The main prizes in the Crystal Palace ceremony of awards are the Golden Shell and the Jury's Grand Prize (films), the Silver Shells (direction and individual performances), and the Donostia and Euskal Media Prizes (for a career in the cinema and a new director, respectively).

See also: film and cinema; film festivals

Further reading

Festival Internacional de Cine de Donostia-San Sebastián: 40 años, 1953–92 (1992) (a detailed chronicle of its history with lists of awards and memorabilia).

XON DE ROS

Sánchez-Albornoz, Claudio

b. 1893, Madrid; d. 1984, Avila

Historian

One of the most important medieval historians of the twentieth century in Spain, Sánchez-Albornoz became professor of Spanish History in Barcelona in 1918, at the age of 25, and was elected to the Royal Academy of History in 1925, though it was to be another half-century before he delivered his inaugural address. A member of the Constituent Cortes of the Second Republic in 1931, he subsequently became a minister and later ambassador to Portugal. After the Civil War he went into **exile** in Argentina, where from 1942 he occupied a chair in the University of Buenos Aires. A liberal Catholic and lifelong Republican, he was head of the Republican government-in-exile between 1959 and 1970.

His name, however, will always be associated with that of Américo **Castro**, with whom he carried on an intense polemic for many years over the interpretation of medieval Spanish history. In works such as *España, un enigma histórico* (Spain, a Historical Enigma) (1956), Sánchez-Albornoz took issue with what he saw as Castro's obsession with genetic inheritance as a factor in the transmission of culture, and accused him of exaggerating Jewish and Muslim influence and playing down the artistic and intellectual contribution of Christians. In Sánchez-Albornoz's view, Castro was excessively pessimistic about Spain's capacity to overcome its inherited disadvantages. His own preferred approach was to emphasize cultural continuity, in line with his liberal belief in progress.

See also: education and research; Francoist culture; historiography

EAMONN RODGERS

Sánchez Ferlosio, Rafael

b. 1927, Rome

Writer

Rafael Sánchez Ferlosio remains one of the major literary figures of the post-Civil War period. His standing is based partly on his first novel *Adventures of the Ingenious Alfanhuí* (*Industrias y Andanzas de Alfanhuí*, 1951), a rich, picaresque fantasy, rooted in recognizable settings, which chronicles a young boy's adventures with strange masters and magical creatures. National recognition came with his second novel, *The One Day of the Week* (*El Jarama*, 1955), **Nadal Prize** winner in 1955, which accurately records the ordinary conversations of eleven working-class youngsters from Madrid as they try to relieve the summer heat and the tedium of the working week with a Sunday picnic on the banks of the river Jarama. Ironically, the only significant event to break an otherwise boring day is the death by drowning of Lucita. The language of the novel successfully combines the banal conversations and *madrileño* slang of the youngsters with very precise, almost scientific descriptions of the geography of the river and the surrounding countryside. Generally regarded at the time of publication as a social realist 'slice of life', offering a critique of working-class existence under the Franco regime, the novel has since given rise to all manner of readings, including historical, social and allegorical interpretations.

In 1974, Sánchez Ferlosio published the first two volumes of *Las semanas del jardín* (Garden Weeks), a collection of essays mainly on language and linguistic theory as well as translations of short stories. In 1986, he finally broke a thirty-year silence in his fictional output with *El testimonio de Yarfoz* (The Testimony of Yarfoz) and in the same year he published two books of essays and one of journalistic writings.

Begun in 1969, *El testimonio de Yarfoz* is presented as a mere appendix to a much larger work, *La historia general de las guerras barcielas* (The History of the Barcielan Wars), dealing with the history of a fictional ancient civilization living alongside the river Barciela. Like *The One Day of the Week*, *El testimonio de Yarfoz* is written in the third person, but in keeping with Cervantine traditions, the narrator of the novel is a mere editor of a text supposedly put together by a certain Ogai el Viejo (Old Ogai). While it seeks to reaffirm the objective validity of history, Yarfoz's chronicle, set against a vast historical canvas and constructed out of heterogenous materials, is complex and demanding, consisting mainly of detailed digressions and sometimes tedious commentaries (e.g. on geological formations).

See also: novel

Further reading

Clarke, S. and A. (1969) *Industrias y Andanzas de Alfanhuí*, London: Harrap (a good edition of Sánchez Ferlosio's first novel, including an informative introduction and textual commentary).

Villanueva, D. (1973) *'El Jarama' de Sánchez Ferlosio: su estructura y significado*, Santiago de Compostela: Universidad de Santiago; 2nd corrected edn Kassel: Reichenberger, 1994, (a very useful study of Sánchez Ferlosio's major text; the second edition contains an updated bibliographical appendix).

d'Ors, I. (1995) *El testimonio de Yarfoz de Rafael Sánchez Ferlosio o, Los Fragmentos del todo*, Kassel: Reichenberger (doctoral thesis on the author's 'come back' novel, including a very detailed bibliographical appendix).

BARRY JORDAN

Sánchez Vicario, Arantxa

b. 1971, Barcelona

Tennis player

The youngest ever Spanish senior tennis champion at the age of fourteen in 1985, Sánchez Vicario became the world number two player in 1993. By then, having turned professional in 1986, she had, among other achievements, won the Roland Garros in 1989, and a bronze and a silver medal for singles and doubles respectively in the Barcelona **Olympic Games** of 1992. In 1994 she gained two more grand slam titles, the Roland Garros and the US open, as well as becoming the ITF World Tennis Champion and retaining her world number two placing. Beaten by her main rival Steffi Graf in the Wimbledon final of 1996, she gained a silver and a bronze medal for singles and doubles respectively at the Atlanta Olympics, and shared the world number two placing with Monica Seles.

See also: tennis

EAMONN RODGERS

Sanchis Sinisterra, José

b. 1940, Valencia

Dramatist

Sanchis Sinisterra combines playwriting and directing with a thorough academic knowledge, and has written widely on the modern **theatre**. His dramatic style draws on historical research and literary sources. In 1990 he won the National Theatre Prize (see also **prizes**). He founded the Teatro Fronterizo in 1977 and the Beckett Theatre in Barcelona in 1989. He has reintroduced classical myth to the modern stage, and reworked masterpieces from the past, often with a contemporary political slant. Many of his plays deal with the discovery of the New World: *Conquistador o El Retablo de Eldorado* (*Conqueror or the Eldorado's Retable*) (1985); *Crímenes y locuras del traidor Lope de Aquirre* (*Crimes and Extravagances of the Traitor Lope de Aquirre*) (1986), and *Naufragios de Álvar Núñez* (*Álvar Núñez's Shipwrecks*) (1991). He has also written works based on or related to modern literature, for instance, Joyce's *Ulysses*, Melville's *Moby Dick* and Cortázar's *Rayuela*. He is the author of *¡Ay Carmela!* (1986), one of the outstanding successes of the contemporary stage, adapted for the cinema by Carlos **Saura** in 1989.

MARÍA FRANCISCA VILCHES DE FRUTOS

Sastre, Alfonso

b. 1926, Madrid

Writer

Sastre ranks among the most openly political and revolutionary Spanish playwrights of the twentieth century. For nearly five decades and in more than fifty plays, he has championed the cause of the oppressed, and openly challenged the institutionalization of cultural expression. In addition to writing for the stage, he founded the Arte Nuevo (New Art) theatre group in 1945, participated in the Teatro de Agitación Social (Theatre of Social Agitation) in 1950, and created the Grupo de Teatro Realista (Realist Theatre Group) in 1960. No other author of his generation confronted the **censorship** of the Franco regime with the same resolve and tenacity. Sastre has also written numerous critical essays on the sociological and political significance of drama. He is also a poet, a novelist and was twice the recipient of the National Theatre Prize (1985 and 1993).

Recognition as a socially committed playwright came initially in 1953, with the début of *Escuadra hacia la muerte* (Death Squad). The play presented embryonically what eventually became characteristic elements of Sastre's writing: the exposure of the human penchant for violence; the condemnation of authoritarian social structures and the abuse of power; the rejection of repressive political tactics and institutionalized codes; the defence of the individual's unconditional right to freedom; and the emphasis on society's need to guard against the spread of tyranny. Sastre's keen social awareness and political commitment are illustrated by his treatment of oppression in *Guillermo Tell tiene los ojos tristes* (Sad are the Eyes of William Tell) (written 1955, banned, produced 1965), *Tierra roja* (Red Earth) (written 1954), *La mordaza* (The Gag) (written and produced 1954), *Ana Kleiber* (written 1959, produced 1960) and *La cornada* (Death Thrust) (written 1959, produced 1960). The importance of social integration is explored in *La taberna fantástica* (The Fantastic Tavern) (written 1966, published 1983, produced 1985) and *La sangre y la ceniza* (Blood and Ashes) (written 1965, banned, produced 1976). The social and political paradoxes of the human condition provide the themes of *Ejercicios de terror* (Exercises in Terror) (written 1970, published 1973, produced 1981), *Los hombres y sus sombras: terrores y miserias del IV Reich* (Men and their Shadows: The Horror and Misery of the Fourth Reich) (written 1983, published 1988), and *Jenofa Juncal* (written 1983, published 1986). **Basque culture** is given sensitive treatment in *Askatasuna!* (Freedom!) (televised Scandinavia 1974), *Las guitarras de la vieja Izaskun* (The Guitars of Old Izaskun) (written 1979) and *Aventura en Euskadi* (Euskadi Adventure) (written 1982).

Sastre has taken subjects from Spain's past, as in *Crónicas romanas* (Roman Chronicles) (written 1968, banned, produced 1982), based plays on classical models, like Euripides' *Medea*, and adapted the works of several foreign playwrights (Langston Hughes' *Mulatto*, Büchner's *Woyzeck*, O'Casey's *The Shadow of a Gunman*), to create a theatre of social and political immediacy. Like the political theatre of Brecht and Piscator, Sastre's work promotes an oppositional stance as a means towards solving social inequity and political injustice.

See also: censorship; Francoist culture; theatre

Further reading

Anderson, F. (1971) *Alfonso Sastre*, New York: Twayne Publishers (an excellent study of the general evolution of Sastre's early theatre).

Bryan, T.A. (1982). *Censorship and Social Conflict in the Spanish Theatre: The Case of Alfonso Sastre*, Washington, D.C.: University Press of America (discussion of the controversial nature of Sastre's life and work).

Sastre, A. (1956). *Drama y sociedad*, Madrid: Taurus (an excellent account of Sastre's views on the sociological importance of drama).

—— (1992) *Prolegómenos a un teatro del porvenir: teoría del drama*, Hondarribia: Hiru (a collection of theoretical essays about theatre).

JOHN P. GABRIELE

Saura, Antonio

b. 1930, Huesca

Painter

Antonio Saura is a major figure in contemporary Spanish **painting**. He was initially drawn to surrealism as a force for freedom and revolt, but on moving to Paris in 1953 he discovered that the movement had stagnated. Between 1953 and 1955 he found his way through a combination of Surrealist automatic techniques and the contemporary gestural painting of *L'art informel*. Late in 1955 he returned to Madrid at the time of the student protests against the regime and took an active part in the cultural life of the city. In February 1956 he burned his books as a sign of his opposition to Franco. In 1957 he was co-founder with the artists Rafael Canogar (b. Toledo 1934), Luis Feito (b. Madrid 1929), and Manolo Millares (b. Las Palmas 1926) of the El Paso group which, like the earlier Dau Al Set started in Barcelona in 1948, served as a forum for contemporary art.

Saura's artistic programme can be seen as a quest to reconcile the present with the past, the modern with cultural memory and the autonomous gestural mark with the image, in a series of dialogues with both old and modern masters and both traditional and contemporary subjects. His paintings can be characterized as a series of portraits, often self-portraits, built up out of a dense network of highly energetic autonomous brushstrokes which contrast starkly with the monochrome flat backgrounds. On one level they are based on a dialogue with a tradition of Spanish portraiture from Velázquez and Goya to Picasso, made explicit by such titles as *Infanta* (1960), *Imaginary portrait of Felipe II no. 181* (1981) and *Dora Maar 20.5.83* (1983), while on another level the fragmentation of the images and dark palette speak of a psychologically dislocated contemporary world. Such paintings as *Hiroshima, mon amour* (1966), *Crucifixion* (1979) and *Great Crucifixion* (1984) deal with suffering and torture. His women series by contrast are compulsively sensual in approach; the very process of painting becomes an act of possession, as he explained: 'When I throw a blob of paint on my canvas I am committing a rape ... My portrait of Brigitte Bardot is at once love and protest'. Saura despises decorative painting and feels that the social function of painters should be to transform life.

NICHOLAS WATKINS

Saura, Carlos

b. 1932, Huesca

Filmmaker

Saura's early work is characterized by a thinly veiled critique of social and political orthodoxies institutionalized in the wake of the Civil War. *La caza* (The Shoot) (1965) and *La prima Angélica* (Cousin Angelica) (1973) are perhaps his most overtly politicized films. *La caza* concentrates on a group of male friends who go hunting rabbits but who end up shooting one another as well, enacting, in their mutual antipathy, unresolved tensions left over from the Civil War. In *La prima Angélica*, a film which provoked violent demonstrations by the far right, the leading male character recalls his childhood and politically motivated family conflicts. The character was played by José López Vázquez, who made several appearances in Saura's films: *Peppermint Frappé* (1967), *El jardín de las delicias* (The Garden of Delights) (1970), and *Ana y los lobos* (Anna and the Wolves) (1972).

Not all of Saura's films, though, are marked by political engagement. A more *intimista* (personal) style, already noticeable in his earliest film, *Los golfos* (The Dropouts) (1959), is increasingly given expression after the restoration of democracy. Films like *Cría cuervos* (Raise Ravens) (1975), *Elisa vida mía* (Elisa, My Love) (1977) and *Dulces horas* (Sweet Hours) (1982) explore the complexities of subjectivity and the relations between the sexes. Many of these films starred Geraldine Chaplin, an actress projecting through her foreignness the dual outsider/insider perspective (through her relationship of many years with Saura, both on and off the screen) on the lives of Spanish women in the 1960s and 1970s.

Whether motivated by political or psychological considerations, Saura's films display from the outset a fascination with formal experiment. Largely unsympathetic to Hollywood conventions and style, these films – until 1981 all produced by Elías **Querejeta** – belong to the European auteurist tradition, especially as represented by **Buñuel**, Bergman and Godard. In its cool analysis of family relations, *Cría Cuervos*, for instance, recalls the portrayal of emotional aridity and solitude of Bergman's *Cries and Whispers*, its use of Geraldine Chaplin exposing the frustrated ambitions and despair of a woman doubly entrapped through ideology by class and gender. All these films reveal a fine eye for detail and composition, not unexpectedly in a director whose first interests lay in still photography.

In the 1980s and 1990s Saura became fascinated by musicals. *Bodas de sangre* (Blood Wedding) (1980), *Carmen* (1983), *El amor brujo* (Love the Magician) (1986), *Sevillanas* (1992) and *Flamenco* (1995) all delight both in formal experimentation and in the exploration of the deeper significance of **flamenco** – its gypsy and Arab roots – beneath its frothier expression in the conventionally 'folkloric' films of the popular Spanish cinema. Perhaps the most brilliant of these, *Carmen*, reworks the conventions of the musical – both in Spain and, to a lesser extent, in Hollywood (with reminiscences of *Carmen Jones*) – producing a narrative that dramatizes, both formally and thematically, the tension in Spain's uneasy relationship with its past, as the country attempts to reconstruct its European future. The past remains a feature of another recent film, *¡Ay Carmela!* (1989). The *intimista* and the politicized Saura combine naturally and elegantly here, in a moving testimony to the unacknowledged heroism of private lives destroyed during the atrocities of the Civil War.

See also: censorship; film and cinema

Further reading

D'Lugo, M. (1991) *The Films of Carlos Saura; the Practice of Seeing*, Princeton, NJ: Princeton University Press.

Sánchez Vidal, A. (1988) *El cine de Carlos Saura*, Zaragoza: Caja de Ahorros de la Inmaculada.

PETER WILLIAM EVANS

science

Scientific activity in Spain has traditionally suffered from chronic under-resourcing, as well as from the tendency to regard universities as primarily teaching, rather than research institutions. Since the mid-1980s, however, there has been a great increase in scientific output, reflected in higher levels of investment, a larger volume of publications, and a higher number of personnel involved in research. In the decade to 1994, the number of research scientists and engineers doubled, rising to 42,000. By the same date, total investment in research, the bulk of which was directed to science and technology, increased five-fold in absolute terms. The Science Law (1986), which set up a framework to co-ordinate the activities of the various bodies involved in scientific research, was followed in 1988 by the first three-year National Plan for Scientific Research and Technological Development. This was an attempt to improve recruitment and training of research personnel, as well as co-ordinating research in agriculture and food science, technology and communication, bioscience, and a category called special programmes, which includes high-energy physics. The third of these national plans was approved in 1995, to run from 1996 to 1999, with a budget of 100,000m pesetas ($794m).

Simultaneously with greater investment, there has been an effort to improve conditions for research workers. It was announced in 1996 that the existing three-year contracts for those employed by **CSIC** was to be extended to five years, with a possible renewal for a further five. Concern has nevertheless been expressed by the scientific community at the scale of the 'brain drain' of Spanish-trained researchers, and of the difficulty experienced by those trained abroad in finding employment when they return to Spain. Many of the most distinguished scientists produced in Spain this century have made their reputations abroad, most notably Severo Ochoa (1905–88), who won the Nobel Prize in 1959 for work in biology carried out in the US. High quality work is nevertheless being carried out in universities and research institutes in Spain, as evidenced by the award of the **Prince of Asturias Prize** in 1995 to Manuel Losada of the University of Seville for work on the photosynthesis of nitrogen, and of the National Research Prize to a geneticist, Antonio García Bellido, of the Centre for Molecular Biology, a joint body of the Autonomous University of Madrid and CSIC.

Despite this overall increase in investment and activity, questions were raised in 1996 about the commitment of the state to scientific development, in view of the fact that the **PP** government elected in March of that year had renamed the former Ministry of Education and Science the Ministry of Education and Culture. A group of leading scientists meeting at their annual summer school in El Escorial published a statement urging that science should continue to be a major government responsibility. Moreover, the objective set by the previous **PSOE** government to increase investment in scientific research to 1 percent of GDP by 1990 has not been met. As a proportion of GDP, spending on research and development has remained static at 0.9 percent, which is less than half the European average.

Scientific research in Spain has benefited considerably from involvement in European programmes, particularly the Fourth Research and Development Framework Programme scheduled for the period 1994–8. In 1994, Spain had an 8 percent share in programmes run by the European Centre for Nuclear Research (CERN), a 4 percent participation in the European Space Agency, and a 6 percent share in the European Science Foundation.

See also: education and research; intellectual life; universities; university education

Further reading

Spain 1995 (1995) Madrid: government publication,

pp. 347–81 (a useful overview of education and research policy).

Yarde, R. (1989) 'Last Rites for the Inquisition', *Times Higher Educational Supplement* 30 June, p. 15 (a compact and clear summary of government-sponsored plans for scientific development).

EAMONN RODGERS

science fiction

There has been a noteworthy increase in the production of science fiction in Spain since the 1950s, though in relative terms it remains a minority interest. The genre has been cultivated by writers whose reputation is based mainly on other literary forms, such as Miguel **Delibes** and Manuel García Viñó, but its expansion since the late 1980s is mainly fuelled by translations of works by, among others, Arthur C. Clarke, Dan Simmons, Lois McMaster Bujold and Paul Anderson. A paperback series, Ultramar, specialized in publishing science fiction by Spanish writers, and a number of titles appeared around 1989, such as Javier Redal's and Juan Miguel Aguilera's *Hijos de la eternidad* (Children of Eternity) (1990) and Angel Torres Quesada's trilogy, *Las islas del infierno* (Islands of Hell) (1989). Spanish writers and publishers, however, found it difficult to compete with the volume of foreign works, and although in 1990 170 new science fiction titles were launched in Spain, none was by a Spanish writer.

Enthusiasm among the reading public nevertheless remained high, reflected in the foundation in 1990 of a magazine for SF devotees, *BEM* (standing for 'Bug-Eyed Monster'), which managed to retain a following despite the collapse of other similar publications. Science fiction writing has also been encouraged by literary competitions organized by the University of the Basque Country (Universidad del País Vasco – UPV) and the Polytechnic University of Catalonia (Universidad Politécnica de Cataluña – UPC). UPV initially awarded a first prize of 1m pesetas in two categories, for writing in Spanish and in Basque, though from 1992 these categories were merged, and the value of the prizes was modified. UPC originally had a similar arrangement for works in Spanish and Catalan, but in 1992 extended eligibility to works in English and French. Prize-winning novels and those gaining second place are commonly published, which has helped to disseminate the work of writers like Rafael Marín Trechera, author of *Mundo de dioses* (World of Gods) (1997), Angel Torres Quesada, author of *El círculo de piedra* (The Stone Circle) (1991), and Javier Negrete Medina, author of *La luna quieta* (Still Moon) (1991).

There is a Spanish Association for Fantasy Literature and Science Fiction (Asociación Española de Fantasía y Ciencia Ficción), which in 1991 held the first conference for many years, at which some hundred people attended. The Association also awards the Ignotus Prize for science fiction, named after the pseudonym 'Coronel Ignotus' used in the 1920s by an early practitioner of the genre, José Elola y Gutiérrez.

Overall, however, science fiction in Spain is more than usually vulnerable to market fluctuations. By 1992 various specialized imprints had ceased publication, most notably the hitherto successful Ultramar. Spanish writers publishing under other imprints had to face increasing delays in publication, and the dominance of the field by translations of British and American works seems set to continue.

Further reading

Pérez, G. and Pérez, J. (eds) (1987) *Monographic Review/Revista Monográfica* 3, 2 (a useful symposium of essays on the genre in the Hispanic world).

EAMONN RODGERS

sculpture

The outcome of the Civil War led to the official encouragement of a pseudo-imperial style in the **visual arts**, including sculpture, where religious and academicist works predominated. Nevertheless, artists such as Angel Ferrant and Antoni **Tàpies** made some attempt to renew the avant-garde spirit of the pre-war years. Ferrant's ludic conception of sculpture, and his freedom in the choice of materials assimilated him to Joan **Miró**.

The 1950s saw the emergence of various artistic groups, which adopted a new idiom in opposition to the contemporary socio-political and cultural climate. *Informalismo* (Informalism) cultivated irrationalism as a violent and despairing protest against the prevailing norms. Two of its major exponents were Martín Chirino and Eduardo **Chillida**. The starkness of Chillida's iron and wooden forms, with their absence of figurative attributes, has revolutionized Spanish sculpture. *Informalismo* had many detractors, such as the eclectic group called *Arte Normativo Español* (Spanish Normative Art), whose leading figure was the sculptor and theorist Jorge de Oteiza, outstanding for his creative energy and original compositions. Oteiza evolved from figuration to abstraction, focusing on the problem of space. His main work is the statuary ensemble for the shrine of the *Virgen de Aránzazu*, which was considered too avant-garde for a religious site and was never exhibited in that location. The influence of Chillida and Oteiza continued into the 1960s, when sculptors in general were producing more statuary and monuments. Significant figures in this period are Marcel Martí and Andreu Alfaro. Alfaro's work expanded the conception of Spanish statuary by developing a form-structure based on the exploitation of planes, complex shapes and volumes, as in his *Homenaje a* ***Picasso*** (Homage to Picasso).

The boom in sculpture since the 1970s has brought fundamental changes in the way sculptors view their activities, leading to freer, more unconventional approaches, inspired by movements such as conceptualism and minimalism, land art and body art. In general, sculptors, rather than creating statuary, increasingly use the facilities provided by large installations, incorporating their works into them. Some artists such as Miquel Navarro, Pepe Espaliú, Pello Irazu and Eva Lootz, even produce statues which look like the installations themselves.

In the 1990s, Spanish sculpture boasted a rich variety of mature artists working with great clarity and precision in their particular idiom, including Adolfo Schlosser, Susana Solano, Angeles Marco, Miquel Navarro and Eva Lootz, renowned for her use of unusual materials such as paraffin wax or mercury. The maturing of a slightly younger generation born in the 1950s, such as Fernando Sinaga, Pepe Espaliú, Txomin Badiloa and Cristina Iglesias, has enriched this artistic domain to an unprecedented extent.

See also: art exhibitions; arts funding; arts policy; Ministry of Culture; painting; Queen Sofia Museum; visual arts

Further reading

Bozal, V. (1994) *Historia del Arte en España II. Desde Goya hasta Nuestros Días*, Madrid: Ediciones Istmo (an account of the evolution of sculpture in relation to artistic and cultural movements from Goya's times to the present).

—— (1995) *Arte del Siglo XX en España. Pintura y Escultura 1939–1990*, Madrid: Espasa Calpe, S.A. (a complete view of the main trends in Spanish sculpture and painting since the Civil War).

Dent Coad, E. (1995) 'Painting and Sculpture: The Rejection of High Art', in H. Graham and J. Labanyi (eds) *Spanish Cultural Studies: An Introduction*, Oxford: Oxford University Press (pp. 299–304 give a concise account of the state of sculpture from the end of the Civil War to the 1970s).

GEMMA BELMONTE TALERO

seafood

With an estimated *per capita* consumption of fish more than twice the EU average, it is to be expected that seafood of all kinds bulks large in the Spanish diet, and this assumption is amply confirmed by a walk through a market or past local shops. Among the favourite fish dishes are cod (*bacalao*), hake (*merluza*), sole (*lenguado*), tuna (*atún*), swordfish (*emperador*) and red mullet (*salmonete*). Squid is particularly popular, in the form of *calamares fritos*, in which the bell is sliced into rings and deep-fried; small octupus (*pulpo*) lends itself to the same treatment. In addition, there is an enormous variety of shellfish and crustaceans, which are incorporated into traditional rice-based dishes like paella, used as an accompaniment to a main fish ingredient, as in Basque cooking, or served as ***tapas*** in bars. The main varieties are shrimp, prawn, crab, crayfish, lobster, mussel, clam, scallop and oyster.

With Spain having the largest fishing fleet in the EU, fishing in coastal and deep waters is an important industry, but it still does not keep pace with domestic demand, and imports of fish and other seafood products account for nearly half of total consumption. In some areas of the peninsula, especially the north and northwest, harvesting of shellfish and crustaceans is still done by traditional methods, either by lowering crab- and lobster-pots from small boats, or, for rock-dwelling species, collecting by hand. More commonly, however, seafood products are farmed on an industrial scale. This can take the form of placing nets across areas of the seabed near the shore to prevent the crustaceans escaping to the open sea, though some losses occur during moulting, when the creatures shed their protective carapace, and can be attacked and eaten by their own kind. An alternative method, more suitable for calm estuaries and fresh water, is to use rafts with suspended cords to which molluscs can cling while they grow prior to harvesting.

See also: fisheries; food and drink; regional cooking

CARLOS ÁLVAREZ ARAGÜÉS

Seat

The motor-vehicle company Seat (Sociedad Española de Automóviles de Turismo) was set up by the government in 1949 under the umbrella of the **National Industrial Institute** (INI) with the participation of Fiat (see also **motor manufacture**). It formed part of an industrialization policy based on import substitution and self-sufficiency. For three decades the company had a protected market, the Seat car was ubiquitous in Spain, and Seat was one of the major employers in Barcelona, and the nucleus of several ancillary industries. In 1967 Fiat took a holding in the company but after substantial losses pulled out in 1981, leaving the state to find a new partner.

The privatization of Seat was the most prominent disposal of a public company in the socialist **PSOE** government's privatization programme in the 1980s. An agreement was reached with Volkswagen (VW) in 1983, which finally led to a majority shareholding in 1986 and full ownership in 1990. The government argued that privatization provided access to international capital, to technological, logistical and commercial expertise and facilities, and achieved economies of scale. However, the company was only sold after a large part of the existing debts had been written off by the government, and the sale placed a significant part of Spain's industrial heritage under foreign control.

Under VW the company thrived in the late 1980s, but then entered a period of crisis, as losses mounted and huge additional liabilities were discovered in 1993. The financial picture was exacerbated by the depreciation of the peseta against the Deutschmark and the sourcing of many components in Germany. This crisis brought Seat near to closure, led to a reduction in the workforce, from almost 24,000 employees in 1988 to some 12,000 in 1996, and precipitated the cessation of car assembly at the Zona Franca site in Barcelona.

Initially, production of Seat cars was centred on this site, but in 1974 Seat took over the former British Leyland plant in Landaben (Pamplona), which became its second major production centre. Following the takeover by VW a major investment programme was begun, including a completely new assembly plant in Martorell, Barcelona. Closure of the Zona Franca plant in the mid-1990s concentrated Spanish production at Martorell, while in 1996 vehicles badged with the Seat name began to be produced in Portugal under a joint venture with Ford.

As part of the negotiations over the future of VW in Barcelona, the company obtained assistance from both the national and regional governments, with the approval of Brussels. In return, VW planned to promote the Zona Franca site as a components supply complex, and began development of a European vehicle design centre in Sitges in 1994. The Landaben plant was also substantially modernized in the early 1990s to produce the VW Polo, and its ownership transferred from Seat to VW.

By 1996 Seat was one of the 'marks' of VW,

along with Audi and Skoda, its future dependent on the international investment strategy of the parent company, the evolving economics of production in the motor-vehicle industry and the on-going relationship between VW and the government in Spain.

Further reading

Salmon, K. (1995) *The Modern Spanish Economy*, 2nd edn, London: Cassell (the development of Seat and its position within the motor-vehicle industry in Spain is covered in pp. 192–8).

KEITH SALMON

secondary education

Between 1970 and the enactment of the **LOGSE** in 1990, the school system consisted of the stages **EGB**, **BUP**, **COU** and **FP**. The full implementation of the LOGSE, planned for 1999, envisages a stage of Compulsory Secondary Education (*Educación Secundaria Obligatoria* – ESO), from age 12 to age 16, and a further optional stage from 16 to 18, which leads either to the more academic school-leaving examination, the baccalaureate (*Bachillerato*), or to the foundation stage of the vocational qualification, FP.

ESO, which is designed as a system of free comprehensive education, is intended to address the educational needs of pupils of different levels of ability and motivation, and diverse interests. It is divided into two stages, from age 12 to age 14, and from 14 to 16, and is structured around a common core curriculum, with an increasing element of choice as pupils advance through the system. More flexible than the system it replaces, it permits pupils to follow different paths in developing the same basic abilities. Completion of ESO qualifies the pupil for the award of the title Graduate in Secondary Education (*Graduado en Educación Secundaria*). The phasing-in of ESO also involves the improvement of school administration and facilities, reduction of class sizes to thirty, better equipment, and the provision of teams, consisting of a psychologist and three teachers, to help pupils with learning difficulties.

The new baccalaureate course lasts two years, from age 16 to age 18. Its purpose, in addition to enhancing pupils' general education, is to prepare them for university or other forms of higher education. Entry to the post-16 cycle is conditional on the award of the title of *Graduado en Educación Secundaria*, or completion of the second stage of BUP. There are four strands: natural and health sciences, technology, arts, and humanities and social sciences. The core syllabus accounts for 40 percent of the marks, more specialist options within each strand for a further 40 percent, and options reflecting the student's individual interests for a further 20. Successful completion of this course leads to the award of the baccalaureate (which carries the title *Bachiller*), which qualifies either for entry to university, subject to passing an entrance examination, called *Selectividad*, or to the advanced level of FP, advanced study of the arts, or the world of work.

The new version of FP also consists of two cycles, intermediate and advanced, both of which qualify for entry to employment. Entry to the first cycle, which lasts for two years, is conditional on completion of ESO. Successful completion of this first cycle qualifies for the award of the grade of Auxiliary Technician (*Técnico Auxiliar*). The second cycle, which lasts for three years, leads to the award of the grade of Specialist Technician (*Técnico Especialista*), which qualifies the recipient to enter either employment or higher education.

ISIDRO FADRIQUE

Segovia, Andrés

b. 1893, Linares (Granada); d. 1987, Madrid

Guitarist

Considered to be probably the leading guitar soloist in any country this century, Segovia, building on the work of Francisco Tárrega, had an important role in consolidating the popularity of the guitar as a concert instrument, transcribing works originally written for lute and vihuela, and composing guitar arrangements of pieces by Bach,

Haydn, Mozart and Schumann, among others (see also **guitar music**).

While studying piano and violin at the Granada Musical Institute, Segovia became interested in the guitar, and decided to specialize in this instrument, despite the opposition of his family, who regarded the guitar as not quite respectable. As a consequence, he was largely self-taught, but he persevered, giving concerts to small audiences in the years 1907 to 1912, when he performed for the first time in Madrid, followed by an appearance in Barcelona in 1916. A successful tour of various Latin American countries began in 1919, and in 1923 he made his début in London, followed by an appearance in Paris in 1924.

By then Segovia was well launched on an international performing career which took him to Germany, Scandinavia, the Soviet Union and the USA. On the outbreak of the Civil War in 1936, he left Spain for Uruguay, where he lived for several years, later moving to the US. It was in Montevideo that in 1939 he gave the world première of Castelnuovo-Tedesco's Guitar Concerto in D. Already, several major composers, with his encouragement, had written new music for the guitar, including Falla, **Rodrigo**, Ponce and Villa-Lobos. Segovia also stimulated interest in the guitar by his teaching activity, which began in Siena in 1914, continued at Santiago de Compostela, and culminated in a series of master-classes given at the University of California at Berkeley. One of his best-known pupils in the English-speaking world is John Williams.

Segovia was awarded many honours, including Spain's Gold Medal for Merit, honorary doctorates from Oxford (1972) and Loyola University, New Orleans (1976), and, in 1978, membership of the Royal Saint Ferdinand Academy of Fine Arts (see also **Royal Academies**).

See also: folk music; music; performing arts

Further reading

Clinton, G. (ed.) (1978) *Andrés Segovia*, London: Musical New Services (a useful collection of essays and interviews).

Purcell, R.C. (1973) *Andrés Segovia: Contributions to the World of the Guitar*, Sherman Oaks, CA: Purcell (includes a list of published works and a discography).

EAMONN RODGERS

Semprún, Jorge

b. 1923, Madrid

Writer

One of the most colourful and versatile members of the Republican left in Spain, Semprún fled to Paris at the end of the Civil War in 1939, joined the Communist Party in 1942, and was active in the Resistance in France during WWII. He was captured and deported to Buchenwald, but survived, and continued to be active in the communist anti-Franco opposition in **exile**, and also within Spain, where, as 'Federico Sánchez', he evaded arrest while operating under the noses of the authorities. In 1965, however, after an acrimonious dispute about ideology and tactics, he was expelled from the **PCE**, along with other prominent intellectuals.

After the restoration of democracy, Semprún devoted his energies increasingly to writing, though he also fulfilled a political role between 1988 and 1991 as Minister of Culture in the socialist **PSOE** government. Already in the 1960s, he had produced the novels *El largo viaje* (The Long Journey) (1963) and *La segunda muerte de Ramón Mercader* (The Second Death of Ramón Mercader) (1969). This was followed by the *Autobiografía de Federico Sánchez* (Federico Sánchez' Autobiography) (1987) and *Federico Sánchez se despide de ustedes* (Federico Sánchez Takes His Leave of You) (1993). Semprún was also responsible for the screenplay of the films *La Guerre est finie* (The War is Over), and *Z*.

EAMONN RODGERS

Sender, Ramón José

b. 1901, Chalamera de Cinca; d. 1982, San Diego (California)

Writer

One of the most famous and prolific Spanish

writers of his generation; his life was split into two by the Civil War and subsequent **exile** in the USA. In his Spanish phase he was a left-wing revolutionary who was celebrated both as a novelist and multifaceted journalist. After 1939 his commitment to radical change gave way to a concern to understand and provoke in others the understanding of a reality that might not be subject to change. While he published articles and novels throughout the western hemisphere, **censorship** in Spain ensured that nothing he wrote was available there for more than twenty-five years. In the twilight of Francoism his works and films of his works became popular in Spain. He returned briefly in 1974.

Sender spent his early life in his beloved Aragon. He saw action during his military service in Spanish Morocco and this radicalized him. Thereafter almost a thousand newspaper articles and six novels allow us to chart the ideological trajectory of this highly heterodox revolutionary up to 1939. Particularly noteworthy are those articles describing the repression of **Casas Viejas** in 1933. The outbreak of the Civil War led to his being separated from his wife and her murder behind the insurgent Nationalists' lines. Subsequently Sender was engaged in pro-Republican government propaganda missions in the USA and France. He broke with the communists and was thereafter to become passionately anti-communist – see the novel *Los cinco libros de Ariadna* (The Five Books of Ariadne). While there is a particular aspect to the dispute – Sender was accused of deserting his post – it is best considered in the broader context of the role of communism during the Civil War, a subject that continues to arouse strong passions. Exile destroyed what remained of his family life; he became estranged from his children when he tried to establish himself in Mexico. In time he regained a relative stability with American citizenship, a second marriage and a post at the University of Albuquerque in 1947, and the period until he moved to Los Angeles in 1963 was particularly productive. Some critics suggest that Sender's powers began to decline after 1970 although he continued writing until his death.

Sender's pre-1939 work is concerned with analysing the immediate Spanish reality surrounding him, discovering what is wrong with it and trying to change it. Personal experiences, military service, imprisonment under Primo de Rivera and the Madrid telephone workers' strike of 1931, provide the material both for newspaper articles and the early novels *Earmarked for Hell* (*Imán*) and *Seven Red Sundays* (*Siete domingos rojos*). The concerns are the same whatever the immediate focus and Sender's prize-winning novel, *Mr Witt Among the Rebels* (*Míster Witt en el cantón*) which explores failures in the First Republic during the nineteenth century, was undoubtedly intended as a warning to his fellow revolutionaries in 1935. It was followed by *The War in Spain* (*Contraataque*), Sender's pro-Republican propaganda work. In the post-1939 exile fiction there was much that was new: American themes – in particular pre-Columbian myths – historical settings far removed in time or space from twentieth-century America or Spain; and some material that defies easy classification; however, a kernel involved the assimilation and reassessment of his recent experience. Autobiographical elements are evident in the nine-novel sequence *Before Noon* (*Crónica del alba*) but they are also there in *Las criaturas saturnianas* (The Children of Saturn) where a host of characters seek values for themselves in a disturbing world they no longer recognize. Moral, philosophical and psychological questions – even in the war novel *Requiem for a Spanish Peasant* (*Réquiem por un campesino español*) – are pre-eminent. While on occasions Sender is evidently dealing with his own internal demons and guilt associated with the death of his first wife, his works subvert cherished beliefs in a manner significant to all readers – he had been to Hell and had returned to speak of it. The form of the novels supports the challenge of the content. Thus the reader has to contend with an eloquent murderer, Saila in *The Sphere* (*La esfera*); a well-intentioned executioner, Ramiro in *The Affable Hangman* (*El verdugo afable*); and a persuasive suicide, Pepe in *Before Noon*. Reality is seen as more confusing than was portrayed in the pre-1939 novels.

In 1995 the Spanish academic world celebrated Sender through two conferences. His rehabilitation is now possible thanks to the work of the Grupo de Estudios del Exilio Literario (Exile Literature Study Group) at the Universidad Autónoma de Barcelona and the Proyecto Sender supported by the Instituto de Estudios Altoaragoneses in Huesca who publish a regular *Boletín Senderiano.*

See also: Aub, Max; Ayala, Francisco; novel

Major works

Sender, R.J. (1930) *Imán*, Madrid: Cenit; trans. J. Cleugh, *Earmarked for Hell*, London: Wishart, 1934 (novel).

—— (1932) *Siete domingos rojos*, Barcelona: Balagué; trans. P. Chalmers Mitchell, *Seven Red Sundays*, London: Faber & Faber, 1936 (novel).

—— (1936) *Míster Witt en el cantón*, Madrid: Espasa-Calpe; trans. P. Chalmers Mitchell, *Mr Witt Among the Rebels*, London: Faber, 1937 (novel).

—— (1938) *The War in Spain*, trans. P. Chalmers Mitchell, London: Faber, 1937; *Counter-Attack in Spain*, Boston, MA: Houghton Mifflin, 1937; *Contraataque*, Madrid and Barcelona: Nuestro Pueblo, 1938 (war report).

—— (1942) *Crónica del alba*, Mexico, 1942; trans. W. Trask *Chronicle of Dawn*, Doubleday, 1944; trans. W. Trask and F. Hall, in *Before Noon*, University of Mexico, 1958 (included in a series of novels); *Crónica del alba*, Barcelona: Delos-Aymá (nine novels).

—— (1968) *Las criaturas saturnianas*, Barcelona: Destino (novel).

—— (1947) *La esfera*, Buenos Aires: Siglo Veinte; trans. F. Giovanelli, *The Sphere*, London: Gray Walls Press, 1950 (novel).

—— (1952) *El verdugo afable*, Santiago de Chile: Nascimiento; trans. F. Hall, *The Affable Hangman*, London: Jonathan Cape, 1954 (novel).

—— (1957) *Los cinco libros de Ariadna*, New York: Iberica (novel).

—— (1992) *Réquiem por un campesino español*, P. McDermott (ed.), Manchester: Manchester University Press (this novel was originally published as *Mosén Millán* in 1953).

Further reading

King, C.L. (1974) *Ramón J. Sender*, New York: Twayne Publishers (the first full-length study in English).

Lough, F. (1996) *Politics and Philosophy in the Early Novels of Ramón J. Sender, 1930–1936: The Impossible Revolution*, Lewiston and Lampeter: Edwin Mellen (this study argues that the early novels are best understood with reference to the philosophy of Schopenhauer; it also analyses three later novels which incorporate pre-Civil War material).

Trippett, A. (1986) *Adjusting to Reality: Philosophical and Psychological Ideas in the Post-Civil War Novels of Ramón J. Sender*, London: Tamesis (an exploration of the impact of defeat and exile).

Vásquez, M.S. (ed.) (1987) *Homenaje a Ramón J. Sender*, Newark, NJ: Delaware.

ANTHONY TRIPPETT

SER

A privately-owned **radio** network in which the PRISA group (the owners of, among other media outlets, the leading daily newspaper *El* ***País***) has a stake, SER commands by far the highest audience of all networks, attracting in 1996, for example, a total of 9.6 million listeners, compared with **COPE**'s 4 million, Radio Nacional's 2.9 million, and Onda Cero's 2.5 million. Its various channels include 40 Principales, dedicated to **rock and pop**, which was the most popular channel during the late 1980s and the first half of the 1990s, and the late-night news programme, Hora 25, which during the transition to democracy provided the first uncensored news, and has retained its very large audience share.

See also: media

EAMONN RODGERS

Serra, Narcís

b. 1943, Barcelona

Politician

Narcís Serra was active in opposition politics during the Franco regime. He quickly rose to power in the ranks of the socialist **PSOE**. He was elected Mayor of Barcelona in the late 1970s, and, to the surprise of many observers, became Defence Minister in the first **González** government in 1982. He rose to the position of Vice-President of the Spanish Government in 1991, but lost popularity thereafter as the ruling party became tainted by **corruption**. Again to the surprise of some observers, Serra was re-elected in the 1996 general elections.

DAVID GEORGE

Serra d'Or

The monthly journal *Serra d'Or* was founded by the Benedictine monks of Montserrat (Catalonia) in 1959. Up to the end of 1963, it described itself as the organ of the Confraternity of Our Lady of Montserrat, but its significance is much greater than this would suggest. As a church publication, it escaped the worst effects of the **censorship** which prevailed throughout the Franco regime, and which bore particularly heavily on publications in **Catalan**. As the only periodical in that language circulating throughout Catalan-speaking areas until the restoration of democracy, it had to fulfil several roles. Though it was the main Catalan religious journal, directly theological articles usually occupied only about 5 percent of the space in the 1960s, the remainder being made up of articles on literary criticism, world affairs, economics, art and archaeology, cinema, architecture, urban development and housing, and industrial design. Its very distinguished range of contributors included Joan Triadú, Joaquim Molas, Josep Maria Castellet, Josep Benet, Joan **Fuster**, Francesc Candel, Jordi **Pujol**, Miquel **Roca** and Francesc Vallverdú. Furthermore, the journal established early a policy of ideological pluralism. Though many of those who wrote regularly in *Serra d'Or* could be described as Catholics who were theologically liberal and politically left-of-centre, others proved subsequently to have been clandestine members of the banned **Catalan United Socialist Party**, the communist PSUC. Its editorial policy is characterized by an international outlook, an openness to dynamism and dialogue in religious matters, and a commitment to democracy and freedom of speech.

These values were difficult to make explicit within the constraints of Francoist censorship, but *Serra d'Or* managed to maintain its distinctive liberal intellectual witness, exploiting to the limits of safety the limited freedom conferred by inconsistencies in the application of censorship. Though it was not possible to question the basic structure of the state or its political methods, social issues like housing could be discussed, especially in the context of events like the flood disaster in Catalonia in 1962.

Serra d'Or was also one of the main sources of liberalizing influences in **Roman Catholicism**, especially in the years after the Second Vatican Council (1962–5), when it championed ecumenical dialogue, co-operation with secular bodies traditionally distanced from the church, such as trade unions and left-wing political parties, and the rights of cultural minorities. Liberal Catholicism thus became closely associated with defence of Catalan cultural identity. New Catalan writing was reviewed at length, and Catalan contributions to **architecture** and the plastic arts were given considerable prominence. The journal has consistently encouraged an international outlook, while at the same time providing a distinctively Catalan perspective on world affairs.

See also: Catalan culture; regional nationalism

EAMONN RODGERS

Serrat, Joan Manuel

b. 1943, Barcelona

Singer

Serrat is one of the most celebrated singer-songwriters in Spain. He appeared on the scene in 1965 in the Catalan ***Nova Cançó*** movement. He was the great discovery of the movement and his songs received considerable exposure on the air, making them chart successes. In 1967 he broke the unity of the *cançó* and recorded songs in Spanish for the first time, although his Catalan identity was always of foremost importance to him (he refused to sing in the Eurovision song contest in 1968 as Catalan was not permissible and he had recurrent problems with state **censorship**).

Serrat has recorded over twenty-five LPs and has a long list of hit records. His seminal work has influenced generations of singer-songwriters.

See also: Catalan culture; folk music; regional nationalism; rock and pop

MIGUEL JIMÉNEZ PINILLA

Sert, José Luis

b. 1902, Barcelona; d. 1983, Barcelona

Architect

After qualifying in 1928 Sert left Barcelona for Paris to work with Le Corbusier until 1930, an experience which was to leave its mark on his professional career. On returning to Spain he helped to found **GATEPAC**, an organization of creative artists who wanted to establish in Spain the avant-garde ideas already being developed in Europe by the Bauhaus school in Germany or by Le Corbusier in France. When he came back to Barcelona he became immersed in the intellectual ferment stimulated by the liberal climate of the Second Republic (1931–9), and was resolutely opposed to any return to historic styles. He evolved an idiom which combined elements of Mediterranean tradition, forms of construction rooted in Catalan culture, and avant-garde elements imported from Europe. Among the works of this period are the Dispensari Central Antituberculós (Central Anti-Tuberculosis Dispensary, with Torres i Clavé) (1935) and the Casa Bloc (1934–6) which display both a revival of architectural form and a use of new techniques. In 1937, a year after the start of the Civil War, Sert designed and constructed (with Luis Lacasa) the Spanish Republic's Pavilion at the International Exhibition in Paris. Exteriors and interiors alternated along the route through the Pavilion where the works of **Picasso** (*Guernica*), Julio González, Juan **Miró** and Calder were displayed. This project was in a sense his artistic manifesto, and he was to take up and develop the architectural themes of the Pavilion in some of his best-known later works.

After the Civil War he went into exile in the United States, and in 1945 he founded, in New York, Town Planning Associates, a firm which specialized in large urbanization projects in Latin America. He was also one of the most active members of the CIAM (International Congress of Modern Architecture), an organization which had been the inspiration for GATEPAC in Spain. He was appointed President of CIAM from 1947 to 1956, and remained a very committed member until its dissolution in 1959. In 1953 he succeeded Walter Gropius as Dean of the School of Architecture at Harvard, a position he held until his retirement in 1968. He also worked in his own practice in partnership with Jackson and Gourley, and from the late 1950s he was regarded as one of the best architects in the US. He constantly strove in his buildings to harmonize the public and private spheres, and to achieve continuity between exteriors and interiors, often through very sensitive placing of light sources. Among his best known American achievements are the US Embassy in Baghdad (1955–60), Holyoke Center (Harvard, 1958–65) and the Welfare Island Housing Project (New York, 1971).

After designing Miró's house-cum-studio in Mallorca (1955), Sert reactivated his links with Europe. Among the prestigious projects that followed, the best-known are the *Fondation Maeght* (Saint Paul de Vence, 1959–64) and the Miró Foundation (Barcelona, 1972–5). Towards the end of his life he returned to Barcelona, where he was showered with honours and awarded the highest distinctions.

See also: architects; architecture; Modernism; *nouocentisme*

Further reading

Freixa, J. (1979) *José Luis Sert*, Barcelona: Gili.

Zevi, B. (1976) *Sert's Architecture in the Miró Foundation*, Barcelona: Polígrafa.

MIHAIL MOLDOVEANU

services

In common with other developed countries Spain has an economy based principally on services. The tertiary sector generates about 63 percent of Spain's GDP as against approximately 25 percent for industry, 8 percent for construction and 4 percent for agriculture and fisheries. The Spanish services sector is in turn characterized by the importance of **tourism** alongside the more conventionally important services of commerce, education (see also **education and research**), **health care**, public administration, **transport** and business services of all kinds. Since the beginning of Spain's economic leap forward in 1960, the tertiary sector has grown far more than the primary and secondary sectors, and this remains true even for the years of **industrial development** (1960–73), when the transfer of surplus agricultural labour was higher to services than to industry. Most services are located in towns and cities, hence the heavy internal **migration** from countryside to town and the rapid **urbanization** of those years. The trend towards employment in services became even more marked during the long recession of 1975–84, when industry underwent a process of shrinkage. The services sector was the only one to show a net gain in employment (by about 450,000 jobs) during these difficult years.

The classical explanation for tertiarization – that as household incomes rise a family will spend proportionately less on material necessities and proportionately more on leisure, education, health and the like – has been reinforced in the case of Spain by other factors. First, there is the obvious fact that Spain has been the beneficiary of other people's leisure spending, hence the importance of its tourism sector. Second, the implantation of democracy and regional devolution brought in its train a major expansion of services provided by the state and the new **autonomous communities**. And third, the opening up of Spain's international trade both immediately before and after accession to the Treaty of Rome led to a very significant increase in the activity of the financial and advertising sub-sectors.

Since the early 1980s, 1,700,000 jobs have been created in services, although different areas have had different fortunes. There has been a loss of jobs in commerce, in repairs, in transport, and in domestic services. On the other hand, there has been a major increase in jobs in hotel and catering, in business services, and in leisure and cultural services, although many of the newly employed have been women on part-time or seasonal contracts. But above all there was, throughout the 1980s, a huge increase in jobs provided by the state, namely in Public Administration, Health, Education, and Social Security, which together more than compensated for losses in other areas of services. But even after public sector spending was curtailed in the mid-1990s, the services sector continued to contribute powerfully to employment: in 1995 and 1996 – years of recovery after the recession of the early 1990s – four out of every five jobs created were in services, due in some measure to the boom in part-time contracts following the 1994 **labour market** reforms.

Since the mid-1980s developments in the services sector have also been affected by the need to adjust to European competition and legislation. Financial and business services have been at the forefront of developments, prompted in part by the arrival of foreign firms, and therefore not always comfortable for native enterprises. The net impact of Europeanization on job creation remains unclear because the shake-out involves mergers and takeovers, which often result in job losses, as well as the implantation of new businesses, which result in job creation. Deregulation, which was initially slow in the services sector, is proceeding apace. The first subsector to be deregulated was banking, with the removal of a variety of compulsory coefficients and a number of other constraints on the private **banks**, as well as the lifting of geographical and other restrictions on the savings banks (**Cajas de Ahorros**). The stock exchanges, too, have been liberalized, reformed and modernized. In real estate services property contracts, rents and leases for all new properties were liberalized in 1985; further legislation, meant to redress the balance by allowing for the revision of existing contracts in the case of older, tenanted property, was approved in 1995. Transport has undergone some minor adjustments, mainly as a result of deregulation in civil aviation: Iberia's loss of its monopoly on domestic flights has brought in new competition and a thorough revision of fare structures. Deregulation of telephone and telecommunication services has been much slower in coming: partial liberalization occurred in 1987 but full deregulation was not due to be achieved until 1998 in accordance with EU requirements. Telefónica, the state-owned telephone company, is being privatized as well as having to face tough competition for the first time. Foreign interest in the Spanish telecommunications sector is intense, and it is expected to be one of the best-performing areas of the entire services sector. Another area of services greatly affected by European integration and showing increasing domination by foreign companies is insurance. Because Spanish households are relatively underinsured, health, life and pensions insurance is expected to undergo substantial expansion.

Distribution and retailing have also had to adapt to the changing pattern of business. The traditional, small to medium size family-owned shops have been adversely affected by competition from large stores, and the numbers declined by 30 percent in the ten years to 1995. Large-scale retailing is now, with one major exception, in the hands of foreign companies, especially French ones such as Continent, Auchamp and Carrefour, although Marks & Spencer has also successfully implanted itself in several major Spanish cities. The one exception to this trend, and the jewel in the crown of Spanish retailing, is the hugely successful El **Corte Inglés** chain of department stores and its hypermarket subsidiary Hipercor, which together constitute the third largest company by turnover in Spain behind Telefónica and Repsol. Within the retailing sector a recent development has been the opening of large shopping malls in the major cities.

The services sector in Spain is still in the throes of adaptive change. Traditionally inefficient, inflationary and fragmented, the process of deregulation, competition and concentration to which it is being subjected is bound to bring about further transformation. Provided that tourism retains its importance, the services sector will continue to provide employment opportunities for two out of every three working Spaniards.

Further reading

Chislett, W. (1996) *Spain 1996. The Central Hispano Handbook*, Madrid (although the handbook lacks a chapter on services, chapters 6 on tourism and property, and 7 on finance, contain much useful information).

Salmon, K. (1995) *The Modern Spanish Economy. Transformation and Integration into Europe*, London: Pinter (chapter 8 contains an informative survey of financial, insurance and other services).

C.A. LONGHURST

sexual behaviour

No-one can doubt that something akin to a sexual revolution has occurred in Spain since the end of the dictatorship; yet the amount of reliable information about the sexual behaviour of Spaniards remains scarce, since surveys often point to contradictory conclusions. The 1980s was the decade when sexual permissiveness became fashionable, and this was evident in the wave of **pornography** that engulfed newspaper stands, theatre and club stages, and cinema and television screens, as well as in the liberated attitudes towards sexual matters reflected in opinion polls. Public, as distinct from private, sexual liberation must largely be ascribed to the waning influence of the Roman Catholic Church in Spain that accompanied, or even antedated, the rediscovery of democracy (see also **Roman Catholicism**). This explains the wide acceptance among Spaniards, and especially the younger generations, of contraception, premarital intercourse, cohabitation, divorce, and even, though less clearly, abortion, practices still outlawed by the Catholic Church. According to the 1975 FOESSA report, by 1973 only 22 percent of the population considered artificial birth control methods to be objectionable.

The key to changes in sexual behaviour, and not simply attitudes, lies almost certainly in the availability of contraceptives, though the precise nature and timing of the change are not easy to gauge. Before the end of the Franco regime the Department of Health and Social Security knew that half-a-million women were being prescribed the contraceptive pill on the pretext of hormonal disorders, the only grounds on which it could legally be prescribed and supplied. Similarly, the sale of condoms was illegal but they could be bought under the counter. Nevertheless the legalization and wide availability of artificial contraceptives after 1978 made an enormous difference, not least to women who could now decide how many children to have and when. Paradoxically, the rate of abortions, estimated at some 300,000 a year under Franco (illegal of course), does not appear to have come down dramatically, suggesting that there has persisted a good deal of ignorance about sexual activity. To some extent this is borne out by the results of a 1993 survey carried out for the fifth FOESSA report: 52 percent of 18 to 21-year-olds declared that they did not use any method of birth control. The corresponding figures for older respondents are much lower (23 percent of 22 to 25-year-olds, 23 percent of 26 to 35, and 32 percent of 36 to 45), but still higher than one would expect considering the extremely low Spanish birthrate. Given that this amounts to nearly one in three of the 18 to 45 population not using birth control, it suggests lower than expected sexual activity. This hypothesis is supported by some surveys: the Durex survey of 1996 (reliability unknown) states that Spanish couples have sex on average 71 times a year compared to 96 in Italy, 124 in Britain and 128 in France.

Other polls, however, have produced contradictory results. A study published in 1986 by the Valencian Institute for Research, of Spanish adolescents between the ages of fourteen and nineteen, discovered that no more than 14 percent had lost their virginity. Yet in a poll carried out that same year by the Instituto Nacional de la Juventud (National Youth Institute), 60 percent of respondents said they had had sex by the age of eighteen (56 percent in the case of girls).

Nevertheless, despite these variations, what these polls indicate is a sea change taking place in Spanish attitudes towards sexual relations between 1970 and 1990, and especially attitudes as they affect **women**. As late as 1975, 80 percent of respondents in a FOESSA III poll indicated their belief that a woman should be a virgin at marriage. By 1992, in a survey by Amando de Miguel's Universidad Complutense team, only 40 percent of housewives, whom one might assume to be among the least permissive, are against pre-marital sex, a figure reduced to just 28 percent in the case of housewives who are university graduates. In the 1970s, no more than one-third of the population indicated acceptance of pre-marital sexual relations, but in a 1989 poll carried out by the Centro de Investigaciones Sociológicas (Centre for Sociological Research), 50 percent of respondents approved of sexual relations between a courting couple, 36 percent disapproved, and 14 percent did not know. In the same poll 66 percent of respondents found a sexual relationship outside marriage acceptable for men and 63 percent found it acceptable for women; a majority of those against were in the 50+ age bracket.

There are, however, grounds for thinking that attitudes have been considerably more daring than actual behaviour. Cohabitation is accepted as normal by two-thirds of Spaniards, but those who practice it remain a tiny minority. The Instituto Nacional de Estadística (National Statistical Institute) published data based on the 1991 population survey, which showed that 1.08 percent of the population aged ten and over had cohabited at some time. These figures are incomplete, because married couples who started off cohabiting are recorded only as married. The figures also show significant geographical variations: the highest incidence of cohabitation is in Barcelona, with twice the national average, followed by Madrid, indicating that this is predominantly a cosmopolitan phenomenon. The cohorts most affected are in the 20 to 29 and 30 to 39 age brackets. The bulk of cohabitants are single, only a quarter being divorced or separated. A significant cultural factor is that there is a positive correlation between cohabitation and both high income levels and a higher than average educational level: the higher the educational level the higher the incidence of cohabitation. Even more revealing is the fact that it is the educational level of the woman, rather than the man, that is the major determining factor: among women graduates the incidence of cohabitation is five times higher than the average, but only three times higher in the case of men. Like so many other social changes in contemporary Spain, this one too appears to be intimately connected to the educational emancipation of Spanish women.

See also: social attitudes; society

Further reading

De Miguel, A. (1994) *La sociedad española 1993–4*, Madrid: Alianza (see pp. 316–32 on sexual relations and attitudes to marriage and cohabitation).

Fundación FOESSA (1994) *V Informe sociológico sobre la situación social en España*, Madrid (vol. 1, chapter 3 contains a section on cohabitation).

Hooper, J. (1995) *The New Spaniards*, Harmondsworth: Penguin (chapter 10 on sex is highly readable).

C.A. LONGHURST

shanty towns

Migration from countryside to town has long been a feature of Spanish life, and was accentuated in the 1940s and 1950s by post-Civil War hardship and by the shift in the economic base from agriculture to industry, with consequent pressure on **housing** in the major cities, especially Madrid and Barcelona. Something like 14 percent of the total population is estimated to have moved residence during these years. Shortage of accommodation gave rise to the phenomenon referred to as *chabolismo*, from the Spanish word *chabola*, an improvised shack made of discarded builder's rubble, wood, corrugated iron, flattened oil-drums and similar materials. The corresponding term in Catalan is *barraca*. When the authorities failed to control the tide of migration, they attempted to regulate the problem by issuing licences and demolishing unlicensed dwellings. Even where permits were obtained, however, the inhabitants were often obliged to wait years for basic services like electricity and refuse collection.

By the 1960s, the numbers of *chabolas* or *barraques* had stabilized, and were beginning to be sold and bought like other immovable properties, especially since with increasing prosperity some of the original migrants were beginning to move on to better accommodation in new apartment blocks. By around 1970, the area covered by shanty towns was beginning to shrink, though they have never been completely eliminated. In the first ten years of the socialist **PSOE** administration (1982–92), the number of *chabolas* was reduced to half, and stood officially at 12,000 in the whole of Spain, but one Madrid suburb still had the largest concentration of shanty-town dwellers in Europe. There has, however, been a significant change in the population, which in the 1990s consisted predominantly of gypsies and **immigrants** from outside Spain, and the shanty-towns have been the scene of some of the most serious occurrences of **racism**.

See also: housing market; planning; urbanization

EAMONN RODGERS

Simó, Isabel-Clara

b. 1943, Alcoi

Writer

Isabel-Clara Simó is one of the best-known contemporary Catalan writers. She is a journalist, short-story writer, novelist and poet, and has written books for children. Three of her crime novels have won awards, while her novels deal with the theme of love as both a creative and a destructive force. Simó is a founding editor of the weekly magazine *Canigó*.

DAVID GEORGE

Sirera, Rodolf

b. 1948, Valencia

Playwright

Rodolf Sirera is the best-known Valencian dramatist of the post-Civil War period. He took a committed political stance during the later years of Francoism, and his plays also confront questions of Valencian cultural and linguistic identity. He was a founding member of the Valencia theatre group El Rogle, which has performed a number of his works, and he has co-authored several plays with his brother Josep-Lluís.

Like **Benet i Jornet**, Sirera was influenced by Brechtian theatre in his early works. An example is *La pau (retorna a Atenes)* (Peace (Returns to Athens)), which was performed by El Rogle in 1973. It contains voiced subtitles for each scene, satirical songs and the projection of slides. However, there is also a good deal of parodic humour, which is characteristic of a number of Sirera's plays, such as *Homenatge a Florentí Montfort* (Homage to Florentí Montfort) (1971).

Sirera's best plays are probably *Plany en la mort d'Enric Ribera* (Lament for the Death of Enric Ribera) (1972) and *The Audition* (*El verí del teatre*) (1978). Although *Plany* is a political play, it is also technically ambitious, and challenging for any director. *The Audition*, Sirera's most successful play to date, is set in Paris in 1784. An aristocrat invites an actor to his home to perform Socrates' death scene. Having been dissatisfied by Gabriel's first performance, the Marquis leads him into believing that the wine he drank earlier was in fact poison and that Gabriel will receive the antidote only if his next performance is adequate. After his second performance, the Marquis gives his victim another drink which is not the antidote, but a real, deadly poison for which there is no cure. The final death scene takes place after the play has ended. *The Audition* subtly and ironically explores questions of identity, and of the theatre itself, which is presented as a form of drug. It is a long way from the social realism of the 1960s, and points the way to the type of drama written since the mid-1980s by such Catalan playwrights as Sergi **Belbel**.

See also: theatre

Further reading

London, J. (1996) 'Josep Lluís and Rodolf Sirera', supplement to Sirera, R., 'Drama and Society', in D. George and J. London (eds) *An Introduction to Contemporary Catalan Theatre*, Sheffield: Anglo-Catalan Society, 1996 (sets Sirera in the context of post-Civil War Catalan social drama).

Sirera, R. (1988) *El verí del teatre*; trans. J. London, *The Audition*, in *Plays International*, 3, 12: 54–8 (English translation of one of Sirera's best plays).

DAVID GEORGE

social attitudes

Although Spanish society is not fundamentally different from other western European societies it does have certain distinctive characteristics. One of the most obvious is the Spaniards' love of nightlife. This is not simply a matter of climate: winters in Castile are cold, but this does not deter most of the inhabitants from slipping in and out of bars and other nightspots until the early hours. Being a naturally gregarious people, Spaniards will spend many hours with friends, preferably in a café or bar, of which there are allegedly as many as one per 300 inhabitants, and which at certain times of the day or week appear to be bursting with clientèle. The habit of going out in the evening and living life in the street is a cultural trait that becomes starkly obvious if one compares adjacent border towns such as Hendaye and Irún: whereas streets on the French side will be deserted by 8 p.m. even on a summer's evening, the streets in Irún are just beginning to throb with life and will remain animated for several hours. It is a curious paradox that hand in hand with this extraordinary addiction to social life Spaniards reveal a high degree of attachment to the family: over 80 percent of Spaniards will cite the family as the most important element in their lives. The continuing strength of family ties across generations probably accounts for the low suicide rate, and certainly gives Spanish society a more cohesive structure than elsewhere, and enables it to cope with levels of **unemployment** (of the order of 1 in 4 of the working population) that would place intolerable strains on the social fabric in Britain, France or Germany. In 1991 only 4.5 percent of Spaniards – the majority of whom were widowed – lived in single-person households (13 percent of all households, roughly half the rate in other western European countries). And while fertility rates have declined, this is balanced by the fact that offspring are remaining longer in the parental home.

Given the Spaniards' love of social life it is surprising that they are also avid watchers of **television**, with a watching time somewhat higher than the average for Europe (although considerably lower than that of the British, who are Europe's leading television addicts by a considerable margin). After devoting their time to family, friends and television, all of which can take place simultaneously, Spaniards have relatively little leisure time left for other activities. Reading (see also **readership**), listening to the **radio**, listening to **music**, going out into the countryside, watching sport, practising sport, and going to the cinema are the most common activities mentioned (see also **sport and leisure**), although with the expected differences between the sexes and level of education.

Foreign travel is still very much a minority activity, although one that has been increasing significantly. About 10 percent of Spaniards are now taking **holidays** abroad; of the vast majority that opt for holidays within Spain itself (including the Canaries and the Balearics), over half stay in property belonging to family or friends. Between 1 in 4 and 1 in 5 Spanish families have a second home, often a seaside flat or a house in the country within a 100 km radius of a large city, and these secondary homes are used for holidays and weekends. The weekend exodus is now a standard phenomenon in large cities, an escape from the metropolis enhanced by the numerous *puentes* (literally 'bridges': a public holiday connecting with a weekend) that prolong the weekend break by one or two days.

Spanish society is one given to conspicuous consumer spending, especially on clothes and eating out (see also **consumerism; fast food outlets; restaurants**). Most of this spending, however, occurs in the context of the family and an inner circle of friends, although Spaniards are also renowned for their lavish hospitality to visitors. The emergence of a strong consumer society has resulted in a watering-down of traditional Catholic attitudes. Rather than turning their backs on **Roman Catholicism**, Spaniards have quietly developed their own pragmatic system of beliefs and attitudes (see also **religion**).

Although there is no evidence that Spanish society is especially promiscuous, there has been a high degree of liberalization of sexual attitudes which the Catholic church finds unpalatable, not to mention the accompanying practice of birth control. The proportion of Spaniards who say they believe in complete sexual freedom is surprisingly high: 48 percent according to a 1990 poll but with 65 percent in the more relevant under-45 age bracket. Co-habitation, though scarcely a norm, is nevertheless widely tolerated. By the end of the 1980s only 30 percent of those polled found co-habitation objectionable. Interestingly, marriage in church remains the most popular option by far when it comes to tying the knot (see also **marriage and divorce**). But if the blessing of the church is still sought upon the occasion of a marriage, a birth or a death, many of its doctrines and injunctions no longer carry weight with the great majority of Spaniards. Abortion, in its present restricted form, commands wide support (and the indications are that a more liberal **abortion law** would still be acceptable), while there is near-universal support for the availability of divorce. Attendance at weekly mass involves about 30 percent of the population, although twice as many people are willing to call themselves religious and 85 percent accept the label 'Catholic'. Thus, while a strong residual religiosity remains, Spaniards have become more choosy about their beliefs. And perhaps most surprising of all, given the *machista* attitudes of yesteryear, only 17 percent declare themselves to be against the ordination of women. What is beyond doubt is that in the public expression of their beliefs and attitudes Spaniards have become tolerant, permissive and relativistic to a degree unthinkable even in the 1960s.

Further reading

De Miguel, A. (1990) *Los españoles*, Madrid: Ediciones Temas de Hoy (highly readable).

—— (1995) *La sociedad española 1994–95*, Madrid: Universidad Complutense, chapter 9 (sociological series based on yearly survey; also relevant are the 1992–3 and 1993–4 reports based on 1991 and 1992 surveys).

Hooper, J. (1995) *The New Spaniards*, Harmondsworth: Penguin (chapters 10–16 give a highly readable account of changes in social attitudes).

Orizo, F.A. (1991) *Los nuevos valores de los españoles*, Madrid: Fundación Santa María (the Spanish part of the European Value System Study Group public opinion polls of 1990; indispensable for those who appreciate statistical information).

C.A. LONGHURST

social security

With the establishment of democracy in the late 1970s Spain rapidly began to assemble a welfare state comparable to those of western Europe. A massive programme of hospital building and the provision of universal free medical assistance (despite the continuation of a strong private sector traditionally patronized by the middle classes) were accompanied by a virtually new system of unemployment insurance and a vastly improved system of state pensions, with pension levels approaching salary level upon retirement and reaching two-thirds of the population. The number of people in receipt of state pensions doubled in twenty years, from three and a half million in the 1970s to seven million in the 1990s. A full pension is payable after 35 years of contributions, with lower entitlements pro-rata, but never falling below an established minimum subject to regular revision. There are in addition non-contributory pensions, both old age and disability, for those who did not have the opportunity to participate in the contributory scheme.

The health service, which is run by the state agency INSALUD, is in principle offered to those who have paid contributions and to their dependants, as well as to those who lack the means to pay for their own medical treatment. In practice it functions as a near-universal free service, although medical appointments are normally held in hospital and outpatient departments rather than in doctors' surgeries, which remain largely in the parallel private sector. Medicines on prescription are normally subject to a charge of 40 percent of the sale price. Coverage of dental treatment is limited to emergencies. A programme for the transference of health services from central government to regional governments began in the mid-1990s.

There are also numerous other welfare benefits, such as temporary incapacity benefit (as a result of illness or accident at work) payable for up to 30 months, permanent disability benefit, maternity benefit (payable for 16 weeks), widow(er)s' pensions, orphans' pensions, death benefit (to help with funeral costs), and indemnity compensation in cases of work-related deaths. To these provisions may be added those afforded by the social services agency INSERSO (dependent on the Ministry of Social Affairs), which not only arranges for home visits to those in need of help but which also has its own centres for occupational therapy and the rehabilitation and training of the physically and mentally handicapped. Increasing attention is being paid to the needs of the elderly and to improvements in their quality of life. In conclusion it can be said that Spain has developed an advanced Social Security system that in terms of cost as a percentage of GDP is approaching the European Union average. However, it is doubtful if the vastly increased costs can continue to be met by the state. The recession of the early 1990s and **labour market** reforms forced the government to curtail what was becoming an over-generous system, and a thoroughgoing review was undertaken with a view to containing costs.

In 1995 spending on Social Security amounted to nearly 11m^2 pesetas (or 16 percent of GDP), whilst income from employers' and employees' contributions was just over 7m^2 pesetas. The gap of about one-third of total cost has to be made up from general government revenues and was a significant contributor to the state's budgetary deficit of some 6.5 percent of GDP in 1995. Although Spain has one of the highest employer contribution rates in Europe (23.6 percent of an employee's salary), it also has one of the worst payment records, even on the part of regional government departments, public corporations and municipalities. Delayed payments and even non-payment are common, but the central government is reluctant to take firm action for fear of worsening the already severe unemployment. In fact, despite the growing number of retired people in receipt of a pension, the overspend so far has been occurring mainly in the health service (three-quarters of whose cost is being borne directly by the state), as a result of which the total separation of pensions from health is under consideration, with the state assuming the major responsibility for funding the health services and guaranteeing the minimum pension, while firms and individuals finance the bulk of the pension system. Additionally, because the workforce is virtually static whereas the number of pensioners is steadily increasing, pensions cannot indefinitely be paid out of revenue from current contributions, and private pension funds, scarcely known in Spain, are expected to experience an explosion over the coming years as an ageing population is increasingly obliged to take over responsibility for its own financial security after retirement.

C.A. LONGHURST

socialism

Spanish socialism has often been characterized by its ideological poverty. No Spanish theorist has made any significant theoretical contribution to **Marxism**. Spanish socialism has been largely derivative, particularly from French socialism, and has also been influenced by Catholicism, which lent it a strong ethical tone. Moreover, the development of socialism in Spain was hampered by the fact that neither the First nor Second International showed much interest in the Iberian peninsula and provided no specific guidance to Spanish socialists. The early Spanish socialists thus lacked any deep understanding of Marxist analysis which resulted in an incoherent programme, combining reformist political practice with a reductionist revolutionary rhetoric.

By failing to provide an adequate framework to analyse the socio-economic and political reality of Spain effectively, the ideological poverty of Spanish socialism also contributed to its organizational weakness. Thus, although the **PSOE**, founded in 1879, is one of the oldest socialist parties in Europe, it initially remained a weak force due to its preoccupation with organizational questions rather than theoretical analysis. Consequently, vital issues such as the agrarian problem and regional diversity in Spain were ignored. Moreover, the socialists' determination to make Madrid the centre of socialist activities rather than Catalonia, the most industrialized region of Spain, which was far more fertile ground for a radical socialist movement, led to the dominance of anarchism, rather than socialism, in that region.

The socialists' essentially incorrect analysis of the political situation in Spain was particularly damaging during the Second Republic (1931–6). By then the socialists were the most important political party in the country, yet they were unable to provide an adequate response to the problems which beset the Republic because they mistakenly believed, in accordance with their own schematic interpretation of Marxism, that the Republic heralded the long-delayed bourgeois revolution. Their misplaced faith in their ability to realize a programme of wide-ranging social reforms by parliamentary means, in a political system where parliamentary democracy remained a façade, thus prevented them from forestalling the military revolt which began the Civil War.

Socialism remained dormant, both ideologically and organizationally, throughout the Francoist dictatorship. With the transition to democracy in 1975–7, however, the PSOE initially displayed its previous inconsistency by emphasizing its radical Marxist heritage whilst simultaneously adopting a reformist political strategy. Subsequently, however, the PSOE dropped its Marxist label in order to achieve electoral success, and, in office from 1982 until 1996, became one of the most cautious social-democratic parties in western Europe. Ironically, therefore, although the PSOE finally enjoyed a hegemonic position within Spanish politics during the 1980s, socialism as an ideology is still arguably deprived of a voice.

See also: political parties; politics

Further reading

Anderson, P. and Camiller, P. (eds) (1994) *Mapping the Western European Left*, London: Verso (includes an excellent chapter on the survival of socialism in Spain).

Gallagher, T. and Williams, A. (eds) (1989) *Southern European Socialism. Parties, Elections and the Challenge of Government*, Manchester: Manchester University Press (there is an excellent detailed chapter on Spain).

Heywood, P. (1990) *Marxism and the Failure of Organised Socialism in Spain, 1879–1936*, Cambridge: Cambridge University Press (an excellent, well-documented study of the early development of Socialism in Spain).

PSOE (1991) *Manifiesto del Programa 2000*, Madrid: Editorial Sistema (this is PSOE's own vision of the future development of Spanish socialism; it contains an introduction and conclusion by Willy Brandt, Felipe González and Alfonso Guerra).

GEORGINA BLAKELEY

society

For about a generation after the end of the Civil War, Spanish society still retained a great deal of its traditional character: conservative in **politics** and **religion**, hierarchical, male-dominated, predominantly rural and economically backward. In all of these respects, and in many others, Spanish society has undergone profound changes, and now displays fewer differences from the societies of other advanced western democracies. These changes cannot be ascribed, however, simply to the ending of the Franco dictatorship in 1975, nor, indeed, to any single factor, but are the result of a complex process of modernization which began during the regime.

Of the various factors that have transformed society and produced significant shifts in **social attitudes**, the most influential was arguably the General Education Law of 1970, which for the first time made education compulsory and free to age 14, and was the starting-point for a series of subsequent reforms over the next twenty years. Chronologically speaking, however, one can date the beginnings of the change from the **Stabilization Plan** of 1959, which began to shift the balance of the Spanish **economy** from **agriculture** to **industry**. The move to an industrial and service base intensified the existing pattern of **migration** from countryside to city, which within a generation resulted in a predominantly urban, rather than rural population distribution: by the 1990s 80 percent lived in towns or cities of 50,000 inhabitants or over.

Nor was mobility of people confined within Spain, for the 1960s saw not only the opening up of the country to **tourism**, but also an increase in the numbers of those seeking work in countries such as France, (West) Germany, Switzerland and Great Britain. This two-way movement led to enhanced awareness of the freedoms enjoyed by citizens who lived in countries with democratic systems, and helped to create a more questioning attitude towards the traditional authoritarian structures of Spanish society. Furthermore, increasing prosperity and the higher earning capacity of those working in new manufacturing, assembly and service sectors produced a realignment of **class** structures, with about half of those defined as working class in 1960 moving up into the middle class by 1980.

The social impact of economic change would, however, have been less dramatic if it had not been accompanied by the wider availability of education (see also **education and research**). Though the 1970 law did not achieve its aim of providing free education to all, it was the first stage in a process of radical reform which embraced all levels of school and university provision. Compared to 1960, there were eight times as many young people receiving secondary education in 1980, and four times as many attending higher education institutions. Legislation such as the **LODE**, **LOGSE** and **LRU** expanded and diversified the curriculum, reduced the gap between academic and vocational education, and gave both pupils and parents a greater say in the running of schools, further eroding the culture of deference which had been a feature of Spanish society not only during the Franco era but long before.

One of the most visible results of the expansion of education has been the profound change in the position of **women**, in terms of participation in the **labour market**, diversification of the kinds of employment open to them, and personal freedom. It is true that women's salaries tend to be about 20 percent lower than men's earnings, and female unemployment is higher, but this is probably not radically different from the position in other countries in western Europe. More significantly, however, the proportion of working women with educational qualifications has undergone a spectacular increase in the twenty years to 1990, with ten times as many educated to secondary level and eleven times as many having degrees.

These changes have been accompanied by rapid secularization and liberalization, particularly in areas such as **sexual behaviour**. Though surveys carried out in the 1990s show that as many as 90 percent profess adherence to **Roman Catholicism**, regular attendance at Sunday worship is only around 30 percent. Even during the Franco period, the church's prohibition of contraception was commonly flouted, as often by practising Catholics as by others, and illegal abortions are estimated to have run at about 40 for every hundred live births. Survey evidence suggests that fewer people have religious or moral objections to premarital sex, cohabitation or divorce than in the 1970s. Furthermore, the lifting of **censorship** in films and printed matter has further intensified the atmosphere of permissiveness in matters of individual behaviour.

This greater freedom is most obvious among the young, whose general lifestyle and attitudes differ little from those of their counterparts elsewhere. The Madrid ***Movida*** of the 1970s has exhausted its initial momentum, but in all of the large towns and cities there is a vibrant **youth culture**, expressed in music (see also **rock and pop**), nightclubbing, fast driving and designer drugs (see also **drug problem**). Not all the drug-taking in Spain is attributable to this group, as marginalized and poverty-stricken individuals of all ages are often users of hard drugs like heroin, and there is widespread use of cocaine. One of the clearest symptoms of the liberalization in attitudes is the fact that the socialist **PSOE** government legalized the private and public use of narcotics in 1983, though it restricted consumption to private use in 1992. Drugs have clearly been a factor in the increase in **crime** and the spread of **AIDS**.

Despite the dramatic nature of the changes which have taken place since 1970, however, there are still respects in which Spain remains relatively traditional. The **family**, for example, is still an important institution. Eight out of every ten respondents to attitude surveys cite the family as an important element in their lives, and the proportion of single-person households is half that of other western European countries, most of these households being occupied by widowed persons. Though sex and parenthood outside marriage have become socially acceptable, the rate of births to single mothers is low by comparison with the rest of western Europe, and the same is true of the divorce rate. For those who do marry, i.e. the vast majority of those living together, the church wedding is still the norm, despite the increased neglect of church teaching and discipline. The residual cultural influence of Catholicism is considerable, as can be seen from the numbers of non-believers who, for example, have their children baptized.

Further reading

Hooper, J. (1995) *The New Spaniards*, Harmondsworth: Penguin (social change is dealt with throughout the book, but the following chapters will be found particularly relevant: 1, 5, 6, 9, and 10–25).

Graham, H. and Labanyi, J. (eds) (1995) *Spanish Cultural Studies, an Introduction: The Struggle for Modernity*, Oxford: Oxford University Press (part IV gives an excellent insight into the subject).

EAMONN RODGERS

sociology

Sociology as a scholarly discipline developed late in Spain, as elsewhere. The foundations were laid by the work of the Instituto de Estudios Políticos (Political Studies Institute), where, from 1948, figures like Javier Conde, Juan José **Linz** and Enrique **Tierno Galván** collaborated on the *Revista de Estudios Políticos* (Political Studies Review). In the 1950s, Spanish culture began to open up to European and American influences, especially in the area of Social Sciences. The 1960s saw the publication of various studies in sociology which had a significant influence, such as Salustiano del Campo's *La Sociología científica* (Scientific Sociology) (1962) and *Introducción a la Sociología* (Introduction to Sociology) (1968), and Salvador Giner's *Historia del pensamiento social* (History of Social Thought) (1967).

Between 1963 and 1965, the Rector's office of the Complutense University of Madrid sponsored courses in Sociology, but the university crisis of 1965 led to their suppression. Owing to an initiative by José Vidal Beneyto, the staff and students involved were able to continue the courses in the Centro de Enseñanza e Investigación (Centre for Teaching and Research), under whose auspices a School of Social Sciences was begun, though this in turn was closed by the authorities in 1968. The immediate response was the foundation of the Escuela Crítica de Ciencias Sociales (Critical School of Social Sciences), which was able to remain functioning until 1970.

It was in the 1970s that sociology really became institutionalized as an academic discipline within the universities. It is to this period that we may date the appearance of most of the specialist professional journals: *Revista de Estudios Sociales* (Social Studies Review), *Revista Española de la Opinión Pública* (The Spanish Review of Public Opinion), *Papers*, and *Trabajos de Sociología* (Papers in Sociology). Gradually sociology was included in the degree programmes of most Faculties of Political Science.

In parallel with university departments, public and private bodies began to foster the development of applied research in sociology, one of the earliest being the Centro de Investigaciones Sociológicas (Centre for Sociological Research), which publishes the journal *Revista de Investigaciones Sociológicas* (Review of Sociological Research). In addition, there are two professional organizations for sociologists: the Colegio Nacional de Licenciados en Ciencias Políticas y Sociología (National College of Graduates in Political Science and Sociology), and the Federación Española de Sociólogos (Federation of Spanish Sociologists).

See also: education and research; UNED; universities; university education

Further reading

Díaz, E. (1983) *Pensamiento español en la era de Franco (1939–1975)*, Madrid: Tecnos (an indispensable classic study).

Díez Nicolás, J. (1989) *Cincuenta años de Sociología en España. Bibliografía de Sociología en lengua castellana*, Málaga: Universidad de Málaga, 2 vols (a fundamental reference work).

Tezanos, J.F. (1996) *La explicación sociológica: una introducción a la Sociología*, Madrid: UNED (a UNED textbook, which contains a section on sociology as a subject in Spain).

ALICIA ALTED

Solana Madariaga, Javier

b. 1942, Madrid

Politician

A graduate in physics from Madrid university, where he was an active opponent of the Franco regime, Solana Madariaga occupied important posts in the socialist **PSOE** continuously between 1974 and 1995. Between 1977 and 1995 he was MP for Madrid and served as minister in all governments of Felipe **González**, occupying portfolios of Culture, Education and Foreign Affairs, and acquiring a reputation for moderation and communication skills. In 1995 he was appointed Secretary General of **NATO**, in spite of having opposed Spanish entry in the early 1980s.

See also: foreign policy; LOGSE

MICHAEL T. NEWTON

Solbes Mira, Pedro

b. 1942, Pinoso (Alicante)

Politician and economist

Solbes Mira took his first degree in economics and a doctorate in politics at Madrid university. Between 1964 and 1979, he held various commercial posts in the civil service, acquiring expertise in **European Union** affairs. He served in important economic posts under Franco, **Calvo Sotelo** and Felipe **González**. Under the latter he was Secretary of State for the European Communities (1985–91), Minister of Agriculture (1991–3) and Minister of Economy and Finance (1993–6). An archetypal **technocrat**, Solbes only joined the **PSOE** in 1996 shortly before winning a parliamentary seat for the party in Alicante.

See also: foreign trade

MICHAEL T. NEWTON

Solchaga Catalán, Carlos

b. 1944, Tafalla (Navarre)

Politician and economist

A Madrid graduate in economics, Solchaga held various posts in the civil service and in banking before entering politics. He joined the socialist **PSOE** in 1974. As Felipe **González**' Minister of Industry and Energy (1982–5) and of Economy and Finance (1985–93), Solchaga played a major role in the government's policy of ***reconversión industrial***, prior to entry into the **European Union**; his austerity measures and right-wing economic views led to conflict with the **trade unions** and left-wing socialists. In 1994 he abandoned politics to work in publishing and higher education.

See also: banks; Guerra, Alfonso; industry; RUMASA; unemployment

MICHAEL T. NEWTON

Soriano Jara, Elena

b. 1917, Fuentidueña de Tajo (Madrid); d. 1997

Writer

Among Spain's most significant feminist intellectuals, Soriano remained essentially unknown during the Franco era, owing to the restrictions of **censorship**. Following a traditional, realist chronicle of family decadence, *Caza menor* (Small Game Hunting) (1951), she produced a trilogy, *Mujer y hombre* (Women and Men) (1955), comprising *La playa de los locos* (Madmen's Beach), *Espejismos* (Mirages), and *Medea* – all treating problematic male–female relationships – characterized by psychological acuity, socioethical preoccupations, and intellectual profundity. *Testimonio materno* (A Mother's Testimony) (1985), both memoir and confessions, recalls the drug-related death of Soriano's only son; *La vida pequeña* (Small Life) (1989) contains short stories.

Soriano founded and oversaw the publication of *El Urogallo*, one of Spain's leading intellectual periodicals, for a quarter of a century.

Further reading

Arkinstall, C. (1992) 'Rewriting Genre, Re-reading Gender in Elena Soriano's *La playa de los locos*', *Monographic Review/Revista Monográfica* 8: 99–113 (a feminist explication concentrating on the novel named).

Winecoff, J. (1964) 'Existentialism in the Novels of Elena Soriano', *Hispania* 47, 2: 309–15 (life and works overview with thematic analysis).

JANET PÉREZ

Sostres, José María

b. 1915, La seu d'Urgell (Catalonia); d. 1984, Barcelona

Architect

Sostres began his professional career by working with Yllescas, one of the few survivors of **GATEPAC** who continued to defend rationalist architecture in Spain in the 1940s. After qualifying in 1946, he travelled to Italy and became acquainted with the work of Giuseppe Terragni, which had a great influence on his thinking. On his return to Barcelona he had an important role as a theorist, defining the principles of the Grupo R of which he was a founder member, along with **Coderch**, **Moragas**, **Bohigas** and others. His architectural projects, though few in number, display great sophistication in their use of modern idiom. Influences ranging from Marcel Breuer to Alvar Aalto can be detected in the much admired Casa Agustí in Sitges (1955) while the Ciudad Diagonal (Barcelona, 1958) recalls the work of the Dutch architect Oud.

MIHAIL MOLDOVEANU

Sota, Alejandro de la

b. 1913, Pontevedra (Galicia)

Architect

Alejandro de la Sota began his career as an architect by working on the creation of new villages in rural areas. The best known example is Esquivel in Andalusia, which was completed in 1955. It is an excellent example of a harmonious combination of traditional techniques and vernacular idiom with the needs of the modern age. During the same period he was developing his abstract geometric style, shown to great advantage in the Gobierno Civil (provincial government headquarters) in Tarragona (1954–7), a major work of contemporary Spanish architecture. Among his other notable achievements are the César Carlos school (Madrid, 1967) and the Caja Postal (post office savings bank) in León (1980–4). In 1972 he was awarded the National Prize for Architecture.

MIHAIL MOLDOVEANU

Spanish

Spanish (or Castilian) is a Romance language, originating in ancient Cantabria, which was adopted by the kingdom of Castile and later extended to be used in the whole of Spain and Spanish-speaking Latin America. It is also spoken in Africa (Equatorial Guinea, Ceuta and Melilla, parts of Morocco), the Far East (the Philippines) and in the Balkans and Israel (by Sephardic Jewish communities, the descendants of those expelled from Spain in 1492), as well as occupying the status of a rapidly expanding minority language in the US. It is an official language of twenty-three countries and should reach 400 million speakers at the beginning of the twenty-first century.

Of all the Romance languages spoken in Spain, Castilian is the one which has most radically innovated from its Latin base, for instance in the reduction to five vowels, the loss of the initial *f* (Latin *filiu* (*hijo* [son])), and the palatalization of initial *pl*, *cl*, and *fl* (Latin *clave* (*llave* [key])). Castilian already had a rich literary tradition by the end of the thirteenth century, which reached its peak in the sixteenth and seventeenth centuries. The thirteenth-century king Alfonso X of Castile promoted Castilian, using it exclusively for affairs of state, and elaborating its function by developing its grammar and vastly increasing its vocabulary (externally, through borrowing from Latin and Arabic, and internally, through word formation). Thus it became the medium for scientific, legal, administrative and other writings. This period of development was captured in Nebrija's *Grammar of the Castilian Language* of 1492. Temporary stability was subsequently followed by a period of rapid expansion and change in the Spanish language over the sixteenth and seventeenth centuries.

The next major reform of Spanish took place in the eighteenth century with the creation, in the service of the crown and hence the state, of the Royal Academy (*Real Academia Española* – RAE) whose role was to purify and preserve the Spanish language (see also **Royal Academies**). Thus, the RAE was to reform its spelling, provide a grammar and produce and periodically update a dictionary (see also **dictionaries and encyclopedias**).

Despite a strong prescriptive tradition aimed at unifying the language, there are differences between varieties of Spanish spoken in different parts of Spain. Nevertheless, the twentieth century has seen considerable dialect levelling, due in large measure to the flight from the land, widening access to education and the presence of the audiovisual media.

There are two principal subvarieties of Castilian, the more conservative northern dialect on which the Spanish prestige standard has been based (the prestige norm being located either in Burgos/Valladolid or Madrid) and the more progressive southern one (where the prestige norm is located in Seville), more closely related to the Spanish spoken in the Canaries and in Latin America. Phonetically, the primary characteristics which differentiate the southern from the northern variety are the elimination of aspiration of the /s/ in certain contexts (*una casa* – do^{h} casa^{h}) and a lack of distinction between θ and s (*caza* [hunt] and *casa* [house] are pronounced alike). The subvarieties which make up southern Spanish are Extremenian, Murcian, Andalusian and Canary Islands Spanish.

See also: language and national identity; language normalization

Further reading

Entwhistle, W. (1936) *The Spanish Language*, London: Faber & Faber (somewhat antiquated, but still very reliable on the history of the language).

García Mouton, P. (1994) *Lenguas y dialectos de España*, Madrid: Arco Libros.

MIRANDA STEWART

sport and leisure

Sports activities are administered centrally by the Sports Council (*Consejo Superior de Deportes* – CSD), which forms part of the Ministry of Education and Culture, and is headed by a Secretary of State, equal in status to the Secretary of State for

Education and the Secretary of State for Universities and Research. One of its major functions is to promote the 'sports for everybody' initiative, principally through its support of school and university sports programmes. Within the framework of the 1990 Sports Law which pledges state support for sporting bodies, and regulates professional competition and international representation, the CSD has invested large sums in the Physical Education Extension Plan for primary and second schools, and in conjunction with the **autonomous communities** has provided sports grounds in schools for use by students by day and the general public by night.

Elsewhere, too, there has been significant investment both in general facilities for sports, and in High Performance Centres such as those in the Sierra Nevada (Granada), Madrid, Seville and Pontevedra. In Barcelona, sports facilities are provided by venues such as the Estadi Olímpic, reopened in 1989 for the 5th World Cup of Athletics; the Palau dels Sports, modernized for the 1992 **Olympic Games**; the Velódrom d'Horta, opened for the World Cycling Championship in 1984, and the home of the Catalan School of Track Cycling; and the Palau Sant Jordi, a high-tec 'smart' building inaugurated in 1990. The range of participation and spectator sports catered for include basketball, handball and volleyball matches, championships in gymnastics, windsurfing, American football, indoor trials, ice and indoor skating, martial arts (judo, karate, taekwondo) and newer sports such as skateboarding, and indoor climbing.

In collaboration with large businesses and the Spanish Olympic Committee (COE) the CSD also supports the programme of the Association for Olympic Sports (Asociación de Deportes Olímpicos – ADO) by which grants are given to leading senior and junior sportsmen and women to train for the Games. The ADO programme undoubtedly contributed to Spanish successes in Barcelona and Atlanta, and also had the effect of greatly increasing the participation and success of **women** in Olympic events. Whereas eleven women participated in the Games in Rome in 1960, ten in 1976 in Montreal, and fifteen in 1984 in Los Angeles, there were 138 women competitors in the Barcelona Games in 1992 and ninety-seven in Atlanta in 1996.

The individual sports are administered by national federations, which receive grants from the CSD, though it is being suggested that they should be made to rely on private sponsorship, leaving the CSD with a purely promotional and coordinating function. Certainly many sporting responsibilities have already devolved onto the autonomous regions, which have their own sports advisory boards and general directors.

Sports clubs are linked to the national federations, and for professional sports such as **football** and **basketball** they operate as private sports companies, and are members of the Professional Football and Professional Basketball Leagues.

Leisure

Spectator and participation sports of all kinds (football, basketball, *pelota*, **athletics**, **golf**, **tennis**, swimming, **cycling**, sailing, chess, etc.) are only some, and not the most widely practised, of the leisure activities engaged in by Spaniards generally. Figures produced in 1995 by the National Statistical Institute suggest that the most popular activity was listening to **music** at 70 percent (though playing an instrument ranked last at a mere 10 percent). Going shopping, at just over 60 percent, and reading, at over 50 percent, were also popular pastimes. Minority pursuits, from 20 to 40 percent, are listed as DIY, going to concerts, going to sporting events, discoteques, open-air excursions, sport, playing cards, going to the **theatre** and cinema, and going for a drink.

Even this list, however, is by no means a full one. Increased leisure-time resulting from large-scale **unemployment** and the progressive ageing of the population, with a rising proportion of retired people, has produced a significant rise in attendance at **museums** and **art exhibitions** from the 1980s onwards. The leisure section of the annual *El País* digest regularly contains articles on holiday travel (see also **holidays**), **fishing**, **hunting**, animals (principally dogs and dog shows), **gardens**, **food and drink**, stamp collecting, coin collecting, antique collecting, and gambling (the **national lottery**, football pools, casinos, bingo, fruit machines). Much leisure-time activity, however, is unstructured, and consists of socializing with friends in cafés and bars, usually in the late evening.

See also: consumerism; social attitudes

EAMONN RODGERS

sporting press

In 1994 the sports paper *Marca* became the daily with the biggest circulation in Spain, pushing ***El País*** into second place. By 1996 it was commanding over 12.5 percent of the market, compared with *El País*'s 10.5 percent. Its success is a prime example of the huge popularity of the sporting press, whose four main dailies, the others being *As*, *Sport* and *El Mundo Deportivo*, account between them for over 20 percent of total sales.

Until 1989 the most popular sports paper was *As*, but although it retains a loyal clientele, its circulation figures continue to drop. More than 30 percent of its readership is over the age of 45, and it has not been attracting as high a proportion of younger readers as some of the other papers. It is most widely read in Murcia, Andalusia and Catalonia.

Marca, which in 1989 supplanted *As* as the leading sports daily, has successfully captured its natural audience of younger male readers across the whole range of social classes, and is widely distributed in the smaller as well as the larger population centres. It is particularly popular in Andalusia, Murcia, and Extremadura.

Sport and *El Mundo Deportivo*, published in Barcelona, have circulations which come close to those of *As*, but concentrate two-thirds of their sales in Catalonia. Based on figures for the social class of their readership produced by the *Estudio General de Medios* (General Media Survey), *El Mundo Deportivo* is more 'upmarket' than either *As* or *Marca*, and *Sport* decidedly so. Launched in 1981, *Sport* also attracts a slightly higher proportion of female readers (23 percent) than the more usual 15–18 percent.

The launch of a new sports daily, *Súper Deporte*, in Valencia in 1995 and the 50 percent increase in its circulation by the following year are further proof of Spain's love affair with the sporting press.

See also: football; media; readership; sport and leisure

EAMONN RODGERS

Stabilization Plan

The Stabilization Plan of July 1959 has often been credited with laying the foundations for Spain's economic take-off in the 1960s. Though it redirected economic policy away from self-sufficiency towards a more internationalized and market-led philosophy, the real factors facilitating rapid economic development were external: a prosperous Europe that sent millions of tourists, remittances from more than one million Spanish emigrants, foreign investment and help from the IMF and World Bank.

The Plan was the work of a small group of **technocrats**, most of whom belonged to the secretive Catholic organization **Opus Dei**, and whom Franco had brought into the government in 1957 to solve the problem of a near-bankrupt economy. The fact that it took two full years for the Plan to be presented reveals the regime's hesitation in adopting liberalising and market-oriented measures associated with western democracies. Nevertheless the technocrats, more conservative in their religious than in their economic philosophy, persuaded Franco's cabinet to apply for membership of the OECD, the IMF and the World Bank, and it was upon the advice of these bodies that the Stabilization Plan was drawn up. The first objective of the Plan, therefore, was to correct the serious deficit in the **balance of payments**.

The Plan was in effect a mixture of deflationary and liberalising measures, with more initial emphasis on the former. The peseta was devalued against the dollar and the previous system of multiple exchange rates abolished. To contain inflation, public sector borrowing was reduced, loans from the Bank of Spain to government agencies slashed, and interest rates raised. The government-controlled prices of public transport, electricity, petroleum products and tobacco rose, provoking a severe, though short-lived, recession, which some commentators have blamed for intensifying the wave of worker emigration that now affected Spain. These attempts at balancing the books were accompanied by other, less immediately obvious steps, which were to be just as significant in the longer term. Although the Spanish **economy** was to remain more protectionist than other western economies, the revision of the Tariff Statute, with the removal of quotas and other trade barriers on a wide range of goods (especially capital goods) amounted to a tacit admission that Spain's international trade needed to expand if the economy was to develop. In addition, incentives were given to foreign investors to set up businesses in Spain, and the Stabilization Plan was, indeed, soon followed by a large increase in inward foreign investment.

The Stabilization Plan has undoubtedly passed into the text books as a key episode of modern Spanish history. While the Franco regime had never before introduced such a comprehensive package of economic measures, the Plan, though it marked the beginnings of Spain's slow integration into the world economy, could not by itself bring about the economic miracle of the 1960s. It merely set the scene.

Further reading

Fuentes Quintana, E. (1984) 'El Plan de Estabilización económica veinticinco años después', *Información Comercial Española*, nos. 612–3: 25–40 (a retrospective assessment by a leading authority).

Harrison, J. (1985) *The Spanish Economy in the Twentieth Century*, London: Croom Helm (a very readable account of Spain's recent economic history).

Wright, A. (1977) *The Spanish Economy 1959–76*, London: Macmillan (a solid, clear, descriptive account of a crucial period in Spain's development).

C.A. LONGHURST

standard of living

Although there is no single agreed measure for comparing living standards across different countries, there can be no doubt that in absolute terms the standard of living of the average Spaniard has improved beyond recognition in the past thirty years. Even in relative terms there has been some improvement in Spain's position. For example, on joining the EC in 1986 Spain's per capita GDP was two-thirds that of the Community average; by 1991 it was 79 percent. After three years of recession it had fallen back to 77 percent by 1994, but it is expected to reach 80 percent by the turn of the century, reflecting the fact that economic downturns and upturns tend to be more marked in Spain than the average for the EU. With a GNP per capita of $14,020 (1992 figures), Spain occupies twelfth position in the EU of fifteen countries, behind the UK in eleventh position with $17,760, and a long way behind Luxembourg at the top with a GNP per capita of $35,260. If, however, we use per capita GDP adjusted for purchasing power parity, the differences between the wealthier and the less wealthy countries are considerably reduced: Spain appears with $12,200 compared to the UK with $15,420 and Luxembourg with $20,540. The differences in standard of living also have a geographical dimension within Spain itself. The wealthiest region by per capita GDP, the Balearics, is well above the EU average, while the next two, Madrid and Catalonia, are very close to the EU average. At the other end of the scale are Extremadura and Andalusia with per capita GDPs which are below 60 percent of the EU average. However, these large differences are attenuated somewhat if we consider disposable income of households (ie. after taxes, social security transfers and purchasing power adjustments), although they do not disappear. Furthermore there are significant differences even within the regions themselves between town and country, city and town, or coast and hinterland.

The standard of living, however, is not simply a matter of income measures. Other considerations affect the quality of life of a nation. The UN index of human development, for example, incorporates such aspects as life expectancy, literacy, educational enrolments, alongside the more usual per capita income adjusted for purchasing power parity. In such an index Spain does remarkably well, appearing in ninth position, ahead of countries such as Sweden, Germany or the UK which have a higher standard of living in purely monetary terms.

Other indicators of living standards suggest that Spain is, if not in the premier division of countries such as USA, Japan and Switzerland, then in the first division alongside most other western European nations. Such indicators include number of consumer durables per 1,000 inhabitants, such as television sets, telephones or cars. All these measures place Spain among the fully developed nations, although not near the very top except for television sets. Figures for life expectancy at birth and infant mortality are among the very best in the world, while homelessness is lower than in the UK, Germany or France. The one major blot on the landscape of a prosperous and contented nation is the continuing high level of **unemployment**.

See also: national income

C.A. LONGHURST

stock exchanges

When Spain had its own version of Big Bang in 1989 the official stockjobbers or *agentes de cambio y bolsa*, who controlled all trading, disappeared and were replaced by private brokers who used computerized systems. Trading can now be done via the so-called *mercado continuo* (continuous computerized system) or physically in the stock exchanges of Madrid, Barcelona, Bilbao and Valencia, the first of these accounting for the bulk of the total trading. All four exchanges are connected by computer and most trading is done on-screen via a sophisticated system known as SIBE. Although with fewer than 400 listed companies the stock market in Spain is narrow compared with London or New York, the volume of trading is comparatively high, as has been profitability over the past ten years, with the index rising some 400 percent, well in excess of inflation. Few foreign companies are quoted, but among them are Volkswagen and Commerzbank. The Spanish stock exchange system is overseen by a national stock exchange commission (*Comisión Nacional del Mercado de Valores* – CNMV) set up in 1989, which tightened inspection procedures, imposed fines for irregularities and expunged the worst cases of insider dealing. This new more professional approach has encouraged foreigners to invest increasingly in the Spanish stock market.

C.A. LONGHURST

student life

Student life during the Franco regime was characterized by a high level of **student protest** against the absence of democratic structures, particularly in the last ten years of Francoism. After the transition to democracy, protests, while still retaining something of their political focus, tended to concentrate increasingly on specifically student problems, especially those created by *masificación*, the overloading of the university system by increased student numbers.

The number of university students doubled during the 1960s and increased approximately nine-fold between 1970 and the mid-1990s. In the academic session 1995–6, there were approximately 1.5 million students in higher education in Spain. At the same time, there were 67,000 university teachers, giving an average national ratio of one member of staff to twenty-two students. This figure, however, conceals the gross imbalance in the system. Law students account for 13.5 percent of all students nationally, as against 8.9 percent following degree courses in Engineering in the *Escuelas Técnicas Superiores* (Higher Technical Schools, the equivalent of Engineering Faculties), and 2 percent studying Chemistry in Faculties of Science. There is serious overcrowding in some traditional disciplines, where classes contain several hundred students, there is little contact with staff, and tutorials are rare. In addition, students frequently complain about the inadequacy of library and other facilities.

Despite relatively low fee levels (e.g. about £450 per annum for a science student) and the provision of grants, the participation rate, measured as a percentage of the population between ages 20 and 24, is around 30 percent, which is not particularly high by European standards. Fewer than 20 percent of students receive grants. The phenomenon of the 'mature student', who returns to full-time education after working for several years, is comparatively rare, as is the student who supports his or her study by holding a part-time job. On the other hand, there is a large number of students in their late twenties, because of the low proportion (around 45 percent) who complete their degrees within the normal time. Many students take up to seven or eight years to complete a first degree.

Traditionally, students have not only come from a similar social background but also from the same geographical area, as government policy required them to study in the university nearest to their home. In the mid-1990s, in an effort to encourage greater competitiveness, the government relaxed this regulation, to enable students to apply to the institution with the best reputation in their chosen area of study.

One of the most visible changes in student life has been the increasing participation of women in higher education. There are more women than men in most areas of study, including, e.g., architecture, where the proportion of female graduates more than doubled in the decade to 1990, from 12 percent to 25 percent. The percentage of women graduates in all faculties increased from 42 in 1980 to 54 in 1990.

See also: LRU; UNED; universities; university education

Further reading

Alted, A. (1995) 'Educational Policy in Democratic Spain', in H. Graham and J. Labanyi (eds) *Spanish Cultural Studies, an Introduction: The Struggle for Modernity*, Oxford: Oxford University Press, pp. 320–5 (a concise overview, with a useful bibliography).

Hooper, J. (1995) *The New Spaniards*, Harmondsworth: Penguin (chapter 19 is a general overview of education, which contains some useful material on higher education).

Montero, R. (1995) 'The Silent Revolution: The Social and Cultural Advances of Women in Democratic Spain', in H. Graham and J. Labanyi (eds) *Spanish Cultural Studies, an Introduction: The Struggle for Modernity*, Oxford: Oxford University Press, pp. 381–5 (considers the participation of women in higher education as part of general changes in women's situation).

EAMONN RODGERS

student protest

Spanish universities were, from the mid-1950s until the demise of Francoism, one of the principal sites of opposition to the dictatorship. The aim of student protest was, first, the democratization of student unions, and ultimately, the democratization of society itself. The events of February 1956, when police and students clashed in the streets of Madrid, were indicative both of the relative vulnerability of the government and of an increasing politicization of students, which facilitated the organization in universities of left-wing and Christian Democrat political groups, simultaneously with the development of worker organizations in the factories.

The regime saw the universities as an important arena for the attempt to mobilize society in support of Francoist ideology, by means of the **Falange**-directed Spanish University Syndicate (Sindicato Español Universitario – SEU). The effectiveness of organizations like the SEU was, however, circumscribed by the relative weakness of the ideas it was charged with propagating, and by the changes occurring in Spanish society, which were often experienced initially among the educated young. As a compulsory state party organization, active in supporting the continuation of Francoism and perpetuating the legacy of the Civil War, the SEU gradually became devoid of meaning for those students who composed the post-war generation. From the mid-1950s, university students increasingly defined their personal and political objectives according to criteria far removed from the retrospective triumphalism of Franco's anti-communist 'crusade'.

The first major political action by students occurred in 1951, when divisions within the local Falange in Barcelona provided an opportunity for the populace at large, led by university students, to protest at the crippling economic conditions. This set the pattern for future protests: a meeting would be held, from which the SEU representatives would be excluded (or expelled) and demands made of the university Rector. Police intervention would follow, and academic sanctions would be imposed on the instigators and their academic sympathizers. Invariably this would bring renewed protests followed by more violent clashes with the police. The faculty, or the university itself, would then be closed. The increasing rejection by students of the SEU led to its abolition by the regime in 1965. By the late 1960s the government was responding to student protest by declaring states of siege and a virtually continuous occupation of campuses.

In the wake of the May events of Paris in 1968, student protest in Spain became increasingly radicalized. Although this radicalization provoked further repression by the regime, the culture of opposition was by then well established in universities, as lecturers and students joined in the wider protest movement calling for democracy. During the transition to democracy, from 1975 to 1982, students were prominent in public demonstrations, such as that called against the attempted military coup in February 1981. Subsequently they participated in other protest movements, such as the campaign against Spain's membership of NATO in 1986. By the late 1980s and the early 1990s, protest tended to concentrate on specifically educational issues, such as overcrowding, fee levels and poor facilities.

See also: education and research; LRU; universities; university education

Further reading

Maravall, J. (1978) *Dictatorship and Political Dissent: Workers and Students in Franco's Spain*, New York: St Martin's Press (the only account in English of student protest under Franco).

Pérez Díaz, V. (1993) *The Return of Civil Society: The Emergence of Democratic Spain*, Harvard University Press.

MICHAEL RICHARDS

Suárez, Adolfo

b. 1932, Cebreros, Avila

Politician

Prime Minister from June 1976 to February 1981, Suárez is the man largely credited with the successful transition to democracy after Franco's death.

Suárez came from relatively humble origins, and his political career began as a clerk in the Civil Governor's office in Avila, working under Fernando Herrero Tejedor, who sponsored Suárez's rise through the ranks of the Franco administration. In 1969 he was appointed Director-General of Spanish **Television**, where he cultivated his media skills as well as forming a friendship with the future King **Juan Carlos I**. In 1975 he was appointed Minister for the **National Movement** in Arias Navarro's government.

On Arias Navarro's resignation, the King surprised the entire nation by appointing the still little-known Suárez as Prime Minister, to overcome the political impasse left by his predecessor. From a position of considerable weakness he skilfully won support for his government's reform programme by forging contacts with the democratic opposition, whilst reassuring reactionary elements of his intention to remain faithful to the institutional structure of Francoism. His success in persuading the Francoist Cortes to vote itself out of existence, and his deftness in legalizing the communist **PCE** without provoking military intervention, are universally recognized as having been fundamental to the achievement of democracy in Spain.

In 1977 Suárez won the first democratic elections with a centre-right coalition, **UCD**, formed with various small groups from the moderate opposition to Franco. Despite its heterogeneous composition, he was successful in transforming UCD into an effective vehicle for the consolidation of the reform programme. However, after its second election victory in 1979, the UCD began to fall apart under the strain of the compromises inherent in the transition process. A movement of internal opposition linked to powerful business interests forced Suárez's resignation early in 1981. Ceding the Prime Ministership to Leopoldo **Calvo Sotelo**, Suárez became disenchanted with the party's direction, and left to form the *Centro Democrático y Social* (Social and Democratic Centre – CDS) in July 1982.

In the mid-1980s the CDS threatened to become a pivotal force in the political centre, as **Fraga**'s **Popular Alliance** failed to improve its standing. In 1986 it won just under 10 percent of the vote, and in 1989 maintained almost the same level of support. However a controversial decision to ally with the centre-right **PP** in local government, and a sharp electoral decline, led to Suárez's resignation and departure from political life in 1991.

Suárez's great achievement was to govern Spain during the most delicate phases of the movement towards democracy, and encourage negotiation and understanding between mutually hostile forces. Though he has been criticized for his ideological inconsistency and failures as leader of two political parties, the UCD and the CDS, few would deny his extraordinary contribution to the peaceful democratization of Spain.

Further reading

Huneeus, C. (1985) *La Unión de Centro Democrático y la transición a la democracia en España*, Madrid: Centro de Investigaciones Sociológicas (the only published monograph on the UCD).

Morán, G. (1979) *Historia de una ambición*, Barcelona: Planeta (a highly critical account of Suárez's political career).

Preston, P. (1986) *The Triumph of Democracy in Spain*, London: Methuen (an account of the transition process which contains a balanced analysis of the Suárez period).

JONATHAN HOPKIN

Suárez, Gonzalo

b. 1934, Oviedo

Filmmaker and novelist

Suárez's first films were associated with the cosmopolitan Barcelona School, a movement influenced by the aesthetics of the Nouvelle Vague. In the late 1970s he retired temporarily to write cult **detective fiction**. After establishing his own production company, *Ditirambo Films*, he returned to cinema with *Epílogo* (Epilogue) (1984), a reflection on the power of the **media**. From *Remando al viento* (Rowing With the Wind) (1988) his films display a visual lavishness unprecedented in Spanish cinema and a determination to make headway within the European art cinema.

See also: *europeísmo*; film and cinema; novel

Further reading

Cercas, J. (1993) *La obra literaria de Gonzalo Suárez*, Barcelona: Sirmio/Cuaderns Crema (a serious study of Suárez's literary career and its significance).

Hernández Ruiz, J. (1991) *Gonzalo Suárez: un combate ganado con la ficción*, Alcalá de Henares: Festival de Cine de Alcalá de Henares (mostly a biographical account; includes an interview with Suárez and a comprehensive filmography).

XON DE ROS

Suquía Goicoechea, Angel

b. 1916, Zaldivia, Guipúzcoa

Cardinal Archbishop

Created Bishop of Almería in 1966, of Málaga in 1969, Archbishop of Santiago de Compostela in 1973, of Madrid in 1983 and designated Cardinal in 1985, Suquía was elected President of the Spanish Bishops' Conference (CEE) from 1987–90, was re-elected from 1990–3, and retired in 1994, having overseen the completion of Madrid's Almudena Cathedral. Considered to be highly conservative, contrasting in attitude and style with his immediate predecessors as CEE Presidents, Díaz Merchán and **Enrique y Tarancón**, both men of dialogue, he was very much in tune with the 'restoration' attitude of Pope John Paul II. During his presidency of the CEE, and with entrenched positions on both sides, church relations with the socialist **PSOE** government were strained.

See also: church and state; religion; Roman Catholicism; social attitudes

AUDREY BRASSLOFF

Suresnes

Suresnes was the location of the 13th Congress of the socialist **PSOE**, notable for the election as Secretary General of Felipe **González**. González, representing the main groups of socialists active within Spain, thus became the dominant force in the party, overturning the 'old guard' of exiled socialists in France led by Rodolfo Llopis. González's victory enabled the PSOE's strategy to be brought up to date with changes in Spanish society, which the old guard had failed to take on board. The congress also established the strategy of *ruptura democrática* (a clean break with Francoism) as the party's objective for the post-Franco period.

See also: Marxism; political parties; politics; socialism

JONATHAN HOPKIN

T

Tácitos

A reformist group, initially composed largely of former **National Movement** officials, which took its name from the alias Tácito, which was used to sign articles advocating political change appearing in the Catholic newspaper *Ya* from 1972. The group's initial objectives did not go beyond the notion of limited concessions designed to ensure that the basic distribution of power after the end of the Franco regime would remain intact. By 1974, it incorporated some Christian Democrats not identified with the regime, and their inclusion in Adolfo **Suárez**'s first cabinet in 1976 enabled him to give it a more broadly reformist character. Some prominent Tácitos, such as Landelino **Lavilla** and Marcelino Oreja, became ministers in the first **UCD** government after 1977.

See also: history; politics

EAMONN RODGERS

Tamames Gómez, Ramón

b. 1933, Madrid

Economist

A graduate both of the Complutense University of Madrid and the London School of Economics, Tamames combined a career as a professional economist and academic with political activism, mainly in the communist **PCE**, of which he was a member between 1956 and 1981, and which he represented in the first **parliament** of the restored democracy from 1977 to 1981. In the latter year, however, he was expelled from the PCE, and gradually evolved towards a more centre-right position, eventually joining the Centro Democrático y Social (Social Democrat Centre) led by Adolfo **Suárez**. He is the author of many distinguished monographs, notably *Estructura económica de España* (The Economic Structure of Spain).

See also: economy; politics

EAMONN RODGERS

Tamayo, José

b. 1920, Granada

Theatrical producer

Tamayo is arguably the most successful Spanish stage producer of the second half of the twentieth century. Since 1944, when he organized Granada's University Theatre, his stage design and management activities have gone from strength to strength, notably his pioneering work in introducing Spanish audiences to contemporary North American theatre, such as *Salem's Lot* and *Death of a Salesman*. From 1946 onwards he was in charge of the Compañía Lope de Vega (Lope de Vega Theatre Company), which he directed in around thirty plays, and led on numerous tours around Spain and abroad, especially in South America (1949–51). For this work he received the *Premio Nacional de Teatro* (National Theatre Prize) (1946, 1947). In 1954 he started his first lyrical productions, such as *La*

Verbena de la Paloma (The Fair of Our Lady of the Dove) in the old Madrid of *La Corrala* (the traditional roofless playhouse of the seventeenth century). During 1955–62, he was director of the Teatro Español (Spanish Theatre), where he staged many plays from the world repertory, such as *The Carmelites' Dialogue* and *Six Characters in Search of an Author.*

Tamayo's interest in the ***zarzuela*** led him to set up the Amadeus Vives company, with which he travelled Spain, performing the most important examples of the genre. In 1961 he took part in the opening of the Teatro de Bellas Artes (Arts Theatre), to which he frequently returned with his Lope de Vega Company. On that occasion, he staged a very successful revival of Valle-Inclán's *Divinas Palabras* (Divine Words). With the Lope de Vega Company he was a frequent visitor to Granada's International Music Festival during the 1970s.

Among Tamayo's more adventurous enterprises has been the staging of *Autos Sacramentales* (morality plays on eucharistic themes) and similar plays at the entrances to cathedrals and in monastery cloisters. Calderón's *Cena del Rey Baltasar* (King Belshazzar's Feast) was performed at Seville Cathedral. He has also produced Spanish classical plays in the most diverse locations: Lope de Vega's *El Caballero de Olmedo* (*The Knight of Olmedo*) in Washington and New York (1962) and other works in the Roman Theatre at Mérida and the Retiro park in Madrid. One of his most ambitious and magnificent projects was the spectacular performance of *Carmen* in Seville's Maestranza bullring.

Tamayo's approach to classical theatre displays both moderation and imagination, and he has combined popularization and innovation in equal measure, as is well illustrated by his productions of *Abelardo y Eloísa* (Hélöise and Abelard), *Divinas Palabras* (1961), *Luces de Bohemia* (Bohemia Lights) (1970) and *Calígula* (1990). In 1970 he returned to his other favourite genre, the lyric, establishing the Compañía Lírica Nacional (National Lyric Company), which has been his major occupation since then. Tamayo has achieved considerable success in several countries with two *Antologías de la Zarzuela* (*zarzuela* collections).

His achievement has been recognized by awards such as the *Premio de la Crítica de Madrid* (Madrid Critics' Prize) (1967, 1969 and 1971), the *Premio de la Crítica de Barcelona* (Barcelona Critics' Prize) (1960), the *Premio El Espectador y la Crítica de Valladolid* (Valladolid Audiences' and Critics' Prize), and decorations such as the *Mérito Civil*, *Isabel la Católica* and *Alfonso X el Sabio*, and the *Medalla de Plata al Mérito Turístico* (silver medal for services to tourism). In 1997 he received from Carlos Valle-Inclán, son of the playwright, a newly created award for pioneering the revival of Valle-Inclán on the Spanish stage.

Tamayo has not only directed a long list of plays and playwrights in Spain, but has trained many theatre professionals who went on to become leading figures on the stage. He once summarized his ambition by saying he tried to achieve three things in the theatre: uneasiness, immensity and wonder.

See also: cultural institutions; Ministry of Culture; performing arts; prizes; society; theatre

Further reading

de la Hoz, Enrique (1973) *Panorámica del Teatro en España*, Madrid: Editora Nacional (a study of the evolution of Spanish theatre, in all its genres. Illustrated with photographs of representative productions).

Molinari, A. (1994) *Pequeño Diccionario del Teatro Andaluz*, Sevilla: Ediciones Alfar (a dictionary of Andalusian theatre terms).

Vilches de Frutos, M.F. (1994) 'Spain: Artistic Profile; Theatre for Young Audiences; Puppet Theatre; Design; Theatre Space and Architecture; Criticism, Scholarship and Publishing', in D. Rubin (ed.) *The World Encyclopedia of Contemporary Theatre. Europe*, London and New York: Routledge, pp. 790–804.

LUIS VICENTE BELMONTE TALERO

tapas

Tapas are nibbles or snacks eaten with a drink before lunch or dinner. The most common *tapas* are simple things such as olives, nuts, small portions of cold sausages, *serrano* (raw cured) ham, potato omelette, vegetable relishes and prawns. However a mini-portion of almost any dish can constitute a *tapa*, and often bar-restaurants offer a *tapa* of any dish on the day's menu. These hot snacks are called *tapas de cocina*, and include such things as fried fish, fritters, tripe stew, paella, croquettes and octopus. *Tapas* are served with *picos* (bread sticks), or bread. *Ir de tapas* (sampling the specialities of different *tapas* bars), is a popular way of socializing.

See also: fast food outlets; food and drink; restaurants; social attitudes

S. SERRANO

Tàpies, Antoni

b. 1923, Barcelona

Artist

The steel wire sculpture on the roof of the Tàpies Foundation in Barcelona traces the image of a chair floating amongst clouds. This is essentially a call to contemplation, for Tàpies is an experimental artist whose work is rooted in ideas.

The Civil War awakened Tàpies' political consciousness and during the Franco era he was strongly identified with the Catalan people and opposition politics, hence his many subsequent renderings of the Catalan flag and images of protest, as in *L'Esperit català* (The Catalan Spirit) and *Coratge del poble* (Courage of the People). Tàpies abandoned his law studies at the age of twenty-three and began experimenting with collage. His use of an obituary article to create a cross in *Creu de paper de diari* (Newspaper Cross), stressed the transcendental nature of life, and symbolized the fusion of the spiritual (vertical) with the terrestial (horizontal). The cross became a recurring image, evolving into the letter T, for Tàpies, and also X, suggesting rejection and/or harmony, depending on the context.

While participating with Joan **Brossa** on the 1940s surrealist magazine *Dau al set* (The Seventh Side of the Die), he became interested in medievalism and magic, seeing artists and alchemists as transformers of reality. A trip to Paris in the 1950s confirmed his allegiance to socialist ideology, but led him to reject the propaganda approach of social realist art, as well as the then fashionable abstract alternatives, which he found cold and geometric. He experimented with natural materials such as sand, marble dust and coloured earth, giving rise to his now famous 'matter paintings'. Inspired by modern scientific theory and oriental philosophy, both of which emphasize the common origin of all matter (quanta/dust), Tàpies successfully fused the medium with the message so that they became indistinguishable in *Terra i pintura* (Earth and Paint) and *Pintura rosa i blava* (Pink and Blue Paint/Painting).

Tàpies is sometimes associated with an artistic movement known as Informalism which was opposed to all intellectual categories (form) and the dualism of western culture (heaven/hell, body/soul). *Informe*'s views on unnecessary waste inspired Tàpies to paint a calloused foot and other objects normally rejected by capitalist society. He called these works *Matèria en forma de peu* (Matter in the Shape of a Foot) and *Matèria en forma d'aixela* (Matter in the Shape of an Armpit), because all organic life is constantly reshaping itself. His own materials did so as well, evolving naturally into the eponymous 'wall paintings' (*tapia* = wall/Tàpies), with associations of separation, enclosure, and the clandestine graffiti of a persecuted people.

Tàpies has been universally acclaimed since the 1950s. Most major art galleries have on display examples of his huge output of more than 7,000 works.

Further reading

Catoir, B. (1991) *Conversations with Antoni Tàpies*, Munich: Prestel (an excellent general introduction followed by interviews).

Gimferrer, P. (1986) *Tàpies and the Catalan Spirit*, Barcelona: Polígrafa (a sensitive account).

Penrose, R. (1977) *Tàpies*, Barcelona: Polígrafa (perceptive and well structured).

HELEN OPPENHEIMER

tax system

Spain's tax system is, from 1998, in the process of being reformed. The number of income tax brackets was reduced from eighteen in 1996 to ten in 1997, and a further reduction to six was proposed in 1998. Prior to these reforms, rates ranged from 20 percent on annual income of 400,000–600,000 pesetas to a top rate of 56 percent on income above 9.55m pesetas. Subject to improvements in the overall budget deficit, the government planned to reduce the top rate further, to between 40 and 50 percent, by 1999. Since 1995, tax tables have been adjusted annually for inflation.

Spain also has a net worth tax which can bring the top marginal rate to 70 percent for high-income taxpayers with large assets. For variable-income investments, tax tables have been adjusted for inflation since 1992, but for fixed-income investments there is no such adjustment. This sets Spain apart from other EU countries.

The corporate tax rate is 35 percent, around the EU average. Profits or dividends generated abroad are taxed in Spain, which is unusual in the EU. While there is no double taxation of dividends for corporations, individuals still face some double taxation. Capital gains are taxed with no period of exemption, and accelerated depreciation is not permitted.

Spain adopted the EU value-added tax (*Impuesto de Valor Añadido* – IVA) in 1986 and the average rate in 1996 was 16 percent. Excise taxes are levied on tobacco and alcoholic beverages, petrol, diesel fuel and some forms of transportation.

Fiscal pressure in Spain, i.e. total tax receipts as a percentage of GDP, has risen faster than in any of the main EU countries since the mid-1980s, but is still slightly below the EU average (35.99 percent in 1994, compared with an EU average of 42.27 percent). The figures are misleading, however: massive tax fraud in Spain (equivalent to about 5 percent of GDP, according to official estimates) leaves the salaried middle class with most of the tax burden.

Spain's regional and local governments administer some specific taxes to help finance their activities, e.g. on property, gambling, legal documents and net worth (except the Basque and Navarre regions, which collect and administer all taxes). Since 1994, each autonomous region has been permitted to administer 15 percent of all withholding tax revenue collected locally, in an effort to encourage the regions to share responsibility for their own financing. This process was accelerated in the Basque country and Catalonia after the accession to power of the minority centre-right **PP** government in 1996. As a condition of support, the Basque nationalist **PNV** consolidated full fiscal autonomy. In Catalonia, the **CiU** obtained an increase in the proportion of tax administered within the region to 30 percent, and continued to press for the same concessions as the Basques.

The tax system is evolving rapidly: between 1986 and 1996, there were some 3,000 changes in the detail of the regulations. Experts have recommended reforms to yield a system of full fiscal co-responsibility, where regions would add their own surcharges to the basic national withholding tax rate, and adjust these according to their needs. The PP has proposed moving in this direction, to avoid the deficit spending inherent in the previous system, where the central government collects most of the taxes and redistributes them to the regions to be spent.

See also: black economy; economy; national income; regional nationalism; taxation

Further reading

Chislett, W. (1998) *Spain: The Central Hispano Handbook*, Madrid: Central Hispano (pp. 23–5 give a concise summary of the tax system, with useful graphs which give a succinct comparison with the EU).

GAYLE ALLARD

taxation

During the Franco regime taxes were low and evasion high. State revenue depended mainly on a wide range of indirect taxes, and taxation of personal income was not pursued with any real vigour: only one in twenty of the workforce paid income tax; many self-employed professionals did not bother to file returns and were left unmolested by the authorities. The calculation of corporation tax was not properly standardized and often depended on theoretical assessments by the inspectorate. Although some reforms were made in 1957 and 1964 which improved revenues and lessened somewhat the regressive nature of the taxation system, it was not until the advent of democracy in 1977 that steps were taken to implement a major overhaul of the entire fiscal system and to expand the revenue service so as to provide both fiscal vigilance and advice to taxpayers. A publicity campaign was launched to encourage returns and tax inspectors were given greater powers to catch offenders.

By the early 1980s tax revenues had gone up from 20 to 25 percent of GDP and direct taxes had overtaken indirect taxes. Tax evasion was still rife, however, and the welfare plans of the new socialist government demanded substantial increases in revenues. Accordingly, between 1985 and 1990 the government made a two-pronged attack on the problem: it forced banks (and later insurance companies) to declare their customers' assets, and it offered tax dodgers a no-questions-asked route into legality via the investment of undeclared monies in low interest-bearing government securities. By the early 1990s tax revenues had risen to 35 percent of GDP and the number of taxpayers had gone up from around the 6 million mark in 1980 to 12.5 million. Direct taxes had continued to outstrip indirect taxes despite the introduction of VAT which, being more effective than the variety of indirect taxes that it replaced, helped to increase revenue. Part of the increase in direct tax revenues is due to the effect of progressive taxation: incomes in Spain have gone up very substantially, which results in payment at higher rates of tax. Nevertheless compared to other EU countries the fiscal burden (tax revenues as a proportion of GDP) in Spain is at the lower end of the scale, close to that of the UK and considerably below those of countries near the EU average such as Italy, France or Austria.

The distribution of the tax burden, however, is open to serious criticism in that employees, whose earnings are easily identified and have income tax deducted at source, are on average paying tax at higher rates than employers and self-employed, which clearly points to massive tax evasion by the better off whose earnings cannot be directly verified because they are not on a payroll. Since this applies to between a fifth and a sixth of the workforce, the problem is a severe and long-standing one which successive governments have failed to tackle with sufficient vigour and which deepens and perpetuates income inequalities in Spain. According to the Spanish Institute for Fiscal Studies about half the income earned in Spain by the self-employed is undeclared and therefore untaxed.

See also: black economy; economy; national income; tax system

Further reading

Chislett, W. (1998) *Spain: The Central Hispano Handbook*, Madrid: Central Hispano (pp. 23–5 give a concise summary of the tax system, with useful graphs which give a succinct comparison with the EU).

Hooper, J. (1995) *The New Spaniards*, Harmondsworth: Penguin (chapter 17 includes several excellent pages on the deficiencies of Spain's taxation system).

C.A. LONGHURST

technocrats

Tecnócratas was the name given to the new breed of professional economists and other university-trained people brought into the government by Franco in 1957 to tackle the disastrous economic situation to which earlier policies of autarky, protectionism and stifling state interventionism had brought the country. The arrival of the technocrats into positions of influence marked a turning point in Franco's regime. Considerably younger, more pragmatic and less politically blinkered than their predecessors, the new ministers and their advisers set about tackling the problems of inflation, balance of payments deficit and trade disincentives. Among the most prominent of these technocrats were Alberto Ullastres, the new Minister of Trade, Mariano Navarro Rubio, Minister of Finance, and Laureano **López Rodó**, Technical Secretary to the Cabinet, all of whom had teams of highly trained economic and technical advisers. Also associated with the technocrats was Gregorio López Bravo, who became Director-General of the International Trade Department in 1959 and Minister of Industry in 1962. The whole thrust of the technocrats was to improve the workings of the Francoist administration from within by importing new management techniques.

Abandoning the by now discredited attempt at self-sufficiency and import substitution, the technocrats cautiously introduced reforms aimed at liberalizing foreign trade, promoting exports and allowing greatly increased imports. The peseta was devalued and Spain joined international economic organizations (OEEC, IMF and World Bank). The new policies culminated in the **Stabilization Plan** of 1959 which administered a sharp deflationary shock to the Spanish economy. For the technocrats, monetary stability at home was an essential pre-requisite of increased foreign trade and inward investment; hence their uncompromising determination, evident in the severe measures of 1959, to cut back on public expenditure and public debt and bring inflation under control. To the extent that it helped to usher in the 'economic miracle' of the 1960s, the technocrats' economic Stabilization Plan may be said to have been successful. Although this remains their main claim to fame, other political initiatives have also been attributed to the technocrats, such as promoting property ownership through subsidized housing schemes, encouraging Spain's abortive application to join the EEC in 1962, and giving their support to the **Juan Carlos** option in the tricky question of choosing Franco's successor.

The technocrats have been very closely associated with the Catholic-cum-capitalist organization **Opus Dei**, and it is true that many of them did belong (including the four named above). While Opus Dei has often been criticized, no doubt rightly, for being excessively secretive and self-seeking, the new breed of technocratic politician that it promoted was largely responsible for bringing about a refreshing change of rhetoric on the part of the Franco regime, from the vacuous, reactionary, xenophobic, self-congratulatory and pretentious propaganda of the 1940s and 1950s to the much less strident and more realistic promotion of sensible economic and social objectives and values of the 1960s, even if within a framework that remained essentially conservative and dirigiste.

Further reading

Fusi, J.P. (1987) *Franco: A biography*, London: Unwin Hyman (chapter 19 deals with the arrival of the technocrats to power and their policies).

Gallo, M. (1973) *Spain under Franco: A History*, London: Allen & Unwin (the English version of an early (1969) but well-informed study by a distinguished French historian; see especially pp. 251–344 for the period of the technocrats).

Payne, S. (1987) *The Franco Regime, 1936–1975*, Madison, WI: University of Wisconsin Press (some information on the technocrats and their policies in chapters 18 and 19).

C.A. LONGHURST

Tejerazo, El

The popular name given to the attempted military coup staged by the army and the **Civil Guard** on 23 February, 1981 (also known as 23-F), *El Tejerazo* takes its name from Antonio **Tejero Molina**, a Civil Guard colonel who led the storming of the **parliament** building while the Congress of Deputies was in session. The coup was the culmination of a long process of military conspiracy which had begun shortly after the beginning of the transition to democracy in 1975. The traditionally right-wing **armed forces** were suspicious of democracy in general, and disturbed by what they perceived as the government's incapacity to control **terrorism**.

The object of the coup was to force King **Juan Carlos I** to annul the **constitution of 1978**, suspend the Cortes, and rule with a military council. Many senior officers expected the King to collaborate with the movement, but the King telephoned the Captains-General of all the military regions, reminding them of their oath to the constitution and their obedience to him as Commander-in-Chief of all the armed forces. The King also appeared on nationwide television on the night of 23–4 February in the uniform of Commander-in-Chief, declaring his support for constitutionalism, and the conspirators soon found themselves isolated. Those most deeply involved were tried by court martial, but received relatively light sentences, increased after an appeal by the state prosecutor. Generals Alfonso Armada and Jaime **Milans del Bosch**, and Colonel Tejero received sentences of 30 years each, but Armada and Milans were released, in 1988 and 1992 respectively, on grounds of age and good conduct. The failure of the attempted coup led to an upsurge of renewed popular support for democracy, and helped to overcome the sense of disillusionment with the state which had set in around 1979, caused by continuing economic problems and terrorism. The other effect of the coup was that it encouraged the government of Leopoldo **Calvo Sotelo** to speed up the negotiations for Spain's entry into **NATO**, a process which eventually produced increased professionalism and depoliticization of the armed forces.

Further reading

Carr, R. and Fusi, J.P. (1979) *Spain: Dictatorship to Democracy*, London: Allen & Unwin (a thorough and scholarly account of the transition to democracy).

Newton, M.T. with Donaghy, P.J. (1997) *Institutions of Modern Spain: A Political and Economic Guide*, Cambridge: Cambridge University Press (a standard reference work).

Preston, P (1986) *The Triumph of Democracy in Spain*, London: Methuen (a lively account of the issues and personalities involved in the political developments of contemporary Spain).

EAMONN RODGERS

Tejero Molina, Antonio

b. 1932, Spain

Paramilitary police officer

Tejero Molina was an obscure **Civil Guard** officer who came to prominence in the right-wing coup of 1981, the ***Tejerazo***, to which his name was attached, and for which he was sentenced to 30 years' imprisonment. From September 1993, he benefitted from an 'open regime' which meant he was allowed home at weekends and could leave the prison between 8 a.m. and midnight on other days. Though he refused to give an undertaking to respect the **constitution of 1978**, in December 1996, having completed half his sentence, with five years' remission for good behaviour, he was deemed to have served three-quarters of his term, and qualified for release.

EAMONN RODGERS

telephones

The Compañía Telefónica de España S.A. is Spain's largest single company by turnover and the biggest employer by a considerable margin. It has long been a favourite with investors. The state has a 20 percent shareholding and the remainder is in the hands of institutional shareholders (including the major banks) and tens of thousands of small investors. Because of EU rules, Telefónica had to lose its monopoly, and a second fixed-line telecommunications company, Retevisión, was set up in 1997, with investment from the Italian telecoms company Stet. In view of the complete liberalization of the telecommunications market planned for late 1998, and the inevitable increase in competition (which already existed in certain areas such as mobile phones and data transmission), Telefónica made large investments in the upgrade and extension of its services by introducing digital exchanges and fibre optic cables, and drastically reduced the waiting list for new lines. The traditional price structure, with expensive trunk and international calls subsidizing cheap local calls, was reviewed, and the new tariff system is expected to bring charges more into line with those of other operators. With under 50 telephones per 100 inhabitants in Spain (compared to between 60 and 70 in France or Germany) there is considerable scope for growth. The mobile phone market, with less than half a million subscribers in the mid-1990s (compared to six million in the UK), has shown very rapid expansion, rising to an estimated 14 percent in 1998, with market penetration reaching EU levels. A number of consortia, of which Airtel is the best known (made up of Airtouch, BT and two Spanish banks), are active in this area as well as in that of data transmission. For its part, Telefónica, through its international arm, Tisa, has turned to the potentially lucrative

Latin American market and is the biggest foreign operator there, an activity that makes an important contribution to the company's healthy profits. In 1997, Telefónica bought out the state's 23.8 percent holding in Tisa, and acquired complete control of the subsidiary. It also owns 30.8 percent of the telecommunications undertaking in Colombia, and 43.6 percent of its Chilean counterpart.

Further reading

Chislett, W. (1998) *Spain: The Central Hispano Handbook*, Madrid: Central Hispano (see pp. 66–9 for a succinct account of Telefónica's development).

C.A. LONGHURST

television

Spanish television has come a long way since first going on air in the mid-1950s. Having been closely controlled – indeed censored – by the Franco regime for the first twenty years of its existence, it shared in the freedoms of democracy from the mid-1970s on. It has also lost its status as a state monopoly with the arrival of three new national commercial stations in the late 1980s, and has been decentralized even further with the creation of a number of regional channels in different **autonomous communities**.

Spain's first television channel, Televisión de España (TVE) first started broadcasting on 28 October 1956, sending only three hours of programming daily to some 600 receivers in Madrid, and being extended to Barcelona in 1958. Funding from advertising – through sponsorship of programmes – was introduced in 1958, and, alone of European countries, Spain has never levied a television licence fee. The second channel (TVE2) was introduced in September 1965, initially in Barcelona and Zaragoza, but, like the first channel (now renamed TVE1), quickly spread to cover the entire country.

Like all other public institutions dealing in ideas and information – the press, cinema, the theatre – television was closely controlled by state **censorship** during the Franco dictatorship. This control was most obvious in news and related kinds of broadcasts, but in fact affected television output as a whole. The result was that many Spaniards took a very jaundiced view of their television service, particularly as regards its information-providing services, which were rightly seen as little more than a mouthpiece for the regime.

Following the death of Franco in 1975 and the transition to a democratic system over the following two years, Spanish Television was given an entirely new statute in December 1978. Although this new statute stated that Spanish Television was to be subject to commercial law in its external relations, it nevertheless did not completely abolish political influence in the running of the company: the members of the board of governors were to be elected by the Spanish parliament, and the director-general was appointed for a five-year term by the government. As a result of this, widespread suspicions remained in the years following the move to democracy that Spanish Television was still essentially controlled by the party in power, and there were high levels of public mistrust, particularly in the early 1980s.

The monopoly status of TVE could not, however, survive indefinitely. As the 1980s wore on, it was in fact undermined from two different directions. The first of these was the appearance of regional television stations in a number of Spain's autonomous communities. The first of these to go on air was the **Basque television** channel (ETB) in 1982, followed by the first **Catalan television** channel (TV3) in 1983. Subsequently, further regional stations to appear were Televisión de Galicia in Galicia (broadcasting in Galician) in 1985, and Canal Sur in Andalusia, Telemadrid in Madrid and Canal 9 in Valencia (broadcasting in Catalan), all in 1989. During the same period both ETB and Catalan Television went on to add second channels in their respective communities. These regional channels, which have their own programming and purchasing policies, can attract very sizeable audiences, and are often the most popular channels in their particular community, particularly where they broadcast in a language other than **Spanish**. In 1989 they joined together to form FORTA (the Federation of Autonomous Radio and Television Organizations) in order to increase their collective strength.

The second major change to the Spanish television landscape was the arrival of the commercial national stations. These were Antena 3, Canal + and Tele 5, set up following a complicated bidding process in 1989, and going on air in 1990. At the outset Antena 3 was owned mostly by Spanish publishing interests, Canal + was owned jointly by the French television company of the same name, the Spanish publishing group PRISA and a number of Spanish banks, while Tele 5 was owned partly by the Italian media magnate Silvio Berlusconi (on whose own Canale 5 it was partly based), partly by the Spanish Organization for the Blind (**ONCE**) and by a number of other investors.

Canal + is the easiest of these new channels to describe since it is – like its sister French company – a subscription channel whose programmes are encrypted, a special decoder having to be purchased in order to view them. It specializes in films, and maintains a fairly high-profile advertising campaign in Spain, encouraging members of the public to become subscribers in order to be able to view films before they become available on the other terrestrial networks.

Antena 3 is a generalist channel very much in the style of TVE1 (now restyled as 'La Primera', TVE2 having become 'La 2'), with the usual mix of programmes ranging from news and current affairs through sport to drama, fiction, sitcoms and games of various kinds. It is now seriously challenging La Primera as the most viewed channel in Spain, and from time to time actually overtakes it.

Tele 5 – sometimes referred to as 'Tele Teta' ('Boobs TV') in view of its profusion of scantily clad game hostesses – is very much in the Berlusconi Orwellian-nightmare mould, offering very downmarket entertainment of various kinds, from tumultuous game shows to often highly confrontational 'reality shows'. Its news service is, quite literally, something of a joke in Spain, and was at one point restricted to one item of news per hour, appearing in the form of a caption with no commentary of any kind.

Overall, since the mid-1950s, Spanish television has developed in the direction of offering greater choice to viewers, and reacting more and more to the demands of its audience as opposed to the wishes of those in political power.

Further reading

Villagrasa, J.M. (1992) 'Spain: The Emergence of Commercial Television', in A. Silj (ed.) *The New Television in Europe*, London: John Libbey (a wide-ranging but very readable account of changes in television throughout Spain since the early 1980s).

HUGH O'DONNELL

Tellado, Corín

b. 1927, Viavélez (Asturias)

Romantic novelist

The most successful and prominent exponent of the genre of the ***novela rosa***, María del Socorro Tellado began to compose romantic fiction in 1946 at the age of 19, and in 1998, though no longer physically able to write because of poor health, she was still dictating novels to her daughter-in-law. The secret of her success has been her capacity to appeal to the desire of the public for escapism and entertainment, and also her sheer industry, which has enabled her to produce some 5,000 titles in fifty years. Even when allowance is made for the fact that she works within a small-scale format of approximately 100 pages per volume, this figure represents an average of two novels per week. At her peak, she would rise at 5 a.m., and, with only two short breaks for refreshment, would work until 3 p.m. It is estimated that her works have sold a total of over 400 million copies, an average of 80,000 per title, which exceeds the sales of many of the most successful 'serious' novels of the 1980s and 1990s. Her novels have been translated into seven languages.

By creating a romantically charged atmosphere without going into explicit sexual detail, Tellado manages not only to sustain a formula which appeals to her readers but was also able to avoid some of the heavy-handed attentions of the Francoist **censorship** apparatus. The fact, however, that her novels end with the reward of virtue and the discomfiture or repentance of the wicked did not always placate the censors. Implied references to adultery or divorce could lead to passages being cut from the text, and on one occasion an entire novel was banned because it showed a landowner distributing his lands among his tenants, something considered too revolutionary by the guardians of the regime.

Despite their formulaic character, Tellado's novels have evolved in certain ways, reflecting the evolution of society, though they still steer clear of a fully realistic portrayal of contemporary life. This is partly because of the need to avoid disturbing the reader in search of an optimistic and comforting plot, but is also a shrewd commercial decision, since too much historical precision might affect sales by causing the novels to become dated. Nevertheless, the English aristocratic protagonists of the 1950s have gradually been replaced by characters from the Spanish professional classes, and, increasingly since the economic boom of the 1960s, by business executives. The style of the novels, however, continues to reflect the traditional fastidiousness of the genre towards anything smacking even remotely of crudity.

Though dismissed by most of the literary establishment, Tellado's work has been the subject of academic study, and she has been praised by distinguished writers such as the Peruvian novelist Mario Vargas Llosa.

See also: kiosk literature; literature; novel; publishing; readership

Further reading

González García, M.T. (1998) *Corín Tellado. Medio siglo de novela de amor (1946–1996)*, Gijón: Pentalfa (the most comprehensive study to date).

Juana, J.M. de (1998) 'Novelas a destajo', *Cambio 16* 15 June: 60–3 (a useful brief overview of Tellado's life and work).

EAMONN RODGERS

tennis

Dubbed 'the year of the Spanish', 1994 saw Sergi **Bruguera** win the men's Roland Garros Championship, Arantxa **Sánchez Vicario** the women's Roland Garros Championship and the US Open, and Conchita **Martínez** the Ladies' Championship at Wimbledon. That same year the Spanish women's team won the Federation Cup for the third time and went on to win again the following year, making it their third consecutive victory.

Within Spain international tournaments are held in Madrid and Barcelona, and the sport is regulated by the Spanish Tennis Federation to which tennis clubs are affiliated. Public tennis courts are also available, especially in recreational areas such as the Casa del Campo in Madrid.

See also: sport and leisure

EAMONN RODGERS

terrorism

Apart from small, professedly left-wing groups like **FRAP** and **GRAPO**, the main terrorist organization in Spain since the late 1960s is **ETA**, which has been responsible for by far the largest number of deaths and injuries. The peak of ETA activity was the late 1970s and early 1980s, during which deaths from terrorism increased steadily. There were 30 fatalities in 1977, 99 in 1978 and 123 in 1979. Although high-profile attacks on military and **Civil Guard** personnel purport to indicate that ETA is an army of liberation fighting an occupying force, by 1979–80 civilians formed the biggest group among its victims. In the year to October 1980, 114 people died as result of terrorism (an average of one every three days). Of these, fifty-seven were civilians, twenty-seven Civil Guards, eleven army officers and nine policemen. Indiscriminate attacks have been made against supermarkets and resort beaches, and kidnappings for ransom have been carried out. Business people who refused to pay the so-called '**revolutionary tax**', and civilian politicians in the Basque country belonging to all-Spain political parties like **PSOE** and **PP** have been murdered. One of the most spectacular (and tragically ironic) terrorist actions claimed by ETA was the murder in February 1996 of the former President of the Constitutional Tribunal, **Tomás y Valiente**, whose commitment to **civil rights** had caused him in 1993 to strike down as unconstitutional certain clauses in the draconian public-order legislation introduced by the then Minister of the Interior, José Luis **Corcuera**.

Some of the murders perpetrated by ETA have been of their own members, for the organization provides an illustration of the classic features of extreme nationalist terrorism. Since 1970, there have been numerous splits in the movement, caused by some members becoming disillusioned by violence, and advocating a combination of political and military activism. These 'moderates' are then pushed aside by younger extremists who see armed activity as the only way to achieve their goals, and who are willing to murder those who show any inclination to compromise. Some of those ETA members who have tried to take advantage of the government's scheme of ***reinserción*** have also been killed by their former associates.

In addition to death, injury and destruction of property, the main effect of terrorism has been to destabilize the political climate by the classic technique of provoking a right-wing backlash, in an attempt to legitimize armed insurrection. Opposition to democracy by the hard right in the period 1976 to 1982 would have existed in any event, but it was intensified by the scale of terrorist attacks on military and police targets, and the apparent inability of the government of the day to maintain order. Not only did this provide far-right elements with an excuse to take the law into their own hands, but they also had considerable fire-power at their disposal. Gun control in Spain during Franco's time had been relatively lax by British standards, and had been administered in a way which favoured civilian supporters of the regime. It is estimated that at the time of Franco's death in 1975, there were 100,000 members of the **Falange** who were licensed to carry firearms. By 1975, shadowy organizations going by names such as the Batallón Vasco-Español (Spanish Basque Batallion) and Alianza Apostólica Anticomunista (Anti-Communist Apostolic Alliance, which had links to a similar group involved in the 'dirty war' in Argentina) were carrying out attacks on targets in the Basque country. In January 1977, after GRAPO had kidnapped the head of the Supreme Military Tribunal, the offices of a left-wing law firm in the Calle de Atocha in the centre of Madrid were machine-gunned, and five people were killed. In August of the same year, groups of right-wing thugs broke up summer festivals in Basque towns and villages. In one of these incidents, local vigilantes captured and disarmed a gang which was found to include an off-duty police officer.

The involvement of the police in episodes like this shows how far the authorities themselves succumbed to the temptation to combat terrorism by illegal means. The police and the Civil Guard perpetuated many of the authoritarian attitudes and heavy-handed methods which they had been able to use with near impunity in Franco's time. In August 1977, the PSOE deputy for Santander, Jaime Blanco, was beaten up by the police at a political meeting. In July 1978, the police went on the rampage in Rentería, a suburb of San Sebastián, looting shops and damaging private apartments. The **GAL** trials of the 1990s indicated clearly that the willingness to use illegal methods persisted long after the restoration of democracy.

The lack of finesse in the attempts by the security forces to control terrorism have interacted with another characteristic feature of physical-force nationalism, namely, the tendency of popular opinion to fluctuate towards and away from terrorism in response to actions by both terrorists and police. When José María Ryan, an engineer working on the Lemóniz nuclear power project, was kidnapped and murdered in February 1981, there was a general strike throughout Basque country, and 300,000 people demonstrated in protest. Only a week later, however, an ETA member, Arregui, died in custody after being beaten and tortured, which led to new demonstrations, this time against the government. This was only one of several incidents in which detainees were subjected to brutal treatment in custody, most commonly by the Civil Guard, though the Policía Nacional were not entirely blameless either.

Despite the frequency of complaints about ill-treatment in custody throughout the 1980s, real progress in changing the attitudes of the security forces was apparent by 1981, when the police helped to defeat the attempted military coup of 23 February, the ***Tejerazo***. The special anti-terrorist units of the police have proved effective against right-wing terrorism as well as against other terrorist organizations. In addition, the Constitutional Defence Law of 1981 provided for the setting up of an integrated anti-terrorist command (the *Mando Unico Antiterrorista*), to co-ordinate the activities of the army, the police and the Civil

Guard. The MUA effectively neutralized the politico-military wing of ETA by capturing its entire arsenal in January 1982. Effective co-operation by the French authorities has led to the capture of leading ETA commanders, and the considerable reduction in terrorist incidents.

The problem is, however, far from solved, as ETA has begun to rely more on what they call *comandos legales*, active units made up of people who have no police records, and are therefore difficult to trace. It is in the nature of terrorism, especially nationalist terrorism, to be resistant to political arguments, and the clear preference for constitutional nationalism displayed repeatedly in elections by the majority of Basques does not by any means guarantee an early end to the problem.

Furthermore, though GRAPO has been dormant for long periods since it first emerged in 1975, it has not disappeared. In an attempt to put pressure on the authorities over the release of prisoners belonging to the organization, GRAPO bombed government offices in Madrid in March 1998.

See also: armed forces; Franco Bahamonde, Francisco; Herri Batasuna; history; policing; politics

Further reading

Preston, P. (1986) *The Triumph of Democracy in Spain*, London and New York: Methuen (the index entries give easy access to the numerous references to terrorism scattered throughout this classic study).

Sullivan, J. (1988) *ETA and Basque Nationalism: the Fight for Euskadi, 1890–1986*, London: Routledge (the standard work on Basque terrorism).

EAMONN RODGERS

tertulias

A group of people who meet regularly for conversation and card or board games, commonly in cafés, but also in shops, especially bookshops, and literary clubs such as the **Ateneo**. In previous periods, the absence of other outlets for socializing, especially in provincial towns and villages, gave the *tertulia* considerable importance as a cultural, and sometimes political institution. It is still a feature of the older bookshops in the larger cities, and especially of famous literary cafés like the Gijón in Madrid.

EAMONN RODGERS

theatre

After the Civil War (1936–9), the theatre, like most other cultural manifestations, was forced to be as non-controversial as possible. There was a return to the light social dramas of, for instance, the Álvarez Quintero brothers and Carlos Arniches, and conservative contemporary playwrights such as José María Pemán, Joaquín Calvo Sotelo, José López Rubio and Víctor Ruiz Iriarte dominated the stage in Madrid with escapist comedies and psychological dramas. Some influences from the innovative period of the early 1930s, however, survived, in the shape of a few independent groups, and some imaginative directors working in the national theatres. Directors like Felipe Lluch, Luis Escobar, Hurberto Pérez de la Ossa, Claudio de la Torre and Cayetano Luca de Tena worked with some success at the Teatro María Guerrero and the Teatro Español, putting on new versions of classical texts, with a sensitive and intelligent approach to design, choreography and music. From the beginning, under Felipe Lluch's direction, artists such as Salvador **Dalí**, and musicians such as Ernesto **Halffter** and Joaquín **Rodrigo** worked for the national theatres. Plays such as Antonio **Buero Vallejo**'s *Historia de una escalera* (Story of a Staircase) (1949) and Alfonso **Sastre**'s *Escuadra hacia la muerte* (Death Squad) (1953) opened the way to political criticism and social commitment.

This emphasis on the social and political function of the theatre was reinforced by the work of independent groups led by figures like Rivas Cherif, José Luis Alonso, Carmen Troitiño, Alfonso Sastre, José María de Quinto, Marta Grau and Arturo Carbonell, to mention only a few. These groups introduced audiences to plays by North American realists and French existentialists, and revived classic works in open-air performances. They also put on works by dissident writers like

Joan **Brossa**, Buero and Sastre, and promoted techniques derived from Craig, Reinhardt and the epic theatre of Brecht: for instance, the use of a narrator's voice, the fragmentation of time, mixing past and present, cinematic methods and the introduction of the author as a character.

The Franco regime could not remain immune to the gradual opening-up of Spain to cultural influences from abroad during the 1950s. In 1954 the Government created the Teatro Nacional de Cámara y Ensayo (National Studio Theatre), sponsored with public donations and directed by Modesto Higueras (who had collaborated with Federico García Lorca in the travelling theatre company La Barraca in the 1930s). José **Tamayo** headed the Teatro Español from 1955 to 1962, while over the same period Claudio de la Torre was in charge at the María Guerrero Theatre (1954–60). These theatres played host to a number of leading Spanish directors, notably Adolfo **Marsillach** and Ricard Salvat, amongst others. Experienced in working with independent studio theatre groups, and familiar with many languages and cultures, they enabled Spanish audiences to see the most important works of European and American drama within a short time of their first performance abroad. The repertoire of the National Studio Theatre included North American naturalist drama, epic theatre, theatre of cruelty, existentialist drama, German expressionism, theatre of the absurd and Living Theatre. At the Español in 1961, Tamayo produced the first performance since the Civil War of the controversial *Divinas palabras* (Divine Words) by Ramón María del Valle-Inclán, and in the following year Lorca's *Bodas de sangre* (*Blood Wedding*). José Luis Alonso's first production on taking over the management of the María Guerrero in 1961 was Ionesco's *Rhinoceros*. Marsillach mounted the first performance in Spain of *Marat Sade* by Peter Weiss (1968). In Catalonia, Ricard Salvat, one of the main promoters of the Catalan National Theatre, together with Maria Aurèlia **Capmany**, founded the Escola d'Art Dramàtic Adrià Gual (Adrià Gual School of Drama), one of the most important Spanish Theatres of the 1960s.

The 1960s also saw the rise of many university and independent groups seeking to bring the theatre within reach of a wider public, but in an idiom different from that of the commercial stage. Many of these groups performed in the National Studio Theatre, and cultivated the alienation and distancing effects practised by Reinhardt, Piscator and Brecht. They also used elements of Artaud's theatre of cruelty, and drew on the improvisational approach advocated by Grotowsky's Laboratory Theatre. They favoured the anti-realistic style of Beck, in which emotional impact is achieved through a blend of political and aesthetic radicalism. The unifying characteristic of these groups is their rejection of the notion that the dramatic text is something fixed and unchangeable. They advocated the reconfiguration of non-dramatic texts for the stage, especially narrative and cinematography, and drew on the resources of parody and farce. They also devised documentary drama based on newspaper texts, and defended the value of an actor's improvisation on a concrete situation. They exploited the expressive capacity of gesture, mimic, music and tonal variations. In common with Living Theatre, they used techniques derived from vaudeville, cabaret and carnival, as well as parody, to transform themes, myths, genres and styles, which they channelled into 'happenings' and street shows.

After Franco's death (1975) the theatre, like the other arts, benefited from the repeal of the **censorship** laws. In 1985, the Instituto Nacional de las Artes Escénicas y de la Música (National Institute for Performing Arts and Music – INAEM) was created, with four theatrical divisions: the Centro Dramático Nacional (The National Drama Centre); the Centro Nacional de Nuevas Tendencias Escénicas (The National Centre for Experimental Theatre); the Compañía Nacional de Teatro Clásico (The Classic Theatre Company); and the Teatro Nacional Lírico de la Zarzuela (The National **Zarzuela** Lyric Theatre). The INAEM's main functions were to protect and promote theatrical activities in Spain and to open up possibilities for co-operation between theatre professionals and public institutions. In 1993, the INAEM created the Red Nacional de Teatros y Auditorios (National Network of Theatres and Auditoria), which represented an important effort to make public theatres available to companies. The reorganization of Spain into **autonomous communities** facilitated the setting up of new regional centres for drama production and study, as well as regional theatre companies and festivals. In 1995 the The National Drama Centre merged with the National Centre for Experimental Theatre.

After the accession to power by the socialist **PSOE** in 1982, producers and playwrights trained in the studio companies and independent groups became managers of the expanding public theatres, among them Hermann Bonninn, Mario Gas, Guillermo Heras, Juan Margallo, Josep Montanyès, Miguel Narros, Lluís Pasqual, José Luis Gómez and José Carlos Plaza, amongst others. Their experience in the independent groups had an important influence on the dramatic idiom of the public theatre, with increasing emphasis on visual elements rather than text. In the 1990s, even the most conservative audiences came to accept some of the complex semiotic codes used by this theatrical approach. Notable examples are *Calderón* by Pier Paolo Pasolini (1986), directed by Guillermo Heras (a complex interpretation of the historical character of the seventeenth-century playwright expressed almost entirely through visual image) and *Azaña, una pasión española* (Azaña, a Spanish Passion) (1988), based on the life and writings of Manuel Azaña, President of the Spanish Republic, which was directed by José Luis Gómez on an empty stage with an effective use of lighting.

The large public theatres gave official support to productions of works by the historic figures of the Spanish avant-garde of the 1920s and 1930s: Valle-Inclán, **Alberti**, José Bergamín, Ramón Gómez de la Serna, Azorín, and especially García Lorca, whose *El público* (The Audience) (1986), directed by Pasqual and designed by Fabià Puigserver, was one of the most memorable performances of the 1980s. A number of important Catalan writers also saw revivals, such as Angel Guimerà, Joan Oliver, Josep **Pla**, Santiago Rusiñol and Josep Maria de Sagarra. In addition, the public theatres staged some of the most significant contemporary Spanish playwrights, such as Fernando **Arrabal**, Josep Maria **Benet i Jornet**, Ángel García Pintado, Agustín Gómez Arcos, Francisco Nieva, Rudolf **Sirera**, Alfonso Sastre, Jordi Teixidor, and Alfonso Vallejo, as well as younger figures such as Sergi **Belbel**, Ernesto Caballero, Rodrigo García, Sara Molina, Ignacio del Moral, Helena Pimienta, Paloma Pedrero and Etelvino Vázquez. Other contemporary playwrights, however, were neglected: Jerónimo López Mozo, José Martín Elizondo, José Martín Recuerda, Domingo Miras, Lauro **Olmo**, José María Rodríguez Méndez, Miguel Romero Esteo and José Ruibal.

At this same time, plays by Buero Vallejo, including *Diálogo secreto* (Secret Dialogue) (1984), *Lázaro en el laberinto* (Lazarus in the Labyrinth) (1986) and *Música cercana* (Familiar Music) (1989), and by Antonio Gala, including *Samarkanda* (1985), *Séneca o elk beneficio de la duda* (Séneca or The Benefit of the Doubt) (1987) and *Los bellos durientes* (1994), were also staged to great acclaim. Many of the playwrights who had worked exclusively for independent groups in the 1960s and 1970s had their works produced regularly by the large companies in the succeeding decades, e.g. José Luis Alonso de Santos, Ignacio Amestoy, Fermín Cabal, Alberto Miralles and José Sanchis Sinisterra, whose *¡Ay, Carmela!* (1988) was turned into a major film by Carlos **Saura**.

The extension of visual culture since the 1960s has led to a growing interest in theatrical design. Projections, and the imaginative use of lighting are now employed regularly in both large and small theatres, because of their ability to suggest space, time and experience. Two examples are *Comedias Bárbaras* (Barbaric Plays) (1992) by Valle-Inclán, where director José Carlos Plaza used lighting very imaginatively, and *Ara que els ametllers ya estan batuts* (Now that the Almond Trees Have Been Picked) (1990), based on texts by Josep Pla, directed and performed by Josep Maria Flotats, using cinematic projection by Alain Poisson. Some groups have a definite predilection for non-traditional stagings, such as old factories, funeral homes, markets, subway platforms, garages, train stations and warehouses. The group Els **Comediants** had great success with *Dimonis* (Devils) (1983), performed outdoors in the Retiro park in Madrid, as did the group La **Fura dels Baus**, which performed *Accions* (1983) in the old Galileo Funeral Home in Madrid.

The increased emphasis on stage-movement has also led many designers to opt for bare spaces in both large and small-scale productions, one prominent example being Andrea d'Odorico, an architect who has a classical and often monumental sense of space. He is fascinated by the relationship between mass and emptiness, and he often utilizes chiaroscuro. His work was shown to good advantage in his very successful design for the revival of Benavente's *La Malquerida* (The Unloved) (1987), directed by Miguel Narros. Designers of the 1980s and 1990s have also been paying more attention to colour, notable examples being Francisco Nieva, Pedro Moreno, Gerardo Vera and Carlos Cytrynovski, especially in productions of the Compañía Nacional de Teatro Clásico. Nieva in particular has used fabrics for special visual and acoustic effects. Moreno played with colour spectra in costume and set designs both for classics such as Calderón's *The Mayor of Zalamea* (1988) and modern plays such as José Bergamín's *La risa en los huesos* (Laughter in the Bones) (1989). The production, a remarkable example of postmodern theatre, was framed by sound and colour, as well as accomplished choreography. Under the influence of eastern aesthetics, some designers have played with the expressive possibilities of the human body, as did Cytrynovski in his designs for Tirso de Molina's *El vergonzoso en palacio* (The Shy Man at Court) (1989), where human actors were used as rugs, trees and tables. Gerardo Vera transformed bodies into a fence in García Lorca's *Don Perlimplín* (1990) directed by José Luis Gómez.

See also: performing arts

Further reading

Fernández Torres, A. (1987) *Documentos sobre el teatro independiente español*, Madrid: CNNTE (an important primary source).

Gallèn, E. (1985) *El teatre a la ciutat de Barcelona durant el règim franquista (1939–1954)*, Barcelona: Diputació de Barcelona (a significant local study).

Oliva, Cèsar (1989) *Teatro desde 1936*, Madrid: Alhambra (a useful analysis of post-war Spanish theatre).

Peláez, A. (ed.) (1993) *Historia de los teatros nacionales*, vol. 1 (1939–62), vol. 2 (1960–75) Madrid: Centro de Documentación Teatral (a very informative source-book).

Ruiz Ramón, F. (1989) *Historia del teatro español. Siglo XX*, Madrid: Cátedra (the contemporary section of a large-scale study by a leading critic).

Vilches de Frutos, M.F. (1994) 'Spain: Artistic Profile; Theatre for Young Audiences; Puppet Theatre; Design; Theatre Space and Architecture; Criticism, Scholarship and Publishing', in D. Rubin (ed.) *The World Encyclopedia of Contemporary Theatre: Europe*, London and New York: Routledge: pp. 790–804 (a comprehensive survey, one of the few in English).

MARÍA FRANCISCA VILCHES DE FRUTOS

theology

Since the Second Vatican Council (1962–5), theology in Spain has evolved from the highly traditional and conservative to the pluralistic. The majority of interventions by the Spanish bishops in the Council debates showed up the poverty of mainstream Spanish theology, which was due largely to the obscurantism and self-induced isolation of Spanish **Roman Catholicism**, which pre-dated even Francoism.

The situation soon changed in the post-conciliar period: theological research and teaching began to reflect the more open attitudes brought by the Council and by the impact of changes in Spanish society. The present spectrum of theological teaching and publications is as broad as anywhere else in the western Catholic world, though the emphasis in seminaries is now on a spirituality in tune with movements such as **Opus Dei**, which tends to lack the kind of social projection which had characterized the earlier post-conciliar period. By contrast, a more radical approach to socio-political issues is taken by other bodies, including the John XXIII Association of Theologians, founded in 1982.

Theology is taught in nine Church University faculties and forty-six other centres affiliated to them. One in five theology students is a woman. Outstanding are biblical studies at the Institución San Jerónimo (St Jerome Institute), work on dialogue with secular culture at the Instituto Fe y Secularidad (Faith and World Institute), social justice issues at the Cristianisme i Justícia (Christianity and Justice) centre and pastoral theology at the Instituto de Pastoral. Pastoral theology also finds expression in such journals as *Sal Terrae* (Salt of the Earth), *Iglesia Viva* (Living Church) and *Frontera* (Frontier), formerly *Pastoral Misionera* (Pastoral Mission Review). As in the rest of the Catholic world there is a plurality of theological voices regarding political, social and economic issues. Conflict sometimes arises between, on the one hand, certain theologians at the leading edge of research and interpretation, and, on the other, the Spanish hierarchy, who are closer to the safe certainties emanating from Rome. This was so even in the time of Paul VI (1963–78) and increasingly during the long pontificate of John Paul II. Symptomatic of the conflict was the dismissal in 1988 of the editor of the pastorally progressive journal *Misión Abierta* (Open Mission), the suspension about the same time of two theologians of Granada University and, later, disagreement following publication of the new international catechism (1992). Conservative theologians favour the traditional kind of church, with strong emphasis on the *magisterium*, the teaching authority of the bishops, and on the parish organization, rather than on small grass-roots communities (*comunidades de base*), often inspired by Latin American liberation theology.

See also: church and state

Further reading

Castillo, J.M. (1985) 'La teología después del Vaticano II', in C. Floristán and J.J. Tamayo (eds) *El Vaticano II, veinte años después*, Madrid: Ediciones Cristiandad (shows the influence of the Second Vatican Council on Spanish theology).

González de Cardedal, O. (1988) 'Teología en España (1965–1987)', in J.M. Laboa (ed.) *El Postconcilio en España*, Madrid: Ediciones Encuentro (gives an overview of different strands of postconciliar theology in Spain).

AUDREY BRASSLOFF

Thyssen-Bornemisza Museum

The museum houses the most important of the works of art collected by Baron Hans Heinrich Thyssen-Bornemisza and his father Heinrich Thyssen. The first works bought by Heinrich Thyssen, son of a German industrialist who was one of the richest men of his time, were from the German renaissance, including Holbein's *Portrait of Henry VIII of England* and Dürer's *Christ among the Doctors*, and it is for works of this period that the museum is particularly distinguished. Further acquisitions before WWII were from the Dutch school, including van Eyck's *Annunciation* and Memling's *Portrait of a Young Man*, and from the Italian renaissance, including Ghirlandaio's *Portrait of Giovanna Tornabouni*, among the most admired works of the collection, and Carpaccio's *Portrait of a Young Gentleman*.

In 1932, having lived for some years in Hungary, where he was created first Baron Thyssen-Bornemisza, and then in Holland, Heinrich moved to Switzerland, to the Villa Favorita on the shores of Lake Lugano, where he built an art gallery to display his collection. After his death in 1947, his son Hans Heinrich bought out his elder brother's and his sisters' shares in the inheritance, and became one of a very small number of major purchasers of art in the 1940s and 1950s. It has been his policy to acquire representative works of modern art, and the collection includes paintings by Corot, Rothko, Picasso, Van Gogh, Gris, Derain, Bacon and Dalí.

In 1988, as the result of an initiative by the former Minister of Culture, Javier **Solana**, 775 works from the collection were entrusted by the official owners, Favorita Trustees Ltd, to Spain for exhibition in the Villahermosa Palace in Madrid and in the Pedralbes Monastery in Barcelona for nine and half years. In 1993, as a result of the generosity of the second Baron and his Spanish wife, that collection was bought by Spain for $350m, a small proportion of its market value and a fraction of the offer made by the Getty Museum. It is officially owned by the Thyssen-Bornemisza Collection Foundation, but cannot be alienated and reverts to the Spanish state should the foundation be wound up. The complete remodelling of the Villahermosa Palace except for its façade was directed by Rafael **Moneo**.

See also: art collections; museums

EAMONN RODGERS

Tierno Galván, Enrique

b. 1918, Madrid; d. 1986, Madrid

Academic and politician

Tierno Galván fought on the Republican side during the Civil War, and was interned in a concentration camp. Between 1948 and 1953, he was professor of Public Law in the University of Murcia, and from 1953 to 1965 occupied a chair in the University of Salamanca, where he helped to found a newsletter, the *Boletín Informativo*, which became the vehicle for popularizing British neo-positivist philosophy. The Salamanca group, as they came to be known, was pro-European in its outlook, and in 1955 launched a Sociedad por la Unidad Funcional de Europa (Society for the Functional Unity of Europe).

In the mid-1950s, Tierno's political stance was close to that of the liberal monarchists of Unión Española, but in the 1960s he moved closer to socialism. Already, in 1957, he had been imprisoned for his opposition to the Franco regime. His support for student demands led in 1965 to his dismissal from his chair, together with José Luis **Aranguren** and Agustín García Calvo. The following two years were spent at Princeton University. In 1967 he return to Spain and joined the still-illegal **PSOE**, but left in the following year to found his own Partido Socialista en el Interior (Spanish-based Socialist Party: the leadership of the PSOE was still located abroad), which in 1974 became the Partido Socialista Popular (Popular Socialist Party). In the first democratic elections (1977) he won a seat in the Cortes, and shortly after, his party merged with PSOE, of which he became for a brief period Honorary President. In 1979 he was elected Mayor of Madrid, with the combined votes of socialists and communists, a post which he occupied until his death. As mayor, 'the old professor', as he was known from his Salamanca days, enjoyed enormous popularity, and gave a considerable boost to cultural life.

Tierno's numerous publications include: *Costa y el regeneracionismo* (Joaquín Costa and the Regenerationist Movement) (1961), *Acotaciones a la historia de la cultura occidental en la Edad Moderna* (Observations on the History of Western Culture in the Modern Period) (1964), *Leyes políticas españolas fundamentales* (Fundamental Public Law in Spain) (1966), and *Democracia, Socialismo y Libertad* (Democracy, Socialism and Freedom) (1977).

Further reading

de los Ríos, C.A. (1997) *La verdad sobre Tierno Galván*, Madrid: Anaya (a critical biography).

ALICIA ALTED

Tomás y Valiente, Francisco

b. 1932, Valencia; d. 1996, Madrid

Judge

Tomás y Valiente held a chair in the history of law at the University of Salamanca from 1964 to 1979. Such a background proved eminently suitable for a post on the **Constitutional Tribunal**. He joined the Tribunal in 1980, proposed by the socialist **PSOE**, which was then in opposition, but also supported by the ruling centre-right **UCD**, and became its President in 1986. His time as President of the Constitutional Tribunal ended in 1992. From a Republican background, he described his ideological position as being close to socialism and was, on occasion, accused of bias by the right. Shortly after being nominated to serve on the Council of State, he was assassinated in his office at the Autonomous University in Madrid on 14 February 1996. The Basque terrorist organization, **ETA**, claimed responsibilty for the atrocity.

See also: terrorism

PAUL HEYWOOD

torero

In **bullfighting** parlance *torero* refers strictly to any performer in a ***corrida*** – e.g. a **matador**, ***novillero***, *banderillero* or *picador* – though it is frequently used as a synonym for matador.

IAN CAMPBELL ROSS

Torrente Ballester, Gonzalo

b. 1910, El Ferrol

Writer

Teacher, newspaper columnist, critic and novelist, Torrente came to maturity under the influence of **Ortega y Gasset**, Unamuno, R. Gómez de la Serna and **Picasso** at the height of literary and artistic experimentation in pre-Civil War Spain. Politically, he was a member of the regional party in Galicia in northwestern Spain, which favoured autonomy for his native region. In order to be able to return to Galicia – from a research fellowship in Paris in 1936 – and to live safely with his wife and young children in this Franco-controlled region during and after the war, Torrente became a member of the **Falange**, though he left the organization in the early 1940s.

Torrente's greatest conflict as a man and an artist has arguably been to form his own individual project of life and creation, when during so many of his best years ideological conformity in art and politics was the key to survival and success. The nature of humanity, the conflict between reason and emotion, role-playing and demythification, and self-reflective creation are the major concerns of his work. In his 1957–62 trilogy *Los gozos y las sombras* (Joys and Sorrows; made into a thirteen-hour Spanish-French television production) it is significant that the main character and his girlfriend leave Spain for Portugal on the eve of the Civil War because they have neither the energy nor the conviction to take sides in the issues over which the war would be fought. In the subsequent 1963 novel *Don Juan*, the protagonist is characterized in general terms by his extreme human perfection and his refusal to be subordinate even to God, the only being whose supremacy to himself he recognizes. This Don Juan's eternal punishment is never to die, to be himself through eternity, and to have to convince succeeding generations that he is the true sixteenth-century figure. In these two novels Torrente, while expressing his own vital concerns, also shares with Ortega y Gasset a preoccupation with the twentieth-century tendency to make the individual subordinate to supposedly great causes and figures, and with the cost borne by the individual who refuses to be absorbed into the mass.

Following the poor reception of those two novels, and the loss of a teaching and newspaper position for having signed a petition protesting against the **censorship** of news coverage in Spain, Torrente accepted in 1966 a distinguished professorship of Spanish at SUNY at Albany in the United States. The climate of intellectual sympathy towards structuralism he experienced there helped him to write *La saga/fuga de J.B.* (The Saga/Flight of J.B.), a humorous vision of the history of Galicia and, symbolically, its resistance to the centralizing forces of Franco's government. This novel made him a public figure in Spain, and won him the 1972 City of Barcelona and Critics Prizes. In conjunction with the two subsequent volumes of the fantastic trilogy, *La saga/fuga* gained him weekly columns in such newspapers as ***ABC***, and paved the way for his election in 1977 to the Royal Academy of Language and the 1985 **Cervantes Prize** (see also **Royal Academies**).

Among his novels of the 1980s and 1990s which deserve notice are *Quizá nos lleve el viento al infinito* (Perhaps the Wind Will Take Us to Infinity) and the winner of the 1988 **Planeta Prize**, *Filomeno a mi pesar* (Filomeno, Despite Myself). In the former novel Torrente carries out a postmodern experiment, using the conventions of both **science fiction** and **detective fiction**, against the backdrop of the Cold War, to explore what makes a human being human. With the 1989 novel *Crónica del rey pasmado* (Chronicle of the Astonished King), Torrente, aware of advancing age and not wishing to leave work unfinished, began to write short, rather schematic novels in which plot, bared almost completely of description and analysis, dominates.

While Torrente has always maintained that his critical and creative activities were two sides of one literary coin, general recognition of his status as a critic only came after the fame of *La saga/fuga* and his first book-length publication following that novel, the critical study *El 'Quijote' como juego* (*Don Quixote* as a Game).

Major works

Torrente Ballester, G. (1943) *Javier Mariño*, Madrid:

Editora Nacional (first novel; best Spanish novel of the 1940s, according to some critics).
—— (1957, 1960, 1962) *Los gozos y las sombras*, Madrid: Arión (this trilogy may be the author's most poetic rendering of the people, places and climate of Galicia).
—— (1963) *Don Juan*, Barcelona: Destino; trans. B. Molloy, *Don Juan*, Madrid: Iberia, 1986 (novel).
—— (1972) *La saga/fuga de J.B.*, Barcelona: Destino (the author's most famous novel).
—— (1977) *Fragmentos de apocalipsis*, Barcelona: Destino (a tour de force in metaliterary creation).
—— (1979) *Las sombras recobradas*, Barcelona: Planeta (best collection of the author's short fiction).
—— (1982) *Teatro*, 2 vols Barcelona: Destino (contains nearly all Torrente's dramatic works).
—— (1982) *Ensayos críticos*, Barcelona: Destino (collection of theatrical and literary criticism).

Further reading

Becerra, C. (1990) *Guardo la voz, cedo la palabra: conversaciones con Gonzalo Torrente Ballester* (I Yield the Floor: Conversations with Gonzalo Torrente Ballester), Barcelona: Anthropos (primary source for Torrente's views on the content, techniques and meanings of his creations).
Blackwell, F.H. (1985) *The Game of Literature: Demythification and Parody in the Novels of Gonzalo Torrente Ballester*, Valencia: Albatrós Ediciones (stresses the ludic element in the author's novels).
Miller, S. (1982, 1983) 'Don Juan's New Trick: Plot, Verisimilitude, Epistemology and Role-Playing in Torrente's *Don Juan*', *Revista de Estudios Hispánicos*, 16: 163–80 (this study was translated and placed as an appendix to the Círculo de Lectores edition of the author's choice as his best novel).
Pérez, J. (1984) *Gonzalo Torrente Ballester*, Boston, MA: Twayne (best introduction to the author and his work to date).
Pérez, J. and Miller, S. (eds) (1989) *Critical Studies on Gonzalo Torrente Ballester*, Boulder, CO: Society of Spanish and Spanish-American Studies (solid collection of essays by diverse hands on Torrente's work; includes an interview on Torrente's politico-literary dimension).

STEPHEN MILLER

tourism

The tourist sector has great importance for the Spanish **economy**, contributing between 8 and 10 percent of GDP and, as an invisible export, making up for the deficit in visible trade. Income from tourism was about $3m^2$ pesetas per annum in 1995, whereas expenditure (by Spanish tourists abroad) was just a fifth of this sum. Approximately 11 percent of the employed population works in the tourist sector, and there are some 10,000 hotels and campsites, 1,100,000 hotel beds, and 5,000 restaurants. Total registered guest capacity is in excess of 2 million beds. In international tourism Spain is the third country in the world by number of visitors, with well over 60 million arrivals a year. Most of them originate from EU countries, about half of all tourists coming from just three countries, France, Germany and the UK in that order; the Portuguese, however, are the most frequent day visitors. Almost 60 percent of all visitors arrive by road, and something over a third arrive by air; comparatively few do so by ship or train.

Despite the large number of visitors who arrive in their own cars, the package holiday remains an important part of the tourist economy in Spain and contributes to a high occupancy rate, of between 80 and 90 percent, of hotels on the coast, as compared to about 60 percent for hotels in inland locations. Nevertheless, there has been a noticeable trend in recent years towards cultural tourism, especially in Madrid and Barcelona. Although there is tourist activity all the year round, one-third of all visitors come to Spain in July and August; September is the next most popular month with about one-tenth of the yearly arrivals. Seasonal fluctuations create employment problems in the sector, while the heavy concentration of visitors from a mere handful of countries makes the Spanish tourist industry highly sensitive to economic conditions in these countries.

The tourist sector is especially important to the economies of certain regions. The Balearics and the Canaries are very heavily dependent on tourism, while Andalusia, one of the poorest of Spain's regions with the worst **unemployment**, receives the third-highest number of foreign tourists after Mallorca and Catalonia, as well as the highest number of visitors from other regions of

Spain. Despite the seasonality of the industry, without the jobs and income that tourism generates, a mass exodus from these regions would be inevitable.

Spanish domestic tourism has experienced an increase in recent times but cannot replace foreign tourism in economic importance: first because it is not a foreign currency earner; second because the numbers of Spanish tourists are so much smaller; and third because Spaniards make rather less use of hotel accommodation, preferring to stay in holiday apartments, with relatives, or in campsites. There has also been an increasing tendency among Spaniards to take **holidays** abroad (mainly in Europe but also in the Spanish-speaking countries of the Caribbean). Nevertheless, the balance of international payments in the sector remains overwhelmingly in Spain's favour. Increasingly, the thrust of government policy has been to increase the quality of inbound tourism rather than the quantity, in other words to generate more income from the same number of visitors. Worries about whether Spain can maintain its share of the tourist market, as well as a wish to exploit the Spaniards' increasing desire for holidays abroad, have prompted major hotel chains such as Sol-Meliá, Occidental Hoteles and Hoteles Barceló (each respectively with 59, 32 and 15 hotels abroad) to invest heavily outside Spain, either by takeovers of existing foreign hotels or even more through opening new establishments. This investment abroad has taken up 40 percent of all direct investment of the major Spanish chains and evinces a determination to maintain Spain as a leading player in the tourist sector. Spanish hotel chains have over 130 hotels abroad, whereas foreign chains have just 34 hotels in Spain.

Further reading

Salmon, K. (1995) *The Modern Spanish Economy. Transformation and Integration into Europe*, London: Pinter (chapter 8 gives a good overall account of the tourist sector).

C.A. LONGHURST

trade unions

Independent unions emerged as part of the transition to democracy. Under Franco there was an official union structure, the **vertical syndicates**, although there did emerge an increasingly significant independent workers' movement, the largest element of which was the Workers' Committees, or **CC OO**.

The **constitution of 1978** established the right to form independent unions and the freedom to join them. The Workers' Statute of 1980 established the framework for post-Franco employer-union relations. Section 2 provided for the election within companies of works committees with the right to negotiate with employers. Resulting agreements are made binding on employers by Section 3 of the Statute. The major unions successfully put forward 'slates' of candidates for these elections and have increasingly dominated the works committees and thus collective bargaining. Success in these elections also determines negotiating rights for the unions at provincial, sectoral or national level and the pattern of distribution of governmental subsidies to the unions.

Not surprisingly, winning elections has become a major objective for each union. The unions are representative rather than membership based (in the UK, for example, the unions depend on their membership for finance and negotiating power rather than on any electoral system). This has contributed to the relatively low union density in Spain (10–20 percent). A Spanish worker can vote for and be represented by a union delegate without joining the union, with the consequence that the mobilizing ability of the unions is greater than their membership would suggest. Other factors contributing to low membership are the high proportion of small firms, which are difficult to organize, the political and manual-worker image of the unions, which has discouraged non-manual workers, and the relative youth of the independent union movement. At national level the two dominant unions are the General Workers Union (**UGT**) and CC OO. However, regional unions are important in Galicia and the Basque country, as are occupationally based unions in certain sectors, such as doctors and pilots. The two major unions are confederations which, through their sectorally based federations, seek to organize all employees in each industrial sector.

Until 1986 the unions participated in social pacts with the government and employers to deliver political stability and salary moderation. From 1986, the unions have sought to strengthen sectoral level bargaining. The disengagement from social pacts (no longer favoured by political and economic circumstances) has been accompanied by more distant relations between the unions and the political parties with which they had been traditionally linked (particularly evident in respect of the UGT and the **PSOE**). This has fostered greater unity between the two major confederations (made more necessary by the difficult economic environment faced by the unions). Despite greater unity, the organizational weakness of the unions at company level prevents them from turning away completely from the political arena. They still seek advances via legislation and involve themselves in sociopolitical campaigns (e.g. on **unemployment**), more than would be typical of union movements in northern Europe.

See also: collective agreements; industrial relations; labour law

Further reading

Lawlor, T. and Rigby, M. (1994) 'Spanish Trade Unions 1986–1993', *Industrial Relations Journal*, 25, 4: 258–71.

Martinez Lucio, M. (1997) 'Spain: Regulating Employment on Social Fragmentation' in Ferner, A. and Hyman, R. *Changing Industrial Relations in Europe*, Oxford: Blackwell.

MICHAEL RIGBY

transport

To anyone accustomed to travelling in Spain in the past, the transformation of the country's transport system must seem almost miraculous. Massive government investment and EC aid have resulted in a vastly improved **roads** network and in significant improvements to the **railways**. The **AVE** high-speed train which cut journey time from Madrid to Seville from six to two-and-a-half hours has turned out to be a commercial success and not merely a prestige project undertaken for **Expo-92**. All major Spanish cities are connected by air, with a frequent shuttle between Madrid and Barcelona. Coach services between Madrid and most provincial capitals are excellent, with modern, fast, air-conditioned coaches.

The greatest improvement has undoubtedly been to the road network. A figure of 160,000 km of main roads appears modest in terms of Spain's area, but is closer to the European average in terms of the country's population. Most motorways have been privately built and are therefore toll roads (except near large cities where they act as ring roads). But the state and the governments of the **autonomous communities** have developed a network of fast dual carriageways (*autovías*) which have cut driving times between major cities virtually by half. It is now possible to drive the length of Spain, from the Franco-Spanish frontier to Gibraltar (1,250 km) in a day, with only the last half-dozen kilometres on a single carriageway road. Alongside these new dual carriageways, numerous ring roads and by-passes have been built, such as the M-40 or Madrid orbital, the SE-30 or Seville by-pass, and the various urban belts (*cinturones*) in Barcelona. Motorways and dual carriageways total about 8,000 km; a further 2,000 are under construction or projected. The radial nature of the fast-track network, with six major routes from Madrid to the periphery, has been complemented by other fast routes: from east to west in Andalusia, and from Santander to Barcelona; from north to south along the Mediterranean coast and in Galicia. Responsibility for much of the non-radial network is now in the hands of the regional governments.

Although investment in the railways has on the whole not been so impressive, timekeeping and journey times have improved immeasurably, and a new high-speed train is planned, linking Madrid to Barcelona, and thence to Paris and the European network. Much of the rail network, however, remains single-track, limiting the possibilities of expansion. Its current limitations are shown by the fact that the railways carry just 4 percent of inland freight and 6 percent of passengers. By contrast, the Madrid underground makes a much more effective contribution to urban transport; without it the streets of the capital would be immobilized by commuter traffic.

Considering its long coastline, Spain has relatively few major ports. The four largest by movement of merchandise are Algeciras (12m tons per annum), Barcelona (8.5m), Valencia (8m) and Bilbao (6m). Algeciras is the biggest container port in the Mediterranean and the second largest in Europe. In terms of passenger traffic, Algeciras again leads with close on four million passengers a year, because of the intense traffic between Spain and Morocco. The other major passenger ports are Ceuta, Santa Cruz de Tenerife and Palma de Mallorca.

In air transport there has been very considerable growth of the domestic market since 1980. Nearly 100 million passengers pass through Spanish airports every year, over 40 percent of whom are on domestic flights. Traffic is particularly intense between Madrid and Barcelona and also between these two cities and the Balearics and Canaries. In international flights about two-thirds of passengers are on charter flights, reflecting the fact that Spain is a major destination for the package holiday industry (see also **tourism**). Some 75 percent of all international flights are to or from other European airports, although Spain is also Europe's principal air link with Latin America.

Further reading

Chislett, W. (1998) *Spain 1998. The Central Hispano Handbook*, Madrid (see p. 32 for a brief section on infrastructure).

Ministerio de la Presidencia (1995) *España 1995* (see the chapter on 'Infraestructuras y Medio Ambiente' (Infrastructure and Environment)).

C.A. LONGHURST

Trueba, Fernando

b. 1955, Madrid

Filmmaker

Winner of an Oscar in 1994 for his film *Belle Epoque* (1993), Trueba had his first success in 1980 with one of the earliest in the genre of 'Madrid comedies', *Opera prima*, whose title means both 'First Effort' and 'Cousin at the (Madrid subway station) Opera'. The lead role was played by a new discovery, Oscar Ladoire, who won the Best Actor award at Venice. Other comedies followed including the box office success *Sé infiel y no mires con quién* (Be Unfaithful and Don't Care With Whom) (1985) and *El año de las luces* (The Year of Enlightenment) (1986) which won the Silver Bear at Berlin. In 1989 he entered the international market with a Spanish-French co-production *Twisted Obsession* (*El sueño del mono loco*), an English language psychological thriller, which won several Goya awards in Spain, but was less successful elsewhere. *Belle Epoque*, on the other hand, a comedy set in the early days of the Republic, brilliantly co-scripted with Rafael Azcona and **García Sánchez**, and starring, among other well-known actors, the veteran **Fernán Gómez**, won both national and international acclaim. His first American film *Two Much* (1995), a romantic comedy based on Westlake's novel and starring Antonio **Banderas** broke box office records in Spain as well as selling well at the international American Film Market in 1996.

See also: film and cinema

EAMONN RODGERS

Tuñón de Lara, Manuel

b. 1915, Madrid; d. 1997, Leoia (Vizcaya)

Historian

One of the most distinguished historians of modern Spain, Tuñón de Lara's professional career was mostly spent outside the country, because of his opposition to the Franco regime. Having fought on the Republican side in the Civil War, and continued his clandestine political activity by reorganizing the Union of Free Intellectuals, he came under constant police surveillance, and was forced to leave for France in 1946. After further studies in the Sorbonne, he taught in Paris until 1970, when he moved to the University of Pau, where he inaugurated courses in Spanish history specifically for students resident in Spain, offering an alternative to the Nationalist **historiography** which still dominated the major Spanish universities.

See also: exile; history; intellectual life; politics

EAMONN RODGERS

Tusquets, Esther

b. 1936, Barcelona

Writer

Tusquets' reputation as one of contemporary Spain's most powerful and original women writers rests largely on four novels and a collection of short stories, each characterized by a search for existential authenticity through heterosexual and lesbian love, and by often biting social satire.

Her highly acclaimed début came in 1978 with *The Same Sea as Every Summer* (*El mismo mar de todos los veranos*). Written (like all Tusquets' creative work) in Spanish rather than Catalan, this linguistically rich and complex novel is the first of three studies of middle-aged women from Barcelona's leisured bourgeoisie, each lonely, dissatisfied with her personal relationships and alienated from the myths and rituals of her social group. The slow, sensual prose evokes a university teacher's attempts to reconstruct her past and substantiate her present through a brief affair with a young woman student. In the 1979 novel *Love is a Solitary Game* (*El amor es un juego solitario*) the relation between love and sex becomes more bitter and ritualized. The self-absorption of the manipulative central character ensures that her affairs with a vulnerable young woman and a young, sexually inexperienced man cannot provide the existential relief she desires. The role-playing dimension is heightened in the 1980 novel *Varada tras el último naufragio* (Beached after the Last Shipwreck) and the focus is fragmented among four characters in crisis, as they reflect on their isolation and the impossibility of absolute intimacy. In the 1981 short-story collection *Siete miradas sobre un mismo paisaje* (Seven Glances at the Same Landscape) this fragmentation intensifies, as different narrators recount a young girl's rites of passage.

Tusquets' 1985 novel *Para no volver* (Never to Return) is a study of social hypocrisy, authority and the impossibility of genuine dialogue, set among the Barcelona bourgeoisie of the Franco years. More recently, her children's writing, occasional journalism and high-profile role as director of publishing-house Lumen have enabled Tusquets to retain a leading role in Catalan intellectual life.

See also: Catalan culture; gay writing; women's writing

Further reading

Molinaro, N.L. (1991) *Foucault, Feminism and Power: Reading Esther Tusquets*, Lewisburg: Buckness University Press (explores Tusquets' aesthetics of power and resistance).

Nichols, G.C. (1989) *Escribir, espacio propio: Laforet, Matute, Moix, Tusquets, Riera y Roig por sí mismas*, Minneapolis, MN: Institute for the Study of Ideologies and Literature, pp. 71–101 (includes a useful interview with Tusquets).

Servodidio, M. (1991) 'Esther Tusquets's Fiction: the Spinning of a Narrative Web' in J.L. Brown (ed.) *Women Writers of Contemporary Spain: Exiles in the Homeland*, London: Associated University Presses, pp. 159–78 (examines the complex interrelations between Tusquets' characters).

Smith, P.J. (1992) *Laws of Desire: Questions of Homosexuality in Spanish Writing and Film 1960–1990*, Oxford: Oxford University Press, chapter three (reads the first three novels as an attempt to represent lesbian desire).

Vásquez, M. (ed.) (1991) *The Sea of Becoming: Approaches to the Fiction of Esther Tusquets*, Westport, CT: Greenwood (excellent selection of essays, with annotated bibliography to 1989).

ANNY BROOKSBANK JONES

Tusquets, Oscar

b. 1941, Barcelona

Architect

Tusquets' background included a training in Arts and Crafts, which influenced his whole professional career. After qualifying at the School of Architecture in Barcelona in 1965 he worked under

Federico **Correa**, and was also the leading light in the *Studio Per*, founded in 1964 with Pep Bonet, Cristian Cirici and Lluis Clotet, which was to have a long-term impact on the Spanish architectural scene. The works of *Studio Per* were noted for their stylistic eclecticism, combining elements of the 'modern' international tradition with borrowings from the past, with contributions from the plastic arts, and with the renewed prominence given to craftwork. Tusquets embarked on a long academic career in 1975, and became the role-model of the architect-artist for some of his colleagues and pupils. His interest in **design** and his achievements in the area of **Interiorism** influenced the development of architecture in the 1970s and 1980s, especially in Catalonia. His contribution to the ***Palau de la Musica*** (1983–9), a prime example of **Modernism**, gave him the authority and prestige which enabled him to undertake a huge programme of activities in the spheres of town-planning, architecture, design and the plastic arts.

On the theoretical level, Tusquets was able to build on the concepts popularized by Robert Venturi and the 'post-modernists' to work out his own ideas on borrowings from the past, the use of traditional techniques and the realization in contemporary architecture of the decorative potential of materials such as glass, wood, stone and metals.

His work has gained him numerous distinctions, including several awards of the FAD Prize and the Delta de Oro (Golden Delta), and other prestigious prizes at both national and international level. The most notable of his achievements, most of them in association with Carlos Díaz since 1987, are the Chandon Complex in Sant Cugat (Barcelona, 1990), his buildings in the Olympic Village (Barcelona, 1991), the International Housing Exhibition (Kashii, Japan, 1987), the Pavillon du Parc de la Villette (Pavillon Tusquets, Paris, 1990) and the Maison Somasaguas (Madrid, 1989). His best known designs are the chairs in the series *Varius* (1984), Gaulino (1989), and *Lucas* (1989), and the *Astrolabio* (1988) and *Vórtice* (1989) tables.

See also: architects; architecture

MIHAIL MOLDOVEANU

U

UCD

The Union of the Democratic Centre (Unión de Centro Democrático) was a centre-right coalition formed under the leadership of Adolfo **Suárez** in 1977 to contest the general elections of June in that year, the first free elections held since 1936. It brought together Christian Democrats such as Alfonso Osorio, liberals like the **Garrigues Walker** brothers, and former officials of the **National Movement**, notably Rodolfo **Martín Villa**, Landelino **Lavilla**, Torcuato **Fernández-Miranda** and Suárez himself. Many of the latter group were simultaneously members of **Opus Dei**. There was also a small number of social democrats under the leadership of Francisco Fernández Ordóñez.

Such a cluster of disparate groups inevitably lacked a clear and coherent ideology, but UCD was nevertheless held together by the personal leadership qualities of Suárez, and, above all, by a common commitment to the gradual evolution of democratic political structures through piecemeal reform of the institutions of Francoism. This strategy was vindicated in the 1977 elections, when, in an exceptionally high turnout of around 80 percent, UCD gained 165 seats in the **parliament**, with 34.3 percent of the vote. This left it comfortably ahead of its nearest competitor, the socialist **PSOE**, which gained 118 seats, or 28.5 percent of the votes cast.

The achievements of UCD in government were considerable, and included the **Moncloa Pacts** with employers and trade unions, agreed in October 1977, and, most significantly, the **constitution of 1978**, which enshrined certain basic **civil rights**, and provided the legal framework for the **autonomous communities** which make up the quasi-federal Spanish state of today. These measures, however, owed more to pragmatism than to ideological conviction, and commitment to them, especially on the right wing of the coalition, was often half-hearted. The promise of economic restructuring contained in the Moncloa Pacts was not implemented, and this led to the resignation in February 1978 of the social democrat Vice-President for Economic Affairs, Enrique **Fuentes Quintana**. His departure, combined with the sacking in 1979 of Fernández Ordóñez, weaked the social democrat element in UCD and accentuated its right-wing complexion. In addition, the government's attempts to slow down the autonomy process, in response to opposition from the **armed forces**, lost it support in the regions, notably in Andalusia.

The results of the 1979 general election, however, suggested that UCD had maintained, or indeed slightly improved its share of the vote, receiving 35 percent, which gave it 168 seats. Nevertheless, its position relative to PSOE (which won 29 percent and 121 seats) remained the same. The results at national level, moreover, were affected by the perception among the electorate that PSOE was still wedded to Marxist–Leninist dogma, and concealed the fact that grassroots support for UCD was declining. The party suffered serious losses in municipal and regional elections over the next three years.

To add to UCD's difficulties, internal divisions among the various disparate elements were becoming more acute, not least because of the decision, in October 1978, to impose a single party organization, which threatened the identity of the separate groups. Suárez's attempt to placate the left wing by bringing Fernández Ordóñez back into the cabinet in 1980 as Minister for Justice proved futile. In addition, Suárez's style of leadership was increasingly resented by party colleagues, as he not only tended to favour the most conservative elements in UCD, but also surrounded himself with a clique of close personal associates from his *Movimiento* days. Eventually, even some of these, such as Lavilla and Martín Villa, turned against him because they considered that his policies were alienating electoral support, and Suárez resigned as head of government in January 1981.

Between then and the general election of October 1982, UCD began to break up. Fernández Ordóñez's group entered into an electoral pact with PSOE, and he eventually joined the socialists, becoming a successful Minister for Foreign Affairs in Felipe **González**'s government, and subsequently a highly regarded ***Defensor del Pueblo***. The conservative Christian Democrats under Oscar Alzaga joined the Alianza Popular and were later absorbed into the **PP** (see also **Popular Alliance**). Suárez himself, embittered by his treatment by the party he had founded, left UCD just prior to the elections and fought under the banner of a new grouping, Centro Democrático y Social (Social Democratic Centre), declaring that he would support PSOE in government. UCD's electoral performance in 1982 was dismal: it suffered the biggest reverse of any governing party in Europe since WWII, with 6 percent of the vote and eleven seats.

UCD was undoubtedly an artificial creation, resulting from the peculiar political circumstances which obtained in Spain after forty years of dictatorship. Its spectacular decline was perhaps inevitable once it had fulfilled its purpose of enabling the establishment of democratic structures, but there can be no doubt that its role in that process was crucial.

See also: history; political parties; politics

Further reading

Heywood, P. (1995) *The Government and Politics of Spain*, London: Macmillan

Preston, P. (1986) *The Triumph of Democracy in Spain*, London and New York: Methuen (the indices to both these volumes enable one to trace the history of UCD).

EAMONN RODGERS

UGT

The General Workers' Union (Unión General de Trabajadores) is one of the two main union confederations in contemporary Spain. It is the only major **trade union** which can trace its history back to pre-Civil War Spain when it had strong links with the socialist **PSOE**. Initially in the post-Franco period, the UGT was in a weaker position than its main rival, the communist-led **CC OO**. Many of its historic leaders had been in exile, whereas activists of CC OO had been the dominant group in the workers' opposition to Franco. Thus, at the time of its congress in 1976, the UGT membership only numbered 6,000.

The next ten years saw the transformation of the UGT into the most supported union in Spain. In the 1986 union elections the UGT had a six-point lead over CC OO. The UGT's growth in power was parallelled by and related to the upward trajectory of PSOE. Despite the dominance of CC OO within the labour movement opposition to Franco, the emergence of a strong socialist trade union during this period is not surprising. The increasing support for PSOE and its entry into government in 1982 also encouraged the filling of 'socialist space' in the union field. PSOE members were expected to join the UGT, and several UGT leaders occupied governmental roles. The UGT became identified as the union of PSOE and was a moderate alternative to many workers who rejected the more oppositional CC OO with its links to the communist **PCE**.

Although the UGT's identification with PSOE undoubtedly benefited the union during this early period, it also gave rise to increasing tension from the mid-1980s. The UGT was expected to co-operate with government policies (e.g. industrial restructuring and the negotiation of social pacts) to a degree which threatened the autonomy of the union. As the government's economic policy became more liberal and unemployment grew, the UGT found it more difficult to maintain the partnership with PSOE. It became sensitive to the negative impact such moderation was having on actual and potential supporters. Hence one of the significant developments in industrial relations during the 1990s has been the growing apart of union and political party, accentuated by interpersonal problems between the leaders of the two organizations.

The divorce of UGT from PSOE and its increasing hostility to government policies has facilitated closer relations with CC OO and the presentation of a more united front to employers and government, although there are still significant minority groups in both unions who want a closer relationship with the political parties. The UGT has found the journey to autonomy more difficult than CC OO. The nature of its growth meant its rank and file organization was weaker than that of CC OO. The retirement of its historic leader, Nicolás **Redondo**, came at a difficult time. Its attempts to modernize itself and offer a range of member services have been handicapped by failures such as the collapse of its housing co-operative PSV. It has currently lost the initiative to CC OO and its electoral performance has suffered.

See also: collective agreements; industrial relations; labour law; Moncloa Pacts; politics; unemployment

MICHAEL RIGBY

Umbral, Francisco

b. 1935, Madrid

Writer and journalist

Umbral is one of the most notable examples of how the profession of **journalism** has developed in contemporary Spain, and how frequently it is exercised by persons who also enjoy a solid reputation in other genres of writing, such as the novel and literary criticism. He began his career on the Valladolid newspaper *El Norte de Castilla*, moving to Madrid in the 1960s to work on the magazine *Vida Mundial*, as well as contributing to the monarchist newspaper ***ABC***, and the illustrated weeklies *Blanco y Negro* and *La Gaceta Ilustrada*. Since 1989 he has contributed a lively regular column to the controversial daily *El* ***Mundo***, which has further consolidated his reputation as one of the most original stylists writing in Spanish.

In parallel with his journalistic writing, Umbral has produced some 75 books, predominantly novels, but also poetry and political commentary, for instance *Guía irracional de España* (Irrational Guide to Spain) (1989) and *El socialfelipismo: la democracia detenida* (Felipe's Brand of Socialism: Democracy on Hold) (1991). Among his most notable publications in book form are *Balada de gamberros* (Ballad of Ruffians) (1965), *Travesía de Madrid* (Across Madrid) (1966), *A Mortal Spring* (*Mortal y rosa*) (1975), inspired by the death of his 5-year-old son, the volume of poems *Crímenes y baladas* (1981), *Leyenda del César visionario* (Legend of the Visionary Caesar) (1991) and *Las señoritas de Aviñón* (The Demoiselles of Avignon) (1994).

Umbral's contribution to Spanish letters has been recognized by the award of numerous **prizes**. In 1975, he was awarded the **Nadal Prize**, and in 1990 the Mariano de Cavía Prize for Journalism. The Critics' Prize for Narrative followed in 1992, and the Francisco Cerecedo Prize for Journalism in 1995. His most notable achievement was the award of the highly prestigious **Prince of Asturias Prize** for Literature in 1996.

See also: novel; press

EAMONN RODGERS

UNED

The National University for Distance Learning (Universidad Nacional de Educación a Distancia) was founded in 1972, at a time when similar institutions were being established in Europe and America. The UNED was set up specifically as a distance learning university on the model of the Open University established in Britain in 1965.

The statutes of the UNED prescribe that its main function is to provide access to university education for suitably qualified applicants who for reasons of work or geographical location cannot enter a conventional university. Applicants are interviewed by staff of the central office of the university in order to establish their qualifications. The UNED has the same status and structure as traditional institutions: faculty organization is similar, courses and subjects have identical or similar titles, and the degrees awarded have the same value. The main innovation is the replacement of direct contact between student and teachers with private study, supported by technology and a minimum level of general guidance by staff.

The UNED is also unique in its geographical organization. The headquarters are located in Madrid, and there are permanent local centres (*centros asociados*), which support the teaching provided by the university, and offer students a range of ancillary services. There are also specialized centres, the function of which is to provide an infrastructure and an operational framework for specific programmes, such as those offered in prisons and in countries outside Spain.

The teaching units are the principal means of disseminating knowledge. These are integrated with multimedia approaches, building increasingly on the use of radio, television, video and computers. Videoconferencing allows contact between a teacher at headquarters and students in different local centres.

The courses offered by the UNED lead either to the official qualifications of Diplomate, Licenciate (equivalent to the Honours B.A. in Britain), and third-cycle courses leading to the doctorate, or to other qualifications outside the national degree system, such as professional training for teachers, open distance learning, or postgraduate courses. In the session 1994–5, there were 118,708 students and 1,037 teachers in the mainstream programmes. The subject area which attracts most students is social and legal sciences, with 86,493, followed by humanities (17,695), engineering and technology (7,580) and natural and exact sciences (6,940).

See also: education and research; science; student life; universities; university education

Further reading

The UNED itself issues a number of useful publications:

Diniz T. (1992) *Universidad abierta/Educación a Distancia. Una alternativa de educación superior*, UNED: Madrid.

Popa Lisseanu, D. (1988) *Un reto mundial: la educación a distancia*, UNED.

Tiana Ferrer, A. (1984) *El modelo español de educación superior a distancia: la UNED*, UNED: Madrid.

García Aretio, L. (ed.) (1996) *La educación a Distancia y la UNED*, UNED: Madrid.

ALICIA ALTED

unemployment

At the time of the oil crisis of 1973, unemployment in Spain stood at just under 2.5 percent of the active population, but with the recession, the estimated one million Spanish workers in Europe began to return. This influx coincided with an increase in the active population, resulting from a 'baby boom' in the 1960s, job losses in agriculture as a consequence of mechanization, and the increasing number of women entering the **labour market**. Official unemployment figures reached 12.4 percent in 1980, and peaked at 24.7 percent in 1994, before falling back to 22 percent in 1996, double the EU average, and the highest in Europe. Moreover, the annual average figures conceal the real scale of the problem in some sectors of society. Female unemployment in 1990, at 24 percent, was double the rate of male unemployment. Youth unemployment is even higher: in 1991, 30.5 percent of those aged between 16 and 24 were unemployed, and the figure rose to 43 percent in 1996.

These figures do not include those working in the **black economy**, which some estimates calculate at a third of those officially unemployed. This is partly offset, however, by the fact that seasonal agricultural workers in Andalusia and Extremadura are not defined as unemployed, even though they often only work for three months in the year. Overall, therefore, the official figures gave a reasonably accurate picture of the true situation, and in any case clearly reflect the worsening trends in employment since 1975. Even when the underground economy is taken into account, a conservative estimate of the real rate would place it at 16 percent, still the highest in the EU.

Job losses were further compounded by the need to restructure the economy to achieve greater competitiveness. The socialist **PSOE** which came to power in 1982 had promised to create 800,000 new jobs, but in the event this proved to be impracticable. The closure of the Sagunto steel works in Valencia in 1982 was an indication of what was to come. The ***reconversión industrial*** of the steel and shipbuilding industries in the Basque country has proved equally controversial.

The problem of unemployment is not confined to Spain, but whereas other countries have a developed system of unemployment benefit, provision in Spain was much less comprehensive. Successive governments have reduced the cost of unemployment benefit by cutting the numbers of those entitled to receive assistance. In 1988, fewer than 30 percent of those unemployed were eligible for benefit, despite the socialists having set a target of 48 percent, which was in any case below the European average. In the wake of the general strike of December 1988, the proportion of those eligible increased, and stood at just under 70 percent in 1993, but new restrictions were introduced again in that year. School-leavers seeking their first job are not entitled to unemployment benefit. Workers who lose their jobs can claim for a maximum of six years, after which unemployment payments are replaced by a system of income support called the *subsidio*, amounting in 1993 to around £3,000 per annum.

See also: industrial relations; labour law

Further reading

Chislett, W. (1997), *Spain 1997: The Central Hispano Handbook*, Madrid: Central Hispano, pp. 18–27 (a brief but clear summary, illustrated with useful graphs).

Heywood, P. (1995) *The Government and Politics of Spain*, London: Macmillan (chapter 10 is an excellent overview of the problems created by convergence with the European economy, illustrated with several useful tables).

Hooper, J. (1995) *The New Spaniards*, Harmondsworth: Penguin (chapter 18 gives a clear and comprehensive account of the unemployment problem).

EAMONN RODGERS

Ungría, Alfonso

b. 1946, Madrid

Filmmaker

Ungría began his career as a director of the officially sponsored newsreels known as NO-DO (*Noticiarios y documentales* – Newsreels and Documentaries), but fell foul of the **censorship** apparatus when he was dismissed after a controversial documentary entitled *La vida en los teleclubs* (Life in the Teleclubs) (1969). He then turned to **television**, but also made a reputation as a film-director with works like his Civil War film *Soldados* (Soldiers) (1978), and art films such as *La conquista de Albania* (The Conquest of Albania) (1983).

See also: film and cinema

EAMONN RODGERS

United Left

The launching of the United Left (Izquierda Unida – IU) in April 1986 was brought about by the convergence of three needs amply felt among political groups standing to the left of the socialist **PSOE**, when the latter was reaching the end of its first period in government. These were: to provide a common platform to unite and strengthen the many small left-wing groups in existence at the time; to revive the Spanish Communist Party (**PCE**) after their abysmal performance at the 1982 elections; and to offer some kind of progressive alternative to a socialist government already committed to a middle-of-the-road programme.

The referendum held on 12 March 1986 to decide the future of Spain's membership of **NATO** was to provide the final impetus for the creation of IU. At the behest of the government a majority of Spaniards voted in favour of remaining in the Atlantic Alliance, but most left-wing and progressive groups in the country wanted Spain out of NATO, and having commanded nearly 40 percent of the vote they felt encouraged to carry their united struggle through to the forthcoming elections. IU was thus born on a wave of enthusiasm and improvisation: an electoral coalition was quickly set up with the PCE – the dominant partner by far – as the central axis, and orbiting around it a number of small parties of varied left-wing hues and an assorted group of independent political figures.

Since its foundation IU has altered considerably, without ever acquiring an identity of its own. What began as an electoral coalition later became a socio-political movement, and subsequently a loose federation of political parties and groupings. But all these transformations have not endowed IU with a clear image, separate from that of the PCE. In spite of official denials, there is a widely held view that IU is no more than an electoral disguise for the communist party – an impression reinforced by the fact that Julio Anguita, PCE's secretary general, is also the leader or co-ordinator of IU.

The relations between the two organizations and the possible – though for the time being not probable – dissolution of the PCE in order to allow IU to become a political party in its own right have been the source of frequent and acerbic disagreements among their leaders. The collapse of the Soviet Union and communism in Eastern Europe exacerbated the situation causing serious confrontations in the ranks of IU at the beginning of the 1990s. The third Federal Congress, held in May 1992, was particularly controversial, with the so-called 'renovators' strongly demanding that IU should be allowed to become an independent party – the corollary being, of course, the disappearance of the PCE – while the official line, supported by Anguita, defended the maintenance of the *status quo*. The latter won the day with 60 percent of the vote. Since then a fragile calm has been maintained though it must be interpreted as a postponement rather than a solution of the real problem.

By the mid-1990s, IU was the third political force in Spain, but despite an improved electoral performance, they still fell short of their initial aspirations. In the March 1996 elections they received 2.6 million votes and won 21 seats in Congress. They have some 100 deputies in the seventeen regional assemblies, more than 3,500 local councillors, and 9 representatives in the European Parliament. Their numerical presence in Spanish politics is significant, but not important enough to threaten the two major contenders, the PSOE and the conservative **PP**, still less to bring about the hoped for breakthrough which would turn IU – following the Italian example – into the major political party on the left, ahead of its socialist rivals. In fact, IU's influence in Spanish public life is considerably reduced by their inability or unwillingness to reach agreements and form coalitions with the PSOE. The antagonism between communists and socialists in Spain has deep historical roots, but the inflexible attitude of Anguita and his followers is making impossible any form of cohabitation on the left.

Further reading

Amodia, J. (1993) 'Requiem for the Spanish Communist Party', in D.S. Bell, *Western Communists and the Collapse of Communism*, Oxford: Berg, pp. 101–19 (a study of the decline of the PCE and the role of IU as possible saviour).

Jáuregui, F. (1992) *Julio Anguita*, Madrid: Grupo Libro 88 (IU seen through the eyes of its leader; some documentary appendices).

Taibo, C. (1996) *Izquierda Unida y sus mundos*, Madrid: Libros de la Catarata (a critical assessment of IU from the extreme left).

JOSÉ AMODIA

United Nations

Spain was excluded from membership of the United Nations in 1945 because of Franco's support for the Axis powers during WWII. It was not long, however, before the attitude of the UN towards Spain was absorbed into the international diplomatic chess-game of the Cold War. Though Britain, the US and France wished to see Franco removed, they shrank from any action which might provoke another Civil War, especially since this could benefit Stalin, whom the western Allies suspected of plotting to destabilize Spain so as to draw it into the communist ambit. Though the

French government decided to close the frontier with Spain in February 1946 in response to the executions of opponents of the Franco regime, Britain and the US would not agree to a proposal from France that the Spanish issue be discussed at the Security Council. Furthermore, a declaration issued by all three governments emphasized that there was no question of intervening in the internal affairs of Spain, and that the eventual removal of Franco would be a matter for the Spanish people. Thereafter the western Allies gradually withdrew support from the Republican opposition in exile.

When the Security Council passed the question of Spain to the General Assembly, the UN was effectively signalling the end of any serious attempt to take effective action against Franco. The resolution agreed by the Assembly in December 1946 did not even call for economic sanctions. Though the resolution excluded Spain from all UN dependent organizations, and advocated that governments break off diplomatic relations, the main effect was to hand Franco an easy propaganda victory by enabling him to appear as the beleaguered victim of a Soviet-led international conspiracy, a stance which united large sections of the populace behind him.

Simultaneously, however, the view was growing in US and British government circles that Franco, despite his rhetorical posturing, did indeed provide a useful bulwark against Soviet intentions in western Europe. In December 1947, the US *chargé d'affaires* in Madrid was instructed to adopt a more friendly attitude towards Spain. Three months later, the American Joint Chiefs of Staff expressed interest in establishing military bases in Spain, and it was decided to include Spain in the Marshall Plan. In October 1950, the Special Ad Hoc Political Committee of the UN voted to rescind the resolution of December 1946, which cleared the way for the resumption of full diplomatic relations by member states. Two years later, Spain was admitted to UNESCO, and in 1953 the **American bases agreement** was concluded. Membership of the United Nations followed in 1955.

Thereafter relations with the UN eased, to the extent that in 1966 resolutions sympathetic to the Spanish claim to Gibraltar were passed. The organization, however, was highly critical of the increased repression which marked the last years of the regime, and in 1975 heard a proposal from the President of Mexico, Luis Echevarría, that Spain should be expelled. With the advent of democracy, the situation was once more normalized, and by 1989 Spain was contributing troops to UN peacekeeping missions. By 1992, Spain had more officers serving under the UN flag than any other country in the world.

See also: foreign policy

Further reading

Preston, P. (1993) *Franco*, London: Harper Collins (a comprehensive index makes it easy to trace references to the United Nations through this very substantial volume).

EAMONN RODGERS

universities

The oldest Spanish universities date from the early thirteenth century, and they reached a peak of prestige in the Renaissance period. In the eighteenth century they came under the influence of the Enlightenment, with the introduction of new syllabi in the 1760s under Charles III, and the loss of their traditional autonomy. This was the beginning of a centralizing and regalist policy under the Bourbons which was continued in the nineteenth century, when the universities became an extension of the state administrative apparatus. This process was complete by 1857, when the so-called Ley Moyano placed the universities fully under the tutelage of the state, represented by the Rector. Thereafter, apart from a brief interlude during the radical liberal regime of 1868 to 1875, when freedom of education became government policy, the universities remained under state control until 1919.

In that year, the universities were granted their autonomy, a decision which reflected the reformist currents of the late nineteenth century, mainly associated with the Institución Libre de Enseñanza (Free Institute of Education), an independent body founded in 1875 by dissident professors who refused to accept the re-imposition of state control of higher education. The Institute continued to exercise considerable intellectual influence until the outbreak of the Civil War.

The work of reform was continued by the government of the Second Republic. It was during the period of the Republic, in the session 1932–3, that the Universidad Popular (People's University) began to function, with staff provided by the *Federación Escolar Universitaria* (University Academic Federation), a body which had considerable influence on government policy on higher education. A systematic overhaul of the universities was planned, but the increasing ideological polarization of the later years of the Republic prevented its implementation. With the outbreak of the Civil War, all academic activity was interrupted, and most of the staff enlisted.

In the 1940s, especially after the University Reform Law of 1943, higher education once more came under the control of the state, and its content was determined by '**National Catholicism**'. Nevertheless, from the 1950s, the gradual acceptance of the Franco regime by other countries, and the progressive opening up of Spain to external influences, brought about a transition, especially in the period 1956–62, from a 'spiritualized' and ideologically determined model of higher education to a more technocratic one. However, the tenure of the Ministry of Education by Lora Tamayo saw a greater influence of the church, and especially of **Opus Dei**, in higher education, and greater support by the government of private Catholic Universities, notably the University of Navarre, founded by Opus Dei.

The most far-reaching reform of the structure and financing of education during the Franco regime was the 1970 legislation introduced by the then Minister, Villar Palasí, which was an attempt to adapt the system to the developing needs of Spanish society. The transition to democracy, in the years 1976–82, was a period of uncertainty, owing to the fragile parliamentary majority commanded by the government party, **UCD**. The **PSOE** victory of 1982 opened the way to a comprehensive reform programme, reflected in legislation on the right to education (the **LODE**), on university reform (the **LRU**) and on the general reorganization of the system of education (the **LOGSE**).

The increase in student numbers in the 1980s and 1990s has necessitated the creation of new universities. About half of the fifty-four universities in Spain (of which ten are private institutions) have been founded since 1970.

See also: education and research; science; student life; UNED; university education

Further reading

Álvarez de Morales, A. (1972) *Génesis de la Universidad española contemporánea*, Madrid: Instituto de Estudios Administrativos (despite its age, still a useful overview).

Carreras Ares, J.J. y Ruiz Carnicer, M.A. (eds) (1991) *La universidad española bajo el régimen de Franco (1939–1975)*, Zaragoza: Institución Fernando el Católico (a symposium of essays which offers the most up-to-date account of this period).

Hooper, J. (1995) *The New Spaniards*, Harmondsworth: Penguin (chapter 19 gives a good overall account of the development of education at all levels).

ALICIA ALTED

university education

Though **universities** have existed in Spain since the Middle Ages, the shape of higher education in modern times really derives from reforms carried out in the late eighteenth and early nineteenth centuries. The main effect of these was to establish standard programmes of study in all institutions, and to consolidate state control. The Complutense University of Madrid, indeed, was initially known as the Central University, created by the transfer of the University of Alcalá de Henares (the original Universidad Complutense, founded in the early sixteenth century) to Madrid in 1836. By 1857, all aspects of university life, academic, administrative and financial were subject to government control. It was at this time that the division into faculties was adopted (philosophy and letters; physical and natural sciences; pharmacy; medicine; law and theology), as well as the three-part structure of degree courses into bachelor, licenciate and doctoral levels.

By the end of the nineteenth century universities had come to be regarded as little more than degree factories, and demand for radical reform grew. Some individual institutions took initiatives in this direction, such as the University of Oviedo, which, in the spirit of renewal associated with the *Institución Libre de Enseñanza* (Free Institute of Education) began a programme of university outreach. Discussion on university autonomy intensified until a decree of 1919 established this principle, which remained in being until the Civil War.

The early governments of the Second Republic evolved a vision of higher education which embraced the professional training of staff, the encouragement of research and the dissemination of culture, though most of the effective initiatives were concentrated in the primary and secondary sectors. The future shape of university education during the Franco period was, however, determined in the Nationalist zone during the Civil War, when in 1938 a scheme was drawn up which established the *bachillerato universitario*, a school-leaving examination conceived as facilitating entry to the university system by a select minority who would form the future ruling class. This notion of forming a kind of intellectual aristocracy was what underlay the University Reform Law of 1943, and it was reinforced by the foundation of the *Sindicato Español Universitario* (Spanish Students' Union), a branch of the **Falange**. Membership of SEU was compulsory for all students, though paradoxically the earliest **student protests** against government control of higher education were mounted by this organization.

From the mid-1950s, it became obvious that economic growth and social changes made it necessary to update the university system. New advanced technical schools were established by legislation enacted in 1964, and were incorporated into the third-level educational sector through the polytechnic universities. The 1960s saw the transition from an élite to a mass system of higher education, and the increasing politicization of students, in response to the social transformations which were taking place elsewhere. Though Spain felt the impact of the revolutionary agitation which began in Paris in May 1968, the student movement in Spain, as in other countries, exhausted itself and turned inward, the banner of protest being handed to junior university staff.

Though significant reforms of education were enacted in 1970, the university system did not assume its present shape until the changes brought about by the **LRU** in 1983, which established the principle of university autonomy in certain aspects of course design, government and financing, and facilitated the foundation of new private universities. Overall, the number of universities in Spain has doubled since 1970.

See also: education and research; science; student life; UNED

Further reading

Carreras Ares, J.J. and Ruiz Carnicer, M.A. (eds) (1991) *La universidad española bajo el régimen de Franco (1939–1975)*, Zaragoza: Institución Fernando el Católico (a symposium of essays which offers the most up-to-date account of this period).

Guereña, J.L. *et al.* (1994) *Historia de la educación en la España Contemporánea. Diez años de investigación*, Madrid: CIDE (a symposium of overview essays; see especially the chapter on higher education).

Hooper, J. (1995) *The New Spaniards*, Harmondsworth: Penguin (chapter 19 gives a good overall account of the development of education at all levels).

Ministerio de Educación (1996) *Guía de la Universidad*, Madrid: Ministerio de Educación (the official reference guide to universities).

ALICIA ALTED

urbanization

Just over half of Spain's population, or 20 million people, live in towns of more than 50,000 inhabitants, and three-quarters in towns of more than 10,000 inhabitants. In two provinces (Madrid and Cádiz) urbanization is above 90 percent, and in ten others it is above 80 percent. Regionally, the greatest density of population is found in the **autonomous community** of Madrid, with 626 inhabitants per square kilometre, the average for

Spain being just 78. The Basque country has a density of 295 inhabitants per square kilometre, and the Canaries of 219. Above average densities of between 100 and 200 are found in the regions of Catalonia (191), Valencia (168), the Balearics (149), Asturias (104), and Cantabria (101). The lowest densities are found in Castile-La Mancha (21), Extremadura (25), Aragon (25), and Castile-León (27). Spain has fifty-five cities of between 50,000 and 100,000 inhabitants and another fifty-five of more than 100,000. The largest conurbations are Madrid (3.1m), Barcelona (1.7m), Valencia (0.77m), Seville (0.72m), Zaragoza (0.61m) and Málaga (0.53m).

The shift of population to urban centres intensified in the 1960s, as agricultural labourers left an impoverished countryside in search of jobs in the industrial and **services** sectors. In the twenty-five years to 1975 the proportion of the population living in cities of more than 100,000 people doubled. The largest cities grew fastest, but virtually all provincial capitals grew at the expense of small towns and villages. Estimates of the number of abandoned villages vary between 2,000 and 3,000. The counterpart of rural depopulation was the near uncontrolled growth of cities, with unsightly apartment blocks and shanty-town-style suburban belts without proper roads, sanitation or other services. It was only in the 1970s and 1980s that corrective action was taken, **planning controls** were established, and the **shanty towns** became less numerous. From 1975 onwards, urbanization continued, but at a moderate pace and with an altered pattern. Whereas during the Francoist period it was the large conurbations of Madrid, Barcelona and Bilbao that had the highest growth rates, in the late 1970s and 1980s it was peripheral provincial capitals like Málaga, Seville, Alicante and Las Palmas that grew fastest, together with certain non-capitals geared to specific roles, such as Algeciras (international maritime trade) or Marbella (**tourism**). Losses from the more isolated rural areas, but also from underdeveloped provincial capitals such as Orense, Teruel or Zamora, continued, but in the late 1980s and 1990s the rural exodus was partly reversed by the tendency of prosperous urban dwellers to acquire country properties for weekends and vacations. Twenty-two percent of house owners in Spain have a second home.

The growth of the cities since the 1950s cannot be divorced from other transformations of the social fabric: changes in the **labour market**, as people move to jobs in services; a massive increase in educational enrolments; improvements in **health care**; and the emergence of a progressive, permissive society with a more homogeneous lifestyle and widely shared **social attitudes**.

Further reading

De Miguel, A. (1992) *La sociedad española 1992–93*, Madrid: Alianza (pp. 112–31 contain an interesting comparison of the urban and rural worlds).

—— (1994) *La sociedad española 1993–94*, Madrid: Alianza (pp. 102–28 contain an important study of the changing nature of the urbanizing process).

Hooper, J. (1995) *The New Spaniards*, Harmondsworth: Penguin (chapter 20, on housing, looks at the way the government tried to cope with the urban explosion).

C.A. LONGHURST

Uribe, Imanol

b. 1950, San Salvador (El Salvador)

Filmmaker and journalist

Uribe's career was initially concerned with the problems of the Basque country, as in his controversial films about the terrorist organization **ETA**: *El proceso de Burgos* (The Burgos Trial) (1979); *La fuga de Segovia* (The Segovia Escape) (1981); and *La muerte de Mikel* (Mikel's Murder) (1983). After some forays into the area of the genre film, both for the screen and for television, his cinema regained its former edge and topicality with *Días contados* (Running Out of Time) (1994) which won the Golden Shell in San Sebastián, as did *Bwana* in 1996.

See also: Basque culture; Basque Left; film and cinema

Further reading

Angulo, J., Heredero, C.F. and Rebordinas, J.L. (eds) (1994) *El cine de Imanol Uribe: entre el documental y la ficción*, San Sebastián: Filmoteca Vasca (a well-documented monograph containing an interview with the filmmaker).

Basque Cinema. Euskal Zinema. Cine Vasco. 1981–89 (1990) Donastia: Euskadiko Filmategia (comprehensive catalogue of the films covering the period of the formalization of Basque cinema in the 1980s).

XON DE ROS

Urretabizkaia, Arantxa

b. 1947, San Sebastián

Writer

At once straightforward and lyrical, the work of Urretabizkaia includes prize-winning works in **Basque**, such as her novel *Zergatik Panpox?* (Why Panpox?) (1979) and her collection of poetry *Maitasunaren Magalean* (1981). In an effort to create accessible literature for a Basque public, she strives for clarity and her work is characterized by an elegant simplicity. Most of her protagonists are female, as she explores such topics as single motherhood, friendship between women, the life of a nun, and memories evoked in old age. Her apprenticeship as a writer was in journalism, and she continues her activities in this field. For her work published in the 1990s she has changed her name from Urretavizcaya to accord with Basque orthography.

KATHLEEN McNERNEY

V

Valente, José Ángel

b. 1929, Orense

Poet and critic

Like other poets who emerged in the mid-1950s, Valente began by reacting against the false attitudes and tired rhetoric which were common features of Spanish poetry in the years immediately following the Civil War. In retrospect, his early poems, from the collections *A modo de esperanza* (By Way of Hope) (1955) to *La memoria y los signos* (Memory and Signs) (1966), can be seen as a necessary preparation for the later work. Even at this stage, however, Valente's originality comes out in his use of language as a moral instrument; the best poems of these years have an austerity of diction and an intensity of verbal concentration which reflect the refusal to compromise with a society whose corruption has infected the roots of language itself.

Where Valente goes further than any of his Spanish contemporaries is in the degree of self-criticism he is prepared to apply to his own activity as a poet. From about 1970 on, this amounts to a re-thinking of his whole way of writing: the poems become deliberately fragmentary, and Valente speaks of the need to avoid the manipulation of language, which for him is an abuse of authority, and to allow poetry to speak *through* the poet. Hence his association of poetry with mysticism: both are forms of heterodoxy, modes of experience which continually challenge existing dogmas, whether religious or linguistic, and which come to share the same kind of alternative language. Moreover, both poetry and mysticism – about which he has written at length in *La piedra y el centro* (The Stone and the Centre) (1982) and *Variaciones sobre el pájaro y la red* (Variations on the Bird and the Net) (1991) – operate on the borders of silence, the silence before language in which the word is 'infinitely available'.

All this is brilliantly summed-up in *Tres lecciones de tinieblas* (Three Lessons of *Tenebrae*), published in 1980, a meditation on the first fourteen letters of the Hebrew alphabet in which the stress on the material nature of the letter or syllable is associated with birth and gestation, and ultimately with the nature of creation itself. In all this, the erotic is crucial: in his next collections, *Mandorla* (1982) and *El fulgor* (The Gleam) (1984), Valente engages not so much in a meditation on the body as in an attempt to break down the kind of detachment this might imply and to create a situation in which the body may 'speak'.

At the very least, Valente offers a myth of origins which, whatever its religious precedents, places poetic creation at the limits of what language can convey and implies that language itself will bear traces of the body. No other contemporary Spanish poet has continued to investigate so seriously the possibilities and limitations of poetic language, nor has so consistently produced poems which successfully embody these preoccupations.

Most of Valente's poems are collected in two volumes, *Punto cero: poesí 1953–79)* (Zero Point) (1980) and *Material memoria* (1989). *El fin de la Edad de la Plata* (The End of the Silver Age), a remarkable collection of prose poems and fables, was published in 1973.

Further reading

Polo, M. (1983) *José Ángel Valente. Poesía y poemas*, Madrid: Narcea.

Valcárcel, E. (1989) *El fulgor o la palabra encarnada*, Barcelona: PPU.

Rodríguez Fer, C. (ed.) (1994) *Material Valente*, Madrid: Ediciones Júcar.

ARTHUR TERRY

Valentí, Helena

b. 1940, Barcelona

Writer

Active in the feminist movement during eleven years' study and writing in England, Valentí began publishing in English. On her return to Barcelona, she began writing in **Catalan** and translating from English. Her works explore intimacy and alternative lifestyles with unusual frankness. In the stories of *Amic, Amat* (Mature Love), women struggle with unwanted pregnancy, failed marriages, economic dependency and identity crises. Comparable conflicts imbue the novel, *La solitud d'Anna* (Anna's Solitude), which examines relationships of power and abuse and the struggle for self-affirmation with delicacy and insight. *La dona errant* (Errant Female) analyses changing sexual mores.

Further reading

Pérez, J. (1988) *Contemporary Women Writers of Spain*, Boston, MA: G.K. Hall, pp. 184–6 (schematic analysis of feminist aspects).

JANET PÉREZ

Vanguardia, La

La Vanguardia, published in Barcelona, is the oldest and most prestigious daily newspaper published in Catalonia, and the only one with a significant circulation in the rest of Spain where it features among the top quality daily publications.

La Vanguardia was founded in 1881 by the Catalan industrialists Carlos and Bartolomé Godó and is still owned by the Godó family today. It has an average daily readership of around 700,000, while the Sunday edition can attract well over one million readers. Though its readership has declined slightly, it is still viewed as Catalonia's leading newspaper in terms of quality, and it has acquired the status of something of an institution in Catalan life. It gives extensive daily coverage to Catalan, Spanish and international news, as well as having substantial business and sports sections, and individual issues – particularly the Sunday editions – can have as many as a hundred pages.

Since its inception *La Vanguardia* has been a newspaper which has espoused what might generally be termed liberal-conservative views. It has always been written in Spanish, even during those moments of Spanish history when publication in **Catalan** would have been possible. Its stance in relation to **language normalization** as regards the use of Catalan within Catalan society as a whole has been to some extent ambiguous. It officially supports the policy, but makes no concessions to it as far as its own language of publication is concerned, and at times it attacks what it sees as the excesses of such a policy. Given its general position as a Spanish rather than a purely Catalan newspaper, there seems little likelihood of it ever allowing the Catalan language to make serious inroads into its columns.

La Vanguardia has traditionally tended to represent the views of those sections of Catalan society – mostly its industrial and business sectors – which have seen their interests as being best served by Catalonia's continuing inclusion within Spain as a whole, a stance which has earned it a certain amount of criticism from more radically nationalistic sectors of Catalan society. In keeping with this general outlook, *La Vanguardia* has at times been critical of aspects of the nationalist politics carried out in the Catalan parliament, the **Generalitat**, by the conservative–nationalist coalition Convergència i Unió (Convergence and Unity – **CiU**), whose official rhetoric suggests a long-term goal of secession from the rest of Spain. Though it has lost some ground to its main competitor *El* ***Periódico de Catalunya***, there can be little doubt that *La Vanguardia* will continue to be a leading newspaper and an important institution within Catalan society as a whole.

See also: media; press

Further reading

Mateo, R. de and Corbella, J.M. (1992) 'Spain', in B.S. Østergaard (ed.) *The Media in Western Europe*, London: Sage (a useful guide to the media in Spain in general, though its coverage of individual newspapers is rather slim).

HUGH O'DONNELL

Vargas, Rafael

b. 1959, Barcelona

Photographer

Rafael Vargas' works are often conceived as works of art in their own right, following to some extent the direction taken by Joan **Fontcuberta**. Vargas generally uses colour and creates a theatrical setting for his models, in which the elements of the decor help to define their characters, their 'story'. He is also a very experienced architectural photographer, particularly attracted to townscapes. Enlargements on a huge scale of three of his photographs depicting the city by night were used by the architect Alfredo **Arribas** in his work '*Gran Velvet*'. These images, 12 metres in length, are remarkable for their abstract, schematic elegance and represent a novel use of photography.

MIHAIL MOLDOVEANU

Vaz de Soto, José María

b. 1938, Paymogo (Huelva)

Novelist

Since his first novel, *Hell and the Breeze* (*El infierno y la brisa*), Vaz de Soto's narrative has been characterized by the autobiographical exploration of the historic conditions that traumatized those who were children during the Spanish Civil War. This novel was made into a film by José María Gutiérrez with the title *¡Viva Hazaña!*. The dialectic analysis of a repressive Spanish society is the leitmotif of the tetralogy *Diálogos del anochecer* (*Dialogues at Dusk*). *Fabián and Sabas* (originally two novels), and *Late Night Dialogues* (*Diálogos de alta noche*). Vaz de Soto is a follower of Pío Baroja in the vitality of his dialogue, directness, ironic tone and the use of many digressions.

Further reading

Ortega, J. (1980) 'Educación, represión y frustración en la narrativa de José María Vaz de Soto', *Cuadernos Hispanoamericanos* 363: 579–89.

JOSÉ ORTEGA

Vázquez Montalbán, Manuel

b. 1939, Barcelona

Writer

Vázquez Montalbán is one of the most prolific, and at the same time, most highly regarded writers in contemporary Spain. Though he has cultivated 'popular' genres like **detective fiction**, he has done so at a level of complexity and sophistication which takes his novels beyond the conventions of the crime mystery and turns them into a sharp-edged and witty commentary on contemporary society. Perhaps his best-known work is the series of novels featuring the detective Pepe Carvalho, where the interest focuses less on solving the crime than on Carvalho's observations on the society he sees around him.

A former member of the **Catalan United Socialist Party** (the communist PSUC), Vázquez Montalbán began his writing career as a journalist in the 1960s. His varied output, embracing novels, essays, books on gastronomy and political memoirs, has won him various **prizes**. His novel *Los mares del sur* (South Seas) (1979) won the **Planeta Prize**, *Galíndez* won the Europa Prize in 1992, and *El estrangulador* (The Strangler) (1995) the Critics' Prize. His work as a whole was honoured by the award of the National Literature Prize in 1995.

See also: literature; novel

EAMONN RODGERS

vertical syndicates

The Sindicatos Verticales, which were also known as the Organización Sindical, were the official state trade unions of the Franco regime. They were set up during the Civil War on the model of the Italian fascist labour organization, and dominated labour relations for forty years. The objective of the *sindicatos* was to organize national production in a system of bodies arranged 'vertically' within each sector of the economy. This meant that workers, administrators and bosses were to be grouped together, thereby avoiding the class solidarity implicit in exclusively worker unions, 'horizontally' organized. In spite of the rhetoric of the 'harmonization of capital and labour', the real effect of the imposition of the state union structure and the outlawing of strikes was to deny the working class the possibility of voicing dissent.

As in fascist Italy, the *sindicatos verticales* were provided with a bureaucracy by the state party, the **Falange**. They also derived from a longer tradition of authoritarian Catholic corporativism which pre-dated the Republic of the 1930s, and which aimed to do away with class conflict, either by incorporating political unions into institutions of the state, or by setting up alternative unions motivated not by class but by other 'superior' interests. At various stages prior to the Civil War the notion of establishing specifically Catholic unions was mooted. The Francoist vertical trade unions were partly influenced by this idea, but in addition the *sindicatos* were now portrayed as an integral part of a broader and more grandiose image of the resurgent nation. The 'superior' interest, above considerations of class, was 'the nation' and national production.

Election to posts of worker representatives (*enlaces*) in the *sindicatos* was officially open only to Falangists. However, despite all the efforts of the regime, the *sindicatos* gradually became significant as a means for voicing protest. Even some Falangists dissented from the official government line or the stance taken by an employer. Moreover, from the very outset, at the end of the Civil War in 1939, militants of the anarchist **CNT** had infiltrated the official state unions in small numbers. Increasingly, other clandestine political groups were adopting a policy of 'entryism', widespread infiltration into the state machinery in order genuinely to fight for worker demands and to subvert the aims of the regime. By the 1960s the state unions were increasingly influenced by the **CC OO**, the clandestine labour organization led jointly by Catholics and communists, which had been practising the strategy of entryism since 1948.

Employers, who had always, in the main, had the ear of the government in the elaboration of economic policy, began to recognize that often a more effective way of negotiating labour disputes was to deal directly with unofficial workers' groups. The official union structure, by the end of the 1960s, was becoming increasingly anachronistic. By the time of its final dismantling in 1977, following the demise of Franco and of his regime in 1975, it had become a vast unwieldy bureaucracy, largely irrelevant to the day-to-day activities of the economy, work and labour agitation.

Further reading

Amsden, J. (1972) *Collective Bargaining and Class Conflict in Spain*, London: Weidenfeld-Nicolson (a useful overview concentrating on the 1960s).

Balfour, S. (1989) *Dictatorship, Workers and the City: Labour in Greater Barcelona Since 1939*, Oxford: Oxford University Press (a regional study giving many insights into relations between the official unions and CC OO).

MICHAEL RICHARDS

Vicens Vives, Jaume

b. 1910, Girona; d. 1960, Barcelona

Historian

Vicens Vives, despite his early death at the age of 50, was one of the most influential historians of Spain working during the Franco period, and formed a school of **historiography** which continues to shape the writing of Spanish history. Vicens was trained in the tradition of erudite documentary historiography, but at an early stage began to question the conventional Castilian-centred view of the past, by giving due prominence to Catalonia's contribution to the cultural and political identity of Spain, hitherto largely ignored by conservative historians. One of his first books, *Política del Rey Católico en Cataluña* (The Catalan Policy of Ferdinand the Catholic) (1940), provided an important corrective to the tendency to interpret Ferdinand's role exclusively in a Castilian context. This was followed by *Historia de los remensas en el siglo XV* (The Catalan Peasantry in the Fifteenth Century) (1945), an in-depth study of a particularly oppressed social group. His comprehensive and nuanced interpretation of the history of the peninsula was popularized in the short 1952 volume *Approach to the History of Spain* (*Aproximación a la historia de España*), still widely read for its lucid insights.

In the 1950s Vicens came under the influence of the French *Annales* school, which provided a powerful stimulus to the development of his interest in social and economic history, and the use of quantitative methods. This had the effect of expanding the scope of his investigation beyond the medieval specialism with which he had begun his career into the nineteenth century, regarded by scholars identified with the Franco regime as a period of decadence provoked by 'foreign' importations such as liberalism, but by revisionist historians like Vicens, Artola, Jover Zamora and **Tuñón de Lara** as the key to the character of contemporary Spain. One of the earliest fruits of this new orientation was his *Industrials i polítics del segle XIX* (Industrialists and Politicians of the Nineteenth Century) (1950), a series of short biographies of representative figures, skilfully placed in their historical context, which illuminates important aspects of the social and economic evolution of nineteenth-century society. This was followed by his monumental five-volume work, *Historia social y económica de España y América* (Social and Economic History of Spain and the Americas) (1958), part of which appeared in English as *An Economic History of Spain* (1969).

See also: education and research; Francoist culture; history; universities

EAMONN RODGERS

Vida Nueva

A Catholic news and views weekly published in Madrid, founded in 1956, *Vida Nueva* has undergone several transformations. Catering first for a 'traditional Catholic' readership, it became ever more progressive in the wake of the Second Vatican Council (1962–5), to the extent that in 1987 its editor was dismissed under pressure from a Spanish hierarchy increasingly in tune with the 'restoration' Catholicism of Pope John Paul II. *Vida Nueva* became more docile to official church attitudes, although it did not exclude reference to the activities of the 'loyal opposition'. In 1993 its image was revamped under a new editor and with a new format.

AUDREY BRASSLOFF

Villarta Tuñón, Ángeles

b. 1921, Belmore (Asturias)

Writer

Educated in Switzerland, Villarta produced her cosmopolitan fiction from the late 1940s to the 1960s. She edited the comic magazine *Don Venerando* and the second series of *La novela corta.* Beginning close to the pulp romance with novels such as *Un pleno de amor* (Dance of Love) (1942), *Por encima de las nieblas* (Above the Mist) (1943), and *Muchachas que trabajan* (Working Girls) (1944), she progressed to politicosocial commitment in *Ahora que soy estraperlista* (Since I'm a Black Marketeer) (1949) and *Con derecho a cocina* (Cooking Privileges) (1950), treating themes favoured by 'critical realists' of the 'Mid-Century Generation'. *Una mujer fea* (An Ugly Woman) (1953) expresses growing feminist preoccupations.

Further reading

Pérez, J. (1988). *Contemporary Women Writers of Spain*, Boston, MA: G.K. Hall, 117 (a brief bio-bibliographical overview).

JANET PÉREZ

Villena, Luis Antonio de

b. 1951, Madrid

Writer

Villena made his reputation as a poet and essayist in the 1970s and – as well as having become a cultural icon, hero and hate-figure – has in the 1980s and 1990s established a second reputation as a short-story writer, novelist and biographer (of renaissance artists and of Byron, winning the 1994 Azorín Prize in the latter case). He has made a sustained attempt to mingle ethics and aesthetics, from his early interest in the figure of the dandy and his convolutedly luxurious poetic style in *Sublime solarium* (1971) and *El viaje a Bizancio* (The Journey to Byzantium) (1978) through to his treatment of suffering, folly, loss and nostalgia in stories in *El tártaro de las estrellas* (The Tartar of the Stars) (1994), the novel *Divino* (Divine) (1994), and the poems of *Marginados* (Marginal Figures) (1993). *Divino* is a harrowing, unforgiving, yet arrestingly beautiful account of a glamorous and intelligent circle of artists and aristocrats drifting through the 1920s into the tragedies of Civil War Madrid, with forgotten songs and lost freedoms left at the end of the novel to signify, in part, Spain of the 1990s, itself torn by disappointments and lost opportunities. *Marginados* looks back on past pleasures almost with a jaundiced eye and represents sharply a contemporary Madrid where sex, drugs, poverty and death cohabit.

The poems in *Hymnica* (1975) and *Huir del invierno* (To Flee from Winter) (1981) seem, with their emphasis on pleasure, to have no hint of the graver preoccupations referred to above. They are complex investigations of desire – usually homoerotic – and of the role of art and beauty. But like *La muerte únicamente* (Death Alone) (1984), they draw on a postmodern blend of tones, styles and subject matter, a mixing of sanctified traditions and radical new conceptualizations of pleasure, desire, pain and death. Death, as a metaphysical construct standing for the possibility of absolute attainment as well as a theme appropriately laden with late romantic and decadent implication, is the focus of the essays of *La tentación de Ícaro* (The Temptation of Icarus) (1986) which might be viewed as a summary of the aesthetic and moral intent of Villena's first two decades of writing. Much of Villena's writing is transgressive and resistant to normalization in matters of taste or behaviour. In parallel, however, he has developed a considerable talent as an almost neo-realist observer of the contemporary cultural scene – especially the social life and certain sectors of the gay scene in Madrid – and its manners, influences, and pretensions are minutely detailed, and often satirized. One of Villena's major talents, indeed, is to combine an inflation of certain values (male beauty, youth, being different) with the deflation of self and others. Early short stories, the novella *Amor Pasión* (Amour Passion) (1983), the 1989 sequence of stories *Chicos* (Boys), and the novel *Fuera del mundo* (Beyond the World) (1990), as well as being sociologically acute miniatures, are brilliant exercises in unreliable narration, calling into question received ideas about love, identity and selfhood.

Further reading

Perriam, C. (1995) *Desire and Dissent: An Introduction to Luis Antonio de Villena*, Oxford: Berg (includes a select bibliography).

CHRIS PERRIAM

VIPS

VIPS is one of the most popular **fast food outlets** in Spain, providing international tourist fare as well as national dishes from Spain, Mexico and Italy. It is owned by CIFRA, Mexico's largest retail company, founded by Jerónimo Arango Arias, the son of a Spanish immigrant. In many of its branches, the restaurant incorporates a shop selling books, magazines, videos, audio cassettes and compact discs, together with a small selection of sports clothing.

EAMONN RODGERS

visual arts

Spain has had a long tradition of excellence in the visual arts, covering the entire range from the Moorish palace of the Alhambra in Granada to the sixteenth- and seventeenth-century flowering of **painting** represented by artists like El Greco and Velázquez, to local **crafts** such as the brightly coloured hand-painted **pottery** from Talavera.

It is, however, to the early 1980s that one may date a significant increase in public awareness. Major **art exhibitions** were mounted, testifying to renewed interest in the artistic heritage of the past, most notably the Velázquez exhibition in the **Prado Museum** in 1990, which was visited by half a million people. In addition, the public showed an increased appetite for attending exhibitions of contemporary art, and acquiring original works. In the mid-1980s, it was estimated that one in five people visited an art gallery twice a month. The International Festival of Contemporary Art, sponsored in 1983 by the ARCO Foundation, was the first of a series of art fairs held in the 1980s and 1990s, which stimulated private purchases of art works. Though sales began to decline after a peak in 1990, this probably reflects a reduction in individual purchasing power rather than a falling-off of interest in art. The number of visitors to galleries and art fairs continued to increase.

The reawakening of public enthusiasm has been paralleled at official level by increased support for the arts, reflected in the improved level of **arts funding** from central and regional government, which increased by some 70 percent in the 1980s. Though there were severe cuts in arts budgets by the mid-1990s, overall support from non-governmental sources is still considerable. Banks, private individuals and **foundations** both own significant **art collections** and also subsidize museums and galleries. The savings banks (***Cajas de Ahorros***) in particular are obliged by law to devote half their profits to community enterprises.

Increased funding from either public or private sources has enabled the refurbishment and extension of the large number of existing **museums**, such as the Prado and the Museum of the Americas, as well as the establishment of new ones, particularly the **Queen Sofia Museum**, **Thyssen-Bornemisza Museum** and the **Guggenheim Museum**, all opened between 1986 and 1997. These developments have not only ensured that major works from the past are preserved using modern standards of conservation, but have also, through enlightened acquisition policies, increased the range of contemporary painting and **sculpture** from other countries which is directly available to the Spanish public. Furthermore, the need to create new installations or upgrade existing ones has provided opportunities for new creative additions to Spain's already flourishing traditions of **architecture**. The Institute of Modern Art in Valencia (IVAM) is a good example of a project which brings together the two enterprises of displaying works of art, and providing an appropriate and striking setting for them.

The burgeoning of interest in the visual arts is attributable in part to the reaction against what was perceived as the cultural impoverishment of the Franco era. The heady excitement of the 1930s, when Spain could boast avant-garde artists of the calibre of **Dalí** and Joan **Miró**, had largely given way, in the years after the Civil War, to an unadventurous academicism, represented in painting principally by Zuloaga, who, having moved in radical circles in the 1930s, became an establishment artist, painting portraits of Franco in heroic poses. This is not to say that the avant-garde tradition disappeared completely. Miró returned to Spain in 1940, and although **Picasso** continued to live in France, he still exercised a powerful influence on Spanish artists. In Catalonia, Joan **Brossa** and Antoni **Tàpies** experimented with new forms and materials, as did Madrid-based painters such as Antonio **Saura**. The sculptor Eduardo **Chillida** departed radically from conventional norms by cultivating a style which became known as Informalism. Nor was avant-garde experimentalism the only approach open to those opposed to the conformist art favoured by the regime. Pastiches of figurative and representative painting could be turned to good account to satirize artistic convention and make a political point, as with the 1973 version of the portrait of Philip II by Equipo Crónica, and the ironic treatment of establishment figures by Eduardo **Arroyo**. Even a figurative sculptor like Jorge de Oteiza transcended his earlier style and evolved towards a degree of abstraction which caused some of his religious statuary to be rejected as too avant-garde, providing eloquent testimony to the rapid development and vitality of the visual arts in contemporary Spain.

See also: Dalí Museum; Ministry of Culture; photography

Further reading

Dent Coad, E. (1995) 'Painting and Sculpture: The Rejection of High Art', in H. Graham and J. Labanyi (eds) *Spanish Cultural Studies, an Introduction: The Struggle for Modernity*, Oxford: Oxford University Press, pp. 299–304 (a useful brief overview of the main trends since the Civil War).

Hooper, J. (1995) *The New Spaniards*, Harmondsworth: Penguin (chapter 23, 'Art and the Possible: The Politics of Culture', places 'art fever' in the context of general changes in the cultural climate).

Wright, P. (1992) 'State of the Nation', *Museums Journal*, June 1992: 25–33 (a very informative and wide-ranging article on the situation in the early 1990s).

EAMONN RODGERS

Vizcaíno Casas, Fernando

b. 1926, Valencia

Writer

After taking degrees in law, journalism and business administration, Vizcaíno Casas embarked on what was to prove a long and prolific career as a writer of plays, essays, novels and film adaptations. His play *La senda iluminada* (The Illuminated Path) dates from 1949, and was followed by, among others, *El escultor de sus sueños* (The Sculptor of his Dreams) (1953), *Las luciérnagas* (The Glow-worms) (1963), and *Los derrotados* (The Defeated). His prose writings are light satirical presentations of contemporary social and political reality, as the titles suggest: *Niñas... al salón* (Girls, to the Drawing-room) (1976), *De camisa vieja a chaqueta nueva: crónica de una evolución ideológica* (From 'Old Shirt' [i.e. member of the old **Falange**] to New Jacket: Chronicle of an Ideological Evolution) (1976), *Y al tercer año resucitó* (And in the Third Year he Rose Again) (1978), *Isabel camisa vieja* (Isabel the 'Old Shirt') (1987), and *El año en que Franco murió en la cama* (The Year Franco Died in his Bed) (1992).

See also: novel

EAMONN RODGERS

water supply

Water is critical for domestic consumption and for sustaining economic activity in Spain, particularly agriculture, which accounts for 80 percent of water demand. Increasing demand, coupled with periods of drought, has led to the realization that water is a scarce resource requiring careful management: ensuring supplies, regulating demand, balancing conflicting uses, and monitoring environmental impact.

There are significant variations in water supply. In the north of Spain there is a surplus, with average annual precipitation in excess of 1,000 mm a year. Across the rest of Spain there is a deficit, owing to low annual average precipitation (varying from less than 600 mm to true desert conditions in the south-east) and substantial water loss resulting from high summer temperatures. Actual precipitation varies from year to year, including droughts where in successive years annual precipitation falls below the average. One such drought occurred between 1990 and 1995, creating serious social, economic and political problems. Crop yields and agricultural employment fell; costs of electricity generation rose as supply was lost from low-cost hydroelectric plant; drinking water was rationed; and the governments of the **autonomous communities** argued over water resources.

Water demand has risen with population growth, the rise in tourism and the increased emphasis on irrigated agriculture. Moreover, these three factors have been most prominent outside of the north of Spain, creating further imbalances in supply and demand.

Responsibilities for water management are shared between the state, regional governments, local authorities and some private utilities. At the strategic level the regions are responsible for co-ordinating water developments. However, water management has developed around public river basin authorities (*Confederaciones Hidrográficas*), which often span different regions. River basin authorities tap surface and underground water supplies, store water underground or in reservoirs, transport water to areas of consumption and frequently treat the water ready for use. Local authorities are generally responsible for local distribution and supply to individual consumers. In Barcelona, water supply is in the hands of the largest water company in Spain, Aguas de Barcelona. More private and foreign capital will enter the industry as the business environment of water supply is liberalized.

Development of water resources depends on the legal arrangements governing use. Until 1985 subterranean water was regarded as part of land ownership, while surface water belonged to the state. This enabled Spain to produce a national water policy, become a pioneer in the management of its rivers and to develop hydroelectric installations. But soaring demand, new pumping techniques and modern knowledge about the water cycle connecting underground and surface water made the old law obsolete. The new law of 1985 included underground water in the public domain (although it left existing wells in private ownership and protected the rights of well owners).

Several critical issues are associated with water supply in Spain, principally that of ensuring supplies to people and industry. This embraces measures such as tapping new sources (including desalination schemes), reducing water losses and developing a national system of supply capable of transferring water from the north to the south. It also embraces the regulation of demand, through the introduction of water charges and critical scrutiny of intensive activities such as irrigated agriculture and golf courses. Other issues are environmental, including reducing water pollution, maintaining water flow in rivers, reducing flood hazards and avoiding desertification.

See also: agriculture; economy; migration

KEITH SALMON

wine

Spain is among the largest wine producers by volume in the world. As well as being the standard accompaniment to food, wine is also drunk as an aperitif in bars, with ***tapas***, and is also widely used in cooking. Picnics in the countryside are frequently complemented with wine carried in the traditional leather wineskin or *bota*, which is often seen at popular ***fiestas*** and ***corridas***. In certain areas in summer, ordinary red table wine is mixed with soda water or white lemonade to make a more refreshing drink.

The wine harvest in Spain extends from September to November, and is commonly the occasion of a village fiesta. Although modern cold-fermentation methods are employed in the preparation of popular white wines such as those produced by Torres in the Penedès region in Catalonia, traditional methods of vinification are still widely used in other regions, especially for reds. Most of Spain is favoured with a dry climate which protects the bloom on the grape from being washed away by rain in the period before the harvest. The vinification process lasts between ten and forty days, depending on the type and quality of wine, red wines receiving a secondary fermentation to reduce acidity.

The wine is matured in casks and in the bottle for varying periods, depending on the final quality to be achieved. *Vinos de crianza* are three-year-old wines, with a minimum of one year in cask for reds and six months for whites. *Vinos de reserva* are wines in their fourth year, with a similar minimum period in cask, but a longer overall ageing than *vinos de crianza*. The superior *gran reserva* wines are laid down from the best vintages, with reds having a minimum age of five years, two in cask and three in the bottle, and whites matured in cask for six months, and at least four years ageing overall. Some of the more famous cellars (*bodegas*) keep stocks from all their vintages for an indefinite period.

The Spanish equivalent of the *Appellation Contrôlée* is the *Denominación de Origen* (DO) or guarantee of origin, which is regulated by a *Consejo Regulador* (Regulatory Council), an agency of the Ministry of Agriculture, Fisheries and Food. Every **autonomous community** except Asturias and Cantabria has DO wines, and some have several famous varieties within their boundaries. Andalusia has the Condado de Huelva and Jérez (sherry) labels, as well as similar fortified wines from Málaga, Moriles and Montilla, amounting to a total of 200m litres. Cariñena, from Aragon, is known all over Spain, and the region also boasts Calatayud, Campo de Borja and Somontano. The world-famous Rioja comes from an area which historically lay within the territory of Aragon but now forms a separate *autonomía*, though the designated wine area overlaps the borders of the provinces of Alava and Burgos, and the autonomous region of Navarre. Northern Navarre also has a DO in its own right, producing well-regarded reds, and is particularly famous for rosés. The Basque provinces produce a popular white called Chacolí. New Castile, including La Mancha, has wines of very variable quality, because of climatic differences across the region, probably the largest wine-producing area in Europe, which yields 200m litres. Valdepeñas is one of the most widely drunk wines in Spain, as well as being exported in volume; other labels are Almansa, La Mancha and Méntrida. Old Castile, producing some 12.5m litres, offers, among others, the well-known variety of Ribera del Duero.

Catalonia, as well as producing much-appreciated wines such as Alella, Ampurdán, Cuenca del Barberá, Penedès, Priorato, Tarragona, Tierra Alta and Segre, is the home of *Cava*, a sparkling white wine produced by the *méthode champenoise*. This was formerly known as *champán*, until **European**

Union regulations restricted the use of the designation. Galicia produces 20m litres, including Rías Bajas, Valdeorras and above all Ribeiro, much appreciated everywhere as an ideal accompaniment to rich Galician cooking. The heady dark red wines of the southeast include the famous Jumilla and Yecla, as well as Utiel-Requena.

As with other wine-producing countries, the obvious categorizations are white, red (*tinto*) and rosé (*rosado* or *claro*). The slightly confusing term *clarete* refers to a light red table wine. Spanish, however, has an exceptionally wide range of terms to describe different grades of sweetness and strength. A wine with less than three grams of sugar per litre is called *seco* (dry). The scale runs all the way to *dulce* (sweet), passing through, in ascending order of sweetness, *generoso*, *generoso seco*, *abocado*, *licoroso*, *semiseco* and *semidulce*. There is a special terminology for sherry: *fino* and *manzanilla* are pale, very dry sherries of an alcoholic content of about 15 percent. The stronger, more deeply coloured *amontillado* is produced by allowing *fino* to age. *Oloroso* has a higher alcohol content, and is rich-tasting and medium-dry to medium-sweet.

See also: agriculture; food and drink

Further reading

Read, J. (1986) *The Wines of Spain*, London: Faber & Faber (an excellent guide to the topic, illustrated with explanatory photographs showing aspects of vinification).

CARLOS ÁLVAREZ ARAGÜÉS

women

The social position of women has undergone a remarkable change in post-Franco Spain. Women hold public office as judges, ambassadors, mayors, government ministers, and university rectors, as well as obtaining jobs in sectors from which they had traditionally been barred or discouraged, such as the police, the armed forces, and public transport. Although pressure from feminist movements cannot be discounted, the fundamental cause of the emancipation of Spanish women is the enormous increase in female participation in education, both secondary and post-compulsory. This began in the late 1960s, accelerated dramatically in the 1970s, and culminated in the 1980s in a higher proportion of females at both secondary school and university. As a result of pressure from *Sección Femenina* (the female section of **Falange**) in the 1960s, early Francoist legislation discriminating against women had been virtually dismantled by the time the dictator died in 1975, and the democratic **constitution of 1978** declared sexual discrimination illegal, as did the Workers' Statute of 1980.

Subsequent democratic governments took more positive steps to redress the balance, through the setting up in 1983 of the publicly financed **Instituto de la Mujer** to conduct research into the economic and social situation of Spanish women, and the establishment of the First Equal Opportunities Plan (1988–90), later followed by the Second Plan. The legalization of the sale of contraceptives (1978) and the de-criminalization of abortion under certain conditions (1985) were further important concessions to women's rights.

Nevertheless, some degree of discrimination appears to remain in the labour market, both in terms of salaries and in offers of employment. Female salaries are on average 20 percent lower than male salaries, while female unemployment hovers around 25 percent of the workforce compared to about 15 percent for males. The high unemployment rate among women is, however, attributable in part to the rapid rise in the female labour force (up from 3.5 million in the mid-1970s to 5.7 million twenty years later), which the economy has been unable to absorb. Despite these difficulties there are now more women than ever in jobs, over 4 million, three-quarters of them being employed in the services sector, especially education, health and welfare, and hotel and catering. Access to jobs in the male-dominated world of business has also improved markedly, partly as a result of an increasing supply of female graduates in economics and business studies. The participation rate among women in the labour market (36 percent overall), is much higher in the 20–30 age group, so it is likely to approach the higher participation rate of countries such as Britain, France or Italy. Spanish women have a much higher life expectancy than Spanish men (81 compared to 74), spend less time in hospital than men, more time on domestic chores whether or not they have jobs, are more likely than their male counterparts to pass their exams first time, and less likely to fall by the wayside in university studies.

See also: abortion law; family; marriage and divorce; sexual behaviour; social attitudes

Further reading

Jones, A.B. (1997) *Women in Contemporary Spain*, Manchester: Manchester University Press (the best, most up-to-date account in English).

Garrido, L. (1993) *Las dos biografías de la mujer en España*, Madrid: Instituto de la Mujer (an interesting account of women's progress and problems).

Hooper, J. (1995) *The New Spaniards*, Harmondsworth: Penguin, pp. 164–75 (highly readable, and well-informed on post-1975 developments).

Instituto de la Mujer (1994) *La mujer en cifras. Una década, 1982–92*, Madrid: Instituto de la Mujer (contains a compendium of essential statistics attractively and accessibly presented).

C.A. LONGHURST

women's writing

Changing social roles and the expanding publishing industry have transformed women's writing and its critical reception in the democratic period. Under Franco, virtually the only woman to feature in post-war literary overviews was Carmen **Laforet**, whose 1945 novel *Andrea* (*Nada*) was taken to mark the birth of neo-realism. Underlying this neglect was the fact that, with notable exceptions like Dolores Medio, Mercedes **Fórmica Corsi** and the early novels of Concha **Alós**, few women produced the socialist realist narrative that influential commentators of the 1950s and 1960s deemed the only effective literary means of opposing the regime. Although the more subjective or psychological focus of Ana María **Matute**, Elena **Soriano** and Mercedes Salisachs, for example, or the ambiguities and stylistic complexities of Elena **Quiroga**'s work, did not preclude a critical dimension – and may in some cases have been cultivated to elude **censorship** – they were generally either ignored or criticized as unengaged. Unsurprisingly, however, given women's restricted horizons, the best-selling women's writing of the post-war period was the ***novela rosa*** (sentimental romance), a genre not marked by dissidence. By the mid-1950s, however, writers like Carmen **Martín Gaite**, Laforet and Carmen Kurtz were among those using its conventions to question the regime's constraints on women.

Within a decade, the effects of Spain's limited modernization and the increased availability of Latin American and European criticism and non-realist narrative was encouraging more experimental writing. Ana María Moix was one of the number of young poets who functioned as cultural mediators between these new and more traditional influences. By the 1970s this experimentalism was visible in the narrative of Lourdes Ortiz, for example, and the more established Martín Gaite. The newer generation was also influenced by the highly acclaimed work produced in **exile** by Mercè **Rodoreda** and Rosa **Chacel**. Despite its increasingly liberal climate, however, innovation was less evident in the **theatre**, where Ana Diosdado was writing the bourgeois comedies that have made her Spain's most commercially successful woman playwright.

The widespread disenchantment that followed the euphoria of the transition to democracy and the fragmentation of organized **feminism** led a number of writers – including Rosa **Montero**, Lidia **Falcón** and Montserrat **Roig** – to rework their experiences as feminist and anti-Franco activists in their writing. Like the dynastic narratives of Roig and Rodoreda in the early 1970s, this reflected an attempt to interpret an uncertain present with reference to the past. Also associated with the prevailing sense of lost bearings was the adoption by some writers of a more introspective, existentially inflected tone usually associated with a search for stable identity, as in the novels of **Tusquets**, Marina **Mayoral**, Soledad **Puértolas** and Mercedes Soriano. The 1980s saw the publication of a number of texts – by Paloma Díaz-Mas, for example, Ortiz, María Xosé Queizán, Carmen **Gómez Ojea** and Pilar Pedraza – which sought alternative identities, or new discursive conditions in which these might emerge, by reconfiguring history or myth. Montero has used science fiction to similar effect. In the theatre, androcentric gender stereotypes (to which certain established women playwrights like Diosdado and María Manuela Reina also had recourse) began to be challenged by younger writers, among them Pilar Pombo, Maribel Lázaro and Paloma Pedrero.

The late 1970s had seen revived interest among some writers – including Puértolas and Ortiz – in plot-driven thriller or **detective fiction** as a focus for interpreting and thus stabilizing the effects of rapid social change. Throughout the 1980s, however, post-structuralist and postmodern critiques contributed to a widespread loss of faith in notions of truth, stability and identity. In her 1983 novel *Te trataré como a una reina* (I'll Treat You Like a Queen) for example, Montero deliberately undermines the distinction between crime reporting and fiction. Five years earlier Martín Gaite's *The Back Room* (*El cuarto de atrás*) had affirmed the constructed nature of autobiography, identity and subject alike. The element of mystery which structures her central character's quest for identity while underlining its illusoriness can also be traced in the work of Carme **Riera** and, more recently, in writing by Cristina **Fernández Cubas**, Mayoral and Adelaida García Morales. The ongoing tension between the seach for authentic identity and the view that truth and identity are effects produced in discourse is evident in recent historical narratives by Angeles Caso and Moix: the first marked by the search for an accurate alternative to androcentric history; the second by an implicit critique of historiography as a project. Among younger novelists like Belén Gopegui, however, there are signs of a desire to move beyond this tension towards a renewed collective project.

The link between the high profile of Spanish women's writing since the 1980s and the expansion of the publishing industry is evident in the vogue for women's *literatura erótica* (erotic literature). Whereas the erotic had been an integral part of more complex narratives by Tusquets, for example, and of poetry by Ana **Rossetti** and Juana Castro since the late 1970s, the 1989 début novels of Almudena Grandes and Mercedes Abad were marketed primarily for their erotic content, although both have been criticized for reproducing male-authored models. More generally, the expansion of locally based publishing has raised the profile of regional writers like the Galician poet and novelist Xohana Torres and the Basque-language writer Arantza **Urretabizkaia**.

See also: Basque culture; Catalan culture; feminist writing; Galician culture; literature

Further reading

Brown, J.L. (ed.) (1991) *Women Writers of Contemporary Spain: Exiles in the Homeland*, London: Associated University Presses (wide-ranging collection, covering some lesser-known writers).

Levine, L.G. (1993) *Spanish Women Writers: a Bio-Bibliographical Source Book*, London: Greenwood (invaluable reference text).

López, F. (1995) *Mito y discurso en la novela femenina de posguerra en España*, Madrid: Pliegos (particularly strong on the pre-1975 novel, usefully contextualized).

Ordoñez, E. (1991) *Voices of Their Own: Contemporary Spanish Narrative by Women*, London: Associated University Presses (impressive range of theoretical feminist readings).

Pérez, J. (1988) *Contemporary Women Writers of Spain*, Boston, MA: Twayne (accessible survey from the beginning of the century).

ANNY BROOKSBANK JONES

Xirinacs, Olga

b. 1936, Tarragona

Writer

Active in the cultural life of her native city, the prolific Catalan Xirinacs has won many prestigious prizes for her poetry, among them the Carles Riba for *Llavis que dansen* (Dancing Lips) (1987) and for her prose, including both the Crítica and the Sant Jordi for *Al meu cap una llosa* (A Gravestone at my Head) (1985). In this latter novel, she pays tribute to Virginia Woolf, one of her favourite writers. Xirinac's themes are often philosophical, exploring such topics as the nature of evil and the creative process. Much of her verse is love poetry, sometimes with an erudite literary base, with quotations from other poets, ranging from Virgil to Giuseppi Ungaretti. Xirinacs is a piano teacher and has studied painting; these aesthetic activities inform her work and are occasionally reflected in titles such as *Interior amb difunts* (Interior with Deceased) (1983) and *Música de cambra* (Chamber Music) (1982). The latter is written in the form of a lyrical diary covering three years (1979–81) with reflections on the past and projections to the future that greatly expand the time period evoked. *Tempesta d'hivern* (Winter Storm) (1990) relies on music for theme as well as imagery: a successful orchestra director returns home after a long absence to find ghosts from the past. The description of her triumphant concert is impeccable.

The protagonist of *Enterments lleugers* (Light Burials) (1991) is a house, in the sort of subgenre used by writers such as Latin America's García Márquez and Allende, and Catalonia's own **Rodoreda**. The wall referred to in the title *La muralla* (The Wall) (1993) is the Roman wall of Tarragona; this long poem is a monument to her historic birthplace and its inhabitants. *Sense malícia* (Without Malice) (1994) is a chilling psychological study of a violent young boy, who 'examines' the suffering of his victims while showing a polite, sweet demeanour to the world.

Based on the newspaper story of an aristocratic double suicide, *Cerimònia privada* (Private Ceremony) (1993) uses wedding guests turned funeral mourners to reflect on meanings and motivations. The novel opens with a quotation from Peter Handke and includes references to Peter Pan. Xirinacs' latest work, *Sucant el melindro* (Dipping the Pastry) (1996), is a collection of realistic, ironic, and tender stories written originally for the Barcelona daily paper ***Avui***. The sea and death are often present in the work of this versatile author. She has also written literature for children, and some of her work has been translated into Russian, German, English and **Spanish**.

See also: Catalan culture; women's writing

KATHLEEN McNERNEY

Xunta de Galicia

Established via a decree of the pre-autonomous Assembly of Galician Parliamentarians in March 1978, article 152 of the **constitution of 1978** and a Statute of Autonomy in April 1981, the Xunta de Galicia is the government of the **autonomous**

community of Galicia, accountable to the Galician parliament which nominates its president, who in turn selects its ministers. A *consellerià de cultura* (culture ministry) promotes *galego* (the **Galician**), subidizes **Galician culture**, venues, the radio and TV station of Galicia (RTVG) and publications.

While some Galician nationalists made demands for self-determination, the Popular Party (Partido Popular, **PP**), which under the leadership of Manuel **Fraga Iribarne** controlled the Xunta after the elections in 1989, 1993 and 1997 stressed cultural autonomy (or *auto-identificacion*).

JOHN P. GIBBONS

youth culture

Though Spain has an ageing population and the lowest fertility rate in Europe (see also **demographic indicators**), the effects of this will only be seen in the twenty-first century, as the birth-rate in the 1970s was relatively high, leading to a substantial proportion of under-25s in the mid to late 1990s. A visitor to the country is therefore likely to receive the impression of a vibrant youth culture. This is due to a number of factors, not least the enthusiasm with which young people in Spain have, since the 1970s, embraced the lifestyles of their counterparts in the US, Britain and other European countries. Dress, tastes in music (see also **rock and pop**), and the numbers of young people observed in bars and discos combine to strengthen the impression of a cosmopolitan, consumer generation identifying with the rest of the developed world.

There are, however, a number of features which for historic reasons are arguably more accentuated in Spain than elsewhere. Though persons under 25 in the year 2000 will by definition have no direct experience of living under Francoism, the feeling that Spain is a young democracy recently emerged from an authoritarian system is still strong. In addition, this generation is considerably better educated than its elders, and, having access to better-paid employment, has more disposable income. There is also a strong libertarian strand to youth culture in Spain, represented in its most characteristic form by the ***Movida*** of the years around 1980. Though this had spent its force by the early 1990s, the element of excess in the lifestyle of the young is perhaps more marked than elsewhere, notably in the phenomenon known as *la ruta del bakalao*, the Spanish equivalent of the 'acid house'. The difference is that in Spain a weekend of disco-dancing and dosing on Ecstasy can be spread over several widely distant venues, entailing long car journeys at reckless speed. At a more general level, resistance to authority is reflected in more relaxed attitudes towards **sexual behaviour**, drug-taking, and the increasing rejection of the obligation of **military service** (see also ***insumisos***).

There is, however, evidence to suggest that external appearances are in some ways deceptive, and that the under-25s have become more conservative in the 1990s. Some surveys indicate that young people's actual sexual behaviour is more cautious than their replies to questionnaires would suggest. A large majority, of the order of 80 percent, declare that the **family** is the most important element in their lives, and Spain has one of the lowest rates in Europe of single-person households, indicating that young people are remaining longer in the parental home. Figures for cohabitation are also very low (slightly over 1 percent, according to a National Statistical Institute survey in the early 1990s), and those who marry prefer to do so in church, despite the fact that church affiliation is lowest among this age cohort. As with other aspects of post-Franco culture, it would appear that the initial exuberance has been replaced by something more moderate.

See also: cultural institutions and movements; gay culture; social attitudes; society

Further reading

Aznárez, M. (1996) 'Juventud: la infancia más larga', *El País 20 Años* (a concise and useful overview included in this supplement, which was published to celebrate the first twenty years of *El País*).

Hooper, J. (1995) *The New Spaniards*, Harmondsworth: Penguin (part three, 'Coming to Terms with Freedom', especially chapter 14, 'A Cult of Excess', gives a reliable picture of youth culture within the context of overall cultural developments).

EAMONN RODGERS

'YOYES' *see* González Cataráin, María Dolores

Z

Zabaleta, Nicanor

b. 1907, San Sebastián; d. 1993, Puerto Rico

Harpist

After studies in San Sebastián and Madrid, Zabaleta went to Paris, studying the harp with Marcel Tournier, and composition with Marcel Samuel Rousseau and Eugène Cools. Zabaleta has arguably done more than any other musician this century to revive and promote interest in the harp as a solo instrument and establish its repertoire, rescuing forgotten compositions for harp by Cabezón, Bach, Handel and Beethoven. He even contributed design innovations, developing an eight-pedal version of the harp. Composers as diverse as Rodolfo **Halffter**, Joaquín **Rodrigo** (who arranged his guitar concerto, *Concierto de Aranjuez*, for the harp at Zabaleta's request), Darius Milhaud and Villa-Lobos have written works specially for performance by him. Zabaleta continued to perform into the 1970s with orchestras all over the world, in Israel, Warsaw, London, Berlin, Salzburg and Philadelphia. His farewell concert tour took place in 1988, when he was 80, and included concerts in Paris, Naples, Palermo, Tel Aviv and Madrid. In 1982, he was awarded the National Prize for Music in recognition of his contribution.

EAMONN RODGERS

Zambrano, María

b. 1904, Vélez-Málaga; d. 1991, Madrid

Philosopher

In 1988, Zambrano became the first woman and first philosopher to receive the **Cervantes Prize**. Influenced by her father, a noted liberal pedagogue and socialist thinker, she lived from childhood at the centre of educational reform, later obtaining her doctorate with Spain's major philosophers – José **Ortega y Gasset**, Xavier Zubiri, Manuel García Morente – and participating in pro-Republican political activities which inspired her first book, *Horizonte del liberalismo* (Horizons of Liberalism). Later works emphasize 'pure' philosophical inquiry rather than politics, but she remained true to the ideals of pacifism, humanitarian socialism and freedom.

Los intelectuales en el drama de España (Intellectuals in Spain's Drama) is partly autobiographical, but forty-five years of post-war exile leave little imprint on her writing. Even such wartime works as *Pensamiento y poesía en la vida española* (Thought and Poetry in Spanish Life) and *Filosofía y poesía* (Philosophy and Poetry) reflect little of contemporary reality, but seek to elucidate similarities and differences between the two genres: she envisages philosophy as search and method, poetry as encounter. *La agonía de Europa* (Europe's Agony) does, however, reflect the global crisis of WWII. *Hacia un saber sobre el alma* (Towards Knowledge of the Soul) initiates lifelong metaphysical preoccupations, pursued in *El hombre y lo divino* (Humanity and the Divine), where she applies the method of 'poetic reason' (her modification of Ortega y Gasset's 'vital reason') to elucidating religious experience. Zambrano commented that the title 'Humanity and the Divine' would aptly suit her complete work.

Especially significant are dreams, viewed in *El sueño creador* (Creative Dreaming) as pregnant with creative potential and revelatory of time's origins. Her theory of dreams reappears in *España, sueño y verdad* (Spain, Dream and Truth) which pursues connections between dreams and metaphysical time, reviving Baroque concepts of life as dream, death as awakening. *Claros del bosque* (Clearings in the Forest) treats themes of being, presence and reality, concealment and revelation, immanent knowledge and passive epiphany, united by ontological seeking.

In 1981, Zambrano received the **Prince of Asturias Prize** for Literature, and following an honorary doctorate from the University of Málaga, established her residence in Madrid in 1984. *Persona y democracia* (Person and Democracy), contrasting individual and collectivity, and *De la Aurora* (Concerning Dawn), among the more significant works of her final years, continue the quest for knowledge metaphorically and poetically as she moves towards mystic passivity, emphasizing the intuitive and spiritual over the analytical, revelation over reason, ultimately closer to Unamuno than to Ortega y Gasset.

See also: philosophy

Further reading

Abellán, J.L. (1967) 'María Zambrano: La "razón poética" en marcha', in *Filosofía española en América (1936–1966)*, Madrid: Guadarrama, pp. 169–89 (discussion by a leading critic of Zambrano's place among exiled philosophers, 'poetic reason' and connections with Ortega y Gasset).

Donahue, D. (1993) 'National History as Autobiography: María Zambrano's *Delirio y destino*', *Monographic Review* 9: 116–24 (discussion of Zambrano's lyric memoir of her involvement at age 20 with the Republican intellectual scene).

Johnson, R. (1998) 'The Context and Achievement of *Delirium and Destiny*', in M. Zambrano, *Delirium and Destiny. A Spaniard in her Twenties*, trans. C. Maier, Albany, NY: State University of New York Press, 1998, pp. 215–35.

—— (1996) 'María Zambrano's Theory of Literature as Knowledge and Contingency', *Hispania* 79, 2 (1996): 215–21.

Marí, A. (1989) 'Poesía y verdad', *Insula* 44, 509: 1–2 (studies her treatment of truth and relationship to antecedents in Ortega y Gasset).

Ortega Muñoz, J.F., (ed.) (1982) *María Zambrano o la metafísica recuperada*, Vélez Málaga: Delegación de Cultura (a collection of critical tributes to Zambrano published by the government of her native city).

Pérez, J. (1999) 'La razón de la sinrazón: Unamuno, Machado and Ortega in the thought of María Zambrano', *Hispania* 82, 4 (1999): 58–67.

JANET PÉREZ

zarzuela

Zarzuela is a species of Spanish opera that combines dialogue with music and song, and whose themes are often of a popular nature. It takes its name from the Zarzuela Palace outside Madrid, an area covered in *zarzas* (brambles), and where some of the first *zarzuelas* were performed in the seventeenth century. There are two principal types of *zarzuela*: *género chico*, a one-act comic operetta, often with a satirical theme, and *zarzuela grande*, normally in three acts and of a more serious nature, whose style approximates to that of romantic opera. Juan Hidalgo was the earliest known composer of *zarzuelas*, and some renowned nineteenth-century composers include Chapí, Bretón, Valverde and Vives.

JUAN SERRANO

zoological gardens

Famous for the birth in 1983 of a giant panda, Chulín, by artificial insemination, and for its collection of other rare and unusual animals, such as the Komodo dragon and a pair of red pandas from Nepal, the modern Madrid Zoo was opened in the Casa del Campo in the early 1970s, when many other zoos and safari parks were also founded. It was, however, the immediate successor to the much older Madrid zoo, the Real Casa de Fieras del Retiro (Royal Animal House of the Retiro Park), founded by Charles III around 1770, as the second oldest in the world after Vienna (1756), rebuilt by Ferdinand VII and closed in 1972. Among its exhibits were lions from the Atlas mountains. Also much older than others in Spain is the Barcelona Municipal Zoo, opened in 1892, which by the 1980s was complete with aquarium, aviary, reptile house and dolphinarium, and which specializes in anthropoid apes, the most famous being the white gorilla Snowflake.

Several safari parks were opened in the 1970s, such as the first of them, the Río-León Safari, Tarragona, the Auto-Safari African Reserve on Mallorca and the Safari del Rincón, Madrid, at that time the largest in Europe. In the 1980s the Valladolid Zoo-Park was founded, combining traditional with open, safari-type enclosures.

A much more specialist centre, the Parque de Rescate de Fauna Sahariana (Rescue Park for Sahara Fauna), Almeria, was established by the **CSIC** in 1971 to preserve Saharan species on the verge of extinction.

See also: environment; gardens; sport and leisure

EAMONN RODGERS

Zulueta, Iván

b. 1949, San Sebastián

Filmmaker and graphic designer.

One of the most iconoclastic filmmakers of the 1970s, who enjoys an avant-garde cult status and was associated with *la* ***Movida***. His career consists of a series of experimental short films in Super 8 format and two long feature films: *Un, dos, tres... al escondite inglés* (Hide and Seek) (1969), a musical parody which combines psychodelia and pop imagery, produced and co-written by his former teacher and mentor, J.L. **Borau**, and *Arrebato* (Rapture) (1979) where he mixes cinematic reflexivity with supernatural and gothic elements. His cinema is introspective, concerned with exploring the language and experience of film.

See also: film and cinema

Further reading

Bonet, E. and Palacio, M. (1982) *Práctica fílmica y vanguardia artística en España: 1925–81*, Madrid: Universidad Complutense (a brief, well-informed historical survey).

Heredero, C.F. (1989) *Iván Zulueta: la vanguardia frente al espejo*, Alcalá de Henares: Festival de cine de Alcalá de Henares (an informative monograph which includes an interview with the filmmaker).

XON DE ROS

Index

Page numbers in **bold** indicate references to the main entry.